AF838563

The Who, What, *and* Where *of* America

Understanding the American Community Survey

Twelfth Edition

2025

Edited by
Shana Hertz Hattis

BLOOMSBURY ACADEMIC
NEW YORK • LONDON • OXFORD • NEW DELHI • SYDNEY

BLOOMSBURY ACADEMIC
Bloomsbury Publishing Inc, 1359 Broadway, New York, NY 10018, USA
Bloomsbury Publishing Plc, 50 Bedford Square, London, WC1B 3DP, UK
Bloomsbury Publishing Ireland, 29 Earlsfort Terrace, Dublin 2, D02 AY28, Ireland

BLOOMSBURY, BLOOMSBURY ACADEMIC and the Diana logo are trademarks of Bloomsbury Publishing Plc

First published in the United States of America 2025

Copyright © Bloomsbury Publishing, 2025

Cover images: © iStock.com/monkeybusinessimages, Starcevic, SergeyIT, Spondylolithesis, and Maksymowicz

All rights reserved. No part of this publication may be: i) reproduced or transmitted in any form, electronic or mechanical, including photocopying, recording or by means of any information storage or retrieval system without prior permission in writing from the publishers; or ii) used or reproduced in any way for the training, development or operation of artificial intelligence (AI) technologies, including generative AI technologies. The rights holders expressly reserve this publication from the text and data mining exception as per Article 4(3) of the Digital Single Market Directive (EU) 2019/790.

Bloomsbury Publishing Inc does not have any control over, or responsibility for, any third-party websites referred to or in this book. All internet addresses given in this book were correct at the time of going to press. The author and publisher regret any inconvenience caused if addresses have changed or sites have ceased to exist, but can accept no responsibility for any such changes.

ISBN: HB: 978-1-63671-431-8
ePDF: 979-8-7651-6495-2

Series: County and City Extra Series

Typeset by Deanta

For product safety related questions contact productsafety@bloomsbury.com.

To find out more about our authors and books visit www.bloomsbury.com and sign up for our newsletters..

Contents

Page

Page

Preface

The 2010 census was different from any census in recent memory. All American households answered a simple questionnaire with ten questions. No longer did some people get the "long form" which included dozens of detailed questions about employment, education, income, previous residence, housing characteristics, and more. The data gleaned from these important questions have long been used by federal, state, and local governments to evaluate their populations and program needs; by large and small businesses and nonprofit organizations for a variety of planning and location purposes; and by academic researchers to study trends in social and economic conditions. However, the cost, timeliness, and quality of the traditional long form data made it necessary to develop a new data collection strategy for gathering economic and demographic characteristics of the nation.

The "long form" has been replaced by the American Community Survey (ACS). Under development for more than a decade, the ACS is an ongoing survey of the American people that ushered in a new era in social and economic data analysis. The census "long form" provided detailed estimates of social and economic characteristics every ten years. The ACS collects this same information on a rolling basis. It takes 5 years of ACS responses to accumulate a sample almost as large as the census "long form" collected at a single point in time. But data users now have the ability to study these characteristics and trends throughout the decade—annually for some areas.

Because the ACS is a sample survey, large numbers of sample cases are needed before reliable estimates can be made for small populations. Each year's sample is large enough to produce estimates for the nation, all the states, most metropolitan areas, and many counties and cities. The tables in this volume include single-year estimates for 2023 (the most current year available) for the United States, all states, all metropolitan areas, as well as counties and cities of 65,000 or more population.

The richness of the ACS data can be accessed in varying degrees. Much more subject matter detail is available for large geographic areas partly because reliable estimates for large areas can be produced with smaller samples, and partly because more data must be suppressed for the smaller areas to protect the confidentiality of the respondents.

This book is designed to include a sampling of key information, but also to guide users through the process of using the Census Bureau's website to expand on the information included here. The state tables in this book include more than 300 data items. The metropolitan area, county, and city tables include 48 data items. The data in the tables are a small selection that show what is available for the geographic areas in the book. Every column includes an ACS Table Number that enables users to find the original data on the Census Bureau's website. The selection in this book is limited because the county and city data are from the less detailed supplemental file. Much more information is available in the standard 1-year file for analysis of larger cities and counties or for analysis of specific racial or ethnic groups if those groups have large populations in a particular city or county. Furthermore, as the 5-year data are also available, additional information can be found for the cities and counties in this book, and for all cities and counties in the nation, no matter how small.

One of the most notable differences between the census "long form" and the ACS is the time frame of the estimates. We are accustomed to the census data that give us specific information every ten years, a snapshot of the country on April 1. The ACS multiyear estimates are different as the Census Bureau surveys nearly 300,000 households every month. The data in this book are from the ACS 1-year 2023 estimates which are produced from the 12 calendar months of survey data collection. The estimates reported here represent an "average" population profile over the 12 months of 2023. The sample cases are spread evenly throughout the year rather than the "point in time" decennial census estimates reported as of April 1.

To help in the understanding of these estimates, we have included a measure of population change for each geographic area. These are from the 2010 census and the 2019 estimates, showing the actual population growth or decline in each geographic area. Each table shows population characteristics as estimated for 2023. It should be remembered that the decennial census and the Census Bureau's Population Estimates Program provide the official population counts that underlie the ACS sample. If an area experienced unusually large population growth or decline, we should understand that these short-term population impacts may not be reflected in the ACS period estimates. Changes due to a city annexing a large tract of land, many people moving into a new development, or many people leaving the area because of a plant closing may be hidden in the short-term.

With the ACS, there is always a trade-off between data currency and data reliability. More current 1-year estimates come from smaller samples and therefore have larger margins of error. Estimates from the 5-year data are based on five times the sample size and have smaller margins of error—but of course, they do not represent as current a period. Earlier editions of *The Who, What, and Where of America* relied on the Census Bureau's 3-year (2010–2012) estimates because of the larger sample size and smaller margins of error inherent in the longer period estimates. Due to the elimination of the 3-year data series, the current volume reports the results of the 1-year 2023 data. Users may want to compare data among the editions but should use caution as there will be more sample variability in the 2023 data and small differences may not be meaningful. Users will also notice that there are a number of geographic areas where the estimates are not available due to the Census Bureau's data disclosure rules.

Finally, it is always critical to remember that all estimates are subject to sampling error. On the Census Bureau's website, every ACS number is accompanied by its margin of error. In the interests of space and simplicity, this book does not include the margins of error, but all users are encouraged to consult the Census Bureau's website and to understand some basics: small differences are very likely to represent no difference at all; do not draw conclusions from small numbers; use these numbers as a starting point to explore the wealth of information from the ACS.

Introduction

The American Community Survey (ACS) has ushered in the most substantial change in the decennial census in more than 60 years. It replaced the decennial census long form in 2010, providing more current data throughout the decade by collecting long-form-type information annually rather than only once every 10 years. The ACS provides annual data for states, metropolitan areas, and large cities and counties, and combines multiple years of survey responses to produce data for midsize communities. Very small communities (under 20,000 population) and statistical areas like census tracts and ZIP code tabulation areas require 5 years of survey responses to yield characteristic estimates.

The ACS gathers demographic, social, economic, housing and financial information about the nation's people and communities on a continuous basis. The ACS is an ongoing survey conducted by the U.S. Census Bureau in every county, American Indian and Alaska Native Area, and Hawaiian Home Land in the United States. The ACS is also conducted as the Puerto Rico Community Survey in every municipality in Puerto Rico. As the largest survey in the United States, it is the only source of small-area data on a wide range of important social and economic characteristics for all communities in the country. After years of planning, development, and a demonstration period, the ACS began nationwide full implementation in 2005.

Information about the ACS is available on the Census Bureau's website. The ACS main page is https://www.census.gov/programs-surveys/acs. Data from the ACS is available at https://data.census.gov.

A vast amount of information is collected in the ACS. In this publication, selections of these data have been assembled in various tables by subject and geographic type.

Volume Organization

The data tables in this book contain a representative selection of information from the ACS.

Part A: Who contains the following subjects: age, race/ethnicity, and household structure, among others.

Part B: What contains the following subject areas: education, employment, and income.

Part C: Where contains the following subject areas: migration, housing, and transportation.

Within each part are four tables. Table 1 has data for the 50 states and the District of Columbia; Table 2 has data for all counties with populations of 65,000 or more. Table 3 has data for all the nation's metropolitan statistical areas; and Table 4 has data for all cities with populations of 65,000 or more. Counties and cities are listed alphabetically by state. Metropolitan areas are listed alphabetically, and metropolitan divisions are listed alphabetically within the metropolitan statistical area of which they are components.

In addition, each part is preceded by highlights and ranking tables that show how areas diverge from the national norm, as well as the differences among small areas. These research aids are invaluable for helping people understand what the census data tell us about who we are, what we do, and where we live.

In the following sections, information about the ACS and how to use the data is included, much of it excerpted from the wealth of information available on the Census Bureau's website. Especially helpful are the instructions, definitions, and guidelines on using the data in the section on "Guidance for Data Users."

Readers are encouraged to explore the Census Bureau's Web site to expand on the information contained here and to keep up to date with this constantly changing dataset.

Shana Hertz Hattis is an editor with over a decade of experience in statistical and government research publications. Past titles include *State Profiles: The Population and Economy of Each U.S. State, Housing Statistics of the United States,* and *Justice Statistics: An Extended Look at Crime in the United States.* She earned her bachelor of science in journalism and master of science in education degrees from Northwestern University.

Understanding the American Community Survey

Every 10 years since 1790, as required by the U.S. Constitution, Congress has authorized funds to conduct a national census of the U.S. population. From 1960 through 2000, censuses have consisted of:

- a "short form," which included basic questions about age, sex, race, Hispanic origin (since 1980), household relationship, and owner/renter status, and
- a "long form" used for a sample of approximately one of every six households that included not only the basic short-form questions but also detailed questions about socioeconomic and housing characteristics.

Beginning with the 2010 census, the American Community Survey (ACS) replaced the decennial census long form by collecting long-form-type information annually rather than only once every 10 years, providing more current data throughout the decade. The 2010 Census counted the population to support the constitutional mandate—to provide population counts needed to apportion the seats in the U.S. House of Representatives. The ACS data now provide, for the first time, a regular stream of updated information for states and local areas, revolutionizing the way we use data to understand our communities. It produces social, housing, and economic characteristics for demographic groups, even for geographic areas as small as census tracts and block groups.

Some Key Facts about the ACS

- The ACS annually provides the same kind of detailed information previously available only every 10 years from the census. The ACS is conducted under the authority of Title 13, United States Code, Sections 141 and 193.
- All answers are confidential. Any Census Bureau employee who violates that confidentiality is subject to a jail term, a fine, or both.
- The Census Bureau may use the information it collects only for statistical purposes.
- Addresses are selected at random from the Master Address File to represent similar households in the area. Nearly 300,000 addresses are selected each month and the survey is conducted by mail, telephone, and personal visit. Response to this survey is required by federal statute Section 221 of Title 13.
- Approximately 3.0 percent of U.S. households are surveyed each year. A sample of group quarters (nursing homes, college dormitories, etc.) is included in the ACS as well.
- While the ACS sample size approximates the traditional long-form census sample, it is a smaller sample resulting in somewhat larger margins of error.

The traditional long-form census taken once a decade provided the socioeconomic portrait of the nation and communities but that portrait was fixed in time for 10 years. Data from the ACS provides a regular update to that portrait which is used for a variety of purposes that include: monitoring the well-being of America's older population, children and families, tracking trends in disability, analyzing the growth in the number of grandparents responsible for their grandchildren, determining the economic well-being of the elderly and working-poor families, or tracking social, economic, and demographic changes in the general U.S. population.

The ACS provides critical information for communities on a current basis when they need it most. But the ACS is still a relatively new data collection instrument and a different measure of the characteristics of the population and households. Researchers are still working to understand the differences from the traditional census data so it is good to be cautious in the interpretation of differences between areas and across time. Small differences may not be meaningful. On the other hand, the ACS provides annual estimates and the frequency of updates and currency of the data far outweigh waiting 10 years for new results.

New Opportunities

The main benefits of the ACS are timeliness and access to annual data for states, local areas, and small population subgroups. The ACS delivers useful, relevant data, similar to data from previous census long forms, but updated every year rather than every 10 years. The ACS provides comparable information across and within states for program evaluation and use in funding formulas.

- ACS information is often used to determine the placement of new schools, senior residential services, hospitals, and highways.
- ACS provides information for tracking the well-being of children, families, and the elderly allowing service providers to better target populations in need.
- The data will improve the distribution of aid through federal, state, and local governments. More than $400 billion in federal program funds are distributed each year based, in whole or in part, on census and ACS data.
- The data are used by community programs, such as those for the elderly, libraries, hospitals, banks, and other organizations.
- The data are used by transportation planners to evaluate peak volumes of traffic in order to reduce congestion, plan for parking, and develop plans for carpooling and flexible work schedules.

- Corporations, small businesses, and individuals use these data to develop business plans, to set strategies for expansion or starting a business, and to determine trends in their service areas to meet current and future needs.
- Small towns and rural communities have much to gain from the ACS. Lacking the staff and resources to conduct their own research, many local communities have relied on decennial census information that became increasingly outdated throughout the decade, or used local administrative records that are not comparable with information collected in neighboring areas.
- The ACS also provides tools for those who want to conduct their own research. The ACS includes a Public Use Microdata Sample (PUMS) file each year that enables researchers to create custom universes and tabulations from individual ACS records that have been stripped of personally identifiable information.
- Because the ACS data collection occurs every month, the Census Bureau uses professional, highly trained, permanent interviewers who have improved the accuracy of ACS data compared with those from the decennial census long-form sample. This strategy has effectively reduced the number of refusals to complete the ACS questionnaire and allows interviewers to obtain more complete information than decennial census interviewers.

New Challenges

The main challenges for ACS data users are understanding and using multiyear estimates and the relatively large margins of error associated with ACS data for smaller geographic areas and subgroups of the population.

- ACS data are produced every year, but the sample size of the ACS is smaller than that of the Census 2000 long form sample. Data users need to pay more attention to the margin of error.
- Data users have access to 5-year estimates of ACS data. The sample size based on 5-year period estimates of ACS data is still smaller than the long-form sample in the decennial census, resulting in larger margins of error in the ACS 5-year estimates.
- Prior to the 2014 data release, the ACS produced 1-year, 3-year, and 5-year estimates so areas of 65,000 population or more received three separate estimates of the same characteristic every year. For example, a large city would receive 1-year, 3-year and 5-year estimates of the number of persons 65 and over in poverty. Data users had to decide which datasets were appropriate for their needs.
- As of 2014, the Census Bureau eliminated all 3-year estimates products as a cost saving measure. The historical 3-year data are still available.
- Data users will need to be aware of the implications of multiyear estimates, particularly in analyzing employment and income data that will span a full year or even a 5-year period.
- The 5-year estimates will not reflect short-term changes in the population or economy of an area. A recession is a good example because the 5-year ACS estimates might span both the fall into recession and the resulting growth coming out.

The ACS includes several questions that are very similar to those collected in other federal surveys—especially the Current Population Survey (CPS), the American Housing Survey, and the Survey of Income and Program Participation. In some cases, there are clear guidelines about which data to use. For example, the CPS is the official source of income and poverty data. It includes detailed questions on these topics and should be used in reporting national trends in these subject areas. The Census Bureau recommends that ACS information on income and poverty be used to supplement CPS data for areas below the state level and for population subgroups (such as age, sex, race, Hispanic origin, type of household) at the state level. More information on income and poverty can be found on the Census website at https://www.census.gov/topics/income-poverty.html. For states, generally the Census Bureau recommends using the ACS, though the CPS is still valuable as a source for examining historical state income and poverty trends.

Data Collection versus Data Reporting

Results from the ACS are reported each year which is a major advantage over the traditional long-form data from the decennial census. But unlike the release of data only once every 10 years in the decennial census, the annual release of data from the ACS can be quite confusing. The ACS sample size is such that the reliability of the data is greatly affected by the length of the data collection period and the size of geographic reporting areas. In survey sampling, it is well understood that larger samples yield more reliable estimates with smaller margins of error. In order to produce reliable estimates from the ACS, it is necessary to collect the data over differing periods of time in order to provide estimates for all areas, including small areas like census tracts.

Each set of period estimates is released each year, generally between September and December, and reflect data collection ending in the previous calendar year. Thus, the collection year 2017 1-year estimates were released in September of 2018, the 1-year Supplemental estimates followed in October, and the 2013–2017 5-year estimates were released in December 2018.

The ACS Sample

The ACS is sent each month to a sample of over 290,000 addresses in the United States and Puerto Rico, or about 3.5 million a year, resulting in more than 2.2 million final interviews. The sample represents all housing units and group quarters in the United States and Puerto Rico. (Group quarters include places such as college dormitories, prisons, military barracks, and nursing homes.) The addresses are selected from the Census Bureau's Master Address File (MAF), which is also the basis for the decennial census.

The annual ACS sample is smaller than that of the Census 2000 long-form sample, which included about 18 million housing units. As a result, the ACS needs to combine population or housing data from multiple years to produce reliable numbers for small counties, neighborhoods, and other local areas. To provide information for communities each year, the ACS provides 1- and 5-year estimates.

The ACS sample is not spread evenly across all areas but includes a larger proportion of addresses in sparsely populated rural communities and American Indian reservations and a lower proportion in densely populated areas. Over a 5-year period, the ACS will sample more than 15 million addresses and complete interviews for about 11 million. This sample is sufficient to produce estimates for small geographic areas, such as neighborhoods and sparsely-populated rural counties though the estimates will have larger margins of error than the census long-form data. In a 5-year period no address will be selected for the ACS more than once, and many addresses will never be selected for the survey. It's important to remember that the sample is address-based so while a given address will not be in sample again for at least five years, it is possible that individuals who move or have a second home could be surveyed more than once.

Geography

The ACS data are tabulated for a variety of geographic areas ranging in size from broad geographic regions (Northeast, Midwest, South, and West) to cities, towns, neighborhoods, and census block groups. Before December 2008, the ACS data were only available for geographic areas with at least 65,000 people, including regions, divisions, states, the District of Columbia, Puerto Rico, congressional districts, Public Use Microdata Areas (PUMAs)—census-constructed geographic areas, each with approximately a population of 100,000—and many large counties, metropolitan areas, cities, school districts, and American Indian areas. Starting in December 2008, 3-year estimates became available for all areas with at least 20,000 residents, and in 2010, 5-year estimates for geographic areas down to the block group level became available. One-, three-, and five-year estimates—three sets of numbers—were available and were refreshed every year up until the 2014 data release. Less populous areas—those under 20,000—receive only 5-year estimates. Areas of 20,000 or more receive 1-year estimates, but areas between 20,000 and 65,000 receive less detailed information in the supplemental estimates while those with populations of 65,000 or more continue to receive the very detailed 1-year estimates.

The data tables in this book contain data from the 1-year 2017 estimates. These tables are based on the 2010 tabulation geography for political and statistical areas, the same definitions as the 2010 Census. Changes in area boundaries can occur as a result of annexation, new incorporation or disincorporation of cities, towns, and places. For multiyear estimates, the Census Bureau reports the data based on the most current geographic boundaries incorporating any changes occurring in the multiyear period.

Data Comparability

Since the ACS data are collected continuously, they are not always comparable with long-form data that was collected from the decennial census. For example, both surveys asked about employment status during the week prior to the survey. However, data from the decennial census were typically collected between March and July with a reference date of April 1st, whereas data from the ACS are collected nearly every day and reflect employment throughout the year. Other factors that may also have an impact on the data include seasonal variation in population and minor differences in question wording and question order.

While the categories of income by source are comparable with the decennial long-form data, the monthly collection of ACS data results in a significant difference in concept. In the decennial census, income referred to the previous calendar year whereas in the ACS it refers to the previous 12-month period. Most people have a better understanding of what their calendar year income is, especially since the census is taken around tax time. With the ACS, individuals have to report income for a different period each month. A response to the survey in October of the year will report income from October of the previous year through September of the current year. This may require respondents to actually compute their 12-month income.

In 2006, the ACS began including samples of the population living in group quarters (e.g., jails, college dormitories, and nursing homes) for the first time. As a result, the ACS data from 2008 through 2017 may not be comparable with data from earlier ACS surveys. This is especially true for estimates of young adults and the elderly, who are more likely than other groups to be living in group quarters facilities.

One of the most important uses of the ACS estimates is to make comparisons between estimates—over time or across areas. Several key types of comparisons are of general interest to users:

- Comparisons of estimates from different geographic areas within the same time period (e.g., comparing the proportion of seniors below the poverty level in two counties).
- Comparisons of estimates for the same geographic area across time periods (e.g., comparing the proportion of people below the poverty level in a metropolitan area for 2015 and 2017).

- Comparisons of ACS estimates with the corresponding estimates from past decennial census samples (e.g., comparing the proportion of people below the poverty level in a county in 2017 compared with 2010 and 2000).

A number of conditions must be met when comparing survey estimates.

- When comparing data for different geographic areas, always use the same period estimates. When comparing data for an area which only have 5-year estimates to an area with 1- and 5-year estimates, it is important to compare only the 5-year estimates.
- When comparing over time for the same geographic area, again, only compare like-year period estimates. For example, it is not appropriate to compare a 1-year estimate for 2017 to a 5-year estimate for 2013-2017.
- Of primary importance is that the comparison takes into account the sampling error associated with each estimate, thus determining whether the observed differences between estimates are statistically significant. Statistical significance means that there is statistical evidence that a true difference exists within the full population, and that the observed difference is unlikely to have occurred by chance due to sampling. A method for determining statistical significance when making comparisons, as well as considerations associated with the various types of comparisons, can be found in Sections 4 and 7 of the *ACS General Handbook*: https://www.census.gov/programs-surveys/acs/guidance/handbooks/general.html
- The statistical properties of survey samples like the ACS are dependent upon independence of samples. In the ACS multiyear period estimates, the estimates are based on the sampled households for each year. That means that when comparing estimates for the period 2009–2011 to 2010–2012, two thirds of the sample cases are the same households—those surveyed in 2010 and 2011. The only different (independent) households are those taken in 2009 and 2012. When comparisons over time are made, it is best to compare non-overlapping samples. That is, compare estimates for 2007–2009 to the period 2010–1012 because both periods contain independent household samples. To meet this criterion for the use of the most recent 5-year estimates (2013-2017), data users should use the 2008-2012 data to make time series comparisons.

Finally, the decennial census and the ACS have different residency rules. In the decennial census, population is tabulated by their "usual place of residence" typically where they spend six months or more of the year. This is subject to some seasonal variation due to persons with dual residences. In the ACS, there is a 2-month residency rule. That is, if the respondent has been in the sampled housing unit for 2 months or expects to be resident there for 2 months they are captured in the survey. This can have an impact on communities with highly seasonal populations and college communities.

Subjects Covered

The topics covered by the ACS focus on demographic, social, economic, and housing characteristics. These topics are virtually the same as those covered by the 2000 census long-form sample data.

Demographic Characteristics

Age, Sex, Hispanic Origin, Race, and Relationship to Householder (e.g., spouse)

Social Characteristics

Marital Status and Marital History; Fertility; Grandparents as Caregivers; Ancestry

Place of Birth; Citizenship and Year of Entry; Language Spoken at Home; Educational Attainment and School Enrollment; Residence One Year Ago; Veteran Status, Period of Military Service, and VA Service-Connected Disability Rating; and Disability

Economic Characteristics

Income, Food Stamps Benefit, Labor Force Status, Industry, Occupation, Class of Worker, Place of Work and Journey to Work, Work Status Last Year, Vehicles Available, and Health Insurance Coverage

Housing Characteristics

Year Structure Built, Units in Structure, Year Moved Into Unit, Rooms, Bedrooms, Kitchen Facilities, Plumbing Facilities, House Heating Fuel, Telephone Service Available, and Farm Residence

Financial Characteristics

Tenure (Owner/Renter), Housing Value, Rent, and Selected Monthly Owner Costs

Availability of ACS Estimates

The ACS began in 1996 and has expanded each subsequent year. From 2000 through 2004, the sample included between 740,000 and 900,000 addresses annually. In 2005, the ACS shifted from a demonstration program to the full sample size and design. It became the largest household survey in the United States, with an annual sample size of about 3 million addresses. Beginning with 2005, the ACS single-year estimates are available for geographic areas with a population of 65,000 or more. Less detailed single-year supplemental estimates were first released in 2014 for areas of 20,000 or more and are expected to continue. Three-year period estimates for areas of 20,000 or more were first released for the 2005–2007 time period and there are annual 3-year estimates through the 2011-2013 period. 5-year estimates for all areas were first released in 2010 and are available for every subsequent year with 2017 being the most current as of this writing. The ACS will continue to accumulate samples over 5-year intervals to produce estimates for smaller geographic areas, including census tracts and block groups.

Annually, the ACS produces updated, single-year estimates of demographic, housing, social, and economic characteristics for all states, as well as for larger counties, cities, metropolitan and urban areas, and congressional districts. Geographic areas must have a minimum population of 65,000 to qualify for detailed estimates based on a single year's sample, and a minimum population of 20,000 to qualify for supplemental estimates. Every state, metropolitan area, and congressional district meets the 65,000 threshold and therefore new single year estimates are released each year for these areas. Some school districts, townships, and American Indian and Alaska Native areas also meet this population threshold.

For areas with populations of at least 20,000, the Census Bureau produces 1-year supplemental estimates, and until 2013 produced estimates using data collected over a 3 year period. The 3-year estimates are available through the 2011-2013 collection period (released in 2014). However, the Census Bureau is no longer producing the 3-year data products. For rural areas and city neighborhoods (including census tracts and block groups) with fewer than 20,000 people, the Census Bureau produces estimates using data collected over a 5-year period and updates these multiyear estimates every year. ACS data are released annually, about nine months after the end of each calendar year of data collection.

For most geographic areas—including three-quarters of all counties, most school districts, and most cities, towns, and American Indian reservations—the only detailed estimates are the 5-year estimates because of their population size. Because some federal grant programs allocate funds directly to these areas, Congress can use the 5-year estimates to evaluate needs at the relevant geographic level, compare characteristics between areas within and among states, and analyze how various formulas distribute funds. The vast majority of areas will receive only 5-year detailed estimates. In partnership with the states, the Census Bureau created *Public Use Microdata Areas* (PUMAs), which are special, non-overlapping areas within a state, each with a population of about 100,000. These areas will have annual 1-year estimates.

Definitions of these geographic areas are at https://www.census.gov/programs-surveys/acs/geography-acs/concepts-definitions.html.

Using the ACS

Differences between the ACS and the Decennial Census

While the main function of the decennial census is to provide *counts* of people for the purpose of congressional apportionment and legislative redistricting, the primary purpose of the ACS is to measure the changing social and economic *characteristics* of the U.S. population. As a result, the ACS does not provide official counts of the population though users of the data will report the estimate results as though they were counts. In non-decennial census years, the Census Bureau's Population Estimates Program continues to be the official source for annual population totals, by age, race, Hispanic origin, and sex. The ACS sample estimates are controlled to match the decennial census and the Census Bureau's annual population estimates by selected age, sex, race, and Hispanic origin categories. For more information about population estimates, visit the Census Bureau's website at https://www.census.gov/programs-surveys/popest.html.

There are many similarities between the methods used in the traditional decennial census sample and the ACS but there are also a number of differences in collection method and concepts. Response to both the ACS and decennial census is required by law, a factor that helps improve overall response. Both the ACS and the decennial census sample data are based on information from a sample of the population. The data from the Census 2000 sample of about one-sixth of the population were collected using a "long-form" questionnaire, whose content was the model for the ACS. The sample for the ACS is somewhat smaller, approximately 1 in 7 households, resulting in larger margins of error.

While some differences exist in the specific Census 2000 long-form question wording and that of the ACS, most questions are identical or nearly identical. Differences in the design and implementation of the two surveys are noted below with references provided to a series of evaluation studies that assess the degree to which these differences are likely to impact the estimates. The ACS produces period estimates (covering one or five years of data collection) so these estimates do not measure characteristics for the same time frame as the decennial census estimates, which are interpreted to be a snapshot as of April 1 of the census year.

Some data items were collected by both the ACS and the Census 2000 long form with slightly different definitions or reference periods that could affect the comparability of the estimates for these items. One example is annual costs for a mobile home. Census 2000 included installment loan costs in the total annual costs but the ACS does not. In this example, the ACS could be expected to yield smaller estimates than Census 2000.

While some differences were a part of the census and survey design objectives, other differences observed between ACS and census results were not by design, but due to nonsampling error—differences related to how well the surveys were conducted. The ACS and the census experience different levels and types of coverage error, different levels and treatment of housing unit and questionnaire item nonresponse, and different instances of measurement and processing error. Both Census 2000 and the ACS had similarly high levels of survey coverage and low levels of unit nonresponse. Higher levels of unit nonresponse were found in the nonresponse follow-up stage of Census 2000 while lower levels of item nonresponse were found in the ACS due to a permanent staff of trained interviewers.

Census Bureau analysts have compared sample estimates from Census 2000 with 1-year ACS estimates based on data collected in 2000 and 3-year ACS estimates based on data collected in 1999–2001 in selected counties. In general, ACS estimates were found to be quite similar to those produced from decennial census data.

Detailed information about the ACS methodology can be found at https://www.census.gov/programs-surveys/acs/methodology.html.

Residence Rules

The fundamentally different purposes of the ACS and the census, and their timing, led to important differences in the choice of data collection methods. For example, the residence rules for a census or survey determine the sample unit's occupancy status and household membership at the time of collection. Defining the rules in a dissimilar way can affect those two very important estimates. The 2010 census residence rules, which determined where people should be counted, were based on the principle of "usual residence" on April 1, 2010, in keeping with the focus of the census on the requirements of congressional apportionment and state redistricting. To accomplish this, the decennial census attempts to restrict and determine a principal place of residence on one specific date for everyone enumerated. The ACS residence rules are based on a "current residence" concept since data are collected continuously throughout the entire year with responses provided relative to the continuously changing survey interview dates. Under this concept, anyone who is living or staying at an address for two months or more is considered a resident of that address. This method is consistent with the goal of the ACS to produce estimates that reflect annual averages of the characteristics of all areas.

Residence rules determine which individuals are considered to be residents of a particular housing unit or group quarters. While many people have definite ties to a single housing unit or group quarters, some people may stay in different places for significant periods of time over the course of the year. The differences in the ACS and census data, as a consequence of the different residence rules, are most likely minimal for most areas and most characteristics. However, for certain segments of the population the usual and current residence concepts could result in different residence decisions. The older population is one of those segments as many retired and active seniors maintain dual residences. Appreciable differences may occur in areas where large proportions of the total population spend several months of the year in what would not be considered their residence under decennial census rules. In particular, data for areas that include large beach, lake, or mountain vacation areas may differ appreciably between the census and the ACS if populations live there for more than two months. In addition, in the decennial census college students are to be counted at the location of the college rather than their parent's home. However, during summer months, college students can meet the two-month residency rule for the ACS and be counted along with their parents rather than at the college.

For the past several censuses, decennial census residence rules were designed to produce an accurate count of the population as of Census Day, April 1, while the ACS residence rules were designed to collect representative information to produce annual average estimates of the characteristics of all types of areas. The residence rules governing the census enumerations of people in group quarters depend on the type of group quarter and, where permitted, whether people claim a "usual residence" elsewhere. The ACS applies a straight de facto residence rule to every type of group quarter. Everyone living or staying in a group quarter on the day it is visited by an ACS interviewer is eligible to be sampled and interviewed for the survey.

Reference Periods

Estimates produced by the ACS are not measuring exactly what decennial samples have been measuring. The ACS yearly samples, spread over 12 months, collect information that is anchored to the day on which the sampled unit was interviewed, whether it is the day that a mail questionnaire is completed or the day that an interview is conducted by telephone or personal visit. Individual questions with time references such as "last week" or "the last 12 months" all begin the reference period as of this interview date. Even the information on types and amounts of income refers to the 12 months prior to the day the question is answered. ACS interviews are conducted just about every day of the year, and all of the estimates that the survey releases are considered to be averages for a specific time period. The 1-year estimates reflect the full calendar year; 5-year estimates reflect the full 60-month period.

Most decennial census sample estimates are anchored in this same way to the reference date of April 1. The most obvious difference between the ACS and the census is the overall time frame in which they are conducted. The census enumeration time period is less than half the time period used to collect data for each single-year ACS estimate. But a more important difference is that the distribution of census enumeration dates are highly clustered in March and April (when most census mail returns were received) with additional, smaller clusters seen in May and June (when nonresponse follow-up activities took place).

This means that the data from the decennial census, intended to reflect the characteristics of the population and housing on April 1, tend to describe the characteristics in the March through June time period (with an overrepresentation of March/April). The ACS data describe the characteristics nearly every day over the full calendar year. For employment and income estimates, the decennial census referred to the prior calendar year for all respondents, while the ACS asks about the 12 months preceding the interview.

Individual tables can be compared with the table comparison tool or you can download the entire comparison table.

Some specific differences in reference periods between the ACS and the decennial census are described below. Users should consider the potential impact these different reference periods could have on distributions when comparing ACS estimates with Census 2000. As we get further and further away from use of the 2000 data and compare current ACS data to prior years' ACS data, these differences have become less important.

- **Income Data**: To estimate annual income, the Census 2000 long-form sample used the calendar year prior to Census Day as the reference period, and the ACS uses the 12 months prior to the interview date as the reference period. Thus, while Census 2000 collected income information for calendar year 1999, the ACS collects income information for the 12 months preceding the interview date. The responses are a mixture of 12 reference periods ranging from, in the case of the 2016 ACS single-year estimates, the full calendar year 2015 through November 2016. The ACS income responses for each of these reference periods are individually inflation-adjusted to represent dollar values for the ACS collection year. Further inflation adjustments are made to the 3- and 5-year estimates to reflect dollar values of the final year of the estimate. It's important to note that the rotating reference period for income can result in misreporting. The calendar year reference period of the decennial census coincides with an individual's annual salary and is also collected around tax time. Respondents will have a good idea of what their annual salary is. In the ACS, the respondent has to calculate their income for the previous 12 months, a figure which can vary considerably throughout the year.

- **School Enrollment**: The school enrollment question on the ACS asks if a person had "at any time in the last 3 months attended a school or college." A consistent 3-month reference period is used for all interviews. In contrast, Census 2000 asked if a person had "at any time since February 1 attended a school or college." Since Census 2000 data were collected from mid-March to late-August, the reference period could have been as short as about 6 weeks or as long as 7 months.
- **Utility Costs**: The reference periods for two utility cost questions—gas and electricity—differ between Census 2000 and the ACS. The census asked for annual costs, while the ACS asks for the utility costs in the previous month.

Period Estimates

The ACS produces period estimates of socioeconomic and housing characteristics. It is designed to provide estimates that describe the average characteristics of an area over a specific time period. In the case of ACS single-year estimates, the period is the calendar year (e.g., the 2017 ACS covers January through December 2017). In the case of ACS five-year estimates, the period is January 2013 through December 2017). The ACS five-year estimates are similar in many ways to the ACS single-year estimates, but they encompass a longer time period.

The differences in time periods between single-year and multiyear ACS estimates affect decisions about which set of estimates should be used for a particular analysis. While one may think of these estimates as representing average characteristics over a single calendar year or multiple calendar years, it must be remembered that the 1-year estimates are not calculated as an average of 12 monthly values and the five-year estimates are not calculated as the average of 60 monthly values, nor are the five-year estimates calculated as the average of five single-year estimates. Rather, the ACS collects survey information continuously nearly every day of the year and then aggregates the results over a specific time period—one year or five years. The data collection is spread evenly across the entire period represented so as not to over-represent any particular month or year within the period.

Because ACS estimates provide information about the characteristics of the population and housing for areas over an entire time frame, ACS single-year and multiyear estimates contrast with "point-in-time" estimates, such as those from the decennial census long-form samples or monthly employment estimates from the Current Population Survey (CPS), which are designed to measure characteristics as of a certain date or narrow time period. For example, Census 2000 was designed to measure the characteristics of the population and housing in the United States based upon data collected around April 1, 2000, and thus its data reflect a narrower time frame than ACS data. The monthly CPS collects data for an even narrower time frame, the week containing the 12th of each month.

Most areas have consistent population characteristics throughout the calendar year, and their period estimates may not look much different from estimates that would be obtained from a "point-in-time" survey design. However, some areas may experience changes in the estimated characteristics of the population, depending on when in the calendar year the measurement occurred. For these areas, the ACS period estimates (even for a single-year) may noticeably differ from "point-in-time" estimates. The impact will be more noticeable in smaller areas where changes such as a factory closing can have a large impact on population characteristics, in areas with seasonal population shifts, and in areas with a large natural event such as Hurricane Katrina's impact on the New Orleans area.

This logic can be extended to better interpret five-year estimates where the periods involved are much longer. If, over the full period of time there have been major or consistent changes in certain population or housing characteristics for an area, a period estimate for that area could differ markedly from estimates based on a "point-in-time" survey. The tables in this book were prepared from the 1-year 2017 survey results. Some areas will have experienced a more rapid recovery from the recession while others still continue to struggle and haven't returned to previous levels of growth. Strong growth between the 2000 and 2010 censuses may be replaced by a slowdown in the most recent years

The important thing to keep in mind is that ACS single-year estimates describe the population and characteristics of an area for the full year, not for any specific day or period within the year. The ACS multiyear estimates describe the population and characteristics of an area for the full five-year period, not for any specific day, period, or year within the multiyear time period.

Deciding Which ACS Estimate to Use

Three primary uses of ACS estimates are:

- to understand the characteristics of the population of an area for local planning needs,
- to make comparisons across areas, and
- to assess change over time in an area.

Single-year estimates provide more current information

Single-year estimates provide more current information about areas that have changing population and/or housing characteristics because they are based on the most current data—survey responses from the past calendar year. In contrast, multiyear estimates provide less current information because they are based on both survey responses from the previous year and responses that are up to five years old. As noted earlier, for many areas with minimal change taking place, using the "less current" sample used to produce the multiyear estimates may not have a substantial influence on the estimates. However, in areas experiencing major changes over a given time period, the multiyear estimates may be quite different from the single-year estimates for any of the individual years. Single-year and multiyear estimates are not expected to be the same because they are based on data from two different time periods. This will be true even if the ACS single year is the midyear of the ACS multiyear period (e.g., 2015 single year, 2013–2017 multiyear).

Multiyear estimates are based on larger sample sizes and are therefore more reliable

The five-year estimates are based on five times as many sample cases as the one-year estimates. For some characteristics this increased sample is needed for the estimates to be reliable enough for use in certain applications. For other characteristics the increased sample may not be necessary.

Multiyear estimates are the only type of detailed estimates available for geographic areas with populations of less than 20,000. Users may think that they only need to use multiyear estimates when they are working with small areas, but this isn't the case. Estimates for large geographic areas benefit from the increased sample, resulting in more precise estimates of population and housing characteristics, especially for subpopulations within those areas. In addition, users may determine that they want to use single-year estimates, despite their reduced reliability, as building blocks to produce estimates for meaningful higher levels of geography. These aggregations will similarly benefit from the increased sample sizes and gain reliability.

Local planning could include making local decisions such as where to place schools or hospitals, determining the need for senior services or transportation, and carrying out other infrastructure analysis. In the past, decennial census sample data provided the most comprehensive information. However, the currency of those data suffered through the intercensal period, and the ability to assess change over time was limited. ACS estimates greatly improve the currency of data for understanding the characteristics of housing and population and enhance the ability to assess change over time. At the same time, small differences between ACS estimates can lead to misinterpretation due to larger margins of error.

Several key factors can help users decide whether to use single-year or multiyear ACS estimates for areas where both are available:

- intended use of the estimates
- required precision, or reliability, of the estimates
- currency of the estimates

All of these factors, along with an understanding of the differences between single-year and multiyear ACS estimates, should be taken into consideration when deciding which set of estimates to use.

For users analyzing estimates for areas of different size and for different time periods, it is important to recognize that three-year estimates for areas of any size were eliminated in the 2014 ACS product release. Three year estimates had been available for areas of 20,000 or more so it is still possible to analyze the 3-year data for time periods prior to 2014. For the smallest of geographic areas (under 20,000 population), the only option is to use the 5-year ACS estimates. When comparing areas of different size, it is critical that users only make comparisons between similar period estimates. Even if the study area has one-year estimates, it is not appropriate to compare the one-year estimate to a five-year estimate from a different area.

The release of one-year supplemental estimates has greatly improved the availability of ACS data for many geographic areas. The supplemental estimates consist of 58 detailed tables tabulated on the one-year microdata for geographies with populations of 20,000 or more. These supplemental estimates are available for the same geographic summary levels as those in the ACS 1-year dataset.

The key trade-off to be made in deciding whether to use single-year or multiyear estimates is between currency and precision. In general, the single-year estimates are preferred, as they will be more relevant to the current conditions. However, the user must take into account the level of uncertainty present in the single-year estimates, which may be large for small subpopulation groups and rare characteristics. While single-year estimates offer more current estimates, they also have higher sampling variability. One measure, the coefficient of variation (CV) can help you determine the fitness for use of a single-year estimate in order to assess if you should opt instead to use the multiyear estimate. The CV is calculated as the ratio of the standard error of the estimate to the estimate, times 100. A single-year estimate with a small CV is usually preferable to a multiyear estimate as it is more up to date. However, multiyear estimates are an alternative option when a single-year estimate has an unacceptably high CV. Single-year estimates for small subpopulations (e.g., grandparents 65 and over who are responsible for grandchildren) will typically have larger CVs. In general, multiyear estimates are preferable to single-year estimates when looking at estimates for small subpopulations.

For the complete discussion on deciding which estimates to use and on calculating the CV, see Section 7 of the *ACS General Handbook*: https://www.census.gov/programs-surveys/acs/guidance/handbooks/general.html.

Users are encouraged to make comparisons between sequential single-year estimates. Comparison profiles are available beginning with the 2007 single-year data. These profiles identify statistically significant differences between each year from 2007 through the most recently released year.

Caution is needed when using multiyear estimates for estimating year-to-year change in a particular characteristic. This is because roughly four-fifths of the respondents in a 5-year estimate overlap with the respondents in the next year's 5-year estimate period. When comparing 5-year estimates from 2011–2015 with those from 2012–2016, the differences in overlapping multiyear estimates are driven by differences in the non-overlapping years (i.e., 2011 and 2016). A more appropriate comparison of change over time would be comparing the 2008–2012 5-year estimate to the 2013–2017 5-year estimate because they include responses from totally independent samples. Comparison of overlapping periods should be made with caution.

Users who are interested in comparing overlapping multiyear period estimates should refer to Section 4 of the *ACS General Handbook* for more information: https://www.census.gov/programs-surveys/acs/guidance/handbooks/general.html.

Multiyear estimates are likely to confuse some data users, in part because of their statistical properties, and in part because this is a new product from the Census Bureau. The ACS will provide all states and communities that have at least 65,000 residents with single-year estimates of demographic, housing, social, and economic characteristics—a boon to government agencies that need to budget and plan for public services like transportation, medical care, and schools. For geographic areas with smaller populations, the one-year supplemental estimates will provide even greater opportunities. For very small communities, several years of data will be pooled together to create reliable five-year estimates.

Multiyear estimates should, in general, be used when single-year estimates have large CVs or when the precision of the estimates is more important than the currency of the data. Multiyear estimates should also be used when analyzing data for smaller geographies and smaller population subgroups in larger geographies. Multiyear estimates are also of value when examining change over non-overlapping time periods and for smoothing data trends over time.

Single-year estimates should, in general, be used for larger geographies and populations when currency is more important than the precision of the estimates. Single-year estimates should be used to examine year-to-year change for estimates with small CVs. Given the availability of a single-year estimate, calculating the CV provides useful information to determine if the single-year estimate should be used. For areas believed to be experiencing rapid changes in a characteristic, single-year estimates should generally be used rather than multiyear estimates as long as the CV for the single-year estimate is reasonable for the specific usage.

Local area variations may occur due to rapidly occurring changes. Multiyear estimates will tend to be insensitive to such changes when they first occur. Single-year estimates, if associated with sufficiently small CVs, can be very valuable in identifying and studying such phenomena.

Data users also need to use caution in looking at trends involving income or other measures that are adjusted for inflation, such as rental costs, home values, and energy costs. Note that inflation adjustment is based on a national-level consumer price index: it does not adjust for differences in costs of living across different geographic areas.

Section 10 of the *ACS General Handbook* provides information on the adjustment of single-year and multiyear ACS estimates for inflation: https://www.census.gov/programs-surveys/acs/guidance/handbooks/general.html.

Margin of Error

All data that are based on samples, such as the ACS and the census long-form samples, include a range of uncertainty. Two broad types of error can occur: sampling error and nonsampling error. Nonsampling errors can result from mistakes in how the data are reported or coded, problems in the sampling frame or survey questionnaires, or problems related to nonresponse or interviewer bias. The Census Bureau tries to minimize nonsampling errors by using trained interviewers and by carefully reviewing the survey's sampling methods, data processing techniques, and questionnaire design.

Section 7 of the *ACS General Handbook* includes a more detailed description of different types of errors in the ACS and other measures of ACS quality: https://www.census.gov/programs-surveys/acs/guidance/handbooks/general.html.

Sampling error occurs when data are based on a sample of a population rather than the full population. Sampling error is easier to measure than nonsampling error and can be used to assess the statistical reliability of survey data. For any given area, the larger the sample and the more months included in the data, the greater the confidence in the estimate. The Census Bureau reports the 90-percent confidence interval on all ACS estimates produced since 2005. Beginning with the release of the 2006 ACS data, *margins of error* (MOE) are now provided for every ACS estimate. Ninety percent confidence intervals define a range expected to contain the *true* value of an estimate with a level of confidence of 90 percent. Margins of error are easily converted into these confidence ranges. By adding and subtracting the margin of error from the point estimate, we can calculate the 90-percent confidence interval for an estimate. Therefore, we can be 90 percent confident that the true number falls between the lower-bound interval and the upper-bound interval.

Detailed information about sampling error and instructions for calculating confidence intervals and margins of error are included in Section 7 of the *ACS General Handbook*. The margin of error around an estimate is important because it helps one draw conclusions about the data. Small differences between two estimates may not be statistically significant if the confidence intervals of those estimates overlap. However, the Census Bureau cautions data users not to rely on overlapping confidence intervals as a test for statistical significance, because this method will not always produce accurate results. Instead, the Census Bureau recommends following the detailed instructions for conducting statistical significance tests in Section 7 of the *ACS General Handbook*.

In some cases, data users will need to construct custom ACS estimates by combining data across multiple geographic areas or population subgroups or it may be necessary to derive a new percentage, proportion, or ratio from published ACS data. In such cases, additional calculations are needed to produce confidence intervals and margins of error for the derived estimates. Section 8 of the *ACS General Handbook* provides detailed instructions on how to make these calculations. Note that these error measures do not tell us about the magnitude of nonsampling errors.

Accessing ACS Data Online

All ACS data are available through the Census Bureau's Data Explorer website at https://data.census.gov/. From the home page, there is a search box that leads to both general and advanced searches, as well as links to lists of tables and maps that can be modified to user preference.

The various ACS data products are described below.

- **Geographic comparison tables.** Those interested in geographic comparisons for areas other than states may be interested in the *geographic comparison tables*, which allow comparison of ACS data across a variety of geographic areas, including metropolitan areas, cities, counties, and congressional districts.
- **Subject tables.** These are similar to *data profiles* but are specific to a more detailed characteristic or topic (e.g., employment, education, and income). *Subject tables* provide pre-tabulated numbers and percentages for a wide variety of topics, often available separately by age (60 and over and 65 and over), gender, or race/ethnicity.
- **Selected population profiles.** The most detailed race/ethnic data are available through the *selected population profiles*, which provide summary tables separately for more than 400 detailed race, ethnic, tribal, ancestry, and country of birth groups.
- **Comparison profiles.** The *comparison profiles* show data side-by-side from multiple years, indicating where there is a statistically significant difference between the two sets of estimates. Comparison profiles are only available for 1-year estimates.
- **Thematic maps.** The *thematic maps* provide graphic displays of the data available through the various tables. Different shades of color are used to display variations in the data across geographic areas. Data users can also highlight areas with statistically different values from a selected state, county, or metropolitan area of interest. If a mapping option is available, it will display as an option when you view a table.

The ACS data are complex and cover a broad range of topics and geographic areas. Because this is a relatively new survey, many people do not fully understand how to interpret and use the ACS data. The key points are summarized below.

- Use caution in comparing ACS data with data from the decennial census or other sources. Every survey uses different methods, which could affect the comparability of the numbers. Some characteristics in the ACS, such as income, reflect a different reference period from the traditional long-form census.
- The ACS was designed to provide estimates of the characteristics of the population, not to provide counts of the population in different geographic areas or population subgroups. However, counts of the population are often what is required by grant applications and researchers and is primarily what is provided in this publication.
- Be careful in drawing conclusions about small differences between two estimates because they may not be statistically different. Statistical testing should always be considered based on the sensitivity of conclusions to differences in the data results. Users can check the table on Census Explorer to review the margin of error.
- Data users need to be careful not to interpret annual fluctuations in the data as long-term trends. Again, statistical testing is necessary to determine if annual fluctuations are real or merely a result of the sample.
- Use caution in comparing data from 2006 and later surveys with data from the 2000–2005 surveys. Unlike earlier surveys, the 2006 and later ACS surveys include samples of the population living in group quarters (e.g., college dorms and nursing homes), so the data may not be comparable, especially for young adults and the elderly, who are more likely than other age groups to be living in group quarters facilities.
- The questionnaire series to define disability changed in 2008 making it impossible to compare disability status for periods before that date.
- Data users should not interpret or refer to multi-year period estimates as estimates of the middle year or last year in the series. For example, a 2013–2017 estimate is not a "2015 average."
- Data users should always be consistent in comparing similar period estimates over time or between geographic areas. Compare 1-year to 1-year, 3-year to 3-year and 5-year to 5-year estimates. Since geographic areas of different population size have different period estimates available, always make comparisons using the same period estimate. Do not compare a 1-year estimate for a large population size area to a 5-year estimate for a small area or census tract.
- Due to reductions in funding authorization for data products, the Census Bureau has eliminated the 3-year ACS estimates. The last set of 3-year estimates covered the period 2011–2013.
- Data users should *not* rely on overlapping confidence intervals as a test for statistical significance because this method will not always provide an accurate result.

PART A

Who

Age, Race/Ethnicity, and Household Structure

Who: Age, Race/Ethnicity, and Household Structure

Every 10 years, the census measures changes in the American population: shifts in race and ethnic groups, changing age patterns, migration among cities and regions, and changes in the predominant household structures. In the years between censuses, the American Community Survey is used to discover the details of these changes and the changes that are occurring in the new decade. In earlier decades, these detailed characteristics could not be updated until the next decennial census. The ACS provides annual detailed information about states, metropolitan areas, and other geographic entities with populations of 65,000 or more. For smaller areas with fewer than 20,000 residents, five-year estimates are available, providing a regular stream of detailed social, housing, and economic characteristics for demographic groups. The number of counties and cities included in this publication is limited, as all have populations of 65,000 or more.

One of the American Community Survey's most valuable aspects is that it allows users to compare their city or town against other local areas or against the United States. It highlights the differences among small areas within the United States. National trends are not mirrored in every community. Some places are changing even faster than the national picture; others are lagging or even going in a different direction. It is important for people to know how their locality fits into the national picture. These tables offer Americans information needed to compare various areas to see how they differ and how they are similar.

Population

Although the ACS has replaced the census long form as the key source of detailed social and economic characteristics, the official population estimates are still developed through the Census Bureau's Population Estimates Program. After the 2010 census, all ACS estimates were adjusted to reflect the new population count. The ACS single-year estimates are based on the official total population estimates from the Population Estimates Program. For states, metropolitan areas, and counties, the ACS total population is usually the same as the official population estimate, but the city populations often differ because of weighting and adjustments. The ACS includes census designated places (CDPs)—and we include them in this book—but they are not included in the Population Estimates Program.

Ten states had populations of 10 million or more in 2023, led by California with nearly 40 million and Texas with just over 30 million. More than half of the nation's population lived in these 10 states. Another five states and the District of Columbia had populations of less than 1 million, representing 1.3 percent of the nation's population. Between 2010 and 2023, the United States' population increased 8.3 percent. Idaho, Utah, and Texas each grew by more than 20 percent, followed closely by Florida (19.9 percent). Due to a boom in oil extraction, North Dakota's population grew by 16.2 percent. The populations of Nevada, Colorado, South Carolina, Arizona, and Washington also increased by more than 15 percent. Overall, 18 states and the District of Columbia had population growth above the national average. Four states had population growth of less than two percent, and three states lost population. West Virginia had the largest decrease at 4.5 percent.

Nearly 37 percent of the U.S. population resided in the 75 most populous counties in 2023. Forty-eight of these counties had populations exceeding 1 million. These 45 large counties were home to just over 29 percent of Americans. Los Angeles County was, by far, the most populous county in the nation, with nearly 10 million residents. New York City consists of five counties which together total nearly 8 million people. Four of these counties are in the top 30.

Almost 292 million people, or about 86 percent of the population, lived in the nation's 393 metropolitan statistical areas (including those in Puerto Rico) in 2023. Nearly one-third of the U.S. population resided in the 15 most populous metropolitan areas, those with 4 million people or more. Fifty-five metropolitan areas had populations of 1 million or more. Thirty metropolitan areas had growth rates of 34 percent or more between 2010 and 2023. About 45 percent of the metropolitan areas had growth rates exceeding the national rate of 8.3 percent, while 83 areas lost population. Six metropolitan areas with over a million residents experienced population losses—San Juan-Bayamón-Caguas, Puerto Rico (17.7 percent Hartford-West Hartford-East Hartford, Connecticut (5.1 percent); Chicago-Naperville-Elgin, IL-IN (2.2 percent); St. Louis, MO-IL (0.7 percent); Los Angeles-Long Beach-Anaheim, California (0.4 percent); and Rochester, New York (0.2 percent).

Thirty-eight cities had populations of 500,000 or more in 2023, including 9 with populations of 1 million or more. With more than 8 million people, New York was, by far, the largest city. Los Angeles was second, with nearly 4 million people, and Chicago's nearly 2.7 million people still outnumbered the fast-growing Houston's 2.3 million.

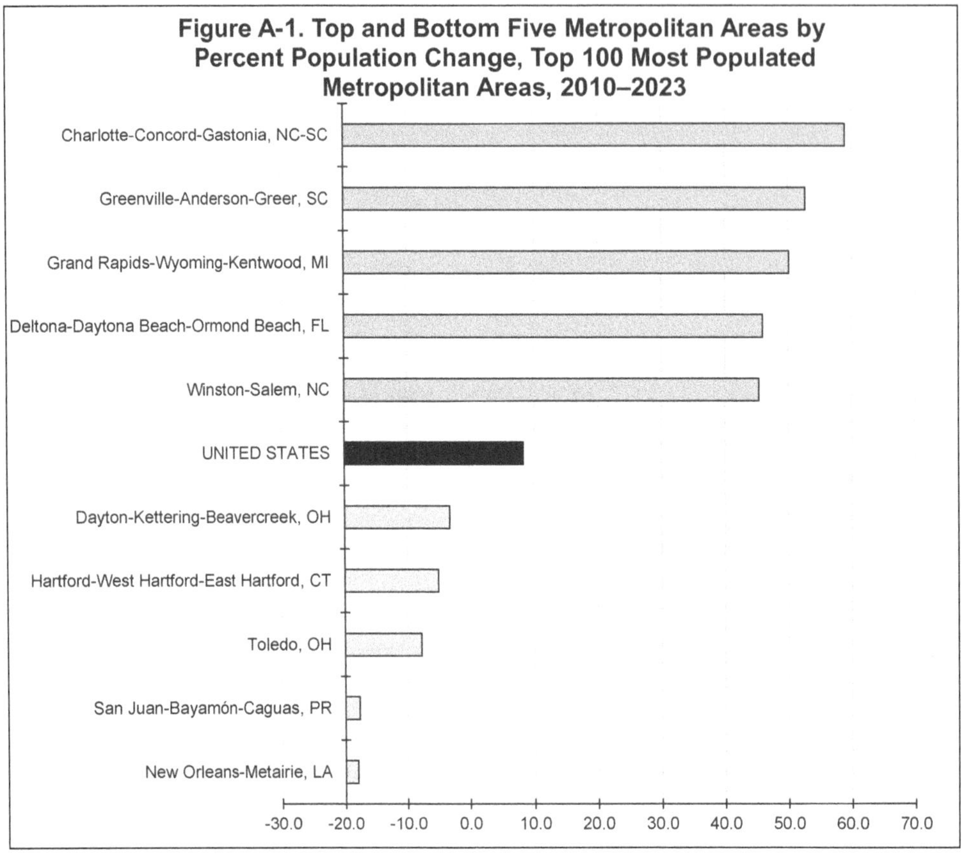

Age

In 2023, the United States' median age was 39.2 years, with half of the people older and half the people younger. Eighteen states had median ages of 40 or higher, topped by Maine at 44.9 years. Utah had the lowest median age, at 32.3 years. Only Utah and the District of Columbia had median ages lower than 35 years. Nearly 30 percent of Utah's population was under age 18, compared with 21.7 percent for the nation as a whole. At the other extreme, only about 18.6 percent of the District of Columbia's population was under 18 years, despite its relatively low median age of 34.9. Over 38 percent of the District of Columbia's population was in the 25- to 44-year old age group, well above the national level of 26.9 percent. In Maine, Vermont, New Hampshire, Rhode Island, the District of Columbia, Massachusetts, Florida, Oregon, and West Virginia, children under 18 years old accounted for less than 20 percent of the population. In Rhode Island, Maryland, Virginia, Georgia, Wisconsin, the District of Columbia, Idaho, New Jersey, Nebraska, and Puerto Rico, over 20 percent of residents were 65 years or older, and 18 other states had levels above the national proportion of 17.7 percent. In Hawaii and Puerto Rico, 2.5 percent or more of the population was 85 years old and over, while only Alaska had less than 1.2 percent in that age group.

Four metropolitan areas had more than 30 percent residents under the age of 18. Three were located in Texas and one was located in Utah. Nine metropolitan areas had at least one in three residents who were over age 65; seven of them in Florida, one in Arizona; and one in Massachusetts. By far, the highest proportion was in Wildwood-The Villages, Florida, where 57.2 percent of residents were age 65 or older.

Eighteen counties had median ages of 50 or older. The most populous was Sarasota County, Florida, with nearly 470,000 residents; Charlotte County, Florida; Mohave County, Arizona; Barnstable County, Massachusetts; Yavapai County, Arizona; Sussex County, Delaware; and Collier County, Florida, all had more than 200,000 residents. Two counties in Utah and one county in Kansas had median ages under 27. In 8 counties, at least 30 percent of the population was under age 18; 5 of these counties were in Texas, 2 were in Utah, and 1 was in Washington.

The median age in 5 of the 649 cities surveyed was 50 years or more. All of these cities were located in Florida. In 2023, 22 cities had 25 percent or more of their populations consisting of people 65 years and older. Nationally, this age group accounted for 17.7 percent of the population. In one city surveyed, more than half of the residents were under 18 years old: Lakewood,

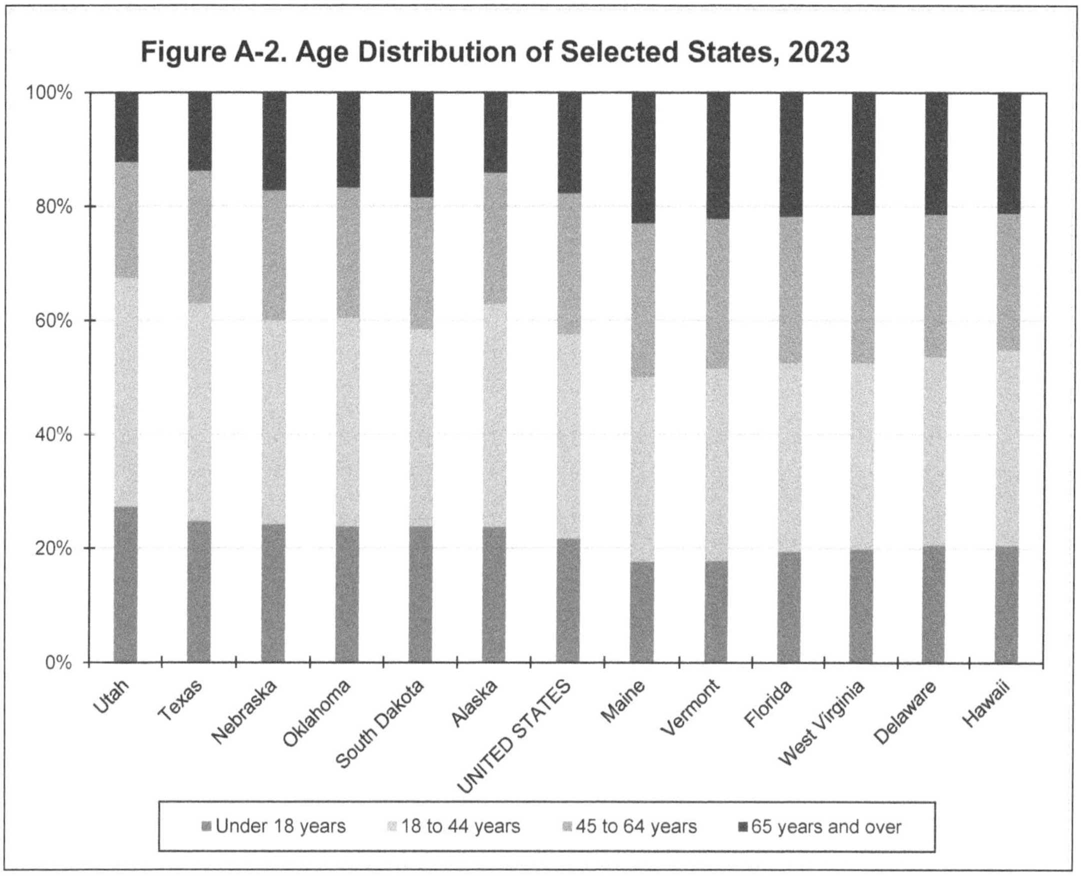

New Jersey, which has large Orthodox Jewish communities. Seventeen cities had between 30 and 37 percent of their populations under 18, with the majority in Utah, California, and Texas.

The working-age population is generally considered to include people between the ages of 16 and 64, but another definition includes only ages 25 to 64 to exclude the many 18- to 24-year-olds who are in school or training situations. Nationally, 51.5 percent of the population was in this latter category. Nineteen surveyed cities had proportions of working-age population that exceeded 60 percent. In 10 cities, fewer than 40 percent of residents were between the ages of 25 and 64. These were mostly retirement communities and college towns.

Race/Ethnicity

Probably the most visible place-based demographic difference is in racial and ethnic composition. Seen from afar, the U.S. population may be a melting pot, but at close range, it varies widely. For example, nearly 90 percent of the population of Maine, Vermont, and West Virginia was non-Hispanic White in 2023. In contrast, Georgia, Maryland, Nevada, Texas, New Mexico, California, Hawaii, and the District of Columbia are all majority minority states, in which non-Hispanic Whites made up less than 50 percent of their populations. Almost half of the District of Columbia's residents were Black. Over 20 percent of Alaskan residents were American Indian or Alaska Native alone or in combination. More than four in five Hawaiian residents were Asian, Native Hawaiian, or Other Pacific Islander. In New Mexico, just under half of the population was Hispanic or Latino.

Seventeen metropolitan areas—all relatively small—had populations consisting of 95 percent or more of White alone or in combination (including both Hispanic and non-Hispanic) in 2023. In the Honolulu metropolitan area, about 87 percent of the population identified as Asian, Native Hawaiian, or Other Pacific Islander[1]. Albany, Georgia, was a majority Black metropolitan area, with more than half of its population identifying as Black alone or in combination. In another 12 metropolitan areas—all in the South—more than 40 percent of the residents were Black. The Memphis, TN-MS-AR, metropolitan area was the only one with more than 1 million residents. Hispanic or Latino residents make up a majority in 20 metropolitan areas outside of Puerto Rico, the largest of which are Riverside-San Bernardino-Ontario, California, and San Antonio-New Braunfels, Texas.[2] In another 11 metropolitan areas, the proportion of Hispanic or

[1] There is some double counting of persons who identified with both groups ("Asian alone or in combination" and "Native Hawaiian or Pacific Islander alone or in combination").

[2] Hispanic or Latino persons may be of any race. Most self-identify as "White" or "some other race."

Figure A-3. Cities and Places with the Highest Combined Populations of Asians and Native Hawaiian, or Pacific Islanders, 2023

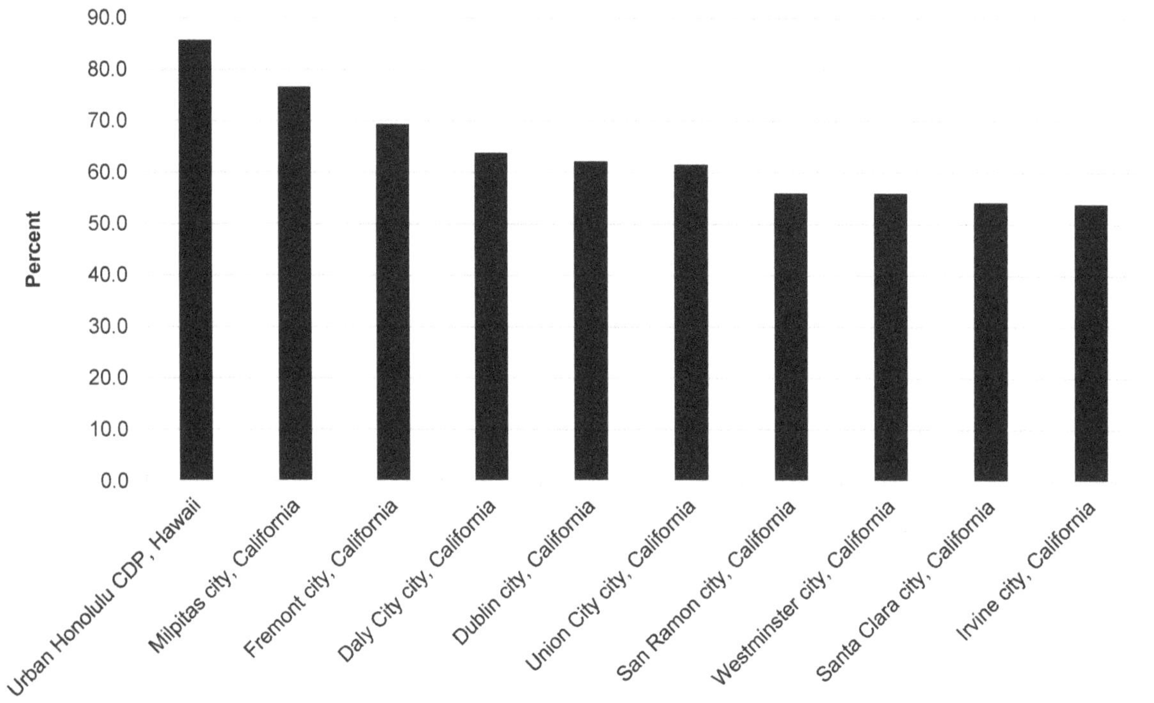

Latino residents is between 40 and 50 percent. These include Los Angeles-Long Beach-Anaheim, California, and Miami-Fort Lauderdale-Pompano Beach, Florida.

Thirty-four of the cities surveyed in 2023 had White populations of 90 percent or higher. Outside of Puerto Rico, there were 6 cities where more than 90 percent of the residents identified as Hispanic or Latino; these were in California, Texas, and Florida. In four cities, more than 80 percent of residents were Black or African American alone. Detroit's population was 78.5 percent Black or African American, the highest level among the largest cities. In six cities—one in Hawaii and five in California—more than 60 percent of residents were Asian or Native Hawaiian or Other Pacific Islander.

Foreign-Born Populations and Foreign Languages

Nationally, 14.3 percent of the population was foreign born in 2023. Over 27 percent of California's population was foreign born, and New York, New Jersey, and Florida had levels at 22 percent or more. West Virginia had the lowest proportion of foreign-born residents at 1.8 percent, while Mississippi and Montana both had levels below three percent.

In 15 counties, one-third or more of the residents were foreign born. Ten of these counties had more than a million residents; the percentage of foreign-born residents were led by Miami-Dade County, Florida, with 54. percent, and Queens County, New York, with 48.4 percent. Thirty-three metropolitan areas had foreign-born populations of 20 percent or more. The Miami and San Jose metropolitan areas had the highest proportions, both at more than 40 percent, and just under one-third of residents in Los Angeles and San Francisco were foreign born.

Of the 649 cities surveyed for 2023, 359 had foreign-born proportions that exceeded the U.S. average. Ten cities had majority foreign-born residents. More than two-thirds of the residents of Hialeah, Florida, and Doral, Florida, were foreign born.

Over one in five American households spoke a language other than English at home (in addition to or instead of English). California had the highest proportion—approximately 47 percent of households—while between 35 and 40 percent of households in New Mexico, Texas, and New Jersey spoke another language at home. Spanish-speaking households were most prevalent in Texas (29.6 percent), New Mexico (29.0 percent), California (27.3 percent), and Florida (22.8 percent). In

Figure A-4. Foreign-Born U.S. Residents, by County, 2023

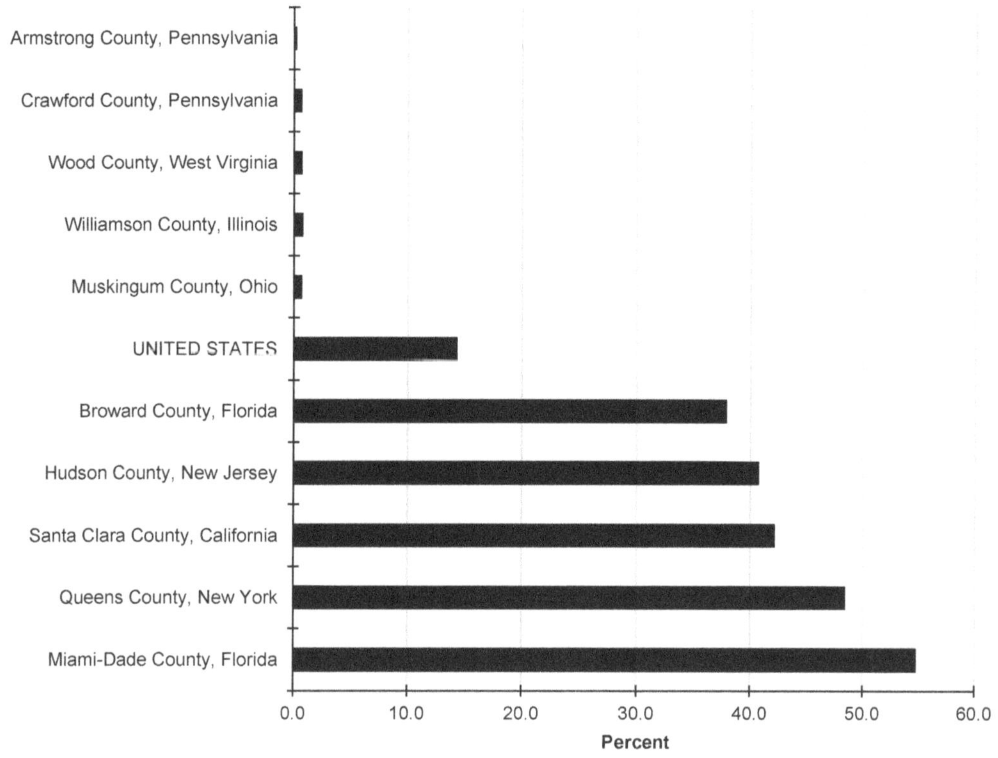

Hawaii, 28.6 percent of households spoke languages other than English and Spanish, and 19.7 percent of California households were in this group. In approximately 8.5 percent of California households, 8.1 percent of New York households, 7.7 percent of New Jersey households, and 7.0 percent of Florida households, no adult spoke English well. West Virginia and Mississippi had the lowest proportions of households speaking a language other than English, both under 6 percent.

Household Structure

Places that differ from the national age portrait also differ from the nation's household portrait. Almost two-thirds of the nation's households were family households in 2023 (people related by birth, marriage, or adoption), and 46.8 percent of all households were married-couple family households. Nonfamily households included people living alone or with unrelated people. In some areas, people lived predominantly in married-couple households, while others were dominated by male- and female-headed family households (no spouse present) or by nonfamily households.

Approximately 36 percent of the nation's households are made up of nonfamily households—people living alone, or with other, unrelated adults. Thirty states, Puerto Rico, and the District of Columbia had proportions of nonfamily households that exceeded this national level. Nearly 60 percent of the District of Columbia's households were nonfamily households, many of them one-person households. Nationally, 28.8 percent of households consisted of a person living alone.

Although there were large numbers of single-person households in every age group, Puerto Rico, West Virginia, New Mexico, and Vermont had the highest proportions of persons over 65 years old living alone (all at or above 13.5 percent).

About 7.2 percent of householders were unmarried partner couples, ranging from 4.6 percent in Mississippi to 9.7 percent in Maine and 10.6 percent in Puerto Rico. Same-sex unmarried couples comprised 0.4 percent of all households, while married same-sex couples were estimated to be about 0.6 percent of all households in 2023.

In the United States, over 34 percent of adults had never married by 2023. The District of Columbia had the highest proportion of never-married residents at 54.4 percent, and 15 states and Puerto Rico had rates above the national level, led by New York, California, and Massachusetts, all at or above 38 percent. Utah and Idaho had the highest percentages of currently married residents, at 56.1 and 55.9 percent, respectively. Nationally, just under half of all persons are currently married, but 18 states, Puerto Rico, and the District of Columbia have lower

Figure A-5. Percent Distribution of Household Types, United States, 2023

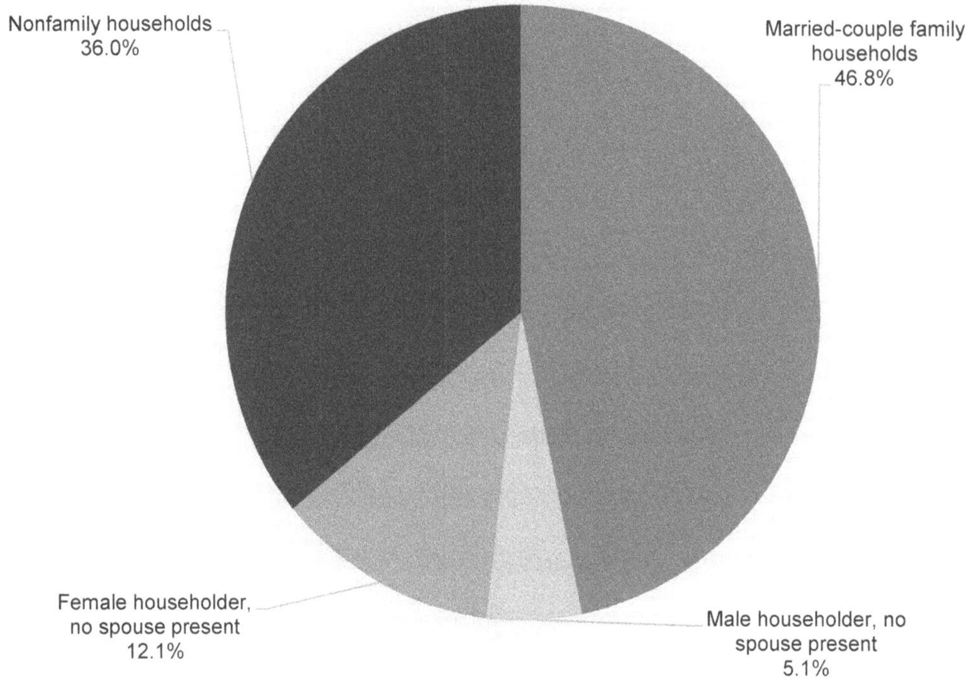

proportions. West Virginia, New Mexico, and Nevada had the highest proportions of divorced residents among states, with all at or exceeding 13 percent, while more than 12 percent of residents were divorced in 8 more states. New York, New Jersey, California, and Utah had the lowest proportions of divorced individuals, all under 9 percent. Puerto Rico had a divorce rate of 14.3 percent.

In four metropolitan areas in the area excluding Puerto Rico, 20 percent or more of households were female-headed families, compared with 12.1 percent for the nation as a whole. Nationally, 46.8 percent of households were married-couple families. In four metropolitan areas, all in Utah and Idaho, married-couple families equaled or exceeded 60 percent of households. The proportion was less than 40 percent in 28 metropolitan areas outside Puerto Rico, some with large student populations.

Among the states in 2023, Utah had the highest average household size—2.88 persons per household, followed by Hawaii and California with 2.82 and 2.78 persons per household, respectively. The District of Columbia (1.92 persons per household), Maine (2.20 persons per household), and North Dakota and Vermont (2.23 persons per household each) had the lowest average household sizes. The national average was 2.49 persons per household.

Approximately 65 percent of households with children were married-couple family households. Utah had the highest proportion—78.1 percent—and the District of Columbia had the lowest proportion (excluding Puerto Rico), 52.6 percent. Just under 29 percent of American households included children under 18 years old in 2023, with proportions ranging from 37.2 percent in Utah and 33.6 percent in Texas to 19.9 percent in the District of Columbia, 21.9 percent in Vermont, and 23.1 percent in Maine.

Nationally, 42.1 percent of households included someone 60 years old or older in 2023. Over half of the states (plus Puerto Rico at 52.6 percent) had higher proportions, led by Hawaii, Delaware, Florida, West Virginia, Vermont, Maine, and New Hampshire, all with more than 46 percent. In the District of Columbia and Utah, less than one-third of households included someone over 60 years of age. In 97 of the counties surveyed in 2023, more than half of the households included someone age 60 years or over, led by Sumter County, Florida, where 82.4 percent of the households included this age group. Arlington County, Virginia; Utah County, Utah; and

Riley County, Kansas, counted fewer than 26 percent of their households with people 60 years old or older. These counties generally have large student and military populations. Among the 75 largest cities, only 5 exceed the national level of 42.1 percent of households with persons age 60 or over: San Juan, Puerto Rico (51.8 percent); Honolulu, Hawaii (48.0 percent); Henderson, Nevada (44.0 percent); New Orleans, Louisiana (43.1 percent); and Mesa, Arizona (43.0 percent). In Austin, Texas, only 22.9 percent of households included this older age group, while Seattle, Washington; Minneapolis, Minnesota; Denver, Colorado; and Washington, District of Columbia, all had levels below 28 percent.

State Rankings, 2023

Selected Rankings

Population rank	State	Total population, [A-1, col 1]	Percent change rank	State	Percent change, 2010–2023 [A-1, col 2]	Percent White alone, not Hispanic or Latino rank	State	Percent White alone, not Hispanic or Latino [A-1, col 11]
	UNITED STATES	334,914,896		**UNITED STATES**	8.3		**UNITED STATES**	57.1
1	California	38,965,193	1	Idaho	25.1	1	Maine	89.5
2	Texas	30,503,301	2	Utah	23.2	2	West Virginia	89.4
3	Florida	22,610,726	3	Texas	20.8	3	Vermont	89.3
4	New York	19,571,216	4	Florida	19.9	4	New Hampshire	86.5
5	Pennsylvania	12,961,683	5	Nevada	18.1	5	Montana	83.3
6	Illinois	12,549,689	6	Colorado	16.4	6	Iowa	82.4
7	Ohio	11,785,935	7	North Dakota	16.2	7	Kentucky	81.5
8	Georgia	11,029,227	8	South Carolina	15.9	7	North Dakota	81.5
9	North Carolina	10,835,491	8	Arizona	15.9	9	Wyoming	81.3
10	Michigan	10,037,261	8	Washington	15.9	10	South Dakota	79.4
11	New Jersey	9,290,841	11	Delaware	14.7	11	Wisconsin	78.4
12	Virginia	8,715,698	12	Montana	14.4	11	Idaho	78.4
13	Washington	7,812,880	13	Georgia	13.5	13	Missouri	76.5
14	Arizona	7,431,344	14	North Carolina	13.3	14	Ohio	75.6
15	Tennessee	7,126,489	15	South Dakota	12.6	14	Minnesota	75.6
16	Massachusetts	7,001,399	16	District of Columbia	12.2	16	Nebraska	75.2
17	Indiana	6,862,199	17	Tennessee	12.1	17	Indiana	75.1
18	Missouri	6,196,156	18	Oregon	10.3	18	Utah	74.5
19	Maryland	6,180,253	19	Virginia	8.6	19	Kansas	72.7
20	Wisconsin	5,910,955	20	Nebraska	8.1	19	Pennsylvania	72.7
21	Colorado	5,877,610	20	Minnesota	8.1	21	Michigan	72.3
22	Minnesota	5,737,915	22	Oklahoma	7.8	22	Tennessee	71.1
23	South Carolina	5,373,555	23	Maryland	6.8	23	Oregon	70.8
24	Alabama	5,108,468	24	Alabama	6.7	24	Rhode Island	67.7
25	Louisiana	4,573,749	24	Massachusetts	6.7	25	Arkansas	67.1
26	Kentucky	4,526,154	26	New Hampshire	6.5	26	Massachusetts	65.9
27	Oregon	4,233,358	27	Indiana	5.7	27	Colorado	64.5
28	Oklahoma	4,053,824	28	New Jersey	5.5	28	Alabama	63.3
29	Connecticut	3,617,176	29	Hawaii	5.2	29	Washington	62.4
30	Utah	3,417,734	29	Maine	5.2	30	South Carolina	61.9
31	Iowa	3,207,004	31	Iowa	5.1	31	Oklahoma	61.7
32	Nevada	3,194,176	32	Arkansas	5.0	32	Connecticut	61.4
33	Arkansas	3,067,732	33	California	4.4	33	North Carolina	59.8
34	Kansas	2,940,547	34	Rhode Island	4.1	34	Virginia	58.1
35	Mississippi	2,939,690	34	Kentucky	4.1	35	Delaware	58.0
36	New Mexico	2,114,371	36	Wisconsin	3.9	36	Illinois	57.9
37	Nebraska	1,978,379	37	Wyoming	3.5	37	Alaska	57.7
38	Idaho	1,964,726	37	Vermont	3.5	38	Louisiana	55.7
39	West Virginia	1,770,071	39	Missouri	3.3	39	Mississippi	55.1
40	Hawaii	1,435,138	40	Kansas	2.9	40	New York	52.8
41	New Hampshire	1,402,054	41	Alaska	2.7	41	Arizona	52.3
42	Maine	1,395,722	42	New Mexico	2.4	42	New Jersey	50.6
43	Montana	1,132,812	43	Ohio	2.1	43	Florida	50.3
44	Rhode Island	1,095,962	44	Pennsylvania	2.0	44	Georgia	48.7
45	Delaware	1,031,890	45	Michigan	1.6	45	Maryland	46.3
46	South Dakota	919,318	46	Connecticut	1.1	46	Nevada	44.4
47	North Dakota	783,926	47	New York	0.9	47	Texas	38.7
48	Alaska	733,406	48	Louisiana	0.6	48	District of Columbia	37.1
49	District of Columbia	678,972	49	Mississippi	-1.0	49	New Mexico	35.9
50	Vermont	647,464	50	Illinois	-2.3	50	California	33.3
51	Wyoming	584,057	51	West Virginia	-4.5	51	Hawaii	20.9

State Rankings, 2023

Selected Rankings

Percent Black or African American rank	State	Percent Black or African American alone or in combination [A-1, col 4]	Percent American Indian/ Alaska Native rank	State	Percent American Indian/ Alaska Native alone or in combination [A-1, col 5]	Percent Asian rank	State	Percent Asian alone or in combination [A-1, col 6]
	UNITED STATES	19.4		**UNITED STATES**	39.2		**UNITED STATES**	2.49
1	New Mexico	48.6	1	Maine	44.9	1	Utah	2.88
2	California	40.4	2	Vermont	43.7	2	Hawaii	2.82
3	Texas	39.8	3	New Hampshire	43.4	3	California	2.78
4	Arizona	31.6	4	Florida	42.8	4	Texas	2.66
5	Nevada	29.9	4	West Virginia	42.8	5	Idaho	2.61
6	Florida	27.4	6	Delaware	42.0	6	Georgia	2.60
7	Colorado	22.7	7	Connecticut	41.5	7	Nevada	2.58
7	New Jersey	22.7	8	Hawaii	41.4	7	New Jersey	2.58
9	New York	19.8	9	Pennsylvania	41.1	9	Alaska	2.54
10	Illinois	19.0	10	Rhode Island	40.8	9	Maryland	2.54
11	Connecticut	18.6	11	Oregon	40.7	11	Arizona	2.50
12	Rhode Island	18.0	12	Montana	40.6	12	Virginia	2.49
13	Utah	16.0	13	Michigan	40.5	13	Oklahoma	2.48
14	Oregon	14.9	13	South Carolina	40.5	14	Florida	2.47
15	Washington	14.6	13	Wisconsin	40.5	14	Washington	2.47
16	Idaho	13.8	16	New Jersey	40.4	16	Delaware	2.45
17	Kansas	13.7	17	Massachusetts	40.3	17	Connecticut	2.44
18	Massachusetts	13.5	18	New York	40.2	17	Mississippi	2.44
19	Nebraska	12.9	19	New Mexico	39.9	19	Indiana	2.43
19	Oklahoma	12.9	19	Ohio	39.9	19	Louisiana	2.43
21	Maryland	12.6	21	Maryland	39.8	19	New York	2.43
22	District of Columbia	12.0	22	Alabama	39.6	22	Alabama	2.42
23	North Carolina	11.4	23	Illinois	39.5	22	Arkansas	2.42
24	Virginia	11.1	24	Nevada	39.4	22	Illinois	2.42
24	Delaware	11.1	24	North Carolina	39.4	22	New Mexico	2.42
24	Georgia	11.1	26	Arizona	39.3	22	Tennessee	2.42
27	Wyoming	10.8	26	Mississippi	39.3	27	Massachusetts	2.41
28	Hawaii	10.1	26	Missouri	39.3	28	Kansas	2.40
29	Arkansas	9.1	26	Virginia	39.3	28	North Carolina	2.40
30	Pennsylvania	8.9	26	Wyoming	39.3	28	South Carolina	2.40
31	Indiana	8.7	31	Kentucky	39.2	31	Michigan	2.39
32	Wisconsin	8.1	32	Iowa	39.1	31	Minnesota	2.39
33	Tennessee	7.5	32	Minnesota	39.1	31	New Hampshire	2.39
33	Alaska	7.5	32	Tennessee	39.1	34	Kentucky	2.38
35	South Carolina	7.4	35	Arkansas	38.9	35	Colorado	2.37
36	Iowa	7.3	36	Louisiana	38.7	35	Nebraska	2.37
37	Louisiana	7.1	37	Washington	38.6	35	Rhode Island	2.37
38	Minnesota	6.4	38	South Dakota	38.5	38	Missouri	2.36
39	Michigan	6.0	39	Indiana	38.3	38	Oregon	2.36
40	Alabama	5.7	40	California	38.2	40	Pennsylvania	2.35
41	Missouri	5.2	41	Colorado	37.9	41	Ohio	2.34
42	South Dakota	5.1	41	Georgia	37.9	41	South Dakota	2.34
43	North Dakota	4.9	41	Kansas	37.9	43	Iowa	2.33
43	Kentucky	4.9	44	Idaho	37.8	43	Montana	2.33
45	Ohio	4.8	45	Nebraska	37.4	45	West Virginia	2.31
46	New Hampshire	4.7	46	Oklahoma	37.1	45	Wisconsin	2.31
47	Montana	4.6	47	Alaska	36.5	47	Wyoming	2.30
48	Mississippi	3.7	48	North Dakota	36.3	48	North Dakota	2.23
49	Vermont	2.5	49	Texas	35.9	48	Vermont	2.23
50	Maine	2.2	50	District of Columbia	34.9	50	Maine	2.20
51	West Virginia	2.1	51	Utah	32.3	51	District of Columbia	1.92

State Rankings, 2023

Selected Rankings

Never married rank	State	Percent never married [A-1, col 33]	Now married (includes separated) rank	State	Percent now married (includes separated) [A-1, col 34]	Divorced rank	State	Percent divorced [A-1, col 36]
	UNITED STATES	34.4		**UNITED STATES**	49.8		**UNITED STATES**	10.4
1	District of Columbia	54.4	1	Utah	56.1	1	West Virginia	13.1
2	New York	38.6	2	Idaho	55.9	1	New Mexico	13.1
3	California	38.4	3	Wyoming	54.6	3	Nevada	13.0
4	Massachusetts	38.0	4	Nebraska	53.5	4	Oklahoma	12.6
5	Rhode Island	36.8	5	Kansas	52.7	4	Kentucky	12.6
6	Illinois	36.4	6	Montana	52.6	4	Maine	12.6
6	Maryland	36.4	6	Iowa	52.6	7	Oregon	12.3
8	Louisiana	36.1	8	New Hampshire	52.5	8	Florida	12.2
8	New Mexico	36.1	9	Maine	52.3	8	Arkansas	12.2
10	Connecticut	35.8	10	South Dakota	52.1	10	Montana	12.1
11	Nevada	35.6	11	Colorado	51.9	10	Indiana	12.1
12	Georgia	35.3	12	Minnesota	51.8	12	Alabama	11.8
13	New Jersey	34.9	13	Virginia	51.7	13	Tennessee	11.7
14	Pennsylvania	34.6	13	Washington	51.7	13	Missouri	11.7
15	Alaska	34.5	15	North Dakota	51.6	13	Mississippi	11.7
16	Arizona	34.3	16	South Carolina	51.5	16	Ohio	11.6
17	Michigan	34.2	17	Kentucky	51.3	16	Alaska	11.6
17	Texas	34.2	17	Texas	51.3	16	New Hampshire	11.6
19	Hawaii	33.9	17	New Jersey	51.3	19	Louisiana	11.5
20	Mississippi	33.8	20	North Carolina	51.2	20	Vermont	11.4
20	Ohio	33.8	21	Tennessee	50.9	21	Arizona	11.3
20	Wisconsin	33.8	21	Hawaii	50.9	22	Washington	11.2
23	North Dakota	33.5	23	Arkansas	50.7	23	Idaho	11.1
24	Minnesota	33.4	23	Missouri	50.7	24	Michigan	11.0
25	Delaware	33.2	25	Vermont	50.6	24	Rhode Island	11.0
26	Colorado	33.1	26	Wisconsin	50.5	26	Georgia	10.9
26	Virginia	33.1	27	Florida	50.1	26	Colorado	10.9
26	Vermont	33.1	28	Alaska	50.0	28	Kansas	10.8
29	Oregon	32.7	28	Delaware	50.0	29	Delaware	10.7
30	North Carolina	32.6	28	Oklahoma	50.0	30	Wyoming	10.6
30	Washington	32.6	31	Oregon	49.9	31	Wisconsin	10.5
32	Indiana	32.5	31	Alabama	49.9	32	North Carolina	10.4
33	South Dakota	32.2	33	Indiana	49.8	32	Connecticut	10.4
34	South Carolina	32.0	34	West Virginia	49.5	34	Iowa	10.3
35	Alabama	31.7	34	Pennsylvania	49.5	35	South Dakota	10.1
35	Missouri	31.7	36	Michigan	49.1	35	Minnesota	10.1
37	Nebraska	31.5	37	Arizona	49.0	37	South Carolina	10.0
38	Utah	31.4	38	Maryland	48.8	37	Nebraska	10.0
38	Iowa	31.4	39	Georgia	48.7	39	Virginia	9.9
40	Florida	31.3	40	Ohio	48.5	40	North Dakota	9.8
40	Tennessee	31.3	40	Connecticut	48.5	40	Texas	9.8
42	Oklahoma	31.1	40	Illinois	48.5	42	Illinois	9.6
42	Kansas	31.1	43	California	48.2	43	Pennsylvania	9.5
44	Arkansas	30.5	44	Massachusetts	47.8	43	Maryland	9.5
44	New Hampshire	30.5	45	Mississippi	47.5	45	Massachusetts	9.4
46	Montana	29.8	46	New York	47.1	46	Hawaii	9.3
47	Kentucky	29.5	47	Rhode Island	46.5	47	Utah	9.1
48	West Virginia	29.3	48	Nevada	46.4	48	New York	8.8
49	Maine	29.1	49	Louisiana	46.1	49	California	8.7
50	Wyoming	28.5	50	New Mexico	44.9	50	New Jersey	8.4
51	Idaho	28.4	51	District of Columbia	33.9	51	District of Columbia	8.1

State Rankings, 2023

Selected Rankings

Foreign born rank	State	Percent foreign born [A-1, col. 37]	Spanish-speaking households rank	State	Percent Spanish-speaking households [A-1, col. 39]	Limited English-speaking household rank	State	Percent Limited English-speaking household [A-1, col. 41]
	UNITED STATES	14.3		**UNITED STATES**	13.3		**UNITED STATES**	4.4
1	California	27.3	1	Texas	29.6	1	California	8.5
2	New Jersey	24.2	2	New Mexico	29.0	2	New York	8.1
3	New York	23.1	3	California	27.3	3	New Jersey	7.7
4	Florida	22.1	4	Florida	22.8	4	Florida	7.0
5	Nevada	19.2	5	Arizona	19.7	5	Texas	6.8
6	Massachusetts	18.0	5	Nevada	19.7	6	Massachusetts	6.0
7	Texas	17.9	7	New Jersey	17.5	7	Rhode Island	5.4
8	Hawaii	17.8	8	New York	15.1	8	Nevada	5.3
9	Maryland	17.0	9	Connecticut	13.8	8	New Mexico	5.3
10	Connecticut	16.3	10	Utah	13.0	10	Hawaii	5.1
11	Washington	15.5	11	Illinois	12.9	11	Connecticut	5.0
12	Illinois	15.0	12	Rhode Island	12.7	12	Illinois	4.2
13	Rhode Island	14.7	13	Colorado	11.5	13	Maryland	3.9
14	District of Columbia	14.1	14	Massachusetts	10.2	14	Washington	3.7
15	Virginia	13.3	15	Maryland	9.0	15	Arizona	3.4
16	Arizona	13.2	16	Oregon	8.9	16	District of Columbia	3.2
17	Georgia	11.6	17	Washington	8.8	17	Pennsylvania	2.9
18	Delaware	11.2	18	District of Columbia	8.7	18	Georgia	2.8
19	New Mexico	10.2	19	Idaho	8.4	19	Virginia	2.7
20	Colorado	9.6	20	Georgia	8.3	20	Delaware	2.6
20	Oregon	9.6	21	Delaware	8.2	20	Kansas	2.6
22	North Carolina	9.2	21	Kansas	8.2	20	Nebraska	2.6
23	Utah	8.9	23	Nebraska	8.1	23	North Carolina	2.5
24	Minnesota	8.6	24	North Carolina	8.0	23	Oregon	2.5
25	Pennsylvania	8.0	25	Oklahoma	7.8	25	Utah	2.4
26	Nebraska	7.7	25	Virginia	7.8	26	Colorado	2.3
27	Alaska	7.4	27	Pennsylvania	6.3	26	Indiana	2.3
28	Michigan	7.3	28	Arkansas	6.0	26	Minnesota	2.3
29	Kansas	7.1	29	Wyoming	5.9	29	Iowa	2.0
30	New Hampshire	6.8	30	Indiana	5.8	29	Louisiana	2.0
31	Indiana	6.3	31	South Carolina	5.3	29	Michigan	2.0
32	Oklahoma	6.1	32	Louisiana	5.1	29	Oklahoma	2.0
32	Tennessee	6.1	32	Tennessee	5.1	33	Alaska	1.8
34	Iowa	5.9	34	Iowa	4.9	33	Tennessee	1.8
34	South Carolina	5.9	34	Wisconsin	4.9	35	Kentucky	1.7
36	Idaho	5.7	36	Alaska	4.5	36	Arkansas	1.6
37	Arkansas	5.3	36	Minnesota	4.5	36	Idaho	1.6
37	Ohio	5.3	38	Alabama	3.8	36	Ohio	1.6
39	Wisconsin	5.2	39	Kentucky	3.7	39	South Carolina	1.5
40	Louisiana	4.9	40	Michigan	3.5	39	Wisconsin	1.5
41	Missouri	4.8	41	Hawaii	3.4	41	North Dakota	1.4
42	Kentucky	4.5	42	Missouri	3.3	41	South Dakota	1.4
42	Vermont	4.5	43	Ohio	3.2	43	Alabama	1.3
44	South Dakota	4.3	44	South Dakota	3.1	43	New Hampshire	1.3
45	Alabama	4.0	45	New Hampshire	3.0	45	Missouri	1.2
45	North Dakota	4.0	46	Mississippi	2.9	46	Wyoming	1.1
47	Maine	3.8	47	Montana	2.6	47	Maine	0.9
48	Wyoming	3.6	47	North Dakota	2.6	48	Mississippi	0.8
49	Mississippi	2.6	49	Vermont	1.9	49	Vermont	0.7
50	Montana	2.2	50	West Virginia	1.4	50	Montana	0.6
51	West Virginia	1.8	51	Maine	1.0	51	West Virginia	0.4

State Rankings, 2023

Selected Rankings

Married-couple families rank	State	Percent married-couple families [A-1, col. 45]	Female householders rank	State	Percent female householders [A-1, col. 47]	One-person households rank	State	Percent one-person households [A-1, col. 49]
	UNITED STATES	46.8		**UNITED STATES**	12.1		**UNITED STATES**	28.8
1	Utah	58.2	1	Mississippi	16.2	1	District of Columbia	47.8
2	Idaho	55.7	2	Louisiana	15.6	2	North Dakota	34.7
3	New Hampshire	51.3	3	Georgia	14.5	3	Ohio	32.2
4	Hawaii	50.4	4	Alabama	14.1	4	South Dakota	32.1
5	New Jersey	49.6	5	New Mexico	13.9	4	West Virginia	32.1
6	Wyoming	49.2	6	New York	13.5	6	Louisiana	32.0
7	Nebraska	49.0	6	South Carolina	13.5	7	New Mexico	31.9
7	Virginia	49.0	8	Delaware	13.3	8	Wisconsin	31.6
9	Kansas	48.9	8	Maryland	13.3	9	New York	31.5
10	Texas	48.7	10	California	13.1	10	Illinois	31.3
10	Washington	48.7	10	District of Columbia	13.1	10	Vermont	31.3
12	Minnesota	48.6	10	Texas	13.1	12	Montana	31.2
13	Montana	48.3	13	Arkansas	12.9	13	Rhode Island	31.0
14	Iowa	48.2	13	Connecticut	12.9	14	Iowa	30.9
15	South Dakota	48.1	13	Nevada	12.9	14	Mississippi	30.9
16	California	48.0	13	New Jersey	12.9	14	Wyoming	30.9
17	Maine	47.9	17	Florida	12.5	17	Michigan	30.8
18	Colorado	47.8	18	Tennessee	12.4	17	Pennsylvania	30.8
19	Delaware	47.6	19	North Carolina	12.3	19	Missouri	30.7
19	South Carolina	47.6	19	Oklahoma	12.3	20	Nebraska	30.3
21	North Carolina	47.4	19	Rhode Island	12.3	21	Alabama	30.2
22	Vermont	47.3	22	Kentucky	12.1	21	Alaska	30.2
23	Florida	47.0	23	Ohio	11.9	21	Minnesota	30.2
24	Wisconsin	46.9	24	Arizona	11.8	24	Arkansas	29.9
25	Arizona	46.8	24	Massachusetts	11.8	24	Indiana	29.9
25	Kentucky	46.8	26	Illinois	11.7	26	Kansas	29.7
27	Arkansas	46.7	27	Hawaii	11.6	26	Maine	29.7
27	Indiana	46.7	27	Virginia	11.6	28	Kentucky	29.6
27	Tennessee	46.7	29	Pennsylvania	11.4	28	Tennessee	29.6
30	Missouri	46.6	30	Michigan	11.3	30	Oklahoma	29.4
31	Georgia	46.4	31	Indiana	11.2	31	Maryland	29.3
32	Alabama	46.3	32	West Virginia	11.0	31	Massachusetts	29.3
32	Alaska	46.3	33	Missouri	10.9	33	Nevada	29.1
32	Connecticut	46.3	34	Oregon	10.4	33	North Carolina	29.1
32	Oklahoma	46.3	35	Alaska	9.9	35	Connecticut	29.0
32	Oregon	46.3	36	Kansas	9.7	36	Colorado	28.6
37	Michigan	46.2	37	Washington	9.5	36	South Carolina	28.6
38	North Dakota	46.0	38	Nebraska	9.3	38	Oregon	28.4
38	Pennsylvania	46.0	38	Utah	9.3	39	Virginia	28.3
40	Maryland	45.8	40	Idaho	9.1	40	Delaware	28.0
41	Massachusetts	45.3	41	Iowa	8.9	40	Washington	28.0
41	West Virginia	45.3	42	Colorado	8.8	42	Florida	27.9
43	Illinois	44.9	42	Wisconsin	8.8	43	Arizona	27.7
44	Ohio	44.2	44	New Hampshire	8.7	43	Georgia	27.7
45	Mississippi	43.5	45	Wyoming	8.6	45	New Hampshire	26.9
45	Rhode Island	43.5	46	Maine	8.5	46	Texas	26.5
47	Nevada	43.1	46	Minnesota	8.5	47	New Jersey	26.2
48	New York	42.1	48	South Dakota	8.1	48	Hawaii	25.1
49	Louisiana	41.8	49	Montana	8.0	49	California	24.7
50	New Mexico	40.9	50	Vermont	7.6	50	Idaho	23.7
51	District of Columbia	25.5	51	North Dakota	6.5	51	Utah	19.7

County Rankings, 2023

Selected Rankings

Population rank	County	Total population [A-2, col 1]	Median age rank	County	Median age [A-2, col 8]
	UNITED STATES	334,914,896		**UNITED STATES**	39.2
1	Los Angeles County, California	9,663,345	1	Sumter County, Florida	68.2
2	Cook County, Illinois	5,087,072	2	Charlotte County, Florida	60.1
3	Harris County, Texas	4,835,125	3	Sarasota County, Florida	57.6
4	Maricopa County, Arizona	4,585,871	3	Brunswick County, North Carolina	57.6
5	San Diego County, California	3,269,973	5	Citrus County, Florida	56.7
6	Orange County, California	3,135,755	6	Barnstable County, Massachusetts	56.3
7	Miami-Dade County, Florida	2,686,867	7	Indian River County, Florida	55.9
8	Dallas County, Texas	2,606,358	8	Yavapai County, Arizona	55.3
9	Kings County, New York	2,561,225	9	Highlands County, Florida	54.4
10	Riverside County, California	2,492,442	10	Collier County, Florida	54.0
11	Clark County, Nevada	2,336,573	11	Mohave County, Arizona	53.7
12	King County, Washington	2,271,380	12	Martin County, Florida	53.4
13	Queens County, New York	2,252,196	13	Flagler County, Florida	52.9
14	San Bernardino County, California	2,195,611	14	Cape May County, New Jersey	52.7
15	Tarrant County, Texas	2,182,947	15	Sussex County, Delaware	52.6
16	Bexar County, Texas	2,087,679	15	Georgetown County, South Carolina	52.6
17	Broward County, Florida	1,962,531	17	Clallam County, Washington	52.4
18	Santa Clara County, California	1,877,592	18	Carteret County, North Carolina	50.4
19	Wayne County, Michigan	1,751,169	19	Nevada County, California	49.9
20	Middlesex County, Massachusetts	1,623,952	20	Manatee County, Florida	49.6
21	Alameda County, California	1,622,188	21	Pinellas County, Florida	49.4
22	New York County, New York	1,597,451	21	Belknap County, New Hampshire	49.4
23	Sacramento County, California	1,584,288	23	Santa Fe County, New Mexico	49.3
24	Philadelphia County, Pennsylvania	1,550,542	23	Horry County, South Carolina	49.3
25	Hillsborough County, Florida	1,535,564	25	Lee County, Florida	49.1
26	Palm Beach County, Florida	1,533,801	26	Monroe County, Florida	48.8
27	Suffolk County, New York	1,523,170	27	Berkshire County, Massachusetts	48.4
28	Orange County, Florida	1,471,416	28	Marin County, California	48.2
29	Nassau County, New York	1,381,715	29	Henderson County, North Carolina	48.1
30	Bronx County, New York	1,356,476	29	Beaufort County, South Carolina	48.1
31	Travis County, Texas	1,334,961	31	Chatham County, North Carolina	47.9
32	Franklin County, Ohio	1,326,063	31	Newport County, Rhode Island	47.9
33	Oakland County, Michigan	1,270,426	33	Marion County, Florida	47.7
34	Hennepin County, Minnesota	1,258,713	33	Franklin County, Massachusetts	47.7
35	Cuyahoga County, Ohio	1,233,088	35	Josephine County, Oregon	47.6
36	Allegheny County, Pennsylvania	1,224,825	36	Northwest Hills Planning Region, Connecticut	47.5
37	Collin County, Texas	1,195,359	36	Aroostook County, Maine	47.5
38	Wake County, North Carolina	1,190,275	36	Westmoreland County, Pennsylvania	47.5
39	Salt Lake County, Utah	1,185,813	39	Hernando County, Florida	47.4
40	Mecklenburg County, North Carolina	1,163,701	40	James City County, Virginia	47.3
41	Contra Costa County, California	1,155,025	41	Oconee County, South Carolina	47.2
42	Fairfax County, Virginia	1,141,878	42	Erie County, Ohio	47.1
43	Fulton County, Georgia	1,079,105	42	Guaynabo Municipio, Puerto Rico	47.1
44	Pima County, Arizona	1,063,162	44	Somerset County, Pennsylvania	47.0
45	Montgomery County, Maryland	1,058,474	44	Bedford County, Virginia	47.0
46	Duval County, Florida	1,030,822	46	Warren County, New York	46.9
47	Fresno County, California	1,017,162	47	Volusia County, Florida	46.8
48	Denton County, Texas	1,007,703	47	Armstrong County, Pennsylvania	46.8
49	Westchester County, New York	990,817	49	Lake County, Florida	46.7
50	Honolulu County, Hawaii	989,408	49	Nassau County, Florida	46.7
51	St. Louis County, Missouri	987,059	49	Douglas County, Oregon	46.7
52	Gwinnett County, Georgia	983,526	52	Brevard County, Florida	46.6
53	Capitol Planning Region, Connecticut	975,328	53	El Dorado County, California	46.5
54	Marion County, Indiana	968,460	54	Crow Wing County, Minnesota	46.4
55	Pinellas County, Florida	961,596	55	Clearfield County, Pennsylvania	46.3
56	Bergen County, New Jersey	957,736	56	Hunterdon County, New Jersey	46.2
57	Prince George's County, Maryland	947,430	57	Hood County, Texas	46.1
58	Erie County, New York	946,147	57	San Juan Municipio, Puerto Rico	46.1
59	Pierce County, Washington	928,696	59	Washington County, Rhode Island	46.0
60	DuPage County, Illinois	921,213	60	Garland County, Arkansas	45.9
61	Fort Bend County, Texas	916,778	60	Rutherford County, North Carolina	45.9
62	Milwaukee County, Wisconsin	916,205	60	Wilkes County, North Carolina	45.9
63	Kern County, California	913,820	60	Fayette County, Pennsylvania	45.9
64	Shelby County, Tennessee	910,042	60	Manitowoc County, Wisconsin	45.9
65	Hidalgo County, Texas	898,471	65	Lower Connecticut River Valley Planning Region, Connecticut	45.8
66	Macomb County, Michigan	875,101	65	Ontario County, New York	45.8
67	El Paso County, Texas	869,880	65	Caldwell County, North Carolina	45.8
68	Montgomery County, Pennsylvania	868,742	65	Carbon County, Pennsylvania	45.8
69	Worcester County, Massachusetts	866,866	69	York County, Maine	45.7
70	Middlesex County, New Jersey	863,623	69	Cambria County, Pennsylvania	45.7
71	Essex County, New Jersey	851,117	69	Island County, Washington	45.7
72	Snohomish County, Washington	844,761	69	Arecibo Municipio, Puerto Rico	45.7
73	Baltimore County, Maryland	844,703	69	Carolina Municipio, Puerto Rico	45.7
74	Lee County, Florida	834,573	74	Palm Beach County, Florida	45.6
75	Ventura County, California	829,590	75	Putnam County, Florida	45.4
			75	Columbiana County, Ohio	45.4
			75	Sullivan County, Tennessee	45.4

County Rankings, 2023

Selected Rankings

Foreign born rank	County	Percent foreign born [A-2, col. 18]	Married-couple families rank	County	Percent married-couple families [A-2, col. 22]
	UNITED STATES	14.3		**UNITED STATES**	46.8
1	Miami-Dade County, Florida	54.8	1	Forsyth County, Georgia	69.7
2	Queens County, New York	48.4	2	Oldham County, Kentucky	69.4
3	Santa Clara County, California	42.2	3	Utah County, Utah	68.2
4	Hudson County, New Jersey	40.7	4	Williamson County, Tennessee	67.1
5	Broward County, Florida	37.8	5	Hood County, Texas	65.8
6	Middlesex County, New Jersey	37.1	6	Loudoun County, Virginia	65.7
7	Bronx County, New York	36.2	6	Davis County, Utah	65.7
8	San Mateo County, California	36.0	8	Christian County, Missouri	65.5
9	Kings County, New York	35.9	9	Union County, North Carolina	65.1
10	Alameda County, California	35.7	9	Chatham County, North Carolina	65.1
11	San Francisco County, California	35.0	11	Fort Bend County, Texas	64.8
12	Montgomery County, Maryland	34.7	12	Cache County, Utah	64.4
13	Passaic County, New Jersey	34.6	13	Cherokee County, Georgia	64.1
14	Union County, New Jersey	33.7	13	Wise County, Texas	64.1
15	Los Angeles County, California	33.5	15	Lincoln County, North Carolina	63.5
16	Imperial County, California	32.2	15	Jackson County, Georgia	63.5
17	Bergen County, New Jersey	31.6	17	Delaware County, Ohio	63.4
18	Fairfax County, Virginia	31.6	18	Calvert County, Maryland	63.3
19	Fort Bend County, Texas	31.0	18	Washington County, Utah	63.3
20	Orange County, California	30.8	20	Rockwall County, Texas	63.1
21	Essex County, New Jersey	30.6	20	Fayette County, Georgia	63.1
22	Gwinnett County, Georgia	29.6	22	Douglas County, Colorado	63.0
23	Monterey County, California	29.5	23	Geauga County, Ohio	62.8
24	New York County, New York	29.3	24	Nassau County, Florida	62.5
25	Suffolk County, Massachusetts	28.7	24	St. Johns County, Florida	62.5
26	Loudoun County, Virginia	28.4	26	Hunterdon County, New Jersey	62.4
27	Starr County, Texas	28.2	27	Carver County, Minnesota	61.8
28	Contra Costa County, California	28.2	28	Hamilton County, Indiana	61.6
29	Somerset County, New Jersey	28.1	28	Kaufman County, Texas	61.6
30	Mercer County, New Jersey	27.8	28	Carroll County, Maryland	61.6
31	Palm Beach County, Florida	27.7	28	St. Croix County, Wisconsin	61.6
32	Harris County, Texas	27.3	32	Wright County, Minnesota	61.2
33	Yuma County, Arizona	27.0	33	Wilson County, Tennessee	61.0
34	San Joaquin County, California	26.6	34	Rockland County, New York	60.9
35	Westchester County, New York	26.3	34	Morris County, New Jersey	60.9
36	Prince William County, Virginia	26.3	36	Fauquier County, Virginia	60.7
37	Osceola County, Florida	25.9	36	El Dorado County, California	60.7
38	Hidalgo County, Texas	25.8	38	Warren County, Ohio	60.6
39	Merced County, California	25.8	39	Livingston County, Michigan	60.5
40	King County, Washington	25.8	39	Nassau County, New York	60.5
41	Orange County, Florida	25.7	41	Cass County, Missouri	60.2
42	Richmond County, New York	25.5	42	Coryell County, Texas	60.0
43	Dallas County, Texas	25.4	42	Stafford County, Virginia	60.0
44	Western Connecticut Planning Region, Connecticut	25.4	44	Scott County, Minnesota	59.9
45	Collier County, Florida	25.2	44	Warrick County, Indiana	59.9
46	Forsyth County, Georgia	25.2	44	Placer County, California	59.9
47	Webb County, Texas	24.9	47	Leavenworth County, Kansas	59.8
48	Alexandria city, Virginia	24.7	47	Putnam County, New York	59.8
49	Prince George's County, Maryland	24.7	49	Limestone County, Alabama	59.6
50	Collin County, Texas	24.2	50	Shelby County, Alabama	59.5
51	Greater Bridgeport Planning Region, Connecticut	23.6	50	Parker County, Texas	59.5
52	Cameron County, Texas	23.4	52	Benton County, Arkansas	59.4
53	Middlesex County, Massachusetts	23.2	52	Collin County, Texas	59.4
54	San Diego County, California	23.1	52	York County, Virginia	59.4
55	Nassau County, New York	23.0	55	Johnson County, Texas	59.3
56	Ventura County, California	22.9	55	Montgomery County, Texas	59.3
57	Sacramento County, California	22.8	57	Johnston County, North Carolina	59.2
58	Sutter County, California	22.7	58	Bedford County, Virginia	59.1
59	San Bernardino County, California	22.6	59	Columbia County, Georgia	59.0
60	El Paso County, Texas	22.5	59	Harnett County, North Carolina	59.0
61	Howard County, Maryland	22.4	59	Wagoner County, Oklahoma	59.0
62	Solano County, California	22.4	62	James City County, Virginia	58.9
63	Whitfield County, Georgia	22.4	63	Comal County, Texas	58.8
64	Santa Barbara County, California	22.3	63	Ottawa County, Michigan	58.8
65	Cook County, Illinois	22.2	65	Clinton County, Michigan	58.7
66	Clark County, Nevada	22.1	65	Hancock County, Indiana	58.7
67	Rockland County, New York	22.1	67	Walton County, Georgia	58.6
68	Riverside County, California	22.1	67	St. Clair County, Alabama	58.6
69	Napa County, California	21.9	69	Sumter County, Florida	58.4
70	Tulare County, California	21.8	70	Bucks County, Pennsylvania	58.3
71	Stanislaus County, California	21.7	70	Will County, Illinois	58.3
72	Yolo County, California	21.5	72	Butler County, Kansas	58.1
73	Kings County, California	21.1	73	Tooele County, Utah	58.0
74	Monroe County, Florida	21.0	73	Chester County, Pennsylvania	58.0
75	Hillsborough County, Florida	20.8	73	McHenry County, Illinois	58.0

County Rankings, 2023

Selected Rankings

Female householders rank	County	Percent female householders [A-2, col. 24]	One-person households rank	County	Percent one-person households [A-2, col. 26]
	UNITED STATES	12.1		**UNITED STATES**	28.8
1	Dougherty County, Georgia	32.7	1	District of Columbia, District of Columbia	47.8
2	McKinley County, New Mexico	31.2	1	New York County, New York	47.8
3	Toa Baja Municipio, Puerto Rico	29.9	3	San Juan Municipio, Puerto Rico	46.4
4	Caguas Municipio, Puerto Rico	28.7	4	St. Louis city, Missouri	45.7
5	Bronx County, New York	26.8	5	Baltimore city, Maryland	45.2
6	Toa Alta Municipio, Puerto Rico	26.1	6	Alexandria city, Virginia	44.3
7	Apache County, Arizona	24.8	7	Richmond city, Virginia	42.5
8	Richmond County, Georgia	24.6	8	Arlington County, Virginia	41.7
8	Bayamón Municipio, Puerto Rico	24.6	9	Orleans Parish, Louisiana	41.6
10	Starr County, Texas	24.3	10	Denver County, Colorado	41.4
11	Ponce Municipio, Puerto Rico	24.0	11	Cuyahoga County, Ohio	41.3
12	Robeson County, North Carolina	23.9	12	Vermilion County, Illinois	40.7
13	Clayton County, Georgia	23.6	13	Vigo County, Indiana	40.3
14	Arecibo Municipio, Puerto Rico	23.3	14	Cass County, North Dakota	39.9
15	Carolina Municipio, Puerto Rico	23.1	15	San Francisco County, California	39.5
16	Jefferson County, Arkansas	22.1	16	Champaign County, Illinois	39.3
17	Troup County, Georgia	21.8	17	Monongalia County, West Virginia	39.3
17	Orangeburg County, South Carolina	21.8	18	Philadelphia County, Pennsylvania	39.0
19	Montgomery County, Alabama	21.2	19	Tompkins County, New York	39.0
20	Webb County, Texas	20.5	20	Mendocino County, California	38.6
21	Passaic County, New Jersey	20.4	21	Macon County, Illinois	38.5
22	Hinds County, Mississippi	20.3	22	Hinds County, Mississippi	38.4
22	Newton County, Georgia	20.3	23	Fulton County, Georgia	38.0
24	Douglas County, Georgia	20.2	24	Caddo Parish, Louisiana	37.8
25	Shelby County, Tennessee	20.1	24	Mayagüez Municipio, Puerto Rico	37.8
25	Lauderdale County, Mississippi	20.1	26	Kanawha County, West Virginia	37.6
27	Bibb County, Georgia	20.0	27	McCracken County, Kentucky	37.5
28	Iberia Parish, Louisiana	19.9	27	Anderson County, Tennessee	37.5
29	Florence County, South Carolina	19.8	29	Roanoke city, Virginia	37.1
30	Hidalgo County, Texas	19.7	30	Lauderdale County, Mississippi	37.0
30	Houston County, Georgia	19.7	30	Newport News city, Virginia	37.0
32	Cameron County, Texas	19.5	32	Lewis and Clark County, Montana	36.9
33	San Juan Municipio, Puerto Rico	19.4	33	Milwaukee County, Wisconsin	36.8
33	Wayne County, North Carolina	19.4	33	Davidson County, Tennessee	36.8
33	Caddo Parish, Louisiana	19.4	35	Hamilton County, Ohio	36.7
36	Sumter County, South Carolina	19.2	36	Pinellas County, Florida	36.6
36	Trujillo Alto Municipio, Puerto Rico	19.2	37	Potter County, Texas	36.4
38	Portsmouth city, Virginia	19.1	37	Sangamon County, Illinois	36.4
38	Essex County, New Jersey	19.1	37	Multnomah County, Oregon	36.4
38	Rockdale County, Georgia	19.1	40	Wayne County, Michigan	36.3
41	Henry County, Georgia	18.7	40	Pulaski County, Arkansas	36.3
42	Wyandotte County, Kansas	18.6	40	Montgomery County, Ohio	36.3
42	Lowndes County, Georgia	18.6	40	Ramsey County, Minnesota	36.3
44	Rapides Parish, Louisiana	18.5	40	Minnehaha County, South Dakota	36.3
45	Baltimore city, Maryland	18.4	45	Muscogee County, Georgia	36.2
45	Mayagüez Municipio, Puerto Rico	18.4	45	Norfolk city, Virginia	36.2
45	Cumberland County, New Jersey	18.4	45	Tom Green County, Texas	36.2
48	Kern County, California	18.3	48	Dane County, Wisconsin	36.2
49	El Paso County, Texas	18.2	49	Ponce Municipio, Puerto Rico	36.1
49	Greenwood County, South Carolina	18.2	49	Lake County, California	36.1
51	Union County, New Jersey	18.1	49	Allegheny County, Pennsylvania	36.1
52	Houston County, Alabama	18.0	52	Montgomery County, Alabama	36.0
53	Madison County, Tennessee	17.9	53	Spalding County, Georgia	35.9
53	Ouachita Parish, Louisiana	17.9	53	Suffolk County, Massachusetts	35.9
53	Prince George's County, Maryland	17.9	53	Vanderburgh County, Indiana	35.9
53	Muscogee County, Georgia	17.9	56	Jackson County, Missouri	35.8
57	San Bernardino County, California	17.8	56	Albany County, New York	35.8
57	Kershaw County, South Carolina	17.8	56	Rock Island County, Illinois	35.8
59	Talladega County, Alabama	17.7	59	Hennepin County, Minnesota	35.8
60	Lafourche Parish, Louisiana	17.6	60	Peoria County, Illinois	35.6
60	Hampton city, Virginia	17.6	61	Marion County, Indiana	35.5
62	Tulare County, California	17.5	61	East Baton Rouge Parish, Louisiana	35.5
63	Philadelphia County, Pennsylvania	17.4	61	Mahoning County, Ohio	35.5
63	Fresno County, California	17.4	61	Cattaraugus County, New York	35.5
63	Yakima County, Washington	17.4	61	St. Lawrence County, New York	35.5
66	Hampden County, Massachusetts	17.3	66	Cole County, Missouri	35.4
67	San Juan County, New Mexico	17.2	67	Trumbull County, Ohio	35.4
67	Christian County, Kentucky	17.2	68	Winnebago County, Wisconsin	35.4
67	Terrebonne Parish, Louisiana	17.2	69	Sullivan County, Tennessee	35.3
70	Jefferson County, Alabama	17.0	69	Oneida County, New York	35.3
70	Floyd County, Georgia	17.0	71	Cambria County, Pennsylvania	35.2
70	Miami-Dade County, Florida	17.0	72	Cook County, Illinois	35.1
73	Mobile County, Alabama	16.9	73	Bronx County, New York	35.0
73	St. Landry Parish, Louisiana	16.9	73	St. Landry Parish, Louisiana	35.0
75	Roanoke city, Virginia	16.8	73	Lee County, Alabama	35.0
75	Cumberland County, North Carolina	16.8			
75	Gregg County, Texas	16.8			
75	Imperial County, California	16.8			

Metropolitan Area Rankings, 2023

Selected Rankings

Population rank	Area name	Total population [A-3, col 1]	Median age rank	Area name	Median age [A-3, col 8]
	UNITED STATES	334,914,896		**UNITED STATES**	39.2
1	New York-Newark-Jersey City, NY-NJ	19,498,249	1	Wildwood-The Villages, FL	68.2
2	Los Angeles-Long Beach-Anaheim, CA	12,799,100	2	Punta Gorda, FL	60.1
3	Chicago-Naperville-Elgin, IL-IN	9,262,559	3	Homosassa Springs, FL	56.7
4	Dallas-Fort Worth-Arlington, TX	8,100,037	4	Barnstable Town, MA	56.3
5	Houston-Pasadena-The Woodlands, TX	7,510,252	5	Sebastian-Vero Beach-West Vero Corridor, FL	55.9
6	Atlanta-Sandy Springs-Roswell, GA	6,305,839	6	Prescott Valley-Prescott, AZ	55.3
7	Washington-Arlington-Alexandria, DC-VA-MD-WV	6,304,449	7	Sebring, FL	54.4
8	Philadelphia-Camden-Wilmington, PA-NJ-DE-MD	6,246,160	8	Naples-Marco Island, FL	54.0
9	Miami-Fort Lauderdale-West Palm Beach, FL	6,183,199	9	North Port-Bradenton-Sarasota, FL	53.8
10	Phoenix-Mesa-Chandler, AZ	5,070,110	10	Lake Havasu City-Kingman, AZ	53.7
11	Boston-Cambridge-Newton, MA-NH	4,919,179	11	Myrtle Beach-Conway-North Myrtle Beach, SC	49.3
12	Riverside-San Bernardino-Ontario, CA	4,688,053	11	Santa Fe, NM	49.3
13	San Francisco-Oakland-Fremont, CA	4,566,961	13	Cape Coral-Fort Myers, FL	49.1
14	Detroit-Warren-Dearborn, MI	4,342,304	14	Sandusky, OH	49.0
15	Seattle-Tacoma-Bellevue, WA	4,044,837	15	Pittsfield, MA	48.4
16	Minneapolis-St. Paul-Bloomington, MN-WI	3,712,020	16	Deltona-Daytona Beach-Ormond Beach, FL	48.1
17	Tampa-St. Petersburg-Clearwater, FL	3,342,963	17	Port St. Lucie, FL	47.8
18	San Diego-Chula Vista-Carlsbad, CA	3,269,973	18	Ocala, FL	47.7
19	Denver-Aurora-Centennial, CO	3,005,131	19	Grants Pass, OR	47.6
20	Baltimore-Columbia-Towson, MD	2,834,316	19	Hilton Head Island-Bluffton-Port Royal, SC	47.6
21	Orlando-Kissimmee-Sanford, FL	2,817,933	21	Palm Bay-Melbourne-Titusville, FL	46.6
22	Charlotte-Concord-Gastonia, NC-SC	2,805,115	21	Traverse City, MI	46.6
23	St. Louis, MO-IL	2,795,504	23	Mayagüez, PR	46.4
24	San Antonio-New Braunfels, TX	2,703,999	24	Glens Falls, NY	46.2
25	Portland-Vancouver-Hillsboro, OR-WA	2,509,925	25	Arecibo, PR	46.1
26	Austin-Round Rock-San Marcos, TX	2,473,275	25	Weirton-Steubenville, WV-OH	46.1
27	Pittsburgh, PA	2,422,725	27	Hot Springs, AR	45.9
28	Sacramento-Roseville-Folsom, CA	2,420,608	27	Wilmington, NC	45.9
29	Las Vegas-Henderson-North Las Vegas, NV	2,336,573	29	Johnstown, PA	45.7
30	Cincinnati, OH-KY-IN	2,272,910	29	Kingsport-Bristol, TN-VA	45.7
31	Kansas City, MO-KS	2,219,865	31	Aguadilla, PR	45.6
32	Columbus, OH	2,180,271	32	Atlantic City-Hammonton, NJ	45.1
33	Cleveland, OH	2,158,932	33	San Juan-Bayamón-Caguas, PR	44.8
34	Indianapolis-Carmel-Greenwood, IN	2,139,689	34	Gettysburg, PA	44.6
35	Nashville-Davidson--Murfreesboro--Franklin, TN	2,104,235	34	Guayama, PR	44.6
36	San Juan-Bayamón-Caguas, PR	2,037,875	34	Ponce, PR	44.6
37	San Jose-Sunnyvale-Santa Clara, CA	1,945,767	34	Wheeling, WV-OH	44.6
38	Virginia Beach-Chesapeake-Norfolk, VA-NC	1,781,671	38	Parkersburg-Vienna, WV	44.5
39	Jacksonville, FL	1,713,240	39	Bay City, MI	44.4
40	Providence-Warwick, RI-MA	1,677,803	40	Daphne-Fairhope-Foley, AL	44.3
41	Milwaukee-Waukesha, WI	1,560,424	40	Kingston, NY	44.3
42	Raleigh-Cary, NC	1,509,231	42	Carson City, NV	44.2
43	Oklahoma City, OK	1,477,926	43	Brunswick-St. Simons, GA	44.0
44	Louisville/Jefferson County, KY-IN	1,364,742	43	Charleston, WV	44.0
45	Richmond, VA	1,350,123	43	Pinehurst-Southern Pines, NC	44.0
46	Memphis, TN-MS-AR	1,335,549	43	Sierra Vista-Douglas, AZ	44.0
47	Salt Lake City-Murray, UT	1,267,864	47	Asheville, NC	43.9
48	Birmingham, AL	1,184,290	48	Portland-South Portland, ME	43.8
49	Fresno, CA	1,180,020	49	Altoona, PA	43.7
50	Grand Rapids-Wyoming-Kentwood, MI	1,162,950	49	Hickory-Lenoir-Morganton, NC	43.7
51	Buffalo-Cheektowaga, NY	1,155,604	51	Napa, CA	43.6
52	Hartford-West Hartford-East Hartford, CT	1,151,543	51	Staunton-Stuarts Draft, VA	43.6
53	Tucson, AZ	1,063,162	53	Johnson City, TN	43.5
54	Rochester, NY	1,052,087	54	Paducah, KY-IL	43.4
55	Tulsa, OK	1,044,287	55	Kahului-Wailuku, HI	43.3
56	Urban Honolulu, HI	989,408	55	Midland, MI	43.3
57	Omaha, NE-IA	984,548	55	Santa Rosa-Petaluma, CA	43.3
58	Greenville-Anderson-Greer, SC	975,480	55	Youngstown-Warren, OH	43.3
59	New Orleans-Metairie, LA	962,165	59	Beckley, WV	43.1
60	Bridgeport-Stamford-Danbury, CT	951,558	60	Niles, MI	43.0
61	Knoxville, TN	947,017	61	Monroe, MI	42.9
62	Albuquerque, NM	923,518	62	Bend, OR	42.8
63	Bakersfield-Delano, CA	913,820	62	Mount Vernon-Anacortes, WA	42.8
64	North Port-Bradenton-Sarasota, FL	910,108	62	Pittsburgh, PA	42.8
65	Albany-Schenectady-Troy, NY	904,682	65	Bangor, ME	42.7
66	McAllen-Edinburg-Mission, TX	898,471	65	Huntington-Ashland, WV-KY-OH	42.7
67	Baton Rouge, LA	873,661	65	Roanoke, VA	42.7
68	Allentown-Bethlehem-Easton, PA-NJ	873,555	68	Sheboygan, WI	42.6
69	El Paso, TX	872,063	69	Elmira, NY	42.5
70	Worcester, MA	866,866	69	Medford, OR	42.5
71	Columbia, SC	856,889	69	Waterbury-Shelton, CT	42.5
72	Charleston-North Charleston, SC	849,417	72	Canton-Massillon, OH	42.4
73	Cape Coral-Fort Myers, FL	834,573	72	Springfield, IL	42.4
74	Oxnard-Thousand Oaks-Ventura, CA	829,590	72	Tampa-St. Petersburg-Clearwater, FL	42.4
75	Boise City, ID	826,521	75	Miami-Fort Lauderdale-West Palm Beach, FL	42.3

Metropolitan Area Rankings, 2023

Selected Rankings

Foreign born rank	Area name	Percent foreign born [A-3, col. 15]	One-person households rank	Area name	Percent one-person households [A-3, col. 22]
	UNITED STATES	14.3		**UNITED STATES**	28.8
1	Miami-Fort Lauderdale-West Palm Beach, FL	42.7	1	Ithaca, NY	39.0
2	San Jose-Sunnyvale-Santa Clara, CA	41.4	2	Decatur, IL	38.5
3	Los Angeles-Long Beach-Anaheim, CA	32.9	3	Champaign-Urbana, IL	37.4
4	San Francisco-Oakland-Fremont, CA	32.8	4	Fargo, ND-MN	37.3
5	El Centro, CA	32.2	5	Terre Haute, IN	37.2
6	Eagle Pass, TX	32.1	6	Morgantown, WV	36.8
7	New York-Newark-Jersey City, NY-NJ	30.5	7	Charleston, WV	36.6
8	Salinas, CA	29.5	8	Springfield, IL	36.4
9	Trenton-Princeton, NJ	27.8	9	San Angelo, TX	36.0
10	Yuma, AZ	27.0	10	Cleveland, OH	35.9
11	Stockton-Lodi, CA	26.6	11	New Orleans-Metairie, LA	35.8
12	McAllen-Edinburg-Mission, TX	25.8	12	Auburn-Opelika, AL	35.7
12	Merced, CA	25.8	13	Shreveport-Bossier City, LA	35.5
14	Naples-Marco Island, FL	25.2	13	Youngstown-Warren, OH	35.5
15	Laredo, TX	24.9	15	Madison, WI	35.4
16	Houston-Pasadena-The Woodlands, TX	24.8	15	Oshkosh-Neenah, WI	35.4
16	Bridgeport-Stamford-Danbury, CT	24.8	17	Staunton-Stuarts Draft, VA	35.3
18	Washington-Arlington-Alexandria, DC-VA-MD-WV	24.6	18	Johnstown, PA	35.2
19	Brownsville-Harlingen, TX	23.4	19	Tuscaloosa, AL	35.0
20	San Diego-Chula Vista-Carlsbad, CA	23.1	20	Altoona, PA	34.7
21	Oxnard-Thousand Oaks-Ventura, CA	22.9	20	Battle Creek, MI	34.7
22	El Paso, TX	22.5	20	Bay City, MI	34.7
23	Vallejo, CA	22.4	20	Mobile, AL	34.7
24	Riverside-San Bernardino-Ontario, CA	22.3	24	Buffalo-Cheektowaga, NY	34.6
24	Santa Maria-Santa Barbara, CA	22.3	25	Columbus, GA-AL	34.5
26	Las Vegas-Henderson-North Las Vegas, NV	22.1	25	Weirton-Steubenville, WV-OH	34.5
27	Orlando-Kissimmee-Sanford, FL	21.9	27	Mayagüez, PR	34.4
27	Napa, CA	21.9	27	Parkersburg-Vienna, WV	34.4
29	Visalia, CA	21.8	29	Bismarck, ND	34.3
30	Modesto, CA	21.7	29	Kingsport-Bristol, TN-VA	34.3
31	Seattle-Tacoma-Bellevue, WA	21.3	31	Santa Fe, NM	34.2
32	Hanford-Corcoran, CA	21.1	32	Iowa City, IA	34.1
33	Dallas-Fort Worth-Arlington, TX	20.0	32	Peoria, IL	34.1
34	Boston-Cambridge-Newton, MA-NH	19.9	34	Pittsfield, MA	34.0
35	Sacramento-Roseville-Folsom, CA	19.8	35	Dayton-Kettering-Beavercreek, OH	33.9
36	Odessa, TX	19.7	35	Pittsburgh, PA	33.9
37	Fresno, CA	19.6	37	Helena, MT	33.8
38	Bakersfield-Delano, CA	19.5	38	Great Falls, MT	33.6
39	Urban Honolulu, HI	19.1	38	Guayama, PR	33.6
40	Chicago-Naperville-Elgin, IL-IN	18.9	40	Sioux Falls, SD-MN	33.5
41	Cape Coral-Fort Myers, FL	18.8	41	Ponce, PR	33.4
42	Kahului-Wailuku, HI	18.7	41	Walla Walla, WA	33.4
43	Wenatchee-East Wenatchee, WA	18.3	43	Bloomington, IN	33.3
44	Santa Cruz-Watsonville, CA	18.2	43	Lincoln, NE	33.3
45	Dalton, GA	18.0	43	Scranton--Wilkes-Barre, PA	33.3
46	Yakima, WA	17.9	43	Utica-Rome, NY	33.3
47	Yuba City, CA	17.1	47	Hot Springs, AR	33.2
48	Port St. Lucie, FL	17.0	47	Texarkana, TX-AR	33.2
49	Santa Rosa-Petaluma, CA	16.8	49	Milwaukee-Waukesha, WI	33.1
50	Gainesville, GA	16.4	49	Paducah, KY-IL	33.1
51	Tampa-St. Petersburg-Clearwater, FL	16.1	51	Amherst Town-Northampton, MA	33.0
52	Austin-Round Rock-San Marcos, TX	16.0	51	Jackson, MS	33.0
53	Atlanta-Sandy Springs-Roswell, GA	15.8	53	San Juan-Bayamón-Caguas, PR	32.9
54	Las Cruces, NM	15.5	53	Tallahassee, FL	32.9
55	Worcester, MA	15.3	53	Valdosta, GA	32.9
56	Santa Fe, NM	15.2	56	Erie, PA	32.8
56	North Port-Bradenton-Sarasota, FL	15.2	56	Rocky Mount, NC	32.8
58	Kiryas Joel-Poughkeepsie-Newburgh, NY	15.0	56	Toledo, OH	32.8
59	Hartford-West Hartford-East Hartford, CT	14.8	59	Kingston, NY	32.7
60	Providence-Warwick, RI-MA	14.5	59	Missoula, MT	32.7
60	Grand Island, NE	14.5	59	Springfield, MA	32.7
62	Raleigh-Cary, NC	14.4	62	Akron, OH	32.6
63	Phoenix-Mesa-Chandler, AZ	14.2	62	Albany-Schenectady-Troy, NY	32.6
63	Vineland, NJ	14.2	64	Albuquerque, NM	32.5
65	Waterbury-Shelton, CT	14.1	64	Ann Arbor, MI	32.5
66	New Haven, CT	13.9	64	Detroit-Warren-Dearborn, MI	32.5
67	Atlantic City-Hammonton, NJ	13.8	64	Greensboro-High Point, NC	32.5
67	Ann Arbor, MI	13.8	64	Monroe, LA	32.5
69	Reno, NV	13.4	64	Sierra Vista-Douglas, AZ	32.5
70	Durham-Chapel Hill, NC	13.2	64	Tucson, AZ	32.5
71	Ithaca, NY	12.9	71	Binghamton, NY	32.4
71	College Station-Bryan, TX	12.9	71	Cape Girardeau, MO-IL	32.4
71	Salt Lake City-Murray, UT	12.9	71	Cheyenne, WY	32.4
74	San Antonio-New Braunfels, TX	12.5	71	Jonesboro, AR	32.4
74	Kennewick-Richland, WA	12.5	71	Lansing-East Lansing, MI	32.4
			71	Montgomery, AL	32.4
			71	Saginaw, MI	32.4

City Rankings, 2023

Selected Rankings

Population rank	City	Total population, [A-4, col 1]	Median age rank	City	Median age [A-4, col 8]
	UNITED STATES	334,914,896		**UNITED STATES**	39.2
1	New York city, New York	8,258,035	1	The Villages CDP, Florida	74.5
2	Los Angeles city, California	3,820,963	2	Delray Beach city, Florida	51.9
3	Chicago city, Illinois	2,664,454	3	Port Charlotte CDP, Florida	51.4
4	Houston city, Texas	2,311,461	4	Palm Coast city, Florida	50.9
5	Phoenix city, Arizona	1,650,051	5	Palm Harbor CDP, Florida	50.8
6	Philadelphia city, Pennsylvania	1,550,542	6	Scottsdale city, Arizona	49.8
7	San Antonio city, Texas	1,495,312	7	Cape Coral city, Florida	49.2
8	San Diego city, California	1,388,312	8	Tamarac city, Florida	48.3
9	Dallas city, Texas	1,302,859	9	Southfield city, Michigan	47.8
10	Jacksonville city, Florida	985,837	10	Mission Viejo city, California	47.2
11	Austin city, Texas	979,700	10	Clearwater city, Florida	47.2
12	Fort Worth city, Texas	976,932	12	Farmington Hills city, Michigan	47.1
13	San Jose city, California	969,615	13	Hialeah city, Florida	46.8
14	Charlotte city, North Carolina	911,307	14	Casas Adobes CDP, Arizona	46.7
15	Columbus city, Ohio	909,074	15	Pembroke Pines city, Florida	46.6
16	Indianapolis city (balance), Indiana	874,182	16	Boca Raton city, Florida	46.3
17	San Francisco city, California	808,988	17	Santa Fe city, New Mexico	46.2
18	Seattle city, Washington	755,081	17	San Juan zona urbana, Puerto Rico	46.2
19	Denver city, Colorado	716,577	19	Port Orange city, Florida	46.1
20	Oklahoma City city, Oklahoma	702,654	20	Yorba Linda city, California	45.8
21	Nashville-Davidson metropolitan government (balance), Tennessee	687,787	21	Ponce zona urbana, Puerto Rico	45.7
22	Washington city, District of Columbia	678,972	22	Walnut Creek city, California	45.4
23	El Paso city, Texas	678,945	23	Thousand Oaks city, California	45.3
24	Las Vegas city, Nevada	660,942	23	Carolina zona urbana, Puerto Rico	45.3
25	Boston city, Massachusetts	652,442	25	Johns Creek city, Georgia	45.2
26	Detroit city, Michigan	633,221	26	North Port city, Florida	45.1
27	Portland city, Oregon	630,395	26	Skokie village, Illinois	45.1
28	Louisville/Jefferson County metro government (balance), Kentucky	622,987	28	Largo city, Florida	45.0
29	Memphis city, Tennessee	618,655	29	Bayamón zona urbana, Puerto Rico	44.8
30	Baltimore city, Maryland	565,239	30	Surprise city, Arizona	44.7
31	Milwaukee city, Wisconsin	561,369	31	Deerfield Beach city, Florida	44.6
32	Albuquerque city, New Mexico	560,283	31	Pompano Beach city, Florida	44.6
33	Tucson city, Arizona	547,232	33	Boynton Beach city, Florida	44.4
34	Fresno city, California	545,717	33	Bethesda CDP, Maryland	44.4
35	Sacramento city, California	526,383	33	Caguas zona urbana, Puerto Rico	44.4
36	Mesa city, Arizona	511,624	36	Spring Hill CDP, Florida	44.2
37	Atlanta city, Georgia	510,826	36	Guaynabo zona urbana, Puerto Rico	44.2
38	Kansas City city, Missouri	510,671	38	Pleasanton city, California	44.1
39	Colorado Springs city, Colorado	488,670	39	Huntington Beach city, California	43.9
40	Omaha city, Nebraska	483,362	40	Camarillo city, California	43.8
41	Raleigh city, North Carolina	482,425	40	Weston city, Florida	43.8
42	Miami city, Florida	455,955	42	Torrance city, California	43.7
43	Virginia Beach city, Virginia	453,649	43	Fort Lauderdale city, Florida	43.6
44	Long Beach city, California	449,496	43	Springfield city, Illinois	43.6
45	Oakland city, California	436,508	43	Parma city, Ohio	43.6
46	Minneapolis city, Minnesota	425,142	46	Santa Monica city, California	43.5
47	Bakersfield city, California	413,376	46	Port St. Lucie city, Florida	43.5
48	Tulsa city, Oklahoma	410,915	46	St. Petersburg city, Florida	43.5
49	Tampa city, Florida	403,361	49	Brentwood city, California	43.4
50	Arlington city, Texas	398,423	49	Carlsbad city, California	43.4
51	Wichita city, Kansas	396,123	49	Napa city, California	43.4
52	Aurora city, Colorado	394,701	49	Alpharetta city, Georgia	43.4
53	New Orleans city, Louisiana	364,136	53	Daly City city, California	43.3
54	Cleveland city, Ohio	362,670	53	Palm Bay city, Florida	43.3
55	Urban Honolulu CDP, Hawaii	341,753	55	Castro Valley CDP, California	43.2
56	Anaheim city, California	340,505	55	Kendall CDP, Florida	43.2
57	Henderson city, Nevada	337,280	57	Newton city, Massachusetts	43.1
58	Orlando city, Florida	320,753	57	Livonia city, Michigan	43.1
59	Lexington-Fayette urban county, Kentucky	320,154	59	Maple Grove city, Minnesota	43.0
60	Stockton city, California	319,537	60	Burbank city, California	42.9
61	Riverside city, California	318,855	60	Simi Valley city, California	42.9
62	Corpus Christi city, Texas	316,603	60	Warwick city, Rhode Island	42.9
63	Irvine city, California	314,615	63	Alameda city, California	42.8
64	San Juan zona urbana, Puerto Rico	312,488	63	Alhambra city, California	42.8
65	Cincinnati city, Ohio	311,112	63	Ellicott City CDP, Maryland	42.8
66	Santa Ana city, California	310,523	63	East Orange city, New Jersey	42.8
67	Newark city, New Jersey	304,943	67	Urban Honolulu CDP, Hawaii	42.7
68	St. Paul city, Minnesota	303,827	67	Naperville city, Illinois	42.7
69	Pittsburgh city, Pennsylvania	303,254	67	Eagan city, Minnesota	42.7
70	Greensboro city, North Carolina	302,307	70	Palo Alto city, California	42.6
71	Durham city, North Carolina	295,845	70	Norwalk city, Connecticut	42.6
72	Lincoln city, Nebraska	294,750	70	Arlington Heights village, Illinois	42.6
73	Jersey City city, New Jersey	291,663	70	Mount Vernon city, New York	42.6
74	Plano city, Texas	288,228	70	Georgetown city, Texas	42.6
75	Anchorage municipality, Alaska	286,075	75	Glendale city, California	42.5

City Rankings, 2023

Selected Rankings

Foreign born rank	City	Percent foreign born [A-4, col. 18]	One-person households rank	City	Percent one-person households [A-4, col. 27]
	UNITED STATES	14.3		**UNITED STATES**	28.8
1	Hialeah city, Florida	76.2	1	Santa Monica city, California	50.5
2	Doral city, Florida	66.7	2	Cleveland city, Ohio	48.0
3	Union City city, New Jersey	59.4	3	Washington city, District of Columbia	47.8
4	Milpitas city, California	57.4	4	Southfield city, Michigan	47.4
5	Miami city, Florida	55.4	5	Atlanta city, Georgia	47.3
6	Fremont city, California	55.3	6	San Juan zona urbana, Puerto Rico	47.0
7	Miami Beach city, Florida	52.6	7	Cincinnati city, Ohio	46.9
8	Daly City city, California	51.3	8	Champaign city, Illinois	46.3
9	Glendale city, California	50.9	9	St. Louis city, Missouri	45.7
10	Sunnyvale city, California	50.5	10	Decatur city, Illinois	45.6
11	Garden Grove city, California	48.9	10	Fargo city, North Dakota	45.6
12	Homestead city, Florida	48.5	12	Minneapolis city, Minnesota	45.5
13	Weston city, Florida	48.0	13	Wilmington city, Delaware	45.4
14	El Monte city, California	47.7	14	Baltimore city, Maryland	45.2
15	Westminster city, California	46.9	15	Pittsburgh city, Pennsylvania	44.6
16	Elizabeth city, New Jersey	46.7	16	Alexandria city, Virginia	44.3
17	Lawrence city, Massachusetts	46.5	17	East Orange city, New Jersey	44.2
18	Gaithersburg city, Maryland	46.4	18	Delray Beach city, Florida	43.7
19	Union City city, California	46.3	18	Detroit city, Michigan	43.7
19	Paterson city, New Jersey	46.3	20	Rochester city, New York	43.1
21	Kendall CDP, Florida	46.2	21	Miami Beach city, Florida	43.0
22	Santa Clara city, California	46.1	21	Seattle city, Washington	43.0
23	Pembroke Pines city, Florida	45.4	23	Evansville city, Indiana	42.9
24	Bellevue city, Washington	44.7	24	Springfield city, Missouri	42.7
25	Deerfield Beach city, Florida	44.6	25	Jackson city, Mississippi	42.6
26	Redmond city, Washington	44.5	25	Dayton city, Ohio	42.6
27	Alhambra city, California	44.3	25	Bellingham city, Washington	42.6
28	Town 'n' Country CDP, Florida	44.2	28	Richmond city, Virginia	42.5
29	Mountain View city, California	44.0	29	Bloomington city, Indiana	42.4
30	Irving city, Texas	43.9	29	Baton Rouge city, Louisiana	42.4
31	Passaic city, New Jersey	43.8	31	Flint city, Michigan	42.3
32	Sunrise city, Florida	43.7	31	Asheville city, North Carolina	42.3
33	South Gate city, California	43.6	33	Albany city, New York	42.0
34	Danbury city, Connecticut	43.2	34	Auburn city, Alabama	41.9
35	Baldwin Park city, California	43.0	34	Iowa City city, Iowa	41.9
36	San Jose city, California	42.8	36	Mobile city, Alabama	41.8
37	Hayward city, California	42.3	36	Tuscaloosa city, Alabama	41.8
38	Tamarac city, Florida	42.1	36	Madison city, Wisconsin	41.8
39	Santa Ana city, California	41.9	39	Syracuse city, New York	41.7
40	Miramar city, Florida	41.7	39	Arlington CDP, Virginia	41.7
41	Hollywood city, Florida	41.1	39	Reston CDP, Virginia	41.7
42	East Los Angeles CDP, California	40.7	42	New Orleans city, Louisiana	41.6
43	Dublin city, California	40.5	43	Birmingham city, Alabama	41.5
44	Malden city, Massachusetts	40.2	43	Muncie city, Indiana	41.5
45	Lauderhill city, Florida	40.0	45	Denver city, Colorado	41.4
45	Cicero town, Illinois	40.0	45	Knoxville city, Tennessee	41.4
47	Palo Alto city, California	39.8	47	Shreveport city, Louisiana	41.3
47	Skokie village, Illinois	39.8	48	Hartford city, Connecticut	41.1
49	Irvine city, California	39.4	48	Westland city, Michigan	41.1
50	Pleasanton city, California	39.3	50	New Haven city, Connecticut	41.0
50	Lynn city, Massachusetts	39.3	50	Pompano Beach city, Florida	41.0
52	Germantown CDP, Maryland	39.1	50	Springfield city, Illinois	41.0
53	San Leandro city, California	38.9	50	Lansing city, Michigan	41.0
54	Jersey City city, New Jersey	38.8	50	Columbia city, South Carolina	41.0
54	Sammamish city, Washington	38.8	55	Santa Fe city, New Mexico	40.9
56	West Covina city, California	38.4	55	Greenville city, South Carolina	40.9
57	Sugar Land city, Texas	38.3	57	Erie city, Pennsylvania	40.7
58	San Ramon city, California	38.2	58	Gainesville city, Florida	40.6
59	Salinas city, California	38.0	58	Topeka city, Kansas	40.6
60	Pine Hills CDP, Florida	37.8	60	Paradise CDP, Nevada	40.5
61	New York city, New York	37.5	60	Buffalo city, New York	40.5
62	Schaumburg village, Illinois	37.3	62	St. Petersburg city, Florida	40.4
63	Chino Hills city, California	36.9	63	Little Rock city, Arkansas	40.3
64	Bridgeport city, Connecticut	36.7	63	Fort Lauderdale city, Florida	40.3
64	Newark city, New Jersey	36.7	63	Gulfport city, Mississippi	40.3
66	Lynwood city, California	36.6	63	Pawtucket city, Rhode Island	40.3
67	Tustin city, California	36.4	67	Chicago city, Illinois	40.2
68	Miami Gardens city, Florida	36.2	68	Oshkosh city, Wisconsin	40.0
69	Burbank city, California	36.1	69	Quincy city, Massachusetts	39.9
69	Carson city, California	36.1	70	Peoria city, Illinois	39.8
69	Yonkers city, New York	36.1	70	Akron city, Ohio	39.8
69	Kent city, Washington	36.1	72	Camden city, New Jersey	39.7
73	San Mateo city, California	35.7	73	Wilmington city, North Carolina	39.6
73	Johns Creek city, Georgia	35.7	74	San Francisco city, California	39.5
75	Buena Park city, California	35.6	74	Bowling Green city, Kentucky	39.5
			74	Toledo city, Ohio	39.5

Table A-1. States — Who: Age, Race/Ethnicity, and Household Structure, 2023

State code	STATE	Total population	Percent change, 2010–2023	Race alone or in combination (percent)						Percent Hispanic or Latino	Percent two or more races	Percent White alone, not Hispanic or Latino
				White	Black or African American	American Indian or Alaska Native	Asian	Native Hawaiian or Pacific Islander	Some other race			
	ACS table number:	B01003	Census PEP	B02008	B02009	B02010	B02011	B02012	B02013	B03003	B02001	B01001H
	Column number:	1	2	3	4	5	6	7	8	9	10	11

Table A-1. States — Who: Age, Race/Ethnicity, and Household Structure, 2023

State code	STATE	Total population	Population by age (percent)							+/- U.S. percent under 18 years	+/- U.S. percent 65 years and over	Percent female
			Under 5 years	5 to 17 years	18 to 24 years	25 to 44 years	45 to 64 years	65 to 84 years	85 years and over			
	ACS table number:	B01001	B01001	B01001	B01001	B01001	B01001	B01001	B01001	B01001	B01001	B01001
	Column number:	12	13	14	15	16	17	18	19	20	21	22

Table A-1. States — Who: Age, Race/Ethnicity, and Household Structure, 2023

State code	STATE	Median age								
		Total population	White alone, not Hispanic or Latino	Black alone	American Indian or Alaska Native alone	Asian alone	Native Hawaiian or Pacific Islander alone	Some other race alone	Two or more races	Hispanic or Latino
	ACS table number:	B01002	B01002H	B01002B	B01002C	B01002D	B01002E	B01002F	B01002G	B01002I
	Column number:	23	24	25	26	27	28	29	30	31

Table A-1. States — Who: Age, Race/Ethnicity, and Household Structure, 2023

State code	STATE	Total population, 15 years and over	Marital status of population 15 years and over (percent)				Foreign born (percent of total population)	Languages spoken (percent of households)			
			Never married	Now married (includes separated)	Widowed	Divorced		English only	Spanish, with or without English	Other languages, with or without English	Limited English-speaking household
	ACS table number:	B12001	B12001	B12001	B12001	B12001	B05002	C16002	C16002	C16002	C16002
	Column number:	32	33	34	35	36	37	38	39	40	41

Table A-1. States — Who: Age, Race/Ethnicity, and Household Structure, 2023

				Household type (percent of all households)										
				Family households				Nonfamily households			Unmarried partner households			
	STATE	Total households	Average household size	Total family households	Married-couple families	Male householder families (no spouse)	Female householder families (no spouse)	Total nonfamily households	Total one-person households	One person households age 65 or over	Total unmarried cohabiting partner households	Same-sex cohabiting partner households		Same-sex married partner households
State code	ACS table number:	B11001	B25010	B11001	B11001	B11001	B11001	B11001	B11001	B11010 / B11001	B11009	B11009		B11009
	Column number:	42	43	44	45	46	47	48	49	50	51	52		53

Table A-1. States — Who: Age, Race/Ethnicity, and Household Structure, 2023

		Households with people under 18 years old				Households with people 60 years and over				
			Household type (percent)				Household type (percent)			
	STATE	Total households with children	Married-couple families	Male householder families (no spouse)	Female householder families (no spouse)	Total households with people 60 years and over	Married-couple families	Male householder families (no spouse)	Female householder families (no spouse)	Nonfamily households
State code	ACS table number:	B11005	B11005	B11005	B11005	B11006	B11006	B11006	B11006	B11006
	Column number:	54	55	56	57	58	59	60	61	62

Table A-2. Counties — Who: Age, Race/Ethnicity, and Household Structure, 2023

				Population by age (percent)						Race alone or in combination (percent)					
	STATE County	Total population	Percent change, 2010–2023	Under 18 years	18 to 24 years	25 to 44 years	45 to 64 years	65 years and over	Median age	White	Black or African American	American Indian and Alaska Native	Asian	Native Hawaiian or Other Pacific Islander	Some other race
STATE County code	ACS table number:	B01003	Census PEP	B01001	B01001	B01001	B01001	B01001	B01002	B02008	B02009	B02010	B02011	B02012	B02013
	Column number:	1	2	3	4	5	6	7	8	9	10	11	12	13	14

Table A-2. Counties — Who: Age, Race/Ethnicity, and Household Structure, 2023

									Household type (percent of all households)						
									Family households				Nonfamily households		
	STATE County	Two or more races (percent)	Hispanic or Latino (percent)	Native, born in state of residence (percent)	Foreign born (percent)	Non-citizens (percent)	Total households	Average household size	Total	Married couple	Male householder	Female householder	Total	One-person households	Percent of households with people age 60 years and over
STATE County code	ACS table number:	B02001	B03003	B05002	B05002	B05002	B11001	B25010	B11001	B11001	B11001	B11001	B11001	B11001	B11006
	Column number:	15	16	17	18	19	20	21	22	23	24	25	26	27	28

Table A-3. Metropolitan Areas — Who: Age, Race/Ethnicity, and Household Structure, 2023

Metropolitan area / division code	Metropolitan area / division	Total population	Percent change, 2010–2023	Population by age (percent): Under 18 years	18 to 24 years	25 to 44 years	45 to 64 years	65 years and over	Median age	Race alone or in combination (percent): White	Black or African American	Asian + Native Hawaiian or Other Pacific Islander	American Indian and Alaska Native + Some other race	Two or more races
	ACS table number:	B01003	Population Estimates	B01001	B01001	B01001	B01001	B01001	B01002	B02008	B02009	B02011 + B02012	B02010 + B02013	B02001
	column number:	1	2	3	4	5	6	7	8	9	10	11	12	13

Table A-3. Metropolitan Areas — Who: Age, Race/Ethnicity, and Household Structure, 2023

Metropolitan area / division code	Metropolitan area / division	Hispanic or Latino (percent)	Born in state of residence (percent)	Foreign born (percent)	Not a U.S. citiz(en (percent)	Total households	Average household size	Household type (percent of all households): Family households: Total	Married-couple	Male householder	Female householder	Nonfamily households: Total	One-person households	Percent of households with people age 60 years and over
	ACS table number:	B03003	B05002	B05002	B05002	B11001	B25010	B11001	B11001	B11001	B11001	B11001	B11001	B11006
	column number:	14	15	16	17	18	19	20	21	22	23	24	25	26

Table A-4. Cities — Who: Age, Race/Ethnicity, and Household Structure, 2023

STATE and place code	STATE Place	Total population	Percent change, 2010–2023	Population by age (percent): Under 18 years	18 to 24 years	25 to 44 years	45 to 64 years	65 years and over	Median age	Race alone or in combination (percent): White	Black	Asian + Native Hawaiian or Other Pacific Islander	American Indian and Alaska Native + Some other race	Two or more races (percent)	Hispanic or Latino (percent)
	ACS table number:	B01003	Census PEP	B01001	B01001	B01001	B01001	B01001	B01002	B02008	B02009	B02011 + B02012	B02010 + B02013	B02001	B03003
FIPS	column number:	1	2	3	4	5	6	7	8	9	10	11	12	13	14

Table A-4. Cities — Who: Age, Race/Ethnicity, and Household Structure, 2023

STATE and place code	STATE Place	Native, born in state of residence (percent)	Foreign born (percent)	Non-citizens (percent)	Total households	Average household size	Household type (percent of all households): Family households: Total	Married-couple	Male house-holder	Female house-holder	Nonfamily households: Total	One-person households	Percent of households with people age 60 years and over
	ACS table number:	B05002	B05002	B05002	B11001	B25010	B11001	B11001	B11001	B11001	B11001	B11001	B11006
FIPS	column number:	15	16	17	18	19	20	21	22	23	24	25	26

Table A-1. States — Who: Age, Race/Ethnicity, and Household Structure, 2023

State code	STATE	Total population	Percent change, 2010–2023	Race alone or in combination (percent)						Percent Hispanic or Latino	Percent two or more races	Percent White alone, not Hispanic or Latino
				White	Black or African American	American Indian or Alaska Native	Asian	Native Hawaiian or Pacific Islander	Some other race			
	ACS table number:	B01003	Census PEP	B02008	B02009	B02010	B02011	B02012	B02013	B03003	B02001	B01001H
	Column number:	1	2	3	4	5	6	7	8	9	10	11
	UNITED STATES	334,914,896	8.3	72.3	14.4	2.6	7.4	0.5	16.4	19.4	12.8	57.1
1	Alabama	5,108,468	6.7	69.7	27.1	2.0	2.1	0.2	4.9	5.7	5.6	63.3
2	Alaska	733,406	2.7	72.2	5.4	20.5	9.1	2.5	5.8	7.5	14.1	57.7
4	Arizona	7,431,344	15.9	77.3	6.7	6.2	5.3	0.6	24.9	31.6	19.9	52.3
5	Arkansas	3,067,732	5.0	80.0	16.1	2.9	2.2	0.5	10.3	9.1	11.5	67.1
6	California	38,965,193	4.4	56.2	7.2	3.3	18.4	0.8	34.4	40.4	19.0	33.3
8	Colorado	5,877,610	16.4	84.5	5.8	3.5	5.1	0.4	16.7	22.7	14.7	64.5
9	Connecticut	3,617,176	1.1	74.3	13.9	1.3	5.9	0.2	16.0	18.6	10.8	61.4
10	Delaware	1,031,890	14.7	66.2	25.8	1.5	5.1	0.3	9.9	11.1	8.2	58.0
11	District of Columbia	678,972	12.2	47.5	45.8	1.5	6.4	0.3	10.8	12.0	10.7	37.1
12	Florida	22,610,726	19.9	73.6	17.7	1.6	4.1	0.2	23.2	27.4	19.3	50.3
13	Georgia	11,029,227	13.5	58.1	33.4	2.2	5.5	0.2	10.0	11.1	8.8	48.7
15	Hawaii	1,435,138	5.2	44.3	3.7	2.9	57.0	27.1	5.4	10.1	28.2	20.9
16	Idaho	1,964,726	25.1	91.1	1.4	3.1	2.8	0.5	11.5	13.8	9.7	78.4
17	Illinois	12,549,689	-2.3	71.1	15.3	2.2	7.1	0.1	16.0	19.0	11.1	57.9
18	Indiana	6,862,199	5.7	83.9	11.2	1.8	3.3	0.1	7.7	8.7	7.7	75.1
19	Iowa	3,207,004	5.1	90.4	5.5	1.9	3.1	0.3	5.9	7.3	6.5	82.4
20	Kansas	2,940,547	2.9	86.4	7.7	3.2	3.9	0.3	10.7	13.7	11.2	72.7
21	Kentucky	4,526,154	4.1	88.7	9.5	2.1	2.1	0.2	4.4	4.9	6.6	81.5
22	Louisiana	4,573,749	0.6	63.8	32.7	2.4	2.5	0.2	7.0	7.1	7.9	55.7
23	Maine	1,395,722	5.2	95.9	2.6	1.7	2.0	0.1	3.8	2.2	5.9	89.5
24	Maryland	6,180,253	6.8	55.3	32.2	2.0	8.2	0.2	11.6	12.6	8.6	46.3
25	Massachusetts	7,001,399	6.7	77.3	10.3	1.1	8.6	0.1	14.8	13.5	11.0	65.9
26	Michigan	10,037,261	1.6	80.5	15.3	1.9	4.3	0.1	5.6	6.0	7.2	72.3
27	Minnesota	5,737,915	8.1	83.3	9.1	2.4	6.4	0.2	6.2	6.4	7.1	75.6
28	Mississippi	2,939,690	-1.0	60.4	37.5	2.2	1.6	0.2	3.8	3.7	5.2	55.1
29	Missouri	6,196,156	3.3	84.6	12.8	2.0	2.9	0.3	5.1	5.2	7.1	76.5
30	Montana	1,132,812	14.4	91.5	1.2	8.4	1.9	0.2	4.6	4.6	7.2	83.3
31	Nebraska	1,978,379	8.1	86.1	7.0	2.6	3.4	0.2	10.3	12.9	9.0	75.2
32	Nevada	3,194,176	18.1	64.7	12.5	3.2	12.2	1.8	23.6	29.9	16.4	44.4
33	New Hampshire	1,402,054	6.5	94.2	2.7	1.2	3.7	0.3	5.6	4.7	7.0	86.5
34	New Jersey	9,290,841	5.5	64.4	15.3	1.9	11.4	0.1	20.0	22.7	12.3	50.6
35	New Mexico	2,114,371	2.4	73.0	3.4	12.0	2.8	0.4	35.7	48.6	26.1	35.9
36	New York	19,571,216	0.9	63.5	17.6	1.8	10.5	0.2	17.9	19.8	10.5	52.8
37	North Carolina	10,835,491	13.3	68.8	22.8	2.5	4.3	0.2	10.3	11.4	8.3	59.8
38	North Dakota	783,926	16.2	89.0	4.3	6.5	2.4	0.3	4.5	4.9	6.7	81.5
39	Ohio	11,785,935	2.1	83.0	14.5	1.6	3.4	0.2	4.7	4.8	6.8	75.6
40	Oklahoma	4,053,824	7.8	78.8	9.7	14.3	3.3	0.5	9.8	12.9	15.0	61.7
41	Oregon	4,233,358	10.3	86.3	3.4	3.8	6.8	0.8	12.8	14.9	12.9	70.8
42	Pennsylvania	12,961,683	2.0	80.6	13.1	1.3	4.7	0.1	8.4	8.9	7.4	72.7
72	Puerto Rico	3,205,691	-13.9	57.4	12.1	2.4	0.3	0.0	69.7	99.0	38.6	0.6
44	Rhode Island	1,095,962	4.1	79.8	10.8	2.5	4.8	0.3	17.1	18.0	13.5	67.7
45	South Carolina	5,373,555	15.9	70.1	26.7	1.7	2.5	0.2	6.2	7.4	7.0	61.9
46	South Dakota	919,318	12.6	86.2	3.4	10.4	2.2	0.1	4.2	5.1	6.1	79.4
47	Tennessee	7,126,489	12.1	79.3	17.2	1.7	2.7	0.2	6.8	7.5	7.4	71.1
48	Texas	30,503,301	20.8	70.1	14.2	2.6	6.8	0.3	30.3	39.8	23.3	38.7
49	Utah	3,417,734	23.2	87.7	2.1	2.3	4.0	1.7	12.4	16.0	9.5	74.5
50	Vermont	647,464	3.5	95.6	2.5	1.7	2.7	0.2	3.7	2.5	5.8	89.3
51	Virginia	8,715,698	8.6	68.7	21.2	1.7	8.8	0.3	9.9	11.1	9.8	58.1
53	Washington	7,812,880	15.9	77.5	6.2	3.5	13.1	1.4	12.7	14.6	13.1	62.4
54	West Virginia	1,770,071	-4.5	94.9	4.7	1.6	1.1	0.1	2.8	2.1	5.0	89.4
55	Wisconsin	5,910,955	3.9	87.2	7.7	2.1	3.8	0.2	7.2	8.1	7.6	78.4
56	Wyoming	584,057	3.5	92.5	1.6	4.5	1.7	0.2	8.5	10.8	8.3	81.3

Table A-1. States — Who: Age, Race/Ethnicity, and Household Structure, 2023—*Continued*

State code	STATE	Total population	Population by age (percent) Under 5 years	5 to 17 years	18 to 24 years	25 to 44 years	45 to 64 years	65 to 84 years	85 years and over	+/- U.S. percent under 18 years	+/- U.S. percent 65 years and over	Percent female
	ACS table number:	B01001	B01001	B01001	B01001	B01001	B01001	B01001	B01001	B01001	B01001	B01001
	Column number:	12	13	14	15	16	17	18	19	20	21	22
	UNITED STATES	334,914,896	5.5	16.2	9.1	26.9	24.6	15.9	1.8	X	X	50.5
1	Alabama	5,108,468	5.6	16.5	9.4	25.3	24.9	16.5	1.7	0.4	0.5	51.6
2	Alaska	733,406	6.2	17.6	8.9	30.3	23.0	13.1	1.0	2.1	-3.7	47.4
4	Arizona	7,431,344	5.3	16.0	9.4	26.5	23.5	17.5	1.9	-0.4	1.6	50.1
5	Arkansas	3,067,732	5.8	17.1	9.4	25.8	24.0	16.2	1.8	1.2	0.3	50.7
6	California	38,965,193	5.4	16.3	9.1	28.6	24.4	14.4	1.8	0.0	-1.5	50.1
8	Colorado	5,877,610	5.2	15.4	9.0	30.7	23.6	14.6	1.5	-1.1	-1.6	49.3
9	Connecticut	3,617,176	5.0	15.0	9.3	25.4	26.3	16.8	2.2	-1.7	1.4	50.9
10	Delaware	1,031,890	5.3	15.3	8.6	24.6	25.0	19.2	2.1	-1.2	3.6	51.6
11	District of Columbia	678,972	5.7	13.0	10.2	38.1	19.9	11.8	1.3	-3.1	-4.6	52.6
12	Florida	22,610,726	5.0	14.4	8.0	25.3	25.6	19.3	2.4	-2.3	4.0	50.8
13	Georgia	11,029,227	5.6	17.3	9.5	27.2	24.9	14.1	1.3	1.3	-2.3	51.2
15	Hawaii	1,435,138	5.4	15.1	8.1	26.4	23.9	18.6	2.5	-1.2	3.4	49.9
16	Idaho	1,964,726	5.6	18.1	9.8	26.1	22.9	15.9	1.5	2.0	-0.3	49.7
17	Illinois	12,549,689	5.3	16.3	9.1	26.8	25.1	15.6	2.0	-0.2	-0.1	50.6
18	Indiana	6,862,199	5.9	17.2	9.7	25.8	24.2	15.5	1.7	1.3	-0.5	50.3
19	Iowa	3,207,004	5.7	16.9	9.8	25.2	23.8	16.3	2.2	0.9	0.8	50.0
20	Kansas	2,940,547	5.8	17.6	10.1	26.0	22.9	15.7	1.9	1.7	-0.1	49.8
21	Kentucky	4,526,154	5.8	16.5	9.0	25.7	25.1	16.2	1.6	0.7	0.1	50.4
22	Louisiana	4,573,749	6.0	17.2	8.9	26.5	24.0	15.8	1.6	1.6	-0.3	51.1
23	Maine	1,395,722	4.3	13.3	7.9	24.6	26.9	20.8	2.2	-4.1	5.2	50.9
24	Maryland	6,180,253	5.6	16.4	8.5	26.6	25.7	15.5	1.8	0.3	-0.4	51.5
25	Massachusetts	7,001,399	4.9	14.3	9.8	27.0	25.5	16.5	2.0	-2.5	0.8	51.1
26	Michigan	10,037,261	5.3	15.8	9.2	25.3	25.2	17.3	1.9	-0.7	1.6	50.5
27	Minnesota	5,737,915	5.7	16.9	8.7	26.6	24.2	15.9	2.0	0.9	0.2	50.0
28	Mississippi	2,939,690	5.7	17.3	9.7	25.2	24.6	16.0	1.6	1.3	-0.1	51.5
29	Missouri	6,196,156	5.6	16.5	9.2	25.9	24.4	16.5	1.9	0.4	0.7	50.7
30	Montana	1,132,812	4.9	15.9	9.0	26.1	23.7	18.6	1.9	-0.9	2.8	49.5
31	Nebraska	1,978,379	6.1	18.1	9.7	26.1	22.7	15.4	1.8	2.5	-0.5	49.8
32	Nevada	3,194,176	5.4	16.1	8.0	28.2	24.9	16.0	1.4	-0.3	-0.3	49.7
33	New Hampshire	1,402,054	4.5	13.4	8.6	25.4	27.5	18.9	1.8	-3.8	3.0	50.1
34	New Jersey	9,290,841	5.6	16.0	8.3	26.1	26.3	15.8	1.9	-0.1	0.0	50.8
35	New Mexico	2,114,371	4.9	16.3	9.2	26.2	23.5	18.0	2.0	-0.5	2.2	50.4
36	New York	19,571,216	5.3	14.9	8.9	27.0	25.4	16.4	2.1	-1.5	0.9	51.2
37	North Carolina	10,835,491	5.5	15.9	9.5	26.3	25.1	16.0	1.6	-0.3	0.0	51.0
38	North Dakota	783,926	5.9	17.0	10.8	28.3	21.0	14.9	2.2	1.2	-0.6	48.9
39	Ohio	11,785,935	5.6	16.3	8.8	25.7	24.8	16.8	2.0	0.1	1.1	50.7
40	Oklahoma	4,053,824	5.9	17.9	10.0	26.6	22.9	15.1	1.6	2.1	-1.0	50.3
41	Oregon	4,233,358	4.7	14.9	8.3	28.2	24.3	17.6	1.9	-2.1	1.9	50.3
42	Pennsylvania	12,961,683	5.1	15.1	9.0	25.5	25.2	17.7	2.3	-1.5	2.3	50.7
72	Puerto Rico	3,205,691	2.9	12.6	9.4	25.1	26.0	20.8	3.2	-6.1	6.3	52.6
44	Rhode Island	1,095,962	4.8	13.7	9.7	27.1	25.3	17.2	2.1	-3.2	1.7	51.1
45	South Carolina	5,373,555	5.3	15.9	9.0	25.4	25.0	17.7	1.6	-0.4	1.6	51.5
46	South Dakota	919,318	6.0	17.8	9.2	25.4	23.1	16.4	2.1	2.1	0.7	49.1
47	Tennessee	7,126,489	5.8	16.2	8.9	26.9	24.9	15.9	1.6	0.2	-0.2	50.9
48	Texas	30,503,301	6.3	18.4	9.6	28.6	23.3	12.5	1.3	3.0	-3.9	50.1
49	Utah	3,417,734	6.7	20.6	11.7	28.5	20.3	10.9	1.2	5.6	-5.5	49.3
50	Vermont	647,464	4.2	13.5	9.5	24.4	26.2	20.2	2.0	-4.0	4.5	50.1
51	Virginia	8,715,698	5.5	16.0	9.2	27.2	24.9	15.5	1.7	-0.2	-0.5	50.6
53	Washington	7,812,880	5.3	15.7	8.4	29.7	23.7	15.5	1.7	-0.6	-0.6	49.6
54	West Virginia	1,770,071	4.9	14.9	9.0	23.7	25.9	19.5	2.0	-1.8	3.8	50.1
55	Wisconsin	5,910,955	5.2	15.8	9.3	25.3	25.2	17.2	2.0	-0.7	1.5	49.9
56	Wyoming	584,057	5.2	17.0	8.6	27.1	22.8	17.2	2.0	0.6	1.5	49.4

Table A-1. States — Who: Age, Race/Ethnicity, and Household Structure, 2023—*Continued*

State code	STATE	Median age: Total population	White alone, not Hispanic or Latino	Black alone	American Indian or Alaska Native alone	Asian alone	Native Hawaiian or Pacific Islander alone	Some other race alone	Two or more races	Hispanic or Latino
	ACS table number:	B01002	B01002H	B01002B	B01002C	B01002D	B01002E	B01002F	B01002G	B01002I
	Column number:	23	24	25	26	27	28	29	30	31
	UNITED STATES	39.2	44.2	35.9	33.4	39.1	33.2	32.3	30.0	31.0
1	Alabama	39.6	43.1	36.3	39.1	37.0	NA	25.6	26.6	24.2
2	Alaska	36.5	40.9	36.8	30.5	40.0	24.5	34.9	23.5	28.5
4	Arizona	39.3	49.2	33.5	32.7	39.5	30.7	32.4	29.4	29.8
5	Arkansas	38.9	43.1	34.9	35.2	35.9	22.6	29.4	27.5	26.7
6	California	38.2	47.2	38.3	34.5	41.0	37.7	32.5	30.9	31.7
8	Colorado	37.9	41.9	34.8	32.1	36.9	32.3	32.7	29.9	29.8
9	Connecticut	41.5	48.5	35.7	41.0	37.4	31.6	32.9	30.1	31.0
10	Delaware	42.0	50.0	37.4	23.7	38.3	48.5	30.3	25.5	27.1
11	District of Columbia	34.9	35.2	36.9	33.2	34.7	33.7	32.1	30.3	32.5
12	Florida	42.8	51.4	35.5	36.0	41.3	36.5	36.1	37.8	37.5
13	Georgia	37.9	42.9	35.8	28.3	37.8	28.1	28.7	26.8	27.8
15	Hawaii	41.4	46.1	34.4	34.2	50.8	35.9	29.5	30.1	26.0
16	Idaho	37.8	40.5	25.1	33.0	37.2	21.6	33.7	27.6	26.4
17	Illinois	39.5	44.2	36.8	34.0	38.9	43.3	33.1	28.2	30.7
18	Indiana	38.3	41.7	33.5	32.5	32.3	26.1	29.4	24.6	26.7
19	Iowa	39.1	42.1	27.4	34.5	34.7	28.3	28.6	24.3	26.0
20	Kansas	37.9	41.5	34.3	36.1	37.2	34.5	32.8	24.4	26.5
21	Kentucky	39.2	41.6	34.2	40.4	35.1	28.8	28.5	26.2	25.5
22	Louisiana	38.7	42.3	35.7	35.1	39.0	NA	29.4	28.6	30.7
23	Maine	44.9	46.6	32.1	36.7	38.4	NA	33.5	32.4	31.4
24	Maryland	39.8	44.8	38.9	30.8	41.4	28.0	30.7	27.1	29.8
25	Massachusetts	40.3	46.0	34.6	30.9	35.8	37.7	32.2	28.9	30.0
26	Michigan	40.5	43.9	35.4	33.8	35.7	NA	31.3	26.7	28.1
27	Minnesota	39.1	43.2	29.0	32.5	33.2	33.8	30.2	23.1	26.6
28	Mississippi	39.3	42.9	36.7	33.2	38.1	25.7	25.4	25.4	26.6
29	Missouri	39.3	41.9	34.4	40.9	35.7	25.8	30.2	26.3	27.1
30	Montana	40.6	42.6	29.4	30.5	42.9	42.5	35.7	30.5	27.4
31	Nebraska	37.4	41.3	32.2	29.4	33.6	20.3	26.0	25.5	25.0
32	Nevada	39.4	48.4	35.5	34.2	43.4	33.4	32.3	27.9	30.4
33	New Hampshire	43.4	46.1	30.1	40.4	38.9	34.7	33.2	31.6	29.9
34	New Jersey	40.4	46.7	37.5	29.3	39.8	43.1	33.9	32.0	33.4
35	New Mexico	39.9	51.9	33.5	35.4	38.5	28.9	37.7	34.6	33.8
36	New York	40.2	44.5	38.0	34.3	39.6	32.2	35.0	33.3	34.4
37	North Carolina	39.4	44.4	37.5	36.9	36.6	35.9	28.1	24.4	26.3
38	North Dakota	36.3	38.9	30.5	29.3	32.3	13.8	28.2	23.1	23.3
39	Ohio	39.9	43.0	34.7	39.5	35.9	28.0	30.0	25.4	27.5
40	Oklahoma	37.1	42.7	33.8	31.3	34.7	19.7	27.7	25.6	24.8
41	Oregon	40.7	45.0	32.5	34.9	39.4	30.9	30.3	29.5	28.2
42	Pennsylvania	41.1	45.4	35.1	35.9	36.9	32.3	30.1	25.4	28.5
72	Puerto Rico	45.0	48.6	48.2	33.8	42.5	61.6	43.0	45.6	45.0
44	Rhode Island	40.8	47.3	35.0	29.3	35.4	50.9	32.0	28.8	29.6
45	South Carolina	40.5	44.9	37.5	30.5	39.0	41.0	30.9	26.3	27.9
46	South Dakota	38.5	41.8	24.6	26.7	33.5	NA	30.4	25.9	23.3
47	Tennessee	39.1	42.5	35.3	27.1	37.9	30.1	26.7	25.7	26.0
48	Texas	35.9	42.7	34.3	33.3	37.4	31.5	32.2	30.8	30.4
49	Utah	32.3	34.4	26.7	31.0	35.3	29.4	29.8	24.2	26.3
50	Vermont	43.7	45.0	44.2	36.7	33.7	56.1	35.3	33.6	34.2
51	Virginia	39.3	43.1	38.0	34.9	39.2	36.7	31.0	26.9	29.8
53	Washington	38.6	43.8	34.3	34.1	36.8	31.6	29.5	26.8	26.8
54	West Virginia	42.8	44.0	39.9	33.2	37.8	NA	30.0	28.7	28.4
55	Wisconsin	40.5	44.5	31.0	32.8	31.5	46.2	30.9	24.3	25.8
56	Wyoming	39.3	41.8	33.9	29.7	47.0	61.4	32.7	29.7	28.7

Table A-1. States — Who: Age, Race/Ethnicity, and Household Structure, 2023—*Continued*

State code	STATE	Total population, 15 years and over	Marital status of population 15 years and over (percent)				Foreign born (percent of total population)	Languages spoken (percent of households)			
			Never married	Now married (includes separated)	Widowed	Divorced		English only	Spanish, with or without English	Other languages, with or without English	Limited English-speaking household
	ACS table number:	B12001	B12001	B12001	B12001	B12001	B05002	C16002	C16002	C16002	C16002
	Column number:	32	33	34	35	36	37	38	39	40	41
	UNITED STATES	275,577,890	34.4	49.8	5.5	10.4	14.3	76.6	13.3	10.0	4.4
1	Alabama	4,183,456	31.7	49.9	6.6	11.8	4.0	93.4	3.8	2.9	1.3
2	Alaska	587,506	34.5	50.0	3.8	11.6	7.4	82.4	4.5	13.1	1.8
4	Arizona	6,149,973	34.3	49.0	5.4	11.3	13.2	71.9	19.7	8.4	3.4
5	Arkansas	2,496,533	30.5	50.7	6.5	12.2	5.3	91.4	6.0	2.6	1.6
6	California	32,099,889	38.4	48.2	4.7	8.7	27.3	53.0	27.3	19.7	8.5
8	Colorado	4,892,956	33.1	51.9	4.1	10.9	9.6	82.0	11.5	6.5	2.3
9	Connecticut	3,033,170	35.8	48.5	5.4	10.4	16.3	73.5	13.8	12.6	5.0
10	Delaware	858,290	33.2	50.0	6.0	10.7	11.2	83.5	8.2	8.3	2.6
11	District of Columbia	569,959	54.4	33.9	3.5	8.1	14.1	78.6	8.7	12.8	3.2
12	Florida	19,035,619	31.3	50.1	6.3	12.2	22.1	67.7	22.8	9.5	7.0
13	Georgia	8,972,322	35.3	48.7	5.1	10.9	11.6	83.6	8.3	8.1	2.8
15	Hawaii	1,188,673	33.9	50.9	5.9	9.3	17.8	68.0	3.4	28.6	5.1
16	Idaho	1,587,304	28.4	55.9	4.6	11.1	5.7	87.5	8.4	4.1	1.6
17	Illinois	10,355,562	36.4	48.5	5.5	9.6	15.0	75.4	12.9	11.7	4.2
18	Indiana	5,574,487	32.5	49.8	5.7	12.1	6.3	88.7	5.8	5.5	2.3
19	Iowa	2,614,371	31.4	52.6	5.7	10.3	5.9	90.7	4.9	4.4	2.0
20	Kansas	2,381,110	31.1	52.7	5.5	10.8	7.1	86.8	8.2	5.0	2.6
21	Kentucky	3,694,195	29.5	51.3	6.5	12.6	4.5	92.7	3.7	3.6	1.7
22	Louisiana	3,698,398	36.1	46.1	6.3	11.5	4.9	89.5	5.1	5.5	2.0
23	Maine	1,196,853	29.1	52.3	6.0	12.6	3.8	92.6	1.0	6.4	0.9
24	Maryland	5,066,739	36.4	48.8	5.3	9.5	17.0	77.8	9.0	13.3	3.9
25	Massachusetts	5,912,054	38.0	47.8	4.9	9.4	18.0	72.3	10.2	17.5	6.0
26	Michigan	8,314,793	34.2	49.1	5.6	11.0	7.3	88.8	3.5	7.7	2.0
27	Minnesota	4,676,415	33.4	51.8	4.8	10.1	8.6	86.8	4.5	8.7	2.3
28	Mississippi	2,396,940	33.8	47.5	7.0	11.7	2.6	94.9	2.9	2.2	0.8
29	Missouri	5,076,786	31.7	50.7	5.9	11.7	4.8	92.0	3.3	4.7	1.2
30	Montana	939,482	29.8	52.6	5.5	12.1	2.2	93.9	2.6	3.6	0.6
31	Nebraska	1,586,300	31.5	53.5	5.0	10.0	7.7	87.0	8.1	4.9	2.6
32	Nevada	2,635,992	35.6	46.4	5.0	13.0	19.2	68.2	19.7	12.1	5.3
33	New Hampshire	1,199,031	30.5	52.5	5.5	11.6	6.8	89.1	3.0	7.9	1.3
34	New Jersey	7,646,402	34.9	51.3	5.4	8.4	24.2	64.2	17.5	18.3	7.7
35	New Mexico	1,750,707	36.1	44.9	5.9	13.1	10.2	62.6	29.0	8.4	5.3
36	New York	16,321,357	38.6	47.1	5.6	8.8	23.1	67.3	15.1	17.5	8.1
37	North Carolina	8,940,919	32.6	51.2	5.8	10.4	9.2	86.3	8.0	5.8	2.5
38	North Dakota	633,643	33.5	51.6	5.2	9.8	4.0	92.3	2.6	5.1	1.4
39	Ohio	9,683,030	33.8	48.5	6.1	11.6	5.3	90.9	3.2	6.0	1.6
40	Oklahoma	3,261,460	31.1	50.0	6.3	12.6	6.1	88.2	7.8	4.1	2.0
41	Oregon	3,560,049	32.7	49.9	5.1	12.3	9.6	84.0	8.9	7.1	2.5
42	Pennsylvania	10,817,285	34.6	49.5	6.4	9.5	8.0	85.8	6.3	7.9	2.9
72	Puerto Rico	2,817,547	41.8	36.1	7.8	14.3	2.6	4.1	95.7	0.2	66.2
44	Rhode Island	928,906	36.8	46.5	5.7	11.0	14.7	76.0	12.7	11.3	5.4
45	South Carolina	4,444,892	32.0	51.5	6.4	10.0	5.9	90.6	5.3	4.1	1.5
46	South Dakota	739,226	32.2	52.1	5.6	10.1	4.3	91.9	3.1	5.0	1.4
47	Tennessee	5,845,145	31.3	50.9	6.1	11.7	6.1	91.0	5.1	4.0	1.8
48	Texas	24,317,743	34.2	51.3	4.8	9.8	17.9	61.9	29.6	8.5	6.8
49	Utah	2,658,577	31.4	56.1	3.5	9.1	8.9	80.1	13.0	6.9	2.4
50	Vermont	554,679	33.1	50.6	4.9	11.4	4.5	92.0	1.9	6.1	0.7
51	Virginia	7,180,123	33.1	51.7	5.3	9.9	13.3	81.2	7.8	11.0	2.7
53	Washington	6,455,198	32.6	51.7	4.5	11.2	15.5	76.9	8.8	14.2	3.7
54	West Virginia	1,483,374	29.3	49.5	8.1	13.1	1.8	96.8	1.4	1.8	0.4
55	Wisconsin	4,901,177	33.8	50.5	5.2	10.5	5.2	90.2	4.9	4.8	1.5
56	Wyoming	478,840	28.5	54.6	6.2	10.6	3.6	90.7	5.9	3.4	1.1

Table A-1. States — Who: Age, Race/Ethnicity, and Household Structure, 2023—*Continued*

State code	STATE	Total households	Average household size	Household type (percent of all households)									
				Family households				Nonfamily households			Unmarried partner households		
				Total family households	Married-couple families	Male householder families (no spouse)	Female householder families (no spouse)	Total nonfamily households	Total one-person households	One person households age 65 or over	Total unmarried cohabiting partner households	Same-sex cohabiting partner households	Same-sex married partner households
	ACS table number:	B11001	B25010	B11001	B11001	B11001	B11001	B11001	B11001	B11010 / B11001	B11009	B11009	B11009
	Column number:	42	43	44	45	46	47	48	49	50	51	52	53
	UNITED STATES	131,332,360	2.49	64.0	46.8	5.1	12.1	36.0	28.8	11.6	7.2	0.4	0.6
1	Alabama	2,051,545	2.42	64.8	46.3	4.4	14.1	35.2	30.2	12.1	5.5	0.3	0.4
2	Alaska	276,852	2.54	61.9	46.3	5.7	9.9	38.1	30.2	10.2	8.7	0.3	0.6
4	Arizona	2,907,014	2.50	63.9	46.8	5.3	11.8	36.1	27.7	12.0	8.1	0.4	0.7
5	Arkansas	1,232,871	2.42	64.7	46.7	5.0	12.9	35.3	29.9	12.0	5.9	0.2	0.4
6	California	13,699,816	2.78	67.4	48.0	6.3	13.1	32.6	24.7	9.9	7.7	0.5	0.8
8	Colorado	2,428,261	2.37	61.2	47.8	4.6	8.8	38.8	28.6	10.1	8.2	0.5	0.7
9	Connecticut	1,442,969	2.44	64.0	46.3	4.8	12.9	36.0	29.0	12.7	7.5	0.4	0.5
10	Delaware	412,048	2.45	65.2	47.6	4.2	13.3	34.8	28.0	12.2	6.3	0.4	1.1
11	District of Columbia	334,673	1.92	41.1	25.5	2.5	13.1	58.9	47.8	11.0	7.7	1.1	1.5
12	Florida	8,966,402	2.47	64.7	47.0	5.2	12.5	35.3	27.9	13.0	7.6	0.4	0.7
13	Georgia	4,150,138	2.60	65.9	46.4	5.0	14.5	34.1	27.7	10.1	6.2	0.4	0.6
15	Hawaii	493,898	2.82	68.2	50.4	6.2	11.6	31.8	25.1	12.0	7.3	0.5	0.7
16	Idaho	733,244	2.61	69.6	55.7	4.8	9.1	30.4	23.7	10.0	6.4	0.3	0.4
17	Illinois	5,071,288	2.42	61.8	44.9	5.3	11.7	38.2	31.3	12.2	7.0	0.5	0.5
18	Indiana	2,754,881	2.43	63.0	46.7	5.0	11.2	37.0	29.9	11.9	7.7	0.3	0.5
19	Iowa	1,337,243	2.33	61.3	48.2	4.2	8.9	38.7	30.9	12.5	7.7	0.3	0.3
20	Kansas	1,188,340	2.40	63.4	48.9	4.7	9.7	36.6	29.7	12.0	6.8	0.4	0.5
21	Kentucky	1,853,603	2.38	64.1	46.8	5.2	12.1	35.9	29.6	11.9	6.8	0.4	0.4
22	Louisiana	1,833,915	2.43	62.8	41.8	5.4	15.6	37.2	32.0	12.6	6.6	0.3	0.4
23	Maine	616,085	2.20	60.9	47.9	4.5	8.5	39.1	29.7	13.4	9.7	0.5	0.9
24	Maryland	2,384,715	2.54	64.3	45.8	5.3	13.3	35.7	29.3	11.4	6.6	0.3	0.6
25	Massachusetts	2,800,984	2.41	61.8	45.3	4.6	11.8	38.2	29.3	12.7	7.8	0.5	0.8
26	Michigan	4,107,809	2.39	62.5	46.2	5.0	11.3	37.5	30.8	12.9	7.2	0.4	0.5
27	Minnesota	2,344,432	2.39	61.7	48.6	4.6	8.5	38.3	30.2	12.3	8.2	0.5	0.7
28	Mississippi	1,166,617	2.44	64.6	43.5	4.9	16.2	35.4	30.9	12.8	4.6	0.2	0.3
29	Missouri	2,556,271	2.36	62.1	46.6	4.6	10.9	37.9	30.7	12.5	7.4	0.4	0.5
30	Montana	472,867	2.33	60.5	48.3	4.2	8.0	39.5	31.2	12.9	7.4	0.4	0.6
31	Nebraska	813,864	2.37	62.4	49.0	4.0	9.3	37.6	30.3	11.6	7.1	0.3	0.3
32	Nevada	1,224,685	2.58	62.7	43.1	6.6	12.9	37.3	29.1	10.7	8.8	0.4	0.9
33	New Hampshire	569,493	2.39	64.5	51.3	4.4	8.7	35.5	26.9	12.5	8.5	0.4	0.7
34	New Jersey	3,538,457	2.58	67.7	49.6	5.2	12.9	32.3	26.2	11.9	7.2	0.3	0.6
35	New Mexico	856,580	2.42	61.2	40.9	6.4	13.9	38.8	31.9	14.0	9.1	0.6	0.6
36	New York	7,809,267	2.43	60.8	42.1	5.2	13.5	39.2	31.5	12.9	7.1	0.4	0.7
37	North Carolina	4,392,669	2.40	64.3	47.4	4.6	12.3	35.7	29.1	11.5	6.5	0.4	0.5
38	North Dakota	338,059	2.23	56.8	46.0	4.4	6.5	43.2	34.7	11.6	8.2	0.3	0.1
39	Ohio	4,917,309	2.34	60.9	44.2	4.8	11.9	39.1	32.2	13.3	7.7	0.3	0.4
40	Oklahoma	1,589,105	2.48	64.1	46.3	5.5	12.3	35.9	29.4	11.9	6.8	0.4	0.4
41	Oregon	1,752,050	2.36	61.8	46.3	5.2	10.4	38.2	28.4	11.9	9.3	0.6	0.8
42	Pennsylvania	5,324,209	2.35	62.3	46.0	5.0	11.4	37.7	30.8	13.4	7.5	0.4	0.5
72	Puerto Rico	1,277,486	2.48	62.5	34.0	6.0	22.4	37.5	32.4	16.7	10.6	0.3	0.2
44	Rhode Island	443,980	2.37	60.6	43.5	4.8	12.3	39.4	31.0	13.4	8.2	0.6	0.8
45	South Carolina	2,177,733	2.40	65.3	47.6	4.3	13.5	34.7	28.6	11.9	5.9	0.3	0.5
46	South Dakota	378,559	2.34	61.2	48.1	4.9	8.1	38.8	32.1	12.7	7.8	0.2	0.3
47	Tennessee	2,889,226	2.42	63.9	46.7	4.8	12.4	36.1	29.6	11.5	6.6	0.3	0.4
48	Texas	11,260,645	2.66	67.4	48.7	5.6	13.1	32.6	26.5	8.7	6.3	0.4	0.6
49	Utah	1,167,591	2.88	72.2	58.2	4.8	9.3	27.8	19.7	7.6	6.2	0.3	0.5
50	Vermont	279,612	2.23	59.3	47.3	4.4	7.6	40.7	31.3	13.7	8.7	0.7	1.0
51	Virginia	3,402,670	2.49	65.2	49.0	4.7	11.6	34.8	28.3	11.0	6.4	0.4	0.5
53	Washington	3,101,265	2.47	63.0	48.7	4.8	9.5	37.0	28.0	10.7	8.4	0.5	0.9
54	West Virginia	743,644	2.31	61.5	45.3	5.2	11.0	38.5	32.1	15.0	6.8	0.3	0.5
55	Wisconsin	2,495,539	2.31	60.2	46.9	4.5	8.8	39.8	31.6	12.6	8.4	0.3	0.4
56	Wyoming	247,368	2.30	62.4	49.2	4.6	8.6	37.6	30.9	13.0	5.9	0.2	0.4

Table A-1. States — Who: Age, Race/Ethnicity, and Household Structure, 2023—*Continued*

State code	STATE	Households with people under 18 years old: Total households with children	Household type (percent): Married-couple families	Male householder families (no spouse)	Female householder families (no spouse)	Households with people 60 years and over: Total households with people 60 years and over	Household type (percent): Married-couple families	Male householder families (no spouse)	Female householder families (no spouse)	Nonfamily households
	ACS table number:	B11005	B11005	B11005	B11005	B11006	B11006	B11006	B11006	B11006
	Column number:	54	55	56	57	58	59	60	61	62
	UNITED STATES	37,780,108	65.0	9.4	24.8	55,315,608	20.0	1.7	4.0	16.3
1	Alabama	587,241	60.1	7.7	31.4	871,051	20.1	1.5	4.3	16.5
2	Alaska	84,415	67.9	11.4	20.0	103,084	17.1	1.7	3.4	15.0
4	Arizona	813,912	62.9	10.6	25.6	1,294,489	22.0	1.7	4.0	16.9
5	Arkansas	364,245	61.4	9.6	27.7	510,891	19.8	1.7	3.7	16.3
6	California	4,313,138	66.8	9.7	22.7	5,797,390	20.6	2.5	5.0	14.3
8	Colorado	658,561	70.3	9.1	19.8	893,598	18.3	1.4	2.8	14.3
9	Connecticut	400,878	64.2	8.5	26.4	649,195	21.1	1.8	4.2	18.0
10	Delaware	110,360	61.9	7.6	29.4	200,017	24.2	1.7	4.7	17.9
11	District of Columbia	66,488	52.6	7.9	39.3	93,528	7.5	0.8	3.9	15.7
12	Florida	2,313,878	63.1	9.6	26.4	4,358,034	23.4	2.0	4.7	18.4
13	Georgia	1,282,709	62.4	8.3	28.5	1,630,761	18.5	1.7	4.6	14.5
15	Hawaii	150,555	69.0	10.1	20.1	253,027	25.5	2.9	6.2	16.7
16	Idaho	234,576	73.8	8.8	17.0	299,132	22.5	1.3	2.7	14.4
17	Illinois	1,389,029	65.5	9.7	24.0	2,097,979	18.8	1.7	3.9	16.8
18	Indiana	791,391	64.3	9.7	24.7	1,112,115	18.8	1.5	3.3	16.7
19	Iowa	374,630	68.4	9.6	21.1	540,341	20.3	0.9	2.0	17.2
20	Kansas	348,400	68.0	9.8	21.5	475,771	19.7	1.1	2.7	16.6
21	Kentucky	550,778	61.9	10.4	26.7	768,094	19.0	1.7	3.7	17.0
22	Louisiana	543,141	55.5	10.5	33.4	768,358	18.2	1.8	4.5	17.4
23	Maine	142,036	66.1	11.1	22.0	289,842	23.5	1.4	2.6	19.5
24	Maryland	714,031	64.9	9.3	24.9	1,014,121	19.8	1.8	4.7	16.2
25	Massachusetts	745,865	66.8	7.8	24.5	1,222,770	20.0	1.9	4.0	17.7
26	Michigan	1,081,999	63.7	10.1	25.3	1,799,332	20.6	1.6	3.7	17.9
27	Minnesota	649,100	69.9	9.5	19.7	954,094	20.3	1.2	2.2	17.0
28	Mississippi	352,411	56.6	8.3	34.2	494,802	18.4	1.7	4.7	17.6
29	Missouri	712,591	65.3	9.0	24.4	1,068,560	19.6	1.4	3.3	17.5
30	Montana	119,054	69.3	11.0	19.3	206,621	22.1	1.0	2.6	18.1
31	Nebraska	239,670	69.5	7.8	21.7	317,904	19.7	1.0	2.2	16.2
32	Nevada	335,893	59.1	12.8	27.2	516,507	19.6	2.2	4.4	16.0
33	New Hampshire	143,891	70.3	9.6	19.1	272,143	24.8	1.4	3.3	18.4
34	New Jersey	1,085,100	68.5	7.8	23.1	1,581,869	21.4	1.9	4.8	16.5
35	New Mexico	238,263	54.2	13.7	31.1	394,076	19.2	2.1	4.8	19.9
36	New York	2,072,766	63.0	9.1	27.2	3,482,743	19.3	2.1	5.2	17.9
37	North Carolina	1,247,155	64.7	8.9	25.7	1,792,947	19.7	1.3	3.9	15.9
38	North Dakota	91,742	70.6	10.8	17.7	121,848	17.4	0.8	1.0	16.9
39	Ohio	1,327,922	61.8	10.2	26.9	2,087,275	18.9	1.4	3.6	18.5
40	Oklahoma	487,823	63.7	10.1	25.3	641,556	18.2	1.6	3.9	16.7
41	Oregon	465,205	63.5	11.2	24.2	739,799	20.3	1.5	3.3	17.0
42	Pennsylvania	1,419,707	63.9	9.7	25.3	2,393,041	21.1	1.7	3.8	18.4
72	Puerto Rico	301,081	38.1	13.0	48.4	671,675	19.2	2.4	8.4	22.5
44	Rhode Island	116,940	63.6	7.4	27.7	200,360	19.6	1.8	4.2	19.5
45	South Carolina	617,752	61.6	8.0	28.9	959,580	21.6	1.5	4.6	16.4
46	South Dakota	110,003	67.3	12.1	19.7	152,888	20.3	1.3	1.7	17.1
47	Tennessee	813,005	63.8	8.8	26.4	1,190,283	19.5	1.6	3.9	16.2
48	Texas	3,785,792	66.3	8.7	24.4	4,057,029	18.1	1.7	3.9	12.3
49	Utah	434,784	78.1	6.5	14.9	382,797	18.6	1.3	2.6	10.3
50	Vermont	61,168	70.2	10.7	18.8	130,446	23.4	1.7	2.3	19.3
51	Virginia	1,015,686	67.4	8.8	23.0	1,403,004	20.6	1.6	3.8	15.3
53	Washington	878,298	69.7	9.3	19.8	1,233,219	19.6	1.5	3.0	15.6
54	West Virginia	194,023	62.4	11.1	25.8	347,024	20.9	1.7	3.9	20.2
55	Wisconsin	632,840	65.9	10.6	22.6	1,044,189	20.8	1.2	2.2	17.6
56	Wyoming	69,268	68.1	10.2	21.2	106,084	21.2	1.2	2.6	18.0

- = Either no sample observations or too few sample observations were available to compute an estimate, or a ratio of medians cannot be calculated because one or both of the median estimates falls in the lowest interval or upper interval of an open-ended distribution.
NA = Not available.
X = Not applicable.

This Page Intentionally Left Blank Page

Table A-2. Counties — Who: Age, Race/Ethnicity, and Household Structure, 2023

STATE County code	STATE County	Total population	Percent change, 2010–2023	Population by age (percent): Under 18 years	18 to 24 years	25 to 44 years	45 to 64 years	65 years and over	Median age	Race alone or in combination (percent): White	Black or African American	American Indian and Alaska Native	Asian	Native Hawaiian or Other Pacific Islander	Some other race
	ACS table number:	B01003	Census PEP	B01001	B01001	B01001	B01001	B01001	B01002	B02008	B02009	B02010	B02011	B02012	B02013
	Column number:	1	2	3	4	5	6	7	8	9	10	11	12	13	14
00000	**UNITED STATES**	334,914,896	8.3	21.7	9.1	26.9	24.6	17.7	39.2	72.3	14.4	2.6	7.4	0.5	16.4
01000	**ALABAMA**	5,108,468	6.7	22.1	9.4	25.3	24.9	18.2	39.6	69.7	27.1	2.0	2.1	0.2	4.9
01003	Baldwin County	253,507	38.4	20.9	6.1	23.7	26.8	22.4	44.3	87.8	9.0	1.3	1.6	NA	5.8
01015	Calhoun County	116,429	-1.8	21.1	11.6	23.4	24.9	19.1	40.5	74.9	23.9	1.3	1.2	NA	2.9
01043	Cullman County	92,016	14.4	22.3	7.8	24.9	25.4	19.6	40.1	96.4	1.8	1.3	0.8	NA	6.9
01049	DeKalb County	72,569	2.0	24.0	9.0	24.0	25.1	17.9	39.9	85.2	2.0	3.0	0.7	NA	14.2
01051	Elmore County	90,441	13.7	21.5	7.9	26.6	26.7	17.3	40.2	77.7	20.9	3.8	NA	NA	3.2
01055	Etowah County	103,241	-1.2	21.9	7.6	25.1	25.2	20.1	41.2	80.7	16.6	1.1	1.0	NA	4.3
01069	Houston County	108,462	6.5	22.8	7.9	24.7	25.6	19.0	39.9	69.1	28.5	1.3	1.6	0.1	4.7
01073	Jefferson County	662,895	0.7	22.8	9.4	26.9	23.7	17.2	38.0	52.5	44.0	1.1	2.3	0.1	5.5
01077	Lauderdale County	96,814	4.5	19.3	13.1	21.9	24.8	20.9	41.3	88.4	8.6	3.9	1.3	NA	4.0
01081	Lee County	183,215	30.1	20.8	17.3	25.6	22.6	13.7	33.8	70.6	23.4	1.9	4.8	NA	3.5
01083	Limestone County	114,654	37.8	22.5	7.7	27.2	26.5	16.0	40.6	80.8	15.1	3.0	3.3	0.5	6.0
01089	Madison County	412,600	22.8	21.4	9.7	27.6	25.2	16.1	37.8	69.0	26.3	2.1	3.8	0.2	6.2
01095	Marshall County	100,756	8.1	25.6	8.4	24.2	24.2	17.6	38.8	86.5	3.8	3.2	1.4	NA	13.8
01097	Mobile County	411,640	-0.4	23.2	8.5	26.5	24.0	17.8	38.5	60.1	37.6	1.8	2.8	NA	2.9
01101	Montgomery County	224,980	-2.1	24.1	9.6	25.8	24.2	16.4	37.3	34.9	61.8	0.8	4.1	0.3	5.0
01103	Morgan County	125,133	4.6	23.3	8.3	24.3	26.2	18.0	40.2	81.8	15.1	4.1	0.8	NA	7.0
01115	St. Clair County	95,552	14.1	22.3	7.3	26.5	25.8	18.1	41.2	88.5	9.7	0.9	1.2	2.5	3.1
01117	Shelby County	233,000	19.0	22.5	8.0	26.4	25.6	17.5	40.7	80.1	15.4	0.9	3.2	NA	6.3
01121	Talladega County	81,132	-1.2	20.0	7.3	25.4	27.5	19.8	42.7	68.4	31.6	3.0	NA	NA	1.8
01125	Tuscaloosa County	237,373	21.7	20.3	19.0	25.3	21.1	14.3	33.3	64.5	31.6	2.4	2.1	NA	4.1
02000	**ALASKA**	733,406	2.7	23.8	8.9	30.3	23.0	14.0	36.5	72.2	5.4	20.5	9.1	2.5	5.8
02020	Anchorage Municipality	286,075	-2.4	23.3	9.2	32.0	22.3	13.2	36.0	69.5	8.2	13.7	13.1	4.7	7.3
02090	Fairbanks North Star Borough	94,840	-3.5	24.0	11.5	32.2	19.7	12.6	33.2	82.0	7.6	12.7	7.0	1.5	5.3
02170	Matanuska-Susitna Borough	115,239	28.4	25.3	8.1	28.8	23.7	14.1	36.9	89.2	2.6	12.9	3.9	0.6	5.5
04000	**ARIZONA**	7,431,344	15.9	21.3	9.4	26.5	23.5	19.3	39.3	77.3	6.7	6.2	5.3	0.6	24.9
04001	Apache County	65,036	-9.3	25.4	8.5	25.0	22.8	18.3	38.8	26.3	1.1	73.3	0.8	NA	1.5
04003	Cochise County	124,640	-5.4	20.3	8.0	23.3	22.9	25.7	44.0	85.4	6.5	3.3	4.2	0.6	29.2
04005	Coconino County	144,472	7.3	18.9	20.1	25.1	20.6	15.4	32.7	67.2	2.3	28.5	3.9	0.3	9.8
04013	Maricopa County	4,585,871	19.8	22.1	9.3	28.1	23.9	16.6	37.8	76.2	8.2	4.2	6.5	0.6	24.9
04015	Mohave County	223,682	11.7	15.9	5.7	19.5	25.9	33.1	53.7	90.5	2.0	3.8	2.1	0.4	12.7
04017	Navajo County	109,175	1.5	24.2	8.1	23.6	23.0	21.1	40.4	51.2	2.0	44.1	1.1	0.6	8.9
04019	Pima County	1,063,162	8.2	19.3	11.6	24.8	22.3	22.0	40.1	80.5	5.4	4.8	4.9	0.6	28.6
04021	Pinal County	484,239	26.2	21.4	7.5	26.7	22.9	21.5	40.7	78.0	7.6	6.5	3.3	0.5	22.6
04025	Yavapai County	249,081	18.0	15.1	6.7	18.5	25.1	34.7	55.3	91.8	1.5	4.1	2.1	0.7	13.1
04027	Yuma County	213,221	8.5	24.3	10.0	25.5	19.0	21.2	37.2	80.2	3.7	3.6	2.0	0.4	55.7
05000	**ARKANSAS**	3,067,732	5.0	22.9	9.4	25.8	24.0	18.0	38.9	80.0	16.1	2.9	2.2	0.5	10.3
05007	Benton County	311,013	39.5	25.1	8.8	29.3	23.1	13.8	35.9	88.9	2.8	3.6	5.4	0.9	30.7
05031	Craighead County	113,993	17.8	25.2	9.8	28.7	22.2	14.1	35.1	81.3	16.1	4.2	1.6	NA	6.6
05045	Faulkner County	129,951	14.0	22.4	14.4	27.0	21.9	14.3	34.6	84.0	13.7	1.4	2.0	NA	4.2
05051	Garland County	99,784	3.8	19.7	6.6	22.4	25.5	25.8	45.9	89.6	9.5	2.6	1.2	NA	3.7
05069	Jefferson County	63,661	-17.7	21.1	10.2	24.8	24.5	19.4	40.5	39.1	59.2	2.6	NA	0.2	2.0
05085	Lonoke County	75,944	10.7	24.3	7.1	28.3	25.1	15.3	39.9	89.7	7.6	1.6	1.8	NA	4.7
05119	Pulaski County	400,009	4.3	23.2	8.8	27.6	23.5	16.9	38.0	57.3	39.2	1.3	3.0	0.2	7.9
05125	Saline County	129,574	20.5	23.0	7.9	25.3	25.2	18.6	41.5	87.0	10.7	1.5	1.8	NA	7.0
05131	Sebastian County	129,098	2.5	23.6	8.9	25.9	23.7	17.9	38.5	76.6	8.4	6.3	5.4	NA	15.4
05143	Washington County	261,549	28.1	23.2	15.5	27.7	21.3	12.3	32.9	86.2	4.8	3.6	3.3	3.1	24.1
05145	White County	78,452	1.4	23.2	10.3	23.9	25.4	17.3	38.3	93.4	6.7	2.8	0.7	NA	2.9
06000	**CALIFORNIA**	38,965,193	4.4	21.7	9.1	28.6	24.4	16.2	38.2	56.2	7.2	3.3	18.4	0.8	34.4
06001	Alameda County	1,622,188	7.1	19.5	7.9	31.0	25.5	16.1	39.5	40.1	12.1	2.4	37.6	1.4	20.4
06007	Butte County	207,172	-5.9	20.4	14.9	25.1	21.0	18.7	35.9	82.2	3.4	3.7	7.7	0.7	18.6
06013	Contra Costa County	1,155,025	9.7	21.7	7.9	26.2	26.5	17.7	40.9	54.5	10.6	2.9	23.5	1.2	25.3
06017	El Dorado County	192,215	6.1	19.4	6.5	22.1	27.7	24.2	46.5	88.5	1.9	2.9	7.8	0.7	13.1
06019	Fresno County	1,017,162	9.0	27.5	9.8	28.4	21.1	13.2	33.9	57.0	6.0	3.7	13.4	0.5	44.4
06023	Humboldt County	133,985	-0.6	18.4	11.6	26.6	22.8	20.6	39.5	85.5	3.4	9.8	5.2	0.7	11.3
06025	Imperial County	179,057	2.2	28.0	10.5	26.9	20.7	13.8	33.4	49.3	2.3	4.3	2.7	0.4	76.8
06029	Kern County	913,820	8.5	28.4	9.8	28.7	20.9	12.2	32.7	64.7	6.8	3.9	6.7	0.4	44.6
06031	Kings County	152,682	-0.3	26.7	10.0	31.8	20.4	11.2	33.2	60.1	7.8	3.7	4.8	0.1	47.4

Table A-2. Counties — Who: Age, Race/Ethnicity, and Household Structure, 2023—*Continued*

STATE County code	STATE County	Two or more races (percent)	Hispanic or Latino (percent)	Native, born in state of residence (percent)	Foreign born (percent)	Non-citizens (percent)	Total households	Average household size	Household type (percent of all households): Family households: Total	Married couple	Male house-holder	Female house-holder	Nonfamily households: Total	One-person house-holds	Percent of households with people age 60 years and over
	ACS table number:	B02001	B03003	B05002	B05002	B05002	B11001	B25010	B11001	B11001	B11001	B11001	B11001	B11001	B11006
	Column number:	15	16	17	18	19	20	21	22	23	24	25	26	27	28
00000	**UNITED STATES**	12.8	19.4	56.9	14.3	6.8	131,332,360	2.49	64.0	46.8	5.1	12.1	36.0	28.8	42.1
01000	**ALABAMA**	5.6	5.7	66.2	4.0	2.4	2,051,545	2.42	64.8	46.3	4.4	14.1	35.2	30.2	42.5
01003	Baldwin County	5.7	5.8	47.8	4.9	3.2	105,698	2.37	70.0	54.4	4.3	11.3	30.0	26.0	48.2
01015	Calhoun County	3.9	4.8	68.2	2.3	1.2	46,310	2.41	63.6	44.4	3.8	15.5	36.4	32.0	43.2
01043	Cullman County	7.1	5.1	76.9	1.6	1.1	35,961	2.53	70.2	55.1	6.1	9.0	29.8	23.7	44.4
01049	DeKalb County	5.4	17.3	66.0	7.2	5.4	27,182	2.64	68.9	51.9	5.6	11.3	31.1	26.1	46.6
01051	Elmore County	5.5	3.5	66.6	1.9	1.1	33,692	2.56	70.1	53.8	4.2	12.2	29.9	25.7	41.9
01055	Etowah County	4.0	5.4	77.1	2.7	1.5	40,027	2.54	68.4	47.9	4.8	15.6	31.6	26.8	44.6
01069	Houston County	5.1	4.8	63.0	3.8	2.6	44,880	2.39	66.1	43.1	4.9	18.0	33.9	29.1	43.3
01073	Jefferson County	5.3	5.5	71.7	4.6	3.0	272,648	2.35	61.8	40.2	4.6	17.0	38.2	31.2	39.0
01077	Lauderdale County	6.1	3.5	66.3	2.5	1.5	41,199	2.27	65.9	50.6	5.0	10.3	34.1	27.3	44.5
01081	Lee County	4.0	5.4	53.0	6.7	4.6	74,799	2.35	55.7	42.6	3.4	9.8	44.3	35.0	33.3
01083	Limestone County	7.9	7.7	57.4	4.0	2.1	43,490	2.57	73.3	59.6	3.7	10.0	26.7	22.5	38.9
01089	Madison County	6.9	6.8	51.1	5.0	2.5	168,996	2.37	63.8	49.2	3.9	10.7	36.2	30.3	38.1
01095	Marshall County	7.4	17.5	66.0	5.9	3.6	36,274	2.75	68.8	50.7	7.1	11.1	31.2	26.9	46.0
01097	Mobile County	5.0	3.5	72.3	3.6	1.5	163,963	2.46	60.3	39.5	3.9	16.9	39.7	34.7	42.6
01101	Montgomery County	6.2	5.0	70.8	6.4	4.3	92,816	2.33	59.1	34.1	3.8	21.2	40.9	36.0	40.8
01103	Morgan County	8.0	10.6	69.4	3.7	2.9	49,759	2.48	68.9	49.3	5.2	14.4	31.1	25.7	43.5
01115	St. Clair County	5.6	3.0	79.4	1.7	0.9	35,354	2.65	74.1	58.6	2.2	13.3	25.9	21.1	45.5
01117	Shelby County	6.2	7.6	60.0	6.8	3.5	88,270	2.60	73.7	59.5	3.8	10.3	26.3	23.6	40.6
01121	Talladega County	5.5	2.4	79.1	2.1	1.4	34,080	2.28	68.1	43.9	6.6	17.7	31.9	29.5	44.1
01125	Tuscaloosa County	4.6	5.5	71.0	4.6	3.4	93,966	2.36	58.9	40.6	5.6	12.8	41.1	33.6	34.9
02000	**ALASKA**	14.1	7.5	42.9	7.4	2.7	276,852	2.54	61.9	46.3	5.7	9.9	38.1	30.2	37.2
02020	Anchorage Municipality	14.7	9.6	40.2	10.7	4.0	109,125	2.55	59.4	45.6	4.9	8.9	40.6	31.1	34.5
02090	Fairbanks North Star Borough	15.6	8.8	32.1	3.9	1.2	37,510	2.43	60.7	47.4	6.4	6.9	39.3	32.2	32.2
02170	Matanuska-Susitna Borough	13.4	5.5	44.1	2.5	0.8	39,870	2.82	68.6	55.3	4.5	8.8	31.4	24.8	39.4
04000	**ARIZONA**	19.9	31.6	39.1	13.2	6.8	2,907,014	2.50	63.9	46.8	5.3	11.8	36.1	27.7	44.5
04001	Apache County	2.5	6.6	73.6	1.0	0.7	24,010	2.65	73.5	42.9	5.8	24.8	26.5	24.0	50.0
04003	Cochise County	27.3	34.8	37.1	11.1	4.7	50,919	2.35	62.9	47.6	4.6	10.8	37.1	32.5	55.1
04005	Coconino County	11.5	15.6	53.0	3.8	2.0	56,954	2.30	58.4	39.9	5.2	13.3	41.6	27.9	36.0
04013	Maricopa County	19.2	31.4	38.3	14.7	7.9	1,753,589	2.57	64.4	47.0	5.5	11.9	35.6	26.8	40.1
04015	Mohave County	11.2	17.6	20.6	5.7	2.5	98,791	2.22	60.7	46.2	4.2	10.2	39.3	32.0	64.5
04017	Navajo County	7.5	11.1	65.7	4.2	2.0	41,945	2.54	68.6	44.9	8.1	15.6	31.4	27.3	51.2
04019	Pima County	23.4	36.6	41.0	12.2	5.5	445,471	2.32	58.3	42.0	4.8	11.5	41.7	32.5	47.2
04021	Pinal County	18.0	30.2	39.6	9.3	4.3	168,479	2.79	71.4	53.8	7.0	10.6	28.6	22.4	50.8
04025	Yavapai County	13.0	15.7	28.9	6.3	3.0	113,784	2.15	63.6	52.2	3.4	8.0	36.4	29.0	65.0
04027	Yuma County	44.9	65.2	33.9	27.0	16.0	83,811	2.45	70.7	53.1	4.6	13.0	29.3	24.1	46.2
05000	**ARKANSAS**	11.5	9.1	60.2	5.3	3.4	1,232,871	2.42	64.7	46.7	5.0	12.9	35.3	29.9	41.4
05007	Benton County	31.5	18.7	41.1	12.9	8.1	117,446	2.62	72.2	59.4	4.0	8.7	27.8	21.6	32.5
05031	Craighead County	9.5	6.5	65.9	4.4	2.7	47,150	2.35	62.5	42.7	4.3	15.5	37.5	31.0	32.8
05045	Faulkner County	5.0	5.8	67.8	2.7	1.6	50,963	2.44	66.3	52.0	5.7	8.6	33.7	26.1	33.3
05051	Garland County	6.5	7.6	56.3	3.3	1.5	45,243	2.17	57.7	43.0	5.2	9.4	42.3	33.2	50.9
05069	Jefferson County	2.9	2.8	75.8	1.6	1.5	23,885	2.44	61.5	35.8	3.6	22.1	38.5	32.8	43.9
05085	Lonoke County	5.4	5.7	60.6	3.3	1.5	29,388	2.56	69.1	52.5	4.7	11.9	30.9	25.6	42.1
05119	Pulaski County	8.5	8.3	65.8	6.4	4.5	169,230	2.31	59.7	39.8	4.1	15.8	40.3	36.3	40.0
05125	Saline County	8.1	7.4	60.0	4.0	2.4	50,684	2.53	67.6	54.0	4.4	9.3	32.4	27.7	40.9
05131	Sebastian County	9.7	16.4	55.8	8.5	4.4	51,596	2.46	60.2	43.9	5.2	11.2	39.8	34.7	42.6
05143	Washington County	24.3	18.7	48.9	11.7	8.5	99,630	2.53	63.6	46.0	5.0	12.5	36.4	26.2	30.2
05145	White County	6.5	5.1	73.1	1.5	0.7	30,920	2.44	71.8	53.9	5.4	12.6	28.2	25.2	42.2
06000	**CALIFORNIA**	19.0	40.4	56.3	27.3	12.4	13,699,816	2.78	67.4	48.0	6.3	13.1	32.6	24.7	42.3
06001	Alameda County	12.4	23.3	46.6	35.7	15.9	608,534	2.60	63.4	48.8	4.9	9.7	36.6	26.8	38.6
06007	Butte County	15.1	20.6	74.0	8.4	3.9	86,279	2.32	58.0	41.7	5.7	10.7	42.0	26.0	42.0
06013	Contra Costa County	16.4	27.8	54.6	28.2	11.9	416,172	2.74	71.5	54.3	5.5	11.7	28.5	22.0	45.6
06017	El Dorado County	13.4	14.7	66.0	8.5	3.4	77,904	2.44	71.9	60.7	3.7	7.5	28.1	21.3	50.8
06019	Fresno County	23.7	54.9	69.8	19.8	10.0	328,895	3.03	71.1	45.5	8.2	17.4	28.9	22.3	39.2
06023	Humboldt County	13.3	14.4	70.5	6.4	2.7	56,130	2.31	56.0	38.4	6.4	11.2	44.0	32.6	42.7
06025	Imperial County	34.1	86.3	59.6	32.2	14.9	50,024	3.45	77.6	53.6	7.2	16.8	22.4	20.7	43.6
06029	Kern County	25.9	57.1	69.2	19.5	11.5	289,845	3.09	72.4	45.3	8.8	18.3	27.6	21.7	37.5
06031	Kings County	22.8	58.8	64.4	21.1	14.2	44,262	3.13	73.4	50.1	8.6	14.8	26.6	22.4	32.8

Table A-2. Counties — Who: Age, Race/Ethnicity, and Household Structure, 2023—*Continued*

STATE County code	STATE County	Total population	Percent change, 2010–2023	Population by age (percent): Under 18 years	18 to 24 years	25 to 44 years	45 to 64 years	65 years and over	Median age	Race alone or in combination (percent): White	Black or African American	American Indian and Alaska Native	Asian	Native Hawaiian or Other Pacific Islander	Some other race
	ACS table number:	B01003	Census PEP	B01001	B01001	B01001	B01001	B01001	B01002	B02008	B02009	B02010	B02011	B02012	B02013
	Column number:	1	2	3	4	5	6	7	8	9	10	11	12	13	14
	CALIFORNIA—Cont.														
06033	Lake County	67,878	4.8	21.6	6.7	25.1	20.5	26.1	43.2	74.1	5.6	5.3	2.7	1.6	23.8
06037	Los Angeles County	9,663,345	-1.7	20.2	8.8	29.8	25.5	15.7	38.6	48.4	9.3	3.3	17.5	0.6	41.8
06039	Madera County	162,858	7.6	26.7	9.7	26.8	22.2	14.6	35.0	56.7	4.2	6.0	3.1	0.9	51.7
06041	Marin County	254,407	0.6	18.9	7.3	19.9	29.1	24.7	48.2	78.8	3.6	1.7	9.8	0.2	19.5
06045	Mendocino County	89,108	1.5	20.0	7.7	22.7	24.1	25.4	44.5	86.1	1.5	5.6	3.1	NA	28.0
06047	Merced County	291,920	13.7	28.4	11.4	27.4	20.8	12.1	32.2	40.8	4.0	4.3	9.3	1.3	56.7
06053	Monterey County	430,723	3.4	25.5	9.9	26.5	22.6	15.5	35.9	47.2	3.1	3.4	7.4	1.0	54.2
06055	Napa County	133,216	-2.7	19.0	8.4	24.8	25.9	22.0	43.6	72.1	4.5	2.6	11.6	NA	28.3
06057	Nevada County	102,037	3.3	16.9	5.9	21.7	25.3	30.1	49.9	91.0	1.1	2.6	3.5	0.3	12.9
06059	Orange County	3,135,755	3.9	20.6	9.0	27.2	26.3	16.9	39.7	58.5	2.6	2.2	25.9	0.7	29.1
06061	Placer County	423,561	21.0	21.5	7.4	24.4	25.6	21.1	42.4	82.0	3.6	2.7	13.2	0.6	14.0
06065	Riverside County	2,492,442	13.1	23.8	9.3	27.4	23.7	15.7	37.1	57.9	8.4	4.0	9.5	0.8	44.5
06067	Sacramento County	1,584,288	11.4	22.6	8.3	29.6	23.7	15.8	38.0	55.7	13.2	3.5	22.0	1.9	20.6
06069	San Benito County	68,175	23.4	23.8	8.5	30.6	23.3	13.9	36.6	72.4	1.9	5.4	9.0	NA	55.0
06071	San Bernardino County	2,195,611	7.5	25.2	9.8	29.0	23.1	12.9	34.9	49.4	9.8	3.3	10.7	0.7	47.5
06073	San Diego County	3,269,973	5.3	20.6	9.7	30.2	23.5	15.9	37.6	67.0	6.9	3.0	16.1	0.9	28.9
06075	San Francisco County	808,988	0.4	13.6	6.4	36.2	25.3	18.5	40.7	49.5	6.7	2.5	39.5	0.7	13.6
06077	San Joaquin County	800,965	16.5	25.9	9.3	28.0	23.1	13.8	36.0	47.1	9.1	4.6	22.5	1.3	35.6
06079	San Luis Obispo County	281,639	4.3	17.2	15.1	22.3	22.6	22.8	41.0	84.7	2.3	3.0	6.1	0.1	21.5
06081	San Mateo County	726,353	0.9	19.1	7.3	28.5	26.6	18.6	41.5	50.6	3.1	2.5	35.7	2.2	21.1
06083	Santa Barbara County	441,257	3.9	22.2	15.0	24.7	20.9	17.1	34.9	73.9	2.9	5.9	7.5	0.5	38.0
06085	Santa Clara County	1,877,592	5.0	19.9	9.1	30.3	25.2	15.4	38.3	42.5	3.6	2.3	44.0	0.9	22.2
06087	Santa Cruz County	261,547	-0.6	17.9	14.8	23.3	24.2	19.8	39.8	72.9	2.2	3.5	6.8	0.5	29.1
06089	Shasta County	180,366	1.7	21.5	7.1	25.5	24.0	21.8	41.2	88.4	2.4	5.5	5.4	0.7	10.6
06095	Solano County	449,218	8.4	21.5	8.2	27.8	24.6	17.9	40.0	51.7	16.2	3.7	21.0	2.6	23.9
06097	Sonoma County	481,812	-0.7	18.7	7.7	25.4	25.9	22.3	43.3	76.9	3.1	4.3	6.8	1.0	25.9
06099	Stanislaus County	551,430	7.0	26.5	9.4	27.3	22.7	14.1	35.1	68.2	4.8	3.6	8.6	1.4	43.9
06101	Sutter County	97,948	3.3	24.1	9.7	26.2	22.9	17.2	38.0	58.5	3.6	5.5	21.2	NA	27.2
06103	Tehama County	64,896	2.3	24.1	8.8	23.9	22.7	20.6	40.2	74.2	1.1	4.9	2.9	0.7	26.4
06107	Tulare County	479,468	8.1	29.4	10.2	27.5	20.8	12.1	32.4	53.0	2.2	3.3	4.2	0.3	60.0
06111	Ventura County	829,590	0.5	21.5	8.7	26.2	25.6	18.1	39.9	75.8	3.2	3.3	10.0	0.5	33.7
06113	Yolo County	220,544	9.6	19.1	20.6	25.8	20.6	13.8	32.6	66.6	4.3	3.6	19.5	0.5	22.7
06115	Yuba County	85,722	18.4	27.0	10.1	27.9	21.6	13.3	34.4	69.0	7.6	5.4	11.0	1.5	23.4
08000	**COLORADO**	5,877,610	16.4	20.6	9.0	30.7	23.6	16.1	37.9	84.5	5.8	3.5	5.1	0.4	16.7
08001	Adams County	533,365	20.2	24.3	9.0	32.2	23.0	11.5	35.1	75.5	5.9	4.9	5.9	0.3	33.4
08005	Arapahoe County	656,061	14.1	22.2	8.2	30.8	23.9	14.9	37.4	72.4	13.6	3.7	8.5	0.6	17.2
08013	Boulder County	326,831	10.7	17.0	15.5	26.0	24.4	17.0	38.2	91.1	2.0	1.5	6.7	0.2	12.4
08014	Broomfield County	76,860	37.5	20.2	7.5	31.3	24.5	16.5	37.9	87.9	2.2	3.2	9.5	NA	12.1
08031	Denver County	716,577	18.6	17.7	8.2	40.5	20.7	12.9	35.4	77.7	11.2	3.6	5.5	0.6	21.7
08035	Douglas County	383,906	33.8	22.9	7.9	27.5	27.4	14.4	39.8	89.5	3.4	2.1	8.4	0.2	8.8
08041	El Paso County	744,215	18.7	22.8	10.2	30.6	22.0	14.4	35.4	83.1	9.1	3.3	5.6	0.8	12.9
08059	Jefferson County	576,366	7.6	18.0	7.5	30.9	25.2	18.4	40.7	92.0	2.2	2.7	4.4	0.2	11.6
08069	Larimer County	370,771	23.3	18.0	14.0	28.4	21.9	17.8	37.3	93.2	2.5	2.1	4.2	0.4	9.7
08077	Mesa County	159,681	9.1	20.1	8.6	26.0	23.8	21.5	41.6	92.1	1.9	3.4	1.6	0.3	13.9
08101	Pueblo County	169,422	6.2	21.4	8.5	25.7	24.5	19.9	41.2	87.8	3.7	5.1	2.3	NA	17.0
08123	Weld County	359,442	41.4	25.3	9.0	30.2	22.4	13.2	35.4	86.0	2.6	3.9	3.1	0.4	20.0
09000	**CONNECTICUT**	3,617,176	1.1	20.0	9.3	25.4	26.3	19.1	41.5	74.3	13.9	1.3	5.9	0.2	16.0
09110	Capitol Planning Region	975,328	NA	20.0	10.1	26.2	25.2	18.6	40.6	73.0	16.1	1.0	7.1	0.4	13.2
09120	Greater Bridgeport Planning Region	327,651	NA	21.8	10.4	24.1	27.1	16.6	40.3	64.0	16.7	1.2	6.0	NA	24.3
09130	Lower Connecticut River Valley Planning Region	176,215	NA	16.4	8.5	24.3	27.9	22.9	45.8	88.1	7.1	1.3	4.3	NA	7.1
09140	Naugatuck Valley Planning Region	456,128	NA	20.1	8.0	26.1	26.0	19.8	42.5	73.8	16.2	2.0	5.0	NA	18.6
09150	Northeastern Connecticut Planning Region	96,692	NA	18.2	6.5	26.6	28.2	20.5	44.2	93.6	3.7	1.9	2.1	NA	4.7
09160	Northwest Hills Planning Region	113,463	NA	17.7	6.5	23.7	28.7	23.5	47.5	89.7	4.6	1.0	3.0	NA	9.5
09170	South Central Connecticut Planning Region	568,158	NA	19.4	10.4	25.6	25.5	19.2	40.5	70.7	16.8	0.8	5.6	0.1	17.4
09180	Southeastern Connecticut Planning Region	279,634	NA	19.0	10.2	25.1	25.5	20.1	40.8	83.0	9.1	3.7	5.0	NA	11.3
09190	Western Connecticut Planning Region	623,907	NA	21.5	8.0	24.9	27.6	18.0	41.7	71.9	12.3	0.8	6.9	0.2	20.4

Table A-2. Counties — Who: Age, Race/Ethnicity, and Household Structure, 2023—*Continued*

STATE County code	STATE County	Two or more races (percent)	Hispanic or Latino (percent)	Native, born in state of residence (percent)	Foreign born (percent)	Non-citizens (percent)	Total households	Average household size	Household type (percent of all households): Family households: Total	Family households: Married couple	Family households: Male householder	Family households: Female householder	Nonfamily households: Total	Nonfamily households: One-person households	Percent of households with people age 60 years and over
	ACS table number:	B02001	B03003	B05002	B05002	B05002	B11001	B25010	B11001	B11001	B11001	B11001	B11001	B11001	B11006
	Column number:	15	16	17	18	19	20	21	22	23	24	25	26	27	28
	CALIFORNIA—Cont.														
06033	Lake County	12.1	25.4	73.2	8.6	4.3	26,092	2.56	57.7	37.1	6.7	13.9	42.3	36.1	58.3
06037	Los Angeles County	19.7	48.6	51.7	33.5	15.0	3,450,470	2.74	64.2	42.4	7.1	14.7	35.8	27.4	41.4
06039	Madera County	21.4	61.3	72.2	18.9	12.6	46,781	3.34	72.6	48.5	8.7	15.4	27.4	22.4	43.4
06041	Marin County	13.0	19.6	52.4	19.9	9.7	101,608	2.44	63.9	51.7	4.5	7.7	36.1	28.0	52.2
06045	Mendocino County	24.3	28.1	66.5	14.0	8.4	34,951	2.49	54.7	36.5	4.6	13.6	45.3	38.6	56.7
06047	Merced County	15.1	63.9	65.8	25.8	16.0	88,053	3.27	67.5	44.5	8.9	14.1	32.5	28.0	38.4
06053	Monterey County	15.3	62.0	56.0	29.5	19.9	132,170	3.10	70.6	47.8	7.3	15.5	29.4	22.7	46.1
06055	Napa County	18.0	36.7	59.6	21.9	8.7	51,167	2.52	68.2	51.0	4.7	12.5	31.8	24.0	50.7
06057	Nevada County	11.1	10.9	67.8	4.8	2.5	42,712	2.35	63.2	54.6	1.6	7.0	36.8	29.8	57.7
06059	Orange County	18.2	34.2	53.4	30.8	12.6	1,092,528	2.82	70.4	53.2	5.7	11.5	29.6	21.8	43.5
06061	Placer County	14.9	16.0	65.6	12.9	3.7	160,315	2.61	72.3	59.9	2.8	9.5	27.7	22.7	49.0
06065	Riverside County	23.2	51.9	62.0	22.1	9.5	791,757	3.10	75.1	53.0	7.3	14.8	24.9	19.3	45.5
06067	Sacramento County	14.9	24.5	60.9	22.8	9.5	573,170	2.72	65.8	46.1	5.9	13.7	34.2	26.8	41.1
06069	San Benito County	41.3	62.5	70.7	19.8	10.1	20,194	3.35	73.7	54.9	4.7	14.1	26.3	19.6	43.7
06071	San Bernardino County	20.2	55.9	65.3	22.6	10.5	682,807	3.16	75.7	49.5	8.4	17.8	24.3	18.3	41.0
06073	San Diego County	21.4	34.9	50.8	23.1	9.3	1,181,259	2.67	66.0	49.3	5.3	11.3	34.0	24.7	40.0
06075	San Francisco County	11.4	16.4	39.8	35.0	13.0	372,027	2.09	46.4	34.7	3.9	7.8	53.6	39.5	36.9
06077	San Joaquin County	18.4	42.7	62.7	26.6	12.7	251,091	3.14	76.0	53.1	6.3	16.7	24.0	19.4	41.0
06079	San Luis Obispo County	16.5	25.2	68.8	10.5	5.0	110,283	2.40	61.9	48.9	2.2	10.8	38.1	25.5	49.5
06081	San Mateo County	13.9	24.8	47.9	36.0	15.7	265,124	2.69	66.1	52.0	4.4	9.7	33.9	26.4	43.4
06083	Santa Barbara County	27.2	48.5	59.5	22.3	13.2	150,932	2.77	63.2	46.2	5.4	11.6	36.8	26.0	43.7
06085	Santa Clara County	14.4	25.0	43.8	42.2	19.8	665,549	2.76	68.6	53.3	5.5	9.8	31.4	22.8	38.7
06087	Santa Cruz County	13.9	35.2	60.7	18.2	9.3	99,069	2.47	64.3	48.2	6.7	9.3	35.7	24.3	47.7
06089	Shasta County	12.2	12.2	69.4	5.3	2.2	72,320	2.44	61.7	44.5	4.5	12.7	38.3	29.2	50.7
06095	Solano County	16.6	30.1	58.6	22.4	10.0	157,766	2.78	69.5	48.4	7.1	14.0	30.5	24.7	45.7
06097	Sonoma County	16.6	30.3	63.0	16.8	9.1	192,765	2.44	62.6	47.1	4.6	10.9	37.4	27.6	49.3
06099	Stanislaus County	28.6	50.9	68.5	21.7	11.0	179,152	3.05	73.9	51.7	7.3	14.8	26.1	20.6	41.0
06101	Sutter County	13.9	33.5	62.9	22.7	9.5	33,325	2.91	75.1	56.1	4.5	14.5	24.9	19.7	48.2
06103	Tehama County	9.6	29.8	69.9	11.8	8.3	24,919	2.56	68.1	53.4	3.5	11.3	31.9	27.7	49.9
06107	Tulare County	22.2	67.0	69.5	21.8	13.3	145,442	3.26	79.8	53.1	9.2	17.5	20.2	15.6	38.3
06111	Ventura County	25.3	44.8	58.4	22.9	10.5	283,718	2.88	72.1	53.8	6.9	11.4	27.9	21.5	47.6
06113	Yolo County	16.1	33.4	62.2	21.5	11.4	77,230	2.71	61.0	48.9	4.2	7.8	39.0	23.6	36.7
06115	Yuba County	16.8	31.5	69.5	10.7	2.7	29,253	2.87	67.9	46.3	6.5	15.1	32.1	26.6	41.2
08000	**COLORADO**	14.7	22.7	41.1	9.6	5.1	2,428,261	2.37	61.2	47.8	4.6	8.8	38.8	28.6	36.8
08001	Adams County	23.1	43.2	49.4	15.7	10.8	192,742	2.75	68.2	49.8	7.3	11.1	31.8	23.0	32.9
08005	Arapahoe County	14.6	22.0	38.8	16.8	8.7	261,161	2.49	64.1	49.2	5.1	9.8	35.9	26.1	35.3
08013	Boulder County	13.5	14.7	31.1	10.4	5.2	137,425	2.28	53.9	43.8	4.0	6.0	46.1	31.1	38.5
08014	Broomfield County	14.2	14.5	37.5	8.8	4.3	33,563	2.28	58.6	48.0	5.2	5.5	41.4	28.7	33.7
08031	Denver County	19.2	27.9	37.1	14.4	7.8	342,996	2.05	43.9	32.4	3.2	8.3	56.1	41.4	27.0
08035	Douglas County	10.9	10.4	36.1	7.8	3.0	145,551	2.63	73.8	63.0	3.5	7.3	26.2	20.2	35.3
08041	El Paso County	13.2	19.1	31.7	6.9	2.8	298,973	2.42	67.2	52.7	4.6	9.9	32.8	25.6	34.4
08059	Jefferson County	12.3	16.2	44.5	6.1	2.6	242,433	2.34	60.7	48.0	4.0	8.7	39.3	28.3	40.4
08069	Larimer County	10.8	13.1	37.2	4.9	2.6	156,498	2.30	58.9	47.2	4.5	7.1	41.1	27.8	37.1
08077	Mesa County	11.3	15.6	48.6	5.3	3.3	68,115	2.27	59.7	42.8	6.4	10.4	40.3	31.8	46.8
08101	Pueblo County	14.1	42.4	59.7	3.8	2.8	68,732	2.38	66.9	46.5	7.7	12.7	33.1	26.9	45.9
08123	Weld County	14.9	31.3	55.9	8.0	4.6	129,057	2.75	71.6	56.8	4.3	10.4	28.4	21.0	35.5
09000	**CONNECTICUT**	10.8	18.6	53.3	16.3	7.4	1,442,969	2.44	64.0	46.3	4.8	12.9	36.0	29.0	45.0
09110	Capitol Planning Region	10.2	17.9	55.6	16.0	6.3	391,422	2.40	62.7	45.0	5.4	12.3	37.3	30.4	43.4
09120	Greater Bridgeport Planning Region	11.7	26.8	46.0	23.6	11.7	119,505	2.65	69.9	48.9	5.7	15.2	30.1	25.6	46.0
09130	Lower Connecticut River Valley Planning Region	7.8	8.0	61.2	8.7	3.5	75,959	2.24	63.3	50.7	3.6	9.0	36.7	28.4	48.6
09140	Naugatuck Valley Planning Region	13.8	20.7	62.9	14.1	6.0	180,851	2.49	64.6	43.9	4.9	15.9	35.4	29.8	46.0
09150	Northeastern Connecticut Planning Region	5.5	5.6	55.6	4.5	1.9	40,349	2.36	68.2	53.1	3.2	11.9	31.8	26.2	45.5
09160	Northwest Hills Planning Region	7.5	9.3	60.8	9.6	3.1	50,297	2.21	64.6	51.1	4.5	9.0	35.4	26.5	48.3
09170	South Central Connecticut Planning Region	10.7	19.9	60.8	13.9	6.7	233,004	2.34	60.1	41.0	4.5	14.7	39.9	31.4	44.6
09180	Southeastern Connecticut Planning Region	10.3	15.2	54.6	9.1	3.5	114,156	2.35	61.2	44.2	3.9	13.1	38.8	30.2	44.3
09190	Western Connecticut Planning Region	12.0	20.9	35.2	25.4	13.0	237,426	2.60	67.2	51.8	4.8	10.6	32.8	26.4	45.1

Table A-2. Counties — Who: Age, Race/Ethnicity, and Household Structure, 2023—*Continued*

STATE County code	STATE County	Total population	Percent change, 2010–2023	Population by age (percent): Under 18 years	18 to 24 years	25 to 44 years	45 to 64 years	65 years and over	Median age	Race alone or in combination (percent): White	Black or African American	American Indian and Alaska Native	Asian	Native Hawaiian or Other Pacific Islander	Some other race
	ACS table number:	B01003	Census PEP	B01001	B01001	B01001	B01001	B01001	B01002	B02008	B02009	B02010	B02011	B02012	B02013
	Column number:	1	2	3	4	5	6	7	8	9	10	11	12	13	14
10000	**DELAWARE**	1,031,890	14.7	20.5	8.6	24.6	25.0	21.3	42.0	66.2	25.8	1.5	5.1	0.3	9.9
10001	Kent County	189,789	16.5	22.6	9.7	25.4	23.5	18.8	39.0	64.2	32.3	1.8	3.4	0.4	6.9
10003	New Castle County	578,592	7.3	21.1	9.0	27.1	25.2	17.6	39.8	59.7	29.5	1.0	7.2	NA	10.8
10005	Sussex County	263,509	33.2	17.7	6.8	18.6	25.6	31.3	52.6	82.0	13.1	2.3	1.8	NA	10.0
11000	**DISTRICT OF COLUMBIA**	678,972	12.3	18.6	10.2	38.1	19.9	13.1	34.9	47.5	45.8	1.5	6.4	0.3	10.8
11001	District of Columbia	678,972	12.3	18.6	10.2	38.1	19.9	13.1	34.9	47.5	45.8	1.5	6.4	0.3	10.8
12000	**FLORIDA**	22,610,726	19.9	19.4	8.0	25.3	25.6	21.7	42.8	73.6	17.7	1.6	4.1	0.2	23.2
12001	Alachua County	285,994	15.6	17.7	21.1	26.0	19.6	15.5	33.4	71.9	19.9	2.5	7.3	NA	10.0
12005	Bay County	190,769	12.7	21.2	7.5	25.7	27.2	18.4	41.4	85.8	10.6	4.4	3.8	0.6	8.1
12009	Brevard County	643,979	18.5	17.9	7.0	23.3	26.9	24.9	46.6	83.7	12.4	1.2	3.7	0.2	10.6
12011	Broward County	1,962,531	11.9	20.5	7.4	26.5	27.0	18.5	41.5	59.1	31.3	1.7	4.8	0.2	30.2
12015	Charlotte County	206,134	28.8	11.8	4.9	16.7	25.7	40.9	60.1	90.3	7.2	0.9	2.0	NA	6.4
12017	Citrus County	166,696	18.1	15.3	4.7	18.0	25.6	36.4	56.7	94.9	4.3	1.4	2.0	NA	5.5
12019	Clay County	232,439	21.4	22.5	7.1	26.7	26.3	17.4	40.7	81.3	15.5	2.2	5.0	NA	9.2
12021	Collier County	404,310	25.4	16.0	6.3	18.5	24.8	34.4	54.0	83.9	8.4	3.1	2.2	0.1	23.2
12023	Columbia County	73,063	8.1	21.0	6.3	28.2	24.4	20.1	41.2	80.5	17.9	1.6	1.4	NA	5.9
12031	Duval County	1,030,822	19.0	22.3	8.8	29.5	23.8	15.7	37.2	60.6	32.4	1.3	6.5	0.3	10.9
12033	Escambia County	326,928	9.7	20.9	10.8	26.2	23.7	18.4	38.2	72.4	23.5	1.7	5.2	0.5	6.8
12035	Flagler County	131,439	37.0	15.9	7.6	17.7	26.3	32.5	52.9	84.3	13.4	1.2	3.5	NA	8.7
12053	Hernando County	212,807	23.0	18.5	7.1	22.0	26.1	26.3	47.4	88.4	6.8	3.3	2.2	NA	13.0
12055	Highlands County	107,614	9.0	16.2	6.6	18.7	21.9	36.6	54.4	79.8	11.8	1.3	1.8	NA	18.4
12057	Hillsborough County	1,535,564	24.5	21.4	9.1	29.2	24.9	15.3	37.9	69.6	19.9	1.6	6.0	0.3	25.7
12061	Indian River County	169,795	22.8	14.8	6.1	17.6	25.8	35.7	55.9	86.8	9.8	1.2	2.3	NA	10.8
12069	Lake County	424,462	42.5	19.0	6.2	23.1	25.1	26.7	46.7	81.5	13.6	1.5	3.3	0.4	17.3
12071	Lee County	834,573	34.6	17.1	7.2	21.5	25.2	29.0	49.1	83.6	10.4	2.3	2.4	NA	21.1
12073	Leon County	296,913	7.6	18.3	21.5	25.2	19.7	15.3	32.6	62.5	33.0	1.0	4.9	0.2	7.3
12081	Manatee County	441,095	36.4	17.2	6.1	21.6	26.1	29.0	49.6	83.0	9.4	2.0	3.3	0.3	15.2
12083	Marion County	409,959	23.7	18.7	6.1	22.2	24.1	28.9	47.7	79.7	14.7	1.5	2.8	NA	15.8
12085	Martin County	163,315	11.6	15.8	5.6	20.0	25.6	33.0	53.4	87.4	5.5	1.6	2.1	NA	12.5
12086	Miami-Dade County	2,686,867	7.2	19.8	8.1	27.1	27.5	17.4	41.0	71.5	16.9	0.8	2.3	0.1	54.9
12087	Monroe County	80,614	10.0	16.0	4.7	25.1	28.8	25.4	48.8	85.1	8.0	1.3	2.5	NA	19.5
12089	Nassau County	101,501	38.1	19.2	5.9	23.5	26.9	24.5	46.7	91.2	7.3	1.2	2.1	NA	5.2
12091	Okaloosa County	218,464	20.9	22.5	8.5	28.3	23.5	17.1	38.6	80.9	12.4	1.6	5.4	0.8	10.1
12095	Orange County	1,471,416	28.0	21.1	10.2	30.6	24.6	13.5	36.9	61.8	23.1	1.7	7.0	0.3	29.7
12097	Osceola County	437,784	62.2	23.7	8.6	29.4	24.7	13.5	37.3	55.1	16.0	1.1	4.4	0.4	44.9
12099	Palm Beach County	1,533,801	15.9	18.7	7.3	23.2	25.3	25.4	45.6	68.6	20.8	1.2	4.2	0.2	23.2
12101	Pasco County	632,996	36.0	20.2	7.2	24.9	25.9	21.8	43.0	83.6	9.1	1.7	4.9	0.3	15.7
12103	Pinellas County	961,596	4.9	15.1	6.3	23.9	27.7	27.0	49.4	82.3	11.5	1.5	4.7	0.2	10.5
12105	Polk County	818,330	35.8	22.0	8.6	26.6	23.4	19.4	39.5	69.1	17.1	1.8	2.9	0.2	25.9
12107	Putnam County	75,955	2.3	21.1	7.5	20.8	26.4	24.2	45.4	84.2	16.7	1.5	0.8	NA	9.9
12109	St. Johns County	320,110	67.3	21.4	6.7	22.9	27.7	21.4	44.0	88.7	6.6	1.1	5.3	NA	9.6
12111	St. Lucie County	373,586	34.1	19.6	6.8	23.5	25.3	24.9	45.2	70.8	25.6	1.1	2.5	0.2	17.0
12113	Santa Rosa County	203,162	33.7	21.6	7.0	28.3	26.1	17.0	40.2	90.1	8.0	2.6	4.1	0.3	7.6
12115	Sarasota County	469,013	23.5	13.8	5.8	16.8	25.9	37.7	57.6	90.7	5.2	1.1	2.6	NA	11.3
12117	Seminole County	484,271	14.3	20.4	8.0	28.8	25.7	17.0	40.1	73.7	15.5	2.0	7.0	0.5	20.6
12119	Sumter County	151,565	61.1	7.3	2.7	11.4	21.4	57.2	68.2	88.7	7.9	0.4	1.4	NA	6.0
12127	Volusia County	590,357	19.4	17.4	7.9	22.8	26.2	25.7	46.8	79.0	12.9	1.4	2.8	0.3	14.9
12131	Walton County	86,354	56.9	20.8	7.1	24.0	28.0	20.1	43.6	88.4	5.6	3.9	2.2	NA	5.3
13000	**GEORGIA**	11,029,227	13.5	23.0	9.5	27.2	24.9	15.4	37.9	58.1	33.4	2.2	5.5	0.2	10.0
13013	Barrow County	92,792	33.1	24.8	8.1	30.2	24.0	12.9	35.2	76.0	16.9	1.4	4.6	NA	11.0
13015	Bartow County	115,041	14.8	22.8	8.4	25.7	27.5	15.5	38.9	84.7	11.9	1.3	1.8	NA	9.1
13021	Bibb County	156,512	0.5	24.5	9.0	26.9	22.9	16.7	36.3	38.4	56.6	1.0	2.7	NA	4.9
13031	Bulloch County	84,327	19.2	19.8	23.1	26.6	17.8	12.6	30.4	67.2	31.0	1.2	1.8	NA	5.2
13045	Carroll County	127,098	14.9	23.6	12.2	25.9	24.0	14.4	35.8	74.0	22.9	1.2	1.6	NA	8.0
13047	Catoosa County	68,910	7.8	22.0	8.5	24.0	26.4	19.0	41.8	96.6	2.4	3.7	2.2	NA	3.9
13051	Chatham County	303,655	14.2	20.4	10.4	29.3	22.7	17.2	37.8	54.0	39.3	2.8	4.4	0.2	8.1
13057	Cherokee County	286,602	33.2	22.3	8.2	26.3	26.7	16.5	40.2	86.0	6.7	4.6	3.3	0.3	10.6
13059	Clarke County	129,933	11.4	16.1	24.7	28.0	18.4	12.8	29.6	64.7	27.7	1.5	4.9	NA	9.6
13063	Clayton County	298,300	14.9	26.4	9.8	28.7	23.7	11.5	34.0	14.7	72.6	1.6	5.6	NA	13.9
13067	Cobb County	776,743	12.6	22.3	9.1	28.7	25.8	14.1	37.9	57.5	30.3	1.7	6.9	0.2	14.7
13073	Columbia County	165,162	32.3	24.6	8.6	27.2	24.2	15.3	37.9	72.3	20.1	3.3	6.3	NA	5.7

Table A-2. Counties — Who: Age, Race/Ethnicity, and Household Structure, 2023—*Continued*

STATE County code	STATE County	Two or more races (percent)	Hispanic or Latino (percent)	Native, born in state of residence (percent)	Foreign born (percent)	Non-citizens (percent)	Total households	Average household size	Household type (percent of all households): Family households: Total	Family households: Married couple	Family households: Male house-holder	Family households: Female house-holder	Nonfamily households: Total	Nonfamily households: One-person house-holds	Percent of households with people age 60 years and over
	ACS table number:	B02001	B03003	B05002	B05002	B05002	B11001	B25010	B11001	B11001	B11001	B11001	B11001	B11001	B11006
	Column number:	15	16	17	18	19	20	21	22	23	24	25	26	27	28
10000	**DELAWARE**	8.2	11.1	42.1	11.2	5.4	412,048	2.45	65.2	47.6	4.2	13.3	34.8	28.0	48.5
10001	Kent County	8.0	8.3	45.1	8.3	3.5	74,183	2.50	67.2	48.8	4.8	13.6	32.8	27.4	48.2
10003	New Castle County	8.0	11.9	43.6	12.9	6.3	226,373	2.48	64.3	45.0	4.8	14.5	35.7	28.4	42.8
10005	Sussex County	8.8	11.4	36.6	9.3	5.0	111,492	2.34	65.5	52.3	2.7	10.6	34.5	27.7	60.5
11000	**DISTRICT OF COLUMBIA**	10.7	12.0	33.4	14.1	6.9	334,673	1.92	41.1	25.5	2.5	13.1	58.9	47.8	27.9
11001	District of Columbia	10.7	12.0	33.4	14.1	6.9	334,673	1.92	41.1	25.5	2.5	13.1	58.9	47.8	27.9
12000	**FLORIDA**	19.3	27.4	35.1	22.1	9.6	8,966,402	2.47	64.7	47.0	5.2	12.5	35.3	27.9	48.6
12001	Alachua County	11.2	12.6	50.2	12.5	5.6	121,753	2.19	50.9	36.7	3.7	10.5	49.1	32.6	33.4
12005	Bay County	12.3	9.3	38.1	8.0	4.8	80,689	2.33	61.9	45.3	5.0	11.6	38.1	31.5	42.1
12009	Brevard County	11.3	12.5	33.5	9.8	3.0	258,656	2.45	64.5	49.7	4.3	10.5	35.5	29.0	53.9
12011	Broward County	25.5	33.0	33.7	37.8	15.0	758,853	2.56	64.3	43.8	5.6	14.9	35.7	29.0	45.9
12015	Charlotte County	6.7	8.3	21.0	8.8	2.9	90,367	2.22	67.1	57.1	3.1	6.9	32.9	27.0	70.3
12017	Citrus County	7.7	7.2	31.3	6.1	1.7	75,745	2.17	62.3	50.0	4.7	7.6	37.7	31.0	64.5
12019	Clay County	11.5	11.7	43.1	6.4	1.4	86,946	2.65	72.7	55.5	5.1	12.1	27.3	21.6	44.0
12021	Collier County	20.2	28.0	22.6	25.2	13.3	166,192	2.40	67.6	54.7	4.7	8.2	32.4	26.8	62.7
12023	Columbia County	6.9	8.0	59.0	5.1	1.5	27,280	2.54	63.6	41.0	9.5	13.1	36.4	33.3	48.9
12031	Duval County	10.8	12.6	47.6	11.7	5.3	428,020	2.36	59.8	39.3	5.1	15.4	40.2	31.7	38.0
12033	Escambia County	9.5	7.0	40.9	6.7	3.3	131,375	2.35	63.9	45.1	4.9	13.9	36.1	29.6	43.1
12035	Flagler County	9.8	11.9	25.6	12.6	2.9	56,177	2.33	67.0	53.2	2.3	11.5	33.0	27.4	63.9
12053	Hernando County	12.5	17.8	35.1	7.8	2.6	85,911	2.45	70.3	48.6	6.6	15.1	29.7	23.8	55.6
12055	Highlands County	12.4	22.7	37.7	10.8	5.6	47,278	2.24	60.5	46.5	4.1	10.0	39.5	29.6	66.4
12057	Hillsborough County	22.2	30.4	37.2	20.8	10.3	593,029	2.54	64.3	44.7	6.4	13.3	35.7	26.9	38.2
12061	Indian River County	10.7	14.1	34.0	8.2	2.5	72,833	2.31	61.5	47.4	4.0	10.1	38.5	32.1	65.8
12069	Lake County	16.6	19.3	34.0	13.0	5.0	172,803	2.43	64.5	51.7	3.3	9.5	35.5	29.7	56.2
12071	Lee County	19.0	25.1	27.2	18.8	10.3	326,338	2.52	64.4	50.2	3.8	10.4	35.6	28.5	57.5
12073	Leon County	8.2	8.3	54.3	8.4	4.1	124,867	2.22	52.1	36.0	3.0	13.0	47.9	33.5	33.4
12081	Manatee County	12.9	18.2	27.6	15.7	7.8	190,091	2.30	63.7	50.7	4.4	8.6	36.3	28.3	57.2
12083	Marion County	13.8	17.6	38.9	10.2	4.6	171,369	2.35	65.6	49.1	4.5	11.9	34.4	29.0	57.7
12085	Martin County	9.3	15.8	31.7	12.3	5.5	69,169	2.30	58.3	48.2	2.4	7.6	41.7	33.5	63.5
12086	Miami-Dade County	45.6	69.1	31.3	54.8	22.6	985,935	2.68	69.0	44.0	8.0	17.0	31.0	24.4	45.0
12087	Monroe County	15.7	24.8	29.0	21.0	10.7	32,559	2.42	62.9	49.0	4.4	9.4	37.1	29.2	53.0
12089	Nassau County	6.9	6.0	42.1	4.9	1.5	41,045	2.45	75.5	62.5	3.2	9.8	24.5	19.1	52.8
12091	Okaloosa County	10.4	11.4	31.3	8.1	3.8	86,541	2.48	68.9	51.9	5.8	11.1	31.1	24.4	39.5
12095	Orange County	21.8	33.8	34.6	25.7	12.6	556,557	2.58	65.5	45.4	5.4	14.8	34.5	24.9	36.2
12097	Osceola County	20.5	56.1	26.8	25.9	12.4	154,722	2.81	75.6	51.5	8.3	15.7	24.4	19.1	38.1
12099	Palm Beach County	17.0	24.5	30.6	27.7	12.0	605,132	2.49	63.9	48.0	4.7	11.3	36.1	29.0	54.6
12101	Pasco County	14.3	19.2	33.2	12.9	5.4	239,952	2.61	65.4	49.7	4.7	11.0	34.6	28.9	49.7
12103	Pinellas County	10.1	11.4	33.1	12.4	4.1	439,896	2.14	55.0	41.3	3.8	9.9	45.0	36.6	52.1
12105	Polk County	15.9	30.3	40.7	12.4	6.4	306,915	2.62	69.2	49.8	6.1	13.3	30.8	24.2	45.9
12107	Putnam County	12.6	11.4	61.6	4.9	2.8	32,487	2.30	69.7	48.5	5.6	15.6	30.3	25.0	57.5
12109	St. Johns County	10.7	9.3	31.8	9.8	2.9	126,240	2.51	72.0	62.5	2.0	7.5	28.0	22.6	47.8
12111	St. Lucie County	16.2	22.3	34.7	19.1	7.1	145,735	2.54	66.2	49.1	5.7	11.4	33.8	26.1	55.3
12113	Santa Rosa County	11.8	7.1	36.6	4.2	1.9	72,969	2.73	70.7	56.8	4.2	9.7	29.3	22.6	43.7
12115	Sarasota County	10.5	10.7	20.8	14.6	6.2	218,010	2.11	63.6	51.8	3.6	8.2	36.4	29.3	65.8
12117	Seminole County	17.3	24.3	39.4	14.6	5.9	189,580	2.52	65.7	49.8	4.5	11.4	34.3	24.7	40.1
12119	Sumter County	4.2	6.6	21.3	5.1	2.4	73,238	1.96	65.6	58.4	1.6	5.6	34.4	28.2	82.4
12127	Volusia County	10.2	16.8	35.2	9.0	3.8	243,904	2.34	62.4	46.2	5.1	11.1	37.6	30.0	54.6
12131	Walton County	5.5	8.5	29.3	8.4	4.9	35,435	2.39	68.6	52.3	5.9	10.4	31.4	25.6	48.6
13000	**GEORGIA**	8.8	11.1	53.0	11.6	5.9	4,150,138	2.60	65.9	46.4	5.0	14.5	34.1	27.7	39.3
13013	Barrow County	10.3	16.3	56.0	12.8	7.1	32,217	2.87	73.3	54.3	7.0	11.9	26.7	20.1	36.2
13015	Bartow County	9.1	10.9	65.1	5.2	2.0	42,225	2.70	70.2	54.4	4.7	11.1	29.8	22.4	39.6
13021	Bibb County	3.5	4.8	71.0	5.1	3.5	60,919	2.46	61.5	37.8	3.6	20.0	38.5	33.8	41.0
13031	Bulloch County	5.9	5.2	72.9	3.7	2.1	30,988	2.54	54.0	32.4	7.9	13.6	46.0	32.9	32.9
13045	Carroll County	7.0	8.8	61.4	6.3	4.4	44,515	2.77	68.0	51.6	3.0	13.4	32.0	24.6	38.0
13047	Catoosa County	8.6	4.3	26.9	2.2	1.4	26,248	2.60	66.3	51.7	4.9	9.7	33.7	29.4	46.6
13051	Chatham County	7.8	8.2	51.2	9.5	5.4	123,272	2.36	58.9	39.0	5.8	14.1	41.1	33.9	40.6
13057	Cherokee County	10.9	12.5	44.2	9.8	4.9	102,811	2.77	77.1	64.1	3.8	9.2	22.9	18.3	41.6
13059	Clarke County	8.1	11.8	56.7	9.3	6.6	55,505	2.15	48.2	30.8	5.2	12.2	51.8	30.0	29.2
13063	Clayton County	7.8	14.5	54.7	15.0	6.9	106,914	2.75	62.0	31.6	6.8	23.6	38.0	30.7	35.6
13067	Cobb County	10.6	15.1	40.5	16.3	8.5	299,074	2.56	66.0	49.3	4.6	12.1	34.0	26.2	35.6
13073	Columbia County	7.4	8.1	46.9	6.7	2.0	57,807	2.84	74.8	59.0	4.0	11.7	25.2	20.7	38.5

Table A-2. Counties — Who: Age, Race/Ethnicity, and Household Structure, 2023—*Continued*

STATE County code	STATE County	Total population	Percent change, 2010–2023	Population by age (percent) Under 18 years	18 to 24 years	25 to 44 years	45 to 64 years	65 years and over	Median age	Race alone or in combination (percent) White	Black or African American	American Indian and Alaska Native	Asian	Native Hawaiian or Other Pacific Islander	Some other race
	ACS table number:	B01003	Census PEP	B01001	B01001	B01001	B01001	B01001	B01002	B02008	B02009	B02010	B02011	B02012	B02013
	Column number:	1	2	3	4	5	6	7	8	9	10	11	12	13	14
	GEORGIA—Cont.														
13077	Coweta County	155,892	21.8	22.7	8.1	25.8	28.0	15.4	39.7	76.4	18.7	5.0	3.2	NA	5.3
13089	DeKalb County	762,992	10.1	22.4	8.5	30.8	24.1	14.2	36.8	36.5	54.0	2.1	7.5	0.5	10.1
13095	Dougherty County	82,645	-12.6	24.0	11.4	23.9	23.2	17.5	36.4	24.1	72.5	1.3	1.1	NA	3.5
13097	Douglas County	149,160	12.4	24.9	9.4	26.8	26.2	12.8	36.3	39.1	54.4	2.8	2.1	NA	13.3
13103	Effingham County	71,541	36.9	26.9	7.6	28.3	24.2	13.0	35.8	82.5	17.2	1.7	1.4	NA	4.3
13113	Fayette County	123,351	15.3	22.2	8.1	22.2	26.4	21.1	43.6	61.0	30.3	1.7	5.5	NA	10.4
13115	Floyd County	100,113	4.0	22.6	9.9	26.2	24.1	17.2	37.8	79.8	14.0	3.2	1.9	NA	10.1
13117	Forsyth County	272,887	54.4	25.2	8.1	25.7	27.8	13.2	39.8	70.7	5.5	0.9	22.7	NA	10.2
13121	Fulton County	1,079,105	16.5	20.6	9.7	31.8	24.8	13.1	36.8	45.1	45.4	1.1	9.3	0.1	8.3
13127	Glynn County	86,172	8.0	20.6	6.2	23.4	26.4	23.4	44.8	71.7	24.5	3.8	2.2	NA	8.3
13135	Gwinnett County	983,526	21.6	25.7	9.5	27.2	25.9	11.8	36.4	43.9	31.8	1.3	15.0	0.3	20.7
13139	Hall County	217,267	20.5	23.4	9.4	25.6	25.0	16.7	38.7	81.0	7.4	3.5	3.8	NA	24.9
13151	Henry County	254,613	24.0	24.9	9.4	25.9	27.2	12.7	37.5	37.3	56.2	2.9	4.0	NA	8.0
13153	Houston County	171,974	22.2	25.3	8.0	29.3	23.0	14.4	36.5	61.7	36.7	1.3	4.6	NA	5.7
13157	Jackson County	88,615	46.5	25.0	8.2	27.3	25.2	14.3	38.1	84.9	11.6	1.7	3.1	NA	8.9
13179	Liberty County	69,210	9.1	27.7	14.5	32.6	14.9	10.1	28.4	48.3	48.7	4.6	4.6	1.2	9.5
13185	Lowndes County	120,712	10.0	24.6	14.4	27.8	19.8	13.4	34.0	57.8	38.4	2.5	2.7	NA	6.3
13215	Muscogee County	201,877	6.0	24.8	9.0	28.5	22.1	15.7	35.4	46.3	50.9	1.2	5.1	NA	7.6
13217	Newton County	120,135	20.0	24.9	10.7	25.0	25.6	13.8	36.4	49.0	51.4	5.0	2.1	NA	7.7
13223	Paulding County	183,164	28.3	25.2	9.0	27.1	26.7	12.0	37.8	68.7	27.5	1.9	2.1	NA	9.0
13245	Richmond County	205,414	2.2	22.6	11.0	28.3	22.4	15.7	35.5	36.9	59.4	1.5	2.4	0.9	5.1
13247	Rockdale County	95,987	12.4	23.2	10.0	23.9	26.9	15.9	40.2	31.1	64.3	2.1	3.3	NA	10.7
13255	Spalding County	69,946	9.2	23.3	9.4	25.1	23.1	19.2	39.5	58.0	38.5	1.4	NA	NA	6.9
13285	Troup County	70,742	5.3	24.3	8.0	24.4	27.3	16.0	39.0	56.8	37.9	0.8	2.6	NA	5.2
13295	Walker County	69,489	1.1	21.6	7.5	25.0	26.1	19.7	41.1	96.6	3.2	4.0	0.5	NA	2.9
13297	Walton County	106,702	27.0	23.5	8.0	25.0	26.5	16.9	39.8	73.2	22.0	0.7	2.3	NA	6.0
13313	Whitfield County	103,687	0.7	24.3	9.4	27.0	23.3	16.0	37.2	70.6	3.2	3.9	1.8	NA	32.3
15000	**HAWAII**	1,435,138	5.2	20.5	8.1	26.4	23.9	21.1	41.4	44.3	3.7	2.9	57.0	27.1	5.4
15001	Hawaii County	207,615	12.0	20.8	7.1	23.2	24.4	24.5	44.3	59.8	2.2	4.5	44.3	35.5	7.5
15003	Honolulu County	989,408	3.5	20.4	8.7	27.3	23.5	20.2	40.2	38.8	4.5	2.8	61.6	25.1	4.8
15007	Kauai County	73,851	9.9	20.9	6.4	24.6	24.7	23.4	43.2	50.9	1.6	2.8	50.8	26.9	4.6
15009	Maui County	164,244	5.8	20.6	6.8	25.5	25.7	21.5	43.3	54.2	1.8	1.9	47.9	28.7	7.0
16000	**IDAHO**	1,964,726	25.1	23.7	9.8	26.1	22.9	17.4	37.8	91.1	1.4	3.1	2.8	0.5	11.5
16001	Ada County	524,673	33.3	21.5	9.0	28.1	24.6	16.9	38.8	91.4	2.2	2.6	4.7	0.5	7.9
16005	Bannock County	90,400	8.8	24.8	10.4	28.2	20.6	15.9	35.7	88.9	0.6	5.1	2.7	NA	9.7
16019	Bonneville County	131,366	25.6	29.1	8.7	27.8	20.4	13.9	34.0	91.5	1.5	2.5	1.9	0.6	12.2
16027	Canyon County	257,674	36.0	26.3	9.3	27.6	22.0	14.8	35.1	86.9	1.4	2.7	2.5	0.4	21.0
16055	Kootenai County	185,010	33.2	22.1	6.7	25.8	24.7	20.6	42.2	95.7	0.9	2.7	2.0	0.1	9.5
16083	Twin Falls County	95,156	22.8	25.6	9.1	26.9	21.5	17.0	36.1	90.3	2.4	2.0	2.1	1.7	13.8
17000	**ILLINOIS**	12,549,689	-2.3	21.5	9.1	26.8	25.1	17.6	39.5	71.1	15.3	2.2	7.1	0.1	16.0
17019	Champaign County	205,644	2.1	19.0	22.5	25.0	18.6	14.9	30.9	73.2	15.9	0.7	12.1	NA	7.8
17031	Cook County	5,087,072	-2.2	20.7	8.6	29.6	24.5	16.6	38.4	55.5	24.1	2.2	9.3	0.1	22.6
17037	DeKalb County	100,288	-4.7	21.3	18.1	24.8	21.3	14.6	34.4	83.7	10.6	0.8	3.6	NA	11.6
17043	DuPage County	921,213	0.3	21.9	8.2	26.0	25.8	18.0	40.6	74.5	6.3	1.3	14.7	0.1	14.6
17089	Kane County	514,982	-0.3	23.4	9.0	25.3	26.1	16.1	39.1	74.7	6.5	3.4	5.4	NA	29.6
17091	Kankakee County	105,940	-6.7	22.6	10.1	24.2	24.6	18.5	38.8	79.8	16.3	1.1	1.5	NA	8.3
17093	Kendall County	139,976	21.4	26.6	9.1	28.5	24.1	11.7	36.0	81.6	9.9	2.5	5.2	NA	21.3
17097	Lake County	708,760	0.6	22.9	10.1	24.3	26.2	16.5	39.6	72.0	8.5	2.3	10.2	0.2	20.3
17099	LaSalle County	108,309	-4.9	20.7	7.7	24.9	26.2	20.5	42.5	91.6	3.5	1.0	1.5	NA	9.2
17111	McHenry County	312,800	1.2	22.4	7.9	24.7	27.8	17.1	41.1	88.8	3.0	1.6	4.2	NA	13.4
17113	McLean County	170,441	0.4	20.9	16.9	24.9	22.8	14.5	35.0	83.9	10.6	1.3	6.3	NA	5.4
17115	Macon County	100,591	-9.1	22.5	8.5	24.7	22.9	21.5	40.2	82.2	19.7	2.7	1.9	0.4	3.0
17119	Madison County	262,752	-2.4	20.8	9.0	25.6	25.6	19.1	41.1	89.3	10.1	2.2	1.7	0.2	3.7
17143	Peoria County	177,513	-4.7	23.8	9.1	24.5	23.7	18.9	39.3	75.0	21.6	2.2	5.6	0.8	5.0
17161	Rock Island County	141,236	-4.3	22.3	9.0	23.6	24.4	20.7	40.7	81.1	12.8	3.0	3.8	NA	10.6
17163	St. Clair County	251,018	-7.2	22.7	7.9	26.4	25.1	17.9	39.7	67.1	30.6	2.3	2.9	0.3	4.9
17167	Sangamon County	193,491	-2.2	21.5	8.0	24.8	25.8	19.9	42.1	82.9	14.0	2.0	3.0	0.5	3.5
17179	Tazewell County	129,541	-4.4	21.5	7.6	25.0	25.7	20.2	42.2	97.0	2.5	0.8	1.4	NA	2.8
17183	Vermilion County	71,652	-12.1	23.2	7.6	23.9	24.2	21.1	41.7	82.2	15.4	1.2	1.2	NA	4.8
17197	Will County	700,728	3.2	23.3	9.0	25.7	26.9	15.1	39.6	73.4	12.7	3.7	7.9	0.0	16.3

Table A-2. Counties — Who: Age, Race/Ethnicity, and Household Structure, 2023—*Continued*

STATE County code	STATE County	Two or more races (percent)	Hispanic or Latino (percent)	Native, born in state of residence (percent)	Foreign born (percent)	Non-citizens (percent)	Total households	Average household size	Household type (percent of all households): Family households: Total	Family households: Married couple	Family households: Male house-holder	Family households: Female house-holder	Nonfamily households: Total	Nonfamily households: One-person house-holds	Percent of households with people age 60 years and over
	ACS table number:	B02001	B03003	B05002	B05002	B05002	B11001	B25010	B11001	B11001	B11001	B11001	B11001	B11001	B11006
	Column number:	15	16	17	18	19	20	21	22	23	24	25	26	27	28
	GEORGIA—Cont.														
13077	Coweta County	8.3	8.4	54.1	5.4	3.0	57,325	2.70	72.9	55.2	5.1	12.6	27.1	23.4	38.7
13089	DeKalb County	10.3	10.4	44.2	18.3	9.3	291,423	2.58	56.6	36.8	4.3	15.4	43.4	34.7	36.3
13095	Dougherty County	2.3	3.4	73.3	2.7	1.6	35,052	2.25	64.6	25.0	7.0	32.7	35.4	29.3	41.3
13097	Douglas County	10.7	12.7	51.1	8.7	4.4	53,350	2.78	72.8	46.3	6.3	20.2	27.2	22.2	36.3
13103	Effingham County	6.8	7.1	50.9	4.1	3.4	25,452	2.80	76.8	55.3	5.8	15.7	23.2	19.3	40.2
13113	Fayette County	8.3	8.9	38.7	12.1	6.1	45,095	2.72	75.5	63.1	2.9	9.5	24.5	21.0	48.3
13115	Floyd County	9.0	12.7	69.1	5.8	2.8	37,835	2.53	69.2	43.6	8.6	17.0	30.8	27.3	40.2
13117	Forsyth County	9.3	10.0	35.8	25.2	12.9	90,635	3.00	80.1	69.7	3.8	6.6	19.9	16.0	36.3
13121	Fulton County	8.6	8.2	42.8	14.2	6.4	458,812	2.28	51.9	36.8	3.9	11.2	48.1	38.0	31.2
13127	Glynn County	9.7	7.8	55.6	6.1	2.8	37,904	2.24	67.6	48.9	6.1	12.7	32.4	25.7	50.8
13135	Gwinnett County	12.5	23.8	36.2	29.6	14.8	330,254	2.96	73.2	52.9	5.4	14.9	26.8	21.4	35.9
13139	Hall County	19.9	29.4	55.2	16.4	10.2	76,413	2.81	73.4	54.2	7.1	12.0	26.6	21.1	43.3
13151	Henry County	7.4	8.5	52.0	10.1	3.6	89,313	2.84	74.5	50.5	5.4	18.7	25.5	21.1	37.8
13153	Houston County	9.8	7.7	55.4	7.1	3.9	65,688	2.59	71.6	46.2	5.7	19.7	28.4	23.5	39.1
13157	Jackson County	9.0	11.5	62.7	8.2	2.1	30,300	2.91	75.8	63.5	3.6	8.7	24.2	19.3	41.6
13179	Liberty County	15.5	13.2	36.0	5.7	2.1	24,654	2.70	62.7	42.5	5.9	14.3	37.3	32.8	32.1
13185	Lowndes County	7.4	7.3	55.8	5.1	2.7	48,322	2.40	60.8	38.3	4.0	18.6	39.2	33.1	31.8
13215	Muscogee County	10.1	8.7	56.0	5.1	1.5	82,007	2.39	57.1	33.1	6.2	17.9	42.9	36.2	36.1
13217	Newton County	12.4	7.4	60.1	7.1	3.2	42,633	2.78	76.4	50.9	5.2	20.3	23.6	18.9	41.4
13223	Paulding County	7.9	9.2	53.0	8.2	3.7	61,401	2.97	78.7	57.7	5.6	15.4	21.3	16.7	36.3
13245	Richmond County	5.6	5.9	61.4	4.2	2.8	77,202	2.55	61.1	30.6	5.9	24.6	38.9	31.9	40.0
13247	Rockdale County	10.4	11.1	55.6	12.5	5.6	35,459	2.68	71.4	44.7	7.6	19.1	28.6	23.8	45.2
13255	Spalding County	5.7	6.5	70.0	4.1	2.0	26,898	2.57	59.9	39.0	6.2	14.7	40.1	35.9	49.2
13285	Troup County	3.2	4.8	64.8	7.1	4.7	28,232	2.45	65.3	41.0	2.6	21.8	34.7	32.5	38.3
13295	Walker County	7.5	3.0	41.8	1.3	0.6	26,020	2.60	65.5	53.8	2.6	9.2	34.5	28.9	47.3
13297	Walton County	5.1	7.2	58.0	9.6	3.7	37,132	2.85	73.9	58.6	5.3	10.0	26.1	21.4	44.7
13313	Whitfield County	11.2	37.5	55.5	22.4	14.8	37,316	2.75	68.9	54.9	3.4	10.6	31.1	26.0	39.2
15000	**HAWAII**	28.2	10.1	53.1	17.8	6.7	493,898	2.82	68.2	50.4	6.2	11.6	31.8	25.1	51.2
15001	Hawaii County	37.1	11.9	56.0	10.8	5.0	73,933	2.77	64.3	45.4	6.9	11.9	35.7	27.8	58.5
15003	Honolulu County	26.3	9.6	53.5	19.1	6.6	338,496	2.82	69.0	51.7	5.9	11.4	31.0	24.7	49.0
15007	Kauai County	26.3	10.6	52.3	18.2	9.0	24,621	2.97	68.7	49.4	8.7	10.6	31.3	22.6	56.9
15009	Maui County	29.6	10.7	47.0	18.7	8.3	56,848	2.84	68.4	49.4	6.3	12.7	31.6	25.0	52.7
16000	**IDAHO**	9.7	13.8	43.4	5.7	3.0	733,244	2.61	69.6	55.7	4.8	9.1	30.4	23.7	40.8
16001	Ada County	8.5	10.1	37.9	6.2	2.6	209,863	2.43	67.3	53.5	4.4	9.5	32.7	23.8	37.3
16005	Bannock County	7.4	10.1	57.1	2.8	1.6	33,729	2.61	64.3	53.0	4.2	7.1	35.7	29.3	34.9
16019	Bonneville County	9.4	14.7	59.6	3.8	1.7	45,245	2.87	69.6	54.5	4.8	10.3	30.4	24.8	35.6
16027	Canyon County	14.2	26.0	44.2	8.2	4.7	88,688	2.87	72.2	56.7	6.1	9.5	27.8	21.0	39.9
16055	Kootenai County	10.6	5.9	28.3	2.9	0.9	74,253	2.47	69.1	53.9	5.7	9.5	30.9	23.8	45.0
16083	Twin Falls County	10.3	18.3	57.0	7.9	4.3	35,050	2.67	68.8	46.9	9.2	12.7	31.2	25.0	39.6
17000	**ILLINOIS**	11.1	19.0	66.4	15.0	7.1	5,071,288	2.42	61.8	44.9	5.3	11.7	38.2	31.3	41.4
17019	Champaign County	9.5	8.2	65.6	13.9	9.4	89,155	2.14	49.4	36.8	3.3	9.3	50.6	39.3	30.0
17031	Cook County	13.0	27.0	60.3	22.2	10.4	2,117,084	2.36	56.9	38.0	5.7	13.3	43.1	35.1	39.2
17037	DeKalb County	10.2	14.9	77.8	6.5	3.4	40,202	2.36	61.0	43.4	6.1	11.5	39.0	28.6	33.0
17043	DuPage County	10.9	16.3	63.5	20.3	8.2	353,618	2.57	68.8	55.3	4.8	8.8	31.2	24.9	42.9
17089	Kane County	18.7	33.5	67.0	17.4	9.2	185,921	2.74	72.2	54.7	6.4	11.1	27.8	21.9	42.3
17091	Kankakee County	6.5	13.0	79.2	6.9	4.3	41,130	2.47	66.1	44.9	6.6	14.7	33.9	26.8	42.4
17093	Kendall County	19.6	23.1	72.9	10.8	4.9	44,934	3.11	77.3	57.5	9.3	10.5	22.7	17.4	33.8
17097	Lake County	12.9	25.1	59.0	20.1	10.3	260,243	2.65	70.9	55.9	5.0	10.0	29.1	23.9	42.7
17099	LaSalle County	6.9	11.5	83.0	4.8	1.7	44,319	2.37	63.2	46.0	5.9	11.2	36.8	31.7	48.6
17111	McHenry County	10.5	16.4	72.1	10.2	4.2	119,150	2.61	70.8	58.0	4.2	8.6	29.2	23.2	41.7
17113	McLean County	6.9	6.6	72.6	7.7	4.3	71,060	2.27	56.4	44.8	3.0	8.6	43.6	32.1	34.3
17115	Macon County	8.9	3.0	78.8	3.3	1.4	43,598	2.24	54.6	39.3	5.2	10.2	45.4	38.5	46.6
17119	Madison County	6.7	4.4	65.8	2.9	1.1	110,909	2.33	63.7	47.1	5.0	11.6	36.3	29.5	43.4
17143	Peoria County	8.7	6.2	73.0	8.1	4.9	77,525	2.23	59.2	42.8	4.4	12.1	40.8	35.6	38.3
17161	Rock Island County	11.2	14.4	63.9	7.9	4.4	62,396	2.18	58.4	41.4	5.4	11.6	41.6	35.8	43.0
17163	St. Clair County	7.9	5.2	58.1	3.3	2.1	102,701	2.40	61.9	43.9	5.9	12.1	38.1	32.8	45.3
17167	Sangamon County	5.7	3.0	80.0	4.1	2.1	85,477	2.22	54.6	41.0	3.5	10.1	45.4	36.4	43.0
17179	Tazewell County	4.3	2.8	82.9	1.2	0.6	54,228	2.33	60.3	46.5	5.5	8.4	39.7	33.8	44.3
17183	Vermilion County	4.7	5.8	80.5	2.2	1.1	30,703	2.23	55.1	36.3	6.0	12.7	44.9	40.7	46.4
17197	Will County	12.6	20.2	72.4	14.4	6.5	246,145	2.81	74.2	58.3	5.2	10.7	25.8	21.6	40.5

Table A-2. Counties — Who: Age, Race/Ethnicity, and Household Structure, 2023—*Continued*

STATE County code	STATE County	Total population	Percent change, 2010–2023	Population by age (percent): Under 18 years	18 to 24 years	25 to 44 years	45 to 64 years	65 years and over	Median age	Race alone or in combination (percent): White	Black or African American	American Indian and Alaska Native	Asian	Native Hawaiian or Other Pacific Islander	Some other race
	ACS table number:	B01003	Census PEP	B01001	B01001	B01001	B01001	B01001	B01002	B02008	B02009	B02010	B02011	B02012	B02013
	Column number:	1	2	3	4	5	6	7	8	9	10	11	12	13	14
	ILLINOIS—Cont.														
17199	Williamson County	66,706	0.5	21.4	6.6	26.7	25.5	19.8	40.8	93.7	6.4	2.6	1.9	NA	2.5
17201	Winnebago County	280,922	-4.8	23.3	8.6	24.6	24.4	19.1	40.1	77.0	14.5	4.0	3.7	0.2	13.7
18000	**INDIANA**	6,862,199	5.7	23.0	9.7	25.8	24.2	17.2	38.3	83.9	11.2	1.8	3.3	0.1	7.7
18003	Allen County	394,545	10.9	25.3	9.4	26.5	22.9	15.9	36.5	79.7	13.9	2.2	6.3	NA	7.9
18005	Bartholomew County	84,003	9.3	23.6	8.9	27.4	22.4	17.8	36.8	84.1	3.4	1.1	6.7	NA	12.2
18011	Boone County	76,120	34.4	25.7	6.6	26.3	24.7	16.8	39.2	93.5	4.2	1.5	4.8	NA	3.0
18019	Clark County	125,467	13.4	21.7	8.2	27.3	24.7	18.1	39.8	88.9	10.2	1.0	2.5	NA	5.2
18035	Delaware County	112,321	-4.5	18.1	19.0	23.0	21.9	18.0	35.4	91.6	7.2	3.3	2.2	NA	3.0
18039	Elkhart County	206,409	4.4	27.1	9.2	24.6	23.5	15.6	36.3	79.5	7.1	2.2	1.5	NA	18.1
18043	Floyd County	80,809	8.2	22.0	8.6	25.9	24.5	18.9	41.2	92.5	6.3	2.9	1.8	NA	4.5
18053	Grant County	66,200	-5.4	21.5	13.1	21.7	24.5	19.1	37.6	92.5	8.6	5.8	1.7	1.0	3.4
18057	Hamilton County	371,645	34.5	25.0	7.8	27.1	25.6	14.5	38.5	86.7	6.1	0.7	8.2	NA	5.6
18059	Hancock County	86,166	22.7	22.6	8.1	25.7	26.1	17.6	41.2	94.4	5.6	0.8	2.0	NA	4.1
18063	Hendricks County	186,387	27.8	24.4	7.8	27.1	25.1	15.5	39.1	83.4	13.3	1.6	4.3	NA	4.2
18067	Howard County	83,831	1.3	22.9	8.5	23.6	24.7	20.3	40.5	91.2	10.1	1.4	1.9	NA	1.2
18081	Johnson County	167,819	19.9	24.1	8.0	28.4	23.5	16.0	37.9	86.9	4.6	0.9	6.9	NA	4.2
18085	Kosciusko County	80,364	3.9	23.4	8.4	24.3	25.5	18.3	38.7	92.2	3.0	0.6	1.7	NA	9.0
18089	Lake County	500,598	0.9	23.0	8.3	25.2	25.1	18.3	39.8	65.2	25.0	1.7	2.2	NA	18.3
18091	LaPorte County	111,706	0.2	21.1	6.8	26.6	25.7	19.8	41.9	85.9	13.5	1.6	1.4	NA	7.2
18095	Madison County	132,504	0.7	21.3	7.5	25.9	26.3	19.0	41.1	91.6	8.2	3.6	1.1	NA	4.5
18097	Marion County	968,460	7.0	24.8	9.4	30.0	22.1	13.6	34.5	60.1	31.4	2.0	5.0	0.1	12.1
18105	Monroe County	139,342	0.7	15.8	25.0	25.0	19.0	15.3	31.7	87.5	5.5	1.2	8.2	NA	3.4
18109	Morgan County	73,227	6.0	21.5	8.1	24.0	28.0	18.5	41.4	98.4	2.0	1.2	1.0	NA	2.3
18127	Porter County	175,335	6.5	21.1	8.4	26.3	25.1	19.0	41.4	91.9	5.7	1.1	2.0	NA	8.1
18141	St. Joseph County	272,848	2.2	23.1	11.7	25.4	22.3	17.4	36.8	80.9	15.8	1.1	3.7	0.1	10.0
18157	Tippecanoe County	188,792	9.2	20.2	23.8	24.2	19.3	12.4	29.0	82.6	8.0	1.0	9.3	NA	9.7
18163	Vanderburgh County	179,810	-0.0	21.7	9.7	26.2	23.6	18.7	39.0	86.2	11.7	2.1	2.0	0.4	4.8
18167	Vigo County	106,153	-1.7	20.1	15.1	25.4	21.6	17.8	35.9	91.5	6.6	3.1	2.7	NA	3.3
18173	Warrick County	65,867	10.4	22.0	7.4	24.4	26.7	19.5	41.0	93.5	3.6	1.8	2.5	NA	3.3
18177	Wayne County	66,127	-4.0	21.4	10.4	22.8	25.5	19.9	40.9	93.0	6.0	3.2	1.6	NA	5.6
19000	**IOWA**	3,207,004	5.1	22.6	9.8	25.2	23.8	18.5	39.1	90.4	5.5	1.9	3.1	0.3	5.9
19013	Black Hawk County	130,471	-0.6	21.6	13.9	25.8	20.7	18.0	36.1	83.7	11.5	1.6	3.3	0.8	4.7
19049	Dallas County	111,092	66.8	26.3	7.5	30.8	22.2	13.2	36.3	90.6	4.4	1.0	5.9	NA	3.6
19061	Dubuque County	98,887	5.3	22.1	8.9	24.8	24.1	20.0	39.5	94.2	5.6	0.6	1.7	NA	2.8
19103	Johnson County	157,528	20.0	19.2	20.5	27.1	19.4	13.7	32.2	84.2	10.0	1.0	7.3	NA	5.8
19113	Linn County	228,972	8.3	22.3	9.0	26.3	24.7	17.8	39.6	90.1	9.0	1.6	3.4	0.2	3.2
19153	Polk County	505,255	16.9	24.1	8.9	29.4	23.4	14.2	36.8	81.9	9.5	1.7	5.9	0.1	8.5
19155	Pottawattamie County	93,179	-0.2	22.7	8.9	24.8	24.3	19.3	41.0	94.1	3.0	1.4	1.6	NA	7.0
19163	Scott County	174,270	5.1	22.8	8.3	26.9	24.4	17.6	39.5	85.7	10.2	1.7	4.5	1.0	6.7
19169	Story County	98,566	10.0	16.5	28.9	24.6	16.5	13.5	27.6	87.6	4.0	1.2	7.7	0.5	3.5
19193	Woodbury County	105,951	3.5	25.2	10.5	23.8	24.5	16.1	37.6	85.2	7.8	2.6	3.5	NA	14.5
20000	**KANSAS**	2,940,547	2.9	23.4	10.1	26.0	22.9	17.6	37.9	86.4	7.7	3.2	3.9	0.3	10.7
20015	Butler County	68,632	4.1	24.4	8.0	25.7	25.0	16.8	39.0	93.4	4.0	4.3	2.4	NA	4.8
20045	Douglas County	120,553	8.5	17.5	21.6	27.2	19.8	13.9	32.6	87.9	6.8	5.2	6.5	NA	5.0
20091	Johnson County	622,237	14.0	23.2	7.9	28.1	24.2	16.6	39.1	87.7	6.7	1.9	6.5	0.2	8.4
20103	Leavenworth County	83,518	13.2	23.6	8.2	27.5	23.7	17.0	38.1	88.4	10.3	2.2	2.6	NA	5.4
20161	Riley County	71,402	-0.1	16.0	34.4	24.7	13.0	11.8	24.9	84.6	9.0	2.5	6.3	NA	6.4
20173	Sedgwick County	528,469	5.8	24.6	9.5	27.0	22.5	16.3	36.4	81.7	11.6	3.0	5.2	0.2	12.8
20177	Shawnee County	177,746	-0.3	22.8	8.3	24.7	24.2	20.0	40.3	87.8	10.7	4.0	2.8	1.0	10.1
20209	Wyandotte County	165,281	4.7	26.9	9.8	26.7	22.0	14.6	34.8	56.9	23.0	4.1	5.8	1.2	27.0
21000	**KENTUCKY**	4,526,154	4.1	22.4	9.0	25.7	25.1	17.8	39.2	88.7	9.5	2.1	2.1	0.2	4.4
21015	Boone County	140,496	17.8	25.3	9.2	24.6	25.8	15.1	36.9	90.6	6.7	1.4	3.3	0.0	6.7
21029	Bullitt County	84,863	14.0	21.3	7.2	25.2	28.6	17.7	42.2	97.4	1.0	3.4	1.2	0.0	2.9
21037	Campbell County	93,702	3.5	19.9	8.7	28.3	25.0	18.1	40.4	96.4	2.0	2.8	1.4	NA	3.1
21047	Christian County	72,032	-2.9	28.7	12.8	29.5	15.7	13.3	28.6	77.3	23.6	1.7	2.4	0.5	7.2
21059	Daviess County	103,458	6.9	24.1	8.2	25.7	23.7	18.4	38.2	89.6	9.1	2.0	NA	NA	3.3
21067	Fayette County	320,154	7.9	20.7	13.6	28.1	22.2	15.3	35.4	77.2	17.7	1.3	5.3	NA	7.5
21093	Hardin County	112,273	5.0	24.2	8.3	26.1	25.4	16.0	38.0	82.8	15.5	3.3	3.4	0.4	5.4
21111	Jefferson County	772,144	4.0	22.1	8.2	27.7	24.2	17.8	38.5	72.6	23.7	2.9	4.2	0.2	8.0
21117	Kenton County	171,321	7.2	23.0	8.3	27.7	24.7	16.4	37.9	91.9	6.6	0.6	1.8	NA	5.3

Table A-2. Counties — Who: Age, Race/Ethnicity, and Household Structure, 2023—*Continued*

STATE County code	STATE County	Two or more races (percent)	Hispanic or Latino (percent)	Native, born in state of residence (percent)	Foreign born (percent)	Non-citizens (percent)	Total households	Average household size	Household type (percent of all households): Family households: Total	Family households: Married couple	Family households: Male house-holder	Family households: Female house-holder	Nonfamily households: Total	Nonfamily households: One-person house-holds	Percent of households with people age 60 years and over
	ACS table number:	B02001	B03003	B05002	B05002	B05002	B11001	B25010	B11001	B11001	B11001	B11001	B11001	B11001	B11006
	Column number:	15	16	17	18	19	20	21	22	23	24	25	26	27	28
	ILLINOIS—Cont.														
17199	Williamson County	5.5	3.0	76.6	0.7	0.2	29,509	2.19	63.6	47.5	2.4	13.7	36.4	30.4	41.0
17201	Winnebago County	12.0	16.1	70.3	8.2	3.7	115,540	2.40	63.1	42.6	5.1	15.4	36.9	30.6	44.2
18000	**INDIANA**	7.7	8.7	66.9	6.3	3.7	2,754,881	2.43	63.0	46.7	5.0	11.2	37.0	29.9	40.4
18003	Allen County	9.7	9.2	66.5	7.6	3.6	160,153	2.43	61.6	44.4	5.1	12.2	38.4	31.6	36.2
18005	Bartholomew County	7.8	9.5	67.3	10.6	8.4	33,777	2.45	66.6	49.7	3.5	13.4	33.4	27.2	37.7
18011	Boone County	6.4	4.4	65.5	5.4	2.2	29,659	2.54	69.3	56.3	6.9	6.1	30.7	27.1	39.9
18019	Clark County	8.1	7.0	46.5	3.3	1.8	52,156	2.37	63.6	46.5	3.8	13.3	36.4	29.1	41.8
18035	Delaware County	6.7	3.3	76.7	3.5	2.3	44,361	2.35	55.6	39.1	6.2	10.3	44.4	32.0	40.1
18039	Elkhart County	8.1	20.4	66.8	9.9	6.2	73,439	2.78	67.9	52.8	3.7	11.4	32.1	27.4	39.4
18043	Floyd County	8.0	4.4	53.3	2.8	1.4	31,833	2.49	62.4	49.7	4.0	8.7	37.6	31.0	40.7
18053	Grant County	9.6	5.7	71.0	2.2	1.3	27,670	2.20	61.9	42.0	6.7	13.2	38.1	31.9	45.0
18057	Hamilton County	7.1	5.7	57.4	10.3	5.2	140,850	2.62	72.2	61.6	3.9	6.7	27.8	21.6	35.0
18059	Hancock County	6.9	3.9	75.9	3.8	1.4	34,114	2.50	72.7	58.7	4.2	9.8	27.3	21.6	40.8
18063	Hendricks County	6.7	5.5	66.8	6.5	3.3	69,367	2.61	69.7	56.9	4.4	8.4	30.3	24.0	37.3
18067	Howard County	5.6	4.3	77.3	1.8	0.6	35,551	2.33	58.2	41.1	5.6	11.5	41.8	31.3	47.5
18081	Johnson County	3.2	4.4	69.7	6.0	3.1	64,079	2.57	73.1	57.3	4.0	11.9	26.9	20.3	38.1
18085	Kosciusko County	5.5	9.9	72.3	5.1	4.5	32,268	2.44	69.7	56.1	4.6	9.0	30.3	26.0	41.9
18089	Lake County	11.8	21.3	51.2	7.0	3.0	197,595	2.51	65.5	44.1	6.3	15.1	34.5	29.8	44.3
18091	LaPorte County	8.3	7.8	66.9	4.3	2.5	45,725	2.29	61.2	41.3	5.7	14.2	38.8	30.0	44.5
18095	Madison County	8.3	5.7	78.4	2.2	1.2	54,317	2.35	59.6	39.8	4.6	15.2	40.4	34.2	44.5
18097	Marion County	10.2	13.9	62.0	13.3	8.6	408,293	2.33	55.9	36.9	4.9	14.1	44.1	35.5	33.8
18105	Monroe County	5.6	4.9	59.6	8.1	5.2	61,400	2.04	47.4	37.0	2.5	7.9	52.6	34.4	31.1
18109	Morgan County	4.5	2.3	79.9	1.4	0.5	29,202	2.48	71.6	55.0	5.7	11.0	28.4	26.7	44.8
18127	Porter County	8.2	12.0	68.2	3.1	1.0	68,120	2.52	64.4	51.6	4.6	8.2	35.6	28.1	45.7
18141	St. Joseph County	11.2	10.9	65.7	7.1	4.3	106,607	2.45	59.3	42.4	4.6	12.2	40.7	33.1	41.6
18157	Tippecanoe County	10.2	10.4	56.7	11.6	8.3	76,240	2.27	54.2	38.5	5.3	10.4	45.8	30.3	30.1
18163	Vanderburgh County	6.4	3.9	72.9	3.2	2.1	77,472	2.24	56.2	42.2	3.0	11.0	43.8	35.9	39.6
18167	Vigo County	6.8	3.3	72.8	2.9	1.7	42,219	2.33	50.0	33.7	4.1	12.2	50.0	40.3	42.9
18173	Warrick County	4.2	2.5	71.8	3.6	1.8	25,278	2.57	73.3	59.9	3.7	9.7	26.7	22.8	45.7
18177	Wayne County	8.1	4.0	67.6	3.4	1.8	26,843	2.41	59.3	40.4	4.3	14.6	40.7	31.9	48.0
19000	**IOWA**	6.5	7.3	69.5	5.9	3.4	1,337,243	2.33	61.3	48.2	4.2	8.9	38.7	30.9	40.4
19013	Black Hawk County	5.0	5.3	73.8	6.2	3.9	53,791	2.33	54.8	41.3	2.2	11.3	45.2	31.8	39.1
19049	Dallas County	5.0	7.0	68.1	10.3	6.3	44,043	2.51	65.8	54.4	4.1	7.3	34.2	26.4	31.3
19061	Dubuque County	5.5	3.4	71.7	2.6	1.8	42,889	2.21	60.8	48.7	2.8	9.3	39.2	31.6	41.7
19103	Johnson County	8.0	6.8	58.6	10.1	4.7	64,076	2.32	51.4	41.3	2.0	8.1	48.6	34.4	30.5
19113	Linn County	6.8	4.2	71.0	6.3	2.7	96,058	2.33	61.0	47.5	4.5	9.1	39.0	32.5	38.8
19153	Polk County	7.2	10.6	66.2	10.4	6.5	207,757	2.39	60.1	45.0	5.1	10.0	39.9	31.6	32.3
19155	Pottawattamie County	6.9	9.5	50.6	3.3	1.2	38,289	2.34	61.5	44.1	4.0	13.4	38.5	32.3	42.1
19163	Scott County	8.7	7.6	57.8	5.5	2.2	75,239	2.27	61.2	48.0	3.5	9.7	38.8	29.5	39.2
19169	Story County	4.4	5.2	61.4	7.8	5.1	38,771	2.23	49.2	41.3	3.1	4.8	50.8	29.7	31.1
19193	Woodbury County	13.8	19.5	65.2	10.1	6.7	40,348	2.56	64.9	46.8	7.3	10.8	35.1	28.9	42.1
20000	**KANSAS**	11.2	13.7	59.3	7.1	3.9	1,188,340	2.40	63.4	48.9	4.7	9.7	36.6	29.7	40.0
20015	Butler County	7.7	6.1	66.7	3.6	2.1	25,801	2.55	72.2	58.1	4.3	9.8	27.8	25.2	43.5
20045	Douglas County	10.2	7.3	51.7	5.7	3.9	51,013	2.20	53.1	38.9	3.7	10.5	46.9	32.0	30.8
20091	Johnson County	10.6	9.4	44.2	8.5	4.2	250,337	2.46	65.1	54.2	3.8	7.1	34.9	27.5	37.2
20103	Leavenworth County	8.4	7.8	50.5	4.6	2.4	30,246	2.61	72.5	59.8	1.7	11.0	27.5	23.4	41.5
20161	Riley County	9.1	9.6	46.2	6.0	2.6	27,875	2.18	50.8	40.2	3.9	6.7	49.2	30.5	24.9
20173	Sedgwick County	13.2	16.7	63.9	8.0	4.5	211,238	2.45	62.2	45.3	5.3	11.6	37.8	31.7	37.8
20177	Shawnee County	13.3	14.0	71.3	3.3	2.2	73,980	2.34	59.5	42.7	5.1	11.6	40.5	34.6	46.6
20209	Wyandotte County	17.3	34.3	54.0	17.9	11.7	62,238	2.63	66.1	40.3	7.2	18.6	33.9	26.3	36.3
21000	**KENTUCKY**	6.6	4.9	68.1	4.5	2.5	1,853,603	2.38	64.1	46.8	5.2	12.1	35.9	29.6	41.4
21015	Boone County	8.5	6.0	49.6	4.7	2.1	51,702	2.69	71.0	54.7	5.3	11.1	29.0	25.0	37.4
21029	Bullitt County	5.7	3.5	78.0	2.0	0.7	32,321	2.62	71.8	56.6	4.9	10.4	28.2	25.3	45.2
21037	Campbell County	5.8	2.6	62.2	2.2	1.4	40,425	2.27	60.6	45.1	5.6	9.9	39.4	30.6	38.8
21047	Christian County	11.9	9.1	45.7	3.8	1.9	25,768	2.61	67.8	44.2	6.4	17.2	32.2	27.8	36.7
21059	Daviess County	4.3	4.2	75.0	2.8	1.9	42,164	2.41	63.2	42.3	5.7	15.2	36.8	33.0	42.0
21067	Fayette County	8.5	9.4	58.5	11.9	6.5	141,680	2.17	54.1	38.5	3.8	11.8	45.9	34.0	33.9
21093	Hardin County	9.0	6.6	58.2	4.6	1.5	45,909	2.38	66.4	45.6	6.0	14.8	33.6	26.6	38.3
21111	Jefferson County	10.7	8.5	65.2	10.0	5.7	331,206	2.29	58.5	40.0	5.2	13.3	41.5	33.9	40.3
21117	Kenton County	6.2	4.7	57.5	4.7	3.3	67,180	2.53	62.6	47.5	4.9	10.3	37.4	29.1	40.1

Table A-2. Counties — Who: Age, Race/Ethnicity, and Household Structure, 2023—*Continued*

STATE County code	STATE County	Total population	Percent change, 2010–2023	Population by age (percent) Under 18 years	18 to 24 years	25 to 44 years	45 to 64 years	65 years and over	Median age	Race alone or in combination (percent) White	Black or African American	American Indian and Alaska Native	Asian	Native Hawaiian or Other Pacific Islander	Some other race
	ACS table number:	B01003	Census PEP	B01001	B01001	B01001	B01001	B01001	B01002	B02008	B02009	B02010	B02011	B02012	B02013
	Column number:	1	2	3	4	5	6	7	8	9	10	11	12	13	14
	KENTUCKY—Cont.														
21145	McCracken County	67,428	2.9	22.0	6.8	25.7	24.2	21.3	41.8	86.1	12.6	0.8	1.8	NA	4.2
21151	Madison County	96,735	16.3	20.8	16.1	25.5	22.7	14.9	34.5	95.0	5.5	1.1	1.6	0.7	2.2
21185	Oldham County	70,183	16.4	24.2	7.8	24.1	29.0	14.9	40.6	93.1	4.3	2.1	2.7	NA	5.2
21199	Pulaski County	66,191	5.0	22.3	7.2	23.6	26.9	20.1	43.1	98.0	2.2	1.0	0.9	NA	2.7
21227	Warren County	142,229	24.6	23.5	15.1	26.3	21.1	14.0	33.0	83.0	12.0	2.2	6.1	0.2	5.1
22000	**LOUISIANA**	4,573,749	0.6	23.3	8.9	26.5	24.0	17.4	38.7	63.8	32.7	2.4	2.5	0.2	7.0
22005	Ascension Parish	131,632	22.0	26.1	7.4	28.5	24.6	13.5	37.3	75.1	24.4	3.2	2.2	NA	8.8
22015	Bossier Parish	129,795	10.4	24.0	8.6	27.2	24.4	15.7	38.8	71.0	25.8	1.7	2.8	NA	9.9
22017	Caddo Parish	226,386	-11.4	23.3	7.8	25.6	23.8	19.5	40.4	46.6	51.0	1.4	2.2	NA	4.1
22019	Calcasieu Parish	203,761	5.4	24.6	8.5	26.1	23.8	17.0	38.0	74.4	25.9	2.1	2.1	NA	6.9
22033	East Baton Rouge Parish	448,467	1.7	22.5	14.6	26.4	20.6	16.0	34.6	47.9	45.5	1.1	4.4	NA	8.4
22045	Iberia Parish	67,659	-7.6	24.6	9.6	22.5	25.6	17.8	40.4	63.6	34.3	1.7	2.9	NA	5.7
22051	Jefferson Parish	421,777	-2.5	22.1	7.3	26.4	24.8	19.4	40.2	60.9	28.0	3.3	5.3	0.0	16.5
22055	Lafayette Parish	249,750	12.5	24.1	7.8	29.8	23.0	15.3	37.1	70.3	27.5	0.6	2.5	NA	7.8
22057	Lafourche Parish	95,056	-1.3	22.6	9.6	25.1	25.4	17.3	40.0	80.3	15.4	5.7	NA	NA	3.5
22063	Livingston Parish	150,145	16.8	25.5	8.1	28.9	23.3	14.0	36.1	86.6	8.2	4.2	1.2	NA	7.4
22071	Orleans Parish	364,136	4.7	19.5	9.1	29.3	23.9	18.1	39.5	38.2	57.9	1.8	3.9	0.2	7.5
22073	Ouachita Parish	157,568	2.4	24.3	9.6	26.5	23.3	16.4	36.6	61.4	36.6	3.1	1.3	NA	3.3
22079	Rapides Parish	126,260	-4.2	24.6	8.6	25.4	23.9	17.4	38.4	64.3	32.6	3.2	2.4	NA	3.8
22097	St. Landry Parish	81,464	-2.4	26.6	7.0	26.0	22.9	17.4	37.7	56.5	42.9	0.7	NA	NA	3.9
22103	St. Tammany Parish	275,583	17.5	23.4	7.7	24.2	25.7	19.0	40.8	83.5	15.7	2.3	2.2	NA	8.2
22105	Tangipahoa Parish	138,064	13.7	24.7	9.7	27.9	21.9	15.8	36.8	71.1	28.5	3.7	1.0	NA	5.7
22109	Terrebonne Parish	103,616	-7.4	24.5	8.4	26.2	24.6	16.3	37.9	71.1	21.6	9.1	1.9	NA	5.8
23000	**MAINE**	1,395,722	5.2	17.6	7.9	24.6	26.9	22.9	44.9	95.9	2.6	1.7	2.0	0.1	3.8
23001	Androscoggin County	113,765	5.7	20.3	10.1	25.5	25.4	18.8	40.7	91.2	7.1	2.0	1.6	NA	2.7
23003	Aroostook County	67,351	-6.1	18.4	6.0	22.2	27.8	25.5	47.5	97.5	1.6	2.7	0.8	0.4	1.9
23005	Cumberland County	310,230	10.2	17.8	8.3	27.2	25.9	20.8	42.5	93.7	4.8	1.1	3.8	0.1	5.5
23011	Kennebec County	127,259	4.2	18.5	8.6	24.1	27.1	21.8	44.1	97.7	1.4	1.5	1.6	NA	2.9
23019	Penobscot County	155,312	1.0	17.2	10.5	25.6	26.0	20.8	42.7	95.8	1.7	1.9	2.0	0.2	2.5
23031	York County	218,586	10.8	17.1	6.8	25.2	27.8	23.2	45.7	96.4	2.0	1.2	2.1	NA	5.2
24000	**MARYLAND**	6,180,253	6.8	22.0	8.5	26.6	25.7	17.3	39.8	55.3	32.2	2.0	8.2	0.2	11.6
24001	Allegany County	67,273	-10.3	17.2	11.0	24.9	25.3	21.5	42.2	88.0	9.0	1.2	1.6	NA	3.8
24003	Anne Arundel County	594,582	10.3	22.5	7.6	28.1	25.3	16.4	39.6	69.9	21.8	1.8	6.4	0.1	9.9
24005	Baltimore County	844,703	4.8	21.7	8.9	26.0	24.8	18.7	39.8	58.2	32.9	1.5	7.5	0.4	7.4
24009	Calvert County	94,728	6.5	23.0	8.2	25.2	26.9	16.6	39.9	83.4	16.7	0.9	4.0	NA	7.9
24013	Carroll County	176,639	5.6	22.2	7.8	24.9	26.8	18.3	40.9	91.0	4.1	2.2	3.5	NA	4.8
24015	Cecil County	105,672	4.4	22.0	7.1	24.8	27.9	18.1	41.2	89.5	10.3	1.1	2.3	NA	4.6
24017	Charles County	171,973	16.9	23.7	7.7	26.6	28.0	14.0	39.2	40.2	55.9	4.1	5.0	0.6	6.6
24021	Frederick County	293,391	25.3	23.4	8.4	27.0	25.7	15.6	38.8	75.4	12.8	3.0	8.0	0.2	11.1
24025	Harford County	264,644	7.9	22.1	7.6	26.0	26.2	18.0	41.0	79.6	16.4	1.9	4.2	NA	5.3
24027	Howard County	336,001	16.5	23.5	8.0	26.3	26.4	15.9	40.2	53.9	23.1	1.7	22.4	0.3	7.9
24031	Montgomery County	1,058,474	8.4	22.6	7.7	25.6	26.4	17.7	40.6	52.5	21.5	2.1	17.6	0.1	19.4
24033	Prince George's County	947,430	9.5	21.8	9.1	27.1	26.4	15.6	39.1	18.6	62.5	2.8	4.9	0.2	20.8
24037	St. Mary's County	115,281	9.0	23.2	9.1	25.8	26.9	15.0	38.7	76.7	17.8	1.5	4.7	NA	6.2
24043	Washington County	155,813	5.6	21.6	8.7	25.2	25.9	18.7	40.6	84.0	14.4	2.3	2.9	0.2	7.4
24045	Wicomico County	104,800	6.0	21.6	13.9	24.4	23.3	16.9	37.0	68.1	28.5	3.1	3.6	NA	8.3
24510	Baltimore city	565,239	-8.9	20.8	9.2	31.8	22.2	16.0	36.5	31.5	62.0	1.7	3.6	0.0	7.5
25000	**MASSACHUSETTS**	7,001,399	6.7	19.2	9.8	27.0	25.5	18.5	40.3	77.3	10.3	1.1	8.6	0.1	14.8
25001	Barnstable County	231,735	7.3	13.6	6.3	18.6	27.2	34.3	56.3	93.2	4.6	1.8	2.2	NA	6.4
25003	Berkshire County	126,818	-3.3	15.8	8.4	22.3	27.4	26.1	48.4	91.7	5.0	1.6	2.5	NA	6.8
25005	Bristol County	581,841	6.1	20.3	8.6	25.9	26.9	18.3	40.8	83.3	9.1	1.2	3.3	0.1	13.7
25009	Essex County	810,089	8.8	20.6	8.9	25.2	26.2	19.1	41.7	76.5	7.2	1.0	4.3	0.1	23.0
25011	Franklin County	70,836	-0.7	16.3	6.4	24.3	27.2	25.8	47.7	93.4	2.9	1.5	2.9	NA	6.0
25013	Hampden County	460,291	-0.7	20.7	9.7	26.1	24.7	18.9	39.9	78.5	13.4	1.4	3.0	0.1	22.0
25015	Hampshire County	162,502	2.8	13.1	25.1	20.1	22.0	19.7	36.8	88.4	4.4	1.7	6.9	NA	7.2
25017	Middlesex County	1,623,952	7.8	19.3	9.5	29.0	25.3	16.8	39.2	74.8	7.3	0.8	15.7	0.2	12.3
25021	Norfolk County	727,473	8.2	20.3	8.6	26.2	26.6	18.3	41.1	75.4	9.7	0.5	14.4	0.1	8.0
25023	Plymouth County	535,308	8.0	20.4	8.2	23.7	27.5	20.3	43.2	81.4	12.4	1.2	2.7	NA	11.1
25025	Suffolk County	768,425	6.2	15.8	13.7	35.6	21.0	13.9	34.3	59.5	25.3	1.4	10.8	0.3	22.8
25027	Worcester County	866,866	8.4	20.4	9.2	26.1	26.7	17.6	40.5	83.1	8.2	1.2	6.4	0.2	15.8

Table A-2. Counties — Who: Age, Race/Ethnicity, and Household Structure, 2023—*Continued*

STATE County code	STATE County	Two or more races (percent)	Hispanic or Latino (percent)	Native, born in state of residence (percent)	Foreign born (percent)	Non-citizens (percent)	Total households	Average household size	Household type (percent of all households): Family households: Total	Family households: Married couple	Family households: Male house-holder	Family households: Female house-holder	Nonfamily households: Total	Nonfamily households: One-person house-holds	Percent of households with people age 60 years and over
	ACS table number:	B02001	B03003	B05002	B05002	B05002	B11001	B25010	B11001	B11001	B11001	B11001	B11001	B11001	B11006
	Column number:	15	16	17	18	19	20	21	22	23	24	25	26	27	28
	KENTUCKY—Cont.														
21145	McCracken County	5.3	3.5	69.3	1.4	0.9	28,934	2.28	56.6	40.8	3.8	12.1	43.4	37.5	43.9
21151	Madison County	5.5	3.6	70.2	2.8	1.7	37,672	2.42	63.0	47.8	4.4	10.8	37.0	25.6	35.6
21185	Oldham County	7.1	5.1	60.5	3.5	1.3	23,415	2.83	80.9	69.4	3.7	7.8	19.1	16.2	40.1
21199	Pulaski County	4.3	3.2	72.1	1.3	0.5	26,203	2.48	67.9	50.1	5.5	12.2	32.1	25.0	45.3
21227	Warren County	8.2	7.1	57.5	8.9	5.5	57,773	2.38	61.1	45.5	5.4	10.2	38.9	30.8	32.4
22000	**LOUISIANA**	7.9	7.1	77.1	4.9	2.9	1,833,915	2.43	62.8	41.8	5.4	15.6	37.2	32.0	41.9
22005	Ascension Parish	11.9	8.4	79.6	6.4	4.3	48,526	2.70	74.8	55.4	5.3	14.1	25.2	21.9	35.4
22015	Bossier Parish	10.4	8.2	65.6	3.8	1.9	54,151	2.35	63.4	46.2	6.2	11.0	36.6	32.2	36.9
22017	Caddo Parish	5.1	4.0	76.6	2.1	0.9	98,864	2.23	58.3	33.8	5.1	19.4	41.7	37.8	44.7
22019	Calcasieu Parish	10.4	5.4	75.0	2.9	1.5	79,222	2.54	67.2	47.0	6.2	14.0	32.8	28.4	41.9
22033	East Baton Rouge Parish	6.6	6.8	74.4	7.8	5.2	177,309	2.44	57.0	38.7	4.1	14.1	43.0	35.5	38.3
22045	Iberia Parish	6.3	5.6	87.1	2.7	0.7	26,439	2.53	69.1	41.0	8.2	19.9	30.9	28.3	45.9
22051	Jefferson Parish	13.1	18.9	69.7	14.0	8.5	176,635	2.37	60.8	40.3	6.2	14.4	39.2	34.5	45.0
22055	Lafayette Parish	8.8	6.5	81.6	5.0	2.5	102,227	2.42	62.5	43.4	5.9	13.1	37.5	31.1	36.5
22057	Lafourche Parish	5.5	5.9	87.4	2.2	1.9	38,393	2.41	73.7	51.5	4.5	17.6	26.3	23.2	40.2
22063	Livingston Parish	7.2	6.6	78.7	4.0	2.8	55,653	2.68	75.0	54.0	6.3	14.7	25.0	19.7	36.6
22071	Orleans Parish	8.7	8.1	67.2	6.7	3.1	155,005	2.26	50.3	30.7	4.0	15.6	49.7	41.6	43.1
22073	Ouachita Parish	5.5	3.7	78.0	2.6	1.9	63,158	2.42	61.3	37.8	5.6	17.9	38.7	34.4	39.9
22079	Rapides Parish	5.5	4.3	78.6	4.0	2.0	50,301	2.43	62.6	38.2	5.9	18.5	37.4	33.4	42.6
22097	St. Landry Parish	4.5	3.2	91.9	1.2	1.0	34,635	2.32	60.0	37.5	5.6	16.9	40.0	35.0	41.9
22103	St. Tammany Parish	11.1	8.2	72.6	3.5	2.0	106,164	2.57	70.5	51.7	4.8	14.1	29.5	24.4	44.0
22105	Tangipahoa Parish	9.9	5.9	80.3	2.9	1.6	54,627	2.45	64.2	41.3	6.8	16.1	35.8	31.3	38.5
22109	Terrebonne Parish	8.5	7.3	83.4	5.4	3.9	42,203	2.43	70.2	46.8	6.2	17.2	29.8	25.2	44.5
23000	**MAINE**	5.9	2.2	58.9	3.8	1.8	616,085	2.20	60.9	47.9	4.5	8.5	39.1	29.7	47.0
23001	Androscoggin County	4.5	2.3	68.5	5.0	2.8	48,239	2.27	63.8	47.5	4.6	11.7	36.2	30.1	38.8
23003	Aroostook County	4.6	1.8	66.1	4.8	2.1	32,671	2.01	62.3	49.7	5.4	7.3	37.7	29.8	49.5
23005	Cumberland County	8.2	2.9	52.6	5.8	2.9	134,326	2.23	60.0	49.4	3.1	7.6	40.0	29.4	42.8
23011	Kennebec County	4.9	2.3	68.2	2.3	1.0	55,601	2.20	59.7	42.5	5.8	11.5	40.3	31.2	47.0
23019	Penobscot County	4.1	2.2	66.4	3.9	2.1	66,556	2.22	57.4	45.1	4.8	7.5	42.6	30.6	46.4
23031	York County	6.9	2.3	46.8	4.0	1.6	93,995	2.29	62.9	50.8	4.1	8.0	37.1	29.2	48.7
24000	**MARYLAND**	8.6	12.6	46.9	17.0	7.6	2,384,715	2.54	64.3	45.8	5.3	13.3	35.7	29.3	42.5
24001	Allegany County	3.4	2.1	70.5	3.0	1.8	28,187	2.18	59.8	41.4	5.7	12.7	40.2	31.1	49.6
24003	Anne Arundel County	8.9	10.7	49.5	11.2	4.9	226,503	2.58	66.5	50.3	5.7	10.5	33.5	26.5	39.9
24005	Baltimore County	7.1	8.0	63.6	14.1	5.6	331,624	2.49	63.1	43.8	5.0	14.3	36.9	30.6	44.4
24009	Calvert County	10.8	5.5	52.8	2.7	0.4	33,642	2.80	77.8	63.3	4.6	9.9	22.2	18.3	48.0
24013	Carroll County	5.5	5.3	66.2	5.6	2.2	64,081	2.69	72.8	61.6	3.3	7.9	27.2	22.8	45.7
24015	Cecil County	7.3	5.7	48.0	2.0	0.7	41,195	2.52	74.5	54.1	5.8	14.6	25.5	21.3	42.8
24017	Charles County	11.0	8.2	40.2	10.0	3.5	62,532	2.73	70.5	48.5	5.7	16.4	29.5	25.6	39.0
24021	Frederick County	10.0	13.2	48.5	14.8	6.0	107,332	2.69	69.0	55.9	4.3	8.8	31.0	25.0	40.0
24025	Harford County	7.1	5.9	64.9	7.8	3.1	103,909	2.53	70.0	53.6	5.1	11.3	30.0	23.9	44.8
24027	Howard County	8.2	8.9	40.3	22.4	7.2	121,399	2.75	72.3	57.2	5.2	9.9	27.7	22.5	39.6
24031	Montgomery County	11.9	21.1	25.6	34.7	14.5	392,629	2.67	67.1	52.2	4.5	10.3	32.9	26.7	43.1
24033	Prince George's County	8.9	22.8	27.2	24.7	13.7	351,460	2.64	63.6	38.1	7.7	17.9	36.4	30.8	43.4
24037	St. Mary's County	6.5	6.3	48.6	4.3	1.7	43,227	2.61	71.2	53.5	5.9	11.9	28.8	23.2	37.3
24043	Washington County	10.6	8.4	64.1	7.8	3.8	59,404	2.51	65.7	45.2	7.8	12.7	34.3	29.5	43.3
24045	Wicomico County	10.9	7.2	59.5	10.4	6.9	39,679	2.53	63.4	46.4	2.7	14.4	36.6	26.2	41.5
24510	Baltimore city	5.6	8.2	64.3	9.1	4.1	259,385	2.10	45.0	22.1	4.5	18.4	55.0	45.2	36.8
25000	**MASSACHUSETTS**	11.0	13.5	58.2	18.0	8.4	2,800,984	2.41	61.8	45.3	4.6	11.8	38.2	29.3	43.7
25001	Barnstable County	7.1	3.8	57.7	10.0	5.5	109,475	2.09	63.9	52.4	3.2	8.4	36.1	30.4	63.7
25003	Berkshire County	6.9	5.9	62.3	6.6	3.3	58,807	2.06	56.6	40.9	4.2	11.5	43.4	34.0	52.8
25005	Bristol County	9.6	10.4	65.9	14.2	6.3	233,990	2.42	64.0	43.1	6.4	14.5	36.0	28.4	43.8
25009	Essex County	10.9	24.5	61.8	19.2	8.1	313,787	2.53	65.3	47.2	4.9	13.2	34.7	28.4	47.2
25011	Franklin County	6.1	5.5	64.7	5.1	2.3	32,430	2.14	57.1	44.5	4.2	8.4	42.9	33.1	51.0
25013	Hampden County	16.2	27.4	63.5	9.6	4.0	184,698	2.42	60.8	38.0	5.5	17.3	39.2	32.7	45.4
25015	Hampshire County	7.8	7.5	62.6	7.8	3.3	61,802	2.26	55.4	42.1	2.6	10.7	44.6	33.0	47.4
25017	Middlesex County	10.2	9.4	51.1	23.2	11.0	632,721	2.47	62.5	49.7	3.7	9.1	37.5	27.7	40.3
25021	Norfolk County	7.7	6.0	58.6	19.0	7.5	286,649	2.47	64.6	49.9	4.8	10.0	35.4	28.8	43.0
25023	Plymouth County	7.7	5.0	72.1	11.6	5.4	203,356	2.58	68.3	52.8	4.0	11.5	31.7	26.1	49.9
25025	Suffolk County	17.0	23.4	42.6	28.7	15.3	332,924	2.16	46.8	27.5	4.6	14.6	53.2	35.9	32.8
25027	Worcester County	13.2	13.9	63.9	15.3	7.5	336,660	2.49	66.0	48.4	5.6	12.0	34.0	25.5	43.5

Table A-2. Counties — Who: Age, Race/Ethnicity, and Household Structure, 2023—*Continued*

				Population by age (percent)						Race alone or in combination (percent)					
STATE County code	STATE County	Total population	Percent change, 2010–2023	Under 18 years	18 to 24 years	25 to 44 years	45 to 64 years	65 years and over	Median age	White	Black or African American	American Indian and Alaska Native	Asian	Native Hawaiian or Other Pacific Islander	Some other race
	ACS table number:	B01003	Census PEP	B01001	B01001	B01001	B01001	B01001	B01002	B02008	B02009	B02010	B02011	B02012	B02013
	Column number:	1	2	3	4	5	6	7	8	9	10	11	12	13	14
26000	**MICHIGAN**	10,037,261	1.6	21.0	9.2	25.3	25.2	19.3	40.5	80.5	15.3	1.9	4.3	0.1	5.6
26005	Allegan County	121,939	9.4	23.0	7.1	24.8	26.1	18.9	41.3	94.1	2.5	1.3	1.4	NA	7.6
26017	Bay County	102,500	-4.8	19.3	7.3	24.0	26.5	22.8	44.4	96.9	3.6	1.6	0.5	NA	2.4
26021	Berrien County	152,261	-2.9	21.1	7.9	23.0	25.8	22.0	43.0	81.4	15.2	1.9	3.0	NA	7.0
26025	Calhoun County	133,366	-2.0	22.8	8.4	24.8	25.1	19.0	40.3	83.8	13.9	1.6	3.7	0.3	6.7
26037	Clinton County	79,720	5.7	21.0	8.8	23.9	26.9	19.5	42.5	92.8	3.1	1.0	2.3	NA	5.3
26045	Eaton County	108,820	0.9	20.3	8.3	25.5	24.9	21.0	41.4	88.6	9.2	1.9	3.0	NA	6.0
26049	Genesee County	401,522	-5.5	22.0	8.2	24.9	25.4	19.6	41.0	77.7	21.9	1.5	1.9	0.1	2.9
26055	Grand Traverse County	96,421	10.8	18.9	7.5	25.3	25.4	22.8	42.9	97.3	1.2	2.3	1.4	NA	4.0
26065	Ingham County	284,637	1.4	19.3	19.7	26.1	19.8	15.2	33.0	79.3	14.9	1.7	7.6	NA	7.4
26067	Ionia County	66,262	3.7	22.9	8.1	26.9	25.7	16.5	37.8	95.4	6.5	1.4	0.8	NA	3.0
26075	Jackson County	159,424	-0.5	20.7	7.9	26.1	25.9	19.5	41.6	90.4	10.0	1.3	1.3	NA	5.6
26077	Kalamazoo County	262,215	4.6	21.2	15.2	25.5	21.7	16.4	34.9	82.8	14.0	2.0	3.6	0.2	6.1
26081	Kent County	661,354	9.6	23.2	9.3	29.3	22.8	15.4	36.5	82.5	12.9	1.7	4.1	0.2	11.5
26087	Lapeer County	88,977	0.9	20.2	6.7	24.1	28.4	20.7	44.3	96.2	2.7	1.7	1.1	NA	4.5
26091	Lenawee County	97,520	-2.2	20.4	8.6	22.6	27.4	21.1	43.5	95.6	3.5	2.1	0.8	NA	5.9
26093	Livingston County	196,757	8.7	20.0	7.6	23.1	28.6	20.8	44.4	97.6	1.1	1.0	1.6	NA	3.0
26099	Macomb County	875,101	4.0	20.5	7.8	26.2	26.7	18.8	41.4	80.2	15.4	1.2	6.5	0.2	3.4
26103	Marquette County	66,999	-0.2	17.1	15.4	24.6	22.4	20.5	39.9	96.9	2.2	3.5	1.2	NA	1.9
26111	Midland County	84,039	0.5	20.7	7.3	24.5	27.0	20.6	43.3	95.2	2.2	0.9	2.7	NA	3.5
26115	Monroe County	155,045	2.0	20.6	7.9	23.9	26.7	20.9	42.9	95.8	4.0	1.9	1.2	NA	4.4
26117	Montcalm County	68,154	7.6	20.8	7.7	25.9	26.9	18.7	40.6	95.1	1.8	4.1	1.2	NA	5.6
26121	Muskegon County	176,564	2.6	22.4	7.6	26.4	24.8	18.9	40.3	85.1	15.5	2.6	1.0	NA	5.4
26125	Oakland County	1,270,426	5.6	20.0	7.8	26.4	26.7	19.1	41.4	76.1	14.8	1.1	9.8	0.3	5.7
26139	Ottawa County	303,372	14.9	22.7	13.1	24.5	22.5	17.3	36.9	90.4	2.8	1.3	3.5	NA	8.8
26145	Saginaw County	187,782	-6.1	21.1	8.8	24.9	23.9	21.2	41.2	78.1	20.5	1.1	1.6	NA	4.5
26147	St. Clair County	159,874	-1.8	20.0	7.0	23.2	28.6	21.1	44.8	94.7	3.9	1.3	1.0	NA	3.4
26155	Shiawassee County	68,025	-3.7	20.4	7.6	24.3	27.3	20.4	42.5	98.0	1.5	1.1	0.9	NA	1.4
26159	Van Buren County	75,798	-0.5	22.8	7.2	23.3	25.7	21.0	42.8	88.5	5.1	2.4	1.0	NA	13.5
26161	Washtenaw County	365,536	5.9	17.9	17.3	25.9	22.5	16.4	35.5	77.9	14.2	1.7	10.8	0.1	5.3
26163	Wayne County	1,751,169	-3.6	23.5	8.3	26.5	24.6	17.1	38.1	55.4	39.4	1.9	4.6	0.1	6.4
27000	**MINNESOTA**	5,737,915	8.1	22.6	8.7	26.6	24.2	17.9	39.1	83.3	9.1	2.4	6.4	0.2	6.2
27003	Anoka County	372,441	12.4	23.6	7.9	26.9	25.6	16.0	39.0	80.9	11.3	1.8	7.2	NA	6.2
27013	Blue Earth County	70,006	9.4	19.6	22.1	24.0	18.5	15.8	31.1	92.4	6.5	0.7	3.5	NA	4.5
27019	Carver County	111,057	21.6	24.8	7.4	26.1	26.5	15.2	40.3	92.4	3.6	1.4	4.5	0.8	4.6
27027	Clay County	66,258	12.3	24.2	14.4	26.4	19.6	15.4	34.1	90.6	7.1	2.3	2.7	NA	4.8
27035	Crow Wing County	68,304	9.3	20.1	6.1	22.6	25.9	25.2	46.4	97.6	1.8	1.8	0.6	NA	2.6
27037	Dakota County	447,440	12.1	23.8	7.8	27.1	25.0	16.4	38.7	80.8	11.0	1.4	6.6	0.4	8.3
27053	Hennepin County	1,258,713	9.0	21.4	8.5	30.4	23.5	16.3	37.8	74.5	16.5	2.4	8.8	0.1	7.3
27109	Olmsted County	164,784	14.0	23.6	7.6	29.0	22.4	17.4	37.7	81.9	9.5	0.7	8.0	NA	6.9
27123	Ramsey County	536,075	5.3	22.8	9.4	29.5	21.9	16.4	36.4	66.6	15.6	2.0	16.9	0.2	7.9
27131	Rice County	67,948	5.9	20.7	15.6	22.8	24.1	16.8	37.3	86.7	7.4	1.7	2.9	NA	9.7
27137	St. Louis County	200,514	0.2	18.3	12.2	23.3	24.2	22.0	41.7	94.8	2.7	3.4	1.9	0.2	2.8
27139	Scott County	155,814	19.4	25.5	7.9	26.3	27.1	13.2	38.4	82.0	8.7	1.8	7.7	NA	5.1
27141	Sherburne County	102,206	15.2	25.8	7.9	27.6	25.9	12.8	36.5	92.8	6.4	1.8	2.5	NA	2.2
27145	Stearns County	160,977	6.8	23.4	14.4	23.0	22.8	16.4	36.0	86.5	11.2	0.8	3.1	0.2	5.4
27163	Washington County	278,936	16.8	23.7	7.8	25.3	25.9	17.3	40.8	83.3	7.6	1.1	8.9	0.2	5.4
27171	Wright County	151,150	20.8	26.9	7.3	26.3	25.5	13.9	37.6	92.2	3.8	1.0	2.7	NA	5.4
28000	**MISSISSIPPI**	2,939,690	-1.0	23.0	9.7	25.2	24.6	17.6	39.3	60.4	37.5	2.2	1.6	0.2	3.8
28033	DeSoto County	193,247	19.5	24.6	8.3	28.1	25.3	13.6	37.2	63.3	32.5	2.9	3.3	NA	6.4
28035	Forrest County	78,208	4.1	22.9	16.1	25.3	22.0	13.8	32.9	60.6	37.6	1.1	1.4	NA	5.0
28047	Harrison County	210,612	12.2	23.3	8.7	26.2	24.8	17.1	40.2	70.3	27.6	1.5	4.1	0.1	6.2
28049	Hinds County	214,870	-12.5	23.2	10.6	25.8	23.5	16.9	37.5	26.3	73.1	1.4	1.0	NA	2.5
28059	Jackson County	146,389	4.8	22.6	8.1	26.0	25.8	17.5	40.9	76.2	18.7	4.9	2.9	NA	7.2
28067	Jones County	66,250	-2.4	23.9	10.2	24.7	22.9	18.2	38.4	67.3	28.4	NA	0.8	NA	4.8
28073	Lamar County	66,217	19.0	22.9	8.2	28.0	25.1	15.8	38.1	75.8	23.9	0.8	1.3	NA	3.4
28075	Lauderdale County	70,527	-12.1	23.2	8.6	24.1	24.9	19.1	39.4	55.4	44.8	2.9	NA	NA	3.3
28081	Lee County	82,799	-0.3	24.7	10.0	24.7	24.7	15.9	38.4	65.1	32.2	2.4	1.5	NA	3.0
28089	Madison County	112,511	17.7	23.9	9.4	25.7	25.4	15.7	37.9	58.0	38.5	1.2	3.2	NA	4.4
28121	Rankin County	160,417	13.0	22.1	7.4	28.5	24.6	17.4	39.8	74.3	22.6	1.4	1.8	NA	3.3
29000	**MISSOURI**	6,196,156	3.3	22.1	9.2	25.9	24.4	18.4	39.3	84.6	12.8	2.0	2.9	0.3	5.1
29019	Boone County	189,463	16.1	20.0	18.9	26.1	21.3	13.7	33.0	84.5	12.1	1.1	6.2	NA	3.6

Table A-2. Counties — Who: Age, Race/Ethnicity, and Household Structure, 2023—*Continued*

STATE County code	STATE County	Two or more races (percent)	Hispanic or Latino (percent)	Native, born in state of residence (percent)	Foreign born (percent)	Non-citizens (percent)	Total households	Average household size	Household type (percent of all households)						Percent of households with people age 60 years and over
									Family households				Nonfamily households		
									Total	Married couple	Male house-holder	Female house-holder	Total	One-person house-holds	
	ACS table number:	B02001	B03003	B05002	B05002	B05002	B11001	B25010	B11001	B11001	B11001	B11001	B11001	B11001	B11006
	Column number:	15	16	17	18	19	20	21	22	23	24	25	26	27	28
26000	**MICHIGAN**	7.2	6.0	75.8	7.3	3.2	4,107,809	2.39	62.5	46.2	5.0	11.3	37.5	30.8	43.8
26005	Allegan County	6.7	8.4	78.4	3.8	2.2	46,317	2.61	69.4	55.0	5.0	9.4	30.6	24.9	46.1
26017	Bay County	4.9	6.0	89.5	1.6	0.9	44,417	2.28	58.2	42.7	3.0	12.4	41.8	34.7	49.5
26021	Berrien County	8.1	6.4	60.1	6.9	3.1	65,129	2.29	64.2	47.6	5.6	10.9	35.8	31.7	46.9
26025	Calhoun County	9.8	6.1	76.1	3.9	2.1	54,568	2.38	58.7	40.4	3.6	14.6	41.3	34.7	44.8
26037	Clinton County	4.4	5.3	83.2	3.0	1.0	31,653	2.49	70.5	58.7	3.6	8.2	29.5	23.9	43.1
26045	Eaton County	7.8	6.5	79.9	2.9	1.3	45,181	2.36	59.4	48.2	3.7	7.6	40.6	33.3	45.4
26049	Genesee County	5.8	4.4	83.8	2.6	0.9	164,086	2.42	63.7	42.1	5.7	15.9	36.3	30.8	45.2
26055	Grand Traverse County	6.0	3.5	76.6	2.1	0.6	42,544	2.23	63.9	52.7	3.1	8.1	36.1	27.5	44.2
26065	Ingham County	10.6	8.7	70.9	8.4	4.8	117,197	2.26	53.7	40.0	4.1	9.5	46.3	34.3	34.2
26067	Ionia County	6.8	5.4	87.8	2.3	1.2	23,600	2.64	66.9	47.9	8.4	10.5	33.1	26.5	42.6
26075	Jackson County	8.2	4.2	82.2	3.2	2.1	61,851	2.44	64.7	47.4	5.1	12.2	35.3	30.9	45.4
26077	Kalamazoo County	7.3	6.1	72.0	5.7	3.3	107,893	2.36	58.9	42.9	5.7	10.3	41.1	29.5	35.3
26081	Kent County	11.4	11.7	73.8	8.9	5.1	257,898	2.52	64.0	49.1	4.6	10.4	36.0	27.7	37.3
26087	Lapeer County	5.5	5.2	87.9	3.0	1.2	34,494	2.54	68.9	52.5	5.9	10.5	31.1	26.8	47.9
26091	Lenawee County	7.5	9.1	74.7	1.8	0.9	40,142	2.32	67.9	51.0	5.7	11.1	32.1	26.1	45.8
26093	Livingston County	4.2	2.9	81.4	2.9	0.9	77,304	2.53	71.1	60.5	4.0	6.5	28.9	22.6	47.8
26099	Macomb County	6.2	3.3	77.2	11.6	3.0	359,464	2.41	63.7	46.4	5.3	12.0	36.3	29.9	44.3
26103	Marquette County	5.7	2.1	76.3	1.5	0.6	28,707	2.17	57.3	46.7	5.5	5.1	42.7	32.2	41.4
26111	Midland County	4.8	3.6	81.7	3.1	1.3	35,761	2.32	65.5	54.8	3.5	7.2	34.5	28.7	44.9
26115	Monroe County	6.7	4.5	60.9	2.3	1.1	62,936	2.44	69.1	51.5	5.5	12.1	30.9	24.8	47.2
26117	Montcalm County	7.4	4.5	85.8	1.5	1.2	24,697	2.65	65.8	50.9	5.8	9.1	34.2	26.4	46.9
26121	Muskegon County	8.8	6.4	83.3	2.3	1.2	70,042	2.44	66.7	47.3	5.6	13.7	33.3	25.9	43.3
26125	Oakland County	7.3	5.1	70.3	13.8	6.2	533,533	2.36	62.3	49.0	4.2	9.1	37.7	31.6	42.2
26139	Ottawa County	6.7	10.4	77.8	5.4	3.3	114,316	2.55	70.2	58.8	3.3	8.1	29.8	22.5	40.2
26145	Saginaw County	5.6	9.3	86.2	2.1	0.9	77,158	2.36	62.0	43.0	4.2	14.7	38.0	32.4	46.1
26147	St. Clair County	4.2	3.8	86.1	2.6	0.7	69,234	2.29	65.5	49.1	5.6	10.8	34.5	28.4	47.5
26155	Shiawassee County	2.8	3.1	87.4	0.9	0.1	26,950	2.50	66.3	48.2	6.3	11.7	33.7	27.3	48.3
26159	Van Buren County	9.9	12.8	73.2	3.6	2.3	31,149	2.40	67.1	50.0	5.0	12.2	32.9	24.9	47.5
26161	Washtenaw County	9.3	5.8	58.5	13.8	7.3	149,379	2.33	56.3	43.9	3.7	8.8	43.7	32.5	36.6
26163	Wayne County	7.4	7.0	75.6	10.7	4.0	696,332	2.49	58.6	36.0	6.0	16.6	41.4	36.3	42.7
27000	**MINNESOTA**	7.1	6.4	67.5	8.6	3.6	2,344,432	2.39	61.7	48.6	4.6	8.5	38.3	30.2	40.7
27003	Anoka County	7.1	6.0	71.3	10.3	3.2	138,924	2.66	69.4	52.7	6.0	10.7	30.6	23.9	42.0
27013	Blue Earth County	7.6	4.8	76.8	4.7	1.8	27,037	2.42	55.3	44.6	4.8	6.0	44.7	28.0	34.0
27019	Carver County	6.1	5.1	70.7	5.8	2.3	42,250	2.60	74.8	61.8	4.2	8.8	25.2	21.3	36.3
27027	Clay County	6.8	5.1	37.8	3.9	1.5	26,890	2.36	61.0	46.0	4.3	10.6	39.0	29.4	34.3
27035	Crow Wing County	4.5	1.7	78.9	1.2	0.8	31,463	2.13	63.4	53.1	4.2	6.1	36.6	26.7	49.2
27037	Dakota County	8.2	8.8	64.9	9.2	4.3	176,865	2.51	65.4	52.0	4.2	9.2	34.6	26.7	38.9
27053	Hennepin County	8.8	7.9	58.1	13.3	6.1	545,627	2.25	54.2	42.0	4.1	8.1	45.8	35.8	36.5
27109	Olmsted County	6.8	6.1	57.8	11.1	3.6	66,425	2.43	62.6	52.4	3.2	7.1	37.4	30.9	37.9
27123	Ramsey County	8.6	8.5	59.8	15.5	5.0	225,183	2.30	52.9	37.5	5.0	10.3	47.1	36.3	37.6
27131	Rice County	8.0	10.5	65.5	9.8	6.4	23,512	2.53	62.2	47.6	4.2	10.3	37.8	31.4	44.1
27137	St. Louis County	5.3	2.0	77.2	2.2	1.1	87,576	2.21	55.5	44.2	3.9	7.4	44.5	33.1	44.0
27139	Scott County	5.0	6.6	66.8	9.9	3.9	55,921	2.76	73.4	59.9	4.7	8.8	26.6	21.6	36.9
27141	Sherburne County	5.7	3.6	78.5	5.5	1.3	35,909	2.78	71.2	55.9	3.5	11.8	28.8	22.0	35.4
27145	Stearns County	6.8	4.9	75.1	9.0	3.5	60,666	2.53	59.2	49.7	3.1	6.4	40.8	30.1	41.9
27163	Washington County	6.4	5.4	68.8	8.2	2.8	109,093	2.53	71.4	57.3	5.0	9.1	28.6	23.5	42.3
27171	Wright County	5.1	3.7	77.6	5.2	1.9	55,367	2.71	73.4	61.2	5.3	6.9	26.6	20.1	37.5
28000	**MISSISSIPPI**	5.2	3.7	70.2	2.6	1.6	1,166,617	2.44	64.6	43.5	4.9	16.2	35.4	30.9	42.4
28033	DeSoto County	7.2	5.9	33.9	4.7	2.0	70,666	2.73	76.0	56.6	5.8	13.7	24.0	21.7	36.1
28035	Forrest County	5.4	4.4	71.8	3.2	2.3	30,255	2.43	58.3	37.1	4.6	16.6	41.7	31.8	35.0
28047	Harrison County	8.6	6.8	54.4	5.2	3.3	86,167	2.39	61.9	41.5	3.7	16.7	38.1	31.8	42.6
28049	Hinds County	4.0	2.2	83.0	1.7	1.3	88,687	2.32	56.7	31.1	5.3	20.3	43.3	38.4	40.9
28059	Jackson County	9.8	7.8	56.1	4.1	2.2	59,347	2.45	65.7	46.9	4.9	13.9	34.3	28.8	40.6
28067	Jones County	2.9	6.2	80.5	1.6	1.1	25,758	2.51	60.3	39.9	4.3	16.1	39.7	34.5	41.1
28073	Lamar County	4.9	3.8	70.6	4.5	3.7	26,301	2.51	62.5	47.1	3.1	12.3	37.5	31.9	38.8
28075	Lauderdale County	8.8	2.5	78.1	2.3	1.7	29,693	2.28	60.7	36.5	4.1	20.1	39.3	37.0	46.9
28081	Lee County	4.1	3.6	76.1	2.9	1.8	32,115	2.55	65.6	50.2	5.2	10.2	34.4	28.7	39.7
28089	Madison County	5.3	3.8	74.7	4.1	3.1	45,674	2.42	67.2	53.1	2.0	12.1	32.8	29.6	37.8
28121	Rankin County	3.6	3.3	76.2	1.8	1.3	60,434	2.56	64.6	47.3	4.3	13.1	35.4	30.4	41.8
29000	**MISSOURI**	7.1	5.2	64.9	4.8	2.4	2,556,271	2.36	62.1	46.6	4.6	10.9	37.9	30.7	41.8
29019	Boone County	7.3	4.5	62.2	6.3	4.0	76,762	2.33	57.8	42.4	3.0	12.3	42.2	28.9	32.3

Table A-2. Counties — Who: Age, Race/Ethnicity, and Household Structure, 2023—*Continued*

				Population by age (percent)						Race alone or in combination (percent)					
STATE County code	STATE County	Total population	Percent change, 2010–2023	Under 18 years	18 to 24 years	25 to 44 years	45 to 64 years	65 years and over	Median age	White	Black or African American	American Indian and Alaska Native	Asian	Native Hawaiian or Other Pacific Islander	Some other race
	ACS table number:	B01003	Census PEP	B01001	B01001	B01001	B01001	B01001	B01002	B02008	B02009	B02010	B02011	B02012	B02013
	Column number:	1	2	3	4	5	6	7	8	9	10	11	12	13	14
	MISSOURI—Cont.														
29021	Buchanan County	82,956	-6.9	22.7	8.9	26.9	23.0	18.5	38.6	88.3	8.2	1.2	2.6	1.7	7.6
29031	Cape Girardeau County	82,984	9.3	21.7	14.2	23.2	22.1	18.8	36.9	89.1	9.6	1.3	1.8	NA	2.1
29037	Cass County	111,732	12.0	23.2	7.7	24.5	26.4	18.3	41.5	92.2	6.9	1.3	1.5	NA	4.9
29043	Christian County	94,422	21.3	25.5	6.7	25.5	24.9	17.5	39.5	97.0	2.0	2.1	1.4	NA	2.0
29047	Clay County	259,772	16.6	23.5	7.3	28.8	25.0	15.5	38.4	85.6	9.4	1.7	3.7	0.6	6.2
29051	Cole County	77,278	1.4	21.3	8.8	26.2	25.1	18.6	40.8	86.8	12.1	2.7	1.8	NA	3.0
29071	Franklin County	106,404	4.8	21.5	7.2	24.7	27.1	19.5	42.7	97.9	2.0	2.0	1.0	NA	8.7
29077	Greene County	304,611	10.6	20.7	12.9	26.7	22.2	17.5	36.6	92.4	5.4	2.5	3.1	0.4	4.4
29095	Jackson County	718,560	6.4	23.0	8.4	29.0	23.3	16.3	37.2	71.0	25.1	2.1	2.8	0.5	9.7
29097	Jasper County	125,056	6.2	24.4	9.8	25.8	23.6	16.4	36.9	92.3	4.0	3.8	1.6	0.4	7.6
29099	Jefferson County	231,230	5.5	22.3	7.8	25.9	26.9	17.1	40.4	96.8	2.1	1.2	1.5	0.2	6.0
29165	Platte County	111,940	24.8	22.9	8.2	27.1	24.2	17.6	38.4	86.0	10.5	1.3	4.2	NA	7.4
29183	St. Charles County	416,659	15.2	22.3	7.9	27.1	25.2	17.6	40.2	90.3	7.3	1.1	4.2	0.1	4.2
29187	St. Francois County	67,058	2.4	20.7	8.1	27.1	26.6	17.6	41.2	94.4	5.8	2.2	0.5	0.1	1.3
29189	St. Louis County	987,059	-1.2	21.8	8.3	25.6	24.6	19.7	40.6	68.7	26.4	1.0	6.0	0.1	4.5
29510	St. Louis city	281,754	-11.7	18.0	8.9	33.8	22.8	16.5	37.2	52.8	44.5	1.7	4.9	0.3	5.2
30000	**MONTANA**	1,132,812	14.4	20.8	9.0	26.1	23.7	20.5	40.6	91.5	1.2	8.4	1.9	0.2	4.6
30013	Cascade County	84,900	4.1	22.1	8.8	26.3	22.9	19.9	39.1	91.8	3.0	7.0	2.1	NA	5.8
30029	Flathead County	113,679	25.1	21.5	6.7	25.7	25.0	21.1	41.7	97.5	1.0	3.5	2.4	NA	3.9
30031	Gallatin County	126,409	41.0	18.3	15.1	31.5	21.1	14.0	34.6	93.7	0.7	2.2	2.7	NA	6.5
30049	Lewis and Clark County	75,011	18.3	21.1	7.5	25.7	24.6	21.0	42.0	97.4	0.8	4.8	1.0	NA	3.7
30063	Missoula County	121,849	11.3	17.6	12.7	30.1	22.1	17.5	37.7	94.8	1.0	5.0	2.9	NA	6.0
30111	Yellowstone County	170,843	15.1	22.7	7.8	27.6	23.0	18.9	39.0	92.9	1.7	6.6	2.2	NA	4.7
31000	**NEBRASKA**	1,978,379	8.1	24.2	9.7	26.1	22.7	17.2	37.4	86.1	7.0	2.6	3.4	0.2	10.3
31055	Douglas County	589,540	13.6	25.1	9.2	28.8	22.4	14.6	36.1	77.6	14.2	2.5	5.6	0.2	11.0
31109	Lancaster County	326,716	14.2	22.2	15.0	25.7	21.2	15.9	34.8	88.8	6.2	1.6	5.6	0.2	6.8
31153	Sarpy County	199,886	25.2	25.9	8.3	29.5	23.2	13.1	36.0	86.7	6.6	2.0	4.0	NA	10.2
32000	**NEVADA**	3,194,176	18.1	21.4	8.0	28.2	24.9	17.4	39.4	64.7	12.5	3.2	12.2	1.8	23.6
32003	Clark County	2,336,573	19.6	21.9	8.0	28.9	24.9	16.3	38.9	58.0	15.7	2.8	14.4	2.0	25.5
32031	Washoe County	498,022	17.9	20.4	8.6	28.5	24.5	18.1	39.1	80.4	4.3	3.9	8.4	1.5	21.2
33000	**NEW HAMPSHIRE**	1,402,054	6.5	17.9	8.6	25.4	27.5	20.7	43.4	94.2	2.7	1.2	3.7	0.3	5.6
33001	Belknap County	65,027	8.2	17.2	6.1	21.9	29.9	24.9	49.4	97.1	0.6	2.4	1.0	NA	3.5
33005	Cheshire County	77,703	0.8	17.3	9.3	24.5	26.0	23.0	44.2	97.6	1.4	1.3	1.8	NA	6.7
33009	Grafton County	93,146	4.5	15.4	12.3	23.4	25.2	23.8	44.2	92.9	1.9	1.1	5.9	NA	3.2
33011	Hillsborough County	427,354	6.6	19.3	8.2	27.7	26.9	17.9	41.1	90.7	4.7	1.0	5.2	NA	8.5
33013	Merrimack County	157,103	7.3	17.9	9.1	26.3	26.3	20.3	42.1	95.5	2.5	1.0	2.9	0.3	3.5
33015	Rockingham County	320,689	8.6	18.3	6.8	24.7	29.4	20.8	45.2	95.7	1.5	1.1	3.2	NA	4.5
33017	Strafford County	133,243	8.2	17.4	14.0	26.2	25.0	17.4	38.4	95.7	3.0	1.7	4.3	NA	4.7
34000	**NEW JERSEY**	9,290,841	5.5	21.6	8.3	26.1	26.3	17.7	40.4	64.4	15.3	1.9	11.4	0.1	20.0
34001	Atlantic County	275,213	0.2	20.6	9.1	22.9	26.8	20.6	42.6	65.5	17.4	2.1	8.8	0.2	17.8
34003	Bergen County	957,736	5.6	20.7	7.9	25.0	27.8	18.7	42.2	65.9	7.9	1.4	18.5	0.1	20.3
34005	Burlington County	469,167	4.5	20.4	7.5	26.1	27.1	18.8	41.8	73.0	20.5	1.3	7.5	0.2	8.3
34007	Camden County	527,196	2.6	22.7	7.9	27.4	25.1	16.9	39.0	62.3	22.7	2.7	7.5	0.2	16.7
34009	Cape May County	94,610	-2.7	16.5	6.3	18.9	27.8	30.5	52.7	91.0	5.2	2.4	1.4	0.3	6.7
34011	Cumberland County	152,326	-3.1	24.2	8.3	25.7	25.6	16.2	39.0	58.8	20.6	3.3	1.5	NA	31.3
34013	Essex County	851,117	8.5	23.4	8.8	27.6	25.6	14.7	37.8	39.8	40.6	1.8	7.5	0.3	24.0
34015	Gloucester County	308,423	6.9	21.1	9.8	25.1	26.6	17.3	40.4	83.7	12.9	2.4	4.7	NA	6.6
34017	Hudson County	705,472	11.0	19.4	7.6	37.4	22.6	13.1	36.0	50.6	15.3	2.4	17.7	0.2	36.6
34019	Hunterdon County	130,183	1.4	19.0	7.2	22.2	30.4	21.2	46.2	89.8	3.3	0.3	6.4	NA	10.0
34021	Mercer County	381,671	4.1	21.9	9.9	25.2	26.3	16.6	40.2	52.6	21.7	3.9	13.7	NA	17.0
34023	Middlesex County	863,623	6.5	21.2	9.4	26.6	26.0	16.7	39.9	47.6	12.9	2.4	26.9	0.1	20.0
34025	Monmouth County	642,799	1.9	20.7	8.2	22.9	28.4	19.8	43.6	83.1	6.5	2.3	6.5	0.1	11.3
34027	Morris County	514,423	4.4	20.5	8.0	24.3	28.4	18.8	43.1	80.3	4.8	0.4	12.8	NA	15.3
34029	Ocean County	659,197	14.1	25.0	7.3	21.5	23.2	23.0	41.1	91.3	3.4	1.7	2.8	NA	9.7
34031	Passaic County	513,395	2.3	23.5	9.2	25.8	25.1	16.4	38.3	62.5	12.6	1.2	6.6	0.1	40.8
34033	Salem County	65,338	-1.1	22.1	7.8	23.9	27.0	19.1	42.4	80.9	16.6	0.4	2.0	NA	9.7
34035	Somerset County	348,842	7.6	20.9	7.5	25.1	28.8	17.7	41.9	59.8	10.9	0.6	22.1	0.1	17.8
34037	Sussex County	146,132	-2.1	19.2	7.3	25.5	28.6	19.5	43.2	89.0	3.6	1.4	3.1	NA	11.5
34039	Union County	572,726	6.5	23.3	8.2	26.4	26.5	15.6	39.5	49.5	23.5	1.8	7.0	0.1	31.8
34041	Warren County	111,252	2.3	19.2	7.7	23.7	28.9	20.4	44.6	84.1	6.7	2.7	3.9	NA	11.0

Table A-2. Counties — Who: Age, Race/Ethnicity, and Household Structure, 2023—*Continued*

STATE County code	STATE County	Two or more races (percent)	Hispanic or Latino (percent)	Native, born in state of residence (percent)	Foreign born (percent)	Non-citizens (percent)	Total households	Average household size	Household type (percent of all households): Family households: Total	Family households: Married couple	Family households: Male house-holder	Family households: Female house-holder	Nonfamily households: Total	Nonfamily households: One-person house-holds	Percent of households with people age 60 years and over
	ACS table number:	B02001	B03003	B05002	B05002	B05002	B11001	B25010	B11001	B11001	B11001	B11001	B11001	B11001	B11006
	Column number:	15	16	17	18	19	20	21	22	23	24	25	26	27	28
	MISSOURI—Cont.														
29021	Buchanan County	8.9	7.6	70.3	4.3	2.1	33,257	2.41	59.1	36.5	6.5	16.1	40.9	34.8	44.3
29031	Cape Girardeau County	3.7	3.1	70.5	2.4	1.4	33,624	2.37	59.1	46.2	4.2	8.7	40.9	32.6	42.2
29037	Cass County	7.0	5.7	59.6	2.8	1.2	44,422	2.49	74.0	60.2	4.0	9.8	26.0	21.8	41.0
29043	Christian County	4.4	3.9	59.5	2.9	0.7	35,654	2.63	76.2	65.5	2.2	8.5	23.8	22.0	40.5
29047	Clay County	6.6	8.2	53.8	6.8	2.4	103,995	2.47	64.9	50.2	5.1	9.6	35.1	28.6	38.7
29051	Cole County	6.4	3.7	74.5	5.0	2.5	31,874	2.31	59.6	49.0	3.3	7.3	40.4	35.4	41.0
29071	Franklin County	10.6	2.4	80.8	1.0	0.7	44,140	2.39	65.8	52.1	6.4	7.4	34.2	26.7	43.3
29077	Greene County	7.1	5.3	62.3	3.4	1.5	132,232	2.24	55.8	41.2	4.1	10.4	44.2	33.6	37.1
29095	Jackson County	10.2	11.5	58.7	6.7	3.4	310,868	2.28	56.4	39.2	4.3	12.9	43.6	35.8	37.7
29097	Jasper County	9.2	10.0	58.0	4.5	3.0	52,000	2.36	63.7	44.6	8.0	11.2	36.3	29.8	37.4
29099	Jefferson County	7.5	2.7	79.4	2.1	0.7	88,836	2.58	71.1	57.1	4.4	9.5	28.9	21.6	41.2
29165	Platte County	9.3	7.3	49.8	4.4	0.9	44,751	2.48	65.3	55.8	1.4	8.1	34.7	27.9	39.8
29183	St. Charles County	6.7	4.2	68.4	5.2	2.5	163,272	2.51	67.8	54.6	3.8	9.5	32.2	25.0	41.2
29187	St. Francois County	4.1	0.9	81.5	0.9	0.3	25,489	2.41	64.1	47.8	7.0	9.3	35.9	28.7	42.4
29189	St. Louis County	6.2	3.9	66.7	9.2	4.2	419,348	2.30	62.6	45.6	4.3	12.6	37.4	31.9	43.3
29510	St. Louis city	7.7	5.3	60.2	8.2	4.5	150,404	1.80	41.4	23.1	4.6	13.7	58.6	45.7	34.9
30000	**MONTANA**	7.2	4.6	51.1	2.2	0.9	472,867	2.33	60.5	48.3	4.2	8.0	39.5	31.2	43.7
30013	Cascade County	8.2	5.4	52.8	3.7	1.2	36,414	2.25	59.4	46.7	3.2	9.5	40.6	33.6	42.7
30029	Flathead County	6.6	3.9	42.4	2.3	0.5	45,510	2.46	64.5	52.6	4.4	7.4	35.5	28.7	47.4
30031	Gallatin County	5.9	5.5	35.9	4.0	2.5	54,621	2.23	58.6	49.3	5.3	4.1	41.4	23.8	30.5
30049	Lewis and Clark County	7.6	4.2	54.2	2.0	0.8	30,756	2.39	55.5	42.6	5.5	7.3	44.5	36.9	47.3
30063	Missoula County	8.9	5.0	46.0	1.9	0.6	55,084	2.15	52.0	38.7	5.3	8.0	48.0	32.6	34.4
30111	Yellowstone County	8.0	6.8	59.1	1.7	1.0	72,668	2.30	62.5	45.7	6.3	10.5	37.5	31.5	39.2
31000	**NEBRASKA**	9.0	12.9	63.9	7.7	4.5	813,864	2.37	62.4	49.0	4.0	9.3	37.6	30.3	39.1
31055	Douglas County	10.3	14.7	58.0	10.5	6.6	242,890	2.38	59.7	43.8	4.6	11.3	40.3	32.7	35.1
31109	Lancaster County	8.7	8.7	65.8	7.6	3.9	138,006	2.26	53.8	43.7	3.0	7.1	46.2	33.5	35.8
31153	Sarpy County	8.9	11.8	54.5	6.5	2.9	75,546	2.63	70.6	57.7	3.4	9.5	29.4	23.9	34.3
32000	**NEVADA**	16.4	29.9	27.2	19.2	8.9	1,224,685	2.58	62.7	43.1	6.6	12.9	37.3	29.1	42.2
32003	Clark County	16.6	32.1	25.6	22.1	10.1	880,604	2.63	63.1	42.0	7.0	14.1	36.9	28.8	40.6
32031	Washoe County	18.2	26.5	33.5	14.2	7.5	201,140	2.44	58.7	43.1	5.8	9.8	41.3	30.6	42.7
33000	**NEW HAMPSHIRE**	7.0	4.7	40.4	6.8	2.6	569,493	2.39	64.5	51.3	4.4	8.7	35.5	26.9	47.8
33001	Belknap County	4.5	2.4	47.1	2.0	0.6	27,150	2.35	69.1	55.3	5.4	8.4	30.9	26.8	54.3
33005	Cheshire County	8.5	2.7	40.1	2.9	1.7	31,921	2.31	67.8	54.1	4.5	9.2	32.2	24.7	49.9
33009	Grafton County	5.3	1.3	41.8	7.9	4.7	40,528	2.10	57.7	47.3	3.4	7.0	42.3	32.0	50.3
33011	Hillsborough County	9.5	8.8	40.0	10.8	4.3	170,761	2.45	64.3	50.4	4.5	9.4	35.7	26.5	43.6
33013	Merrimack County	5.1	2.8	52.3	5.2	1.8	62,305	2.44	63.4	51.8	5.2	6.5	36.6	26.4	47.6
33015	Rockingham County	5.5	3.8	28.9	6.1	2.2	127,021	2.51	69.0	54.6	4.0	10.5	31.0	24.0	50.2
33017	Strafford County	7.6	3.3	48.4	5.0	1.5	53,495	2.34	60.7	48.5	4.1	8.1	39.3	28.2	39.9
34000	**NEW JERSEY**	12.3	22.7	50.4	24.2	10.7	3,538,457	2.58	67.7	49.6	5.2	12.9	32.3	26.2	44.7
34001	Atlantic County	11.0	20.5	57.5	16.8	7.2	111,158	2.42	66.0	48.4	5.8	11.8	34.0	27.4	51.0
34003	Bergen County	13.2	23.3	41.5	31.6	10.3	356,438	2.66	70.6	54.7	5.3	10.5	29.4	25.0	47.7
34005	Burlington County	9.9	10.0	55.0	11.0	3.7	179,477	2.55	68.4	51.3	3.8	13.3	31.6	25.6	44.9
34007	Camden County	10.8	19.5	54.2	13.2	6.2	201,670	2.58	63.9	44.1	4.7	15.1	36.1	30.0	42.0
34009	Cape May County	6.4	8.4	44.8	5.1	2.7	47,516	1.96	63.5	49.8	5.4	8.3	36.5	29.0	53.3
34011	Cumberland County	13.6	36.1	65.5	14.2	9.2	54,482	2.68	67.5	40.4	8.7	18.4	32.5	27.5	48.0
34013	Essex County	13.1	25.3	46.1	30.6	15.8	322,456	2.58	65.0	38.5	7.4	19.1	35.0	29.7	40.3
34015	Gloucester County	9.1	8.7	60.2	6.2	2.3	113,391	2.66	68.8	51.4	4.8	12.6	31.2	25.5	44.6
34017	Hudson County	21.6	40.8	34.9	40.7	20.4	305,743	2.28	56.8	38.5	5.2	13.1	43.2	31.7	31.6
34019	Hunterdon County	9.7	9.6	61.4	11.6	3.8	51,186	2.50	72.5	62.4	2.7	7.4	27.5	21.7	49.5
34021	Mercer County	8.5	23.3	48.1	27.8	15.2	146,258	2.49	66.7	46.4	6.2	14.1	33.3	28.1	43.5
34023	Middlesex County	9.3	24.0	41.4	37.1	16.9	311,100	2.69	72.0	53.4	5.9	12.7	28.0	22.4	43.5
34025	Monmouth County	9.4	13.0	56.9	13.8	5.7	252,995	2.51	67.4	55.3	3.8	8.3	32.6	26.5	49.0
34027	Morris County	13.0	16.3	57.2	19.8	7.4	193,192	2.62	71.6	60.9	3.3	7.4	28.4	23.5	44.9
34029	Ocean County	8.3	11.0	65.8	8.5	3.2	245,827	2.65	67.1	54.1	4.4	8.6	32.9	27.8	54.5
34031	Passaic County	23.0	44.7	49.1	34.6	15.3	178,277	2.83	71.5	45.4	5.7	20.4	28.5	23.3	47.4
34033	Salem County	9.4	11.9	64.6	2.9	1.6	25,207	2.53	63.4	47.5	3.1	12.8	36.6	29.6	45.7
34035	Somerset County	10.8	17.9	51.8	28.1	10.3	132,047	2.61	71.6	57.6	4.2	9.7	28.4	22.6	43.6
34037	Sussex County	8.0	12.7	68.1	10.2	2.9	58,679	2.47	69.5	55.0	3.8	10.7	30.5	22.3	48.7
34039	Union County	12.8	35.3	45.2	33.7	16.3	206,095	2.76	73.8	48.6	7.2	18.1	26.2	21.2	43.0
34041	Warren County	8.0	13.7	63.7	11.8	3.9	45,263	2.41	61.1	48.5	3.2	9.4	38.9	29.6	46.3

Table A-2. Counties — Who: Age, Race/Ethnicity, and Household Structure, 2023—*Continued*

STATE County code	STATE County	Total population	Percent change, 2010–2023	Population by age (percent): Under 18 years	Population by age (percent): 18 to 24 years	Population by age (percent): 25 to 44 years	Population by age (percent): 45 to 64 years	Population by age (percent): 65 years and over	Median age	Race alone or in combination (percent): White	Race alone or in combination (percent): Black or African American	Race alone or in combination (percent): American Indian and Alaska Native	Race alone or in combination (percent): Asian	Race alone or in combination (percent): Native Hawaiian or Other Pacific Islander	Race alone or in combination (percent): Some other race
	ACS table number:	B01003	Census PEP	B01001	B01001	B01001	B01001	B01001	B01002	B02008	B02009	B02010	B02011	B02012	B02013
	Column number:	1	2	3	4	5	6	7	8	9	10	11	12	13	14
35000	**NEW MEXICO**	2,114,371	2.4	21.2	9.2	26.2	23.5	19.9	39.9	73.0	3.4	12.0	2.8	0.4	35.7
35001	Bernalillo County	671,586	1.0	19.8	9.0	28.1	24.2	18.9	39.8	73.6	4.7	7.5	4.3	0.4	36.1
35013	Doña Ana County	225,210	7.0	22.5	14.2	24.7	21.0	17.7	34.8	77.1	2.9	2.9	2.0	NA	53.7
35025	Lea County	72,101	11.4	28.8	10.6	28.8	19.7	12.1	33.5	79.5	2.9	2.9	2.1	NA	45.7
35031	McKinley County	68,797	-4.2	26.5	8.3	27.9	22.7	14.7	35.0	14.5	2.0	80.9	1.6	0.7	7.2
35035	Otero County	68,835	7.9	21.4	12.3	26.0	22.3	17.9	36.7	76.3	5.6	7.7	2.3	0.6	29.6
35043	Sandoval County	155,936	17.8	20.9	8.4	25.5	24.8	20.5	40.8	74.5	4.5	16.1	2.7	1.2	28.7
35045	San Juan County	120,675	-7.3	24.9	8.1	26.8	22.6	17.5	38.3	50.8	1.9	43.1	1.5	NA	13.5
35049	Santa Fe County	155,956	7.8	15.5	7.1	22.5	25.8	29.1	49.3	85.7	1.7	5.1	2.4	NA	37.8
35061	Valencia County	79,141	3.1	22.7	8.1	25.2	25.2	18.8	40.4	85.2	3.0	7.2	1.2	0.8	43.8
36000	**NEW YORK**	19,571,216	0.9	20.2	8.9	27.0	25.4	18.6	40.2	63.5	17.6	1.8	10.5	0.2	17.9
36001	Albany County	316,659	4.2	17.9	14.4	25.7	23.4	18.7	38.9	76.1	15.1	2.0	8.7	0.1	7.5
36005	Bronx County	1,356,476	-2.2	23.9	9.4	27.4	24.0	15.3	36.7	20.4	40.8	3.4	5.0	0.4	46.0
36007	Broome County	196,077	-2.1	19.0	14.3	23.1	23.1	20.6	38.5	86.4	8.5	0.6	6.6	NA	5.4
36009	Cattaraugus County	75,600	-5.8	21.9	8.2	22.6	26.0	21.3	42.5	94.4	2.9	4.0	1.4	NA	4.0
36011	Cayuga County	74,485	-6.9	18.9	7.1	24.9	27.1	21.9	44.0	93.7	5.5	0.9	1.2	NA	5.7
36013	Chautauqua County	124,891	-7.3	20.4	9.1	22.6	25.9	22.0	43.0	92.4	4.7	1.3	0.9	NA	7.4
36015	Chemung County	81,325	-8.4	20.7	7.8	24.8	26.1	20.6	42.5	89.7	8.8	0.7	2.2	NA	2.2
36019	Clinton County	78,115	-4.9	18.1	11.3	24.1	26.7	19.7	43.2	95.1	2.5	3.1	1.3	NA	3.6
36027	Dutchess County	297,150	-0.1	18.2	10.0	25.1	26.8	19.9	42.3	79.1	13.1	2.6	4.8	0.1	13.4
36029	Erie County	946,147	3.0	20.0	8.9	26.4	24.8	19.9	40.7	79.2	14.7	1.2	5.8	0.2	5.5
36045	Jefferson County	114,787	-1.5	24.0	11.5	28.0	21.0	15.6	34.1	88.9	6.9	3.5	2.9	0.5	6.1
36047	Kings County	2,561,225	2.1	21.8	7.6	31.7	22.8	16.2	37.0	45.7	32.3	1.4	14.2	0.1	18.2
36053	Madison County	66,921	-8.9	18.4	13.4	21.2	25.8	21.3	42.1	95.5	2.8	1.0	1.9	NA	3.0
36055	Monroe County	748,482	0.5	20.1	9.7	26.4	24.5	19.3	39.8	76.6	17.6	1.2	4.9	0.1	8.1
36059	Nassau County	1,381,715	3.0	21.4	8.2	24.2	27.0	19.2	42.4	65.5	13.4	1.0	14.3	NA	17.7
36061	New York County	1,597,451	0.7	13.5	8.9	35.3	23.5	18.8	39.3	58.9	18.6	1.5	14.6	0.1	21.1
36063	Niagara County	209,457	-3.3	19.7	7.6	24.4	27.2	21.1	43.4	89.4	9.5	2.6	2.1	NA	4.9
36065	Oneida County	227,555	-3.1	21.3	8.9	24.2	25.4	20.3	41.2	85.7	8.4	0.5	5.2	NA	7.3
36067	Onondaga County	467,873	0.1	20.8	10.1	25.6	24.3	19.2	39.8	81.7	13.9	1.9	5.2	0.3	4.6
36069	Ontario County	112,494	4.0	18.5	8.2	22.6	27.5	23.2	45.8	93.7	3.6	0.9	2.0	NA	5.9
36071	Orange County	407,470	9.1	25.6	10.1	24.7	24.7	15.0	37.0	70.9	14.7	4.3	3.9	0.1	19.0
36075	Oswego County	118,162	-3.2	19.9	11.9	23.5	26.2	18.6	40.7	96.9	2.2	0.8	1.3	0.1	2.9
36079	Putnam County	98,060	-1.7	19.0	6.7	25.2	29.0	20.0	44.3	85.2	5.0	1.4	3.0	NA	18.4
36081	Queens County	2,252,196	0.8	19.1	7.3	28.2	26.6	18.7	41.3	35.6	20.4	2.0	28.4	0.2	27.1
36083	Rensselaer County	159,305	-0.1	18.8	10.6	26.7	24.9	19.0	40.3	87.3	9.2	1.4	3.8	NA	6.6
36085	Richmond County	490,687	4.5	21.4	8.1	25.7	27.0	17.7	40.7	68.3	11.4	1.7	15.3	NA	15.6
36087	Rockland County	340,807	9.2	29.9	9.2	22.6	22.3	16.0	34.7	68.6	13.2	1.1	6.9	NA	19.4
36089	St. Lawrence County	106,940	-4.4	19.5	13.3	22.5	25.1	19.6	39.9	95.5	2.6	1.6	1.7	NA	3.0
36091	Saratoga County	238,711	8.5	18.9	7.3	25.0	28.0	20.9	43.9	93.6	2.9	1.5	3.1	0.2	5.1
36093	Schenectady County	159,902	3.2	21.4	9.6	26.3	24.7	18.1	38.8	74.9	15.9	1.4	7.9	NA	11.3
36101	Steuben County	92,162	-6.8	21.0	7.2	23.5	26.8	21.6	43.7	95.1	3.8	0.7	2.1	NA	2.2
36103	Suffolk County	1,523,170	1.9	20.5	8.9	24.2	27.8	18.5	42.1	75.3	9.8	1.6	5.6	0.1	20.8
36105	Sullivan County	79,920	3.1	21.6	8.2	25.0	26.2	19.1	41.5	77.8	13.5	4.8	2.6	NA	15.7
36109	Tompkins County	103,558	1.9	13.5	27.8	22.4	19.0	17.3	32.2	81.1	6.0	0.9	12.0	0.2	8.2
36111	Ulster County	182,333	-0.1	16.9	8.9	25.1	27.2	21.9	44.3	84.3	8.1	2.3	2.9	NA	11.7
36113	Warren County	65,380	-0.5	16.9	6.3	24.7	26.9	25.2	46.9	97.2	2.2	0.6	1.4	NA	2.6
36117	Wayne County	90,829	-3.1	20.5	6.3	24.5	27.3	21.4	43.6	94.2	4.3	1.8	1.2	NA	5.3
36119	Westchester County	990,817	4.2	21.0	8.5	24.4	27.4	18.8	42.2	63.0	16.7	2.1	7.9	NA	24.3
37000	**NORTH CAROLINA**	10,835,491	13.3	21.4	9.5	26.3	25.1	17.7	39.4	68.8	22.8	2.5	4.3	0.2	10.3
37001	Alamance County	179,165	18.2	21.9	10.7	24.4	25.7	17.3	39.4	66.3	23.3	1.6	2.4	NA	15.1
37019	Brunswick County	159,964	48.1	13.5	4.7	19.1	28.3	34.4	57.6	87.3	9.7	1.4	1.2	NA	6.6
37021	Buncombe County	275,901	15.5	17.5	7.7	28.1	24.6	22.0	42.7	92.7	6.8	1.8	1.8	0.4	8.6
37023	Burke County	88,338	-2.7	18.3	7.8	23.8	28.0	22.2	45.2	85.8	5.7	2.9	3.9	NA	7.8
37025	Cabarrus County	240,016	34.4	24.9	8.1	27.6	25.5	14.0	38.1	65.1	23.4	1.9	7.4	NA	11.9
37027	Caldwell County	80,574	-2.9	19.3	6.6	23.7	28.2	22.3	45.8	90.8	6.5	0.9	1.0	NA	5.8
37031	Carteret County	69,615	4.4	14.3	6.3	23.4	28.5	27.5	50.4	90.9	6.6	2.9	1.6	0.0	4.7
37035	Catawba County	164,645	6.6	21.5	8.2	24.3	26.8	19.2	42.4	80.7	10.3	1.2	5.5	NA	9.4
37037	Chatham County	81,624	28.5	18.6	6.0	20.6	28.5	26.4	47.9	77.6	12.2	1.4	3.1	NA	12.6
37045	Cleveland County	101,378	3.4	22.2	7.9	23.4	27.5	19.0	42.6	78.0	19.4	3.0	1.4	NA	4.4
37049	Craven County	102,391	-1.5	21.2	9.8	25.1	22.2	21.7	39.0	74.6	21.7	1.8	3.8	0.2	8.4
37051	Cumberland County	337,890	5.5	25.2	12.4	29.2	19.9	13.3	32.1	51.5	42.9	3.9	4.6	0.9	8.6
37057	Davidson County	174,804	7.3	21.3	7.7	24.7	26.3	20.0	42.4	83.9	11.7	1.9	2.6	NA	9.7

Table A-2. Counties — Who: Age, Race/Ethnicity, and Household Structure, 2023—*Continued*

STATE County code	STATE County	Two or more races (percent)	Hispanic or Latino (percent)	Native, born in state of residence (percent)	Foreign born (percent)	Non-citizens (percent)	Total households	Average household size	Household type (percent of all households): Family households: Total	Family households: Married couple	Family households: Male house-holder	Family households: Female house-holder	Nonfamily households: Total	Nonfamily households: One-person house-holds	Percent of households with people age 60 years and over
	ACS table number:	B02001	B03003	B05002	B05002	B05002	B11001	B25010	B11001	B11001	B11001	B11001	B11001	B11001	B11006
	Column number:	15	16	17	18	19	20	21	22	23	24	25	26	27	28
35000	**NEW MEXICO**	26.1	48.6	51.4	10.2	5.7	856,580	2.42	61.2	40.9	6.4	13.9	38.8	31.9	46.0
35001	Bernalillo County	25.3	49.1	51.8	10.4	5.5	285,796	2.31	56.8	37.2	6.6	13.0	43.2	34.8	42.8
35013	Doña Ana County	37.5	68.0	41.7	15.5	8.1	87,688	2.51	63.4	43.6	5.9	14.0	36.6	28.3	42.3
35025	Lea County	33.1	63.2	41.0	17.1	13.4	24,812	2.83	68.2	50.0	3.6	14.6	31.8	27.9	38.4
35031	McKinley County	5.8	12.4	74.8	3.1	1.4	21,312	3.17	70.2	25.3	13.7	31.2	29.8	23.1	46.8
35035	Otero County	21.9	40.0	34.0	13.0	8.0	25,289	2.58	62.2	43.1	4.9	14.2	37.8	30.3	44.6
35043	Sandoval County	25.5	40.5	52.8	5.5	2.4	58,731	2.64	70.6	50.0	6.6	14.0	29.4	23.7	49.5
35045	San Juan County	10.5	19.9	59.1	3.7	1.6	42,670	2.80	70.3	45.6	7.5	17.2	29.7	24.6	45.8
35049	Santa Fe County	31.8	47.7	43.2	15.2	9.7	71,322	2.16	58.2	42.9	4.4	11.0	41.8	34.2	53.8
35061	Valencia County	38.5	61.1	57.3	9.8	5.2	29,932	2.59	69.2	46.7	5.9	16.6	30.8	25.6	45.9
36000	**NEW YORK**	10.5	19.8	62.1	23.1	9.4	7,809,267	2.43	60.8	42.1	5.2	13.5	39.2	31.5	44.6
36001	Albany County	8.8	7.3	72.6	11.9	5.7	134,971	2.21	51.6	36.8	3.0	11.9	48.4	35.8	41.3
36005	Bronx County	14.2	55.0	50.7	36.2	17.0	537,953	2.43	60.6	25.2	8.6	26.8	39.4	35.0	42.7
36007	Broome County	6.8	5.7	77.1	6.1	3.4	80,001	2.30	57.4	42.7	5.1	9.6	42.6	33.8	46.0
36009	Cattaraugus County	6.6	2.5	82.7	1.7	0.4	32,376	2.24	58.1	41.3	5.5	11.3	41.9	35.5	48.1
36011	Cayuga County	6.9	3.7	84.6	2.3	1.4	32,786	2.17	64.6	44.8	6.4	13.3	35.4	29.4	46.4
36013	Chautauqua County	6.7	9.8	74.2	2.6	1.3	54,284	2.21	61.2	42.2	5.9	13.0	38.8	34.0	47.2
36015	Chemung County	3.6	3.9	74.3	3.5	1.3	35,591	2.20	60.4	39.4	7.2	13.7	39.6	32.1	44.1
36019	Clinton County	5.3	3.4	74.5	4.0	2.0	34,639	2.10	60.8	46.0	5.8	9.0	39.2	28.2	40.5
36027	Dutchess County	12.0	15.9	66.9	12.9	5.0	115,529	2.41	63.8	48.1	5.2	10.5	36.2	30.3	48.2
36029	Erie County	6.2	6.4	79.9	7.4	2.9	410,430	2.24	57.4	40.3	4.5	12.6	42.6	34.9	44.3
36045	Jefferson County	8.3	8.0	64.7	4.5	1.7	50,542	2.18	64.1	46.2	4.9	13.0	35.9	29.3	35.7
36047	Kings County	11.0	18.9	47.4	35.9	13.7	1,035,549	2.43	57.4	36.1	5.3	15.9	42.6	32.2	39.0
36053	Madison County	4.2	2.7	81.7	2.7	1.4	26,755	2.29	61.1	46.0	5.3	9.8	38.9	31.7	49.3
36055	Monroe County	7.9	10.1	74.5	7.4	2.6	317,369	2.27	57.8	40.4	4.5	12.9	42.2	33.5	42.9
36059	Nassau County	11.3	18.8	70.0	23.0	7.1	458,162	2.97	76.8	60.5	4.0	12.3	23.2	18.9	51.6
36061	New York County	13.3	24.4	42.0	29.3	13.9	787,747	1.93	40.8	28.6	3.1	9.1	59.2	47.8	38.0
36063	Niagara County	7.7	4.1	85.3	4.0	1.3	91,894	2.23	59.9	42.6	5.7	11.6	40.1	33.4	46.3
36065	Oneida County	6.8	7.2	80.4	8.1	2.9	96,767	2.22	58.3	40.9	5.8	11.6	41.7	35.3	44.5
36067	Onondaga County	7.2	6.1	74.1	8.2	3.2	198,699	2.23	57.3	41.0	4.6	11.7	42.7	33.1	43.0
36069	Ontario County	5.9	5.8	78.3	5.4	2.0	48,610	2.22	61.2	48.4	5.6	7.2	38.8	30.3	48.6
36071	Orange County	11.6	24.4	67.2	16.5	7.1	138,856	2.84	72.2	55.8	5.1	11.3	27.8	23.1	42.5
36075	Oswego County	4.1	3.4	86.3	1.7	0.3	48,010	2.37	62.5	45.4	6.3	10.8	37.5	27.4	43.6
36079	Putnam County	12.6	20.8	70.6	12.7	4.3	36,405	2.63	72.1	59.8	3.8	8.5	27.9	23.1	50.6
36081	Queens County	12.7	28.1	43.3	48.4	19.6	863,975	2.57	66.1	42.6	7.0	16.6	33.9	26.9	47.8
36083	Rensselaer County	8.0	6.2	76.8	5.4	2.9	66,583	2.28	59.7	42.6	5.4	11.7	40.3	31.1	43.3
36085	Richmond County	12.0	19.5	67.2	25.5	8.1	169,526	2.85	71.9	50.2	5.2	16.5	28.1	24.1	49.2
36087	Rockland County	8.8	20.8	63.7	22.1	9.7	104,325	3.20	75.3	60.9	5.1	9.3	24.7	21.4	46.9
36089	St. Lawrence County	4.0	2.6	81.1	4.1	1.9	42,945	2.24	55.6	38.0	6.3	11.3	44.4	35.5	45.3
36091	Saratoga County	6.2	4.0	76.8	5.2	1.9	103,758	2.26	61.6	47.6	4.0	10.1	38.4	29.9	44.2
36093	Schenectady County	11.1	8.3	72.6	10.7	3.8	68,172	2.27	59.2	40.1	5.3	13.8	40.8	32.3	41.7
36101	Steuben County	3.6	0.8	80.1	2.0	0.7	38,764	2.33	62.1	48.4	5.0	8.8	37.9	31.6	46.3
36103	Suffolk County	12.1	23.1	74.3	17.2	6.9	508,809	2.94	71.1	55.1	4.8	11.2	28.9	22.9	51.1
36105	Sullivan County	12.5	19.3	68.6	12.9	6.2	30,971	2.45	62.5	47.3	5.2	10.1	37.5	31.2	48.8
36109	Tompkins County	7.7	6.5	57.0	12.9	8.7	43,054	2.03	45.8	36.6	2.0	7.2	54.2	39.0	38.4
36111	Ulster County	9.3	12.4	72.3	8.7	3.3	73,895	2.27	58.1	45.5	3.6	9.1	41.9	32.7	49.6
36113	Warren County	4.0	3.1	78.8	3.4	0.9	31,013	2.07	58.4	46.3	3.0	9.1	41.6	33.2	47.9
36117	Wayne County	6.6	5.4	85.2	3.0	1.4	39,094	2.26	62.9	47.2	4.9	10.8	37.1	29.5	47.4
36119	Westchester County	12.8	27.5	58.1	26.3	10.3	374,012	2.58	66.6	49.8	4.3	12.6	33.4	28.6	45.5
37000	**NORTH CAROLINA**	8.3	11.4	52.9	9.2	5.2	4,392,669	2.40	64.3	47.4	4.6	12.3	35.7	29.1	40.8
37001	Alamance County	8.2	15.4	61.0	9.4	6.3	70,911	2.43	65.2	47.0	4.0	14.2	34.8	31.1	44.4
37019	Brunswick County	5.9	5.7	41.1	4.2	1.6	72,932	2.18	68.9	56.9	3.7	8.2	31.1	25.3	62.5
37021	Buncombe County	11.3	8.6	47.1	6.7	3.9	104,181	2.57	58.7	46.1	5.1	7.5	41.3	32.2	46.0
37023	Burke County	5.9	8.6	74.6	3.5	1.1	37,485	2.29	69.4	51.3	5.3	12.8	30.6	26.3	50.4
37025	Cabarrus County	9.4	13.0	47.8	11.2	6.9	90,254	2.64	69.4	53.7	4.0	11.6	30.6	25.5	33.4
37027	Caldwell County	4.8	6.8	75.6	4.6	3.7	34,367	2.32	68.2	47.5	7.8	12.9	31.8	26.0	47.8
37031	Carteret County	5.6	4.9	54.5	4.9	2.0	34,497	1.98	62.5	54.6	3.3	4.5	37.5	27.7	52.5
37035	Catawba County	6.9	11.7	65.9	5.9	1.9	68,126	2.38	65.2	47.6	6.4	11.3	34.8	29.4	43.7
37037	Chatham County	6.3	13.4	45.5	10.3	5.3	33,971	2.38	75.4	65.1	3.7	6.6	24.6	22.8	49.0
37045	Cleveland County	6.2	5.0	70.2	4.5	2.0	39,314	2.53	72.1	55.2	3.7	13.2	27.9	23.7	46.1
37049	Craven County	10.0	7.8	51.7	4.5	1.8	41,100	2.39	66.3	47.7	4.9	13.7	33.7	29.7	46.7
37051	Cumberland County	10.7	13.1	44.1	7.0	2.9	131,421	2.43	63.4	42.1	4.5	16.8	36.6	30.7	34.9
37057	Davidson County	8.9	9.2	68.6	6.0	3.6	71,400	2.42	65.3	48.0	5.9	11.4	34.7	29.3	47.5

Table A-2. Counties — Who: Age, Race/Ethnicity, and Household Structure, 2023—*Continued*

STATE County code	STATE County	Total population	Percent change, 2010–2023	Population by age (percent): Under 18 years	18 to 24 years	25 to 44 years	45 to 64 years	65 years and over	Median age	Race alone or in combination (percent): White	Black or African American	American Indian and Alaska Native	Asian	Native Hawaiian or Other Pacific Islander	Some other race
	ACS table number:	B01003	Census PEP	B01001	B01001	B01001	B01001	B01001	B01002	B02008	B02009	B02010	B02011	B02012	B02013
	Column number:	1	2	3	4	5	6	7	8	9	10	11	12	13	14
	NORTH CAROLINA—Cont.														
37063	Durham County	336,892	25.5	19.3	10.7	32.4	22.8	14.8	36.0	50.1	35.2	2.0	7.4	0.7	14.7
37067	Forsyth County	392,921	11.8	22.4	10.2	25.4	24.9	17.2	37.8	62.4	28.4	1.4	3.3	0.1	13.0
37069	Franklin County	77,001	27.0	21.4	7.1	27.2	26.6	17.7	40.9	67.3	26.4	2.9	1.4	NA	10.8
37071	Gaston County	237,242	15.0	22.3	8.2	26.6	26.1	16.9	39.0	73.8	21.0	1.6	2.4	0.1	8.9
37081	Guilford County	549,866	12.3	21.8	12.1	25.5	24.3	16.3	37.8	54.1	37.5	2.2	6.7	0.1	9.2
37085	Harnett County	141,477	22.2	25.2	9.2	28.2	23.2	14.1	36.3	70.3	22.3	1.4	2.8	0.0	14.9
37089	Henderson County	119,230	11.5	18.2	6.4	21.7	26.4	27.3	48.1	88.0	4.3	1.9	1.5	NA	12.8
37097	Iredell County	199,710	25.0	22.1	7.7	24.7	28.3	17.2	40.8	81.2	13.3	1.1	3.0	0.2	10.1
37101	Johnston County	241,955	42.5	24.5	8.4	26.7	26.8	13.6	38.6	71.8	19.5	2.1	1.6	NA	14.0
37105	Lee County	67,059	15.9	23.2	7.6	25.8	25.3	18.1	40.5	73.1	20.7	0.7	2.1	NA	13.4
37109	Lincoln County	95,675	22.0	20.4	7.0	23.7	28.4	20.4	44.3	89.9	7.2	0.7	1.6	NA	7.5
37119	Mecklenburg County	1,163,701	26.0	22.5	9.2	31.9	24.0	12.3	35.6	53.2	33.0	1.4	7.7	0.3	15.4
37125	Moore County	106,898	20.7	21.4	5.8	25.1	23.4	24.3	44.0	84.5	11.6	3.9	2.6	NA	7.4
37127	Nash County	96,551	0.6	22.1	7.4	23.4	27.7	19.4	42.0	50.7	42.8	1.7	1.7	NA	8.3
37129	New Hanover County	238,852	17.5	17.6	12.6	24.7	25.6	19.4	41.3	83.5	12.9	1.5	2.5	0.1	7.7
37133	Onslow County	213,676	19.1	24.7	20.1	28.6	15.9	10.8	27.8	79.8	16.2	4.7	3.6	0.5	11.0
37135	Orange County	150,626	12.2	17.9	19.7	22.1	23.8	16.5	36.7	76.1	13.0	1.2	9.3	NA	8.3
37141	Pender County	68,521	31.2	22.5	7.1	25.8	26.2	18.4	40.6	83.6	10.2	3.5	1.5	NA	7.5
37147	Pitt County	175,119	3.7	21.3	16.8	25.4	21.4	15.1	34.1	56.5	37.4	1.0	3.0	NA	8.2
37151	Randolph County	147,458	3.9	22.1	8.3	23.7	26.5	19.5	41.2	83.1	10.3	1.1	0.3	NA	10.0
37155	Robeson County	117,365	-12.7	26.0	10.3	24.1	23.5	16.1	35.8	27.8	26.3	42.4	1.1	NA	8.3
37157	Rockingham County	92,518	-1.2	20.1	7.2	23.7	26.8	22.2	43.8	78.7	20.0	1.4	1.0	NA	6.2
37159	Rowan County	151,661	9.5	21.6	9.5	24.4	26.4	18.1	41.0	77.5	17.4	2.4	1.5	NA	10.5
37161	Rutherford County	65,507	-3.3	19.9	7.3	21.7	28.5	22.6	45.9	87.3	11.4	0.7	0.3	NA	6.8
37167	Stanly County	65,699	8.4	21.3	8.1	24.3	27.2	19.1	41.6	85.5	11.2	0.6	2.2	NA	4.3
37171	Surry County	71,462	-3.0	20.8	7.7	23.5	27.0	21.0	44.2	91.4	3.1	2.2	0.9	NA	8.2
37179	Union County	256,452	26.8	25.3	9.2	23.9	27.8	13.8	39.9	74.6	13.4	1.2	6.1	NA	12.9
37183	Wake County	1,190,275	31.2	22.7	8.7	29.7	25.6	13.4	37.7	65.8	21.0	1.5	10.3	0.2	11.2
37191	Wayne County	118,686	-3.4	23.4	9.8	26.1	22.9	17.7	37.4	66.5	33.9	0.9	2.1	NA	12.3
37193	Wilkes County	66,013	-4.7	19.7	8.1	20.4	28.2	23.6	45.9	91.5	6.0	1.3	NA	NA	6.1
37195	Wilson County	78,970	-2.9	22.7	8.2	23.7	26.2	19.2	41.2	51.9	40.9	1.2	NA	NA	11.3
38000	**NORTH DAKOTA**	783,926	16.2	22.9	10.8	28.3	21.0	17.1	36.3	89.0	4.3	6.5	2.4	0.3	4.5
38015	Burleigh County	100,012	22.5	22.9	8.9	27.6	21.9	18.6	38.7	91.4	1.9	7.6	1.4	NA	2.6
38017	Cass County	196,362	30.7	22.1	14.8	30.7	18.9	13.5	32.6	88.2	8.1	2.3	4.1	NA	3.9
38035	Grand Forks County	72,708	8.5	20.3	19.7	27.5	17.7	14.8	30.8	91.0	6.1	3.6	3.8	NA	4.9
38101	Ward County	68,332	10.8	24.1	10.1	29.7	20.9	15.3	34.4	89.7	6.1	3.6	3.9	NA	6.4
39000	**OHIO**	11,785,935	2.1	21.8	8.8	25.7	24.8	18.8	39.9	83.0	14.5	1.6	3.4	0.2	4.7
39003	Allen County	100,838	-5.1	23.4	8.7	23.9	24.7	19.2	40.1	88.7	13.6	3.2	1.2	NA	2.8
39007	Ashtabula County	96,845	-4.5	21.8	7.7	23.1	26.6	20.7	43.3	93.5	5.4	1.3	0.7	NA	4.6
39013	Belmont County	64,918	-7.7	18.6	7.7	23.9	27.3	22.5	44.8	95.1	5.9	0.8	NA	NA	3.1
39017	Butler County	393,043	6.6	23.0	12.3	23.8	24.2	16.7	37.5	83.6	11.9	1.1	5.7	0.1	6.4
39023	Clark County	134,610	-2.6	22.6	7.8	23.6	25.4	20.7	41.3	90.9	9.0	3.4	1.2	0.3	5.1
39025	Clermont County	211,972	7.3	21.8	7.7	25.6	25.8	19.1	41.8	96.3	1.9	2.4	2.0	NA	3.1
39029	Columbiana County	100,182	-7.1	19.8	7.1	22.7	27.3	23.2	45.4	97.0	3.5	1.4	0.6	NA	1.6
39035	Cuyahoga County	1,233,088	-3.5	20.3	8.2	26.9	24.6	20.0	40.7	63.7	31.9	1.2	4.3	0.1	6.4
39041	Delaware County	231,636	32.2	24.4	8.6	24.9	26.4	15.7	39.7	84.8	5.6	0.7	10.5	NA	4.2
39043	Erie County	74,035	-3.9	19.4	6.1	22.8	27.2	24.5	47.1	89.8	10.5	1.1	1.1	NA	5.7
39045	Fairfield County	165,360	13.0	23.8	8.0	25.3	25.7	17.2	39.7	85.4	12.1	1.4	4.1	NA	2.1
39049	Franklin County	1,326,063	13.7	23.1	9.5	31.7	22.2	13.5	35.1	66.4	27.1	1.5	6.7	0.2	7.3
39055	Geauga County	95,407	2.1	21.9	8.0	19.8	27.3	23.0	45.2	97.9	2.1	0.9	1.1	NA	2.7
39057	Greene County	169,691	5.0	20.4	11.1	25.8	23.6	19.2	39.4	91.5	7.5	2.9	4.2	0.4	3.7
39061	Hamilton County	827,058	3.1	22.8	9.4	27.8	23.0	17.0	37.0	70.8	26.7	2.2	3.8	0.4	5.3
39063	Hancock County	74,704	-0.0	20.4	9.0	27.4	23.6	19.5	39.5	92.6	2.0	2.8	2.4	NA	6.9
39085	Lake County	231,640	0.7	19.0	7.7	23.9	27.1	22.3	44.5	91.0	7.1	0.7	2.0	0.1	5.2
39089	Licking County	183,201	9.9	22.7	8.6	25.0	25.3	18.3	40.0	91.1	4.9	2.3	5.1	0.2	3.5
39093	Lorain County	317,910	5.5	21.2	8.3	23.5	26.4	20.5	42.4	87.6	10.7	1.2	2.1	NA	9.0
39095	Lucas County	425,484	-3.6	22.6	8.8	26.2	24.2	18.2	38.5	76.3	23.2	1.7	2.5	0.1	5.5
39099	Mahoning County	225,596	-5.3	20.2	7.9	24.0	25.0	22.8	43.3	83.0	14.9	3.6	1.6	0.2	6.9
39101	Marion County	64,851	-2.5	21.2	7.1	26.8	25.8	19.1	41.2	93.2	7.3	1.9	1.3	NA	2.5
39103	Medina County	184,042	6.6	21.1	7.3	23.1	27.9	20.6	43.9	97.2	2.3	0.5	2.3	NA	2.6
39109	Miami County	110,876	8.2	22.5	7.2	24.6	25.5	20.2	41.5	95.2	4.3	0.6	2.3	NA	2.8
39113	Montgomery County	533,796	-0.2	22.1	9.2	26.0	23.9	18.9	38.6	74.5	23.9	1.3	3.3	0.1	5.0
39119	Muskingum County	86,305	0.2	22.6	8.7	24.6	24.8	19.3	39.6	96.3	6.3	1.5	0.9	NA	1.5

Table A-2. Counties — Who: Age, Race/Ethnicity, and Household Structure, 2023—*Continued*

STATE County code	STATE County	Two or more races (percent)	Hispanic or Latino (percent)	Native, born in state of residence (percent)	Foreign born (percent)	Non-citizens (percent)	Total households	Average household size	Household type (percent of all households): Family households: Total	Family households: Married couple	Family households: Male house-holder	Family households: Female house-holder	Nonfamily households: Total	Nonfamily households: One-person house-holds	Percent of households with people age 60 years and over
	ACS table number:	B02001	B03003	B05002	B05002	B05002	B11001	B25010	B11001	B11001	B11001	B11001	B11001	B11001	B11006
	Column number:	15	16	17	18	19	20	21	22	23	24	25	26	27	28
	NORTH CAROLINA—Cont.														
37063	Durham County	8.9	15.4	43.2	15.2	9.5	143,466	2.26	56.8	41.5	4.1	11.1	43.2	33.6	32.4
37067	Forsyth County	8.1	15.3	55.8	9.5	5.7	166,028	2.30	61.7	41.8	5.0	14.9	38.3	32.2	41.5
37069	Franklin County	8.7	11.6	56.0	5.7	3.5	31,057	2.44	71.6	54.8	4.3	12.5	28.4	26.6	43.1
37071	Gaston County	7.2	10.2	59.3	6.7	3.9	97,287	2.40	67.8	46.3	6.2	15.4	32.2	25.1	41.1
37081	Guilford County	9.0	10.2	54.9	11.7	5.8	222,927	2.35	60.0	39.6	6.1	14.3	40.0	34.0	38.9
37085	Harnett County	11.5	15.6	48.0	8.3	4.4	49,285	2.81	74.7	59.0	3.2	12.5	25.3	20.7	40.8
37089	Henderson County	8.3	13.0	45.0	8.5	5.3	52,492	2.24	66.3	51.1	4.5	10.6	33.7	26.7	50.7
37097	Iredell County	8.6	9.6	50.0	6.6	3.1	77,592	2.56	71.3	57.5	5.4	8.5	28.7	23.5	44.9
37101	Johnston County	8.5	16.9	51.1	10.8	6.3	87,955	2.73	73.8	59.2	4.4	10.1	26.2	21.9	35.9
37105	Lee County	9.6	21.8	57.4	10.4	7.0	25,961	2.55	68.1	47.9	4.2	16.0	31.9	26.8	45.2
37109	Lincoln County	6.6	8.4	60.4	4.4	2.5	37,618	2.52	76.1	63.5	4.7	7.9	23.9	20.5	47.6
37119	Mecklenburg County	10.1	15.9	38.4	16.9	10.1	474,611	2.42	58.0	42.1	3.9	12.1	42.0	33.6	30.0
37125	Moore County	9.4	7.8	46.4	6.1	3.1	46,385	2.28	64.5	51.4	4.6	8.5	35.5	30.6	48.1
37127	Nash County	4.8	8.4	73.1	3.9	2.4	39,349	2.41	64.1	43.1	5.9	15.1	35.9	32.5	42.5
37129	New Hanover County	7.5	7.9	46.7	7.0	4.3	106,358	2.20	54.7	39.4	3.3	12.0	45.3	33.3	40.7
37133	Onslow County	14.6	14.2	32.2	4.3	1.5	76,788	2.50	72.7	55.1	4.4	13.3	27.3	22.4	28.8
37135	Orange County	7.2	10.5	44.9	12.8	6.6	59,771	2.33	57.9	48.3	2.2	7.4	42.1	29.5	37.5
37141	Pender County	6.3	8.8	53.8	5.1	3.8	27,256	2.47	66.9	50.4	6.1	10.4	33.1	27.8	44.8
37147	Pitt County	5.4	8.0	62.3	6.0	3.0	74,443	2.28	58.3	37.7	4.0	16.6	41.7	29.2	33.0
37151	Randolph County	4.8	14.3	70.2	5.8	4.5	59,646	2.44	62.5	44.8	4.5	13.3	37.5	31.3	44.7
37155	Robeson County	6.1	11.1	77.8	5.8	4.3	43,590	2.61	66.5	35.7	6.9	23.9	33.5	29.2	41.7
37157	Rockingham County	6.5	7.3	72.5	3.2	2.0	39,251	2.33	69.1	51.4	5.2	12.4	30.9	26.0	47.4
37159	Rowan County	9.0	12.2	63.0	5.0	3.0	60,965	2.43	67.7	47.8	4.9	14.9	32.3	27.0	43.0
37161	Rutherford County	6.1	6.0	62.8	3.6	2.5	26,805	2.39	62.6	46.7	2.4	13.5	37.4	30.3	51.4
37167	Stanly County	5.5	6.0	72.1	4.6	2.2	25,371	2.52	68.1	51.6	4.2	12.3	31.9	27.2	49.1
37171	Surry County	5.7	12.6	68.0	4.0	2.6	30,752	2.29	65.4	45.5	9.3	10.7	34.6	30.4	48.3
37179	Union County	8.0	13.6	45.7	12.8	5.9	87,714	2.89	77.8	65.1	4.7	8.0	22.2	18.6	37.8
37183	Wake County	9.1	11.5	41.1	15.7	8.3	481,294	2.43	64.2	51.0	3.7	9.5	35.8	27.0	32.2
37191	Wayne County	15.0	14.0	60.7	8.3	6.1	47,035	2.46	66.8	40.9	6.5	19.4	33.2	27.6	41.6
37193	Wilkes County	4.7	7.6	77.6	3.8	3.1	26,154	2.48	66.8	48.9	4.4	13.5	33.2	29.3	52.9
37195	Wilson County	6.4	12.7	74.0	5.4	3.7	34,524	2.25	61.4	40.4	4.4	16.6	38.6	30.7	41.8
38000	**NORTH DAKOTA**	6.7	4.9	61.0	4.0	2.0	338,059	2.23	56.8	46.0	4.4	6.5	43.2	34.7	36.0
38015	Burleigh County	5.0	3.4	74.2	1.8	1.2	42,486	2.26	61.3	48.4	6.5	6.3	38.7	33.9	39.9
38017	Cass County	6.5	3.8	52.6	6.5	3.6	84,603	2.24	48.8	39.1	2.8	6.9	51.2	39.9	27.9
38035	Grand Forks County	8.4	5.7	50.9	5.9	2.5	32,099	2.11	52.1	43.3	3.2	5.7	47.9	32.5	29.0
38101	Ward County	9.8	7.4	57.7	3.0	1.2	28,565	2.32	61.5	51.4	4.0	6.2	38.5	30.7	32.5
39000	**OHIO**	6.8	4.8	74.3	5.3	2.6	4,917,309	2.34	60.9	44.2	4.8	11.9	39.1	32.2	42.4
39003	Allen County	8.5	3.7	81.6	1.8	0.8	42,147	2.34	61.2	43.8	4.3	13.1	38.8	31.1	43.2
39007	Ashtabula County	5.2	5.1	72.0	1.5	0.5	37,507	2.49	66.7	48.2	6.8	11.7	33.3	28.1	47.3
39013	Belmont County	5.3	1.4	44.8	1.2	0.6	27,281	2.24	63.5	46.3	6.3	10.9	36.5	31.7	48.0
39017	Butler County	8.2	7.0	68.5	8.1	3.5	148,804	2.56	67.3	51.4	4.2	11.7	32.7	27.0	41.7
39023	Clark County	9.7	4.3	78.1	2.6	1.8	55,322	2.39	63.9	43.0	6.3	14.6	36.1	31.2	47.1
39025	Clermont County	5.1	2.6	75.8	2.2	1.0	87,429	2.40	68.5	52.4	5.4	10.8	31.5	25.3	43.0
39029	Columbiana County	3.9	2.0	77.7	1.3	1.0	42,415	2.28	61.0	46.4	6.4	8.2	39.0	34.0	50.0
39035	Cuyahoga County	7.1	7.2	72.9	7.9	3.1	551,306	2.19	52.6	33.7	3.9	14.9	47.4	41.3	43.1
39041	Delaware County	5.5	3.5	66.1	9.3	5.1	84,413	2.72	74.0	63.4	3.5	7.2	26.0	21.5	38.0
39043	Erie County	8.2	4.7	80.0	1.6	0.9	33,608	2.13	64.2	43.7	7.4	13.1	35.8	32.2	50.3
39045	Fairfield County	4.7	2.9	78.2	3.4	0.9	62,834	2.57	75.2	57.4	7.5	10.3	24.8	19.9	41.0
39049	Franklin County	8.4	7.5	64.2	13.2	6.8	561,634	2.31	55.5	36.4	5.5	13.6	44.5	33.8	33.1
39055	Geauga County	4.2	2.1	81.6	2.4	0.3	36,405	2.59	72.2	62.8	3.9	5.6	27.8	22.1	51.2
39057	Greene County	9.5	3.4	64.1	4.1	1.3	70,169	2.32	65.5	52.1	4.5	8.9	34.5	28.1	41.1
39061	Hamilton County	8.6	4.9	71.6	6.2	3.7	360,340	2.24	54.5	38.4	4.3	11.8	45.5	36.7	37.8
39063	Hancock County	6.8	6.2	75.1	6.4	5.3	31,675	2.30	57.8	47.5	5.5	4.7	42.2	34.6	42.4
39085	Lake County	6.0	5.4	79.0	4.6	1.3	103,532	2.21	62.7	47.2	4.3	11.2	37.3	29.9	47.6
39089	Licking County	6.9	2.5	74.2	4.6	1.2	68,568	2.62	65.5	49.4	5.6	10.5	34.5	27.5	45.8
39093	Lorain County	10.5	11.2	76.1	3.4	1.5	128,887	2.40	64.4	46.5	4.9	13.0	35.6	29.5	46.2
39095	Lucas County	8.4	8.0	76.3	3.9	1.7	182,625	2.29	58.2	38.6	4.0	15.6	41.8	34.1	41.1
39099	Mahoning County	9.7	7.1	77.4	2.5	1.2	98,872	2.22	57.5	38.2	5.4	14.0	42.5	35.5	48.0
39101	Marion County	6.2	3.3	80.9	2.1	0.7	24,957	2.37	61.7	44.4	7.0	10.2	38.3	32.7	46.6
39103	Medina County	4.7	2.8	81.5	3.8	2.2	73,675	2.47	69.2	56.3	2.9	10.1	30.8	25.4	46.6
39109	Miami County	5.2	2.2	82.4	2.0	1.0	44,756	2.46	65.5	51.4	5.7	8.4	34.5	30.2	44.7
39113	Montgomery County	7.5	4.3	71.2	5.0	2.7	235,734	2.19	56.6	37.8	4.9	14.0	43.4	36.3	42.0
39119	Muskingum County	5.8	1.4	86.8	0.7	0.3	32,776	2.57	65.1	45.7	4.4	15.0	34.9	27.9	45.3

Table A-2. Counties — Who: Age, Race/Ethnicity, and Household Structure, 2023—*Continued*

STATE County code	STATE County	Total population	Percent change, 2010–2023	Population by age (percent): Under 18 years	18 to 24 years	25 to 44 years	45 to 64 years	65 years and over	Median age	Race alone or in combination (percent): White	Black or African American	American Indian and Alaska Native	Asian	Native Hawaiian or Other Pacific Islander	Some other race
	ACS table number:	B01003	Census PEP	B01001	B01001	B01001	B01001	B01001	B01002	B02008	B02009	B02010	B02011	B02012	B02013
	Column number:	1	2	3	4	5	6	7	8	9	10	11	12	13	14
	OHIO—Cont.														
39133	Portage County	162,665	0.8	17.5	15.8	23.4	24.6	18.6	38.8	91.9	6.7	1.7	2.9	NA	2.9
39139	Richland County	125,064	0.7	21.5	7.0	26.1	24.3	21.1	41.6	91.1	9.3	2.9	1.3	NA	2.7
39141	Ross County	76,501	-2.0	21.4	7.3	26.3	26.8	18.2	40.4	93.6	5.1	3.8	1.0	NA	1.7
39145	Scioto County	71,969	-9.5	21.1	8.9	25.7	25.3	19.0	41.3	96.8	3.8	1.6	1.1	NA	1.7
39151	Stark County	372,716	-0.7	21.5	8.1	24.1	25.2	21.0	42.2	91.4	8.0	3.0	1.4	NA	3.5
39153	Summit County	535,733	-1.1	20.5	8.0	25.9	25.6	19.9	41.3	79.9	17.5	1.1	5.4	0.1	3.1
39155	Trumbull County	200,373	-4.6	20.5	7.5	23.7	25.7	22.6	43.3	90.4	11.0	0.8	1.0	NA	3.2
39157	Tuscarawas County	91,874	-0.7	23.0	7.9	23.0	25.4	20.7	42.5	96.1	1.5	1.3	NA	NA	3.4
39159	Union County	69,637	33.1	23.7	7.1	29.8	26.3	13.1	37.9	90.7	4.2	2.6	5.7	NA	4.2
39165	Warren County	252,148	18.3	23.6	7.3	25.9	26.9	16.3	40.3	87.9	4.8	0.9	8.5	NA	4.3
39169	Wayne County	116,510	1.8	23.8	9.9	23.0	23.9	19.5	38.5	97.5	3.3	1.5	1.6	NA	3.0
39173	Wood County	132,650	5.7	20.0	15.8	24.8	22.4	16.9	36.1	93.0	4.4	0.8	2.9	NA	5.5
40000	**OKLAHOMA**	4,053,824	7.8	23.8	10.0	26.6	22.9	16.7	37.1	78.8	9.7	14.3	3.3	0.5	9.8
40017	Canadian County	175,829	51.3	25.4	8.5	29.8	22.3	14.0	35.9	83.0	6.9	8.2	4.7	NA	11.4
40027	Cleveland County	301,193	17.2	20.0	15.4	27.1	21.9	15.6	35.5	84.0	8.3	9.5	6.3	0.1	8.5
40031	Comanche County	121,574	-3.0	23.7	11.3	29.9	20.7	14.4	33.9	73.3	20.2	11.0	4.5	1.1	9.2
40037	Creek County	73,332	4.6	22.5	9.1	23.7	25.5	19.2	41.3	84.2	3.7	16.7	1.4	0.1	5.2
40101	Muskogee County	66,677	-6.2	24.3	8.9	25.7	23.6	17.5	38.8	68.3	12.4	27.6	0.9	NA	5.1
40109	Oklahoma County	808,866	12.2	25.2	9.4	28.5	22.0	14.8	35.4	72.6	17.5	7.9	4.7	1.0	16.0
40119	Payne County	83,352	7.6	18.5	27.6	23.6	17.3	13.0	27.8	86.9	5.5	9.8	5.4	0.2	3.8
40125	Pottawatomie County	73,791	6.0	23.2	9.6	26.1	24.0	17.1	38.3	84.2	6.2	18.2	1.5	NA	4.5
40131	Rogers County	100,248	15.2	23.1	9.0	24.8	25.3	17.7	39.0	82.8	2.6	20.9	2.8	0.3	4.3
40143	Tulsa County	682,868	12.8	24.9	9.2	27.8	22.6	15.5	36.2	75.1	13.0	12.1	4.9	0.4	12.3
40145	Wagoner County	89,280	21.7	23.5	7.6	27.5	24.4	17.2	39.5	83.9	6.0	16.9	2.8	NA	7.3
41000	**OREGON**	4,233,358	10.3	19.6	8.3	28.2	24.3	19.6	40.7	86.3	3.4	3.8	6.8	0.8	12.8
41003	Benton County	97,713	14.2	15.1	22.4	23.9	20.6	18.1	34.7	87.2	2.7	2.7	8.4	NA	10.1
41005	Clackamas County	423,173	12.3	20.7	7.0	25.9	26.0	20.5	42.7	87.5	2.3	2.5	7.5	0.6	10.2
41017	Deschutes County	208,513	32.1	18.5	6.4	27.4	26.4	21.3	43.1	95.1	1.3	2.3	2.8	1.1	7.2
41019	Douglas County	112,435	4.5	19.2	6.6	22.8	24.2	27.2	46.7	95.8	1.0	5.8	2.2	0.2	5.9
41029	Jackson County	220,768	8.5	20.2	7.6	25.2	23.3	23.8	42.5	92.4	1.6	3.9	3.2	0.4	13.6
41033	Josephine County	87,821	6.1	18.9	6.0	22.6	25.0	27.5	47.6	95.6	0.4	4.3	2.1	0.5	6.4
41035	Klamath County	70,003	8.2	22.1	7.2	26.1	22.7	21.9	40.5	88.4	1.8	7.0	2.2	NA	13.5
41039	Lane County	381,181	8.3	17.2	12.3	25.8	23.2	21.5	40.4	89.8	3.0	4.1	5.1	0.5	10.2
41043	Linn County	131,496	12.5	22.0	7.1	26.8	24.4	19.7	40.4	94.1	1.6	4.6	2.5	NA	9.0
41047	Marion County	346,741	9.7	23.3	9.0	27.6	23.1	17.1	37.5	84.4	2.5	4.3	3.8	1.5	23.1
41051	Multnomah County	789,698	7.0	17.3	7.8	35.0	24.7	15.2	39.2	81.0	8.2	3.2	10.3	1.3	12.1
41053	Polk County	89,805	18.8	20.9	12.1	24.2	23.5	19.2	38.1	87.4	1.8	3.7	4.5	0.6	15.4
41059	Umatilla County	80,053	5.2	24.2	7.4	29.5	21.8	17.1	36.4	82.8	0.9	6.2	1.5	NA	26.2
41067	Washington County	598,865	12.6	21.1	8.0	31.0	24.6	15.3	38.6	75.7	4.4	2.9	15.7	1.2	16.0
41071	Yamhill County	108,644	9.3	20.3	9.9	27.2	22.8	19.7	39.3	90.9	1.8	3.9	4.1	NA	15.4
42000	**PENNSYLVANIA**	12,961,683	2.0	20.2	9.0	25.5	25.2	20.0	41.1	80.6	13.1	1.3	4.7	0.1	8.4
42001	Adams County	106,748	5.2	19.1	9.8	21.7	26.6	22.7	44.6	93.5	1.9	2.0	1.3	NA	6.6
42003	Allegheny County	1,224,825	0.1	18.5	8.7	28.1	23.9	20.8	40.6	81.3	15.0	1.0	5.2	0.0	4.0
42005	Armstrong County	64,074	-6.9	18.8	6.3	22.5	27.7	24.7	46.8	99.0	2.1	1.1	NA	NA	1.6
42007	Beaver County	165,631	-2.9	19.3	7.2	23.8	26.5	23.2	44.8	92.8	7.7	1.5	1.0	NA	4.3
42011	Berks County	432,821	5.1	21.8	9.6	24.8	25.5	18.4	39.5	83.8	12.8	2.3	2.0	0.1	21.9
42013	Blair County	120,273	-5.3	19.8	8.1	23.6	26.2	22.3	43.7	96.1	4.2	0.7	1.2	NA	4.0
42017	Bucks County	645,984	3.3	19.7	7.7	23.4	27.8	21.3	44.3	87.5	5.2	1.0	6.5	0.1	7.5
42019	Butler County	198,413	7.8	19.2	8.9	23.7	27.0	21.2	43.4	96.8	2.2	0.7	2.1	NA	2.4
42021	Cambria County	130,668	-8.9	19.2	8.8	21.4	26.0	24.7	45.7	96.2	5.6	1.6	0.8	NA	1.9
42025	Carbon County	65,458	0.4	18.6	6.7	23.3	27.7	23.7	45.8	92.6	3.1	2.1	1.1	NA	7.0
42027	Centre County	157,795	2.4	14.2	24.6	22.8	21.8	16.5	34.3	88.1	5.1	1.2	7.4	NA	3.6
42029	Chester County	549,784	10.0	21.7	9.0	24.5	26.3	18.4	40.6	83.5	7.3	0.9	8.1	0.0	8.3
42033	Clearfield County	77,090	-5.5	18.4	7.0	23.3	28.4	22.9	46.3	96.1	2.9	0.7	0.3	NA	2.8
42037	Columbia County	65,439	-2.7	16.9	15.4	22.5	25.0	20.2	40.8	95.3	3.3	0.6	1.7	NA	3.3
42039	Crawford County	82,001	-7.5	20.5	7.8	22.8	25.6	23.2	43.9	97.7	2.7	0.6	0.9	NA	2.5
42041	Cumberland County	270,738	14.8	20.3	10.8	25.2	24.2	19.4	40.2	87.0	7.7	1.2	7.0	0.1	4.9
42043	Dauphin County	289,234	7.8	22.2	8.0	27.6	23.7	18.5	39.9	69.6	22.7	1.4	7.7	NA	8.3
42045	Delaware County	576,720	3.1	21.9	9.8	25.8	24.6	17.9	39.5	67.5	24.7	0.8	7.7	0.1	5.2
42049	Erie County	267,571	-4.7	20.5	10.3	24.1	24.6	20.5	41.3	88.3	10.1	0.7	2.7	NA	4.5
42051	Fayette County	123,915	-9.2	18.9	6.9	23.3	27.4	23.5	45.9	95.0	5.4	1.5	0.7	NA	2.1
42055	Franklin County	157,854	5.4	21.6	7.1	24.9	25.6	20.8	41.6	91.2	4.4	2.1	1.8	NA	7.4

Table A-2. Counties — Who: Age, Race/Ethnicity, and Household Structure, 2023—*Continued*

STATE County code	STATE County	Two or more races (percent)	Hispanic or Latino (percent)	Native, born in state of residence (percent)	Foreign born (percent)	Non-citizens (percent)	Total households	Average household size	Household type (percent of all households): Family households: Total	Family households: Married couple	Family households: Male house-holder	Family households: Female house-holder	Nonfamily households: Total	Nonfamily households: One-person house-holds	Percent of households with people age 60 years and over
	ACS table number:	B02001	B03003	B05002	B05002	B05002	B11001	B25010	B11001	B11001	B11001	B11001	B11001	B11001	B11006
	Column number:	15	16	17	18	19	20	21	22	23	24	25	26	27	28
	OHIO—Cont.														
39133	Portage County	5.1	2.4	76.3	4.7	3.0	65,601	2.37	58.0	45.1	3.7	9.1	42.0	31.6	43.4
39139	Richland County	7.0	2.3	78.8	1.8	0.8	51,046	2.31	64.1	47.3	3.4	13.4	35.9	30.7	45.4
39141	Ross County	4.9	1.5	86.2	0.8	0.3	28,870	2.47	64.7	48.2	5.0	11.6	35.3	31.4	43.5
39145	Scioto County	4.3	1.6	82.1	1.3	0.6	30,143	2.28	63.2	43.4	6.1	13.8	36.8	31.7	42.0
39151	Stark County	7.6	3.1	82.4	2.1	0.7	156,143	2.34	61.4	45.4	4.9	11.1	38.6	31.8	44.5
39153	Summit County	6.4	2.8	76.2	6.4	2.9	232,592	2.26	59.6	43.0	4.7	11.9	40.4	32.9	43.1
39155	Trumbull County	5.8	2.4	78.3	1.7	0.5	87,955	2.23	57.9	38.8	5.4	13.7	42.1	35.4	48.9
39157	Tuscarawas County	2.5	4.7	85.4	3.1	2.4	39,110	2.32	61.1	47.3	7.1	6.7	38.9	33.2	47.0
39159	Union County	6.9	3.7	74.1	6.5	3.7	25,554	2.63	75.1	57.5	7.5	10.1	24.9	20.3	34.4
39165	Warren County	6.1	3.6	65.5	9.8	5.4	93,271	2.65	73.1	60.6	3.7	8.8	26.9	23.0	39.4
39169	Wayne County	4.5	2.5	81.5	2.6	0.8	44,453	2.52	67.6	55.3	5.1	7.3	32.4	27.0	43.8
39173	Wood County	6.2	6.6	78.9	3.5	1.8	54,408	2.33	60.4	45.9	4.6	9.9	39.6	29.4	39.0
40000	**OKLAHOMA**	15.0	12.9	59.6	6.1	3.6	1,589,105	2.48	64.1	46.3	5.5	12.3	35.9	29.4	40.4
40017	Canadian County	13.2	12.5	61.8	5.2	2.1	58,214	2.98	70.1	55.8	4.8	9.5	29.9	25.0	37.3
40027	Cleveland County	15.1	11.3	59.1	7.0	3.6	118,062	2.45	61.5	46.7	5.1	9.7	38.5	29.1	36.8
40031	Comanche County	17.0	15.0	45.1	5.0	2.3	45,945	2.43	64.0	43.2	5.5	15.3	36.0	29.2	36.4
40037	Creek County	10.5	5.7	71.0	2.0	1.2	28,988	2.50	67.0	49.9	6.4	10.7	33.0	28.3	46.3
40101	Muskogee County	13.5	7.8	70.3	2.2	0.8	26,362	2.38	60.6	42.8	3.7	14.2	39.4	32.2	44.4
40109	Oklahoma County	18.1	20.4	57.5	10.2	6.1	335,473	2.37	59.4	40.8	5.2	13.4	40.6	32.6	36.0
40119	Payne County	11.1	6.5	55.8	4.6	3.5	32,739	2.26	54.1	38.5	5.5	10.2	45.9	29.4	32.8
40125	Pottawatomie County	13.2	6.5	72.3	2.3	1.4	27,150	2.57	66.6	47.7	6.1	12.8	33.4	28.6	43.7
40131	Rogers County	12.7	6.4	62.1	2.6	1.3	37,082	2.65	71.6	55.8	5.2	10.7	28.4	24.8	44.6
40143	Tulsa County	16.4	15.8	56.1	10.1	6.4	275,702	2.44	61.8	42.9	6.1	12.8	38.2	31.2	37.4
40145	Wagoner County	15.6	9.2	61.1	5.2	2.6	31,633	2.81	73.9	59.0	5.2	9.7	26.1	21.5	42.0
41000	**OREGON**	12.9	14.9	45.2	9.6	4.8	1,752,050	2.36	61.8	46.3	5.2	10.4	38.2	28.4	42.2
41003	Benton County	10.6	9.4	41.6	9.7	6.4	38,306	2.39	49.7	40.4	3.6	5.7	50.3	32.3	40.6
41005	Clackamas County	10.1	10.2	53.3	9.3	3.6	167,319	2.50	70.7	56.5	4.8	9.4	29.3	22.2	44.7
41017	Deschutes County	8.9	9.3	37.7	4.8	2.9	88,597	2.34	66.3	52.5	3.6	10.2	33.7	22.9	44.5
41019	Douglas County	10.3	6.9	49.0	2.8	1.5	47,733	2.31	61.9	44.5	6.4	11.1	38.1	29.7	54.8
41029	Jackson County	13.9	15.1	39.9	5.9	2.7	92,225	2.35	63.9	46.5	5.6	11.8	36.1	29.3	51.3
41033	Josephine County	8.8	9.1	38.6	3.4	1.1	37,241	2.32	67.3	46.7	8.9	11.7	32.7	26.1	55.3
41035	Klamath County	12.7	14.4	45.5	5.4	2.9	30,395	2.28	62.6	45.0	4.7	13.0	37.4	30.2	48.1
41039	Lane County	11.1	10.8	48.0	4.4	1.8	162,001	2.29	59.8	44.6	4.5	10.8	40.2	27.8	43.5
41043	Linn County	10.9	11.0	57.1	4.5	2.2	51,636	2.52	63.8	50.0	3.9	9.9	36.2	26.8	46.6
41047	Marion County	18.3	29.3	52.8	13.6	9.0	129,087	2.61	66.7	46.3	6.7	13.7	33.3	26.3	41.3
41051	Multnomah County	14.6	13.7	39.5	12.9	5.5	354,646	2.17	49.4	36.2	4.6	8.6	50.6	36.4	31.5
41053	Polk County	12.6	16.0	52.5	5.0	2.5	33,113	2.64	66.6	51.0	4.8	10.8	33.4	24.1	43.3
41059	Umatilla County	17.4	30.0	39.0	12.7	10.0	30,821	2.48	72.7	48.6	9.0	15.1	27.3	22.1	37.8
41067	Washington County	14.6	18.7	41.3	17.4	8.9	237,507	2.49	66.3	50.2	5.3	10.9	33.7	23.9	35.3
41071	Yamhill County	14.9	18.0	50.0	8.1	4.2	40,380	2.54	69.3	54.1	5.2	10.0	30.7	25.1	48.8
42000	**PENNSYLVANIA**	7.4	8.9	70.1	8.0	3.6	5,324,209	2.35	62.3	46.0	5.0	11.4	37.7	30.8	44.9
42001	Adams County	5.4	7.7	60.1	3.4	1.9	41,810	2.44	68.4	53.5	7.4	7.5	31.6	25.4	51.4
42003	Allegheny County	5.9	3.0	74.1	6.7	3.2	547,396	2.17	55.9	41.9	3.7	10.3	44.1	36.1	42.2
42005	Armstrong County	3.9	0.4	90.5	0.1	0.1	28,117	2.25	67.4	54.6	4.6	8.3	32.6	27.7	48.9
42007	Beaver County	7.2	2.5	82.1	1.8	0.5	73,220	2.23	61.0	46.6	4.1	10.3	39.0	33.8	48.7
42011	Berks County	16.8	25.3	71.0	10.5	5.2	163,307	2.56	68.2	49.4	6.0	12.8	31.8	25.2	44.4
42013	Blair County	6.0	0.9	85.8	2.1	0.8	50,651	2.28	58.3	43.0	5.0	10.2	41.7	34.7	49.3
42017	Bucks County	7.3	6.7	63.7	10.9	4.2	249,189	2.55	71.8	58.3	4.3	9.2	28.2	23.1	49.2
42019	Butler County	4.0	2.1	80.8	2.4	0.7	81,535	2.37	63.3	52.2	4.2	6.9	36.7	30.8	46.5
42021	Cambria County	5.5	2.2	86.3	1.0	0.4	57,282	2.16	59.7	44.2	5.5	10.1	40.3	35.2	52.2
42025	Carbon County	5.8	7.4	72.4	5.5	1.4	28,934	2.23	63.1	43.4	6.7	13.0	36.9	30.9	50.0
42027	Centre County	4.7	3.7	63.9	8.1	5.1	62,175	2.17	55.7	43.0	4.6	8.1	44.3	30.0	38.3
42029	Chester County	7.5	8.3	61.4	10.9	5.6	205,426	2.60	70.6	58.0	4.2	8.3	29.4	23.4	41.3
42033	Clearfield County	2.9	2.7	84.3	2.3	1.3	33,554	2.18	60.5	47.4	5.5	7.7	39.5	32.1	49.3
42037	Columbia County	4.2	4.3	77.9	4.1	1.3	25,929	2.37	58.0	45.1	5.6	7.3	42.0	33.2	47.0
42039	Crawford County	4.3	1.6	82.4	0.6	0.3	34,813	2.23	62.4	48.2	5.0	9.2	37.6	29.9	49.5
42041	Cumberland County	7.1	5.3	68.1	7.8	3.2	107,981	2.39	61.8	50.5	3.6	7.8	38.2	31.0	44.5
42043	Dauphin County	7.7	12.0	65.9	10.5	4.3	121,773	2.32	59.3	40.9	4.9	13.5	40.7	32.7	42.2
42045	Delaware County	5.7	5.1	67.3	11.9	4.3	215,645	2.57	65.1	45.5	6.6	13.0	34.9	29.7	45.0
42049	Erie County	5.9	4.9	76.2	4.6	2.0	111,118	2.29	61.0	42.8	5.8	12.5	39.0	32.8	46.3
42051	Fayette County	5.0	1.5	81.8	0.9	0.3	55,724	2.15	60.5	43.7	5.4	11.4	39.5	33.0	49.3
42055	Franklin County	5.8	7.7	61.4	4.8	3.0	62,966	2.48	69.1	52.9	5.3	11.0	30.9	26.8	44.1

Table A-2. Counties — Who: Age, Race/Ethnicity, and Household Structure, 2023—*Continued*

STATE County code	STATE County	Total population	Percent change, 2010–2023	Population by age (percent): Under 18 years	18 to 24 years	25 to 44 years	45 to 64 years	65 years and over	Median age	Race alone or in combination (percent): White	Black or African American	American Indian and Alaska Native	Asian	Native Hawaiian or Other Pacific Islander	Some other race
	ACS table number:	B01003	Census PEP	B01001	B01001	B01001	B01001	B01001	B01002	B02008	B02009	B02010	B02011	B02012	B02013
	Column number:	1	2	3	4	5	6	7	8	9	10	11	12	13	14
	PENNSYLVANIA—Cont.														
42063	Indiana County	83,094	-6.5	18.6	15.8	21.1	23.5	20.9	39.7	96.9	3.8	0.5	1.3	NA	1.5
42069	Lackawanna County	216,123	0.8	20.2	9.2	24.5	25.0	21.1	41.2	85.9	5.8	1.2	3.9	NA	10.3
42071	Lancaster County	558,589	7.4	22.9	8.9	24.8	23.2	20.2	39.1	87.7	6.2	0.9	3.1	0.4	10.1
42073	Lawrence County	84,472	-7.1	19.7	7.7	22.6	25.9	24.2	45.1	92.6	5.8	0.7	0.8	NA	3.9
42075	Lebanon County	144,252	7.9	22.2	7.2	25.6	24.0	21.0	41.4	87.7	4.8	0.6	2.5	NA	12.4
42077	Lehigh County	377,754	7.9	22.2	8.9	26.2	24.7	18.1	39.8	72.5	9.5	2.4	4.4	NA	25.2
42079	Luzerne County	327,388	2.1	20.3	8.6	24.7	26.0	20.4	41.9	83.4	8.2	1.0	1.6	0.3	16.8
42081	Lycoming County	112,724	-2.9	20.1	9.0	24.8	25.0	21.0	41.4	94.3	5.5	2.4	1.2	NA	2.9
42085	Mercer County	108,503	-6.9	18.9	9.3	22.2	26.2	23.3	44.5	94.4	5.6	2.5	1.1	NA	2.5
42089	Monroe County	166,053	-2.3	18.8	9.2	22.8	28.9	20.3	44.5	73.2	18.5	2.1	3.6	NA	16.9
42091	Montgomery County	868,742	8.5	21.1	7.9	25.9	25.7	19.4	41.4	78.9	11.6	0.9	9.4	0.1	6.7
42095	Northampton County	319,091	7.0	18.9	10.5	23.8	25.8	20.9	42.1	84.1	8.3	2.6	3.9	NA	15.3
42097	Northumberland County	90,120	-4.5	19.7	6.6	23.4	27.8	22.5	45.2	95.1	2.7	1.6	0.9	NA	6.3
42101	Philadelphia County	1,550,542	1.5	20.9	9.9	32.1	21.8	15.2	35.6	42.0	43.0	1.8	9.1	0.1	13.8
42107	Schuylkill County	143,786	-3.0	19.7	7.6	24.0	27.2	21.5	44.0	92.0	5.4	0.7	0.9	NA	7.4
42111	Somerset County	72,197	-7.0	18.1	6.8	23.1	27.6	24.4	47.0	96.6	2.3	1.2	0.8	NA	1.6
42125	Washington County	210,232	1.1	19.5	7.6	23.7	26.7	22.4	44.0	95.1	4.0	1.9	1.9	0.2	2.5
42129	Westmoreland County	351,163	-3.8	18.0	7.2	22.2	27.6	25.0	47.5	95.8	4.1	0.7	1.5	0.1	1.8
42133	York County	464,640	6.7	21.7	7.9	25.2	26.1	19.2	41.1	87.1	8.7	1.4	2.4	NA	8.8
44000	**RHODE ISLAND**	1,095,962	4.1	18.5	9.7	27.1	25.3	19.4	40.8	79.8	10.8	2.5	4.8	0.3	17.1
44003	Kent County	171,278	3.1	17.7	6.2	28.4	26.4	21.3	43.4	92.4	4.5	2.4	4.0	0.2	7.7
44005	Newport County	83,832	1.2	15.4	7.7	24.3	25.8	26.8	47.9	93.2	4.5	2.4	3.2	NA	5.5
44007	Providence County	660,615	5.3	20.0	10.0	28.7	24.5	16.8	38.4	70.5	15.5	2.8	5.6	0.4	24.4
44009	Washington County	129,982	2.3	14.6	14.1	20.1	26.9	24.2	46.0	95.2	2.7	1.6	3.1	NA	4.5
45000	**SOUTH CAROLINA**	5,373,555	15.9	21.3	9.0	25.4	25.0	19.3	40.5	70.1	26.7	1.7	2.5	0.2	6.2
45003	Aiken County	177,130	10.3	21.5	8.0	25.1	24.4	21.0	41.7	71.7	25.5	1.6	1.6	NA	6.4
45007	Anderson County	213,076	13.8	22.4	7.7	26.1	25.2	18.5	40.0	84.8	13.8	4.0	2.0	NA	4.3
45013	Beaufort County	198,979	22.1	16.7	9.9	20.6	23.4	29.4	48.1	77.4	17.6	1.1	2.2	NA	9.9
45015	Berkeley County	255,217	42.8	23.4	9.3	28.1	24.2	15.0	36.6	69.4	25.7	1.8	3.6	NA	6.6
45019	Charleston County	424,367	20.7	19.2	8.3	29.9	24.2	18.4	39.7	72.8	23.8	1.1	2.5	NA	6.2
45035	Dorchester County	169,833	23.5	24.1	8.1	27.9	24.4	15.4	38.2	68.9	27.6	1.3	3.1	NA	6.8
45041	Florence County	137,214	0.1	23.0	9.2	24.3	25.1	18.4	39.5	52.6	44.6	1.0	1.9	NA	3.1
45043	Georgetown County	65,731	9.3	16.5	7.7	17.7	26.4	31.7	52.6	69.4	29.0	0.7	NA	NA	2.7
45045	Greenville County	558,036	23.2	22.8	8.1	27.6	24.4	17.1	38.5	76.9	19.0	1.5	3.4	0.4	9.1
45047	Greenwood County	69,460	-0.3	22.3	9.4	26.1	22.8	19.4	37.9	65.4	31.9	1.0	1.4	NA	3.1
45051	Horry County	397,478	47.0	16.7	7.5	21.1	27.5	27.3	49.3	83.8	13.3	1.7	2.1	0.2	6.5
45055	Kershaw County	69,905	13.3	23.2	8.3	22.8	26.6	19.1	40.8	70.0	27.0	0.7	1.3	NA	4.8
45057	Lancaster County	108,215	40.7	21.6	5.9	25.8	25.0	21.8	42.6	75.1	20.5	0.6	4.1	NA	7.1
45059	Laurens County	68,873	3.6	21.8	7.7	24.6	26.7	19.3	42.2	72.5	25.2	1.3	0.4	NA	6.9
45063	Lexington County	309,528	17.5	22.8	7.3	26.5	25.8	17.6	40.8	79.9	17.3	2.6	2.9	0.3	7.2
45073	Oconee County	81,221	9.2	19.0	6.9	22.0	26.9	25.1	47.2	86.9	7.7	0.7	1.1	NA	6.8
45075	Orangeburg County	82,820	-10.3	21.1	11.5	21.8	24.1	21.4	41.2	36.1	61.6	2.7	NA	NA	2.6
45077	Pickens County	135,495	13.7	18.3	17.9	22.6	22.9	18.3	36.7	90.5	6.9	2.1	2.4	0.4	5.0
45079	Richland County	425,138	10.2	21.4	15.0	26.6	22.6	14.4	34.6	46.6	49.6	1.5	4.0	0.9	5.5
45083	Spartanburg County	356,698	25.3	23.3	8.9	27.0	24.3	16.4	37.7	74.2	21.5	0.8	3.2	NA	8.9
45085	Sumter County	104,165	-3.2	23.7	10.2	24.5	23.5	18.1	38.2	50.4	49.4	1.1	2.1	NA	2.5
45091	York County	298,320	31.4	23.5	8.1	26.3	26.5	15.6	40.3	75.6	20.8	1.7	4.2	NA	6.2
46000	**SOUTH DAKOTA**	919,318	12.6	23.8	9.2	25.4	23.1	18.4	38.5	86.2	3.4	10.4	2.2	0.1	4.2
46083	Lincoln County	73,238	63.4	25.7	8.6	28.5	21.8	15.4	35.9	95.3	3.4	2.3	2.4	NA	3.6
46099	Minnehaha County	206,930	21.7	25.2	8.6	28.7	22.9	14.5	36.7	85.4	8.7	3.8	3.0	NA	5.7
46103	Pennington County	115,903	14.4	21.3	8.8	24.9	24.7	20.3	40.2	88.0	2.3	13.6	2.4	NA	4.4
47000	**TENNESSEE**	7,126,489	12.1	21.9	8.9	26.9	24.9	17.5	39.1	79.3	17.2	1.7	2.7	0.2	6.8
47001	Anderson County	80,234	6.8	21.0	7.4	26.0	25.3	20.2	41.6	91.9	7.1	1.9	0.4	NA	2.8
47009	Blount County	141,456	14.9	19.7	7.5	24.0	27.5	21.4	43.8	95.2	3.7	0.8	1.3	NA	4.9
47011	Bradley County	111,579	12.6	21.8	9.2	26.1	25.5	17.5	38.0	91.3	7.6	1.0	1.6	NA	7.4
47037	Davidson County	712,334	13.4	20.4	9.8	35.0	21.5	13.3	34.8	66.5	26.9	2.0	4.8	0.4	12.2
47059	Greene County	72,577	5.5	17.8	8.8	23.5	27.6	22.4	44.9	94.2	3.3	1.8	0.8	NA	3.5
47063	Hamblen County	66,216	5.9	22.8	5.3	26.4	25.7	19.8	40.1	88.6	5.2	1.0	1.3	NA	14.3
47065	Hamilton County	379,864	12.6	21.1	8.3	27.5	24.2	18.9	40.2	75.8	19.0	1.3	2.7	0.2	7.6
47093	Knox County	500,669	15.6	20.8	12.0	27.1	23.6	16.5	37.5	86.4	9.9	1.0	3.1	0.1	6.9
47113	Madison County	99,193	0.8	22.2	9.1	26.3	23.9	18.5	39.0	59.5	37.4	2.3	1.8	NA	5.0

Table A-2. Counties — Who: Age, Race/Ethnicity, and Household Structure, 2023—*Continued*

STATE County code	STATE County	Two or more races (percent)	Hispanic or Latino (percent)	Native, born in state of residence (percent)	Foreign born (percent)	Non-citizens (percent)	Total households	Average household size	Household type (percent of all households): Family households: Total	Family households: Married couple	Family households: Male householder	Family households: Female householder	Nonfamily households: Total	Nonfamily households: One-person households	Percent of households with people age 60 years and over
	ACS table number:	B02001	B03003	B05002	B05002	B05002	B11001	B25010	B11001	B11001	B11001	B11001	B11001	B11001	B11006
	Column number:	15	16	17	18	19	20	21	22	23	24	25	26	27	28
	PENNSYLVANIA—Cont.														
42063	Indiana County	3.8	1.9	83.5	2.5	2.0	32,454	2.41	61.8	47.7	6.1	8.0	38.2	31.7	46.0
42069	Lackawanna County	6.2	10.4	71.7	7.7	4.3	88,871	2.34	60.0	38.0	8.0	14.0	40.0	34.0	48.2
42071	Lancaster County	8.1	11.7	73.4	6.2	2.6	211,669	2.56	66.7	54.1	4.3	8.4	33.3	26.2	47.0
42073	Lawrence County	3.6	2.3	84.1	1.5	0.8	36,638	2.24	62.6	46.3	4.8	11.5	37.4	32.7	50.7
42075	Lebanon County	7.2	15.6	74.8	5.1	2.2	58,012	2.42	70.1	50.1	5.9	14.1	29.9	24.5	45.6
42077	Lehigh County	12.5	28.6	57.6	14.9	6.9	147,524	2.50	69.6	46.2	7.2	16.2	30.4	23.6	43.5
42079	Luzerne County	10.6	18.4	70.4	10.3	5.4	136,046	2.33	61.3	40.9	5.4	15.0	38.7	32.7	46.4
42081	Lycoming County	6.1	2.4	81.2	1.1	0.5	46,849	2.28	63.3	48.2	4.7	10.4	36.7	30.0	44.6
42085	Mercer County	6.1	1.8	80.0	1.3	0.4	47,517	2.14	60.8	45.4	4.4	11.0	39.2	34.4	49.6
42089	Monroe County	13.3	18.7	37.5	11.7	3.5	61,129	2.66	69.7	50.7	5.9	13.2	30.3	23.2	51.8
42091	Montgomery County	7.2	6.8	68.6	11.6	4.9	338,467	2.50	65.4	52.4	4.3	8.6	34.6	28.5	44.8
42095	Northampton County	13.5	15.9	60.1	8.6	3.3	123,536	2.47	67.3	51.6	4.6	11.1	32.7	26.3	47.0
42097	Northumberland County	6.5	5.5	85.2	2.3	1.4	37,343	2.32	62.6	48.5	6.8	7.4	37.4	30.9	46.9
42101	Philadelphia County	8.9	15.8	62.2	15.1	7.2	688,112	2.18	51.3	28.5	5.3	17.4	48.7	39.0	36.7
42107	Schuylkill County	6.3	8.6	82.8	3.0	2.0	58,809	2.32	61.3	42.0	7.0	12.2	38.7	31.6	46.7
42111	Somerset County	2.4	1.6	85.7	1.1	0.7	29,435	2.31	63.1	51.2	3.5	8.4	36.9	32.1	50.3
42125	Washington County	4.8	2.1	81.1	2.4	1.0	89,091	2.30	64.2	50.4	3.6	10.3	35.8	29.7	47.4
42129	Westmoreland County	3.7	1.6	85.4	1.9	0.6	155,459	2.21	62.3	48.6	3.6	10.0	37.7	32.1	51.8
42133	York County	8.1	9.9	65.8	4.3	2.1	183,864	2.48	66.8	51.9	4.3	10.5	33.2	26.3	44.8
44000	**RHODE ISLAND**	13.5	18.0	53.6	14.7	6.8	443,980	2.37	60.6	43.5	4.8	12.3	39.4	31.0	45.1
44003	Kent County	9.4	7.5	68.1	6.2	2.5	73,493	2.30	64.6	49.8	6.7	8.1	35.4	28.5	48.7
44005	Newport County	8.3	6.7	33.2	7.2	3.5	36,932	2.16	61.5	49.1	1.7	10.7	38.5	29.6	53.1
44007	Providence County	17.1	26.0	52.4	20.5	9.9	259,528	2.44	58.6	38.6	5.5	14.6	41.4	32.4	41.5
44009	Washington County	6.6	3.9	57.1	5.0	1.3	53,307	2.29	62.3	52.0	2.1	8.2	37.7	29.4	52.5
45000	**SOUTH CAROLINA**	7.0	7.4	51.8	5.9	3.4	2,177,733	2.40	65.3	47.6	4.3	13.5	34.7	28.6	44.1
45003	Aiken County	6.6	7.3	33.7	4.4	2.5	70,920	2.46	67.7	48.8	4.7	14.2	32.3	27.6	46.2
45007	Anderson County	9.1	5.3	61.4	3.5	2.0	86,773	2.41	67.4	50.0	2.2	15.2	32.6	26.4	43.5
45013	Beaufort County	7.9	12.1	23.2	9.0	5.2	87,165	2.18	69.2	57.1	4.5	7.5	30.8	26.1	56.7
45015	Berkeley County	6.5	9.2	48.1	8.0	4.7	97,713	2.57	68.6	52.6	4.8	11.2	31.4	25.5	39.4
45019	Charleston County	6.1	7.0	44.6	6.8	4.2	183,800	2.25	56.4	44.4	3.2	8.8	43.6	32.4	40.1
45035	Dorchester County	7.5	7.3	48.7	6.0	3.0	65,532	2.56	66.5	45.5	6.4	14.6	33.5	25.9	38.7
45041	Florence County	3.2	3.4	71.3	2.9	1.2	53,651	2.50	65.9	40.9	5.2	19.8	34.1	31.2	43.3
45043	Georgetown County	NA	3.6	49.5	3.2	1.5	28,720	2.27	68.2	52.3	4.9	11.0	31.8	28.4	59.6
45045	Greenville County	9.7	11.7	47.7	8.7	4.9	226,571	2.41	67.3	53.0	3.8	10.5	32.7	26.2	38.6
45047	Greenwood County	2.6	7.4	74.3	3.9	1.9	29,676	2.21	63.6	42.1	3.3	18.2	36.4	32.0	43.1
45051	Horry County	7.1	7.3	32.4	6.2	3.3	168,080	2.32	65.0	50.3	3.2	11.5	35.0	29.8	54.7
45055	Kershaw County	3.7	6.1	60.3	2.5	1.4	27,356	2.54	70.2	48.1	4.3	17.8	29.8	24.3	45.8
45057	Lancaster County	7.3	7.6	40.9	9.5	5.3	42,439	2.51	67.1	52.1	2.7	12.2	32.9	30.4	46.3
45059	Laurens County	6.2	6.9	72.2	4.1	3.2	28,833	2.32	64.0	46.4	5.3	12.3	36.0	30.8	44.5
45063	Lexington County	8.7	8.1	57.3	6.3	3.9	126,509	2.42	68.2	50.9	4.7	12.6	31.8	25.6	40.5
45073	Oconee County	3.2	6.3	54.7	4.8	3.0	34,416	2.34	72.7	54.0	5.2	13.5	27.3	22.9	54.5
45075	Orangeburg County	3.9	2.8	71.3	2.5	1.6	34,120	2.32	65.2	37.9	5.5	21.8	34.8	31.2	51.5
45077	Pickens County	6.9	5.5	58.2	3.0	1.6	54,412	2.33	62.0	44.7	4.7	12.6	38.0	28.3	43.2
45079	Richland County	7.3	6.5	55.8	5.5	3.1	169,715	2.35	57.1	38.1	4.2	14.7	42.9	34.4	35.5
45083	Spartanburg County	8.3	9.5	58.0	9.0	4.5	134,559	2.59	68.6	50.5	3.8	14.4	31.4	25.8	39.9
45085	Sumter County	5.4	4.5	60.8	2.5	1.0	40,059	2.52	68.0	42.8	6.0	19.2	32.0	26.2	44.8
45091	York County	8.1	7.6	34.7	7.2	4.3	113,164	2.61	71.1	52.4	5.8	12.9	28.9	24.3	39.9
46000	**SOUTH DAKOTA**	6.1	5.1	62.3	4.3	2.2	378,559	2.34	61.2	48.1	4.9	8.1	38.8	32.1	40.4
46083	Lincoln County	6.1	3.3	59.4	2.7	0.8	28,842	2.53	67.7	56.2	3.5	8.0	32.3	26.2	30.8
46099	Minnehaha County	6.2	6.8	61.5	9.8	5.0	87,657	2.29	56.3	42.4	4.8	9.1	43.7	36.3	34.0
46103	Pennington County	10.5	5.9	55.8	1.9	0.5	48,946	2.29	63.6	48.0	7.1	8.6	36.4	31.2	44.5
47000	**TENNESSEE**	7.4	7.5	56.8	6.1	3.8	2,889,226	2.42	63.9	46.7	4.8	12.4	36.1	29.6	41.2
47001	Anderson County	4.1	4.3	61.9	2.5	1.3	33,521	2.36	56.6	38.1	7.4	11.1	43.4	37.5	45.8
47009	Blount County	6.0	4.8	57.3	3.1	2.1	56,548	2.47	70.9	55.5	5.0	10.4	29.1	23.3	47.8
47011	Bradley County	8.8	8.6	53.6	6.7	3.7	42,712	2.55	65.7	51.8	3.0	10.9	34.3	28.4	43.0
47037	Davidson County	12.0	13.7	42.8	15.5	9.7	341,597	2.03	52.4	36.5	5.5	10.3	47.6	36.8	29.1
47059	Greene County	3.6	4.0	63.5	2.7	0.8	28,214	2.52	65.3	49.5	4.9	10.9	34.7	29.1	52.2
47063	Hamblen County	10.1	15.1	59.0	8.4	7.1	27,311	2.41	63.3	44.7	6.2	12.4	36.7	29.0	46.9
47065	Hamilton County	6.2	8.2	54.9	5.5	3.1	157,992	2.34	62.0	44.7	4.5	12.8	38.0	30.4	41.1
47093	Knox County	7.3	6.4	56.3	6.6	3.9	200,022	2.44	60.4	47.2	2.5	10.6	39.6	30.3	38.0
47113	Madison County	5.6	5.4	68.0	4.8	3.0	40,525	2.35	63.2	43.1	2.1	17.9	36.8	31.4	44.5

Table A-2. Counties — Who: Age, Race/Ethnicity, and Household Structure, 2023—*Continued*

STATE County code	STATE County	Total population	Percent change, 2010–2023	Population by age (percent) Under 18 years	18 to 24 years	25 to 44 years	45 to 64 years	65 years and over	Median age	Race alone or in combination (percent) White	Black or African American	American Indian and Alaska Native	Asian	Native Hawaiian or Other Pacific Islander	Some other race
	ACS table number:	B01003	Census PEP	B01001	B01001	B01001	B01001	B01001	B01002	B02008	B02009	B02010	B02011	B02012	B02013
	Column number:	1	2	3	4	5	6	7	8	9	10	11	12	13	14
	TENNESSEE—Cont.														
47119	Maury County	110,760	36.5	23.1	6.9	28.9	23.4	17.7	37.9	87.1	10.2	3.7	2.2	NA	5.2
47125	Montgomery County	239,872	38.4	26.6	10.5	32.4	20.2	10.2	32.5	73.2	25.6	2.2	4.7	0.3	8.0
47141	Putnam County	83,844	15.5	20.5	14.3	25.2	23.5	16.6	36.5	89.4	3.3	1.5	1.5	NA	8.7
47147	Robertson County	76,776	15.5	23.9	7.7	27.4	25.8	15.2	38.9	89.3	8.6	1.1	1.1	NA	8.9
47149	Rutherford County	367,101	39.2	24.5	11.7	29.2	23.0	11.6	34.6	76.0	17.9	1.1	5.0	0.6	12.4
47155	Sevier County	99,415	10.4	20.2	7.5	24.3	26.9	21.1	43.4	95.2	0.8	3.4	1.7	NA	8.9
47157	Shelby County	910,042	-2.0	25.4	8.6	27.5	23.2	15.3	36.0	39.3	54.4	1.2	3.6	0.1	8.6
47163	Sullivan County	162,135	3.4	18.8	7.1	23.7	27.9	22.5	45.4	97.3	2.1	2.2	1.2	NA	0.8
47165	Sumner County	207,994	29.0	22.9	7.5	26.7	26.2	16.7	39.4	85.7	9.7	1.5	2.2	NA	6.8
47179	Washington County	138,420	12.2	18.4	12.2	24.4	25.8	19.2	41.4	93.7	5.3	0.7	2.8	NA	4.9
47187	Williamson County	264,460	43.7	25.5	8.0	23.0	28.0	15.5	40.8	89.3	5.0	1.6	6.5	NA	6.2
47189	Wilson County	163,674	42.9	23.2	6.6	27.5	26.3	16.4	40.3	86.6	9.2	1.6	3.8	NA	5.4
48000	**TEXAS**	30,503,301	20.8	24.7	9.6	28.6	23.3	13.8	35.9	70.1	14.2	2.6	6.8	0.3	30.3
48005	Angelina County	87,319	0.4	25.3	8.5	25.7	23.1	17.4	37.6	81.5	14.0	6.7	1.3	NA	19.8
48021	Bastrop County	110,778	48.9	25.9	9.6	25.2	23.6	15.7	37.6	84.6	7.4	2.6	1.7	NA	37.2
48027	Bell County	393,193	25.6	27.3	10.2	30.0	20.2	12.2	32.5	63.2	27.8	2.4	5.0	1.3	18.9
48029	Bexar County	2,087,679	21.1	24.5	10.1	30.1	22.3	13.1	35.0	73.8	10.3	4.0	4.9	0.4	41.9
48037	Bowie County	91,687	-1.1	23.5	7.9	26.8	23.9	17.9	39.4	71.2	26.4	1.8	1.7	1.2	5.7
48039	Brazoria County	398,938	26.9	25.4	8.3	28.9	24.3	13.0	36.8	67.1	18.5	2.4	8.2	0.2	27.0
48041	Brazos County	244,703	25.0	20.2	26.3	25.7	17.1	10.7	27.3	76.7	12.2	2.8	7.1	0.3	18.1
48061	Cameron County	426,710	4.6	28.0	10.9	24.7	21.9	14.4	33.4	87.0	0.7	1.4	1.1	0.1	65.2
48085	Collin County	1,195,359	51.6	24.4	8.5	29.2	26.0	11.9	37.6	64.0	12.9	2.0	21.3	0.1	12.5
48091	Comal County	193,928	77.3	22.1	7.0	25.1	26.8	19.0	42.2	87.9	4.4	2.3	3.1	NA	21.7
48099	Coryell County	84,878	12.2	21.7	11.9	31.7	23.2	11.5	33.4	75.0	19.9	5.3	4.6	1.6	16.5
48113	Dallas County	2,606,358	9.6	24.8	9.7	30.3	23.0	12.2	34.3	53.7	24.2	2.4	8.1	0.4	33.0
48121	Denton County	1,007,703	51.1	23.0	8.9	30.4	25.8	12.0	37.3	69.8	13.8	2.1	13.3	0.4	16.7
48135	Ector County	164,494	19.9	30.4	9.7	29.0	20.7	10.2	31.6	72.9	5.7	1.7	1.6	NA	48.0
48139	Ellis County	222,829	48.1	26.4	8.3	28.1	24.1	13.1	36.4	72.7	16.7	3.4	1.5	NA	21.9
48141	El Paso County	869,880	8.1	25.7	10.7	28.5	21.7	13.5	33.9	73.4	4.8	2.9	2.3	0.3	62.8
48157	Fort Bend County	916,778	55.3	26.4	8.4	27.0	25.2	13.0	37.6	47.7	23.6	1.8	24.1	0.1	20.1
48167	Galveston County	361,744	23.6	23.4	8.4	26.7	25.4	16.2	39.3	78.9	14.5	2.4	4.8	NA	18.6
48181	Grayson County	146,907	21.3	24.1	8.3	24.3	25.6	17.7	39.6	89.1	7.3	2.8	2.8	NA	13.3
48183	Gregg County	126,243	3.6	25.5	9.7	25.5	23.2	16.1	35.8	75.8	19.8	3.7	1.8	NA	18.2
48187	Guadalupe County	188,454	42.3	23.7	8.4	28.4	24.2	15.3	38.1	80.1	8.5	3.4	3.5	0.8	30.3
48201	Harris County	4,835,125	17.6	25.6	9.4	29.8	23.0	12.1	34.8	55.2	21.6	2.9	8.5	0.3	35.6
48203	Harrison County	70,895	7.8	23.9	9.0	26.3	22.6	18.2	38.8	73.4	21.7	1.2	1.3	NA	11.5
48209	Hays County	280,486	77.2	22.1	14.7	29.2	21.4	12.6	34.2	80.1	5.1	3.2	3.8	NA	27.4
48213	Henderson County	86,158	9.6	21.2	7.8	20.8	26.7	23.5	45.2	90.7	6.7	2.4	1.0	NA	13.6
48215	Hidalgo County	898,471	15.2	30.5	11.3	25.9	20.5	11.8	30.9	87.5	1.0	1.0	1.3	0.1	70.0
48221	Hood County	67,774	32.4	20.4	6.4	21.8	25.1	26.3	46.1	93.3	1.3	1.6	2.6	NA	13.8
48231	Hunt County	113,347	31.3	24.3	10.1	26.0	24.1	15.5	37.2	77.7	10.3	2.9	1.9	NA	19.9
48245	Jefferson County	251,496	-0.4	24.6	8.6	27.7	23.0	16.1	37.5	47.7	33.9	3.0	4.4	NA	21.0
48251	Johnson County	202,906	34.2	25.6	8.8	27.3	24.2	14.1	37.3	86.4	7.1	2.1	2.1	0.3	20.8
48257	Kaufman County	185,690	78.7	28.8	8.6	31.1	21.1	10.5	33.7	66.5	23.3	5.2	3.0	0.6	21.2
48291	Liberty County	108,272	42.7	30.3	8.9	27.1	21.8	11.9	32.8	66.2	8.2	5.8	1.1	NA	32.7
48303	Lubbock County	320,940	14.5	23.4	16.1	27.2	19.7	13.6	32.1	82.4	9.2	2.4	2.7	0.1	22.8
48309	McLennan County	268,583	13.8	23.9	14.0	25.3	21.2	15.6	34.2	79.0	15.8	1.5	2.6	NA	23.7
48329	Midland County	177,108	29.3	28.8	8.2	33.5	18.6	10.9	32.9	73.4	9.4	2.7	2.6	NA	31.6
48339	Montgomery County	711,354	55.0	25.8	8.2	27.4	24.5	14.0	37.3	82.0	8.6	2.5	4.3	0.3	19.5
48347	Nacogdoches County	65,375	1.3	23.1	17.9	22.4	20.2	16.3	32.8	73.2	17.7	2.5	2.0	NA	15.8
48355	Nueces County	352,289	3.5	23.6	9.7	27.1	23.2	16.4	37.3	85.7	4.8	2.3	3.1	NA	47.0
48361	Orange County	85,722	4.6	25.5	8.6	24.7	24.2	17.0	38.6	86.0	11.4	1.5	1.5	NA	7.2
48367	Parker County	173,494	47.9	24.5	7.6	26.3	25.6	16.0	38.3	94.4	2.3	1.6	1.4	0.9	13.3
48375	Potter County	114,647	-5.6	24.2	10.2	27.3	23.7	14.5	35.4	74.4	11.4	2.0	5.0	0.6	27.6
48381	Randall County	148,255	22.3	23.9	10.7	26.3	23.3	15.8	37.0	89.9	5.2	1.6	2.5	NA	15.4
48397	Rockwall County	131,307	66.2	26.5	8.9	26.9	25.0	12.7	37.6	76.9	11.2	1.8	4.9	NA	18.2
48409	San Patricio County	70,660	9.4	25.2	5.7	31.3	22.6	15.2	38.4	85.7	2.9	2.0	3.6	NA	43.1
48423	Smith County	245,209	16.5	24.0	9.8	25.8	22.7	17.7	38.2	75.3	18.6	1.4	2.3	NA	13.9
48427	Starr County	65,934	8.1	32.0	11.2	24.6	20.8	11.4	29.9	78.4	NA	NA	NA	NA	64.5
48439	Tarrant County	2,182,947	20.1	25.1	9.5	29.1	23.6	12.7	35.3	66.4	20.4	2.1	7.6	0.4	23.9
48441	Taylor County	146,836	11.3	24.2	13.8	27.0	19.0	16.0	34.0	84.0	8.7	2.0	2.9	1.9	18.2
48451	Tom Green County	119,057	7.6	23.3	10.0	28.5	20.9	17.4	37.2	88.5	5.0	2.8	2.6	NA	28.0
48453	Travis County	1,334,961	29.5	19.7	9.0	36.6	23.2	11.4	36.1	74.6	10.2	2.6	10.2	0.2	24.3
48469	Victoria County	91,664	5.5	25.0	9.3	26.4	22.0	17.2	37.2	78.4	8.2	1.7	2.6	NA	39.6

Table A-2. Counties — Who: Age, Race/Ethnicity, and Household Structure, 2023—*Continued*

STATE County code	STATE County	Two or more races (percent)	Hispanic or Latino (percent)	Native, born in state of residence (percent)	Foreign born (percent)	Non-citizens (percent)	Total households	Average household size	Household type (percent of all households): Family households: Total	Family households: Married couple	Family households: Male householder	Family households: Female householder	Nonfamily households: Total	Nonfamily households: One-person households	Percent of households with people age 60 years and over
	ACS table number:	B02001	B03003	B05002	B05002	B05002	B11001	B25010	B11001	B11001	B11001	B11001	B11001	B11001	B11006
	Column number:	15	16	17	18	19	20	21	22	23	24	25	26	27	28
	TENNESSEE—Cont.														
47119	Maury County	8.8	8.3	52.4	2.0	1.2	45,571	2.40	66.2	45.8	6.7	13.7	33.8	29.4	40.4
47125	Montgomery County	11.8	11.6	36.1	6.7	4.2	91,893	2.55	70.6	53.2	5.7	11.7	29.4	23.3	28.2
47141	Putnam County	4.3	8.6	58.8	6.1	4.7	34,727	2.31	60.4	46.7	3.8	9.9	39.6	33.3	40.9
47147	Robertson County	8.7	10.2	59.7	4.6	3.9	29,522	2.57	73.0	56.6	3.7	12.7	27.0	19.9	43.6
47149	Rutherford County	12.4	12.4	51.2	12.0	6.8	134,245	2.70	65.7	50.9	4.1	10.8	34.3	26.8	30.8
47155	Sevier County	9.7	9.6	53.7	6.6	5.8	42,727	2.31	65.5	48.4	4.8	12.3	34.5	29.5	47.3
47157	Shelby County	6.6	8.9	63.6	7.9	5.3	362,776	2.47	60.7	35.0	5.5	20.1	39.3	34.5	39.0
47163	Sullivan County	3.5	2.8	58.4	1.9	0.5	68,655	2.33	59.9	44.8	2.8	12.3	40.1	35.3	50.7
47165	Sumner County	5.7	7.5	55.3	5.5	3.6	80,536	2.56	69.1	54.9	3.8	10.3	30.9	25.1	39.6
47179	Washington County	7.1	5.0	57.9	3.6	2.6	57,629	2.32	59.9	47.2	4.1	8.6	40.1	31.6	44.0
47187	Williamson County	7.6	6.0	41.7	7.6	4.6	95,439	2.76	77.2	67.1	3.1	7.1	22.8	18.2	39.6
47189	Wilson County	6.8	6.7	53.1	5.8	2.4	60,911	2.66	74.8	61.0	1.8	12.0	25.2	20.9	40.2
48000	**TEXAS**	23.3	39.8	57.7	17.9	10.3	11,260,645	2.66	67.4	48.7	5.6	13.1	32.6	26.5	36.0
48005	Angelina County	21.3	23.8	71.6	8.8	6.6	31,996	2.62	68.7	48.5	4.0	16.2	31.3	28.0	40.8
48021	Bastrop County	33.1	45.9	63.7	14.5	11.0	38,591	2.78	71.8	52.3	5.5	14.0	28.2	21.4	44.3
48027	Bell County	16.9	26.6	45.9	9.0	4.2	145,863	2.64	66.2	47.5	4.7	14.0	33.8	27.9	32.8
48029	Bexar County	33.2	59.8	60.1	14.4	7.9	758,070	2.70	64.8	44.2	5.9	14.7	35.2	28.8	35.8
48037	Bowie County	7.5	8.7	62.8	6.1	3.4	36,110	2.38	62.8	44.6	6.0	12.2	37.2	33.7	43.1
48039	Brazoria County	22.1	31.8	62.4	15.7	6.0	138,692	2.77	75.0	55.6	6.0	13.5	25.0	21.1	35.7
48041	Brazos County	15.6	27.5	64.2	13.6	8.4	92,216	2.47	53.3	38.6	2.9	11.7	46.7	31.0	26.2
48061	Cameron County	55.1	89.2	65.7	23.4	13.9	143,033	2.96	75.0	49.1	6.4	19.5	25.0	21.6	41.1
48085	Collin County	12.0	16.1	41.4	24.2	11.7	431,746	2.75	72.5	59.4	4.2	8.8	27.5	23.2	32.0
48091	Comal County	18.4	28.8	57.1	7.7	2.6	75,234	2.55	70.8	58.8	1.8	10.2	29.2	23.1	43.5
48099	Coryell County	20.0	21.1	49.3	6.5	2.8	28,070	2.43	74.5	60.0	2.5	12.0	25.5	19.5	34.7
48113	Dallas County	20.9	41.4	52.9	25.4	16.6	993,312	2.59	61.2	41.3	5.9	14.0	38.8	31.7	32.6
48121	Denton County	15.1	20.5	45.0	18.1	8.8	370,503	2.69	70.6	57.4	4.2	9.0	29.4	22.8	30.8
48135	Ector County	29.4	64.5	60.4	19.7	12.9	66,937	2.43	67.9	47.2	8.5	12.1	32.1	26.3	29.3
48139	Ellis County	15.7	28.4	64.7	9.6	5.6	75,570	2.92	77.2	57.5	5.9	13.8	22.8	18.4	38.1
48141	El Paso County	45.2	82.8	59.6	22.5	10.9	301,198	2.84	70.7	45.2	7.2	18.2	29.3	24.8	38.8
48157	Fort Bend County	16.6	24.7	46.8	31.0	13.3	303,900	3.00	81.7	64.8	4.8	12.1	18.3	15.3	38.3
48167	Galveston County	18.2	26.7	63.4	10.1	4.4	142,199	2.51	67.3	50.6	5.4	11.3	32.7	27.3	38.9
48181	Grayson County	14.1	16.7	61.3	7.3	4.4	56,267	2.56	68.7	51.4	5.1	12.2	31.3	26.0	44.8
48183	Gregg County	19.2	20.5	69.9	8.3	5.8	47,550	2.58	67.1	43.2	7.1	16.8	32.9	27.2	38.5
48187	Guadalupe County	24.9	39.5	60.5	6.2	2.8	69,236	2.69	71.4	54.9	4.2	12.3	28.6	20.7	38.7
48201	Harris County	22.9	44.1	51.6	27.3	16.2	1,791,013	2.67	66.4	44.9	6.8	14.8	33.6	27.4	33.1
48203	Harrison County	9.1	15.1	67.2	5.5	2.9	26,811	2.56	66.2	46.7	4.4	15.2	33.8	26.6	43.5
48209	Hays County	18.9	39.6	60.0	8.7	4.1	105,917	2.56	63.9	49.5	4.1	10.3	36.1	24.3	32.6
48213	Henderson County	14.2	15.4	74.2	5.7	3.5	33,957	2.50	66.6	50.0	5.5	11.1	33.4	30.1	52.3
48215	Hidalgo County	60.5	91.9	63.7	25.8	18.0	277,001	3.22	77.3	49.9	7.8	19.7	22.7	18.9	37.2
48221	Hood County	12.5	14.2	63.8	3.2	2.0	25,660	2.61	72.4	65.8	2.4	4.2	27.6	22.3	52.5
48231	Hunt County	12.3	22.2	66.5	8.5	5.7	40,067	2.73	67.8	53.1	4.7	10.0	32.2	25.8	41.5
48245	Jefferson County	9.8	24.6	69.6	12.7	8.1	94,005	2.52	66.1	44.6	6.0	15.5	33.9	28.5	39.7
48251	Johnson County	18.1	25.9	65.5	7.5	3.4	65,934	3.04	73.9	59.3	5.0	9.5	26.1	21.4	39.9
48257	Kaufman County	18.1	28.1	61.0	14.6	7.1	52,963	3.48	78.2	61.6	6.3	10.3	21.8	17.6	31.9
48291	Liberty County	13.4	41.8	70.7	16.1	11.5	32,959	3.12	72.4	55.5	3.7	13.2	27.6	20.4	40.0
48303	Lubbock County	18.5	36.6	74.2	5.6	3.5	128,053	2.41	60.4	39.2	6.0	15.2	39.6	28.6	31.3
48309	McLennan County	22.3	27.2	71.0	8.8	6.2	96,965	2.68	64.3	47.1	4.9	12.3	35.7	29.7	39.1
48329	Midland County	19.3	47.1	64.0	12.2	6.6	70,890	2.47	63.6	47.6	7.2	8.8	36.4	31.2	29.2
48339	Montgomery County	16.4	28.3	51.0	16.9	10.0	262,273	2.70	74.5	59.3	3.8	11.4	25.5	19.8	37.3
48347	Nacogdoches County	10.0	21.8	73.3	7.8	4.3	25,074	2.43	61.5	46.0	2.9	12.5	38.5	32.2	37.8
48355	Nueces County	42.4	62.9	74.4	7.8	4.6	132,759	2.59	68.5	46.3	6.2	16.0	31.5	24.1	40.4
48361	Orange County	7.5	10.0	70.0	4.5	2.4	33,271	2.56	67.3	48.3	6.0	13.0	32.7	29.8	43.0
48367	Parker County	13.4	15.1	61.2	5.9	3.7	57,996	2.96	75.2	59.5	3.9	11.9	24.8	19.8	42.5
48375	Potter County	20.6	39.9	70.3	12.9	7.2	42,674	2.55	57.0	37.9	5.1	13.9	43.0	36.4	38.7
48381	Randall County	14.6	25.3	70.1	5.0	1.7	56,279	2.59	66.6	51.3	5.2	10.1	33.4	28.8	36.5
48397	Rockwall County	12.7	21.5	58.8	9.6	3.2	43,259	3.02	74.8	63.1	5.1	6.6	25.2	21.2	36.1
48409	San Patricio County	36.6	56.6	72.6	9.5	7.2	25,735	2.72	69.4	50.5	4.2	14.7	30.6	26.3	42.8
48423	Smith County	10.8	21.1	68.6	8.1	4.7	81,987	2.92	70.4	52.8	5.6	12.1	29.6	24.5	45.4
48427	Starr County	NA	97.0	68.6	28.2	20.0	19,004	3.45	83.7	54.4	5.0	24.3	16.3	14.1	39.3
48439	Tarrant County	19.8	30.5	53.2	17.6	10.2	801,716	2.69	66.5	47.5	5.1	13.9	33.5	27.0	34.2
48441	Taylor County	17.1	25.4	66.0	6.5	2.3	54,805	2.56	66.1	47.1	6.2	12.8	33.9	27.7	35.9
48451	Tom Green County	26.2	41.2	69.4	6.8	3.5	47,638	2.41	58.5	39.6	4.8	14.0	41.5	36.2	40.6
48453	Travis County	20.7	32.4	48.8	17.8	9.8	608,921	2.15	52.0	39.9	4.4	7.7	48.0	34.8	26.3
48469	Victoria County	29.4	48.4	75.0	8.8	5.2	34,484	2.62	72.6	52.2	7.7	12.7	27.4	22.7	42.9

Table A-2. Counties — Who: Age, Race/Ethnicity, and Household Structure, 2023—*Continued*

STATE County code	STATE County	Total population	Percent change, 2010–2023	Population by age (percent): Under 18 years	18 to 24 years	25 to 44 years	45 to 64 years	65 years and over	Median age	Race alone or in combination (percent): White	Black or African American	American Indian and Alaska Native	Asian	Native Hawaiian or Other Pacific Islander	Some other race
	ACS table number:	B01003	Census PEP	B01001	B01001	B01001	B01001	B01001	B01002	B02008	B02009	B02010	B02011	B02012	B02013
	Column number:	1	2	3	4	5	6	7	8	9	10	11	12	13	14
	TEXAS—Cont.														
48471	Walker County	81,268	19.2	14.7	20.6	25.5	25.7	13.4	36.9	71.4	22.5	3.1	0.6	NA	13.4
48479	Webb County	269,148	7.0	30.7	11.5	26.3	20.7	10.8	30.5	87.5	0.7	0.5	0.4	NA	79.8
48485	Wichita County	130,180	-1.1	22.9	12.0	27.6	22.0	15.4	35.6	80.9	13.2	2.1	3.0	NA	12.3
48491	Williamson County	697,191	63.4	23.7	7.8	31.9	23.5	13.1	37.4	74.3	9.3	1.9	12.7	0.3	19.8
48497	Wise County	78,097	32.1	24.1	7.8	25.5	26.4	16.1	40.6	88.5	2.9	2.4	1.0	NA	14.7
49000	**UTAH**	3,417,734	23.2	27.3	11.7	28.5	20.3	12.2	32.3	87.7	2.1	2.3	4.0	1.7	12.4
49005	Cache County	142,393	25.5	29.1	18.5	25.7	16.6	10.1	26.6	90.6	2.9	2.3	3.3	0.9	9.8
49011	Davis County	373,207	21.2	29.5	9.6	28.8	20.8	11.4	32.9	92.6	2.1	1.3	4.1	1.2	9.3
49035	Salt Lake County	1,185,813	14.7	24.7	10.0	31.0	22.0	12.3	34.4	80.7	3.0	2.4	6.0	2.7	17.6
49045	Tooele County	82,051	40.9	31.5	9.0	29.1	20.7	9.7	32.0	91.9	1.7	2.1	2.1	1.3	7.3
49049	Utah County	719,174	38.3	31.1	16.7	27.7	16.4	8.1	26.2	91.0	1.7	1.7	3.6	1.8	11.4
49053	Washington County	202,452	46.2	24.1	9.8	23.3	20.4	22.5	40.1	91.3	1.2	2.4	2.0	1.7	10.1
49057	Weber County	271,926	17.1	26.0	10.0	29.5	21.9	12.6	33.8	90.8	2.2	1.5	2.7	0.7	10.4
50000	**VERMONT**	647,464	3.5	17.7	9.5	24.4	26.2	22.2	43.7	95.6	2.5	1.7	2.7	0.2	3.7
50007	Chittenden County	169,481	8.2	16.9	14.3	28.0	23.5	17.3	38.0	91.2	4.2	1.4	5.9	0.4	3.6
51000	**VIRGINIA**	8,715,698	8.6	21.5	9.2	27.2	24.9	17.2	39.3	68.7	21.2	1.7	8.8	0.3	9.9
51003	Albemarle County	115,676	16.7	19.1	11.0	24.6	24.2	21.2	42.1	82.4	11.8	0.9	7.1	0.3	6.1
51013	Arlington County	234,162	11.8	18.0	8.3	38.4	23.0	12.4	35.7	71.8	11.4	2.6	13.4	0.1	14.5
51015	Augusta County	78,247	5.5	18.0	6.9	24.8	26.7	23.7	45.3	92.5	5.7	0.6	1.1	NA	3.8
51019	Bedford County	81,525	18.6	19.3	6.9	21.4	28.7	23.7	47.0	92.9	8.2	0.9	2.0	0.4	2.7
51041	Chesterfield County	383,876	21.1	23.5	8.8	26.0	25.4	16.3	39.5	65.6	26.2	1.5	4.9	NA	11.6
51059	Fairfax County	1,141,878	5.1	22.6	8.2	27.6	26.1	15.6	39.5	61.1	12.0	1.4	23.2	0.2	16.5
51061	Fauquier County	75,165	19.4	22.9	8.3	24.7	26.7	17.5	41.2	90.5	7.7	3.6	2.8	NA	8.2
51069	Frederick County	95,994	22.3	22.3	7.8	25.0	24.8	20.0	41.8	84.1	5.2	2.0	2.7	NA	13.2
51085	Hanover County	114,148	14.2	21.5	8.1	23.3	27.7	19.4	42.7	86.1	10.3	0.8	3.5	NA	4.3
51087	Henrico County	334,760	8.9	21.6	7.8	28.2	24.6	17.8	39.8	55.9	31.5	1.2	11.1	0.3	6.4
51095	James City County	82,654	22.9	18.8	5.3	22.8	25.9	27.2	47.3	80.1	15.7	1.2	4.7	NA	6.4
51107	Loudoun County	436,347	38.5	26.1	8.0	27.1	27.3	11.4	38.3	64.9	9.6	1.1	25.4	0.2	13.1
51121	Montgomery County	98,666	4.4	15.0	28.9	22.6	18.9	14.6	29.8	87.9	5.3	1.1	7.6	NA	3.8
51153	Prince William County	489,640	20.6	26.2	8.9	27.5	25.6	11.8	36.7	56.0	23.6	1.6	13.2	0.5	22.4
51161	Roanoke County	97,026	5.0	19.3	7.1	26.0	25.2	22.4	42.9	88.5	8.5	0.8	4.4	NA	4.5
51165	Rockingham County	86,568	13.3	22.3	9.0	24.1	23.9	20.6	40.6	92.0	4.4	0.5	1.0	NA	8.8
51177	Spotsylvania County	149,588	21.8	24.2	8.4	26.1	25.5	15.7	39.3	72.7	21.4	1.7	4.6	NA	12.8
51179	Stafford County	165,428	27.5	25.9	9.3	27.5	25.7	11.5	36.4	64.5	24.4	1.1	6.2	NA	15.6
51199	York County	70,952	8.4	22.7	8.0	26.7	24.4	18.2	40.5	78.4	16.3	1.6	9.8	1.8	6.0
51510	Alexandria city	155,230	10.2	18.0	6.2	39.2	22.9	13.7	38.2	65.8	24.3	3.3	8.3	0.1	15.2
51550	Chesapeake city	253,886	13.9	24.0	8.0	28.9	24.2	15.0	38.4	63.9	33.0	1.7	6.1	0.5	6.1
51650	Hampton city	137,098	-0.2	21.8	10.4	29.9	21.0	17.0	35.9	43.1	55.7	3.7	3.8	0.3	5.6
51680	Lynchburg city	79,535	5.1	19.3	25.3	24.6	16.5	14.4	28.2	68.4	28.5	2.4	3.2	NA	3.8
51700	Newport News city	183,118	1.3	23.2	11.8	28.9	21.5	14.6	34.7	50.1	46.6	1.8	4.6	1.1	10.1
51710	Norfolk city	230,930	-5.0	20.2	14.7	32.0	19.4	13.7	33.0	52.3	43.0	3.1	5.6	0.6	8.5
51740	Portsmouth city	96,793	1.1	22.9	9.1	30.4	22.2	15.3	35.6	42.4	57.0	1.1	2.7	NA	7.0
51760	Richmond city	229,247	12.2	17.4	11.7	35.5	20.8	14.6	34.9	49.4	44.9	1.7	3.4	NA	9.1
51770	Roanoke city	97,171	0.2	22.5	7.0	28.7	24.4	17.5	38.9	64.0	30.3	1.2	4.3	NA	8.0
51800	Suffolk city	100,659	18.6	23.4	6.9	28.8	25.4	15.4	39.8	52.2	45.5	1.8	3.0	NA	6.7
51810	Virginia Beach city	453,649	3.3	21.7	8.3	29.5	24.0	16.5	38.2	69.1	22.4	1.7	10.3	0.8	7.1
53000	**WASHINGTON**	7,812,880	15.9	21.1	8.4	29.7	23.7	17.1	38.6	77.5	6.2	3.5	13.1	1.4	12.7
53005	Benton County	215,219	22.0	25.9	8.3	27.3	22.3	16.1	36.2	84.3	2.7	4.4	4.5	0.5	22.3
53007	Chelan County	79,997	10.0	22.1	7.4	24.4	24.1	22.0	42.4	82.3	1.1	3.0	1.7	NA	28.8
53009	Clallam County	77,616	8.5	15.7	5.1	21.8	25.0	32.5	52.4	90.9	2.3	9.0	3.4	0.3	5.2
53011	Clark County	521,150	22.0	22.2	8.0	27.8	24.8	17.1	39.2	85.8	3.8	2.4	7.6	2.0	10.5
53015	Cowlitz County	112,864	10.1	22.2	7.9	25.1	25.1	19.7	41.4	91.3	1.8	3.6	2.8	1.8	9.1
53021	Franklin County	99,034	25.0	30.6	10.3	28.7	19.5	10.9	31.3	75.2	3.0	1.5	3.5	NA	45.8
53025	Grant County	102,678	14.4	27.6	10.5	25.5	21.5	14.9	34.0	77.9	2.8	3.5	2.0	NA	40.3
53027	Grays Harbor County	77,290	6.0	19.9	7.5	23.7	24.7	24.1	43.4	85.3	2.0	7.5	2.6	0.6	9.3
53029	Island County	86,267	9.6	17.4	7.6	24.2	22.2	28.6	45.7	90.3	5.0	1.8	9.0	0.3	8.2
53033	King County	2,271,380	17.2	19.1	8.1	34.3	23.9	14.5	37.7	65.2	9.0	2.5	25.2	1.4	10.2
53035	Kitsap County	277,658	10.3	19.2	8.6	27.9	23.9	20.4	40.4	88.0	4.7	4.1	9.1	2.1	7.4
53041	Lewis County	86,154	14.1	21.6	6.2	26.0	24.5	21.7	42.6	92.5	2.1	3.5	2.2	0.5	9.7
53045	Mason County	68,389	12.7	19.4	6.5	24.5	24.1	25.5	43.9	84.7	1.3	10.8	2.9	0.6	9.2
53053	Pierce County	928,696	16.7	22.8	8.5	30.2	23.3	15.2	37.5	78.0	11.9	3.6	11.8	3.1	10.8

Table A-2. Counties — Who: Age, Race/Ethnicity, and Household Structure, 2023—*Continued*

STATE County code	STATE County	Two or more races (percent)	Hispanic or Latino (percent)	Native, born in state of residence (percent)	Foreign born (percent)	Non-citizens (percent)	Total households	Average household size	Household type (percent of all households): Family households: Total	Family households: Married couple	Family households: Male house-holder	Family households: Female house-holder	Nonfamily households: Total	Nonfamily households: One-person house-holds	Percent of households with people age 60 years and over
	ACS table number:	B02001	B03003	B05002	B05002	B05002	B11001	B25010	B11001	B11001	B11001	B11001	B11001	B11001	B11006
	Column number:	15	16	17	18	19	20	21	22	23	24	25	26	27	28
	TEXAS—Cont.														
48471	Walker County	10.7	21.7	71.4	6.8	4.5	26,539	2.34	53.8	36.2	2.5	15.1	46.2	33.7	39.1
48479	Webb County	68.9	94.9	68.2	24.9	17.1	83,045	3.21	79.0	48.9	9.6	20.5	21.0	18.2	36.8
48485	Wichita County	10.8	20.9	64.4	7.0	3.3	49,403	2.42	63.1	43.2	5.4	14.6	36.9	30.6	40.1
48491	Williamson County	17.2	24.9	48.3	15.4	8.4	264,986	2.61	68.8	55.4	4.9	8.5	31.2	24.1	32.1
48497	Wise County	9.0	21.5	63.7	7.7	5.4	26,319	2.91	77.6	64.1	5.4	8.1	22.4	18.8	45.3
49000	**UTAH**	9.5	16.0	60.7	8.9	5.1	1,167,591	2.88	72.2	58.2	4.8	9.3	27.8	19.7	32.8
49005	Cache County	8.9	11.9	63.6	7.6	4.7	46,318	2.96	75.3	64.4	2.1	8.8	24.7	13.6	26.8
49011	Davis County	10.0	12.0	64.8	5.2	2.5	118,498	3.13	78.5	65.7	4.2	8.6	21.5	16.6	32.2
49035	Salt Lake County	11.4	20.7	56.8	13.5	7.9	436,181	2.68	65.0	49.5	5.3	10.2	35.0	25.0	32.2
49045	Tooele County	6.2	15.9	72.3	3.9	1.5	24,796	3.29	78.8	58.0	8.6	12.1	21.2	17.3	31.9
49049	Utah County	10.3	14.6	60.8	8.2	5.0	214,806	3.28	79.7	68.2	4.2	7.3	20.3	11.6	25.3
49053	Washington County	8.4	12.4	54.7	5.4	3.1	72,315	2.76	75.3	63.3	4.6	7.4	24.7	19.8	47.8
49057	Weber County	7.8	19.4	64.2	7.6	4.1	97,783	2.74	71.1	54.6	5.2	11.3	28.9	21.0	33.5
50000	**VERMONT**	5.8	2.5	46.5	4.5	1.5	279,612	2.23	59.3	47.3	4.4	7.6	40.7	31.3	46.7
50007	Chittenden County	6.2	2.9	41.6	8.2	2.2	73,216	2.16	57.0	46.3	4.1	6.5	43.0	27.1	35.6
51000	**VIRGINIA**	9.8	11.1	48.6	13.3	5.7	3,402,670	2.49	65.2	49.0	4.7	11.6	34.8	28.3	41.2
51003	Albemarle County	8.3	7.4	46.4	10.2	5.3	46,900	2.31	64.8	52.0	2.4	10.3	35.2	27.2	45.0
51013	Arlington County	13.0	16.0	23.6	20.7	9.5	114,097	2.03	43.9	37.6	1.9	4.4	56.1	41.7	25.5
51015	Augusta County	3.7	4.2	70.1	3.4	2.7	32,169	2.35	64.8	51.4	5.8	7.7	35.2	29.9	53.5
51019	Bedford County	6.1	3.0	62.0	2.9	1.9	33,205	2.44	71.0	59.1	3.2	8.7	29.0	25.4	52.1
51041	Chesterfield County	9.8	12.2	53.4	10.1	4.6	143,255	2.65	72.6	56.2	3.8	12.6	27.4	22.4	39.6
51059	Fairfax County	13.6	17.7	28.2	31.6	12.4	414,946	2.72	69.9	57.2	4.5	8.2	30.1	24.3	38.9
51061	Fauquier County	12.4	13.2	53.2	8.6	2.6	26,954	2.78	75.7	60.7	5.1	10.0	24.3	21.0	44.5
51069	Frederick County	7.0	13.1	52.2	8.5	4.1	35,341	2.68	68.2	56.4	5.6	6.2	31.8	25.3	47.1
51085	Hanover County	5.1	4.1	66.9	3.5	1.8	43,496	2.56	73.7	57.4	4.6	11.6	26.3	20.7	45.3
51087	Henrico County	5.7	7.0	55.5	15.8	8.1	137,529	2.40	64.3	45.9	5.0	13.4	35.7	29.5	39.6
51095	James City County	7.7	7.4	39.6	7.3	2.4	33,898	2.39	72.7	58.9	4.6	9.1	27.3	21.7	54.1
51107	Loudoun County	13.1	14.2	33.8	28.4	10.1	145,601	2.99	76.3	65.7	3.5	7.1	23.7	18.3	33.9
51121	Montgomery County	5.8	4.6	55.3	8.8	5.9	37,229	2.38	52.1	43.2	0.9	8.0	47.9	29.6	37.0
51153	Prince William County	16.0	26.3	37.2	26.3	11.3	158,620	3.06	75.4	57.5	5.3	12.6	24.6	19.3	36.9
51161	Roanoke County	6.2	4.3	62.4	8.3	3.3	40,176	2.36	70.1	54.8	5.2	10.1	29.9	25.6	46.0
51165	Rockingham County	6.6	9.6	69.4	5.6	2.8	32,827	2.58	69.2	56.0	3.6	9.7	30.8	26.8	47.2
51177	Spotsylvania County	12.0	14.0	47.0	10.6	4.2	55,487	2.69	71.3	56.0	5.8	9.5	28.7	21.9	41.1
51179	Stafford County	11.5	17.1	40.0	13.3	4.9	53,938	3.00	79.6	60.0	5.6	14.0	20.4	16.2	36.9
51199	York County	12.2	8.1	35.6	8.0	2.4	27,654	2.49	76.2	59.4	5.8	11.1	23.8	19.9	46.1
51510	Alexandria city	15.9	18.1	21.7	24.7	13.0	76,890	2.00	45.7	34.5	3.6	7.6	54.3	44.3	28.1
51550	Chesapeake city	10.0	7.9	53.9	6.0	1.8	94,056	2.65	73.4	53.4	3.9	16.1	26.6	21.0	41.5
51650	Hampton city	10.4	7.2	52.8	5.3	0.6	57,645	2.32	58.8	36.2	5.0	17.6	41.2	33.7	41.1
51680	Lynchburg city	6.2	5.1	52.6	4.5	2.2	28,916	2.37	56.4	39.2	6.1	11.0	43.6	33.1	36.0
51700	Newport News city	12.7	11.0	50.9	7.6	3.2	76,086	2.33	56.7	33.9	6.4	16.4	43.3	37.0	36.8
51710	Norfolk city	11.2	10.3	48.1	8.0	4.0	94,056	2.28	56.4	34.1	6.2	16.2	43.6	36.2	33.8
51740	Portsmouth city	9.8	5.8	66.4	3.5	1.8	40,661	2.33	60.8	36.3	5.4	19.1	39.2	31.9	38.1
51760	Richmond city	7.6	10.6	55.5	9.4	6.4	104,332	2.09	45.5	26.8	3.9	14.8	54.5	42.5	33.0
51770	Roanoke city	7.7	8.9	61.0	9.3	6.4	45,061	2.12	56.6	35.2	4.7	16.8	43.4	37.1	35.3
51800	Suffolk city	8.0	5.5	55.2	5.7	2.5	39,203	2.55	65.4	50.7	2.2	12.5	34.6	30.3	39.4
51810	Virginia Beach city	9.8	9.2	41.0	8.7	2.7	179,291	2.49	65.3	47.9	4.7	12.7	34.7	28.0	39.5
53000	**WASHINGTON**	13.1	14.6	46.1	15.5	7.9	3,101,265	2.47	63.0	48.7	4.8	9.5	37.0	28.0	39.8
53005	Benton County	17.6	26.4	53.7	9.9	5.2	78,748	2.70	67.1	51.3	4.0	11.8	32.9	26.5	39.4
53007	Chelan County	16.8	29.2	53.0	17.0	12.4	32,915	2.37	68.2	55.8	4.6	7.8	31.8	26.5	48.1
53009	Clallam County	10.2	7.0	44.1	4.1	1.4	34,807	2.18	61.1	47.9	4.9	8.2	38.9	31.8	62.2
53011	Clark County	11.2	12.6	34.6	10.0	4.1	202,217	2.56	65.3	51.7	5.2	8.4	34.7	25.6	41.8
53015	Cowlitz County	10.0	10.8	52.6	5.0	3.3	44,694	2.50	69.4	48.6	6.2	14.6	30.6	24.1	48.0
53021	Franklin County	28.9	55.6	56.6	18.0	12.2	30,733	3.12	77.0	52.8	8.8	15.4	23.0	18.9	32.8
53025	Grant County	26.0	44.2	57.2	16.2	12.7	34,911	2.82	68.5	45.5	7.7	15.3	31.5	25.1	40.6
53027	Grays Harbor County	6.9	11.4	63.9	6.3	4.6	30,498	2.46	54.2	36.6	4.4	13.2	45.8	34.4	52.8
53029	Island County	13.8	8.9	35.7	8.3	2.3	35,431	2.39	71.0	57.3	5.3	8.5	29.0	23.2	55.9
53033	King County	12.2	11.1	38.7	25.8	13.1	949,792	2.35	57.4	46.2	3.7	7.5	42.6	32.0	32.5
53035	Kitsap County	13.3	9.6	42.3	6.6	2.6	109,652	2.47	68.4	53.3	5.3	9.9	31.6	24.4	44.4
53041	Lewis County	10.0	11.7	59.4	5.7	3.6	33,672	2.54	63.7	47.6	7.2	9.0	36.3	30.0	51.7
53045	Mason County	9.3	13.2	53.7	9.0	6.5	25,161	2.64	66.6	54.6	4.6	7.4	33.4	29.0	60.5
53053	Pierce County	16.4	13.1	49.8	11.1	4.9	356,066	2.54	65.2	47.9	6.3	11.0	34.8	25.5	37.8

Table A-2. Counties — Who: Age, Race/Ethnicity, and Household Structure, 2023—*Continued*

				Population by age (percent)							Race alone or in combination (percent)					
	STATE County	Total population	Percent change, 2010–2023	Under 18 years	18 to 24 years	25 to 44 years	45 to 64 years	65 years and over	Median age	White	Black or African American	American Indian and Alaska Native	Asian	Native Hawaiian or Other Pacific Islander	Some other race
STATE County code	ACS table number:	B01003	Census PEP	B01001	B01001	B01001	B01001	B01001	B01002	B02008	B02009	B02010	B02011	B02012	B02013
	Column number:	1	2	3	4	5	6	7	8	9	10	11	12	13	14
	WASHINGTON—Cont.														
53057	Skagit County	131,417	12.2	20.6	6.9	25.7	23.2	23.7	42.8	81.7	1.6	3.6	3.8	0.9	19.3
53061	Snohomish County	844,761	18.1	21.8	7.2	30.8	24.9	15.3	38.5	73.8	5.7	3.1	17.4	1.3	10.4
53063	Spokane County	551,455	16.8	21.3	9.0	28.4	23.5	17.8	38.7	90.5	4.1	3.5	4.2	1.0	6.6
53067	Thurston County	299,003	18.1	20.5	7.1	29.5	23.5	19.3	40.3	83.1	6.1	3.7	9.6	1.6	9.4
53073	Whatcom County	231,919	15.0	18.2	12.8	27.0	22.8	19.2	38.5	86.0	2.6	3.7	7.0	0.7	9.6
53077	Yakima County	256,643	5.0	28.5	9.5	26.2	20.9	14.9	33.8	72.2	1.8	6.0	2.3	0.3	45.5
54000	**WEST VIRGINIA**	1,770,071	-4.5	19.9	9.0	23.7	25.9	21.5	42.8	94.9	4.7	1.6	1.1	0.1	2.8
54003	Berkeley County	132,440	26.6	23.0	7.5	28.3	25.8	15.3	38.4	86.5	11.0	0.9	1.9	NA	6.9
54011	Cabell County	92,082	-4.5	19.6	14.0	22.6	23.4	20.3	39.5	93.7	6.6	0.8	1.9	NA	1.6
54033	Harrison County	64,639	-6.6	20.6	7.2	25.5	26.1	20.5	43.1	96.2	3.0	0.9	1.0	NA	3.1
54039	Kanawha County	174,805	-9.4	19.8	7.8	23.3	26.2	22.9	44.2	93.7	7.7	2.9	1.6	NA	1.7
54061	Monongalia County	107,718	11.3	15.8	22.9	27.3	20.2	13.7	32.6	91.6	5.2	0.6	4.3	NA	3.0
54081	Raleigh County	72,356	-8.3	21.2	7.6	24.4	24.4	22.3	42.4	92.0	8.3	1.8	1.4	NA	0.8
54107	Wood County	83,052	-4.5	21.2	6.9	23.3	26.5	22.1	43.8	98.4	1.0	2.3	1.0	NA	2.4
55000	**WISCONSIN**	5,910,955	3.9	21.0	9.3	25.3	25.2	19.2	40.5	87.2	7.7	2.1	3.8	0.2	7.2
55009	Brown County	271,417	9.2	22.7	9.7	26.0	24.5	17.2	38.5	86.9	4.6	4.9	4.2	0.2	8.3
55017	Chippewa County	66,970	7.3	21.1	6.6	26.0	25.9	20.4	42.3	96.0	1.3	1.4	3.1	NA	2.0
55025	Dane County	575,347	17.6	19.4	13.8	29.5	22.0	15.4	35.9	84.5	7.6	1.3	7.6	0.1	7.4
55027	Dodge County	88,231	-0.6	19.1	7.9	25.9	27.6	19.5	43.2	94.7	3.5	1.4	1.1	NA	5.5
55035	Eau Claire County	107,903	9.1	19.7	15.7	26.3	21.0	17.2	35.7	93.0	2.6	1.6	4.9	NA	2.7
55039	Fond du Lac County	103,948	2.2	20.1	10.1	23.8	25.0	21.0	41.6	93.0	3.7	1.3	2.7	NA	5.6
55055	Jefferson County	85,743	2.4	19.6	10.0	25.0	26.2	19.2	40.8	95.1	1.5	1.7	1.5	NA	7.0
55059	Kenosha County	167,488	0.5	21.3	9.6	26.2	26.1	16.9	39.5	86.4	9.5	1.4	2.7	NA	14.4
55063	La Crosse County	120,486	4.9	19.2	15.5	24.2	22.7	18.4	38.3	92.1	2.8	0.7	5.4	NA	2.4
55071	Manitowoc County	81,331	-0.0	20.0	6.4	22.9	27.6	23.2	45.9	94.9	2.0	1.2	3.1	NA	5.8
55073	Marathon County	138,612	3.4	22.3	7.1	24.8	26.1	19.6	41.4	91.3	1.8	1.4	7.0	0.3	3.8
55079	Milwaukee County	916,205	-3.5	23.5	9.4	29.6	22.3	15.2	35.7	62.5	28.6	2.1	6.1	0.2	14.7
55087	Outagamie County	193,234	9.2	22.7	8.1	27.0	24.8	17.5	39.8	90.7	3.5	2.5	4.5	NA	4.8
55089	Ozaukee County	93,460	8.2	20.6	9.3	21.3	26.5	22.3	44.3	94.7	2.5	0.9	3.6	NA	3.5
55097	Portage County	71,024	1.4	18.8	15.4	24.1	23.1	18.6	37.9	94.3	1.8	1.0	3.7	NA	4.6
55101	Racine County	196,613	0.6	22.3	8.3	24.7	26.0	18.6	40.6	84.7	13.4	2.1	2.1	NA	11.9
55105	Rock County	164,278	2.5	21.8	8.2	25.2	26.1	18.8	40.1	89.6	6.6	2.3	1.9	NA	9.0
55109	St. Croix County	96,763	14.6	23.3	7.5	25.4	27.2	16.5	40.9	96.3	2.3	1.0	2.0	0.3	3.7
55111	Sauk County	65,920	6.4	21.9	7.1	24.0	26.6	20.4	42.2	93.5	1.8	1.8	1.1	NA	10.0
55117	Sheboygan County	117,752	2.0	21.0	7.6	24.0	27.0	20.3	42.6	89.3	3.6	1.1	6.7	NA	7.5
55127	Walworth County	105,822	3.5	19.2	12.5	21.5	26.1	20.7	41.8	93.3	2.0	1.4	1.5	NA	10.0
55131	Washington County	138,168	4.7	20.8	6.9	23.2	28.3	20.9	44.1	94.8	2.4	0.6	2.3	NA	3.3
55133	Waukesha County	412,591	5.8	20.7	7.4	23.6	27.3	20.9	43.5	92.5	2.8	0.7	4.9	NA	5.1
55139	Winnebago County	171,735	2.8	20.0	11.4	25.7	24.8	18.1	38.9	92.3	4.6	1.9	4.0	NA	2.9
55141	Wood County	73,939	-1.1	21.7	7.0	22.9	25.9	22.4	43.7	96.9	1.7	1.1	1.7	0.7	3.8
56000	**WYOMING**	584,057	3.5	22.3	8.6	27.1	22.8	19.2	39.3	92.5	1.6	4.5	1.7	0.2	8.5
56021	Laramie County	100,984	9.6	22.3	8.6	28.3	22.4	18.5	38.3	89.7	3.4	4.5	2.6	0.6	11.3
56025	Natrona County	79,941	5.9	23.0	7.9	28.0	23.7	17.3	39.0	95.2	2.3	2.9	1.0	NA	6.3
72000	**PUERTO RICO**	3,205,691	-13.9	15.6	9.4	25.1	26.0	24.0	45.0	57.4	12.1	2.4	0.3	0.0	69.7
72013	Arecibo Municipio	85,641	-11.1	15.4	8.8	24.6	26.8	24.4	45.7	75.6	3.2	NA	NA	NA	83.5
72021	Bayamón Municipio	180,835	-13.0	14.9	8.9	26.5	24.7	25.0	44.8	41.6	6.7	1.0	0.5	NA	85.3
72025	Caguas Municipio	124,608	-12.7	15.3	8.9	26.2	26.5	23.1	44.8	61.1	11.8	1.8	0.4	NA	64.8
72031	Carolina Municipio	150,843	-14.6	15.0	8.8	25.3	25.7	25.2	45.7	50.5	21.0	1.4	0.4	NA	71.3
72061	Guaynabo Municipio	89,039	-9.0	13.4	8.0	25.7	26.4	26.5	47.1	43.3	5.9	NA	NA	NA	74.9
72097	Mayagüez Municipio	69,798	-21.6	15.2	15.7	21.0	21.0	27.0	44.0	24.0	5.2	NA	NA	NA	83.9
72113	Ponce Municipio	130,251	-21.6	16.6	9.1	24.2	24.0	26.0	45.0	76.5	11.2	0.9	NA	NA	71.0
72127	San Juan Municipio	333,005	-15.7	14.8	8.9	24.8	25.3	26.2	46.1	58.8	14.9	1.3	0.2	NA	71.2
72135	Toa Alta Municipio	65,957	-10.8	15.8	9.4	28.6	28.4	17.8	42.6	73.1	8.4	NA	NA	NA	90.5
72137	Toa Baja Municipio	71,888	-19.7	15.5	9.1	26.9	25.7	22.9	44.3	37.9	9.4	0.5	0.3	NA	86.9
72139	Trujillo Alto Municipio	66,705	-10.8	15.1	10.2	25.4	26.5	22.7	44.4	63.6	27.1	6.9	NA	NA	80.2

Table A-2. Counties — Who: Age, Race/Ethnicity, and Household Structure, 2023—*Continued*

STATE County code	STATE County	Two or more races (percent)	Hispanic or Latino (percent)	Native, born in state of residence (percent)	Foreign born (percent)	Non-citizens (percent)	Total households	Average household size	Household type (percent of all households)							Percent of households with people age 60 years and over
									Family households				Nonfamily households			
									Total	Married couple	Male householder	Female householder	Total	One-person households		
	ACS table number:	B02001	B03003	B05002	B05002	B05002	B11001	B25010	B11001	B11001	B11001	B11001	B11001	B11001		B11006
	Column number:	15	16	17	18	19	20	21	22	23	24	25	26	27		28
	WASHINGTON—Cont.															
53057	Skagit County	10.5	19.7	54.3	10.2	5.6	53,087	2.44	68.9	54.3	5.2	9.4	31.1	23.7		50.8
53061	Snohomish County	10.7	12.3	48.6	20.4	10.5	321,835	2.60	68.4	53.0	5.7	9.7	31.6	23.8		38.7
53063	Spokane County	8.8	7.3	53.2	6.1	2.4	219,230	2.45	61.0	46.6	4.5	9.9	39.0	30.1		41.9
53067	Thurston County	12.4	11.0	46.4	8.4	2.9	119,786	2.46	65.3	50.6	3.4	11.4	34.7	25.6		43.1
53073	Whatcom County	9.2	10.8	51.1	9.3	3.6	93,449	2.43	57.4	46.8	4.0	6.6	42.6	31.2		42.9
53077	Yakima County	27.3	53.0	62.0	17.9	12.6	89,414	2.82	70.6	44.4	8.8	17.4	29.4	24.1		40.7
54000	**WEST VIRGINIA**	5.0	2.1	67.2	1.8	0.9	743,644	2.31	61.5	45.3	5.2	11.0	38.5	32.1		46.7
54003	Berkeley County	7.1	6.7	36.7	4.6	2.0	51,094	2.57	66.4	45.4	5.2	15.8	33.6	22.6		38.7
54011	Cabell County	4.7	1.8	73.8	1.9	0.8	39,720	2.19	56.4	41.3	4.4	10.6	43.6	34.4		41.7
54033	Harrison County	3.8	2.3	80.5	1.3	0.4	27,161	2.35	62.8	45.8	7.2	9.8	37.2	33.8		46.6
54039	Kanawha County	7.0	1.6	81.1	1.7	0.3	76,963	2.23	54.5	37.8	5.0	11.7	45.5	37.6		48.6
54061	Monongalia County	4.5	3.2	60.6	5.0	2.7	44,307	2.30	47.6	36.5	3.0	8.1	52.4	39.3		32.1
54081	Raleigh County	NA	1.8	75.2	1.0	0.6	28,275	2.43	67.1	47.5	6.1	13.5	32.9	29.3		48.4
54107	Wood County	5.1	1.5	71.9	0.7	0.1	36,936	2.22	60.4	45.3	3.6	11.4	39.6	34.3		47.5
55000	**WISCONSIN**	7.6	8.1	70.1	5.2	2.7	2,495,539	2.31	60.2	46.9	4.5	8.8	39.8	31.6		41.8
55009	Brown County	7.9	10.5	76.2	6.1	2.9	112,027	2.36	60.9	47.1	4.3	9.4	39.1	30.4		38.6
55017	Chippewa County	3.8	2.0	80.2	1.7	0.3	27,846	2.29	65.4	51.3	2.9	11.3	34.6	24.5		42.6
55025	Dane County	8.1	7.8	58.7	9.1	5.9	257,528	2.17	51.5	42.2	2.9	6.4	48.5	36.2		31.2
55027	Dodge County	5.8	6.9	82.0	1.9	0.8	35,795	2.32	63.7	48.8	5.8	9.1	36.3	29.8		46.5
55035	Eau Claire County	5.0	3.2	72.5	1.8	0.9	44,769	2.31	57.1	41.7	4.7	10.7	42.9	32.2		37.3
55039	Fond du Lac County	6.0	7.0	79.7	3.4	1.2	44,262	2.27	60.2	48.8	4.7	6.6	39.8	29.8		42.2
55055	Jefferson County	6.4	8.5	76.3	3.5	2.4	34,914	2.36	65.8	51.4	5.8	8.6	34.2	25.9		45.3
55059	Kenosha County	13.5	15.4	48.4	7.7	3.4	69,907	2.34	61.3	44.6	5.4	11.2	38.7	31.6		41.8
55063	La Crosse County	3.4	2.8	70.2	3.2	1.0	51,283	2.26	55.7	44.1	3.3	8.3	44.3	32.3		36.1
55071	Manitowoc County	6.8	5.7	81.6	3.4	2.1	35,669	2.24	60.2	49.5	5.2	5.6	39.8	34.0		49.7
55073	Marathon County	5.0	3.6	79.2	4.3	2.3	58,104	2.36	61.4	49.7	4.8	6.9	38.6	30.9		43.2
55079	Milwaukee County	13.4	17.2	66.7	10.1	5.6	388,165	2.31	53.6	33.8	5.3	14.5	46.4	36.8		35.6
55087	Outagamie County	6.1	5.4	76.4	4.6	1.9	78,027	2.44	66.0	54.5	4.2	7.3	34.0	26.6		38.6
55089	Ozaukee County	4.8	3.9	70.4	5.6	1.0	38,030	2.41	66.2	56.1	4.4	5.8	33.8	29.5		47.1
55097	Portage County	5.4	4.3	77.8	3.3	1.5	30,620	2.22	60.3	47.9	5.3	7.2	39.7	29.7		40.0
55101	Racine County	13.1	15.4	72.5	4.1	2.1	79,066	2.43	62.2	45.4	4.3	12.4	37.8	30.2		42.3
55105	Rock County	9.2	10.3	69.9	4.5	2.2	66,220	2.44	64.5	47.1	5.4	12.0	35.5	28.9		44.1
55109	St. Croix County	5.2	3.1	42.9	2.1	1.0	38,606	2.48	73.8	61.6	4.0	8.2	26.2	23.0		38.5
55111	Sauk County	8.2	6.9	75.7	3.0	1.6	28,295	2.30	62.2	51.6	3.4	7.2	37.8	27.9		41.8
55117	Sheboygan County	7.8	7.9	75.5	5.2	1.8	49,852	2.30	63.1	48.6	5.1	9.4	36.9	29.7		43.0
55127	Walworth County	8.0	12.1	56.0	5.9	3.1	43,005	2.39	64.6	50.9	5.1	8.6	35.4	27.5		46.2
55131	Washington County	3.4	3.9	82.0	3.7	1.7	56,641	2.42	68.3	56.9	6.1	5.2	31.7	25.7		44.9
55133	Waukesha County	5.8	5.9	74.0	5.4	2.6	168,150	2.43	65.6	56.0	3.3	6.3	34.4	28.0		46.1
55139	Winnebago County	5.6	5.2	78.4	3.2	1.6	71,563	2.32	56.2	44.6	3.8	7.8	43.8	35.4		41.5
55141	Wood County	5.7	3.9	81.0	3.1	1.3	32,099	2.27	57.9	47.8	1.8	8.3	42.1	32.4		47.3
56000	**WYOMING**	8.3	10.8	41.9	3.6	2.0	247,368	2.30	62.4	49.2	4.6	8.6	37.6	30.9		42.9
56021	Laramie County	10.7	15.9	40.1	3.1	1.2	44,460	2.24	62.8	47.6	5.6	9.7	37.2	32.4		41.8
56025	Natrona County	7.4	9.6	46.7	3.3	1.6	34,332	2.29	64.1	50.9	4.7	8.5	35.9	29.2		41.2
72000	**PUERTO RICO**	38.6	99.0	0.0	2.6	1.3	1,277,486	2.48	62.5	34.0	6.0	22.4	37.5	32.4		52.6
72013	Arecibo Municipio	62.4	98.8	NA	NA	NA	33,466	2.49	62.8	32.9	6.6	23.3	37.2	34.0		53.9
72021	Bayamón Municipio	33.8	98.9	0.0	2.6	1.1	76,203	2.31	61.4	31.2	5.5	24.6	38.6	33.1		51.0
72025	Caguas Municipio	39.3	98.9	0.0	1.9	0.9	51,579	2.40	68.3	32.8	6.8	28.7	31.7	29.0		48.5
72031	Carolina Municipio	42.5	99.0	0.0	5.8	2.3	63,447	2.37	60.3	33.6	3.6	23.1	39.7	33.7		55.0
72061	Guaynabo Municipio	23.8	97.0	0.0	7.2	4.2	34,184	2.56	60.8	42.2	3.8	14.7	39.2	32.1		53.8
72097	Mayagüez Municipio	13.9	98.4	0.0	2.2	1.1	31,111	2.19	53.3	30.2	4.7	18.4	46.7	37.8		49.9
72113	Ponce Municipio	58.8	99.2	0.0	0.8	0.6	56,772	2.22	60.7	28.9	7.8	24.0	39.3	36.1		52.4
72127	San Juan Municipio	45.3	98.1	0.0	10.3	5.1	150,969	2.16	48.3	24.3	4.5	19.4	51.7	46.4		52.0
72135	Toa Alta Municipio	NA	99.6	NA	NA	NA	24,486	2.67	73.9	41.2	6.6	26.1	26.1	19.8		45.0
72137	Toa Baja Municipio	33.6	99.3	0.0	2.8	1.4	30,304	2.36	65.2	30.2	5.1	29.9	34.8	30.4		52.0
72139	Trujillo Alto Municipio	61.6	99.4	NA	NA	NA	27,299	2.41	70.6	46.2	5.1	19.2	29.4	23.6		49.5

NA = Not available.
X= Not applicable.
- = Indicates that either no sample observations or too few sample observations were available to compute an estimate, or a ratio of medians cannot be calculated because one or both of the median estimates falls in the lowest interval or upper interval of an open-ended distribution, or the margin of error associated with a median was larger than the median itself.

Table A-3. Metropolitan Areas — Who: Age, Race/Ethnicity, and Household Structure, 2023

Metropolitan area / division code	Metropolitan area / division	Total population	Percent change, 2010–2023	Population by age (percent): Under 18 years	18 to 24 years	25 to 44 years	45 to 64 years	65 years and over	Median age	Race alone or in combination (percent): White	Black or African American	Asian + Native Hawaiian or Other Pacific Islander	American Indian and Alaska Native + Some other race	Two or more races
	ACS table number:	B01003	Population Estimates	B01001	B01001	B01001	B01001	B01001	B01002	B02008	B02009	B02011 + B02012	B02010 + B02013	B02001
	column number:	1	2	3	4	5	6	7	8	9	10	11	12	13
10180	Abilene, TX	180,224	9.3	22.7	13.2	26.8	20.5	16.8	35.9	83.5	9.0	4.1	20.6	16.5
10380	Aguadilla, PR	250,435	-18.2	15.8	9.2	24.2	26.6	24.3	45.6	66.7	20.7	0.1	60.3	27.7
10420	Akron, OH	698,398	-0.6	19.8	9.8	25.3	25.4	19.6	40.8	82.7	14.9	4.9	4.2	6.1
10500	Albany, GA	147,062	-9.6	24.0	9.2	25.0	24.4	17.5	38.3	43.5	54.0	1.6	5.1	4.0
10540	Albany, OR	131,496	11.3	22.0	7.1	26.8	24.4	19.7	40.4	94.1	1.6	2.5	13.6	10.9
10580	Albany-Schenectady-Troy, NY	904,682	3.9	18.9	10.9	25.7	25.2	19.4	41.0	83.2	10.6	6.1	9.0	8.3
10740	Albuquerque, NM	923,518	3.5	20.3	8.8	27.4	24.4	19.1	40.0	74.8	4.5	4.2	44.2	26.3
10780	Alexandria, LA	148,171	-3.9	24.0	8.2	26.6	24.2	17.0	38.5	66.9	30.6	2.1	6.6	5.3
10900	Allentown-Bethlehem-Easton, PA-NJ	873,555	6.3	20.3	9.2	24.8	25.9	19.8	41.7	79.7	8.2	3.9	20.9	11.8
11020	Altoona, PA	120,273	-5.3	19.8	8.1	23.6	26.2	22.3	43.7	96.1	4.2	1.2	4.7	6.0
11100	Amarillo, TX	273,100	8.4	24.2	10.5	26.5	23.6	15.3	36.3	83.6	7.7	3.9	21.9	16.9
11180	Ames, IA	125,156	39.7	17.3	24.3	24.9	18.4	15.0	30.5	90.0	3.6	6.8	4.6	4.8
11200	Amherst Town-Northampton, MA	162,502	NA	13.1	25.1	20.1	22.0	19.7	36.8	88.4	4.4	6.9	8.9	7.8
11260	Anchorage, AK	401,314	4.8	23.9	8.9	31.0	22.7	13.5	36.3	75.1	6.6	13.9	20.3	14.3
11460	Ann Arbor, MI	365,536	5.9	17.9	17.3	25.9	22.5	16.4	35.5	77.9	14.2	10.9	7.0	9.3
11500	Anniston-Oxford, AL	116,429	-1.8	21.1	11.6	23.4	24.9	19.1	40.5	74.9	23.9	1.2	4.1	3.9
11540	Appleton, WI	246,433	9.1	22.3	8.0	26.5	25.5	17.8	40.3	91.5	3.1	4.4	7.3	6.1
11640	Arecibo, PR	179,470	NA	14.4	10.5	23.9	27.3	24.0	46.1	71.8	3.1	0.0	60.8	35.0
11700	Asheville, NC	417,202	-1.3	17.7	7.5	26.0	25.3	23.4	43.9	91.6	5.9	1.9	11.3	10.1
12020	Athens-Clarke County, GA	219,870	14.1	19.3	18.6	26.4	20.6	15.1	32.8	72.1	20.7	4.8	9.5	6.8
12060	Atlanta-Sandy Springs-Roswell, GA	6,305,839	19.2	23.2	9.2	28.1	25.6	13.9	37.6	52.2	36.5	8.1	13.5	9.6
1206012054	Atlanta-Sandy Springs-Roswell, GA Metro Division	4,910,474	NA	23.4	9.3	28.2	22.5	10.5	37.3	47.7	40.3	8.9	13.2	9.5
1206031924	Marietta, GA Metro Division	1,395,365	NA	22.8	8.8	27.8	23.1	11.2	38.4	67.9	23.0	5.2	14.7	10.1
12100	Atlantic City-Hammonton, NJ	369,823	34.6	19.5	8.4	21.9	27.1	23.1	45.1	72.0	14.3	7.1	17.1	9.8
12220	Auburn-Opelika, AL	202,676	44.0	20.6	17.8	24.9	22.5	14.2	33.9	66.0	28.6	4.3	5.5	4.1
12260	Augusta-Richmond County, GA-SC	628,186	12.1	22.5	9.3	26.7	24.0	17.5	38.5	58.9	36.8	3.4	7.4	6.1
12420	Austin-Round Rock-San Marcos, TX	2,473,275	43.1	21.4	9.3	33.8	23.1	12.3	36.3	75.6	9.1	9.9	26.9	20.3
12540	Bakersfield-Delano, CA	913,820	8.5	28.4	9.8	28.7	20.9	12.2	32.7	64.7	6.8	7.1	48.5	25.9
12580	Baltimore-Columbia-Towson, MD	2,834,316	4.4	22.0	8.3	27.5	24.9	17.3	39.4	59.4	31.4	7.8	9.3	7.2
12620	Bangor, ME	155,312	1.0	17.2	10.5	25.6	26.0	20.8	42.7	95.8	1.7	2.2	4.4	4.1
12700	Barnstable Town, MA	231,735	7.3	13.6	6.3	18.6	27.2	34.3	56.3	93.2	4.6	2.2	8.2	7.1
12940	Baton Rouge, LA	873,661	8.6	23.2	11.2	27.4	22.4	15.8	36.8	60.0	35.2	3.0	9.4	6.9
12980	Battle Creek, MI	133,366	-2.0	22.8	8.4	24.8	25.1	19.0	40.3	83.8	13.9	4.1	8.4	9.8
13020	Bay City, MI	102,500	-4.8	19.3	7.3	24.0	26.5	22.8	44.4	96.9	3.6	0.5	4.1	4.9
13140	Beaumont-Port Arthur, TX	395,479	1.6	24.8	8.4	26.5	23.8	16.5	38.1	62.6	24.9	3.7	18.6	9.2
13220	Beckley, WV	111,428	40.8	21.1	8.3	22.5	25.6	22.5	43.1	93.0	7.4	1.0	2.8	4.0
13380	Bellingham, WA	231,919	15.0	18.2	12.8	27.0	22.8	19.2	38.5	86.0	2.6	7.7	13.3	9.2
13460	Bend, OR	260,919	65.2	19.3	6.8	26.6	26.2	21.1	42.8	92.7	1.1	3.4	11.9	8.3
13740	Billings, MT	191,435	21.7	22.3	7.6	26.9	23.4	19.8	40.1	93.5	1.7	2.4	11.1	8.0
13780	Binghamton, NY	243,792	-3.0	19.1	12.9	23.1	23.9	21.0	39.7	88.6	7.1	5.5	5.8	6.4
13820	Birmingham, AL	1,184,290	4.9	22.6	8.7	26.4	24.7	17.6	39.4	66.9	29.6	2.6	6.5	5.4
13900	Bismarck, ND	135,589	24.1	23.0	8.1	28.2	22.3	18.4	38.9	92.5	1.8	1.4	10.1	5.9
13980	Blacksburg-Christiansburg-Radford, VA	180,890	11.8	16.2	21.0	22.6	22.7	17.4	35.5	91.0	5.2	4.8	4.1	5.0
14010	Bloomington, IL	170,441	0.4	20.9	16.9	24.9	22.8	14.5	35.0	83.9	10.6	6.3	6.7	6.9
14020	Bloomington, IN	160,874	-16.5	16.0	22.4	24.7	20.2	16.7	33.6	88.9	4.9	7.2	4.9	5.7
14260	Boise City, ID	826,521	33.4	22.9	9.1	27.6	23.8	16.6	38.0	89.9	1.9	4.3	15.1	10.4
14460	Boston-Cambridge-Newton, MA-NH	4,919,179	7.9	19.1	9.7	28.1	25.5	17.6	39.7	75.4	10.5	10.5	15.2	10.3
1446014454	Boston, MA Metro Division	2,031,206	NA	18.6	10.4	29.1	21.3	13.1	38.6	71.0	16.3	10.1	15.5	11.2
1446015764	Cambridge-Newton-Framingham, MA Metro Division	2,434,041	NA	19.8	9.3	27.7	22.2	13.4	39.9	75.4	7.2	12.1	16.7	10.4
1446040484	Rockingham County-Strafford County, NH Metro Division	453,932	NA	18.0	8.9	25.2	23.8	15.0	43.4	95.7	1.9	3.8	5.8	6.1
14500	Boulder, CO	326,831	10.7	17.0	15.5	26.0	24.4	17.0	38.2	91.1	2.0	6.9	14.0	13.5
14540	Bowling Green, KY	192,191	51.0	22.7	12.9	26.5	22.8	15.1	35.2	86.7	9.1	4.8	6.9	7.3
14580	Bozeman, MT	126,409	NA	18.3	15.1	31.5	21.1	14.0	34.6	93.7	0.7	2.7	8.7	5.9
14740	Bremerton-Silverdale-Port Orchard, WA	277,658	10.3	19.2	8.6	27.9	23.9	20.4	40.4	88.0	4.7	11.2	11.4	13.3
14860	Bridgeport-Stamford-Danbury, CT	951,558	3.6	21.6	8.8	24.6	27.4	17.5	41.2	69.2	13.8	6.7	22.7	11.9
15180	Brownsville-Harlingen, TX	426,710	4.6	28.0	10.9	24.7	21.9	14.4	33.4	87.0	0.7	1.2	66.6	55.1
15260	Brunswick-St. Simons, GA	115,087	6.7	20.5	7.1	23.7	25.6	23.1	44.0	75.2	22.5	1.7	10.1	8.9
15380	Buffalo-Cheektowaga, NY	1,155,604	1.8	20.0	8.6	26.1	25.2	20.1	41.2	81.1	13.8	5.3	6.8	6.5

Table A-3. Metropolitan Areas — Who: Age, Race/Ethnicity, and Household Structure, 2023—*Continued*

Metropolitan area / division code	Metropolitan area / division	Hispanic or Latino (percent)	Born in state of residence (percent)	Foreign born (percent)	Not a U.S. citizen (percent)	Total households	Average household size	Household type (percent of all households): Family households: Total	Family households: Married-couple	Family households: Male householder	Family households: Female householder	Nonfamily households: Total	Nonfamily households: One-person households	Percent of households with people age 60 years and over
	ACS table number:	B03003	B05002	B05002	B05002	B11001	B25010	B11001	B11001	B11001	B11001	B11001	B11001	B11006
	column number:	14	15	16	17	18	19	20	21	22	23	24	25	26
10180	Abilene, TX	24.8	68.2	5.6	2.0	66,460	2.53	66.3	48.1	5.3	12.9	33.7	27.4	37.8
10380	Aguadilla, PR	98.5	0.0	1.3	0.6	89,374	2.77	65.1	41.5	4.5	19.2	34.9	31.2	55.7
10420	Akron, OH	2.7	76.2	6.0	2.9	298,193	2.29	59.3	43.5	4.5	11.3	40.7	32.6	43.2
10500	Albany, GA	3.3	73.6	2.7	1.3	59,228	2.39	66.6	35.3	5.4	25.9	33.4	28.0	40.6
10540	Albany, OR	11.0	57.1	4.5	2.2	51,636	2.52	63.8	50.0	3.9	9.9	36.2	26.8	46.6
10580	Albany-Schenectady-Troy, NY	6.3	74.6	8.5	3.7	386,690	2.25	57.4	41.6	4.2	11.6	42.6	32.6	42.9
10740	Albuquerque, NM	48.6	52.6	9.4	5.0	381,326	2.38	59.7	39.9	6.5	13.3	40.3	32.5	44.0
10780	Alexandria, LA	4.6	77.3	3.9	2.2	58,235	2.42	64.3	39.5	6.1	18.7	35.7	32.1	42.4
10900	Allentown-Bethlehem-Easton, PA-NJ	20.5	60.4	11.5	4.8	345,257	2.45	67.1	48.2	5.7	13.2	32.9	26.0	45.6
11020	Altoona, PA	0.9	85.8	2.1	0.8	50,651	2.28	58.3	43.0	5.0	10.2	41.7	34.7	49.3
11100	Amarillo, TX	31.0	70.0	8.2	4.0	102,739	2.57	62.6	45.9	5.1	11.5	37.4	32.1	37.7
11180	Ames, IA	4.4	63.9	6.2	4.0	49,962	2.26	53.8	44.2	3.6	6.0	46.2	27.8	33.6
11200	Amherst Town-Northampton, MA	7.5	62.6	7.8	3.3	61,802	2.26	55.4	42.1	2.6	10.7	44.6	33.0	47.4
11260	Anchorage, AK	8.4	41.3	8.3	3.1	148,995	2.62	61.9	48.2	4.8	8.9	38.1	29.4	35.8
11460	Ann Arbor, MI	5.8	58.5	13.8	7.3	149,379	2.33	56.3	43.9	3.7	8.8	43.7	32.5	36.6
11500	Anniston-Oxford, AL	4.8	68.2	2.3	1.2	46,310	2.41	63.6	44.4	3.8	15.5	36.4	32.0	43.2
11540	Appleton, WI	5.5	77.4	4.4	1.8	99,606	2.44	65.9	55.3	4.0	6.7	34.1	27.0	39.4
11640	Arecibo, PR	99.0	0.0	0.5	0.1	65,668	2.68	68.4	38.8	5.0	24.6	31.6	28.7	55.5
11700	Asheville, NC	9.4	47.6	6.9	4.1	164,757	2.47	61.4	47.8	5.0	8.6	38.6	30.4	47.6
12020	Athens-Clarke County, GA	9.8	61.4	7.6	5.2	87,635	2.38	58.3	41.5	5.2	11.6	41.7	25.7	33.9
12060	Atlanta-Sandy Springs-Roswell, GA	12.5	46.3	15.8	7.7	2,341,283	2.66	65.8	47.4	4.7	13.6	34.2	27.2	36.6
1206012054	Atlanta-Sandy Springs-Roswell, GA Metro Division	12.3	46.4	16.7	8.1	1,823,623	2.65	64.5	45.6	4.8	14.1	35.5	28.4	36.5
1206031924	Marietta, GA Metro Division	13.2	45.9	12.6	6.4	517,660	2.67	70.1	53.8	4.5	11.9	29.9	23.2	37.2
12100	Atlantic City-Hammonton, NJ	17.4	54.3	13.8	6.0	158,674	2.28	65.3	48.8	5.7	10.8	34.7	27.9	51.7
12220	Auburn-Opelika, AL	5.3	55.3	6.3	4.2	81,935	2.36	55.5	40.9	3.5	11.0	44.5	35.7	35.4
12260	Augusta-Richmond County, GA-SC	6.7	50.1	4.7	2.3	236,371	2.60	67.0	45.3	4.8	16.9	33.0	27.7	42.4
12420	Austin-Round Rock-San Marcos, TX	32.2	50.9	16.0	8.8	1,036,074	2.34	58.5	45.5	4.6	8.5	41.5	30.4	29.3
12540	Bakersfield-Delano, CA	57.1	69.2	19.5	11.5	289,845	3.09	72.4	45.3	8.8	18.3	27.6	21.7	37.5
12580	Baltimore-Columbia-Towson, MD	8.3	58.3	12.2	4.9	1,127,320	2.46	61.9	43.7	4.9	13.3	38.1	31.0	41.5
12620	Bangor, ME	2.2	66.4	3.9	2.1	66,556	2.22	57.4	45.1	4.8	7.5	42.6	30.6	46.4
12700	Barnstable Town, MA	3.8	57.7	10.0	5.5	109,475	2.09	63.9	52.4	3.2	8.4	36.1	30.4	63.7
12940	Baton Rouge, LA	6.4	78.0	5.8	3.9	334,402	2.53	62.7	43.5	4.7	14.4	37.3	31.2	38.6
12980	Battle Creek, MI	6.1	76.1	3.9	2.1	54,568	2.38	58.7	40.4	3.6	14.6	41.3	34.7	44.8
13020	Bay City, MI	6.0	89.5	1.6	0.9	44,417	2.28	58.2	42.7	3.0	12.4	41.8	34.7	49.5
13140	Beaumont-Port Arthur, TX	18.9	70.0	9.5	5.8	150,294	2.53	67.9	48.0	5.8	14.1	32.1	27.8	40.4
13220	Beckley, WV	1.6	77.2	0.9	0.4	44,847	2.39	64.2	47.1	4.8	12.2	35.8	32.2	47.7
13380	Bellingham, WA	10.8	51.1	9.3	3.6	93,449	2.43	57.4	46.8	4.0	6.6	42.6	31.2	42.9
13460	Bend, OR	11.4	40.6	4.8	2.7	107,729	2.40	67.4	52.7	4.2	10.5	32.6	22.4	46.1
13740	Billings, MT	6.4	58.0	1.5	0.9	81,750	2.30	62.9	47.1	5.8	10.0	37.1	31.5	40.8
13780	Binghamton, NY	5.1	75.3	5.3	2.9	99,826	2.31	59.0	43.7	5.7	9.6	41.0	32.4	46.4
13820	Birmingham, AL	6.0	70.8	4.7	2.9	471,767	2.44	66.2	47.4	4.4	14.4	33.8	28.2	40.6
13900	Bismarck, ND	3.7	73.2	2.0	1.3	57,951	2.26	60.6	48.5	6.0	6.1	39.4	34.3	39.7
13980	Blacksburg-Christiansburg-Radford, VA	3.4	61.8	5.3	3.3	71,419	2.33	56.2	44.3	3.3	8.5	43.8	30.7	41.9
14010	Bloomington, IL	6.6	72.6	7.7	4.3	71,060	2.27	56.4	44.8	3.0	8.6	43.6	32.1	34.3
14020	Bloomington, IN	4.8	62.6	7.2	4.5	70,681	2.08	50.5	38.5	3.7	8.3	49.5	33.3	34.2
14260	Boise City, ID	15.2	40.3	6.7	3.3	314,846	2.57	68.9	54.9	4.7	9.3	31.1	23.2	38.9
14460	Boston-Cambridge-Newton, MA-NH	12.6	53.4	19.9	9.2	1,949,953	2.44	61.6	46.1	4.3	11.1	38.4	29.0	42.2
1446014454	Boston, MA Metro Division	12.3	56.1	20.8	9.9	822,929	2.37	58.3	41.6	4.5	12.2	41.7	31.0	40.6
1446015764	Cambridge-Newton-Framingham, MA Metro Division	14.4	54.7	21.9	10.1	946,508	2.49	63.4	48.8	4.1	10.5	36.6	27.9	42.6
1446040484	Rockingham County-Strafford County, NH Metro Division	3.7	34.6	5.8	2.0	180,516	2.46	66.5	52.8	4.0	9.8	33.5	25.3	47.2
14500	Boulder, CO	14.7	31.1	10.4	5.2	137,425	2.28	53.9	43.8	4.0	6.0	46.1	31.1	38.5
14540	Bowling Green, KY	5.7	61.3	7.0	4.3	77,804	2.40	62.2	47.2	5.5	9.4	37.8	31.1	35.3
14580	Bozeman, MT	5.5	35.9	4.0	2.5	54,621	2.23	58.6	49.3	5.3	4.1	41.4	23.8	30.5
14740	Bremerton-Silverdale-Port Orchard, WA	9.6	42.3	6.6	2.6	109,652	2.47	68.4	53.3	5.3	9.9	31.6	24.4	44.4
14860	Bridgeport-Stamford-Danbury, CT	22.9	38.9	24.8	12.6	356,931	2.62	68.1	50.8	5.1	12.1	31.9	26.1	45.4
15180	Brownsville-Harlingen, TX	89.2	65.7	23.4	13.9	143,033	2.96	75.0	49.1	6.4	19.5	25.0	21.6	41.1
15260	Brunswick-St. Simons, GA	6.4	59.7	4.9	2.1	48,281	2.36	68.6	49.0	6.4	13.2	31.4	25.5	50.5
15380	Buffalo-Cheektowaga, NY	6.0	80.9	6.8	2.6	502,324	2.24	57.8	40.7	4.7	12.4	42.2	34.6	44.7

Table A-3. Metropolitan Areas — Who: Age, Race/Ethnicity, and Household Structure, 2023—*Continued*

Metropolitan area / division code	Metropolitan area / division	Total population	Percent change, 2010–2023	Population by age (percent)					Median age	Race alone or in combination (percent)				
				Under 18 years	18 to 24 years	25 to 44 years	45 to 64 years	65 years and over		White	Black or African American	Asian + Native Hawaiian or Other Pacific Islander	American Indian and Alaska Native + Some other race	Two or more races
	ACS table number:	B01003	Population Estimates	B01001	B01001	B01001	B01001	B01001	B01002	B02008	B02009	B02011 + B02012	B02010 + B02013	B02001
	column number:	1	2	3	4	5	6	7	8	9	10	11	12	13
15500	Burlington, NC	179,165	18.2	21.9	10.7	24.4	25.7	17.3	39.4	66.3	23.3	2.4	16.7	8.2
15540	Burlington-South Burlington, VT	227,719	7.9	17.9	12.4	27.5	24.3	17.9	39.3	92.7	3.6	5.1	5.4	6.2
15940	Canton-Massillon, OH	399,474	-0.9	21.4	8.1	23.9	25.5	21.1	42.4	91.9	7.6	1.9	6.2	7.4
15980	Cape Coral-Fort Myers, FL	834,573	34.6	17.1	7.2	21.5	25.2	29.0	49.1	83.6	10.4	2.4	23.4	19.0
16020	Cape Girardeau, MO-IL	97,947	-0.1	21.7	13.4	22.9	22.9	19.2	38.3	88.9	10.1	1.6	3.1	3.5
16180	Carson City, NV	58,036	5.1	19.2	6.1	25.8	28.2	20.7	44.2	81.0	3.0	3.7	25.1	13.0
16220	Casper, WY	79,941	5.9	23.0	7.9	28.0	23.7	17.3	39.0	95.2	2.3	1.0	9.2	7.4
16300	Cedar Rapids, IA	275,668	6.8	22.1	8.7	25.8	25.1	18.4	40.3	91.4	7.8	3.0	4.4	6.0
16540	Chambersburg, PA	157,854	4.7	21.6	7.1	24.9	25.6	20.8	41.6	91.2	4.4	1.8	9.4	5.8
16580	Champaign-Urbana, IL	237,052	1.1	19.7	20.4	24.7	19.5	15.7	32.5	76.3	14.1	10.6	8.1	8.8
16620	Charleston, WV	203,259	-33.3	20.0	7.4	23.6	25.9	23.0	44.0	94.3	6.8	1.4	4.1	6.1
16700	Charleston-North Charleston, SC	849,417	27.2	21.5	8.6	29.0	24.2	16.8	38.6	71.0	25.1	3.0	7.8	6.5
16740	Charlotte-Concord-Gastonia, NC-SC	2,805,115	59.0	22.8	8.6	28.2	25.6	14.8	38.0	65.8	24.7	5.7	13.3	8.9
16820	Charlottesville, VA	224,932	12.6	18.5	11.6	25.1	23.7	21.1	41.6	81.8	12.5	6.4	7.2	7.5
16860	Chattanooga, TN-GA	580,353	9.5	20.8	8.3	26.3	25.2	19.3	41.0	82.9	13.4	2.3	8.1	6.5
16940	Cheyenne, WY	100,984	9.6	22.3	8.6	28.3	22.4	18.5	38.3	89.7	3.4	3.2	15.8	10.7
16980	Chicago-Naperville-Elgin, IL-IN	9,262,559	-2.2	21.7	8.8	27.7	25.2	16.6	39.0	64.5	17.7	8.8	22.6	12.8
1698016984	Chicago-Naperville-Schaumburg, IL Metro Division	7,075,391	NA	21.2	8.6	28.5	21.7	12.6	38.9	61.5	19.6	9.7	22.6	12.5
1698020994	Elgin, IL Metro Division	755,246	NA	23.7	10.2	25.8	22.1	11.6	37.8	77.2	7.7	5.1	28.5	17.8
1698029404	Lake County, IL Metro Division	708,760	NA	22.9	10.1	24.3	23.0	12.4	39.6	72.0	8.5	10.4	22.6	12.9
1698029414	Lake County-Porter County-Jasper County, IN Metro Division	723,162	NA	22.5	8.3	25.3	21.6	14.3	40.4	73.7	18.7	2.1	16.7	10.5
17020	Chico, CA	207,172	-5.9	20.4	14.9	25.1	21.0	18.7	35.9	82.2	3.4	8.4	22.4	15.1
17140	Cincinnati, OH-KY-IN	2,272,910	6.5	22.8	9.2	26.2	24.6	17.1	38.4	83.3	13.6	4.1	6.7	7.3
17300	Clarksville, TN-KY	336,861	22.6	26.3	10.8	31.0	19.9	12.0	32.5	75.5	24.0	4.3	9.4	11.4
17420	Cleveland, OH	2,158,932	4.0	20.5	8.0	25.3	25.6	20.6	41.9	75.9	21.1	3.4	7.2	7.1
17460	Cleveland, TN	129,612	12.0	21.2	8.4	26.3	26.4	17.7	38.8	92.2	6.7	1.5	8.8	9.1
17660	Coeur d'Alene, ID	185,010	33.2	22.1	6.7	25.8	24.7	20.6	42.2	95.7	0.9	2.1	12.2	10.6
17780	College Station-Bryan, TX	280,939	22.1	20.8	23.4	25.2	18.8	11.9	29.1	76.7	12.9	6.6	20.3	15.2
17820	Colorado Springs, CO	768,832	18.5	22.5	9.9	30.4	22.4	14.8	35.8	83.4	8.8	6.3	16.0	13.0
17860	Columbia, MO	215,811	25.2	20.1	17.8	25.7	21.8	14.6	34.0	85.7	11.2	5.5	4.4	6.7
17900	Columbia, SC	856,889	11.2	21.9	11.2	26.0	24.4	16.5	38.3	61.6	35.3	3.7	8.1	7.6
17980	Columbus, GA-AL	329,047	12.6	24.3	9.0	27.8	22.8	16.0	36.2	51.2	46.2	3.8	8.2	8.8
18020	Columbus, IN	84,003	9.3	23.6	8.9	27.4	22.4	17.8	36.8	84.1	3.4	6.7	13.3	7.8
18140	Columbus, OH	2,180,271	18.5	23.1	8.9	29.3	23.8	14.8	36.9	75.5	18.9	6.3	7.3	7.4
18580	Corpus Christi, TX	446,041	4.2	23.2	8.7	27.3	23.5	17.2	38.5	85.9	4.6	3.3	46.9	40.0
18700	Corvallis, OR	97,713	14.2	15.1	22.4	23.9	20.6	18.1	34.7	87.2	2.7	8.4	12.8	10.6
18880	Crestview-Fort Walton Beach-Destin, FL	304,818	68.7	22.0	8.1	27.1	24.8	18.0	40.0	83.0	10.5	5.2	11.0	9.0
19100	Dallas-Fort Worth-Arlington, TX	8,100,037	26.5	24.7	9.2	29.5	24.1	12.5	35.8	64.2	18.5	10.1	25.8	17.8
1910019124	Dallas-Plano-Irving, TX Metro Division	5,462,593	NA	24.6	9.2	29.9	21.4	9.2	35.8	61.2	18.9	11.6	26.4	17.2
1910023104	Fort Worth-Arlington-Grapevine, TX Metro Division	2,637,444	NA	25.0	9.3	28.7	20.8	10.0	35.8	70.4	17.7	7.0	24.7	18.9
19140	Dalton, GA	144,722	1.6	24.0	9.4	26.4	24.5	15.7	37.5	76.0	2.7	1.3	30.8	10.3
19300	Daphne-Fairhope-Foley, AL	253,507	35.8	20.9	6.1	23.7	26.8	22.4	44.3	87.8	9.0	1.6	7.1	5.7
19340	Davenport-Moline-Rock Island, IA-IL	379,869	-0.7	22.4	8.3	25.2	24.6	19.4	40.4	85.8	9.7	4.1	10.5	9.5
19380	Dayton-Kettering-Beavercreek, OH	814,363	-3.2	21.8	9.3	25.7	24.0	19.1	39.2	80.9	17.8	3.5	5.9	7.6
19460	Decatur, AL	158,635	3.0	23.0	7.8	24.4	26.6	18.2	40.7	82.7	14.3	1.0	11.1	8.5
19500	Decatur, IL	100,591	-9.1	22.5	8.5	24.7	22.9	21.5	40.2	82.2	19.7	2.3	5.7	8.9
19660	Deltona-Daytona Beach-Ormond Beach, FL	721,796	46.0	17.1	7.9	21.9	26.2	26.9	48.1	79.9	13.0	3.1	15.1	10.1
19740	Denver-Aurora-Centennial, CO	3,005,131	17.4	20.6	8.1	32.8	23.9	14.6	37.5	81.0	7.6	6.8	22.1	16.2
19780	Des Moines-West Des Moines, IA	737,164	29.2	24.3	8.6	28.8	23.5	14.8	37.3	85.7	7.3	5.2	8.4	6.3
19820	Detroit-Warren-Dearborn, MI	4,342,304	1.2	21.5	7.9	26.1	26.0	18.4	40.5	70.6	23.6	6.3	6.7	6.8
1982019804	Detroit-Dearborn-Livonia, MI Metro Division	1,751,169	NA	23.5	8.3	26.5	21.1	13.0	38.1	55.4	39.4	4.8	8.3	7.4
1982047664	Warren-Troy-Farmington Hills, MI Metro Division	2,591,135	NA	20.2	7.7	25.8	23.3	14.6	42.0	81.0	12.9	7.4	5.7	6.4
20020	Dothan, AL	153,349	5.0	22.3	7.9	24.2	25.7	19.9	41.4	74.6	23.7	1.3	5.8	5.0
20100	Dover, DE	189,789	16.5	22.6	9.7	25.4	23.5	18.8	39.0	64.2	32.3	3.8	8.7	8.0
20220	Dubuque, IA	98,887	5.3	22.1	8.9	24.8	24.1	20.0	39.5	94.2	5.6	1.7	3.4	5.5

Table A-3. Metropolitan Areas — Who: Age, Race/Ethnicity, and Household Structure, 2023—*Continued*

Metropolitan area / division code	Metropolitan area / division	Hispanic or Latino (percent)	Born in state of residence (percent)	Foreign born (percent)	Not a U.S. citizen (percent)	Total households	Average household size	Household type (percent of all households): Family households: Total	Family households: Married-couple	Family households: Male householder	Family households: Female householder	Nonfamily households: Total	Nonfamily households: One-person households	Percent of households with people age 60 years and over
	ACS table number:	B03003	B05002	B05002	B05002	B11001	B25010	B11001	B11001	B11001	B11001	B11001	B11001	B11006
	column number:	14	15	16	17	18	19	20	21	22	23	24	25	26
15500	Burlington, NC	15.4	61.0	9.4	6.3	70,911	2.43	65.2	47.0	4.0	14.2	34.8	31.1	44.4
15540	Burlington-South Burlington, VT	2.7	48.6	6.9	2.0	96,541	2.23	59.5	48.4	4.1	7.0	40.5	26.7	37.9
15940	Canton-Massillon, OH	2.9	82.6	1.9	0.7	168,115	2.33	61.5	45.5	5.1	11.0	38.5	31.8	45.0
15980	Cape Coral-Fort Myers, FL	25.1	27.2	18.8	10.3	326,338	2.52	64.4	50.2	3.8	10.4	35.6	28.5	57.5
16020	Cape Girardeau, MO-IL	2.7	70.1	2.1	1.2	39,485	2.39	60.2	47.7	4.1	8.3	39.8	32.4	44.2
16180	Carson City, NV	26.7	30.3	11.7	6.0	24,562	2.26	64.6	46.2	6.7	11.7	35.4	31.9	43.8
16220	Casper, WY	9.6	46.7	3.3	1.6	34,332	2.29	64.1	50.9	4.7	8.5	35.9	29.2	41.2
16300	Cedar Rapids, IA	3.8	72.8	5.3	2.2	114,563	2.35	62.2	48.5	4.6	9.1	37.8	31.5	39.7
16540	Chambersburg, PA	7.7	61.4	4.8	3.0	62,966	2.48	69.1	52.9	5.3	11.0	30.9	26.8	44.1
16580	Champaign-Urbana, IL	7.7	67.6	12.3	8.2	102,205	2.17	52.2	38.9	4.0	9.3	47.8	37.4	31.6
16620	Charleston, WV	1.5	82.0	1.5	0.2	89,395	2.24	56.4	39.5	5.4	11.5	43.6	36.6	48.4
16700	Charleston-North Charleston, SC	7.7	46.5	7.0	4.1	347,045	2.40	61.7	46.9	4.3	10.6	38.3	29.2	39.7
16740	Charlotte-Concord-Gastonia, NC-SC	12.6	45.0	11.7	6.8	1,103,360	2.51	65.4	48.8	4.5	12.1	34.6	28.2	36.2
16820	Charlottesville, VA	6.3	50.4	8.0	4.4	92,687	2.29	62.2	48.9	3.1	10.1	37.8	27.7	44.6
16860	Chattanooga, TN-GA	6.6	49.9	4.2	2.4	235,003	2.41	63.8	47.3	4.2	12.3	36.2	29.8	43.8
16940	Cheyenne, WY	15.9	40.1	3.1	1.2	44,460	2.24	62.8	47.6	5.6	9.7	37.2	32.4	41.8
16980	Chicago-Naperville-Elgin, IL-IN	24.3	62.5	18.9	8.8	3,671,659	2.48	62.5	44.8	5.5	12.1	37.5	30.5	40.4
1698016984	Chicago-Naperville-Schaumburg, IL Metro Division	24.3	62.6	20.5	9.4	2,856,546	2.44	60.5	42.8	5.4	12.3	39.5	32.1	39.9
1698020994	Elgin, IL Metro Division	29.1	69.5	14.8	7.6	271,057	2.75	71.4	53.5	6.8	11.0	28.6	22.1	39.5
1698029404	Lake County, IL Metro Division	25.1	59.0	20.1	10.3	260,243	2.65	70.9	55.9	5.0	10.0	29.1	23.9	42.7
1698029414	Lake County-Porter County-Jasper County, IN Metro Division	18.1	56.9	5.8	2.5	283,813	2.52	65.7	46.8	5.9	13.0	34.3	29.1	45.0
17020	Chico, CA	20.6	74.0	8.4	3.9	86,279	2.32	58.0	41.7	5.7	10.7	42.0	26.0	42.0
17140	Cincinnati, OH-KY-IN	4.6	67.4	5.8	3.1	921,306	2.42	62.8	47.1	4.6	11.0	37.2	30.3	39.8
17300	Clarksville, TN-KY	10.2	39.5	5.6	3.4	129,593	2.52	68.5	50.5	5.7	12.3	31.5	25.7	32.2
17420	Cleveland, OH	6.9	75.1	6.0	2.4	931,312	2.27	58.0	40.5	4.1	13.4	42.0	35.9	44.8
17460	Cleveland, TN	8.4	54.0	6.0	3.2	50,001	2.54	64.8	51.3	2.8	10.7	35.2	29.6	43.0
17660	Coeur d'Alene, ID	5.9	28.3	2.9	0.9	74,253	2.47	69.1	53.9	5.7	9.5	30.9	23.8	45.0
17780	College Station-Bryan, TX	26.6	66.5	12.9	8.0	107,713	2.45	55.9	39.8	3.1	13.0	44.1	30.4	28.7
17820	Colorado Springs, CO	18.8	31.5	6.8	2.8	311,530	2.40	67.5	53.4	4.6	9.6	32.5	25.5	35.0
17860	Columbia, MO	4.0	64.3	5.8	3.6	87,256	2.34	57.8	43.0	3.1	11.6	42.2	29.9	33.7
17900	Columbia, SC	7.2	57.7	5.5	3.2	346,000	2.39	62.9	44.3	4.5	14.1	37.1	29.9	39.5
17980	Columbus, GA-AL	8.0	49.6	4.0	1.1	131,169	2.42	60.6	37.4	5.5	17.7	39.4	34.5	38.7
18020	Columbus, IN	9.5	67.3	10.6	8.4	33,777	2.45	66.6	49.7	3.5	13.4	33.4	27.2	37.7
18140	Columbus, OH	5.6	68.6	10.0	5.0	879,910	2.42	61.1	43.6	5.3	12.1	38.9	30.1	36.1
18580	Corpus Christi, TX	59.7	73.5	7.9	4.9	170,701	2.56	68.5	47.2	6.1	15.2	31.5	24.9	42.1
18700	Corvallis, OR	9.4	41.6	9.7	6.4	38,306	2.39	49.7	40.4	3.6	5.7	50.3	32.3	40.6
18880	Crestview-Fort Walton Beach-Destin, FL	10.6	30.7	8.2	4.1	121,976	2.45	68.8	52.0	5.8	10.9	31.2	24.7	42.1
19100	Dallas-Fort Worth-Arlington, TX	29.7	51.7	20.0	11.6	2,959,385	2.70	67.1	49.8	5.1	12.2	32.9	26.7	33.5
1910019124	Dallas-Plano-Irving, TX Metro Division	30.1	50.1	22.1	12.8	2,007,420	2.69	66.8	50.0	5.2	11.6	33.2	27.0	32.6
1910023104	Fort Worth-Arlington-Grapevine, TX Metro Division	28.9	55.0	15.7	9.1	951,965	2.73	67.8	49.5	5.0	13.3	32.2	26.0	35.4
19140	Dalton, GA	31.6	57.2	18.0	11.9	52,722	2.72	72.0	54.5	5.2	12.3	28.0	23.2	39.8
19300	Daphne-Fairhope-Foley, AL	5.8	47.8	4.9	3.2	105,698	2.37	70.0	54.4	4.3	11.3	30.0	26.0	48.2
19340	Davenport-Moline-Rock Island, IA-IL	9.9	63.6	5.7	2.7	164,230	2.26	61.4	46.8	4.5	10.1	38.6	31.5	42.1
19380	Dayton-Kettering-Beavercreek, OH	3.8	71.2	4.4	2.2	350,659	2.25	59.5	42.4	4.9	12.3	40.5	33.9	42.1
19460	Decatur, AL	9.1	71.0	3.4	2.7	64,526	2.42	69.6	49.9	5.1	14.5	30.4	25.2	43.9
19500	Decatur, IL	3.0	78.8	3.3	1.4	43,598	2.24	54.6	39.3	5.2	10.2	45.4	38.5	46.6
19660	Deltona-Daytona Beach-Ormond Beach, FL	15.9	33.4	9.7	3.6	300,081	2.34	63.3	47.5	4.6	11.2	36.7	29.5	56.4
19740	Denver-Aurora-Centennial, CO	24.1	41.0	12.4	6.7	1,244,895	2.39	59.7	46.3	4.5	8.9	40.3	29.5	33.9
19780	Des Moines-West Des Moines, IA	8.8	68.6	8.9	5.5	299,784	2.42	62.4	48.3	4.8	9.4	37.6	30.0	33.8
19820	Detroit-Warren-Dearborn, MI	5.4	75.3	11.0	4.2	1,770,361	2.43	61.7	43.9	5.2	12.6	38.3	32.5	43.4
1982019804	Detroit-Dearborn-Livonia, MI Metro Division	7.0	75.6	10.7	4.0	696,332	2.49	58.6	36.0	6.0	16.6	41.4	36.3	42.7
1982047664	Warren-Troy-Farmington Hills, MI Metro Division	4.3	75.0	11.2	4.2	1,074,029	2.39	63.8	49.1	4.7	10.0	36.2	30.0	43.9
20020	Dothan, AL	6.1	63.0	3.3	2.4	62,401	2.43	67.1	45.8	4.4	16.9	32.9	28.9	45.7
20100	Dover, DE	8.3	45.1	8.3	3.5	74,183	2.50	67.2	48.8	4.8	13.6	32.8	27.4	48.2
20220	Dubuque, IA	3.4	71.7	2.6	1.8	42,889	2.21	60.8	48.7	2.8	9.3	39.2	31.6	41.7

Table A-3. Metropolitan Areas — Who: Age, Race/Ethnicity, and Household Structure, 2023—*Continued*

Metropolitan area / division code	Metropolitan area / division	Total population	Percent change, 2010–2023	Population by age (percent) Under 18 years	18 to 24 years	25 to 44 years	45 to 64 years	65 years and over	Median age	Race alone or in combination (percent) White	Black or African American	Asian + Native Hawaiian or Other Pacific Islander	American Indian and Alaska Native + Some other race	Two or more races
	ACS table number:	B01003	Population Estimates	B01001	B01001	B01001	B01001	B01001	B01002	B02008	B02009	B02011 + B02012	B02010 + B02013	B02001
	column number:	1	2	3	4	5	6	7	8	9	10	11	12	13
20260	Duluth, MN-WI	281,603	0.6	18.8	11.0	23.7	25.0	21.5	41.9	94.5	2.5	1.9	6.9	5.4
20500	Durham-Chapel Hill, NC	608,879	20.3	18.7	12.2	27.5	24.4	17.3	38.4	61.8	25.9	7.2	14.1	8.1
20580	Eagle Pass, TX	57,762	NA	29.7	10.9	26.4	20.5	12.5	31.3	91.3	0.0	0.0	85.5	78.1
20740	Eau Claire, WI	174,873	8.3	20.2	12.2	26.2	22.9	18.4	38.4	94.1	2.1	4.2	4.0	4.5
20940	El Centro, CA	179,057	2.2	28.0	10.5	26.9	20.7	13.8	33.4	49.3	2.3	3.1	81.0	34.1
21060	Elizabethtown, KY	129,403	5.8	24.5	8.1	26.0	25.5	16.0	37.8	84.8	13.8	3.3	8.3	8.6
21140	Elkhart-Goshen, IN	206,409	4.4	27.1	9.2	24.6	23.5	15.6	36.3	79.5	7.1	1.5	20.4	8.1
21300	Elmira, NY	81,325	-8.4	20.7	7.8	24.8	26.1	20.6	42.5	89.7	8.8	2.2	3.0	3.6
21340	El Paso, TX	872,063	8.4	25.6	10.7	28.5	21.7	13.4	33.9	73.4	4.8	2.6	65.8	45.2
21420	Enid, OK	62,023	NA	26.2	10.2	25.4	20.8	17.3	36.1	83.1	5.0	7.2	17.1	10.3
21500	Erie, PA	267,571	-4.7	20.5	10.3	24.1	24.6	20.5	41.3	88.3	10.1	2.7	5.3	5.9
21660	Eugene-Springfield, OR	381,181	8.3	17.2	12.3	25.8	23.2	21.5	40.4	89.8	3.0	5.6	14.3	11.1
21780	Evansville, IN	270,717	-24.4	21.6	8.9	25.5	24.7	19.3	39.8	88.9	8.8	2.3	6.5	5.8
21820	Fairbanks-College, AK	94,840	-3.5	24.0	11.5	32.2	19.7	12.6	33.2	82.0	7.6	8.5	18.0	15.6
22020	Fargo, ND-MN	262,620	25.6	22.6	14.7	29.6	19.1	13.9	32.9	88.8	7.9	3.7	6.4	6.6
22140	Farmington, NM	120,675	-7.3	24.9	8.1	26.8	22.6	17.5	38.3	50.8	1.9	1.5	56.6	10.5
22180	Fayetteville, NC	392,336	6.7	25.4	11.7	29.4	20.3	13.2	32.5	50.8	42.2	5.1	14.1	10.6
22220	Fayetteville-Springdale-Rogers, AR	590,295	26.7	24.1	11.8	28.5	22.3	13.3	34.9	87.9	3.6	6.2	31.2	28.2
22380	Flagstaff, AZ	144,472	7.3	18.9	20.1	25.1	20.6	15.4	32.7	67.2	2.3	4.2	38.4	11.5
22420	Flint, MI	401,522	-5.5	22.0	8.2	24.9	25.4	19.6	41.0	77.7	21.9	2.0	4.5	5.8
22500	Florence, SC	199,630	-3.0	22.7	9.2	24.0	25.1	19.0	40.2	54.0	44.2	1.3	3.8	3.2
22520	Florence-Muscle Shoals, AL	155,175	5.5	20.1	10.9	22.8	25.2	20.9	41.9	86.5	11.7	1.4	6.7	6.0
22540	Fond du Lac, WI	103,948	2.2	20.1	10.1	23.8	25.0	21.0	41.6	93.0	3.7	2.7	6.9	6.0
22660	Fort Collins-Loveland, CO	370,771	23.3	18.0	14.0	28.4	21.9	17.8	37.3	93.2	2.5	4.5	11.8	10.8
22900	Fort Smith, AR-OK	231,280	-22.8	23.6	8.3	25.4	24.2	18.5	39.4	80.3	6.2	3.8	24.5	12.9
23060	Fort Wayne, IN	457,842	10.3	25.1	9.3	26.1	23.2	16.4	37.2	82.1	12.2	5.8	9.2	8.8
23420	Fresno, CA	1,180,020	26.4	27.4	9.8	28.1	21.3	13.4	34.0	57.0	5.7	12.5	49.5	23.4
23460	Gadsden, AL	103,241	-1.2	21.9	7.6	25.1	25.2	20.1	41.2	80.7	16.6	1.0	5.4	4.0
23540	Gainesville, FL	350,203	31.5	18.3	18.6	25.3	20.7	17.2	35.0	75.0	18.0	6.2	11.6	10.5
23580	Gainesville, GA	217,267	20.5	23.4	9.4	25.6	25.0	16.7	38.7	81.0	7.4	3.8	28.4	19.9
23900	Gettysburg, PA	106,748	5.2	19.1	9.8	21.7	26.6	22.7	44.6	93.5	1.9	1.3	8.6	5.4
24020	Glens Falls, NY	125,427	-2.8	17.4	6.3	24.5	27.9	23.9	46.2	95.4	2.2	1.2	6.0	4.9
24140	Goldsboro, NC	118,686	-3.4	23.4	9.8	26.1	22.9	17.7	37.4	66.5	33.9	2.1	13.1	15.0
24220	Grand Forks, ND-MN	103,120	3.5	21.3	16.5	26.1	19.8	16.3	33.6	91.6	5.4	3.1	9.6	8.8
24260	Grand Island, NE	76,479	4.3	26.3	8.1	25.0	24.3	16.4	36.8	76.8	4.3	1.4	25.3	7.4
24300	Grand Junction, CO	159,681	9.1	20.1	8.6	26.0	23.8	21.5	41.6	92.1	1.9	2.0	17.2	11.3
24340	Grand Rapids-Wyoming-Kentwood, MI	1,162,950	50.1	22.8	10.0	27.4	23.3	16.4	37.1	86.9	8.7	3.5	11.3	9.5
24420	Grants Pass, OR	87,821	5.8	18.9	6.0	22.6	25.0	27.5	47.6	95.6	0.4	2.6	10.8	8.8
24500	Great Falls, MT	84,900	4.1	22.1	8.8	26.3	22.9	19.9	39.1	91.8	3.0	2.1	12.8	8.2
24540	Greeley, CO	359,442	41.4	25.3	9.0	30.2	22.4	13.2	35.4	86.0	2.6	3.4	23.8	14.9
24580	Green Bay, WI	331,882	8.2	22.2	9.1	25.3	25.2	18.3	39.9	88.7	3.8	3.7	11.7	7.1
24660	Greensboro-High Point, NC	789,842	8.9	21.6	10.8	24.9	25.0	17.6	39.0	62.4	30.4	4.9	10.9	7.9
24780	Greenville, NC	175,119	-7.9	21.3	16.8	25.4	21.4	15.1	34.1	56.5	37.4	3.0	9.2	5.4
24860	Greenville-Anderson-Greer, SC	975,480	52.8	22.0	9.4	26.3	24.5	17.7	39.0	80.2	16.6	3.1	9.4	8.9
25020	Guayama, PR	64,758	-22.9	16.7	9.3	24.5	25.3	24.2	44.6	45.3	19.4	0.0	58.9	24.5
25060	Gulfport-Biloxi, MS	421,916	68.6	22.1	8.1	25.9	25.6	18.4	41.2	74.9	22.2	3.4	9.3	8.8
25180	Hagerstown-Martinsburg, MD-WV	304,506	13.9	22.0	8.0	26.3	25.9	17.8	39.8	85.9	12.2	2.5	8.6	8.8
25220	Hammond, LA	138,064	12.6	24.7	9.7	27.9	21.9	15.8	36.8	71.1	28.5	1.0	9.4	9.9
25260	Hanford-Corcoran, CA	152,682	-0.3	26.7	10.0	31.8	20.4	11.2	33.2	60.1	7.8	5.0	51.0	22.8
25420	Harrisburg-Carlisle, PA	606,055	10.2	21.3	9.2	26.2	24.3	19.1	40.3	79.5	14.4	6.9	7.6	7.2
25500	Harrisonburg, VA	137,650	9.7	19.9	19.2	22.7	20.9	17.2	34.8	88.4	6.8	2.7	14.0	11.2
25540	Hartford-West Hartford-East Hartford, CT	1,151,543	-5.1	19.5	9.8	25.9	25.6	19.2	41.2	75.3	14.7	7.1	13.4	9.8
25620	Hattiesburg, MS	155,835	6.6	22.6	12.3	25.9	24.3	14.8	36.8	68.5	31.0	1.2	5.1	5.5
25740	Helena, MT	95,185	22.4	21.7	6.6	25.3	25.0	21.4	42.2	97.6	0.7	0.8	8.4	7.3
25860	Hickory-Lenoir-Morganton, NC	370,030	1.3	19.8	7.9	24.0	27.6	20.7	43.7	85.0	8.0	3.7	9.5	6.0
25940	Hilton Head Island-Bluffton-Port Royal, SC	232,523	22.5	16.9	9.7	21.2	23.4	28.7	47.6	74.7	19.1	2.2	12.4	8.0
25980	Hinesville, GA	88,753	18.7	28.0	14.4	32.2	16.0	9.5	28.8	51.1	44.6	4.6	15.1	14.1

Table A-3. Metropolitan Areas — Who: Age, Race/Ethnicity, and Household Structure, 2023—*Continued*

Metropolitan area / division code	Metropolitan area / division	Hispanic or Latino (percent)	Born in state of residence (percent)	Foreign born (percent)	Not a U.S. citizen (percent)	Total households	Average household size	Household type (percent of all households): Family households: Total	Family households: Married-couple	Family households: Male householder	Family households: Female householder	Nonfamily households: Total	Nonfamily households: One-person households	Percent of households with people age 60 years and over
	ACS table number:	B03003	B05002	B05002	B05002	B11001	B25010	B11001	B11001	B11001	B11001	B11001	B11001	B11006
	column number:	14	15	16	17	18	19	20	21	22	23	24	25	26
20260	Duluth, MN-WI	2.0	71.5	1.8	0.9	120,943	2.24	57.2	45.5	4.0	7.7	42.8	32.0	43.7
20500	Durham-Chapel Hill, NC	13.4	45.6	13.2	7.8	253,951	2.30	60.6	46.6	3.9	10.1	39.4	30.4	36.9
20580	Eagle Pass, TX	94.7	56.4	32.1	19.7	18,890	3.03	72.8	47.6	4.3	21.0	27.2	25.9	38.1
20740	Eau Claire, WI	2.8	75.5	1.8	0.6	72,615	2.31	60.3	45.4	4.0	10.9	39.7	29.2	39.4
20940	El Centro, CA	86.3	59.6	32.2	14.9	50,024	3.45	77.6	53.6	7.2	16.8	22.4	20.7	43.6
21060	Elizabethtown, KY	5.8	60.6	4.1	1.4	51,413	2.46	67.0	46.0	5.9	15.0	33.0	26.1	39.2
21140	Elkhart-Goshen, IN	20.4	66.8	9.9	6.2	73,439	2.78	67.9	52.8	3.7	11.4	32.1	27.4	39.4
21300	Elmira, NY	3.9	74.3	3.5	1.3	35,591	2.20	60.4	39.4	7.2	13.7	39.6	32.1	44.1
21340	El Paso, TX	82.8	59.6	22.5	10.9	301,927	2.84	70.7	45.3	7.2	18.2	29.3	24.8	38.8
21420	Enid, OK	15.6	60.8	4.6	2.9	23,645	2.55	65.0	44.5	7.5	13.0	35.0	30.8	42.1
21500	Erie, PA	4.9	76.2	4.6	2.0	111,118	2.29	61.0	42.8	5.8	12.5	39.0	32.8	46.3
21660	Eugene-Springfield, OR	10.8	48.0	4.4	1.8	162,001	2.29	59.8	44.6	4.5	10.8	40.2	27.8	43.5
21780	Evansville, IN	3.3	73.1	3.1	1.8	113,389	2.32	61.4	47.8	3.2	10.4	38.6	31.9	41.7
21820	Fairbanks-College, AK	8.8	32.1	3.9	1.2	37,510	2.43	60.7	47.4	6.4	6.9	39.3	32.2	32.2
22020	Fargo, ND-MN	4.1	48.9	5.9	3.1	111,493	2.27	51.7	40.7	3.2	7.8	48.3	37.3	29.4
22140	Farmington, NM	19.9	59.1	3.7	1.6	42,670	2.80	70.3	45.6	7.5	17.2	29.7	24.6	45.8
22180	Fayetteville, NC	13.5	44.7	7.3	3.3	150,658	2.48	64.6	42.9	4.8	17.0	35.4	29.7	34.8
22220	Fayetteville-Springdale-Rogers, AR	18.4	45.2	12.1	8.1	224,357	2.57	68.7	53.5	4.7	10.5	31.3	23.5	31.6
22380	Flagstaff, AZ	15.6	53.0	3.8	2.0	56,954	2.30	58.4	39.9	5.2	13.3	41.6	27.9	36.0
22420	Flint, MI	4.4	83.8	2.6	0.9	164,086	2.42	63.7	42.1	5.7	15.9	36.3	30.8	45.2
22500	Florence, SC	3.1	72.5	2.2	1.0	78,453	2.49	64.0	38.7	5.0	20.3	36.0	32.2	44.2
22520	Florence-Muscle Shoals, AL	3.6	68.4	2.3	1.0	67,774	2.23	66.3	49.3	4.1	12.8	33.7	28.5	44.1
22540	Fond du Lac, WI	7.0	79.7	3.4	1.2	44,262	2.27	60.2	48.8	4.7	6.6	39.8	29.8	42.2
22660	Fort Collins-Loveland, CO	13.1	37.2	4.9	2.6	156,498	2.30	58.9	47.2	4.5	7.1	41.1	27.8	37.1
22900	Fort Smith, AR-OK	12.5	54.8	6.4	3.5	90,483	2.52	66.1	47.7	5.8	12.6	33.9	30.0	43.2
23060	Fort Wayne, IN	8.3	68.3	6.6	3.1	186,586	2.42	62.4	45.9	4.8	11.7	37.6	31.3	37.1
23420	Fresno, CA	55.8	70.1	19.6	10.4	375,676	3.07	71.3	45.9	8.2	17.2	28.7	22.3	39.7
23460	Gadsden, AL	5.4	77.1	2.7	1.5	40,027	2.54	68.4	47.9	4.8	15.6	31.6	26.8	44.6
23540	Gainesville, FL	12.3	50.8	10.8	4.8	146,910	2.24	52.9	38.2	3.7	11.0	47.1	32.1	37.4
23580	Gainesville, GA	29.4	55.2	16.4	10.2	76,413	2.81	73.4	54.2	7.1	12.0	26.6	21.1	43.3
23900	Gettysburg, PA	7.7	60.1	3.4	1.9	41,810	2.44	68.4	53.5	7.4	7.5	31.6	25.4	51.4
24020	Glens Falls, NY	3.0	75.3	3.8	2.1	55,835	2.17	60.8	47.9	3.4	9.5	39.2	31.2	49.2
24140	Goldsboro, NC	14.0	60.7	8.3	6.1	47,035	2.46	66.8	40.9	6.5	19.4	33.2	27.6	41.6
24220	Grand Forks, ND-MN	6.1	50.1	4.6	1.9	44,443	2.18	54.9	45.4	3.1	6.4	45.1	31.8	32.8
24260	Grand Island, NE	27.8	66.3	14.5	9.6	30,614	2.46	66.3	50.3	4.1	11.9	33.7	28.0	38.7
24300	Grand Junction, CO	15.6	48.6	5.3	3.3	68,115	2.27	59.7	42.8	6.4	10.4	40.3	31.8	46.8
24340	Grand Rapids-Wyoming-Kentwood, MI	10.1	76.8	6.9	4.0	445,882	2.54	66.2	52.0	4.6	9.5	33.8	26.0	39.3
24420	Grants Pass, OR	9.1	38.6	3.4	1.1	37,241	2.32	67.3	46.7	8.9	11.7	32.7	26.1	55.3
24500	Great Falls, MT	5.4	52.8	3.7	1.2	36,414	2.25	59.4	46.7	3.2	9.5	40.6	33.6	42.7
24540	Greeley, CO	31.3	55.9	8.0	4.6	129,057	2.75	71.6	56.8	4.3	10.4	28.4	21.0	35.5
24580	Green Bay, WI	9.1	77.8	5.3	2.5	137,111	2.36	61.8	48.4	4.5	8.9	38.2	29.9	40.6
24660	Greensboro-High Point, NC	10.6	59.8	9.6	5.1	321,824	2.36	61.6	42.0	5.7	13.9	38.4	32.5	41.0
24780	Greenville, NC	8.0	62.3	6.0	3.0	74,443	2.28	58.3	37.7	4.0	16.6	41.7	29.2	33.0
24860	Greenville-Anderson-Greer, SC	9.1	53.9	6.5	3.7	396,589	2.40	66.4	50.7	3.7	12.0	33.6	26.9	40.8
25020	Guayama, PR	100.0	0.0	1.4	0.5	27,480	2.29	57.7	27.0	7.0	23.7	42.3	33.6	54.8
25060	Gulfport-Biloxi, MS	6.9	54.1	4.4	2.6	174,612	2.38	63.9	44.9	4.5	14.5	36.1	30.7	43.4
25180	Hagerstown-Martinsburg, MD-WV	7.4	50.7	6.1	2.8	117,709	2.52	65.9	45.6	6.4	13.8	34.1	26.7	41.8
25220	Hammond, LA	5.9	80.3	2.9	1.6	54,627	2.45	64.2	41.3	6.8	16.1	35.8	31.3	38.5
25260	Hanford-Corcoran, CA	58.8	64.4	21.1	14.2	44,262	3.13	73.4	50.1	8.6	14.8	26.6	22.4	32.8
25420	Harrisburg-Carlisle, PA	8.3	68.5	8.6	3.6	248,403	2.36	60.8	45.6	4.5	10.7	39.2	31.8	43.7
25500	Harrisonburg, VA	14.8	62.7	9.3	5.6	50,113	2.56	62.4	48.7	2.9	10.7	37.6	27.8	41.0
25540	Hartford-West Hartford-East Hartford, CT	16.4	56.5	14.8	5.8	467,381	2.38	62.8	45.9	5.1	11.8	37.2	30.0	44.2
25620	Hattiesburg, MS	4.1	71.7	3.6	2.8	61,290	2.46	60.4	41.9	3.8	14.7	39.6	32.0	36.7
25740	Helena, MT	3.8	52.8	1.7	0.6	38,384	2.43	59.1	47.9	4.7	6.6	40.9	33.8	47.2
25860	Hickory-Lenoir-Morganton, NC	9.3	70.2	4.7	2.0	155,168	2.33	66.9	48.3	6.2	12.3	33.1	28.0	46.9
25940	Hilton Head Island-Bluffton-Port Royal, SC	13.1	25.2	9.3	5.8	100,794	2.20	69.8	57.2	4.3	8.3	30.2	26.0	56.4
25980	Hinesville, GA	15.2	38.1	5.2	2.3	31,349	2.73	65.6	43.1	7.3	15.2	34.4	29.7	30.1

Table A-3. Metropolitan Areas — Who: Age, Race/Ethnicity, and Household Structure, 2023—*Continued*

Metropolitan area / division code	Metropolitan area / division	Total population	Percent change, 2010–2023	Population by age (percent): Under 18 years	18 to 24 years	25 to 44 years	45 to 64 years	65 years and over	Median age	Race alone or in combination (percent): White	Black or African American	Asian + Native Hawaiian or Other Pacific Islander	American Indian and Alaska Native + Some other race	Two or more races
	ACS table number:	B01003	Population Estimates	B01001	B01001	B01001	B01001	B01001	B01002	B02008	B02009	B02011 + B02012	B02010 + B02013	B02001
	column number:	1	2	3	4	5	6	7	8	9	10	11	12	13
26140	Homosassa Springs, FL	166,696	-36.9	15.3	4.7	18.0	25.6	36.4	56.7	94.9	4.3	2.0	6.8	7.7
26300	Hot Springs, AR	99,784	3.8	19.7	6.6	22.4	25.5	25.8	45.9	89.6	9.5	1.2	6.3	6.5
26380	Houma-Bayou Cane-Thibodaux, LA	198,672	-4.6	23.6	9.0	25.6	25.0	16.8	38.7	75.5	18.6	1.3	12.2	7.1
26420	Houston-Pasadena-The Woodlands, TX	7,510,252	25.7	25.7	9.1	28.9	23.7	12.7	35.7	59.1	19.8	9.8	33.3	20.9
26580	Huntington-Ashland, WV-KY-OH	367,192	27.7	20.6	9.1	23.5	26.1	20.7	42.7	97.0	3.1	1.0	2.9	3.9
26620	Huntsville, AL	527,254	25.8	21.7	9.3	27.5	25.5	16.1	38.4	71.5	23.9	3.9	8.5	7.1
26820	Idaho Falls, ID	167,609	26.4	29.5	8.7	27.3	20.8	13.7	34.1	92.7	1.3	2.2	14.0	9.4
26900	Indianapolis-Carmel-Greenwood, IN	2,139,689	21.6	24.2	8.5	28.1	24.0	15.1	37.1	76.0	17.8	5.2	9.7	8.0
26980	Iowa City, IA	180,088	17.8	19.9	18.8	26.7	20.0	14.6	33.2	85.4	9.1	6.4	6.9	7.5
27060	Ithaca, NY	103,558	1.9	13.5	27.8	22.4	19.0	17.3	32.2	81.1	6.0	12.2	9.1	7.7
27100	Jackson, MI	159,424	-0.5	20.7	7.9	26.1	25.9	19.5	41.6	90.4	10.0	1.3	7.0	8.2
27140	Jackson, MS	609,582	12.9	23.2	9.5	26.1	24.6	16.6	38.5	48.8	48.8	1.8	5.1	4.4
27180	Jackson, TN	181,826	59.2	22.9	8.4	26.1	24.4	18.2	39.0	70.1	26.9	1.3	8.6	6.7
27260	Jacksonville, FL	1,713,240	26.9	21.9	8.0	27.4	25.1	17.6	39.5	71.0	23.5	6.0	11.3	10.6
27340	Jacksonville, NC	213,676	19.1	24.7	20.1	28.6	15.9	10.8	27.8	79.8	16.2	4.0	15.8	14.6
27500	Janesville-Beloit, WI	164,278	2.5	21.8	8.2	25.2	26.1	18.8	40.1	89.6	6.6	1.9	11.2	9.2
27620	Jefferson City, MO	150,447	0.4	21.8	9.4	25.4	25.4	18.1	39.9	90.8	8.0	1.4	6.1	6.1
27740	Johnson City, TN	212,561	6.8	17.7	10.6	24.1	26.7	20.8	43.5	94.9	4.4	2.0	5.3	6.4
27780	Johnstown, PA	130,668	-8.9	19.2	8.8	21.4	26.0	24.7	45.7	96.2	5.6	0.8	3.4	5.5
27860	Jonesboro, AR	136,390	13.3	24.6	9.7	27.9	22.8	14.9	36.3	82.9	15.1	1.3	9.9	9.0
27900	Joplin, MO-KS	204,787	16.4	23.9	9.2	24.5	24.4	18.0	39.1	92.6	3.2	2.8	11.3	9.3
27980	Kahului-Wailuku, HI	164,264	4.8	20.6	6.8	25.5	25.7	21.5	43.3	54.2	1.8	76.6	8.8	29.6
28020	Kalamazoo-Portage, MI	262,215	-19.8	21.2	15.2	25.5	21.7	16.4	34.9	82.8	14.0	3.8	8.1	7.3
28100	Kankakee, IL	105,940	-6.7	22.6	10.1	24.2	24.6	18.5	38.8	79.8	16.3	1.5	9.5	6.5
28140	Kansas City, MO-KS	2,219,865	9.0	23.4	8.1	27.8	24.1	16.6	38.4	80.6	14.3	4.4	11.3	9.8
28420	Kennewick-Richland, WA	314,253	22.9	27.4	8.9	27.7	21.4	14.5	34.7	81.4	2.8	4.6	33.2	21.2
28450	Kenosha, WI	167,488	NA	21.3	9.6	26.2	26.1	16.9	39.5	86.4	9.5	2.7	15.8	13.5
28660	Killeen-Temple, TX	501,334	22.8	26.1	10.4	30.0	21.1	12.4	33.2	66.4	25.5	6.2	21.3	17.4
28700	Kingsport-Bristol, TN-VA	312,490	0.6	18.8	7.3	23.1	27.9	23.0	45.7	96.9	2.3	1.2	3.4	3.6
28740	Kingston, NY	182,333	-0.1	16.9	8.9	25.1	27.2	21.9	44.3	84.3	8.1	2.9	14.0	9.3
28880	Kiryas Joel-Poughkeepsie-Newburgh, NY	704,620	5.0	22.5	10.1	24.8	25.6	17.1	39.5	74.4	14.0	4.4	20.2	11.8
28940	Knoxville, TN	947,017	35.4	20.4	9.7	25.5	25.2	19.2	40.7	90.9	6.9	2.2	6.8	6.6
29020	Kokomo, IN	83,831	-16.6	22.9	8.5	23.6	24.7	20.3	40.5	91.2	10.1	1.9	2.6	5.6
29100	La Crosse-Onalaska, WI-MN	170,238	27.1	20.3	13.0	23.1	23.6	20.0	40.7	93.7	2.2	4.3	3.0	3.2
29180	Lafayette, LA	414,288	51.1	24.5	8.2	27.6	23.7	15.9	37.6	73.7	24.7	2.1	7.0	7.5
29200	Lafayette-West Lafayette, IN	226,830	11.9	20.7	21.2	24.3	20.5	13.3	30.7	85.0	6.8	7.8	9.7	9.0
29340	Lake Charles, LA	240,210	20.9	24.6	8.3	25.7	24.1	17.2	38.1	76.4	24.0	1.9	9.0	10.3
29420	Lake Havasu City-Kingman, AZ	223,682	11.7	15.9	5.7	19.5	25.9	33.1	53.7	90.5	2.0	2.5	16.5	11.2
29460	Lakeland-Winter Haven, FL	818,330	35.8	22.0	8.6	26.6	23.4	19.4	39.5	69.1	17.1	3.0	27.7	15.9
29540	Lancaster, PA	558,589	7.4	22.9	8.9	24.8	23.2	20.2	39.1	87.7	6.2	3.5	11.0	8.1
29620	Lansing-East Lansing, MI	473,177	2.0	19.8	15.2	25.6	22.1	17.2	36.3	83.7	11.6	5.8	8.4	8.9
29700	Laredo, TX	269,148	7.0	30.7	11.5	26.3	20.7	10.8	30.5	87.5	0.7	0.4	80.3	68.9
29740	Las Cruces, NM	225,210	7.0	22.5	14.2	24.7	21.0	17.7	34.8	77.1	2.9	2.0	56.6	37.5
29820	Las Vegas-Henderson-North Las Vegas, NV	2,336,573	19.6	21.9	8.0	28.9	24.9	16.3	38.9	58.0	15.7	16.4	28.3	16.6
29940	Lawrence, KS	120,553	8.5	17.5	21.6	27.2	19.8	13.9	32.6	87.9	6.8	6.5	10.2	10.2
30020	Lawton, OK	126,687	1.1	23.6	11.0	29.8	21.0	14.6	34.3	74.0	19.5	5.3	20.3	16.9
30140	Lebanon, PA	144,252	7.9	22.2	7.2	25.6	24.0	21.0	41.4	87.7	4.8	2.5	13.0	7.2
30300	Lewiston, ID-WA	65,536	7.5	20.7	9.7	23.9	23.4	22.3	40.7	92.3	0.4	2.6	12.3	7.4
30340	Lewiston-Auburn, ME	113,765	5.7	20.3	10.1	25.5	25.4	18.8	40.7	91.2	7.1	1.6	4.8	4.5
30460	Lexington-Fayette, KY	520,045	9.8	21.5	11.6	27.1	23.7	16.1	37.0	83.2	13.2	4.0	8.0	7.9
30500	Lexington Park, MD	210,009	NA	23.1	8.7	25.5	26.9	15.7	39.2	79.7	17.3	4.4	8.2	8.5
30620	Lima, OH	100,838	-5.1	23.4	8.7	23.9	24.7	19.2	40.1	88.7	13.6	1.2	6.0	8.5
30700	Lincoln, NE	343,620	13.3	22.3	14.9	25.4	21.3	16.2	35.1	89.1	6.0	5.6	8.3	8.6
30780	Little Rock-North Little Rock-Conway, AR	764,582	9.0	23.0	9.4	27.1	23.8	16.7	38.3	71.7	25.5	2.6	7.9	7.4
30860	Logan, UT-ID	157,164	24.9	28.9	17.3	25.8	17.2	10.7	27.4	91.4	2.6	3.9	11.4	8.4
30980	Longview, TX	293,498	36.8	24.1	9.0	25.9	23.9	17.1	38.2	79.1	17.7	1.5	18.2	15.9

Table A-3. Metropolitan Areas — Who: Age, Race/Ethnicity, and Household Structure, 2023—*Continued*

Metropolitan area / division code	Metropolitan area / division	Hispanic or Latino (percent)	Born in state of residence (percent)	Foreign born (percent)	Not a U.S. citizen (percent)	Total households	Average household size	Household type (percent of all households): Family households: Total	Family households: Married-couple	Family households: Male householder	Family households: Female householder	Nonfamily households: Total	Nonfamily households: One-person households	Percent of households with people age 60 years and over
	ACS table number:	B03003	B05002	B05002	B05002	B11001	B25010	B11001	B11001	B11001	B11001	B11001	B11001	B11006
	column number:	14	15	16	17	18	19	20	21	22	23	24	25	26
26140	Homosassa Springs, FL	7.2	31.3	6.1	1.7	75,745	2.17	62.3	50.0	4.7	7.6	37.7	31.0	64.5
26300	Hot Springs, AR	7.6	56.3	3.3	1.5	45,243	2.17	57.7	43.0	5.2	9.4	42.3	33.2	50.9
26380	Houma-Bayou Cane-Thibodaux, LA	6.6	85.3	3.9	3.0	80,596	2.42	71.8	49.1	5.4	17.4	28.2	24.2	42.5
26420	Houston-Pasadena-The Woodlands, TX	38.3	52.7	24.8	13.9	2,731,843	2.72	69.7	49.8	6.1	13.8	30.3	24.7	34.7
26580	Huntington-Ashland, WV-KY-OH	1.3	65.5	1.2	0.6	156,188	2.29	63.6	47.0	5.5	11.2	36.4	30.3	44.9
26620	Huntsville, AL	7.0	52.5	4.8	2.4	212,486	2.41	65.8	51.3	3.9	10.6	34.2	28.7	38.3
26820	Idaho Falls, ID	13.8	60.6	3.8	1.8	56,728	2.92	73.2	57.5	5.3	10.4	26.8	21.9	35.2
26900	Indianapolis-Carmel-Greenwood, IN	9.0	65.1	9.5	5.6	862,092	2.44	63.2	46.9	4.7	11.6	36.8	29.7	36.6
26980	Iowa City, IA	6.9	61.1	9.2	4.3	73,376	2.33	53.0	41.9	2.2	8.8	47.0	34.1	32.5
27060	Ithaca, NY	6.5	57.0	12.9	8.7	43,054	2.03	45.8	36.6	2.0	7.2	54.2	39.0	38.4
27100	Jackson, MI	4.2	82.2	3.2	2.1	61,851	2.44	64.7	47.4	5.1	12.2	35.3	30.9	45.4
27140	Jackson, MS	3.9	79.3	2.5	1.9	240,218	2.44	62.6	41.2	4.3	17.1	37.4	33.0	40.9
27180	Jackson, TN	5.2	69.4	3.8	2.3	73,444	2.39	65.0	44.1	4.4	16.4	35.0	29.3	42.4
27260	Jacksonville, FL	11.3	44.2	10.0	4.0	693,081	2.43	64.7	47.3	4.4	13.1	35.3	27.9	41.4
27340	Jacksonville, NC	14.2	32.2	4.3	1.5	76,788	2.50	72.7	55.1	4.4	13.3	27.3	22.4	28.8
27500	Janesville-Beloit, WI	10.3	69.9	4.5	2.2	66,220	2.44	64.5	47.1	5.4	12.0	35.5	28.9	44.1
27620	Jefferson City, MO	3.6	76.1	3.4	1.5	59,911	2.36	62.8	48.6	5.2	9.0	37.2	32.1	42.3
27740	Johnson City, TN	4.7	60.5	2.8	2.1	91,198	2.26	60.9	47.5	3.3	10.2	39.1	31.5	46.7
27780	Johnstown, PA	2.2	86.3	1.0	0.4	57,282	2.16	59.7	44.2	5.5	10.1	40.3	35.2	52.2
27860	Jonesboro, AR	6.0	67.4	3.8	2.4	56,301	2.36	60.9	42.2	3.9	14.8	39.1	32.4	34.2
27900	Joplin, MO-KS	8.6	55.4	4.5	2.9	83,470	2.41	66.8	47.6	7.1	12.2	33.2	27.6	40.9
27980	Kahului-Wailuku, HI	10.7	47.0	18.7	8.3	56,848	2.84	68.4	49.4	6.3	12.7	31.6	25.0	52.7
28020	Kalamazoo-Portage, MI	6.1	72.0	5.7	3.3	107,893	2.36	58.9	42.9	5.7	10.3	41.1	29.5	35.3
28100	Kankakee, IL	13.0	79.2	6.9	4.3	41,130	2.47	66.1	44.9	6.6	14.7	33.9	26.8	42.4
28140	Kansas City, MO-KS	11.0	53.8	7.3	3.7	906,504	2.42	63.0	48.3	4.2	10.5	37.0	29.9	38.5
28420	Kennewick-Richland, WA	35.6	54.7	12.5	7.4	109,481	2.82	69.9	51.7	5.3	12.8	30.1	24.4	37.6
28450	Kenosha, WI	15.4	48.4	7.7	3.4	69,907	2.34	61.3	44.6	5.4	11.2	38.7	31.6	41.8
28660	Killeen-Temple, TX	25.6	47.1	8.5	4.0	182,336	2.61	67.5	49.8	4.4	13.3	32.5	26.7	33.5
28700	Kingsport-Bristol, TN-VA	2.4	55.6	1.4	0.5	132,975	2.31	61.2	44.6	3.8	12.8	38.8	34.3	50.9
28740	Kingston, NY	12.4	72.3	8.7	3.3	73,895	2.27	58.1	45.5	3.6	9.1	41.9	32.7	49.6
28880	Kiryas Joel-Poughkeepsie-Newburgh, NY	20.9	67.1	15.0	6.2	254,385	2.64	68.4	52.3	5.1	11.0	31.6	26.4	45.1
28940	Knoxville, TN	5.6	57.9	4.7	2.8	380,978	2.44	63.1	49.1	3.8	10.1	36.9	29.1	43.4
29020	Kokomo, IN	4.3	77.3	1.8	0.6	35,551	2.33	58.2	41.1	5.6	11.5	41.8	31.3	47.5
29100	La Crosse-Onalaska, WI-MN	2.5	67.1	2.8	0.7	72,276	2.28	58.2	48.1	3.2	7.0	41.8	31.3	39.9
29180	Lafayette, LA	5.5	84.3	3.8	2.1	166,896	2.46	63.9	42.8	6.3	14.9	36.1	29.7	38.2
29200	Lafayette-West Lafayette, IN	9.3	60.1	10.0	7.1	91,594	2.30	56.8	41.0	5.4	10.4	43.2	29.7	32.1
29340	Lake Charles, LA	4.9	77.0	2.6	1.3	93,049	2.55	68.3	47.0	6.5	14.9	31.7	27.5	41.7
29420	Lake Havasu City-Kingman, AZ	17.6	20.6	5.7	2.5	98,791	2.22	60.7	46.2	4.2	10.2	39.3	32.0	64.5
29460	Lakeland-Winter Haven, FL	30.3	40.7	12.4	6.4	306,915	2.62	69.2	49.8	6.1	13.3	30.8	24.2	45.9
29540	Lancaster, PA	11.7	73.4	6.2	2.6	211,669	2.56	66.7	54.1	4.3	8.4	33.3	26.2	47.0
29620	Lansing-East Lansing, MI	7.6	75.0	6.2	3.4	194,031	2.32	57.8	45.0	3.9	8.8	42.2	32.4	38.3
29700	Laredo, TX	94.9	68.2	24.9	17.1	83,045	3.21	79.0	48.9	9.6	20.5	21.0	18.2	36.8
29740	Las Cruces, NM	68.0	41.7	15.5	8.1	87,688	2.51	63.4	43.6	5.9	14.0	36.6	28.3	42.3
29820	Las Vegas-Henderson-North Las Vegas, NV	32.1	25.6	22.1	10.1	880,604	2.63	63.1	42.0	7.0	14.1	36.9	28.8	40.6
29940	Lawrence, KS	7.3	51.7	5.7	3.9	51,013	2.20	53.1	38.9	3.7	10.5	46.9	32.0	30.8
30020	Lawton, OK	14.7	45.9	4.8	2.2	48,105	2.43	64.4	43.9	5.5	15.0	35.6	29.0	37.0
30140	Lebanon, PA	15.6	74.8	5.1	2.2	58,012	2.42	70.1	50.1	5.9	14.1	29.9	24.5	45.6
30300	Lewiston, ID-WA	6.5	41.0	1.6	0.5	26,723	2.40	64.3	45.2	6.8	12.3	35.7	26.6	47.1
30340	Lewiston-Auburn, ME	2.3	68.5	5.0	2.8	48,239	2.27	63.8	47.5	4.6	11.7	36.2	30.1	38.8
30460	Lexington-Fayette, KY	7.9	62.6	9.1	4.9	222,167	2.26	59.0	43.4	4.4	11.2	41.0	31.5	36.8
30500	Lexington Park, MD	5.9	50.5	3.6	1.1	76,869	2.69	74.1	57.8	5.3	11.0	25.9	21.1	42.0
30620	Lima, OH	3.7	81.6	1.8	0.8	42,147	2.34	61.2	43.8	4.3	13.1	38.8	31.1	43.2
30700	Lincoln, NE	8.5	66.5	7.3	3.7	144,767	2.27	54.4	44.2	3.2	7.0	45.6	33.3	36.0
30780	Little Rock-North Little Rock-Conway, AR	7.2	65.1	4.8	3.2	310,926	2.40	63.2	45.6	4.5	13.1	36.8	32.0	39.4
30860	Logan, UT-ID	11.2	61.2	7.1	4.3	51,478	2.95	76.0	65.6	2.2	8.2	24.0	13.7	27.5
30980	Longview, TX	17.6	69.2	6.6	4.1	108,309	2.60	67.9	48.8	4.7	14.5	32.1	26.4	41.7

Table A-3. Metropolitan Areas — Who: Age, Race/Ethnicity, and Household Structure, 2023—*Continued*

Metropolitan area / division code	Metropolitan area / division	Total population	Percent change, 2010–2023	Population by age (percent): Under 18 years	18 to 24 years	25 to 44 years	45 to 64 years	65 years and over	Median age	Race alone or in combination (percent): White	Black or African American	Asian + Native Hawaiian or Other Pacific Islander	American Indian and Alaska Native + Some other race	Two or more races
	ACS table number:	B01003	Population Estimates	B01001	B01001	B01001	B01001	B01001	B01002	B02008	B02009	B02011 + B02012	B02010 + B02013	B02001
	column number:	1	2	3	4	5	6	7	8	9	10	11	12	13
31020	Longview-Kelso, WA	112,864	10.1	22.2	7.9	25.1	25.1	19.7	41.4	91.3	1.8	4.6	12.7	10.0
31080	Los Angeles-Long Beach-Anaheim, CA	12,799,100	-0.4	20.3	8.9	29.2	25.7	16.0	38.9	50.9	7.7	20.2	41.8	19.4
3108011244	Anaheim-Santa Ana-Irvine, CA Metro Division	3,135,755	NA	20.6	9.0	27.2	23.1	12.6	39.7	58.5	2.6	26.6	31.4	18.2
3108031084	Los Angeles-Long Beach-Glendale, CA Metro Division	9,663,345	NA	20.2	8.8	29.8	22.3	11.8	38.6	48.4	9.3	18.1	45.1	19.7
31140	Louisville/Jefferson County, KY-IN	1,364,742	6.0	22.1	8.1	26.7	25.4	17.7	39.5	81.7	15.6	3.2	9.1	9.1
31180	Lubbock, TX	360,342	24.9	23.6	15.4	27.2	19.8	14.0	32.6	82.3	8.8	2.6	27.4	20.0
31340	Lynchburg, VA	265,565	5.8	20.0	12.3	23.8	24.2	19.8	39.5	81.4	18.1	2.3	5.8	6.8
31420	Macon-Bibb County, GA	233,020	2.3	23.3	8.6	25.6	24.1	18.4	38.7	50.8	45.2	2.2	5.9	3.9
31540	Madison, WI	694,345	21.8	19.5	12.7	28.6	22.9	16.3	37.1	86.5	6.6	6.7	8.0	7.4
31700	Manchester-Nashua, NH	427,354	6.6	19.3	8.2	27.7	26.9	17.9	41.1	90.7	4.7	5.2	9.5	9.5
31740	Manhattan, KS	132,831	3.9	22.4	23.3	27.0	15.1	12.1	27.2	83.9	10.4	6.2	11.1	10.5
31860	Mankato, MN	104,248	7.6	20.1	19.0	24.4	20.0	16.6	33.9	91.8	6.2	2.8	6.0	6.6
31900	Mansfield, OH	125,064	0.7	21.5	7.0	26.1	24.3	21.1	41.6	91.1	9.3	1.3	5.6	7.0
32420	Mayagüez, PR	205,345	94.6	14.8	11.6	22.0	24.5	27.1	46.4	54.9	5.7	0.0	51.0	11.2
32580	McAllen-Edinburg-Mission, TX	898,471	15.2	30.5	11.3	25.9	20.5	11.8	30.9	87.5	1.0	1.4	71.0	60.5
32780	Medford, OR	220,768	8.5	20.2	7.6	25.2	23.3	23.8	42.5	92.4	1.6	3.6	17.4	13.9
32820	Memphis, TN-MS-AR	1,335,549	1.4	24.8	8.5	27.3	23.8	15.6	37.0	47.0	48.0	3.1	9.3	6.8
32900	Merced, CA	291,920	13.7	28.4	11.4	27.4	20.8	12.1	32.2	40.8	4.0	10.6	61.0	15.1
33100	Miami-Fort Lauderdale-West Palm Beach, FL	6,183,199	10.8	19.8	7.7	26.0	26.8	19.7	42.3	66.8	22.4	3.8	40.4	32.1
3310022744	Fort Lauderdale-Pompano Beach-Sunrise, FL Metro Division	1,962,531	NA	20.5	7.4	26.5	23.6	13.8	41.5	59.1	31.3	5.1	31.9	25.5
3310033124	Miami-Miami Beach-Kendall, FL Metro Division	2,686,867	NA	19.8	8.1	27.1	24.2	13.2	41.0	71.5	16.9	2.4	55.7	45.6
3310048424	West Palm Beach-Boca Raton-Delray Beach, FL Metro Division	1,533,801	NA	18.7	7.3	23.2	21.5	18.3	45.6	68.6	20.8	4.4	24.4	17.0
33140	Michigan City-La Porte, IN	111,706	0.2	21.1	6.8	26.6	25.7	19.8	41.9	85.9	13.5	1.4	8.7	8.3
33220	Midland, MI	84,039	-0.0	20.7	7.3	24.5	27.0	20.6	43.3	95.2	2.2	2.7	4.4	4.8
33260	Midland, TX	182,432	33.2	28.9	8.1	33.3	18.7	11.0	33.0	74.2	9.2	2.6	33.7	19.1
33340	Milwaukee-Waukesha, WI	1,560,424	0.2	22.4	8.7	26.9	24.4	17.6	38.8	75.2	17.9	5.5	12.0	10.0
33460	Minneapolis-St. Paul-Bloomington, MN-WI	3,712,020	13.0	23.0	8.3	28.1	24.5	16.1	38.3	79.2	11.8	8.6	8.5	7.6
33500	Minot, ND	75,489	3.4	24.5	9.3	29.1	21.4	15.8	34.9	90.2	5.7	3.6	9.7	9.2
33540	Missoula, MT	125,744	14.8	17.6	12.5	29.9	22.1	18.0	38.0	94.8	1.0	2.9	10.9	8.8
33660	Mobile, AL	411,640	-0.4	23.2	8.5	26.5	24.0	17.8	38.5	60.1	37.6	2.8	4.7	5.0
33700	Modesto, CA	551,430	7.0	26.5	9.4	27.3	22.7	14.1	35.1	68.2	4.8	10.0	47.5	28.6
33740	Monroe, LA	222,341	25.9	23.6	9.1	25.6	24.0	17.7	38.1	61.8	36.7	1.0	5.6	4.8
33780	Monroe, MI	155,045	2.0	20.6	7.9	23.9	26.7	20.9	42.9	95.8	4.0	1.2	6.3	6.7
33860	Montgomery, AL	385,463	2.5	23.2	8.9	25.7	25.2	16.9	38.3	51.3	46.4	2.8	5.5	5.4
34060	Morgantown, WV	141,817	8.8	16.4	19.0	27.4	21.7	15.5	35.1	91.6	6.1	3.3	3.2	4.1
34100	Morristown, TN	124,054	-9.3	21.2	6.6	24.9	26.9	20.3	41.5	91.4	3.5	1.1	11.6	7.3
34580	Mount Vernon-Anacortes, WA	131,417	12.2	20.6	6.9	25.7	23.2	23.7	42.8	81.7	1.6	4.7	22.9	10.5
34620	Muncie, IN	112,321	-4.5	18.1	19.0	23.0	21.9	18.0	35.4	91.6	7.2	2.2	6.4	6.7
34740	Muskegon-Norton Shores, MI	176,564	2.6	22.4	7.6	26.4	24.8	18.9	40.3	85.1	15.5	1.0	7.9	8.8
34820	Myrtle Beach-Conway-North Myrtle Beach, SC	397,478	47.0	16.7	7.5	21.1	27.5	27.3	49.3	83.8	13.3	2.3	8.2	7.1
34900	Napa, CA	133,216	-2.7	19.0	8.4	24.8	25.9	22.0	43.6	72.1	4.5	11.6	31.0	18.0
34940	Naples-Marco Island, FL	404,310	25.4	16.0	6.3	18.5	24.8	34.4	54.0	83.9	8.4	2.4	26.3	20.2
34980	Nashville-Davidson--Murfreesboro--Franklin, TN	2,104,235	32.1	22.7	9.1	29.7	24.0	14.6	37.0	79.1	15.8	4.4	10.9	9.6
35300	New Haven, CT	568,158	-34.2	19.4	10.4	25.6	25.5	19.2	40.5	70.7	16.8	5.7	18.2	10.7
35380	New Orleans-Metairie, LA	962,165	-18.0	21.5	7.9	27.4	24.9	18.3	40.0	52.3	40.5	4.5	14.2	10.6
35620	New York-Newark-Jersey City, NY-NJ	19,498,249	3.1	20.9	8.2	27.6	25.7	17.7	39.9	55.7	19.1	13.8	25.0	12.6
3562029484	Lakewood-New Brunswick, NJ Metro Division	2,514,461	NA	22.0	8.3	24.1	22.7	14.5	41.4	69.8	8.5	14.8	16.7	9.3
3562035004	Nassau County-Suffolk County, NY Metro Division	2,904,885	NA	20.9	8.6	24.2	23.9	14.3	42.3	70.6	11.5	9.9	20.7	11.7
3562035084	Newark, NJ Metro Division	2,214,581	NA	22.1	8.3	26.0	23.5	12.5	40.2	57.9	23.2	8.4	23.7	12.5

Table A-3. Metropolitan Areas — Who: Age, Race/Ethnicity, and Household Structure, 2023—*Continued*

Metropolitan area / division code	Metropolitan area / division	Hispanic or Latino (percent)	Born in state of residence (percent)	Foreign born (percent)	Not a U.S. citizen (percent)	Total households	Average household size	Household type (percent of all households): Family households: Total	Family households: Married-couple	Family households: Male householder	Family households: Female householder	Nonfamily households: Total	Nonfamily households: One-person households	Percent of households with people age 60 years and over
	ACS table number:	B03003	B05002	B05002	B05002	B11001	B25010	B11001	B11001	B11001	B11001	B11001	B11001	B11006
	column number:	14	15	16	17	18	19	20	21	22	23	24	25	26
31020	Longview-Kelso, WA	10.8	52.6	5.0	3.3	44,694	2.50	69.4	48.6	6.2	14.6	30.6	24.1	48.0
31080	Los Angeles-Long Beach-Anaheim, CA	45.1	52.2	32.9	14.4	4,542,998	2.76	65.7	45.0	6.8	13.9	34.3	26.0	41.9
3108011244	Anaheim-Santa Ana-Irvine, CA Metro Division	34.2	53.4	30.8	12.6	1,092,528	2.82	70.4	53.2	5.7	11.5	29.6	21.8	43.5
3108031084	Los Angeles-Long Beach-Glendale, CA Metro Division	48.6	51.7	33.5	15.0	3,450,470	2.74	64.2	42.4	7.1	14.7	35.8	27.4	41.4
31140	Louisville/Jefferson County, KY-IN	7.0	64.2	6.8	3.8	563,933	2.38	62.8	45.5	5.0	12.3	37.2	30.8	41.0
31180	Lubbock, TX	38.0	74.9	6.0	3.8	143,229	2.41	62.0	40.9	6.1	15.0	38.0	27.9	32.1
31340	Lynchburg, VA	3.9	63.4	3.0	1.5	104,544	2.41	63.9	48.6	4.6	10.6	36.1	30.3	46.0
31420	Macon-Bibb County, GA	4.1	74.0	3.7	2.4	89,842	2.50	64.4	44.9	3.9	15.6	35.6	31.1	45.7
31540	Madison, WI	7.2	61.4	8.0	5.1	308,244	2.19	53.3	43.4	3.2	6.6	46.7	35.4	33.6
31700	Manchester-Nashua, NH	8.8	40.0	10.8	4.3	170,761	2.45	64.3	50.4	4.5	9.4	35.7	26.5	43.6
31740	Manhattan, KS	10.9	46.7	6.2	2.2	51,764	2.34	58.8	46.7	4.1	8.0	41.2	28.0	27.1
31860	Mankato, MN	5.1	75.8	4.9	2.0	40,152	2.40	56.1	45.6	3.9	6.6	43.9	30.3	36.4
31900	Mansfield, OH	2.3	78.8	1.8	0.8	51,046	2.31	64.1	47.3	3.4	13.4	35.9	30.7	45.4
32420	Mayagüez, PR	99.2	0.0	1.7	1.0	83,931	2.42	58.2	32.2	4.9	21.1	41.8	34.4	53.5
32580	McAllen-Edinburg-Mission, TX	91.9	63.7	25.8	18.0	277,001	3.22	77.3	49.9	7.8	19.7	22.7	18.9	37.2
32780	Medford, OR	15.1	39.9	5.9	2.7	92,225	2.35	63.9	46.5	5.6	11.8	36.1	29.3	51.3
32820	Memphis, TN-MS-AR	7.6	58.6	6.4	4.2	523,295	2.51	63.9	39.6	5.6	18.7	36.1	31.9	39.8
32900	Merced, CA	63.9	65.8	25.8	16.0	88,053	3.27	67.5	44.5	8.9	14.1	32.5	28.0	38.4
33100	Miami-Fort Lauderdale-West Palm Beach, FL	46.6	31.9	42.7	17.5	2,349,920	2.59	66.2	45.0	6.4	14.8	33.8	27.1	47.7
3310022744	Fort Lauderdale-Pompano Beach-Sunrise, FL Metro Division	33.0	33.7	37.8	15.0	758,853	2.56	64.3	43.8	5.6	14.9	35.7	29.0	45.9
3310033124	Miami-Miami Beach-Kendall, FL Metro Division	69.1	31.3	54.8	22.6	985,935	2.68	69.0	44.0	8.0	17.0	31.0	24.4	45.0
3310048424	West Palm Beach-Boca Raton-Delray Beach, FL Metro Division	24.5	30.6	27.7	12.0	605,132	2.49	63.9	48.0	4.7	11.3	36.1	29.0	54.6
33140	Michigan City-La Porte, IN	7.8	66.9	4.3	2.5	45,725	2.29	61.2	41.3	5.7	14.2	38.8	30.0	44.5
33220	Midland, MI	3.6	81.7	3.1	1.3	35,761	2.32	65.5	54.8	3.5	7.2	34.5	28.7	44.9
33260	Midland, TX	46.6	64.5	12.0	6.5	73,012	2.47	64.3	47.7	7.9	8.7	35.7	30.6	29.0
33340	Milwaukee-Waukesha, WI	12.2	70.2	8.0	4.2	650,986	2.36	58.7	42.8	4.8	11.1	41.3	33.1	39.8
33460	Minneapolis-St. Paul-Bloomington, MN-WI	6.9	63.7	10.6	4.3	1,501,453	2.43	61.6	48.1	4.6	8.9	38.4	30.1	38.4
33500	Minot, ND	7.2	58.7	2.9	1.1	31,532	2.33	62.1	52.0	3.9	6.2	37.9	30.5	33.5
33540	Missoula, MT	4.8	45.6	1.9	0.6	56,810	2.15	52.3	39.1	5.3	7.9	47.7	32.7	35.2
33660	Mobile, AL	3.5	72.3	3.6	1.5	163,963	2.46	60.3	39.5	3.9	16.9	39.7	34.7	42.6
33700	Modesto, CA	50.9	68.5	21.7	11.0	179,152	3.05	73.9	51.7	7.3	14.8	26.1	20.6	41.0
33740	Monroe, LA	3.0	78.5	1.9	1.4	87,927	2.45	63.9	39.3	6.1	18.5	36.1	32.5	43.0
33780	Monroe, MI	4.5	60.9	2.3	1.1	62,936	2.44	69.1	51.5	5.5	12.1	30.9	24.8	47.2
33860	Montgomery, AL	4.3	69.9	4.6	2.9	153,926	2.42	63.2	41.0	4.2	18.0	36.8	32.4	41.8
34060	Morgantown, WV	3.0	60.4	4.2	2.4	57,621	2.28	51.7	39.5	3.0	9.1	48.3	36.8	36.4
34100	Morristown, TN	10.3	58.5	5.1	4.1	49,910	2.45	68.7	50.6	5.7	12.4	31.3	24.6	48.0
34580	Mount Vernon-Anacortes, WA	19.7	54.3	10.2	5.6	53,087	2.44	68.9	54.3	5.2	9.4	31.1	23.7	50.8
34620	Muncie, IN	3.3	76.7	3.5	2.3	44,361	2.35	55.6	39.1	6.2	10.3	44.4	32.0	40.1
34740	Muskegon-Norton Shores, MI	6.4	83.3	2.3	1.2	70,042	2.44	66.7	47.3	5.6	13.7	33.3	25.9	43.3
34820	Myrtle Beach-Conway-North Myrtle Beach, SC	7.3	32.4	6.2	3.3	168,080	2.32	65.0	50.3	3.2	11.5	35.0	29.8	54.7
34900	Napa, CA	36.7	59.6	21.9	8.7	51,167	2.52	68.2	51.0	4.7	12.5	31.8	24.0	50.7
34940	Naples-Marco Island, FL	28.0	22.6	25.2	13.3	166,192	2.40	67.6	54.7	4.7	8.2	32.4	26.8	62.7
34980	Nashville-Davidson--Murfreesboro--Franklin, TN	10.0	49.7	9.7	5.9	863,464	2.39	63.3	48.2	4.5	10.5	36.7	28.9	34.6
35300	New Haven, CT	19.9	60.8	13.9	6.7	233,004	2.34	60.1	41.0	4.5	14.7	39.9	31.4	44.6
35380	New Orleans-Metairie, LA	13.1	71.1	9.6	5.3	399,198	2.36	58.1	37.5	5.2	15.3	41.9	35.8	44.1
35620	New York-Newark-Jersey City, NY-NJ	25.7	52.3	30.5	12.6	7,490,498	2.55	63.9	44.5	5.3	14.1	36.1	29.2	44.4
3562029484	Lakewood-New Brunswick, NJ Metro Division	16.9	53.2	22.4	9.5	941,969	2.62	69.4	54.7	4.7	10.0	30.6	24.9	47.9
3562035004	Nassau County-Suffolk County, NY Metro Division	21.0	72.3	19.9	7.0	966,971	2.95	73.8	57.6	4.4	11.8	26.2	21.0	51.3
3562035084	Newark, NJ Metro Division	24.0	50.8	26.4	12.4	831,608	2.62	69.5	48.8	5.9	14.8	30.5	25.1	43.2

Table A-3. Metropolitan Areas — Who: Age, Race/Ethnicity, and Household Structure, 2023—*Continued*

Metropolitan area / division code	Metropolitan area / division	Total population	Percent change, 2010–2023	Population by age (percent): Under 18 years	18 to 24 years	25 to 44 years	45 to 64 years	65 years and over	Median age	Race alone or in combination (percent): White	Black or African American	Asian + Native Hawaiian or Other Pacific Islander	American Indian and Alaska Native + Some other race	Two or more races
	ACS table number:	B01003	Population Estimates	B01001	B01001	B01001	B01001	B01001	B01002	B02008	B02009	B02011 + B02012	B02010 + B02013	B02001
	column number:	1	2	3	4	5	6	7	8	9	10	11	12	13
3562035614	New York-Jersey City-White Plains, NY-NJ Metro Division	11,864,322	NA	20.4	8.1	29.4	21.6	13.1	39.1	48.7	22.4	15.5	28.0	13.5
35660	Niles, MI	152,261	-2.9	21.1	7.9	23.0	25.8	22.0	43.0	81.4	15.2	3.0	8.9	8.1
35840	North Port-Bradenton-Sarasota, FL	910,108	29.4	15.5	5.9	19.1	26.0	33.5	53.8	87.0	7.2	3.2	14.7	11.7
35980	Norwich-New London-Willimantic, CT	279,634	2.0	19.0	10.2	25.1	25.5	20.1	40.8	83.0	9.1	5.0	15.0	10.3
36100	Ocala, FL	409,959	23.7	18.7	6.1	22.2	24.1	28.9	47.7	79.7	14.7	2.8	17.4	13.8
36220	Odessa, TX	164,494	19.9	30.4	9.7	29.0	20.7	10.2	31.6	72.9	5.7	1.6	49.7	29.4
36260	Ogden, UT	658,013	19.4	28.1	9.7	29.0	21.3	11.9	33.3	91.9	2.1	4.5	11.1	9.0
36420	Oklahoma City, OK	1,477,926	17.5	23.9	10.4	28.0	22.4	15.2	36.0	78.6	12.7	5.3	21.4	16.3
36500	Olympia-Lacey-Tumwater, WA	299,003	18.1	20.5	7.1	29.5	23.5	19.3	40.3	83.1	6.1	11.2	13.0	12.4
36540	Omaha, NE-IA	984,548	13.4	24.9	8.7	28.0	23.1	15.3	37.0	83.2	10.3	4.6	12.0	9.3
36740	Orlando-Kissimmee-Sanford, FL	2,817,933	31.6	21.1	9.0	29.0	24.9	16.1	38.9	65.8	19.3	6.4	30.3	20.0
36780	Oshkosh-Neenah, WI	171,735	2.8	20.0	11.4	25.7	24.8	18.1	38.9	92.3	4.6	4.0	4.8	5.6
36980	Owensboro, KY	112,258	-3.1	23.4	8.4	25.0	24.4	18.8	38.9	90.3	8.4	0.0	4.9	4.1
37100	Oxnard-Thousand Oaks-Ventura, CA	829,590	0.5	21.5	8.7	26.2	25.6	18.1	39.9	75.8	3.2	10.5	37.0	25.3
37140	Paducah, KY-IL	101,900	2.5	22.2	6.8	23.4	25.6	22.0	43.4	88.7	11.0	1.5	5.3	6.3
37340	Palm Bay-Melbourne-Titusville, FL	643,979	18.5	17.9	7.0	23.3	26.9	24.9	46.6	83.7	12.4	3.9	11.9	11.3
37460	Panama City-Panama City Beach, FL	216,371	27.8	21.0	7.5	25.5	27.5	18.5	41.6	85.6	11.2	4.0	11.6	11.6
37620	Parkersburg-Vienna, WV	87,628	-46.1	20.7	7.0	22.9	27.1	22.2	44.5	98.5	0.9	1.1	4.8	5.3
37860	Pensacola-Ferry Pass-Brent, FL	530,090	17.8	21.2	9.4	27.0	24.6	17.9	39.1	79.2	17.5	5.2	9.2	10.4
37900	Peoria, IL	361,989	-4.4	22.9	8.4	24.4	24.6	19.6	40.8	86.4	11.7	3.8	5.4	6.5
37980	Philadelphia-Camden-Wilmington, PA-NJ-DE-MD	6,246,160	4.6	21.2	8.8	27.2	25.0	17.8	39.5	66.8	22.9	7.9	11.3	8.2
3798015804	Camden, NJ Metro Division	1,304,786	NA	21.5	8.2	26.4	22.9	13.3	40.3	71.2	19.6	7.0	13.4	10.1
3798033874	Montgomery County-Bucks County-Chester County, PA Metro Division	2,064,510	NA	20.8	8.1	24.8	23.0	14.9	42.1	82.8	8.5	8.2	8.3	7.3
3798037964	Philadelphia, PA Metro Division	2,127,262	NA	21.2	9.9	30.4	19.2	12.3	36.4	48.9	38.1	8.8	13.0	8.1
3798048864	Wilmington, DE-MD-NJ Metro Division	749,602	NA	21.3	8.7	26.5	22.0	13.5	40.2	65.7	25.7	6.5	10.8	8.0
38060	Phoenix-Mesa-Chandler, AZ	5,070,110	20.4	22.0	9.1	27.9	23.8	17.1	38.0	76.3	8.1	6.8	29.1	19.1
38420	Pinehurst-Southern Pines, NC	106,898	19.6	21.4	5.8	25.1	23.4	24.3	44.0	84.5	11.6	2.6	11.3	9.4
38300	Pittsburgh, PA	2,422,725	2.8	18.7	8.1	25.6	25.5	22.1	42.8	88.2	9.7	3.4	4.3	5.2
38340	Pittsfield, MA	126,818	-3.3	15.8	8.4	22.3	27.4	26.1	48.4	91.7	5.0	2.5	8.4	6.9
38540	Pocatello, ID	90,400	-0.0	24.8	10.4	28.2	20.6	15.9	35.7	88.9	0.6	2.7	14.7	7.4
38660	Ponce, PR	266,237	9.6	16.7	9.4	24.4	25.2	24.3	44.6	80.9	9.2	0.0	62.4	51.6
38860	Portland-South Portland, ME	566,329	10.2	17.5	7.5	26.3	26.6	22.0	43.8	95.0	3.5	3.0	6.6	7.8
38900	Portland-Vancouver-Hillsboro, OR-WA	2,509,925	12.4	20.1	7.7	30.5	24.9	16.8	39.8	82.6	4.9	11.3	15.3	13.0
38940	Port St. Lucie, FL	536,901	26.3	18.4	6.4	22.4	25.4	27.4	47.8	75.9	19.4	2.7	16.8	14.1
39140	Prescott Valley-Prescott, AZ	249,081	18.0	15.1	6.7	18.5	25.1	34.7	55.3	91.8	1.5	2.8	17.2	13.0
39300	Providence-Warwick, RI-MA	1,677,803	4.8	19.2	9.3	26.7	25.9	19.0	40.8	81.0	10.2	4.5	17.9	12.1
39340	Provo-Orem-Lehi, UT	733,218	38.4	31.2	16.6	27.6	16.5	8.2	26.3	91.2	1.6	5.3	12.8	10.1
39380	Pueblo, CO	169,422	6.2	21.4	8.5	25.7	24.5	19.9	41.2	87.8	3.7	2.3	22.1	14.1
39460	Punta Gorda, FL	206,134	28.8	11.8	4.9	16.7	25.7	40.9	60.1	90.3	7.2	2.0	7.3	6.7
39540	Racine-Mount Pleasant, WI	196,613	0.6	22.3	8.3	24.7	26.0	18.6	40.6	84.7	13.4	2.1	14.0	13.1
39580	Raleigh-Cary, NC	1,509,231	32.7	23.0	8.5	29.0	25.8	13.6	38.0	66.8	21.0	8.6	13.3	9.0
39660	Rapid City, SD	156,686	23.6	21.6	8.8	25.2	24.7	19.8	40.2	89.5	2.5	2.1	15.5	9.4
39740	Reading, PA	432,821	5.1	21.8	9.6	24.8	25.5	18.4	39.5	83.8	12.8	2.1	24.2	16.8
39820	Redding, CA	180,366	1.7	21.5	7.1	25.5	24.0	21.8	41.2	88.4	2.4	6.1	16.1	12.2
39900	Reno, NV	564,527	32.4	20.3	8.2	28.3	24.4	18.8	39.7	81.5	4.0	9.2	24.4	17.7
40060	Richmond, VA	1,350,123	7.0	21.0	9.1	28.1	24.6	17.2	39.0	62.0	30.6	5.9	9.2	7.1
40140	Riverside-San Bernardino-Ontario, CA	4,688,053	10.4	24.5	9.6	28.2	23.4	14.4	36.1	53.9	9.0	10.8	49.6	21.8
40220	Roanoke, VA	313,786	1.6	19.9	8.0	25.0	25.6	21.6	42.7	82.1	14.6	3.2	6.6	6.1
40340	Rochester, MN	229,077	23.0	23.5	7.3	27.4	23.3	18.5	39.0	85.9	7.4	6.1	6.9	6.1
40380	Rochester, NY	1,052,087	-0.2	19.7	9.4	25.5	25.3	20.1	41.1	81.6	13.6	4.1	8.5	7.2
40420	Rockford, IL	334,124	-4.3	23.2	8.7	24.1	25.2	18.7	40.5	77.2	12.8	3.5	19.1	11.4
40580	Rocky Mount, NC	145,383	-4.7	22.4	7.7	23.6	26.2	20.1	41.7	47.4	48.5	1.2	8.3	5.3
40660	Rome, GA	100,113	4.0	22.6	9.9	26.2	24.1	17.2	37.8	79.8	14.0	1.9	13.3	9.0
40900	Sacramento-Roseville-Folsom, CA	2,420,608	12.4	21.8	9.1	27.7	24.1	17.2	38.9	63.9	9.8	20.5	22.4	14.9
40980	Saginaw, MI	187,782	-6.1	21.1	8.8	24.9	23.9	21.2	41.2	78.1	20.5	1.6	5.6	5.6
41060	St. Cloud, MN	202,577	7.0	23.8	13.3	23.8	23.1	16.0	36.2	87.7	10.3	3.1	5.8	6.5

Table A-3. Metropolitan Areas — Who: Age, Race/Ethnicity, and Household Structure, 2023—*Continued*

Metropolitan area / division code	Metropolitan area / division	Hispanic or Latino (percent)	Born in state of residence (percent)	Foreign born (percent)	Not a U.S. citizen (percent)	Total households	Average household size	Household type (percent of all households): Family households: Total	Family households: Married-couple	Family households: Male householder	Family households: Female householder	Nonfamily households: Total	Nonfamily households: One-person households	Percent of households with people age 60 years and over
	ACS table number:	B03003	B05002	B05002	B05002	B11001	B25010	B11001	B11001	B11001	B11001	B11001	B11001	B11006
	column number:	14	15	16	17	18	19	20	21	22	23	24	25	26
3562035614	New York-Jersey City-White Plains, NY-NJ Metro Division	29.1	47.5	35.5	14.7	4,749,950	2.44	59.8	39.0	5.5	15.3	40.2	32.3	42.5
35660	Niles, MI	6.4	60.1	6.9	3.1	65,129	2.29	64.2	47.6	5.6	10.9	35.8	31.7	46.9
35840	North Port-Bradenton-Sarasota, FL	14.3	24.1	15.2	7.0	408,101	2.20	63.7	51.3	4.0	8.4	36.3	28.8	61.8
35980	Norwich-New London-Willimantic, CT	15.2	54.6	9.1	3.5	114,156	2.35	61.2	44.2	3.9	13.1	38.8	30.2	44.3
36100	Ocala, FL	17.6	38.9	10.2	4.6	171,369	2.35	65.6	49.1	4.5	11.9	34.4	29.0	57.7
36220	Odessa, TX	64.5	60.4	19.7	12.9	66,937	2.43	67.9	47.2	8.5	12.1	32.1	26.3	29.3
36260	Ogden, UT	14.8	64.8	6.2	3.1	220,388	2.96	75.4	61.0	4.7	9.7	24.6	18.5	32.8
36420	Oklahoma City, OK	16.0	59.6	7.9	4.5	581,140	2.49	62.6	45.7	5.0	11.8	37.4	29.9	37.3
36500	Olympia-Lacey-Tumwater, WA	11.0	46.4	8.4	2.9	119,786	2.46	65.3	50.6	3.4	11.4	34.7	25.6	43.1
36540	Omaha, NE-IA	12.4	57.4	8.0	4.7	397,769	2.43	62.8	47.7	4.2	10.9	37.2	30.4	36.7
36740	Orlando-Kissimmee-Sanford, FL	33.4	34.1	21.9	10.2	1,073,662	2.58	66.9	48.1	5.3	13.5	33.1	24.8	40.4
36780	Oshkosh-Neenah, WI	5.2	78.4	3.2	1.6	71,563	2.32	56.2	44.6	3.8	7.8	43.8	35.4	41.5
36980	Owensboro, KY	4.4	75.8	2.6	1.8	45,814	2.40	64.1	43.5	5.5	15.0	35.9	32.2	42.9
37100	Oxnard-Thousand Oaks-Ventura, CA	44.8	58.4	22.9	10.5	283,718	2.88	72.1	53.8	6.9	11.4	27.9	21.5	47.6
37140	Paducah, KY-IL	3.5	64.7	1.5	1.0	43,021	2.32	61.4	45.3	3.9	12.2	38.6	33.1	46.7
37340	Palm Bay-Melbourne-Titusville, FL	12.5	33.5	9.8	3.0	258,656	2.45	64.5	49.7	4.3	10.5	35.5	29.0	53.9
37460	Panama City-Panama City Beach, FL	8.9	39.8	7.5	4.4	89,699	2.35	62.5	45.8	4.8	12.0	37.5	30.8	42.6
37620	Parkersburg-Vienna, WV	1.4	71.8	0.6	0.1	38,866	2.23	60.6	45.7	3.4	11.5	39.4	34.4	48.1
37860	Pensacola-Ferry Pass-Brent, FL	7.0	39.2	5.8	2.8	204,344	2.48	66.3	49.3	4.7	12.4	33.7	27.1	43.3
37900	Peoria, IL	4.4	77.8	4.7	2.7	153,577	2.29	60.6	45.5	4.9	10.2	39.4	34.1	41.7
37980	Philadelphia-Camden-Wilmington, PA-NJ-DE-MD	10.9	60.4	12.0	5.3	2,484,152	2.45	62.8	44.7	4.9	13.2	37.2	30.2	42.3
3798015804	Camden, NJ Metro Division	13.5	55.9	10.8	4.4	494,538	2.59	66.7	48.4	4.4	13.9	33.3	27.3	43.7
3798033874	Montgomery County-Bucks County-Chester County, PA Metro Division	7.2	65.1	11.2	4.8	793,082	2.54	68.7	55.7	4.3	8.7	31.3	25.5	45.3
3798037964	Philadelphia, PA Metro Division	12.9	63.6	14.2	6.4	903,757	2.28	54.6	32.6	5.7	16.4	45.4	36.8	38.7
3798048864	Wilmington, DE-MD-NJ Metro Division	11.0	46.1	10.5	5.1	292,775	2.49	65.7	46.5	4.8	14.4	34.3	27.5	43.0
38060	Phoenix-Mesa-Chandler, AZ	31.3	38.4	14.2	7.5	1,922,068	2.59	65.1	47.6	5.6	11.8	34.9	26.4	41.0
38420	Pinehurst-Southern Pines, NC	7.8	46.4	6.1	3.1	46,385	2.28	64.5	51.4	4.6	8.5	35.5	30.6	48.1
38300	Pittsburgh, PA	2.4	78.6	4.3	1.9	1,067,180	2.21	59.2	45.3	3.9	10.1	40.8	33.9	45.7
38340	Pittsfield, MA	5.9	62.3	6.6	3.3	58,807	2.06	56.6	40.9	4.2	11.5	43.4	34.0	52.8
38540	Pocatello, ID	10.1	57.1	2.8	1.6	33,729	2.61	64.3	53.0	4.2	7.1	35.7	29.3	34.9
38660	Ponce, PR	99.5	0.0	0.5	0.4	105,603	2.47	63.4	32.9	7.2	23.4	36.6	33.4	52.9
38860	Portland-South Portland, ME	2.5	50.6	4.9	2.4	244,997	2.25	61.5	50.1	3.6	7.8	38.5	29.1	45.6
38900	Portland-Vancouver-Hillsboro, OR-WA	14.1	41.9	12.3	5.5	1,028,651	2.40	61.3	47.0	5.0	9.4	38.7	28.3	37.6
38940	Port St. Lucie, FL	20.3	33.8	17.0	6.6	214,904	2.46	63.7	48.8	4.7	10.2	36.3	28.5	57.9
39140	Prescott Valley-Prescott, AZ	15.7	28.9	6.3	3.0	113,784	2.15	63.6	52.2	3.4	8.0	36.4	29.0	65.0
39300	Providence-Warwick, RI-MA	15.4	57.9	14.5	6.6	677,970	2.39	61.7	43.4	5.3	13.0	38.3	30.1	44.7
39340	Provo-Orem-Lehi, UT	14.4	61.2	8.1	4.9	219,263	3.28	79.8	68.3	4.1	7.3	20.2	11.7	25.8
39380	Pueblo, CO	42.4	59.7	3.8	2.8	68,732	2.38	66.9	46.5	7.7	12.7	33.1	26.9	45.9
39460	Punta Gorda, FL	8.3	21.0	8.8	2.9	90,367	2.22	67.1	57.1	3.1	6.9	32.9	27.0	70.3
39540	Racine-Mount Pleasant, WI	15.4	72.5	4.1	2.1	79,066	2.43	62.2	45.4	4.3	12.4	37.8	30.2	42.3
39580	Raleigh-Cary, NC	12.4	43.5	14.4	7.7	600,306	2.47	66.0	52.4	3.9	9.8	34.0	26.2	33.3
39660	Rapid City, SD	5.6	56.3	2.0	0.7	65,028	2.33	65.5	50.8	6.2	8.5	34.5	29.3	43.1
39740	Reading, PA	25.3	71.0	10.5	5.2	163,307	2.56	68.2	49.4	6.0	12.8	31.8	25.2	44.4
39820	Redding, CA	12.2	69.4	5.3	2.2	72,320	2.44	61.7	44.5	4.5	12.7	38.3	29.2	50.7
39900	Reno, NV	25.7	32.5	13.4	7.0	227,132	2.45	60.2	44.0	6.2	10.0	39.8	29.6	43.6
40060	Richmond, VA	8.4	57.4	9.7	4.9	536,542	2.44	64.6	46.3	4.5	13.8	35.4	28.7	40.0
40140	Riverside-San Bernardino-Ontario, CA	53.7	63.5	22.3	10.0	1,474,564	3.13	75.4	51.4	7.8	16.2	24.6	18.9	43.4
40220	Roanoke, VA	5.6	63.7	6.6	3.5	134,105	2.28	64.6	46.8	4.9	12.9	35.4	30.2	43.9
40340	Rochester, MN	5.3	63.3	8.4	2.7	92,141	2.44	64.4	54.0	3.1	7.3	35.6	29.6	40.0
40380	Rochester, NY	8.7	76.7	6.5	2.4	446,704	2.26	59.3	42.8	4.8	11.8	40.7	32.2	44.3
40420	Rockford, IL	17.7	69.8	8.4	3.8	135,255	2.44	65.5	45.0	5.7	14.7	34.5	28.6	43.4
40580	Rocky Mount, NC	7.7	76.3	3.3	1.8	59,997	2.38	63.3	41.0	6.0	16.4	36.7	32.8	42.8
40660	Rome, GA	12.7	69.1	5.8	2.8	37,835	2.53	69.2	43.6	8.6	17.0	30.8	27.3	40.2
40900	Sacramento-Roseville-Folsom, CA	23.0	62.2	19.8	8.2	888,619	2.68	67.1	50.1	5.0	11.9	32.9	25.3	43.0
40980	Saginaw, MI	9.3	86.2	2.1	0.9	77,158	2.36	62.0	43.0	4.2	14.7	38.0	32.4	46.1
41060	St. Cloud, MN	4.7	76.8	8.0	3.3	77,652	2.50	59.3	47.8	4.1	7.3	40.7	30.5	40.6

Table A-3. Metropolitan Areas — Who: Age, Race/Ethnicity, and Household Structure, 2023—*Continued*

Metropolitan area / division code	Metropolitan area / division	Total population	Percent change, 2010–2023	Population by age (percent)					Median age	Race alone or in combination (percent)				
				Under 18 years	18 to 24 years	25 to 44 years	45 to 64 years	65 years and over		White	Black or African American	Asian + Native Hawaiian or Other Pacific Islander	American Indian and Alaska Native + Some other race	Two or more races
	ACS table number:	B01003	Population Estimates	B01001	B01001	B01001	B01001	B01001	B01002	B02008	B02009	B02011 + B02012	B02010 + B02013	B02001
	column number:	1	2	3	4	5	6	7	8	9	10	11	12	13
41100	St. George, UT	202,452	46.2	24.1	9.8	23.3	20.4	22.5	40.1	91.3	1.2	3.6	12.6	8.4
41140	St. Joseph, MO-KS	118,666	-8.5	22.6	8.5	25.5	24.0	19.4	39.6	91.0	7.0	3.1	7.3	7.8
41180	St. Louis, MO-IL	2,795,504	-0.7	21.4	8.2	26.6	25.1	18.6	40.2	78.1	19.1	4.1	6.1	6.7
41420	Salem, OR	436,546	11.4	22.8	9.6	26.9	23.2	17.6	37.7	85.0	2.4	5.3	25.7	17.1
41500	Salinas, CA	430,723	3.4	25.5	9.9	26.5	22.6	15.5	35.9	47.2	3.1	8.4	57.6	15.3
41540	Salisbury, MD	129,710	3.5	20.8	12.8	25.8	23.5	17.1	37.4	65.9	30.9	3.0	10.5	9.6
41620	Salt Lake City-Murray, UT	1,267,864	12.3	25.1	9.9	30.9	21.9	12.1	34.2	81.5	3.0	8.3	19.3	11.0
41660	San Angelo, TX	120,055	6.7	23.2	9.9	28.3	21.1	17.6	37.3	88.5	5.0	2.5	30.8	26.1
41700	San Antonio-New Braunfels, TX	2,703,999	25.3	24.1	9.4	29.3	23.0	14.3	36.2	75.9	9.0	4.7	42.5	30.4
41740	San Diego-Chula Vista-Carlsbad, CA	3,269,973	5.3	20.6	9.7	30.2	23.5	15.9	37.6	67.0	6.9	17.0	31.9	21.4
41780	Sandusky, OH	113,838	47.7	18.3	5.3	22.5	27.6	26.3	49.0	92.0	7.0	1.4	6.0	6.3
41860	San Francisco-Oakland-Fremont, CA	4,566,961	5.1	18.9	7.5	29.7	26.1	17.8	40.7	49.2	8.8	33.8	23.0	13.5
4186036084	Oakland-Fremont-Berkeley, CA Metro Division	2,777,213	NA	20.4	7.9	29.0	22.8	12.6	40.0	46.1	11.5	33.0	25.0	14.1
4186041884	San Francisco-San Mateo-Redwood City, CA Metro Division	1,535,341	NA	16.2	6.8	32.5	22.8	13.9	41.0	50.0	5.0	39.2	19.7	12.6
4186042034	San Rafael, CA Metro Division	254,407	NA	18.9	7.3	19.9	25.3	17.5	48.2	78.8	3.6	10.0	21.3	13.0
41940	San Jose-Sunnyvale-Santa Clara, CA	1,945,767	5.6	20.1	9.1	30.3	25.2	15.3	38.2	43.5	3.6	43.7	25.8	15.3
41980	San Juan-Bayamón-Caguas, PR	2,037,875	-17.7	15.4	9.1	25.8	26.0	23.7	44.8	52.0	12.3	0.4	79.1	41.3
42020	San Luis Obispo-Paso Robles, CA	281,639	4.3	17.2	15.1	22.3	22.6	22.8	41.0	84.7	2.3	6.2	24.5	16.5
42100	Santa Cruz-Watsonville, CA	261,547	-0.6	17.9	14.8	23.3	24.2	19.8	39.8	72.9	2.2	7.3	32.6	13.9
42140	Santa Fe, NM	155,956	7.8	15.5	7.1	22.5	25.8	29.1	49.3	85.7	1.7	2.4	42.9	31.8
42200	Santa Maria-Santa Barbara, CA	441,257	3.9	22.2	15.0	24.7	20.9	17.1	34.9	73.9	2.9	7.9	43.9	27.2
42220	Santa Rosa-Petaluma, CA	481,812	-0.7	18.7	7.7	25.4	25.9	22.3	43.3	76.9	3.1	7.9	30.3	16.6
42340	Savannah, GA	424,935	21.9	22.5	9.4	29.3	22.9	15.9	37.0	61.7	33.1	4.1	9.5	7.5
42540	Scranton--Wilkes-Barre, PA	569,413	0.9	20.2	8.9	24.5	25.6	20.8	41.9	85.0	7.0	2.7	14.7	8.6
42660	Seattle-Tacoma-Bellevue, WA	4,044,837	17.3	20.5	8.0	32.6	24.0	14.8	37.8	69.9	9.0	22.3	13.3	12.9
4266021794	Everett, WA Metro Division	844,761	NA	21.8	7.2	30.8	21.6	11.6	38.5	73.8	5.7	18.7	13.5	10.7
4266042644	Seattle-Bellevue-Kent, WA Metro Division	2,271,380	NA	19.1	8.1	34.3	21.1	11.0	37.7	65.2	9.0	26.7	12.7	12.2
4266045104	Tacoma-Lakewood, WA Metro Division	928,696	NA	22.8	8.5	30.2	20.3	11.4	37.5	78.0	11.9	14.9	14.4	16.4
42680	Sebastian-Vero Beach-West Vero Corridor, FL	169,795	22.8	14.8	6.1	17.6	25.8	35.7	55.9	86.8	9.8	2.3	12.0	10.7
42700	Sebring, FL	107,614	9.1	16.2	6.6	18.7	21.9	36.6	54.4	79.8	11.8	1.8	19.7	12.4
43100	Sheboygan, WI	117,752	2.0	21.0	7.6	24.0	27.0	20.3	42.6	89.3	3.6	6.7	8.6	7.8
43300	Sherman-Denison, TX	146,907	21.3	24.1	8.3	24.3	25.6	17.7	39.6	89.1	7.3	2.8	16.0	14.1
43340	Shreveport-Bossier City, LA	383,295	-4.1	23.6	8.1	25.8	24.3	18.2	40.2	56.0	41.5	2.3	7.4	6.8
43420	Sierra Vista-Douglas, AZ	124,640	-6.5	20.3	8.0	23.3	22.9	25.7	44.0	85.4	6.5	4.8	32.6	27.3
43580	Sioux City, IA-NE-SD	143,885	0.0	25.3	10.0	23.7	24.6	16.3	37.3	83.2	7.8	3.2	19.5	13.8
43620	Sioux Falls, SD-MN	303,827	32.5	25.2	8.5	28.1	22.9	15.2	37.1	88.7	6.8	2.7	8.3	5.9
43640	Slidell-Mandeville-Covington, LA	275,583	NA	23.4	7.7	24.2	25.7	19.0	40.8	83.5	15.7	2.2	10.5	11.1
43780	South Bend-Mishawaka, IN-MI	324,490	1.7	22.6	11.2	24.7	23.3	18.2	38.1	83.0	14.4	3.4	10.0	10.5
43900	Spartanburg, SC	383,327	34.6	23.2	8.9	26.7	24.5	16.8	38.1	73.8	22.2	3.0	9.3	8.0
44060	Spokane-Spokane Valley, WA	600,292	27.1	21.3	8.7	27.8	23.7	18.4	39.2	90.7	3.8	4.9	10.3	8.8
44100	Springfield, IL	205,111	-2.5	21.4	7.9	24.4	26.0	20.4	42.4	83.8	13.3	3.4	5.4	5.7
44140	Springfield, MA	460,291	-33.6	20.7	9.7	26.1	24.7	18.9	39.9	78.5	13.4	3.1	23.4	16.2
44180	Springfield, MO	490,886	12.8	22.4	11.0	26.0	23.1	17.6	37.4	94.4	3.9	2.6	6.2	6.4
44220	Springfield, OH	134,610	-2.6	22.6	7.8	23.6	25.4	20.7	41.3	90.9	9.0	1.5	8.5	9.7
44300	State College, PA	157,795	2.4	14.2	24.6	22.8	21.8	16.5	34.3	88.1	5.1	7.4	4.8	4.7
44420	Staunton-Stuarts Draft, VA	127,344	3.9	18.7	7.1	25.8	25.5	23.0	43.6	89.3	9.3	1.4	5.6	5.3
44700	Stockton-Lodi, CA	800,965	16.5	25.9	9.3	28.0	23.1	13.8	36.0	47.1	9.1	23.8	40.2	18.4
44940	Sumter, SC	104,165	-3.2	23.7	10.2	24.5	23.5	18.1	38.2	50.4	49.4	2.1	3.6	5.4
45060	Syracuse, NY	652,956	-1.5	20.4	10.8	24.7	24.8	19.3	40.1	85.9	10.7	4.4	5.8	6.3
45220	Tallahassee, FL	393,414	6.9	19.2	17.4	25.0	21.8	16.6	35.6	61.3	34.2	4.1	8.7	7.8
45300	Tampa-St. Petersburg-Clearwater, FL	3,342,963	19.9	19.2	7.8	26.4	26.0	20.6	42.4	77.1	14.6	5.4	20.3	16.6
4530041304	St. Petersburg-Clearwater-Largo, FL Metro Division	961,596	NA	15.1	6.3	23.9	23.5	19.6	49.4	82.3	11.5	5.0	12.0	10.1
4530045294	Tampa, FL Metro Division	2,381,367	NA	20.9	8.4	27.4	22.0	13.4	40.0	75.0	15.9	5.6	23.7	19.2
45460	Terre Haute, IN	167,429	-3.3	20.7	12.2	25.4	23.4	18.4	38.2	93.8	5.2	1.9	5.3	5.8
45500	Texarkana, TX-AR	146,363	7.4	24.0	7.4	26.4	23.8	18.4	39.2	72.3	25.8	2.3	6.6	6.6
45780	Toledo, OH	600,141	-7.8	22.1	10.3	25.7	23.9	18.1	38.3	81.2	17.4	2.6	7.1	7.6
45820	Topeka, KS	232,322	-1.7	22.9	8.0	24.1	24.8	20.2	41.1	89.6	8.5	3.2	12.9	11.9

Table A-3. Metropolitan Areas — Who: Age, Race/Ethnicity, and Household Structure, 2023—*Continued*

Metropolitan area / division code	Metropolitan area / division	Hispanic or Latino (percent)	Born in state of residence (percent)	Foreign born (percent)	Not a U.S. citizen (percent)	Total households	Average household size	Household type (percent of all households): Family households: Total	Family households: Married-couple	Family households: Male householder	Family households: Female householder	Nonfamily households: Total	Nonfamily households: One-person households	Percent of households with people age 60 years and over
	ACS table number:	B03003	B05002	B05002	B05002	B11001	B25010	B11001	B11001	B11001	B11001	B11001	B11001	B11006
	column number:	14	15	16	17	18	19	20	21	22	23	24	25	26
41100	St. George, UT	12.4	54.7	5.4	3.1	72,315	2.76	75.3	63.3	4.6	7.4	24.7	19.8	47.8
41140	St. Joseph, MO-KS	6.4	69.1	3.5	1.6	47,529	2.38	62.7	42.4	6.2	14.1	37.3	32.2	45.6
41180	St. Louis, MO-IL	3.9	67.8	5.7	2.8	1,179,884	2.32	62.0	45.9	4.5	11.5	38.0	31.0	42.2
41420	Salem, OR	26.6	52.7	11.8	7.7	162,200	2.61	66.7	47.2	6.3	13.1	33.3	25.8	41.8
41500	Salinas, CA	62.0	56.0	29.5	19.9	132,170	3.10	70.6	47.8	7.3	15.5	29.4	22.7	46.1
41540	Salisbury, MD	6.9	60.9	9.2	5.8	48,542	2.47	62.9	45.1	2.7	15.1	37.1	27.3	43.7
41620	Salt Lake City-Murray, UT	20.4	57.8	12.9	7.5	460,977	2.71	65.7	49.9	5.5	10.3	34.3	24.6	32.2
41660	San Angelo, TX	41.1	69.4	6.8	3.5	48,119	2.41	58.7	40.1	4.8	13.9	41.3	36.0	40.9
41700	San Antonio-New Braunfels, TX	54.7	60.6	12.5	6.7	986,961	2.69	66.3	47.2	5.3	13.8	33.7	27.4	37.8
41740	San Diego-Chula Vista-Carlsbad, CA	34.9	50.8	23.1	9.3	1,181,259	2.67	66.0	49.3	5.3	11.3	34.0	24.7	40.0
41780	Sandusky, OH	4.9	80.2	1.4	0.7	53,716	2.07	63.8	46.9	5.8	11.1	36.2	31.4	51.1
41860	San Francisco-Oakland-Fremont, CA	23.3	47.9	32.8	14.0	1,763,465	2.53	62.2	47.7	4.8	9.7	37.8	28.3	41.4
4186036084	Oakland-Fremont-Berkeley, CA Metro Division	25.2	49.9	32.5	14.3	1,024,706	2.66	66.7	51.0	5.2	10.5	33.3	24.8	41.4
4186041884	San Francisco-San Mateo-Redwood City, CA Metro Division	20.4	43.6	35.5	14.3	637,151	2.34	54.6	41.9	4.1	8.6	45.4	34.0	39.6
4186042034	San Rafael, CA Metro Division	19.6	52.4	19.9	9.7	101,608	2.44	63.9	51.7	4.5	7.7	36.1	28.0	52.2
41940	San Jose-Sunnyvale-Santa Clara, CA	26.3	44.7	41.4	19.5	685,743	2.78	68.7	53.3	5.5	10.0	31.3	22.7	38.9
41980	San Juan-Bayamón-Caguas, PR	98.9	0.0	3.6	1.7	827,522	2.44	61.8	33.3	6.1	22.5	38.2	32.9	51.7
42020	San Luis Obispo-Paso Robles, CA	25.2	68.8	10.5	5.0	110,283	2.40	61.9	48.9	2.2	10.8	38.1	25.5	49.5
42100	Santa Cruz-Watsonville, CA	35.2	60.7	18.2	9.3	99,069	2.47	64.3	48.2	6.7	9.3	35.7	24.3	47.7
42140	Santa Fe, NM	47.7	43.2	15.2	9.7	71,322	2.16	58.2	42.9	4.4	11.0	41.8	34.2	53.8
42200	Santa Maria-Santa Barbara, CA	48.5	59.5	22.3	13.2	150,932	2.77	63.2	46.2	5.4	11.6	36.8	26.0	43.7
42220	Santa Rosa-Petaluma, CA	30.3	63.0	16.8	9.1	192,765	2.44	62.6	47.1	4.6	10.9	37.4	27.6	49.3
42340	Savannah, GA	7.6	49.4	8.0	4.6	165,394	2.49	63.8	43.7	5.7	14.3	36.2	29.8	40.1
42540	Scranton--Wilkes-Barre, PA	14.6	71.3	9.0	4.8	236,141	2.33	60.6	40.0	6.3	14.3	39.4	33.3	47.3
42660	Seattle-Tacoma-Bellevue, WA	11.8	43.3	21.3	10.6	1,627,693	2.44	61.3	47.9	4.7	8.7	38.7	29.0	34.9
4266021794	Everett, WA Metro Division	12.3	48.6	20.4	10.5	321,835	2.60	68.4	53.0	5.7	9.7	31.6	23.8	38.7
4266042644	Seattle-Bellevue-Kent, WA Metro Division	11.1	38.7	25.8	13.1	949,792	2.35	57.4	46.2	3.7	7.5	42.6	32.0	32.5
4266045104	Tacoma-Lakewood, WA Metro Division	13.1	49.8	11.1	4.9	356,066	2.54	65.2	47.9	6.3	11.0	34.8	25.5	37.8
42680	Sebastian-Vero Beach-West Vero Corridor, FL	14.1	34.0	8.2	2.5	72,833	2.31	61.5	47.4	4.0	10.1	38.5	32.1	65.8
42700	Sebring, FL	22.7	37.7	10.8	5.6	47,278	2.24	60.5	46.5	4.1	10.0	39.5	29.6	66.4
43100	Sheboygan, WI	7.9	75.5	5.2	1.8	49,852	2.30	63.1	48.6	5.1	9.4	36.9	29.7	43.0
43300	Sherman-Denison, TX	16.7	61.3	7.3	4.4	56,267	2.56	68.7	51.4	5.1	12.2	31.3	26.0	44.8
43340	Shreveport-Bossier City, LA	5.2	72.9	2.5	1.2	164,006	2.29	60.4	38.7	5.3	16.4	39.6	35.5	42.2
43420	Sierra Vista-Douglas, AZ	34.8	37.1	11.1	4.7	50,919	2.35	62.9	47.6	4.6	10.8	37.1	32.5	55.1
43580	Sioux City, IA-NE-SD	20.9	54.1	11.4	6.4	55,198	2.56	66.3	47.7	8.0	10.6	33.7	28.1	41.8
43620	Sioux Falls, SD-MN	5.8	61.4	7.5	3.8	126,616	2.35	59.7	46.8	4.4	8.5	40.3	33.5	33.7
43640	Slidell-Mandeville-Covington, LA	8.2	72.6	3.5	2.0	106,164	2.57	70.5	51.7	4.8	14.1	29.5	24.4	44.0
43780	South Bend-Mishawaka, IN-MI	9.9	62.0	6.5	3.8	128,897	2.42	61.1	44.1	4.7	12.2	38.9	31.8	43.2
43900	Spartanburg, SC	9.0	59.8	8.4	4.2	146,672	2.56	67.6	49.2	3.7	14.7	32.4	27.1	40.5
44060	Spokane-Spokane Valley, WA	7.1	53.4	5.8	2.3	239,251	2.45	61.8	47.7	4.4	9.8	38.2	29.4	43.3
44100	Springfield, IL	2.9	80.7	4.0	2.0	91,114	2.21	55.0	41.5	3.6	9.9	45.0	36.4	43.5
44140	Springfield, MA	27.4	63.5	9.6	4.0	184,698	2.42	60.8	38.0	5.5	17.3	39.2	32.7	45.4
44180	Springfield, MO	4.5	62.2	2.8	1.1	200,832	2.38	62.4	49.1	3.6	9.7	37.6	29.6	38.8
44220	Springfield, OH	4.3	78.1	2.6	1.8	55,322	2.39	63.9	43.0	6.3	14.6	36.1	31.2	47.1
44300	State College, PA	3.7	63.9	8.1	5.1	62,175	2.17	55.7	43.0	4.6	8.1	44.3	30.0	38.3
44420	Staunton-Stuarts Draft, VA	4.6	64.9	3.6	3.1	54,483	2.25	58.4	43.8	5.9	8.7	41.6	35.3	49.7
44700	Stockton-Lodi, CA	42.7	62.7	26.6	12.7	251,091	3.14	76.0	53.1	6.3	16.7	24.0	19.4	41.0
44940	Sumter, SC	4.5	60.8	2.5	1.0	40,059	2.52	68.0	42.8	6.0	19.2	32.0	26.2	44.8
45060	Syracuse, NY	5.2	77.1	6.4	2.5	273,464	2.26	58.6	42.3	4.9	11.4	41.4	31.9	43.7
45220	Tallahassee, FL	8.2	56.0	7.3	3.7	163,838	2.23	54.7	36.8	3.4	14.5	45.3	32.9	36.4
45300	Tampa-St. Petersburg-Clearwater, FL	22.0	35.1	16.1	7.1	1,358,788	2.41	61.9	44.7	5.3	11.9	38.1	30.2	45.8
4530041304	St. Petersburg-Clearwater-Largo, FL Metro Division	11.4	33.1	12.4	4.1	439,896	2.14	55.0	41.3	3.8	9.9	45.0	36.6	52.1
4530045294	Tampa, FL Metro Division	26.3	36.0	17.6	8.3	918,892	2.55	65.1	46.4	5.9	12.8	34.9	27.1	42.8
45460	Terre Haute, IN	2.6	75.2	2.1	1.1	67,572	2.32	54.3	38.0	4.6	11.7	45.7	37.2	44.6
45500	Texarkana, TX-AR	7.0	51.9	4.2	2.2	59,815	2.33	62.5	42.1	5.8	14.6	37.5	33.2	41.6
45780	Toledo, OH	7.8	77.0	3.7	1.7	254,228	2.31	59.2	41.3	4.1	13.8	40.8	32.8	41.0
45820	Topeka, KS	11.5	71.8	2.7	1.8	95,618	2.37	61.8	45.9	5.4	10.5	38.2	32.3	46.9

Table A-3. Metropolitan Areas — Who: Age, Race/Ethnicity, and Household Structure, 2023—*Continued*

Metropolitan area / division code	Metropolitan area / division	Total population	Percent change, 2010–2023	Population by age (percent): Under 18 years	18 to 24 years	25 to 44 years	45 to 64 years	65 years and over	Median age	Race alone or in combination (percent): White	Black or African American	Asian + Native Hawaiian or Other Pacific Islander	American Indian and Alaska Native + Some other race	Two or more races
	ACS table number:	B01003	Population Estimates	B01001	B01001	B01001	B01001	B01001	B01002	B02008	B02009	B02011 + B02012	B02010 + B02013	B02001
	column number:	1	2	3	4	5	6	7	8	9	10	11	12	13
45900	Traverse City, MI	156,371	6.4	18.0	6.7	23.4	26.2	25.6	46.6	97.1	0.9	1.3	6.8	5.8
45940	Trenton-Princeton, NJ	381,671	4.1	21.9	9.9	25.2	26.3	16.6	40.2	52.6	21.7	13.7	20.9	8.5
46060	Tucson, AZ	1,063,162	8.2	19.3	11.6	24.8	22.3	22.0	40.1	80.5	5.4	5.5	33.4	23.4
46140	Tulsa, OK	1,044,287	11.2	24.1	9.1	26.8	23.4	16.6	37.6	77.4	10.4	4.3	24.4	15.3
46220	Tuscaloosa, AL	271,223	23.4	20.3	17.3	25.3	21.6	15.5	34.9	63.1	33.4	1.9	6.1	4.3
46300	Twin Falls, ID	120,060	19.2	26.2	9.0	25.9	22.7	16.1	36.1	87.4	2.0	3.1	19.6	10.6
46340	Tyler, TX	245,209	16.5	24.0	9.8	25.8	22.7	17.7	38.2	75.3	18.6	2.3	15.3	10.8
46520	Urban Honolulu, HI	989,408	3.5	20.4	8.7	27.3	23.5	20.2	40.2	38.8	4.5	86.7	7.6	26.3
46540	Utica-Rome, NY	287,039	-4.1	21.0	8.6	23.9	25.8	20.7	41.9	87.8	7.2	4.4	7.3	6.4
46660	Valdosta, GA	151,923	10.4	24.2	13.0	26.4	21.7	14.7	34.7	59.1	36.3	2.8	9.4	7.2
46700	Vallejo, CA	449,218	8.4	21.5	8.2	27.8	24.6	17.9	40.0	51.7	16.2	23.6	27.6	16.6
47020	Victoria, TX	99,982	-13.4	25.1	8.9	26.8	21.5	17.8	37.2	79.6	7.9	2.4	39.8	28.8
47220	Vineland, NJ	152,326	-3.1	24.2	8.3	25.7	25.6	16.2	39.0	58.8	20.6	1.5	34.6	13.6
47260	Virginia Beach-Chesapeake-Norfolk, VA-NC	1,781,671	6.3	21.9	9.5	28.7	23.3	16.7	37.7	61.9	33.6	6.7	8.9	9.8
47300	Visalia, CA	479,468	8.1	29.4	10.2	27.5	20.8	12.1	32.4	53.0	2.2	4.5	63.3	22.2
47380	Waco, TX	305,370	29.4	23.4	13.4	25.3	21.1	16.7	35.3	79.9	15.1	2.4	24.2	21.3
47460	Walla Walla, WA	61,568	NA	19.8	12.7	24.7	21.5	21.3	39.3	87.0	2.4	3.1	15.2	7.0
47580	Warner Robins, GA	200,779	42.7	24.4	8.5	29.2	23.0	14.9	36.7	60.6	38.2	4.0	7.3	9.9
47900	Washington-Arlington-Alexandria, DC-VA-MD-WV	6,304,449	12.4	22.5	8.5	28.8	25.4	14.8	38.3	53.8	27.5	13.4	18.4	12.0
4790011694	Arlington-Alexandria-Reston, VA-WV Metro Division	3,154,209	NA	23.4	8.4	28.6	22.9	10.4	38.3	64.9	15.0	16.8	17.9	13.5
4790023224	Frederick-Gaithersburg-Bethesda, MD Metro Division	1,351,865	NA	22.7	7.9	25.9	22.8	12.9	40.3	57.4	19.6	15.7	19.9	11.5
4790047764	Washington, DC-MD Metro Division	1,798,375	NA	20.8	9.4	31.2	20.9	11.2	37.1	31.6	55.6	5.8	18.1	9.8
47930	Waterbury-Shelton, CT	456,128	NA	20.1	8.0	26.1	26.0	19.8	42.5	73.8	16.2	5.0	20.5	13.8
47940	Waterloo-Cedar Falls, IA	168,162	1.9	21.9	13.4	25.0	21.3	18.5	37.0	86.4	9.3	3.5	5.8	4.5
48060	Watertown-Fort Drum, NY	114,787	-2.6	24.0	11.5	28.0	21.0	15.6	34.1	88.9	6.9	3.4	9.7	8.3
48140	Wausau, WI	138,612	3.4	22.3	7.1	24.8	26.1	19.6	41.4	91.3	1.8	7.2	5.2	5.0
48260	Weirton-Steubenville, WV-OH	114,106	-8.2	18.2	8.6	22.3	26.4	24.5	46.1	94.7	5.6	1.2	4.2	5.3
48300	Wenatchee-East Wenatchee, WA	124,795	12.1	22.7	8.1	24.7	23.4	21.1	42.1	82.4	1.1	2.2	33.5	19.1
48540	Wheeling, WV-OH	135,517	-8.3	18.9	8.2	23.3	26.6	23.0	44.6	95.9	4.8	0.4	4.2	5.3
48620	Wichita, KS	652,939	4.9	24.5	9.2	26.7	22.8	16.9	37.3	83.9	10.1	4.8	14.6	12.2
48660	Wichita Falls, TX	149,947	-1.5	22.6	11.5	26.7	22.8	16.4	37.0	82.8	11.8	2.8	13.3	10.2
48680	Wildwood-The Villages, FL	151,565	55.0	7.3	2.7	11.4	21.4	57.2	68.2	88.7	7.9	1.4	6.3	4.2
48700	Williamsport, PA	112,724	-2.9	20.1	9.0	24.8	25.0	21.0	41.4	94.3	5.5	1.2	5.3	6.1
48900	Wilmington, NC	467,337	28.5	16.9	9.1	23.0	26.6	24.4	45.9	84.8	11.4	2.0	9.0	6.8
49020	Winchester, VA-WV	148,656	15.5	22.1	8.4	24.6	25.3	19.6	41.5	86.3	7.3	2.0	13.9	9.1
49180	Winston-Salem, NC	695,630	45.4	21.6	8.9	24.8	25.8	18.9	40.7	73.1	19.9	3.3	12.7	8.4
49340	Worcester, MA	866,866	8.4	20.4	9.2	26.1	26.7	17.6	40.5	83.1	8.2	6.6	17.0	13.2
49420	Yakima, WA	256,643	5.0	28.5	9.5	26.2	20.9	14.9	33.8	72.2	1.8	2.6	51.5	27.3
49620	York-Hanover, PA	464,640	6.7	21.7	7.9	25.2	26.1	19.2	41.1	87.1	8.7	2.4	10.2	8.1
49660	Youngstown-Warren, OH	425,969	-24.6	20.3	7.7	23.8	25.4	22.7	43.3	86.5	13.0	1.4	7.4	7.8
49700	Yuba City, CA	183,670	9.9	25.4	9.9	27.0	22.3	15.4	35.9	63.4	5.4	17.4	30.9	15.3
49740	Yuma, AZ	213,221	8.5	24.3	10.0	25.5	19.0	21.2	37.2	80.2	3.7	2.4	59.3	44.9

Table A-3. Metropolitan Areas — Who: Age, Race/Ethnicity, and Household Structure, 2023—*Continued*

Metropolitan area / division code	Metropolitan area / division	Hispanic or Latino (percent)	Born in state of residence (percent)	Foreign born (percent)	Not a U.S. citizen (percent)	Total households	Average house-hold size	Household type (percent of all households)						Percent of house-holds with people age 60 years and over
								Family households				Nonfamily house-holds		
								Total	Married-couple	Male house-holder	Female house-holder	Total	One-per-son house-holds	
	ACS table number:	B03003	B05002	B05002	B05002	B11001	B25010	B11001	B11001	B11001	B11001	B11001	B11001	B11006
	column number:	14	15	16	17	18	19	20	21	22	23	24	25	26
45900	Traverse City, MI	3.2	77.4	2.2	0.7	69,457	2.21	64.7	53.2	3.5	7.9	35.3	28.3	49.6
45940	Trenton-Princeton, NJ	23.3	48.1	27.8	15.2	146,258	2.49	66.7	46.4	6.2	14.1	33.3	28.1	43.5
46060	Tucson, AZ	36.6	41.0	12.2	5.5	445,471	2.32	58.3	42.0	4.8	11.5	41.7	32.5	47.2
46140	Tulsa, OK	12.6	59.5	7.6	4.7	411,320	2.50	64.5	46.4	5.8	12.3	35.5	29.4	40.0
46220	Tuscaloosa, AL	5.2	71.6	4.2	3.1	108,078	2.35	58.1	40.1	5.4	12.7	41.9	35.0	38.0
46300	Twin Falls, ID	22.8	56.5	9.4	5.6	43,326	2.73	69.6	49.6	8.7	11.3	30.4	24.4	40.4
46340	Tyler, TX	21.1	68.6	8.1	4.7	81,987	2.92	70.4	52.8	5.6	12.1	29.6	24.5	45.4
46520	Urban Honolulu, HI	9.6	53.5	19.1	6.6	338,496	2.82	69.0	51.7	5.9	11.4	31.0	24.7	49.0
46540	Utica-Rome, NY	6.4	80.5	7.1	2.5	124,085	2.20	59.6	42.2	5.7	11.7	40.4	33.3	44.8
46660	Valdosta, GA	8.1	58.0	5.2	3.1	60,298	2.42	61.8	41.0	3.6	17.2	38.2	32.9	34.7
46700	Vallejo, CA	30.1	58.6	22.4	10.0	157,766	2.78	69.5	48.4	7.1	14.0	30.5	24.7	45.7
47020	Victoria, TX	46.4	75.8	8.3	4.8	37,816	2.61	72.6	53.2	7.0	12.3	27.4	23.0	43.3
47220	Vineland, NJ	36.1	65.5	14.2	9.2	54,482	2.68	67.5	40.4	8.7	18.4	32.5	27.5	48.0
47260	Virginia Beach-Chesapeake-Norfolk, VA-NC	8.1	48.6	6.8	2.4	710,613	2.44	64.5	45.5	4.9	14.0	35.5	29.2	40.6
47300	Visalia, CA	67.0	69.5	21.8	13.3	145,442	3.26	79.8	53.1	9.2	17.5	20.2	15.6	38.3
47380	Waco, TX	26.8	71.8	8.5	5.8	111,745	2.64	65.4	47.8	5.4	12.2	34.6	29.2	40.8
47460	Walla Walla, WA	24.4	51.6	11.1	7.0	23,887	2.36	61.7	48.6	4.2	8.9	38.3	33.4	45.8
47580	Warner Robins, GA	7.5	56.4	6.6	3.7	77,061	2.57	70.7	46.0	5.7	19.1	29.3	23.7	39.8
47900	Washington-Arlington-Alexandria, DC-VA-MD-WV	18.2	31.9	24.6	10.7	2,409,575	2.57	63.5	47.6	4.7	11.2	36.5	29.5	37.5
4790011694	Arlington-Alexandria-Reston, VA-WV Metro Division	18.2	33.2	25.1	10.2	1,160,949	2.69	67.8	54.4	4.5	8.9	32.2	25.5	36.3
4790023224	Frederick-Gaithersburg-Bethesda, MD Metro Division	19.4	30.6	30.3	12.6	499,961	2.68	67.5	53.0	4.5	10.0	32.5	26.3	42.4
4790047764	Washington, DC-MD Metro Division	17.3	30.8	19.3	10.2	748,665	2.32	54.1	33.3	5.2	15.6	45.9	37.9	36.1
47930	Waterbury-Shelton, CT	20.7	62.9	14.1	6.0	180,851	2.49	64.6	43.9	4.9	15.9	35.4	29.8	46.0
47940	Waterloo-Cedar Falls, IA	4.6	75.4	5.0	3.0	68,791	2.34	56.9	43.8	2.6	10.5	43.1	31.3	39.9
48060	Watertown-Fort Drum, NY	8.0	64.7	4.5	1.7	50,542	2.18	64.1	46.2	4.9	13.0	35.9	29.3	35.7
48140	Wausau, WI	3.6	79.2	4.3	2.3	58,104	2.36	61.4	49.7	4.8	6.9	38.6	30.9	43.2
48260	Weirton-Steubenville, WV-OH	2.0	55.4	1.5	0.6	50,285	2.19	59.8	41.9	5.5	12.4	40.2	34.5	52.3
48300	Wenatchee-East Wenatchee, WA	31.6	52.8	18.3	13.2	49,671	2.46	66.3	54.3	4.1	7.9	33.7	28.5	45.6
48540	Wheeling, WV-OH	1.2	59.7	1.7	0.8	59,980	2.15	63.2	46.6	5.8	10.8	36.8	30.6	47.9
48620	Wichita, KS	15.0	65.2	7.1	3.9	260,885	2.45	63.6	47.2	5.0	11.4	36.4	30.7	39.0
48660	Wichita Falls, TX	19.3	65.4	6.4	3.0	57,000	2.44	64.7	45.9	4.8	13.9	35.3	29.3	41.3
48680	Wildwood-The Villages, FL	6.6	21.3	5.1	2.4	73,238	1.96	65.6	58.4	1.6	5.6	34.4	28.2	82.4
48700	Williamsport, PA	2.4	81.2	1.1	0.5	46,849	2.28	63.3	48.2	4.7	10.4	36.7	30.0	44.6
48900	Wilmington, NC	7.3	45.8	5.7	3.3	206,546	2.23	61.3	47.1	3.8	10.5	38.7	29.8	49.0
49020	Winchester, VA-WV	11.5	48.3	6.9	3.5	56,287	2.59	66.9	53.4	5.0	8.5	33.1	27.6	46.7
49180	Winston-Salem, NC	12.2	61.4	7.6	4.4	292,187	2.33	64.0	45.8	5.1	13.1	36.0	30.6	44.7
49340	Worcester, MA	13.9	63.9	15.3	7.5	336,660	2.49	66.0	48.4	5.6	12.0	34.0	25.5	43.5
49420	Yakima, WA	53.0	62.0	17.9	12.6	89,414	2.82	70.6	44.4	8.8	17.4	29.4	24.1	40.7
49620	York-Hanover, PA	9.9	65.8	4.3	2.1	183,864	2.48	66.8	51.9	4.3	10.5	33.2	26.3	44.8
49660	Youngstown-Warren, OH	4.9	77.8	2.1	0.9	186,827	2.23	57.7	38.4	5.4	13.8	42.3	35.5	48.4
49700	Yuba City, CA	32.5	66.0	17.1	6.3	62,578	2.89	71.7	51.5	5.4	14.8	28.3	22.9	44.9
49740	Yuma, AZ	65.2	33.9	27.0	16.0	83,811	2.45	70.7	53.1	4.6	13.0	29.3	24.1	46.2

NA = Not available.

X = Not applicable.

Table A-4. Cities — Who: Age, Race/Ethnicity, and Household Structure, 2023

STATE and place code	STATE Place	Total population	Percent change, 2010–2023	Population by age (percent): Under 18 years	18 to 24 years	25 to 44 years	45 to 64 years	65 years and over	Median age	Race alone or in combination (percent): White	Black	Asian + Native Hawaiian or Other Pacific Islander	American Indian and Alaska Native + Some other race	Two or more races (percent)	Hispanic or Latino (percent)
	ACS table number:	B01003	Census PEP	B01001	B01001	B01001	B01001	B01001	B01002	B02008	B02009	B02011 + B02012	B02010 + B02013	B02001	B03003
	column number:	1	2	3	4	5	6	7	8	9	10	11	12	13	14
00000	**UNITED STATES**	333,287,562	7.7	21.7	9.4	26.8	24.8	17.3	39.0	72.5	14.4	7.8	18.8	19.1	12.5
01000	**ALABAMA**	5,074,296	6.0	21.9	9.6	25.3	25.2	18.0	39.6	69.8	27.3	2.5	6.0	4.9	5.1
0103076	Auburn city	82,030	53.7	20.8	30.3	24.5	15.7	8.8	24.6	69.8	21.0	8.7	4.1	3.7	5.3
0107000	Birmingham city	196,518	-7.2	18.3	12.4	29.7	22.7	16.9	35.7	27.9	71.0	1.2	5.5	5.0	4.3
0121184	Dothan city	71,577	8.3	22.1	8.8	24.1	26.0	19.1	40.6	59.1	38.5	2.2	5.5	5.1	5.2
0135896	Hoover city	92,459	15.0	23.7	7.8	27.4	24.9	16.2	39.8	73.5	17.6	8.4	4.9	4.2	3.3
0137000	Huntsville city	227,571	25.6	18.4	12.4	27.7	23.4	18.1	37.5	62.8	32.1	3.2	9.3	6.5	8.8
0150000	Mobile city	182,594	-6.5	19.7	11.1	27.4	23.5	18.3	38.6	43.4	53.1	4.0	3.2	3.6	2.9
0151000	Montgomery city	195,275	-5.5	24.0	9.6	26.3	23.7	16.5	37.0	30.8	65.5	4.4	5.9	5.9	5.2
0177256	Tuscaloosa city	111,339	22.8	18.7	32.1	24.7	13.9	10.5	24.7	51.9	44.1	3.0	6.2	5.0	4.3
02000	**ALASKA**	733,583	2.7	24.0	9.4	29.8	23.0	13.8	35.9	72.6	5.3	12.0	26.0	7.7	14.2
0203000	Anchorage municipality	286,075	-2.4	23.3	9.2	32.0	22.3	13.2	36.0	69.5	8.2	17.7	21.0	14.7	9.6
04000	**ARIZONA**	7,359,197	14.9	21.6	9.8	26.4	23.5	18.8	38.8	76.5	6.4	5.5	31.9	32.5	19.4
0404720	Avondale city	93,555	22.4	26.0	9.0	29.5	27.1	8.3	35.8	61.1	12.1	6.2	47.6	26.6	50.4
0407940	Buckeye city	108,900	114.0	24.7	10.7	28.0	23.2	13.4	35.3	64.2	5.3	2.0	41.9	12.6	43.6
0410670	Casas Adobes CDP	70,641	5.8	17.7	6.9	23.6	27.3	24.6	46.7	88.2	2.6	6.3	23.9	19.2	26.5
0412000	Chandler city	280,171	18.3	23.5	8.6	28.6	25.8	13.4	37.4	76.0	5.8	13.7	22.1	16.9	26.7
0423620	Flagstaff city	76,595	16.1	16.0	32.0	27.4	15.9	8.6	26.0	74.2	3.2	5.5	28.1	10.0	18.8
0427400	Gilbert town	275,408	31.8	27.7	7.7	30.0	23.9	10.6	36.1	79.2	6.2	12.2	20.7	15.8	19.3
0427820	Glendale city	253,868	11.7	26.6	9.4	28.1	22.9	13.0	34.8	73.3	10.2	5.5	35.1	23.2	41.6
0428380	Goodyear city	111,807	70.8	24.1	6.5	28.0	23.6	17.8	39.2	74.9	8.9	5.6	30.5	18.6	31.8
0444410	Maricopa city	71,021	63.3	26.3	8.5	24.6	25.1	15.5	38.2	65.0	19.3	6.5	23.8	13.7	24.1
0446000	Mesa city	511,624	16.2	21.9	8.6	27.9	22.2	19.4	38.3	82.9	6.9	5.7	24.5	19.0	27.5
0454050	Peoria city	198,753	28.7	23.0	7.2	24.2	24.6	20.9	41.6	84.2	5.7	7.4	14.9	10.7	17.3
0455000	Phoenix city	1,650,051	13.8	23.2	10.2	30.9	23.5	12.2	34.9	70.5	11.3	6.8	38.4	25.5	41.8
0458150	Queen Creek town	76,046	188.5	29.3	6.6	27.7	22.9	13.5	36.8	86.7	3.6	3.5	15.2	9.3	20.7
0464210	San Tan Valley CDP	119,497	59.4	28.3	7.8	32.0	20.0	11.9	34.2	83.0	5.6	5.4	21.5	15.4	26.1
0465000	Scottsdale city	244,421	12.1	14.3	7.0	24.3	27.5	27.0	49.8	90.3	2.5	5.7	10.4	8.5	8.8
0471510	Surprise city	158,282	34.3	18.9	8.5	22.8	26.8	23.0	44.7	82.5	7.2	5.9	17.3	12.2	17.4
0473000	Tempe city	189,839	17.1	12.4	24.4	32.3	20.3	10.7	30.5	69.7	10.4	14.5	22.6	15.0	22.4
0477000	Tucson city	547,232	5.0	19.1	14.9	27.9	21.6	16.5	35.6	78.1	7.5	5.2	35.6	25.4	42.8
0485540	Yuma city	100,861	8.0	25.6	13.0	28.6	15.6	17.1	32.4	71.1	5.2	3.3	51.3	30.1	62.6
05000	**ARKANSAS**	3,045,637	4.2	22.8	9.6	25.4	24.5	17.7	38.9	79.3	16.3	3.0	12.7	8.4	10.8
0515190	Conway city	69,577	18.1	20.9	18.2	30.5	16.6	13.8	32.0	76.6	19.4	2.7	8.4	6.3	9.9
0523290	Fayetteville city	101,694	37.5	17.6	26.8	27.5	16.8	11.3	27.6	87.6	8.1	5.9	18.1	19.6	7.2
0524550	Fort Smith city	89,771	4.0	24.7	8.4	26.9	21.7	18.4	36.5	69.9	11.4	7.1	27.1	12.0	19.8
0535710	Jonesboro city	80,655	19.5	26.6	11.3	30.8	19.1	12.2	32.0	74.0	22.2	1.8	13.7	11.4	8.3
0541000	Little Rock city	203,844	5.1	21.8	9.2	28.9	22.2	18.0	38.3	53.6	41.2	4.6	12.2	10.9	11.0
0560410	Rogers city	74,047	32.3	26.0	8.4	33.6	19.5	12.5	34.7	88.5	2.8	4.2	48.8	45.0	32.9
0566080	Springdale city	89,394	26.4	32.2	10.2	29.3	19.7	8.6	31.3	77.0	2.6	11.7	48.9	39.0	43.2
06000	**CALIFORNIA**	39,029,342	4.6	21.8	9.4	28.5	24.5	15.8	37.9	56.6	7.3	19.0	37.5	40.3	19.0
0600562	Alameda city	75,344	1.8	21.3	5.1	26.8	27.0	19.8	42.8	60.3	8.7	33.9	18.3	20.3	17.6
0600884	Alhambra city	79,798	-4.1	14.8	6.8	30.0	25.4	22.9	42.8	22.7	3.2	51.1	34.5	11.6	39.8
0602000	Anaheim city	340,505	1.0	20.2	10.3	29.1	26.1	14.3	37.1	57.5	3.7	23.2	42.8	26.3	50.4
0602252	Antioch city	117,097	14.0	23.6	7.8	27.1	26.6	14.9	39.5	46.5	19.0	21.4	37.4	21.3	36.1
0602364	Apple Valley town	75,040	8.1	24.3	9.8	26.4	21.0	18.5	36.8	77.5	9.5	6.2	32.2	24.0	39.0
0602553	Arden-Arcade CDP	90,934	4.2	22.1	6.7	35.0	19.0	17.2	35.9	69.0	16.1	13.8	22.0	18.1	22.4
0603526	Bakersfield city	413,376	18.6	29.5	10.4	28.7	20.0	11.4	31.9	60.7	8.8	9.1	46.4	23.7	56.6
0603666	Baldwin Park city	68,799	-8.9	22.3	8.9	28.2	25.2	15.4	38.8	34.6	0.7	24.5	66.1	24.6	72.4
0604982	Bellflower city	75,111	-2.1	21.4	11.1	27.8	27.7	12.0	36.4	36.9	11.2	13.0	53.2	13.6	59.8
0606000	Berkeley city	118,962	5.4	10.6	28.1	25.9	18.4	16.9	32.9	62.2	11.0	30.3	11.3	13.1	11.0
0608142	Brentwood city	65,115	26.5	24.5	7.6	20.5	28.3	19.1	43.4	66.6	10.8	23.4	19.0	18.3	19.1
0608786	Buena Park city	81,965	1.5	23.8	7.3	31.1	25.1	12.7	36.7	48.0	3.1	32.8	38.4	21.4	45.4
0608954	Burbank city	102,768	-0.7	17.1	6.5	29.2	26.8	20.3	42.9	71.1	4.4	14.9	26.0	15.9	28.6
0610046	Camarillo city	69,514	6.3	18.2	7.0	25.9	22.5	26.3	43.8	78.7	4.4	12.1	21.5	15.8	30.5
0611194	Carlsbad city	113,491	7.4	23.5	5.9	23.1	28.5	19.0	43.4	85.6	2.0	11.7	14.4	13.2	15.5
0611390	Carmichael CDP	75,718	22.6	17.3	8.0	28.4	23.2	23.1	41.6	79.1	10.0	10.9	14.4	12.3	11.3
0611530	Carson city	91,122	-0.8	19.8	8.7	27.1	25.6	18.9	40.4	22.5	23.9	32.1	33.4	10.8	40.2
0611964	Castro Valley CDP	65,354	6.5	20.6	5.7	26.6	27.9	19.2	43.2	46.4	11.5	37.6	19.9	14.6	19.9

Table A-4. Cities — Who: Age, Race/Ethnicity, and Household Structure, 2023

STATE and place code	STATE Place	Native, born in state of residence (percent)	Foreign born (percent)	Non-citizens (percent)	Total households	Average household size	Household type (percent of all households): Family households: Total	Family households: Married-couple	Family households: Male householder	Family households: Female householder	Nonfamily households: Total	Nonfamily households: One-person households	Percent of households with people age 60 years and over
	ACS table number:	B05002	B05002	B05002	B11001	B25010	B11001	B11001	B11001	B11001	B11001	B11001	B11006
	column number:	15	16	17	18	19	20	21	22	23	24	25	26
00000	**UNITED STATES**	57.3	13.9	6.5	129,870,928	2.50	64.1	46.9	5.1	12.1	35.9	28.6	41.7
01000	**ALABAMA**	67.7	3.8	2.2	2,016,448	2.45	64.9	46.7	4.5	13.7	35.1	30.4	42.6
0103076	Auburn city	53.5	9.9	7.2	32,859	2.30	44.7	34.7	3.1	7.0	55.3	41.9	21.1
0107000	Birmingham city	76.4	3.8	2.8	91,740	2.05	49.5	23.2	5.6	20.8	50.5	41.5	37.3
0121184	Dothan city	63.2	4.8	3.1	30,920	2.28	62.0	37.5	5.0	19.5	38.0	31.9	41.4
0135896	Hoover city	56.8	8.3	4.0	38,178	2.40	70.1	55.6	3.5	10.9	29.9	25.3	34.9
0137000	Huntsville city	50.0	5.9	3.1	99,557	2.17	56.6	39.8	4.7	12.1	43.4	36.9	38.2
0150000	Mobile city	72.5	4.3	2.0	79,383	2.22	52.7	30.9	2.7	19.2	47.3	41.8	41.2
0151000	Montgomery city	70.7	6.6	4.4	82,966	2.27	56.7	30.6	4.1	22.0	43.3	37.9	40.0
0177256	Tuscaloosa city	63.7	5.4	4.2	42,870	2.26	46.1	26.3	6.6	13.2	53.9	41.8	27.5
02000	**ALASKA**	41.9	7.5	2.8	274,574	2.56	64.0	47.2	6.4	10.5	36.0	27.8	36.0
0203000	Anchorage municipality	40.2	10.7	4.0	109,125	2.55	59.4	45.6	4.9	8.9	40.6	31.1	34.5
04000	**ARIZONA**	39.6	13.1	6.6	2,850,377	2.53	64.7	46.7	6.1	11.8	35.3	27.2	43.7
0404720	Avondale city	46.8	18.2	8.0	32,208	2.89	73.8	46.2	13.0	14.6	26.2	18.2	29.2
0407940	Buckeye city	35.1	13.9	9.4	32,161	3.21	82.2	65.0	5.9	11.2	17.8	12.4	44.5
0410670	Casas Adobes CDP	36.7	8.8	3.3	32,025	2.15	56.9	43.7	4.4	8.8	43.1	31.2	44.8
0412000	Chandler city	37.1	15.0	6.6	105,611	2.64	68.5	52.0	3.2	13.2	31.5	22.6	35.3
0423620	Flagstaff city	48.7	4.1	2.8	30,080	2.14	47.6	32.0	4.6	11.0	52.4	31.0	20.6
0427400	Gilbert town	39.4	9.7	3.6	94,016	2.91	75.2	61.1	4.3	9.8	24.8	18.4	29.8
0427820	Glendale city	44.8	17.2	7.8	89,664	2.79	68.4	46.5	6.4	15.6	31.6	26.8	37.3
0428380	Goodyear city	34.4	10.7	4.8	38,956	2.76	74.4	56.7	6.4	11.4	25.6	19.7	44.8
0444410	Maricopa city	39.1	10.4	3.0	23,278	3.05	72.6	55.3	7.4	9.9	27.4	21.3	42.4
0446000	Mesa city	39.2	11.3	6.9	203,676	2.48	61.6	44.5	6.1	11.1	38.4	29.5	43.0
0454050	Peoria city	39.1	10.4	3.4	74,637	2.63	72.0	55.2	4.6	12.3	28.0	21.4	47.6
0455000	Phoenix city	42.0	19.6	11.7	621,234	2.61	61.1	40.5	6.6	14.1	38.9	28.8	33.1
0458150	Queen Creek town	38.0	8.0	2.7	24,749	3.07	85.3	73.9	3.0	8.4	14.7	13.3	34.1
0464210	San Tan Valley CDP	37.1	6.6	3.7	36,966	3.23	83.6	60.4	10.6	12.6	16.4	10.7	34.7
0465000	Scottsdale city	25.0	9.7	3.3	118,561	2.04	55.3	44.6	3.3	7.3	44.7	35.3	49.0
0471510	Surprise city	30.1	6.6	2.5	59,045	2.65	73.3	57.6	3.7	12.0	26.7	21.1	53.8
0473000	Tempe city	36.9	15.6	10.7	76,512	2.34	47.4	32.5	4.2	10.7	52.6	28.5	24.7
0477000	Tucson city	44.9	13.9	6.7	233,257	2.23	51.1	32.1	4.6	14.4	48.9	37.8	38.8
0485540	Yuma city	36.9	18.4	8.4	41,742	2.35	64.3	44.1	6.3	13.9	35.7	28.7	36.8
05000	**ARKANSAS**	60.1	5.1	3.3	1,216,207	2.44	64.0	47.1	4.7	12.1	36.0	30.8	41.6
0515190	Conway city	67.3	4.6	2.8	28,356	2.27	54.8	45.3	3.5	5.9	45.2	35.2	27.0
0523290	Fayetteville city	46.4	6.2	3.4	42,333	2.20	48.7	32.9	4.5	11.3	51.3	34.9	24.9
0524550	Fort Smith city	55.6	11.2	6.0	36,439	2.43	55.7	39.7	4.0	11.9	44.3	39.3	40.0
0535710	Jonesboro city	63.2	5.3	3.5	32,817	2.36	59.0	36.4	4.7	17.9	41.0	32.5	28.1
0541000	Little Rock city	64.1	9.8	7.2	89,358	2.22	56.0	37.4	3.5	15.2	44.0	40.3	39.0
0560410	Rogers city	42.3	19.1	13.5	27,613	2.66	67.9	53.2	3.4	11.2	32.1	27.5	28.9
0566080	Springdale city	45.9	26.7	21.7	29,550	2.99	76.5	52.3	7.9	16.3	23.5	18.8	24.6
06000	**CALIFORNIA**	56.8	26.7	12.2	13,550,586	2.82	67.5	48.1	6.4	13.0	32.5	24.3	41.9
0600562	Alameda city	48.8	27.0	8.4	30,642	2.42	63.6	47.2	6.9	9.5	36.4	27.8	41.5
0600884	Alhambra city	48.0	44.3	14.1	30,242	2.62	65.9	41.4	8.4	16.1	34.1	23.2	48.4
0602000	Anaheim city	54.1	35.3	17.1	109,885	3.04	70.7	48.9	7.1	14.7	29.3	20.6	40.8
0602252	Antioch city	58.3	28.6	12.9	37,645	3.09	76.5	50.4	6.5	19.6	23.5	15.3	46.5
0602364	Apple Valley town	73.3	10.5	3.3	26,684	2.80	76.6	54.1	5.8	16.7	23.4	20.6	44.0
0602553	Arden-Arcade CDP	61.6	19.9	11.4	37,548	2.39	59.5	41.1	3.3	15.1	40.5	32.7	39.1
0603526	Bakersfield city	70.7	18.4	9.9	130,761	3.12	73.5	46.3	8.3	18.8	26.5	20.5	34.8
0603666	Baldwin Park city	51.9	43.0	17.0	18,805	3.62	86.8	59.9	10.9	16.0	13.2	10.8	49.9
0604982	Bellflower city	59.8	30.5	14.0	23,352	3.17	78.0	49.6	7.8	20.5	22.0	14.3	43.6
0606000	Berkeley city	44.0	23.2	13.5	49,088	2.15	40.0	31.4	2.3	6.2	60.0	38.3	37.0
0608142	Brentwood city	65.1	17.7	6.2	22,600	2.87	81.0	66.1	2.9	12.0	19.0	16.5	49.0
0608786	Buena Park city	56.0	35.6	13.9	23,777	3.42	83.0	55.5	10.0	17.4	17.0	13.5	39.2
0608954	Burbank city	43.9	36.1	11.1	43,209	2.36	59.1	44.8	5.4	8.9	40.9	31.8	44.4
0610046	Camarillo city	55.5	19.0	7.8	26,253	2.63	69.9	53.9	8.7	7.3	30.1	22.2	57.0
0611194	Carlsbad city	54.4	11.9	4.1	43,752	2.57	69.7	57.1	2.8	9.7	30.3	22.3	43.6
0611390	Carmichael CDP	61.5	19.2	7.7	30,982	2.39	60.3	41.7	8.6	10.0	39.7	32.8	51.7
0611530	Carson city	51.8	36.1	9.9	27,512	3.28	75.3	51.3	8.5	15.5	24.7	19.6	57.9
0611964	Castro Valley CDP	55.3	32.4	10.9	23,198	2.77	76.0	59.8	4.1	12.1	24.0	17.4	45.6

Table A-4. Cities — Who: Age, Race/Ethnicity, and Household Structure, 2023—*Continued*

STATE and place code	STATE Place	Total population	Percent change, 2010–2023	Population by age (percent)					Median age	Race alone or in combination (percent)				Two or more races (percent)	Hispanic or Latino (percent)
				Under 18 years	18 to 24 years	25 to 44 years	45 to 64 years	65 years and over		White	Black	Asian + Native Hawaiian or Other Pacific Islander	American Indian and Alaska Native + Some other race		
	ACS table number:	B01003	Census PEP	B01001	B01001	B01001	B01001	B01001	B01002	B02008	B02009	B02011 + B02012	B02010 + B02013	B02001	B03003
	column number:	1	2	3	4	5	6	7	8	9	10	11	12	13	14
	CALIFORNIA—Cont.														
0613014	Chico city	101,296	17.5	17.9	24.3	26.5	16.5	14.8	29.6	83.3	4.5	9.4	22.1	18.0	22.8
0613210	Chino city	93,122	19.0	24.9	7.8	31.8	22.6	12.8	36.0	43.3	7.3	24.0	46.8	21.3	53.3
0613214	Chino Hills city	77,237	2.9	21.7	9.6	28.1	29.8	10.8	39.6	35.7	6.9	42.4	24.4	9.6	29.0
0613392	Chula Vista city	274,344	12.1	25.2	8.0	28.8	23.7	14.2	37.8	60.6	5.5	19.7	53.0	37.4	61.3
0613588	Citrus Heights city	86,238	3.3	20.2	7.3	29.9	23.4	19.3	39.1	81.5	5.3	6.4	24.9	16.3	23.1
0614218	Clovis city	125,833	31.2	30.3	7.2	26.6	23.5	12.5	36.3	70.0	3.0	20.3	24.5	16.4	30.4
0615044	Compton city	91,004	-5.8	26.2	10.5	27.4	24.6	11.4	33.0	28.8	24.2	2.2	71.8	26.6	73.5
0616000	Concord city	122,325	-0.1	20.4	8.5	28.0	25.3	17.8	39.4	61.4	7.2	20.4	29.8	17.6	30.9
0616350	Corona city	160,255	4.5	22.6	10.4	26.9	27.2	12.8	37.8	54.4	6.6	17.5	43.6	20.4	47.6
0616532	Costa Mesa city	108,367	-1.7	19.5	8.6	35.9	23.8	12.3	36.5	72.0	3.4	12.7	35.2	22.8	36.5
0617918	Daly City city	99,838	-1.5	13.6	8.3	31.1	24.6	22.4	43.3	23.6	3.9	63.6	20.4	11.0	20.8
0618100	Davis city	65,837	0.1	13.2	31.4	26.4	15.6	13.4	27.1	68.3	3.1	29.0	12.8	12.6	15.8
0619766	Downey city	108,795	-2.8	21.0	7.7	28.8	27.1	15.4	38.2	40.2	4.1	9.6	70.9	22.2	76.7
0620018	Dublin city	69,129	50.2	23.6	6.6	35.8	24.6	9.3	36.9	37.5	5.6	62.1	9.8	13.6	11.4
0620802	East Los Angeles CDP	106,903	-16.0	25.4	9.8	30.7	22.3	11.8	35.7	27.8	NA	1.3	90.6	19.5	96.5
0621230	Eastvale city	70,514	31.4	29.0	7.5	30.9	24.3	8.3	36.0	41.5	5.0	35.0	41.7	20.9	46.9
0621712	El Cajon city	102,989	3.2	27.7	8.9	30.1	19.8	13.5	34.2	74.2	8.4	12.9	27.4	22.1	29.5
0622020	Elk Grove city	178,425	16.3	26.3	8.5	24.9	25.3	15.1	39.4	44.3	15.6	40.0	16.4	14.3	16.5
0622230	El Monte city	103,782	-8.7	23.0	8.2	26.8	24.7	17.3	38.4	31.0	0.8	26.6	70.8	28.8	67.7
0622804	Escondido city	148,119	2.6	22.9	7.9	31.4	22.7	15.1	37.0	58.3	4.5	14.1	46.8	21.9	51.3
0623182	Fairfield city	120,764	14.4	23.3	11.0	27.7	23.8	14.2	37.7	43.6	21.7	24.1	30.2	16.2	33.3
0624638	Folsom city	84,775	17.2	23.8	4.5	27.9	27.7	16.0	42.2	65.5	4.9	28.0	11.3	9.3	11.6
0624680	Fontana city	215,485	9.5	25.6	10.1	30.1	24.0	10.2	34.5	33.1	7.5	12.3	65.6	17.6	70.0
0626000	Fremont city	226,211	5.4	20.9	5.0	31.5	26.8	15.9	40.3	22.8	3.1	69.1	10.6	5.2	11.6
0627000	Fresno city	545,717	10.0	26.9	10.5	30.4	19.5	12.7	32.8	51.5	9.4	17.8	47.7	24.7	51.4
0628000	Fullerton city	139,254	2.7	20.9	9.3	28.3	25.7	15.9	38.6	46.9	2.7	30.3	39.3	19.3	42.1
0629000	Garden Grove city	168,246	-1.8	20.3	8.8	25.5	27.8	17.6	40.8	39.3	2.9	46.2	30.7	18.2	35.3
0630000	Glendale city	187,032	-2.6	17.7	6.7	28.6	26.4	20.5	42.5	73.8	2.1	15.2	18.4	8.8	18.9
0632548	Hawthorne city	83,386	-1.2	22.3	7.8	34.3	22.4	13.2	36.3	38.9	29.4	8.3	48.5	26.1	48.0
0633000	Hayward city	155,672	7.7	19.6	7.9	30.7	27.2	14.6	38.9	26.1	9.7	39.5	37.6	12.4	39.2
0633182	Hemet city	92,385	16.7	23.6	8.0	24.9	22.3	21.2	38.9	52.2	10.9	8.8	49.4	22.7	53.8
0633434	Hesperia city	100,631	11.2	27.2	11.7	27.7	21.2	12.3	33.4	51.6	8.4	3.0	58.8	20.7	63.8
0636000	Huntington Beach city	192,151	0.8	17.7	7.7	25.8	28.5	20.4	43.9	78.2	2.9	17.2	19.4	16.2	20.1
0636448	Indio city	93,045	21.6	22.5	9.2	25.5	21.5	21.2	37.8	76.6	2.9	3.4	65.4	46.8	71.1
0636546	Inglewood city	102,857	-6.3	17.1	9.9	29.5	26.5	17.0	40.1	25.8	38.7	2.5	51.8	18.1	54.9
0636770	Irvine city	314,615	47.7	22.7	14.1	29.6	23.2	10.5	33.9	43.9	3.1	53.7	10.5	10.4	10.4
0637692	Jurupa Valley city	107,333	NA	23.7	10.4	29.2	23.1	13.6	35.4	45.1	3.3	6.8	66.9	21.1	71.9
0639486	Lake Elsinore city	73,017	40.9	25.4	11.3	30.8	20.7	11.8	34.7	60.4	4.6	6.7	50.3	21.7	57.8
0639496	Lake Forest city	85,835	10.8	23.1	6.7	27.9	26.9	15.5	39.5	56.0	2.4	31.0	25.2	13.4	28.1
0639892	Lakewood city	78,132	-2.5	22.6	8.6	28.3	27.7	12.7	38.6	56.4	8.5	21.3	41.6	24.8	43.2
0640130	Lancaster city	166,220	6.0	26.7	9.6	25.5	24.4	13.8	35.3	58.7	19.3	7.4	39.1	23.4	46.6
0641992	Livermore city	82,899	2.1	27.9	4.7	26.6	25.9	14.9	38.8	70.8	2.4	24.7	19.3	15.8	18.6
0642202	Lodi city	67,675	8.9	27.5	10.2	26.7	20.2	15.4	34.6	60.3	2.9	13.6	39.4	14.3	39.3
0643000	Long Beach city	449,496	-2.9	17.7	10.9	31.3	26.3	13.9	37.6	50.2	13.4	17.8	35.0	15.0	43.5
0644000	Los Angeles city	3,820,963	0.6	18.9	9.8	32.9	24.1	14.4	37.2	50.6	10.7	15.2	44.2	19.6	46.8
0644574	Lynwood city	63,223	-9.5	25.3	9.1	32.4	23.2	10.0	33.8	32.0	7.0	0.9	85.1	23.3	90.8
0645022	Madera city	68,083	10.9	27.5	10.7	28.5	20.2	13.1	33.6	47.5	3.8	2.9	67.9	21.6	77.4
0645484	Manteca city	91,055	35.2	23.2	6.9	30.5	24.8	14.5	37.3	65.4	6.5	17.5	35.6	23.7	39.2
0646842	Menifee city	113,425	45.4	25.2	7.6	29.1	21.2	16.9	36.9	67.6	12.3	10.6	36.2	24.5	44.0
0646898	Merced city	93,687	18.2	30.0	13.7	27.4	19.9	8.9	28.9	40.1	8.1	18.3	51.8	17.3	55.2
0647766	Milpitas city	77,321	15.4	16.7	9.2	33.0	23.8	17.3	38.6	13.6	2.5	76.4	13.2	5.9	13.9
0648256	Mission Viejo city	90,615	-3.2	18.7	5.5	22.9	28.0	24.8	47.2	77.7	1.5	20.1	18.3	16.3	19.1
0648354	Modesto city	218,909	8.6	25.3	8.9	26.3	23.3	16.2	36.5	64.6	7.8	13.2	42.0	24.6	45.5
0649270	Moreno Valley city	212,416	9.2	26.3	11.4	30.4	22.8	9.1	31.6	36.7	15.2	7.6	57.3	16.2	65.0
0649670	Mountain View city	81,790	10.1	17.8	6.6	41.2	22.2	12.2	34.7	46.3	3.1	45.0	19.0	11.1	16.9
0650076	Murrieta city	111,870	7.5	24.1	8.4	27.4	27.1	12.9	39.3	69.8	8.5	14.4	29.0	18.7	29.2
0650258	Napa city	77,486	0.5	18.0	7.8	27.2	26.7	20.2	43.4	76.2	3.9	5.4	34.7	19.7	40.5
0651182	Newport Beach city	82,627	-3.3	18.9	5.3	28.9	24.3	22.6	42.4	88.8	1.9	8.1	7.7	6.3	8.0
0652526	Norwalk city	98,084	-7.2	23.1	8.4	29.5	26.0	13.0	39.0	37.9	5.1	13.9	66.6	22.3	75.5
0653000	Oakland city	436,508	11.4	17.4	7.1	36.0	23.9	15.6	38.6	40.7	24.2	20.8	30.3	14.0	30.2
0653322	Oceanside city	170,042	1.4	17.9	8.6	26.8	26.7	20.0	41.7	71.2	7.1	13.4	33.9	23.6	36.4
0653896	Ontario city	182,432	10.9	24.1	9.6	32.8	22.8	10.7	34.2	37.5	7.8	10.8	66.3	22.4	70.7
0653980	Orange city	138,332	1.1	22.5	11.2	29.1	22.7	14.5	36.7	73.2	2.1	14.5	37.3	26.0	43.9
0654652	Oxnard city	198,499	0.0	26.4	9.9	29.2	21.5	13.0	34.1	69.6	3.6	7.7	63.4	43.4	76.0

Table A-4. Cities — Who: Age, Race/Ethnicity, and Household Structure, 2023

STATE and place code	STATE Place	Native, born in state of residence (percent)	Foreign born (percent)	Non-citizens (percent)	Total households	Average household size	Household type (percent of all households): Family households: Total	Married-couple	Male householder	Female householder	Nonfamily households: Total	One-person households	Percent of households with people age 60 years and over
	ACS table number:	B05002	B05002	B05002	B11001	B25010	B11001	B11001	B11001	B11001	B11001	B11001	B11006
	column number:	15	16	17	18	19	20	21	22	23	24	25	26
	CALIFORNIA—Cont.												
0613014	Chico city	76.4	6.9	3.1	44,270	2.19	46.9	32.6	3.1	11.2	53.1	28.8	30.4
0613210	Chino city	64.4	27.4	8.8	26,314	3.39	83.7	61.6	7.4	14.6	16.3	13.0	40.4
0613214	Chino Hills city	53.1	36.9	14.4	24,476	3.14	81.0	65.0	3.8	12.1	19.0	14.2	34.9
0613392	Chula Vista city	52.8	29.4	11.8	88,029	3.10	77.4	54.8	6.3	16.4	22.6	17.8	39.7
0613588	Citrus Heights city	65.4	16.3	7.1	34,364	2.49	57.4	37.4	6.4	13.7	42.6	30.4	46.5
0614218	Clovis city	75.6	11.5	2.7	44,194	2.83	66.5	47.4	5.8	13.3	33.5	24.8	35.8
0615044	Compton city	58.0	35.4	21.8	23,447	3.87	78.7	38.5	12.4	27.8	21.3	18.8	43.8
0616000	Concord city	57.8	27.0	14.0	47,248	2.55	68.0	46.4	7.0	14.6	32.0	25.5	42.6
0616350	Corona city	63.1	26.0	9.8	51,110	3.11	76.2	56.6	5.4	14.2	23.8	20.3	42.4
0616532	Costa Mesa city	56.9	25.0	16.1	42,336	2.51	56.0	42.8	3.3	9.9	44.0	29.8	30.9
0617918	Daly City city	40.7	51.3	15.0	33,137	2.98	67.7	46.3	6.7	14.7	32.3	25.2	51.6
0618100	Davis city	54.1	21.9	9.9	25,542	2.47	46.2	38.8	1.8	5.6	53.8	21.4	28.5
0619766	Downey city	59.3	33.4	11.4	33,472	3.21	81.9	51.3	11.3	19.3	18.1	14.7	47.6
0620018	Dublin city	44.5	40.5	18.8	23,439	2.79	77.4	66.7	2.5	8.2	22.6	17.4	26.3
0620802	East Los Angeles CDP	56.7	40.7	24.1	29,208	3.65	80.5	43.1	13.5	23.9	19.5	15.2	43.3
0621230	Eastvale city	60.0	32.0	10.7	18,433	3.82	92.1	73.3	6.2	12.6	7.9	6.3	29.4
0621712	El Cajon city	52.1	31.7	11.8	32,145	3.08	71.4	45.0	10.0	16.4	28.6	21.4	36.9
0622020	Elk Grove city	60.0	24.0	3.9	53,383	3.32	82.3	64.3	6.1	12.0	17.7	13.2	42.9
0622230	El Monte city	48.4	47.7	23.9	29,314	3.48	79.2	45.7	9.4	24.1	20.8	16.9	49.6
0622804	Escondido city	52.6	29.5	13.9	47,740	3.05	71.0	51.8	6.3	12.9	29.0	21.5	44.5
0623182	Fairfield city	58.1	24.9	11.3	38,515	3.09	74.5	54.2	4.6	15.7	25.5	21.1	41.6
0624638	Folsom city	56.7	23.7	10.0	32,761	2.49	70.2	58.9	4.3	7.0	29.8	25.6	39.8
0624680	Fontana city	60.8	32.5	15.2	59,598	3.61	82.7	55.6	9.4	17.7	17.3	12.8	37.8
0626000	Fremont city	35.6	55.3	24.6	81,639	2.74	77.6	66.2	4.6	6.9	22.4	17.4	39.8
0627000	Fresno city	69.8	20.2	9.4	180,634	2.96	69.5	42.0	8.4	19.1	30.5	23.6	38.4
0628000	Fullerton city	54.5	32.1	14.1	49,425	2.75	66.4	47.7	8.5	10.2	33.6	25.3	40.7
0629000	Garden Grove city	42.8	48.9	18.0	50,343	3.30	77.5	55.2	6.8	15.5	22.5	15.4	50.7
0630000	Glendale city	35.4	50.9	17.9	76,375	2.42	64.9	45.7	5.8	13.4	35.1	30.4	46.7
0632548	Hawthorne city	50.4	35.4	19.6	32,299	2.56	60.4	35.4	6.4	18.6	39.6	31.6	32.6
0633000	Hayward city	46.5	42.3	17.6	49,029	3.11	73.0	52.1	7.0	13.9	27.0	20.3	42.4
0633182	Hemet city	58.2	23.4	9.6	33,674	2.72	66.2	44.0	5.9	16.4	33.8	28.6	53.0
0633434	Hesperia city	70.6	18.7	7.7	29,608	3.39	78.2	48.4	9.6	20.3	21.8	17.3	42.4
0636000	Huntington Beach city	60.7	15.7	5.3	75,314	2.54	68.7	51.2	6.3	11.2	31.3	23.7	43.4
0636448	Indio city	56.3	26.9	14.5	31,048	2.97	73.1	50.4	7.3	15.3	26.9	20.9	52.2
0636546	Inglewood city	54.1	29.0	14.5	37,918	2.69	68.2	34.8	7.4	26.0	31.8	25.6	45.4
0636770	Irvine city	43.0	39.4	16.8	111,471	2.67	66.0	51.1	4.7	10.2	34.0	24.1	29.0
0637692	Jurupa Valley city	62.2	29.9	14.2	30,398	3.50	79.9	54.5	10.8	14.7	20.1	14.5	48.7
0639486	Lake Elsinore city	63.5	21.0	7.4	20,252	3.61	87.2	64.1	5.7	17.4	12.8	8.3	41.1
0639496	Lake Forest city	51.7	27.7	10.4	29,721	2.87	77.6	64.3	5.7	7.7	22.4	15.6	37.9
0639892	Lakewood city	69.9	20.4	7.0	25,033	3.11	78.2	56.9	7.5	13.8	21.8	16.3	41.8
0640130	Lancaster city	69.9	15.6	5.6	52,431	3.08	70.7	45.7	6.9	18.2	29.3	23.6	44.6
0641992	Livermore city	61.0	20.5	8.3	29,208	2.81	76.5	65.5	3.0	8.1	23.5	19.0	39.3
0642202	Lodi city	70.2	15.4	9.4	23,274	2.86	67.5	48.8	3.4	15.3	32.5	27.5	42.6
0643000	Long Beach city	59.0	25.3	11.8	176,407	2.48	54.9	37.8	4.7	12.4	45.1	33.4	35.4
0644000	Los Angeles city	46.8	35.4	17.4	1,460,167	2.54	55.9	35.7	6.7	13.6	44.1	33.1	36.1
0644574	Lynwood city	59.6	36.6	22.6	16,131	3.81	83.6	43.7	12.8	27.1	16.4	12.8	36.8
0645022	Madera city	71.1	22.2	15.6	19,945	3.38	73.7	42.2	10.3	21.2	26.3	21.5	40.1
0645484	Manteca city	68.1	19.5	6.6	30,532	2.96	79.1	56.3	6.8	16.0	20.9	18.1	41.9
0646842	Menifee city	67.1	12.4	3.9	39,358	2.88	70.9	52.8	7.0	11.2	29.1	24.7	43.2
0646898	Merced city	70.6	20.9	12.0	27,221	3.41	71.4	34.8	14.3	22.3	28.6	22.8	29.6
0647766	Milpitas city	32.6	57.4	24.5	25,653	2.92	74.2	57.3	6.5	10.4	25.8	16.0	37.9
0648256	Mission Viejo city	52.4	24.2	4.7	34,477	2.58	72.9	59.9	2.6	10.5	27.1	23.8	57.0
0648354	Modesto city	68.4	19.9	8.6	76,577	2.82	68.2	46.0	6.6	15.6	31.8	26.3	44.0
0649270	Moreno Valley city	66.2	22.1	10.3	56,294	3.76	81.8	48.9	10.5	22.4	18.2	13.6	37.0
0649670	Mountain View city	35.7	44.0	26.0	35,859	2.27	54.4	43.9	2.3	8.3	45.6	32.5	26.2
0650076	Murrieta city	60.7	16.8	4.2	36,867	3.02	79.8	63.9	4.6	11.4	20.2	15.4	41.4
0650258	Napa city	60.4	21.2	9.6	30,838	2.46	65.5	49.3	4.8	11.4	34.5	25.9	48.0
0651182	Newport Beach city	54.3	15.2	5.0	36,300	2.26	55.0	44.4	3.6	6.9	45.0	33.0	43.7
0652526	Norwalk city	61.7	32.4	13.8	27,925	3.46	77.6	47.1	8.6	21.9	22.4	16.1	46.9
0653000	Oakland city	48.9	27.8	13.7	182,014	2.36	50.5	33.7	5.9	11.0	49.5	35.6	34.2
0653322	Oceanside city	50.1	22.1	9.0	63,683	2.65	66.8	48.9	6.4	11.5	33.2	22.4	47.1
0653896	Ontario city	64.8	28.1	15.7	54,719	3.32	80.0	52.1	11.3	16.6	20.0	15.2	35.5
0653980	Orange city	65.6	20.5	8.1	46,584	2.83	68.5	50.5	7.2	10.8	31.5	20.1	39.2
0654652	Oxnard city	55.9	34.0	18.9	55,777	3.51	79.9	53.1	9.5	17.3	20.1	16.3	44.2

Table A-4. Cities — Who: Age, Race/Ethnicity, and Household Structure, 2023—*Continued*

STATE and place code	STATE Place	Total population	Percent change, 2010–2023	Population by age (percent) Under 18 years	18 to 24 years	25 to 44 years	45 to 64 years	65 years and over	Median age	Race alone or in combination (percent) White	Black	Asian + Native Hawaiian or Other Pacific Islander	American Indian and Alaska Native + Some other race	Two or more races (percent)	Hispanic or Latino (percent)
	ACS table number:	B01003	Census PEP	B01001	B01001	B01001	B01001	B01001	B01002	B02008	B02009	B02011 + B02012	B02010 + B02013	B02001	B03003
	column number:	1	2	3	4	5	6	7	8	9	10	11	12	13	14
	CALIFORNIA—Cont.														
0655156	Palmdale city	161,412	5.5	27.7	10.2	25.1	26.2	10.9	34.0	43.9	18.0	6.0	58.1	24.8	66.3
0655282	Palo Alto city	65,881	2.3	20.6	5.9	26.5	26.7	20.4	42.6	54.8	4.7	42.9	5.5	8.0	5.0
0656000	Pasadena city	133,573	-2.7	17.6	7.3	33.0	24.0	18.1	39.6	52.9	11.5	21.6	31.8	16.8	31.7
0656700	Perris city	80,606	17.1	26.9	12.2	30.4	20.8	9.6	32.6	44.3	11.5	5.4	70.2	30.8	77.0
0657456	Pittsburg city	75,790	19.3	24.4	9.3	28.8	24.5	13.1	36.5	38.1	18.7	25.3	44.2	25.3	45.6
0657792	Pleasanton city	74,660	6.0	24.9	4.7	22.3	30.8	17.3	44.1	48.3	5.0	49.3	13.1	13.7	14.1
0658072	Pomona city	145,489	-2.5	20.3	8.8	32.9	24.7	13.2	37.0	33.8	8.8	13.8	63.1	18.6	68.5
0659444	Rancho Cordova city	82,608	27.5	26.2	6.1	27.1	28.4	12.2	38.4	61.7	13.5	17.0	24.0	16.0	23.4
0659451	Rancho Cucamonga city	174,403	5.2	23.8	8.3	26.8	25.6	15.5	38.0	54.0	13.7	18.7	31.6	16.6	38.6
0659920	Redding city	92,718	3.1	22.5	7.7	29.3	20.2	20.3	38.3	86.0	3.9	6.8	16.9	12.7	13.6
0659962	Redlands city	72,552	5.2	22.5	8.1	28.6	25.9	14.8	37.0	67.6	9.3	13.2	32.0	20.1	37.6
0660018	Redondo Beach city	67,750	1.4	21.0	4.6	30.1	27.0	17.3	42.0	76.3	5.1	24.7	15.7	18.1	13.8
0660102	Redwood City city	80,992	5.2	20.3	7.3	30.3	25.5	16.6	39.4	51.3	3.7	30.4	30.7	13.0	34.0
0660466	Rialto city	103,383	3.9	29.7	9.4	28.1	20.8	11.8	32.6	35.1	14.1	3.6	75.6	26.8	76.2
0660620	Richmond city	114,104	9.7	18.9	8.4	28.9	25.9	18.0	40.7	33.0	17.6	17.6	47.1	16.1	46.9
0662000	Riverside city	318,855	4.3	23.2	13.0	29.1	22.6	12.0	33.6	45.7	10.4	11.0	50.6	16.2	54.1
0662364	Rocklin city	73,470	29.0	24.4	9.9	23.9	26.5	15.2	38.3	80.2	2.7	16.5	17.3	16.0	15.1
0662938	Roseville city	159,126	33.3	21.9	6.8	27.2	25.2	18.9	41.0	78.3	5.1	18.0	17.7	16.9	17.6
0664000	Sacramento city	526,383	12.6	21.3	9.2	33.2	21.9	14.4	36.2	46.9	16.3	27.8	28.3	17.0	29.9
0664224	Salinas city	159,521	5.6	30.1	11.0	27.3	21.2	10.4	32.1	26.4	2.0	7.5	77.2	12.0	82.3
0665000	San Bernardino city	223,706	6.2	28.0	10.7	30.1	21.6	9.6	31.9	25.9	12.0	7.1	68.9	13.3	74.1
0665042	San Buenaventura (Ventura) city	109,056	2.2	18.7	6.8	28.8	26.8	18.9	40.8	79.2	3.8	9.3	30.1	20.6	35.4
0666000	San Diego city	1,388,312	5.8	18.2	11.1	33.9	22.4	14.4	36.0	63.1	8.1	22.1	27.8	19.6	30.4
0667000	San Francisco city	808,988	0.4	13.6	6.4	36.2	25.3	18.5	40.7	49.5	6.7	40.3	16.1	11.4	16.4
0668000	San Jose city	969,615	2.2	20.3	9.4	30.3	25.0	15.0	38.1	38.0	3.8	43.9	30.9	15.3	31.5
0668084	San Leandro city	85,785	0.7	19.2	5.8	28.6	27.5	18.9	42.1	34.0	13.4	39.5	27.0	12.5	29.6
0668196	San Marcos city	94,197	12.0	23.2	11.3	26.7	26.8	11.9	36.8	67.7	4.9	17.3	35.6	23.8	37.8
0668252	San Mateo city	101,328	4.0	16.7	8.6	31.2	27.1	16.5	40.0	52.6	2.9	34.2	25.9	15.0	26.7
0668378	San Ramon city	84,942	17.3	25.2	6.4	23.5	32.1	12.9	42.0	41.8	4.6	55.9	4.8	8.0	4.7
0669000	Santa Ana city	310,523	-4.6	21.6	10.6	31.1	25.0	11.6	35.4	37.9	0.9	12.1	75.3	25.7	79.2
0669070	Santa Barbara city	86,495	-2.4	16.1	7.2	29.5	24.0	23.3	41.6	77.1	1.1	6.8	31.3	15.9	36.7
0669084	Santa Clara city	131,075	12.2	16.2	11.2	39.9	20.6	12.1	34.4	38.9	4.4	54.0	13.6	10.6	14.3
0669088	Santa Clarita city	224,039	26.9	23.3	7.2	27.1	27.4	15.0	40.1	68.3	5.4	18.5	31.5	22.8	35.5
0669196	Santa Maria city	109,985	10.3	31.5	13.3	26.7	18.7	9.8	29.1	70.4	2.0	4.7	72.6	47.6	79.3
0670000	Santa Monica city	89,939	0.1	13.2	3.3	34.9	26.1	22.5	43.5	76.9	5.3	17.8	13.3	12.4	13.1
0670098	Santa Rosa city	175,861	4.5	19.4	7.2	27.4	25.5	20.6	41.6	66.5	4.2	9.0	37.0	14.9	37.3
0672016	Simi Valley city	125,100	0.4	19.6	8.2	24.1	30.0	18.2	42.9	73.6	2.8	15.3	26.3	17.2	30.5
0673080	South Gate city	90,068	-4.7	20.1	9.5	29.6	26.6	14.1	38.4	39.9	1.2	1.6	88.2	30.9	94.9
0675000	Stockton city	319,537	9.2	26.1	9.3	29.8	20.9	13.8	34.1	36.5	14.8	24.8	43.4	17.4	47.2
0677000	Sunnyvale city	151,973	8.1	20.2	7.4	38.4	23.6	10.4	35.8	37.8	5.1	53.4	13.2	9.0	13.6
0678120	Temecula city	110,696	9.9	27.2	6.6	28.7	23.7	13.8	36.7	67.3	10.9	16.1	21.4	14.9	22.9
0678582	Thousand Oaks city	123,458	-2.8	18.2	9.9	21.5	29.9	20.6	45.3	81.5	2.7	13.6	21.1	17.4	20.6
0680000	Torrance city	139,232	-4.4	19.9	5.9	26.2	26.3	21.6	43.7	46.9	5.3	42.8	17.2	11.4	17.5
0680238	Tracy city	98,006	17.8	24.8	11.2	25.0	26.5	12.5	37.3	43.5	9.6	30.8	39.0	20.6	41.8
0680644	Tulare city	71,093	19.9	31.3	10.4	28.6	21.1	8.6	29.1	60.8	2.5	4.4	66.8	33.8	69.0
0680812	Turlock city	72,099	5.0	24.4	10.9	27.4	20.8	16.4	35.0	66.1	3.5	10.1	40.6	18.9	41.7
0680854	Tustin city	77,693	2.5	22.9	8.5	29.8	27.5	11.3	36.8	44.8	6.6	25.3	37.7	15.1	41.0
0681204	Union City city	65,416	-6.1	20.5	4.9	30.5	24.7	19.4	41.1	25.7	8.6	61.4	14.9	8.8	16.2
0681344	Upland city	78,707	6.4	21.0	8.6	29.8	26.1	14.5	38.4	63.1	5.3	15.2	37.8	20.5	43.7
0681554	Vacaville city	102,533	10.7	21.5	7.3	27.9	25.5	17.8	40.9	61.6	12.1	21.1	21.6	14.8	27.1
0681666	Vallejo city	122,796	5.7	18.6	7.4	30.4	25.3	18.3	40.1	39.2	19.3	33.0	30.7	19.0	31.2
0682590	Victorville city	138,871	19.4	29.2	10.8	27.5	21.1	11.3	32.7	55.3	16.5	4.4	52.1	28.8	59.0
0682954	Visalia city	145,005	16.1	28.1	8.5	30.1	21.4	11.9	33.8	64.9	2.8	7.1	49.2	23.4	52.2
0682996	Vista city	98,336	4.4	25.8	8.1	28.6	24.6	12.9	37.4	72.0	4.3	9.7	47.1	30.9	48.2
0683346	Walnut Creek city	69,151	7.8	15.0	6.0	28.2	22.1	28.7	45.4	74.6	4.6	19.9	16.6	13.7	15.2
0684200	West Covina city	105,617	-0.6	19.5	8.3	27.7	27.9	16.5	41.0	24.7	3.9	33.2	56.6	16.1	57.5
0684550	Westminster city	88,737	-1.4	20.6	7.8	25.0	25.0	21.6	42.0	29.4	0.8	55.8	24.7	10.0	25.8
0685292	Whittier city	84,149	-1.5	27.1	8.8	25.3	24.9	13.8	37.2	46.1	1.7	6.1	65.2	18.7	68.9
0686832	Yorba Linda city	66,163	2.7	21.2	7.7	19.8	29.4	21.9	45.8	63.5	2.0	33.9	13.4	12.5	13.7
0686972	Yuba City city	68,662	5.8	23.6	10.4	26.2	21.9	17.9	38.6	54.4	4.7	25.2	32.9	14.0	32.7
08000	**COLORADO**	5,839,926	15.7	20.7	9.3	30.4	23.8	15.7	37.7	84.3	5.7	5.4	20.2	22.5	14.6
0803455	Arvada city	123,517	14.8	18.6	7.8	30.2	26.6	16.7	40.5	91.9	2.0	5.3	11.8	10.3	15.1
0804000	Aurora city	394,701	20.8	22.9	9.6	31.5	22.9	13.1	35.3	60.5	19.1	9.3	30.1	17.2	32.8

Table A-4. Cities — Who: Age, Race/Ethnicity, and Household Structure, 2023

STATE and place code	STATE Place	Native, born in state of residence (percent)	Foreign born (percent)	Non-citizens (percent)	Total households	Average household size	Household type (percent of all households)						Percent of households with people age 60 years and over
							Family households				Nonfamily households		
							Total	Married-couple	Male householder	Female householder	Total	One-person households	
	ACS table number:	B05002	B05002	B05002	B11001	B25010	B11001	B11001	B11001	B11001	B11001	B11001	B11006
	column number:	15	16	17	18	19	20	21	22	23	24	25	26
	CALIFORNIA—Cont.												
0655156	Palmdale city	65.4	25.3	10.4	47,380	3.40	80.2	50.8	9.0	20.4	19.8	15.8	39.7
0655282	Palo Alto city	33.1	39.8	18.3	27,768	2.35	60.8	52.2	0.8	7.8	39.2	33.1	41.4
0656000	Pasadena city	48.4	28.7	12.2	57,025	2.26	54.1	36.5	4.7	12.9	45.9	34.3	35.7
0656700	Perris city	66.3	28.1	11.9	20,943	3.84	88.6	54.7	9.1	24.8	11.4	8.7	31.6
0657456	Pittsburg city	59.4	31.9	13.2	24,968	2.99	73.0	48.9	7.1	17.0	27.0	20.9	41.4
0657792	Pleasanton city	42.3	39.3	21.2	26,569	2.77	77.0	67.2	3.7	6.1	23.0	19.3	42.2
0658072	Pomona city	58.6	32.8	15.5	42,390	3.33	75.7	44.1	12.5	19.0	24.3	15.1	41.4
0659444	Rancho Cordova city	57.0	25.3	12.7	28,916	2.83	69.7	50.0	5.9	13.8	30.3	23.0	40.1
0659451	Rancho Cucamonga city	65.0	20.3	5.8	58,173	2.94	71.1	51.9	5.9	13.3	28.9	19.5	44.2
0659920	Redding city	68.1	4.3	1.6	37,380	2.40	58.4	40.4	4.8	13.3	41.6	31.0	45.4
0659962	Redlands city	63.9	17.1	7.1	27,161	2.57	66.0	44.5	5.2	16.2	34.0	25.3	39.4
0660018	Redondo Beach city	50.1	15.5	5.2	29,220	2.31	55.1	44.6	1.6	8.9	44.9	33.4	38.9
0660102	Redwood City city	48.5	35.2	22.2	29,831	2.64	62.1	49.5	3.8	8.8	37.9	30.7	38.5
0660466	Rialto city	68.0	25.0	13.0	26,568	3.87	79.4	49.9	7.7	21.8	20.6	16.0	45.1
0660620	Richmond city	49.4	34.3	19.4	45,299	2.49	57.6	38.1	7.5	12.0	42.4	34.4	47.9
0662000	Riverside city	66.2	22.5	10.0	96,201	3.20	73.0	47.6	6.7	18.8	27.0	19.0	38.4
0662364	Rocklin city	65.4	14.7	5.5	27,308	2.64	69.4	55.7	4.2	9.5	30.6	24.6	40.6
0662938	Roseville city	61.9	16.1	4.4	61,142	2.57	71.7	58.3	2.6	10.8	28.3	23.5	44.9
0664000	Sacramento city	62.9	21.9	9.5	202,421	2.55	58.8	38.9	5.7	14.2	41.2	32.1	36.0
0664224	Salinas city	56.4	38.0	28.6	43,233	3.63	75.7	42.7	10.5	22.6	24.3	18.4	42.1
0665000	San Bernardino city	66.5	26.0	14.8	64,370	3.39	72.9	40.8	10.5	21.6	27.1	17.8	37.3
0665042	San Buenaventura (Ventura) city	63.2	13.9	6.4	43,032	2.47	63.7	44.5	7.7	11.5	36.3	25.3	44.0
0666000	San Diego city	46.5	25.7	10.7	537,532	2.46	58.4	43.6	4.8	10.0	41.6	29.5	34.5
0667000	San Francisco city	39.8	35.0	13.0	372,027	2.09	46.4	34.7	3.9	7.8	53.6	39.5	36.9
0668000	San Jose city	45.8	42.8	18.6	331,229	2.88	70.4	51.4	7.1	11.9	29.6	21.7	40.0
0668084	San Leandro city	48.7	38.9	14.6	31,539	2.69	62.5	44.1	5.5	12.9	37.5	28.0	45.6
0668196	San Marcos city	54.0	23.1	9.4	31,360	2.93	74.0	53.8	5.7	14.4	26.0	17.4	40.7
0668252	San Mateo city	47.2	35.7	18.5	39,795	2.50	60.9	48.7	3.7	8.5	39.1	26.0	36.8
0668378	San Ramon city	46.1	38.2	11.0	30,872	2.75	75.3	67.4	0.9	6.9	24.7	20.9	36.1
0669000	Santa Ana city	52.8	41.9	23.6	83,498	3.68	78.9	50.7	9.3	18.8	21.1	14.4	41.5
0669070	Santa Barbara city	54.7	22.8	13.3	38,553	2.17	50.6	40.2	2.3	8.1	49.4	35.7	46.5
0669084	Santa Clara city	40.0	46.1	28.0	51,014	2.48	60.4	48.7	5.0	6.7	39.6	26.3	30.0
0669088	Santa Clarita city	59.3	24.6	8.1	76,446	2.92	76.1	63.2	3.9	8.9	23.9	17.4	43.6
0669196	Santa Maria city	60.4	32.1	23.8	28,422	3.82	81.1	51.0	9.8	20.3	18.9	13.8	33.3
0670000	Santa Monica city	36.7	22.7	7.8	48,189	1.82	42.1	32.4	2.5	7.2	57.9	50.5	38.7
0670098	Santa Rosa city	63.2	19.3	11.6	70,361	2.43	61.6	42.8	5.0	13.8	38.4	28.9	45.7
0672016	Simi Valley city	62.3	18.5	5.4	44,629	2.78	71.8	57.2	6.5	8.2	28.2	22.6	47.7
0673080	South Gate city	52.5	43.6	23.7	27,422	3.28	74.3	42.7	10.9	20.7	25.7	16.2	42.4
0675000	Stockton city	60.6	29.8	14.8	101,924	3.09	72.7	45.3	7.3	20.1	27.3	21.3	38.7
0677000	Sunnyvale city	34.3	50.5	30.3	58,756	2.56	60.1	51.7	2.7	5.8	39.9	25.6	28.1
0678120	Temecula city	58.3	15.1	4.2	35,801	3.09	80.7	58.9	7.6	14.2	19.3	14.2	40.3
0678582	Thousand Oaks city	56.0	19.1	7.0	46,158	2.61	68.3	55.2	6.4	6.7	31.7	23.6	48.5
0680000	Torrance city	50.7	30.1	13.3	55,836	2.46	66.3	53.6	3.5	9.2	33.7	28.7	46.6
0680238	Tracy city	57.8	31.0	12.9	27,880	3.51	83.5	66.2	6.5	10.8	16.5	12.5	43.7
0680644	Tulare city	72.1	20.6	12.2	20,967	3.37	78.6	53.7	9.1	15.8	21.4	15.9	36.3
0680812	Turlock city	67.4	22.9	9.0	25,660	2.77	68.0	47.9	5.8	14.3	32.0	25.5	40.0
0680854	Tustin city	52.4	36.4	19.8	26,025	2.97	73.4	55.4	5.8	12.2	26.6	21.0	36.0
0681204	Union City city	43.9	46.3	13.2	21,920	2.93	76.2	58.1	7.0	11.1	23.8	20.2	48.3
0681344	Upland city	69.3	17.9	7.4	28,043	2.77	74.0	47.1	6.5	20.3	26.0	17.0	38.5
0681554	Vacaville city	60.7	16.0	6.8	35,647	2.69	70.7	50.9	5.6	14.2	29.3	23.6	42.6
0681666	Vallejo city	53.0	29.3	12.9	44,936	2.69	67.7	42.7	9.9	15.0	32.3	25.2	46.6
0682590	Victorville city	67.9	20.2	10.5	38,786	3.44	80.3	44.3	13.5	22.5	19.7	15.6	39.8
0682954	Visalia city	72.7	14.7	7.6	48,446	2.96	76.4	49.9	7.9	18.6	23.6	18.6	35.7
0682996	Vista city	58.6	23.6	12.2	31,866	3.00	76.3	52.8	5.7	17.7	23.7	16.3	36.0
0683346	Walnut Creek city	44.3	27.3	9.6	32,550	2.09	58.1	47.4	3.3	7.4	41.9	33.3	50.0
0684200	West Covina city	53.6	38.4	13.2	31,349	3.34	82.5	53.5	10.2	18.8	17.5	12.7	49.1
0684550	Westminster city	45.1	46.9	12.8	28,524	3.09	76.2	50.7	8.5	17.0	23.8	17.9	57.9
0685292	Whittier city	71.5	18.1	6.3	27,466	3.00	72.2	49.2	5.5	17.5	27.8	24.6	39.9
0686832	Yorba Linda city	58.6	24.5	6.1	22,960	2.86	81.5	66.7	6.0	8.8	18.5	13.7	53.2
0686972	Yuba City city	61.9	25.1	10.2	23,521	2.89	74.9	54.8	2.9	17.2	25.1	18.5	48.9
08000	**COLORADO**	41.7	9.5	4.9	2,384,584	2.40	61.4	48.0	4.6	8.8	38.6	28.3	36.6
0803455	Arvada city	47.5	6.5	2.2	49,987	2.46	66.7	52.7	2.9	11.1	33.3	23.2	37.1
0804000	Aurora city	38.5	22.8	13.2	149,344	2.62	64.5	44.3	7.4	12.8	35.5	25.6	34.0

Table A-4. Cities — Who: Age, Race/Ethnicity, and Household Structure, 2023—*Continued*

STATE and place code	STATE Place	Total population	Percent change, 2010–2023	Population by age (percent): Under 18 years	18 to 24 years	25 to 44 years	45 to 64 years	65 years and over	Median age	Race alone or in combination (percent): White	Black	Asian + Native Hawaiian or Other Pacific Islander	American Indian and Alaska Native + Some other race	Two or more races (percent)	Hispanic or Latino (percent)
	ACS table number:	B01003	Census PEP	B01001	B01001	B01001	B01001	B01001	B01002	B02008	B02009	B02011 + B02012	B02010 + B02013	B02001	B03003
	column number:	1	2	3	4	5	6	7	8	9	10	11	12	13	14
	COLORADO—Cont.														
0807850	Boulder city	105,893	8.5	11.5	31.3	27.4	16.8	12.9	28.6	91.3	2.8	8.4	9.8	11.9	11.2
0809280	Broomfield city	76,860	37.5	20.2	7.5	31.3	24.5	16.5	37.9	87.9	2.2	9.5	15.3	14.2	14.5
0812415	Castle Rock town	81,401	68.8	24.9	7.4	28.9	25.1	13.7	39.4	90.5	5.5	5.9	15.1	13.5	12.8
0812815	Centennial city	106,873	5.9	24.5	4.7	28.4	23.3	19.0	40.5	88.5	4.6	9.5	13.3	14.7	13.4
0816000	Colorado Springs city	488,670	16.5	21.6	9.7	31.7	21.8	15.2	36.4	83.9	8.9	6.0	16.6	13.7	19.3
0816495	Commerce City city	68,248	48.6	30.1	7.2	30.6	24.5	7.7	34.1	70.6	10.2	3.2	38.7	23.5	48.1
0820000	Denver city	716,577	18.6	17.7	8.2	40.5	20.7	12.9	35.4	77.7	11.2	6.1	25.3	19.2	27.9
0827425	Fort Collins city	170,368	17.9	15.7	22.3	30.9	17.2	13.9	30.9	92.0	2.5	6.0	11.3	10.2	12.2
0831660	Grand Junction city	69,406	18.5	18.5	11.4	26.8	22.1	21.2	40.5	92.1	2.4	2.0	15.0	10.5	14.2
0832155	Greeley city	112,614	20.6	25.1	13.5	27.0	19.5	14.8	33.5	81.0	4.1	2.2	29.1	15.0	43.1
0836410	Highlands Ranch CDP	103,195	8.1	22.1	8.9	27.0	26.3	15.7	40.0	89.6	1.4	10.2	9.6	10.1	9.8
0843000	Lakewood city	155,973	8.9	14.8	10.0	34.5	22.5	18.3	38.8	90.3	2.0	5.1	18.9	15.6	22.0
0845970	Longmont city	99,306	14.9	19.4	9.8	26.5	24.6	19.7	40.0	89.7	2.6	5.5	22.7	20.4	24.9
0846465	Loveland city	79,353	18.3	18.9	9.0	27.5	25.2	19.4	41.3	91.9	3.2	4.4	13.8	11.2	15.0
0862000	Pueblo city	111,081	3.9	21.5	9.4	27.7	22.6	18.7	38.4	85.1	3.9	2.0	25.4	14.3	49.7
0877290	Thornton city	144,889	21.4	22.8	9.0	30.7	25.6	11.8	36.5	82.7	6.6	5.5	31.3	22.9	33.0
0883835	Westminster city	114,882	7.9	17.9	7.6	33.3	23.0	18.3	38.5	86.9	2.2	8.1	21.5	16.7	25.1
09000	**CONNECTICUT**	3,626,205	1.3	20.1	9.7	25.1	26.8	18.3	40.9	75.2	13.8	6.1	17.5	18.2	11.4
0908000	Bridgeport city	148,006	2.4	21.8	12.4	28.5	23.7	13.6	35.9	41.2	29.7	3.9	44.0	18.1	47.5
0918430	Danbury city	86,125	6.3	20.7	9.4	27.7	26.6	15.7	41.3	55.7	17.8	4.0	39.6	17.2	34.6
0937000	Hartford city	119,674	-4.1	24.1	13.5	28.2	21.2	13.1	33.2	40.7	44.2	4.7	28.9	19.5	44.7
0950370	New Britain city	74,064	1.1	20.3	13.1	30.0	22.1	14.6	34.1	66.2	15.6	2.7	27.0	11.8	45.1
0952000	New Haven city	135,307	4.2	20.2	14.8	33.3	18.7	12.9	33.1	42.6	34.3	8.0	27.2	11.5	28.8
0955990	Norwalk city	92,460	7.8	18.8	6.9	26.8	27.7	19.9	42.6	64.0	18.3	7.5	27.9	17.5	30.9
0973000	Stamford city	136,212	10.8	16.0	9.2	31.5	25.6	17.7	39.0	61.4	19.3	8.3	22.6	11.3	25.1
0980000	Waterbury city	114,994	4.1	25.7	8.1	27.7	22.3	16.2	36.9	51.2	30.8	3.2	39.8	22.1	41.5
10000	**DELAWARE**	1,018,396	13.2	20.4	8.5	25.1	25.1	20.8	41.5	68.2	25.3	5.4	11.5	10.3	9.6
1077580	Wilmington city	71,672	1.1	22.4	9.9	32.4	19.5	15.8	33.5	35.8	55.8	3.5	11.4	6.3	10.6
11000	**DISTRICT OF COLUMBIA**	678,972	12.3	18.6	10.2	38.1	19.9	13.1	34.9	47.5	45.8	6.7	12.3	10.7	12.0
1150000	Washington city	678,972	12.3	18.6	10.2	38.1	19.9	13.1	34.9	47.5	45.8	6.7	12.3	10.7	12.0
12000	**FLORIDA**	22,244,823	18.0	19.3	8.3	25.1	25.7	21.6	42.7	73.9	17.7	4.1	24.2	27.1	19.1
1200410	Alafaya CDP	94,330	11.2	20.5	12.9	27.6	28.5	10.6	37.1	68.5	11.1	12.2	34.7	24.2	37.7
1207300	Boca Raton city	99,973	18.2	15.7	13.5	19.0	26.3	25.6	46.3	92.0	5.0	5.0	16.6	17.0	16.5
1207875	Boynton Beach city	81,252	18.8	20.0	6.7	23.9	27.0	22.4	44.4	61.2	37.7	3.2	12.5	14.5	15.2
1208150	Brandon CDP	116,754	13.4	21.8	9.0	30.3	23.7	15.2	37.4	66.1	22.7	6.8	24.6	19.3	30.6
1210275	Cape Coral city	224,452	45.1	16.0	6.1	22.6	30.3	25.0	49.2	83.4	9.9	2.0	24.0	18.8	26.7
1212875	Clearwater city	116,868	8.5	15.5	5.9	26.7	26.6	25.3	47.2	79.4	11.9	3.1	16.3	10.3	15.2
1214400	Coral Springs city	134,913	11.0	27.1	7.5	26.3	26.6	12.6	38.3	56.8	28.5	8.3	29.2	22.3	30.5
1216475	Davie town	107,814	16.8	23.2	12.0	25.1	25.2	14.5	36.6	76.2	14.9	6.3	36.8	32.2	40.9
1216525	Daytona Beach city	82,493	35.2	19.8	13.7	21.1	22.8	22.6	40.7	62.2	34.7	2.8	11.0	10.1	9.8
1216725	Deerfield Beach city	87,322	16.1	18.3	7.5	24.7	28.1	21.4	44.6	62.0	27.7	2.9	32.0	24.2	23.0
1217100	Delray Beach city	67,542	11.6	13.2	6.5	24.8	27.0	28.5	51.9	62.2	32.9	4.4	10.8	9.9	9.7
1217200	Deltona city	98,749	15.9	23.6	7.6	28.5	26.1	14.2	39.0	63.7	15.7	2.1	39.5	19.8	44.4
1217935	Doral city	79,359	73.6	24.9	9.7	27.7	30.3	7.5	37.8	89.4	2.2	1.5	61.6	54.2	88.1
1224000	Fort Lauderdale city	184,263	11.0	16.8	6.4	28.2	26.6	22.0	43.6	61.0	33.2	2.8	20.8	16.4	20.4
1224125	Fort Myers city	97,369	56.0	19.6	8.3	28.9	21.9	21.3	38.6	71.2	21.6	3.0	24.8	19.9	24.9
1224581	Four Corners CDP		72,275	176.7	21.1	9.9	31.2	22.9	14.9	34.6	79.2	12.4	4.1	29.9	26.0
1225175	Gainesville city	145,800	17.2	11.7	34.1	25.8	14.6	13.8	28.0	66.9	22.8	9.1	11.4	9.7	13.5
1230000	Hialeah city	221,318	-1.8	15.7	7.7	23.9	30.7	22.0	46.8	82.5	2.2	1.3	81.0	66.8	95.2
1232000	Hollywood city	153,864	9.0	18.8	7.7	26.4	25.4	21.7	42.3	66.2	22.4	6.2	36.9	30.5	39.7
1232275	Homestead city	81,672	35.0	24.8	10.7	31.2	23.6	9.8	34.2	72.0	12.6	0.4	45.2	29.2	77.9
1232610	Horizon West CDP	75,002	435.7	23.5	8.1	35.9	22.4	10.0	36.5	85.2	11.9	8.2	26.8	27.2	25.0
1235000	Jacksonville city	985,837	19.7	22.2	9.0	29.8	23.5	15.5	36.9	59.4	33.5	7.1	12.3	10.9	12.9
1236100	Kendall CDP	73,368	-11.1	19.5	5.7	26.6	27.5	20.6	43.2	85.4	6.1	2.7	54.5	48.1	70.4
1236950	Kissimmee city	81,268	36.2	25.2	7.4	32.5	23.3	11.5	35.4	46.0	12.6	5.0	59.3	20.6	69.9
1238250	Lakeland city	122,246	25.3	19.6	12.5	25.8	20.9	21.1	37.2	69.0	20.5	2.2	22.4	12.0	24.7
1239425	Largo city	82,238	5.9	15.2	9.7	25.1	23.6	26.5	45.0	81.1	11.4	3.7	11.3	8.2	13.6
1239550	Lauderhill city	73,986	10.3	24.0	6.4	30.1	21.9	17.7	36.5	18.9	79.3	1.0	11.3	9.5	10.1
1239925	Lehigh Acres CDP	130,548	48.0	24.8	8.9	25.8	24.8	15.7	37.0	75.6	20.4	1.3	46.7	42.2	53.4
1243975	Melbourne city	86,956	14.3	19.7	8.2	26.8	23.4	22.0	40.0	79.8	15.6	5.5	11.0	11.7	11.4

Table A-4. Cities — Who: Age, Race/Ethnicity, and Household Structure, 2023

STATE and place code	STATE Place	Native, born in state of residence (percent)	Foreign born (percent)	Non-citizens (percent)	Total households	Average household size	Household type (percent of all households)							Percent of households with people age 60 years and over
							Family households				Nonfamily households		
							Total	Married-couple	Male householder	Female householder	Total	One-person households	
	ACS table number:	B05002	B05002	B05002	B11001	B25010	B11001	B11001	B11001	B11001	B11001	B11001	B11006
	column number:	15	16	17	18	19	20	21	22	23	24	25	26
	COLORADO—Cont.												
0807850	Boulder city	28.1	10.5	5.8	44,722	2.10	35.4	29.2	2.3	3.9	64.6	39.3	28.2
0809280	Broomfield city	37.5	8.8	4.3	33,563	2.28	58.6	48.0	5.2	5.5	41.4	28.7	33.7
0812415	Castle Rock town	36.2	5.4	1.6	29,100	2.78	78.4	62.4	4.9	11.1	21.6	18.4	34.4
0812815	Centennial city	38.0	10.0	4.2	41,393	2.55	72.7	64.1	2.4	6.2	27.3	23.2	41.6
0816000	Colorado Springs city	32.0	7.1	2.9	208,035	2.30	62.1	48.4	4.1	9.6	37.9	29.5	34.2
0816495	Commerce City city	64.6	9.6	6.7	21,705	3.12	83.9	62.3	9.3	12.4	16.1	9.2	25.5
0820000	Denver city	37.1	14.4	7.8	342,996	2.05	43.9	32.4	3.2	8.3	56.1	41.4	27.0
0827425	Fort Collins city	34.7	5.9	3.3	72,318	2.23	49.6	39.6	4.1	5.9	50.4	29.5	27.1
0831660	Grand Junction city	46.8	4.3	2.4	31,087	2.09	51.8	36.2	6.0	9.6	48.2	36.7	42.0
0832155	Greeley city	59.3	11.3	8.0	42,813	2.53	62.0	46.9	4.0	11.1	38.0	28.4	37.5
0836410	Highlands Ranch CDP	35.5	7.9	3.5	39,866	2.58	72.8	65.5	2.1	5.2	27.2	19.5	36.4
0843000	Lakewood city	43.5	8.6	4.9	71,477	2.14	49.9	36.1	4.6	9.2	50.1	37.0	38.7
0845970	Longmont city	37.3	11.5	4.9	42,201	2.32	59.6	44.1	6.0	9.5	40.4	27.9	42.6
0846465	Loveland city	40.3	2.4	1.0	35,134	2.24	58.1	45.9	3.3	9.0	41.9	32.2	45.2
0862000	Pueblo city	61.8	4.2	3.3	46,921	2.25	62.0	38.4	8.6	15.1	38.0	31.0	42.9
0877290	Thornton city	47.5	12.9	8.0	52,600	2.74	69.5	55.5	3.6	10.4	30.5	21.2	33.3
0883835	Westminster city	47.1	7.5	3.5	51,565	2.22	54.6	42.6	5.3	6.6	45.4	33.9	36.1
09000	**CONNECTICUT**	52.7	15.7	7.0	1,433,635	2.45	63.0	46.0	4.9	12.1	37.0	29.9	44.3
0908000	Bridgeport city	37.3	36.7	21.2	54,695	2.63	63.9	32.8	9.0	22.1	36.1	30.6	43.5
0918430	Danbury city	30.6	43.2	28.1	32,993	2.54	67.5	43.1	8.1	16.2	32.5	28.2	42.1
0937000	Hartford city	40.5	26.1	14.3	49,229	2.30	52.5	25.1	4.9	22.5	47.5	41.1	35.4
0950370	New Britain city	53.0	21.7	9.1	30,047	2.35	54.0	26.6	9.5	17.9	46.0	37.2	35.1
0952000	New Haven city	50.7	18.4	10.9	57,392	2.19	45.6	21.5	5.2	18.9	54.4	41.0	30.5
0955990	Norwalk city	38.7	28.6	13.2	37,777	2.43	59.8	39.7	5.8	14.3	40.2	33.6	48.3
0973000	Stamford city	37.7	29.3	14.4	55,324	2.44	56.9	41.4	4.1	11.4	43.1	30.7	39.9
0980000	Waterbury city	52.3	19.6	11.3	45,898	2.47	59.0	27.9	6.0	25.2	41.0	36.3	39.5
10000	**DELAWARE**	42.5	9.9	4.3	402,334	2.47	65.6	49.0	4.8	11.8	34.4	28.6	48.4
1077580	Wilmington city	52.0	9.0	5.6	32,131	2.15	47.5	21.2	5.4	21.0	52.5	45.4	37.8
11000	**DISTRICT OF COLUMBIA**	33.4	14.1	6.9	334,673	1.92	41.1	25.5	2.5	13.1	58.9	47.8	27.9
1150000	Washington city	33.4	14.1	6.9	334,673	1.92	41.1	25.5	2.5	13.1	58.9	47.8	27.9
12000	**FLORIDA**	35.2	21.7	9.1	8,826,394	2.47	64.4	46.7	5.2	12.5	35.6	28.1	47.8
1200410	Alafaya CDP	35.6	23.0	7.0	34,029	2.77	73.8	51.9	5.9	16.0	26.2	20.8	34.5
1207300	Boca Raton city	24.7	24.7	9.9	41,274	2.26	58.7	49.2	2.5	7.0	41.3	32.6	51.4
1207875	Boynton Beach city	30.3	34.7	13.5	31,874	2.50	59.7	42.0	4.2	13.5	40.3	34.5	51.6
1208150	Brandon CDP	39.2	17.8	8.4	44,579	2.55	70.7	43.7	7.7	19.4	29.3	21.8	38.7
1210275	Cape Coral city	25.0	19.6	9.2	83,021	2.69	71.0	55.4	4.8	10.8	29.0	23.8	55.4
1212875	Clearwater city	34.3	14.8	5.1	52,536	2.16	56.0	39.9	5.5	10.6	44.0	37.1	49.5
1214400	Coral Springs city	31.4	32.3	13.8	46,223	2.91	77.3	55.6	5.9	15.9	22.7	18.4	40.4
1216475	Davie town	41.8	31.7	13.7	38,969	2.68	70.4	48.7	6.7	15.1	29.6	23.7	37.3
1216525	Daytona Beach city	39.8	8.1	3.1	33,906	2.19	56.0	29.1	8.5	18.5	44.0	35.8	50.1
1216725	Deerfield Beach city	25.9	44.6	26.3	34,846	2.48	64.4	43.6	4.7	16.1	35.6	28.3	50.8
1217100	Delray Beach city	29.8	22.7	8.5	30,118	2.22	44.7	31.8	2.4	10.5	55.3	43.7	56.7
1217200	Deltona city	35.2	11.9	5.7	33,155	2.97	73.9	50.9	8.4	14.6	26.1	20.6	44.0
1217935	Doral city	22.0	66.7	36.0	26,222	3.03	84.7	62.0	6.2	16.5	15.3	9.6	26.3
1224000	Fort Lauderdale city	32.7	29.2	12.3	81,232	2.22	48.8	33.3	4.2	11.3	51.2	40.3	46.4
1224125	Fort Myers city	32.1	21.0	13.0	39,447	2.40	55.1	36.5	5.3	13.2	44.9	35.6	44.3
1224581	Four Corners CDP	32.2	22.5	17.8	9.5	27,549	2.61	67.1	50.5	3.5	13.1	32.9	22.9
1225175	Gainesville city	47.9	14.8	7.2	65,576	1.94	35.5	22.4	2.7	10.3	64.5	40.6	26.8
1230000	Hialeah city	18.7	76.2	34.8	78,792	2.79	76.3	46.7	9.6	20.0	23.7	17.5	54.3
1232000	Hollywood city	33.0	41.1	16.9	61,197	2.49	60.9	39.0	6.1	15.8	39.1	32.8	50.8
1232275	Homestead city	37.7	48.5	24.0	26,901	3.01	74.5	46.8	8.2	19.6	25.5	19.1	28.3
1232610	Horizon West CDP	21.6	30.4	13.4	24,678	3.04	79.1	68.8	3.3	6.9	20.9	13.5	30.5
1235000	Jacksonville city	47.8	12.0	5.4	409,221	2.36	59.7	38.8	5.2	15.8	40.3	31.8	37.6
1236100	Kendall CDP	35.3	46.2	15.3	28,984	2.49	65.6	44.3	6.0	15.3	34.4	27.0	48.3
1236950	Kissimmee city	20.1	32.6	16.6	28,697	2.81	77.0	44.8	10.7	21.5	23.0	18.8	31.2
1238250	Lakeland city	42.6	10.7	5.6	51,663	2.19	55.8	38.1	5.1	12.6	44.2	34.3	46.3
1239425	Largo city	35.1	11.1	3.9	37,626	2.15	51.1	37.8	2.9	10.4	48.9	38.0	49.9
1239550	Lauderhill city	39.1	40.0	14.3	27,832	2.64	58.7	30.3	5.6	22.8	41.3	34.2	44.3
1239925	Lehigh Acres CDP	36.8	33.7	20.0	40,585	3.21	70.8	44.9	7.3	18.6	29.2	21.5	41.7
1243975	Melbourne city	33.0	9.3	3.7	36,223	2.29	53.3	36.0	4.7	12.5	46.7	35.9	48.8

Table A-4. Cities — Who: Age, Race/Ethnicity, and Household Structure, 2023—*Continued*

STATE and place code	STATE Place	Total population	Percent change, 2010–2023	Population by age (percent)					Median age	Race alone or in combination (percent)				Two or more races (percent)	Hispanic or Latino (percent)
				Under 18 years	18 to 24 years	25 to 44 years	45 to 64 years	65 years and over		White	Black	Asian + Native Hawaiian or Other Pacific Islander	American Indian and Alaska Native + Some other race		
	ACS table number:	B01003	Census PEP	B01001	B01001	B01001	B01001	B01001	B01002	B02008	B02009	B02011 + B02012	B02010 + B02013	B02001	B03003
	column number:	1	2	3	4	5	6	7	8	9	10	11	12	13	14
	FLORIDA—Cont.														
1245000	Miami city	455,955	13.7	16.7	7.3	34.4	25.7	15.9	39.3	70.9	17.0	3.1	60.4	50.3	66.9
1245025	Miami Beach city	79,616	-9.6	19.8	4.6	29.1	27.8	18.7	42.4	83.4	5.4	1.9	39.4	29.7	55.0
1245060	Miami Gardens city	110,714	2.9	26.3	8.3	26.9	23.8	14.7	36.9	29.7	66.0	1.7	26.5	23.5	32.7
1245975	Miramar city	138,330	13.0	25.4	7.3	28.0	26.3	13.1	38.2	42.8	47.2	6.8	36.3	32.2	41.9
1249675	North Port city	88,931	55.0	20.4	7.8	21.7	24.7	25.4	45.1	88.3	6.5	2.1	14.6	10.7	14.1
1250750	Ocala city		68,424	21.5	21.3	5.6	26.4	23.6	23.1	41.0	73.4	17.3	6.1	15.8	12.6
1253000	Orlando city	320,753	34.2	20.6	8.7	36.1	22.8	11.8	35.3	59.6	26.8	7.0	34.5	26.4	34.9
1254000	Palm Bay city	135,570	31.3	18.7	7.3	26.5	26.1	21.3	43.3	74.2	20.1	3.4	21.2	18.2	21.3
1254200	Palm Coast city	102,106	31.8	15.8	8.7	19.7	25.8	30.1	50.9	82.5	15.0	3.9	10.9	10.8	14.3
1254350	Palm Harbor CDP		62,105	8.1	16.8	6.1	19.3	30.4	27.4	50.8	93.9	2.3	4.6	7.9	8.5
1255775	Pembroke Pines city	171,105	10.2	14.6	9.5	24.0	30.8	21.1	46.6	67.3	22.5	4.8	46.9	37.5	54.1
1256825	Pine Hills CDP	79,274	32.0	27.0	9.9	23.3	27.1	12.5	35.7	15.8	82.2	2.7	3.9	4.8	9.9
1257425	Plantation city	96,537	13.3	18.9	7.6	30.4	27.8	15.2	41.6	60.7	26.4	7.7	31.0	25.4	32.7
1257900	Poinciana CDP	78,799	48.1	26.4	7.1	27.7	18.0	20.8	37.2	38.2	36.1	2.4	46.3	21.8	53.6
1258050	Pompano Beach city	113,613	13.4	17.9	6.8	25.7	25.6	24.0	44.6	59.9	29.3	3.1	26.7	16.5	24.4
1258350	Port Charlotte CDP	64,797	19.1	13.9	9.0	21.4	26.2	29.5	51.4	83.1	11.8	3.7	10.8	9.1	13.7
1258575	Port Orange city	65,965	17.7	20.0	5.8	23.7	25.0	25.6	46.1	90.1	7.0	4.5	9.7	10.0	5.9
1258715	Port St. Lucie city	245,036	48.4	21.3	6.5	24.0	26.4	21.7	43.5	69.9	26.9	2.8	17.4	15.8	22.5
1260950	Riverview CDP	119,714	80.3	24.6	7.2	31.7	25.0	11.6	37.1	75.4	19.3	7.6	23.6	24.7	26.0
1262625	St. Cloud city	66,441	88.8	24.4	8.3	30.7	25.4	11.1	36.9	60.3	11.4	1.9	49.0	21.1	58.1
1263000	St. Petersburg city	263,546	7.6	16.4	6.8	29.1	24.7	23.0	43.5	75.0	20.0	5.0	11.8	10.8	11.0
1263650	Sanford city	65,397	22.1	19.8	8.3	32.7	25.9	13.3	38.1	62.5	27.9	6.7	23.8	19.9	28.8
1268350	Spring Hill CDP	121,939	25.6	19.1	7.0	24.8	25.9	23.1	44.2	85.2	8.6	2.9	20.5	15.7	22.7
1269700	Sunrise city	96,808	14.3	21.5	7.2	27.2	27.4	16.7	41.8	51.3	33.7	6.0	34.4	24.5	38.7
1270600	Tallahassee city	202,222	11.3	15.9	28.9	26.2	16.6	12.4	28.2	57.3	37.6	6.1	8.8	9.1	9.5
1270675	Tamarac city	72,360	19.7	13.5	6.6	25.7	26.6	27.6	48.3	53.4	43.7	3.5	23.1	24.7	27.4
1271000	Tampa city	403,361	19.7	19.2	11.1	32.6	23.4	13.7	35.9	66.3	24.4	7.1	24.1	20.8	26.0
1271625	The Villages CDP	79,772	55.1	1.5	0.4	2.7	13.1	82.4	74.5	94.9	3.2	0.8	2.4	1.4	1.8
1272145	Town 'n' Country CDP	78,974	-2.7	16.2	7.1	31.2	28.1	17.4	42.0	79.0	9.7	5.5	51.1	45.3	55.2
1275875	Wesley Chapel CDP	82,087	86.2	27.4	8.9	26.5	25.1	12.1	36.7	70.7	16.2	11.2	22.0	18.9	24.8
1276582	Weston city	68,168	4.0	26.4	8.4	17.3	36.3	11.7	43.8	80.4	6.4	8.9	54.4	46.5	58.0
1276600	West Palm Beach city	124,148	23.9	18.6	8.4	29.5	22.2	21.3	41.4	58.0	35.3	4.9	26.8	21.7	26.2
13000	**GEORGIA**	10,912,876	12.4	23.0	9.8	27.1	25.1	15.1	37.6	58.7	33.6	5.6	11.1	10.4	8.3
1301052	Albany city	67,373	-14.7	24.2	12.5	26.0	21.7	15.6	34.8	18.5	79.3	1.2	3.4	2.3	2.4
1301696	Alpharetta city	67,054	16.5	21.9	6.3	24.7	33.7	13.4	43.4	62.3	13.6	22.1	10.8	8.1	10.2
1303440	Athens-Clarke County unified government (balance)	128,423	11.2	16.1	25.0	28.0	18.2	12.7	29.5	64.5	27.8	5.0	11.2	8.2	12.0
1304000	Atlanta city	510,826	21.0	17.5	13.3	35.9	21.1	12.2	34.5	44.7	49.4	6.5	7.3	7.4	6.5
1304204	Augusta-Richmond County consolidated government (balance)	202,629	3.2	22.7	11.1	28.3	22.4	15.5	35.3	36.9	59.3	3.3	6.7	5.6	5.9
1319000	Columbus city	201,877	6.0	24.8	9.0	28.5	22.1	15.7	35.4	46.3	50.9	5.1	8.9	10.1	8.7
1342425	Johns Creek city	81,119	5.1	24.4	6.1	19.2	35.5	14.8	45.2	54.1	13.7	34.0	9.2	10.8	7.7
1349008	Macon-Bibb County	156,512	71.3	24.5	9.0	26.9	22.9	16.7	36.3	38.4	56.6	2.7	5.8	3.5	4.8
1367284	Roswell city	91,708	3.1	23.9	7.2	25.1	29.7	14.0	40.5	81.4	9.8	7.4	18.4	15.7	16.3
1368516	Sandy Springs city	105,803	12.0	16.1	7.3	39.0	24.2	13.5	36.9	64.0	25.8	10.3	13.8	13.3	12.3
1369000	Savannah city	147,751	8.1	19.5	13.7	31.1	21.8	13.9	34.4	44.1	49.0	5.5	7.6	6.0	5.7
1372122	South Fulton city	110,911	NA	27.2	8.6	26.8	24.7	12.7	35.7	3.8	95.8	0.8	3.2	3.1	2.5
1380508	Warner Robins city	84,151	26.1	26.1	8.7	32.0	19.3	13.9	33.2	51.4	45.1	5.1	8.6	10.2	11.4
15000	**HAWAII**	1,440,196	5.6	20.6	8.3	26.5	24.1	20.5	40.8	43.8	4.0	84.5	9.0	11.1	28.7
1571550	Urban Honolulu CDP	341,753	0.8	15.8	8.1	28.9	25.0	22.3	42.7	31.8	4.1	85.5	5.9	19.8	7.1
16000	**IDAHO**	1,939,033	23.4	24.0	10.0	26.1	22.9	17.0	37.5	91.4	1.5	3.0	14.7	13.5	9.8
1608830	Boise City city	235,416	14.1	17.6	10.6	29.0	26.3	16.5	39.0	89.5	2.6	5.5	10.9	7.8	9.5
1612250	Caldwell city		68,339	47.8	29.3	9.8	31.4	18.5	11.0	31.4	77.0	NA	4.0	38.2	18.6
1639700	Idaho Falls city	67,996	19.7	31.1	10.6	28.9	18.4	11.0	31.1	88.8	2.0	3.3	17.4	10.3	17.3
1652120	Meridian city	134,794	79.0	24.6	9.6	27.7	21.1	16.9	36.6	94.6	1.0	6.5	7.8	9.4	9.6
1656260	Nampa city	114,261	39.7	25.0	9.6	29.1	20.8	15.5	35.3	88.7	2.6	3.2	20.5	14.1	22.5
17000	**ILLINOIS**	12,582,032	-2.0	21.6	9.3	26.7	25.2	17.2	39.1	71.3	15.3	7.2	17.7	18.3	10.9
1702154	Arlington Heights village	77,699	0.9	21.1	6.2	25.3	27.3	20.1	42.6	83.3	4.2	8.9	12.6	8.9	10.9
1703012	Aurora city	179,355	-7.3	25.7	11.1	27.6	25.9	9.8	34.5	61.4	11.3	14.4	38.4	24.9	40.4
1706587	Bloomington city	78,591	2.4	24.9	8.9	29.0	23.8	13.4	36.5	76.9	13.2	11.7	11.0	11.4	9.4

Table A-4. Cities — Who: Age, Race/Ethnicity, and Household Structure, 2023

STATE and place code	STATE Place	Native, born in state of residence (percent)	Foreign born (percent)	Non-citizens (percent)	Total households	Average household size	Household type (percent of all households): Family households: Total	Family households: Married-couple	Family households: Male householder	Family households: Female householder	Nonfamily households: Total	Nonfamily households: One-person households	Percent of households with people age 60 years and over
	ACS table number:	B05002	B05002	B05002	B11001	B25010	B11001	B11001	B11001	B11001	B11001	B11001	B11006
	column number:	15	16	17	18	19	20	21	22	23	24	25	26
	FLORIDA—Cont.												
1245000	Miami city	27.6	55.4	27.1	201,102	2.23	55.1	32.9	8.0	14.1	44.9	35.4	35.7
1245025	Miami Beach city	23.3	52.6	27.1	37,894	2.08	51.1	36.2	7.1	7.9	48.9	43.0	40.7
1245060	Miami Gardens city	53.8	36.2	14.7	34,688	3.16	72.0	39.8	8.4	23.8	28.0	22.7	48.9
1245975	Miramar city	42.4	41.7	10.0	44,827	3.08	77.6	51.4	5.2	20.9	22.4	17.0	37.6
1249675	North Port city	23.7	15.0	7.1	35,320	2.51	73.8	57.7	4.6	11.4	26.2	19.5	53.6
1250750	Ocala city	15.3	47.6	13.7	9.5	29,755	2.22	56.7	42.6	6.4	7.7	43.3	39.1
1253000	Orlando city	35.9	27.2	16.2	141,669	2.24	54.9	31.4	7.2	16.3	45.1	33.1	29.7
1254000	Palm Bay city	32.1	17.1	3.8	50,448	2.66	67.2	48.4	4.7	14.1	32.8	26.6	50.7
1254200	Palm Coast city	24.9	14.8	3.5	43,003	2.36	66.4	51.7	2.8	12.0	33.6	27.5	59.5
1254350	Palm Harbor CDP	9.8	23.9	14.0	3.9	27,659	2.21	68.9	56.0	3.1	9.8	31.1	27.6
1255775	Pembroke Pines city	30.8	45.4	14.3	63,065	2.70	72.4	50.6	5.8	15.9	27.6	21.7	53.6
1256825	Pine Hills CDP	42.5	37.8	19.0	24,671	3.20	77.5	47.2	6.5	23.9	22.5	16.0	42.5
1257425	Plantation city	36.1	34.2	12.4	36,927	2.60	66.2	51.9	3.3	11.1	33.8	25.8	39.6
1257900	Poinciana CDP	28.9	23.7	10.8	26,064	3.02	76.4	52.0	9.2	15.2	23.6	18.9	50.5
1258050	Pompano Beach city	32.6	32.5	17.3	51,440	2.16	49.7	32.2	5.8	11.7	50.3	41.0	50.3
1258350	Port Charlotte CDP	29.6	12.2	4.2	26,105	2.45	66.2	51.1	4.5	10.6	33.8	28.3	59.4
1258575	Port Orange city	35.2	8.8	2.1	27,070	2.42	62.8	47.3	3.1	12.3	37.2	29.7	56.1
1258715	Port St. Lucie city	34.0	19.9	6.3	90,069	2.71	72.4	55.0	5.9	11.5	27.6	22.2	51.9
1260950	Riverview CDP	33.5	16.0	6.5	44,076	2.71	71.9	52.8	4.3	14.7	28.1	20.8	33.0
1262625	St. Cloud city	26.1	21.0	7.2	23,749	2.78	75.7	51.3	7.2	17.1	24.3	20.3	36.3
1263000	St. Petersburg city	39.1	11.6	4.2	123,605	2.08	49.8	35.9	4.1	9.9	50.2	40.4	44.4
1263650	Sanford city	43.9	16.2	8.9	26,511	2.39	60.6	38.9	4.6	17.1	39.4	29.3	32.7
1268350	Spring Hill CDP	33.9	9.9	3.4	47,821	2.51	72.5	48.2	7.9	16.3	27.5	21.8	50.1
1269700	Sunrise city	35.1	43.7	15.4	34,455	2.78	67.7	44.9	6.9	15.9	32.3	28.8	46.7
1270600	Tallahassee city	54.6	9.5	5.0	87,824	2.08	42.5	26.0	2.7	13.8	57.5	38.7	28.0
1270675	Tamarac city	28.2	42.1	7.3	32,913	2.19	59.4	38.1	7.4	13.9	40.6	32.8	56.1
1271000	Tampa city	37.4	21.4	10.0	169,317	2.27	52.0	34.3	6.5	11.2	48.0	35.7	32.2
1271625	The Villages CDP	5.2	3.4	0.7	45,000	1.77	64.9	61.7	0.5	2.7	35.1	31.2	94.5
1272145	Town 'n' Country CDP	24.4	44.2	26.7	31,323	2.51	58.6	38.7	7.8	12.1	41.4	27.5	39.3
1275875	Wesley Chapel CDP	30.9	19.2	6.7	26,661	3.08	76.5	61.7	4.3	10.5	23.5	17.6	31.4
1276582	Weston city	24.8	48.0	23.0	22,243	3.06	85.0	72.3	3.1	9.6	15.0	12.8	36.4
1276600	West Palm Beach city	34.3	28.2	11.9	50,890	2.37	56.9	32.0	9.9	15.0	43.1	31.8	44.4
13000	**GEORGIA**	53.2	10.7	5.3	4,092,467	2.61	66.8	46.9	4.9	15.0	33.2	27.1	38.7
1301052	Albany city	75.5	2.7	1.6	28,379	2.24	62.9	19.7	7.9	35.3	37.1	29.8	39.0
1301696	Alpharetta city	27.9	25.9	11.5	26,224	2.53	72.1	63.4	3.0	5.7	27.9	21.8	34.5
1303440	Athens-Clarke County unified government (balance)	56.7	9.4	6.6	54,856	2.15	47.9	30.4	5.3	12.2	52.1	30.2	29.0
1304000	Atlanta city	46.5	9.8	4.7	233,047	2.05	40.5	25.4	3.5	11.5	59.5	47.3	28.0
1304204	Augusta-Richmond County consolidated government (balance)	61.4	4.2	2.8	76,232	2.55	60.9	30.5	5.5	24.8	39.1	32.0	39.7
1319000	Columbus city	56.0	5.1	1.5	82,007	2.39	57.1	33.1	6.2	17.9	42.9	36.2	36.1
1342425	Johns Creek city	24.0	35.7	14.9	28,800	2.81	82.9	70.4	3.6	8.8	17.1	14.5	40.8
1349008	Macon-Bibb County	71.0	5.1	3.5	60,919	2.46	61.5	37.8	3.6	20.0	38.5	33.8	41.0
1367284	Roswell city	35.7	15.7	6.8	35,275	2.59	67.4	59.8	1.9	5.7	32.6	24.8	37.5
1368516	Sandy Springs city	33.9	18.9	9.6	50,453	2.08	50.7	41.9	2.5	6.4	49.3	37.8	27.2
1369000	Savannah city	51.4	9.0	4.6	60,129	2.28	53.1	31.7	5.4	16.0	46.9	38.7	35.2
1372122	South Fulton city	57.6	7.3	2.0	40,298	2.74	61.8	35.8	5.5	20.6	38.2	32.0	35.0
1380508	Warner Robins city	52.3	10.1	5.6	33,527	2.50	66.4	36.3	5.6	24.4	33.6	28.1	36.8
15000	**HAWAII**	53.3	17.1	6.5	494,827	2.83	67.7	48.6	5.5	13.5	32.3	25.3	50.1
1571550	Urban Honolulu CDP	47.8	27.4	10.9	137,203	2.42	56.2	39.7	5.7	10.8	43.8	35.0	48.0
16000	**IDAHO**	43.3	6.0	3.2	717,151	2.63	68.5	55.3	4.5	8.7	31.5	24.3	40.7
1608830	Boise City city	39.3	8.4	4.3	104,336	2.18	58.6	44.0	4.5	10.1	41.4	30.8	35.9
1612250	Caldwell city	40.8	43.5	14.0	9.1	21,765	3.08	70.7	54.5	6.3	9.9	29.3	23.4
1639700	Idaho Falls city	58.6	3.0	1.7	24,008	2.77	62.2	42.7	5.0	14.5	37.8	31.6	32.2
1652120	Meridian city	37.2	4.0	1.0	50,116	2.67	73.8	59.7	5.1	9.0	26.2	18.4	37.2
1656260	Nampa city	45.0	7.4	4.1	41,060	2.73	70.9	52.9	7.2	10.8	29.1	20.3	37.4
17000	**ILLINOIS**	66.6	14.4	6.7	5,056,360	2.43	62.1	45.1	4.9	12.0	37.9	31.0	40.7
1702154	Arlington Heights village	61.3	24.2	8.2	32,370	2.37	66.0	54.2	1.9	9.9	34.0	24.8	42.6
1703012	Aurora city	62.7	22.4	12.7	61,278	2.90	71.8	45.7	9.7	16.4	28.2	21.2	30.7
1706587	Bloomington city	69.0	10.5	7.1	33,447	2.30	56.7	44.7	2.7	9.3	43.3	35.4	32.1

Table A-4. Cities — Who: Age, Race/Ethnicity, and Household Structure, 2023—*Continued*

STATE and place code	STATE Place	Total population	Percent change, 2010–2023	Population by age (percent): Under 18 years	18 to 24 years	25 to 44 years	45 to 64 years	65 years and over	Median age	Race alone or in combination (percent): White	Black	Asian + Native Hawaiian or Other Pacific Islander	American Indian and Alaska Native + Some other race	Two or more races (percent)	Hispanic or Latino (percent)
	ACS table number:	B01003	Census PEP	B01001	B01001	B01001	B01001	B01001	B01002	B02008	B02009	B02011 + B02012	B02010 + B02013	B02001	B03003
	column number:	1	2	3	4	5	6	7	8	9	10	11	12	13	14
	ILLINOIS—Cont.														
1707133	Bolingbrook village	75,121	2.9	19.7	11.3	26.2	30.1	12.7	38.2	55.3	15.6	16.4	31.6	17.0	31.5
1712385	Champaign city	89,191	9.9	15.0	31.6	23.9	16.8	12.7	28.1	67.7	19.9	14.9	8.1	10.3	7.5
1714000	Chicago city	2,664,454	-1.3	18.9	9.5	34.5	22.7	14.4	36.4	48.7	30.5	9.2	26.6	14.1	29.5
1714351	Cicero town	81,006	-3.6	23.0	14.9	25.3	23.8	13.0	33.5	30.3	4.1	0.1	84.5	18.2	89.2
1718823	Decatur city	66,594	-12.7	20.5	10.1	25.8	21.0	22.6	39.4	75.6	27.9	1.6	6.5	10.6	3.2
1723074	Elgin city	118,799	9.7	24.5	9.1	29.0	24.1	13.3	36.8	61.1	7.8	7.8	49.9	24.6	51.3
1724582	Evanston city	75,073	0.7	19.5	15.7	23.9	21.8	19.2	38.0	73.5	12.6	12.5	14.3	11.9	14.9
1738570	Joliet city	147,944	-1.9	22.7	9.3	29.1	26.2	12.7	37.9	65.5	18.7	2.9	32.6	17.5	35.3
1751622	Naperville city	151,220	6.9	23.7	7.9	22.3	30.7	15.5	42.7	69.3	4.1	26.7	8.8	8.6	7.3
1757225	Palatine village	65,176	-5.0	22.7	7.5	27.8	27.0	15.0	39.5	66.8	4.4	13.0	25.3	9.7	26.3
1759000	Peoria city	113,442	-1.3	24.6	11.9	24.2	22.6	16.7	36.3	66.1	28.7	8.0	8.5	8.9	7.6
1765000	Rockford city	146,219	-3.9	22.6	8.9	25.4	23.2	19.9	39.6	66.1	21.7	5.1	22.3	14.3	22.0
1768003	Schaumburg village	76,128	3.9	23.2	5.8	27.2	23.4	20.4	41.5	65.9	6.9	25.9	8.1	8.8	11.1
1770122	Skokie village	64,939	0.1	22.2	7.9	19.8	26.6	23.6	45.1	55.0	11.3	32.8	11.5	8.5	8.1
1772000	Springfield city	112,327	-3.3	18.6	9.6	23.7	26.3	21.8	43.6	77.0	17.9	4.8	6.6	6.0	2.9
1779293	Waukegan city	89,097	1.6	23.2	8.7	29.3	26.1	12.6	36.2	48.1	16.4	5.6	51.1	21.3	62.6
18000	**INDIANA**	6,833,037	5.3	23.0	9.9	25.7	24.5	16.9	38.2	84.1	11.3	3.3	8.7	7.8	7.0
1805860	Bloomington city	74,028	-8.7	9.8	42.1	26.9	11.0	10.2	24.2	79.5	7.4	13.6	6.7	6.9	7.0
1810342	Carmel city	102,091	28.5	26.1	8.8	25.2	26.0	14.0	37.5	83.3	4.2	14.9	4.3	6.3	5.0
1822000	Evansville city	113,291	-2.2	22.7	9.4	26.8	24.0	17.1	37.5	82.3	16.2	2.3	8.3	7.9	3.8
1823278	Fishers city	101,789	31.2	26.1	6.9	27.5	25.2	14.3	38.9	85.5	10.3	6.1	7.9	9.8	5.8
1825000	Fort Wayne city	271,629	7.1	24.1	11.2	28.1	21.7	14.9	35.0	74.8	17.9	7.6	11.4	10.9	10.5
1827000		Gary city	68,269	-15.6	29.7	7.8	23.7	19.3	19.6	34.8	17.6	78.4	0.0	9.2	5.5
1831000	Hammond city	76,181	-5.7	22.8	12.0	26.5	25.5	13.2	36.1	48.2	22.1	2.2	44.7	15.8	48.8
1836003	Indianapolis city (balance)	874,182	6.1	24.7	9.6	30.0	22.0	13.6	34.3	60.0	31.2	5.2	14.4	10.2	14.4
1840788	Lafayette city	67,406	3.3	23.6	11.1	30.1	21.5	13.7	34.2	85.0	11.8	3.7	14.7	15.2	15.2
1851876	Muncie city		64,599	-5.9	14.1	26.7	22.5	20.7	16.1	31.1	88.1	9.9	3.2	7.3	7.4
1854180	Noblesville city	76,124	46.5	25.4	8.0	28.7	22.9	15.0	37.7	87.9	8.6	3.1	4.9	4.1	5.9
1871000	South Bend city	100,715	-5.9	22.8	9.9	29.6	21.7	16.1	36.1	70.2	25.6	2.8	18.4	16.6	18.5
19000	**IOWA**	3,200,517	4.9	22.4	10.1	25.2	23.9	18.4	38.9	90.7	5.3	3.5	7.5	6.8	6.4
1901855	Ames city	65,676	11.4	10.7	41.1	22.7	13.5	11.9	24.4	83.2	5.3	11.5	4.2	4.0	4.8
1902305	Ankeny city	74,455	63.3	25.4	9.5	29.2	23.5	12.4	34.9	90.2	5.4	2.5	5.1	3.1	4.6
1912000	Cedar Rapids city	135,960	7.5	20.7	11.3	27.9	24.4	15.8	36.5	86.2	12.9	4.7	6.0	8.8	5.1
1919000	Davenport city	100,361	0.3	21.2	10.8	27.4	25.4	15.1	37.9	80.9	15.0	5.8	11.0	10.9	9.8
1921000	Des Moines city	210,363	3.0	22.5	11.3	31.7	22.5	12.0	34.4	72.6	16.0	7.0	16.9	11.6	17.1
1938595	Iowa City city	75,671	11.2	14.3	34.8	25.7	13.6	11.6	25.6	81.3	11.5	7.1	8.8	8.4	8.9
1973335	Sioux City city	85,172	3.4	25.3	11.6	24.4	23.8	15.0	37.0	82.7	9.2	3.4	19.3	14.6	23.2
1982425	Waterloo city	66,604	-2.7	26.1	8.0	28.5	20.4	16.9	37.5	74.4	18.6	5.0	9.4	6.2	8.7
1983910	West Des Moines city	72,161	27.5	19.7	7.6	32.1	22.6	18.0	38.4	83.5	1.8	12.5	5.6	3.2	7.0
20000	**KANSAS**	2,937,150	2.8	23.4	10.4	25.9	23.1	17.2	37.6	85.8	7.6	4.2	13.3	13.0	10.0
2036000	Kansas City city	149,918	1.4	26.5	9.4	26.8	22.2	15.0	35.1	55.2	23.4	7.7	32.5	18.2	35.8
2038900	Lawrence city	96,209	3.8	16.1	24.9	27.9	18.6	12.4	30.6	85.7	8.2	7.8	12.1	12.2	8.5
2052575	Olathe city	147,466	16.8	26.5	8.5	27.7	23.0	14.2	37.4	85.9	8.2	6.4	13.0	12.9	12.7
2053775	Overland Park city	197,062	13.3	22.4	7.6	28.5	24.9	16.7	39.6	84.1	7.4	8.8	10.0	9.3	8.5
2064500	Shawnee city	69,417	11.6	21.4	9.7	28.1	23.2	17.6	38.9	89.0	5.6	5.1	11.7	10.6	12.3
2071000	Topeka city	125,480	-1.8	20.5	10.2	26.4	23.8	19.1	39.2	83.5	13.5	3.4	16.5	16.0	16.8
2079000	Wichita city	396,123	3.4	23.3	10.0	27.3	22.7	16.7	36.8	78.5	13.6	6.3	18.2	15.2	19.9
21000	**KENTUCKY**	4,512,310	3.8	22.3	9.2	25.6	25.4	17.5	39.4	88.8	9.6	2.2	5.9	4.2	6.0
2108902	Bowling Green city	76,215	31.3	21.5	23.8	26.5	15.5	12.7	28.1	75.1	16.3	8.4	10.9	10.5	12.8
2146027	Lexington-Fayette urban county	320,154	7.9	20.7	13.6	28.1	22.2	15.3	35.4	77.2	17.7	5.3	8.8	8.5	9.4
2148006	Louisville/Jefferson County metro government (balance)	622,987	4.1	22.4	8.7	27.4	24.6	16.9	38.0	71.1	25.2	4.3	11.8	11.4	9.4
22000	**LOUISIANA**	4,590,241	1.0	23.1	9.5	26.2	24.2	17.0	38.2	63.9	33.3	2.4	7.9	5.7	6.9
2205000	Baton Rouge city	219,563	-4.5	22.0	19.8	25.3	17.9	15.0	30.6	39.0	53.3	5.1	9.9	6.3	6.4
2239475	Kenner city	63,339	-5.0	24.2	6.6	23.5	24.7	20.9	41.0	62.6	23.1	7.0	23.8	18.4	28.6
2240735	Lafayette city	121,452	0.5	20.0	9.9	28.6	23.5	17.9	37.3	65.1	32.7	1.7	11.3	10.8	8.2
2241155	Lake Charles city	79,647	10.4	20.9	14.1	24.4	23.0	17.6	37.6	55.8	42.9	1.8	5.5	5.0	3.3
2250115	Metairie CDP	136,597	2.8	20.7	6.7	26.6	23.6	22.4	41.9	79.2	10.2	4.4	24.7	17.8	24.0

Table A-4. Cities — Who: Age, Race/Ethnicity, and Household Structure, 2023

STATE and place code	STATE Place	Native, born in state of residence (percent)	Foreign born (percent)	Non-citizens (percent)	Total households	Average household size	Household type (percent of all households) — Family households — Total	Family households — Married-couple	Family households — Male householder	Family households — Female householder	Nonfamily households — Total	Nonfamily households — One-person households	Percent of households with people age 60 years and over
	ACS table number:	B05002	B05002	B05002	B11001	B25010	B11001	B11001	B11001	B11001	B11001	B11001	B11006
	column number:	15	16	17	18	19	20	21	22	23	24	25	26
	ILLINOIS—Cont.												
1707133	Bolingbrook village	56.8	26.8	11.4	25,142	2.98	80.7	59.3	9.8	11.6	19.3	16.8	41.6
1712385	Champaign city	61.7	15.6	10.7	40,599	1.99	42.0	30.1	2.0	9.9	58.0	46.3	25.1
1714000	Chicago city	57.8	21.0	10.8	1,179,081	2.22	49.2	30.1	5.6	13.5	50.8	40.2	33.4
1714351	Cicero town	50.7	40.0	24.7	24,167	3.32	77.3	49.5	14.0	13.8	22.7	14.8	45.3
1718823	Decatur city	77.9	3.1	1.0	30,783	2.07	46.3	28.3	6.3	11.7	53.7	45.6	47.3
1723074	Elgin city	58.6	29.5	15.7	41,062	2.85	72.4	51.8	6.3	14.3	27.6	21.7	36.7
1724582	Evanston city	45.9	19.0	10.5	31,310	2.18	52.7	40.8	4.7	7.2	47.3	38.7	43.0
1738570	Joliet city	73.1	17.0	11.2	52,512	2.76	68.1	48.9	5.3	13.9	31.9	23.9	34.6
1751622	Naperville city	55.5	22.3	8.8	55,580	2.67	73.3	67.0	2.1	4.3	26.7	20.7	37.4
1757225	Palatine village	60.6	24.7	13.2	27,531	2.35	60.2	42.6	5.8	11.8	39.8	32.3	35.5
1759000	Peoria city	70.0	11.0	7.3	49,577	2.21	56.2	39.5	4.6	12.1	43.8	39.8	34.0
1765000	Rockford city	70.0	11.8	5.9	62,552	2.28	60.3	36.1	5.6	18.6	39.7	32.6	43.0
1768003	Schaumburg village	51.1	37.3	19.5	31,791	2.38	63.9	52.3	3.8	7.9	36.1	30.9	43.3
1770122	Skokie village	45.3	39.8	8.8	23,942	2.68	74.4	52.7	5.1	16.6	25.6	21.1	56.0
1772000	Springfield city	78.0	5.3	2.7	51,843	2.10	49.5	35.0	3.4	11.1	50.5	41.0	43.9
1779293	Waukegan city	52.4	33.2	22.0	31,784	2.75	64.9	38.3	7.8	18.7	35.1	28.3	39.1
18000	**INDIANA**	67.0	6.1	3.4	2,726,489	2.44	63.8	48.0	4.9	11.0	36.2	29.6	39.9
1805860	Bloomington city	48.8	13.4	9.4	33,738	1.80	28.7	21.5	1.8	5.4	71.3	42.4	20.4
1810342	Carmel city	53.3	12.5	6.8	38,523	2.64	69.9	61.4	4.2	4.3	30.1	24.4	33.2
1822000	Evansville city	72.5	3.0	1.7	51,696	2.12	49.0	32.0	3.3	13.7	51.0	42.9	38.1
1823278	Fishers city	52.6	12.2	5.1	38,270	2.64	76.1	64.4	3.9	7.7	23.9	20.9	32.9
1825000	Fort Wayne city	65.2	8.8	4.2	115,195	2.32	56.1	36.9	6.3	13.0	43.9	35.9	34.0
1827000		11.4	58.8	2.8	1.2	27,688	2.45	58.0	18.0	8.2	31.9	42.0	36.8
1831000	Hammond city	42.5	12.6	7.8	29,271	2.58	62.9	36.9	8.9	17.1	37.1	30.4	39.8
1836003	Indianapolis city (balance)	62.1	12.9	8.4	368,064	2.33	55.6	36.9	4.9	13.7	44.4	36.0	33.7
1840788	Lafayette city	61.9	11.8	8.5	31,331	2.10	53.6	31.1	7.6	14.9	46.4	39.0	31.3
1851876	Muncie city	3.9	73.7	4.8	3.6	26,505	2.15	43.3	27.8	4.4	11.1	56.7	41.5
1854180	Noblesville city	67.0	6.8	3.5	28,543	2.64	67.9	54.8	3.2	9.8	32.1	20.1	36.8
1871000	South Bend city	65.3	8.4	5.9	42,331	2.33	52.1	31.2	5.2	15.7	47.9	39.3	37.2
19000	**IOWA**	70.1	6.0	3.3	1,330,995	2.33	61.8	48.6	4.5	8.7	38.2	30.6	40.5
1901855	Ames city	53.3	11.1	7.5	26,633	2.03	37.5	31.6	3.0	2.9	62.5	34.6	26.5
1902305	Ankeny city	70.8	4.3	3.1	30,257	2.43	64.1	54.0	4.0	6.1	35.9	26.7	25.1
1912000	Cedar Rapids city	68.3	8.9	3.7	58,123	2.28	55.5	40.2	5.7	9.6	44.5	35.8	35.2
1919000	Davenport city	56.9	6.0	1.8	44,171	2.20	58.2	40.8	4.6	12.8	41.8	30.0	35.0
1921000	Des Moines city	61.8	14.6	9.7	90,465	2.27	53.5	34.0	6.8	12.7	46.5	37.1	29.3
1938595	Iowa City city	50.9	11.2	5.9	30,588	2.22	38.3	28.5	2.4	7.4	61.7	41.9	26.3
1973335	Sioux City city	61.6	11.9	8.2	32,278	2.56	63.4	43.7	7.3	12.4	36.6	30.0	40.3
1982425	Waterloo city	70.9	9.8	6.9	28,471	2.30	52.5	33.8	2.3	16.4	47.5	35.6	38.9
1983910	West Des Moines city	62.1	15.1	11.1	33,094	2.17	55.1	44.8	3.2	7.2	44.9	34.6	36.0
20000	**KANSAS**	59.3	7.1	4.1	1,175,294	2.43	63.0	48.9	4.6	9.5	37.0	30.3	40.0
2036000	Kansas City city	52.1	19.4	12.9	57,487	2.59	64.9	38.4	7.5	19.0	35.1	27.6	36.9
2038900	Lawrence city	49.3	7.0	4.8	41,551	2.14	47.0	31.7	3.5	11.9	53.0	35.2	27.0
2052575	Olathe city	50.7	9.4	4.2	53,252	2.74	70.3	58.0	4.7	7.5	29.7	23.3	35.3
2053775	Overland Park city	37.3	10.3	6.0	85,022	2.30	59.8	49.3	3.1	7.5	40.2	32.3	36.4
2064500	Shawnee city	50.1	8.4	3.0	28,168	2.45	68.1	53.7	4.2	10.1	31.9	23.6	35.9
2071000	Topeka city	70.7	4.2	3.0	55,148	2.19	52.3	34.6	4.8	12.8	47.7	40.6	44.6
2079000	Wichita city	61.6	9.9	5.7	163,555	2.37	58.5	41.5	5.0	12.0	41.5	34.6	38.3
21000	**KENTUCKY**	67.2	4.0	2.2	1,828,680	2.40	64.1	47.1	5.0	12.0	35.9	29.7	41.8
2108902	Bowling Green city	52.4	13.0	8.9	32,904	2.17	50.2	31.5	7.5	11.2	49.8	39.5	27.9
2146027	Lexington-Fayette urban county	58.5	11.9	6.5	141,680	2.17	54.1	38.5	3.8	11.8	45.9	34.0	33.9
2148006	Louisville/Jefferson County metro government (balance)	66.2	10.3	6.0	264,694	2.31	58.4	38.8	5.5	14.1	41.6	34.1	39.3
22000	**LOUISIANA**	77.5	4.2	2.3	1,816,902	2.46	62.3	41.5	5.2	15.6	37.7	31.5	41.9
2205000	Baton Rouge city	74.2	8.3	5.8	86,978	2.36	48.5	28.4	3.6	16.4	51.5	42.4	36.6
2239475	Kenner city	61.3	20.5	10.0	23,924	2.63	66.8	46.9	7.0	13.0	33.2	30.4	49.4
2240735	Lafayette city	76.6	7.2	3.1	53,953	2.22	55.1	36.6	5.0	13.5	44.9	37.5	39.1
2241155	Lake Charles city	74.4	3.1	2.0	33,140	2.35	59.3	36.8	6.4	16.1	40.7	33.8	38.8
2250115	Metairie CDP	68.2	15.0	10.1	61,486	2.21	57.8	41.2	5.5	11.0	42.2	38.7	46.1

Table A-4. Cities — Who: Age, Race/Ethnicity, and Household Structure, 2023—*Continued*

STATE and place code	STATE Place	Total population	Percent change, 2010–2023	Population by age (percent): Under 18 years	18 to 24 years	25 to 44 years	45 to 64 years	65 years and over	Median age	Race alone or in combination (percent): White	Black	Asian + Native Hawaiian or Other Pacific Islander	American Indian and Alaska Native + Some other race	Two or more races (percent)	Hispanic or Latino (percent)
	ACS table number:	B01003	Census PEP	B01001	B01001	B01001	B01001	B01001	B01002	B02008	B02009	B02011 + B02012	B02010 + B02013	B02001	B03003
	column number:	1	2	3	4	5	6	7	8	9	10	11	12	13	14
	LOUISIANA—Cont.														
2255000	New Orleans city	364,136	4.7	19.5	9.1	29.3	23.9	18.1	39.5	38.2	57.9	4.0	9.3	8.7	8.1
2270000	Shreveport city	177,225	-10.9	24.1	7.6	26.9	21.9	19.4	39.0	38.9	58.1	2.6	5.7	5.1	4.5
23000	**MAINE**	1,385,340	4.3	17.7	7.9	24.2	27.5	22.6	45.1	96.0	2.6	2.0	5.1	2.1	5.2
2360545	Portland city	69,104	4.5	13.8	10.5	37.9	20.9	16.9	37.7	90.1	9.8	2.8	10.0	11.7	4.2
24000	**MARYLAND**	6,164,660	6.5	21.8	8.6	26.7	25.9	16.9	39.7	55.4	32.6	8.4	12.6	11.4	8.2
2404000	Baltimore city	565,239	-8.9	20.8	9.2	31.8	22.2	16.0	36.5	31.5	62.0	3.7	9.2	5.6	8.2
2407125	Bethesda CDP	69,966	15.0	21.7	9.0	19.7	29.9	19.7	44.4	74.0	8.7	19.3	9.6	10.3	9.0
2419125	Columbia CDP	101,379	-0.8	21.5	9.2	28.4	24.4	16.4	39.4	53.0	33.8	15.0	9.5	10.3	9.4
2426000	Ellicott City CDP	74,574	10.9	25.4	6.7	22.0	24.7	21.1	42.8	53.9	13.1	33.8	3.5	3.8	2.5
2430325	Frederick city	85,803	31.1	22.0	9.2	30.5	22.9	15.4	37.7	60.8	18.8	6.8	20.7	7.4	23.3
2431175	Gaithersburg city	69,572	16.1	25.9	5.7	31.5	20.8	16.2	36.8	43.8	16.5	15.8	30.6	9.3	38.9
2432025	Germantown CDP	96,698	16.0	20.4	10.3	23.3	31.3	14.6	40.7	36.4	29.4	24.7	19.9	10.3	19.5
2432650	Glen Burnie CDP	79,598	17.7	25.9	8.0	32.3	20.7	13.1	34.6	54.8	26.9	7.7	21.9	10.2	21.7
2467675	Rockville city	67,298	9.9	22.3	7.4	26.0	27.0	17.3	40.6	57.1	19.0	24.4	15.2	12.7	15.5
2472450	Silver Spring CDP	84,996	11.1	21.8	8.0	39.1	20.2	10.9	33.7	42.1	32.5	10.4	23.7	8.2	26.1
2481175	Waldorf CDP	82,770	20.0	25.9	6.4	30.1	26.5	11.0	37.0	23.2	70.5	7.6	12.4	11.8	10.6
25000	**MASSACHUSETTS**	6,981,974	6.3	19.1	10.0	26.9	25.9	18.0	40.3	77.8	10.2	8.5	15.1	13.0	10.7
2507000	Boston city	652,442	5.0	14.4	15.1	36.3	20.8	13.4	33.7	56.6	26.6	12.4	20.7	14.2	19.4
2509000	Brockton city	104,884	11.6	24.6	8.2	27.3	24.1	15.7	37.5	34.2	48.8	4.1	31.9	15.9	12.9
2511000	Cambridge city	118,208	12.2	11.7	21.4	40.2	15.1	11.6	30.4	67.3	11.6	22.8	10.9	11.8	11.1
2523000	Fall River city	93,864	5.6	22.2	7.5	31.6	22.0	16.6	37.3	80.3	6.9	4.9	17.1	8.4	13.1
2524960	Framingham city	71,866	5.0	23.4	9.8	29.0	24.5	13.2	36.0	67.8	17.7	8.9	33.9	22.2	20.0
2529405	Haverhill city	67,398	10.7	22.3	9.0	22.6	29.4	16.7	41.8	80.7	6.8	1.9	28.0	16.9	26.9
2534550	Lawrence city	88,174	15.2	21.8	11.6	28.2	27.2	11.3	35.5	29.7	5.9	1.6	77.4	14.3	82.0
2537000	Lowell city	114,289	7.1	18.6	12.2	29.2	23.5	16.5	37.5	49.0	16.9	23.0	21.9	10.2	19.5
2537490	Lynn city	101,250	11.9	22.7	9.8	26.7	23.6	17.1	38.7	52.8	19.7	7.3	40.3	16.5	41.0
2537875	Malden city	65,136	9.6	17.7	6.0	36.6	26.1	13.7	37.4	50.7	18.2	27.2	15.4	10.9	9.0
2545000	New Bedford city	100,683	5.8	24.4	8.6	28.6	22.5	15.9	36.6	67.8	18.7	2.1	35.6	22.2	24.7
2545560	Newton city	88,415	3.6	21.0	10.9	20.5	25.6	22.1	43.1	75.6	4.0	23.4	7.5	10.9	7.3
2555745	Quincy city	101,607	9.9	13.9	9.2	35.7	22.7	18.5	38.8	58.4	6.3	34.2	7.0	5.8	5.7
2562535	Somerville city	80,407	5.9	8.6	12.9	52.4	16.0	10.0	32.0	73.4	9.2	14.9	13.0	9.9	10.8
2567000	Springfield city	153,672	0.4	24.5	11.5	28.8	20.9	14.3	34.3	63.1	27.7	2.3	40.4	29.8	48.0
2582000	Worcester city	207,629	14.5	18.9	15.0	29.2	21.9	14.9	33.9	70.8	15.5	8.0	25.8	17.9	23.3
26000	**MICHIGAN**	10,034,118	1.6	21.0	9.5	25.3	25.6	18.7	40.3	80.7	15.3	4.3	7.2	5.7	7.1
2603000	Ann Arbor city	119,380	4.6	14.8	28.3	26.0	17.6	13.3	28.3	76.8	10.1	16.9	7.2	10.3	6.2
2621000	Dearborn city	105,818	8.1	26.0	9.7	24.1	22.6	17.6	35.5	95.1	3.4	2.4	4.2	4.9	3.5
2622000	Detroit city	633,221	-11.1	25.2	9.0	27.6	22.7	15.5	35.2	16.0	78.5	2.4	9.9	6.5	8.2
2627440	Farmington Hills city	82,539	3.5	16.1	7.3	23.9	27.5	25.2	47.1	63.8	18.8	16.4	4.7	3.9	4.7
2629000	Flint city	79,654	-22.1	24.9	9.4	27.5	24.0	14.2	36.5	36.2	63.4	2.1	2.7	4.2	3.0
2634000	Grand Rapids city	196,587	4.4	19.5	14.7	33.6	18.6	13.6	32.3	71.1	23.1	2.4	17.4	12.1	16.9
2642160	Kalamazoo city	73,122	-1.7	18.4	24.5	26.4	16.8	13.9	29.0	72.8	23.6	3.4	6.9	6.0	7.0
2646000	Lansing city	111,269	-2.4	18.5	12.5	31.4	22.3	15.3	35.5	70.4	27.3	6.1	11.7	14.7	13.4
2649000	Livonia city	92,184	-4.7	21.2	5.3	25.9	25.4	22.1	43.1	89.3	5.4	6.3	5.7	6.7	3.2
2659440	Novi city	66,320	20.1	23.2	5.5	28.9	24.3	18.2	40.0	62.2	6.6	28.5	9.1	5.6	5.4
2669035	Rochester Hills city	75,995	7.0	19.9	10.6	24.5	28.3	16.7	40.6	81.5	4.4	12.4	11.2	8.6	7.8
2674900	Southfield city	75,699	5.5	15.0	7.6	25.3	26.3	25.8	47.8	31.8	65.3	4.6	3.1	4.6	1.4
2676460	Sterling Heights city	133,308	2.8	20.3	8.5	26.0	25.3	19.8	41.0	79.6	10.5	11.0	4.1	5.2	2.8
2680700	Troy city	87,338	7.8	21.6	5.5	26.1	29.1	17.6	42.4	65.3	5.1	31.6	4.1	6.5	3.2
2684000	Warren city	136,660	1.9	22.2	7.5	29.5	24.2	16.6	38.0	59.6	27.8	15.5	4.0	5.8	2.8
2686000	Westland city	82,558	-1.6	17.8	8.9	27.9	27.0	18.4	40.9	72.0	27.7	6.2	5.5	10.8	5.7
2688940	Wyoming city	77,452	7.3	24.1	7.3	32.9	22.3	13.4	34.4	80.0	14.6	3.6	27.0	22.7	25.5
27000	**MINNESOTA**	5,717,184	7.6	22.5	8.9	26.7	24.5	17.4	39.0	83.5	8.8	6.5	8.4	5.8	6.7
2706382	Blaine city	73,762	29.0	26.4	9.0	27.2	22.2	15.2	37.5	70.9	15.3	12.8	12.2	10.2	8.3
2706616	Bloomington city	87,378	5.2	18.3	9.1	28.7	20.9	23.0	40.0	75.7	14.9	6.6	11.7	8.6	11.6
2707966	Brooklyn Park city	82,027	8.0	27.4	6.7	25.6	25.2	15.1	37.8	45.1	41.5	16.5	6.9	8.6	6.4
2717000	Duluth city	87,693	1.7	16.0	18.5	26.1	20.9	18.6	37.0	92.2	5.1	4.0	7.0	7.6	2.8
2717288	Eagan city	67,401	5.0	20.4	7.0	26.6	27.2	18.9	42.7	75.9	18.3	7.8	7.3	9.0	6.6
2735180	Lakeville city	76,235	36.2	27.4	8.0	27.1	26.9	10.7	37.4	82.4	6.7	10.0	7.0	7.5	7.3
2740166	Maple Grove city	71,275	15.8	21.7	4.5	26.1	29.0	18.7	43.0	84.2	7.6	9.5	3.9	5.0	3.1

Table A-4. Cities — Who: Age, Race/Ethnicity, and Household Structure, 2023

STATE and place code	STATE Place	Native, born in state of residence (percent)	Foreign born (percent)	Non-citizens (percent)	Total households	Average household size	Household type (percent of all households): Family households: Total	Family households: Married-couple	Family households: Male householder	Family households: Female householder	Nonfamily households: Total	Nonfamily households: One-person households	Percent of households with people age 60 years and over
	ACS table number:	B05002	B05002	B05002	B11001	B25010	B11001	B11001	B11001	B11001	B11001	B11001	B11006
	column number:	15	16	17	18	19	20	21	22	23	24	25	26
	LOUISIANA—Cont.												
2255000	New Orleans city	67.2	6.7	3.1	155,005	2.26	50.3	30.7	4.0	15.6	49.7	41.6	43.1
2270000	Shreveport city	77.2	2.4	1.3	78,443	2.19	54.8	28.4	5.8	20.6	45.2	41.3	43.1
23000	**MAINE**	59.1	4.1	1.8	605,338	2.23	61.3	48.4	4.4	8.5	38.7	30.0	46.7
2360545	Portland city	46.5	8.3	4.4	34,067	1.97	44.9	36.1	3.2	5.7	55.1	36.7	30.2
24000	**MARYLAND**	47.2	16.7	7.6	2,375,984	2.54	65.1	46.5	5.3	13.3	34.9	28.5	42.3
2404000	Baltimore city	64.3	9.1	4.1	259,385	2.10	45.0	22.1	4.5	18.4	55.0	45.2	36.8
2407125	Bethesda CDP	13.1	28.0	11.7	28,973	2.40	63.4	55.0	1.9	6.5	36.6	30.6	43.2
2419125	Columbia CDP	39.2	17.9	6.1	42,978	2.35	61.7	42.9	6.0	12.8	38.3	33.1	37.6
2426000	Ellicott City CDP	38.7	27.0	7.2	25,715	2.87	78.5	69.1	1.7	7.7	21.5	17.6	49.3
2430325	Frederick city	43.2	22.3	10.7	34,562	2.42	55.3	40.4	5.2	9.7	44.7	34.5	38.6
2431175	Gaithersburg city	26.6	46.4	25.7	25,813	2.68	61.0	41.9	8.8	10.3	39.0	33.8	39.5
2432025	Germantown CDP	29.6	39.1	14.7	34,372	2.81	73.9	53.7	3.0	17.3	26.1	23.3	45.2
2432650	Glen Burnie CDP	57.2	18.2	11.3	29,159	2.70	64.4	40.5	7.4	16.5	35.6	28.1	33.9
2467675	Rockville city	23.3	34.1	14.1	26,261	2.52	66.2	50.9	5.6	9.6	33.8	26.2	40.4
2472450	Silver Spring CDP	22.4	33.3	16.9	35,086	2.42	49.7	32.5	5.9	11.3	50.3	34.1	26.6
2481175	Waldorf CDP	34.9	14.3	5.3	31,345	2.63	71.3	44.5	7.5	19.3	28.7	26.6	34.1
25000	**MASSACHUSETTS**	58.6	18.0	8.1	2,797,776	2.41	61.6	45.2	4.7	11.8	38.4	29.1	43.1
2507000	Boston city	41.9	26.6	13.1	288,129	2.10	44.7	26.5	4.1	14.1	55.3	36.8	31.6
2509000	Brockton city	52.9	34.4	17.7	35,485	2.91	66.9	43.4	4.3	19.1	33.1	27.1	44.2
2511000	Cambridge city	29.6	27.8	17.1	49,310	2.05	38.9	31.1	1.4	6.4	61.1	38.1	26.9
2523000	Fall River city	60.0	22.0	12.1	43,425	2.12	52.1	28.4	7.8	15.9	47.9	38.1	34.8
2524960	Framingham city	50.0	31.1	21.8	25,727	2.66	63.1	47.9	5.8	9.4	36.9	29.6	35.8
2529405	Haverhill city	71.2	13.5	3.8	27,274	2.43	62.2	40.8	3.3	18.1	37.8	30.5	41.8
2534550	Lawrence city	34.7	46.5	26.0	32,631	2.68	65.5	30.6	6.0	29.0	34.5	28.5	35.4
2537000	Lowell city	50.2	33.5	13.7	43,220	2.52	61.7	36.6	6.0	19.1	38.3	29.4	41.4
2537490	Lynn city	51.6	39.3	17.8	36,403	2.76	66.9	45.8	5.2	15.9	33.1	29.0	45.5
2537875	Malden city	40.9	40.2	17.9	27,716	2.34	54.7	39.6	3.1	11.9	45.3	29.7	31.5
2545000	New Bedford city	63.3	21.4	11.7	41,300	2.40	60.5	30.8	7.8	22.0	39.5	33.1	39.0
2545560	Newton city	41.9	26.5	9.4	32,074	2.58	74.5	64.0	4.8	5.6	25.5	20.3	50.0
2555745	Quincy city	52.3	32.0	14.0	46,448	2.16	48.4	33.8	3.9	10.7	51.6	39.9	35.8
2562535	Somerville city	35.3	24.5	13.1	37,108	2.10	37.2	29.9	3.3	4.1	62.8	35.6	21.4
2567000	Springfield city	55.9	8.8	4.0	56,229	2.63	61.1	30.3	7.1	23.7	38.9	33.0	38.7
2582000	Worcester city	55.3	24.1	13.4	81,973	2.36	56.7	33.0	6.7	17.0	43.3	29.9	37.6
26000	**MICHIGAN**	76.0	6.9	3.0	4,089,794	2.40	62.3	45.7	4.9	11.7	37.7	30.5	43.5
2603000	Ann Arbor city	46.8	19.4	12.4	49,077	2.22	45.6	37.3	2.6	5.7	54.4	36.7	27.6
2621000	Dearborn city	55.3	34.3	8.6	38,777	2.72	62.6	50.4	3.5	8.7	37.4	32.8	44.8
2622000	Detroit city	77.8	6.8	3.6	255,857	2.43	51.8	19.3	7.7	24.8	48.2	43.7	40.5
2627440	Farmington Hills city	62.3	22.2	10.4	37,173	2.20	65.6	54.4	3.6	7.6	34.4	28.8	50.3
2629000	Flint city	82.1	1.1	0.5	33,879	2.29	52.7	18.1	7.9	26.7	47.3	42.3	41.3
2634000	Grand Rapids city	71.0	11.0	7.4	80,311	2.36	52.5	33.0	5.2	14.4	47.5	32.4	32.9
2642160	Kalamazoo city	70.1	5.8	4.6	30,482	2.18	45.3	25.6	4.7	14.9	54.7	38.0	30.1
2646000	Lansing city	72.4	8.9	4.7	52,849	2.08	47.6	30.0	5.0	12.6	52.4	41.0	33.7
2649000	Livonia city	77.5	7.7	2.2	38,023	2.40	64.4	53.4	3.2	7.8	35.6	30.7	48.6
2659440	Novi city	54.4	27.9	15.9	26,962	2.44	68.5	56.6	4.2	7.7	31.5	29.1	40.2
2669035	Rochester Hills city	64.7	19.4	9.1	28,914	2.55	71.2	60.6	3.7	6.9	28.8	24.3	41.6
2674900	Southfield city	70.9	8.4	3.3	35,348	2.09	48.0	31.8	3.0	13.1	52.0	47.4	54.4
2676460	Sterling Heights city	64.1	26.4	5.7	52,105	2.54	66.5	49.0	7.4	10.1	33.5	28.5	47.2
2680700	Troy city	52.8	35.0	16.3	34,743	2.51	69.0	60.7	3.5	4.8	31.0	28.0	40.3
2684000	Warren city	73.4	15.3	4.6	54,644	2.48	63.4	42.6	6.3	14.5	36.6	32.4	42.5
2686000	Westland city	78.9	8.6	3.4	35,723	2.29	53.8	32.1	5.3	16.4	46.2	41.1	42.5
2688940	Wyoming city	69.0	13.5	7.7	30,586	2.50	60.9	42.1	5.2	13.5	39.1	30.8	34.3
27000	**MINNESOTA**	67.2	8.7	3.6	2,322,190	2.40	62.7	49.4	4.6	8.7	37.3	29.5	40.1
2706382	Blaine city	65.9	17.1	4.3	25,670	2.86	73.4	53.6	8.2	11.6	26.6	21.4	41.1
2706616	Bloomington city	63.8	14.6	6.7	39,370	2.17	56.0	46.0	3.3	6.7	44.0	36.0	44.3
2707966	Brooklyn Park city	56.9	21.0	8.4	29,325	2.77	69.2	46.5	9.4	13.4	30.8	25.3	44.1
2717000	Duluth city	72.2	3.4	1.9	38,843	2.15	49.6	37.4	3.7	8.4	50.4	35.5	34.9
2717288	Eagan city	58.5	13.2	6.7	27,978	2.40	63.6	52.6	4.8	6.2	36.4	29.3	42.7
2735180	Lakeville city	64.2	10.5	5.5	25,289	3.01	83.2	74.2	3.6	5.4	16.8	11.6	33.6
2740166	Maple Grove city	60.8	12.9	4.2	29,987	2.37	68.2	55.0	5.3	7.9	31.8	27.9	45.3

Table A-4. Cities — Who: Age, Race/Ethnicity, and Household Structure, 2023—*Continued*

STATE and place code	STATE Place	Total population	Percent change, 2010–2023	Population by age (percent): Under 18 years	18 to 24 years	25 to 44 years	45 to 64 years	65 years and over	Median age	Race alone or in combination (percent): White	Black	Asian + Native Hawaiian or Other Pacific Islander	American Indian and Alaska Native + Some other race	Two or more races (percent)	Hispanic or Latino (percent)
	ACS table number:	B01003	Census PEP	B01001	B01001	B01001	B01001	B01001	B01002	B02008	B02009	B02011 + B02012	B02010 + B02013	B02001	B03003
	column number:	1	2	3	4	5	6	7	8	9	10	11	12	13	14
	LOUISIANA—Cont.														
2743000	Minneapolis city	425,142	10.9	18.6	13.0	37.2	19.6	11.6	33.3	70.0	20.7	7.7	12.7	9.8	10.2
2751730	Plymouth city	77,638	9.8	26.3	5.1	26.0	25.7	16.8	39.9	82.1	9.7	10.8	6.1	8.4	4.0
2754880	Rochester city	122,404	14.4	22.1	8.3	31.8	20.3	17.5	36.3	77.6	11.9	9.8	7.4	6.7	6.2
2756896	St. Cloud city	68,399	3.8	22.7	18.8	25.4	20.5	12.6	31.9	72.2	24.7	3.5	6.0	6.8	5.5
2758000	St. Paul city	303,827	6.4	23.0	11.0	31.4	21.6	13.0	34.6	58.6	20.0	20.3	10.0	8.5	8.9
2771428	Woodbury city	79,530	28.4	25.1	8.0	26.7	25.5	14.7	38.8	76.4	12.2	12.8	5.1	6.3	4.6
28000	**MISSISSIPPI**	2,940,057	-1.0	23.0	10.2	24.9	24.4	17.5	38.9	59.8	38.2	1.5	5.4	3.3	4.6
2829700	Gulfport city	72,824	7.0	24.1	9.0	24.8	25.7	16.5	40.3	56.6	41.5	3.2	6.4	7.3	6.2
2836000	Jackson city	143,633	-17.1	23.4	10.7	27.5	22.8	15.6	36.0	15.3	83.8	0.0	4.3	3.3	2.7
29000	**MISSOURI**	6,177,957	3.0	22.1	9.4	26.0	24.6	18.0	39.1	84.6	12.5	3.2	7.5	4.7	7.3
2915670	Columbia city	129,328	18.8	16.9	23.9	27.7	18.5	13.0	31.4	80.3	15.0	7.4	4.0	6.4	4.4
2935000	Independence city	120,931	3.3	24.3	6.3	26.9	21.6	20.8	38.0	84.1	12.3	3.6	15.3	13.6	14.6
2938000	Kansas City city	510,671	10.9	21.5	8.8	31.0	23.9	14.9	36.5	65.1	29.0	4.1	11.6	9.0	12.5
2941348	Lee's Summit city	104,352	14.4	26.1	10.1	27.2	23.8	12.8	36.8	83.1	14.1	4.3	7.9	8.3	6.8
2954074	O'Fallon city	94,073	18.2	24.8	7.1	28.1	25.4	14.7	38.7	90.5	8.0	4.6	5.7	7.6	4.3
2964082	St. Charles city	71,802	8.8	17.5	14.2	27.1	22.0	19.3	38.7	85.7	10.8	3.5	7.6	7.6	7.4
2964550	St. Joseph city	70,702	-5.5	23.4	9.2	27.6	22.5	17.3	37.2	87.5	9.3	4.9	9.3	10.2	7.8
2965000	St. Louis city	281,754	-11.7	18.0	8.9	33.8	22.8	16.5	37.2	52.8	44.5	5.2	6.9	7.7	5.3
2970000	Springfield city	170,178	6.6	17.8	17.8	27.6	20.4	16.5	34.2	90.9	7.4	3.6	7.1	7.5	6.3
30000	**MONTANA**	1,122,867	13.3	20.9	9.2	26.0	23.8	20.1	40.2	91.7	0.9	2.1	12.7	4.4	6.8
3006550	Billings city	120,874	15.7	22.7	8.1	29.7	20.5	19.0	38.2	93.5	1.4	2.4	12.0	8.9	7.2
3050200	Missoula city	77,763	16.2	17.2	15.5	31.3	19.6	16.5	34.6	96.8	1.2	3.4	9.4	9.8	4.1
31000	**NEBRASKA**	1,967,923	7.6	24.1	9.8	26.2	22.9	17.0	37.4	86.8	6.5	3.6	12.6	12.3	8.9
3128000	Lincoln city	294,750	13.8	21.3	16.2	26.3	20.6	15.6	33.8	87.7	6.7	6.4	9.0	9.3	8.9
3137000	Omaha city	483,362	17.8	23.7	10.4	28.7	22.4	14.8	35.9	76.2	16.0	4.9	14.6	10.8	16.1
32000	**NEVADA**	3,177,772	17.6	21.7	8.3	28.2	24.8	16.9	39.0	65.2	12.2	13.5	28.4	30.3	17.7
3223770	Enterprise CDP	243,802	105.4	21.9	7.7	33.6	25.6	11.2	37.5	53.5	13.2	33.5	17.2	15.5	18.5
3231900	Henderson city	337,280	30.7	21.0	5.6	27.7	24.9	20.8	42.2	73.9	11.3	15.8	13.3	12.8	15.2
3240000	Las Vegas city	660,942	13.1	22.2	8.4	27.7	24.9	16.8	39.2	61.2	15.5	11.8	31.9	18.0	35.9
3251800	North Las Vegas city	284,772	31.0	25.4	8.8	29.1	24.0	12.7	35.0	49.1	26.1	10.6	32.8	17.3	41.2
3254600	Paradise CDP	177,413	-17.7	18.1	9.3	30.9	26.6	15.0	39.0	60.8	14.3	14.8	33.5	21.6	39.4
3260600	Reno city	274,937	21.8	19.6	10.0	30.2	23.2	17.1	37.6	79.2	4.6	10.6	27.7	20.6	29.0
3268400	Sparks city	110,301	21.9	21.2	8.5	29.9	24.9	15.6	37.4	75.9	6.0	12.6	26.5	18.6	29.5
3268585	Spring Valley CDP	198,326	10.3	17.1	8.7	32.7	23.5	18.1	39.5	52.7	13.7	30.1	21.7	17.1	26.5
3271400	Sunrise Manor CDP	213,644	15.3	27.9	9.2	27.1	24.7	11.2	33.9	36.1	15.5	11.2	53.3	15.3	56.5
33000	**NEW HAMPSHIRE**	1,395,231	6.0	18.0	8.5	25.4	27.9	20.2	43.3	93.9	2.4	3.9	6.8	4.5	6.5
3345140	Manchester city	115,473	5.3	17.1	10.7	30.1	24.8	17.2	39.3	87.7	7.8	5.7	12.3	11.9	13.3
3350260	Nashua city	90,997	5.1	20.4	7.4	31.2	25.1	15.9	38.9	86.3	6.5	7.8	16.6	16.1	17.0
34000	**NEW JERSEY**	9,261,699	5.3	21.5	8.5	26.1	26.5	17.4	40.4	64.8	15.2	11.5	21.4	21.9	12.2
3403580	Bayonne city	70,303	11.5	23.7	6.9	29.3	24.5	15.5	36.9	64.5	16.8	9.9	29.7	20.1	29.4
3410000	Camden city	71,099	-8.1	22.4	10.3	28.8	24.7	13.7	38.3	15.9	46.9	3.8	49.5	14.8	50.3
3413690	Clifton city	88,478	5.0	20.3	6.4	29.9	25.0	18.4	40.8	68.6	7.0	10.4	37.0	22.2	44.4
3419390	East Orange city	69,553	8.2	17.5	9.5	25.8	28.7	18.6	42.8	8.9	86.2	2.3	10.0	7.1	10.7
3421000	Elizabeth city	135,836	8.5	27.7	10.8	27.6	23.4	10.5	33.9	38.0	21.5	3.0	58.3	19.3	66.5
3436000	Jersey City city	291,663	17.6	19.2	7.7	40.3	19.9	12.9	34.8	38.4	22.8	28.2	27.0	15.4	26.7
3438580	Lakewood CDP	67,764	25.9	51.4	11.0	25.6	8.4	3.6	17.1	NA	NA	NA	NA	NA	NA
3451000	Newark city	304,943	10.0	25.3	9.4	30.8	23.9	10.6	34.9	24.8	50.5	1.6	39.7	15.9	38.6
3456550	Passaic city	68,917	-1.4	29.3	11.8	25.4	21.9	11.5	32.6	63.1	9.1	5.6	70.1	46.5	71.3
3457000	Paterson city	156,419	6.9	26.0	10.3	26.4	24.0	13.3	34.6	31.4	24.8	5.7	61.4	22.4	64.0
3473110	Toms River CDP	95,515	6.9	22.7	6.4	24.5	26.1	20.3	41.8	84.6	7.6	7.8	9.7	8.9	10.3
3474000	Trenton city	89,607	5.4	26.3	11.3	27.0	23.3	12.2	33.7	21.1	43.4	1.2	46.7	11.1	52.1
3474630	Union City city	64,470	-3.1	20.5	9.7	31.4	26.5	11.9	38.5	52.8	8.3	5.9	73.2	37.8	81.1
35000	**NEW MEXICO**	2,113,344	2.4	21.6	9.7	26.0	23.6	19.2	39.4	70.8	3.4	3.1	49.2	50.2	25.3
3502000	Albuquerque city	560,283	2.3	19.7	9.0	29.3	23.4	18.5	39.2	73.2	5.1	5.1	42.4	24.6	47.7
3539380	Las Cruces city	114,891	17.0	20.8	14.5	26.8	20.7	17.2	33.6	78.3	4.5	3.0	47.8	32.1	58.6

Table A-4. Cities — Who: Age, Race/Ethnicity, and Household Structure, 2023

STATE and place code	STATE Place	Native, born in state of residence (percent)	Foreign born (percent)	Non-citizens (percent)	Total households	Average household size	Household type (percent of all households)						Percent of households with people age 60 years and over
							Family households				Nonfamily households		
							Total	Married-couple	Male householder	Female householder	Total	One-person households	
	ACS table number:	B05002	B05002	B05002	B11001	B25010	B11001	B11001	B11001	B11001	B11001	B11001	B11006
	column number:	15	16	17	18	19	20	21	22	23	24	25	26
	LOUISIANA—Cont.												
2743000	Minneapolis city	51.8	13.7	6.5	198,866	2.04	38.7	27.4	2.9	8.3	61.3	45.5	26.1
2751730	Plymouth city	59.7	13.9	6.3	29,393	2.61	71.4	61.7	4.3	5.4	28.6	20.7	38.2
2754880	Rochester city	53.1	13.6	4.4	51,184	2.33	57.9	48.2	2.5	7.2	42.1	34.7	35.4
2756896	St. Cloud city	63.9	15.9	6.3	25,769	2.44	47.1	32.3	4.6	10.2	52.9	33.5	35.1
2758000	St. Paul city	56.0	18.2	5.0	126,409	2.31	49.0	32.8	5.1	11.1	51.0	39.4	32.6
2771428	Woodbury city	62.4	13.1	4.7	31,280	2.54	68.4	55.8	3.7	9.0	31.6	25.7	39.2
28000	**MISSISSIPPI**	70.7	2.2	1.3	1,148,340	2.48	65.7	43.8	5.2	16.7	34.3	29.9	43.3
2829700	Gulfport city	58.6	4.2	2.6	31,011	2.29	52.5	29.6	3.5	19.4	47.5	40.3	42.9
2836000	Jackson city	85.6	1.0	0.8	60,636	2.28	52.1	22.5	6.2	23.4	47.9	42.6	38.8
29000	**MISSOURI**	65.8	4.1	2.0	2,521,832	2.38	62.2	46.3	4.9	11.0	37.8	30.9	41.8
2915670	Columbia city	57.3	7.6	4.5	53,894	2.21	52.0	35.0	3.3	13.7	48.0	32.0	29.6
2935000	Independence city	64.9	5.9	3.7	51,311	2.33	58.0	42.7	2.5	12.8	42.0	34.7	44.5
2938000	Kansas City city	51.7	9.1	3.8	227,773	2.21	52.4	36.1	4.1	12.3	47.6	39.3	35.2
2941348	Lee's Summit city	59.6	3.7	1.0	40,435	2.57	69.1	54.6	5.7	8.8	30.9	22.5	31.8
2954074	O'Fallon city	69.7	4.8	2.9	34,714	2.70	71.9	59.2	3.0	9.7	28.1	23.4	37.3
2964082	St. Charles city	66.2	8.2	4.7	31,316	2.12	53.6	39.2	3.0	11.5	46.4	33.1	37.7
2964550	St. Joseph city	70.0	3.8	2.4	28,196	2.41	56.5	31.5	7.3	17.6	43.5	36.4	43.2
2965000	St. Louis city	60.2	8.2	4.5	150,404	1.80	41.4	23.1	4.6	13.7	58.6	45.7	34.9
2970000	Springfield city	61.2	3.6	1.8	79,707	2.03	44.4	30.1	4.1	10.2	55.6	42.7	33.7
30000	**MONTANA**	51.0	2.3	1.1	464,072	2.36	60.8	48.1	4.5	8.2	39.2	30.5	44.0
3006550	Billings city	57.5	1.7	1.1	52,878	2.22	59.6	41.8	6.3	11.5	40.4	35.0	38.0
3050200	Missoula city	46.0	1.5	0.7	35,775	2.08	46.6	31.3	5.6	9.7	53.4	36.6	30.4
31000	**NEBRASKA**	64.5	7.2	4.0	803,157	2.39	62.5	48.6	4.2	9.6	37.5	30.8	38.9
3128000	Lincoln city	64.5	8.2	4.3	126,828	2.21	51.3	40.9	3.1	7.3	48.7	35.3	34.7
3137000	Omaha city	57.2	10.9	7.2	204,135	2.31	56.7	40.4	4.6	11.7	43.3	35.1	34.8
32000	**NEVADA**	27.4	18.9	8.7	1,198,356	2.62	64.6	44.2	7.0	13.3	35.4	27.5	41.8
3223770	Enterprise CDP	24.5	23.8	7.7	90,011	2.71	62.6	40.9	8.0	13.6	37.4	26.2	31.7
3231900	Henderson city	23.3	14.0	4.2	136,680	2.46	64.1	46.9	6.0	11.3	35.9	27.5	44.0
3240000	Las Vegas city	26.8	21.9	10.6	252,848	2.59	62.3	40.1	7.6	14.7	37.7	29.9	40.3
3251800	North Las Vegas city	30.0	18.9	9.3	92,288	3.07	71.8	48.2	7.2	16.4	28.2	21.9	39.3
3254600	Paradise CDP	21.0	26.3	13.9	74,847	2.34	51.0	30.1	7.9	13.0	49.0	40.5	38.3
3260600	Reno city	31.9	16.4	8.7	114,623	2.34	53.5	36.9	6.2	10.3	46.5	34.4	40.1
3268400	Sparks city	37.1	13.6	7.5	41,595	2.64	62.1	46.4	5.3	10.4	37.9	24.9	37.9
3268585	Spring Valley CDP	23.2	31.1	11.8	82,320	2.40	57.9	38.2	6.2	13.4	42.1	31.9	39.7
3271400	Sunrise Manor CDP	33.1	30.3	17.9	67,326	3.17	70.3	42.8	6.1	21.3	29.7	23.6	38.7
33000	**NEW HAMPSHIRE**	41.1	6.2	2.4	557,220	2.44	64.3	51.2	4.6	8.5	35.7	27.6	46.7
3345140	Manchester city	45.9	14.5	6.2	50,053	2.23	54.7	38.6	4.1	11.9	45.3	32.2	37.6
3350260	Nashua city	36.1	16.9	8.9	36,451	2.46	61.5	42.9	5.7	12.9	38.5	28.3	39.7
34000	**NEW JERSEY**	50.7	23.5	9.9	3,516,978	2.59	67.6	49.9	5.2	12.6	32.4	26.5	44.3
3403580	Bayonne city	50.3	31.1	14.9	30,335	2.31	56.7	32.3	6.4	18.0	43.3	37.5	43.3
3410000	Camden city	50.6	23.8	15.8	27,511	2.50	52.9	19.7	4.9	28.3	47.1	39.7	39.7
3413690	Clifton city	48.8	35.0	9.9	31,968	2.74	70.9	53.0	3.9	14.0	29.1	23.2	51.2
3419390	East Orange city	47.3	30.4	12.5	30,360	2.26	49.2	22.3	6.9	20.0	50.8	44.2	47.7
3421000	Elizabeth city	37.1	46.7	28.1	45,491	2.97	75.5	34.9	8.7	31.9	24.5	19.9	35.5
3436000	Jersey City city	33.8	38.8	20.4	130,020	2.23	52.5	36.0	4.3	12.2	47.5	34.0	28.2
3438580	Lakewood CDP	56.7	9.2	6.5	13,406	4.95	94.1	84.0	5.3	4.8	5.9	5.7	17.7
3451000	Newark city	46.4	36.7	23.4	114,599	2.54	61.2	22.7	10.8	27.7	38.8	32.8	34.4
3456550	Passaic city	38.9	43.8	23.9	21,234	3.23	73.8	32.0	6.4	35.4	26.2	23.2	43.4
3457000	Paterson city	41.1	46.3	26.0	51,969	2.99	74.6	33.0	9.0	32.5	25.4	20.4	42.2
3473110	Toms River CDP	67.1	12.7	4.1	36,998	2.54	64.1	48.3	5.7	10.2	35.9	29.7	48.4
3474000	Trenton city	47.7	34.8	27.2	32,131	2.69	63.0	23.5	14.4	25.1	37.0	30.5	39.9
3474630	Union City city	28.2	59.4	32.0	25,001	2.56	67.6	37.8	11.5	18.3	32.4	23.5	35.9
35000	**NEW MEXICO**	53.1	9.3	5.2	848,218	2.44	60.9	40.6	6.5	13.9	39.1	32.3	44.8
3502000	Albuquerque city	49.9	11.0	5.8	243,664	2.26	54.7	34.8	6.7	13.2	45.3	36.4	41.5
3539380	Las Cruces city	49.4	10.1	4.1	50,409	2.26	53.7	36.2	6.7	10.7	46.3	37.1	38.2

Table A-4. Cities — Who: Age, Race/Ethnicity, and Household Structure, 2023—*Continued*

STATE and place code	STATE Place	Total population	Percent change, 2010–2023	Population by age (percent): Under 18 years	18 to 24 years	25 to 44 years	45 to 64 years	65 years and over	Median age	Race alone or in combination (percent): White	Black	Asian + Native Hawaiian or Other Pacific Islander	American Indian and Alaska Native + Some other race	Two or more races (percent)	Hispanic or Latino (percent)
	ACS table number:	B01003	Census PEP	B01001	B01001	B01001	B01001	B01001	B01002	B02008	B02009	B02011 + B02012	B02010 + B02013	B02001	B03003
	column number:	1	2	3	4	5	6	7	8	9	10	11	12	13	14
	NEW MEXICO—Cont.														
3563460	Rio Rancho city	110,660	25.8	21.6	9.4	27.8	24.2	17.0	37.7	82.8	6.1	4.7	37.7	28.6	40.5
3570500	Santa Fe city	89,157	30.8	15.4	8.3	25.3	23.9	27.1	46.2	86.2	1.8	3.3	46.9	37.0	53.0
36000	**NEW YORK**	19,677,151	1.4	20.2	9.2	26.9	25.6	18.1	40.0	63.4	17.6	10.5	19.5	19.7	10.1
3601000	Albany city	101,220	3.6	14.1	23.2	28.2	19.8	14.7	32.4	59.6	29.3	8.8	12.8	8.8	10.6
3611000	Buffalo city	274,686	5.2	21.4	10.4	30.2	22.4	15.7	35.7	52.5	36.7	9.3	11.2	9.1	12.2
3615000	Cheektowaga CDP	75,443	0.6	17.8	9.5	27.3	24.2	21.3	40.4	78.7	15.3	6.1	6.1	5.8	5.7
3649121	Mount Vernon city	71,168	5.6	21.1	7.4	25.0	28.2	18.3	42.6	24.5	65.9	2.4	21.4	13.9	20.6
3650617	New Rochelle city	83,737	8.5	18.8	11.3	24.5	26.8	18.5	41.3	60.5	21.4	6.8	33.1	20.5	32.3
3651000	New York city	8,258,035	0.9	19.8	8.1	30.4	24.4	17.3	38.8	42.7	26.6	16.9	27.5	12.5	28.4
3663000	Rochester city	207,264	-1.6	19.7	12.0	32.0	22.2	14.2	34.2	51.4	42.3	3.8	15.9	12.2	19.3
3665508	Schenectady city	68,545	3.5	20.5	14.5	26.0	22.8	16.2	36.1	56.9	28.9	12.3	20.7	18.6	11.1
3673000	Syracuse city	145,573	0.2	20.2	18.8	28.8	16.9	15.4	31.3	60.4	32.0	7.6	8.9	8.7	10.1
3684000	Yonkers city	207,644	5.8	19.8	10.2	27.2	26.4	16.4	39.2	44.1	23.0	6.9	42.4	15.4	45.7
37000	**NORTH CAROLINA**	10,698,973	11.7	21.4	9.7	26.1	25.3	17.4	39.2	69.4	22.8	4.3	12.1	10.4	7.9
3701520	Apex town		72,213	92.7	30.3	4.7	29.2	26.2	9.6	38.3	73.2	5.3	22.4	7.1	7.2
3702140	Asheville city	95,053	13.7	16.0	9.2	30.9	24.8	19.1	41.3	90.9	9.2	1.5	8.9	9.7	6.7
3710740	Cary town	178,883	32.1	22.3	7.5	27.1	28.7	14.3	39.9	67.8	9.4	20.9	12.5	10.0	11.5
3712000	Charlotte city	911,307	24.1	22.0	10.1	33.1	23.4	11.4	34.7	48.9	35.8	8.2	18.0	10.2	17.3
3714100	Concord city	110,097	38.8	25.8	7.5	28.8	25.2	12.7	37.3	58.0	27.0	10.5	13.7	9.2	13.7
3719000	Durham city	295,845	29.2	19.9	10.9	33.8	21.6	13.7	35.0	49.5	35.8	8.8	16.9	9.7	15.5
3722920	Fayetteville city	209,751	4.3	24.1	14.1	30.4	18.5	12.9	31.2	48.3	47.0	6.0	12.8	12.1	14.8
3725580	Gastonia city	83,949	16.9	24.2	9.0	27.4	23.4	16.0	36.4	58.5	38.3	2.1	11.7	9.6	12.1
3728000	Greensboro city	302,307	11.8	21.3	14.1	27.5	22.0	15.1	34.9	49.9	42.4	5.7	12.0	9.5	10.6
3728080	Greenville city	90,059	6.1	20.1	22.9	29.0	15.0	13.0	29.3	56.0	39.3	2.7	8.6	5.6	7.6
3731400	High Point city	116,205	12.1	21.0	14.6	26.3	21.3	16.8	35.4	44.1	39.9	11.1	14.5	8.8	13.6
3734200	Jacksonville city	72,867	3.1	19.2	38.3	24.0	8.8	9.8	23.3	77.9	17.9	5.9	17.2	17.2	15.1
3755000	Raleigh city	482,425	18.6	20.1	11.7	32.5	23.0	12.7	34.9	61.0	29.2	7.0	12.9	9.1	12.2
3774440	Wilmington city	122,695	14.9	15.3	15.9	25.6	23.4	19.8	39.3	80.3	15.7	2.3	8.5	6.5	8.3
3775000	Winston-Salem city	252,970	10.0	23.2	12.1	25.7	23.5	15.6	36.1	57.0	34.0	3.4	15.4	9.1	16.3
38000	**NORTH DAKOTA**	779,261	15.5	23.2	10.7	28.1	21.2	16.7	36.2	88.2	4.2	2.8	10.2	4.4	5.2
3807200	Bismarck city	75,102	22.6	19.6	9.7	27.2	22.6	21.0	39.8	89.3	2.3	1.9	12.4	5.8	4.1
3825700	Fargo city	132,400	24.2	19.6	17.1	31.0	18.3	13.9	31.5	87.6	8.9	4.2	6.4	7.0	4.5
39000	**OHIO**	11,756,058	1.9	21.8	9.1	25.6	25.1	18.4	39.9	83.1	14.5	3.3	6.0	4.4	6.5
3901000	Akron city	188,692	-5.2	21.9	11.0	27.5	23.1	16.5	37.1	63.3	36.2	5.7	5.6	9.9	4.9
3912000	Canton city	69,196	-5.2	22.8	10.3	26.1	21.4	19.4	37.0	74.7	23.7	1.2	10.2	12.6	4.5
3915000	Cincinnati city	311,112	4.8	19.8	13.0	32.4	20.9	14.0	34.1	57.5	39.4	4.6	8.1	9.0	5.4
3916000	Cleveland city	362,670	-8.5	20.4	10.4	30.2	22.4	16.6	36.3	42.5	51.5	3.5	13.0	9.6	13.6
3918000	Columbus city	909,074	15.1	22.0	11.6	34.0	20.5	11.8	33.4	59.6	33.5	7.0	9.6	9.0	8.3
3921000	Dayton city	135,507	-4.2	22.2	15.1	25.9	22.7	14.0	33.6	59.9	39.3	1.8	7.9	8.0	6.4
3944856	Lorain city	65,330	1.9	22.9	9.1	21.0	27.7	19.3	42.4	75.8	20.1	0.9	22.1	20.3	25.7
3961000	Parma city	78,952	-3.1	17.4	7.1	27.4	27.9	20.2	43.6	88.1	8.3	3.3	7.5	7.3	8.8
3977000	Toledo city	265,306	-7.6	22.9	9.9	28.1	22.6	16.6	35.5	67.6	32.5	2.4	8.7	10.2	9.6
40000	**OKLAHOMA**	4,019,800	6.9	23.7	10.1	26.6	23.2	16.5	37.1	78.6	9.8	3.6	23.5	12.1	14.4
4009050	Broken Arrow city	119,666	21.5	25.3	7.1	28.5	22.5	16.5	37.4	81.0	7.9	6.4	21.3	15.8	12.1
4023200	Edmond city	98,113	20.1	23.6	11.5	23.0	24.0	17.9	39.0	86.2	7.6	7.9	11.2	12.0	5.1
4041850	Lawton city	90,226	-7.8	22.8	13.0	32.9	18.2	13.2	32.2	69.8	24.8	6.3	19.3	17.6	15.0
4052500	Norman city	130,052	16.7	15.3	24.2	24.9	18.7	16.9	32.9	85.4	7.4	5.2	15.2	12.0	7.8
4055000	Oklahoma City city	702,654	20.7	25.4	8.9	30.3	21.9	13.6	34.9	71.4	16.8	6.8	25.5	18.5	22.7
4075000	Tulsa city	410,915	4.4	23.5	10.3	28.5	22.2	15.6	35.7	68.9	17.8	5.5	27.2	17.7	20.4
41000	**OREGON**	4,240,137	10.5	19.6	8.6	28.1	24.5	19.3	40.5	85.8	3.3	7.7	16.2	14.4	11.9
4105350	Beaverton city	96,946	7.5	19.2	7.4	35.2	23.9	14.3	37.6	78.4	4.8	14.5	18.3	15.3	18.1
4105800	Bend city	104,554	36.3	18.7	7.2	28.3	28.1	17.6	41.7	96.1	1.5	5.7	9.0	10.7	9.2
4123850	Eugene city	177,900	13.8	13.7	17.4	27.6	21.9	19.4	37.2	87.4	4.2	8.5	13.0	11.2	10.7
4131250	Gresham city	110,678	4.4	22.2	8.5	28.6	26.1	14.6	37.1	77.5	6.4	8.3	22.2	14.1	21.6
4134100	Hillsboro city	107,726	17.2	19.0	9.5	35.2	23.2	13.0	35.6	72.0	3.8	18.1	25.5	18.2	24.5
4147000	Medford city	85,100	13.5	22.2	6.6	28.5	22.0	20.7	40.4	92.9	2.5	5.5	20.8	19.1	17.4
4159000	Portland city	630,395	7.7	16.1	7.9	36.5	24.6	14.9	39.4	81.6	8.7	12.2	14.2	14.8	12.2
4164900	Salem city	177,423	14.5	21.4	10.5	30.0	22.3	15.8	36.4	83.1	3.2	7.7	25.8	18.1	26.3

Table A-4. Cities — Who: Age, Race/Ethnicity, and Household Structure, 2023

STATE and place code	STATE Place	Native, born in state of residence (percent)	Foreign born (percent)	Non-citizens (percent)	Total households	Average household size	Household type (percent of all households): Family households: Total	Family households: Married-couple	Family households: Male house-holder	Family households: Female house-holder	Nonfamily households: Total	Nonfamily households: One-person households	Percent of house-holds with people age 60 years and over
	ACS table number:	B05002	B05002	B05002	B11001	B25010	B11001	B11001	B11001	B11001	B11001	B11001	B11006
	column number:	15	16	17	18	19	20	21	22	23	24	25	26
	NEW MEXICO—Cont.												
3563460	Rio Rancho city	47.8	5.7	2.5	42,054	2.62	69.9	47.2	7.6	15.1	30.1	23.0	44.8
3570500	Santa Fe city	42.4	19.7	13.2	42,397	2.07	51.6	35.2	4.2	12.2	48.4	40.9	48.4
36000	**NEW YORK**	62.5	22.7	8.9	7,774,308	2.45	60.9	42.3	5.1	13.5	39.1	31.2	43.9
3601000	Albany city	66.6	14.3	9.2	44,875	2.00	39.8	25.7	2.2	12.0	60.2	42.0	32.8
3611000	Buffalo city	73.7	10.4	5.0	123,347	2.17	49.5	24.8	5.3	19.4	50.5	40.5	37.4
3615000	Cheektowaga CDP	82.4	6.8	2.5	34,150	2.12	55.4	33.6	6.1	15.7	44.6	38.4	47.5
3649121	Mount Vernon city	61.4	28.0	9.1	27,369	2.58	64.3	34.8	5.9	23.5	35.7	29.2	48.8
3650617	New Rochelle city	53.2	33.7	12.7	29,052	2.74	69.9	54.6	3.9	11.5	30.1	25.7	44.6
3651000	New York city	47.0	37.5	15.5	3,394,750	2.37	57.0	35.0	5.8	16.3	43.0	34.5	42.1
3663000	Rochester city	67.9	7.9	3.4	91,471	2.16	44.4	17.8	5.5	21.1	55.6	43.1	34.7
3665508	Schenectady city	67.4	15.0	4.0	28,730	2.25	56.6	30.5	6.6	19.5	43.4	34.0	36.4
3673000	Syracuse city	63.5	11.7	6.1	60,652	2.09	44.4	23.2	6.4	14.8	55.6	41.7	35.9
3684000	Yonkers city	53.7	36.1	14.1	79,190	2.58	62.8	35.4	5.6	21.9	37.2	32.0	42.1
37000	**NORTH CAROLINA**	53.6	8.6	4.8	4,299,266	2.42	64.8	47.9	4.4	12.5	35.2	28.8	40.5
3701520	Apex town	5.8	32.2	20.4	10.3	27,306	2.64	74.1	64.5	2.6	6.9	25.9	21.3
3702140	Asheville city	43.4	5.0	2.9	39,811	2.30	46.6	34.9	5.3	6.5	53.4	42.3	40.1
3710740	Cary town	28.3	24.7	14.1	71,248	2.50	70.1	61.8	2.8	5.6	29.9	24.0	33.3
3712000	Charlotte city	39.3	18.1	11.1	375,680	2.39	55.1	37.8	4.2	13.1	44.9	35.5	28.4
3714100	Concord city	44.9	13.9	8.6	42,777	2.54	66.0	49.6	3.9	12.5	34.0	28.2	28.1
3719000	Durham city	42.7	15.4	9.3	127,514	2.24	54.7	39.0	3.9	11.7	45.3	34.9	30.3
3722920	Fayetteville city	40.8	7.0	2.9	83,410	2.31	59.3	37.9	3.7	17.7	40.7	34.9	33.8
3725580	Gastonia city	57.9	8.2	4.4	33,496	2.45	68.6	40.1	9.1	19.3	31.4	23.9	38.5
3728000	Greensboro city	53.0	11.8	6.1	125,752	2.27	54.5	32.4	6.6	15.4	45.5	37.9	35.9
3728080	Greenville city	59.1	5.4	2.4	41,037	2.08	43.9	27.2	4.1	12.6	56.1	37.2	23.4
3731400	High Point city	52.5	17.1	9.0	45,442	2.36	60.4	38.2	7.8	14.3	39.6	35.5	39.7
3734200	Jacksonville city	25.8	6.4	1.9	24,538	2.23	70.0	48.6	3.6	17.8	30.0	25.9	22.7
3755000	Raleigh city	46.6	14.3	7.5	211,433	2.20	52.3	37.5	4.3	10.4	47.7	35.2	28.8
3774440	Wilmington city	45.3	6.1	3.2	59,730	1.99	44.8	30.3	2.8	11.8	55.2	39.6	39.3
3775000	Winston-Salem city	55.8	9.8	6.1	107,693	2.26	57.5	37.0	4.1	16.4	42.5	37.5	39.2
38000	**NORTH DAKOTA**	62.1	4.9	2.9	331,481	2.26	58.5	47.1	3.9	7.5	41.5	33.3	36.1
3807200	Bismarck city	73.1	2.2	1.5	34,598	2.10	56.0	42.0	7.6	6.3	44.0	39.1	41.8
3825700	Fargo city	49.2	7.2	4.2	60,510	2.08	43.7	33.1	3.0	7.6	56.3	45.6	26.9
39000	**OHIO**	74.8	5.0	2.3	4,878,206	2.35	61.2	44.6	4.7	11.9	38.8	31.8	41.9
3901000	Akron city	75.9	7.3	4.0	85,349	2.16	50.6	28.4	4.9	17.3	49.4	39.8	37.8
3912000	Canton city	81.0	2.1	1.4	29,864	2.25	52.4	25.9	8.5	18.0	47.6	39.3	39.4
3915000	Cincinnati city	69.6	6.5	4.2	149,698	1.97	40.4	23.7	3.5	13.2	59.6	46.9	31.5
3916000	Cleveland city	71.8	6.9	4.1	168,307	2.08	44.0	18.0	4.7	21.2	56.0	48.0	38.5
3918000	Columbus city	61.9	15.1	8.2	394,905	2.24	50.5	30.1	5.8	14.6	49.5	36.9	29.1
3921000	Dayton city	68.6	6.3	4.4	57,882	2.12	49.2	24.1	6.3	18.8	50.8	42.6	39.6
3944856	Lorain city	74.5	3.4	1.7	27,930	2.32	55.1	31.6	4.2	19.3	44.9	38.2	44.7
3961000	Parma city	76.5	12.1	3.7	34,406	2.26	58.8	36.0	5.7	17.1	41.2	34.5	40.9
3977000	Toledo city	75.6	4.4	2.3	117,902	2.21	52.1	28.4	4.0	19.7	47.9	39.5	39.1
40000	**OKLAHOMA**	59.6	6.0	3.6	1,573,180	2.48	64.7	47.5	5.4	11.8	35.3	28.9	39.7
4009050	Broken Arrow city	53.0	8.0	3.6	44,802	2.65	72.0	55.9	4.9	11.2	28.0	22.2	40.9
4023200	Edmond city	51.7	6.9	3.2	39,282	2.44	68.2	55.7	3.9	8.6	31.8	25.7	39.1
4041850	Lawton city	44.4	5.4	2.7	34,205	2.36	59.4	35.7	6.3	17.4	40.6	32.3	32.7
4052500	Norman city	53.9	6.6	4.0	54,715	2.23	51.8	39.3	4.6	8.0	48.2	33.8	34.7
4055000	Oklahoma City city	58.4	11.2	6.6	284,755	2.43	59.7	41.4	5.0	13.4	40.3	32.6	34.0
4075000	Tulsa city	54.3	12.8	8.8	173,905	2.31	55.8	35.8	6.2	13.7	44.2	36.2	36.8
41000	**OREGON**	45.2	9.9	5.2	1,726,340	2.40	60.3	45.7	4.8	9.9	39.7	29.3	42.4
4105350	Beaverton city	38.7	18.7	10.7	43,874	2.19	55.5	41.4	5.3	8.8	44.5	34.1	31.7
4105800	Bend city	34.0	4.2	2.2	46,318	2.24	57.7	44.9	3.9	8.9	42.3	28.1	38.5
4123850	Eugene city	40.5	5.4	2.1	78,974	2.15	52.2	40.0	4.4	7.8	47.8	32.2	38.6
4131250	Gresham city	53.3	16.3	8.5	42,173	2.57	61.3	44.1	9.2	8.1	38.7	29.1	37.2
4134100	Hillsboro city	39.9	19.9	12.8	42,575	2.50	63.0	45.4	6.2	11.4	37.0	22.0	30.6
4147000	Medford city	39.0	7.9	3.9	34,867	2.38	61.5	41.9	4.6	15.1	38.5	32.7	46.3
4159000	Portland city	36.0	12.5	4.9	292,037	2.09	46.3	33.8	3.9	8.7	53.7	38.2	29.8
4164900	Salem city	49.7	13.1	8.5	68,817	2.46	61.1	42.6	5.8	12.8	38.9	29.5	38.2

Table A-4. Cities — Who: Age, Race/Ethnicity, and Household Structure, 2023—*Continued*

STATE and place code	STATE Place	Total population	Percent change, 2010–2023	Population by age (percent)					Median age	Race alone or in combination (percent)				Two or more races (percent)	Hispanic or Latino (percent)
				Under 18 years	18 to 24 years	25 to 44 years	45 to 64 years	65 years and over		White	Black	Asian + Native Hawaiian or Other Pacific Islander	American Indian and Alaska Native + Some other race		
	ACS table number:	B01003	Census PEP	B01001	B01001	B01001	B01001	B01001	B01002	B02008	B02009	B02011 + B02012	B02010 + B02013	B02001	B03003
	column number:	1	2	3	4	5	6	7	8	9	10	11	12	13	14
42000	**PENNSYLVANIA**	12,972,008	2.1	20.2	9.2	25.4	25.5	19.6	40.9	80.9	12.9	4.8	9.4	8.6	7.2
4202000	Allentown city	124,871	5.6	26.8	12.9	27.3	19.2	13.8	32.4	48.7	16.8	3.1	54.8	20.8	60.1
4206088	Bethlehem city	77,841	3.5	18.6	14.9	29.1	19.5	17.9	36.3	73.9	12.1	3.9	31.0	19.4	32.4
4224000	Erie city	92,953	-8.7	22.9	12.9	26.5	21.5	16.2	35.5	76.5	23.1	3.2	8.0	9.8	9.0
4260000	Philadelphia city	1,550,542	1.5	20.9	9.9	32.1	21.8	15.2	35.6	42.0	43.0	9.2	15.6	8.9	15.8
4261000	Pittsburgh city	303,254	-0.8	14.4	17.9	32.7	18.5	16.4	34.1	70.0	22.6	7.6	6.2	6.0	4.8
4263624	Reading city	94,897	7.6	30.2	11.8	28.2	20.0	9.7	30.6	63.6	39.4	0.6	70.8	49.3	74.7
4269000	Scranton city	75,803	-0.3	18.8	12.8	26.7	20.9	20.8	38.3	71.9	9.1	5.1	20.5	6.1	20.5
44000	**RHODE ISLAND**	1,093,734	-13.4	18.6	10.3	26.4	25.9	18.8	40.7	80.1	10.2	4.6	18.7	17.6	12.1
4419180	Cranston city	82,640	2.8	20.4	6.3	30.4	26.1	16.8	39.1	75.8	13.4	7.9	11.6	9.1	14.4
4454640	Pawtucket city	75,312	5.8	19.6	5.2	29.7	27.5	18.1	41.7	69.0	17.9	4.0	30.9	19.5	29.2
4459000	Providence city	190,791	7.1	19.7	16.7	31.0	21.8	10.8	32.7	51.3	21.5	7.2	44.7	22.7	44.9
4474300	Warwick city	82,997	0.4	17.4	4.9	30.1	25.2	22.4	42.9	90.7	5.6	4.1	9.8	9.1	7.7
45000	**SOUTH CAROLINA**	5,282,634	3.8	21.1	9.5	25.2	25.1	19.1	40.5	69.5	26.9	2.5	7.9	6.5	6.4
4513330	Charleston city	155,988	30.2	18.7	11.0	33.1	22.6	14.7	36.2	81.9	17.5	3.6	4.9	7.6	4.2
4516000	Columbia city	142,083	10.0	14.6	23.5	28.9	19.2	13.9	31.7	56.2	40.1	7.3	6.0	8.8	4.7
4530850	Greenville city	72,822	24.7	17.2	13.7	34.8	19.6	14.7	34.3	72.5	21.7	4.3	7.6	6.2	7.1
4548535	Mount Pleasant town	95,229	39.8	22.9	5.2	27.4	24.8	19.7	41.3	94.8	3.8	1.8	4.7	4.9	3.5
4550875	North Charleston city	121,463	27.1	20.3	11.8	30.5	22.1	15.4	36.0	52.9	36.6	3.7	13.1	6.0	14.3
4561405	Rock Hill city	75,641	13.9	17.3	11.4	28.5	26.9	16.0	41.0	51.9	43.8	4.5	4.8	4.8	6.2
46000	**SOUTH DAKOTA**	909,824	14.0	24.1	9.4	25.0	23.4	18.2	38.5	86.7	3.5	2.4	14.2	4.7	6.3
4652980	Rapid City city	79,409	16.4	21.8	9.4	25.7	23.7	19.3	39.4	85.3	2.8	2.8	19.7	10.2	6.1
4659020	Sioux Falls city	206,405	34.1	23.8	9.2	29.9	21.6	15.5	36.5	84.7	9.1	3.4	10.2	6.7	7.3
47000	**TENNESSEE**	7,051,339	11.5	21.8	9.2	26.6	25.2	17.3	39.2	79.5	17.3	2.8	7.6	6.3	6.9
4714000	Chattanooga city	187,023	11.3	21.1	9.9	29.6	22.6	16.9	37.2	64.6	28.7	2.5	9.5	5.1	9.3
4715160	Clarksville city	180,705	35.2	25.6	11.5	34.2	18.9	9.7	31.4	68.7	31.0	4.8	12.7	14.3	14.7
4727740	Franklin city	88,558	41.7	21.4	9.2	26.2	26.1	17.2	40.4	84.0	6.3	8.8	12.0	9.9	11.0
4737640	Jackson city	68,262	4.6	21.6	10.5	26.6	22.5	18.7	38.5	52.8	45.4	2.4	4.6	4.7	3.0
4738320	Johnson City city	73,440	16.3	18.0	17.0	25.6	20.6	18.7	35.3	88.9	8.6	2.9	6.0	6.7	4.3
4740000	Knoxville city	198,175	10.6	16.8	18.8	29.9	18.8	15.7	33.7	80.8	17.0	2.7	9.1	9.1	8.7
4748000	Memphis city	618,655	-4.5	25.4	9.4	28.7	22.0	14.6	33.9	27.8	65.1	3.0	10.5	6.0	9.8
4751560	Murfreesboro city	165,423	51.5	23.2	14.9	30.6	20.2	11.2	32.5	73.6	23.6	6.1	10.8	13.2	9.4
4752006	Nashville-Davidson metropolitan government (balance)	687,787	14.1	20.3	9.9	35.4	21.4	13.0	34.7	66.0	27.2	5.3	14.5	12.2	14.1
48000	**TEXAS**	30,029,572	10.9	24.8	10.0	28.5	23.3	13.4	35.6	70.6	13.9	6.8	33.4	40.2	23.8
4801000	Abilene city	130,093	8.7	22.3	14.6	28.8	19.4	14.9	34.3	80.5	11.0	5.2	22.4	18.3	27.5
4801924	Allen city	111,627	31.5	24.4	8.1	26.2	28.5	12.9	40.5	63.1	10.6	24.0	13.5	10.9	13.7
4803000	Amarillo city	203,042	4.6	23.4	10.8	26.7	23.2	15.8	36.1	81.0	8.6	4.9	24.7	18.9	34.3
4804000	Arlington city	398,423	8.5	24.7	10.7	28.8	23.5	12.4	34.5	56.0	27.4	9.8	29.3	21.4	33.2
4804462	Atascocita CDP	119,502	67.7	31.3	9.4	28.2	22.0	9.1	33.4	52.5	34.5	6.6	27.6	18.0	33.5
4805000	Austin city	979,700	23.2	17.2	10.5	40.4	21.6	10.3	34.9	74.5	9.4	11.8	27.4	21.7	32.6
4806128	Baytown city	85,651	18.3	26.8	8.0	31.9	21.4	11.9	32.7	46.4	26.7	2.8	40.7	16.0	44.6
4807000	Beaumont city	112,196	-5.2	25.5	9.1	27.0	20.8	17.6	36.6	37.8	47.0	5.5	19.5	10.3	18.0
4810768	Brownsville city	190,166	8.2	26.1	11.9	25.1	23.1	13.9	33.3	86.4	0.2	0.8	68.7	55.9	94.5
4810912	Bryan city	89,606	17.1	24.1	13.8	29.5	20.4	12.2	31.7	72.5	18.8	3.2	28.8	21.3	40.3
4813024	Carrollton city	132,357	10.5	20.4	9.1	28.4	28.5	13.6	40.1	61.3	9.2	21.2	27.2	17.5	31.6
4813552	Cedar Park city	78,969	61.4	26.0	8.7	27.5	24.9	12.9	38.1	71.6	6.8	22.3	14.2	13.8	18.6
4815976	College Station city	125,199	32.8	16.0	40.0	23.0	13.0	8.0	23.0	76.8	9.6	11.4	15.7	12.5	19.4
4816432	Conroe city	108,244	92.6	24.8	11.9	34.6	17.3	11.5	30.9	77.8	14.4	3.3	23.9	18.5	30.6
4817000	Corpus Christi city	316,603	3.7	23.8	10.1	27.3	23.1	15.8	36.8	85.1	5.1	3.4	48.2	41.4	62.0
4819000	Dallas city	1,302,859	8.3	23.4	9.7	33.3	21.7	12.0	33.5	54.0	25.5	4.5	37.6	21.5	41.8
4819972	Denton city	158,361	38.8	16.8	19.5	30.4	20.8	12.4	32.2	77.3	13.8	7.3	23.2	20.5	25.5
4822660	Edinburg city	105,803	36.3	26.9	14.6	29.3	20.1	9.0	28.8	86.4	1.3	2.4	64.9	54.9	87.5
4824000	El Paso city	678,945	4.1	24.2	10.2	28.3	22.2	15.1	35.3	72.8	5.0	2.8	64.6	43.9	81.4
4826232	Flower Mound town	79,292	19.7	24.8	6.3	23.4	32.1	13.4	42.1	75.6	6.4	15.1	14.6	11.5	15.0
4827000	Fort Worth city	976,932	31.3	26.2	10.2	30.4	22.3	10.8	33.7	64.4	21.8	7.6	30.9	23.5	34.7
4827684	Frisco city	225,009	90.9	27.1	6.4	27.6	29.7	9.1	39.3	57.3	9.6	34.2	11.1	11.7	10.9
4829000	Garland city	243,536	7.0	26.8	9.5	28.3	24.2	11.1	34.4	63.7	14.3	12.6	48.0	37.3	51.2
4829336	Georgetown city	96,317	103.2	18.3	4.9	29.1	20.7	27.0	42.6	79.1	9.0	5.8	16.1	9.8	19.8

Table A-4. Cities — Who: Age, Race/Ethnicity, and Household Structure, 2023

STATE and place code	STATE Place	Native, born in state of residence (percent)	Foreign born (percent)	Non-citizens (percent)	Total households	Average household size	Household type (percent of all households): Family households: Total	Family households: Married-couple	Family households: Male house-holder	Family households: Female house-holder	Nonfamily households: Total	Nonfamily households: One-person households	Percent of households with people age 60 years and over
	ACS table number:	B05002	B05002	B05002	B11001	B25010	B11001	B11001	B11001	B11001	B11001	B11001	B11006
	column number:	15	16	17	18	19	20	21	22	23	24	25	26
42000	**PENNSYLVANIA**	70.5	7.5	3.3	5,294,065	2.37	62.2	46.5	4.5	11.2	37.8	30.6	44.6
4202000	Allentown city	41.4	24.3	12.8	46,104	2.59	65.8	26.5	9.6	29.7	34.2	26.8	37.0
4206088	Bethlehem city	56.1	11.2	6.1	32,208	2.21	58.0	34.4	6.6	17.0	42.0	36.0	39.8
4224000	Erie city	71.2	6.1	2.6	39,704	2.19	51.2	27.3	6.8	17.2	48.8	40.7	38.0
4260000	Philadelphia city	62.2	15.1	7.2	688,112	2.18	51.3	28.5	5.3	17.4	48.7	39.0	36.7
4261000	Pittsburgh city	63.5	9.9	5.6	140,615	1.99	42.0	28.9	3.4	9.7	58.0	44.6	33.4
4263624	Reading city	41.8	26.3	16.2	31,358	2.92	66.6	27.3	11.9	27.5	33.4	27.9	32.8
4269000	Scranton city	60.5	14.3	9.1	31,094	2.25	55.2	30.9	7.9	16.5	44.8	38.8	46.0
44000	**RHODE ISLAND**	52.3	14.4	6.9	446,688	2.35	59.8	42.1	6.2	11.4	40.2	31.3	45.2
4419180	Cranston city	60.2	17.9	5.1	31,571	2.51	64.2	48.3	3.0	12.9	35.8	29.0	40.4
4454640	Pawtucket city	48.0	26.0	7.9	33,667	2.22	51.7	30.5	3.9	17.3	48.3	40.3	42.7
4459000	Providence city	37.7	30.4	18.3	71,374	2.47	49.9	27.4	8.6	13.9	50.1	35.3	32.9
4474300	Warwick city	67.2	5.6	1.8	36,989	2.22	60.0	45.1	7.0	7.9	40.0	33.1	49.4
45000	**SOUTH CAROLINA**	52.8	5.2	2.7	2,136,080	2.41	65.5	47.7	4.4	13.4	34.5	28.8	43.6
4513330	Charleston city	42.6	5.7	3.3	69,588	2.15	50.4	40.9	2.7	6.7	49.6	33.2	34.3
4516000	Columbia city	51.4	7.2	4.2	58,713	2.01	46.4	29.7	3.1	13.6	53.6	41.0	32.1
4530850	Greenville city	46.5	8.8	5.4	35,609	1.94	48.3	37.1	2.3	8.9	51.7	40.9	30.1
4548535	Mount Pleasant town	31.9	3.8	1.9	40,023	2.36	64.1	56.4	2.7	5.0	35.9	29.8	39.6
4550875	North Charleston city	49.0	12.2	7.2	53,710	2.20	52.5	34.1	3.8	14.7	47.5	36.1	34.6
4561405	Rock Hill city	54.7	7.1	4.2	31,189	2.35	57.8	38.9	5.0	13.9	42.2	33.5	38.8
46000	**SOUTH DAKOTA**	62.0	3.5	1.6	368,300	2.38	61.1	48.3	5.0	7.7	38.9	31.8	41.5
4652980	Rapid City city	55.6	1.9	0.4	33,880	2.23	61.5	42.6	8.5	10.4	38.5	33.2	41.5
4659020	Sioux Falls city	59.0	10.3	5.2	90,489	2.22	53.7	40.0	4.3	9.4	46.3	38.3	33.6
47000	**TENNESSEE**	57.3	5.6	3.3	2,846,684	2.43	64.9	47.1	4.9	12.8	35.1	28.6	40.4
4714000	Chattanooga city	56.5	5.4	3.5	81,086	2.23	54.3	34.9	4.5	14.9	45.7	37.0	37.3
4715160	Clarksville city	35.4	6.8	4.4	71,172	2.46	68.2	49.4	5.9	12.9	31.8	25.3	26.7
4727740	Franklin city	34.9	12.6	9.9	35,730	2.45	67.7	57.7	4.0	6.1	32.3	26.1	37.4
4737640	Jackson city	67.4	3.7	1.5	28,458	2.26	59.5	38.2	1.6	19.7	40.5	36.2	43.6
4738320	Johnson City city	52.7	4.3	3.6	31,162	2.24	50.6	37.9	3.0	9.6	49.4	36.9	41.0
4740000	Knoxville city	57.8	7.4	5.3	87,036	2.16	43.1	28.3	3.3	11.5	56.9	41.4	34.3
4748000	Memphis city	66.8	8.3	5.9	257,188	2.36	55.3	25.3	6.1	23.8	44.7	39.2	37.4
4751560	Murfreesboro city	51.3	10.6	5.0	63,223	2.55	59.1	45.8	2.9	10.4	40.9	31.0	26.9
4752006	Nashville-Davidson metropolitan government (balance)	42.5	15.9	10.0	330,506	2.02	51.9	36.0	5.6	10.3	48.1	37.1	28.8
48000	**TEXAS**	58.3	17.2	9.7	11,087,708	2.65	67.5	48.7	5.5	13.3	32.5	26.3	35.5
4801000	Abilene city	65.2	7.2	2.4	47,511	2.49	63.3	43.3	5.7	14.2	36.7	30.0	34.1
4801924	Allen city	39.2	27.3	13.4	38,830	2.86	77.0	64.0	3.0	10.0	23.0	19.7	35.0
4803000	Amarillo city	70.1	10.2	5.0	80,754	2.48	58.9	41.8	4.7	12.4	41.1	35.2	37.2
4804000	Arlington city	51.0	21.7	13.0	150,945	2.59	63.8	40.4	6.8	16.7	36.2	28.8	33.7
4804462	Atascocita CDP	55.4	12.5	6.6	38,628	3.02	78.9	57.1	8.7	13.0	21.1	15.9	24.5
4805000	Austin city	47.7	18.3	10.9	475,680	2.01	45.4	34.2	4.3	6.9	54.6	39.2	22.9
4806128	Baytown city	67.5	18.0	10.7	31,402	2.71	67.3	43.8	8.7	14.8	32.7	27.5	32.7
4807000	Beaumont city	71.3	10.3	6.2	44,169	2.49	66.1	39.5	5.5	21.1	33.9	29.0	40.0
4810768	Brownsville city	64.3	28.3	16.5	64,083	2.93	76.3	48.7	4.9	22.7	23.7	21.4	40.5
4810912	Bryan city	65.3	15.7	10.6	33,775	2.57	58.7	37.1	3.5	18.1	41.3	33.1	31.2
4813024	Carrollton city	44.5	26.4	11.5	52,503	2.50	66.9	51.1	5.7	10.2	33.1	28.5	35.3
4813552	Cedar Park city	45.9	18.8	9.7	27,998	2.80	74.2	59.5	3.8	10.9	25.8	21.1	34.2
4815976	College Station city	63.2	12.9	7.5	47,029	2.37	45.6	35.4	1.9	8.3	54.4	31.5	20.0
4816432	Conroe city	53.2	17.7	11.6	42,134	2.53	69.8	55.6	3.7	10.6	30.2	19.2	28.4
4817000	Corpus Christi city	73.3	8.2	4.9	118,392	2.61	68.8	46.4	5.8	16.6	31.2	23.5	39.4
4819000	Dallas city	53.6	23.9	16.5	536,727	2.40	53.2	34.4	5.6	13.1	46.8	38.3	29.6
4819972	Denton city	55.6	10.0	6.7	59,711	2.49	54.4	43.3	3.3	7.7	45.6	31.4	33.1
4822660	Edinburg city	69.8	17.7	10.8	34,958	2.91	70.0	43.9	9.9	16.2	30.0	22.4	30.4
4824000	El Paso city	59.7	21.7	10.1	249,362	2.70	68.0	42.8	6.6	18.6	32.0	27.2	40.0
4826232	Flower Mound town	39.8	17.9	6.9	29,171	2.71	76.7	65.1	4.3	7.3	23.3	19.5	36.0
4827000	Fort Worth city	53.9	18.6	11.6	346,392	2.78	66.0	46.3	5.4	14.4	34.0	27.8	30.3
4827684	Frisco city	34.8	29.5	13.6	80,665	2.78	78.2	65.2	5.2	7.8	21.8	19.3	25.5
4829000	Garland city	49.5	34.4	21.1	80,786	3.00	71.8	52.0	7.1	12.7	28.2	22.3	35.5
4829336	Georgetown city	48.0	8.8	4.5	42,239	2.23	63.8	53.2	3.4	7.2	36.2	30.5	51.6

Table A-4. Cities — Who: Age, Race/Ethnicity, and Household Structure, 2023—*Continued*

STATE and place code	STATE Place	Total population	Percent change, 2010–2023	Population by age (percent): Under 18 years	18 to 24 years	25 to 44 years	45 to 64 years	65 years and over	Median age	Race alone or in combination (percent): White	Black	Asian + Native Hawaiian or Other Pacific Islander	American Indian and Alaska Native + Some other race	Two or more races (percent)	Hispanic or Latino (percent)
	ACS table number:	B01003	Census PEP	B01001	B01001	B01001	B01001	B01001	B01002	B02008	B02009	B02011 + B02012	B02010 + B02013	B02001	B03003
	column number:	1	2	3	4	5	6	7	8	9	10	11	12	13	14
	TEXAS—Cont.														
4830464	Grand Prairie city	202,092	14.8	26.6	9.5	28.9	24.3	10.7	33.8	43.5	27.8	7.4	41.0	19.7	47.5
4832372	Harlingen city	71,512	9.8	28.8	10.6	28.6	17.9	14.1	32.2	88.8	2.7	1.9	64.6	57.4	82.6
4835000	Houston city	2,311,461	9.7	23.2	10.0	32.2	21.7	12.8	34.5	51.7	25.6	8.0	38.9	23.1	43.9
4837000	Irving city	254,392	17.2	26.4	11.2	33.3	20.0	9.1	31.8	52.5	11.6	23.9	23.8	10.5	45.4
4839148	Killeen city	159,635	23.7	27.6	10.3	32.2	20.1	9.8	31.0	45.8	44.5	7.4	22.3	18.2	27.2
4841464	Laredo city	252,974	6.6	30.4	11.4	26.5	20.9	10.8	30.9	87.1	0.8	0.5	79.8	68.0	94.7
4841980	League City city	117,520	40.2	28.6	6.3	28.4	23.6	13.3	38.1	81.6	10.2	6.4	17.5	14.8	21.8
4842016	Leander city	79,853	201.1	27.6	7.0	34.4	22.0	9.0	36.2	66.9	6.1	22.3	17.6	12.1	21.4
4842508	Lewisville city	133,779	39.8	21.7	8.5	34.0	24.8	11.1	35.7	60.3	16.5	13.1	25.8	15.0	30.4
4843888	Longview city	84,418	5.2	25.2	11.1	26.4	20.6	16.7	34.9	71.0	23.9	2.5	23.5	20.8	23.7
4845000	Lubbock city	266,878	15.7	23.5	17.6	28.0	18.5	12.3	30.6	80.6	10.2	3.4	25.3	18.7	37.5
4845384	McAllen city	146,599	12.1	26.4	10.1	26.3	23.7	13.5	35.3	81.0	1.3	3.4	61.5	46.9	86.2
4845744	McKinney city	213,504	61.6	26.8	8.1	29.3	24.4	11.3	36.5	66.8	16.1	15.5	15.5	12.6	16.6
4846452	Mansfield city	79,775	41.5	30.5	8.8	27.3	23.6	9.8	34.7	65.9	24.8	4.9	17.9	12.5	21.9
4847892	Mesquite city	147,522	5.2	27.8	9.4	26.4	23.4	13.1	34.1	52.5	29.1	5.6	39.3	25.3	45.3
4848072	Midland city	138,362	24.4	30.2	8.8	32.6	17.9	10.6	32.2	74.1	10.5	2.1	32.3	18.6	46.2
4848768	Mission city	87,288	12.5	29.7	8.9	25.4	21.2	14.8	34.3	89.0	1.8	2.4	76.5	69.0	89.0
4848804	Missouri City city	71,820	4.0	20.2	9.7	26.7	24.9	18.4	37.8	32.9	39.5	19.4	21.1	12.7	25.2
4850820	New Braunfels city	110,961	92.2	22.1	9.0	33.2	22.2	13.5	36.1	86.5	4.1	3.0	27.1	19.8	34.0
4852356	North Richland Hills city	70,671	11.0	22.3	7.4	30.9	23.8	15.6	36.6	84.7	9.4	4.3	9.3	7.6	17.2
4853388	Odessa city	121,604	22.1	28.2	8.6	32.6	19.5	11.0	31.9	72.1	8.1	2.4	47.1	28.8	62.3
4856000	Pasadena city	146,705	-2.0	28.1	11.2	25.5	23.5	11.8	33.6	67.0	3.5	4.2	60.7	35.2	72.9
4856348	Pearland city	127,216	40.1	26.7	8.5	25.9	25.5	13.5	37.6	58.5	21.9	16.7	23.4	19.3	22.9
4857176	Pflugerville city	65,127	38.8	22.3	6.1	31.8	27.9	11.8	38.4	64.9	21.1	11.3	21.4	18.0	32.9
4857200	Pharr city	80,409	13.4	32.7	11.8	25.5	18.5	11.5	29.0	NA	NA	NA	NA	NA	NA
4858016	Plano city	288,228	10.1	20.2	8.4	29.3	25.9	16.1	40.4	63.5	9.3	26.1	15.2	12.9	16.3
4861796	Richardson city	117,445	17.8	16.8	17.0	30.1	20.4	15.7	34.2	63.2	12.7	22.1	17.2	14.3	20.3
4863500	Round Rock city	131,735	28.6	24.0	9.3	33.8	22.2	10.8	35.4	72.4	11.0	10.3	29.4	21.6	32.5
4863572	Rowlett city		66,736	18.7	24.3	9.0	27.3	27.4	12.1	36.4	67.0	21.7	9.7	19.3	15.1
4864472	San Angelo city	97,183	3.6	23.7	10.5	29.1	19.8	16.9	35.8	87.7	5.6	2.8	33.8	29.0	44.6
4865000	San Antonio city	1,495,312	12.1	23.0	11.0	29.9	22.4	13.6	35.4	74.5	8.9	4.5	49.3	35.5	64.6
4865600	San Marcos city	71,566	59.4	12.7	39.5	25.0	13.4	9.5	24.6	80.7	5.5	3.9	27.1	16.2	39.6
4869596	Spring CDP	67,562	24.4	28.9	7.2	33.1	19.1	11.6	34.1	59.5	23.6	5.7	38.7	25.3	48.2
4870808	Sugar Land city	108,511	36.5	25.5	6.0	23.7	26.3	18.5	41.9	47.8	14.5	38.7	13.6	14.2	14.5
4872176	Temple city	93,101	39.6	25.3	10.0	28.8	21.4	14.6	34.1	72.6	18.4	4.5	24.4	18.2	30.7
4872656	The Woodlands CDP	121,514	32.0	27.4	5.8	23.0	27.2	16.6	40.8	81.6	7.5	8.4	21.2	18.9	22.8
4874144	Tyler city	110,325	13.4	24.7	11.2	28.1	21.0	15.1	34.9	66.4	25.1	3.5	19.3	12.8	26.0
4875428	Victoria city	65,800	5.1	25.4	10.7	26.6	20.4	16.9	35.5	76.3	8.7	3.4	44.2	31.1	53.8
4876000	Waco city	144,820	15.5	24.3	19.1	26.7	16.8	13.2	28.8	71.7	22.5	2.6	29.9	26.4	32.1
4879000	Wichita Falls city	102,683	-1.9	21.9	13.7	27.8	20.8	15.8	34.4	76.9	16.3	3.4	15.8	11.7	24.5
49000	**UTAH**	3,380,800	19.0	27.5	12.0	28.3	20.2	11.9	32.1	87.7	2.2	5.6	14.2	15.1	8.8
4943660	Layton city	83,523	23.5	29.0	7.6	30.4	20.4	12.5	32.8	94.5	1.7	3.3	14.7	13.5	17.5
4944320	Lehi city	90,229	90.3	36.7	10.6	29.7	16.0	7.1	26.6	93.6	1.0	6.9	11.3	12.1	12.1
4955980	Ogden city	87,272	4.9	25.4	11.9	31.7	19.0	12.1	32.0	86.4	4.1	3.2	16.6	10.1	36.5
4957300	Orem city	95,514	7.4	25.1	20.3	26.3	17.7	10.7	26.8	85.3	2.6	10.2	15.6	12.0	21.8
4962470	Provo city	113,355	0.1	19.7	38.9	24.0	9.8	7.5	23.8	83.7	2.0	7.6	19.1	10.6	18.9
4965330	St. George city	104,592	43.1	22.4	10.2	24.6	21.1	21.8	40.5	92.1	0.9	2.6	12.4	7.4	11.5
4967000	Salt Lake City city	209,606	12.0	16.5	16.5	34.2	19.8	13.1	33.2	79.8	2.7	9.0	20.0	10.8	22.7
4967440	Sandy city	91,934	4.7	22.8	7.7	27.1	23.9	18.5	39.0	89.9	1.6	9.0	11.3	10.4	11.0
4970850	South Jordan city	84,508	67.6	28.9	7.2	27.7	24.7	11.6	37.4	94.4	0.8	5.8	15.1	14.8	14.6
4982950	West Jordan city	114,908	10.3	28.6	9.9	28.1	22.7	10.7	33.9	82.3	4.6	7.7	19.8	13.1	21.5
4983470	West Valley City city	134,466	3.4	26.7	10.4	29.9	23.7	9.3	33.3	57.4	3.4	11.3	41.6	13.0	43.7
50000	**VERMONT**	647,064	21.8	17.6	10.2	24.4	26.3	21.6	43.2	96.2	2.1	2.6	5.1	2.3	5.5
51000	**VIRGINIA**	8,683,619	3.4	21.4	9.7	26.9	25.1	16.8	39.0	68.6	21.3	8.9	11.3	10.4	9.2
5101000	Alexandria city	155,230	10.2	18.0	6.2	39.2	22.9	13.7	38.2	65.8	24.3	8.4	18.5	15.9	18.1
5103000	Arlington CDP	234,162	11.8	18.0	8.3	38.4	23.0	12.4	35.7	71.8	11.4	13.5	17.1	13.0	16.0
5114440	Centreville CDP	71,374	-7.3	22.5	9.8	32.7	24.6	10.4	34.9	57.5	9.7	32.1	17.0	17.9	20.5
5116000	Chesapeake city	253,886	13.9	24.0	8.0	28.9	24.2	15.0	38.4	63.9	33.0	6.6	7.8	10.0	7.9
5121088	Dale City CDP	70,529	13.7	28.1	9.0	27.6	24.3	11.0	35.5	43.6	27.3	12.3	36.3	19.2	40.5
5135000	Hampton city	137,098	-0.2	21.8	10.4	29.9	21.0	17.0	35.9	43.1	55.7	4.1	9.2	10.4	7.2
5147672	Lynchburg city	79,535	5.1	19.3	25.3	24.6	16.5	14.4	28.2	68.4	28.5	3.2	6.2	6.2	5.1

Table A-4. Cities — Who: Age, Race/Ethnicity, and Household Structure, 2023

STATE and place code	STATE Place	Native, born in state of residence (percent)	Foreign born (percent)	Non-citizens (percent)	Total households	Average household size	Household type (percent of all households)							Percent of households with people age 60 years and over
							Family households				Nonfamily households		
							Total	Married-couple	Male householder	Female householder	Total	One-person households	
	ACS table number:	B05002	B05002	B05002	B11001	B25010	B11001	B11001	B11001	B11001	B11001	B11001	B11006
	column number:	15	16	17	18	19	20	21	22	23	24	25	26
	TEXAS—Cont.												
4830464	Grand Prairie city	49.0	27.1	16.1	70,750	2.85	70.4	49.4	6.4	14.6	29.6	25.4	33.0
4832372	Harlingen city	73.0	12.3	7.2	25,629	2.76	65.7	42.9	8.4	14.4	34.3	27.8	35.3
4835000	Houston city	50.5	29.3	19.4	942,146	2.41	57.6	36.3	6.6	14.7	42.4	34.8	31.9
4837000	Irving city	37.4	43.9	32.8	95,909	2.64	62.1	45.3	4.4	12.3	37.9	29.8	25.0
4839148	Killeen city	36.3	10.8	4.6	64,777	2.46	62.1	40.2	5.2	16.7	37.9	32.3	25.5
4841464	Laredo city	68.0	24.9	17.2	79,072	3.16	79.0	48.6	10.0	20.4	21.0	18.1	36.7
4841980	League City city	59.3	11.0	3.6	41,978	2.78	75.1	62.6	4.4	8.1	24.9	21.3	35.5
4842016	Leander city	42.9	20.8	11.0	28,615	2.79	79.0	69.5	3.5	6.0	21.0	16.8	24.1
4842508	Lewisville city	45.2	26.4	15.5	50,672	2.63	66.5	47.5	6.1	12.9	33.5	26.8	28.5
4843888	Longview city	68.5	9.1	6.5	32,201	2.53	64.6	37.4	6.5	20.7	35.4	30.5	39.9
4845000	Lubbock city	73.3	5.9	3.6	108,609	2.35	58.1	37.8	5.6	14.8	41.9	30.2	29.4
4845384	McAllen city	60.1	27.8	17.4	51,319	2.84	73.5	49.0	7.0	17.6	26.5	20.9	38.1
4845744	McKinney city	43.9	20.3	8.9	74,833	2.83	74.9	57.2	4.3	13.3	25.1	20.1	30.1
4846452	Mansfield city	50.0	14.1	4.9	26,245	3.02	78.1	55.8	3.0	19.3	21.9	17.4	33.0
4847892	Mesquite city	61.0	23.7	14.4	49,690	2.96	73.6	45.1	8.9	19.6	26.4	23.4	40.5
4848072	Midland city	62.7	12.3	7.5	53,640	2.55	67.0	49.0	8.3	9.7	33.0	27.8	28.2
4848768	Mission city	59.7	25.5	15.8	29,183	2.98	74.9	51.2	7.1	16.6	25.1	21.3	41.2
4848804	Missouri City city	57.7	20.9	7.4	26,271	2.71	77.7	53.0	7.9	16.8	22.3	18.3	48.3
4850820	New Braunfels city	64.0	6.8	2.3	42,756	2.56	64.4	50.2	1.6	12.5	35.6	26.9	32.6
4852356	North Richland Hills city	60.5	7.9	4.2	27,385	2.57	68.0	52.9	3.9	11.1	32.0	23.8	37.1
4853388	Odessa city	57.8	19.3	12.2	54,163	2.21	63.5	43.6	6.9	12.9	36.5	31.1	26.9
4856000	Pasadena city	58.9	27.6	17.3	49,618	2.94	77.3	51.0	8.8	17.5	22.7	19.5	37.9
4856348	Pearland city	53.0	18.7	5.3	45,686	2.77	71.5	56.7	4.2	10.5	28.5	24.1	35.6
4857176	Pflugerville city	48.2	21.1	6.4	24,333	2.66	70.2	54.5	4.9	10.9	29.8	22.7	31.4
4857200	Pharr city	60.1	27.7	19.7	23,919	3.36	76.4	48.3	6.8	21.3	23.6	20.3	36.8
4858016	Plano city	37.4	29.7	15.2	114,555	2.50	66.7	55.1	3.8	7.8	33.3	28.5	38.5
4861796	Richardson city	45.8	21.2	10.0	45,822	2.43	57.9	45.1	4.2	8.7	42.1	31.8	35.4
4863500	Round Rock city	47.7	16.8	9.8	48,682	2.69	68.1	47.8	8.0	12.3	31.9	24.9	29.2
4863572	Rowlett city	21.8	58.7	11.8	3.0	23,939	2.78	75.8	55.7	5.3	14.8	24.2	20.1
4864472	San Angelo city	68.3	7.3	4.1	39,231	2.39	56.5	36.1	5.5	15.0	43.5	38.0	38.8
4865000	San Antonio city	62.5	15.4	9.2	558,796	2.62	61.8	39.2	6.4	16.2	38.2	31.4	36.9
4865600	San Marcos city	67.0	7.5	3.5	28,741	2.22	42.6	28.2	2.9	11.5	57.4	31.7	25.0
4869596	Spring CDP	49.3	23.7	11.6	22,132	3.05	74.2	55.9	6.8	11.5	25.8	16.7	35.6
4870808	Sugar Land city	38.2	38.3	13.5	36,977	2.93	82.7	73.0	3.0	6.6	17.3	16.0	46.1
4872176	Temple city	54.1	7.7	4.0	35,445	2.59	65.1	45.2	6.8	13.2	34.9	28.3	36.9
4872656	The Woodlands CDP	36.9	22.4	8.9	44,480	2.72	75.3	68.0	1.1	6.2	24.7	21.7	40.3
4874144	Tyler city	70.0	10.7	6.7	36,292	2.91	63.7	45.6	5.2	12.9	36.3	28.2	39.7
4875428	Victoria city	73.5	10.2	6.8	25,267	2.56	69.1	49.0	6.0	14.1	30.9	25.8	39.4
4876000	Waco city	68.8	11.5	8.4	52,857	2.60	57.9	38.6	4.4	15.0	42.1	34.1	33.4
4879000	Wichita Falls city	63.8	8.3	4.1	38,473	2.40	61.5	40.5	6.0	15.0	38.5	31.6	39.2
49000	**UTAH**	60.8	8.6	5.0	1,129,660	2.95	73.5	59.5	5.1	8.9	26.5	19.5	32.9
4943660	Layton city	61.1	6.1	3.4	28,387	2.92	73.5	60.0	4.4	9.2	26.5	22.8	32.3
4944320	Lehi city	62.1	7.0	3.7	25,416	3.55	82.4	74.1	2.2	6.0	17.6	10.5	22.8
4955980	Ogden city	53.5	13.8	8.1	32,848	2.56	62.8	39.4	7.1	16.3	37.2	29.8	31.6
4957300	Orem city	55.6	10.5	6.3	31,948	2.92	72.8	57.5	3.8	11.5	27.2	15.9	29.4
4962470	Provo city	45.4	12.8	10.2	36,198	2.85	67.0	56.8	3.9	6.3	33.0	13.4	21.6
4965330	St. George city	55.2	5.9	4.1	38,886	2.64	70.7	59.1	5.0	6.6	29.3	23.4	48.1
4967000	Salt Lake City city	45.5	15.2	9.1	92,626	2.13	45.3	34.3	4.1	7.0	54.7	38.1	28.8
4967440	Sandy city	54.8	9.2	4.3	35,081	2.61	69.2	57.7	3.7	7.8	30.8	24.3	41.9
4970850	South Jordan city	64.3	7.3	4.4	27,610	3.06	81.7	70.5	2.5	8.7	18.3	15.8	33.8
4982950	West Jordan city	62.1	11.3	5.3	36,479	3.13	79.1	58.2	6.9	14.0	20.9	12.7	31.1
4983470	West Valley City city	53.9	28.5	17.8	43,539	3.08	73.6	47.1	10.2	16.3	26.4	18.5	32.2
50000	**VERMONT**	46.9	4.2	1.5	277,090	2.25	59.4	47.4	4.7	7.8	40.6	30.3	46.8
51000	**VIRGINIA**	48.7	12.7	5.3	3,380,607	2.50	64.8	48.6	4.7	11.6	35.2	28.2	40.7
5101000	Alexandria city	21.7	24.7	13.0	76,890	2.00	45.7	34.5	3.6	7.6	54.3	44.3	28.1
5103000	Arlington CDP	23.6	20.7	9.5	114,097	2.03	43.9	37.6	1.9	4.4	56.1	41.7	25.5
5114440	Centreville CDP	30.7	33.1	13.6	25,109	2.84	72.6	54.5	5.8	12.3	27.4	19.4	31.0
5116000	Chesapeake city	53.9	6.0	1.8	94,056	2.65	73.4	53.4	3.9	16.1	26.6	21.0	41.5
5121088	Dale City CDP	38.2	32.7	13.9	19,694	3.58	85.8	63.3	6.7	15.7	14.2	10.0	42.4
5135000	Hampton city	52.8	5.3	0.6	57,645	2.32	58.8	36.2	5.0	17.6	41.2	33.7	41.1
5147672	Lynchburg city	52.6	4.5	2.2	28,916	2.37	56.4	39.2	6.1	11.0	43.6	33.1	36.0

Table A-4. Cities — Who: Age, Race/Ethnicity, and Household Structure, 2023—*Continued*

STATE and place code	STATE Place	Total population	Percent change, 2010–2023	Population by age (percent): Under 18 years	18 to 24 years	25 to 44 years	45 to 64 years	65 years and over	Median age	Race alone or in combination (percent): White	Black	Asian + Native Hawaiian or Other Pacific Islander	American Indian and Alaska Native + Some other race	Two or more races (percent)	Hispanic or Latino (percent)
	ACS table number:	B01003	Census PEP	B01001	B01001	B01001	B01001	B01001	B01002	B02008	B02009	B02011 + B02012	B02010 + B02013	B02001	B03003
	column number:	1	2	3	4	5	6	7	8	9	10	11	12	13	14
	VIRGINIA—Cont.														
5156000	Newport News city	183,118	1.3	23.2	11.8	28.9	21.5	14.6	34.7	50.1	46.6	5.7	11.8	12.7	11.0
5157000	Norfolk city	230,930	-5.0	20.2	14.7	32.0	19.4	13.7	33.0	52.3	43.0	6.2	11.6	11.2	10.3
5164000	Portsmouth city	96,793	1.1	22.9	9.1	30.4	22.2	15.3	35.6	42.4	57.0	2.7	8.1	9.8	5.8
5166672	Reston CDP		66,070	13.1	18.0	8.9	31.5	26.5	15.0	39.3	69.1	13.6	12.5	18.1	11.6
5167000	Richmond city	229,247	12.2	17.4	11.7	35.5	20.8	14.6	34.9	49.4	44.9	3.4	10.7	7.6	10.6
5168000	Roanoke city	97,171	0.2	22.5	7.0	28.7	24.4	17.5	38.9	64.0	30.3	4.3	9.2	7.7	8.9
5176432	Suffolk city	100,659	18.6	23.4	6.9	28.8	25.4	15.4	39.8	52.2	45.5	3.0	8.5	8.0	5.5
5182000	Virginia Beach city	453,649	3.3	21.7	8.3	29.5	24.0	16.5	38.2	69.1	22.4	11.1	8.8	9.8	9.2
53000	**WASHINGTON**	7,785,786	8.2	21.1	8.6	29.4	24.0	16.8	38.4	77.7	6.1	14.1	15.9	14.0	12.6
5303180	Auburn city	84,887	19.8	23.3	9.5	28.9	25.0	13.3	36.6	64.6	7.6	22.8	21.7	15.7	19.1
5305210	Bellevue city	151,579	23.4	20.0	6.8	35.1	23.4	14.8	38.4	48.9	2.4	49.8	7.7	8.4	5.9
5305280	Bellingham city	94,712	16.8	15.4	19.8	29.2	19.6	16.1	34.2	85.6	4.1	8.9	12.1	10.7	11.1
5322640	Everett city	111,147	7.6	18.6	7.8	33.7	23.8	16.1	37.8	73.9	9.1	13.9	14.1	10.7	14.7
5323515	Federal Way city	97,689	9.0	20.1	8.6	27.7	26.3	17.3	38.6	48.0	23.8	25.1	17.8	13.3	18.9
5335275	Kennewick city	85,155	14.4	28.4	9.5	26.0	20.3	15.9	35.1	80.3	2.8	3.1	37.4	23.6	35.5
5335415	Kent city	133,381	43.9	20.3	9.3	28.9	27.6	13.9	37.6	48.6	18.2	29.5	18.1	12.2	15.8
5335940	Kirkland city	91,190	86.9	18.9	6.8	36.9	24.8	12.6	37.1	73.0	2.1	27.0	7.9	9.4	8.4
5343955	Marysville city	72,922	21.5	20.7	7.2	31.2	26.2	14.7	38.2	81.8	6.3	11.2	17.9	15.9	18.4
5353545	Pasco city	81,415	36.2	31.1	10.6	28.8	18.8	10.6	31.1	74.1	2.6	3.6	48.9	29.0	58.6
5357535	Redmond city	80,275	48.3	19.7	6.7	44.9	19.4	9.4	35.0	52.6	4.1	42.8	8.6	7.9	5.8
5357745	Renton city	104,505	14.5	19.7	7.5	34.1	25.2	13.5	37.8	56.8	13.2	30.2	15.9	14.7	16.0
5361115	Sammamish city	65,126	42.3	28.9	5.6	24.2	31.4	10.0	41.3	55.8	3.9	44.4	5.1	8.8	5.6
5363000	Seattle city	755,081	23.6	14.5	10.2	41.7	20.7	12.9	35.6	71.6	8.8	22.8	10.7	12.4	8.7
5365922	South Hill CDP	67,851	29.4	26.8	9.7	28.6	22.7	12.2	35.3	76.7	14.5	19.4	14.3	21.1	11.2
5367000	Spokane city	229,451	9.6	21.0	9.1	31.3	21.8	16.8	36.7	89.0	5.0	4.6	10.7	8.9	8.0
5367167	Spokane Valley city	108,232	20.4	18.1	8.8	30.5	26.9	15.7	39.5	91.7	2.6	6.3	9.0	8.7	6.7
5370000	Tacoma city	222,932	12.3	18.7	8.6	33.5	24.5	14.7	37.9	73.2	14.7	15.7	15.5	17.5	14.8
5374060	Vancouver city	196,441	20.9	19.5	9.0	30.0	23.8	17.7	38.1	79.8	5.0	10.3	16.5	10.8	17.9
5380010	Yakima city	96,739	5.7	24.8	9.6	26.8	20.4	18.5	35.9	78.2	2.6	3.4	45.6	29.2	48.2
54000	**WEST VIRGINIA**	1,775,156	15.5	19.8	9.1	23.9	26.1	21.2	42.9	94.9	4.7	1.3	4.0	1.9	4.7
55000	**WISCONSIN**	5,892,539	-4.3	21.1	9.5	25.1	25.6	18.7	40.4	88.0	7.6	3.8	8.9	7.6	7.9
5502375	Appleton city	75,861	5.7	21.0	9.0	28.0	23.7	18.4	40.1	86.3	3.7	8.2	8.3	6.5	5.6
5522300	Eau Claire city	70,469	7.6	16.7	20.1	27.2	19.4	16.6	34.2	90.8	2.2	6.6	5.5	5.5	3.1
5531000	Green Bay city	105,734	1.4	22.5	10.4	28.4	23.1	15.6	36.7	79.3	6.1	6.8	20.7	11.9	16.0
5537825	Janesville city	66,113	4.0	19.5	10.6	24.9	26.5	18.5	40.5	88.6	4.7	2.3	11.3	6.7	9.6
5539225	Kenosha city	98,210	-1.2	20.9	10.9	27.7	25.7	14.8	38.1	83.1	14.0	2.1	18.3	16.6	21.6
5548000	Madison city	280,307	19.9	14.8	20.7	32.1	19.3	13.1	32.5	80.1	9.7	10.2	10.7	10.2	10.4
5553000	Milwaukee city	561,369	-5.7	25.0	11.8	30.2	20.6	12.4	32.6	49.0	40.5	6.8	21.2	16.3	22.0
5560500	Oshkosh city	66,184	0.1	16.9	15.8	27.4	20.9	19.1	36.6	89.1	7.2	4.5	5.7	6.4	5.7
5566000	Racine city	76,608	-2.9	25.8	8.7	26.4	23.4	15.7	36.8	72.9	25.4	0.0	21.6	18.9	26.0
5584250	Waukesha city	70,452	-0.4	20.4	9.4	26.4	25.7	18.0	40.5	90.3	4.0	2.9	9.6	6.6	10.7
56000	**WYOMING**	581,381	3.5	22.3	8.9	26.5	23.7	18.6	39.1	92.6	1.4	2.0	12.9	10.8	8.3
5613900	Cheyenne city	65,163	9.6	19.5	8.0	30.4	22.7	19.3	39.2	92.1	4.1	3.3	14.2	13.0	15.8
72000	**PUERTO RICO**	3,221,789	3.0	16.1	9.3	25.0	26.2	23.5	44.7	60.7	13.1	0.3	68.7	99.0	38.2
7206593	Bayamón zona urbana	162,976	-12.9	14.7	8.8	26.9	23.9	25.8	44.8	41.0	7.0	0.6	85.1	32.5	98.8
7210334	Caguas zona urbana		70,683	-13.4	15.3	7.8	28.1	24.3	24.5	44.4	60.9	12.7	0.5	60.3	33.7
7214290	Carolina zona urbana	138,375	-13.7	15.1	9.2	25.4	25.7	24.7	45.3	50.2	21.4	0.5	72.5	42.2	98.9
7232522	Guaynabo zona urbana		68,737	-4.9	15.3	8.9	27.7	23.4	24.6	44.2	47.1	6.3	0.0	71.7	24.5
7263820	Ponce zona urbana	106,498	-21.0	16.1	8.9	24.0	23.7	27.3	45.7	74.2	11.9	0.0	68.0	53.0	99.0
7276770	San Juan zona urbana	312,488	-18.4	14.4	8.9	25.1	25.4	26.2	46.2	59.6	14.6	0.2	72.5	45.7	98.1

Table A-4. Cities — Who: Age, Race/Ethnicity, and Household Structure, 2023

STATE and place code	STATE Place	Native, born in state of residence (percent)	Foreign born (percent)	Non-citizens (percent)	Total households	Average household size	Household type (percent of all households): Family households: Total	Family households: Married-couple	Family households: Male householder	Family households: Female householder	Nonfamily households: Total	Nonfamily households: One-person households	Percent of households with people age 60 years and over
	ACS table number:	B05002	B05002	B05002	B11001	B25010	B11001	B11001	B11001	B11001	B11001	B11001	B11006
	column number:	15	16	17	18	19	20	21	22	23	24	25	26
	VIRGINIA—Cont.												
5156000	Newport News city	50.9	7.6	3.2	76,086	2.33	56.7	33.9	6.4	16.4	43.3	37.0	36.8
5157000	Norfolk city	48.1	8.0	4.0	94,056	2.28	56.4	34.1	6.2	16.2	43.6	36.2	33.8
5164000	Portsmouth city	66.4	3.5	1.8	40,661	2.33	60.8	36.3	5.4	19.1	39.2	31.9	38.1
5166672	Reston CDP	16.7	25.5	28.2	11.2	29,528	2.23	51.4	39.7	3.2	8.5	48.6	41.7
5167000	Richmond city	55.5	9.4	6.4	104,332	2.09	45.5	26.8	3.9	14.8	54.5	42.5	33.0
5168000	Roanoke city	61.0	9.3	6.4	45,061	2.12	56.6	35.2	4.7	16.8	43.4	37.1	35.3
5176432	Suffolk city	55.2	5.7	2.5	39,203	2.55	65.4	50.7	2.2	12.5	34.6	30.3	39.4
5182000	Virginia Beach city	41.0	8.7	2.7	179,291	2.49	65.3	47.9	4.7	12.7	34.7	28.0	39.5
53000	**WASHINGTON**	46.4	15.3	7.8	3,079,953	2.48	62.8	48.7	4.7	9.4	37.2	27.9	39.0
5303180	Auburn city	47.6	23.2	11.6	30,938	2.71	69.3	46.2	5.2	17.9	30.7	26.2	37.0
5305210	Bellevue city	26.6	44.7	27.9	62,868	2.39	64.5	55.5	1.7	7.4	35.5	27.6	32.6
5305280	Bellingham city	48.8	7.9	3.2	42,207	2.14	39.3	29.2	3.6	6.4	60.7	42.6	34.3
5322640	Everett city	42.4	21.4	11.0	46,726	2.32	55.1	40.7	5.0	9.3	44.9	33.1	39.4
5323515	Federal Way city	38.6	31.1	16.4	37,759	2.57	64.2	45.7	5.5	13.0	35.8	27.1	41.3
5335275	Kennewick city	52.5	12.9	7.8	30,295	2.77	62.9	46.2	5.1	11.6	37.1	30.1	39.4
5335415	Kent city	39.4	36.1	16.1	50,481	2.61	62.4	44.4	7.7	10.3	37.6	28.2	37.6
5335940	Kirkland city	39.6	26.8	13.6	39,893	2.25	57.3	48.9	2.2	6.1	42.7	31.8	29.4
5343955	Marysville city	60.9	13.8	6.0	27,002	2.68	70.4	48.9	6.4	15.0	29.6	22.8	40.3
5353545	Pasco city	57.8	17.2	10.6	26,284	3.08	76.4	50.9	9.2	16.3	23.6	18.9	31.0
5357535	Redmond city	28.9	44.5	28.5	36,551	2.18	52.7	44.7	3.0	4.9	47.3	37.3	20.2
5357745	Renton city	43.3	29.2	8.7	40,968	2.53	63.2	45.1	6.2	11.9	36.8	28.6	37.7
5361115	Sammamish city	30.1	38.8	21.4	21,792	2.98	83.7	78.1	1.7	4.0	16.3	13.4	29.2
5363000	Seattle city	35.4	19.4	10.2	364,627	2.00	42.1	35.2	2.3	4.6	57.9	43.0	25.4
5365922	South Hill CDP	50.8	12.6	6.6	23,059	2.94	74.1	56.9	5.3	11.8	25.9	17.3	32.3
5367000	Spokane city	53.8	7.3	3.4	95,061	2.35	54.4	38.2	5.6	10.6	45.6	35.5	39.7
5367167	Spokane Valley city	53.9	6.0	3.1	45,025	2.37	59.8	42.1	5.4	12.3	40.2	31.1	41.2
5370000	Tacoma city	48.0	13.6	6.5	97,027	2.24	55.3	37.0	7.6	10.7	44.7	33.0	35.3
5374060	Vancouver city	29.9	10.9	6.0	84,778	2.29	54.7	40.1	6.0	8.6	45.3	34.1	40.9
5380010	Yakima city	59.5	16.1	10.7	37,918	2.50	64.4	38.2	9.7	16.5	35.6	29.6	44.8
54000	**WEST VIRGINIA**	67.1	1.8	0.8	736,341	2.34	62.9	46.0	5.3	11.6	37.1	31.0	47.0
55000	**WISCONSIN**	70.3	5.0	2.6	2,491,121	2.31	60.7	47.0	4.5	9.1	39.3	31.0	41.5
5502375	Appleton city	67.9	8.6	3.2	30,831	2.38	62.1	48.4	5.5	8.3	37.9	30.3	36.7
5522300	Eau Claire city	68.0	2.4	1.4	30,280	2.20	51.5	36.5	3.4	11.5	48.5	35.4	34.4
5531000	Green Bay city	72.3	8.8	4.2	45,483	2.26	54.9	37.1	4.9	12.9	45.1	36.1	34.3
5537825	Janesville city	68.7	4.6	1.6	27,361	2.39	63.4	45.0	5.8	12.6	36.6	27.4	42.3
5539225	Kenosha city	52.5	9.4	4.8	42,461	2.24	57.1	38.7	5.6	12.7	42.9	35.3	38.2
5548000	Madison city	50.4	12.4	8.3	134,512	1.98	40.8	32.0	2.9	5.9	59.2	41.8	25.6
5553000	Milwaukee city	64.2	11.7	7.1	227,173	2.41	52.2	27.1	6.0	19.1	47.8	37.2	32.2
5560500	Oshkosh city	76.6	3.8	2.5	28,147	2.17	50.0	37.0	3.7	9.3	50.0	40.0	39.1
5566000	Racine city	70.0	4.3	3.0	31,700	2.39	54.1	32.5	4.0	17.6	45.9	37.8	38.3
5584250	Waukesha city	71.2	6.3	3.9	30,668	2.25	56.2	44.9	3.4	7.8	43.8	33.9	37.3
56000	**WYOMING**	43.4	3.1	1.6	243,321	2.33	63.0	49.0	5.2	8.8	37.0	30.4	41.9
5613900	Cheyenne city	43.0	1.9	0.4	30,643	2.11	57.0	40.7	6.4	10.0	43.0	37.6	42.3
72000	**PUERTO RICO**	X	2.6	1.2	1,289,311	2.47	63.7	34.9	6.9	21.9	36.3	31.1	51.7
7206593	Bayamón zona urbana	0.0	2.8	1.2	69,470	2.28	60.8	30.0	5.7	25.0	39.2	33.8	51.4
7210334	Caguas zona urbana	98.7	0.0	2.8	1.5	30,465	2.31	65.0	27.4	5.4	32.3	35.0	31.9
7214290	Carolina zona urbana	0.0	6.2	2.4	58,026	2.38	59.5	32.7	3.4	23.4	40.5	34.2	54.2
7232522	Guaynabo zona urbana	96.2	0.0	9.0	5.3	26,800	2.51	58.1	40.8	3.1	14.2	41.9	34.8
7263820	Ponce zona urbana	0.0	0.9	0.7	48,343	2.17	59.9	28.9	6.1	24.9	40.1	37.0	52.3
7276770	San Juan zona urbana	0.0	10.0	4.8	143,453	2.13	47.7	23.9	4.4	19.4	52.3	47.0	51.8

NA = Not available.

PART B

What

Education, Employment, and Income

What: Education, Employment, and Income

What do Americans do? In 2023, over 173 million Americans were in the labor force and nearly 80 million were enrolled in school. Many people were in both groups at the same time. Americans' employment and income potential are closely related to their educational attainment. Educational differences among states, cities, and metropolitan areas can influence location decisions of both workers and employers. Employers with low-wage jobs might seek locations with lower education levels, while locations with highly educated work forces might be sought out by other employers.

Education

Just over 36 percent of Americans (age 25 years and over) held bachelor's degrees and/or advanced degrees, and another 27.7 percent had attended some college or held associate degrees. Nearly two-thirds (65.9 percent) of residents of the District of Columbia held bachelor's and/or advanced degrees, while Massachusetts had the highest level of the 50 states (47.8 percent). In Colorado, New Jersey, Maryland, Vermont, Connecticut, Virginia, New Hampshire, New York, and Washington, more than 40 percent of the population held bachelor's and/or advanced degrees, while less than 26 percent of people in West Virginia and Mississippi were college educated. More than half of the seven metropolitan areas with the highest proportions of college-educated residents—more than half of their populations—Boulder, Colorado; Ithaca, New York; Ann Arbor, Michigan; Corvallis, Oregon; and Charlottesville, Virginia— were relatively small metropolitan areas with large universities. More than half of the population held bachelor's degrees or higher in four of the largest metropolitan areas: Washington-Arlington-Alexandria, DC-MD-VA-WV; San Jose-Sunnyvale-Santa Clara and San Francisco-Oakland-Berkey, CA; and Boston-Cambridge-Newton, MA-NH. In 28 more metropolitan areas, more than 45 percent of the residents had college degrees. In 78 of the counties surveyed in 2023, more than half of residents had bachelor's or advanced degrees, with 6 of the top 10 counties being suburbs of Washington, DC. More than three-quarters of the people in 13 cities were college educated. Some were university cities, while others were suburbs of large metropolitan areas.

Figure B-1. Educational Attainment in the United States, Percent Distribution, 2023

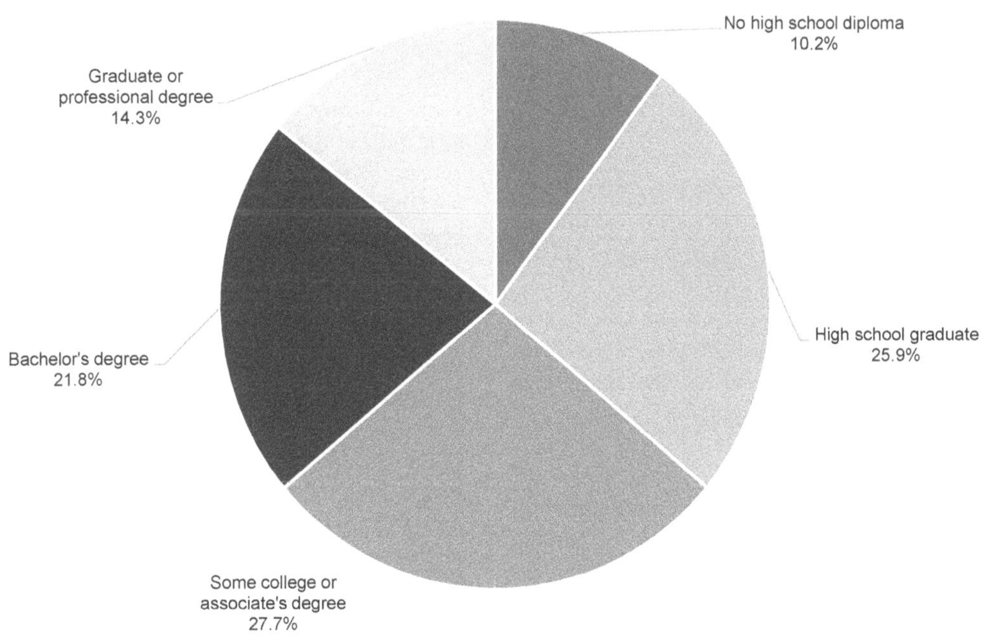

(The number of counties and cities in this book is limited due to raising of the population threshold for the ACS 1-Year Estimates from 20,000 to 65,000.)

In addition to those who have earned bachelor's or advanced degrees, 27.7 percent of Americans have received associate degrees or attended college but did not graduate. This group includes more than one-third of residents of three states — Wyoming, North Dakota, and Idaho. The ACS measure of educational attainment specifically excludes vocational programs, but many adults have earned non-degree credentials such as certificates and licenses.

In the United States in 2023, 10.2 percent of adults had not graduated from high school. Another 25.9 percent had a high school diploma but no further education in regular 2-year or 4-year colleges. Thus, over 35 percent of the American people were in the group with a high school diploma or less. In West Virginia, just over half of the people had not attended college, and nearly half of residents in Louisiana, Arkansas, Puerto Rico, and Kentucky had completed their education with a high school diploma or less. In eight metropolitan areas, 55 percent or more of residents had not attended college: Eagle Pass, Texas; Merced, California; Vineland, New Jersey; Odessa, Texas; Houma-Bayou Cane-Thibodaux, Louisiana; Dalton, Georgia; Beckley, West Virginia; and Yakima, Washington. In five cities—including two in California, one in New Jersey, one in Pennsylvania, and one in Illinois—more than two-thirds of the people had a high school education or less, while 13 cities had levels below 10 percent. In 7 counties (2 in Louisiana, 2 in Texas, and 1 each in Ohio, Pennsylvania, and California), more than 58 percent of residents had a high school diploma or less: Starr County; Texas; Somerset County, Pennsylvania; Merced County, California; Iberia Parish, Louisiana; Liberty County, Texas; Terrebonne Parish, Louisiana; and Tuscarawas County, Ohio.

Among 16- to 19-year-olds in the United States in 2023, 1.9 percent were not enrolled in school, not high school graduates, and not in the labor force. This measure provides one way to use ACS data to identify unemployed high school dropouts. Twenty-four states and the District of Columbia exceeded the national level, led by Alaska (4.1 percent), Montana (4.0 percent), and West Virginia, Arkansas, and Louisiana (3.2 percent each) in this high-risk category. New Mexico saw 3.0 percent of its 16- to 19-year-olds in this group, while New Hampshire (0.5 percent) was the only state under 1 percent.

Of the nearly 80 million people enrolled in school in the United States in 2023, 67.8 were in kindergarten through 12th grade, 26.3 percent were in college or graduate school, and the remaining 5.9 percent were in preschool. Overall, 18.0 percent of the students were in private schools, but this varied by level of school and by location. Approximately 40 percent of both preschoolers and graduate students were in private schools, but private schools enrolled only about 11.5 percent of high school students and 22.4 percent of undergraduate college students. Excluding Puerto Rico and the District of Columbia, which both slightly exceeded the highest state, the proportion of high school students in private schools ranged from 19.8 percent in Hawaii to 6.4 percent in Wyoming. In some states with large numbers of private colleges, higher education attracts many students from other states. Approximately three-quarters of the college undergraduates in the District of Columbia were in private schools, as were more than half in Massachusetts, over 45 percent in Rhode Island, and nearly 40 percent in New York and Pennsylvania. Private school proportions were even higher for medical, law, and graduate school enrollment, with over 72 percent of students in private schools in Puerto Rico, and over 50 percent of students in private schools in the District of Columbia, Massachusetts, Rhode Island, New York, New Hampshire, Pennsylvania, and Connecticut.

Employment

Approximately 63.8 percent of adults (age 16 years and over) in the United States were in the labor force in 2023—the civilian labor force or the armed forces. Those who were not in the labor force might be retired, in school, disabled, homemakers, or formerly employed individuals who have become discouraged from seeking work. Labor force participation was highest in the District of Columbia and Utah, where more than 70 percent of adults were in the labor force, with just under 70 percent participating in Nebraska, Minnesota, North Dakota, and Colorado. In 6 states and Puerto Rico, labor force participation was below 60 percent, with the lowest levels in West Virginia, at only 54.4 percent, and Puerto Rico, with only 47.1 percent. But labor force participation does not mean full-time permanent work. Only 68.6 percent of adults age 16 and over worked 35 hours or more per week for 50 to 52 weeks—full-year, full-time workers—in the past 12 months. These full-year, full-time workers included 56.2 percent of men and 43.8 percent of women. Texas, Alabama, Arkansas, Maryland, and the District of Columbia had the highest levels at more than 71 percent. Hawaii, Alaska, and Puerto Rico had the lowest levels of full-year, full-time workers—all below 64 percent. At least 56 percent of men worked full-year, full-time jobs in 29 states, with the highest levels—over 59 percent—in Utah, Idaho, and Wyoming. The lowest level was in the District of Columbia (49.6 percent). Full-year, full-time work among women was lower, with the highest level of 50.4 percent in the District of Columbia, followed by Delaware, Mississippi, Maryland, and Puerto Rico, where 46 percent or more of women worked full-year, full-time. In Utah, Wyoming, and Idaho, less than 41 percent of women were employed at full-year, full-time jobs.

In 2023, in 5 metropolitan areas (all in Florida and Arizona, which have significant numbers of retirees), less than 30

Figure B-2. Highest and Lowest Proportions of Persons, Age 16 Years and Over, Who Worked Year-Round, Full-Time, by County, 2023

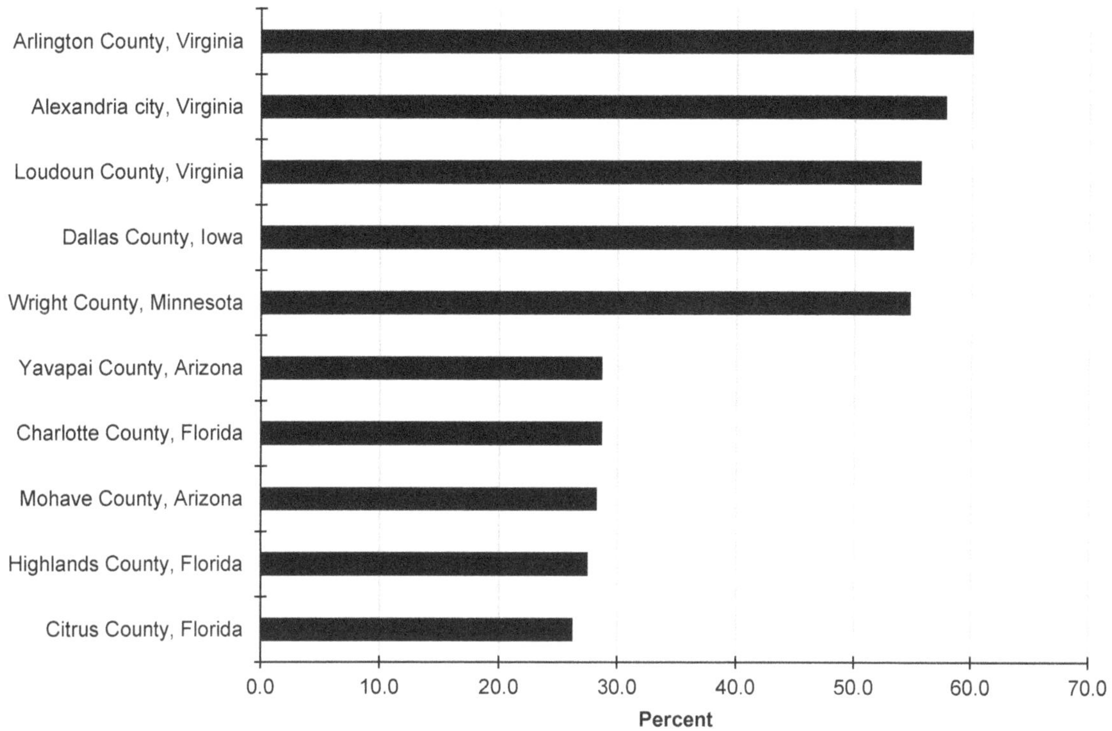

percent of the population age 16 years and old had full-year, full-time employment. At the county level in 2023, Arlington County, Virginia, had the highest proportion of full-year, full-time workers age 16 years and over. Among cities, Arlington CDP, Virginia, had the highest level at 60.1 percent. These levels are not comparable to those presented in editions of this volume before that containing the 2021 data, as previous editions only measured the population age 16 to 64 years.

In 2023, the national unemployment rate, as measured in the ACS, was 4.3 percent, but 17 states, Puerto Rico, and the District of Columbia had higher levels. Puerto Rico, New York, California, and the District of Columbia had unemployment rates at or above 5 percent, and 7 more states had rates above 4.5 percent. Nebraska's unemployment rate was 2.6 percent and 7 other states had rates below 3 percent. Three metropolitan areas outside of Puerto Rico had unemployment rates over 5 percent: Hinesville, Georgia (5.5 percent); Merced, California (5.5 percent); and Bakersfield-Delano, California (5.1 percent). Five cities had unemployment rates over 7 percent, topped by Reading, Pennsylvania, at 8.9 percent.

In the United States, there were just under 69 million children under the age of 18 years old, with just under two-thirds of them living in families with two parents. Both parents were in the labor force for 44.1 percent of children. Another 20.8 percent lived with both parents but only one parent was in the labor force. About 28 percent lived with a single parent who was in the labor force. In eleven states, at least half of the children had two parents in the labor force, with the highest levels in North Dakota, Vermont, and Minnesota, all over 55 percent.

Nearly four out of five employed civilians age 16 years and over worked for private employers in 2023. Twenty-one states had higher levels of private employment, led by Indiana, Michigan, and Pennsylvania, all above 82 percent. Alaska, Wyoming, and the District of Columbia had the lowest levels of private sector employment, all with less than 70 percent of their labor forces employed in the private sector. Nationally, 14.4 percent worked for federal, state, or local government agencies, but in Alaska, New Mexico, and the District of Columbia, government employment provided more than 23 percent of jobs. Wyoming, Maryland, West Virginia, Hawaii, and Virginia also had high levels of government employment, all over 20 percent. Government employment was lowest—under 12 percent—in Michigan, Pennsylvania, and Florida. At the national level, 6.1 percent of workers were self-employed or unpaid family workers. In Puerto Rico, Montana, Maine,

Figure B-3. Class of Worker, Percent Distribution, by States with Greatest and Smallest Numbers of Private Wage and Salary Workers, 2023

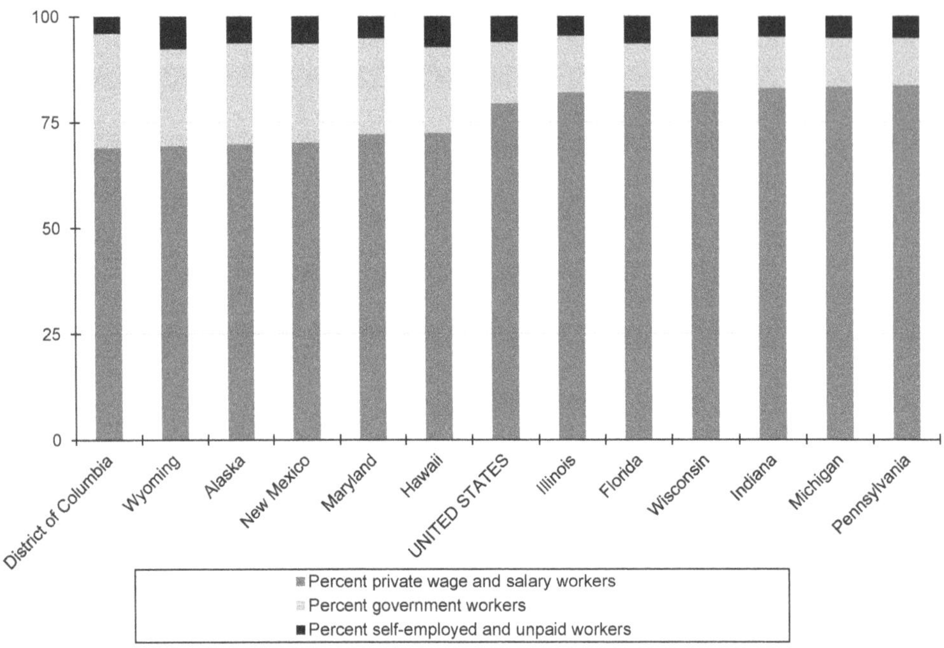

and Vermont, the proportion was over 8 percent. The District of Columbia had the lowest level of self-employment, at 3.9 percent.

Income

The median income for all American households in 2023 inflation-adjusted dollars was $77,719, ranging from highs of $108,210 in the District of Columbia and $96,346 in New Jersey to lows of $54,203 in Mississippi and $26,621 in Puerto Rico. The San Jose-Sunnyvale-Santa Clara, California, metropolitan area had the highest median income of all metropolitan areas, at $153,202. Eight other metropolitan areas had median household incomes above $105,000, including San Francisco-Oakland-Fremont, California; Washington-Arlington-Alexandria, DC-VA-MD-WV; Lexington Park, Maryland; Seattle-Tacoma-Bellevue, Washington; Boston-Cambridge-Newton, MA-NH; Oxnard-Thousand Oaks-Ventura, CA; and Santa Cruz-Watsonville, CA. Excluding Puerto Rico, Eagle Pass, Texas, had the lowest median income, at $46,657. Five other metropolitan areas among the states had median incomes below $51,000, mainly concentrated in the South: Florence, SC; Monroe, LA; Texarkana, TX-AR; Anniston-Oxford, AL; and Terre Haute, IN. Fifty-two of the surveyed counties had 2023 median incomes over $110,000, topped by Loudoun County, Virginia, with a median income of $174,148, and Santa Clara County, California, with a median income of $154,954. Excluding Puerto Rico, McKinley County, New Mexico ($40,108); Apache County, Arizona ($40,539); and Robeson County, North Carolina ($40,996), had the lowest median incomes. In 24 of the 649 cities surveyed, the median household income was over $150,000, topped by Sammamish, Washington; Dublin, California; and San Ramon, California. Cities at the lower end of the income spectrum among the states included Flint, Michigan; Gary, Indiana; Camden, New Jersey; Detroit, Michigan; and Reading, Pennsylvania, all under $39,000.

In the United States in 2023, households headed by 45- to 64-year-olds had higher incomes than other households. Among households of different race and Hispanic origin groups, Asian-headed households had the highest median incomes, followed by non-Hispanic White households. Among household types, married-couple families with children under 18 years old had the highest median incomes. Among individuals, the median income for men was higher than the median income for women. Per capita income is the total aggregate income in the geographic area, divided by the population of the area, resulting in a measure of the income for every man, woman, and child. The per capita income for the United States was $43,313. The District of Columbia had the highest per capita income, at $78,479 (partly because it has a very high proportion of one-person household, and a high proportion of prime working-age residents), followed by Massachusetts, Connecticut, New Jersey, Washington, Colorado, New

Hampshire, Maryland, New York, Virginia, and California, all over $48,000. The lowest per capita incomes were in Puerto Rico, Mississippi, Arkansas, and West Virginia, all under $34,000.

Most American households (75.1 percent) had some wage and salary income in 2023, ranging from 82.9 percent of Utah's households to 64.9 percent of West Virginia's households and 52.0 percent of Puerto Rico's households. Social Security income was reported by 31.3 percent of households. West Virginia had the highest level among states at 40.4 percent, while more than 35 percent of households in 8 other states and Puerto Rico collected Social Security. With younger populations, less than 25 percent of households in the District of Columbia and Utah had income from Social Security.

In 2023, 12.9 percent of households reported income from cash public assistance or SNAP (Supplemental Assistance Nutrition Program, or Food Stamps.) Puerto Rico had a rate of 47.0 percent, while New Mexico (20.8 percent) and West Virginia (18.9 percent) had the highest proportions of households in this group among states. Louisiana, Oregon, New York, Massachusetts, Pennsylvania, Oklahoma, and the District of Columbia all had levels above 15 percent. The lowest levels were in Wyoming, Utah, New Hampshire, North Dakota, and Kansas, all under 8 percent. Interest, dividend, and net rental income were reported by 18.9 percent of households. The highest level, by far, was 47.8 percent of households in Alaska, where many residents receive an annual dividend payment from the state. The lowest level among states was in Mississippi, where only 11.2 percent of households had any income in this category.

About 12.4 percent of American households had incomes over $200,000 in 2023. In the District of Columbia, Massachusetts, New Jersey, California, Maryland, Connecticut, Washington, and Hawaii, the proportion in this income bracket was 17 percent or higher. West Virginia, Puerto Rico, and Mississippi had levels below 6 percent.

In the United States in 2023, 21.5 percent of households had incomes of $150,000 or more. In 16 metropolitan areas, 30 percent or more of households had incomes of $150,000 or more, topped by the San Jose-Sunnyvale-Santa Clara, California, metropolitan area at 49.7 percent and the San

Figure B-4. Top and Bottom Median Household Incomes, by City, 2023

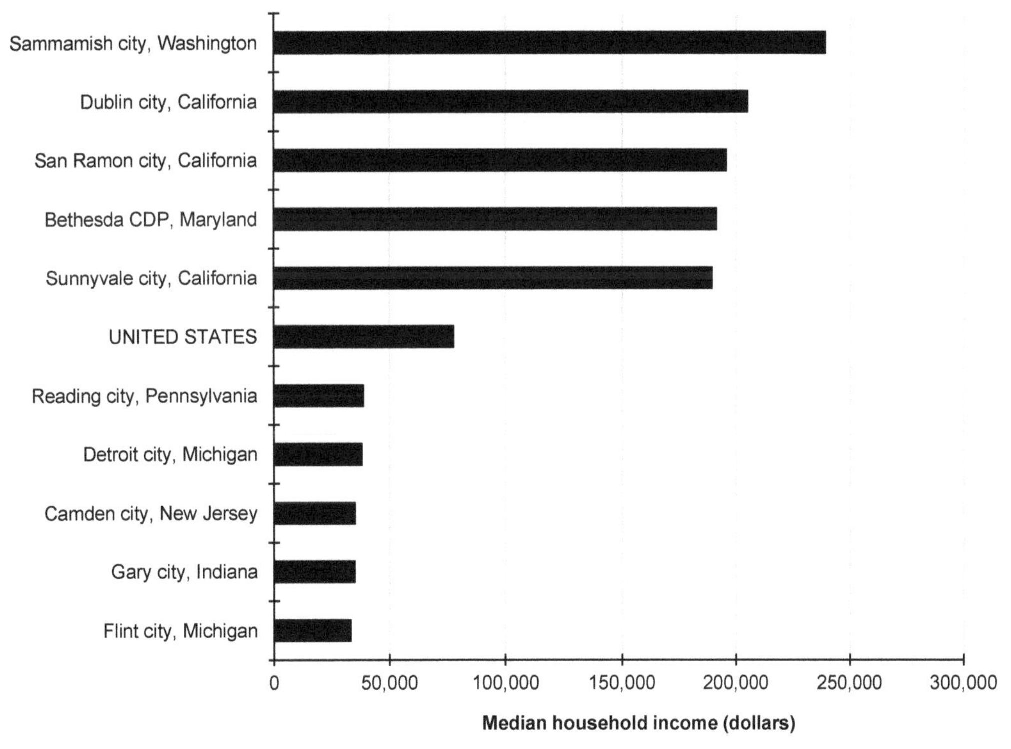

Francisco-Oakland-Berkeley, California, metropolitan area at 43.7 percent. In the Pine Bluff, Arkansas, metropolitan area, only 5 percent of households had incomes in that range. In 30 of the counties supplying 2023 data, more than 40 percent of all households had incomes of $150,000 or more. In 27 additional counties, the proportion of $150,000 households was more than one-third. In 21 counties, including those in Puerto Rico, less than 7 percent of households had incomes in this high range. In 19 cities, more than half of households had incomes of $150,000 or more, with the highest proportion—just over 70 percent—in Sammamish, Washington. Fourteen of the remaining seventeen cities were located in California. In 10 cities, including Flint, Michigan; Canton, Ohio; Albany, Georgia; Reading, Pennsylvania; Camden, New Jersey; and Bowling Green, Kentucky, less than 5 percent of households had these high incomes.

Poverty status is determined by a standard national definition that includes a household or family's income and number of household or family members. In the 2023 ACS, an estimated 12.7 percent of households were below the poverty level. The poverty measure does not vary from state to state despite variations in the cost of living. In Mississippi, Louisiana, New Mexico, and West Virginia, 17 percent or more of households had incomes below the poverty level, with Mississippi and Louisiana at over 19 percent of households. Less than 10 percent of households in Minnesota, Colorado, Utah, and New Hampshire were below the poverty level. In Puerto Rico, 42.2 percent of households were below the poverty level. In all states, poverty rates were higher for female-headed family households.

About 15.2 percent of American households had incomes under $25,000 in 2023, below the weighted average poverty level for a family of four. The proportion was over 20 percent in Puerto Rico, Mississippi, West Virginia, Louisiana, Kentucky, Arkansas, New Mexico, and Alabama, and under 12 percent in Utah, New Hampshire, Colorado, and Maryland. There were 23 cities where more than 30 percent of all households had incomes below $25,000. Flint, Michigan, had the highest level outside of Puerto Rico at just over 41 percent. In 17 cities, this low-income proportion was less than 5 percent of households. In Starr County, Texas; Apache County, Arizona; McKinley County, New Mexico; St, Landry Parish, Louisiana; Bronx County, New York; Robeson County, North Carolina; and Lauderdale County, Mississippi, over 31 percent of households had incomes below $25,000.

Figure B-5. Type of Health Insurance as a Percentage of All Persons, by State, 2023

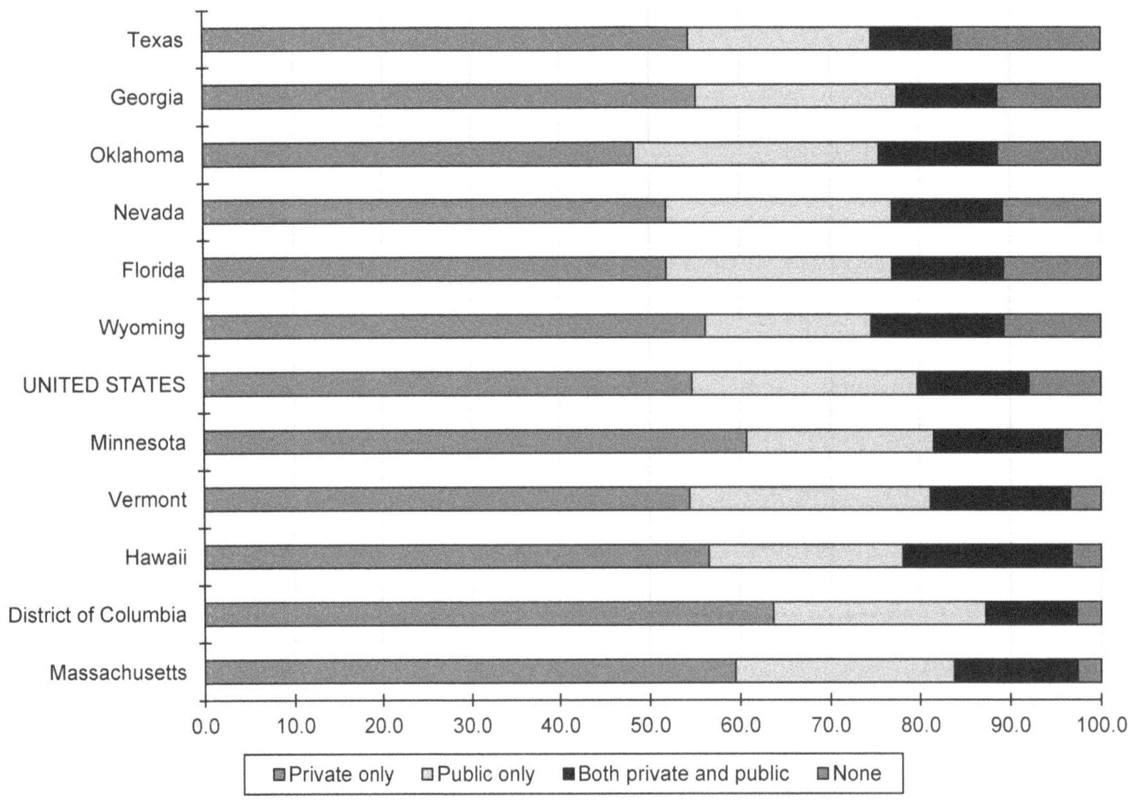

Health Care Coverage

More than 90 percent of Americans had some type of health care coverage (public, private, or both), while nearly 8.0 percent of all Americans had no health care coverage. Massachusetts had the highest percentage of residents with some type of health care coverage, at 97.4 percent. More than 90 percent of residents in 42 other states, Puerto Rico, and the District of Columbia had some health insurance coverage. Texas had the highest percentage of residents with no health care coverage, at 16.4 percent, while about 11.4 percent of residents in Oklahoma and Georgia (respectively) had no health insurance.

A little more than half of all Americans (54.7 percent) had only private health care coverage, while 25.1 percent had only public coverage, and 12.4 percent had both private and public health care coverage. Private insurance is most often employment related but also includes insurance purchased directly by individuals, while public health insurance includes Medicare (primarily for persons age 65 and older), and Medicaid (mainly for low-income persons). Utah and North Dakota had the highest proportions of private health insurance, both over 66 percent, while New Mexico and Puerto Rico had the lowest proportion of private health insurance, at 38.7 percent and 31.7 percent, respectively. New Mexico had the highest proportion of public-only health care coverage among the states, at 36.9 percent. Hawaii had the highest proportion of residents carrying both private and public health care coverage (18.7 percent). Many Medicare recipients carry supplemental private insurance, and several states with large older populations had high proportions with both public and private insurance. The lowest proportions were in Texas, Utah, and Puerto Rico, all under 10 percent.

State Rankings, 2023

Selected Rankings

High school diploma or less rank	State	Percent with a high school diploma or less [B-1, cols. 2 + 3]	Bachelor's degree or more rank	State	Percent with a bachelor's degree or more [B-1, cols. 5 + 6]	Labor force participation rate rank	State	Labor force participation rate [B-1, col. 20]
	UNITED STATES	36.2		**UNITED STATES**	36.2		**UNITED STATES**	63.8
1	West Virginia	50.7	1	District of Columbia	65.9	1	District of Columbia	72.8
2	Louisiana	45.3	2	Massachusetts	47.8	2	Utah	70.2
3	Arkansas	44.9	3	Colorado	46.4	3	North Dakota	69.4
4	Kentucky	43.5	4	New Jersey	43.8	4	Colorado	69.0
5	Indiana	41.7	5	Maryland	43.7	4	Nebraska	69.0
5	Mississippi	41.7	5	Vermont	43.7	6	Minnesota	68.4
7	Alabama	40.9	7	Connecticut	42.9	7	Maryland	67.5
7	Oklahoma	40.9	8	Virginia	42.4	8	South Dakota	67.3
7	Pennsylvania	40.9	9	New Hampshire	40.7	9	Massachusetts	67.2
7	Tennessee	40.9	10	New York	40.6	10	New Jersey	66.9
11	Ohio	39.9	11	Washington	40.5	11	Alaska	66.8
12	Nevada	39.1	12	Minnesota	40.0	12	New Hampshire	66.5
13	South Carolina	38.0	13	Rhode Island	39.0	13	Connecticut	66.4
14	Texas	37.9	14	Utah	38.4	14	Iowa	66.3
15	New Mexico	37.6	15	Illinois	38.3	15	Kansas	66.2
16	Missouri	37.4	16	Oregon	37.7	16	Texas	66.0
17	Delaware	37.1	17	California	37.5	17	Illinois	65.4
18	Georgia	36.9	18	Maine	37.0	18	Virginia	65.3
19	Rhode Island	36.8	18	Hawaii	37.0	19	Wisconsin	65.2
20	Iowa	36.7	20	North Carolina	36.8	20	Washington	65.1
21	Florida	36.6	21	Delaware	36.5	21	Vermont	64.9
22	New York	35.9	22	Kansas	35.8	22	Rhode Island	64.6
22	Alaska	35.9	23	Georgia	35.4	23	Indiana	64.4
24	Wisconsin	35.8	24	Pennsylvania	35.3	24	California	64.3
25	Michigan	35.7	24	Nebraska	35.3	25	Georgia	64.1
26	California	35.6	26	Florida	34.9	26	Missouri	63.9
27	Illinois	34.7	27	Montana	34.6	27	Nevada	63.5
28	New Jersey	34.5	28	Texas	34.2	27	Ohio	63.5
28	Maine	34.5	29	Wisconsin	33.8	27	Wyoming	63.5
30	South Dakota	34.2	30	North Dakota	33.6	30	North Carolina	63.2
31	Arizona	34.0	31	Arizona	33.5	31	New York	63.0
32	North Carolina	33.9	32	South Dakota	33.3	31	Hawaii	63.0
33	Connecticut	33.8	33	Missouri	33.2	31	Montana	63.0
33	Idaho	33.8	34	South Carolina	32.9	34	Pennsylvania	62.8
35	Wyoming	33.6	35	Michigan	32.7	35	Tennessee	62.7
35	Montana	33.6	36	Alaska	32.2	36	Oregon	62.6
37	Kansas	33.4	37	Idaho	32.1	36	Idaho	62.6
38	Hawaii	33.3	38	Ohio	32.0	38	Delaware	62.2
39	Maryland	32.7	39	Tennessee	31.7	39	Maine	62.1
39	New Hampshire	32.7	40	New Mexico	31.6	40	Michigan	61.7
41	Virginia	32.6	41	Iowa	31.5	41	Oklahoma	61.2
42	Nebraska	32.1	42	Wyoming	30.4	42	South Carolina	61.1
43	Vermont	31.6	43	Indiana	30.2	43	Arizona	60.7
44	Massachusetts	31.4	44	Alabama	28.9	44	Kentucky	60.3
45	Oregon	30.1	45	Oklahoma	28.7	45	Florida	60.0
46	North Dakota	29.8	45	Nevada	28.7	46	Louisiana	59.2
47	Washington	29.2	47	Kentucky	27.8	47	Arkansas	58.8
48	Utah	29.1	48	Louisiana	27.0	48	New Mexico	58.6
49	Minnesota	29.0	49	Arkansas	26.2	48	Alabama	58.6
50	Colorado	26.0	50	Mississippi	25.5	50	Mississippi	57.6
51	District of Columbia	20.4	51	West Virginia	24.0	51	West Virginia	54.4

State Rankings, 2023

Selected Rankings

Unemployment rate rank	State	Unemployment rate [B-1, col. 23]	Veterans rank	State	Veterans as a percent of population 18 years and over [B-1, col. 84]	Families with income below poverty rank	State	Percent of households with income below poverty [B-1, col. 138]
	UNITED STATES	4.3		**UNITED STATES**	6.1		**UNITED STATES**	12.7
1	California	5.5	1	Alaska	10.5	1	Mississippi	19.5
2	District of Columbia	5.2	2	Virginia	9.1	2	Louisiana	19.4
3	New York	5.0	3	Montana	8.9	3	New Mexico	17.2
4	Louisiana	4.8	4	Wyoming	8.7	3	West Virginia	17.2
4	Mississippi	4.8	5	South Carolina	8.4	5	Kentucky	16.9
6	Rhode Island	4.7	6	Maine	8.0	6	Arkansas	16.3
6	New Mexico	4.7	7	South Dakota	7.8	7	Oklahoma	16.1
6	New Jersey	4.7	8	Nevada	7.7	8	Alabama	16.0
6	Illinois	4.7	8	Oklahoma	7.7	9	New York	14.5
10	Connecticut	4.6	10	Alabama	7.6	10	South Carolina	14.3
11	Alaska	4.5	10	Idaho	7.6	11	Tennessee	14.2
11	Oklahoma	4.5	10	Washington	7.6	12	Michigan	13.8
11	Nevada	4.5	13	Arizona	7.5	13	Georgia	13.7
11	West Virginia	4.5	13	Delaware	7.5	14	Ohio	13.6
11	Michigan	4.5	13	Hawaii	7.5	15	District of Columbia	13.4
16	Washington	4.4	13	New Hampshire	7.5	16	Texas	13.3
16	Georgia	4.4	17	New Mexico	7.4	17	North Carolina	12.8
16	Texas	4.4	18	Florida	7.3	18	Arizona	12.6
19	Pennsylvania	4.2	18	North Carolina	7.3	18	Florida	12.6
19	Arizona	4.2	20	Colorado	7.2	18	Indiana	12.6
19	South Carolina	4.2	20	Georgia	7.2	21	Missouri	12.5
22	Arkansas	4.1	20	North Dakota	7.2	21	Pennsylvania	12.5
22	Oregon	4.1	20	West Virginia	7.2	23	Illinois	12.3
22	Kentucky	4.1	24	Missouri	7.1	24	Montana	12.2
22	Florida	4.1	24	Tennessee	7.1	24	Oregon	12.2
26	Ohio	4.0	26	Arkansas	7.0	24	Rhode Island	12.2
26	Alabama	4.0	27	Mississippi	6.9	27	California	12.0
26	North Carolina	4.0	28	Oregon	6.8	28	Nevada	11.9
29	Tennessee	3.9	29	Maryland	6.6	29	Kansas	11.7
29	Massachusetts	3.9	29	Nebraska	6.6	30	Iowa	11.6
29	Maryland	3.9	31	Iowa	6.5	30	South Dakota	11.6
32	Colorado	3.7	31	Ohio	6.5	30	Wyoming	11.6
33	Indiana	3.6	33	Kansas	6.4	33	Nebraska	11.5
33	Idaho	3.6	34	Vermont	6.3	34	Massachusetts	11.3
33	Virginia	3.6	35	Kentucky	6.2	35	Connecticut	11.1
36	Delaware	3.4	36	Texas	6.1	35	Maine	11.1
36	Missouri	3.4	37	Indiana	6.0	35	North Dakota	11.1
38	Utah	3.3	38	Pennsylvania	5.9	35	Wisconsin	11.1
38	Hawaii	3.3	38	Wisconsin	5.9	39	Vermont	11.0
40	Kansas	3.2	40	Louisiana	5.8	40	Virginia	10.7
40	Wyoming	3.2	41	Minnesota	5.7	41	Delaware	10.5
40	Maine	3.2	42	Michigan	5.6	42	Alaska	10.4
43	Minnesota	3.0	43	Illinois	4.7	42	Washington	10.4
44	North Dakota	2.8	44	Connecticut	4.5	44	Hawaii	10.3
44	Iowa	2.8	44	Rhode Island	4.5	45	New Jersey	10.2
44	Wisconsin	2.8	46	Utah	4.4	46	Idaho	10.1
47	Montana	2.7	47	California	4.1	47	Maryland	10.0
48	Nebraska	2.6	47	Massachusetts	4.1	48	Minnesota	9.8
48	Vermont	2.6	49	New Jersey	3.6	49	Colorado	9.7
48	South Dakota	2.6	49	New York	3.6	50	Utah	9.2
48	New Hampshire	2.6	51	District of Columbia	3.2	51	New Hampshire	8.3

State Rankings, 2023

Selected Rankings

Median household income rank	State	Median household income (dollars) [B-1. col. 85]	Households with income of less than $25,000 rank	State	Percent of households with income of less than $25,000 [B-1, cols. 123 + 124 + 125]	Households with income of $100,000 or more rank	State	Percent of households with income of $100,000 or more [B-1, col. 130+131+132]
	UNITED STATES	77,719		**UNITED STATES**	15.2		**UNITED STATES**	38.9
1	District of Columbia	108,210	1	Mississippi	24.1	1	District of Columbia	53.0
2	Massachusetts	99,858	2	Louisiana	23.0	2	Massachusetts	49.9
3	New Jersey	99,781	3	West Virginia	22.0	2	New Jersey	49.9
4	Maryland	98,678	4	Kentucky	20.8	4	Maryland	49.5
5	New Hampshire	96,838	5	Arkansas	20.6	5	New Hampshire	48.3
6	California	95,521	6	New Mexico	20.5	6	California	48.1
7	Hawaii	95,322	7	Alabama	20.2	6	Hawaii	48.1
8	Washington	94,605	8	Oklahoma	19.1	8	Washington	47.5
9	Utah	93,421	9	Tennessee	17.2	9	Colorado	46.7
10	Colorado	92,911	9	South Carolina	17.2	10	Utah	46.6
11	Connecticut	91,665	11	Michigan	16.9	11	Connecticut	46.2
12	Virginia	89,931	12	Ohio	16.8	12	Virginia	45.2
13	Alaska	86,631	13	New York	16.7	13	Alaska	43.3
14	Minnesota	85,086	14	Georgia	16.2	14	New York	42.1
15	Rhode Island	84,972	15	Pennsylvania	16.1	14	Minnesota	42.1
16	New York	82,095	16	North Carolina	15.8	16	Rhode Island	42.0
17	Delaware	81,361	16	Missouri	15.8	17	Illinois	40.3
18	Vermont	81,211	16	Montana	15.8	17	Delaware	40.3
19	Illinois	80,306	16	Indiana	15.8	17	Vermont	40.3
20	Oregon	80,160	20	District of Columbia	15.6	20	Oregon	39.6
21	Arizona	77,315	21	Florida	15.1	21	Arizona	38.0
22	North Dakota	76,525	22	Rhode Island	15.0	22	Texas	37.8
23	Nevada	76,364	22	Illinois	15.0	23	Georgia	37.1
24	Texas	75,780	22	Maine	15.0	23	Nevada	37.1
25	Idaho	74,942	25	Texas	14.9	25	North Dakota	37.0
26	Georgia	74,632	25	South Dakota	14.9	26	Pennsylvania	36.5
27	Wisconsin	74,631	25	Wyoming	14.9	27	Wisconsin	36.0
28	Nebraska	74,590	28	Oregon	14.8	28	Maine	35.9
29	Pennsylvania	73,824	28	Kansas	14.8	29	Florida	35.8
30	Maine	73,733	30	North Dakota	14.6	29	Nebraska	35.8
31	Florida	73,311	31	Arizona	14.3	29	Idaho	35.8
32	Wyoming	72,415	31	Wisconsin	14.3	32	North Carolina	34.2
33	South Dakota	71,810	31	Iowa	14.3	33	South Dakota	34.0
34	Iowa	71,433	34	Nebraska	14.2	33	Wyoming	34.0
35	Montana	70,804	35	Vermont	14.1	35	Iowa	33.6
35	North Carolina	70,804	36	Massachusetts	14.0	36	Kansas	33.4
37	Kansas	70,333	36	Nevada	14.0	37	Michigan	33.2
38	Indiana	69,477	38	Connecticut	13.7	37	Montana	33.2
39	Michigan	69,183	39	Virginia	13.0	39	Missouri	32.8
40	Missouri	68,545	40	California	12.9	40	Tennessee	32.7
41	South Carolina	67,804	41	Idaho	12.6	40	Ohio	32.7
42	Ohio	67,769	42	Hawaii	12.4	42	Indiana	32.4
43	Tennessee	67,631	43	Alaska	12.3	43	South Carolina	32.2
44	New Mexico	62,268	44	Minnesota	12.2	44	New Mexico	29.0
45	Alabama	62,212	45	New Jersey	12.1	44	Alabama	29.0
46	Oklahoma	62,138	45	Washington	12.1	44	Oklahoma	29.0
47	Kentucky	61,118	45	Delaware	12.1	47	Kentucky	28.4
48	Arkansas	58,700	48	Maryland	11.8	48	Louisiana	27.8
49	Louisiana	58,229	49	Colorado	11.6	49	Arkansas	26.5
50	West Virginia	55,948	50	New Hampshire	10.7	50	West Virginia	25.0
51	Mississippi	54,203	51	Utah	9.4	51	Mississippi	24.7

County Rankings, 2023

Selected Rankings

High school diploma or less rank	County	Percent with a high school diploma or less [B-2, col. 2]	Bachelor's degree or more rank	County	Percent with a bachelor's degree or more [B-2, col. 3]	Unemployment rate rank	County	Unemployment rate [B-2, col. 6]
	UNITED STATES	36.2		**UNITED STATES**	36.2		**UNITED STATES**	4.3
1	Starr County, Texas	65.1	1	Arlington County, Virginia	78.0	1	Dougherty County, Georgia	6.4
2	Somerset County, Pennsylvania	60.6	2	Alexandria city, Virginia	66.1	2	Walker County, Texas	5.9
3	Merced County, California	59.6	3	District of Columbia, District of Columbia	65.9	3	Liberty County, Georgia	5.7
4	Iberia Parish, Louisiana	58.9	4	Boulder County, Colorado	65.4	4	Merced County, California	5.5
5	Liberty County, Texas	58.6	5	Loudoun County, Virginia	65.2	4	Bronx County, New York	5.5
6	Terrebonne Parish, Louisiana	58.4	6	New York County, New York	64.9	6	Mendocino County, California	5.3
7	Tuscarawas County, Ohio	58.1	7	Fairfax County, Virginia	63.8	7	McKinley County, New Mexico	5.2
8	Northumberland County, Pennsylvania	57.9	8	Hamilton County, Indiana	63.6	8	Kern County, California	5.1
9	Marion County, Ohio	57.8	9	Orange County, North Carolina	63.0	9	Tulare County, California	5.0
10	Cumberland County, New Jersey	57.4	10	Howard County, Maryland	62.5	9	Imperial County, California	5.0
10	Columbiana County, Ohio	57.4	10	Williamson County, Tennessee	62.5	11	Houston County, Georgia	4.9
12	Fayette County, Pennsylvania	56.9	12	Albemarle County, Virginia	61.8	11	Pitt County, North Carolina	4.9
13	Carbon County, Pennsylvania	56.6	13	Douglas County, Colorado	61.7	11	Kings County, California	4.9
14	DeKalb County, Alabama	56.5	14	Montgomery County, Maryland	61.0	14	Wayne County, Indiana	4.8
14	Ector County, Texas	56.5	15	Tompkins County, New York	60.6	14	Apache County, Arizona	4.8
16	Lea County, New Mexico	56.4	16	San Francisco County, California	60.4	16	New York County, New York	4.7
17	Robeson County, North Carolina	56.1	17	Washtenaw County, Michigan	60.2	16	Yuba County, California	4.7
18	Laurens County, South Carolina	55.9	18	Middlesex County, Massachusetts	60.0	18	Jackson County, Mississippi	4.6
19	St. Landry Parish, Louisiana	55.7	19	Marin County, California	59.9	18	Essex County, New Jersey	4.6
19	Schuylkill County, Pennsylvania	55.7	20	Norfolk County, Massachusetts	59.7	18	Wayne County, North Carolina	4.6
21	Yakima County, Washington	55.1	21	Fulton County, Georgia	59.5	21	Fresno County, California	4.5
22	Whitfield County, Georgia	54.8	22	Delaware County, Ohio	59.1	21	Greater Bridgeport Planning Region, Connecticut	4.5
22	Raleigh County, West Virginia	54.8	23	Broomfield County, Colorado	58.8	21	Richmond County, Georgia	4.5
24	Imperial County, California	54.7	23	Wake County, North Carolina	58.8	24	Kershaw County, South Carolina	4.4
25	McKinley County, New Mexico	54.6	25	Hunterdon County, New Jersey	58.7	24	Mason County, Washington	4.4
25	Hidalgo County, Texas	54.6	25	Travis County, Texas	58.7	24	Iberia Parish, Louisiana	4.4
27	Livingston Parish, Louisiana	54.5	27	King County, Washington	58.3	24	Lauderdale County, Mississippi	4.4
28	Blair County, Pennsylvania	54.4	28	Somerset County, New Jersey	58.0	24	Grant County, Washington	4.4
29	Elkhart County, Indiana	54.2	29	Denver County, Colorado	57.9	29	Polk County, Oregon	4.3
30	Madera County, California	53.9	29	Chester County, Pennsylvania	57.9	29	Clayton County, Georgia	4.3
31	Muskingum County, Ohio	53.8	31	Johnson County, Kansas	57.4	29	Madera County, California	4.3
32	Trumbull County, Ohio	53.7	32	Morris County, New Jersey	57.1	29	Kaufman County, Texas	4.3
33	Clearfield County, Pennsylvania	53.6	33	Santa Clara County, California	57.0	33	Shelby County, Tennessee	4.2
34	Potter County, Texas	53.4	33	Durham County, North Carolina	57.0	33	Ouachita Parish, Louisiana	4.2
35	Lebanon County, Pennsylvania	53.3	35	Western Connecticut Planning Region, Connecticut	56.4	33	Vermilion County, Illinois	4.2
36	Mayagüez Municipio, Puerto Rico	53.1	35	Benton County, Oregon	56.4	33	Wayne County, Michigan	4.2
37	Lafourche Parish, Louisiana	52.9	37	Cumberland County, Maine	55.5	33	San Joaquin County, California	4.2
37	Richland County, Ohio	52.9	37	Collin County, Texas	55.5	33	Stanislaus County, California	4.2
39	Tulare County, California	52.8	39	Hennepin County, Minnesota	55.2	33	Bibb County, Georgia	4.2
40	Kings County, California	52.7	40	Forsyth County, Georgia	55.1	40	Sumter County, South Carolina	4.1
41	Ross County, Ohio	52.6	41	San Mateo County, California	54.8	40	Genesee County, Michigan	4.1
41	Greene County, Tennessee	52.6	42	Johnson County, Iowa	54.6	40	Butte County, California	4.1
43	Jefferson County, Arkansas	52.5	43	Chittenden County, Vermont	54.4	40	Atlantic County, New Jersey	4.1
43	Allegany County, Maryland	52.5	44	Washington County, Rhode Island	54.3	40	Peoria County, Illinois	4.1
45	Putnam County, Florida	52.4	45	Monroe County, Indiana	54.2	40	Sacramento County, California	4.1
46	Spalding County, Georgia	52.2	46	Westchester County, New York	54.1	46	Leon County, Florida	4.0
46	Bronx County, New York	52.2	47	Dane County, Wisconsin	53.9	46	Monroe County, Pennsylvania	4.0
46	Creek County, Oklahoma	52.2	48	Story County, Iowa	53.8	46	Harris County, Texas	4.0
49	Ashtabula County, Ohio	51.8	49	Boone County, Indiana	53.7	46	Hinds County, Mississippi	4.0
49	Armstrong County, Pennsylvania	51.8	50	Bergen County, New Jersey	53.3	46	Philadelphia County, Pennsylvania	4.0
51	Vermilion County, Illinois	51.6	51	Douglas County, Kansas	53.2	46	Charles County, Maryland	4.0
52	Lawrence County, Pennsylvania	51.5	52	Jefferson County, Colorado	52.9	52	Bulloch County, Georgia	3.9
52	Cameron County, Texas	51.5	52	Larimer County, Colorado	52.9	52	Hunt County, Texas	3.9
54	Randolph County, North Carolina	51.4	54	Carver County, Minnesota	52.7	52	San Bernardino County, California	3.9
55	Caldwell County, North Carolina	51.3	55	St. Johns County, Florida	52.6	52	Comanche County, Oklahoma	3.9
55	Crawford County, Pennsylvania	51.3	56	Montgomery County, Pennsylvania	52.5	52	Calhoun County, Michigan	3.9
57	San Patricio County, Texas	51.2	57	DuPage County, Illinois	52.4	52	Bradley County, Tennessee	3.9
58	Yuma County, Arizona	50.9	57	Ozaukee County, Wisconsin	52.4	58	Mercer County, New Jersey	3.8
59	Troup County, Georgia	50.8	59	Boone County, Missouri	52.3	58	Providence County, Rhode Island	3.8
59	Scioto County, Ohio	50.8	60	Alameda County, California	51.9	58	Los Angeles County, California	3.8
59	Rockingham County, Virginia	50.8	61	James City County, Virginia	51.8	58	Richland County, South Carolina	3.8
62	Kern County, California	50.7	61	Guaynabo Municipio, Puerto Rico	51.8	58	Ingham County, Michigan	3.8
63	LaPorte County, Indiana	50.6	63	Suffolk County, Massachusetts	51.7	58	Franklin County, Washington	3.8
63	Buchanan County, Missouri	50.6	63	Newport County, Rhode Island	51.7	58	Orange County, Texas	3.8
65	Talladega County, Alabama	50.4	63	Charleston County, South Carolina	51.7	58	Humboldt County, California	3.8
65	Orangeburg County, South Carolina	50.4	66	Cobb County, Georgia	51.6	58	Union County, New Jersey	3.8
65	Angelina County, Texas	50.4	66	Mecklenburg County, North Carolina	51.6	58	Delaware County, Pennsylvania	3.8

County Rankings, 2023—*Continued*

Selected Rankings

High school diploma or less rank	County	Percent with a high school diploma or less [B-2, col. 2]	Bachelor's degree or more rank	County	Percent with a bachelor's degree or more [B-2, col. 3]	Unemployment rate rank	County	Unemployment rate [B-2, col. 6]
68	Pulaski County, Kentucky	50.3	68	Madison County, Mississippi	51.4	58	District of Columbia, District of Columbia	3.8
68	Cattaraugus County, New York	50.3	69	Washington County, Minnesota	51.3	58	Kings County, New York	3.8
70	Wyandotte County, Kansas	50.2	69	Monmouth County, New Jersey	51.3	58	Vigo County, Indiana	3.8
70	Franklin County, Pennsylvania	50.2	71	Oakland County, Michigan	51.1	58	Cook County, Illinois	3.8
70	Augusta County, Virginia	50.2	71	York County, Virginia	51.1	58	East Baton Rouge Parish, Louisiana	3.8
73	Webb County, Texas	50.1	73	Gallatin County, Montana	51.0	73	Rockdale County, Georgia	3.7
74	Jefferson County, Texas	50.0	73	Davidson County, Tennessee	51.0	73	Sutter County, California	3.7
75	Barrow County, Georgia	49.8	75	Alachua County, Florida	50.4	73	Rockingham County, North Carolina	3.7
75	Kosciusko County, Indiana	49.8				73	Cumberland County, New Jersey	3.7
						73	Newton County, Georgia	3.7
						73	Walton County, Georgia	3.7
						73	Prince George's County, Maryland	3.7
						73	Madison County, Tennessee	3.7
						73	Santa Barbara County, California	3.7
						73	Cuyahoga County, Ohio	3.7
						73	Henry County, Georgia	3.7
						73	Navajo County, Arizona	3.7
						73	Christian County, Kentucky	3.7
						73	Saginaw County, Michigan	3.7
						73	Lucas County, Ohio	3.7
						73	Douglas County, Georgia	3.7

County Rankings, 2023

Selected Rankings

Households who received cash public assistance or food stamps/ SNAP rank	County	Percent of households who received cash public assistance or food stamps/ SNAP [B-2, col. 12]	Households with income of less than $25,000 rank	County	Percent of households with income of less than $25,000 [B-2, col. 10]	Households with income of $150,000 or more rank	County	Percent of households with income of $150,000 or more [B-2, col. 11]
	UNITED STATES	12.9		**UNITED STATES**	15.2		**UNITED STATES**	21.5
1	Starr County, Texas	44.1	1	Apache County, Arizona	36.6	1	Loudoun County, Virginia	57.8
2	McKinley County, New Mexico	42.7	1	Starr County, Texas	36.6	2	Santa Clara County, California	51.6
3	Bronx County, New York	40.6	3	McKinley County, New Mexico	36.5	3	San Mateo County, California	50.6
4	Dougherty County, Georgia	37.7	4	St. Landry Parish, Louisiana	31.8	4	Douglas County, Colorado	48.2
5	Robeson County, North Carolina	35.0	4	Bronx County, New York	31.8	5	Howard County, Maryland	47.5
6	Apache County, Arizona	32.7	6	Robeson County, North Carolina	31.7	6	Somerset County, New Jersey	47.4
7	Klamath County, Oregon	30.8	7	Lauderdale County, Mississippi	31.1	7	Nassau County, New York	47.2
8	Imperial County, California	29.5	8	Dougherty County, Georgia	29.6	7	Fairfax County, Virginia	47.2
9	Hampden County, Massachusetts	29.3	9	Iberia Parish, Louisiana	27.4	9	Arlington County, Virginia	46.9
10	Valencia County, New Mexico	27.8	10	Bibb County, Georgia	26.8	10	Marin County, California	46.6
11	Philadelphia County, Pennsylvania	27.7	11	Orleans Parish, Louisiana	26.7	11	Morris County, New Jersey	45.5
12	Hidalgo County, Texas	27.3	12	Jefferson County, Arkansas	26.6	12	Hunterdon County, New Jersey	45.3
13	Fayette County, Pennsylvania	27.2	12	Vigo County, Indiana	26.6	13	Forsyth County, Georgia	44.6
14	Lake County, California	26.9	14	St. Lawrence County, New York	26.5	14	Stafford County, Virginia	44.3
15	Tulare County, California	26.0	15	Navajo County, Arizona	26.4	15	San Francisco County, California	44.2
15	Otero County, New Mexico	26.0	15	Ouachita Parish, Louisiana	26.4	16	Williamson County, Tennessee	44.1
15	Orangeburg County, South Carolina	26.0	17	Anderson County, Tennessee	26.2	17	Prince William County, Virginia	43.2
18	Humboldt County, California	25.9	18	Orangeburg County, South Carolina	26.0	18	Montgomery County, Maryland	42.8
19	Madera County, California	25.8	19	Payne County, Oklahoma	25.9	19	Norfolk County, Massachusetts	42.4
20	Bibb County, Georgia	25.5	19	Klamath County, Oregon	25.9	19	Delaware County, Ohio	42.4
21	Iberia Parish, Louisiana	25.3	21	Lake County, California	25.8	21	Carver County, Minnesota	42.1
22	Doña Ana County, New Mexico	25.1	21	Hinds County, Mississippi	25.8	22	Western Connecticut Planning Region, Connecticut	42.0
23	Vermilion County, Illinois	25.0	21	Putnam County, Tennessee	25.8	23	Middlesex County, Massachusetts	41.7
24	Josephine County, Oregon	24.8	24	Cochise County, Arizona	25.7	24	Oldham County, Kentucky	41.3
25	Lea County, New Mexico	24.7	24	Clarke County, Georgia	25.7	25	Contra Costa County, California	41.2
26	Fresno County, California	24.6	24	Angelina County, Texas	25.7	26	Alameda County, California	40.8
27	Kings County, New York	24.3	27	Lowndes County, Georgia	25.6	27	Calvert County, Maryland	40.7
27	Cameron County, Texas	24.3	27	Forrest County, Mississippi	25.6	28	King County, Washington	40.5
29	Yakima County, Washington	24.2	29	Caddo Parish, Louisiana	25.5	29	Westchester County, New York	40.2
30	Macon County, Illinois	24.1	29	Hidalgo County, Texas	25.5	30	Suffolk County, New York	40.1
31	Wayne County, Michigan	23.9	31	Richmond County, Georgia	25.3	31	Chester County, Pennsylvania	39.8
32	Butte County, California	23.7	32	DeKalb County, Alabama	25.2	32	Putnam County, New York	39.6
33	Portsmouth city, Virginia	23.6	32	Grant County, Indiana	25.2	33	Hamilton County, Indiana	39.5
34	Webb County, Texas	23.5	32	Columbiana County, Ohio	25.2	34	Monmouth County, New Jersey	39.4
35	Winnebago County, Illinois	23.4	35	White County, Arkansas	25.1	35	Bergen County, New Jersey	39.1
36	Polk County, Oregon	23.2	35	Vermilion County, Illinois	25.1	36	Collin County, Texas	38.6
37	Kern County, California	22.8	35	Rapides Parish, Louisiana	25.1	37	District of Columbia, District of Columbia	38.1
37	Douglas County, Oregon	22.8	35	Muskogee County, Oklahoma	25.1	38	New York County, New York	38.0
39	Kings County, California	22.6	39	Garland County, Arkansas	24.9	39	Frederick County, Maryland	37.5
39	Linn County, Oregon	22.6	39	Fayette County, Pennsylvania	24.9	40	Fauquier County, Virginia	37.1
41	Bristol County, Massachusetts	22.5	41	Walker County, Texas	24.8	41	Napa County, California	36.5
42	Baltimore city, Maryland	22.4	42	Lackawanna County, Pennsylvania	24.7	41	Anne Arundel County, Maryland	36.5
43	Umatilla County, Oregon	22.3	43	Lee County, Alabama	24.6	43	Alexandria city, Virginia	36.2
44	Ouachita Parish, Louisiana	22.2	43	Muscogee County, Georgia	24.6	44	Rockingham County, New Hampshire	36.1
44	Muskegon County, Michigan	22.2	45	Bulloch County, Georgia	24.5	45	Carroll County, Maryland	35.9
46	Suffolk County, Massachusetts	22.0	45	Jones County, Mississippi	24.5	46	Orange County, California	35.7
47	Muskingum County, Ohio	21.9	45	Nacogdoches County, Texas	24.5	47	Placer County, California	35.6
47	Blair County, Pennsylvania	21.9	48	Etowah County, Alabama	24.4	48	Rockland County, New York	35.1
49	Miami-Dade County, Florida	21.8	48	Baltimore city, Maryland	24.4	49	Broomfield County, Colorado	35.0
49	Caddo Parish, Louisiana	21.8	48	Montgomery County, Virginia	24.4	50	Denton County, Texas	34.6
49	Raleigh County, West Virginia	21.8	51	Scioto County, Ohio	24.3	51	Ventura County, California	34.4
52	Allegany County, Maryland	21.7	52	Hamblen County, Tennessee	24.2	51	Lake County, Illinois	34.4
53	Wayne County, North Carolina	21.6	53	Brazos County, Texas	24.1	51	Bucks County, Pennsylvania	34.4
54	Muskogee County, Oklahoma	21.5	54	Lafourche Parish, Louisiana	24.0	54	Middlesex County, New Jersey	34.3
55	Lafourche Parish, Louisiana	21.4	54	St. Louis city, Missouri	24.0	55	Montgomery County, Pennsylvania	34.2
55	Androscoggin County, Maine	21.4	54	Cattaraugus County, New York	24.0	56	DuPage County, Illinois	34.0
55	San Juan County, New Mexico	21.4	54	Philadelphia County, Pennsylvania	24.0	56	Plymouth County, Massachusetts	34.0
55	Wilson County, North Carolina	21.4	58	Champaign County, Illinois	23.8	58	Williamson County, Texas	33.5
59	Merced County, California	21.3	58	Wayne County, Michigan	23.8	59	Boone County, Indiana	33.4
59	Clayton County, Georgia	21.3	58	Greenwood County, South Carolina	23.8	59	Washington County, Minnesota	33.4
61	Mendocino County, California	21.2	58	Raleigh County, West Virginia	23.8	59	Fort Bend County, Texas	33.4
61	Erie County, Pennsylvania	21.2	62	Mohave County, Arizona	23.7	59	Spotsylvania County, Virginia	33.4
63	Luzerne County, Pennsylvania	21.1	62	Tangipahoa Parish, Louisiana	23.7	63	York County, Virginia	33.3
64	Pueblo County, Colorado	21.0	62	Doña Ana County, New Mexico	23.7	64	St. Johns County, Florida	33.2
64	Richmond County, Georgia	21.0	65	Wayne County, Indiana	23.6	65	San Diego County, California	33.1
64	Aroostook County, Maine	21.0	65	Portsmouth city, Virginia	23.6	66	El Dorado County, California	32.9
64	St. Francois County, Missouri	21.0	67	Highlands County, Florida	23.4	66	James City County, Virginia	32.9
64	Chautauqua County, New York	21.0	67	Muskingum County, Ohio	23.4	68	Snohomish County, Washington	32.8
69	Surry County, North Carolina	20.9	69	Citrus County, Florida	23.3	69	Boulder County, Colorado	32.7
70	Shiawassee County, Michigan	20.8	69	Creek County, Oklahoma	23.3	69	Jefferson County, Colorado	32.7
71	Cleveland County, North Carolina	20.7	69	Cameron County, Texas	23.3	69	Union County, New Jersey	32.7
72	Lackawanna County, Pennsylvania	20.5	72	Tuscaloosa County, Alabama	23.2	72	Santa Cruz County, California	32.6
72	Nacogdoches County, Texas	20.5	72	Walker County, Georgia	23.2	73	Sussex County, New Jersey	32.5
74	Lane County, Oregon	20.4	72	Trumbull County, Ohio	23.2	73	Wake County, North Carolina	32.5
74	Milwaukee County, Wisconsin	20.4	72	Pottawatomie County, Oklahoma	23.2	73	Hanover County, Virginia	32.5

Metropolitan Area Rankings, 2023

Selected Rankings

High school diploma or less rank	Area name	Percent with a high school diploma or less [B-3, col. 2]	Bachelor's degree or more rank	Area name	Percent with a bachelor's degree or more [B-3, col. 3]
	UNITED STATES	36.2		**UNITED STATES**	36.2
1	Eagle Pass, TX	60.9	1	Boulder, CO	65.4
2	Merced, CA	59.6	2	Ithaca, NY	60.6
3	Vineland, NJ	57.4	3	Ann Arbor, MI	60.2
4	Odessa, TX	56.5	4	Corvallis, OR	56.4
5	Houma-Bayou Cane-Thibodaux, LA	55.7	5	San Jose-Sunnyvale-Santa Clara, CA	55.8
6	Dalton, GA	55.3	6	Charlottesville, VA	55.5
7	Beckley, WV	55.1	7	Washington-Arlington-Alexandria, DC-VA-MD-WV	54.8
7	Yakima, WA	55.1	8	Durham-Chapel Hill, NC	54.7
9	El Centro, CA	54.7	9	Lawrence, KS	53.2
10	McAllen-Edinburg-Mission, TX	54.6	10	San Francisco-Oakland-Fremont, CA	53.1
11	Altoona, PA	54.4	11	Fort Collins-Loveland, CO	52.9
12	Elkhart-Goshen, IN	54.2	12	Raleigh-Cary, NC	52.7
13	Lebanon, PA	53.3	13	Boston-Cambridge-Newton, MA-NH	52.2
14	Mansfield, OH	52.9	14	Austin-Round Rock-San Marcos, TX	52.1
15	Visalia, CA	52.8	15	Bridgeport-Stamford-Danbury, CT	51.9
16	Hanford-Corcoran, CA	52.7	16	Bozeman, MT	51.0
17	Aguadilla, PR	52.4	17	Iowa City, IA	50.7
18	Brownsville-Harlingen, TX	51.5	18	Amherst Town-Northampton, MA	50.2
19	Texarkana, TX-AR	51.1	19	Denver-Aurora-Centennial, CO	49.9
20	Yuma, AZ	50.9	20	Barnstable Town, MA	49.8
21	Bakersfield-Delano, CA	50.7	21	Bloomington, IL	49.6
22	Guayama, PR	50.6	22	Madison, WI	49.2
22	Michigan City-La Porte, IN	50.6	23	Columbia, MO	49.0
24	Chambersburg, PA	50.2	24	Seattle-Tacoma-Bellevue, WA	48.6
25	Laredo, TX	50.1	25	Burlington-South Burlington, VT	48.5
25	Rocky Mount, NC	50.1	26	Ames, IA	48.3
27	Morristown, TN	49.7	27	Portland-South Portland, ME	48.0
28	Weirton-Steubenville, WV-OH	49.6	28	Bloomington, IN	47.7
29	Reading, PA	49.5	29	State College, PA	47.6
29	Youngstown-Warren, OH	49.5	30	Hilton Head Island-Bluffton-Port Royal, SC	47.0
31	Johnstown, PA	49.4	31	Missoula, MT	46.8
31	St. Joseph, MO-KS	49.4	32	Athens-Clarke County, GA	46.7
33	Alexandria, LA	49.3	33	Minneapolis-St. Paul-Bloomington, MN-WI	46.2
33	Florence, SC	49.3	34	Santa Fe, NM	45.9
35	Beaumont-Port Arthur, TX	49.2	35	Provo-Orem-Lehi, UT	45.4
36	Mayagüez, PR	49.1	36	Champaign-Urbana, IL	45.3
37	Salinas, CA	49.0	37	Trenton-Princeton, NJ	45.2
38	Jackson, TN	48.9	38	Asheville, NC	44.7
39	Terre Haute, IN	48.7	39	Huntsville, AL	44.6
40	Gettysburg, PA	48.6	39	New York-Newark-Jersey City, NY-NJ	44.6
41	Dothan, AL	48.5	41	Lexington-Fayette, KY	44.5
41	Lima, OH	48.5	42	Baltimore-Columbia-Towson, MD	44.4
41	Modesto, CA	48.5	42	Santa Cruz-Watsonville, CA	44.4
44	Hammond, LA	48.3	44	Colorado Springs, CO	44.2
45	Lafayette, LA	48.2	45	Pinehurst-Southern Pines, NC	44.1
46	Hagerstown-Martinsburg, MD-WV	47.7	46	Portland-Vancouver-Hillsboro, OR-WA	43.8
47	Homosassa Springs, FL	47.4	47	San Diego-Chula Vista-Carlsbad, CA	43.5
48	Huntington-Ashland, WV-KY-OH	47.3	48	Gainesville, FL	43.3
48	Lake Havasu City-Kingman, AZ	47.3	49	Fargo, ND-MN	42.9
50	Albany, GA	47.2	50	Manchester-Nashua, NH	42.8
50	Grand Island, NE	47.2	50	Rochester, MN	42.8
50	Lancaster, PA	47.2	52	Atlanta-Sandy Springs-Roswell, GA	42.6
50	Staunton-Stuarts Draft, VA	47.2	52	Kalamazoo-Portage, MI	42.6
54	Lewiston-Auburn, ME	47.1	54	Hartford-West Hartford-East Hartford, CT	42.5
54	Salisbury, MD	47.1	55	Nashville-Davidson--Murfreesboro--Franklin, TN	42.4
56	Fort Smith, AR-OK	46.9	55	New Haven, CT	42.4
56	Goldsboro, NC	46.9	57	Philadelphia-Camden-Wilmington, PA-NJ-DE-MD	42.3
56	Springfield, OH	46.9	58	Charleston-North Charleston, SC	42.2
59	Stockton-Lodi, CA	46.8	59	Bend, OR	42.1
59	Victoria, TX	46.8	59	Chicago-Naperville-Elgin, IL-IN	42.1
61	Enid, OK	46.7	59	San Luis Obispo-Paso Robles, CA	42.1
61	Gadsden, AL	46.7	62	Lincoln, NE	42.0
63	Decatur, AL	46.6	63	Richmond, VA	41.9
63	Kokomo, IN	46.6	64	Logan, UT-ID	41.6
65	Charleston, WV	46.5	65	Worcester, MA	41.4
66	Arecibo, PR	46.2	66	Albany-Schenectady-Troy, NY	41.3
66	Gainesville, GA	46.2	66	Charlotte-Concord-Gastonia, NC-SC	41.3
66	Ponce, PR	46.2	68	Olympia-Lacey-Tumwater, WA	41.0
69	Scranton--Wilkes-Barre, PA	46.1	69	Traverse City, MI	40.9
70	Harrisonburg, VA	46.0	70	Kansas City, MO-KS	40.8
70	York-Hanover, PA	46.0	71	Wilmington, NC	40.7
72	Fresno, CA	45.9	72	Milwaukee-Waukesha, WI	40.5
72	Lake Charles, LA	45.9	72	Tallahassee, FL	40.5
74	Springfield, MA	45.7	74	Columbus, OH	40.3
75	Parkersburg-Vienna, WV	45.6	75	Naples-Marco Island, FL	40.1
75	Sebring, FL	45.6	75	Omaha, NE-IA	40.1
75	Sumter, SC	45.6			

Metropolitan Area Rankings, 2023

Selected Rankings

Unemploy-ment rate rank	Area name	Unemployment rate [B-3, col. 6]	Households who received cash public assistance or food stamps/SNAP rank	Area name	Percent of households who received cash public assistance or food stamps/SNAP [B-2, col. 12]
	UNITED STATES	4.3		**UNITED STATES**	12.9
1	Ponce, PR	6.9	1	Ponce, PR	54.2
2	Mayagüez, PR	6.7	2	Arecibo, PR	53.5
3	Hinesville, GA	5.5	3	Aguadilla, PR	53.3
3	Merced, CA	5.5	4	Guayama, PR	52.9
5	Bakersfield-Delano, CA	5.1	5	Mayagüez, PR	48.3
6	El Centro, CA	5.0	6	San Juan-Bayamón-Caguas, PR	43.3
6	Visalia, CA	5.0	7	Eagle Pass, TX	33.2
8	Aguadilla, PR	4.9	8	Albany, GA	30.7
8	Greenville, NC	4.9	9	El Centro, CA	29.5
8	Hanford-Corcoran, CA	4.9	10	Springfield, MA	29.3
11	Arecibo, PR	4.7	11	McAllen-Edinburg-Mission, TX	27.3
11	Warner Robins, GA	4.7	12	Visalia, CA	26.0
13	Goldsboro, NC	4.6	13	Las Cruces, NM	25.1
14	Albany, GA	4.5	14	Fresno, CA	24.8
14	Fresno, CA	4.5	14	Grants Pass, OR	24.8
16	Eagle Pass, TX	4.3	16	Brownsville-Harlingen, TX	24.3
17	Modesto, CA	4.2	17	Yakima, WA	24.2
17	Monroe, LA	4.2	18	Decatur, IL	24.1
17	Stockton-Lodi, CA	4.2	19	Chico, CA	23.7
17	Yuba City, CA	4.2	20	Laredo, TX	23.5
21	Chico, CA	4.1	21	Monroe, LA	23.3
21	Flint, MI	4.1	22	Bakersfield-Delano, CA	22.8
21	Sumter, SC	4.1	23	Rocky Mount, NC	22.7
24	Battle Creek, MI	3.9	24	Albany, OR	22.6
25	Florence, SC	3.8	24	Hanford-Corcoran, CA	22.6
25	Trenton-Princeton, NJ	3.8	26	Rockford, IL	22.3
27	Atlantic City-Hammonton, NJ	3.7	27	Muskegon-Norton Shores, MI	22.2
27	Grand Island, NE	3.7	28	Altoona, PA	21.9
27	Jackson, TN	3.7	29	Goldsboro, NC	21.6
27	Lawton, OK	3.7	30	Farmington, NM	21.4
27	Memphis, TN-MS-AR	3.7	30	Lewiston-Auburn, ME	21.4
27	Sacramento-Roseville-Folsom, CA	3.7	32	Merced, CA	21.3
27	Saginaw, MI	3.7	33	Erie, PA	21.2
27	San Juan-Bayamón-Caguas, PR	3.7	34	Pueblo, CO	21.0
27	Santa Maria-Santa Barbara, CA	3.7	35	Macon-Bibb County, GA	20.7
27	Vineland, NJ	3.7	35	Scranton--Wilkes-Barre, PA	20.7
37	Cleveland, TN	3.6	37	Salem, OR	20.6
37	Los Angeles-Long Beach-Anaheim, CA	3.6	38	Eugene-Springfield, OR	20.4
37	Macon-Bibb County, GA	3.6	39	Johnstown, PA	20.3
37	Mansfield, OH	3.6	39	Vineland, NJ	20.3
37	Rockford, IL	3.6	41	Saginaw, MI	20.1
37	Santa Cruz-Watsonville, CA	3.6	42	El Paso, TX	20.0
37	Tallahassee, FL	3.6	42	Flint, MI	20.0
44	Bridgeport-Stamford-Danbury, CT	3.5	42	Parkersburg-Vienna, WV	20.0
44	Decatur, IL	3.5	45	Rome, GA	19.9
44	Fayetteville, NC	3.5	46	Beckley, WV	19.8
44	Gadsden, AL	3.5	47	Alexandria, LA	19.7
44	Hammond, LA	3.5	47	Charleston, WV	19.7
44	Houston-Pasadena-The Woodlands, TX	3.5	47	Gadsden, AL	19.7
44	Lawrence, KS	3.5	50	Walla Walla, WA	19.6
44	Riverside-San Bernardino-Ontario, CA	3.5	51	Hammond, LA	19.5
44	Tuscaloosa, AL	3.5	52	Fayetteville, NC	19.3
44	Waterbury-Shelton, CT	3.5	52	Longview-Kelso, WA	19.3
54	Corvallis, OR	3.4	52	Medford, OR	19.3
54	Eugene-Springfield, OR	3.4	55	Salisbury, MD	19.2
54	Farmington, NM	3.4	56	Albuquerque, NM	19.1
54	Flagstaff, AZ	3.4	57	Kankakee, IL	19.0
54	Janesville-Beloit, WI	3.4	57	Lawton, OK	19.0
54	New York-Newark-Jersey City, NY-NJ	3.4	59	Houma-Bayou Cane-Thibodaux, LA	18.9
54	Oxnard-Thousand Oaks-Ventura, CA	3.4	60	Dothan, AL	18.8

Metropolitan Area Rankings, 2023—*Continued*

Selected Rankings

Unemploy-ment rate rank	Area name	Unemployment rate [B-3, col. 6]	Households who received cash public assistance or food stamps/SNAP rank	Area name	Percent of households who received cash public assistance or food stamps/SNAP [B-2, col. 12]
54	Terre Haute, IN	3.4	61	Shreveport-Bossier City, LA	18.7
54	Walla Walla, WA	3.4	62	Worcester, MA	18.6
63	Auburn-Opelika, AL	3.3	63	Mansfield, OH	18.5
63	Brownsville-Harlingen, TX	3.3	63	Pittsfield, MA	18.5
63	Cheyenne, WY	3.3	65	Lake Charles, LA	18.2
63	Chicago-Naperville-Elgin, IL-IN	3.3	65	Springfield, OH	18.2
63	Columbia, SC	3.3	67	Anniston-Oxford, AL	18.1
63	Elmira, NY	3.3	67	Sumter, SC	18.1
63	Gulfport-Biloxi, MS	3.3	67	Weirton-Steubenville, WV-OH	18.1
63	Kennewick-Richland, WA	3.3	67	Yuma, AZ	18.1
63	Las Cruces, NM	3.3	71	Bay City, MI	18.0
63	Lima, OH	3.3	71	Enid, OK	18.0
63	Manhattan, KS	3.3	71	Utica-Rome, NY	18.0
63	McAllen-Edinburg-Mission, TX	3.3	74	Valdosta, GA	17.9
63	San Francisco-Oakland-Fremont, CA	3.3	75	Bangor, ME	17.8
63	Yuma, AZ	3.3			

Metropolitan Area Rankings, 2023

Selected Rankings

Households with income of less than $25,000 rank	County	Percent of households with income of less than $25,000 [B-3, col. 10]	Households with income of $150,000 or more rank	Area name	Percent of households with income of $150,000 or more [B-3, col. 11]
	UNITED STATES	15.2		**UNITED STATES**	21.5
1	Mayagüez, PR	56.6	1	San Jose-Sunnyvale-Santa Clara, CA	51.0
2	Guayama, PR	55.6	2	San Francisco-Oakland-Fremont, CA	43.4
2	Ponce, PR	55.6	3	Washington-Arlington-Alexandria, DC-VA-MD-WV	40.3
4	Aguadilla, PR	54.7	4	Bridgeport-Stamford-Danbury, CT	38.3
5	Arecibo, PR	46.8	5	Boston-Cambridge-Newton, MA-NH	36.8
6	San Juan-Bayamón-Caguas, PR	45.9	6	Napa, CA	36.5
7	Eagle Pass, TX	29.0	7	Seattle-Tacoma-Bellevue, WA	36.1
8	Monroe, LA	28.2	8	Lexington Park, MD	35.7
9	Auburn-Opelika, AL	25.8	9	Oxnard-Thousand Oaks-Ventura, CA	34.4
10	Sierra Vista-Douglas, AZ	25.7	10	San Diego-Chula Vista-Carlsbad, CA	33.1
11	Valdosta, GA	25.6	11	Boulder, CO	32.7
12	McAllen-Edinburg-Mission, TX	25.5	12	Santa Cruz-Watsonville, CA	32.6
13	Albany, GA	25.4	13	Denver-Aurora-Centennial, CO	32.3
14	Hot Springs, AR	24.9	14	New York-Newark-Jersey City, NY-NJ	31.7
15	Tuscaloosa, AL	24.8	15	Manchester-Nashua, NH	31.5
16	Texarkana, TX-AR	24.6	16	Santa Rosa-Petaluma, CA	31.3
17	Alexandria, LA	24.5	17	Urban Honolulu, HI	31.1
18	Florence, SC	24.4	18	Austin-Round Rock-San Marcos, TX	30.4
18	Gadsden, AL	24.4	19	Trenton-Princeton, NJ	30.3
20	Terre Haute, IN	24.2	20	Vallejo, CA	29.7
21	Columbus, GA-AL	23.9	21	Raleigh-Cary, NC	29.3
22	Hammond, LA	23.7	22	Los Angeles-Long Beach-Anaheim, CA	29.1
22	Lake Havasu City-Kingman, AZ	23.7	23	Baltimore-Columbia-Towson, MD	28.7
22	Las Cruces, NM	23.7	24	Kiryas Joel-Poughkeepsie-Newburgh, NY	28.6
25	Huntington-Ashland, WV-KY-OH	23.6	25	Bremerton-Silverdale-Port Orchard, WA	28.3
25	Weirton-Steubenville, WV-OH	23.6	26	Anchorage, AK	28.2
27	Sebring, FL	23.4	27	Worcester, MA	28.0
28	Brownsville-Harlingen, TX	23.3	28	Sacramento-Roseville-Folsom, CA	27.9
28	Homosassa Springs, FL	23.3	29	Hartford-West Hartford-East Hartford, CT	27.5
30	Charleston, WV	23.2	30	Barnstable Town, MA	27.4
30	College Station-Bryan, TX	23.2	30	Minneapolis-St. Paul-Bloomington, MN-WI	27.4
30	Hattiesburg, MS	23.2	30	Santa Maria-Santa Barbara, CA	27.4
33	Elmira, NY	23.1	33	Portland-Vancouver-Hillsboro, OR-WA	27.2
33	Youngstown-Warren, OH	23.1	34	Charlottesville, VA	26.6
35	Sumter, SC	23.0	34	Naples-Marco Island, FL	26.6
36	Altoona, PA	22.9	36	Ogden, UT	26.3
36	El Centro, CA	22.9	36	Provo-Orem-Lehi, UT	26.3
38	Lafayette, LA	22.7	36	Salt Lake City-Murray, UT	26.3
38	Shreveport-Bossier City, LA	22.7	36	San Luis Obispo-Paso Robles, CA	26.3
40	New Orleans-Metairie, LA	22.6	40	Philadelphia-Camden-Wilmington, PA-NJ-DE-MD	26.1
41	Anniston-Oxford, AL	22.5	41	Chicago-Naperville-Elgin, IL-IN	25.6
41	Macon-Bibb County, GA	22.5	41	Salinas, CA	25.6
43	Champaign-Urbana, IL	22.4	43	Ann Arbor, MI	25.5
43	Merced, CA	22.4	43	Kahului-Wailuku, HI	25.5
45	Dothan, AL	22.3	45	Dallas-Fort Worth-Arlington, TX	25.3
45	Kingsport-Bristol, TN-VA	22.3	46	Durham-Chapel Hill, NC	25.1
45	San Angelo, TX	22.3	46	Stockton-Lodi, CA	25.1
48	Scranton--Wilkes-Barre, PA	22.2	48	Fort Collins-Loveland, CO	25.0
49	El Paso, TX	22.1	49	Atlanta-Sandy Springs-Roswell, GA	24.8
50	Johnson City, TN	21.9	50	Burlington-South Burlington, VT	24.7
50	Mobile, AL	21.9	51	Bend, OR	24.2
52	Laredo, TX	21.8	51	Riverside-San Bernardino-Ontario, CA	24.2
52	Morgantown, WV	21.8	53	Colorado Springs, CO	24.1
54	Blacksburg-Christiansburg-Radford, VA	21.7	53	Corvallis, OR	24.1
55	Beckley, WV	21.6	53	Greeley, CO	24.1
56	Chico, CA	21.5	56	New Haven, CT	24.0
56	Greenville, NC	21.5	57	Mount Vernon-Anacortes, WA	23.8
56	Jackson, MS	21.5	58	Bozeman, MT	23.7
56	Parkersburg-Vienna, WV	21.5	58	Portland-South Portland, ME	23.7
60	Athens-Clarke County, GA	21.3	60	Amherst Town-Northampton, MA	23.3
61	Waco, TX	21.1	60	Norwich-New London-Willimantic, CT	23.3
62	Lake Charles, LA	21.0	60	Providence-Warwick, RI-MA	23.3
63	Cape Girardeau, MO-IL	20.9	63	Phoenix-Mesa-Chandler, AZ	23.1
63	Springfield, MA	20.9	63	Rochester, MN	23.1
65	Jackson, TN	20.8	65	Midland, TX	23.0
65	Johnstown, PA	20.8	65	Richmond, VA	23.0
65	Rocky Mount, NC	20.8	67	Waterbury-Shelton, CT	22.8

Metropolitan Area Rankings, 2023—*Continued*

Selected Rankings

Households with income of less than $25,000 rank	County	Percent of households with income of less than $25,000 [B-3, col. 10]	Households with income of $150,000 or more rank	Area name	Percent of households with income of $150,000 or more [B-3, col. 11]
68	Rome, GA	20.7	68	Charlotte-Concord-Gastonia, NC-SC	22.5
69	Bay City, MI	20.6	68	Nashville-Davidson--Murfreesboro--Franklin, TN	22.5
70	Muncie, IN	20.5	70	Houston-Pasadena-The Woodlands, TX	22.4
71	Houma-Bayou Cane-Thibodaux, LA	20.4	70	Huntsville, AL	22.4
71	Wheeling, WV-OH	20.4	72	Atlantic City-Hammonton, NJ	22.3
73	Brunswick-St. Simons, GA	20.3	73	Bloomington, IL	22.1
73	Cleveland, TN	20.3	73	Madison, WI	22.1
73	Farmington, NM	20.3	73	Santa Fe, NM	22.1

City Rankings, 2023

Selected Rankings

High school diploma or less rank	City	Percent with a high school diploma or less [B-4, col. 2]	Bachelor's degree or more rank	City	Percent with a bachelor's degree or more [B-4, col. 3]	Unemployment rate rank	City	Unemployment rate [B-4, col. 6]
	UNITED STATES	36.2		**UNITED STATES**	36.2		**UNITED STATES**	4.3
1	Cicero town, Illinois	71.4	1	Bethesda CDP, Maryland	85.0	1	Reading city, Pennsylvania	8.9
2	South Gate city, California	70.1	2	Sammamish city, Washington	83.4	2	Flint city, Michigan	7.7
3	Reading city, Pennsylvania	69.5	3	Cambridge city, Massachusetts	82.7	3	Victorville city, California	7.6
4	Paterson city, New Jersey	69.1	4	Palo Alto city, California	82.4	4	Albany city, Georgia	7.3
5	East Los Angeles CDP, California	68.0	5	Newton city, Massachusetts	82.0	5	Ponce zona urbana, Puerto Rico	7.2
6	Lawrence city, Massachusetts	66.3	6	Ann Arbor city, Michigan	78.4	6	Greenville city, North Carolina	6.9
7	Lynwood city, California	65.6	7	Arlington CDP, Virginia	78.0	6	Pawtucket city, Rhode Island	6.9
8	Salinas city, California	64.2	8	Bellevue city, Washington	76.4	8	Camden city, New Jersey	6.7
9	Madera city, California	63.6	8	Redmond city, Washington	76.4	9	Merced city, California	6.5
10	Trenton city, New Jersey	63.4	10	Carmel city, Indiana	76.0	10	El Cajon city, California	6.4
11	Camden city, New Jersey	63.3	11	Boulder city, Colorado	75.9	11	Newark city, New Jersey	6.3
12	Compton city, California	63.0	12	San Ramon city, California	75.8	12	Trenton city, New Jersey	6.2
13	Passaic city, New Jersey	62.6	13	Berkeley city, California	75.5	13	Bridgeport city, Connecticut	6.1
14	El Monte city, California	62.3	14	Johns Creek city, Georgia	74.8	13	Waterbury city, Connecticut	6.1
15	Rialto city, California	61.2	15	Mountain View city, California	74.3	15	Rancho Cordova city, California	5.9
16	Sunrise Manor CDP, Nevada	61.1	16	Apex town, North Carolina	73.8	15	Detroit city, Michigan	5.9
17	Baldwin Park city, California	60.8	17	Newport Beach city, California	73.1	15	Bethlehem city, Pennsylvania	5.9
17	Santa Ana city, California	60.8	18	Evanston city, Illinois	73.0	18	Hartford city, Connecticut	5.8
19	Jurupa Valley city, California	60.3	19	Davis city, California	72.8	19	Warner Robins city, Georgia	5.7
20	Perris city, California	59.9	20	Santa Monica city, California	71.9	19	Elizabeth city, New Jersey	5.7
21	Newark city, New Jersey	59.4	20	Sunnyvale city, California	71.9	19	Cleveland city, Ohio	5.7
22	San Bernardino city, California	59.3	22	Irvine city, California	71.8	22	New Rochelle city, New York	5.4
22	Bridgeport city, Connecticut	59.3	23	Naperville city, Illinois	71.6	22	Akron city, Ohio	5.4
24	Allentown city, Pennsylvania	59.2	23	Mount Pleasant town, South Carolina	71.6	24	Tuscaloosa city, Alabama	5.3
25	New Bedford city, Massachusetts	59.1	25	Cary town, North Carolina	71.5	24	Lynwood city, California	5.3
26	Lehigh Acres CDP, Florida	58.4	26	Reston CDP, Virginia	70.9	24	Madera city, California	5.3
26	Springfield city, Massachusetts	58.4	27	Highlands Ranch CDP, Colorado	70.8	24	Hammond city, Indiana	5.3
26	Elizabeth city, New Jersey	58.4	28	Alpharetta city, Georgia	70.5	24	Quincy city, Massachusetts	5.3
29	Santa Maria city, California	58.3	29	Dublin city, California	70.3	24	Paradise CDP, Nevada	5.3
30	Pine Hills CDP, Florida	58.2	30	Somerville city, Massachusetts	69.9	30	Hawthorne city, California	5.2
31	New Britain city, Connecticut	57.9	31	Seattle city, Washington	69.8	30	East Orange city, New Jersey	5.2
31	Waukegan city, Illinois	57.9	32	Walnut Creek city, California	69.7	30	Providence city, Rhode Island	5.2
33	Pharr city, Texas	57.7	33	Pleasanton city, California	69.6	33	Hesperia city, California	5.1
34	Pasadena city, Texas	57.1	34	Roswell city, Georgia	69.5	34	Citrus Heights city, California	5.0
34	West Valley City city, Utah	57.1	35	Sandy Springs city, Georgia	68.6	34	Peoria city, Illinois	5.0
36	Hartford city, Connecticut	56.8	36	Kirkland city, Washington	68.4	34	Toledo city, Ohio	5.0
37	Hialeah city, Florida	56.5	37	Frisco city, Texas	67.5	37	Carmichael CDP, California	4.9
37	Flint city, Michigan	56.5	38	Santa Clara city, California	67.2	37	Chula Vista city, California	4.9
39	Oxnard city, California	55.7	39	Plymouth city, Minnesota	66.2	37	Tallahassee city, Florida	4.9
40	Fall River city, Massachusetts	55.6	40	Ellicott City CDP, Maryland	66.1	37	Jackson city, Mississippi	4.9
41	Lauderhill city, Florida	55.2	40	Alexandria city, Virginia	66.1	37	Rochester city, New York	4.9
42	Springdale city, Arkansas	55.1	42	Washington city, District of Columbia	65.9	42	Lodi city, California	4.8
43	Hammond city, Indiana	54.6	42	Horizon West CDP, Florida	65.9	42	Palmdale city, California	4.8
44	Hesperia city, California	54.3	44	Fremont city, California	65.8	42	Pittsburg city, California	4.8
45	Pomona city, California	54.2	45	Weston city, Florida	65.7	42	Alpharetta city, Georgia	4.8
46	Miami Gardens city, Florida	54.1	46	Franklin city, Tennessee	65.6	42	New Bedford city, Massachusetts	4.8
47	Moreno Valley city, California	53.7	47	Fishers city, Indiana	65.3	42	Albany city, New York	4.8
47	Scranton city, Pennsylvania	53.7	48	Troy city, Michigan	65.1	42	Yonkers city, New York	4.8
49	Victorville city, California	53.3	49	Fort Collins city, Colorado	64.5	42	Concord city, North Carolina	4.8
49	Lynn city, Massachusetts	53.3	50	Flower Mound town, Texas	64.4	42	Memphis city, Tennessee	4.8
51	Odessa city, Texas	53.0	51	Bloomington city, Indiana	64.0	42	San Juan zona urbana, Puerto Rico	4.8
52	Palmdale city, California	52.6	51	The Woodlands CDP, Texas	64.0	52	Vallejo city, California	4.7
52	Gary city, Indiana	52.6	53	Auburn city, Alabama	63.8	52	Danbury city, Connecticut	4.7
54	St. Joseph city, Missouri	52.2	54	Carlsbad city, California	63.6	52	Clifton city, New Jersey	4.7
55	Baytown city, Texas	52.0	54	Rockville city, Maryland	63.6	55	Oakland city, California	4.6
56	Waterbury city, Connecticut	51.9	56	Silver Spring CDP, Maryland	63.3	55	Mount Vernon city, New York	4.6
57	Hemet city, California	51.7	57	Hoover city, Alabama	63.1	55	Parma city, Ohio	4.6
57	Kansas City city, Kansas	51.7	57	Overland Park city, Kansas	63.1	55	Rock Hill city, South Carolina	4.6
59	Canton city, Ohio	51.4	59	Boca Raton city, Florida	62.8	59	Los Angeles city, California	4.5
60	Norwalk city, California	51.3	60	Centennial city, Colorado	62.5	59	Boulder city, Colorado	4.5
60	Union City city, New Jersey	51.3	61	Arlington Heights village, Illinois	62.2	59	Augusta-Richmond County consolidated government (balance), Georgia	4.5
62	Stockton city, California	51.1	61	Novi city, Michigan	62.2	59	Union City city, New Jersey	4.5
62	Garland city, Texas	51.1	63	Iowa City city, Iowa	62.0	59	Eugene city, Oregon	4.5
64	Indio city, California	50.7	64	Portland city, Maine	61.8	59	Allentown city, Pennsylvania	4.5

City Rankings, 2023—*Continued*

Selected Rankings

High school diploma or less rank	City	Percent with a high school diploma or less [B-4, col. 2]	Bachelor's degree or more rank	City	Percent with a bachelor's degree or more [B-4, col. 3]	Unemployment rate rank	City	Unemployment rate [B-4, col. 6]
64	Erie city, Pennsylvania	50.7	65	Austin city, Texas	61.7	59	Pasadena city, Texas	4.5
66	Cleveland city, Ohio	50.6	66	Doral city, Florida	61.4	59	Auburn city, Washington	4.5
67	Tulare city, California	50.5	66	Sugar Land city, Texas	61.4	67	Compton city, California	4.4
67	Caldwell city, Idaho	50.5	68	Charleston city, South Carolina	61.2	67	Corona city, California	4.4
69	Yakima city, Washington	50.4	69	Woodbury city, Minnesota	61.0	67	Elk Grove city, California	4.4
70	Brownsville city, Texas	50.3	70	Scottsdale city, Arizona	60.9	67	El Monte city, California	4.4
71	Merced city, California	50.1	71	Milpitas city, California	60.8	67	Fresno city, California	4.4
71	Lorain city, Ohio	50.1	71	Plano city, Texas	60.8	67	Rancho Cucamonga city, California	4.4
73	Ontario city, California	50.0	73	San Francisco city, California	60.4	67	Rialto city, California	4.4
74	Decatur city, Illinois	49.7	74	Guaynabo zona urbana, Puerto Rico	60.3	67	Stockton city, California	4.4
75	Westland city, Michigan	49.1	75	Alameda city, California	60.1	67	Chicago city, Illinois	4.4
						67	Bloomington city, Indiana	4.4
						67	Haverhill city, Massachusetts	4.4
						67	Lawton city, Oklahoma	4.4
						67	Baytown city, Texas	4.4
						67	Redmond city, Washington	4.4

City Rankings, 2023

Selected Rankings

Households who received cash public assistance or food stamps/ SNAP rank	City	Percent of households who received cash public assistance or food stamps/ SNAP [B-2, col. 12]	Households with income of less than $25,000 rank	City	Percent of households with income of less than $25,000 [B-4, col. 10]	Households with income of $150,000 or more rank	City	Percent of households with income of $150,000 or more [B-4, col. 11]
	UNITED STATES	12.9		**UNITED STATES**	15.2		**UNITED STATES**	21.5
1	Ponce zona urbana, Puerto Rico	53.4	1	Ponce zona urbana, Puerto Rico	59.1	1	Sammamish city, Washington	70.7
2	Camden city, New Jersey	50.5	2	San Juan zona urbana, Puerto Rico	47.0	2	San Ramon city, California	62.4
3	Springfield city, Massachusetts	49.2	3	Caguas zona urbana, Puerto Rico	46.8	3	Eastvale city, California	61.1
4	Caguas zona urbana, Puerto Rico	48.1	4	Bayamón zona urbana, Puerto Rico	43.2	3	Sunnyvale city, California	61.1
5	Lawrence city, Massachusetts	45.0	5	Flint city, Michigan	41.1	5	Pleasanton city, California	60.7
6	Passaic city, New Jersey	43.8	6	Detroit city, Michigan	36.2	6	Newton city, Massachusetts	59.3
7	Hialeah city, Florida	42.4	7	Waterbury city, Connecticut	35.9	7	Bethesda CDP, Maryland	58.3
8	Albany city, Georgia	41.6	8	Carolina zona urbana, Puerto Rico	35.7	8	Milpitas city, California	57.3
9	Flint city, Michigan	40.9	9	Cleveland city, Ohio	34.2	9	Redmond city, Washington	57.1
10	Bayamón zona urbana, Puerto Rico	38.7	10	Scranton city, Pennsylvania	34.0	10	Mountain View city, California	56.9
11	Detroit city, Michigan	38.4	11	Tuscaloosa city, Alabama	33.9	11	Palo Alto city, California	55.7
12	Hartford city, Connecticut	37.3	12	Camden city, New Jersey	33.2	12	Fremont city, California	55.6
13	New Bedford city, Massachusetts	37.1	13	Auburn city, Alabama	32.3	13	Santa Clara city, California	54.0
13	Reading city, Pennsylvania	37.1	13	Gary city, Indiana	32.3	14	Bellevue city, Washington	53.7
15	Waterbury city, Connecticut	37.0	15	Dayton city, Ohio	32.2	15	Redondo Beach city, California	53.2
16	Fall River city, Massachusetts	36.4	16	Reading city, Pennsylvania	32.0	16	Newport Beach city, California	52.6
17	Pine Hills CDP, Florida	36.2	17	Bloomington city, Indiana	31.4	17	San Mateo city, California	51.4
18	Paterson city, New Jersey	35.2	18	Jackson city, Mississippi	31.2	17	Highlands Ranch CDP, Colorado	51.4
19	Brockton city, Massachusetts	34.7	19	Champaign city, Illinois	30.9	19	Naperville city, Illinois	51.3
20	San Juan zona urbana, Puerto Rico	34.4	19	Springfield city, Massachusetts	30.9	20	Livermore city, California	50.9
21	El Cajon city, California	33.7	21	Syracuse city, New York	30.7	21	Johns Creek city, Georgia	50.7
22	Rochester city, New York	33.5	22	Baton Rouge city, Louisiana	30.6	22	Redwood City city, California	50.6
23	Allentown city, Pennsylvania	32.7	23	Canton city, Ohio	30.3	22	Apex town, North Carolina	50.6
24	Victorville city, California	32.2	23	Erie city, Pennsylvania	30.3	24	Yorba Linda city, California	49.6
25	Gary city, Indiana	32.0	25	Lorain city, Ohio	30.1	24	Flower Mound town, Texas	49.6
26	Madera city, California	31.6	26	Hartford city, Connecticut	30.0	26	Ellicott City CDP, Maryland	49.5
27	Cleveland city, Ohio	31.4	27	Peoria city, Illinois	29.9	27	Lakeville city, Minnesota	49.3
28	Lynwood city, California	31.3	28	Birmingham city, Alabama	29.7	28	The Woodlands CDP, Texas	48.7
29	Syracuse city, New York	31.0	29	Albany city, Georgia	29.5	29	Kirkland city, Washington	48.6
30	Erie city, Pennsylvania	30.9	30	College Station city, Texas	29.0	30	Carmel city, Indiana	48.2
31	Rockford city, Illinois	30.7	31	Buffalo city, New York	28.8	31	Horizon West CDP, Florida	48.0
32	Lynn city, Massachusetts	30.4	32	Dearborn city, Michigan	28.7	32	Frisco city, Texas	47.6
32	Buffalo city, New York	30.4	33	Waco city, Texas	28.4	33	Walnut Creek city, California	47.3
34	Decatur city, Illinois	30.0	34	Iowa City city, Iowa	28.1	34	Arlington CDP, Virginia	46.9
34	Scranton city, Pennsylvania	30.0	34	Passaic city, New Jersey	28.1	35	Castle Rock town, Colorado	46.7
36	Compton city, California	29.9	36	New Haven city, Connecticut	27.7	36	Thousand Oaks city, California	46.4
36	Carolina zona urbana, Puerto Rico	29.9	37	Muncie city, Indiana	27.6	37	San Jose city, California	46.2
38	Dearborn city, Michigan	29.4	37	Fall River city, Massachusetts	27.6	38	New Rochelle city, New York	45.7
39	Sunrise Manor CDP, Nevada	29.0	39	Rochester city, New York	27.4	39	Carlsbad city, California	45.6
39	Schenectady city, New York	29.0	40	New Bedford city, Massachusetts	27.2	40	Weston city, Florida	45.4
41	Merced city, California	28.9	41	Toledo city, Ohio	27.1	41	Alpharetta city, Georgia	45.2
42	Milwaukee city, Wisconsin	28.8	42	Allentown city, Pennsylvania	27.0	42	Brentwood city, California	44.9
43	East Los Angeles CDP, California	28.7	43	Macon-Bibb County, Georgia	26.8	43	Roswell city, Georgia	44.6
44	El Monte city, California	28.6	43	Guaynabo zona urbana, Puerto Rico	26.8	44	Castro Valley CDP, California	44.5
44	Pharr city, Texas	28.6	45	Gainesville city, Florida	26.7	44	Cambridge city, Massachusetts	44.5
46	Worcester city, Massachusetts	28.4	45	New Orleans city, Louisiana	26.7	46	Plymouth city, Minnesota	44.4
47	Brownsville city, Texas	27.9	47	Greenville city, North Carolina	26.6	47	Centreville CDP, Virginia	44.3
48	Lowell city, Massachusetts	27.7	48	Schenectady city, New York	26.3	48	San Francisco city, California	44.2
48	Canton city, Ohio	27.7	49	Hammond city, Indiana	26.2	48	Leander city, Texas	44.2
48	Philadelphia city, Pennsylvania	27.7	49	Shreveport city, Louisiana	26.2	50	Irvine city, California	43.9
51	Fresno city, California	27.5	49	Trenton city, New Jersey	26.2	51	South Jordan city, Utah	43.2
52	Edinburg city, Texas	27.0	52	Gulfport city, Mississippi	26.1	52	Cary town, North Carolina	43.1
53	Bridgeport city, Connecticut	26.9	53	Athens-Clarke County unified government (balance), Georgia	25.9	53	Lake Forest city, California	42.3
54	Rancho Cordova city, California	26.6	54	Fayetteville city, Arkansas	25.5	53	Reston CDP, Virginia	42.3
55	Racine city, Wisconsin	26.3	54	Augusta-Richmond County consolidated government (balance), Georgia	25.5	55	Allen city, Texas	42.2
56	San Bernardino city, California	25.8	56	Akron city, Ohio	25.4	56	Folsom city, California	42.1
57	Macon-Bibb County, Georgia	25.5	56	Jackson city, Tennessee	25.4	57	Queen Creek town, Arizona	41.7
58	Newark city, New Jersey	25.4	56	Knoxville city, Tennessee	25.4	58	Temecula city, California	41.5

City Rankings, 2023—*Continued*

Selected Rankings

Households who received cash public assistance or food stamps/ SNAP rank	City	Percent of households who received cash public assistance or food stamps/ SNAP [B-2, col. 12]	Households with income of less than $25,000 rank	City	Percent of households with income of less than $25,000 [B-4, col. 10]	Households with income of $150,000 or more rank	City	Percent of households with income of $150,000 or more [B-4, col. 11]
59	Glendale city, California	25.3	59	Paterson city, New Jersey	25.3	59	Lehi city, Utah	41.4
59	Miami Gardens city, Florida	25.3	59	Memphis city, Tennessee	25.3	60	Fishers city, Indiana	41.0
59	Akron city, Ohio	25.3	61	Newark city, New Jersey	24.9	61	Mount Pleasant town, South Carolina	40.9
62	Pueblo city, Colorado	25.1	62	Lauderhill city, Florida	24.7	62	Seattle city, Washington	40.8
62	Kissimmee city, Florida	25.1	63	Columbus city, Georgia	24.6	63	Sugar Land city, Texas	40.7
64	Indio city, California	24.9	63	Las Cruces city, New Mexico	24.6	64	Camarillo city, California	40.2
65	Chico city, California	24.7	65	Baltimore city, Maryland	24.4	65	Santa Monica city, California	39.9
65	New Haven city, Connecticut	24.7	65	Cincinnati city, Ohio	24.4	65	Somerville city, Massachusetts	39.9
67	Las Cruces city, New Mexico	24.5	67	Madera city, California	24.3	67	Mission Viejo city, California	39.7
67	Yakima city, Washington	24.5	68	South Bend city, Indiana	24.2	68	Stamford city, Connecticut	39.6
69	Toledo city, Ohio	24.4	68	Pawtucket city, Rhode Island	24.2	68	Columbia CDP, Maryland	39.6
70	Perris city, California	24.3	70	Mobile city, Alabama	24.1	70	Santa Clarita city, California	39.5
70	Wilmington city, Delaware	24.3	70	Lake Charles city, Louisiana	24.1	71	Orange city, California	39.4
72	Birmingham city, Alabama	24.2	70	San Marcos city, Texas	24.1	71	Union City city, California	39.4
73	Palmdale city, California	24.1	73	St. Louis city, Missouri	24.0	73	Centennial city, Colorado	39.3
73	Union City city, New Jersey	24.1	73	Philadelphia city, Pennsylvania	24.0	73	Cedar Park city, Texas	39.3
75	Lorain city, Ohio	23.9	75	Decatur city, Illinois	23.9	75	Rockville city, Maryland	39.0

Table B-1. States — What: Education, Employment, and Income, 2023

State code	STATE	Total population 25 years and over	Educational attainment (percent): No high school diploma	High school graduate	Some college or associate's degree	Bachelor's degree	Graduate or professional degree	Total enrolled in school	School enrollment by level of school (percent): Enrolled in preschool	Enrolled in grades K–12	Enrolled in college or graduate school
	ACS table number:	C15003	C15003	C15003	C15003	C15003	C15003	C14002	C14002	C14002	C14002
	Column number:	1	2	3	4	5	6	7	8	9	10

Table B-1. States — What: Education, Employment, and Income, 2023

State code	STATE	Percent enrolled in private schools by level of school: All levels	Preschool, nursery school	Kindergarten	Grades 1–8	Grades 9–12	College, under-graduate	Graduate or professional school	Total population, 16 years and over	Total labor force
	ACS table number:	C14002	C14002	C14002	C14002	C14002	C14002	C14002	C23001	C23001
	Column number:	11	12	13	14	15	16	17	18	19

Table B-1. States — What: Education, Employment, and Income, 2023

State code	STATE	Labor force participation (percent): Total	Men	Women	Unemployment rates by age (percent unemployed): Total labor force	16 to 24 years	25 to 64 years	65 years and over	Total labor force, 25 to 64 years
	ACS table number:	C23001	C23001	C23001	C23001	C23001	C23001	C23001	B23006
	Column number:	20	21	22	23	24	25	26	27

Table B-1. States — What: Education, Employment, and Income, 2023

State code	STATE	Unemployment rates for the labor force age 25 to 64 by educational attainment — Unemployment rate (percent unemployed): Total, 25 to 64 years	No high school diploma	High school graduate	Some college or associate's degree	Bachelor's degree or higher	Total population, 16 to 19 years	16 to 19 years, not enrolled in school, not high school graduate, not in labor force	Total labor force
	ACS table number:	B23006	B23006	B23006	B23006	B23006	C14005	C14005	C23001
	Column number:	28	29	30	31	32	33	34	35

Table B-1. States — What: Education, Employment, and Income, 2023

State code	STATE	Percent of population age 16 years and over who worked full-time, year-round in the past 12 months: Total	Male	Female	Total households	Percent of households with no workers	Family status of children under 18 years, by employment status of parents and age of children — Children under 18 years in families: Number	Living with two parents (percent of total): Both in labor force	One parent in labor force	Percent of total living with one parent who is in labor force
	ACS table number:	S2402	S2402	S2402	B08202	B08202	C23008	C23008	C23008	C23008
	Column number:	36	37	38	39	40	41	42	43	44

Table B-1. States — What: Education, Employment, and Income, 2023

State code	STATE	Family status of children under 18 years, by employment status of parents and age of children — Children under 6 years in families: Number	Living with two parents (percent of total): Both in labor force	One parent in labor force	Percent of total living with one parent who is in labor force	Children 6–17 years in families: Number	Living with two parents (percent of total): Both in labor force	One parent in labor force	Percent of total living with one parent who is in labor force
	ACS table number:	C23008	C23008	C23008	C23008	C23008	C23008	C23008	C23008
	Column number:	45	46	47	48	49	50	51	52

Table B-1. States — What: Education, Employment, and Income, 2023

State code	STATE	Employment status of family householders: Total families with children under 18	Opposite-sex married-couple families: Total	Opposite-sex married-couple families: Both in labor force (percent)	Families maintained by women and men with no spouse present: Total	Families maintained by women and men with no spouse present: Householder in labor force (percent)	Women 20 to 64 years in households, by presence of children and labor force status: Total women 20 to 64 years in households	Percent with children under 18 years	Percent in labor force with children under 18 years
	ACS table number:	C23007	C23007	C23007	C23007	C23007	B23003	B23003	B23003
	Column number:	53	54	55	56	57	58	59	60

Table B-1. States — What: Education, Employment, and Income, 2023

State code	STATE	Class of worker for employed civilians 16 years and over: Civilian employed population 16 years and over	Percent private wage and salary workers	Percent government workers	Percent self-employed and unpaid workers	Civilian employed population 16 years and over	Occupation (percent): Management, business, science, and arts	Service	Sales and office	Natural resources, construction, and maintenance	Production, transportation, and material moving
	ACS table number:	C24080	C24080	C24080	C24080	C24060	C24060	C24060	C24060	C24060	C24060
	Column number:	61	62	63	64	65	66	67	68	69	70

Table B-1. States — What: Education, Employment, and Income, 2023

State code	STATE	Industry (percent): Agriculture, forestry, fishing and hunting, and mining	Construction	Manufacturing	Wholesale trade	Retail trade	Transportation and warehousing, and utilities	Information	Finance and insurance, real estate, and rental and leasing
	ACS table number:	C24070	C24070	C24070	C24070	C24070	C24070	C24070	C24070
	Column number:	71	72	73	74	75	76	77	78

Table B-1. States — What: Education, Employment, and Income, 2023

State code	STATE	Industry (percent): Professional, scientific, and management, and administrative and waste management services	Educational services, and health care and social assistance	Arts, entertainment, and recreation, and accommodation and food services	Other services, except public administration	Public administration	Veterans as a percent of the civilian population 18 years and over	Median income in the past 12 months (in 2023 inflation-adjusted dollars) — Median household income by age of householder: All households	Householder under 25 years	Householder 25 to 44 years	Householder 45 to 64 years	Householder 65 years and over
	ACS table number:	C24070	C24070	C24070	C24070	C24070	B21001	B19049	B19049	B19049	B19049	B19049
	Column number:	79	80	81	82	83	84	85	86	87	88	89

Table B-1. States — What: Education, Employment, and Income, 2023

State code	STATE	Median income in the past 12 months (in 2023 inflation-adjusted dollars) — Median household income by race and Hispanic origin of householder: White alone	Black or African American alone	American Indian and Alaska Native alone	Asian alone	Native Hawaiian and other Pacific Islander alone	Some other race alone	Two or more races	White alone, not Hispanic or Latino	Hispanic or Latino
	ACS table number:	B19013A	B19013B	B19013C	B19013D	B19013E	B19013F	B19013G	B19013H	B19013I
	Column number:	90	91	92	93	94	95	96	97	98

Table B-1. States — What: Education, Employment, and Income, 2023

		Median income in the past 12 months (in 2023 inflation-adjusted dollars)											
		Median family income, by type of family							Median nonfamily household income			Median individual income	
										Living alone, 65 years and over		Persons 15 years and over who worked full-time, year-round	
	STATE	All families	Married-couple families with children under 18	Married-couple families, no children under 18	Male householder with children under 18	Male householder, no children under 18	Female householder with children under 18	Female householder, no children under 18	All nonfamily households	Male	Female	Male	Female
State code	ACS table number:	B19126	B19126	B19126	B19126	B19126	B19126	B19126	B19215	B19215	B19215	B19326	B19326
	Column number:	99	100	101	102	103	104	105	106	107	108	109	110

Table B-1. States — What: Education, Employment, and Income, 2023

				Households, by type of income (percent)								
	STATE	Per capita income in the past 12 months (in 2023 inflation-adjusted dollars)	Total number of households	With wage or salary income	With self-employment income	With interest, dividends, or net rental income	With Social Security	With Supplemental Security Income (SSI)	With public assistance income	With cash public assistance or food stamps/ SNAP	With retirement income	With other types of income
State code	ACS table number:	B19301	B19052	B19052	B19053	B19054	B19055	B19056	B19057	B19058	B19059	B19060
	Column number:	111	112	113	114	115	116	117	118	119	120	121

Table B-1. States — What: Education, Employment, and Income, 2023

		Household income in the past 12 months (in 2023 inflation-adjusted dollars)										
			Households by income group (percent)									
	STATE	Total number of housholds	Less than $10,000	$10,000 to $14,999	$15,000 to $24,999	$25,000 to $34,999	$35,000 to $49,999	$50,000 to $74,999	$75,000 to $99,999	$100,000 to $149,999	$150,000 to $199,999	$200,000 or more
State code	ACS table number:	B19001	B19001	B19001	B19001	B19001	B19001	B19001	B19001	B19001	B19001	B19001
	Column number:	122	123	124	125	126	127	128	129	130	131	132

Table B-1. States — What: Education, Employment, and Income, 2023

		Households with income over $100,000, by age of householder (as a percent of all households in age group)					Households with income below poverty (as a percent of all households in household-type group)						
	STATE	All households	Householder under 25 years	Householder 25 to 44 years	Householder 45 to 64 years	Householder 65 years and over	All households	Family households	Married-couple family households	Male householder family households	Female householder family households	Male householder nonfamily households	Female householder nonfamily households
State code	ACS table number:	B19001	B19037	B19037	B19037	B19037	C17017	C17017	C17017	C17017	C17017	C17017	C17017
	Column number:	133	134	135	136	137	138	139	140	141	142	143	144

Table B-1. States — What: Education, Employment, and Income, 2023

			Persons with income below poverty by age (as a percent of all persons in age group)				Persons with income below poverty by selected race and Hispanic origin groups (as a percent of all persons in race/Hispanic group)			
	STATE	Population for whom poverty status is determined	All ages	Under 18 years	18 to 64 years	65 years and over	White alone, not Hispanic or Latino	Black or African American alone	Asian alone	Hispanic or Latino
State code	ACS table number:	C17001	C17001	C17001	C17001	C17001	C17001H	C17001B	C17001D	C17001I
	Column number:	145	146	147	148	149	150	151	152	153

Table B-1. States — What: Education, Employment, and Income, 2023

State code	STATE	Total civilian non-institutionalized population	Type of health insurance (as a percent of all persons)			
			Private only	Public only	Both private and public	None
	ACS table number:	C27010	C27010	C27010	C27010	C27010
	Column number:	154	155	156	157	158

Table B-2. Counties — What: Education, Employment, and Income, 2023

STATE County code	STATE County	Educational attainment			Employment status				Household income and benefits				
		Total population 25 years and over	Percent with a high school diploma or less	Percent with a bachelor's degree or more	Total population 16 years and over	Labor force participation (percent)	Percent unemployed	Percent of persons age 16 years and over who worked full-time year-round in the past 12 months	Total households	Median household income in the past 12 months (in 2023 inflation-adjusted dollars)	Income less than $25,000 (percent)	Income greater than $150,000 (percent)	Percent who received cash public assistance or food stamps/ SNAP
	ACS table number:	C15003	C15003	C15003	C23001	C23001	C23001	S2402	B19001	B19049	B19001	B19001	B19058
	Column number:	1	2	3	4	5	6	7	8	9	10	11	12

Table B-3. Metropolitan Areas — What: Education, Employment, and Income, 2023

Metropolitan area / division code	Metropolitan area / division	Educational attainment			Employment status				Household income and benefits				
		Total population 25 years and over	Percent with a high school diploma or less	Percent with a bachelor's degree or more	Total population 16 years and over	Labor force participation (percent)	Percent unemployed	Percent of persons age 16 years and over who worked full-time year-round in the past 12 months (percent of total population)	Total households	Median household income in the past 12 months (in 2023 inflation-adjusted dollars)	Income less than $25,000 (percent)	Income greater than $150,000 (percent)	Percent who received cash public assistance or food stamps/ SNAP
	ACS table number:	C15003	C15003	C15003	C23001	C23001	C23001	S2402	B19001	B19049	B19001	B19001	B19058
	Column number:	1	2	3	4	5	6	7	8	9	10	11	12

Table B-4. Cities — What: Education, Employment, and Income, 2023

STATE and place code	STATE Place	Educational attainment			Employment status				Household income and benefits				
		Total population 25 years and over	Percent with a high school diploma or less	Percent with a bachelor's degree or more	Total population 16 years and over	Labor force participation (percent)	Percent unemployed	Percent of persons age 16 years and over who worked full-time year-round in the past 12 months	Total households	Median household income in the past 12 months (in 2023 inflation-adjusted dollars)	Income less than $25,000 (percent)	Income greater than $150,000 (percent)	Percent who received cash public assistance or food stamps/ SNAP
	ACS table number:	C15003	C15003	C15003	C23001	C23001	C23001	S2402	B19001	B19049	B19001	B19001	B19058
	column number:	1	2	3	4	5	6	7	8	9	10	11	12

Table B-1. States — What: Education, Employment, and Income, 2023

State code	STATE	Total population 25 years and over	Educational attainment (percent)					Total enrolled in school	School enrollment by level of school (percent)		
			No high school diploma	High school graduate	Some college or associate's degree	Bachelor's degree	Graduate or professional degree		Enrolled in preschool	Enrolled in grades K–12	Enrolled in college or graduate school
	ACS table number:	C15003	C15003	C15003	C15003	C15003	C15003	C14002	C14002	C14002	C14002
	Column number:	1	2	3	4	5	6	7	8	9	10
	UNITED STATES	231,791,117	10.2	25.9	27.7	21.8	14.3	79,814,912	5.9	67.8	26.3
01	Alabama	3,498,967	10.9	30.1	30.2	17.6	11.3	1,214,871	6.2	68.8	25.1
02	Alaska	493,892	6.8	29.1	31.9	20.1	12.2	171,455	5.8	74.5	19.7
04	Arizona	5,150,254	10.6	23.4	32.5	20.4	13.1	1,738,316	4.8	68.8	26.4
05	Arkansas	2,078,254	10.7	34.2	28.9	16.6	9.5	698,717	6.0	72.2	21.8
06	California	26,969,649	15.2	20.4	26.9	22.8	14.7	9,829,642	5.0	64.9	30.1
08	Colorado	4,135,123	6.7	19.3	27.5	28.3	18.1	1,371,780	6.0	66.1	27.9
09	Connecticut	2,559,922	8.2	25.5	23.3	23.1	19.8	861,958	6.3	64.5	29.2
10	Delaware	731,427	8.6	28.5	26.5	21.0	15.5	231,967	5.6	67.8	26.6
11	District of Columbia	482,919	7.3	13.1	13.7	26.9	39.0	160,220	8.6	54.9	36.5
12	Florida	16,421,870	9.8	26.8	28.5	21.6	13.3	4,916,196	6.2	66.2	27.6
13	Georgia	7,448,119	10.7	26.3	27.7	21.3	14.1	2,765,792	5.9	69.8	24.4
15	Hawaii	1,024,897	7.0	26.3	29.7	23.1	13.9	321,417	7.0	65.7	27.3
16	Idaho	1,305,704	7.8	25.9	34.1	21.6	10.6	489,359	5.0	71.3	23.7
17	Illinois	8,710,996	9.4	25.3	27.0	22.8	15.5	3,000,482	6.3	67.7	26.0
18	Indiana	4,614,970	9.6	32.2	28.1	19.1	11.1	1,655,241	5.9	70.2	23.9
19	Iowa	2,166,425	6.7	29.9	31.8	20.9	10.7	783,658	6.5	68.7	24.8
20	Kansas	1,956,252	8.3	25.1	30.8	22.4	13.4	746,968	6.2	68.7	25.2
21	Kentucky	3,107,275	10.5	33.0	28.7	16.3	11.5	1,026,118	5.5	71.1	23.4
22	Louisiana	3,102,893	12.2	33.1	27.7	16.9	10.1	1,116,155	7.1	69.6	23.3
23	Maine	1,039,460	5.1	29.4	28.6	23.2	13.7	278,330	5.3	66.5	28.2
24	Maryland	4,297,439	8.8	23.9	23.6	22.4	21.3	1,515,915	5.8	67.4	26.7
25	Massachusetts	4,975,152	8.6	22.8	20.8	25.4	22.4	1,649,701	6.0	61.3	32.6
26	Michigan	7,007,856	8.0	27.7	31.6	19.9	12.8	2,292,853	5.9	68.7	25.4
27	Minnesota	3,941,575	5.7	23.3	31.0	25.9	14.0	1,387,871	6.2	69.7	24.0
28	Mississippi	1,980,147	12.2	29.4	32.8	15.5	10.0	721,843	5.8	70.0	24.2
29	Missouri	4,255,810	8.0	29.4	29.4	20.2	13.0	1,437,172	6.2	69.9	24.0
30	Montana	795,845	5.6	28.0	31.8	22.7	12.0	245,479	3.6	72.5	23.9
31	Nebraska	1,307,246	7.3	24.8	32.6	22.9	12.4	514,983	6.4	69.0	24.6
32	Nevada	2,253,253	12.3	26.8	32.2	18.7	10.0	707,027	4.7	72.2	23.1
33	New Hampshire	1,030,965	5.6	27.0	26.6	24.6	16.2	289,802	5.6	65.6	28.8
34	New Jersey	6,511,081	9.3	25.2	21.7	26.3	17.5	2,249,812	7.5	66.7	25.9
35	New Mexico	1,471,057	12.5	25.1	30.7	17.5	14.1	501,307	5.2	69.6	25.2
36	New York	13,885,155	11.7	24.2	23.4	22.6	18.1	4,552,603	6.3	64.3	29.5
37	North Carolina	7,487,552	9.4	24.5	29.3	23.0	13.8	2,537,953	5.5	67.3	27.2
38	North Dakota	520,006	5.5	24.3	36.6	23.3	10.2	194,812	4.4	65.5	30.0
39	Ohio	8,172,692	8.1	31.8	28.1	19.3	12.7	2,695,998	6.1	70.2	23.8
40	Oklahoma	2,684,421	10.3	30.6	30.4	18.6	10.1	1,019,247	5.9	71.6	22.6
41	Oregon	3,050,675	8.0	22.1	32.3	23.5	14.2	897,965	5.8	69.0	25.2
42	Pennsylvania	9,171,006	7.8	33.1	23.8	21.0	14.4	2,882,066	6.2	66.9	26.9
72	Puerto Rico	2,407,254	18.0	27.2	24.1	21.8	9.0	658,523	4.3	62.1	33.6
44	Rhode Island	786,493	10.4	26.4	24.1	23.1	15.9	257,233	4.7	59.2	36.0
45	South Carolina	3,745,394	9.8	28.2	29.1	20.4	12.5	1,227,809	5.9	69.6	24.6
46	South Dakota	615,517	6.5	27.7	32.5	22.9	10.4	218,063	6.0	73.3	20.7
47	Tennessee	4,931,967	9.9	31.0	27.4	19.3	12.4	1,599,497	5.4	70.6	24.0
48	Texas	20,029,447	13.7	24.2	27.9	21.6	12.6	7,964,042	5.9	70.5	23.7
49	Utah	2,085,019	6.9	22.2	32.5	24.6	13.8	1,028,225	5.7	68.1	26.2
50	Vermont	471,255	4.5	27.1	24.7	25.2	18.5	139,321	6.8	61.4	31.7
51	Virginia	6,037,339	8.6	24.1	25.0	24.0	18.5	2,096,813	5.7	66.3	28.0
53	Washington	5,511,197	7.6	21.6	30.3	24.3	16.1	1,765,252	6.4	69.2	24.4
54	West Virginia	1,259,219	11.0	39.7	25.3	14.5	9.5	367,695	5.6	70.0	24.4
55	Wisconsin	4,116,216	6.3	29.5	30.4	22.2	11.5	1,339,010	5.6	69.7	24.7
56	Wyoming	403,853	6.1	27.5	36.0	19.3	11.2	138,901	6.1	70.7	23.2

Table B-1. States — What: Education, Employment, and Income, 2023—*Continued*

State code	STATE	Percent enrolled in private schools by level of school: All levels	Preschool, nursery school	Kindergarten	Grades 1–8	Grades 9–12	College, undergraduate	Graduate or professional school	Total population, 16 years and over	Total labor force
	ACS table number:	C14002	C14002	C14002	C14002	C14002	C14002	C14002	C23001	C23001
	Column number:	11	12	13	14	15	16	17	18	19
	UNITED STATES	18.0	41.0	15.7	13.1	11.5	22.4	39.2	271,122,729	173,038,795
01	Alabama	16.6	33.4	17.4	14.9	14.6	15.5	22.0	4,115,279	2,410,315
02	Alaska	17.6	41.5	15.1	14.1	10.3	24.1	37.3	577,598	385,948
04	Arizona	14.4	39.2	12.4	10.7	9.8	17.7	29.7	6,049,109	3,674,799
05	Arkansas	14.6	30.8	12.8	11.3	10.1	22.2	22.1	2,452,773	1,441,034
06	California	14.8	43.4	12.9	10.0	8.8	15.3	43.9	31,584,340	20,298,562
08	Colorado	13.7	36.6	13.3	10.9	8.5	12.7	29.9	4,818,044	3,322,899
09	Connecticut	19.8	38.1	11.0	8.6	10.3	34.8	50.2	2,987,218	1,983,295
10	Delaware	17.5	40.5	9.9	13.9	14.1	17.1	45.4	846,414	526,726
11	District of Columbia	38.8	31.3	11.1	17.9	22.4	75.0	64.9	564,543	410,840
12	Florida	21.2	45.8	19.2	17.1	14.5	22.9	43.1	18,768,460	11,267,928
13	Georgia	15.8	39.4	14.8	12.0	11.6	17.5	33.5	8,818,867	5,652,842
15	Hawaii	25.2	60.9	17.6	20.7	19.8	24.2	38.7	1,172,357	738,940
16	Idaho	18.8	47.9	21.2	15.5	11.5	25.8	23.7	1,558,313	976,225
17	Illinois	18.8	35.5	16.0	12.4	10.4	27.7	46.6	10,192,179	6,665,114
18	Indiana	18.6	42.4	18.7	15.8	11.6	23.0	28.4	5,470,753	3,521,827
19	Iowa	16.2	31.3	14.1	13.0	8.9	22.4	31.8	2,570,587	1,703,217
20	Kansas	15.7	39.1	20.3	14.3	12.3	12.3	21.1	2,339,516	1,549,558
21	Kentucky	18.3	36.6	18.3	16.1	16.5	17.5	27.9	3,633,664	2,190,697
22	Louisiana	21.2	41.0	20.7	20.0	17.8	17.7	33.3	3,635,137	2,153,263
23	Maine	21.2	45.5	7.4	12.9	10.6	37.1	45.9	1,180,683	733,298
24	Maryland	19.6	51.2	16.4	15.4	12.9	20.8	37.6	4,979,552	3,360,696
25	Massachusetts	27.8	47.8	11.3	10.6	14.5	50.2	63.4	5,828,175	3,917,076
26	Michigan	14.0	33.6	12.5	12.4	10.2	14.4	21.2	8,186,295	5,053,867
27	Minnesota	17.4	36.7	16.6	14.0	8.7	23.1	37.9	4,602,443	3,146,576
28	Mississippi	17.5	35.9	16.5	16.8	16.4	12.4	26.6	2,354,139	1,355,540
29	Missouri	19.8	37.4	13.3	15.9	13.9	25.9	38.9	4,997,010	3,195,524
30	Montana	14.3	48.2	13.0	13.6	11.6	11.5	22.2	924,869	582,371
31	Nebraska	17.3	35.5	13.9	14.2	12.6	21.8	25.3	1,558,006	1,075,249
32	Nevada	14.6	35.5	14.1	12.0	9.5	15.1	37.5	2,594,279	1,646,984
33	New Hampshire	25.3	55.9	17.3	15.2	15.7	37.2	55.2	1,184,596	787,493
34	New Jersey	21.0	41.5	14.5	12.4	12.5	33.5	47.1	7,520,182	5,032,256
35	New Mexico	10.8	23.7	16.9	8.6	8.5	11.2	17.0	1,723,938	1,010,975
36	New York	25.1	36.9	19.1	14.8	15.0	39.6	57.9	16,085,030	10,132,536
37	North Carolina	18.2	48.6	16.4	15.2	12.1	17.5	37.6	8,792,430	5,555,824
38	North Dakota	12.6	51.5	17.3	10.0	9.4	9.7	19.8	622,500	432,302
39	Ohio	18.5	40.4	17.3	15.7	12.9	21.7	30.0	9,520,298	6,042,703
40	Oklahoma	13.6	23.4	11.5	11.8	10.5	17.0	22.4	3,201,739	1,958,603
41	Oregon	17.3	50.2	17.4	14.9	9.0	18.3	32.0	3,506,067	2,193,069
42	Pennsylvania	24.0	48.8	19.3	14.8	13.5	38.5	52.5	10,658,635	6,690,945
72	Puerto Rico	40.2	35.9	30.0	29.9	27.9	58.6	72.1	2,777,060	1,307,588
44	Rhode Island	27.5	41.4	28.4	10.5	12.5	46.5	62.7	916,988	592,054
45	South Carolina	17.6	47.8	16.5	13.6	11.6	20.6	31.5	4,370,726	2,671,185
46	South Dakota	12.9	22.0	13.3	11.5	12.5	11.9	20.5	725,788	488,674
47	Tennessee	20.4	45.2	17.9	16.2	17.2	23.2	34.6	5,747,865	3,603,424
48	Texas	13.3	36.3	13.1	9.7	8.3	15.6	29.1	23,857,262	15,735,802
49	Utah	15.7	39.0	10.9	9.2	6.6	29.2	30.8	2,600,950	1,825,335
50	Vermont	19.8	36.4	8.0	12.0	15.0	28.7	34.2	547,286	355,375
51	Virginia	19.3	56.9	16.9	13.7	11.8	21.1	42.1	7,066,427	4,611,949
53	Washington	17.6	52.2	21.9	13.3	10.5	18.4	33.4	6,357,108	4,136,441
54	West Virginia	12.8	23.0	6.4	11.1	10.7	15.8	19.9	1,464,056	795,817
55	Wisconsin	18.0	32.8	22.1	17.3	11.3	17.7	34.6	4,822,901	3,146,602
56	Wyoming	10.8	35.8	8.0	9.1	6.4	10.7	19.4	469,355	298,221

Table B-1. States — What: Education, Employment, and Income, 2023—*Continued*

State code	STATE	Labor force participation (percent)			Unemployment rates by age (percent unemployed)				Total labor force, 25 to 64 years
		Total	Men	Women	Total labor force	16 to 24 years	25 to 64 years	65 years and over	
	ACS table number:	C23001	C23001	C23001	C23001	C23001	C23001	C23001	B23006
	Column number:	20	21	22	23	24	25	26	27
	UNITED STATES	63.8	68.4	59.4	4.3	9.4	3.3	2.8	137,830,738
01	Alabama	58.6	63.2	54.3	4.0	9.8	2.8	1.9	1,901,240
02	Alaska	66.8	70.6	62.6	4.5	6.0	4.0	4.4	307,937
04	Arizona	60.7	65.4	56.2	4.2	8.5	3.2	3.6	2,887,567
05	Arkansas	58.8	63.5	54.3	4.1	8.4	3.2	2.2	1,135,162
06	California	64.3	69.7	59.0	5.5	12.1	4.3	3.6	16,505,891
08	Colorado	69.0	73.1	64.7	3.7	8.3	2.9	2.5	2,665,730
09	Connecticut	66.4	70.2	62.8	4.6	10.5	3.6	2.8	1,559,114
10	Delaware	62.2	66.0	58.8	3.4	8.8	2.6	1.4	414,286
11	District of Columbia	72.8	75.0	70.8	5.2	12.0	4.3	2.6	344,645
12	Florida	60.0	64.5	55.8	4.1	9.2	3.2	3.3	9,068,996
13	Georgia	64.1	68.9	59.6	4.4	9.5	3.4	2.4	4,527,724
15	Hawaii	63.0	66.9	59.2	3.3	6.6	2.8	2.1	582,267
16	Idaho	62.6	67.7	57.5	3.6	9.2	2.2	2.3	752,894
17	Illinois	65.4	69.6	61.3	4.7	9.4	3.9	2.7	5,316,099
18	Indiana	64.4	69.2	59.7	3.6	7.2	2.8	2.5	2,750,495
19	Iowa	66.3	69.9	62.7	2.8	5.9	2.1	1.4	1,314,485
20	Kansas	66.2	71.0	61.5	3.2	6.5	2.5	1.7	1,173,806
21	Kentucky	60.3	64.5	56.2	4.1	9.3	3.0	2.1	1,717,791
22	Louisiana	59.2	62.9	55.8	4.8	11.8	3.6	2.2	1,712,523
23	Maine	62.1	66.1	58.3	3.2	6.3	2.6	2.3	575,041
24	Maryland	67.5	71.8	63.5	3.9	10.3	3.0	2.3	2,700,466
25	Massachusetts	67.2	70.9	63.7	3.9	8.0	3.2	3.2	3,087,618
26	Michigan	61.7	65.5	58.1	4.5	10.1	3.3	3.0	3,965,069
27	Minnesota	68.4	71.8	65.0	3.0	6.2	2.4	2.4	2,481,180
28	Mississippi	57.6	60.9	54.5	4.8	11.7	3.5	1.9	1,080,269
29	Missouri	63.9	67.8	60.3	3.4	7.8	2.5	2.1	2,500,643
30	Montana	63.0	66.6	59.2	2.7	6.2	2.0	1.5	449,982
31	Nebraska	69.0	73.3	64.7	2.6	6.6	1.8	1.5	821,816
32	Nevada	63.5	68.0	59.0	4.5	8.3	3.7	4.0	1,339,603
33	New Hampshire	66.5	70.2	62.8	2.6	6.5	1.8	2.8	611,916
34	New Jersey	66.9	71.9	62.2	4.7	11.4	3.7	3.7	4,054,071
35	New Mexico	58.6	63.1	54.3	4.7	8.6	3.9	2.1	781,937
36	New York	63.0	67.0	59.3	5.0	11.8	4.0	3.1	8,238,371
37	North Carolina	63.2	68.2	58.5	4.0	8.7	3.0	2.8	4,410,552
38	North Dakota	69.4	73.3	65.4	2.8	5.2	2.2	3.0	333,127
39	Ohio	63.5	67.5	59.6	4.0	9.3	3.0	2.6	4,763,745
40	Oklahoma	61.2	66.4	56.1	4.5	9.5	3.4	2.2	1,522,180
41	Oregon	62.6	67.0	58.2	4.1	9.4	3.1	2.9	1,765,567
42	Pennsylvania	62.8	67.1	58.6	4.2	9.9	3.3	2.3	5,289,355
72	Puerto Rico	47.1	52.0	42.8	9.1	19.9	7.2	5.0	1,094,032
44	Rhode Island	64.6	69.6	59.8	4.7	9.5	3.9	2.9	468,126
45	South Carolina	61.1	65.6	56.9	4.2	10.6	3.0	1.8	2,099,360
46	South Dakota	67.3	70.6	64.0	2.6	6.7	1.8	1.5	370,587
47	Tennessee	62.7	67.7	58.0	3.9	8.8	3.0	2.1	2,861,334
48	Texas	66.0	71.9	60.2	4.4	9.5	3.3	2.9	12,611,010
49	Utah	70.2	76.6	63.7	3.3	7.1	2.2	1.8	1,371,495
50	Vermont	64.9	67.0	62.9	2.6	6.7	2.0	1.2	273,213
51	Virginia	65.3	69.7	61.0	3.6	8.9	2.6	2.1	3,680,875
53	Washington	65.1	70.2	59.9	4.4	10.1	3.4	3.1	3,360,890
54	West Virginia	54.4	57.5	51.3	4.5	9.4	3.4	3.1	628,128
55	Wisconsin	65.2	68.4	62.1	2.8	5.9	2.1	1.8	2,460,177
56	Wyoming	63.5	67.9	59.0	3.2	7.6	2.3	2.6	234,383

Table B-1. States — What: Education, Employment, and Income, 2023—*Continued*

State code	STATE	Unemployment rates for the labor force age 25 to 64 by educational attainment — Unemployment rate (percent unemployed): Total, 25 to 64 years	No high school diploma	High school graduate	Some college or associate's degree	Bachelor's degree or higher	Total population, 16 to 19 years	16 to 19 years, not enrolled in school, not high school graduate, not in labor force	Total labor force
	ACS table number:	B23006	B23006	B23006	B23006	B23006	C14005	C14005	C23001
	Column number:	28	29	30	31	32	33	34	35
	UNITED STATES	3.5	6.5	4.7	3.6	2.3	17,713,229	1.9	173,038,795
01	Alabama	3.1	7.6	4.3	2.9	1.4	282,517	1.8	2,410,315
02	Alaska	4.3	11.3	6.9	3.4	2.1	33,972	4.1	385,948
04	Arizona	3.4	5.6	4.7	3.5	2.2	400,258	2.8	3,674,799
05	Arkansas	3.5	6.8	4.0	3.9	1.8	170,804	3.2	1,441,034
06	California	4.6	6.5	5.6	5.0	3.4	2,099,391	1.4	20,298,562
08	Colorado	3.1	4.7	4.6	3.5	2.1	303,575	1.7	3,322,899
09	Connecticut	3.7	9.8	5.3	4.2	2.1	195,079	1.7	1,983,295
10	Delaware	2.7	3.8	4.6	1.8	2.0	53,584	1.3	526,726
11	District of Columbia	4.5	16.6	14.6	7.6	2.1	30,696	2.5	410,840
12	Florida	3.4	5.3	4.3	3.5	2.4	1,060,983	2.2	11,267,928
13	Georgia	3.6	5.7	4.8	4.1	2.3	626,394	2.4	5,652,842
15	Hawaii	2.9	6.8	3.8	2.4	2.3	61,727	1.8	738,940
16	Idaho	2.4	4.9	2.7	2.3	2.0	119,327	2.5	976,225
17	Illinois	4.1	8.3	5.8	4.5	2.3	664,110	1.8	6,665,114
18	Indiana	3.0	8.1	3.8	2.8	1.6	382,197	1.9	3,521,827
19	Iowa	2.2	5.3	3.5	1.9	1.1	181,686	1.9	1,703,217
20	Kansas	2.6	3.3	4.1	2.9	1.6	169,019	1.5	1,549,558
21	Kentucky	3.2	8.9	4.3	3.3	1.4	226,190	1.6	2,190,697
22	Louisiana	3.9	8.6	4.7	3.7	2.1	238,858	3.2	2,153,263
23	Maine	2.7	5.8	3.8	2.8	1.8	63,816	1.1	733,298
24	Maryland	3.1	5.8	4.8	3.8	1.7	314,408	1.6	3,360,696
25	Massachusetts	3.3	6.6	5.2	3.7	2.2	373,679	1.0	3,917,076
26	Michigan	3.5	8.3	5.1	3.5	1.9	518,524	2.0	5,053,867
27	Minnesota	2.5	5.2	4.0	2.4	1.7	312,030	1.1	3,146,576
28	Mississippi	3.7	7.7	5.5	3.1	2.0	181,090	2.6	1,355,540
29	Missouri	2.7	5.9	3.5	2.9	1.5	335,200	2.0	3,195,524
30	Montana	2.1	5.2	3.1	2.2	1.2	53,752	4.0	582,371
31	Nebraska	1.9	6.5	3.2	1.7	0.7	110,161	1.9	1,075,249
32	Nevada	4.0	6.4	4.9	3.7	2.7	157,676	2.6	1,646,984
33	New Hampshire	1.8	6.7	2.8	1.3	1.3	69,829	0.5	787,493
34	New Jersey	3.9	6.1	5.6	4.2	2.7	456,431	1.2	5,032,256
35	New Mexico	4.2	6.7	5.4	4.8	2.2	113,373	3.0	1,010,975
36	New York	4.2	7.5	5.7	4.1	3.0	967,565	1.6	10,132,536
37	North Carolina	3.2	7.0	4.6	3.0	2.1	580,962	2.5	5,555,824
38	North Dakota	2.3	7.9	1.8	2.6	1.6	43,229	1.4	432,302
39	Ohio	3.2	7.5	5.0	2.9	1.6	612,790	2.1	6,042,703
40	Oklahoma	3.7	8.0	4.9	3.9	1.5	233,582	2.3	1,958,603
41	Oregon	3.3	6.2	4.6	3.3	2.3	202,035	1.8	2,193,069
42	Pennsylvania	3.4	6.4	5.0	3.7	1.9	688,694	1.2	6,690,945
72	Puerto Rico	7.8	15.0	12.0	8.2	4.2	150,959	1.7	1,307,588
44	Rhode Island	4.1	7.2	4.8	4.7	2.9	59,317	1.2	592,054
45	South Carolina	3.2	7.6	4.3	3.2	1.8	287,022	2.4	2,671,185
46	South Dakota	1.9	5.7	2.4	2.2	0.8	52,364	1.9	488,674
47	Tennessee	3.2	7.9	4.3	3.3	1.5	355,609	1.1	3,603,424
48	Texas	3.5	5.5	4.7	3.6	2.3	1,737,907	2.4	15,735,802
49	Utah	2.4	3.2	3.9	2.4	1.5	224,458	2.2	1,825,335
50	Vermont	2.0	5.1	2.7	2.1	1.5	35,332	2.0	355,375
51	Virginia	2.8	5.8	4.3	2.9	1.8	466,323	1.2	4,611,949
53	Washington	3.6	6.8	4.6	3.4	2.8	370,788	1.6	4,136,441
54	West Virginia	3.7	8.4	4.8	3.3	2.1	92,827	3.2	795,817
55	Wisconsin	2.2	3.6	3.3	2.5	1.2	311,157	1.6	3,146,602
56	Wyoming	2.4	6.9	2.5	2.8	1.2	30,932	1.9	298,221

Table B-1. States — What: Education, Employment, and Income, 2023—*Continued*

State code	STATE	Percent of population age 16 years and over who worked full-time, year-round in the past 12 months			Total households	Percent of households with no workers	Family status of children under 18 years, by employment status of parents and age of children			
							Children under 18 years in families			
								Living with two parents (percent of total)		
		Total	Male	Female			Number	Both in labor force	One parent in labor force	Percent of total living with one parent who is in labor force
	ACS table number:	S2402	S2402	S2402	B08202	B08202	C23008	C23008	C23008	C23008
	Column number:	36	37	38	39	40	41	42	43	44
	UNITED STATES	68.6	56.2	43.8	131,332,360	26.0	68,850,977	42.8	23.0	26.4
01	Alabama	71.2	55.5	44.5	2,051,545	30.4	1,051,555	36.5	22.5	29.7
02	Alaska	59.1	55.2	44.8	276,852	23.5	164,928	39.9	30.6	21.6
04	Arizona	69.1	56.9	43.1	2,907,014	28.7	1,498,225	36.7	25.4	28.5
05	Arkansas	71.3	55.3	44.7	1,232,871	30.4	649,952	39.8	23.4	27.2
06	California	65.7	57.5	42.5	13,699,816	23.1	8,051,477	42.1	23.5	25.8
08	Colorado	68.7	56.8	43.2	2,428,261	22.0	1,159,138	48.3	24.3	22.0
09	Connecticut	66.2	55.6	44.4	1,442,969	25.2	695,468	49.1	17.6	26.3
10	Delaware	69.9	53.8	46.2	412,048	27.8	198,246	43.7	16.4	32.0
11	District of Columbia	73.8	49.6	50.4	334,673	22.0	119,075	56.7	9.4	27.6
12	Florida	69.9	55.2	44.8	8,966,402	29.8	4,146,106	39.5	22.4	29.7
13	Georgia	70.6	54.5	45.5	4,150,138	24.6	2,374,837	40.7	21.3	29.7
15	Hawaii	63.5	54.4	45.6	493,898	25.5	272,196	44.6	22.7	26.8
16	Idaho	65.5	59.9	40.1	733,244	26.8	451,213	38.5	33.8	22.5
17	Illinois	68.8	55.9	44.1	5,071,288	25.9	2,577,450	46.1	19.8	27.7
18	Indiana	69.5	57.0	43.0	2,754,881	26.1	1,491,199	42.4	24.8	25.7
19	Iowa	70.0	56.8	43.2	1,337,243	25.7	695,370	51.4	19.9	23.5
20	Kansas	69.4	56.7	43.3	1,188,340	24.5	655,899	49.2	24.1	21.4
21	Kentucky	69.9	56.1	43.9	1,853,603	30.7	938,300	42.0	21.2	26.4
22	Louisiana	69.5	54.5	45.5	1,833,915	30.4	988,061	33.9	18.5	36.8
23	Maine	66.2	55.8	44.2	616,085	30.4	234,816	44.0	23.2	26.0
24	Maryland	72.2	53.5	46.5	2,384,715	22.6	1,294,689	47.7	19.2	27.5
25	Massachusetts	67.1	55.0	45.0	2,800,984	24.4	1,287,169	51.9	17.7	23.8
26	Michigan	66.7	56.9	43.1	4,107,809	29.9	2,010,071	42.5	22.8	26.8
27	Minnesota	67.7	56.9	43.1	2,344,432	24.8	1,249,021	54.9	20.1	20.7
28	Mississippi	70.6	53.4	46.6	1,166,617	31.6	624,255	34.0	20.1	35.4
29	Missouri	69.6	55.1	44.9	2,556,271	27.0	1,287,389	45.5	22.5	25.9
30	Montana	65.2	57.8	42.2	472,867	28.0	221,336	46.8	27.5	21.2
31	Nebraska	70.6	57.2	42.8	813,864	23.0	459,891	52.6	21.8	21.8
32	Nevada	68.5	56.0	44.0	1,224,685	25.3	652,124	34.8	23.8	30.2
33	New Hampshire	69.8	57.0	43.0	569,493	25.2	240,209	55.8	20.5	18.6
34	New Jersey	68.8	56.7	43.3	3,538,457	22.8	1,933,494	47.6	21.0	26.5
35	New Mexico	65.7	56.1	43.9	856,580	31.0	421,339	34.7	20.1	31.2
36	New York	67.6	54.6	45.4	7,809,267	27.0	3,724,616	45.3	21.0	25.5
37	North Carolina	69.1	55.2	44.8	4,392,669	26.7	2,189,107	41.6	23.2	27.3
38	North Dakota	68.3	57.4	42.6	338,059	24.0	170,038	59.7	19.9	16.2
39	Ohio	68.7	55.9	44.1	4,917,309	28.3	2,422,869	41.8	21.7	28.7
40	Oklahoma	69.6	56.4	43.6	1,589,105	27.9	902,002	39.0	26.2	25.1
41	Oregon	65.7	57.3	42.7	1,752,050	28.3	794,825	43.9	23.9	24.6
42	Pennsylvania	69.3	56.4	43.6	5,324,209	28.4	2,482,611	44.0	20.7	27.6
72	Puerto Rico	63.3	53.8	46.2	1,277,486	46.6	478,701	22.2	9.1	45.8
44	Rhode Island	66.4	55.8	44.2	443,980	27.9	193,265	45.8	20.2	23.0
45	South Carolina	68.7	55.0	45.0	2,177,733	29.2	1,066,284	38.9	25.1	28.5
46	South Dakota	69.8	57.6	42.4	378,559	24.5	207,344	48.9	19.1	26.7
47	Tennessee	70.4	56.0	44.0	2,889,226	27.3	1,452,426	37.6	25.6	26.7
48	Texas	71.1	57.1	42.9	11,260,645	20.7	7,151,739	38.3	26.3	27.1
49	Utah	65.3	61.7	38.3	1,167,591	18.1	902,433	47.2	35.8	13.8
50	Vermont	66.4	54.3	45.7	279,612	28.0	108,872	60.3	19.0	14.8
51	Virginia	69.8	55.1	44.9	3,402,670	23.9	1,774,658	47.2	22.9	22.6
53	Washington	66.6	58.3	41.7	3,101,265	25.3	1,572,037	42.2	30.0	21.4
54	West Virginia	69.7	56.3	43.7	743,644	36.5	322,938	39.2	22.3	26.7
55	Wisconsin	69.8	56.7	43.3	2,495,539	27.4	1,194,895	48.1	21.5	25.1
56	Wyoming	66.9	59.1	40.9	247,368	28.9	123,520	48.8	23.2	22.4

Table B-1. States — What: Education, Employment, and Income, 2023—*Continued*

State code	STATE	Children under 6 years in families: Number	Children under 6: Living with two parents (percent of total): Both in labor force	Children under 6: Living with two parents (percent of total): One parent in labor force	Children under 6: Percent of total living with one parent who is in labor force	Children 6–17 years in families: Number	Children 6–17: Living with two parents (percent of total): Both in labor force	Children 6–17: Living with two parents (percent of total): One parent in labor force	Children 6–17: Percent of total living with one parent who is in labor force
	ACS table number:	C23008	C23008	C23008	C23008	C23008	C23008	C23008	C23008
	Column number:	45	46	47	48	49	50	51	52
	UNITED STATES	21,177,904	44.1	20.8	28.3	47,673,073	44.6	19.8	29.2
01	Alabama	334,310	39.3	20.6	30.5	717,245	40.6	19.7	30.8
02	Alaska	52,163	41.1	25.9	25.6	112,765	41.6	23.7	27.5
04	Arizona	452,345	38.9	23.8	29.6	1,045,880	39.9	23.1	30.0
05	Arkansas	204,281	41.3	20.8	28.8	445,671	42.0	19.6	29.6
06	California	2,408,194	41.7	22.6	28.1	5,643,283	41.6	22.2	29.1
08	Colorado	356,954	49.6	21.1	24.8	802,184	50.2	19.7	26.1
09	Connecticut	211,169	48.3	16.9	29.1	484,299	48.0	16.6	30.3
10	Delaware	61,794	44.6	14.2	35.7	136,452	45.1	13.2	37.3
11	District of Columbia	44,380	43.5	9.0	38.6	74,695	35.7	8.8	45.2
12	Florida	1,295,758	41.6	20.4	30.7	2,850,348	42.5	19.4	31.2
13	Georgia	718,421	41.3	19.8	31.3	1,656,416	41.5	19.2	32.1
15	Hawaii	85,641	46.1	19.2	28.0	186,555	46.8	17.6	28.6
16	Idaho	132,173	45.3	29.9	20.7	319,040	48.0	28.3	19.9
17	Illinois	772,580	46.1	18.5	29.3	1,804,870	46.1	17.9	30.0
18	Indiana	466,683	45.1	21.3	27.7	1,024,516	46.3	19.7	28.6
19	Iowa	214,756	53.0	17.1	25.6	480,614	53.7	15.9	26.6
20	Kansas	196,961	50.3	19.8	25.3	458,938	50.8	17.9	27.0
21	Kentucky	298,888	42.8	19.5	27.8	639,412	43.2	18.8	28.5
22	Louisiana	316,265	36.6	16.9	36.3	671,796	37.9	16.2	36.0
23	Maine	69,895	47.2	19.0	26.1	164,921	48.5	17.2	26.2
24	Maryland	402,372	48.8	16.0	30.3	892,317	49.3	14.6	31.6
25	Massachusetts	398,149	51.1	15.8	27.0	889,020	50.7	14.9	28.4
26	Michigan	613,817	44.5	20.2	28.1	1,396,254	45.4	19.1	28.7
27	Minnesota	379,362	55.5	16.8	23.9	869,659	55.7	15.3	25.3
28	Mississippi	185,119	35.7	18.8	35.2	439,136	36.4	18.2	35.1
29	Missouri	402,293	47.6	19.6	27.0	885,096	48.5	18.3	27.5
30	Montana	62,791	50.5	20.2	23.9	158,545	52.0	17.2	25.0
31	Nebraska	139,685	54.0	17.4	24.6	320,206	54.6	15.5	25.8
32	Nevada	200,022	36.1	23.0	32.9	452,102	36.7	22.7	34.1
33	New Hampshire	72,655	54.2	18.7	22.4	167,554	53.5	17.9	24.0
34	New Jersey	604,274	49.1	19.2	26.9	1,329,220	49.8	18.4	27.0
35	New Mexico	121,486	34.7	19.2	34.8	299,853	34.7	18.9	36.2
36	New York	1,177,259	44.4	19.1	28.6	2,547,357	44.0	18.2	30.1
37	North Carolina	682,712	42.8	20.9	29.1	1,506,395	43.3	19.8	29.9
38	North Dakota	53,766	59.5	16.5	20.0	116,272	59.4	14.9	21.8
39	Ohio	755,463	44.8	18.4	29.9	1,667,406	46.1	16.8	30.5
40	Oklahoma	276,235	40.4	24.3	27.8	625,767	41.1	23.5	29.0
41	Oregon	233,300	43.4	22.1	28.1	561,525	43.2	21.3	29.5
42	Pennsylvania	771,711	45.7	18.3	29.2	1,710,900	46.5	17.2	29.9
72	Puerto Rico	117,017	23.7	10.6	46.4	361,684	24.2	11.1	46.6
44	Rhode Island	64,502	45.0	19.2	28.0	128,763	44.7	18.7	30.5
45	South Carolina	325,593	40.7	21.4	30.1	740,691	41.5	19.8	30.8
46	South Dakota	63,711	52.5	16.5	26.5	143,633	54.1	15.4	26.4
47	Tennessee	469,951	40.4	23.1	28.2	982,475	41.8	21.8	28.9
48	Texas	2,197,421	40.4	24.3	28.5	4,954,318	41.3	23.5	29.1
49	Utah	273,817	49.2	30.6	16.5	628,616	50.1	28.3	17.7
50	Vermont	31,514	58.1	14.5	22.2	77,358	57.2	12.7	25.3
51	Virginia	543,426	47.9	19.8	26.1	1,231,232	48.2	18.4	27.6
53	Washington	487,577	45.1	25.5	23.7	1,084,460	46.3	23.4	24.7
54	West Virginia	98,380	42.6	20.8	26.2	224,558	44.2	20.1	26.0
55	Wisconsin	360,117	49.5	17.7	27.5	834,778	50.2	16.0	28.6
56	Wyoming	35,813	51.5	18.4	23.3	87,707	52.6	16.5	23.7

Family status of children under 18 years, by employment status of parents and age of children

Table B-1. States — What: Education, Employment, and Income, 2023—*Continued*

State code	STATE	Employment status of family householders: Total families with children under 18	Opposite-sex married-couple families: Total	Opposite-sex married-couple families: Both in labor force (percent)	Families maintained by women and men with no spouse present: Total	Families maintained by women and men with no spouse present: Householder in labor force (percent)	Women 20 to 64 years in households, by presence of children and labor force status: Total women 20 to 64 years in households	Percent with children under 18 years	Percent in labor force with children under 18 years
	ACS table number:	C23007	C23007	C23007	C23007	C23007	B23003	B23003	B23003
	Column number:	53	54	55	56	57	58	59	60
	UNITED STATES	33,505,905	22,740,970	69.7	10,764,935	86.7	95,653,296	34.2	26.1
01	Alabama	506,309	321,443	66.7	184,866	82.7	1,463,190	35.4	26.0
02	Alaska	74,822	52,641	62.3	22,181	85.6	202,116	34.7	25.3
04	Arizona	708,283	472,770	64.4	235,513	88.0	2,061,177	33.7	24.6
05	Arkansas	318,040	205,743	67.7	112,297	82.3	852,725	36.4	27.4
06	California	3,754,747	2,623,259	65.6	1,131,488	86.0	11,278,179	33.3	24.4
08	Colorado	598,132	435,373	72.0	162,759	90.3	1,714,471	33.1	26.0
09	Connecticut	366,806	245,790	75.2	121,016	88.4	1,038,837	33.8	27.4
10	Delaware	94,355	60,899	75.7	33,456	91.0	290,137	33.6	27.4
11	District of Columbia	59,706	33,647	82.3	26,059	83.8	225,650	25.7	21.5
12	Florida	2,024,312	1,330,714	68.1	693,598	87.1	6,367,104	31.3	24.0
13	Georgia	1,114,663	732,261	68.7	382,402	86.6	3,278,556	34.6	26.4
15	Hawaii	121,564	87,531	71.7	34,033	89.3	386,171	33.3	26.2
16	Idaho	215,049	163,290	63.0	51,759	91.7	531,547	39.5	28.2
17	Illinois	1,242,445	849,507	72.5	392,938	88.6	3,616,375	33.3	26.2
18	Indiana	705,942	476,228	70.9	229,714	87.9	1,920,753	35.3	27.2
19	Iowa	349,529	244,570	77.9	104,959	90.3	870,543	37.3	30.7
20	Kansas	321,392	224,221	73.5	97,171	89.5	799,969	38.2	30.1
21	Kentucky	477,143	309,820	70.6	167,323	81.0	1,279,026	36.3	27.3
22	Louisiana	470,135	273,364	69.6	196,771	84.4	1,307,009	35.1	26.6
23	Maine	128,428	86,847	72.1	41,581	85.8	395,371	30.3	23.4
24	Maryland	630,138	426,973	76.3	203,165	90.7	1,816,230	33.8	27.8
25	Massachusetts	676,307	469,192	77.1	207,115	86.0	2,051,589	31.9	26.1
26	Michigan	970,174	645,226	70.4	324,948	86.1	2,834,600	33.2	25.6
27	Minnesota	605,300	435,960	79.5	169,340	89.6	1,586,587	35.9	30.0
28	Mississippi	296,728	177,411	68.0	119,317	83.6	843,812	36.1	27.4
29	Missouri	638,686	434,611	73.5	204,075	89.0	1,744,813	34.9	27.9
30	Montana	108,221	77,700	73.1	30,521	89.1	307,616	32.9	25.8
31	Nebraska	222,842	158,920	77.5	63,922	90.3	537,785	39.1	32.2
32	Nevada	294,818	180,898	63.7	113,920	87.2	922,146	31.1	22.4
33	New Hampshire	128,273	94,261	75.6	34,012	86.0	400,901	30.4	24.4
34	New Jersey	982,603	699,403	73.4	283,200	88.7	2,685,339	35.3	28.4
35	New Mexico	205,167	116,533	65.4	88,634	80.6	580,806	33.8	24.5
36	New York	1,827,974	1,212,292	71.5	615,682	84.8	5,680,940	31.3	24.4
37	North Carolina	1,106,237	746,362	68.5	359,875	86.5	3,152,881	34.1	26.0
38	North Dakota	86,281	62,771	80.6	23,510	87.1	208,273	37.1	31.0
39	Ohio	1,189,556	765,340	73.2	424,216	85.9	3,305,002	34.4	27.1
40	Oklahoma	435,193	289,386	65.1	145,807	84.0	1,119,689	37.3	27.0
41	Oregon	420,170	276,157	68.0	144,013	86.8	1,211,837	32.5	24.7
42	Pennsylvania	1,273,532	846,200	73.4	427,332	86.3	3,601,210	33.7	26.6
72	Puerto Rico	261,159	99,886	66.9	161,273	75.8	960,812	28.2	20.4
44	Rhode Island	103,369	68,531	71.7	34,838	81.4	316,952	32.3	25.1
45	South Carolina	535,088	353,059	67.2	182,029	84.7	1,542,419	34.8	26.1
46	South Dakota	100,902	69,789	76.6	31,113	90.3	239,123	38.1	31.9
47	Tennessee	707,155	471,716	67.2	235,439	84.9	2,076,119	33.9	25.0
48	Texas	3,345,214	2,310,977	64.5	1,034,237	87.8	8,818,698	37.4	27.2
49	Utah	395,598	318,746	65.1	76,852	88.6	950,784	41.7	29.6
50	Vermont	56,502	40,171	82.3	16,331	84.7	178,322	29.4	25.1
51	Virginia	906,183	635,259	72.2	270,924	87.5	2,526,643	34.8	27.2
53	Washington	790,296	575,633	66.0	214,663	86.4	2,243,617	33.8	24.7
54	West Virginia	168,308	109,192	66.4	59,116	79.4	481,607	33.3	24.3
55	Wisconsin	584,147	398,047	76.5	186,100	89.1	1,652,276	32.9	26.8
56	Wyoming	63,141	44,336	77.0	18,805	85.2	155,774	38.0	29.7

Table B-1. States — What: Education, Employment, and Income, 2023—*Continued*

State code	STATE	Class of worker for employed civilians 16 years and over: Civilian employed population 16 years and over	Percent private wage and salary workers	Percent government workers	Percent self-employed and unpaid workers	Civilian employed population 16 years and over	Occupation (percent): Management, business, science, and arts	Service	Sales and office	Natural resources, construction, and maintenance	Production, transportation, and material moving
	ACS table number:	C24080	C24080	C24080	C24080	C24060	C24060	C24060	C24060	C24060	C24060
	Column number:	61	62	63	64	65	66	67	68	69	70
	UNITED STATES	164,346,993	79.5	14.4	6.1	164,346,993	43.2	16.4	19.1	8.4	12.9
01	Alabama	2,297,941	77.5	16.8	5.7	2,297,941	39.7	14.9	19.3	9.3	16.9
02	Alaska	345,460	69.9	23.8	6.3	345,460	41.2	16.7	18.6	10.9	12.7
04	Arizona	3,493,543	79.6	14.0	6.4	3,493,543	42.1	16.8	20.9	8.9	11.3
05	Arkansas	1,375,551	78.8	14.6	6.6	1,375,551	37.0	15.5	20.7	10.2	16.6
06	California	19,026,566	77.7	14.8	7.5	19,026,566	43.4	17.8	18.5	8.5	11.9
08	Colorado	3,151,694	79.3	14.6	6.1	3,151,694	49.3	15.2	18.3	8.4	8.8
09	Connecticut	1,884,125	80.5	13.3	6.2	1,884,125	47.4	16.7	18.5	7.0	10.4
10	Delaware	504,329	80.2	15.6	4.2	504,329	44.3	16.6	18.6	7.9	12.5
11	District of Columbia	385,274	69.0	27.1	3.9	385,274	72.8	12.3	10.9	1.3	2.6
12	Florida	10,731,195	82.2	11.3	6.5	10,731,195	40.6	18.2	21.8	8.7	10.8
13	Georgia	5,346,554	80.0	14.0	5.9	5,346,554	42.3	15.1	20.4	8.2	14.1
15	Hawaii	667,835	72.5	20.2	7.4	667,835	39.3	22.2	20.3	8.7	9.5
16	Idaho	936,279	77.2	14.8	8.0	936,279	39.7	16.3	19.4	11.4	13.2
17	Illinois	6,329,130	82.0	13.3	4.7	6,329,130	43.8	15.7	19.1	6.8	14.7
18	Indiana	3,387,230	83.0	12.1	4.8	3,387,230	39.1	14.8	18.5	8.7	18.8
19	Iowa	1,654,280	78.6	14.8	6.6	1,654,280	39.7	15.1	18.7	10.1	16.3
20	Kansas	1,477,593	77.0	16.9	6.2	1,477,593	42.6	15.3	19.0	9.1	14.1
21	Kentucky	2,085,354	79.6	14.9	5.5	2,085,354	38.9	15.4	19.5	8.7	17.5
22	Louisiana	2,030,949	77.6	15.6	6.8	2,030,949	38.9	18.0	20.1	10.3	12.8
23	Maine	708,660	77.4	14.1	8.5	708,660	43.0	16.2	19.1	9.5	12.1
24	Maryland	3,194,028	72.2	22.6	5.2	3,194,028	50.7	16.0	17.2	7.5	8.7
25	Massachusetts	3,754,447	81.9	12.4	5.7	3,754,447	51.4	16.0	16.8	6.9	8.8
26	Michigan	4,822,997	83.3	11.5	5.3	4,822,997	40.8	15.9	19.4	7.9	16.0
27	Minnesota	3,048,320	81.2	13.2	5.5	3,048,320	45.7	15.1	17.8	7.7	13.7
28	Mississippi	1,278,422	76.0	17.9	6.1	1,278,422	35.6	16.8	20.4	9.8	17.4
29	Missouri	3,071,350	81.0	13.1	5.9	3,071,350	42.1	15.5	19.7	8.4	14.3
30	Montana	562,372	74.2	17.1	8.7	562,372	40.8	18.4	18.9	11.1	10.8
31	Nebraska	1,041,138	78.1	15.0	6.9	1,041,138	42.5	14.9	19.8	9.5	13.3
32	Nevada	1,556,587	82.0	12.2	5.8	1,556,587	35.0	21.6	20.7	8.8	13.9
33	New Hampshire	765,872	81.6	12.4	6.0	765,872	46.1	14.3	18.8	8.7	12.0
34	New Jersey	4,785,505	80.7	14.0	5.3	4,785,505	47.4	15.5	19.0	6.9	11.2
35	New Mexico	947,670	70.2	23.3	6.5	947,670	41.6	19.4	19.0	10.2	9.8
36	New York	9,600,693	78.1	16.1	5.8	9,600,693	46.2	19.0	18.4	6.6	9.7
37	North Carolina	5,230,146	80.5	13.6	5.9	5,230,146	43.6	15.4	18.8	8.6	13.6
38	North Dakota	410,066	74.0	19.0	7.0	410,066	42.5	15.4	18.8	10.0	13.3
39	Ohio	5,784,101	81.9	12.9	5.2	5,784,101	41.3	15.8	18.8	7.7	16.3
40	Oklahoma	1,847,746	75.9	17.5	6.6	1,847,746	38.6	16.3	20.4	10.7	14.0
41	Oregon	2,099,913	78.2	14.8	7.0	2,099,913	44.9	16.4	18.7	8.3	11.7
42	Pennsylvania	6,400,011	83.7	11.1	5.2	6,400,011	43.4	16.3	18.4	7.8	14.2
72	Puerto Rico	1,185,629	71.2	17.5	11.2	1,185,629	34.1	20.7	23.7	9.8	11.8
44	Rhode Island	559,742	81.3	12.7	5.9	559,742	45.1	16.6	18.3	7.0	12.9
45	South Carolina	2,516,719	79.2	14.7	6.1	2,516,719	39.4	16.3	20.5	9.0	14.7
46	South Dakota	472,581	76.3	15.9	7.8	472,581	40.7	16.5	18.7	10.7	13.4
47	Tennessee	3,442,420	79.1	14.0	7.0	3,442,420	40.3	15.6	19.6	8.3	16.2
48	Texas	14,926,761	79.1	13.9	6.9	14,926,761	41.3	15.8	20.0	9.9	13.0
49	Utah	1,758,060	79.7	15.1	5.2	1,758,060	44.4	14.6	20.0	9.2	11.8
50	Vermont	345,752	75.9	15.4	8.7	345,752	47.3	15.0	17.3	9.6	10.8
51	Virginia	4,318,000	74.7	20.1	5.2	4,318,000	49.2	15.3	17.6	7.3	10.6
53	Washington	3,887,150	78.5	15.8	5.8	3,887,150	47.0	15.7	17.0	9.1	11.3
54	West Virginia	757,305	75.6	20.2	4.2	757,305	37.1	18.4	18.9	11.3	14.2
55	Wisconsin	3,056,531	82.3	12.8	4.9	3,056,531	41.2	14.7	18.4	8.7	17.1
56	Wyoming	285,046	69.5	22.8	7.8	285,046	38.5	17.6	17.9	13.7	12.3

Table B-1. States — What: Education, Employment, and Income, 2023—*Continued*

State code	STATE	Industry (percent)							
		Agriculture, forestry, fishing and hunting, and mining	Construction	Manufacturing	Wholesale trade	Retail trade	Transportation and warehousing, and utilities	Information	Finance and insurance, real estate, and rental and leasing
	ACS table number:	C24070	C24070	C24070	C24070	C24070	C24070	C24070	C24070
	Column number:	71	72	73	74	75	76	77	78
	UNITED STATES	1.6	6.9	9.9	2.0	10.6	6.0	1.9	6.6
01	Alabama	1.2	6.8	14.6	2.1	11.0	6.3	1.2	5.4
02	Alaska	5.3	7.3	4.2	2.3	10.3	8.0	1.5	3.0
04	Arizona	1.2	7.9	7.6	1.8	11.5	5.8	1.7	8.8
05	Arkansas	2.2	7.4	12.6	1.8	13.6	6.7	1.3	5.7
06	California	2.0	6.6	8.9	2.1	9.9	6.2	2.9	5.3
08	Colorado	1.9	7.9	6.7	1.9	9.9	5.1	2.6	6.9
09	Connecticut	0.5	6.1	10.6	1.7	9.8	4.8	2.0	8.2
10	Delaware	0.8	6.7	8.7	1.5	10.2	6.7	1.0	9.6
11	District of Columbia	0.1	2.2	1.6	0.6	3.6	2.0	2.9	6.3
12	Florida	0.9	8.1	5.4	2.2	11.6	6.5	1.5	8.4
13	Georgia	1.0	7.1	9.6	2.3	11.1	7.3	2.2	6.5
15	Hawaii	1.2	7.3	2.9	2.2	11.3	6.8	1.4	6.1
16	Idaho	3.6	9.5	9.9	1.9	11.1	5.3	1.5	5.5
17	Illinois	1.1	5.3	11.6	2.4	10.1	7.0	1.6	7.3
18	Indiana	1.2	6.6	17.7	2.1	10.5	5.9	1.2	5.4
19	Iowa	3.6	7.3	14.8	2.4	11.0	5.3	1.4	7.3
20	Kansas	3.3	6.4	12.1	2.2	10.7	5.8	1.8	6.8
21	Kentucky	1.7	6.6	14.1	1.7	11.8	6.6	1.1	5.8
22	Louisiana	3.1	8.4	7.4	2.0	11.0	6.3	1.4	5.1
23	Maine	2.4	7.3	9.0	1.5	12.6	4.4	1.7	6.0
24	Maryland	0.5	7.0	4.6	1.4	8.8	5.3	1.8	5.7
25	Massachusetts	0.4	6.5	8.8	1.6	9.6	4.0	1.8	7.3
26	Michigan	1.2	6.0	18.2	1.9	10.9	4.7	1.2	5.7
27	Minnesota	2.1	6.5	13.5	2.5	10.4	4.8	1.4	6.9
28	Mississippi	2.1	6.3	12.7	2.0	11.5	7.7	1.1	4.7
29	Missouri	1.7	6.8	11.1	2.2	11.4	5.8	1.6	7.3
30	Montana	5.5	9.4	5.0	2.0	10.8	5.3	1.3	6.3
31	Nebraska	4.4	6.7	10.4	2.3	10.1	6.3	1.4	7.8
32	Nevada	1.5	7.6	5.4	1.8	10.9	8.0	1.6	5.8
33	New Hampshire	0.5	7.4	12.4	2.1	11.8	4.1	1.8	7.0
34	New Jersey	0.3	6.3	8.3	2.5	9.9	6.6	2.6	8.5
35	New Mexico	3.5	7.2	4.7	1.4	10.3	4.5	1.6	4.5
36	New York	0.5	5.6	5.9	1.7	9.3	5.8	2.7	8.0
37	North Carolina	1.0	7.3	11.7	1.9	10.9	5.4	1.5	7.2
38	North Dakota	8.1	5.9	7.7	3.3	10.4	6.1	1.7	6.5
39	Ohio	1.0	6.0	14.5	2.0	11.1	6.0	1.3	6.4
40	Oklahoma	3.6	7.1	9.1	2.0	12.2	6.2	1.3	5.7
41	Oregon	2.8	6.7	11.0	2.1	11.9	4.7	1.7	5.1
42	Pennsylvania	1.2	6.2	11.4	2.1	10.9	6.3	1.6	6.2
72	Puerto Rico	1.3	7.0	9.0	2.2	12.2	4.0	1.5	6.3
44	Rhode Island	0.8	6.3	10.9	1.5	11.9	4.8	1.2	6.6
45	South Carolina	0.9	7.4	13.5	2.0	10.8	5.5	1.3	6.5
46	South Dakota	6.7	7.5	9.9	2.2	11.1	4.0	1.6	6.3
47	Tennessee	0.9	7.0	12.4	2.1	11.2	7.5	1.7	5.7
48	Texas	2.3	8.4	8.7	2.2	10.8	6.8	1.7	7.1
49	Utah	1.5	8.1	10.1	1.9	11.1	5.1	1.6	6.8
50	Vermont	2.5	8.5	9.9	1.4	10.4	3.6	1.5	4.3
51	Virginia	0.8	6.5	7.1	1.4	9.8	5.3	1.7	6.5
53	Washington	2.4	6.9	8.9	2.0	11.1	5.8	2.6	5.2
54	West Virginia	3.4	7.3	7.9	1.3	11.2	6.3	1.4	4.7
55	Wisconsin	2.0	6.5	18.2	2.1	10.9	4.9	1.2	6.0
56	Wyoming	9.5	8.4	4.8	1.5	10.0	6.1	1.6	5.1

Table B-1. States — What: Education, Employment, and Income, 2023—*Continued*

State code	STATE	Industry (percent): Professional, scientific, and management, and administrative and waste management services	Industry (percent): Educational services, and health care and social assistance	Industry (percent): Arts, entertainment, and recreation, and accommodation and food services	Industry (percent): Other services, except public administration	Industry (percent): Public administration	Veterans as a percent of the civilian population 18 years and over	Median income in the past 12 months (in 2023 inflation-adjusted dollars): Median household income by age of householder: All households	Householder under 25 years	Householder 25 to 44 years	Householder 45 to 64 years	Householder 65 years and over
	ACS table number:	C24070	C24070	C24070	C24070	C24070	B21001	B19049	B19049	B19049	B19049	B19049
	Column number:	79	80	81	82	83	84	85	86	87	88	89
	UNITED STATES	12.8	23.5	8.8	4.8	4.6	6.1	77,719	44,846	87,673	94,612	56,038
01	Alabama	10.3	22.9	7.8	4.8	5.4	7.6	62,212	34,332	70,078	76,467	47,884
02	Alaska	8.6	25.4	8.2	4.6	11.2	10.5	86,631	60,357	94,507	102,948	67,208
04	Arizona	12.6	22.3	9.5	4.6	4.8	7.5	77,315	47,859	87,263	95,741	57,753
05	Arkansas	8.7	23.6	7.6	4.7	4.2	7.0	58,700	42,076	67,141	69,232	44,695
06	California	14.6	22.3	9.7	4.8	4.6	4.1	95,521	49,485	103,915	111,822	68,292
08	Colorado	16.0	21.8	9.6	4.9	4.8	7.2	92,911	51,162	103,962	115,759	64,210
09	Connecticut	12.7	27.9	8.0	4.1	3.5	4.5	91,665	53,325	99,293	112,847	66,407
10	Delaware	11.1	24.8	9.0	3.9	5.9	7.5	81,361	43,277	88,282	97,151	65,590
11	District of Columbia	26.2	18.4	8.0	9.4	18.6	3.2	108,210	53,134	133,688	119,244	65,937
12	Florida	14.4	20.7	11.1	5.2	4.0	7.3	73,311	46,813	82,093	87,666	55,569
13	Georgia	13.8	21.0	8.6	4.9	4.7	7.2	74,632	42,642	81,615	91,228	53,005
15	Hawaii	11.0	22.3	14.6	5.0	8.0	7.5	95,322	48,701	102,016	115,890	78,353
16	Idaho	10.9	22.3	9.2	4.6	4.7	7.6	74,942	42,170	81,817	94,738	57,539
17	Illinois	13.0	23.7	8.3	4.7	3.8	4.7	80,306	41,140	92,276	96,691	56,316
18	Indiana	9.4	23.8	7.7	4.8	3.7	6.0	69,477	42,739	78,303	83,597	50,047
19	Iowa	7.8	24.2	7.2	4.3	3.4	6.5	71,433	42,602	81,928	87,896	51,575
20	Kansas	10.3	24.8	7.1	4.1	4.7	6.4	70,333	42,348	79,130	88,788	52,955
21	Kentucky	8.9	24.7	8.3	4.5	4.4	6.2	61,118	38,278	73,109	71,563	44,617
22	Louisiana	9.9	25.4	9.5	5.2	5.1	5.8	58,229	33,612	66,854	69,068	44,495
23	Maine	11.1	26.7	8.4	4.6	4.2	8.0	73,733	52,463	86,904	88,380	54,821
24	Maryland	16.7	23.7	8.1	5.4	11.0	6.6	98,678	50,194	102,451	119,029	72,118
25	Massachusetts	15.8	27.9	7.9	4.5	3.9	4.1	99,858	60,718	116,038	123,206	63,240
26	Michigan	10.5	23.0	8.7	4.5	3.6	5.6	69,183	42,081	78,329	84,982	52,764
27	Minnesota	10.5	25.9	7.3	4.4	3.8	5.7	85,086	50,349	98,830	106,624	57,685
28	Mississippi	8.0	25.2	8.7	5.3	4.8	6.9	54,203	39,496	60,349	65,243	41,712
29	Missouri	10.8	24.1	8.1	4.9	4.2	7.1	68,545	41,471	80,649	83,262	50,535
30	Montana	9.8	23.4	10.3	5.4	5.6	8.9	70,804	41,657	81,050	83,785	54,222
31	Nebraska	9.5	24.6	7.8	4.8	4.0	6.6	74,590	40,461	85,170	92,464	55,124
32	Nevada	12.6	16.5	20.0	4.2	4.1	7.7	76,364	50,217	77,911	91,875	59,338
33	New Hampshire	12.9	24.0	7.7	4.1	4.0	7.5	96,838	49,394	107,834	117,129	63,279
34	New Jersey	14.4	24.2	7.7	4.4	4.3	3.6	99,781	60,250	110,632	121,275	67,177
35	New Mexico	13.7	25.6	11.0	5.1	6.9	7.4	62,268	41,168	66,883	74,364	50,637
36	New York	13.5	29.0	8.5	4.8	4.7	3.6	82,095	47,582	97,035	97,221	57,125
37	North Carolina	13.0	22.5	8.7	5.0	4.1	7.3	70,804	43,589	78,793	85,121	51,285
38	North Dakota	6.9	26.1	7.0	4.5	5.8	7.2	76,525	45,715	90,366	91,183	53,059
39	Ohio	10.6	24.3	8.3	4.5	4.0	6.5	67,769	41,503	78,434	83,622	49,869
40	Oklahoma	9.4	23.0	9.2	5.2	6.2	7.7	62,138	39,459	71,237	73,921	49,495
41	Oregon	12.1	23.9	8.5	4.8	4.9	6.8	80,160	49,459	91,175	97,116	58,852
42	Pennsylvania	11.5	26.3	7.8	4.5	3.9	5.9	73,824	42,038	85,860	91,601	52,474
72	Puerto Rico	11.4	20.9	10.3	6.7	7.2	2.2	25,621	12,769	30,843	31,124	20,742
44	Rhode Island	11.9	26.1	9.0	4.5	4.5	4.5	84,972	55,148	92,029	104,176	57,865
45	South Carolina	11.7	21.8	8.9	5.3	4.3	8.4	67,804	39,231	75,064	80,165	52,841
46	South Dakota	7.5	25.6	7.8	4.9	5.0	7.8	71,810	40,749	78,443	89,755	53,981
47	Tennessee	11.2	22.2	8.9	4.8	4.4	7.1	67,631	42,080	77,123	80,786	50,271
48	Texas	13.1	21.7	8.5	4.8	3.9	6.1	75,780	42,996	81,680	91,255	55,533
49	Utah	13.3	23.4	8.2	4.4	4.6	4.4	93,421	57,091	100,018	115,528	67,374
50	Vermont	11.4	28.5	9.1	3.9	4.9	6.3	81,211	53,539	95,660	99,437	55,201
51	Virginia	16.8	22.1	8.0	5.2	8.7	9.1	89,931	50,670	97,400	110,074	64,938
53	Washington	15.0	21.8	8.6	4.5	5.1	7.6	94,605	55,753	108,739	113,460	63,963
54	West Virginia	8.5	27.6	8.4	4.4	7.6	7.2	55,948	37,368	66,827	66,064	44,465
55	Wisconsin	9.9	23.3	7.2	4.2	3.6	5.9	74,631	43,898	86,477	92,701	52,916
56	Wyoming	8.4	24.5	7.9	5.4	6.7	8.7	72,415	51,397	81,607	87,701	53,962

Table B-1. States — What: Education, Employment, and Income, 2023—*Continued*

State code	STATE	Median income in the past 12 months (in 2023 inflation-adjusted dollars) — Median household income by race and Hispanic origin of householder								
		White alone	Black or African American alone	American Indian and Alaska Native alone	Asian alone	Native Hawaiian and other Pacific Islander alone	Some other race alone	Two or more races	White alone, not Hispanic or Latino	Hispanic or Latino
	ACS table number:	B19013A	B19013B	B19013C	B19013D	B19013E	B19013F	B19013G	B19013H	B19013I
	Column number:	90	91	92	93	94	95	96	97	98
	UNITED STATES	82,531	53,927	61,061	111,817	74,257	66,250	73,382	83,121	69,467
01	Alabama	71,058	43,339	56,971	96,502	50,596	49,533	60,127	71,245	54,430
02	Alaska	93,216	60,170	60,691	97,145	97,679	101,032	76,718	94,122	78,246
04	Arizona	81,415	59,504	47,592	104,805	52,442	67,687	72,904	81,954	70,990
05	Arkansas	62,859	35,920	65,812	79,176	67,892	62,973	60,649	63,281	57,612
06	California	103,675	67,476	81,901	123,928	95,404	75,016	87,233	106,214	79,187
08	Colorado	97,154	65,056	62,924	114,156	82,250	72,466	86,351	98,965	76,580
09	Connecticut	101,124	63,020	65,190	128,344	NA	61,174	75,813	102,325	61,081
10	Delaware	86,843	62,176	49,986	139,224	-	53,659	77,325	87,049	65,662
11	District of Columbia	164,990	60,446	115,028	112,244	-	109,427	136,866	169,247	119,186
12	Florida	78,094	57,820	71,447	94,927	83,540	64,279	71,015	78,525	69,286
13	Georgia	84,303	58,739	59,239	105,203	70,188	60,949	75,417	84,582	69,033
15	Hawaii	92,015	80,338	76,154	105,595	73,464	70,586	97,153	91,629	85,833
16	Idaho	76,230	53,548	58,876	71,031	55,716	72,957	69,559	76,406	69,777
17	Illinois	86,538	50,338	68,526	105,723	NA	70,377	80,163	86,932	75,954
18	Indiana	72,483	46,997	57,897	84,849	37,991	55,778	66,109	72,501	63,527
19	Iowa	73,308	42,890	50,847	81,459	50,943	60,562	64,253	73,511	61,264
20	Kansas	73,653	49,801	65,234	72,207	72,664	56,859	62,333	74,390	59,363
21	Kentucky	63,226	41,439	55,489	69,113	NA	51,508	55,017	63,356	53,375
22	Louisiana	70,658	38,115	63,803	68,389	NA	58,693	62,875	70,828	62,639
23	Maine	74,221	50,105	43,949	74,185	-	80,143	71,053	74,258	78,446
24	Maryland	109,807	78,926	91,387	128,472	67,036	79,977	101,661	110,111	86,729
25	Massachusetts	105,911	73,976	72,876	131,406	NA	60,011	71,747	106,631	62,838
26	Michigan	73,345	44,632	58,558	99,146	63,337	62,988	66,345	73,460	66,479
27	Minnesota	86,950	59,261	51,990	102,642	122,847	71,731	81,152	87,150	72,456
28	Mississippi	67,230	38,488	37,704	72,527	41,820	56,931	56,207	67,477	47,188
29	Missouri	72,246	48,226	60,838	84,844	59,930	61,186	64,717	72,392	62,953
30	Montana	72,079	51,270	49,167	93,913	-	75,599	61,409	72,166	68,529
31	Nebraska	77,606	47,293	40,963	81,096	-	77,685	66,301	78,106	65,948
32	Nevada	82,302	55,514	65,762	87,210	78,920	62,422	75,089	83,099	67,693
33	New Hampshire	96,593	96,606	175,388	101,831	-	100,510	94,285	96,488	94,104
34	New Jersey	108,609	68,896	63,869	151,483	145,773	73,665	83,659	110,147	76,104
35	New Mexico	69,148	52,263	44,034	95,186	33,718	48,997	59,255	73,336	56,071
36	New York	91,863	60,927	59,982	93,218	NA	57,191	76,517	92,545	61,724
37	North Carolina	78,232	52,219	45,691	110,382	52,987	56,857	65,305	78,439	60,703
38	North Dakota	80,062	55,075	56,819	55,461	-	60,451	53,169	80,100	56,909
39	Ohio	72,690	43,809	58,733	95,221	NA	50,447	58,750	72,847	55,841
40	Oklahoma	66,012	43,527	52,393	72,144	83,518	55,743	59,936	66,452	56,613
41	Oregon	80,637	56,575	70,278	103,745	68,895	69,897	76,997	80,816	73,475
42	Pennsylvania	78,815	47,841	54,956	99,052	50,347	53,216	63,179	79,044	57,743
72	Puerto Rico	25,827	28,228	28,989	16,870	-	24,941	25,673	50,451	25,573
44	Rhode Island	92,137	57,837	97,861	96,608	-	60,993	65,882	92,561	62,235
45	South Carolina	78,208	45,558	55,411	105,794	NA	60,364	60,964	78,545	60,206
46	South Dakota	75,162	42,220	37,200	67,411	-	56,788	70,195	75,470	59,104
47	Tennessee	72,327	50,060	70,912	101,642	55,495	54,506	63,270	72,268	63,574
48	Texas	85,747	57,762	71,559	113,899	74,013	61,047	65,125	90,486	62,906
49	Utah	95,487	91,321	71,469	104,027	94,263	73,619	89,258	96,337	81,233
50	Vermont	81,771	50,454	87,993	105,558	-	101,601	66,893	81,752	101,001
51	Virginia	95,427	62,307	66,572	135,217	81,889	78,410	96,353	95,411	87,675
53	Washington	94,715	74,492	68,212	138,163	88,771	71,048	88,336	94,973	77,756
54	West Virginia	56,531	36,265	56,458	65,846	-	70,252	50,830	56,662	55,861
55	Wisconsin	77,570	42,358	54,418	79,047	NA	60,858	67,048	77,684	63,306
56	Wyoming	74,331	45,918	48,514	53,223	-	62,297	65,941	74,681	54,239

Table B-1. States — What: Education, Employment, and Income, 2023—*Continued*

State code	STATE	Median income in the past 12 months (in 2023 inflation-adjusted dollars): Median family income, by type of family: All families	Married-couple families with children under 18	Married-couple families, no children under 18	Male householder with children under 18	Male householder, no children under 18	Female householder with children under 18	Female householder, no children under 18	Median nonfamily household income: All nonfamily households	Living alone, 65 years and over: Male	Living alone, 65 years and over: Female	Median individual income: Persons 15 years and over who worked full-time, year-round: Male	Female
	ACS table number:	B19126	B19126	B19126	B19126	B19126	B19126	B19126	B19215	B19215	B19215	B19326	B19326
	Column number:	99	100	101	102	103	104	105	106	107	108	109	110
	UNITED STATES	96,401	125,977	106,751	59,464	76,186	39,121	65,303	47,090	34,198	29,266	66,402	54,393
01	Alabama	79,940	107,403	91,354	50,444	64,149	29,497	48,916	34,218	30,092	24,801	60,683	44,855
02	Alaska	105,752	125,462	121,171	66,992	81,984	46,867	69,431	56,638	33,845	34,086	70,691	60,740
04	Arizona	93,553	119,616	102,161	59,214	77,860	44,148	68,295	49,360	36,705	32,443	62,716	52,419
05	Arkansas	74,179	100,841	84,524	43,658	58,933	31,747	49,552	33,635	24,988	24,028	53,130	43,808
06	California	109,349	138,719	127,578	66,673	85,771	45,721	78,219	61,493	38,074	32,754	71,583	62,279
08	Colorado	115,335	147,124	122,656	71,873	95,882	48,348	75,633	60,009	40,159	32,815	75,433	61,735
09	Connecticut	115,351	157,187	132,597	65,620	90,639	43,073	80,110	53,431	36,431	31,625	80,078	66,420
10	Delaware	100,727	131,254	112,366	74,533	73,872	45,405	67,381	49,863	39,886	35,526	66,118	56,319
11	District of Columbia	157,210	250,000+	214,198	147,938	81,711	55,536	72,511	89,007	41,961	36,291	111,499	96,508
12	Florida	88,238	113,290	98,927	56,802	72,908	41,114	62,836	45,957	35,026	28,369	59,629	49,983
13	Georgia	91,058	119,792	105,837	53,723	74,276	38,311	62,456	45,317	30,691	26,689	61,677	50,737
15	Hawaii	113,856	134,710	124,184	74,583	87,138	49,190	87,850	53,331	38,461	32,983	66,238	56,982
16	Idaho	91,098	107,726	93,737	55,444	77,800	41,533	66,344	42,022	32,006	27,207	61,667	46,922
17	Illinois	101,886	137,283	111,357	62,103	81,948	41,288	67,374	48,842	36,096	31,139	70,797	57,279
18	Indiana	87,851	114,341	96,345	57,057	66,651	35,871	59,766	41,309	33,363	28,212	61,827	49,327
19	Iowa	92,352	120,779	96,821	55,273	70,176	39,543	60,399	42,048	33,942	30,061	62,277	50,444
20	Kansas	90,492	114,128	97,887	56,485	67,855	37,850	60,662	41,087	32,182	29,651	60,905	49,329
21	Kentucky	77,935	106,973	86,313	51,640	58,093	28,400	50,473	36,323	27,738	24,812	58,380	47,560
22	Louisiana	75,974	111,196	88,173	52,158	55,450	27,790	50,541	32,837	27,044	23,943	61,147	44,524
23	Maine	91,546	119,024	98,776	57,416	68,836	40,736	61,751	45,735	33,439	27,491	64,345	54,263
24	Maryland	121,875	159,911	137,790	71,333	93,827	52,696	83,614	60,660	44,657	36,055	78,458	67,088
25	Massachusetts	126,104	177,034	138,058	71,831	95,789	42,380	85,115	59,594	39,037	29,833	85,660	72,113
26	Michigan	88,499	120,797	97,066	52,368	69,375	35,603	60,494	41,497	34,663	30,209	65,284	51,774
27	Minnesota	108,215	142,517	110,861	67,796	80,485	44,713	76,431	50,692	37,480	32,060	71,399	60,685
28	Mississippi	72,259	103,063	86,131	50,000	52,457	26,911	46,230	30,283	24,451	21,980	54,537	41,299
29	Missouri	88,850	115,991	96,134	57,320	69,302	39,986	60,325	41,014	33,641	28,513	61,725	50,164
30	Montana	88,591	112,896	90,743	66,397	74,860	41,602	54,978	41,938	33,980	27,443	63,021	48,633
31	Nebraska	96,439	119,896	101,274	56,506	79,798	42,047	64,775	42,849	33,579	29,204	61,745	51,237
32	Nevada	90,232	112,561	105,667	64,942	74,180	39,499	70,659	50,647	37,221	31,438	60,310	50,180
33	New Hampshire	116,546	150,029	123,428	63,814	90,274	45,086	74,306	55,035	41,495	30,798	77,975	59,401
34	New Jersey	121,944	167,018	134,164	71,707	92,925	44,800	79,934	58,033	39,809	33,048	81,332	66,956
35	New Mexico	75,197	97,703	94,516	42,127	52,376	29,382	53,951	42,058	33,126	28,605	57,038	47,548
36	New York	102,038	141,123	117,910	55,880	81,564	40,903	70,959	51,619	34,170	28,519	72,480	63,676
37	North Carolina	87,911	117,287	98,672	52,565	64,105	36,181	58,107	43,431	30,453	27,728	60,677	51,040
38	North Dakota	103,823	131,059	104,774	70,086	90,545	35,660	63,424	45,661	32,504	28,541	68,565	51,352
39	Ohio	89,221	124,688	97,971	55,066	70,334	34,414	58,268	41,286	32,488	28,780	63,037	51,945
40	Oklahoma	80,417	101,609	91,399	53,204	64,383	31,574	53,263	37,256	31,704	26,936	57,226	44,706
41	Oregon	97,946	125,549	106,761	58,627	76,605	41,753	65,558	50,157	33,450	31,727	70,002	58,164
42	Pennsylvania	94,367	129,691	102,897	57,933	73,125	37,131	62,073	43,501	32,940	28,387	66,843	54,788
72	Puerto Rico	32,091	56,058	39,409	22,966	29,977	14,495	28,050	15,409	13,132	11,718	27,915	28,438
44	Rhode Island	110,143	141,221	125,025	62,988	77,171	39,134	76,820	51,650	29,485	29,584	72,040	64,363
45	South Carolina	83,747	110,894	96,465	50,647	63,720	35,510	52,654	41,014	32,909	27,409	60,453	47,532
46	South Dakota	94,560	115,205	102,356	51,888	84,067	37,415	60,507	41,971	38,742	27,765	61,030	50,330
47	Tennessee	85,440	111,879	96,034	49,191	71,980	32,391	57,938	41,407	29,310	26,654	60,557	50,005
48	Texas	91,467	116,166	105,112	56,096	73,775	38,384	61,049	47,822	32,793	28,297	62,200	51,027
49	Utah	107,507	121,946	112,943	69,111	86,990	44,502	76,575	53,736	41,932	32,195	71,244	51,586
50	Vermont	104,756	133,818	107,381	85,135	70,263	43,136	69,534	46,744	27,366	28,549	65,703	57,225
51	Virginia	109,947	146,806	121,386	61,795	89,689	42,879	70,452	53,526	39,790	32,371	74,484	60,191
53	Washington	113,053	145,513	120,800	73,619	86,461	42,108	78,405	59,147	36,898	32,878	81,283	65,428
54	West Virginia	73,421	100,188	79,625	48,254	57,401	29,974	50,631	32,846	27,215	25,027	60,030	45,544
55	Wisconsin	96,999	129,130	101,197	60,767	75,357	40,428	65,816	45,567	33,329	29,151	64,382	52,384
56	Wyoming	91,428	112,093	94,633	50,375	75,174	33,303	62,689	43,817	39,315	27,100	65,091	47,334

Table B-1. States — What: Education, Employment, and Income, 2023—*Continued*

State code	STATE	Per capita income in the past 12 months (in 2023 inflation-adjusted dollars)	Total number of households	Households, by type of income (percent)								
				With wage or salary income	With self-employment income	With interest, dividends, or net rental income	With Social Security	With Supplemental Security Income (SSI)	With public assistance income	With cash public assistance or food stamps/ SNAP	With retirement income	With other types of income
	ACS table number:	B19301	B19052	B19052	B19053	B19054	B19055	B19056	B19057	B19058	B19059	B19060
	Column number:	111	112	113	114	115	116	117	118	119	120	121
	UNITED STATES	43,313	131,332,360	75.1	11.0	18.9	31.3	5.0	2.4	12.9	24.2	8.5
01	Alabama	35,046	2,051,545	70.8	9.2	14.3	35.2	6.3	1.7	14.3	26.1	9.7
02	Alaska	45,792	276,852	78.3	13.3	47.8	25.3	3.7	5.7	12.0	24.5	32.9
04	Arizona	41,290	2,907,014	72.1	10.9	18.6	33.7	4.2	1.7	10.7	26.2	8.2
05	Arkansas	33,012	1,232,871	70.3	9.7	16.1	34.8	6.3	1.4	8.7	22.8	9.3
06	California	48,013	13,699,816	77.4	13.5	20.8	28.5	5.8	3.6	14.6	21.6	8.0
08	Colorado	51,768	2,428,261	79.5	13.1	22.5	25.6	2.9	2.1	9.8	22.4	8.8
09	Connecticut	53,119	1,442,969	76.0	11.5	22.1	32.5	4.4	2.7	12.9	25.6	7.3
10	Delaware	44,350	412,048	73.8	8.3	21.0	37.1	5.2	2.6	12.1	31.8	7.6
11	District of Columbia	78,479	334,673	80.4	10.4	25.4	17.8	3.7	3.0	15.4	16.7	5.4
12	Florida	41,902	8,966,402	70.9	10.8	19.1	36.7	4.9	1.9	12.4	25.9	8.6
13	Georgia	39,685	4,150,138	76.8	10.7	14.9	29.4	5.2	1.7	13.0	22.5	9.4
15	Hawaii	43,794	493,898	74.6	13.4	28.6	38.5	4.7	3.3	12.2	31.0	9.9
16	Idaho	37,426	733,244	74.7	14.5	20.0	32.3	4.2	2.4	8.0	25.3	10.2
17	Illinois	45,043	5,071,288	75.9	9.3	19.2	29.3	4.4	2.4	14.8	24.1	6.6
18	Indiana	37,299	2,754,881	75.5	9.3	15.7	31.6	4.9	1.7	9.3	25.1	8.2
19	Iowa	39,518	1,337,243	75.2	12.5	19.8	31.4	4.2	1.5	9.3	24.8	9.2
20	Kansas	38,361	1,188,340	76.5	11.8	19.3	30.7	3.6	1.4	7.3	24.2	8.4
21	Kentucky	34,676	1,853,603	71.1	9.6	13.8	34.2	6.4	1.7	13.6	25.4	8.4
22	Louisiana	34,102	1,833,915	70.5	10.3	13.7	32.3	7.0	1.1	17.7	22.0	7.7
23	Maine	42,936	616,085	70.9	14.2	21.5	37.0	5.9	3.0	13.5	27.2	10.3
24	Maryland	50,728	2,384,715	78.7	10.9	20.2	28.7	4.4	2.2	10.9	26.1	7.7
25	Massachusetts	55,897	2,800,984	76.7	11.3	23.1	30.2	5.8	3.5	16.6	23.2	7.7
26	Michigan	38,952	4,107,809	72.1	9.2	17.8	34.8	5.7	2.5	14.6	27.8	7.9
27	Minnesota	46,530	2,344,432	76.6	11.7	21.4	29.9	3.7	2.7	8.8	24.3	9.3
28	Mississippi	30,807	1,166,617	70.0	9.3	11.2	35.3	7.6	1.5	13.3	23.7	9.3
29	Missouri	38,699	2,556,271	74.4	10.6	17.4	32.9	4.8	1.6	10.2	25.5	8.9
30	Montana	40,197	472,867	72.5	14.9	25.5	33.8	3.6	1.6	8.1	25.3	10.5
31	Nebraska	41,436	813,864	78.4	13.4	19.1	28.8	4.5	1.5	8.3	21.4	9.7
32	Nevada	40,463	1,224,685	75.5	10.7	16.7	30.6	4.4	2.8	13.9	24.7	9.0
33	New Hampshire	51,587	569,493	75.6	11.4	23.5	35.0	3.9	1.9	7.3	27.6	7.8
34	New Jersey	52,583	3,538,457	78.1	10.6	22.0	31.6	4.6	2.1	10.4	24.6	7.4
35	New Mexico	35,510	856,580	69.7	10.5	18.5	36.1	6.1	3.3	20.8	26.1	8.6
36	New York	48,847	7,809,267	74.4	10.5	19.4	32.2	6.3	3.9	17.2	24.9	6.4
37	North Carolina	40,414	4,392,669	74.7	10.2	17.4	31.7	4.6	1.6	13.0	24.9	8.9
38	North Dakota	42,814	338,059	77.8	13.1	21.7	27.3	2.9	1.7	7.7	19.8	10.1
39	Ohio	39,395	4,917,309	73.6	9.4	16.8	32.3	5.4	2.0	13.0	26.4	8.3
40	Oklahoma	34,206	1,589,105	73.0	11.0	16.5	32.0	5.5	2.5	15.7	22.2	10.5
41	Oregon	44,623	1,752,050	73.1	12.7	22.7	33.0	4.8	3.2	17.6	25.0	9.3
42	Pennsylvania	42,605	5,324,209	73.0	9.3	20.7	34.9	5.7	3.2	15.7	27.2	7.5
72	Puerto Rico	17,976	1,277,486	52.0	10.5	4.6	46.2	0.6	2.9	47.0	18.3	10.7
44	Rhode Island	46,525	443,980	74.2	10.7	21.7	33.8	6.4	2.9	14.0	24.8	8.0
45	South Carolina	38,097	2,177,733	72.0	9.6	15.1	35.0	4.7	1.1	11.1	26.8	9.5
46	South Dakota	40,263	378,559	75.9	14.6	21.8	31.1	4.1	2.0	8.2	22.6	10.2
47	Tennessee	38,538	2,889,226	73.5	11.6	16.0	32.8	5.3	1.7	10.4	24.1	9.1
48	Texas	39,775	11,260,645	79.6	12.4	15.3	25.5	4.4	1.6	11.8	19.4	8.9
49	Utah	40,096	1,167,591	82.9	13.1	19.5	23.9	3.1	1.4	5.8	20.5	8.1
50	Vermont	46,029	279,612	72.0	16.0	26.9	35.1	4.1	3.2	11.0	25.8	7.1
51	Virginia	48,689	3,402,670	77.2	10.4	21.6	30.0	4.2	1.9	10.5	26.5	10.0
53	Washington	52,011	3,101,265	76.1	11.0	23.4	29.1	4.2	3.4	13.0	23.9	9.6
54	West Virginia	32,766	743,644	64.9	6.6	15.1	40.4	7.4	3.4	18.9	28.3	9.5
55	Wisconsin	41,785	2,495,539	74.3	9.5	20.9	32.3	4.2	1.8	12.0	26.8	8.3
56	Wyoming	39,966	247,368	72.6	12.2	23.8	33.7	3.4	1.2	5.8	27.0	10.3

Table B-1. States — What: Education, Employment, and Income, 2023—*Continued*

State code	STATE	Household income in the past 12 months (in 2023 inflation-adjusted dollars)										
			Households by income group (percent)									
		Total number of housholds	Less than $10,000	$10,000 to $14,999	$15,000 to $24,999	$25,000 to $34,999	$35,000 to $49,999	$50,000 to $74,999	$75,000 to $99,999	$100,000 to $149,999	$150,000 to $199,999	$200,000 or more
	ACS table number:	B19001	B19001	B19001	B19001	B19001	B19001	B19001	B19001	B19001	B19001	B19001
	Column number:	122	123	124	125	126	127	128	129	130	131	132
	UNITED STATES	131,332,360	5.3	3.5	6.4	6.8	10.3	16.1	12.7	17.4	9.1	12.4
01	Alabama	2,051,545	6.4	4.8	9.0	8.9	11.4	17.3	13.2	15.6	6.7	6.7
02	Alaska	276,852	4.1	2.5	5.7	5.4	10.6	15.2	13.3	19.4	10.4	13.5
04	Arizona	2,907,014	5.5	2.9	5.9	6.7	10.8	16.7	13.5	18.0	9.2	10.8
05	Arkansas	1,232,871	6.3	5.2	9.0	9.3	12.8	18.2	12.5	14.6	5.6	6.3
06	California	13,699,816	4.8	3.0	5.2	5.4	8.2	13.5	11.9	17.8	11.2	19.1
08	Colorado	2,428,261	4.2	2.5	4.9	5.1	8.5	15.1	13.0	19.1	11.8	15.9
09	Connecticut	1,442,969	4.9	3.2	5.6	5.6	8.5	13.9	12.1	17.8	11.0	17.5
10	Delaware	412,048	4.0	2.9	5.2	6.5	11.3	16.3	13.5	18.1	10.5	11.7
11	District of Columbia	334,673	7.9	2.9	4.8	3.1	5.8	12.3	10.2	14.9	12.2	25.9
12	Florida	8,966,402	5.4	3.3	6.4	7.4	11.2	17.4	13.2	17.2	8.0	10.6
13	Georgia	4,150,138	5.9	3.6	6.8	6.9	10.7	16.4	12.7	17.5	8.6	11.0
15	Hawaii	493,898	4.6	2.9	5.0	5.2	7.6	14.2	12.5	19.8	11.4	17.0
16	Idaho	733,244	3.9	2.7	6.1	7.3	11.5	18.6	14.2	18.7	8.5	8.6
17	Illinois	5,071,288	5.6	3.4	5.9	6.5	10.0	15.7	12.4	18.1	9.6	12.6
18	Indiana	2,754,881	5.2	3.5	7.0	7.9	11.7	18.7	13.6	17.1	7.8	7.6
19	Iowa	1,337,243	4.2	3.3	6.8	8.0	12.2	17.8	14.1	17.8	8.3	7.5
20	Kansas	1,188,340	4.6	3.2	7.0	8.2	12.2	17.9	13.6	17.2	8.0	8.2
21	Kentucky	1,853,603	6.8	5.2	8.9	8.3	12.8	17.1	12.6	15.5	6.4	6.5
22	Louisiana	1,833,915	7.7	6.1	9.2	8.8	12.4	16.0	12.0	14.1	6.8	7.0
23	Maine	616,085	4.4	3.6	7.0	7.0	11.3	17.4	13.4	19.4	7.7	8.8
24	Maryland	2,384,715	5.1	2.5	4.3	4.9	8.0	13.9	11.9	19.1	11.7	18.7
25	Massachusetts	2,800,984	4.7	3.5	5.8	5.1	7.4	12.6	10.9	17.7	11.1	21.1
26	Michigan	4,107,809	5.8	3.9	7.2	7.3	11.8	17.7	13.1	16.8	7.9	8.6
27	Minnesota	2,344,432	3.8	2.9	5.5	5.8	9.7	16.2	14.0	19.4	10.4	12.3
28	Mississippi	1,166,617	7.4	6.4	10.3	9.2	13.0	16.8	12.2	13.9	5.3	5.5
29	Missouri	2,556,271	4.9	3.6	7.2	8.0	12.4	17.9	13.1	17.3	7.4	8.1
30	Montana	472,867	4.7	3.6	7.6	8.1	11.3	18.1	13.5	17.8	7.4	8.0
31	Nebraska	813,864	4.5	3.2	6.5	6.7	11.2	18.2	14.0	18.3	8.3	9.2
32	Nevada	1,224,685	5.5	2.5	6.0	7.2	10.6	17.4	13.7	18.2	8.8	10.2
33	New Hampshire	569,493	3.5	2.4	4.8	5.9	7.9	14.2	13.0	20.2	12.5	15.7
34	New Jersey	3,538,457	4.3	2.8	5.1	5.2	7.9	13.2	11.6	18.1	11.4	20.4
35	New Mexico	856,580	6.7	5.0	8.8	8.3	11.8	17.6	12.7	14.6	7.1	7.3
36	New York	7,809,267	6.4	4.0	6.4	6.4	9.2	14.1	11.5	16.4	9.8	15.9
37	North Carolina	4,392,669	5.2	3.6	7.0	7.5	11.9	17.5	13.0	16.5	7.9	9.7
38	North Dakota	338,059	4.6	3.3	6.7	7.2	10.5	16.6	14.0	19.2	8.8	9.0
39	Ohio	4,917,309	5.6	3.8	7.4	7.8	12.1	17.8	12.8	16.4	7.8	8.4
40	Oklahoma	1,589,105	6.6	4.2	8.3	8.5	12.6	17.7	13.1	15.9	6.6	6.5
41	Oregon	1,752,050	5.0	3.4	6.4	6.2	9.9	16.0	13.5	18.4	9.4	11.8
42	Pennsylvania	5,324,209	5.4	3.7	7.0	7.2	10.6	16.8	12.8	17.3	8.6	10.7
72	Puerto Rico	1,277,486	21.1	10.6	17.4	12.5	12.7	12.2	5.6	4.8	1.6	1.6
44	Rhode Island	443,980	5.0	4.3	5.7	5.6	8.5	15.4	13.5	18.7	10.2	13.1
45	South Carolina	2,177,733	6.1	3.9	7.2	7.9	11.6	17.9	13.1	16.8	7.2	8.1
46	South Dakota	378,559	4.3	3.5	7.1	7.5	11.8	18.0	13.8	18.6	7.6	7.8
47	Tennessee	2,889,226	5.6	4.1	7.5	7.6	12.0	17.4	13.1	16.9	7.2	8.6
48	Texas	11,260,645	5.3	3.3	6.4	6.8	10.7	17.0	12.7	17.4	8.8	11.6
49	Utah	1,167,591	3.2	2.1	4.2	5.2	8.7	15.5	14.6	22.0	11.5	13.0
50	Vermont	279,612	4.8	2.7	6.6	6.3	10.3	16.4	12.6	19.9	9.9	10.5
51	Virginia	3,402,670	4.7	3.0	5.3	5.9	8.9	14.5	12.6	18.0	10.7	16.5
53	Washington	3,101,265	4.5	2.7	4.9	5.1	8.3	14.4	12.8	19.1	11.0	17.3
54	West Virginia	743,644	6.5	5.7	9.9	9.2	13.8	17.6	12.3	14.3	5.6	5.1
55	Wisconsin	2,495,539	4.5	3.3	6.5	6.9	11.4	17.6	13.8	18.8	8.7	8.5
56	Wyoming	247,368	4.8	3.5	6.7	8.0	11.1	17.5	14.4	18.7	8.0	7.3

Table B-1. States — What: Education, Employment, and Income, 2023—*Continued*

State code	STATE	Households with income over $100,000, by age of householder (as a percent of all households in age group)					Households with income below poverty (as a percent of all households in household-type group)						
		All households	Householder under 25 years	Householder 25 to 44 years	Householder 45 to 64 years	Householder 65 years and over	All households	Family households	Married-couple family households	Male householder family households	Female householder family households	Male householder nonfamily households	Female householder nonfamily households
	ACS table number:	B19001	B19037	B19037	B19037	B19037	C17017	C17017	C17017	C17017	C17017	C17017	C17017
	Column number:	133	134	135	136	137	138	139	140	141	142	143	144
	UNITED STATES	38.9	13.0	43.6	47.6	25.9	12.7	8.8	4.7	12.1	23.2	17.6	21.8
01	Alabama	29.0	8.7	30.9	37.7	19.7	16.0	11.3	4.7	14.1	32.1	22.5	26.8
02	Alaska	43.3	17.5	47.1	51.7	31.4	10.4	7.2	3.5	15.0	19.7	16.8	14.3
04	Arizona	38.0	14.0	42.5	48.1	25.8	12.6	8.7	5.1	12.1	21.4	17.4	21.3
05	Arkansas	26.5	7.0	31.0	33.6	16.5	16.3	11.2	5.6	15.9	29.5	22.2	28.6
06	California	48.1	21.3	52.6	55.4	34.9	12.0	8.5	5.2	11.0	19.5	16.9	21.4
08	Colorado	46.7	15.4	52.5	57.1	30.4	9.7	5.9	3.4	8.9	17.9	14.4	17.1
09	Connecticut	46.2	17.4	49.7	55.6	33.0	11.1	7.4	3.4	11.0	20.4	16.6	18.6
10	Delaware	40.3	8.1	43.4	48.9	30.5	10.5	7.4	3.8	8.5	20.1	15.7	16.7
11	District of Columbia	53.0	21.0	63.0	54.3	36.2	13.4	11.1	4.6	9.8	23.9	14.4	15.5
12	Florida	35.8	13.8	40.2	43.8	25.3	12.6	8.6	5.5	11.5	19.4	17.7	21.8
13	Georgia	37.1	9.2	39.8	46.2	24.5	13.7	9.8	4.9	12.0	24.6	18.9	23.1
15	Hawaii	48.1	12.0	51.5	56.6	39.4	10.3	6.6	4.0	11.6	14.9	17.0	19.7
16	Idaho	35.8	12.7	38.2	46.9	24.0	10.1	6.5	4.7	9.2	16.4	16.4	20.3
17	Illinois	40.3	12.1	46.5	48.6	26.4	12.3	8.0	4.2	10.3	21.8	17.5	20.6
18	Indiana	32.4	9.8	36.9	41.9	19.2	12.6	8.4	4.0	10.7	25.9	17.0	22.0
19	Iowa	33.6	11.2	39.0	43.4	20.8	11.6	6.9	3.5	11.6	23.0	16.6	21.4
20	Kansas	33.4	7.9	37.6	44.3	21.5	11.7	7.6	4.0	10.3	24.3	17.7	20.0
21	Kentucky	28.4	7.2	34.0	36.1	16.2	16.9	12.6	6.8	17.4	32.6	21.3	27.7
22	Louisiana	27.8	5.2	31.8	34.5	18.3	19.4	13.7	5.8	17.5	33.6	25.8	31.9
23	Maine	35.9	13.7	41.7	45.3	22.7	11.1	6.8	3.3	13.1	23.0	15.0	20.4
24	Maryland	49.5	18.3	52.2	58.9	36.5	10.0	6.4	3.3	9.2	15.8	14.4	18.3
25	Massachusetts	49.9	25.6	57.6	59.2	32.1	11.3	7.0	3.4	9.9	19.7	15.7	20.5
26	Michigan	33.2	8.6	37.6	42.9	20.7	13.8	9.2	4.7	14.2	25.1	19.8	23.4
27	Minnesota	42.1	13.2	49.2	53.3	24.3	9.8	5.4	2.8	7.4	19.2	15.1	18.6
28	Mississippi	24.7	10.0	27.7	31.0	15.4	19.5	13.7	5.5	17.1	34.9	27.1	32.5
29	Missouri	32.8	8.0	38.4	41.5	20.4	12.5	7.9	4.5	10.6	21.0	17.3	22.4
30	Montana	33.2	9.7	38.4	42.1	22.2	12.2	7.0	4.1	16.7	19.8	18.3	21.9
31	Nebraska	35.8	9.9	40.8	46.5	22.6	11.5	6.6	3.4	11.1	21.4	16.7	22.7
32	Nevada	37.1	14.0	37.1	46.4	27.8	11.9	8.6	4.8	10.4	20.4	16.5	18.4
33	New Hampshire	48.3	20.7	55.6	58.3	31.0	8.3	4.8	2.3	10.5	16.5	12.2	16.8
34	New Jersey	49.9	19.7	55.4	59.0	33.8	10.2	7.1	3.6	8.9	19.9	14.0	18.4
35	New Mexico	29.0	9.2	29.9	37.1	22.9	17.2	14.3	6.7	22.5	32.7	19.5	24.2
36	New York	42.1	17.8	48.6	48.9	28.9	14.5	10.3	5.9	13.8	22.6	18.8	22.8
37	North Carolina	34.2	11.8	37.7	43.1	22.0	12.8	9.1	4.7	13.7	24.1	17.8	20.9
38	North Dakota	37.0	11.7	45.1	46.3	22.6	11.1	5.3	2.7	13.5	18.7	14.6	23.1
39	Ohio	32.7	8.5	38.1	42.0	19.1	13.6	9.2	3.8	13.6	27.2	18.2	22.5
40	Oklahoma	29.0	7.6	32.7	35.8	20.5	16.1	11.6	6.2	14.8	30.5	22.3	25.9
41	Oregon	39.6	12.9	45.3	48.6	26.6	12.2	7.7	4.2	13.2	20.9	18.4	20.5
42	Pennsylvania	36.5	11.6	42.1	46.2	22.5	12.5	8.3	4.1	11.5	24.1	17.4	21.4
72	Puerto Rico	7.9	1.3	10.0	10.8	4.3	42.2	36.0	24.0	43.4	52.3	48.5	55.4
44	Rhode Island	42.0	20.2	45.6	51.8	28.5	12.2	7.3	3.0	9.8	21.5	15.4	23.2
45	South Carolina	32.2	10.0	34.7	40.2	23.1	14.3	10.0	4.8	14.5	27.3	20.0	24.5
46	South Dakota	34.0	9.4	36.9	44.6	22.8	11.6	7.6	3.7	13.2	27.1	16.2	19.7
47	Tennessee	32.7	10.9	36.7	40.5	21.4	14.2	10.2	5.2	15.0	27.1	19.1	23.0
48	Texas	37.8	12.2	40.5	46.1	26.0	13.3	10.3	5.9	13.3	25.6	16.9	21.9
49	Utah	46.6	17.2	50.0	58.3	32.1	9.2	6.0	3.5	10.3	19.4	17.5	17.3
50	Vermont	40.3	17.7	47.8	49.8	26.1	11.0	4.5	2.0	6.2	18.5	19.8	21.0
51	Virginia	45.2	15.6	48.6	54.7	32.0	10.7	7.1	3.5	10.7	20.7	15.2	19.3
53	Washington	47.5	20.6	54.9	56.5	29.5	10.4	6.6	3.5	9.3	20.8	14.4	19.6
54	West Virginia	25.0	7.0	30.7	32.3	15.1	17.2	11.6	6.1	17.0	31.6	23.4	28.7
55	Wisconsin	36.0	12.2	42.4	46.5	20.5	11.1	6.6	3.3	10.2	22.4	16.3	19.4
56	Wyoming	34.0	13.9	38.9	43.1	21.7	11.6	7.3	3.2	12.6	28.1	16.5	20.9

Table B-1. States — What: Education, Employment, and Income, 2023—*Continued*

State code	STATE	Population for whom poverty status is determined	Persons with income below poverty by age (as a percent of all persons in age group)				Persons with income below poverty by selected race and Hispanic origin groups (as a percent of all persons in race/Hispanic group)			
			All ages	Under 18 years	18 to 64 years	65 years and over	White alone, not Hispanic or Latino	Black or African American alone	Asian alone	Hispanic or Latino
	ACS table number:	C17001	C17001	C17001	C17001	C17001	C17001H	C17001B	C17001D	C17001I
	Column number:	145	146	147	148	149	150	151	152	153
	UNITED STATES	327,076,658	12.5	16.0	11.5	11.3	9.4	20.8	9.9	16.6
01	Alabama	4,960,839	15.6	21.1	14.6	11.9	10.9	26.0	9.3	23.5
02	Alaska	717,303	10.4	12.1	10.4	7.2	7.3	21.4	12.0	11.8
04	Arizona	7,274,129	12.4	15.4	11.7	11.4	9.2	17.8	9.3	16.0
05	Arkansas	2,980,358	15.7	20.9	14.7	12.1	12.8	28.2	10.9	14.6
06	California	38,249,686	12.0	14.9	11.0	12.0	9.2	19.7	9.5	14.4
08	Colorado	5,757,114	9.3	10.7	8.9	9.2	7.3	16.6	9.3	13.6
09	Connecticut	3,521,952	10.3	13.3	9.5	9.4	6.3	17.7	6.9	21.1
10	Delaware	1,007,022	10.5	15.2	9.8	7.9	7.4	15.3	4.3	20.5
11	District of Columbia	649,438	14.0	17.1	12.4	17.7	4.2	26.1	11.8	5.2
12	Florida	22,139,460	12.3	15.7	11.3	12.1	9.3	18.0	10.4	15.0
13	Georgia	10,765,238	13.6	18.4	12.1	12.1	9.5	18.9	10.1	17.8
15	Hawaii	1,398,532	10.1	11.4	9.7	10.1	10.4	14.8	6.9	13.4
16	Idaho	1,915,282	10.1	11.5	9.7	9.5	9.3	27.7	9.8	14.1
17	Illinois	12,268,020	11.6	14.7	10.8	10.6	8.3	23.0	10.4	14.1
18	Indiana	6,672,209	12.3	15.4	11.8	9.8	9.8	23.9	12.3	19.3
19	Iowa	3,108,670	11.3	13.6	11.0	9.4	9.7	24.3	10.6	19.5
20	Kansas	2,854,559	11.2	13.2	11.0	9.3	9.2	18.9	13.8	16.7
21	Kentucky	4,402,485	16.4	21.0	15.6	12.9	14.9	24.9	15.3	25.8
22	Louisiana	4,448,119	18.9	25.0	17.8	14.2	13.2	29.1	18.7	19.7
23	Maine	1,355,422	10.4	12.6	10.1	9.4	9.9	21.2	11.4	10.9
24	Maryland	6,048,665	9.5	10.6	9.1	9.5	6.6	13.5	6.8	12.5
25	Massachusetts	6,780,372	10.4	12.6	9.6	10.8	7.4	18.5	11.5	20.6
26	Michigan	9,827,315	13.5	17.6	13.0	10.6	10.9	25.7	11.2	18.2
27	Minnesota	5,617,947	9.3	10.1	8.9	9.5	7.3	22.5	8.3	14.1
28	Mississippi	2,841,691	18.0	23.2	16.6	15.8	11.5	27.5	10.9	25.2
29	Missouri	6,025,993	12.0	14.4	11.4	10.8	10.2	21.5	12.6	15.1
30	Montana	1,107,806	11.7	12.2	12.3	9.5	10.3	NA	7.9	18.6
31	Nebraska	1,931,461	10.5	11.1	10.2	10.3	8.3	30.4	9.3	15.5
32	Nevada	3,154,850	12.0	16.1	11.0	10.4	9.3	19.1	9.5	14.0
33	New Hampshire	1,362,544	7.2	8.0	6.8	7.6	6.9	14.5	3.9	11.2
34	New Jersey	9,131,628	9.7	12.9	8.5	10.1	6.6	16.1	5.5	15.5
35	New Mexico	2,075,116	17.8	25.3	16.4	13.7	10.8	22.9	10.9	20.7
36	New York	19,068,409	14.2	18.6	12.7	14.3	10.0	20.5	15.1	21.1
37	North Carolina	10,549,944	12.8	17.6	11.6	10.9	9.3	19.4	10.3	19.1
38	North Dakota	755,048	9.8	8.7	9.9	10.9	8.5	8.5	19.6	14.6
39	Ohio	11,479,820	13.3	17.7	12.5	10.7	10.5	25.8	12.2	20.0
40	Oklahoma	3,932,800	15.9	20.8	15.1	11.7	13.1	28.1	13.5	21.5
41	Oregon	4,159,215	12.2	13.6	12.2	10.6	11.0	24.8	9.4	16.2
42	Pennsylvania	12,535,767	12.0	15.7	11.2	10.4	9.1	23.1	11.8	22.4
72	Puerto Rico	3,177,647	39.6	54.3	35.8	39.4	25.8	34.0	NA	39.7
44	Rhode Island	1,055,352	10.8	13.4	9.7	11.8	8.8	13.6	11.5	17.4
45	South Carolina	5,231,370	13.9	19.1	13.0	11.0	9.4	23.0	8.6	22.0
46	South Dakota	890,853	11.8	14.6	11.5	8.8	7.8	30.2	13.8	21.4
47	Tennessee	6,969,478	14.0	19.7	12.5	12.2	11.5	22.6	7.7	20.5
48	Texas	29,889,559	13.7	18.4	12.1	12.3	8.3	18.3	9.1	18.4
49	Utah	3,363,147	9.0	9.5	9.0	8.2	7.5	16.1	12.8	13.1
50	Vermont	624,370	9.7	9.0	9.9	9.6	9.6	10.7	6.9	8.1
51	Virginia	8,472,782	10.2	12.7	9.5	9.5	8.2	16.8	6.6	12.4
53	Washington	7,678,825	10.3	12.2	9.9	9.6	8.9	17.0	7.7	15.2
54	West Virginia	1,716,152	16.7	20.1	17.2	12.0	15.7	30.2	17.5	16.0
55	Wisconsin	5,781,514	10.7	12.8	10.1	10.0	8.7	24.7	14.0	17.1
56	Wyoming	571,028	11.3	14.8	11.2	7.4	10.6	NA	NA	15.7

Table B-1. States — What: Education, Employment, and Income, 2023—*Continued*

State code	STATE	Total civilian non-institutionalized population	Type of health insurance (as a percent of all persons)			
			Private only	Public only	Both private and public	None
	ACS table number:	C27010	C27010	C27010	C27010	C27010
	Column number:	154	155	156	157	158
	UNITED STATES	329,987,997	54.7	25.1	12.4	7.9
01	Alabama	5,022,427	52.9	24.5	14.1	8.5
02	Alaska	702,315	51.8	23.6	14.2	10.4
04	Arizona	7,321,507	51.7	26.1	12.3	9.9
05	Arkansas	3,013,015	48.1	30.8	12.1	8.9
06	California	38,495,524	53.3	30.2	10.0	6.4
08	Colorado	5,776,484	59.4	23.0	11.0	6.7
09	Connecticut	3,573,821	56.0	26.4	11.9	5.7
10	Delaware	1,017,865	52.2	24.4	16.9	6.5
11	District of Columbia	669,458	63.6	23.6	10.0	2.7
12	Florida	22,276,397	51.8	25.1	12.4	10.7
13	Georgia	10,832,829	55.1	22.4	11.1	11.4
15	Hawaii	1,378,162	56.5	21.5	18.7	3.2
16	Idaho	1,938,023	55.4	22.4	13.4	8.9
17	Illinois	12,378,557	58.2	24.2	11.4	6.2
18	Indiana	6,764,280	55.8	25.3	12.0	6.9
19	Iowa	3,162,048	57.2	23.2	14.6	5.0
20	Kansas	2,876,621	60.0	18.4	13.2	8.4
21	Kentucky	4,442,248	49.4	31.8	13.4	5.4
22	Louisiana	4,477,873	45.2	35.4	12.5	6.9
23	Maine	1,378,322	52.2	26.6	15.3	5.9
24	Maryland	6,087,312	59.1	20.6	14.0	6.3
25	Massachusetts	6,934,075	59.5	24.3	13.7	2.6
26	Michigan	9,931,639	54.1	25.6	15.7	4.5
27	Minnesota	5,678,023	60.7	20.8	14.3	4.2
28	Mississippi	2,874,290	49.6	27.6	12.5	10.3
29	Missouri	6,094,536	56.5	24.1	11.9	7.5
30	Montana	1,115,486	50.5	26.2	14.9	8.4
31	Nebraska	1,951,731	61.2	19.8	12.8	6.1
32	Nevada	3,154,027	51.8	25.1	12.3	10.8
33	New Hampshire	1,386,016	61.9	19.4	14.0	4.7
34	New Jersey	9,204,137	58.7	22.7	11.4	7.2
35	New Mexico	2,076,456	38.7	36.9	15.3	9.1
36	New York	19,372,405	51.8	30.0	13.3	4.8
37	North Carolina	10,623,208	54.3	23.5	13.0	9.2
38	North Dakota	763,538	66.2	14.7	14.6	4.5
39	Ohio	11,616,141	54.6	26.6	12.7	6.1
40	Oklahoma	3,967,096	48.3	27.1	13.2	11.4
41	Oregon	4,193,025	53.1	27.6	13.8	5.5
42	Pennsylvania	12,779,387	55.1	24.5	15.0	5.4
72	Puerto Rico	3,180,620	31.7	56.3	6.8	5.3
44	Rhode Island	1,079,737	56.7	25.0	13.8	4.5
45	South Carolina	5,276,214	51.8	24.1	15.0	9.1
46	South Dakota	900,264	59.5	18.4	13.9	8.3
47	Tennessee	7,033,220	53.8	24.4	12.5	9.3
48	Texas	30,020,476	54.3	20.3	9.1	16.4
49	Utah	3,391,381	69.5	13.9	8.6	8.0
50	Vermont	642,064	54.4	26.7	15.5	3.4
51	Virginia	8,489,257	58.7	20.8	14.1	6.4
53	Washington	7,693,927	57.2	23.6	13.0	6.3
54	West Virginia	1,736,140	46.8	30.8	16.5	5.9
55	Wisconsin	5,851,267	59.2	22.4	13.6	4.9
56	Wyoming	573,746	56.2	18.4	14.8	10.7

NOTE: High school graduate includes equivalency (e.g., GED), unless otherwise specified.
NA = Not available.
'- = Indicates that either no sample observations or too few sample observations were available to compute an estimate, or a ratio of medians cannot be calculated because one or both of the median estimates falls in the lowest interval or upper interval of an open-ended distribution, or the margin of error associated with a median was larger than the median itself.

Table B-2. Counties — What: Education, Employment, and Income, 2023

STATE County code	STATE County	Educational attainment			Employment status				Household income and benefits				
		Total population 25 years and over	Percent with a high school diploma or less	Percent with a bachelor's degree or more	Total population 16 years and over	Labor force participation (percent)	Percent unemployed	Percent of persons age 16 years and over who worked full-time year-round in the past 12 months (percent of total population)	Total households	Median household income in the past 12 months (in 2023 inflation-adjusted dollars)	Income less than $25,000 (percent)	Income greater than $150,000 (percent)	Percent who received cash public assistance or food stamps/ SNAP
	ACS table number:	C15003	C15003	C15003	C23001	C23001	C23001	S2402	B19001	B19049	B19001	B19001	B19058
	Column number:	1	2	3	4	5	6	7	8	9	10	11	12
00000	**UNITED STATES**	231,791,117	36.2	36.2	271,122,729	63.8	4.3	68.6	131,332,360	77,719	15.2	21.5	12.9
01000	**ALABAMA**	3,498,967	40.9	28.9	4,115,279	58.6	4.0	71.2	2,051,545	62,212	20.2	13.4	14.3
01003	Baldwin County	184,852	36.3	32.0	206,994	57.4	1.1	42.8	105,698	72,915	12.2	17.3	6.2
01015	Calhoun County	78,420	42.3	23.7	95,233	55.5	2.9	36.7	46,310	50,780	22.5	7.5	18.1
01043	Cullman County	64,307	46.2	17.2	73,980	58.4	2.2	40.7	35,961	58,923	20.8	10.7	12.7
01049	DeKalb County	48,611	56.5	13.5	56,881	53.8	2.0	NA	27,182	43,509	25.2	4.0	18.4
01051	Elmore County	63,874	42.8	27.5	72,745	57.1	1.5	42.7	33,692	72,478	18.5	16.3	11.3
01055	Etowah County	72,785	46.7	18.0	83,519	52.8	3.5	38.1	40,027	52,192	24.4	10.5	19.7
01069	Houston County	75,141	45.4	22.9	86,645	59.9	2.4	43.3	44,880	59,335	21.8	9.4	18.6
01073	Jefferson County	449,622	33.3	36.7	528,221	61.3	2.1	45.2	272,648	64,623	19.3	17.5	15.6
01077	Lauderdale County	65,471	42.0	31.7	81,646	56.7	2.7	38.0	41,199	64,864	17.6	10.7	9.0
01081	Lee County	113,445	30.2	41.6	150,605	60.6	3.2	39.9	74,799	60,358	24.6	14.5	12.1
01083	Limestone County	79,975	33.1	33.6	91,935	59.6	2.0	45.5	43,490	81,942	10.1	21.7	7.7
01089	Madison County	284,230	26.0	47.7	335,208	65.6	1.8	47.0	168,996	86,192	13.0	22.5	7.5
01095	Marshall County	66,443	48.8	22.0	77,926	58.9	1.9	43.1	36,274	60,298	21.8	11.7	13.7
01097	Mobile County	281,188	43.6	27.1	327,693	59.0	1.8	43.0	163,963	55,352	21.9	11.4	17.5
01101	Montgomery County	149,322	37.5	34.3	177,604	59.6	2.6	40.8	92,816	60,739	21.0	9.8	19.8
01103	Morgan County	85,702	44.1	25.2	99,909	61.6	2.1	43.1	49,759	75,028	17.9	16.0	10.0
01115	St. Clair County	67,264	44.9	23.6	77,644	60.3	2.1	47.3	35,354	81,334	14.7	15.3	8.3
01117	Shelby County	161,917	27.8	42.9	187,982	65.5	1.9	49.5	88,270	88,070	10.9	24.4	5.8
01121	Talladega County	58,972	50.4	17.8	66,131	56.0	2.2	NA	34,080	61,111	22.8	8.1	19.8
01125	Tuscaloosa County	144,051	37.3	32.4	194,638	61.2	3.5	40.9	93,966	60,926	23.2	12.6	11.5
02000	**ALASKA**	493,892	35.9	32.2	577,598	66.8	4.5	59.1	276,852	86,631	12.3	23.9	12.0
02020	Anchorage Municipality	193,169	30.0	40.0	226,057	70.6	2.8	44.4	109,125	94,437	9.2	29.1	10.5
02090	Fairbanks North Star Borough	61,164	32.7	32.1	73,843	70.5	2.1	NA	37,510	86,391	11.0	21.1	8.6
02170	Matanuska-Susitna Borough	76,765	42.1	26.5	89,929	60.5	1.4	38.8	39,870	93,673	12.9	25.5	10.6
04000	**ARIZONA**	5,150,254	34.0	33.5	6,049,109	60.7	4.2	69.1	2,907,014	77,315	14.3	20.0	10.7
04001	Apache County	42,999	48.2	16.7	51,707	42.6	4.8	30.4	24,010	40,539	36.6	4.5	32.7
04003	Cochise County	89,455	35.0	25.6	103,202	46.3	2.7	NA	50,919	52,025	25.7	10.5	16.2
04005	Coconino County	88,138	29.4	39.8	120,612	62.8	3.4	37.7	56,954	71,738	16.9	19.7	10.7
04013	Maricopa County	3,145,001	32.1	37.0	3,698,830	65.2	2.4	46.5	1,753,589	87,048	11.7	24.0	9.2
04015	Mohave County	175,513	47.3	15.6	192,575	42.3	2.4	28.3	98,791	55,954	23.7	9.0	12.7
04017	Navajo County	73,922	47.9	16.9	85,292	45.6	3.7	NA	41,945	50,754	26.4	8.1	19.5
04019	Pima County	735,290	31.2	36.8	883,691	59.4	2.7	37.9	445,471	69,758	17.1	16.9	11.8
04021	Pinal County	344,391	39.5	22.2	393,294	54.1	2.7	39.0	168,479	77,143	13.4	13.5	11.2
04025	Yavapai County	194,914	29.3	32.0	217,297	47.7	2.0	28.7	113,784	67,245	16.3	16.9	8.5
04027	Yuma County	140,123	50.9	17.4	167,599	51.5	3.3	32.5	83,811	62,888	16.9	8.3	18.1
05000	**ARKANSAS**	2,078,254	44.9	26.2	2,452,773	58.8	4.1	71.3	1,232,871	58,700	20.6	11.9	8.7
05007	Benton County	205,780	35.4	37.9	240,338	68.5	2.6	50.9	117,446	92,759	9.4	24.8	4.0
05031	Craighead County	74,075	39.5	28.4	88,237	64.1	3.4	44.3	47,150	59,776	15.9	9.1	9.5
05045	Faulkner County	82,109	34.7	36.1	104,388	64.2	2.0	47.8	50,963	67,786	12.0	16.2	5.2
05051	Garland County	73,545	40.5	29.9	82,619	53.0	2.3	36.9	45,243	52,275	24.9	10.1	7.0
05069	Jefferson County	43,748	52.5	21.9	51,878	51.0	3.0	NA	23,885	49,045	26.6	9.2	17.3
05085	Lonoke County	52,158	46.2	22.6	59,912	62.3	3.0	44.7	29,388	75,327	13.0	13.6	6.7
05119	Pulaski County	272,078	34.1	36.2	317,265	60.9	1.9	44.9	169,230	61,129	18.9	14.8	7.7
05125	Saline County	89,559	40.5	30.0	103,535	62.8	1.7	49.1	50,684	77,278	13.8	18.6	4.0
05131	Sebastian County	87,145	42.6	24.2	103,295	61.7	2.9	43.8	51,596	57,949	17.3	10.2	6.2
05143	Washington County	160,396	40.7	36.5	208,922	66.2	2.0	46.9	99,630	65,465	17.2	15.9	5.0
05145	White County	52,190	48.8	22.4	62,139	56.2	2.4	NA	30,920	53,688	25.1	9.2	7.7
06000	**CALIFORNIA**	26,969,649	35.6	37.5	31,584,340	64.3	5.5	65.7	13,699,816	95,521	12.9	30.3	14.6
06001	Alameda County	1,178,124	27.0	51.9	1,344,616	67.1	3.5	46.2	608,534	119,931	11.5	40.8	12.6
06007	Butte County	134,129	32.1	29.9	170,637	59.8	4.1	32.6	86,279	63,222	21.5	15.5	23.7
06013	Contra Costa County	812,770	27.3	46.2	937,941	65.3	3.6	43.1	416,172	122,794	8.6	41.2	10.5
06017	El Dorado County	142,409	23.3	40.7	160,407	59.2	3.0	36.5	77,904	108,594	8.6	32.9	9.1
06019	Fresno County	638,160	44.6	24.8	772,330	61.4	4.5	38.4	328,895	71,689	17.0	17.7	24.6

Table B-2. Counties — What: Education, Employment, and Income, 2023—*Continued*

STATE County code	STATE County	Educational attainment			Employment status				Household income and benefits				
		Total population 25 years and over	Percent with a high school diploma or less	Percent with a bachelor's degree or more	Total population 16 years and over	Labor force participation (percent)	Percent unemployed	Percent of persons age 16 years and over who worked full-time year-round in the past 12 months (percent of total population)	Total households	Median household income in the past 12 months (in 2023 inflation-adjusted dollars)	Income less than $25,000 (percent)	Income greater than $150,000 (percent)	Percent who received cash public assistance or food stamps/ SNAP
	ACS table number:	C15003	C15003	C15003	C23001	C23001	C23001	S2402	B19001	B19049	B19001	B19001	B19058
	Column number:	1	2	3	4	5	6	7	8	9	10	11	12
	CALIFORNIA—Cont.												
06023	Humboldt County	93,805	27.3	36.1	112,428	57.4	3.8	29.6	56,130	61,621	21.5	13.4	25.9
06025	Imperial County	110,055	54.7	16.6	134,491	53.4	5.0	33.5	50,024	60,243	22.9	14.1	29.5
06029	Kern County	564,499	50.7	18.0	687,933	60.6	5.1	38.5	289,845	68,893	17.8	16.6	22.8
06031	Kings County	96,746	52.7	10.4	117,359	54.7	4.9	30.1	44,262	66,429	16.7	11.7	22.6
06033	Lake County	48,642	42.9	16.8	54,298	51.9	3.1	NA	26,092	59,444	25.8	15.2	26.9
06037	Los Angeles County	6,857,511	38.9	36.5	7,952,949	65.2	3.8	43.0	3,450,470	86,587	14.9	27.0	17.1
06039	Madera County	103,594	53.9	15.6	124,330	55.6	4.3	33.5	46,781	66,553	20.2	17.1	25.8
06041	Marin County	187,579	18.9	59.9	212,386	61.1	2.9	36.9	101,608	139,644	10.0	46.6	7.3
06045	Mendocino County	64,380	37.6	28.4	73,631	57.0	5.3	NA	34,951	67,454	16.2	15.2	21.2
06047	Merced County	175,907	59.6	14.5	220,588	60.3	5.5	38.6	88,053	57,570	22.4	13.1	21.3
06053	Monterey County	278,259	49.0	28.9	334,728	59.9	2.1	36.6	132,170	88,035	13.6	25.6	11.1
06055	Napa County	96,806	29.6	39.5	112,327	64.9	2.4	43.2	51,167	104,686	10.4	36.5	9.2
06057	Nevada County	78,720	23.9	41.0	87,257	51.1	2.9	30.0	42,712	87,998	16.9	26.9	11.7
06059	Orange County	2,209,117	30.1	44.5	2,571,553	65.9	2.7	44.6	1,092,528	110,042	10.7	35.7	10.1
06061	Placer County	301,066	21.2	44.3	343,508	61.1	2.9	40.3	160,315	109,713	10.8	35.6	7.3
06065	Riverside County	1,666,754	43.4	26.5	1,974,740	61.9	3.1	41.7	791,757	90,527	12.5	25.8	15.6
06067	Sacramento County	1,094,785	33.8	35.1	1,267,572	64.2	4.1	41.7	573,170	90,252	13.2	25.1	16.3
06069	San Benito County	46,157	42.5	22.6	53,737	68.0	3.0	NA	20,194	107,324	10.5	31.4	12.5
06071	San Bernardino County	1,426,384	45.8	23.6	1,710,161	63.6	3.9	41.3	682,807	85,069	12.9	22.2	18.0
06073	San Diego County	2,277,584	28.4	43.5	2,674,564	66.9	3.0	42.8	1,181,259	103,674	10.2	33.1	11.9
06075	San Francisco County	646,934	22.8	60.4	712,427	69.3	3.4	48.8	372,027	126,730	14.2	44.2	13.1
06077	San Joaquin County	519,374	46.8	23.6	620,747	63.7	4.2	41.3	251,091	87,418	12.5	25.1	15.2
06079	San Luis Obispo County	190,654	24.9	42.1	239,129	58.9	2.6	35.0	110,283	90,670	13.0	26.3	9.9
06081	San Mateo County	535,027	24.4	54.8	606,156	66.3	2.5	47.3	265,124	151,485	8.3	50.6	6.7
06083	Santa Barbara County	276,896	35.3	36.1	354,923	61.9	3.7	36.9	150,932	91,197	14.3	27.4	12.4
06085	Santa Clara County	1,331,885	23.9	57.0	1,553,552	68.1	2.9	47.8	665,549	154,954	8.1	51.6	8.7
06087	Santa Cruz County	176,094	26.8	44.4	220,775	62.6	3.6	35.8	99,069	105,631	12.3	32.6	11.8
06089	Shasta County	128,758	37.0	22.9	146,301	55.5	2.5	37.4	72,320	75,949	16.5	19.0	15.6
06095	Solano County	315,777	36.0	29.1	363,912	62.1	3.0	41.3	157,766	100,027	12.0	29.7	13.6
06097	Sonoma County	354,748	32.8	37.4	403,547	65.1	2.6	40.7	192,765	100,707	10.7	31.3	10.9
06099	Stanislaus County	353,213	48.5	21.0	423,711	63.0	4.2	40.1	179,152	82,758	12.4	19.2	16.9
06101	Sutter County	64,915	44.8	19.1	77,819	58.6	3.7	36.7	33,325	74,727	14.4	18.9	15.9
06103	Tehama County	43,569	41.8	22.2	NA	NA	NA	NA	24,919	55,128	15.0	9.3	13.2
06107	Tulare County	289,766	52.8	16.9	355,039	61.0	5.0	38.9	145,442	73,097	15.8	15.8	26.0
06111	Ventura County	579,642	34.5	37.9	675,002	64.5	3.4	42.4	283,718	107,667	9.4	34.4	10.0
06113	Yolo County	132,967	27.4	46.2	184,580	63.8	3.1	38.5	77,230	93,203	16.5	27.5	12.4
06115	Yuba County	53,869	42.6	16.5	64,604	61.6	4.7	NA	29,253	80,396	18.1	18.8	18.2
08000	**COLORADO**	4,135,123	26.0	46.4	4,818,044	69.0	3.7	68.7	2,428,261	92,911	11.6	27.7	9.8
08001	Adams County	355,595	42.3	29.8	417,273	72.3	2.3	53.9	192,742	97,706	10.9	26.7	12.0
08005	Arapahoe County	456,556	26.5	46.3	527,080	72.2	3.1	50.2	261,161	98,239	9.8	29.4	9.4
08013	Boulder County	220,529	15.7	65.4	279,688	67.0	3.1	41.9	137,425	95,363	14.4	32.7	5.8
08014	Broomfield County	55,576	16.7	58.8	63,536	69.8	2.2	50.3	33,563	112,139	7.2	35.0	3.9
08031	Denver County	530,935	21.4	57.9	603,435	75.1	2.8	54.4	342,996	94,157	13.4	30.5	10.0
08035	Douglas County	265,972	13.0	61.7	308,251	72.9	2.8	51.7	145,551	143,150	5.7	48.2	3.3
08041	El Paso County	498,502	23.0	44.3	593,394	69.9	2.7	43.3	298,973	89,549	10.6	24.2	9.5
08059	Jefferson County	429,619	21.4	52.9	486,912	69.3	2.0	49.1	242,433	102,231	8.6	32.7	6.3
08069	Larimer County	252,129	19.1	52.9	314,119	66.5	3.0	43.0	156,498	88,182	12.1	25.0	10.6
08077	Mesa County	113,815	33.9	32.2	131,775	59.2	2.6	37.7	68,115	64,722	16.9	12.9	15.6
08101	Pueblo County	118,828	39.7	24.2	138,328	57.1	2.0	40.4	68,732	65,161	17.3	14.6	21.0
08123	Weld County	236,202	35.6	33.7	279,428	70.1	2.8	49.0	129,057	91,047	9.8	24.1	11.1
09000	**CONNECTICUT**	2,559,922	33.8	42.9	2,987,718	66.4	4.6	66.2	1,442,969	91,665	13.7	28.5	12.9
09110	Capitol Planning Region	681,931	34.4	41.5	802,624	66.5	3.0	45.1	391,422	91,005	13.6	26.9	13.0
09120	Greater Bridgeport Planning Region	222,075	38.7	42.9	266,209	67.1	4.5	43.2	119,505	95,085	14.6	31.0	15.9
09130	Lower Connecticut River Valley Planning Region	132,227	28.5	47.7	151,009	64.8	1.8	42.3	75,959	99,275	11.0	30.3	8.7
09140	Naugatuck Valley Planning Region	327,868	38.3	33.0	376,640	65.3	3.5	44.4	180,851	81,326	16.0	22.8	16.9

Table B-2. Counties — What: Education, Employment, and Income, 2023—*Continued*

STATE County code	STATE County	Educational attainment: Total population 25 years and over	Educational attainment: Percent with a high school diploma or less	Educational attainment: Percent with a bachelor's degree or more	Employment status: Total population 16 years and over	Employment status: Labor force participation (percent)	Employment status: Percent unemployed	Employment status: Percent of persons age 16 years and over who worked full-time year-round in the past 12 months (percent of total population)	Household income and benefits: Total households	Household income and benefits: Median household income in the past 12 months (in 2023 inflation-adjusted dollars)	Household income and benefits: Income less than $25,000 (percent)	Household income and benefits: Income greater than $150,000 (percent)	Household income and benefits: Percent who received cash public assistance or food stamps/ SNAP
	ACS table number:	C15003	C15003	C15003	C23001	C23001	C23001	S2402	B19001	B19049	B19001	B19001	B19058
	Column number:	1	2	3	4	5	6	7	8	9	10	11	12
	CONNECTICUT—Cont.												
09150	Northeastern Connecticut Planning Region	72,831	41.5	29.2	81,492	67.0	1.5	48.0	40,349	88,806	11.6	20.8	9.7
09160	Northwest Hills Planning Region	86,102	33.7	40.9	96,475	65.1	3.1	42.5	50,297	91,020	11.5	26.4	9.7
09170	South Central Connecticut Planning Region	399,012	36.0	42.4	472,284	65.7	2.7	42.8	233,004	80,733	15.4	24.0	13.5
09180	Southeastern Connecticut Planning Region	198,000	34.8	37.9	233,071	64.4	3.0	38.9	114,156	82,652	15.2	23.3	15.9
09190	Western Connecticut Planning Region	439,876	24.8	56.4	507,414	68.8	2.9	45.9	237,426	121,429	10.8	42.0	8.6
10000	**DELAWARE**	731,427	37.1	36.5	846,414	62.2	3.4	69.9	412,048	81,361	12.1	22.2	12.1
10001	Kent County	128,492	42.1	27.2	152,652	64.4	2.1	43.6	74,183	72,910	15.0	14.9	15.8
10003	New Castle County	404,062	34.6	40.7	470,792	64.9	2.0	46.7	226,373	86,961	11.9	26.1	11.3
10005	Sussex County	198,873	39.0	33.8	222,970	55.1	2.4	36.7	111,492	78,061	10.5	19.2	11.3
11000	**DISTRICT OF COLUMBIA**	482,919	20.4	65.9	564,543	72.8	3.8	53.7	334,673	108,210	15.6	38.1	15.4
11001	District of Columbia	482,919	20.4	65.9	564,543	72.8	3.8	53.7	334,673	108,210	15.6	38.1	15.4
12000	**FLORIDA**	16,421,870	36.6	34.9	18,768,460	60.0	4.1	69.9	8,966,402	73,311	15.1	18.6	12.4
12001	Alachua County	174,855	22.4	50.4	240,199	62.3	2.3	39.3	121,753	61,488	18.4	17.1	9.0
12005	Bay County	136,032	37.3	31.1	155,402	65.6	1.9	42.7	80,689	71,696	14.6	16.5	11.0
12009	Brevard County	483,552	33.7	33.0	542,027	57.3	2.9	39.7	258,656	78,575	13.6	19.7	8.5
12011	Broward County	1,413,273	36.1	36.6	1,605,669	66.6	2.8	47.2	758,853	74,531	16.0	20.2	12.3
12015	Charlotte County	171,699	37.8	27.7	184,349	43.5	1.6	28.6	90,367	71,806	14.3	13.9	6.2
12017	Citrus County	133,412	47.4	21.8	144,572	40.8	2.5	26.2	75,745	53,777	23.3	10.1	10.7
12019	Clay County	163,582	32.3	31.6	187,458	62.5	2.2	44.2	86,946	81,758	10.6	20.0	8.2
12021	Collier County	314,086	34.0	40.1	347,227	50.8	1.0	35.9	166,192	90,072	11.1	26.6	7.0
12023	Columbia County	53,112	46.9	16.8	NA	NA	NA	NA	27,280	60,812	21.8	11.2	17.6
12031	Duval County	710,924	35.7	34.3	827,685	65.4	2.7	45.2	428,020	69,436	16.8	15.6	14.3
12033	Escambia County	223,120	36.6	31.8	267,357	62.9	2.7	38.8	131,375	72,037	14.2	15.7	12.0
12035	Flagler County	100,561	32.4	33.2	113,922	49.4	2.0	32.2	56,177	71,682	13.6	15.8	9.0
12053	Hernando County	158,359	45.0	20.7	179,027	51.3	3.0	35.2	85,911	64,508	15.0	11.3	11.6
12055	Highlands County	83,072	45.6	22.7	92,345	43.0	2.7	27.5	47,278	51,165	23.4	8.5	17.4
12057	Hillsborough County	1,066,931	35.9	38.0	1,246,318	65.7	2.5	46.6	593,029	76,687	15.7	20.6	14.2
12061	Indian River County	134,235	38.8	33.2	148,025	47.4	1.0	31.9	72,833	72,920	16.2	16.7	8.6
12069	Lake County	317,737	40.9	30.5	354,019	54.4	2.2	38.1	172,803	70,730	17.2	14.4	9.2
12071	Lee County	632,549	38.3	31.9	710,288	52.9	2.0	36.6	326,338	71,547	14.2	18.1	8.3
12073	Leon County	178,590	24.6	48.8	249,287	66.1	4.0	41.8	124,867	65,981	18.6	17.0	10.8
12081	Manatee County	338,521	33.5	37.8	373,829	55.4	2.1	36.8	190,091	79,524	13.4	21.7	6.3
12083	Marion County	308,262	45.3	22.5	342,111	50.7	2.6	34.4	171,369	58,606	16.7	9.1	13.4
12085	Martin County	128,394	29.5	41.6	139,908	51.5	2.5	35.5	69,169	74,601	15.0	22.5	8.5
12086	Miami-Dade County	1,935,393	41.4	35.9	2,219,875	65.0	2.5	48.1	985,935	72,311	16.9	20.1	21.8
12087	Monroe County	63,921	31.6	37.8	68,917	60.7	1.0	41.1	32,559	88,870	12.2	26.3	6.9
12089	Nassau County	76,000	32.8	36.7	84,017	56.2	2.0	39.9	41,045	90,671	11.2	23.7	8.6
12091	Okaloosa County	150,761	29.1	35.4	175,994	63.1	1.7	37.5	86,541	83,024	10.4	19.8	7.4
12095	Orange County	1,010,918	32.0	40.7	1,195,190	68.1	2.8	47.6	556,557	79,053	13.8	20.6	14.9
12097	Osceola County	296,082	34.8	32.0	347,115	68.0	3.3	48.0	154,722	77,466	12.1	16.5	16.4
12099	Palm Beach County	1,135,018	32.6	41.7	1,284,051	59.9	2.6	41.2	605,132	84,921	13.1	25.6	9.6
12101	Pasco County	459,482	40.6	29.9	521,422	58.2	2.4	41.1	239,952	72,317	16.0	17.7	10.6
12103	Pinellas County	755,873	32.9	37.0	834,531	59.4	2.4	42.2	439,896	70,768	14.5	17.8	9.5
12105	Polk County	567,736	42.5	26.5	658,879	59.3	2.2	42.1	306,915	66,909	14.6	13.1	14.6
12107	Putnam County	54,258	52.4	16.7	62,224	48.0	2.1	NA	32,487	52,256	21.3	9.2	19.9
12109	St. Johns County	230,163	19.6	52.6	259,759	60.8	1.7	43.2	126,240	105,153	10.7	33.2	4.4
12111	St. Lucie County	274,988	42.0	24.6	311,440	56.1	2.8	39.8	145,735	66,530	15.3	12.8	11.8
12113	Santa Rosa County	145,046	32.2	32.8	165,327	58.9	2.5	37.8	72,969	87,862	10.7	21.0	8.8
12115	Sarasota County	376,944	31.0	41.5	412,659	49.3	2.0	33.1	218,010	77,705	12.0	20.0	6.1
12117	Seminole County	346,689	28.3	42.7	398,575	65.5	2.8	47.1	189,580	80,547	11.2	21.3	10.6
12119	Sumter County	136,372	31.9	37.0	141,239	26.2	2.0	NA	73,238	74,715	11.8	12.8	4.4
12127	Volusia County	441,220	37.4	29.3	502,021	55.1	2.1	38.5	243,904	66,273	15.8	12.9	12.2
12131	Walton County	62,270	38.0	35.6	71,236	59.5	2.4	NA	35,435	78,801	12.7	24.2	9.5

Table B-2. Counties — What: Education, Employment, and Income, 2023—*Continued*

STATE County code	STATE County	Educational attainment: Total population 25 years and over	Educational attainment: Percent with a high school diploma or less	Educational attainment: Percent with a bachelor's degree or more	Employment status: Total population 16 years and over	Employment status: Labor force participation (percent)	Employment status: Percent unemployed	Employment status: Percent of persons age 16 years and over who worked full-time year-round in the past 12 months (percent of total population)	Household income and benefits: Total households	Household income and benefits: Median household income in the past 12 months (in 2023 inflation-adjusted dollars)	Household income and benefits: Income less than $25,000 (percent)	Household income and benefits: Income greater than $150,000 (percent)	Household income and benefits: Percent who received cash public assistance or food stamps/ SNAP
	ACS table number:	C15003	C15003	C15003	C23001	C23001	C23001	S2402	B19001	B19049	B19001	B19001	B19058
	Column number:	1	2	3	4	5	6	7	8	9	10	11	12
13000	**GEORGIA**	7,448,119	36.9	35.4	8,818,867	64.1	4.4	70.6	4,150,138	74,632	16.2	19.6	13.0
13013	Barrow County	62,243	49.8	15.9	73,470	67.5	1.5	50.1	32,217	65,914	13.9	13.9	13.0
13015	Bartow County	79,138	44.6	27.4	92,341	63.9	1.8	47.7	42,225	80,511	13.3	16.5	6.8
13021	Bibb County	104,066	41.8	26.3	122,742	57.7	4.2	37.7	60,919	51,254	26.8	12.7	25.5
13031	Bulloch County	48,129	36.6	34.5	69,624	56.1	3.9	NA	30,988	54,007	24.5	10.6	17.2
13045	Carroll County	81,712	42.5	25.2	101,175	62.8	2.3	44.4	44,515	71,891	15.6	14.7	15.2
13047	Catoosa County	47,854	40.7	23.4	55,835	63.8	2.6	NA	26,248	70,653	15.8	15.9	12.6
13051	Chatham County	210,165	32.1	39.1	250,147	62.8	2.5	43.7	123,272	70,904	16.9	16.0	12.4
13057	Cherokee County	199,126	28.5	41.3	231,167	67.7	2.1	48.6	102,811	103,691	8.5	28.3	4.3
13059	Clarke County	76,931	28.2	50.1	111,024	64.2	2.8	40.3	55,505	54,352	25.7	11.1	9.2
13063	Clayton County	190,473	44.8	26.0	229,456	67.2	4.3	46.0	106,914	58,359	17.1	8.0	21.3
13067	Cobb County	532,843	25.5	51.6	625,149	71.6	2.4	52.0	299,074	99,382	10.1	30.2	7.0
13073	Columbia County	110,259	29.2	37.2	130,282	62.5	2.5	43.3	57,807	96,540	9.2	28.9	6.0
13077	Coweta County	107,861	30.1	37.1	124,784	63.1	1.4	45.7	57,325	92,150	11.9	26.4	7.9
13089	DeKalb County	527,323	28.4	48.6	613,188	68.6	3.6	48.2	291,423	77,861	15.5	23.9	12.8
13095	Dougherty County	53,427	47.2	22.0	64,832	57.2	6.4	NA	35,052	45,769	29.6	6.0	37.7
13097	Douglas County	98,073	35.1	33.4	116,928	68.9	3.7	51.2	53,350	81,339	12.2	18.3	13.0
13103	Effingham County	46,873	38.4	28.4	53,824	70.5	3.4	53.2	25,452	81,733	9.6	19.0	9.7
13113	Fayette County	86,013	24.4	49.2	100,912	60.3	2.2	44.8	45,095	106,849	7.5	32.3	4.0
13115	Floyd County	67,591	39.3	30.0	79,701	60.2	2.1	42.1	37,835	62,098	20.7	13.0	19.9
13117	Forsyth County	181,829	23.0	55.1	213,638	68.6	1.4	51.0	90,635	134,821	7.3	44.6	2.8
13121	Fulton County	752,285	20.1	59.5	884,526	70.5	3.1	50.5	458,812	95,371	15.1	30.8	10.7
13127	Glynn County	63,106	35.0	33.8	70,902	54.8	1.9	39.4	37,904	71,914	19.6	18.8	13.4
13135	Gwinnett County	638,037	36.9	37.6	763,674	69.7	2.9	50.2	330,254	83,917	10.9	21.6	8.8
13139	Hall County	146,015	46.2	30.0	172,144	62.5	1.6	43.7	76,413	77,891	13.3	22.0	9.0
13151	Henry County	167,438	34.3	33.1	198,905	69.1	3.7	48.2	89,313	80,374	10.7	19.8	10.1
13153	Houston County	114,700	35.6	32.6	134,584	64.7	4.9	45.2	65,688	75,825	13.7	15.0	11.1
13157	Jackson County	59,208	40.0	26.2	NA	NA	NA	NA	30,300	84,749	9.2	18.4	9.6
13179	Liberty County	39,940	39.8	20.5	52,025	67.3	5.7	NA	24,654	58,308	18.9	6.7	17.8
13185	Lowndes County	73,687	41.3	29.9	94,522	61.0	2.7	37.9	48,322	54,509	25.6	11.1	18.4
13215	Muscogee County	133,684	38.4	28.2	157,561	59.7	3.6	37.7	82,007	51,835	24.6	9.6	15.1
13217	Newton County	77,359	42.5	24.7	94,111	66.3	3.7	47.0	42,633	79,640	10.2	16.8	14.8
13223	Paulding County	120,574	39.7	27.6	143,983	68.0	2.4	50.6	61,401	94,126	8.7	20.8	8.2
13245	Richmond County	136,374	42.8	24.3	165,144	62.7	4.5	38.7	77,202	51,985	25.3	8.1	21.0
13247	Rockdale County	64,063	35.0	36.5	77,810	63.1	3.7	43.0	35,459	82,339	12.4	22.6	14.2
13255	Spalding County	47,107	52.2	18.2	NA	NA	NA	NA	26,898	56,169	17.7	9.9	17.3
13285	Troup County	47,894	50.8	26.9	NA	NA	NA	NA	28,232	64,728	21.5	13.7	19.9
13295	Walker County	49,213	49.2	18.9	56,185	54.3	1.7	NA	26,020	58,594	23.2	9.3	12.8
13297	Walton County	73,056	45.7	26.0	84,998	63.2	3.7	42.5	37,132	77,346	14.8	20.9	10.6
13313	Whitfield County	68,806	54.8	21.3	82,150	63.6	1.7	46.9	37,316	62,824	16.7	15.8	15.4
15000	**HAWAII**	1,024,897	33.3	37.0	1,172,357	63.0	3.3	63.5	493,898	95,322	12.4	28.4	12.2
15001	Hawaii County	149,785	35.5	31.7	168,674	54.2	2.3	34.4	73,933	74,580	18.5	18.7	16.3
15003	Honolulu County	702,068	32.1	39.6	809,175	64.7	2.1	40.6	338,496	103,131	11.4	31.1	11.3
15007	Kauai County	53,710	36.6	30.7	59,939	64.9	2.0	44.1	24,621	103,564	9.7	27.2	12.9
15009	Maui County	119,314	36.2	31.2	134,549	62.9	1.9	42.0	56,848	83,691	11.8	25.5	11.9
16000	**IDAHO**	1,305,704	33.8	32.1	1,558,313	62.6	3.6	65.5	733,244	74,942	12.6	17.1	8.0
16001	Ada County	364,782	25.2	44.2	426,808	65.6	2.0	44.7	209,863	90,526	9.6	23.8	5.5
16005	Bannock County	58,521	32.4	34.5	70,596	61.5	1.5	38.7	33,729	68,495	14.8	11.7	14.2
16019	Bonneville County	81,587	32.8	32.4	97,443	65.1	1.2	43.8	45,245	73,649	11.9	17.6	12.2
16027	Canyon County	166,039	41.4	25.8	198,354	66.9	2.5	46.0	88,688	72,007	10.6	14.0	8.1
16055	Kootenai County	131,650	33.2	32.1	148,541	60.1	2.4	39.9	74,253	73,456	13.4	18.1	7.9
16083	Twin Falls County	62,141	37.5	19.8	73,982	65.5	1.7	45.0	35,050	66,643	12.4	8.5	9.6
17000	**ILLINOIS**	8,710,996	34.7	38.3	10,192,179	65.4	4.7	68.8	5,071,288	80,306	15.0	22.2	14.8
17019	Champaign County	120,365	26.3	48.2	171,246	60.0	2.0	40.4	89,155	59,574	23.8	13.9	9.8
17031	Cook County	3,593,408	33.3	43.6	4,166,654	67.0	3.8	45.9	2,117,084	80,579	16.0	23.6	17.0
17037	DeKalb County	60,811	34.7	30.6	81,733	68.7	3.3	41.8	40,202	67,697	17.4	17.5	16.8
17043	DuPage County	643,799	25.8	52.4	744,743	67.8	2.7	48.3	353,618	106,961	8.6	34.0	8.3

Table B-2. Counties — What: Education, Employment, and Income, 2023—*Continued*

STATE County code	STATE County	Educational attainment			Employment status				Household income and benefits				
		Total population 25 years and over	Percent with a high school diploma or less	Percent with a bachelor's degree or more	Total population 16 years and over	Labor force participation (percent)	Percent unemployed	Percent of persons age 16 years and over who worked full-time year-round in the past 12 months (percent of total population)	Total households	Median household income in the past 12 months (in 2023 inflation-adjusted dollars)	Income less than $25,000 (percent)	Income greater than $150,000 (percent)	Percent who received cash public assistance or food stamps/ SNAP
	ACS table number:	C15003	C15003	C15003	C23001	C23001	C23001	S2402	B19001	B19049	B19001	B19001	B19058
	Column number:	1	2	3	4	5	6	7	8	9	10	11	12
	ILLINOIS—Cont.												
17089	Kane County	347,943	35.1	39.4	409,988	69.0	2.6	48.4	185,921	97,633	9.0	27.8	8.8
17091	Kankakee County	71,260	45.4	20.9	85,327	61.6	2.1	41.7	41,130	66,788	13.9	16.2	19.0
17093	Kendall County	89,967	30.3	36.5	107,517	73.3	2.8	52.2	44,934	111,349	4.2	29.0	8.6
17097	Lake County	475,104	29.3	47.8	569,460	68.6	3.0	47.0	260,243	108,364	10.4	34.4	8.7
17099	LaSalle County	77,513	45.4	19.3	89,407	61.2	3.2	40.6	44,319	72,737	13.5	16.6	15.8
17111	McHenry County	217,828	34.5	36.0	252,199	70.3	2.0	49.6	119,150	100,884	7.8	28.3	6.8
17113	McLean County	105,999	26.4	49.6	139,667	65.7	1.7	43.9	71,060	77,200	17.5	22.1	12.7
17115	Macon County	69,473	44.0	23.5	80,710	59.0	3.5	38.8	43,598	58,297	19.2	13.7	24.1
17119	Madison County	184,548	32.5	33.7	214,764	63.4	2.2	45.2	110,909	73,041	16.9	16.5	14.4
17143	Peoria County	119,035	34.6	36.1	139,863	62.2	4.1	38.2	77,525	61,488	22.8	17.6	18.1
17161	Rock Island County	96,929	39.6	25.0	114,162	60.1	1.9	41.6	62,396	63,087	20.6	13.2	16.9
17163	St. Clair County	174,283	35.2	30.8	200,975	61.8	2.7	39.9	102,701	65,546	17.4	17.5	18.8
17167	Sangamon County	136,462	31.4	38.0	157,080	62.4	2.8	44.6	85,477	72,496	14.8	18.3	13.2
17179	Tazewell County	91,925	34.3	30.4	104,928	64.6	2.3	43.7	54,228	72,056	14.8	16.8	10.0
17183	Vermilion County	49,592	51.6	16.6	56,799	53.5	4.2	37.9	30,703	46,507	25.1	7.9	25.0
17197	Will County	474,369	34.5	36.6	558,651	68.7	2.5	47.9	246,145	103,482	9.3	29.7	11.1
17199	Williamson County	47,976	36.7	25.0	54,136	57.7	2.4	37.7	29,509	60,135	20.6	11.3	19.7
17201	Winnebago County	191,390	43.5	23.4	222,893	62.9	3.5	40.8	115,540	65,513	17.1	11.8	23.4
18000	**INDIANA**	4,614,970	41.7	30.2	5,470,753	64.4	3.6	69.5	2,754,881	69,477	15.8	15.3	9.3
18003	Allen County	257,647	35.9	32.9	306,139	66.5	2.9	45.3	160,153	65,704	15.7	13.3	8.7
18005	Bartholomew County	56,725	36.6	35.6	66,694	67.2	2.3	NA	33,777	81,832	17.0	20.5	8.5
18011	Boone County	51,586	26.1	53.7	NA	NA	NA	NA	29,659	103,592	9.3	33.4	2.7
18019	Clark County	87,928	42.6	26.6	102,082	66.0	2.4	49.6	52,156	71,711	13.6	13.3	7.1
18035	Delaware County	70,595	44.0	27.2	94,346	61.3	2.3	35.4	44,361	55,206	20.5	9.0	16.2
18039	Elkhart County	131,519	54.2	20.5	157,825	65.4	1.8	44.6	73,439	67,188	14.6	11.6	5.3
18043	Floyd County	56,075	36.2	28.8	65,369	64.8	1.9	45.6	31,833	80,023	13.7	16.7	5.4
18053	Grant County	43,250	47.6	20.7	53,964	55.0	2.4	NA	27,670	52,214	25.2	7.0	19.0
18057	Hamilton County	249,571	16.0	63.6	290,479	71.3	1.7	52.8	140,850	118,777	7.8	39.5	3.4
18059	Hancock County	59,735	38.0	35.3	69,795	66.6	1.2	48.4	34,114	93,906	10.8	24.3	6.9
18063	Hendricks County	126,226	30.8	38.4	146,833	67.8	1.9	49.2	69,367	93,440	7.6	23.7	4.1
18067	Howard County	57,508	46.6	23.9	66,503	60.1	3.0	40.7	35,551	61,267	15.3	12.9	13.2
18081	Johnson County	113,991	36.0	35.3	131,807	68.8	1.9	52.1	64,079	92,231	9.1	22.2	8.1
18085	Kosciusko County	54,804	49.8	25.5	NA	NA	NA	NA	32,268	70,140	13.8	13.7	5.1
18089	Lake County	343,623	43.7	25.6	396,719	61.5	3.0	42.4	197,595	69,166	16.7	16.4	11.9
18091	LaPorte County	80,471	50.6	23.4	91,245	55.5	1.9	38.7	45,725	62,868	15.7	11.1	12.9
18095	Madison County	94,336	49.4	20.3	108,374	60.2	2.7	39.9	54,317	62,012	17.7	12.0	13.5
18097	Marion County	636,500	37.3	36.5	754,132	70.2	3.0	48.7	408,293	66,582	16.7	14.1	11.3
18105	Monroe County	82,529	23.4	54.2	120,016	61.7	2.9	36.9	61,400	58,970	21.3	13.8	5.4
18109	Morgan County	51,561	48.4	21.2	59,825	62.8	2.4	45.3	29,202	71,723	11.8	17.8	8.3
18127	Porter County	123,509	41.7	29.3	142,894	64.2	2.4	44.7	68,120	77,410	11.5	18.7	6.1
18141	St. Joseph County	177,774	38.6	32.9	217,634	64.1	3.2	41.3	106,607	65,751	17.8	12.9	10.2
18157	Tippecanoe County	105,669	34.0	42.2	155,012	65.7	1.8	41.5	76,240	60,762	21.1	14.6	6.6
18163	Vanderburgh County	123,255	43.5	27.1	144,907	63.0	2.4	44.1	77,472	60,459	17.2	11.5	11.9
18167	Vigo County	68,759	45.2	27.0	87,107	56.8	3.8	39.1	42,219	47,659	26.6	8.5	16.0
18173	Warrick County	46,506	35.2	35.5	52,867	63.8	1.9	44.7	25,278	85,260	16.1	24.0	4.8
18177	Wayne County	45,089	48.8	20.8	53,753	59.2	4.8	NA	26,843	51,798	23.6	8.7	17.5
19000	**IOWA**	2,166,425	36.7	31.5	2,570,587	66.3	2.8	70.0	1,337,243	71,433	14.3	15.8	9.3
19013	Black Hawk County	84,166	39.5	29.0	105,278	65.1	2.3	42.6	53,791	59,707	16.4	12.3	11.7
19049	Dallas County	73,562	21.3	47.8	85,115	73.7	1.7	55.0	44,043	97,895	10.3	26.0	3.8
19061	Dubuque County	68,189	37.8	34.0	79,142	67.2	1.5	47.0	42,889	71,940	13.5	13.5	10.2
19103	Johnson County	94,942	19.2	54.6	129,795	69.3	1.5	42.3	64,076	71,563	18.2	18.3	5.2
19113	Linn County	157,480	32.0	35.2	184,559	66.2	2.1	46.5	96,058	72,279	12.7	17.4	9.8
19153	Polk County	338,655	32.1	41.1	398,683	71.8	2.3	51.5	207,757	78,979	11.4	21.2	10.6
19155	Pottawattamie County	63,739	45.0	21.8	74,358	66.0	2.2	49.9	38,289	70,640	14.8	15.9	9.5
19163	Scott County	120,022	31.7	38.0	138,276	66.7	2.2	46.7	75,239	76,822	13.4	18.4	9.4
19169	Story County	53,827	19.5	53.8	84,268	65.5	2.1	37.8	38,771	68,527	14.6	17.0	3.9
19193	Woodbury County	68,098	45.3	20.6	82,740	64.3	1.7	43.4	40,348	64,913	17.5	12.5	17.7

Table B-2. Counties — What: Education, Employment, and Income, 2023—*Continued*

STATE County code	STATE County	Educational attainment			Employment status				Household income and benefits				
		Total population 25 years and over	Percent with a high school diploma or less	Percent with a bachelor's degree or more	Total population 16 years and over	Labor force participation (percent)	Percent unemployed	Percent of persons age 16 years and over who worked full-time year-round in the past 12 months (percent of total population)	Total households	Median household income in the past 12 months (in 2023 inflation-adjusted dollars)	Income less than $25,000 (percent)	Income greater than $150,000 (percent)	Percent who received cash public assistance or food stamps/ SNAP
	ACS table number:	C15003	C15003	C15003	C23001	C23001	C23001	S2402	B19001	B19049	B19001	B19001	B19058
	Column number:	1	2	3	4	5	6	7	8	9	10	11	12
20000	**KANSAS**	1,956,252	33.4	35.8	2,339,516	66.2	3.2	69.4	1,188,340	70,333	14.8	16.1	7.3
20015	Butler County	46,333	33.7	35.1	54,241	61.6	1.2	45.1	25,801	74,566	12.7	16.4	4.8
20045	Douglas County	73,419	21.9	53.2	101,812	67.3	3.5	40.4	51,013	66,997	18.7	14.3	6.4
20091	Johnson County	428,400	18.0	57.4	497,158	71.5	1.7	52.0	250,337	102,702	8.0	31.8	2.2
20103	Leavenworth County	56,980	29.9	37.3	66,276	60.0	1.5	41.3	30,246	81,921	10.8	18.5	7.6
20161	Riley County	35,396	23.7	48.4	60,967	71.5	2.4	33.9	27,875	62,623	20.2	8.9	5.1
20173	Sedgwick County	347,915	35.6	31.7	412,744	66.5	2.4	46.2	211,238	66,646	15.6	14.3	10.5
20177	Shawnee County	122,407	38.5	31.8	142,447	61.0	2.3	42.6	73,980	62,512	16.4	12.8	10.6
20209	Wyandotte County	104,602	50.2	20.6	126,604	65.6	3.3	46.8	62,238	61,766	17.9	10.2	11.5
21000	**KENTUCKY**	3,107,275	43.5	27.8	3,633,664	60.3	4.1	69.9	1,853,603	61,118	20.8	12.9	13.6
21015	Boone County	92,091	33.7	37.1	108,109	68.4	2.1	48.4	51,702	87,550	11.9	21.6	10.0
21029	Bullitt County	60,665	48.3	19.0	69,468	67.6	2.5	48.0	32,321	73,901	15.9	15.2	5.1
21037	Campbell County	66,926	36.4	38.0	77,592	67.9	2.0	49.4	40,425	81,451	10.9	19.2	8.1
21047	Christian County	42,113	41.4	24.1	52,554	63.6	3.7	NA	25,768	55,458	20.7	7.8	11.1
21059	Daviess County	70,103	44.1	25.6	82,716	65.4	2.6	44.3	42,164	61,922	19.3	10.0	13.2
21067	Fayette County	210,210	25.8	49.8	261,590	68.6	2.9	45.1	141,680	66,392	17.0	18.2	8.3
21093	Hardin County	75,776	40.3	24.0	88,647	64.0	2.8	44.9	45,909	63,502	19.1	12.5	13.0
21111	Jefferson County	537,814	34.7	36.8	619,563	63.6	2.9	44.1	331,206	64,542	18.6	15.7	12.3
21117	Kenton County	117,639	35.4	38.9	136,566	67.3	2.1	48.9	67,180	79,392	12.5	17.3	8.0
21145	McCracken County	48,018	40.6	25.3	NA	NA	NA	NA	28,934	60,720	22.5	14.6	13.3
21151	Madison County	61,066	37.2	36.8	79,416	65.4	2.3	44.5	37,672	65,502	16.2	15.5	14.2
21185	Oldham County	47,689	27.3	45.8	55,516	63.5	1.5	46.3	23,415	119,553	8.9	41.3	2.9
21199	Pulaski County	46,664	50.3	18.2	53,618	51.2	2.2	NA	26,203	55,667	20.9	9.6	12.7
21227	Warren County	87,359	33.5	33.8	112,521	68.2	2.7	46.9	57,773	61,067	17.4	10.2	9.4
22000	**LOUISIANA**	3,102,893	45.3	27.0	3,635,137	59.2	4.8	69.5	1,833,915	58,229	23.0	13.7	17.7
22005	Ascension Parish	87,606	42.7	26.2	101,610	68.6	2.5	51.5	48,526	90,190	16.6	23.9	11.0
22015	Bossier Parish	87,444	35.1	26.4	100,948	63.9	2.5	45.4	54,151	71,365	16.5	16.1	13.3
22017	Caddo Parish	155,876	43.8	27.4	180,296	56.6	3.2	39.2	98,864	50,375	25.5	7.7	21.8
22019	Calcasieu Parish	136,294	43.5	27.2	160,051	60.5	2.0	43.0	79,222	63,890	20.8	16.1	16.2
22033	East Baton Rouge Parish	282,303	35.0	37.6	359,803	62.5	3.8	42.0	177,309	59,443	22.3	15.9	16.4
22045	Iberia Parish	44,566	58.9	17.8	52,561	56.0	4.4	NA	26,439	53,352	27.4	10.5	25.3
22051	Jefferson Parish	297,835	42.2	30.0	339,033	62.4	3.2	43.0	176,635	61,085	20.4	14.7	12.2
22055	Lafayette Parish	169,993	40.0	32.7	195,421	64.9	2.2	47.0	102,227	63,116	19.0	14.2	12.8
22057	Lafourche Parish	64,446	52.9	22.4	76,786	55.5	1.5	37.6	38,393	55,926	24.0	13.3	21.4
22063	Livingston Parish	99,581	54.5	17.9	115,780	62.3	1.9	44.6	55,653	72,725	15.4	17.4	14.5
22071	Orleans Parish	259,764	29.8	44.7	301,119	61.7	3.2	40.5	155,005	55,580	26.7	17.0	18.6
22073	Ouachita Parish	104,281	37.8	31.4	124,007	60.0	4.2	41.1	63,158	52,695	26.4	11.3	22.2
22079	Rapides Parish	84,329	47.6	22.9	99,124	56.0	2.5	39.8	50,301	51,301	25.1	9.6	18.8
22097	St. Landry Parish	54,091	55.7	14.2	62,282	50.3	1.4	NA	34,635	41,393	31.8	5.8	15.5
22103	St. Tammany Parish	189,919	34.0	37.1	219,870	63.8	2.9	42.1	106,164	76,420	14.9	21.6	10.2
22105	Tangipahoa Parish	90,573	48.3	22.8	108,154	60.3	3.5	41.4	54,627	54,417	23.7	12.5	19.5
22109	Terrebonne Parish	69,539	58.4	19.0	81,444	58.2	1.4	NA	42,203	64,084	17.1	9.3	16.7
23000	**MAINE**	1,039,460	34.5	37.0	1,180,683	62.1	3.2	66.2	616,085	73,733	15.0	16.5	13.5
23001	Androscoggin County	79,199	47.1	23.4	93,583	63.1	2.6	39.1	48,239	63,404	18.4	12.1	21.4
23003	Aroostook County	50,889	42.9	27.1	56,386	56.4	1.8	39.9	32,671	57,030	22.1	10.0	21.0
23005	Cumberland County	229,213	21.2	55.5	261,875	69.5	1.6	46.5	134,326	98,369	9.8	25.8	6.6
23011	Kennebec County	92,825	35.3	30.2	105,979	61.7	3.0	41.5	55,601	64,083	15.2	11.3	16.3
23019	Penobscot County	112,335	38.3	30.6	132,205	58.3	1.4	39.1	66,556	66,333	17.5	13.3	17.8
23031	York County	166,506	33.1	37.9	186,121	65.0	1.9	44.5	93,995	86,430	11.7	21.9	9.9
24000	**MARYLAND**	4,297,439	32.7	43.7	4,979,552	67.5	3.9	72.2	2,384,715	98,678	11.8	30.4	10.9
24001	Allegany County	48,254	52.5	20.2	56,508	49.8	2.4	31.1	28,187	54,384	20.8	6.8	21.7
24003	Anne Arundel County	415,575	29.7	46.2	475,932	69.6	2.3	50.4	226,503	117,650	7.3	36.5	6.9
24005	Baltimore County	586,604	32.3	42.7	682,165	66.0	2.6	47.8	331,624	87,056	12.1	24.0	10.1
24009	Calvert County	65,162	32.1	36.6	75,683	71.7	2.0	53.8	33,642	126,358	4.4	40.7	7.4
24013	Carroll County	123,601	31.6	42.3	142,983	68.7	1.7	49.1	64,081	114,974	8.8	35.9	5.0
24015	Cecil County	74,890	43.4	25.1	85,244	62.6	2.1	47.3	41,195	90,762	12.1	27.5	14.8

Table B-2. Counties — What: Education, Employment, and Income, 2023—*Continued*

STATE County code	STATE County	Educational attainment: Total population 25 years and over	Educational attainment: Percent with a high school diploma or less	Educational attainment: Percent with a bachelor's degree or more	Employment status: Total population 16 years and over	Employment status: Labor force participation (percent)	Employment status: Percent unemployed	Employment status: Percent of persons age 16 years and over who worked full-time year-round in the past 12 months (percent of total population)	Household income and benefits: Total households	Household income and benefits: Median household income in the past 12 months (in 2023 inflation-adjusted dollars)	Household income and benefits: Income less than $25,000 (percent)	Household income and benefits: Income greater than $150,000 (percent)	Household income and benefits: Percent who received cash public assistance or food stamps/SNAP
	ACS table number:	C15003	C15003	C15003	C23001	C23001	C23001	S2402	B19001	B19049	B19001	B19001	B19058
	Column number:	1	2	3	4	5	6	7	8	9	10	11	12
	MARYLAND—Cont.												
24017	Charles County	117,994	39.1	31.8	136,896	70.5	4.0	50.9	62,532	105,087	11.5	31.0	10.4
24021	Frederick County	200,124	30.4	47.9	232,205	69.4	1.3	51.3	107,332	114,360	6.7	37.5	7.0
24025	Harford County	185,817	32.0	41.4	212,904	67.0	3.0	50.0	103,909	105,029	9.7	29.2	6.9
24027	Howard County	230,165	18.4	62.5	266,714	69.2	1.8	52.1	121,399	141,159	6.6	47.5	6.3
24031	Montgomery County	737,675	22.3	61.0	848,459	70.0	2.7	50.1	392,629	125,371	8.6	42.8	7.2
24033	Prince George's County	654,845	38.8	37.6	764,861	70.2	3.7	51.0	351,460	98,027	11.2	28.7	11.5
24037	St. Mary's County	78,000	35.9	36.0	90,738	68.6	1.8	48.7	43,227	102,282	8.3	31.9	11.2
24043	Washington County	108,673	46.5	22.4	126,193	60.5	2.2	43.0	59,404	71,848	16.1	16.7	14.0
24045	Wicomico County	67,633	45.1	26.5	84,732	64.6	2.0	43.4	39,679	73,834	15.1	13.6	16.9
24510	Baltimore city	395,443	38.6	37.1	459,130	64.1	3.2	45.5	259,385	59,579	24.4	16.4	22.4
25000	**MASSACHUSETTS**	4,975,152	31.4	47.8	5,828,175	67.2	3.9	67.1	2,800,984	99,858	14.0	32.3	16.6
25001	Barnstable County	185,612	26.4	49.8	204,803	57.9	1.9	36.2	109,475	89,893	13.0	27.4	11.1
25003	Berkshire County	96,090	36.5	38.0	110,207	60.7	3.0	38.4	58,807	77,498	19.2	19.1	18.5
25005	Bristol County	413,553	43.3	31.3	477,886	65.5	2.9	44.9	233,990	81,148	17.1	23.3	22.5
25009	Essex County	570,391	35.7	42.7	663,229	67.3	2.8	45.9	313,787	96,874	14.5	31.3	17.7
25011	Franklin County	54,756	32.7	42.3	60,846	62.7	3.3	40.6	32,430	71,296	16.6	16.0	17.3
25013	Hampden County	320,476	45.7	28.8	377,389	60.4	2.4	40.4	184,698	66,997	20.9	15.7	29.3
25015	Hampshire County	100,358	26.5	50.2	145,445	61.5	2.5	34.1	61,802	79,969	17.2	23.3	12.3
25017	Middlesex County	1,155,381	24.0	60.0	1,349,992	70.2	2.4	48.4	632,721	123,705	10.4	41.7	10.3
25021	Norfolk County	517,290	21.9	59.7	597,760	69.6	2.8	48.0	286,649	123,903	11.6	42.4	11.3
25023	Plymouth County	382,359	32.4	41.1	440,122	66.7	2.9	43.0	203,356	108,742	11.3	34.0	15.5
25025	Suffolk County	541,956	31.5	51.7	659,415	71.1	3.0	46.6	332,924	93,360	18.3	32.1	22.0
25027	Worcester County	610,716	35.4	41.4	712,225	66.2	2.6	44.5	336,660	94,099	13.1	28.0	18.6
26000	**MICHIGAN**	7,007,856	35.7	32.7	8,186,295	61.7	4.5	66.7	4,107,809	69,183	16.9	16.5	14.6
26005	Allegan County	85,182	43.9	29.8	97,584	63.1	1.3	47.4	46,317	78,779	13.4	15.4	7.9
26017	Bay County	75,140	40.2	23.1	84,838	57.4	2.6	40.3	44,417	58,675	20.6	8.5	18.0
26021	Berrien County	108,008	35.3	31.6	124,435	59.1	2.6	38.9	65,129	62,460	17.5	15.6	13.3
26025	Calhoun County	91,769	44.9	22.1	108,028	60.6	3.9	40.2	54,568	57,514	19.2	9.4	15.2
26037	Clinton County	55,976	24.8	40.6	65,031	65.9	1.2	47.1	31,653	92,503	7.4	23.7	5.5
26045	Eaton County	77,645	35.4	29.4	89,241	62.9	1.9	44.5	45,181	71,686	15.1	14.9	11.3
26049	Genesee County	280,373	42.4	22.8	323,633	59.8	4.1	37.7	164,086	60,027	20.1	11.2	20.0
26055	Grand Traverse County	70,886	26.9	42.9	80,693	64.3	1.9	41.1	42,544	83,650	8.2	19.4	6.8
26065	Ingham County	173,721	26.9	40.8	237,003	64.6	3.8	37.8	117,197	62,998	20.6	15.2	11.7
26067	Ionia County	45,757	44.2	21.5	53,006	58.3	2.5	39.9	23,600	69,951	17.6	18.1	16.6
26075	Jackson County	113,820	41.0	24.2	129,329	56.2	2.6	37.9	61,851	63,338	17.1	11.7	15.7
26077	Kalamazoo County	166,805	25.1	42.6	213,008	66.5	2.0	44.1	107,893	67,191	14.5	17.2	11.4
26081	Kent County	446,380	29.7	42.0	526,715	69.7	2.4	46.9	257,898	79,756	11.8	18.9	11.4
26087	Lapeer County	65,063	46.7	19.7	72,582	60.9	2.6	41.1	34,494	68,556	14.0	12.6	11.6
26091	Lenawee County	69,276	44.8	22.2	80,385	58.2	1.7	38.1	40,142	63,952	13.6	11.3	13.9
26093	Livingston County	142,500	28.2	39.4	162,839	63.7	1.3	46.7	77,304	102,508	9.1	30.7	5.9
26099	Macomb County	628,007	37.1	27.5	718,712	64.3	2.4	44.2	359,464	73,807	13.4	16.7	13.8
26103	Marquette County	45,244	30.2	38.2	57,138	57.8	2.5	34.8	28,707	62,115	20.9	10.6	13.2
26111	Midland County	60,551	33.8	33.7	69,045	59.9	2.5	39.6	35,761	73,074	16.7	17.9	14.1
26115	Monroe County	110,907	40.5	24.9	127,769	59.5	1.1	40.5	62,936	71,506	15.6	17.3	9.9
26117	Montcalm County	48,731	47.6	16.3	55,382	58.7	1.4	40.5	24,697	65,331	15.5	11.7	13.5
26121	Muskegon County	123,629	39.7	21.7	142,541	59.5	2.9	38.8	70,042	61,189	18.5	9.3	22.2
26125	Oakland County	916,971	22.6	51.1	1,048,056	66.7	2.5	47.2	533,533	92,015	11.6	28.9	8.8
26139	Ottawa County	194,862	31.1	39.9	242,612	67.2	1.6	43.2	114,316	81,513	10.8	18.3	6.8
26145	Saginaw County	131,616	42.4	22.2	152,882	58.8	3.7	37.8	77,158	59,265	19.7	11.2	20.1
26147	St. Clair County	116,573	43.0	20.0	132,004	61.7	3.3	41.1	69,234	68,513	17.5	13.2	15.4
26155	Shiawassee County	48,976	40.9	19.2	56,110	58.8	2.6	42.1	26,950	62,093	18.7	12.8	20.8
26159	Van Buren County	53,101	43.7	26.4	60,798	56.7	2.1	40.7	31,149	66,424	17.1	10.4	16.9
26161	Washtenaw County	236,534	17.0	60.2	306,889	63.6	2.1	40.4	149,379	83,754	14.8	25.5	9.4
26163	Wayne County	1,195,048	41.3	27.1	1,388,089	59.8	4.2	39.0	696,332	57,281	23.8	13.1	23.9
27000	**MINNESOTA**	3,941,575	29.0	40.0	4,602,443	68.4	3.0	67.7	2,344,432	85,086	12.2	22.7	8.8
27003	Anoka County	254,868	33.0	33.8	295,536	70.6	2.2	50.8	138,924	96,812	8.2	25.4	7.9
27013	Blue Earth County	40,829	28.9	35.7	57,506	66.8	2.5	39.0	27,037	66,249	17.1	14.8	8.6

Table B-2. Counties — What: Education, Employment, and Income, 2023—*Continued*

STATE County code	STATE County	Educational attainment: Total population 25 years and over	Educational attainment: Percent with a high school diploma or less	Educational attainment: Percent with a bachelor's degree or more	Employment status: Total population 16 years and over	Employment status: Labor force participation (percent)	Employment status: Percent unemployed	Employment status: Percent of persons age 16 years and over who worked full-time year-round in the past 12 months (percent of total population)	Household income and benefits: Total households	Household income and benefits: Median household income in the past 12 months (in 2023 inflation-adjusted dollars)	Household income and benefits: Income less than $25,000 (percent)	Household income and benefits: Income greater than $150,000 (percent)	Household income and benefits: Percent who received cash public assistance or food stamps/SNAP
	ACS table number:	C15003	C15003	C15003	C23001	C23001	C23001	S2402	B19001	B19049	B19001	B19001	B19058
	Column number:	1	2	3	4	5	6	7	8	9	10	11	12
	MINNESOTA—Cont.												
27019	Carver County	75,289	20.5	52.7	87,061	74.3	1.4	53.9	42,250	129,581	6.4	42.1	2.9
27027	Clay County	40,667	27.1	41.6	52,030	70.9	2.8	45.3	26,890	70,942	15.5	17.0	11.2
27035	Crow Wing County	50,359	30.0	30.5	56,185	61.7	2.6	41.0	31,463	76,050	13.0	14.8	12.1
27037	Dakota County	306,412	24.4	45.1	353,441	70.6	1.9	50.4	176,865	99,830	8.2	29.1	6.0
27053	Hennepin County	882,791	20.7	55.2	1,020,978	71.6	2.4	48.6	545,627	93,668	12.2	28.5	8.9
27109	Olmsted County	113,310	24.2	50.0	130,272	69.2	2.1	47.7	66,425	87,856	11.1	25.2	6.6
27123	Ramsey County	363,251	27.1	47.4	429,010	69.4	2.3	45.5	225,183	77,812	13.2	20.2	11.7
27131	Rice County	43,282	39.8	28.0	55,803	64.2	1.3	37.7	23,512	81,455	15.8	19.1	13.1
27137	St. Louis County	139,262	30.0	33.6	168,567	63.5	1.9	38.4	87,576	67,269	16.5	15.0	10.3
27139	Scott County	103,742	28.5	39.9	121,665	74.0	1.9	49.9	55,921	106,181	7.4	32.2	4.1
27141	Sherburne County	67,786	29.0	29.9	79,069	70.1	1.1	49.0	35,909	101,214	7.9	23.1	5.2
27145	Stearns County	100,128	34.6	30.2	127,926	68.0	2.2	44.4	60,666	74,709	12.0	16.3	8.2
27163	Washington County	191,056	20.6	51.3	221,553	68.3	1.8	48.1	109,093	110,729	6.1	33.4	5.2
27171	Wright County	99,434	30.2	33.9	115,430	74.4	1.0	54.8	55,367	104,269	7.6	30.0	6.4
28000	**MISSISSIPPI**	1,980,147	41.7	25.5	2,354,139	57.6	4.8	70.6	1,166,617	54,203	24.1	10.8	13.3
28033	DeSoto County	129,730	36.3	30.1	151,547	68.2	1.5	49.8	70,666	81,486	13.1	19.1	5.3
28035	Forrest County	47,765	35.5	34.8	62,670	61.7	1.8	NA	30,255	52,157	25.6	8.3	12.1
28047	Harrison County	143,352	39.6	28.4	167,394	60.9	3.0	38.7	86,167	56,159	20.6	11.5	14.8
28049	Hinds County	142,202	38.1	30.8	171,612	61.9	4.0	44.0	88,687	50,904	25.8	9.8	14.7
28059	Jackson County	101,465	34.9	26.8	117,299	64.4	4.6	45.5	59,347	67,472	17.4	16.3	9.2
28067	Jones County	43,649	41.6	20.6	NA	NA	NA	NA	25,758	48,503	24.5	11.7	12.8
28073	Lamar County	45,630	30.1	35.4	53,401	60.3	1.7	NA	26,301	59,716	20.6	12.3	9.4
28075	Lauderdale County	48,045	39.1	22.4	55,837	58.9	4.4	NA	29,693	50,542	31.1	7.0	16.4
28081	Lee County	54,041	37.1	30.5	65,047	62.7	2.6	44.7	32,115	68,233	19.1	13.1	11.7
28089	Madison County	75,081	22.6	51.4	89,908	65.6	2.0	49.7	45,674	78,784	12.5	22.0	7.0
28121	Rankin County	113,094	29.8	31.5	129,763	61.5	2.2	43.1	60,434	69,208	16.3	13.0	5.4
29000	**MISSOURI**	4,255,810	37.4	33.2	4,997,010	63.9	3.4	69.6	2,556,271	68,545	15.8	15.5	10.2
29019	Boone County	115,647	23.1	52.3	155,552	66.7	2.0	44.2	76,762	69,218	16.9	15.6	6.8
29021	Buchanan County	56,730	50.6	20.4	66,557	60.1	1.6	41.9	33,257	60,950	19.2	9.8	16.0
29031	Cape Girardeau County	53,135	40.3	33.1	67,561	66.4	1.3	44.9	33,624	68,094	20.0	13.8	8.1
29037	Cass County	77,298	35.8	31.3	89,717	67.7	2.6	46.3	44,422	84,774	8.6	20.3	6.7
29043	Christian County	64,050	29.5	33.3	73,219	63.2	2.4	44.0	35,654	80,781	10.5	15.5	8.2
29047	Clay County	179,871	32.8	38.0	206,825	69.8	1.8	52.1	103,995	84,378	10.2	22.2	6.9
29051	Cole County	53,975	32.7	41.6	63,104	63.9	2.4	49.5	31,874	74,415	13.1	15.6	4.9
29071	Franklin County	75,837	39.7	27.3	86,457	65.1	2.7	46.7	44,140	68,440	12.0	10.6	8.2
29077	Greene County	202,291	34.1	30.9	248,954	64.9	1.6	44.2	132,232	59,499	16.3	11.4	10.0
29095	Jackson County	492,567	34.0	35.6	572,886	67.1	2.3	48.7	310,868	66,055	15.6	14.2	10.5
29097	Jasper County	82,266	44.4	25.5	98,260	65.3	2.4	43.5	52,000	54,109	21.3	9.3	16.9
29099	Jefferson County	161,658	37.9	25.8	187,184	67.2	2.2	47.6	88,836	81,843	11.7	19.4	6.4
29165	Platte County	77,060	22.9	49.4	88,937	68.8	1.7	48.5	44,751	93,091	11.9	28.2	5.0
29183	St. Charles County	290,987	27.4	41.9	336,289	69.7	1.5	49.9	163,272	98,390	8.0	26.1	3.9
29187	St. Francois County	47,753	48.2	16.7	55,129	55.3	2.9	34.3	25,489	55,042	20.4	9.7	21.0
29189	St. Louis County	689,546	25.6	48.7	797,741	66.6	2.7	46.1	419,348	81,441	11.9	23.6	7.3
29510	St. Louis city	205,959	30.4	45.1	237,461	69.1	3.2	47.3	150,404	56,245	24.0	14.4	17.5
30000	**MONTANA**	795,845	33.6	34.6	924,869	63.0	2.7	65.2	472,867	70,804	15.8	15.4	8.1
30013	Cascade County	58,681	36.2	30.2	68,656	62.4	1.3	39.5	36,414	66,454	13.3	16.0	11.0
30029	Flathead County	81,667	32.2	37.4	92,442	64.1	1.3	42.5	45,510	74,274	12.5	17.0	5.5
30031	Gallatin County	84,207	21.1	51.0	106,871	72.4	1.7	45.6	54,621	91,158	11.8	23.7	2.8
30049	Lewis and Clark County	53,556	30.6	38.9	61,577	60.5	1.2	37.6	30,756	77,405	13.0	16.8	5.4
30063	Missoula County	84,883	22.5	47.5	103,202	68.9	1.6	45.2	55,084	73,429	16.7	16.9	9.3
30111	Yellowstone County	118,721	38.1	31.3	135,846	66.2	2.1	45.2	72,668	68,914	12.7	16.1	8.4
31000	**NEBRASKA**	1,307,246	32.1	35.3	1,558,006	69.0	2.6	70.6	813,864	74,590	14.2	17.5	8.3
31055	Douglas County	387,846	27.5	44.3	459,630	70.8	2.1	50.4	242,890	77,457	14.0	21.3	10.2
31109	Lancaster County	205,157	25.1	42.4	262,567	68.7	2.0	45.2	138,006	70,637	15.3	16.8	8.5
31153	Sarpy County	131,560	25.3	41.3	153,870	73.9	1.5	53.1	75,546	101,932	7.4	24.9	4.9

Table B-2. Counties — What: Education, Employment, and Income, 2023—*Continued*

STATE County code	STATE County	Educational attainment			Employment status				Household income and benefits				
		Total population 25 years and over	Percent with a high school diploma or less	Percent with a bachelor's degree or more	Total population 16 years and over	Labor force participation (percent)	Percent unemployed	Percent of persons age 16 years and over who worked full-time year-round in the past 12 months (percent of total population)	Total households	Median household income in the past 12 months (in 2023 inflation-adjusted dollars)	Income less than $25,000 (percent)	Income greater than $150,000 (percent)	Percent who received cash public assistance or food stamps/ SNAP
	ACS table number:	C15003	C15003	C15003	C23001	C23001	C23001	S2402	B19001	B19049	B19001	B19001	B19058
	Column number:	1	2	3	4	5	6	7	8	9	10	11	12
32000	**NEVADA**	2,253,253	39.1	28.7	2,594,279	63.5	4.5	68.5	1,224,685	76,364	14.0	19.0	13.9
32003	Clark County	1,637,673	40.2	28.7	1,887,864	64.3	3.1	44.2	880,604	75,065	14.5	18.6	15.2
32031	Washoe County	353,801	32.1	35.3	409,162	65.2	2.4	44.3	201,140	84,183	11.8	22.8	9.2
33000	**NEW HAMPSHIRE**	1,030,965	32.7	40.7	1,184,596	66.5	2.6	69.8	569,493	96,838	10.7	28.2	7.3
33001	Belknap County	49,898	32.4	34.9	55,694	61.1	0.6	43.5	27,150	97,692	13.4	24.0	6.1
33005	Cheshire County	57,057	37.1	37.6	66,305	66.6	1.7	45.8	31,921	89,314	10.6	22.0	7.0
33009	Grafton County	67,375	29.5	47.4	80,456	61.5	2.1	40.2	40,528	82,059	11.5	22.5	7.1
33011	Hillsborough County	309,642	31.7	42.8	354,965	71.0	1.5	51.2	170,761	103,727	8.9	31.5	7.1
33013	Merrimack County	114,613	32.6	40.4	132,208	65.3	1.7	45.6	62,305	92,110	9.9	25.4	7.5
33015	Rockingham County	240,442	29.1	45.7	270,773	67.2	2.0	46.4	127,021	109,770	9.2	36.1	5.0
33017	Strafford County	91,334	35.5	35.7	113,140	66.7	2.2	47.0	53,495	84,869	14.4	23.8	10.0
34000	**NEW JERSEY**	6,511,081	34.5	43.8	7,520,182	66.9	4.7	68.8	3,538,457	99,781	12.1	31.9	10.4
34001	Atlantic County	193,545	40.1	33.3	224,652	64.9	4.1	40.2	111,158	77,053	14.4	19.9	15.2
34003	Bergen County	684,037	27.0	53.3	785,281	67.6	2.8	47.2	356,438	116,709	9.9	39.1	6.6
34005	Burlington County	338,116	30.9	42.4	385,610	67.0	2.7	46.0	179,477	102,532	8.8	31.1	5.4
34007	Camden County	365,883	39.2	35.9	421,111	66.9	3.2	44.9	201,670	83,763	14.4	23.6	15.8
34009	Cape May County	73,025	35.2	41.2	80,472	58.7	2.7	36.8	47,516	84,364	11.9	28.0	5.8
34011	Cumberland County	102,814	57.4	18.3	119,942	60.1	3.7	42.0	54,482	64,908	19.2	14.0	20.3
34013	Essex County	577,271	40.3	40.3	676,204	67.4	4.6	45.5	322,456	80,463	17.3	27.6	16.9
34015	Gloucester County	212,917	35.8	35.6	250,952	66.7	2.7	44.4	113,391	97,474	11.2	28.9	7.2
34017	Hudson County	515,006	32.9	49.5	582,463	71.3	3.2	52.0	305,743	89,272	16.0	28.7	16.3
34019	Hunterdon County	96,075	22.1	58.7	109,144	65.8	2.2	47.5	51,186	137,275	8.0	45.3	3.6
34021	Mercer County	260,234	32.8	45.2	308,614	65.2	3.8	44.7	146,258	96,152	13.6	30.3	10.1
34023	Middlesex County	598,957	34.4	45.6	702,136	67.1	3.6	46.0	311,100	105,055	11.2	34.3	9.1
34025	Monmouth County	457,264	28.3	51.3	527,247	66.5	2.8	44.8	252,995	118,008	9.7	39.4	6.0
34027	Morris County	367,791	23.6	57.1	422,166	69.7	2.7	50.3	193,192	134,579	7.0	45.5	4.1
34029	Ocean County	446,156	40.8	34.3	508,981	58.6	2.0	38.0	245,827	85,464	11.8	24.7	7.5
34031	Passaic County	345,750	49.0	31.0	407,017	65.8	3.0	43.7	178,277	82,825	17.0	24.3	19.9
34033	Salem County	45,779	43.9	26.9	52,840	61.6	2.6	39.7	25,207	87,294	15.8	18.1	13.4
34035	Somerset County	249,716	24.4	58.0	286,676	69.9	2.7	51.9	132,047	142,092	7.6	47.4	5.3
34037	Sussex County	107,439	29.8	41.4	121,485	68.3	2.5	48.7	58,679	110,785	7.3	32.5	5.2
34039	Union County	392,042	39.3	38.4	454,395	70.7	3.8	50.2	206,095	101,146	9.9	32.7	9.8
34041	Warren County	81,264	33.3	36.9	92,794	69.9	2.7	49.2	45,263	100,532	10.5	26.9	7.6
35000	**NEW MEXICO**	1,471,057	37.6	31.6	1,723,938	58.6	4.7	65.7	856,580	62,268	20.5	14.4	20.8
35001	Bernalillo County	477,915	31.9	38.2	555,752	63.3	2.7	42.1	285,796	68,372	17.6	16.1	19.0
35013	Doña Ana County	142,574	41.2	31.8	181,728	59.3	3.3	36.5	87,688	56,451	23.7	11.6	25.1
35025	Lea County	43,682	56.4	15.0	54,088	64.2	1.3	NA	24,812	55,736	20.9	19.8	24.7
35031	McKinley County	44,879	54.6	11.7	52,869	48.0	5.2	31.1	21,312	40,108	36.5	5.6	42.7
35035	Otero County	45,594	42.7	21.7	55,046	61.4	2.7	NA	25,289	50,762	21.4	8.8	26.0
35043	Sandoval County	110,305	30.8	35.0	128,202	56.7	2.5	39.3	58,731	82,026	12.6	22.3	13.9
35045	San Juan County	80,773	44.5	20.4	94,401	56.4	3.4	38.6	42,670	57,324	20.3	11.1	21.4
35049	Santa Fe County	120,801	30.3	45.9	135,708	57.0	2.6	38.5	71,322	78,731	13.9	22.1	11.7
35061	Valencia County	54,774	47.0	20.2	62,961	55.6	2.9	37.8	29,932	54,665	21.1	9.9	27.8
36000	**NEW YORK**	13,885,155	35.9	40.6	16,085,030	63.0	5.0	67.6	7,809,267	82,095	16.7	25.6	17.2
36001	Albany County	214,441	28.1	45.2	266,793	64.1	2.8	43.4	134,971	81,335	13.9	20.8	11.6
36005	Bronx County	904,321	52.2	23.5	1,064,629	59.4	5.5	35.8	537,953	46,838	31.8	10.0	40.6
36007	Broome County	130,860	37.9	31.6	164,638	56.5	2.8	35.6	80,001	63,876	19.9	13.1	15.4
36009	Cattaraugus County	52,825	50.3	20.7	61,121	54.0	2.7	35.2	32,376	54,250	24.0	8.0	19.3
36011	Cayuga County	55,059	42.4	25.6	61,718	59.3	1.7	42.3	32,786	66,166	13.8	12.0	13.2
36013	Chautauqua County	87,982	43.9	24.4	102,481	57.5	3.5	36.5	54,284	55,234	21.4	8.8	21.0
36015	Chemung County	58,185	43.3	27.5	66,186	60.0	3.3	38.2	35,591	59,617	23.1	11.9	15.7
36019	Clinton County	55,085	41.5	27.4	65,792	57.1	1.0	39.8	34,639	62,717	18.1	12.8	18.6
36027	Dutchess County	213,395	32.9	40.8	250,548	62.5	2.6	43.0	115,529	96,824	9.7	29.6	9.6
36029	Erie County	672,911	34.3	37.8	778,314	62.5	2.1	42.4	410,430	70,492	17.7	16.9	17.0
36045	Jefferson County	74,117	42.9	26.0	89,797	66.5	2.5	35.0	50,542	61,512	14.0	11.2	16.6
36047	Kings County	1,809,652	37.2	43.5	2,062,593	65.0	3.8	42.8	1,035,549	76,912	19.9	25.2	24.3

Table B-2. Counties — What: Education, Employment, and Income, 2023—*Continued*

STATE County code	STATE County	Educational attainment			Employment status				Household income and benefits				
		Total population 25 years and over	Percent with a high school diploma or less	Percent with a bachelor's degree or more	Total population 16 years and over	Labor force participation (percent)	Percent unemployed	Percent of persons age 16 years and over who worked full-time year-round in the past 12 months (percent of total population)	Total households	Median household income in the past 12 months (in 2023 inflation-adjusted dollars)	Income less than $25,000 (percent)	Income greater than $150,000 (percent)	Percent who received cash public assistance or food stamps/ SNAP
	ACS table number:	C15003	C15003	C15003	C23001	C23001	C23001	S2402	B19001	B19049	B19001	B19001	B19058
	Column number:	1	2	3	4	5	6	7	8	9	10	11	12
	NEW YORK—Cont.												
36053	Madison County	45,676	36.6	31.2	56,568	59.3	2.4	39.5	26,755	74,125	14.4	18.1	12.6
36055	Monroe County	525,326	31.0	41.5	615,900	63.3	2.7	42.2	317,369	73,211	16.3	18.1	16.8
36059	Nassau County	972,762	27.8	48.9	1,124,103	63.4	2.5	44.7	458,162	141,568	7.7	47.2	6.6
36061	New York County	1,239,152	22.1	64.9	1,406,087	67.7	4.7	46.5	787,747	101,078	18.7	38.0	15.8
36063	Niagara County	152,239	43.0	26.5	174,041	61.2	2.7	42.5	91,894	65,875	18.1	14.5	15.9
36065	Oneida County	158,943	42.0	27.1	184,710	58.3	2.6	39.6	96,767	61,118	20.2	13.0	18.7
36067	Onondaga County	323,311	30.8	40.9	381,967	64.0	2.3	42.6	198,699	74,704	16.2	19.7	15.2
36069	Ontario County	82,485	31.5	39.5	94,251	60.1	1.5	40.3	48,610	79,450	10.8	19.0	9.0
36071	Orange County	262,181	38.6	32.4	316,308	64.8	3.2	42.9	138,856	94,364	11.1	27.8	14.3
36075	Oswego County	80,682	45.5	21.4	98,056	57.7	3.2	39.7	48,010	70,076	15.7	13.2	16.1
36079	Putnam County	72,801	29.6	47.6	82,480	66.1	1.7	45.2	36,405	122,777	10.1	39.6	3.2
36081	Queens County	1,657,169	42.0	36.6	1,867,832	63.6	3.2	44.1	863,975	81,929	16.0	23.6	18.9
36083	Rensselaer County	112,496	32.7	37.3	133,048	64.1	3.0	43.0	66,583	84,278	12.1	22.3	9.5
36085	Richmond County	345,758	41.8	35.5	399,442	59.5	2.7	42.7	169,526	95,543	16.1	29.4	15.8
36087	Rockland County	207,397	35.0	41.6	249,675	62.9	2.0	41.0	104,325	106,589	12.4	35.1	11.9
36089	St. Lawrence County	71,910	39.9	27.6	88,863	52.3	1.6	32.9	42,945	56,872	26.5	10.6	19.2
36091	Saratoga County	176,190	29.3	44.2	199,085	64.4	1.6	45.2	103,758	94,330	9.5	26.2	6.5
36093	Schenectady County	110,464	34.3	36.6	129,502	60.6	2.7	42.5	68,172	74,969	15.1	19.2	15.1
36101	Steuben County	66,231	45.6	24.9	75,236	57.7	2.3	39.5	38,764	64,238	19.5	13.2	14.0
36103	Suffolk County	1,075,208	33.3	40.4	1,249,135	64.6	2.3	45.3	508,809	124,045	8.7	40.1	9.5
36105	Sullivan County	56,173	42.6	30.0	64,792	58.4	2.1	41.9	30,971	69,453	20.6	16.5	18.3
36109	Tompkins County	60,770	20.7	60.6	91,530	59.7	2.8	35.0	43,054	67,247	18.8	20.1	8.5
36111	Ulster County	135,460	36.0	39.1	156,207	59.1	2.8	37.8	73,895	85,878	12.9	21.9	10.4
36113	Warren County	50,266	34.1	37.3	55,611	63.3	1.6	45.4	31,013	73,802	13.3	17.0	9.6
36117	Wayne County	66,514	40.2	26.6	74,588	60.5	1.2	42.5	39,094	73,065	15.1	12.7	14.7
36119	Westchester County	698,558	29.4	54.1	809,822	66.1	3.5	45.0	374,012	114,457	12.3	40.2	10.2
37000	**NORTH CAROLINA**	7,487,552	33.9	36.8	8,792,430	63.2	4.0	69.1	4,392,669	70,804	15.8	17.7	13.0
37001	Alamance County	120,632	39.6	29.3	143,807	65.5	3.0	45.8	70,911	65,633	17.3	10.5	15.1
37019	Brunswick County	130,743	33.6	35.0	141,076	49.1	2.4	31.6	72,932	76,221	14.6	16.0	9.6
37021	Buncombe County	206,190	26.8	48.3	234,093	59.2	1.9	39.3	104,181	71,525	16.4	19.2	12.0
37023	Burke County	65,335	47.9	19.9	74,520	57.2	2.3	40.4	37,485	53,739	19.6	9.4	16.5
37025	Cabarrus County	160,935	30.9	38.2	187,502	71.2	2.9	52.0	90,254	85,810	9.9	24.1	11.6
37027	Caldwell County	59,736	51.3	17.6	67,738	61.0	1.4	42.9	34,367	55,766	15.0	10.5	14.6
37031	Carteret County	55,275	29.0	36.6	61,036	57.1	1.6	39.7	34,497	78,256	15.6	19.1	8.7
37035	Catawba County	115,705	39.1	25.4	134,343	62.5	1.4	46.6	68,126	64,214	15.5	13.2	11.3
37037	Chatham County	61,593	25.6	49.2	68,776	57.9	1.9	NA	33,971	97,219	8.8	28.8	7.4
37045	Cleveland County	70,879	42.6	26.7	80,890	59.2	1.8	43.8	39,314	62,186	18.6	12.2	20.7
37049	Craven County	70,552	37.9	25.7	82,736	58.7	3.4	34.7	41,100	59,399	20.6	11.9	16.2
37051	Cumberland County	210,887	33.3	28.7	261,952	66.2	3.4	35.2	131,421	61,643	17.0	11.9	19.1
37057	Davidson County	123,989	42.2	22.9	141,556	61.1	2.4	43.1	71,400	63,189	17.5	11.4	13.9
37063	Durham County	235,826	23.2	57.0	279,562	69.2	2.1	49.2	143,466	81,545	13.5	23.7	6.6
37067	Forsyth County	265,007	31.0	41.3	316,739	62.7	3.0	42.8	166,028	65,062	16.2	14.0	13.0
37069	Franklin County	55,012	39.8	25.3	62,222	62.4	1.8	NA	31,057	70,548	17.4	11.0	9.6
37071	Gaston County	164,829	38.7	28.3	189,960	63.6	1.9	46.6	97,287	66,906	16.3	14.4	15.5
37081	Guilford County	363,450	31.4	38.0	443,007	64.1	2.2	45.0	222,927	65,413	16.8	15.8	16.4
37085	Harnett County	92,806	39.9	28.0	108,699	57.2	2.8	37.3	49,285	70,664	13.8	14.4	13.2
37089	Henderson County	89,872	33.9	38.2	100,887	53.7	1.3	38.3	52,492	61,974	11.4	14.1	10.5
37097	Iredell County	140,226	35.6	35.3	160,777	66.3	2.1	47.9	77,592	85,298	12.3	22.2	7.8
37101	Johnston County	162,375	37.4	31.3	189,768	66.8	2.8	48.0	87,955	79,592	12.5	18.5	11.0
37105	Lee County	46,432	40.6	22.5	53,024	59.9	2.2	NA	25,961	60,140	17.4	12.8	15.3
37109	Lincoln County	69,443	36.3	28.9	78,412	61.6	1.3	44.7	37,618	77,776	16.4	19.4	10.5
37119	Mecklenburg County	793,990	24.3	51.6	933,250	71.8	2.4	53.5	474,611	84,593	11.4	25.2	9.2
37125	Moore County	77,870	26.5	44.1	86,222	54.4	1.8	33.6	46,385	78,057	16.7	18.9	8.7
37127	Nash County	68,053	48.6	23.2	77,619	59.1	1.9	46.8	39,349	66,121	17.5	13.2	19.4
37129	New Hanover County	166,553	21.6	47.2	202,524	65.6	2.5	41.8	106,358	79,547	15.5	20.1	9.8
37133	Onslow County	118,073	37.0	23.6	165,735	70.1	2.2	33.0	76,788	67,597	14.6	12.0	15.6
37135	Orange County	94,015	18.1	63.0	127,768	63.5	1.8	40.6	59,771	86,381	16.0	29.2	4.8
37141	Pender County	48,229	36.5	34.2	54,898	63.5	3.4	NA	27,256	71,487	14.3	19.0	11.7
37147	Pitt County	108,419	33.1	34.9	142,449	63.4	4.9	39.8	74,443	59,946	21.5	12.2	14.2

STATE County code	STATE County	Educational attainment			Employment status				Household income and benefits					
		Total population 25 years and over	Percent with a high school diploma or less	Percent with a bachelor's degree or more	Total population 16 years and over	Labor force participation (percent)	Percent unemployed	Percent of persons age 16 years and over who worked full-time year-round in the past 12 months (percent of total population)	Total households	Median household income in the past 12 months (in 2023 inflation-adjusted dollars)	Income less than $25,000 (percent)	Income greater than $150,000 (percent)	Percent who received cash public assistance or food stamps/ SNAP
	ACS table number:	C15003	C15003	C15003	C23001	C23001	C23001	S2402	B19001	B19049	B19001	B19001	B19058
	Column number:	1	2	3	4	5	6	7	8	9	10	11	12
	NORTH CAROLINA—Cont.												
37151	Randolph County	102,719	51.4	20.3	119,402	60.9	3.1	42.0	59,646	56,310	20.6	8.5	16.5
37155	Robeson County	74,858	56.1	14.1	90,394	50.0	2.4	37.1	43,590	40,996	31.7	6.2	35.0
37157	Rockingham County	67,324	47.6	18.3	76,169	59.5	3.7	41.3	39,251	59,434	19.1	10.6	15.6
37159	Rowan County	104,520	41.1	24.8	123,055	61.4	3.1	43.5	60,965	65,904	18.3	12.6	15.2
37161	Rutherford County	47,677	43.7	20.9	NA	NA	NA	NA	26,805	47,557	18.9	7.5	17.3
37167	Stanly County	46,385	42.9	19.2	53,376	56.9	1.4	42.9	25,371	65,456	17.6	12.0	16.8
37171	Surry County	51,117	41.1	21.7	58,507	55.8	2.4	NA	30,752	58,291	22.1	10.0	20.9
37179	Union County	167,990	33.3	41.1	200,712	67.1	2.2	45.9	87,714	98,215	9.4	26.6	8.8
37183	Wake County	816,613	19.2	58.8	951,610	70.5	2.4	51.5	481,294	102,918	8.9	32.5	6.0
37191	Wayne County	79,276	46.9	22.4	93,719	60.3	4.6	36.4	47,035	55,461	19.3	9.6	21.6
37193	Wilkes County	47,621	45.9	18.7	55,142	57.3	3.0	NA	26,154	47,022	18.6	4.3	13.8
37195	Wilson County	54,537	46.6	20.8	63,525	56.9	3.6	39.0	34,524	51,247	21.3	8.2	21.4
38000	**NORTH DAKOTA**	520,006	29.8	33.6	622,500	69.4	2.8	68.3	338,059	76,525	14.6	17.9	7.7
38015	Burleigh County	68,141	24.9	39.9	79,866	67.4	1.5	48.6	42,486	85,172	16.5	20.8	6.5
38017	Cass County	123,920	20.6	43.4	156,623	75.2	2.7	51.7	84,603	73,742	13.9	18.1	6.6
38035	Grand Forks County	43,613	23.9	34.9	59,718	72.3	2.2	41.9	32,099	72,536	15.7	16.3	9.3
38101	Ward County	44,983	30.2	30.2	52,925	70.4	1.0	43.9	28,565	72,370	8.2	17.6	6.4
39000	**OHIO**	8,172,692	39.9	32.0	9,520,298	63.5	4.0	68.7	4,917,309	67,769	16.8	16.3	13.0
39003	Allen County	68,452	48.5	19.9	79,960	63.2	3.3	43.4	42,147	66,891	17.4	8.9	12.5
39007	Ashtabula County	68,261	51.8	18.8	77,896	57.8	2.4	38.9	37,507	57,577	18.7	9.2	20.0
39013	Belmont County	47,815	46.4	23.9	54,467	56.5	2.5	39.4	27,281	56,361	21.3	8.6	15.8
39017	Butler County	254,202	40.7	32.3	312,632	63.9	2.2	44.7	148,804	80,135	14.8	19.3	11.5
39023	Clark County	93,767	46.9	18.7	108,312	57.5	3.2	37.9	55,322	57,910	19.4	10.9	18.2
39025	Clermont County	149,457	39.5	32.1	170,611	64.4	1.6	46.5	87,429	81,173	12.0	21.5	7.9
39029	Columbiana County	73,316	57.4	14.2	82,865	56.1	2.2	37.8	42,415	53,455	25.2	10.8	17.5
39035	Cuyahoga County	881,523	35.5	37.4	1,013,158	64.3	3.7	42.5	551,306	61,862	20.1	16.1	16.2
39041	Delaware County	155,193	18.8	59.1	181,680	69.5	1.8	49.3	84,413	126,513	4.9	42.4	3.3
39043	Erie County	55,188	43.4	27.7	NA	NA	NA	NA	33,608	61,648	17.5	13.7	10.2
39045	Fairfield County	112,784	40.9	30.7	131,615	62.9	1.5	45.4	62,834	84,759	10.2	19.9	9.3
39049	Franklin County	893,378	32.0	43.6	1,051,776	70.0	2.7	49.3	561,634	71,680	15.4	18.6	11.1
39055	Geauga County	66,917	37.1	36.0	77,327	63.3	2.0	42.0	36,405	99,305	8.6	30.3	4.5
39057	Greene County	116,302	29.3	42.3	138,424	64.3	1.7	41.2	70,169	83,866	13.3	25.3	7.0
39061	Hamilton County	560,823	30.2	44.2	660,192	66.8	2.9	45.8	360,340	68,519	16.7	19.1	13.4
39063	Hancock County	52,725	36.5	34.3	NA	NA	NA	NA	31,675	70,736	18.4	12.3	9.5
39085	Lake County	169,725	36.4	33.4	192,351	66.2	2.4	46.6	103,532	72,620	13.2	18.2	8.5
39089	Licking County	125,853	40.8	26.8	147,063	64.1	2.1	45.5	68,568	75,976	13.9	18.7	13.5
39093	Lorain County	224,008	37.2	29.4	258,093	63.3	2.3	43.8	128,887	75,461	14.1	18.0	10.8
39095	Lucas County	291,778	39.7	29.9	339,987	63.1	3.7	42.1	182,625	60,426	20.8	13.7	17.8
39099	Mahoning County	162,089	45.8	25.8	184,786	57.3	2.5	36.4	98,872	51,738	22.9	9.4	19.1
39101	Marion County	46,515	57.8	12.4	52,914	54.5	2.9	NA	24,957	53,995	20.3	8.0	19.1
39103	Medina County	131,761	36.1	35.0	150,408	64.4	1.8	43.7	73,675	89,647	9.4	22.7	8.9
39109	Miami County	77,994	45.8	26.9	88,522	60.8	2.8	43.2	44,756	75,366	15.2	14.5	11.1
39113	Montgomery County	366,667	34.4	32.5	429,553	64.1	3.2	41.4	235,734	62,450	19.5	13.5	13.7
39119	Muskingum County	59,260	53.8	19.1	69,067	56.9	2.8	39.2	32,776	56,654	23.4	7.3	21.9
39133	Portage County	108,426	40.6	31.0	137,410	63.9	1.7	42.4	65,601	73,220	16.3	14.0	10.2
39139	Richland County	89,346	52.9	18.9	101,917	56.2	3.6	37.7	51,046	56,664	18.2	7.7	18.5
39141	Ross County	54,546	52.6	19.7	61,593	52.4	2.0	37.6	28,870	60,666	17.7	9.4	15.3
39145	Scioto County	50,382	50.8	17.3	58,551	55.5	3.6	37.8	30,143	52,159	24.3	12.8	18.5
39151	Stark County	262,385	42.2	26.5	303,245	61.4	1.9	42.1	156,143	63,145	17.3	10.7	13.3
39153	Summit County	382,690	33.9	38.2	440,217	65.3	3.0	44.3	232,592	69,577	16.1	18.2	14.1
39155	Trumbull County	144,310	53.7	20.6	164,141	56.1	2.0	38.4	87,955	51,016	23.2	10.4	15.9
39157	Tuscarawas County	63,441	58.1	18.1	73,502	59.6	1.9	39.9	39,110	60,604	22.6	10.5	15.6
39159	Union County	48,168	33.9	38.0	NA	NA	NA	NA	25,554	101,968	8.0	30.8	8.7
39165	Warren County	174,225	28.1	48.1	201,321	68.1	2.1	50.5	93,271	107,541	10.2	31.2	4.5
39169	Wayne County	77,279	48.0	26.5	91,602	64.1	1.5	42.0	44,453	69,101	12.5	12.3	8.9
39173	Wood County	85,052	33.9	35.6	109,100	64.2	2.2	44.4	54,408	72,947	14.1	17.9	6.7

Table B-2. Counties — What: Education, Employment, and Income, 2023—*Continued*

STATE County code	STATE County	Educational attainment: Total population 25 years and over	Educational attainment: Percent with a high school diploma or less	Educational attainment: Percent with a bachelor's degree or more	Employment status: Total population 16 years and over	Employment status: Labor force participation (percent)	Employment status: Percent unemployed	Employment status: Percent of persons age 16 years and over who worked full-time year-round in the past 12 months (percent of total population)	Household income and benefits: Total households	Household income and benefits: Median household income in the past 12 months (in 2023 inflation-adjusted dollars)	Household income and benefits: Income less than $25,000 (percent)	Household income and benefits: Income greater than $150,000 (percent)	Household income and benefits: Percent who received cash public assistance or food stamps/ SNAP
	ACS table number:	C15003	C15003	C15003	C23001	C23001	C23001	S2402	B19001	B19049	B19001	B19001	B19058
	Column number:	1	2	3	4	5	6	7	8	9	10	11	12
40000	**OKLAHOMA**	2,684,421	40.9	28.7	3,201,739	61.2	4.5	69.6	1,589,105	62,138	19.1	13.1	15.7
40017	Canadian County	116,259	33.6	32.7	136,050	66.6	1.9	49.1	58,214	86,061	11.6	20.2	8.0
40027	Cleveland County	194,423	33.6	34.4	248,563	63.3	2.3	42.1	118,062	74,495	14.1	16.8	11.0
40031	Comanche County	79,021	41.7	25.8	95,685	60.4	3.9	31.9	45,945	56,706	19.5	8.8	19.0
40037	Creek County	50,156	52.2	18.3	58,995	57.6	1.8	42.7	28,988	55,857	23.3	10.4	16.1
40101	Muskogee County	44,527	47.8	16.7	52,459	52.1	3.1	39.5	26,362	52,484	25.1	7.1	21.5
40109	Oklahoma County	528,587	33.8	38.3	627,681	66.0	3.4	45.8	335,473	65,948	17.5	15.5	15.8
40119	Payne County	44,892	32.7	43.5	69,330	57.9	2.1	33.6	32,739	56,371	25.9	12.3	11.2
40125	Pottawatomie County	49,581	48.9	20.2	58,878	53.8	1.4	40.3	27,150	56,579	23.2	8.8	19.9
40131	Rogers County	68,007	41.6	27.6	80,139	60.9	2.1	43.8	37,082	70,200	13.4	14.3	11.9
40143	Tulsa County	450,351	34.1	34.7	531,774	65.8	3.2	45.8	275,702	65,479	17.3	14.9	14.6
40145	Wagoner County	61,598	39.4	26.9	70,944	63.8	2.5	46.0	31,633	80,372	15.0	14.5	10.5
41000	**OREGON**	3,050,675	30.1	37.7	3,506,067	62.6	4.1	65.7	1,752,050	80,160	14.8	21.1	17.6
41003	Benton County	61,110	14.7	56.4	84,543	61.8	3.4	33.0	38,306	73,047	17.7	24.1	14.1
41005	Clackamas County	306,243	25.2	40.7	347,666	64.7	1.6	43.8	167,319	100,675	8.6	28.9	10.5
41017	Deschutes County	156,709	22.9	47.3	174,387	64.0	2.0	41.6	88,597	97,163	12.0	26.6	11.2
41019	Douglas County	83,419	41.0	19.3	93,277	50.7	2.0	32.8	47,733	60,889	19.6	10.4	22.8
41029	Jackson County	159,533	36.5	29.8	181,887	57.3	2.5	35.4	92,225	71,666	15.3	14.4	19.3
41033	Josephine County	65,953	40.0	20.8	73,091	48.1	3.0	NA	37,241	64,170	18.6	12.5	24.8
41035	Klamath County	49,467	40.9	21.4	56,835	50.6	3.5	NA	30,395	52,547	25.9	4.9	30.8
41039	Lane County	268,607	29.2	33.2	322,130	60.1	3.4	36.8	162,001	70,374	18.1	15.1	20.4
41043	Linn County	93,289	35.4	23.4	106,171	60.1	2.3	41.8	51,636	70,548	16.1	14.6	22.6
41047	Marion County	234,997	39.9	27.9	276,202	63.3	2.9	40.6	129,087	73,417	15.4	18.4	20.0
41051	Multnomah County	591,613	23.8	50.3	671,165	69.6	2.7	47.1	354,646	83,583	15.3	25.4	17.4
41053	Polk County	60,133	35.9	30.0	72,854	60.0	4.3	37.3	33,113	80,328	15.9	19.9	23.2
41059	Umatilla County	54,752	47.0	18.4	63,541	56.3	1.6	NA	30,821	60,582	16.9	8.8	22.3
41067	Washington County	424,964	23.0	49.7	488,124	69.9	2.5	48.8	237,507	103,713	8.6	30.4	13.2
41071	Yamhill County	75,844	38.1	32.2	88,938	57.6	3.5	37.0	40,380	89,160	16.4	24.0	17.9
42000	**PENNSYLVANIA**	9,171,006	40.9	35.3	10,658,635	62.8	4.2	69.3	5,324,209	73,824	16.1	19.3	15.7
42001	Adams County	75,880	48.6	23.9	88,724	64.1	2.0	42.9	41,810	76,725	10.6	18.0	11.9
42003	Allegheny County	891,599	28.5	46.9	1,026,131	65.1	2.5	45.4	547,396	76,615	16.0	21.4	13.1
42005	Armstrong County	47,992	51.8	20.3	53,309	56.6	1.6	41.2	28,117	61,836	18.0	10.1	16.4
42007	Beaver County	121,837	40.4	30.2	137,798	62.6	1.9	43.0	73,220	66,768	15.3	14.7	15.5
42011	Berks County	297,165	49.5	26.9	351,051	63.9	3.2	44.4	163,307	75,675	15.2	17.9	14.9
42013	Blair County	86,686	54.4	22.3	99,594	58.2	2.0	40.9	50,651	54,002	22.9	9.0	21.9
42017	Bucks County	469,067	32.5	44.2	535,385	65.1	2.3	46.7	249,189	107,221	9.6	34.4	9.8
42019	Butler County	142,804	37.8	37.7	164,790	62.1	2.5	43.9	81,535	80,379	14.0	23.7	11.0
42021	Cambria County	94,077	49.4	24.0	108,883	56.3	2.1	39.4	57,282	55,748	20.8	11.0	20.3
42025	Carbon County	48,933	56.6	18.3	54,445	59.3	3.6	40.7	28,934	64,229	15.9	11.1	15.2
42027	Centre County	96,558	33.8	47.6	138,031	55.7	2.0	33.8	62,175	69,101	18.4	17.2	8.7
42029	Chester County	380,770	24.3	57.9	446,199	68.4	2.0	48.2	205,426	120,903	8.4	39.8	6.6
42033	Clearfield County	57,517	53.6	21.3	64,970	56.2	2.0	39.8	33,554	60,711	20.5	9.4	19.9
42037	Columbia County	44,306	48.4	27.6	55,824	63.1	3.6	41.5	25,929	63,683	18.3	12.7	9.4
42039	Crawford County	58,754	51.3	24.8	67,396	56.9	1.6	40.5	34,813	60,797	19.3	7.6	19.8
42041	Cumberland County	186,391	36.8	41.6	221,379	65.7	1.8	43.7	107,981	82,174	11.6	21.2	8.5
42043	Dauphin County	201,713	39.8	35.9	232,217	65.6	2.9	46.3	121,773	74,170	14.9	17.2	15.4
42045	Delaware County	393,927	33.9	42.9	465,191	64.4	3.8	44.8	215,645	84,085	13.2	25.4	12.3
42049	Erie County	185,141	44.7	29.3	220,063	58.4	2.2	39.5	111,118	60,663	20.1	12.3	21.2
42051	Fayette County	91,907	56.9	19.1	103,333	52.3	1.9	39.0	55,724	54,523	24.9	8.5	27.2
42055	Franklin County	112,505	50.2	25.5	128,120	62.1	3.0	43.7	62,966	75,875	14.4	16.0	11.2
42063	Indiana County	54,468	48.1	25.6	69,871	55.3	3.0	35.3	32,454	57,505	21.9	10.3	19.7
42069	Lackawanna County	152,591	44.4	29.4	177,839	57.7	1.8	40.2	88,871	56,002	24.7	11.1	20.5
42071	Lancaster County	380,837	47.2	31.6	445,133	66.0	2.1	43.5	211,669	80,067	11.1	18.8	12.0
42073	Lawrence County	61,355	51.5	25.6	70,344	57.3	2.4	39.6	36,638	62,754	20.8	10.3	19.0
42075	Lebanon County	101,861	53.3	25.3	116,139	65.0	1.5	46.4	58,012	78,824	11.7	16.5	13.7
42077	Lehigh County	260,568	42.2	34.1	304,486	64.2	3.1	45.0	147,524	76,508	14.5	20.9	16.0
42079	Luzerne County	232,643	46.5	24.6	267,938	59.3	2.7	42.1	136,046	60,380	20.7	13.0	21.1
42081	Lycoming County	79,843	44.8	26.4	92,986	60.9	2.8	40.5	46,849	62,135	19.9	14.4	15.2

Table B-2. Counties — What: Education, Employment, and Income, 2023—*Continued*

STATE County code	STATE County	Educational attainment: Total population 25 years and over	Educational attainment: Percent with a high school diploma or less	Educational attainment: Percent with a bachelor's degree or more	Employment status: Total population 16 years and over	Employment status: Labor force participation (percent)	Employment status: Percent unemployed	Employment status: Percent of persons age 16 years and over who worked full-time year-round in the past 12 months (percent of total population)	Household income and benefits: Total households	Household income and benefits: Median household income in the past 12 months (in 2023 inflation-adjusted dollars)	Household income and benefits: Income less than $25,000 (percent)	Household income and benefits: Income greater than $150,000 (percent)	Household income and benefits: Percent who received cash public assistance or food stamps/ SNAP
	ACS table number:	C15003	C15003	C15003	C23001	C23001	C23001	S2402	B19001	B19049	B19001	B19001	B19058
	Column number:	1	2	3	4	5	6	7	8	9	10	11	12
	PENNSYLVANIA—Cont.												
42085	Mercer County	77,861	48.7	24.3	89,875	56.6	2.6	38.0	47,517	61,669	16.8	9.8	18.1
42089	Monroe County	119,562	46.0	26.8	139,010	59.6	4.0	40.5	61,129	71,087	12.5	17.6	17.6
42091	Montgomery County	616,584	26.3	52.5	709,914	67.4	2.3	47.5	338,467	106,748	10.1	34.2	8.5
42095	Northampton County	225,041	39.2	34.3	266,251	61.7	2.7	42.3	123,536	84,229	10.8	21.1	12.1
42097	Northumberland County	66,434	57.9	19.3	75,266	55.5	1.7	38.4	37,343	59,046	18.6	9.6	17.9
42101	Philadelphia County	1,072,210	42.3	35.7	1,262,049	64.3	4.0	43.9	688,112	60,302	24.0	14.6	27.7
42107	Schuylkill County	104,568	55.7	20.1	119,058	56.7	3.2	40.9	58,809	64,276	21.1	9.6	20.2
42111	Somerset County	54,240	60.6	16.2	60,817	56.9	2.9	37.9	29,435	60,515	20.3	7.4	14.8
42125	Washington County	153,112	39.8	32.7	174,345	62.7	1.9	44.0	89,091	77,450	13.6	18.8	15.3
42129	Westmoreland County	262,496	40.4	32.8	295,764	61.6	2.2	42.2	155,459	71,081	15.8	16.7	15.0
42133	York County	327,185	46.0	29.2	376,041	66.7	2.6	46.3	183,864	81,362	10.9	18.2	12.5
44000	**RHODE ISLAND**	786,493	36.8	39.0	916,988	64.6	4.7	66.4	443,980	84,972	15.0	23.3	14.0
44003	Kent County	130,292	34.8	39.0	144,706	64.7	2.1	45.4	73,493	91,821	13.2	25.9	12.7
44005	Newport County	64,469	24.8	51.7	72,396	64.1	2.6	38.0	36,932	104,880	14.9	28.7	10.3
44007	Providence County	462,443	42.3	33.3	543,431	65.4	3.8	43.6	259,528	77,170	16.7	19.4	16.6
44009	Washington County	92,632	24.6	54.3	113,698	61.8	1.6	38.9	53,307	102,108	10.8	30.8	7.3
45000	**SOUTH CAROLINA**	3,745,394	38.0	32.9	4,370,726	61.1	4.2	68.7	2,177,733	67,804	17.2	15.4	11.1
45003	Aiken County	124,842	40.2	33.5	144,075	58.7	2.6	40.4	70,920	67,480	19.7	13.1	10.1
45007	Anderson County	148,795	41.4	27.1	171,023	62.5	1.9	45.2	86,773	64,645	17.6	12.4	11.3
45013	Beaufort County	146,080	27.3	49.7	170,596	56.3	1.1	32.9	87,165	81,111	10.1	22.6	5.3
45015	Berkeley County	171,750	35.6	32.8	203,431	67.8	2.7	47.0	97,713	83,372	11.4	17.2	7.4
45019	Charleston County	307,483	23.0	51.7	352,879	66.6	1.9	46.5	183,800	89,083	12.8	23.9	6.6
45035	Dorchester County	115,071	35.1	30.8	134,742	65.4	2.2	46.2	65,532	78,137	13.6	16.3	11.5
45041	Florence County	93,028	46.6	23.5	109,025	59.2	3.6	41.3	53,651	54,014	21.7	10.0	15.2
45043	Georgetown County	49,831	39.3	33.4	56,598	47.4	1.5	NA	28,720	71,313	16.5	15.3	8.7
45045	Greenville County	385,479	30.4	42.0	445,412	66.5	2.5	46.2	226,571	76,334	13.7	20.1	7.5
45047	Greenwood County	47,463	42.0	27.7	55,665	61.0	1.4	45.4	29,676	56,420	23.8	10.5	10.7
45051	Horry County	301,342	37.9	29.1	338,261	53.3	1.9	34.6	168,080	68,988	16.3	12.7	7.9
45055	Kershaw County	47,871	46.3	26.0	55,807	62.9	4.4	NA	27,356	71,375	12.8	16.7	13.0
45057	Lancaster County	78,516	40.1	34.2	87,679	62.4	3.1	47.6	42,439	73,942	17.8	21.2	7.2
45059	Laurens County	48,579	55.9	16.0	55,515	59.7	3.0	43.2	28,833	56,394	18.5	8.0	16.4
45063	Lexington County	216,231	35.2	33.0	247,462	64.4	2.7	45.4	126,509	76,447	13.6	16.7	10.1
45073	Oconee County	60,139	44.5	29.6	67,815	53.9	3.2	34.7	34,416	67,124	19.0	13.3	12.3
45075	Orangeburg County	55,803	50.4	18.4	68,057	52.4	3.0	NA	34,120	51,863	26.0	6.5	26.0
45077	Pickens County	86,451	40.5	28.7	113,273	58.0	1.4	38.4	54,412	57,110	20.4	10.7	9.8
45079	Richland County	270,085	29.2	41.8	345,095	65.1	3.8	41.0	169,715	61,079	18.5	15.6	11.3
45083	Spartanburg County	241,752	42.9	25.8	283,376	62.0	2.6	44.0	134,559	63,899	15.2	12.1	12.0
45085	Sumter County	68,894	45.6	19.9	81,755	58.7	4.1	37.1	40,059	55,982	23.0	11.4	18.1
45091	York County	204,289	30.7	39.6	237,118	67.0	2.1	48.6	113,164	81,356	10.9	23.7	7.2
46083	Lincoln County	48,101	23.8	46.3	NA	NA	NA	NA	28,842	98,015	6.2	24.6	3.8
46000	**SOUTH DAKOTA**	615,517	34.2	33.3	725,788	67.3	2.6	69.8	378,559	71,810	14.9	15.4	8.2
46099	Minnehaha County	136,920	32.7	37.4	159,332	74.6	1.7	54.0	87,657	71,326	13.0	17.0	7.2
46103	Pennington County	80,984	28.2	36.3	93,904	62.8	1.3	41.0	48,946	74,893	14.8	14.3	7.6
47000	**TENNESSEE**	4,931,967	40.9	31.7	5,747,865	62.7	3.9	70.4	2,889,226	67,631	17.2	15.8	10.4
47001	Anderson County	57,408	41.7	29.6	65,384	58.0	2.2	40.8	33,521	57,652	26.2	10.6	11.5
47009	Blount County	102,938	42.1	29.3	117,157	62.0	1.3	44.4	56,548	78,504	12.5	17.3	5.9
47011	Bradley County	77,055	43.5	24.2	89,993	62.1	3.9	42.7	42,712	61,107	18.9	9.9	9.3
47037	Davidson County	497,353	27.7	51.0	581,955	72.7	2.2	52.4	341,597	80,379	13.0	21.1	8.1
47059	Greene County	53,273	52.6	16.5	62,003	52.6	1.6	37.9	28,214	54,261	18.6	10.4	13.3
47063	Hamblen County	47,607	48.9	22.9	NA	NA	NA	NA	27,311	53,210	24.2	9.6	12.9
47065	Hamilton County	268,209	31.3	37.7	307,873	65.3	2.7	45.4	157,992	73,611	14.2	18.3	9.8
47093	Knox County	336,560	31.9	42.0	407,877	66.0	2.3	44.8	200,022	70,265	16.4	19.1	8.7
47113	Madison County	68,155	47.8	23.6	79,348	61.6	3.7	42.3	40,525	58,702	22.0	11.0	16.4
47119	Maury County	77,558	43.2	28.5	88,121	65.2	2.2	47.6	45,571	72,651	16.7	17.2	8.1
47125	Montgomery County	150,785	34.7	33.4	182,404	65.1	3.1	40.6	91,893	75,361	13.8	12.6	9.2
47141	Putnam County	54,713	42.2	31.9	69,098	60.1	2.1	36.8	34,727	56,368	25.8	12.7	10.9

Table B-2. Counties — What: Education, Employment, and Income, 2023—*Continued*

STATE County code	STATE County	Educational attainment			Employment status				Household income and benefits				
		Total population 25 years and over	Percent with a high school diploma or less	Percent with a bachelor's degree or more	Total population 16 years and over	Labor force participation (percent)	Percent unemployed	Percent of persons age 16 years and over who worked full-time year-round in the past 12 months (percent of total population)	Total households	Median household income in the past 12 months (in 2023 inflation-adjusted dollars)	Income less than $25,000 (percent)	Income greater than $150,000 (percent)	Percent who received cash public assistance or food stamps/ SNAP
	ACS table number:	C15003	C15003	C15003	C23001	C23001	C23001	S2402	B19001	B19049	B19001	B19001	B19058
	Column number:	1	2	3	4	5	6	7	8	9	10	11	12
	TENNESSEE—Cont.												
47147	Robertson County	52,521	48.0	23.0	60,239	68.5	2.0	49.7	29,522	83,355	11.3	14.5	5.3
47149	Rutherford County	234,106	35.9	36.8	287,978	73.1	2.0	53.8	134,245	81,628	9.8	18.0	5.6
47155	Sevier County	71,840	45.5	22.3	81,714	62.9	2.1	41.4	42,727	59,665	18.0	9.8	7.2
47157	Shelby County	600,485	37.0	34.8	704,636	65.6	4.2	46.2	362,776	62,413	20.6	15.2	15.5
47163	Sullivan County	120,174	40.9	28.0	136,133	56.8	2.7	39.7	68,655	56,481	19.2	11.0	11.7
47165	Sumner County	144,753	35.3	35.8	166,157	69.8	1.4	49.0	80,536	86,081	12.2	23.3	4.3
47179	Washington County	96,050	40.2	32.6	116,162	58.6	2.3	39.8	57,629	60,729	20.8	13.0	8.5
47187	Williamson County	176,009	15.8	62.5	206,391	67.1	1.2	48.8	95,439	133,990	6.5	44.1	2.8
47189	Wilson County	114,891	33.2	37.2	131,656	66.6	1.2	48.9	60,911	96,171	8.0	26.2	3.6
48000	**TEXAS**	20,029,447	37.9	34.2	23,857,262	66.0	4.4	71.1	11,260,645	75,780	14.9	20.4	11.8
48005	Angelina County	57,803	50.4	16.0	67,453	58.5	2.0	NA	31,996	56,864	25.7	9.4	18.4
48021	Bastrop County	71,419	48.8	21.4	85,969	62.2	3.6	44.7	38,591	76,522	10.7	15.6	9.9
48027	Bell County	245,652	35.1	27.7	296,949	66.0	3.1	42.6	145,863	69,890	14.6	13.9	12.6
48029	Bexar County	1,366,294	38.3	32.8	1,635,584	66.6	3.0	45.5	758,070	69,807	15.1	16.1	13.5
48037	Bowie County	62,874	47.9	21.8	72,854	55.6	2.3	41.1	36,110	53,212	20.3	11.5	17.8
48039	Brazoria County	264,253	34.3	32.3	310,703	64.1	2.7	48.0	138,692	93,680	10.7	25.8	9.4
48041	Brazos County	130,932	32.7	43.4	200,976	63.0	3.2	36.9	92,216	53,123	24.1	15.0	11.7
48061	Cameron County	260,622	51.5	22.7	322,341	60.0	3.3	40.6	143,033	52,210	23.3	9.5	24.3
48085	Collin County	802,532	19.8	55.5	939,610	71.4	2.4	52.6	431,746	119,155	7.7	38.6	3.8
48091	Comal County	137,598	23.7	43.9	156,604	62.6	2.1	44.5	75,234	99,193	9.0	29.5	4.9
48099	Coryell County	56,339	42.0	24.8	68,843	58.9	2.1	NA	28,070	75,559	13.7	14.8	15.1
48113	Dallas County	1,706,644	39.7	36.5	2,034,431	69.2	2.9	51.0	993,312	74,350	13.5	19.4	10.3
48121	Denton County	686,189	22.5	49.7	804,561	71.7	2.7	52.7	370,503	106,695	7.3	34.6	5.2
48135	Ector County	98,624	56.5	17.2	118,551	68.8	1.3	53.9	66,937	66,608	13.3	15.3	11.9
48139	Ellis County	145,553	41.8	29.4	171,913	69.9	2.5	51.8	75,570	89,488	8.6	24.3	8.6
48141	El Paso County	553,666	44.9	25.9	672,443	62.9	2.5	42.0	301,198	58,971	22.1	11.4	20.0
48157	Fort Bend County	597,895	24.8	49.4	708,280	66.5	2.4	48.4	303,900	105,441	9.6	33.4	7.2
48167	Galveston County	246,855	31.2	35.0	286,591	64.3	3.1	47.7	142,199	83,514	14.7	24.2	10.8
48181	Grayson County	99,292	43.3	25.7	115,573	60.2	1.7	46.1	56,267	69,019	12.6	19.0	8.6
48183	Gregg County	81,812	37.7	21.0	97,947	62.5	2.7	45.4	47,550	61,569	17.2	10.5	12.9
48187	Guadalupe County	127,901	38.6	33.2	149,298	68.0	2.0	48.0	69,236	95,953	9.9	25.0	7.2
48201	Harris County	3,139,846	39.9	34.2	3,742,132	68.5	4.0	48.1	1,791,013	72,336	15.9	19.7	14.2
48203	Harrison County	47,572	44.5	22.7	56,002	62.8	2.4	NA	26,811	65,263	20.8	10.8	14.7
48209	Hays County	177,125	25.2	45.5	226,205	70.3	2.8	46.6	105,917	87,296	11.9	25.2	6.2
48213	Henderson County	61,206	45.2	21.0	70,316	56.1	2.9	39.9	33,957	59,391	18.9	14.7	12.2
48215	Hidalgo County	523,021	54.6	20.7	657,525	59.9	3.3	39.3	277,001	53,661	25.5	9.4	27.3
48221	Hood County	49,614	36.3	31.4	NA	NA	NA	NA	25,660	80,682	11.1	17.2	4.3
48231	Hunt County	74,357	44.3	24.2	88,519	63.6	3.9	42.6	40,067	71,045	13.0	15.8	12.0
48245	Jefferson County	167,998	50.0	17.2	196,429	56.6	2.9	38.9	94,005	59,725	21.8	12.1	18.9
48251	Johnson County	133,242	46.3	25.8	157,706	65.2	2.6	48.2	65,934	83,737	11.9	22.9	8.4
48257	Kaufman County	116,200	40.8	28.1	137,700	69.8	4.3	48.7	52,963	90,793	8.9	21.7	11.7
48291	Liberty County	65,781	58.6	10.9	78,451	57.9	2.3	NA	32,959	77,535	14.7	15.1	14.9
48303	Lubbock County	194,204	38.4	31.7	254,895	67.0	2.5	45.4	128,053	57,149	19.6	12.8	13.1
48309	McLennan County	166,837	37.9	27.9	212,263	62.9	2.4	44.3	96,965	63,553	21.3	15.2	13.7
48329	Midland County	111,564	38.1	34.2	130,591	70.3	1.6	52.9	70,890	93,269	12.0	23.2	8.5
48339	Montgomery County	469,208	32.7	39.3	550,208	65.1	2.8	47.8	262,273	91,841	10.4	27.0	7.6
48347	Nacogdoches County	38,569	45.6	28.8	51,969	60.6	3.3	NA	25,074	51,718	24.5	10.1	20.5
48355	Nueces County	234,866	43.6	25.6	277,889	62.9	2.7	43.8	132,759	64,034	17.4	14.6	16.6
48361	Orange County	56,536	47.9	18.2	65,833	64.2	3.8	44.3	33,271	65,521	19.7	13.0	15.9
48367	Parker County	117,908	35.2	30.6	135,278	65.9	2.1	46.7	57,996	98,174	12.2	27.9	7.1
48375	Potter County	75,154	53.4	17.6	89,566	62.2	2.4	43.1	42,674	50,743	22.1	10.2	18.3
48381	Randall County	96,949	31.0	33.6	116,645	68.5	1.6	49.4	56,279	80,940	13.2	18.7	8.6
48397	Rockwall County	84,746	26.7	45.2	101,161	67.1	3.2	46.4	43,259	112,250	4.7	32.2	4.4
48409	San Patricio County	48,825	51.2	15.9	55,207	66.1	3.1	NA	25,735	60,494	19.2	10.1	11.0
48423	Smith County	162,282	35.2	29.7	194,370	59.3	2.1	43.1	81,987	72,313	15.0	17.4	11.0
48427	Starr County	37,449	65.1	14.2	NA	NA	NA	NA	19,004	41,566	36.6	5.8	44.1
48439	Tarrant County	1,427,698	35.6	35.9	1,702,054	70.0	2.6	50.8	801,716	80,043	12.1	21.5	9.8
48441	Taylor County	90,960	40.9	29.2	115,178	63.6	1.9	42.7	54,805	61,816	18.1	10.6	10.6
48451	Tom Green County	79,474	40.4	25.3	94,218	63.8	2.1	43.2	47,638	57,268	22.3	10.6	12.5

Table B-2. Counties — What: Education, Employment, and Income, 2023—*Continued*

STATE County code	STATE County	Educational attainment: Total population 25 years and over	Educational attainment: Percent with a high school diploma or less	Educational attainment: Percent with a bachelor's degree or more	Employment status: Total population 16 years and over	Employment status: Labor force participation (percent)	Employment status: Percent unemployed	Employment status: Percent of persons age 16 years and over who worked full-time year-round in the past 12 months (percent of total population)	Household income and benefits: Total households	Household income and benefits: Median household income in the past 12 months (in 2023 inflation-adjusted dollars)	Household income and benefits: Income less than $25,000 (percent)	Household income and benefits: Income greater than $150,000 (percent)	Household income and benefits: Percent who received cash public assistance or food stamps/ SNAP
	ACS table number:	C15003	C15003	C15003	C23001	C23001	C23001	S2402	B19001	B19049	B19001	B19001	B19058
	Column number:	1	2	3	4	5	6	7	8	9	10	11	12
	TEXAS—Cont.												
48453	Travis County	952,169	20.5	58.7	1,102,124	73.7	3.0	53.8	608,921	97,543	11.1	31.4	6.4
48469	Victoria County	60,170	47.6	18.9	71,578	60.6	2.5	43.4	34,484	72,075	18.1	12.5	12.5
48471	Walker County	52,503	44.1	27.1	71,349	49.8	5.9	NA	26,539	55,134	24.8	8.7	9.0
48479	Webb County	155,484	50.1	22.9	196,486	62.3	2.8	44.2	83,045	60,204	21.8	9.1	23.5
48485	Wichita County	84,649	42.1	25.3	104,154	62.4	1.6	39.9	49,403	61,983	17.3	12.9	10.9
48491	Williamson County	477,751	23.5	48.6	551,357	71.4	2.2	51.8	264,986	110,415	8.1	33.5	4.5
48497	Wise County	53,168	45.4	23.4	61,634	63.4	3.5	44.2	26,319	91,920	9.7	25.7	11.7
49000	**UTAH**	2,085,019	29.1	38.4	2,600,950	70.2	3.3	65.3	1,167,591	93,421	9.4	24.5	5.8
49005	Cache County	74,636	25.0	43.0	105,950	70.3	1.6	39.5	46,318	83,695	8.4	16.8	4.7
49011	Davis County	227,570	26.4	39.1	277,192	70.7	1.7	48.7	118,498	111,778	7.0	29.8	5.1
49035	Salt Lake County	774,308	30.8	40.3	930,195	72.5	2.6	49.4	436,181	94,439	9.3	26.6	5.7
49045	Tooele County	48,831	36.1	22.6	NA	NA	NA	NA	24,796	94,201	10.0	21.3	6.1
49049	Utah County	375,054	20.8	46.0	521,701	72.1	2.6	42.5	214,806	100,895	8.3	26.5	5.1
49053	Washington County	133,975	30.1	33.7	159,907	59.7	2.5	34.1	72,315	77,480	12.8	16.7	5.9
49057	Weber County	174,083	32.8	29.7	210,323	71.2	1.9	49.9	97,783	87,565	9.8	21.5	6.7
50000	**VERMONT**	471,255	31.6	43.7	547,286	64.9	2.6	66.4	279,612	81,211	14.1	20.4	11.0
50007	Chittenden County	116,572	22.3	54.4	145,268	70.2	1.6	47.0	73,216	99,578	10.3	27.2	7.9
51000	**VIRGINIA**	6,037,339	32.6	42.4	7,066,427	65.3	3.6	69.8	3,402,670	89,931	13.0	27.2	10.5
51003	Albemarle County	80,889	21.0	61.8	95,932	62.7	1.6	43.5	46,900	103,413	11.5	31.5	8.1
51013	Arlington County	172,764	12.1	78.0	196,649	78.3	2.7	60.1	114,097	140,219	8.4	46.9	4.3
51015	Augusta County	58,804	50.2	24.7	65,718	60.3	1.6	41.7	32,169	71,346	17.7	13.9	8.5
51019	Bedford County	60,181	38.6	32.5	68,237	58.0	2.4	38.2	33,205	73,456	15.9	18.1	6.2
51041	Chesterfield County	259,908	27.0	44.6	303,600	68.8	3.3	50.2	143,255	99,658	7.8	26.8	7.2
51059	Fairfax County	790,040	19.2	63.8	916,511	70.6	2.2	50.8	414,946	141,553	6.1	47.2	5.2
51061	Fauquier County	51,756	32.0	41.4	59,979	67.7	1.6	49.7	26,954	110,358	6.3	37.1	3.6
51069	Frederick County	67,038	38.9	33.4	76,392	66.3	2.4	48.0	35,341	92,640	8.8	25.0	6.0
51085	Hanover County	80,342	30.8	43.8	93,347	66.0	1.0	49.6	43,496	112,243	7.8	32.5	6.2
51087	Henrico County	236,577	29.3	46.0	272,423	67.0	2.3	48.7	137,529	85,817	10.4	23.5	10.5
51095	James City County	62,781	23.3	51.8	68,999	56.4	1.5	NA	33,898	110,137	11.1	32.9	7.2
51107	Loudoun County	287,280	18.2	65.2	336,068	73.4	2.6	55.7	145,601	174,148	5.8	57.8	3.3
51121	Montgomery County	55,388	27.5	48.9	85,600	56.3	2.4	35.0	37,229	68,079	24.4	19.7	6.3
51153	Prince William County	317,779	31.1	45.5	378,680	71.9	3.0	51.3	158,620	131,047	6.4	43.2	8.4
51161	Roanoke County	71,413	35.4	35.5	80,478	59.4	2.3	42.3	40,176	80,809	11.0	21.8	8.1
51165	Rockingham County	59,430	50.8	25.6	69,315	62.6	1.5	45.5	32,827	80,935	15.6	18.1	9.3
51177	Spotsylvania County	100,786	36.2	36.8	117,792	67.7	1.6	49.5	55,487	112,595	6.7	33.4	6.6
51179	Stafford County	107,144	29.0	42.7	128,062	70.8	1.9	50.5	53,938	134,619	4.8	44.3	6.8
51199	York County	49,182	20.6	51.1	56,706	66.5	2.6	41.6	27,654	101,351	10.7	33.3	9.5
51510	Alexandria city	117,655	19.8	66.1	129,362	78.6	2.7	57.8	76,890	110,294	9.1	36.2	5.5
51550	Chesapeake city	172,684	31.2	36.6	199,843	66.1	1.9	44.2	94,056	92,633	12.8	27.9	8.6
51650	Hampton city	93,018	37.0	29.0	110,874	66.5	3.5	39.8	57,645	70,238	15.2	13.2	16.7
51680	Lynchburg city	44,115	34.3	42.3	65,737	57.4	1.5	34.8	28,916	61,693	22.7	11.8	16.2
51700	Newport News city	119,123	37.9	30.5	145,834	66.7	3.5	46.5	76,086	64,962	17.4	12.3	15.3
51710	Norfolk city	150,391	36.8	33.1	188,652	70.2	3.2	39.6	94,056	62,382	19.6	15.0	17.8
51740	Portsmouth city	65,762	42.2	28.3	77,216	67.0	3.5	44.8	40,661	57,109	23.6	11.0	23.6
51760	Richmond city	162,645	31.7	46.7	192,612	67.9	2.6	47.7	104,332	65,650	19.7	18.5	13.1
51770	Roanoke city	68,568	42.7	29.9	77,529	60.9	1.8	44.5	45,061	51,038	22.0	10.2	17.4
51800	Suffolk city	70,100	33.4	35.9	80,189	65.5	2.8	43.5	39,203	81,154	15.4	21.2	9.7
51810	Virginia Beach city	317,353	29.3	40.5	366,903	68.2	2.6	43.4	179,291	91,141	9.6	24.2	8.7
53000	**WASHINGTON**	5,511,197	29.2	40.5	6,357,108	65.1	4.4	66.6	3,101,265	94,605	12.1	28.3	13.0
53005	Benton County	141,560	35.0	33.8	165,385	62.2	3.1	40.8	78,748	82,304	12.9	21.1	15.2
53007	Chelan County	56,435	35.8	31.1	64,938	61.0	3.3	41.6	32,915	76,722	12.4	19.1	15.5
53009	Clallam County	61,520	32.6	29.6	66,686	47.6	2.4	29.7	34,807	65,990	18.7	15.1	15.5
53011	Clark County	363,723	30.7	34.4	419,406	65.7	2.7	44.0	202,217	97,678	9.2	26.5	14.2
53015	Cowlitz County	78,889	39.4	19.4	90,659	57.3	3.0	36.1	44,694	70,959	14.7	14.8	19.3
53021	Franklin County	58,536	47.6	20.9	72,377	63.9	3.8	42.6	30,733	84,366	11.1	19.8	18.2
53025	Grant County	63,517	47.7	19.1	78,233	63.3	4.4	40.0	34,911	75,586	16.8	16.6	16.2

Table B-2. Counties — What: Education, Employment, and Income, 2023—*Continued*

STATE County code	STATE County	Educational attainment			Employment status				Household income and benefits				
		Total population 25 years and over	Percent with a high school diploma or less	Percent with a bachelor's degree or more	Total population 16 years and over	Labor force participation (percent)	Percent unemployed	Percent of persons age 16 years and over who worked full-time year-round in the past 12 months (percent of total population)	Total households	Median household income in the past 12 months (in 2023 inflation-adjusted dollars)	Income less than $25,000 (percent)	Income greater than $150,000 (percent)	Percent who received cash public assistance or food stamps/ SNAP
	ACS table number:	C15003	C15003	C15003	C23001	C23001	C23001	S2402	B19001	B19049	B19001	B19001	B19058
	Column number:	1	2	3	4	5	6	7	8	9	10	11	12
	WASHINGTON—Cont.												
53027	Grays Harbor County	56,077	44.2	17.1	63,152	51.3	3.2	NA	30,498	67,221	19.0	12.0	19.0
53029	Island County	64,690	26.5	36.8	73,171	54.4	1.7	NA	35,431	90,308	11.8	20.8	10.2
53033	King County	1,653,274	19.6	58.3	1,886,532	71.0	3.0	49.3	949,792	120,824	10.3	40.5	9.4
53035	Kitsap County	200,493	25.7	38.9	229,642	63.6	3.1	36.7	109,652	99,609	10.1	28.3	10.8
53041	Lewis County	62,213	40.5	20.5	69,631	54.0	3.6	NA	33,672	67,169	17.4	12.3	16.7
53045	Mason County	50,651	38.4	23.3	56,681	48.4	4.4	NA	25,161	74,508	16.9	16.6	19.5
53053	Pierce County	637,780	34.8	32.0	742,598	66.4	2.9	43.4	356,066	98,174	10.4	27.2	13.5
53057	Skagit County	95,334	31.2	30.3	107,746	59.5	2.6	39.7	53,087	91,234	12.4	23.8	13.9
53061	Snohomish County	599,577	28.8	39.6	682,299	67.2	2.4	47.1	321,835	106,269	9.7	32.8	11.2
53063	Spokane County	384,222	31.0	32.4	447,576	62.4	2.5	40.3	219,230	73,583	15.6	17.6	17.8
53067	Thurston County	216,268	27.7	41.0	244,086	62.2	2.5	40.9	119,786	93,170	11.7	21.6	13.6
53073	Whatcom County	160,027	26.0	40.0	194,452	63.3	2.6	38.8	93,449	74,884	15.4	20.5	12.5
53077	Yakima County	159,107	55.1	18.3	191,722	62.9	2.9	43.0	89,414	69,525	17.3	13.2	24.2
54000	**WEST VIRGINIA**	1,259,219	50.7	24.0	1,464,056	54.4	4.5	69.7	743,644	55,948	22.0	10.7	18.9
54003	Berkeley County	91,954	48.1	23.7	105,737	66.3	3.6	47.4	51,094	79,625	14.1	14.8	14.2
54011	Cabell County	61,087	37.3	37.1	76,076	58.3	2.6	36.9	39,720	56,415	22.4	10.8	16.4
54033	Harrison County	46,671	49.4	26.3	53,075	55.2	1.6	40.7	27,161	58,646	21.8	12.5	20.3
54039	Kanawha County	126,601	44.4	30.0	145,315	55.5	3.1	37.9	76,963	56,469	22.4	9.9	17.3
54061	Monongalia County	66,000	32.0	47.8	92,379	64.3	2.9	41.6	44,307	61,009	22.6	16.1	11.1
54081	Raleigh County	51,501	54.8	22.2	NA	NA	NA	NA	28,275	55,189	23.8	8.4	21.8
54107	Wood County	59,726	45.5	24.3	67,871	57.4	3.0	38.6	36,936	54,750	21.1	10.6	20.1
55000	**WISCONSIN**	4,116,216	35.8	33.8	4,822,901	65.2	2.8	69.8	2,495,539	74,631	14.3	17.2	12.0
55009	Brown County	183,656	35.1	32.6	217,072	68.6	1.4	48.0	112,027	77,146	13.4	16.6	11.8
55017	Chippewa County	48,385	38.8	24.9	54,873	64.2	1.8	47.1	27,846	77,617	11.8	14.6	12.0
55025	Dane County	384,543	22.0	53.9	477,135	70.6	1.6	48.1	257,528	82,838	12.2	23.2	8.9
55027	Dodge County	64,434	48.1	19.6	73,793	63.4	2.0	45.7	35,795	72,736	11.1	14.2	10.8
55035	Eau Claire County	69,700	31.8	34.7	89,021	66.5	1.9	46.4	44,769	72,563	12.1	13.2	11.3
55039	Fond du Lac County	72,551	41.5	23.9	85,658	64.3	1.6	46.9	44,262	71,285	13.5	14.6	9.4
55055	Jefferson County	60,377	38.4	31.5	70,631	67.3	2.4	48.4	34,914	82,864	13.3	18.3	10.1
55059	Kenosha County	115,871	35.8	32.4	136,826	67.7	2.1	47.4	69,907	74,886	15.5	18.9	12.5
55063	La Crosse County	78,646	27.5	39.1	100,734	69.1	2.5	42.2	51,283	70,010	13.6	15.1	10.7
55071	Manitowoc County	59,899	47.2	19.8	67,548	61.9	1.1	45.3	35,669	68,297	13.4	13.9	12.5
55073	Marathon County	97,756	39.4	27.9	111,623	65.3	1.4	47.9	58,104	74,141	12.5	14.5	11.0
55079	Milwaukee County	614,512	37.0	35.9	726,608	65.9	2.6	45.3	388,165	63,185	19.5	14.9	20.4
55087	Outagamie County	133,767	35.7	31.4	154,531	68.4	1.2	49.4	78,027	85,784	10.5	19.1	8.5
55089	Ozaukee County	65,471	20.6	52.4	76,989	66.6	2.2	45.8	38,030	96,961	11.2	28.1	6.9
55097	Portage County	46,737	36.5	34.7	59,175	66.3	1.8	45.1	30,620	69,391	13.3	15.1	9.9
55101	Racine County	136,329	40.2	26.9	158,004	64.2	2.3	45.4	79,066	73,978	14.0	15.4	16.1
55105	Rock County	115,060	40.9	26.6	132,906	66.3	3.4	44.7	66,220	73,440	14.1	14.1	16.3
55109	St. Croix County	66,932	29.0	40.7	77,268	68.9	0.9	49.9	38,606	102,475	7.1	29.0	6.5
55111	Sauk County	46,784	38.9	27.5	53,179	68.0	1.4	48.5	28,295	80,070	12.2	16.5	9.1
55117	Sheboygan County	84,017	39.6	26.8	96,040	65.1	0.9	47.9	49,852	72,902	10.6	14.9	8.3
55127	Walworth County	72,291	34.8	34.1	88,732	63.9	2.5	42.9	43,005	75,229	13.9	19.9	7.9
55131	Washington County	99,962	31.5	35.9	112,601	68.6	0.8	50.4	56,641	93,287	11.1	23.7	6.0
55133	Waukesha County	296,292	23.4	48.9	338,244	66.2	1.3	47.9	168,150	98,630	10.9	29.2	5.2
55139	Winnebago County	117,801	35.3	35.3	141,036	66.3	1.5	46.5	71,563	69,957	13.9	16.0	11.2
55141	Wood County	52,662	43.2	23.6	60,230	60.4	2.2	42.1	32,099	66,461	14.6	10.6	14.4
56000	**WYOMING**	403,853	33.6	30.4	469,355	63.5	3.2	66.9	247,368	72,415	14.9	15.2	5.8
56021	Laramie County	69,819	29.8	33.4	80,908	65.4	3.3	43.3	44,460	75,112	11.1	16.1	6.1
56025	Natrona County	55,239	35.2	29.2	63,496	65.0	2.1	42.2	34,332	73,203	14.5	15.3	6.8
72000	**PUERTO RICO**	2,407,254	45.2	30.8	2,777,060	47.1	9.1	63.3	1,277,486	25,621	49.1	3.1	47.0
72013	Arecibo Municipio	64,883	43.4	32.5	73,805	43.6	5.3	NA	33,466	25,496	49.1	0.6	51.6
72021	Bayamón Municipio	137,753	36.4	34.9	157,057	48.7	3.1	32.3	76,203	30,660	43.6	3.1	39.0
72025	Caguas Municipio	94,481	41.9	35.4	108,183	50.7	4.3	32.9	51,579	30,589	42.7	4.8	42.3
72031	Carolina Municipio	115,011	37.4	36.1	131,602	52.2	4.2	39.2	63,447	35,391	36.0	3.8	30.4
72061	Guaynabo Municipio	70,029	31.3	51.8	78,908	52.1	2.4	38.6	34,184	48,084	30.6	16.4	25.0

Table B-2. Counties — What: Education, Employment, and Income, 2023—*Continued*

STATE County code	STATE County	Educational attainment			Employment status				Household income and benefits				
		Total population 25 years and over	Percent with a high school diploma or less	Percent with a bachelor's degree or more	Total population 16 years and over	Labor force participation (percent)	Percent unemployed	Percent of persons age 16 years and over who worked full-time year-round in the past 12 months (percent of total population)	Total households	Median household income in the past 12 months (in 2023 inflation-adjusted dollars)	Income less than $25,000 (percent)	Income greater than $150,000 (percent)	Percent who received cash public assistance or food stamps/ SNAP
	ACS table number:	C15003	C15003	C15003	C23001	C23001	C23001	S2402	B19001	B19049	B19001	B19001	B19058
	Column number:	1	2	3	4	5	6	7	8	9	10	11	12
	PUERTO RICO—Cont.												
72097	Mayagüez Municipio	48,230	53.1	26.9	60,646	42.5	8.4	NA	31,111	16,836	65.1	1.9	49.4
72113	Ponce Municipio	96,698	44.2	31.4	111,911	43.0	7.3	24.0	56,772	18,889	58.5	1.4	54.2
72127	San Juan Municipio	253,950	32.1	42.6	290,600	50.7	4.6	33.1	150,969	27,403	47.2	6.1	35.0
72135	Toa Alta Municipio	49,326	39.7	31.5	NA	NA	NA	NA	24,486	31,635	41.9	2.6	39.6
72137	Toa Baja Municipio	54,219	43.4	29.6	62,293	55.2	2.8	39.7	30,304	31,814	39.4	1.5	38.4
72139	Trujillo Alto Municipio	49,793	24.6	43.3	NA	NA	NA	NA	27,299	49,261	27.3	10.2	29.2

NA = Not available.

Table B-3. Metropolitan Areas — What: Education, Employment, and Income, 2023

Metropolitan area / division code	Metropolitan area / division	Educational attainment: Total population 25 years and over	Educational attainment: Percent with a high school diploma or less	Educational attainment: Percent with a bachelor's degree or more	Employment status: Total population 16 years and over	Employment status: Labor force participation (percent)	Employment status: Percent unemployed	Employment status: Percent of persons age 16 years and over who worked full-time year-round in the past 12 months (percent of total population)	Household income and benefits: Total households	Household income and benefits: Median household income in the past 12 months (in 2023 inflation-adjusted dollars)	Household income and benefits: Income less than $25,000 (percent)	Household income and benefits: Income greater than $150,000 (percent)	Household income and benefits: Percent who received cash public assistance or food stamps/ SNAP
	ACS table number:	C15003	C15003	C15003	C23001	C23001	C23001	S2402	B19001	B19049	B19001	B19001	B19058
	Column number:	1	2	3	4	5	6	7	8	9	10	11	12
10180	Abilene, TX	115,546	43.9	27.0	143,966	60.4	2.0	40.9	66,460	61,262	18.7	10.8	11.5
10380	Aguadilla, PR	188,006	52.4	26.9	216,898	44.8	4.9	25.5	89,374	21,290	54.7	2.0	53.3
10420	Akron, OH	491,116	35.4	36.6	577,627	65.0	2.7	43.8	298,193	70,125	16.1	17.3	13.3
10500	Albany, GA	98,247	47.2	20.9	115,705	57.2	4.5	38.9	59,228	53,056	25.4	8.6	30.7
10540	Albany, OR	93,289	35.4	23.4	106,171	60.1	2.3	41.8	51,636	70,548	16.1	14.6	22.6
10580	Albany-Schenectady-Troy, NY	635,772	30.7	41.3	754,092	63.3	2.5	43.4	386,690	82,410	12.7	22.0	10.6
10740	Albuquerque, NM	654,871	33.3	35.7	760,848	61.4	2.8	41.1	381,326	67,640	17.4	16.4	19.1
10780	Alexandria, LA	100,418	49.3	21.1	117,081	55.2	2.5	40.0	58,235	52,390	24.5	9.3	19.7
10900	Allentown-Bethlehem-Easton, PA-NJ	615,806	41.0	33.3	717,976	63.7	3.0	44.2	345,257	81,159	12.8	20.9	13.4
11020	Altoona, PA	86,686	54.4	22.3	99,594	58.2	2.0	40.9	50,651	54,002	22.9	9.0	21.9
11100	Amarillo, TX	178,518	40.6	26.5	214,066	65.7	1.9	46.9	102,739	63,994	17.0	15.3	12.5
11180	Ames, IA	72,987	22.9	48.3	106,176	65.5	2.0	40.4	49,962	72,007	13.4	16.9	3.6
11200	Amherst Town-Northampton, MA	100,358	26.5	50.2	145,445	61.5	2.5	34.1	61,802	79,969	17.2	23.3	12.3
11260	Anchorage, AK	269,934	33.4	36.2	315,986	67.7	2.4	42.8	148,995	94,150	10.2	28.2	10.5
11460	Ann Arbor, MI	236,534	17.0	60.2	306,889	63.6	2.1	40.4	149,379	83,754	14.8	25.5	9.4
11500	Anniston-Oxford, AL	78,420	42.3	23.7	95,233	55.5	2.9	36.7	46,310	50,780	22.5	7.5	18.1
11540	Appleton, WI	171,791	36.1	31.6	198,037	67.8	1.2	49.4	99,606	83,966	9.8	18.6	8.0
11640	Arecibo, PR	134,921	46.2	29.7	156,715	42.7	4.7	24.8	65,668	27,118	46.8	0.7	53.5
11700	Asheville, NC	312,000	29.4	44.7	353,926	57.5	1.8	39.0	164,757	67,837	14.9	17.2	11.8
12020	Athens-Clarke County, GA	136,500	30.8	46.7	182,588	62.9	2.1	41.8	87,635	67,364	21.3	15.2	7.8
12060	Atlanta-Sandy Springs-Roswell, GA	4,261,178	31.6	42.6	5,031,031	68.0	2.9	48.8	2,341,283	86,505	12.8	24.8	10.3
1206012054	Atlanta-Sandy Springs-Roswell, GA Metro Division	3,306,870	32.0	42.3	3,912,465	67.6	3.0	48.3	1,823,623	83,631	13.5	24.0	11.2
1206031924	Marietta, GA Metro Division	954,308	30.1	43.6	1,118,566	69.4	2.3	50.6	517,660	97,719	10.2	27.3	6.9
12100	Atlantic City-Hammonton, NJ	266,570	38.7	35.5	305,124	63.3	3.7	39.3	158,674	80,073	13.6	22.3	12.4
12220	Auburn-Opelika, AL	124,809	31.8	39.7	166,451	59.8	3.3	39.1	81,935	57,580	25.8	13.6	12.8
12260	Augusta-Richmond County, GA-SC	428,472	40.1	29.9	506,129	60.4	3.1	40.5	236,371	67,152	19.3	15.2	13.9
12420	Austin-Round Rock-San Marcos, TX	1,712,279	23.7	52.1	2,004,890	71.9	2.8	51.9	1,036,074	98,508	10.4	30.4	6.0
12540	Bakersfield-Delano, CA	564,499	50.7	18.0	687,933	60.6	5.1	38.5	289,845	68,893	17.8	16.6	22.8
12580	Baltimore-Columbia-Towson, MD	1,974,988	31.3	44.4	2,282,776	67.0	2.5	48.7	1,127,320	94,289	12.9	28.7	11.3
12620	Bangor, ME	112,335	38.3	30.6	132,205	58.3	1.4	39.1	66,556	66,333	17.5	13.3	17.8
12700	Barnstable Town, MA	185,612	26.4	49.8	204,803	57.9	1.9	36.2	109,475	89,893	13.0	27.4	11.1
12940	Baton Rouge, LA	573,192	43.3	29.0	693,804	61.5	2.8	43.3	334,402	64,550	20.1	17.2	15.1
12980	Battle Creek, MI	91,769	44.9	22.1	108,028	60.6	3.9	40.2	54,568	57,514	19.2	9.4	15.2
13020	Bay City, MI	75,140	40.2	23.1	84,838	57.4	2.6	40.3	44,417	58,675	20.6	8.5	18.0
13140	Beaumont-Port Arthur, TX	264,000	49.2	18.5	307,548	58.8	3.2	41.0	150,294	62,896	19.6	13.8	17.0
13220	Beckley, WV	78,712	55.1	20.2	91,251	48.9	1.6	33.1	44,847	52,437	21.6	7.2	19.8
13380	Bellingham, WA	160,027	26.0	40.0	194,452	63.3	2.6	38.8	93,449	74,884	15.4	20.5	12.5
13460	Bend, OR	192,886	26.7	42.1	216,223	63.3	2.4	40.9	107,729	91,658	12.1	24.2	12.6
13740	Billings, MT	134,160	38.0	30.9	153,158	66.0	2.1	44.8	81,750	70,849	12.9	16.3	8.3
13780	Binghamton, NY	165,738	40.0	30.0	204,080	56.5	2.9	36.2	99,826	64,035	18.6	13.8	15.7
13820	Birmingham, AL	813,624	36.4	33.4	949,416	60.9	2.1	45.3	471,767	69,284	17.6	17.4	13.1
13900	Bismarck, ND	93,390	27.2	38.5	107,850	68.5	1.3	49.3	57,951	83,440	14.9	19.2	5.6
13980	Blacksburg-Christiansburg-Radford, VA	113,530	36.7	35.4	155,235	56.5	2.3	35.8	71,419	61,309	21.7	15.3	12.5
14010	Bloomington, IL	105,999	26.4	49.6	139,667	65.7	1.7	43.9	71,060	77,200	17.5	22.1	12.7
14020	Bloomington, IN	99,102	28.7	47.7	138,167	60.8	2.7	37.2	70,681	58,666	20.2	13.1	5.7
14260	Boise City, ID	561,972	31.2	37.4	662,492	65.2	2.1	44.4	314,846	82,526	10.2	20.5	6.3
14460	Boston-Cambridge-Newton, MA-NH	3,499,153	28.3	52.2	4,094,431	69.1	2.6	46.9	1,949,953	110,697	12.7	36.8	13.8
1446014454	Boston, MA Metro Division	1,441,605	28.3	51.8	1,697,297	69.4	2.9	46.2	822,929	107,974	14.2	36.2	16.7
1446015764	Cambridge-Newton-Framingham, MA Metro Division	1,725,772	27.9	54.3	2,013,221	69.2	2.5	47.6	946,508	114,644	11.7	38.3	12.7
1446040484	Rockingham County-Strafford County, NH Metro Division	331,776	30.9	42.9	383,913	67.0	2.1	46.6	180,516	102,464	10.7	32.5	6.5
14500	Boulder, CO	220,529	15.7	65.4	279,688	67.0	3.1	41.9	137,425	95,363	14.4	32.7	5.8
14540	Bowling Green, KY	123,740	40.9	27.6	153,499	65.4	2.8	46.1	77,804	60,620	18.0	9.5	10.9
14580	Bozeman, MT	84,207	21.1	51.0	106,871	72.4	1.7	45.6	54,621	91,158	11.8	23.7	2.8
14740	Bremerton-Silverdale-Port Orchard, WA	200,493	25.7	38.9	229,642	63.6	3.1	36.7	$109,652	$99,609	10.1	28.3	10.8
14860	Bridgeport-Stamford-Danbury, CT	661,951	29.5	51.9	773,623	68.2	3.5	44.9	356,931	111,058	12.1	38.3	11.1
15180	Brownsville-Harlingen, TX	260,622	51.5	22.7	322,341	60.0	3.3	40.6	143,033	52,210	23.3	9.5	24.3
15260	Brunswick-St. Simons, GA	83,379	39.4	29.9	95,105	53.0	1.6	38.6	48,281	69,235	20.3	16.9	15.9

Table B-3. Metropolitan Areas — What: Education, Employment, and Income, 2023—*Continued*

Metropolitan area / division code	Metropolitan area / division	Educational attainment			Employment status				Household income and benefits				
		Total population 25 years and over	Percent with a high school diploma or less	Percent with a bachelor's degree or more	Total population 16 years and over	Labor force participation (percent)	Percent unemployed	Percent of persons age 16 years and over who worked full-time year-round in the past 12 months (percent of total population)	Total households	Median household income in the past 12 months (in 2023 inflation-adjusted dollars)	Income less than $25,000 (percent)	Income greater than $150,000 (percent)	Percent who received cash public assistance or food stamps/ SNAP
	ACS table number:	C15003	C15003	C15003	C23001	C23001	C23001	S2402	B19001	B19049	B19001	B19001	B19058
	Column number:	1	2	3	4	5	6	7	8	9	10	11	12
15380	Buffalo-Cheektowaga, NY	825,150	35.9	35.7	952,355	62.3	2.2	42.4	502,324	69,861	17.8	16.5	16.8
15500	Burlington, NC	120,632	39.6	29.3	143,807	65.5	3.0	45.8	70,911	65,633	17.3	10.5	15.1
15540	Burlington-South Burlington, VT	158,737	27.1	48.5	192,474	69.4	1.3	47.6	96,541	95,497	10.7	24.7	8.3
15940	Canton-Massillon, OH	281,653	43.3	25.7	325,255	61.2	2.0	42.3	168,115	63,774	17.1	10.9	13.1
15980	Cape Coral-Fort Myers, FL	632,549	38.3	31.9	710,288	52.9	2.0	36.6	326,338	71,547	14.2	18.1	8.3
16020	Cape Girardeau, MO-IL	63,570	43.9	30.4	79,633	64.7	1.143	44.0	39,485	66,427	20.9	13.0	9.2
16180	Carson City, NV	43,375	39.0	21.9	NA	NA	NA	NA	24,562	73,077	13.0	13.0	13.4
16220	Casper, WY	55,239	35.2	29.2	63,496	65.0	2.1	42.2	34,332	73,203	14.5	15.3	6.8
16300	Cedar Rapids, IA	190,800	33.5	33.3	222,109	65.9	1.9	47.1	114,563	73,569	12.5	17.5	9.6
16540	Chambersburg, PA	112,505	50.2	25.5	128,120	62.1	3.0	43.7	62,966	75,875	14.4	16.0	11.2
16580	Champaign-Urbana, IL	141,962	28.5	45.3	196,180	60.1	2.0	40.5	102,205	62,092	22.4	13.8	9.7
16620	Charleston, WV	147,402	46.5	27.7	168,751	53.9	2.8	37.2	89,395	55,415	23.2	9.8	19.7
16700	Charleston-North Charleston, SC	594,304	29.0	42.2	691,052	66.7	2.2	46.6	347,045	85,165	12.6	20.6	7.7
16740	Charlotte-Concord-Gastonia, NC-SC	1,923,968	31.1	41.3	2,243,091	68.1	2.4	49.8	1,103,360	81,262	12.7	22.5	10.3
16820	Charlottesville, VA	157,294	24.3	55.5	187,406	61.3	1.4	42.5	92,687	92,265	15.4	26.6	9.2
16860	Chattanooga, TN-GA	410,996	36.5	32.0	473,186	62.5	2.7	43.0	235,003	68,677	16.3	16.2	10.9
16940	Cheyenne, WY	69,819	29.8	33.4	80,908	65.4	3.3	43.3	44,460	75,112	11.1	16.1	6.1
16980	Chicago-Naperville-Elgin, IL-IN	6,439,543	33.4	42.1	7,510,444	67.3	3.3	46.4	3,671,659	87,071	13.6	25.6	13.8
1698016984	Chicago-Naperville-Schaumburg, IL Metro Division	4,965,716	32.6	43.6	5,764,318	67.4	3.4	46.6	2,856,546	86,599	14.1	25.6	15.0
1698020994	Elgin, IL Metro Division	498,721	34.2	37.8	599,238	69.7	2.7	48.1	271,057	95,301	9.4	26.5	9.9
1698029404	Lake County, IL Metro Division	475,104	29.3	47.8	569,460	68.6	3.0	47.0	260,243	108,364	10.4	34.4	8.7
1698029414	Lake County-Porter County-Jasper County, IN Metro Division	500,002	44.3	25.7	577,428	62.5	2.7	43.0	283,813	71,466	15.4	16.7	10.4
17020	Chico, CA	134,129	32.1	29.9	170,637	59.8	4.1	32.6	86,279	63,222	21.5	15.5	23.7
17140	Cincinnati, OH-KY-IN	1,544,869	35.2	38.4	1,814,807	66.1	2.3	46.5	921,306	77,844	14.4	20.1	10.5
17300	Clarksville, TN-KY	211,730	37.1	30.3	256,255	63.6	3.1	38.5	129,593	67,082	16.0	11.2	9.8
17420	Cleveland, OH	1,542,195	36.7	34.7	1,769,233	64.0	3.1	43.1	931,312	67,586	17.1	17.4	13.7
17460	Cleveland, TN	91,327	45.5	23.0	105,164	60.5	3.6	42.2	50,001	61,033	20.3	10.5	9.1
17660	Coeur d'Alene, ID	131,650	33.2	32.1	148,541	60.1	2.4	39.9	74,253	73,456	13.4	18.1	7.9
17780	College Station-Bryan, TX	156,676	35.5	39.7	229,067	62.8	3.0	38.1	107,713	54,680	23.2	14.6	12.1
17820	Colorado Springs, CO	519,590	23.1	44.2	615,316	69.5	2.7	43.2	311,530	89,792	10.5	24.1	9.5
17860	Columbia, MO	134,102	26.8	49.0	177,148	66.1	1.9	44.6	87,256	69,375	17.0	15.2	7.0
17900	Columbia, SC	573,218	34.3	35.8	692,181	64.1	3.3	42.6	346,000	67,189	16.5	15.8	11.2
17980	Columbus, GA-AL	219,385	39.5	26.6	259,337	59.5	2.8	37.4	131,169	54,661	23.9	11.1	16.2
18020	Columbus, IN	56,725	36.6	35.6	66,694	67.2	2.3	NA	33,777	81,832	17.0	20.5	8.5
18140	Columbus, OH	1,481,139	34.1	40.3	1,733,868	67.8	2.4	48.1	879,910	77,390	13.7	21.1	10.5
18580	Corpus Christi, TX	303,374	44.4	24.5	354,018	62.3	2.7	43.1	170,701	62,499	18.4	14.0	15.8
18700	Corvallis, OR	61,110	14.7	56.4	84,543	61.8	3.4	33.0	38,306	73,047	17.7	24.1	14.1
18880	Crestview-Fort Walton Beach-Destin, FL	213,031	31.7	35.5	247,230	62.1	1.9	37.4	121,976	81,996	11.1	21.1	8.0
19100	Dallas-Fort Worth-Arlington, TX	5,348,237	33.5	40.0	6,334,567	69.8	2.7	50.9	2,959,385	86,860	11.0	25.3	8.4
1910019124	Dallas-Plano-Irving, TX Metro Division	3,616,221	31.9	42.6	4,277,895	70.0	2.8	51.3	2,007,420	89,752	10.6	26.8	7.9
1910023104	Fort Worth-Arlington-Grapevine, TX Metro Division	1,732,016	36.7	34.4	2,056,672	69.2	2.6	50.1	951,965	81,361	12.0	22.1	9.6
19140	Dalton, GA	96,430	55.3	19.8	115,219	63.5	1.9	47.5	52,722	65,143	17.2	13.5	14.5
19300	Daphne-Fairhope-Foley, AL	184,852	36.3	32.0	206,994	57.4	1.1	42.8	105,698	72,915	12.2	17.3	6.2
19340	Davenport-Moline-Rock Island, IA-IL	263,097	35.9	30.6	304,561	63.9	2.0	44.7	164,230	71,262	15.9	15.8	12.3
19380	Dayton-Kettering-Beavercreek, OH	560,963	35.0	33.8	656,499	63.7	2.8	41.6	350,659	67,070	17.7	16.0	12.0
19460	Decatur, AL	109,855	46.6	22.7	126,654	61.0	1.8	42.8	64,526	72,956	17.3	14.6	10.3
19500	Decatur, IL	69,473	44.0	23.5	80,710	59.0	3.5	38.8	43,598	58,297	19.2	13.7	24.1
19660	Deltona-Daytona Beach-Ormond Beach, FL	541,781	36.4	30.0	615,943	54.0	2.1	37.4	300,081	67,176	15.4	13.4	11.6
19740	Denver-Aurora-Centennial, CO	2,142,068	24.8	49.9	2,458,738	72.2	2.6	51.7	1,244,895	103,055	10.1	32.3	8.4
19780	Des Moines-West Des Moines, IA	495,000	31.7	39.8	580,360	71.1	2.2	51.5	299,784	82,728	11.1	21.7	9.0
19820	Detroit-Warren-Dearborn, MI	3,064,162	34.4	34.5	3,522,282	63.1	3.1	43.0	1,770,361	72,574	17.0	19.4	15.9
1982019804	Detroit-Dearborn-Livonia, MI Metro Division	1,195,048	41.3	27.1	1,388,089	59.8	4.2	39.0	696,332	57,281	23.8	13.1	23.9
1982047664	Warren-Troy-Farmington Hills, MI Metro Division	1,869,114	30.0	39.3	2,134,193	65.2	2.4	45.6	1,074,029	83,445	12.5	23.4	10.8

Table B-3. Metropolitan Areas — What: Education, Employment, and Income, 2023—*Continued*

Metropolitan area / division code	Metropolitan area / division	Educational attainment: Total population 25 years and over	Educational attainment: Percent with a high school diploma or less	Educational attainment: Percent with a bachelor's degree or more	Employment status: Total population 16 years and over	Employment status: Labor force participation (percent)	Employment status: Percent unemployed	Employment status: Percent of persons age 16 years and over who worked full-time year-round in the past 12 months (percent of total population)	Household income and benefits: Total households	Household income and benefits: Median household income in the past 12 months (in 2023 inflation-adjusted dollars)	Household income and benefits: Income less than $25,000 (percent)	Household income and benefits: Income greater than $150,000 (percent)	Household income and benefits: Percent who received cash public assistance or food stamps/ SNAP
	ACS table number:	C15003	C15003	C15003	C23001	C23001	C23001	S2402	B19001	B19049	B19001	B19001	B19058
	Column number:	1	2	3	4	5	6	7	8	9	10	11	12
20020	Dothan, AL	107,048	48.5	20.7	123,248	58.2	2.5	40.8	62,401	57,405	22.3	7.8	18.8
20100	Dover, DE	128,492	42.1	27.2	152,652	64.4	2.1	43.6	74,183	72,910	15.0	14.9	15.8
20220	Dubuque, IA	68,189	37.8	34.0	79,142	67.2	1.5	47.0	$42,889	$71,940	13.5	13.5	10.2
20260	Duluth, MN-WI	197,619	31.6	31.9	235,668	63.0	1.8	40.3	120,943	70,208	15.0	14.8	10.1
20500	Durham-Chapel Hill, NC	421,100	24.0	54.7	510,383	65.8	2.1	45.3	253,951	83,280	14.0	25.1	7.2
20580	Eagle Pass, TX	34,297	60.9	12.1	41,982	55.2	4.3	NA	18,890	46,657	29.0	6.1	33.2
20740	Eau Claire, WI	118,085	34.7	30.7	143,894	65.6	1.9	46.7	72,615	75,183	12.0	13.7	11.6
20940	El Centro, CA	110,055	54.7	16.6	134,491	53.4	5.0	33.5	50,024	60,243	22.9	14.1	29.5
21060	Elizabethtown, KY	87,285	42.3	22.5	101,472	64.3	2.5	46.0	51,413	64,904	19.7	12.8	13.6
21140	Elkhart-Goshen, IN	131,519	54.2	20.5	157,825	65.4	1.8	44.6	73,439	67,188	14.6	11.6	5.3
21300	Elmira, NY	58,185	43.3	27.5	66,186	60.0	3.3	38.2	35,591	59,617	23.1	11.9	15.7
21340	El Paso, TX	555,267	44.9	25.9	674,381	62.9	2.5	41.9	301,927	59,037	22.1	11.4	20.0
21420	Enid, OK	39,431	46.7	22.5	47,964	65.0	2.8	NA	23,645	63,161	18.0	14.7	18.0
21500	Erie, PA	185,141	44.7	29.3	220,063	58.4	2.2	39.5	111,118	60,663	20.1	12.3	21.2
21660	Eugene-Springfield, OR	268,607	29.2	33.2	322,130	60.1	3.4	36.8	162,001	70,374	18.1	15.1	20.4
21780	Evansville, IN	188,154	41.3	29.0	218,418	62.8	2.2	44.4	$113,389	$65,073	16.7	14.8	10.1
21820	Fairbanks-College, AK	61,164	32.7	32.1	73,843	70.5	2.1	NA	37,510	86,391	11.0	21.1	8.6
22020	Fargo, ND-MN	164,587	22.2	42.9	208,653	74.1	2.7	50.1	111,493	72,889	14.3	17.9	7.7
22140	Farmington, NM	80,773	44.5	20.4	94,401	56.4	3.4	38.6	42,670	57,324	20.3	11.1	21.4
22180	Fayetteville, NC	246,661	34.5	28.0	303,153	65.7	3.5	35.2	150,658	61,220	17.6	11.7	19.3
22220	Fayetteville-Springdale-Rogers, AR	378,298	38.5	36.6	463,601	67.2	2.4	48.8	224,357	77,695	13.1	20.2	4.7
22380	Flagstaff, AZ	88,138	29.4	39.8	120,612	62.8	3.4	37.7	56,954	71,738	16.9	19.7	10.7
22420	Flint, MI	280,373	42.4	22.8	323,633	59.8	4.1	37.7	164,086	60,027	20.1	11.2	20.0
22500	Florence, SC	135,924	49.3	22.5	159,812	57.6	3.8	39.4	78,453	49,974	24.4	9.0	17.5
22520	Florence-Muscle Shoals, AL	106,984	41.5	29.4	128,925	56.7	2.7	39.4	67,774	61,606	19.3	9.8	11.9
22540	Fond du Lac, WI	72,551	41.5	23.9	85,658	64.3	1.6	46.9	44,262	71,285	13.5	14.6	9.4
22660	Fort Collins-Loveland, CO	252,129	19.1	52.9	314,119	66.5	3.0	43.0	156,498	88,182	12.1	25.0	10.6
22900	Fort Smith, AR-OK	157,395	46.9	21.4	184,421	58.1	2.2	41.9	90,483	58,609	19.9	9.4	8.7
23060	Fort Wayne, IN	300,552	37.0	31.3	355,569	66.8	2.6	45.5	186,586	66,317	15.6	13.3	8.4
23420	Fresno, CA	741,754	45.9	23.5	896,660	60.6	4.5	37.7	375,676	71,140	17.4	17.6	24.8
23460	Gadsden, AL	72,785	46.7	18.0	83,519	52.8	3.5	38.1	40,027	52,192	24.4	10.5	19.7
23540	Gainesville, FL	221,219	28.0	43.3	292,461	59.5	2.4	37.8	146,910	59,290	19.4	15.8	10.6
23580	Gainesville, GA	146,015	46.2	30.0	172,144	62.5	1.6	43.7	76,413	77,891	13.3	22.0	9.0
23900	Gettysburg, PA	75,880	48.6	23.9	88,724	64.1	2.0	42.9	41,810	76,725	10.6	18.0	11.9
24020	Glens Falls, NY	95,628	40.4	30.8	106,218	59.7	2.3	41.8	55,835	73,247	14.0	15.3	12.7
24140	Goldsboro, NC	79,276	46.9	22.4	93,719	60.3	4.6	36.4	47,035	55,461	19.3	9.6	21.6
24220	Grand Forks, ND-MN	64,072	27.3	32.0	84,006	71.2	2.1	42.2	44,443	71,529	15.7	16.4	10.2
24260	Grand Island, NE	50,233	47.2	20.9	59,048	69.3	3.7	53.0	30,614	70,919	14.8	14.2	6.6
24300	Grand Junction, CO	113,815	33.9	32.2	131,775	59.2	2.6	37.7	68,115	64,722	16.9	12.9	15.6
24340	Grand Rapids-Wyoming-Kentwood, MI	781,206	32.8	37.7	929,534	67.4	2.1	45.0	445,882	77,979	12.0	18.0	10.7
24420	Grants Pass, OR	65,953	40.0	20.8	73,091	48.1	3.0	NA	37,241	64,170	18.6	12.5	24.8
24500	Great Falls, MT	58,681	36.2	30.2	68,656	62.4	1.3	39.5	36,414	66,454	13.3	16.0	11.0
24540	Greeley, CO	236,202	35.6	33.7	279,428	70.1	2.8	49.0	129,057	91,047	9.8	24.1	11.1
24580	Green Bay, WI	228,064	37.1	30.1	266,970	66.9	1.4	47.1	137,111	76,171	13.5	15.9	11.4
24660	Greensboro-High Point, NC	533,493	37.3	32.1	638,578	63.0	2.6	44.0	321,824	63,280	17.8	13.8	16.3
24780	Greenville, NC	108,419	33.1	34.9	142,449	63.4	4.9	39.8	74,443	59,946	21.5	12.2	14.2
24860	Greenville-Anderson-Greer, SC	669,304	36.0	35.1	785,223	63.9	2.2	44.6	396,589	69,413	15.9	16.3	9.3
25020	Guayama, PR	47,905	50.6	22.1	NA	NA	NA	NA	27,480	21,345	55.6	0.7	52.9
25060	Gulfport-Biloxi, MS	294,585	38.4	26.7	339,808	60.9	3.3	40.9	174,612	60,114	20.2	13.4	12.1
25180	Hagerstown-Martinsburg, MD-WV	213,094	47.7	22.6	245,387	62.6	2.7	44.9	117,709	75,369	15.0	15.9	14.3
25220	Hammond, LA	90,573	48.3	22.8	108,154	60.3	3.5	41.4	54,627	54,417	23.7	12.5	19.5
25260	Hanford-Corcoran, CA	96,746	52.7	10.4	117,359	54.7	4.9	30.1	44,262	66,429	16.7	11.7	22.6
25420	Harrisburg-Carlisle, PA	421,552	39.8	37.1	491,189	65.3	2.3	45.0	248,403	76,758	13.4	18.6	12.4
25500	Harrisonburg, VA	83,839	46.0	30.8	113,418	61.4	1.9	40.2	50,113	76,250	17.4	16.3	9.5
25540	Hartford-West Hartford-East Hartford, CT	814,158	33.4	42.5	953,633	66.3	2.8	44.7	467,381	92,176	13.2	27.5	12.3
25620	Hattiesburg, MS	101,429	33.8	33.7	125,755	60.7	1.7	41.7	61,290	55,336	23.2	10.0	10.6

Table B-3. Metropolitan Areas — What: Education, Employment, and Income, 2023—*Continued*

Metropolitan area / division code	Metropolitan area / division	Educational attainment			Employment status				Household income and benefits				
		Total population 25 years and over	Percent with a high school diploma or less	Percent with a bachelor's degree or more	Total population 16 years and over	Labor force participation (percent)	Percent unemployed	Percent of persons age 16 years and over who worked full-time year-round in the past 12 months (percent of total population)	Total households	Median household income in the past 12 months (in 2023 inflation-adjusted dollars)	Income less than $25,000 (percent)	Income greater than $150,000 (percent)	Percent who received cash public assistance or food stamps/ SNAP
	ACS table number:	C15003	C15003	C15003	C23001	C23001	C23001	S2402	B19001	B19049	B19001	B19001	B19058
	Column number:	1	2	3	4	5	6	7	8	9	10	11	12
25740	Helena, MT	68,277	31.7	37.8	77,313	61.1	1.1	39.4	38,384	76,866	13.0	18.1	5.3
25860	Hickory-Lenoir-Morganton, NC	267,664	45.1	21.1	307,944	60.2	1.6	43.5	155,168	58,164	16.6	11.3	13.5
25940	Hilton Head Island-Bluffton-Port Royal, SC	170,601	29.2	47.0	198,748	55.9	1.2	33.6	100,794	80,683	12.1	21.2	6.3
25980	Hinesville, GA	51,173	44.4	18.3	66,470	66.2	5.5	NA	31,349	60,732	17.2	5.9	16.9
26140	Homosassa Springs, FL	133,412	47.4	21.8	144,572	40.8	2.5	26.2	75,745	53,777	23.3	10.1	10.7
26300	Hot Springs, AR	73,545	40.5	29.9	82,619	53.0	2.3	36.9	45,243	52,275	24.9	10.1	7.0
26380	Houma-Bayou Cane-Thibodaux, LA	133,985	55.7	20.7	158,230	56.9	1.5	39.8	80,596	60,119	20.4	11.2	18.9
26420	Houston-Pasadena-The Woodlands, TX	4,901,672	37.0	36.0	5,816,909	67.2	3.5	47.9	2,731,843	79,463	14.3	22.4	12.3
26580	Huntington-Ashland, WV-KY-OH	258,301	47.3	23.9	300,670	55.5	2.2	38.7	156,188	57,815	23.6	10.5	17.3
26620	Huntsville, AL	364,205	27.5	44.6	427,143	64.4	1.8	46.6	212,486	84,929	12.4	22.4	7.5
26820	Idaho Falls, ID	103,499	32.5	32.1	123,939	64.7	1.3	43.6	56,728	75,824	11.0	17.3	12.0
26900	Indianapolis-Carmel-Greenwood, IN	1,439,570	34.1	39.7	1,683,738	68.7	2.3	48.9	862,092	77,947	13.3	20.6	8.7
26980	Iowa City, IA	110,362	22.2	50.7	147,443	68.8	1.6	42.9	73,376	71,905	17.9	17.6	5.6
27060	Ithaca, NY	60,770	20.7	60.6	91,530	59.7	2.8	35.0	43,054	67,247	18.8	20.1	8.5
27100	Jackson, MI	113,820	41.0	24.2	129,329	56.2	2.6	37.9	61,851	63,338	17.1	11.7	15.7
27140	Jackson, MS	410,075	36.0	31.7	488,098	60.8	3.1	43.6	240,218	58,592	21.5	12.6	11.7
27180	Jackson, TN	124,874	48.9	20.7	144,908	60.0	3.7	43.0	73,444	59,532	20.8	9.3	15.3
27260	Jacksonville, FL	1,201,032	32.2	37.4	1,383,125	63.4	2.4	44.3	693,081	77,044	14.5	19.7	11.3
27340	Jacksonville, NC	118,073	37.0	23.6	165,735	70.1	2.2	33.0	76,788	67,597	14.6	12.0	15.6
27500	Janesville-Beloit, WI	115,060	40.9	26.6	132,906	66.3	3.4	44.7	66,220	73,440	14.1	14.1	16.3
27620	Jefferson City, MO	103,531	39.8	32.3	121,727	60.8	1.9	45.7	59,911	68,629	16.8	13.4	8.2
27740	Johnson City, TN	152,400	43.8	27.9	179,226	55.6	2.1	38.2	91,198	56,846	21.9	10.6	9.7
27780	Johnstown, PA	94,077	49.4	24.0	108,883	56.3	2.1	39.4	57,282	55,748	20.8	11.0	20.3
27860	Jonesboro, AR	89,544	43.2	25.7	106,695	62.4	3.2	43.3	56,301	58,550	17.3	8.5	9.5
27900	Joplin, MO-KS	137,042	43.7	24.4	161,241	63.0	2.8	42.0	83,470	57,887	19.3	10.0	16.9
27980	Kahului-Wailuku, HI	119,334	36.2	31.2	134,569	62.9	1.9	42.0	56,848	83,691	11.8	25.5	11.9
28020	Kalamazoo-Portage, MI	166,805	25.1	42.6	213,008	66.5	2.0	44.1	107,893	67,191	14.5	17.2	11.4
28100	Kankakee, IL	71,260	45.4	20.9	85,327	61.6	2.1	41.7	41,130	66,788	13.9	16.2	19.0
28140	Kansas City, MO-KS	1,519,857	30.3	40.8	1,766,300	68.1	2.0	49.2	906,504	79,842	12.3	20.9	7.1
28420	Kennewick-Richland, WA	200,096	38.7	30.0	237,762	62.7	3.3	41.4	109,481	83,053	12.4	20.7	16.1
28450	Kenosha, WI	115,871	35.8	32.4	136,826	67.7	2.1	47.4	69,907	74,886	15.5	18.9	12.5
28660	Killeen-Temple, TX	318,541	36.8	27.0	384,463	64.3	2.9	40.5	182,336	71,013	14.4	14.1	12.8
28700	Kingsport-Bristol, TN-VA	230,985	45.4	25.2	261,705	54.1	2.4	38.0	132,975	53,794	22.3	11.1	14.8
28740	Kingston, NY	135,460	36.0	39.1	156,207	59.1	2.8	37.8	73,895	85,878	12.9	21.9	10.4
28880	Kiryas Joel-Poughkeepsie-Newburgh, NY	475,576	36.0	36.2	566,856	63.8	2.9	42.9	254,385	95,839	10.4	28.6	12.2
28940	Knoxville, TN	662,548	38.8	33.6	776,827	61.4	1.9	42.5	380,978	69,872	17.5	16.5	9.0
29020	Kokomo, IN	57,508	46.6	23.9	66,503	60.1	3.0	40.7	35,551	61,267	15.3	12.9	13.2
29100	La Crosse-Onalaska, WI-MN	113,653	31.6	35.4	140,482	66.3	2.1	42.2	72,276	71,312	14.1	15.6	9.8
29180	Lafayette, LA	278,725	48.2	25.9	323,431	62.9	2.4	44.6	166,896	57,311	22.7	12.2	16.2
29200	Lafayette-West Lafayette, IN	131,826	36.9	37.4	185,326	65.4	1.9	43.1	91,594	61,349	20.1	14.3	7.0
29340	Lake Charles, LA	161,001	45.9	25.3	188,749	60.3	2.4	42.7	93,049	65,122	21.0	16.3	18.2
29420	Lake Havasu City-Kingman, AZ	175,513	47.3	15.6	192,575	42.3	2.4	28.3	98,791	55,954	23.7	9.0	12.7
29460	Lakeland-Winter Haven, FL	567,736	42.5	26.5	658,879	59.3	2.2	42.1	306,915	66,909	14.6	13.1	14.6
29540	Lancaster, PA	380,837	47.2	31.6	445,133	66.0	2.1	43.5	211,669	80,067	11.1	18.8	12.0
29620	Lansing-East Lansing, MI	307,342	28.6	37.9	391,275	64.4	3.0	40.9	194,031	70,007	17.2	16.5	10.6
29700	Laredo, TX	155,484	50.1	22.9	196,486	62.3	2.8	44.2	83,045	60,204	21.8	9.1	23.5
29740	Las Cruces, NM	142,574	41.2	31.8	181,728	59.3	3.3	36.5	87,688	56,451	23.7	11.6	25.1
29820	Las Vegas-Henderson-North Las Vegas, NV	1,637,673	40.2	28.7	1,887,864	64.3	3.1	44.2	880,604	75,065	14.5	18.6	15.2
29940	Lawrence, KS	73,419	21.9	53.2	101,812	67.3	3.5	40.4	51,013	66,997	18.7	14.3	6.4
30020	Lawton, OK	82,776	41.6	25.7	99,874	60.1	3.7	32.2	48,105	56,680	19.3	8.9	19.0
30140	Lebanon, PA	101,861	53.3	25.3	116,139	65.0	1.5	46.4	58,012	78,824	11.7	16.5	13.7
30300	Lewiston, ID-WA	45,592	36.1	23.3	53,679	57.2	3.0	NA	26,723	71,005	16.2	12.9	12.0
30340	Lewiston-Auburn, ME	79,199	47.1	23.4	93,583	63.1	2.6	39.1	48,239	63,404	18.4	12.1	21.4
30460	Lexington-Fayette, KY	347,616	30.3	44.5	421,433	66.6	2.5	45.4	222,167	70,027	16.3	18.3	9.1

Table B-3. Metropolitan Areas — What: Education, Employment, and Income, 2023—*Continued*

Metropolitan area / division code	Metropolitan area / division	Educational attainment: Total population 25 years and over	Educational attainment: Percent with a high school diploma or less	Educational attainment: Percent with a bachelor's degree or more	Employment status: Total population 16 years and over	Employment status: Labor force participation (percent)	Employment status: Percent unemployed	Employment status: Percent of persons age 16 years and over who worked full-time year-round in the past 12 months (percent of total population)	Household income and benefits: Total households	Household income and benefits: Median household income in the past 12 months (in 2023 inflation-adjusted dollars)	Household income and benefits: Income less than $25,000 (percent)	Household income and benefits: Income greater than $150,000 (percent)	Household income and benefits: Percent who received cash public assistance or food stamps/ SNAP
	ACS table number:	C15003	C15003	C15003	C23001	C23001	C23001	S2402	B19001	B19049	B19001	B19001	B19058
	Column number:	1	2	3	4	5	6	7	8	9	10	11	12
30500	Lexington Park, MD	143,162	34.2	36.3	166,421	70.0	1.9	51.0	76,869	116,297	6.6	35.7	9.5
30620	Lima, OH	68,452	48.5	19.9	79,960	63.2	3.3	43.4	42,147	66,891	17.4	8.9	12.5
30700	Lincoln, NE	215,916	25.5	42.0	276,283	68.7	1.9	45.5	144,767	71,163	15.0	17.0	8.2
30780	Little Rock-North Little Rock-Conway, AR	516,798	37.4	33.2	608,808	61.9	2.1	46.0	310,926	66,225	16.4	15.4	6.6
30860	Logan, UT-ID	84,485	26.4	41.6	117,304	69.8	1.7	39.9	51,478	85,111	7.9	18.0	4.4
30980	Longview, TX	196,463	42.5	20.2	231,982	60.6	2.5	43.4	108,309	63,956	18.5	11.5	13.5
31020	Longview-Kelso, WA	78,889	39.4	19.4	90,659	57.3	3.0	36.1	44,694	70,959	14.7	14.8	19.3
31080	Los Angeles-Long Beach-Anaheim, CA	9,066,628	36.7	38.5	10,524,502	65.4	3.6	43.4	4,542,998	91,960	13.9	29.1	15.4
3108011244	Anaheim-Santa Ana-Irvine, CA Metro Division	2,209,117	30.1	44.5	2,571,553	65.9	2.7	44.6	1,092,528	110,042	10.7	35.7	10.1
3108031084	Los Angeles-Long Beach-Glendale, CA Metro Division	6,857,511	38.9	36.5	7,952,949	65.2	3.8	43.0	3,450,470	86,587	14.9	27.0	17.1
31140	Louisville/Jefferson County, KY-IN	952,578	38.1	32.3	1,099,066	63.8	2.6	45.1	563,933	68,921	17.0	16.2	10.3
31180	Lubbock, TX	219,860	39.8	30.1	285,704	66.1	2.6	44.8	143,229	57,093	19.5	13.4	13.0
31340	Lynchburg, VA	179,982	39.6	31.5	219,032	59.5	1.7	39.1	104,544	67,050	17.6	14.4	11.9
31420	Macon-Bibb County, GA	158,679	44.8	25.0	186,308	57.5	3.6	38.9	89,842	59,750	22.5	13.0	20.7
31540	Madison, WI	470,708	25.0	49.2	575,053	69.5	1.6	47.9	308,244	82,132	12.6	22.1	9.1
31700	Manchester-Nashua, NH	309,642	31.7	42.8	354,965	71.0	1.5	51.2	170,761	103,727	8.9	31.5	7.1
31740	Manhattan, KS	72,112	27.0	38.9	106,495	71.3	3.3	35.3	51,764	63,033	16.0	9.6	7.0
31860	Mankato, MN	63,571	30.6	34.3	85,393	66.5	1.9	40.3	40,152	69,016	17.1	15.2	8.3
31900	Mansfield, OH	89,346	52.9	18.9	101,917	56.2	3.6	37.7	51,046	56,664	18.2	7.7	18.5
32420	Mayagüez, PR	151,074	49.1	27.9	179,340	42.7	6.7	24.5	83,931	20,939	56.6	1.5	48.3
32580	McAllen-Edinburg-Mission, TX	523,021	54.6	20.7	657,525	59.9	3.3	39.3	277,001	53,661	25.5	9.4	27.3
32780	Medford, OR	159,533	36.5	29.8	181,887	57.3	2.5	35.4	92,225	71,666	15.3	14.4	19.3
32820	Memphis, TN-MS-AR	890,397	39.0	31.5	1,041,680	64.6	3.7	46.1	523,295	64,025	19.8	15.3	13.9
32900	Merced, CA	175,907	59.6	14.5	220,588	60.3	5.5	38.6	88,053	57,570	22.4	13.1	21.3
33100	Miami-Fort Lauderdale-West Palm Beach, FL	4,483,684	37.5	37.6	5,109,595	64.2	2.6	46.1	2,349,920	76,271	15.6	21.5	15.6
3310022744	Fort Lauderdale-Pompano Beach-Sunrise, FL Metro Division	1,413,273	36.1	36.6	1,605,669	66.6	2.8	47.2	758,853	74,531	16.0	20.2	12.3
3310033124	Miami-Miami Beach-Kendall, FL Metro Division	1,935,393	41.4	35.9	2,219,875	65.0	2.5	48.1	985,935	72,311	16.9	20.1	21.8
3310048424	West Palm Beach-Boca Raton-Delray Beach, FL Metro Division	1,135,018	32.6	41.7	1,284,051	59.9	2.6	41.2	605,132	84,921	13.1	25.6	9.6
33140	Michigan City-La Porte, IN	80,471	50.6	23.4	91,245	55.5	1.9	38.7	45,725	62,868	15.7	11.1	12.9
33220	Midland, MI	60,551	33.8	33.7	69,045	59.9	2.5	39.6	35,761	73,074	16.7	17.9	14.1
33260	Midland, TX	114,931	38.4	33.7	134,665	69.9	1.5	52.7	73,012	92,934	11.8	23.0	8.5
33340	Milwaukee-Waukesha, WI	1,076,237	31.7	40.5	1,254,442	66.3	2.1	46.5	650,986	77,006	16.1	20.1	14.4
33460	Minneapolis-St. Paul-Bloomington, MN-WI	2,551,194	25.4	46.2	2,963,757	70.8	2.1	48.9	1,501,453	95,102	10.3	27.4	8.0
33500	Minot, ND	49,977	31.2	29.5	58,285	69.8	1.0	43.5	31,532	72,073	8.5	16.9	6.8
33540	Missoula, MT	87,914	23.2	46.8	106,595	68.4	1.7	44.8	$56,810	$73,324	16.9	16.9	9.4
33660	Mobile, AL	281,188	43.6	27.1	327,693	59.0	1.8	43.0	$163,963	$55,352	21.9	11.4	17.5
33700	Modesto, CA	353,213	48.5	21.0	423,711	63.0	4.2	40.1	179,152	82,758	12.4	19.2	16.9
33740	Monroe, LA	149,545	44.2	26.9	176,438	57.2	4.2	38.6	87,927	50,286	28.2	10.4	23.3
33780	Monroe, MI	110,907	40.5	24.9	127,769	59.5	1.1	40.5	62,936	71,506	15.6	17.3	9.9
33860	Montgomery, AL	261,528	40.8	30.8	306,509	58.4	2.3	40.6	153,926	62,362	20.2	11.6	17.1
34060	Morgantown, WV	91,645	40.7	38.9	120,889	60.7	2.6	39.4	57,621	59,045	21.8	14.8	12.7
34100	Morristown, TN	89,499	49.7	21.3	101,812	59.2	2.1	41.4	49,910	58,401	18.8	10.5	11.2
34580	Mount Vernon-Anacortes, WA	95,334	31.2	30.3	107,746	59.5	2.6	39.7	53,087	91,234	12.4	23.8	13.9
34620	Muncie, IN	70,595	44.0	27.2	94,346	61.3	2.3	35.4	44,361	55,206	20.5	9.0	16.2
34740	Muskegon-Norton Shores, MI	123,629	39.7	21.7	142,541	59.5	2.9	38.8	70,042	61,189	18.5	9.3	22.2
34820	Myrtle Beach-Conway-North Myrtle Beach, SC	301,342	37.9	29.1	338,261	53.3	1.9	34.6	168,080	68,988	16.3	12.7	7.9
34900	Napa, CA	96,806	29.6	39.5	112,327	64.9	2.4	43.2	51,167	104,686	10.4	36.5	9.2
34940	Naples-Marco Island, FL	314,086	34.0	40.1	347,227	50.8	1.0	35.9	166,192	90,072	11.1	26.6	7.0
34980	Nashville-Davidson--Murfreesboro--Franklin, TN	1,435,725	32.8	42.4	1,683,685	69.6	1.8	50.5	863,464	84,685	11.5	22.5	6.3

Table B-3. Metropolitan Areas — What: Education, Employment, and Income, 2023—*Continued*

Metropolitan area / division code	Metropolitan area / division	Educational attainment: Total population 25 years and over	Educational attainment: Percent with a high school diploma or less	Educational attainment: Percent with a bachelor's degree or more	Employment status: Total population 16 years and over	Employment status: Labor force participation (percent)	Employment status: Percent unemployed	Employment status: Percent of persons age 16 years and over who worked full-time year-round in the past 12 months (percent of total population)	Household income and benefits: Total households	Household income and benefits: Median household income in the past 12 months (in 2023 inflation-adjusted dollars)	Household income and benefits: Income less than $25,000 (percent)	Household income and benefits: Income greater than $150,000 (percent)	Household income and benefits: Percent who received cash public assistance or food stamps/ SNAP
	ACS table number:	C15003	C15003	C15003	C23001	C23001	C23001	S2402	B19001	B19049	B19001	B19001	B19058
	Column number:	1	2	3	4	5	6	7	8	9	10	11	12
35300	New Haven, CT	399,012	36.0	42.4	472,284	65.7	2.7	42.8	233,004	80,733	15.4	24.0	13.5
35380	New Orleans-Metairie, LA	679,297	37.9	34.5	778,895	61.7	3.1	42.6	399,198	61,000	22.6	16.0	15.5
35620	New York-Newark-Jersey City, NY-NJ	13,820,282	34.8	44.6	15,898,993	65.3	3.4	44.6	7,490,498	95,220	15.3	31.7	15.8
3562029484	Lakewood-New Brunswick, NJ Metro Division	1,752,093	33.0	46.0	2,025,040	65.2	2.9	44.5	941,969	106,566	10.4	35.0	7.3
3562035004	Nassau County-Suffolk County, NY Metro Division	2,047,970	30.7	44.4	2,373,238	64.1	2.4	45.0	966,971	132,080	8.2	43.5	8.1
3562035084	Newark, NJ Metro Division	1,540,618	34.2	45.1	1,783,394	68.7	3.6	48.2	831,608	103,182	11.8	34.5	10.5
3562035614	New York-Jersey City-White Plains, NY-NJ Metro Division	8,479,601	36.3	44.3	9,717,321	65.0	3.7	43.9	4,749,950	83,787	18.3	28.2	19.9
35660	Niles, MI	108,008	35.3	31.6	124,435	59.1	2.6	38.9	65,129	62,460	17.5	15.6	13.3
35840	North Port-Bradenton-Sarasota, FL	715,465	32.2	39.7	786,488	52.2	2.0	34.8	$408,101	$78,914	12.6	20.8	6.2
35980	Norwich-New London-Willimantic, CT	198,000	34.8	37.9	233,071	64.4	3.0	38.9	$114,156	$82,652	15.2	23.3	15.9
36100	Ocala, FL	308,262	45.3	22.5	342,111	50.7	2.6	34.4	$171,369	$58,606	16.7	9.1	13.4
36220	Odessa, TX	98,624	56.5	17.2	118,551	68.8	1.3	53.9	66,937	66,608	13.3	15.3	11.9
36260	Ogden, UT	409,337	29.0	35.3	496,458	70.9	1.8	49.3	220,388	100,461	8.2	26.3	5.8
36420	Oklahoma City, OK	970,651	35.4	34.8	1,166,025	64.7	2.9	44.9	581,140	69,895	16.2	16.2	13.9
36500	Olympia-Lacey-Tumwater, WA	216,268	27.7	41.0	244,086	62.2	2.5	40.9	119,786	93,170	11.7	21.6	13.6
36540	Omaha, NE-IA	654,241	29.4	40.1	768,316	70.5	1.8	50.7	397,769	81,376	12.5	21.4	8.7
36740	Orlando-Kissimmee-Sanford, FL	1,971,426	33.2	38.1	2,294,899	65.5	2.8	46.1	1,073,662	77,378	13.7	19.1	13.4
36780	Oshkosh-Neenah, WI	117,801	35.3	35.3	141,036	66.3	1.5	46.5	71,563	69,957	13.9	16.0	11.2
36980	Owensboro, KY	76,568	45.0	25.0	90,420	64.7	2.7	43.9	45,814	61,761	19.5	10.2	13.2
37100	Oxnard-Thousand Oaks-Ventura, CA	579,642	34.5	37.9	675,002	64.5	3.4	42.4	283,718	107,667	9.4	34.4	10.0
37140	Paducah, KY-IL	72,307	42.6	22.0	81,720	60.2	0.8	41.6	43,021	61,699	20.0	12.3	14.4
37340	Palm Bay-Melbourne-Titusville, FL	483,552	33.7	33.0	542,027	57.3	2.9	39.7	258,656	78,575	13.6	19.7	8.5
37460	Panama City-Panama City Beach, FL	154,783	39.6	29.0	176,759	62.7	1.8	41.1	89,699	69,690	14.6	15.4	10.7
37620	Parkersburg-Vienna, WV	63,347	45.6	23.9	71,967	57.2	3.0	38.5	38,866	54,906	21.5	10.6	20.0
37860	Pensacola-Ferry Pass-Brent, FL	368,166	34.8	32.2	432,684	61.4	2.6	38.5	204,344	78,315	12.9	17.6	10.9
37900	Peoria, IL	248,585	34.5	33.2	288,518	62.9	3.2	40.9	153,577	68,504	18.5	17.2	14.1
37980	Philadelphia-Camden-Wilmington, PA-NJ-DE-MD	4,374,205	34.5	42.3	5,085,287	65.7	2.9	45.7	2,484,152	86,867	14.6	26.1	14.8
3798015804	Camden, NJ Metro Division	916,916	35.3	38.2	1,057,673	66.9	2.9	45.1	494,538	94,120	11.6	27.5	10.1
3798033874	Montgomery County-Bucks County-Chester County, PA Metro Division	1,466,421	27.8	51.2	1,691,498	66.9	2.2	47.4	793,082	110,476	9.5	35.7	8.4
3798037964	Philadelphia, PA Metro Division	1,466,137	40.1	37.6	1,727,240	64.3	3.9	44.2	903,757	65,014	21.4	17.2	24.0
3798048864	Wilmington, DE-MD-NJ Metro Division	524,731	36.6	37.3	608,876	64.3	2.1	46.2	292,775	87,213	12.3	25.6	11.9
38060	Phoenix-Mesa-Chandler, AZ	3,489,392	32.8	35.5	4,092,124	64.2	2.4	45.8	1,922,068	85,700	11.8	23.1	9.4
38420	Pinehurst-Southern Pines, NC	77,870	26.5	44.1	86,222	54.4	1.8	33.6	46,385	78,057	16.7	18.9	8.7
38300	Pittsburgh, PA	1,773,102	35.7	38.8	2,025,814	62.8	2.3	43.9	1,067,180	72,532	16.2	18.9	14.6
38340	Pittsfield, MA	96,090	36.5	38.0	110,207	60.7	3.0	38.4	58,807	77,498	19.2	19.1	18.5
38540	Pocatello, ID	58,521	32.4	34.5	70,596	61.5	1.5	38.7	33,729	68,495	14.8	11.7	14.2
38660	Ponce, PR	196,795	46.2	30.3	228,463	46.1	6.9	26.1	105,603	20,978	55.6	1.2	54.2
38860	Portland-South Portland, ME	424,615	26.3	48.0	479,392	67.1	1.6	45.4	244,997	92,117	10.7	23.7	8.2
38900	Portland-Vancouver-Hillsboro, OR-WA	1,812,226	26.3	43.8	2,070,357	67.2	2.5	45.7	1,028,651	94,925	11.5	27.2	14.7
38940	Port St. Lucie, FL	403,382	38.0	30.0	451,348	54.7	2.7	38.5	214,904	68,316	15.2	15.9	10.8
39140	Prescott Valley-Prescott, AZ	194,914	29.3	32.0	217,297	47.7	2.0	28.7	$113,784	$67,245	16.3	16.9	8.5
39300	Providence-Warwick, RI-MA	1,200,046	39.0	36.4	1,394,874	64.9	3.0	43.6	$677,970	$83,330	15.7	23.3	16.9
39340	Provo-Orem-Lehi, UT	383,142	21.1	45.4	531,622	72.0	2.6	42.6	$219,263	$100,791	8.4	26.3	5.1
39380	Pueblo, CO	118,828	39.7	24.2	138,328	57.1	2.0	40.4	$68,732	$65,161	17.3	14.6	21.0
39460	Punta Gorda, FL	171,699	37.8	27.7	184,349	43.5	1.6	28.6	90,367	71,806	14.3	13.9	6.2
39540	Racine-Mount Pleasant, WI	136,329	40.2	26.9	158,004	64.2	2.3	45.4	79,066	73,978	14.0	15.4	16.1
39580	Raleigh-Cary, NC	1,034,000	23.2	52.7	1,203,600	69.5	2.4	50.7	600,306	96,096	9.8	29.3	6.9
39660	Rapid City, SD	109,077	30.0	34.3	126,989	64.4	1.4	43.0	65,028	77,164	13.9	16.6	7.2
39740	Reading, PA	297,165	49.5	26.9	351,051	63.9	3.2	44.4	163,307	75,675	15.2	17.9	14.9
39820	Redding, CA	128,758	37.0	22.9	146,301	55.5	2.5	37.4	72,320	75,949	16.5	19.0	15.6
39900	Reno, NV	403,751	33.4	33.6	464,158	64.4	2.4	43.8	227,132	83,759	11.8	22.0	9.6
40060	Richmond, VA	944,268	31.5	41.9	1,100,725	66.5	2.5	47.1	536,542	84,332	12.1	23.0	10.5
40140	Riverside-San Bernardino-Ontario, CA	3,093,138	44.5	25.2	3,684,901	62.7	3.5	41.6	1,474,564	87,843	12.7	24.2	16.7

Table B-3. Metropolitan Areas — What: Education, Employment, and Income, 2023—*Continued*

Metropolitan area / division code	Metropolitan area / division	Educational attainment			Employment status				Household income and benefits				
		Total population 25 years and over	Percent with a high school diploma or less	Percent with a bachelor's degree or more	Total population 16 years and over	Labor force participation (percent)	Percent unemployed	Percent of persons age 16 years and over who worked full-time year-round in the past 12 months (percent of total population)	Total households	Median household income in the past 12 months (in 2023 inflation-adjusted dollars)	Income less than $25,000 (percent)	Income greater than $150,000 (percent)	Percent who received cash public assistance or food stamps/ SNAP
	ACS table number:	C15003	C15003	C15003	C23001	C23001	C23001	S2402	B19001	B19049	B19001	B19001	B19058
	Column number:	1	2	3	4	5	6	7	8	9	10	11	12
40220	Roanoke, VA	226,486	39.9	30.8	258,988	58.9	1.9	42.1	134,105	65,537	16.4	15.2	11.9
40340	Rochester, MN	158,543	28.4	42.8	181,361	68.7	1.9	47.1	92,141	85,213	11.3	23.1	6.8
40380	Rochester, NY	746,240	33.2	38.5	870,818	62.1	2.4	41.7	446,704	73,294	15.4	17.2	15.5
40420	Rockford, IL	227,333	42.9	24.2	265,384	63.3	3.6	41.1	135,255	66,960	16.6	13.7	22.3
40580	Rocky Mount, NC	101,604	50.1	19.7	116,380	59.7	2.7	45.5	59,997	61,388	20.8	11.4	22.7
40660	Rome, GA	67,591	39.3	30.0	79,701	60.2	2.1	42.1	37,835	62,098	20.7	13.0	19.9
40900	Sacramento-Roseville-Folsom, CA	1,671,227	30.1	38.1	1,956,067	63.2	3.7	40.7	888,619	94,992	12.6	27.9	13.7
40980	Saginaw, MI	131,616	42.4	22.2	152,882	58.8	3.7	37.8	77,158	59,265	19.7	11.2	20.1
41060	St. Cloud, MN	127,435	35.6	29.5	160,831	68.1	2.5	44.4	77,652	73,963	14.2	16.2	9.5
41100	St. George, UT	133,975	30.1	33.7	159,907	59.7	2.5	34.1	72,315	77,480	12.8	16.7	5.9
41140	St. Joseph, MO-KS	81,744	49.4	21.3	95,160	60.0	1.6	42.2	47,529	62,682	17.8	10.9	12.5
41180	St. Louis, MO-IL	1,966,576	31.1	39.1	2,271,997	66.2	2.4	46.2	1,179,884	78,224	13.9	20.3	10.0
41420	Salem, OR	295,130	39.1	28.3	349,056	62.6	3.2	39.9	162,200	74,554	15.5	18.7	20.6
41500	Salinas, CA	278,259	49.0	28.9	334,728	59.9	2.1	36.6	$132,170	$88,035	13.6	25.6	11.1
41540	Salisbury, MD	86,108	47.1	25.6	105,563	59.9	2.2	40.7	$48,542	$70,528	17.9	12.4	19.2
41620	Salt Lake City-Murray, UT	823,139	31.1	39.3	989,228	72.5	2.5	49.8	$460,977	$94,409	9.4	26.3	5.7
41660	San Angelo, TX	80,352	40.6	25.3	95,188	63.5	2.0	43.1	$48,119	$56,569	22.3	10.6	12.6
41700	San Antonio-New Braunfels, TX	1,797,820	37.4	33.1	2,128,355	65.3	2.8	45.1	986,961	73,195	14.5	17.9	12.1
41740	San Diego-Chula Vista-Carlsbad, CA	2,277,584	28.4	43.5	2,674,564	66.9	3.0	42.8	1,181,259	103,674	10.2	33.1	11.9
41780	Sandusky, OH	86,973	41.5	29.0	95,663	59.8	1.8	40.6	53,716	65,177	15.1	16.1	9.8
41860	San Francisco-Oakland-Fremont, CA	3,360,434	25.4	53.1	3,813,526	66.6	3.3	45.6	1,763,465	127,792	10.8	43.4	11.0
4186036084	Oakland-Fremont-Berkeley, CA Metro Division	1,990,894	27.2	49.6	2,282,557	66.4	3.6	44.9	1,024,706	121,327	10.3	40.9	11.8
4186041884	San Francisco-San Mateo-Redwood City, CA Metro Division	1,181,961	23.5	57.9	1,318,583	67.9	3.0	48.1	637,151	138,562	11.8	46.9	10.4
4186042034	San Rafael, CA Metro Division	187,579	18.9	59.9	212,386	61.1	2.9	36.9	101,608	139,644	10.0	46.6	7.3
41940	San Jose-Sunnyvale-Santa Clara, CA	1,378,042	24.6	55.8	1,607,289	68.1	2.9	47.8	685,743	153,202	8.1	51.0	8.8
41980	San Juan-Bayamón-Caguas, PR	1,538,195	42.3	33.1	1,768,274	49.1	3.7	32.6	827,522	27,981	45.9	4.2	43.3
42020	San Luis Obispo-Paso Robles, CA	190,654	24.9	42.1	239,129	58.9	2.6	35.0	110,283	90,670	13.0	26.3	9.9
42100	Santa Cruz-Watsonville, CA	176,094	26.8	44.4	220,775	62.6	3.6	35.8	99,069	105,631	12.3	32.6	11.8
42140	Santa Fe, NM	120,801	30.3	45.9	135,708	57.0	2.6	38.5	71,322	78,731	13.9	22.1	11.7
42200	Santa Maria-Santa Barbara, CA	276,896	35.3	36.1	354,923	61.9	3.7	36.9	150,932	91,197	14.3	27.4	12.4
42220	Santa Rosa-Petaluma, CA	354,748	32.8	37.4	403,547	65.1	2.6	40.7	192,765	100,707	10.7	31.3	10.9
42340	Savannah, GA	289,253	32.5	37.2	340,351	64.7	2.6	45.9	165,394	75,196	15.3	17.5	11.5
42540	Scranton--Wilkes-Barre, PA	404,019	46.1	26.3	467,491	58.7	2.4	41.3	236,141	58,834	22.2	12.3	20.7
42660	Seattle-Tacoma-Bellevue, WA	2,890,631	24.9	48.6	3,311,429	69.2	2.9	47.5	1,627,693	110,744	10.2	36.1	10.6
4266021794	Everett, WA Metro Division	599,577	28.8	39.6	682,299	67.2	2.4	47.1	321,835	106,269	9.7	32.8	11.2
4266042644	Seattle-Bellevue-Kent, WA Metro Division	1,653,274	19.6	58.3	1,886,532	71.0	3.0	49.3	949,792	120,824	10.3	40.5	9.4
4266045104	Tacoma-Lakewood, WA Metro Division	637,780	34.8	32.0	742,598	66.4	2.9	43.4	356,066	98,174	10.4	27.2	13.5
42680	Sebastian-Vero Beach-West Vero Corridor, FL	134,235	38.8	33.2	148,025	47.4	1.0	31.9	72,833	72,920	16.2	16.7	8.6
42700	Sebring, FL	83,072	45.6	22.7	92,345	43.0	2.7	27.5	47,278	51,165	23.4	8.5	17.4
43100	Sheboygan, WI	84,017	39.6	26.8	96,040	65.1	0.9	47.9	49,852	72,902	10.6	14.9	8.3
43300	Sherman-Denison, TX	99,292	43.3	25.7	115,573	60.2	1.7	46.1	56,267	69,019	12.6	19.0	8.6
43340	Shreveport-Bossier City, LA	261,805	41.3	26.0	302,481	59.1	3.0	41.3	164,006	54,904	22.7	11.1	18.7
43420	Sierra Vista-Douglas, AZ	89,455	35.0	25.6	103,202	46.3	2.7	NA	50,919	52,025	25.7	10.5	16.2
43580	Sioux City, IA-NE-SD	93,047	44.7	21.1	111,811	65.5	2.0	45.5	55,198	70,718	16.7	13.9	14.7
43620	Sioux Falls, SD-MN	201,433	31.0	38.5	234,875	74.2	1.5	54.2	126,616	76,226	11.6	18.7	6.3
43640	Slidell-Mandeville-Covington, LA	189,919	34.0	37.1	219,870	63.8	2.9	42.1	106,164	76,420	14.9	21.6	10.2
43780	South Bend-Mishawaka, IN-MI	214,872	39.4	31.4	260,330	62.9	2.9	41.2	128,897	65,834	17.4	13.5	11.5
43900	Spartanburg, SC	260,579	43.6	24.9	304,847	61.4	2.6	43.5	146,672	61,196	16.4	11.4	13.1
44060	Spokane-Spokane Valley, WA	420,367	31.7	31.6	487,906	61.3	2.5	39.6	239,251	72,819	15.7	17.3	17.7
44100	Springfield, IL	145,060	32.4	37.0	166,761	61.5	2.7	44.0	91,114	72,201	15.3	17.9	13.7
44140	Springfield, MA	320,476	45.7	28.8	377,389	60.4	2.4	40.4	184,698	66,997	20.9	15.7	29.3
44180	Springfield, MO	327,238	35.6	29.3	394,405	63.3	1.8	43.3	200,832	62,921	15.1	12.2	9.5
44220	Springfield, OH	93,767	46.9	18.7	108,312	57.5	3.2	37.9	55,322	57,910	19.4	10.9	18.2
44300	State College, PA	96,558	33.8	47.6	138,031	55.7	2.0	33.8	62,175	69,101	18.4	17.2	8.7
44420	Staunton-Stuarts Draft, VA	94,607	47.2	26.9	106,188	59.3	2.0	40.7	54,483	63,275	17.1	11.7	9.2
44700	Stockton-Lodi, CA	519,374	46.8	23.6	620,747	63.7	4.2	41.3	251,091	87,418	12.5	25.1	15.2

Table B-3. Metropolitan Areas — What: Education, Employment, and Income, 2023—*Continued*

Metropolitan area / division code	Metropolitan area / division	Educational attainment: Total population 25 years and over	Educational attainment: Percent with a high school diploma or less	Educational attainment: Percent with a bachelor's degree or more	Employment status: Total population 16 years and over	Employment status: Labor force participation (percent)	Employment status: Percent unemployed	Employment status: Percent of persons age 16 years and over who worked full-time year-round in the past 12 months (percent of total population)	Household income and benefits: Total households	Household income and benefits: Median household income in the past 12 months (in 2023 inflation-adjusted dollars)	Household income and benefits: Income less than $25,000 (percent)	Household income and benefits: Income greater than $150,000 (percent)	Household income and benefits: Percent who received cash public assistance or food stamps/SNAP
	ACS table number:	C15003	C15003	C15003	C23001	C23001	C23001	S2402	B19001	B19049	B19001	B19001	B19058
	Column number:	1	2	3	4	5	6	7	8	9	10	11	12
44940	Sumter, SC	68,894	45.6	19.9	81,755	58.7	4.1	37.1	40,059	55,982	23.0	11.4	18.1
45060	Syracuse, NY	449,669	34.1	36.4	536,591	62.4	2.5	41.7	273,464	73,268	15.9	18.4	15.1
45220	Tallahassee, FL	249,311	32.9	40.5	327,722	62.9	3.6	41.1	163,838	63,993	19.6	16.2	13.2
45300	Tampa-St. Petersburg-Clearwater, FL	2,440,645	36.4	35.0	2,781,298	61.5	2.5	43.5	1,358,788	72,743	15.3	18.6	11.9
4530041304	St. Petersburg-Clearwater-Largo, FL Metro Division	755,873	32.9	37.0	834,531	59.4	2.4	42.2	439,896	70,768	14.5	17.8	9.5
4530045294	Tampa, FL Metro Division	1,684,772	38.0	34.1	1,946,767	62.4	2.5	44.1	918,892	74,031	15.7	18.9	13.0
45460	Terre Haute, IN	112,407	48.7	23.0	136,961	57.0	3.4	39.2	67,572	50,992	24.2	8.8	13.5
45500	Texarkana, TX-AR	100,435	51.1	19.8	115,870	55.1	2.6	40.0	59,815	50,711	24.6	10.2	15.9
45780	Toledo, OH	406,034	38.8	30.3	482,598	63.8	3.2	42.8	254,228	63,074	18.8	14.8	14.7
45820	Topeka, KS	160,622	39.2	29.7	186,433	61.6	2.0	43.3	95,618	65,301	15.6	13.3	9.8
45900	Traverse City, MI	117,618	28.3	40.9	131,581	60.5	1.9	38.3	69,457	78,073	10.6	17.3	7.5
45940	Trenton-Princeton, NJ	260,234	32.8	45.2	308,614	65.2	3.8	44.7	146,258	96,152	13.6	30.3	10.1
46060	Tucson, AZ	735,290	31.2	36.8	883,691	59.4	2.7	37.9	445,471	69,758	17.1	16.9	11.8
46140	Tulsa, OK	697,459	37.8	30.9	821,798	63.1	2.9	44.6	411,320	65,561	17.6	14.1	14.5
46220	Tuscaloosa, AL	169,423	39.8	29.8	222,913	59.1	3.5	40.0	$108,078	$58,193	24.8	12.0	13.2
46300	Twin Falls, ID	77,822	40.6	19.0	92,627	65.0	1.6	44.9	$43,326	$66,078	13.7	9.7	9.1
46340	Tyler, TX	162,282	35.2	29.7	194,370	59.3	2.1	43.1	$81,987	$72,313	15.0	17.4	11.0
46520	Urban Honolulu, HI	702,068	32.1	39.6	809,175	64.7	2.1	40.6	338,496	103,131	11.4	31.1	11.3
46540	Utica-Rome, NY	201,951	41.9	27.1	234,026	59.0	2.7	40.7	124,085	61,799	19.7	12.9	18.0
46660	Valdosta, GA	95,420	43.9	27.2	119,224	60.3	2.8	38.7	60,298	54,924	25.6	11.1	17.9
46700	Vallejo, CA	315,777	36.0	29.1	363,912	62.1	3.0	41.3	157,766	100,027	12.0	29.7	13.6
47020	Victoria, TX	66,056	46.8	19.5	77,823	59.3	2.4	42.5	37,816	69,490	18.3	12.1	12.9
47220	Vineland, NJ	102,814	57.4	18.3	119,942	60.1	3.7	42.0	54,482	64,908	19.2	14.0	20.3
47260	Virginia Beach-Chesapeake-Norfolk, VA-NC	1,222,685	33.2	36.1	1,437,081	66.4	2.6	42.6	710,613	79,325	14.0	20.6	12.0
47300	Visalia, CA	289,766	52.8	16.9	355,039	61.0	5.0	38.9	145,442	73,097	15.8	15.8	26.0
47380	Waco, TX	192,949	38.4	27.3	242,933	61.1	2.2	42.7	111,745	62,743	21.1	15.0	13.0
47460	Walla Walla, WA	41,546	34.6	30.3	50,989	58.0	3.4	NA	23,887	72,812	18.2	14.9	19.6
47580	Warner Robins, GA	134,729	35.8	31.3	158,321	64.4	4.7	44.9	77,061	75,680	13.9	15.8	12.5
47900	Washington-Arlington-Alexandria, DC-VA-MD-WV	4,347,638	26.0	54.8	5,054,720	71.1	2.8	51.8	2,409,575	121,469	9.1	40.3	8.3
4790011694	Arlington-Alexandria-Reston, VA-WV Metro Division	2,154,081	23.6	57.4	2,507,756	71.6	2.4	52.2	1,160,949	133,525	6.9	44.3	5.7
4790023224	Frederick-Gaithersburg-Bethesda, MD Metro Division	937,799	24.0	58.2	1,080,664	69.9	2.4	50.4	499,961	123,516	8.2	41.6	7.2
4790047764	Washington, DC-MD Metro Division	1,255,758	31.7	48.0	1,466,300	71.2	3.8	52.0	748,665	102,239	13.2	33.1	13.2
47930	Waterbury-Shelton, CT	327,868	38.3	33.0	376,640	65.3	3.5	44.4	$180,851	$81,326	16.0	22.8	16.9
47940	Waterloo-Cedar Falls, IA	108,862	37.9	30.6	135,330	65.1	1.9	43.0	68,791	62,381	15.4	12.9	10.3
48060	Watertown-Fort Drum, NY	74,117	42.9	26.0	89,797	66.5	2.5	35.0	50,542	61,512	14.0	11.2	16.6
48140	Wausau, WI	97,756	39.4	27.9	111,623	65.3	1.4	47.9	58,104	74,141	12.5	14.5	11.0
48260	Weirton-Steubenville, WV-OH	83,531	49.6	19.6	95,648	56.0	3.0	37.6	50,285	53,422	23.6	8.0	18.1
48300	Wenatchee-East Wenatchee, WA	86,442	36.0	28.2	100,288	60.8	3.2	41.4	49,671	73,601	13.1	19.6	16.3
48540	Wheeling, WV-OH	98,753	45.4	25.8	113,507	57.9	2.8	39.4	59,980	59,180	20.4	10.8	17.4
48620	Wichita, KS	433,247	35.5	32.2	511,972	65.7	2.3	45.9	260,885	67,434	15.1	14.2	9.5
48660	Wichita Falls, TX	98,823	42.7	25.5	120,430	61.8	1.6	40.6	57,000	63,502	16.5	13.0	10.3
48680	Wildwood-The Villages, FL	136,372	31.9	37.0	141,239	26.2	2.0	NA	73,238	74,715	11.8	12.8	4.4
48700	Williamsport, PA	79,843	44.8	26.4	92,986	60.9	2.8	40.5	46,849	62,135	19.9	14.4	15.2
48900	Wilmington, NC	345,525	28.2	40.7	398,498	59.5	2.6	38.3	206,546	76,904	15.0	18.5	10.0
49020	Winchester, VA-WV	103,237	43.4	31.6	119,100	63.5	2.5	45.7	56,287	81,272	14.6	21.1	9.5
49180	Winston-Salem, NC	483,002	36.5	33.1	564,623	61.6	2.6	42.4	292,187	64,406	16.6	13.2	13.2
49340	Worcester, MA	610,716	35.4	41.4	712,225	66.2	2.6	44.5	336,660	94,099	13.1	28.0	18.6
49420	Yakima, WA	159,107	55.1	18.3	191,722	62.9	2.9	43.0	89,414	69,525	17.3	13.2	24.2
49620	York-Hanover, PA	327,185	46.0	29.2	376,041	66.7	2.6	46.3	183,864	81,362	10.9	18.2	12.5
49660	Youngstown-Warren, OH	306,399	49.5	23.4	348,927	56.7	2.3	37.4	186,827	51,350	23.1	9.9	17.6
49700	Yuba City, CA	118,784	43.8	17.9	142,423	59.9	4.2	37.6	62,578	77,335	16.1	18.8	17.0
49740	Yuma, AZ	140,123	50.9	17.4	167,599	51.5	3.3	32.5	83,811	62,888	16.9	8.3	18.1

NA = Not available.

Table B-4. Cities — What: Education, Employment, and Income, 2023

STATE and place code	STATE Place	Educational attainment			Employment status				Household income and benefits				
		Total population 25 years and over	Percent with a high school diploma or less	Percent with a bachelor's degree or more	Total population 16 years and over	Labor force participation (percent)	Percent unemployed	Percent of persons age 16 years and over who worked full-time year-round in the past 12 months	Total households	Median household income in the past 12 months (in 2022 inflation-adjusted dollars)	Income less than $25,000 (percent)	Income greater than $150,000 (percent)	Percent who received cash public assistance or food stamps/ SNAP
	ACS table number:	C15003	C15003	C15003	C23001	C23001	C23001	S2402	B19001	B19049	B19001	B19001	B19058
	column number:	1	2	3	4	5	6	7	8	9	10	11	12
00000	**UNITED STATES**	231,791,117	36.2	36.2	271,122,729	63.8	4.3	68.6	131,332,360	77,719	15.2	21.5	12.9
01000	**ALABAMA**	3,498,967	40.9	28.9	4,115,279	58.6	4.0	71.2	2,051,545	62,212	20.2	13.4	14.3
0103076	Auburn city	40,161	16.6	63.8	67,424	60.7	3.5	NA	32,859	52,259	32.3	14.1	10.8
0107000	Birmingham city	136,205	38.4	30.8	164,645	58.3	2.0	42.6	91,740	44,951	29.7	8.4	24.2
0121184	Dothan city	49,513	40.3	27.6	57,757	59.6	2.0	42.7	30,920	54,598	23.2	10.3	20.4
0135896	Hoover city	63,343	15.4	63.1	74,430	68.9	1.3	52.3	38,178	102,009	9.5	28.9	4.2
0137000	Huntsville city	157,348	25.2	47.7	190,614	64.0	2.2	44.5	99,557	73,319	15.3	19.6	9.0
0150000	Mobile city	126,280	35.3	35.2	150,600	60.7	1.8	44.0	79,383	50,156	24.1	10.2	18.0
0151000	Montgomery city	129,713	37.8	33.1	154,698	59.6	2.7	40.4	82,966	57,300	21.8	8.1	21.0
0177256	Tuscaloosa city	54,715	30.7	38.8	92,388	57.7	5.3	31.6	42,870	43,235	33.9	8.3	16.1
02000	**ALASKA**	493,892	35.9	32.2	577,598	66.8	4.5	59.1	276,852	86,631	12.3	23.9	12.0
0203000	Anchorage municipality	193,169	30.0	40.0	226,057	70.6	2.8	44.4	109,125	94,437	9.2	29.1	10.5
04000	**ARIZONA**	5,150,254	34.0	33.5	6,049,109	60.7	4.2	69.1	2,907,014	77,315	14.3	20.0	10.7
0404720	Avondale city	60,753	43.1	19.4	72,056	69.0	2.5	53.3	32,208	86,428	14.0	19.0	14.7
0407940	Buckeye city	70,315	39.2	22.4	84,016	58.6	1.3	47.7	32,161	99,178	5.4	20.5	8.9
0410670	Casas Adobes CDP	53,322	24.1	39.4	60,268	61.4	2.1	42.3	32,025	79,754	11.1	18.6	5.9
0412000	Chandler city	190,069	20.8	48.5	223,401	70.6	2.0	52.2	105,611	105,393	8.7	33.2	6.6
0423620	Flagstaff city	39,773	18.2	51.1	66,224	70.2	3.5	38.3	30,080	71,402	16.6	18.6	10.0
0427400	Gilbert town	177,782	18.9	48.4	208,814	73.0	1.9	53.4	94,016	122,445	4.8	38.5	3.4
0427820	Glendale city	162,582	41.1	25.6	193,688	65.8	1.9	46.3	89,664	70,600	15.2	16.9	16.2
0428380	Goodyear city	77,562	25.4	41.4	NA	NA	NA	NA	38,956	105,160	5.0	26.9	5.9
0444410	Maricopa city	46,324	31.5	26.6	NA	NA	NA	NA	23,278	83,604	6.5	13.3	8.1
0446000	Mesa city	355,736	32.3	34.0	411,381	63.1	2.4	44.4	203,676	79,145	11.7	20.0	8.8
0454050	Peoria city	138,583	29.6	34.4	159,179	61.1	1.7	44.3	74,637	97,296	10.3	27.7	7.8
0455000	Phoenix city	1,098,979	38.4	33.5	1,318,211	68.9	3.0	49.4	621,234	79,664	13.5	21.5	12.7
0458150	Queen Creek town	48,770	23.6	45.5	NA	NA	NA	NA	24,749	135,444	3.1	41.7	2.3
0464210	San Tan Valley CDP	76,329	34.9	24.6	89,782	67.5	2.5	50.2	36,966	92,963	3.0	18.2	8.5
0465000	Scottsdale city	192,390	14.2	60.9	212,687	60.4	1.8	44.6	118,561	106,058	9.5	35.3	3.1
0471510	Surprise city	114,920	33.9	29.7	131,747	59.6	2.2	41.0	59,045	89,560	12.4	18.6	6.1
0473000	Tempe city	120,080	22.1	52.1	169,057	74.1	3.3	47.1	76,512	91,079	11.6	19.4	6.2
0477000	Tucson city	361,199	36.2	31.3	454,605	63.9	3.2	39.0	233,257	55,708	22.2	11.2	16.4
0485540	Yuma city	61,874	45.1	20.8	77,872	60.5	3.5	36.6	41,742	61,977	16.3	8.2	16.0
05000	**ARKANSAS**	2,078,254	44.9	26.2	2,452,773	58.8	4.1	71.3	1,232,871	58,700	20.6	11.9	8.7
0515190	Conway city	42,373	29.4	43.4	57,091	64.6	2.5	NA	28,356	62,886	14.7	18.1	6.9
0523290	Fayetteville city	56,483	27.9	49.5	86,514	62.8	2.0	39.8	42,333	51,513	25.5	15.3	6.6
0524550	Fort Smith city	60,109	45.7	24.3	70,793	60.0	2.9	41.9	36,439	54,009	20.0	7.7	6.7
0535710	Jonesboro city	50,100	32.7	30.5	61,504	66.1	3.8	NA	32,817	57,264	16.7	9.7	11.7
0541000	Little Rock city	140,745	29.3	43.1	164,241	60.4	1.9	43.5	89,358	59,762	19.7	18.0	7.9
0560410	Rogers city	48,574	41.8	33.3	NA	NA	NA	NA	27,613	84,093	9.5	19.6	4.8
0566080	Springdale city	51,433	55.1	25.5	63,549	70.7	3.2	53.6	29,550	68,544	13.8	12.5	5.1
06000	**CALIFORNIA**	26,969,649	35.6	37.5	31,584,340	64.3	5.5	65.7	13,699,816	95,521	12.9	30.3	14.6
0600562	Alameda city	55,453	17.1	60.1	61,286	66.2	3.2	41.9	30,642	121,817	8.8	38.8	6.4
0600884	Alhambra city	62,529	35.6	39.6	68,899	63.2	3.3	44.0	30,242	79,637	14.0	22.0	17.2
0602000	Anaheim city	236,535	42.6	30.6	280,300	66.6	3.2	46.7	109,885	84,872	15.4	24.1	15.7
0602252	Antioch city	80,335	41.4	27.2	93,912	64.1	3.1	40.8	37,645	91,256	9.8	29.0	16.0
0602364	Apple Valley town	49,443	39.8	21.2	59,770	54.1	3.0	NA	26,684	77,159	9.7	16.5	21.0
0602553	Arden-Arcade CDP	64,780	30.3	39.8	72,811	64.0	4.0	43.7	37,548	89,781	14.3	24.6	17.4
0603526	Bakersfield city	248,506	46.2	22.2	306,295	63.0	3.8	42.4	130,761	79,355	15.9	18.6	21.0
0603666	Baldwin Park city	47,333	60.8	16.8	55,918	63.0	3.1	42.8	18,805	78,662	13.0	17.6	20.2
0604982	Bellflower city	50,687	46.9	20.9	61,541	68.9	3.7	45.9	23,352	76,296	12.4	17.0	21.7
0606000	Berkeley city	72,876	11.4	75.5	108,232	62.5	3.3	33.6	49,088	98,086	20.7	34.4	14.3
0608142	Brentwood city	44,212	22.4	40.3	50,631	62.4	4.1	NA	22,600	140,312	9.0	44.9	12.5
0608786	Buena Park city	56,480	43.9	31.9	65,276	71.2	2.8	49.9	23,777	115,247	7.2	35.9	12.9
0608954	Burbank city	78,485	23.1	45.8	86,849	61.6	3.2	42.6	43,209	91,926	15.9	32.1	14.1
0610046	Camarillo city	51,970	25.3	44.2	59,067	59.1	2.5	NA	26,253	111,847	5.8	40.2	5.4
0611194	Carlsbad city	80,105	11.3	63.6	90,320	64.4	2.7	41.4	43,752	131,257	6.8	45.6	6.5

Table B-4. Cities — What: Education, Employment, and Income, 2023—*Continued*

STATE and place code	STATE Place	Educational attainment			Employment status				Household income and benefits				
		Total population 25 years and over	Percent with a high school diploma or less	Percent with a bachelor's degree or more	Total population 16 years and over	Labor force participation (percent)	Percent unemployed	Percent of persons age 16 years and over who worked full-time year-round in the past 12 months	Total households	Median household income in the past 12 months (in 2022 inflation-adjusted dollars)	Income less than $25,000 (percent)	Income greater than $150,000 (percent)	Percent who received cash public assistance or food stamps/ SNAP
	ACS table number:	C15003	C15003	C15003	C23001	C23001	C23001	S2402	B19001	B19049	B19001	B19001	B19058
	column number:	1	2	3	4	5	6	7	8	9	10	11	12
	CALIFORNIA—Cont.												
0611390	Carmichael CDP	56,567	28.6	35.7	63,975	62.0	4.9	38.6	30,982	86,754	13.6	26.0	20.7
0611530	Carson city	65,200	38.6	27.7	75,435	58.9	3.3	41.3	27,512	100,041	12.0	27.8	18.8
0611964	Castro Valley CDP	48,151	24.8	48.0	NA	NA	NA	NA	23,198	132,000	6.7	44.5	6.9
0613014	Chico city	58,544	22.8	38.4	86,649	67.5	4.2	34.6	44,270	61,464	20.9	15.3	24.7
0613210	Chino city	62,666	38.4	30.1	72,099	66.9	3.5	43.6	26,314	104,185	7.2	31.4	12.8
0613214	Chino Hills city	53,103	29.5	45.4	63,101	64.9	4.0	44.8	24,476	127,294	8.4	37.7	9.1
0613392	Chula Vista city	183,259	31.2	34.1	213,917	67.2	4.9	44.6	88,029	106,623	9.8	33.7	12.1
0613588	Citrus Heights city	62,558	38.3	21.7	70,405	64.8	5.0	NA	34,364	81,123	10.7	13.8	12.9
0614218	Clovis city	78,673	25.5	37.8	93,361	62.5	2.3	44.0	44,194	88,828	9.6	27.0	16.2
0615044	Compton city	57,664	63.0	8.6	69,750	63.8	4.4	41.1	23,447	69,965	18.2	18.1	29.9
0616000	Concord city	87,054	30.0	38.6	100,549	66.9	3.5	42.4	47,248	100,442	10.3	31.7	11.5
0616350	Corona city	107,337	37.6	32.6	129,307	68.2	4.4	48.2	51,110	104,871	11.6	30.6	12.2
0616532	Costa Mesa city	77,920	26.4	47.8	91,214	74.7	2.8	51.5	42,336	101,433	7.0	34.0	9.9
0617918	Daly City city	77,979	32.0	38.2	88,334	66.4	2.1	47.5	33,137	104,079	11.2	37.5	14.2
0618100	Davis city	36,499	11.4	72.8	58,758	64.6	2.8	35.7	25,542	89,386	21.5	30.9	12.9
0619766	Downey city	77,539	44.2	24.8	88,430	66.0	2.9	45.6	33,472	96,699	7.9	26.8	20.8
0620018	Dublin city	48,195	13.6	70.3	54,348	69.5	2.4	NA	null	204,946	NA	NA	3.2
0620802	East Los Angeles CDP	69,228	68.0	10.5	83,354	63.0	3.7	42.6	29,208	69,891	15.3	14.9	28.7
0621230	Eastvale city	44,753	29.1	47.7	NA	NA	NA	NA	18,433	162,853	1.8	61.1	5.6
0621712	El Cajon city	65,297	47.1	19.7	78,447	60.7	6.4	34.9	32,145	67,773	19.5	17.9	33.7
0622020	Elk Grove city	116,310	25.9	39.6	137,348	64.9	4.4	42.4	53,383	119,330	7.6	36.3	11.8
0622230	El Monte city	71,409	62.3	17.9	82,751	61.2	4.4	37.2	29,314	64,991	19.4	12.7	28.6
0622804	Escondido city	102,421	44.1	29.0	118,641	66.0	3.0	43.8	47,740	95,052	12.3	27.4	15.8
0623182	Fairfield city	79,344	37.2	26.9	95,908	63.6	1.3	41.4	38,515	100,126	9.2	29.9	15.4
0624638	Folsom city	60,724	15.3	58.5	NA	NA	NA	NA	32,761	124,531	11.4	42.1	5.0
0624680	Fontana city	138,463	48.1	21.9	167,926	67.0	3.5	46.6	59,598	100,890	9.2	30.1	13.4
0626000	Fremont city	167,765	17.8	65.8	185,439	66.5	3.2	50.3	81,639	170,934	7.6	55.6	6.2
0627000	Fresno city	341,230	43.8	26.0	416,299	63.2	4.4	39.0	180,634	67,603	19.0	15.9	27.5
0628000	Fullerton city	97,214	29.0	41.4	113,390	69.2	3.6	44.9	49,425	97,427	11.0	28.3	12.4
0629000	Garden Grove city	119,202	48.3	26.7	138,218	61.1	2.3	39.6	50,343	87,407	14.9	20.9	19.6
0630000	Glendale city	141,333	28.6	48.2	158,561	62.0	3.1	42.0	76,375	81,365	20.2	26.4	25.3
0632548	Hawthorne city	58,308	43.5	27.8	66,674	71.4	5.2	49.6	32,299	65,166	19.3	15.6	19.8
0633000	Hayward city	112,823	42.1	33.1	128,774	67.0	3.7	49.4	49,029	112,121	8.4	36.9	15.3
0633182	Hemet city	63,221	51.7	16.2	73,283	49.2	1.7	NA	33,674	52,824	19.2	9.8	18.1
0633434	Hesperia city	61,498	54.3	13.4	76,217	60.8	5.1	39.1	29,608	67,348	14.5	14.5	21.8
0636000	Huntington Beach city	143,474	24.0	44.5	162,369	65.0	2.2	42.0	75,314	120,231	10.0	38.1	8.6
0636448	Indio city	63,534	50.7	22.2	73,750	62.2	0.7	42.8	31,048	83,107	10.4	20.1	24.9
0636546	Inglewood city	75,110	45.4	25.2	87,280	65.6	3.6	43.1	37,918	72,900	14.0	15.7	17.1
0636770	Irvine city	199,044	9.8	71.8	251,119	67.7	3.0	44.6	111,471	127,989	11.2	43.9	8.1
0637692	Jurupa Valley city	70,751	60.3	14.7	86,199	60.3	3.3	39.0	30,398	87,809	14.7	23.8	15.3
0639486	Lake Elsinore city	46,246	48.8	21.2	NA	NA	NA	NA	20,252	109,010	10.9	36.0	19.0
0639496	Lake Forest city	60,323	20.4	51.9	67,141	74.0	3.5	51.4	29,721	126,234	6.9	42.3	5.5
0639892	Lakewood city	53,684	34.1	31.9	62,399	69.0	3.5	46.9	25,033	117,970	8.4	35.2	10.2
0640130	Lancaster city	105,798	42.1	20.4	126,768	53.7	3.6	37.1	52,431	74,991	18.7	17.1	22.5
0641992	Livermore city	55,821	19.0	52.4	62,807	66.1	2.7	47.6	29,208	151,705	7.7	50.9	9.9
0642202	Lodi city	42,157	45.0	25.1	50,903	61.1	4.8	41.1	23,274	82,342	15.1	16.8	13.0
0643000	Long Beach city	320,905	35.9	36.8	382,628	66.2	3.3	45.0	176,407	81,606	15.5	22.8	16.7
0644000	Los Angeles city	2,725,450	38.0	39.2	3,180,295	67.3	4.5	42.8	1,460,167	79,701	17.4	25.1	18.2
0644574	Lynwood city	41,485	65.6	12.3	49,544	64.7	5.3	NA	16,131	65,432	13.6	10.3	31.3
0645022	Madera city	42,108	63.6	10.8	51,723	56.4	5.3	NA	19,945	55,622	24.3	11.4	31.6
0645484	Manteca city	63,605	37.8	24.1	NA	NA	NA	NA	30,532	91,533	12.6	28.9	13.1
0646842	Menifee city	76,211	37.6	23.8	87,684	61.1	3.7	40.2	39,358	82,402	16.9	21.3	14.7
0646898	Merced city	52,692	50.1	20.5	69,769	63.8	6.5	37.4	27,221	53,931	21.0	13.0	28.9
0647766	Milpitas city	57,293	22.1	60.8	66,455	65.1	1.6	49.4	25,653	179,727	5.3	57.3	8.8
0648256	Mission Viejo city	68,679	20.9	51.1	75,766	60.8	1.9	40.4	34,477	122,135	8.6	39.7	7.4
0648354	Modesto city	144,050	44.5	21.6	169,231	61.5	2.9	40.0	76,577	80,471	13.3	18.6	17.6
0649270	Moreno Valley city	132,411	53.7	16.3	163,543	65.7	4.2	44.5	56,294	91,021	8.3	21.1	18.8
0649670	Mountain View city	61,882	12.9	74.3	NA	NA	NA	NA	35,859	181,671	7.9	56.9	4.3
0650076	Murrieta city	75,487	29.0	36.7	88,021	65.8	3.7	45.4	36,867	108,703	7.8	35.0	9.2
0650258	Napa city	57,450	29.9	39.1	65,453	67.4	2.2	45.6	30,838	103,601	9.6	36.3	9.5
0651182	Newport Beach city	62,637	10.2	73.1	68,871	63.4	2.6	NA	36,300	156,434	8.9	52.6	3.5

Table B-4. Cities — What: Education, Employment, and Income, 2023—*Continued*

STATE and place code	STATE Place	Educational attainment: Total population 25 years and over	Educational attainment: Percent with a high school diploma or less	Educational attainment: Percent with a bachelor's degree or more	Employment status: Total population 16 years and over	Employment status: Labor force participation (percent)	Employment status: Percent unemployed	Employment status: Percent of persons age 16 years and over who worked full-time year-round in the past 12 months	Household income and benefits: Total households	Household income and benefits: Median household income in the past 12 months (in 2022 inflation-adjusted dollars)	Household income and benefits: Income less than $25,000 (percent)	Household income and benefits: Income greater than $150,000 (percent)	Household income and benefits: Percent who received cash public assistance or food stamps/ SNAP
	ACS table number:	C15003	C15003	C15003	C23001	C23001	C23001	S2402	B19001	B19049	B19001	B19001	B19058
	column number:	1	2	3	4	5	6	7	8	9	10	11	12
	CALIFORNIA—Cont.												
0652526	Norwalk city	67,191	51.3	19.3	78,473	69.1	3.0	49.3	27,925	103,071	11.1	23.9	19.5
0653000	Oakland city	329,736	31.9	47.2	369,177	69.8	4.6	45.7	182,014	96,828	16.5	32.2	18.8
0653322	Oceanside city	125,016	33.0	34.4	142,934	66.4	2.4	42.5	63,683	99,108	12.3	27.5	11.4
0653896	Ontario city	120,905	50.0	22.5	142,883	67.3	4.2	45.4	54,719	84,566	11.0	21.0	14.3
0653980	Orange city	91,774	31.7	39.8	112,000	67.3	2.6	45.3	46,584	117,707	11.5	39.4	8.1
0654652	Oxnard city	126,456	55.7	19.6	152,610	66.0	4.0	42.9	55,777	87,975	10.8	22.9	16.9
0655156	Palmdale city	100,255	52.6	15.8	122,259	64.1	4.8	41.9	47,380	78,743	14.7	20.9	24.1
0655282	Palo Alto city	48,443	10.2	82.4	53,688	61.3	3.4	NA	27,768	184,068	9.8	55.7	6.0
0656000	Pasadena city	100,329	21.9	56.8	112,933	65.7	2.7	45.4	57,025	103,282	13.8	35.1	12.0
0656700	Perris city	49,111	59.9	15.9	61,554	63.5	2.8	NA	20,943	77,365	9.7	18.2	24.3
0657456	Pittsburg city	50,277	45.2	24.6	59,576	68.7	4.8	NA	24,968	92,506	12.7	28.3	18.1
0657792	Pleasanton city	52,566	14.8	69.6	58,878	63.3	2.8	NA	26,569	177,535	5.8	60.7	5.7
0658072	Pomona city	103,152	54.2	22.1	118,479	64.9	3.3	42.8	42,390	78,317	12.4	21.1	23.5
0659444	Rancho Cordova city	55,935	33.7	33.2	62,906	66.8	5.9	42.7	28,916	76,948	19.7	23.6	26.6
0659451	Rancho Cucamonga city	118,453	32.9	33.9	138,600	66.7	4.4	41.8	58,173	103,358	9.5	31.4	12.8
0659920	Redding city	64,730	33.9	24.7	73,808	58.2	1.9	38.4	37,380	71,114	16.3	17.6	18.5
0659962	Redlands city	50,331	25.5	44.7	58,404	68.2	2.8	46.6	27,161	97,943	9.8	29.4	10.3
0660018	Redondo Beach city	null	NA	NA	NA	NA	NA	NA	29,220	159,676	7.3	53.2	5.2
0660102	Redwood City city	58,665	26.7	55.3	66,363	66.7	2.3	47.0	29,831	151,234	7.0	50.6	4.4
0660466	Rialto city	62,875	61.2	12.5	76,760	65.5	4.4	42.7	26,568	80,321	10.9	18.5	22.5
0660620	Richmond city	82,954	36.0	34.9	95,080	67.2	4.3	44.2	45,299	89,052	12.4	24.6	15.3
0662000	Riverside city	203,292	45.1	28.8	254,281	66.1	2.7	44.6	96,201	88,175	12.2	23.2	14.9
0662364	Rocklin city	48,271	19.0	49.5	58,574	62.2	3.4	NA	27,308	106,408	10.5	35.3	10.3
0662938	Roseville city	113,343	20.8	44.3	127,962	62.6	3.0	43.4	61,142	107,888	10.5	35.9	9.3
0664000	Sacramento city	365,775	34.3	37.9	427,188	66.2	4.1	43.5	202,421	85,928	14.2	23.9	16.5
0664224	Salinas city	93,993	64.2	15.3	118,599	60.1	2.2	38.6	43,233	80,580	15.1	18.9	14.9
0665000	San Bernardino city	137,224	59.3	14.3	168,473	62.7	3.2	41.0	64,370	63,328	19.1	12.7	25.8
0665042	San Buenaventura (Ventura) city	81,301	26.6	42.6	91,475	65.1	2.9	42.2	43,032	97,970	11.8	30.0	10.3
0666000	San Diego city	981,161	24.1	52.0	1,162,512	69.5	2.6	44.9	537,532	105,780	10.7	34.0	11.2
0667000	San Francisco city	646,934	22.8	60.4	712,427	69.3	3.4	48.8	372,027	126,730	14.2	44.2	13.1
0668000	San Jose city	681,739	30.9	47.6	800,943	68.2	2.8	47.5	331,229	136,229	9.5	46.2	11.5
0668084	San Leandro city	64,303	41.1	31.0	70,528	64.8	3.3	44.3	31,539	84,657	12.5	22.7	16.5
0668196	San Marcos city	61,645	30.0	42.5	75,846	67.0	3.5	45.2	31,360	96,214	10.0	29.9	11.0
0668252	San Mateo city	75,730	21.5	58.3	87,011	68.2	2.0	50.4	39,795	152,913	10.5	51.4	5.5
0668378	San Ramon city	58,111	8.7	75.8	67,185	69.3	2.5	NA	30,872	195,491	6.1	62.4	3.3
0669000	Santa Ana city	210,378	60.8	16.5	252,759	66.6	2.3	47.0	83,498	85,914	12.2	23.3	13.3
0669070	Santa Barbara city	66,318	23.6	49.5	73,930	65.5	4.1	43.1	38,553	100,041	14.6	34.9	7.0
0669084	Santa Clara city	95,169	14.9	67.2	112,544	72.9	3.1	51.0	51,014	166,228	8.1	54.0	5.7
0669088	Santa Clarita city	155,831	27.7	40.9	179,789	65.8	2.4	46.2	76,446	118,489	6.2	39.5	11.1
0669196	Santa Maria city	60,713	58.3	16.8	80,660	66.0	4.1	38.3	28,422	77,564	13.0	17.3	17.9
0670000	Santa Monica city	75,080	12.0	71.9	79,916	69.4	3.4	NA	48,189	109,503	14.5	39.9	7.8
0670098	Santa Rosa city	129,124	37.1	34.0	145,186	67.1	2.7	43.5	70,361	93,106	11.4	28.1	14.9
0672016	Simi Valley city	90,415	28.1	41.9	103,136	66.4	2.9	45.8	44,629	117,351	8.6	38.0	8.8
0673080	South Gate city	63,370	70.1	10.3	74,167	64.7	3.5	43.1	27,422	71,760	13.1	10.7	22.5
0675000	Stockton city	206,243	51.1	20.6	246,821	63.4	4.4	40.3	101,924	76,191	15.1	18.4	19.0
0677000	Sunnyvale city	110,098	13.6	71.9	123,836	76.9	2.6	56.1	58,756	189,443	4.9	61.1	4.6
0678120	Temecula city	73,271	24.7	39.8	84,048	70.8	3.0	48.2	35,801	121,795	6.8	41.5	9.0
0678582	Thousand Oaks city	88,827	20.0	55.2	104,800	64.1	3.8	40.8	46,158	139,172	6.4	46.4	4.1
0680000	Torrance city	103,228	21.5	52.9	114,082	63.1	2.6	44.1	55,836	109,019	8.6	36.3	8.3
0680238	Tracy city	62,704	46.1	26.5	78,076	67.0	2.6	45.9	27,880	123,525	4.5	36.8	12.9
0680644	Tulare city	41,458	50.5	12.3	51,492	67.0	3.6	NA	20,967	77,286	12.2	19.0	23.0
0680812	Turlock city	46,623	42.8	26.2	NA	NA	NA	NA	25,660	81,595	10.4	19.1	16.8
0680854	Tustin city	53,343	34.2	43.1	61,589	70.6	2.7	52.4	26,025	107,537	7.8	33.0	13.3
0681204	Union City city	48,797	31.4	44.5	53,254	66.0	3.2	50.3	21,920	124,383	7.7	39.4	10.5
0681344	Upland city	55,431	32.7	38.8	65,196	66.9	3.2	47.2	28,043	114,165	9.1	36.6	12.8
0681554	Vacaville city	73,010	37.2	29.4	83,529	59.6	2.5	40.4	35,647	104,278	9.4	33.3	11.3
0681666	Vallejo city	90,859	37.3	28.7	102,736	63.2	4.7	42.7	44,936	91,800	14.2	25.8	16.9
0682590	Victorville city	83,232	53.3	13.3	102,509	60.5	7.6	36.6	38,786	67,099	18.8	17.7	32.2
0682954	Visalia city	91,986	40.7	24.6	108,776	63.8	3.6	44.7	48,446	79,777	11.0	17.7	22.5
0682996	Vista city	64,973	41.9	26.8	76,454	69.5	2.7	47.8	31,866	92,224	5.9	26.2	10.7

Table B-4. Cities — What: Education, Employment, and Income, 2023—*Continued*

STATE and place code	STATE Place	Educational attainment: Total population 25 years and over	Educational attainment: Percent with a high school diploma or less	Educational attainment: Percent with a bachelor's degree or more	Employment status: Total population 16 years and over	Employment status: Labor force participation (percent)	Employment status: Percent unemployed	Employment status: Percent of persons age 16 years and over who worked full-time year-round in the past 12 months	Household income and benefits: Total households	Household income and benefits: Median household income in the past 12 months (in 2022 inflation-adjusted dollars)	Household income and benefits: Income less than $25,000 (percent)	Household income and benefits: Income greater than $150,000 (percent)	Household income and benefits: Percent who received cash public assistance or food stamps/ SNAP
	ACS table number:	C15003	C15003	C15003	C23001	C23001	C23001	S2402	B19001	B19049	B19001	B19001	B19058
	column number:	1	2	3	4	5	6	7	8	9	10	11	12
	CALIFORNIA—Cont.												
0683346	Walnut Creek city	54,673	10.3	69.7	NA	NA	NA	NA	32,550	134,770	8.5	47.3	5.2
0684200	West Covina city	76,278	43.1	25.2	87,585	65.8	3.2	45.9	31,349	96,525	10.1	24.8	17.5
0684550	Westminster city	63,549	43.4	29.5	71,631	61.4	2.6	38.3	28,524	81,443	18.3	23.5	21.9
0685292	Whittier city	53,958	35.7	32.1	64,219	65.8	2.7	48.6	27,466	95,895	12.4	24.5	10.0
0686832	Yorba Linda city	47,073	15.3	57.2	53,868	65.5	1.6	NA	22,960	146,923	5.9	49.6	4.5
0686972	Yuba City city	45,332	47.1	17.4	54,799	59.8	3.4	NA	23,521	74,210	14.6	19.1	15.4
08000	**COLORADO**	4,135,123	26.0	46.4	4,818,044	69.0	3.7	68.7	2,428,261	92,911	11.6	27.7	9.8
0803455	Arvada city	90,864	23.5	53.7	103,882	71.1	2.5	52.7	49,987	114,384	8.8	36.7	7.1
0804000	Aurora city	266,246	36.9	33.6	313,755	73.4	3.7	50.8	149,344	89,300	11.2	24.1	12.9
0807850	Boulder city	60,544	11.2	75.9	95,260	63.3	4.5	33.8	44,722	75,923	22.1	29.7	4.2
0809280	Broomfield city	55,576	16.7	58.8	63,536	69.8	2.2	50.3	33,563	112,139	7.2	35.0	3.9
0812415	Castle Rock town	55,071	16.4	55.2	NA	NA	NA	NA	29,100	137,383	7.6	46.7	5.3
0812815	Centennial city	75,662	13.7	62.5	83,977	68.7	2.2	48.8	41,393	121,531	5.2	39.3	4.6
0816000	Colorado Springs city	335,406	23.1	44.8	394,603	69.5	3.0	45.1	208,035	83,215	11.0	21.7	9.0
0816495	Commerce City city	42,807	45.0	23.0	NA	NA	NA	NA	21,705	124,884	6.5	34.3	10.2
0820000	Denver city	530,935	21.4	57.9	603,435	75.1	2.8	54.4	342,996	94,157	13.4	30.5	10.0
0827425	Fort Collins city	105,572	13.9	64.5	147,831	68.4	3.9	41.2	72,318	81,883	16.0	22.2	11.1
0831660	Grand Junction city	48,614	24.8	41.0	58,213	63.0	2.9	39.2	31,087	67,887	15.4	14.7	16.1
0832155	Greeley city	69,099	43.6	26.3	87,894	65.3	4.1	41.5	42,813	63,526	14.2	13.4	18.1
0836410	Highlands Ranch CDP	71,201	8.0	70.8	83,686	71.8	3.5	49.7	39,866	153,336	5.8	51.4	1.9
0843000	Lakewood city	117,427	25.7	45.6	136,091	70.9	2.7	49.0	71,477	83,987	10.0	23.4	8.2
0845970	Longmont city	70,303	23.9	49.4	82,863	68.6	3.2	45.7	42,201	82,984	12.4	23.4	9.4
0846465	Loveland city	57,210	24.9	36.5	66,377	66.2	2.4	46.7	35,134	77,160	10.3	19.5	11.0
0862000	Pueblo city	76,708	42.8	23.0	90,838	56.5	2.1	40.0	46,921	57,170	20.6	10.9	25.1
0877290	Thornton city	98,731	38.7	35.4	115,186	72.6	2.3	52.0	52,600	101,679	10.5	27.0	12.4
0883835	Westminster city	85,598	24.0	47.2	96,434	72.0	1.2	54.5	51,565	92,101	10.4	27.5	5.6
09000	**CONNECTICUT**	2,559,922	33.8	42.9	2,987,218	66.4	4.6	66.2	1,442,969	91,665	13.7	28.5	12.9
0908000	Bridgeport city	97,456	59.3	21.2	121,228	67.4	6.1	38.9	54,695	58,515	23.2	12.5	26.9
0918430	Danbury city	60,259	45.1	32.7	71,710	72.1	4.7	43.6	32,993	79,358	15.7	22.0	16.0
0937000	Hartford city	74,708	56.8	18.4	94,919	58.7	5.8	37.7	49,229	42,397	30.0	7.7	37.3
0950370	New Britain city	49,355	57.9	17.0	60,217	66.9	3.7	NA	30,047	58,780	18.4	9.1	21.7
0952000	New Haven city	87,869	44.9	37.3	110,931	63.3	4.3	37.4	57,392	51,158	27.7	12.3	24.7
0955990	Norwalk city	68,782	30.3	49.9	77,776	69.7	2.7	46.7	37,777	102,195	11.9	32.8	12.7
0973000	Stamford city	101,915	25.7	54.7	116,482	72.6	2.7	47.2	55,324	106,552	11.6	39.6	11.0
0980000	Waterbury city	76,125	51.9	18.1	89,291	57.0	6.1	34.1	45,898	43,420	35.9	6.7	37.0
10000	**DELAWARE**	731,427	37.1	36.5	846,414	62.2	3.4	69.9	412,048	81,361	12.1	22.2	12.1
1077580	Wilmington city	48,539	43.8	34.4	57,865	64.8	2.7	42.1	32,131	50,420	22.9	13.4	24.3
11000	**DISTRICT OF COLUMBIA**	482,919	20.4	65.9	564,543	72.8	3.8	53.7	334,673	108,210	15.6	38.1	15.4
1150000	Washington city	482,919	20.4	65.9	564,543	72.8	3.8	53.7	334,673	108,210	15.6	38.1	15.4
12000	**FLORIDA**	16,421,870	36.6	34.9	18,768,460	60.0	4.1	69.9	8,966,402	73,311	15.1	18.6	12.4
1200410	Alafaya CDP	62,827	24.7	48.6	77,428	73.9	2.0	55.5	34,029	102,898	7.2	24.2	10.2
1207300	Boca Raton city	70,789	13.5	62.8	86,217	57.8	2.4	35.5	41,274	110,593	13.2	37.1	2.8
1207875	Boynton Beach city	59,535	40.4	34.4	67,275	61.9	2.7	NA	31,874	67,247	18.6	17.6	13.5
1208150	Brandon CDP	80,807	34.2	31.7	NA	NA	NA	NA	44,579	82,027	12.1	16.3	11.1
1210275	Cape Coral city	174,950	40.4	29.4	192,820	56.7	2.3	39.1	83,021	74,634	14.2	17.8	10.2
1212875	Clearwater city	91,836	35.3	35.1	100,972	61.4	2.8	44.4	52,536	73,178	15.4	18.4	10.0
1214400	Coral Springs city	88,327	28.5	41.4	102,891	71.9	2.2	50.8	46,223	85,615	8.9	27.7	5.7
1216475	Davie town	69,860	32.8	37.2	86,304	68.0	2.3	47.0	38,969	82,514	14.0	21.3	10.9
1216525	Daytona Beach city	54,855	41.3	28.1	67,557	49.0	3.1	NA	33,906	50,442	22.9	6.4	21.2
1216725	Deerfield Beach city	64,801	42.6	27.8	NA	NA	NA	NA	34,846	59,148	23.8	11.5	11.9
1217100	Delray Beach city	54,217	34.6	44.1	NA	NA	NA	NA	30,118	76,803	20.3	21.2	10.6
1217200	Deltona city	67,924	41.1	21.1	79,533	64.1	1.3	45.8	33,155	71,107	13.8	11.3	14.1
1217935	Doral city	51,912	16.1	61.4	NA	NA	NA	NA	26,222	98,058	10.2	26.7	9.3
1224000	Fort Lauderdale city	141,540	36.6	37.6	157,859	65.5	3.3	45.3	81,232	80,539	15.5	23.4	13.7
1224125	Fort Myers city	70,192	35.8	34.9	79,601	58.8	2.2	44.2	39,447	61,894	15.0	17.0	10.6
1224581	Four Corners CDP		49,875	29.0	36.3	NA	NA	NA	NA	27,549	73,951	8.7	15.6
1225175	Gainesville city	78,965	17.8	58.3	130,283	60.0	2.7	32.2	65,576	47,099	26.7	9.9	11.0

Table B-4. Cities — What: Education, Employment, and Income, 2023—*Continued*

STATE and place code	STATE Place	Educational attainment			Employment status				Household income and benefits				
		Total population 25 years and over	Percent with a high school diploma or less	Percent with a bachelor's degree or more	Total population 16 years and over	Labor force participation (percent)	Percent unemployed	Percent of persons age 16 years and over who worked full-time year-round in the past 12 months	Total households	Median household income in the past 12 months (in 2022 inflation-adjusted dollars)	Income less than $25,000 (percent)	Income greater than $150,000 (percent)	Percent who received cash public assistance or food stamps/ SNAP
	ACS table number:	C15003	C15003	C15003	C23001	C23001	C23001	S2402	B19001	B19049	B19001	B19001	B19058
	column number:	1	2	3	4	5	6	7	8	9	10	11	12
	FLORIDA—Cont.												
1230000	Hialeah city	169,704	56.5	23.8	191,810	62.6	2.8	45.1	78,792	55,310	21.1	10.6	42.4
1232000	Hollywood city	113,037	35.6	34.4	128,511	62.6	3.9	41.7	61,197	60,630	19.6	13.5	14.0
1232275	Homestead city	52,720	48.4	28.6	NA	NA	NA	NA	26,901	71,901	13.7	14.3	15.9
1232610	Horizon West CDP	51,267	12.1	65.9	NA	NA	NA	NA	24,678	144,193	6.8	48.0	3.3
1235000	Jacksonville city	678,498	36.4	33.2	792,677	65.4	2.8	45.2	409,221	68,069	17.1	14.7	14.6
1236100	Kendall CDP	54,859	24.2	49.2	61,024	62.9	2.0	45.5	28,984	75,301	16.4	27.7	8.5
1236950	Kissimmee city	54,781	38.4	30.8	NA	NA	NA	NA	28,697	59,142	19.2	8.2	25.1
1238250	Lakeland city	82,906	37.9	31.0	101,494	59.5	2.0	36.2	51,663	57,131	22.1	13.1	15.0
1239425	Largo city	61,755	41.7	27.1	70,810	62.2	2.5	43.0	37,626	66,220	14.8	11.7	10.7
1239550	Lauderhill city	51,524	55.2	17.2	NA	NA	NA	NA	27,832	45,454	24.7	8.7	22.0
1239925	Lehigh Acres CDP	86,590	58.4	14.9	103,221	58.6	2.2	43.1	40,585	59,645	16.1	7.2	17.5
1243975	Melbourne city	62,739	34.1	32.5	72,089	58.6	2.7	NA	36,223	63,726	17.7	14.0	11.1
1245000	Miami city	346,526	42.5	38.6	389,463	68.4	3.1	51.7	201,102	68,635	20.7	20.9	21.9
1245025	Miami Beach city	60,190	25.0	57.8	65,782	66.9	2.5	44.8	37,894	71,073	22.9	26.8	13.3
1245060	Miami Gardens city	72,379	54.1	17.5	84,609	65.3	4.0	48.4	34,688	67,169	15.3	9.8	25.3
1245975	Miramar city	93,184	30.3	43.1	108,469	68.0	3.4	48.9	44,827	92,097	12.0	27.9	16.2
1249675	North Port city	63,881	35.1	30.0	73,223	58.4	3.0	NA	35,320	82,495	8.3	17.1	14.5
1250750	Ocala city	50,041	41	33	NA	NA	NA	NA	29,755	52,121	22.2	9.1	17.9
1253000	Orlando city	226,644	29.2	41.2	260,045	72.7	3.8	48.7	141,669	69,414	15.9	15.5	16.2
1254000	Palm Bay city	100,277	46.0	21.7	112,928	61.4	4.0	42.2	50,448	67,928	15.8	15.4	12.1
1254200	Palm Coast city	77,129	32.5	31.5	88,992	50.2	1.8	NA	43,003	70,037	14.5	12.1	10.2
1254350	Palm Harbor CDP	47,887	26.1	45.6	NA	NA	NA	NA	27,659	73,852	11.6	21.6	5.3
1255775	Pembroke Pines city	129,920	32.8	40.9	148,301	67.0	2.7	49.9	63,065	86,135	15.8	24.2	12.6
1256825	Pine Hills CDP	49,966	58.2	13.9	NA	NA	NA	NA	24,671	71,735	13.9	6.4	36.2
1257425	Plantation city	70,890	25.0	47.7	80,307	71.5	2.0	55.3	36,927	95,965	11.1	29.5	7.4
1257900	Poinciana CDP	52,359	41.7	23.7	NA	NA	NA	NA	26,064	71,150	8.7	7.8	20.0
1258050	Pompano Beach city	85,530	43.9	30.0	95,113	62.6	1.8	39.8	51,440	61,419	18.9	13.6	9.6
1258350	Port Charlotte CDP	49,965	44.8	19.5	NA	NA	NA	NA	26,105	60,501	16.7	9.1	8.5
1258575	Port Orange city	48,990	34.8	27.6	NA	NA	NA	NA	27,070	67,241	17.8	14.1	11.4
1258715	Port St. Lucie city	176,759	40.5	25.7	200,996	58.1	2.7	42.4	90,069	74,928	11.3	15.0	10.2
1260950	Riverview CDP	81,716	27.2	41.0	NA	NA	NA	NA	44,076	100,475	13.0	24.3	7.8
1262625	St. Cloud city	44,692	29.9	32.9	NA	NA	NA	NA	23,749	91,228	10.9	20.4	13.3
1263000	St. Petersburg city	202,205	28.5	43.0	225,962	65.0	3.1	45.8	123,605	71,743	14.4	18.2	10.1
1263650	Sanford city	47,054	34.9	33.7	NA	NA	NA	NA	26,511	63,643	19.6	9.8	16.9
1268350	Spring Hill CDP	90,071	45.2	19.9	102,220	55.5	3.3	38.4	47,821	68,872	13.4	13.3	13.0
1269700	Sunrise city	69,008	36.5	36.0	79,341	70.2	2.2	48.3	34,455	76,722	18.4	17.8	18.9
1270600	Tallahassee city	111,607	25.4	50.6	174,339	67.8	4.9	40.1	87,824	56,146	21.5	15.0	12.5
1270675	Tamarac city	57,822	42.3	27.8	NA	NA	NA	NA	32,913	56,910	15.4	10.5	10.7
1271000	Tampa city	281,050	32.4	46.2	335,086	67.0	2.5	47.1	169,317	72,851	18.2	23.6	16.0
1271625	The Villages CDP	78,325	23.9	44.6	NA	NA	NA	NA	45,000	73,805	10.7	12.9	2.3
1272145	Town 'n' Country CDP	60,555	47.8	32.6	68,427	67.9	3.6	47.5	31,323	66,969	15.8	14.4	19.8
1275875	Wesley Chapel CDP	52,265	25.2	45.1	NA	NA	NA	NA	26,661	112,045	9.0	32.4	5.9
1276582	Weston city	44,501	14.5	65.7	53,539	68.8	1.9	NA	22,243	135,764	7.1	45.4	4.1
1276600	West Palm Beach city	90,620	35.8	39.1	103,275	69.0	2.8	48.1	50,890	83,205	12.0	22.6	11.5
13000	**GEORGIA**	7,448,119	36.9	35.4	8,818,867	64.1	4.4	70.6	4,150,138	74,632	16.2	19.6	13.0
1301052	Albany city	42,644	48.6	22.4	52,492	57.4	7.3	NA	28,379	45,624	29.5	4.2	41.6
1301696	Alpharetta city	48,151	11.2	70.5	54,790	72.8	4.8	53.1	26,224	140,188	7.7	45.2	2.3
1303440	Athens-Clarke County unified government (balance)	75,728	28.3	49.9	109,772	64.1	2.8	40.2	54,856	53,775	25.9	10.8	9.3
1304000	Atlanta city	353,754	22.1	59.6	430,772	69.7	4.0	48.6	233,047	85,880	20.2	27.8	13.8
1304204	Augusta-Richmond County consolidated government (balance)	134,074	43.1	24.1	162,710	62.9	4.5	38.7	76,232	51,943	25.5	8.0	20.9
1319000	Columbus city	133,684	38.4	28.2	157,561	59.7	3.6	37.7	82,007	51,835	24.6	9.6	15.1
1342425	Johns Creek city	56,370	11.4	74.8	64,416	67.5	3.1	48.8	28,800	151,344	5.3	50.7	5.5
1349008	Macon-Bibb County	104,066	41.8	26.3	122,742	57.7	4.2	37.7	60,919	51,254	26.8	12.7	25.5
1367284	Roswell city	63,156	12.1	69.5	72,885	71.1	1.3	49.7	35,275	119,657	10.5	44.6	2.6
1368516	Sandy Springs city	81,079	13.3	68.6	91,036	76.4	1.4	57.7	50,453	110,401	7.8	32.5	2.9
1369000	Savannah city	98,649	34.7	36.6	122,251	63.9	2.9	42.6	60,129	56,823	22.5	11.1	15.6

Table B-4. Cities — What: Education, Employment, and Income, 2023—*Continued*

STATE and place code	STATE Place	Educational attainment: Total population 25 years and over	Educational attainment: Percent with a high school diploma or less	Educational attainment: Percent with a bachelor's degree or more	Employment status: Total population 16 years and over	Employment status: Labor force participation (percent)	Employment status: Percent unemployed	Employment status: Percent of persons age 16 years and over who worked full-time year-round in the past 12 months	Household income and benefits: Total households	Household income and benefits: Median household income in the past 12 months (in 2022 inflation-adjusted dollars)	Household income and benefits: Income less than $25,000 (percent)	Household income and benefits: Income greater than $150,000 (percent)	Household income and benefits: Percent who received cash public assistance or food stamps/ SNAP
	ACS table number:	C15003	C15003	C15003	C23001	C23001	C23001	S2402	B19001	B19049	B19001	B19001	B19058
	column number:	1	2	3	4	5	6	7	8	9	10	11	12
	GEORGIA—Cont.												
1372122	South Fulton city	71,226	22.8	43.1	84,013	69.9	2.0	53.1	40,298	79,871	10.1	21.0	11.8
1380508	Warner Robins city	54,879	36.8	33.0	65,051	63.4	5.7	41.1	33,527	59,646	16.6	9.8	13.3
15000	**HAWAII**	1,024,897	33.3	37.0	1,172,357	63.0	3.3	63.5	493,898	95,322	12.4	28.4	12.2
1571550	Urban Honolulu CDP	260,232	31.6	43.0	292,496	65.7	2.0	43.2	137,203	84,907	15.0	26.2	12.5
16000	**IDAHO**	1,305,704	33.8	32.1	1,558,313	62.6	3.6	65.5	733,244	74,942	12.6	17.1	8.0
1608830	Boise City city	169,035	24.9	47.9	199,964	66.7	2.3	45.1	104,336	79,977	11.9	20.8	7.3
1612250	Caldwell city		41,599	50.5	18.4	50,532	70.4	4.2	NA	21,765	67,117	14.6	10.7
1639700	Idaho Falls city	39,681	34.7	34.1	NA	NA	NA	NA	24,008	63,049	15.8	15.5	15.8
1652120	Meridian city	88,650	23.5	41.1	105,177	68.1	2.1	46.9	50,116	100,307	7.6	26.1	3.7
1656260	Nampa city	74,697	38.0	28.7	89,026	70.0	2.3	49.7	41,060	71,752	9.7	12.1	8.0
17000	**ILLINOIS**	8,710,996	34.7	38.3	10,192,179	65.4	4.7	68.8	5,071,288	80,306	15.0	22.2	14.8
1702154	Arlington Heights village	56,472	15.9	62.2	NA	NA	NA	NA	32,370	106,051	7.9	33.5	4.1
1703012	Aurora city	113,417	34.5	40.8	138,587	73.7	4.1	52.0	61,278	89,658	9.8	25.7	13.9
1706587	Bloomington city	52,052	24.7	54.4	62,139	68.1	1.6	50.3	33,447	77,577	15.0	24.0	13.5
1707133	Bolingbrook village	51,851	34.6	40.5	NA	NA	NA	NA	25,142	114,296	4.6	32.1	7.8
1712385	Champaign city	47,600	20.5	56.6	77,792	57.5	1.5	36.0	40,599	46,232	30.9	11.7	9.8
1714000	Chicago city	1,907,364	32.9	45.7	2,223,686	68.5	4.4	46.4	1,179,081	74,474	18.8	21.9	20.1
1714351	Cicero town	50,269	71.4	8.0	65,804	68.5	2.5	NA	24,167	74,353	8.8	19.4	22.4
1718823	Decatur city	46,189	49.7	18.4	54,452	55.6	4.2	36.5	30,783	46,564	23.9	7.4	30.0
1723074	Elgin city	78,897	48.0	26.6	94,791	68.3	3.4	46.6	41,062	83,539	10.0	21.1	12.0
1724582	Evanston city	48,710	14.5	73.0	62,465	58.9	3.6	34.1	31,310	97,085	14.3	31.2	10.5
1738570	Joliet city	100,574	45.7	23.3	119,408	69.6	3.0	46.4	52,512	86,054	14.7	17.2	20.0
1751622	Naperville city	103,493	11.5	71.6	121,120	67.2	2.0	48.1	55,580	152,181	6.0	51.3	5.3
1757225	Palatine village	45,510	30.7	47.6	NA	NA	NA	NA	27,531	89,725	11.1	26.6	11.3
1759000	Peoria city	71,985	34.2	38.8	87,809	63.1	5.0	37.0	49,577	52,796	29.9	17.5	21.5
1765000	Rockford city	100,100	45.2	22.9	116,871	61.5	4.2	38.4	62,552	59,451	22.3	9.0	30.7
1768003	Schaumburg village	54,055	21.7	53.5	NA	NA	NA	NA	31,791	87,202	9.0	26.1	8.5
1770122	Skokie village	45,410	28.9	52.0	52,528	60.5	1.9	NA	23,942	86,125	11.1	24.2	12.5
1772000	Springfield city	80,626	32.1	37.5	94,060	59.3	2.9	40.9	51,843	63,849	18.4	15.8	14.1
1779293	Waukegan city	60,629	57.9	20.6	70,990	69.5	3.5	NA	31,784	72,841	13.1	15.4	12.7
18000	**INDIANA**	4,614,970	41.7	30.2	5,470,753	64.4	3.6	69.5	2,754,881	69,477	15.8	15.3	9.3
1805860	Bloomington city	35,578	17.3	64.0	67,123	59.5	4.4	28.9	33,738	41,799	31.4	8.1	5.2
1810342	Carmel city	66,447	9.4	76.0	79,364	73.2	1.6	52.8	38,523	143,676	4.6	48.2	2.0
1822000	Evansville city	76,961	46.9	24.0	90,598	63.0	3.1	44.3	51,696	52,318	20.1	8.4	15.9
1823278	Fishers city	68,157	14.3	65.3	NA	NA	NA	NA	38,270	121,382	6.1	41.0	4.3
1825000	Fort Wayne city	175,944	37.3	30.4	212,461	66.9	3.4	44.2	115,195	57,138	17.7	8.7	11.0
1827000		Gary city	42,683	52.6	14.3	NA	NA	NA	NA	27,688	35,033	32.3	6.3
1831000	Hammond city	49,640	54.6	15.2	60,422	58.4	5.3	39.2	29,271	51,773	26.2	8.0	20.5
1836003	Indianapolis city (balance)	574,198	37.2	36.6	681,439	70.1	3.1	48.5	368,064	66,629	16.9	14.1	11.7
1840788	Lafayette city	44,012	46.2	28.8	53,377	64.6	1.8	45.7	31,331	51,328	21.0	5.8	11.0
1851876	Muncie city		38,297	47.4	26.6	56,845	59.6	3.3	NA	26,505	43,507	27.6	5.3
1854180	Noblesville city	50,689	22.3	52.0	NA	NA	NA	NA	28,543	107,177	11.7	30.0	5.1
1871000	South Bend city	67,841	43.8	28.6	80,931	65.9	4.3	41.5	42,331	55,767	24.2	8.6	17.3
19000	**IOWA**	2,166,425	36.7	31.5	2,570,587	66.3	2.8	70.0	1,337,243	71,433	14.3	15.8	9.3
1901855	Ames city	null	NA	NA	59,477	63.7	2.5	31.6	26,633	58,693	18.0	13.4	3.4
1902305	Ankeny city	48,465	21.4	51.9	NA	NA	NA	NA	30,257	105,862	6.1	29.6	7.3
1912000	Cedar Rapids city	92,504	34.0	31.9	112,403	67.4	2.5	45.0	58,123	66,720	14.0	12.7	12.7
1919000	Davenport city	68,155	36.0	31.5	81,203	67.6	2.9	45.2	44,171	69,595	14.8	12.4	12.2
1921000	Des Moines city	139,269	42.3	31.2	169,347	72.0	2.9	50.6	90,465	60,882	15.4	11.4	15.8
1938595	Iowa City city	38,490	17.1	62.0	65,862	66.8	1.2	33.7	30,588	50,135	28.1	13.2	5.2
1973335	Sioux City city	53,781	47.7	18.9	66,659	65.1	2.1	42.8	32,278	62,350	17.9	11.2	20.2
1982425	Waterloo city	43,838	46.8	20.1	51,173	63.5	1.7	43.3	28,471	52,320	21.2	7.3	15.1
1983910	West Des Moines city	52,510	20.3	54.8	59,062	69.3	2.0	49.7	33,094	83,637	12.9	21.9	6.7
20000	**KANSAS**	1,956,252	33.4	35.8	2,339,516	66.2	3.2	69.4	1,188,340	70,333	14.8	16.1	7.3
2036000	Kansas City city	96,085	52	20	115,456	64.7	3.0	45.7	57,487	60,739	18.2	8.9	12.0
2038900	Lawrence city	56,697	18.2	56.9	82,350	67.4	3.6	39.9	41,551	62,608	21.4	13.9	7.3

Table B-4. Cities — What: Education, Employment, and Income, 2023—*Continued*

STATE and place code	STATE Place	Educational attainment			Employment status				Household income and benefits				
		Total population 25 years and over	Percent with a high school diploma or less	Percent with a bachelor's degree or more	Total population 16 years and over	Labor force participation (percent)	Percent unemployed	Percent of persons age 16 years and over who worked full-time year-round in the past 12 months	Total households	Median household income in the past 12 months (in 2022 inflation-adjusted dollars)	Income less than $25,000 (percent)	Income greater than $150,000 (percent)	Percent who received cash public assistance or food stamps/ SNAP
	ACS table number:	C15003	C15003	C15003	C23001	C23001	C23001	S2402	B19001	B19049	B19001	B19001	B19058
	column number:	1	2	3	4	5	6	7	8	9	10	11	12
	KANSAS—Cont.												
2052575	Olathe city	95,824	22.4	49.4	113,730	73.7	0.9	52.7	53,252	105,915	7.1	31.3	1.3
2053775	Overland Park city	137,934	15.2	63.1	158,484	70.7	2.0	52.4	85,022	97,176	9.3	31.7	2.5
2064500	Shawnee city	47,856	19.4	54.2	56,895	72.8	2.0	52.6	28,168	100,016	7.1	30.1	0.9
2071000	Topeka city	87,020	41.5	28.5	103,228	60.3	2.4	41.9	55,148	52,417	20.4	8.3	13.3
2079000	Wichita city	264,126	36.7	31.9	314,550	66.2	2.7	45.4	163,555	61,281	17.1	12.9	11.8
21000	**KENTUCKY**	3,107,275	43.5	27.8	3,633,664	60.3	4.1	69.9	1,853,603	61,118	20.8	12.9	13.6
2108902	Bowling Green city	41,752	32.9	36.0	61,670	66.9	2.8	NA	32,904	47,813	22.6	4.8	8.9
2146027	Lexington-Fayette urban county	210,210	25.8	49.8	261,590	68.6	2.9	45.1	141,680	66,392	17.0	18.2	8.3
2148006	Louisville/Jefferson County metro government (balance)	429,182	37.6	33.1	498,152	63.2	2.8	43.8	264,694	61,488	19.8	14.0	14.0
22000	**LOUISIANA**	3,102,893	45.3	27.0	3,635,137	59.2	4.8	69.5	1,833,915	58,229	23.0	13.7	17.7
2205000	Baton Rouge city	127,825	39.8	33.9	177,008	58.9	4.3	36.7	86,978	41,651	30.6	10.9	20.1
2239475	Kenner city	43,800	47.9	25.0	49,250	57.9	2.6	NA	23,924	68,166	19.7	12.2	10.8
2240735	Lafayette city	85,108	36.8	37.5	99,364	63.3	1.5	45.4	53,953	61,258	20.8	12.9	11.5
2241155	Lake Charles city	51,816	34.2	36.6	65,551	62.2	2.4	NA	33,140	55,420	24.1	12.0	18.2
2250115	Metairie CDP	99,121	31.8	39.9	110,633	66.6	2.0	46.2	61,486	65,465	14.8	18.0	6.6
2255000	New Orleans city	259,764	29.8	44.7	301,119	61.7	3.2	40.5	155,005	55,580	26.7	17.0	18.6
2270000	Shreveport city	120,946	44.1	27.9	139,537	56.9	2.9	38.9	78,443	48,486	26.2	7.6	23.7
23000	**MAINE**	1,039,460	34.5	37.0	1,180,683	62.1	3.2	66.2	616,085	73,733	15.0	16.5	13.5
2360545	Portland city	52,337	17.2	61.8	60,595	73.2	2.1	48.5	34,067	83,399	9.1	20.8	9.9
24000	**MARYLAND**	4,297,439	32.7	43.7	4,979,552	67.5	3.9	72.2	2,384,715	98,678	11.8	30.4	10.9
2404000	Baltimore city	395,443	38.6	37.1	459,130	64.1	3.2	45.5	259,385	59,579	24.4	16.4	22.4
2407125	Bethesda CDP	48,491	6.4	85.0	56,498	71.6	2.0	NA	28,973	191,198	5.3	58.3	4.0
2419125	Columbia CDP	70,238	14.3	59.3	82,143	72.5	3.0	50.8	42,978	115,564	10.4	39.6	8.6
2426000	Ellicott City CDP	50,590	17.9	66.1	58,235	59.6	1.1	NA	25,715	148,677	5.3	49.5	4.2
2430325	Frederick city	59,049	33.0	47.9	68,347	71.4	1.3	50.8	34,562	96,084	8.4	28.0	9.8
2431175	Gaithersburg city	47,646	30.9	53.4	NA	NA	NA	NA	25,813	100,387	10.2	31.4	12.8
2432025	Germantown CDP	66,982	29.5	48.8	79,978	70.7	2.4	48.4	34,372	101,446	10.2	31.4	6.7
2432650	Glen Burnie CDP	52,681	49.0	24.4	61,009	69.4	3.3	45.3	29,159	77,549	15.7	16.1	16.0
2467675	Rockville city	47,289	21.3	63.6	NA	NA	NA	NA	26,261	122,294	9.0	39.0	5.9
2472450	Silver Spring CDP	59,668	23.5	63.3	68,170	79.2	3.7	55.2	35,086	100,116	10.8	31.7	8.3
2481175	Waldorf CDP	55,972	37.6	31.7	NA	NA	NA	NA	31,345	96,304	15.5	23.3	10.5
25000	**MASSACHUSETTS**	4,975,152	31.4	47.8	5,828,175	67.2	3.9	67.1	2,800,984	99,858	14.0	32.3	16.6
2507000	Boston city	460,213	27.9	55.8	568,366	71.3	3.0	46.8	288,129	96,931	18.4	33.2	22.1
2509000	Brockton city	70,423	48.9	20.1	81,446	66.0	4.2	43.3	35,485	79,990	18.6	20.8	34.7
2511000	Cambridge city	79,055	9.1	82.7	106,018	69.6	2.3	46.5	49,310	134,307	10.6	44.5	6.9
2523000	Fall River city	65,972	55.6	19.7	75,783	63.4	2.5	42.7	43,425	52,978	27.6	10.9	36.4
2524960	Framingham city	47,997	36.9	46.7	56,180	74.8	2.2	51.6	25,727	103,841	10.6	31.5	11.2
2529405	Haverhill city	46,344	38.4	36.8	54,110	71.7	4.4	50.1	27,274	87,309	13.3	23.5	21.1
2534550	Lawrence city	58,807	66.3	15.3	70,785	68.4	3.3	NA	32,631	58,079	23.6	12.5	45.0
2537000	Lowell city	79,104	46.3	32.6	95,448	67.1	3.9	41.9	43,220	73,083	20.4	17.3	27.7
2537490	Lynn city	68,335	53.3	25.3	82,172	64.0	2.1	44.1	36,403	73,723	19.7	23.7	30.4
2537875	Malden city	49,720	39.6	45.4	NA	NA	NA	NA	27,716	88,003	13.8	25.8	19.8
2545000	New Bedford city	67,401	59.1	17.4	78,259	60.1	4.8	35.6	41,300	53,583	27.2	8.6	37.1
2545560	Newton city	60,281	7.2	82.0	73,351	65.4	2.0	42.7	32,074	185,154	8.7	59.3	4.9
2555745	Quincy city	78,115	28.8	52.6	88,848	71.1	5.3	46.2	46,448	92,085	17.7	27.0	17.3
2562535	Somerville city	63,101	17.9	69.9	74,036	79.1	3.2	58.8	37,108	126,619	13.7	39.9	13.0
2567000	Springfield city	98,360	58.4	18.1	120,902	55.2	2.6	32.6	56,229	47,101	30.9	9.2	49.2
2582000	Worcester city	137,169	41.5	38.3	172,195	64.9	3.5	40.1	81,973	69,262	19.9	15.9	28.4
26000	**MICHIGAN**	7,007,856	35.7	32.7	8,186,295	61.7	4.5	66.7	4,107,809	69,183	16.9	16.5	14.6
2603000	Ann Arbor city	67,938	9.2	78.4	103,053	61.3	1.9	35.3	49,077	76,207	19.2	26.4	6.9
2621000	Dearborn city	68,022	41.4	31.3	81,877	52.8	3.7	32.1	38,777	51,670	28.7	12.5	29.4
2622000	Detroit city	416,566	46.5	18.7	491,892	55.1	5.9	34.2	255,857	38,080	36.2	5.7	38.4
2627440	Farmington Hills city	63,202	21.0	56.5	70,626	64.5	3.0	45.1	37,173	90,598	13.4	31.9	8.3

Table B-4. Cities — What: Education, Employment, and Income, 2023—*Continued*

STATE and place code	STATE Place	Educational attainment			Employment status				Household income and benefits				
		Total population 25 years and over	Percent with a high school diploma or less	Percent with a bachelor's degree or more	Total population 16 years and over	Labor force participation (percent)	Percent unemployed	Percent of persons age 16 years and over who worked full-time year-round in the past 12 months	Total households	Median household income in the past 12 months (in 2022 inflation-adjusted dollars)	Income less than $25,000 (percent)	Income greater than $150,000 (percent)	Percent who received cash public assistance or food stamps/ SNAP
	ACS table number:	C15003	C15003	C15003	C23001	C23001	C23001	S2402	B19001	B19049	B19001	B19001	B19058
	column number:	1	2	3	4	5	6	7	8	9	10	11	12
	MICHIGAN—Cont.												
2629000	Flint city	52,322	56.5	13.2	61,724	57.9	7.7	NA	33,879	33,141	41.1	2.4	40.9
2634000	Grand Rapids city	129,223	30.0	41.6	163,533	70.2	3.9	44.3	80,311	70,258	18.2	13.5	17.9
2642160	Kalamazoo city	41,741	24.8	41.7	61,096	66.3	2.6	36.2	30,482	50,044	22.1	7.0	18.7
2646000	Lansing city	76,681	34.3	30.9	93,281	69.4	4.3	42.9	52,849	55,197	22.3	8.5	18.7
2649000	Livonia city	67,713	25.8	45.4	75,093	63.8	1.0	46.6	38,023	95,003	11.8	23.7	3.5
2659440	Novi city	47,293	18.3	62.2	NA	NA	NA	NA	26,962	97,092	8.0	32.4	4.8
2669035	Rochester Hills city	52,828	19.0	59.0	62,672	64.3	2.4	44.2	28,914	105,784	9.0	32.2	6.1
2674900	Southfield city	58,529	24.4	44.3	65,299	63.0	3.9	44.3	35,348	65,497	19.2	15.7	15.8
2676460	Sterling Heights city	94,885	40.1	30.1	109,770	61.3	2.5	40.1	52,105	73,702	15.2	14.8	14.9
2680700	Troy city	63,635	18.2	65.1	72,177	68.2	2.6	50.7	34,743	106,965	7.8	34.6	4.8
2684000	Warren city	96,014	45.1	19.5	108,936	62.7	3.0	42.4	54,644	60,572	16.6	8.4	22.3
2686000	Westland city	60,476	49.1	18.8	68,814	65.6	3.3	44.7	35,723	55,821	17.7	7.7	12.8
2688940	Wyoming city	53,133	39.0	29.7	NA	NA	NA	NA	30,586	73,950	7.1	10.2	12.1
27000	**MINNESOTA**	3,941,575	29.0	40.0	4,602,443	68.4	3.0	67.7	2,344,432	85,086	12.2	22.7	8.8
2706382	Blaine city	47,589	29.1	40.1	NA	NA	NA	NA	25,670	100,172	5.4	27.3	9.0
2706616	Bloomington city	63,446	28.3	44.3	72,877	67.7	1.9	43.4	39,370	86,206	12.6	23.5	7.0
2707966	Brooklyn Park city	54,104	34.1	31.5	NA	NA	NA	NA	29,325	87,532	12.5	26.2	12.8
2717000	Duluth city	57,484	24.0	44.4	75,652	68.0	2.3	39.4	38,843	61,163	17.5	13.8	12.5
2717288	Eagan city	48,979	21.6	52.1	55,776	67.7	3.1	47.2	27,978	101,896	8.0	29.4	6.0
2735180	Lakeville city	49,274	19.3	53.0	NA	NA	NA	NA	25,289	147,992	3.8	49.3	2.6
2740166	Maple Grove city	52,598	16.5	56.1	NA	NA	NA	NA	29,987	104,200	7.5	34.5	6.3
2743000	Minneapolis city	290,863	20.4	58.8	355,335	74.9	2.9	47.6	198,866	81,001	16.0	22.5	12.3
2751730	Plymouth city	53,229	12.7	66.2	59,103	72.2	1.5	50.5	29,393	130,793	7.1	44.4	4.3
2754880	Rochester city	85,181	23.1	52.6	98,234	69.5	2.1	47.6	51,184	85,240	12.3	24.1	6.9
2756896	St. Cloud city	40,012	33.3	33.1	54,838	66.4	3.7	37.3	25,769	60,782	18.3	12.0	17.2
2758000	St. Paul city	200,626	31.1	46.5	243,293	71.2	2.8	45.4	126,409	73,975	16.3	18.1	16.1
2771428	Woodbury city	53,183	17.0	61.0	NA	NA	NA	NA	31,280	120,588	4.3	38.1	5.7
28000	**MISSISSIPPI**	1,980,147	41.7	25.5	2,354,139	57.6	4.8	70.6	1,166,617	54,203	24.1	10.8	13.3
2829700	Gulfport city	48,760	47.1	20.6	57,086	56.5	3.2	38.7	31,011	47,564	26.1	6.4	22.0
2836000	Jackson city	94,645	43.0	29.0	114,951	62.6	4.9	43.7	60,636	42,336	31.2	8.4	18.9
29000	**MISSOURI**	4,255,810	37.4	33.2	4,997,010	63.9	3.4	69.6	2,556,271	68,545	15.8	15.5	10.2
2915670	Columbia city	76,563	21.4	55.9	109,480	65.3	2.2	41.3	53,894	62,972	20.1	14.5	6.7
2935000	Independence city	83,879	40.5	25.1	93,999	62.6	2.3	45.3	51,311	61,432	15.9	8.2	12.3
2938000	Kansas City city	356,133	32.2	40.3	413,554	68.5	2.3	49.4	227,773	65,225	17.1	16.0	11.1
2941348	Lee's Summit city	66,605	17.4	51.8	82,368	72.8	1.9	55.1	40,435	100,625	6.4	28.0	2.4
2954074	O'Fallon city	64,118	26.1	43.1	NA	NA	NA	NA	34,714	103,301	7.3	30.3	3.1
2964082	St. Charles city	49,070	29.6	42.1	NA	NA	NA	NA	31,316	78,359	11.5	18.5	7.1
2964550	St. Joseph city	47,659	52.2	19.0	55,841	60.6	1.8	41.7	28,196	57,205	20.0	8.4	18.5
2965000	St. Louis city	205,959	30.4	45.1	237,461	69.1	3.2	47.3	150,404	56,245	24.0	14.4	17.5
2970000	Springfield city	109,693	34.7	28.8	143,587	64.0	1.9	40.5	79,707	47,728	20.2	7.7	13.4
30000	**MONTANA**	795,845	33.6	34.6	924,869	63.0	2.7	65.2	472,867	70,804	15.8	15.4	8.1
3006550	Billings city	83,641	35.3	34.6	95,724	65.7	1.5	44.8	52,878	67,028	15.0	15.0	9.4
3050200	Missoula city	52,389	19.4	53.2	66,145	70.1	2.0	44.0	35,775	70,277	18.1	14.9	10.1
31000	**NEBRASKA**	1,307,246	32.1	35.3	1,558,006	69.0	2.6	70.6	813,864	74,590	14.2	17.5	8.3
3128000	Lincoln city	184,415	25.6	42.5	239,098	69.1	2.1	44.9	126,828	68,050	15.9	15.3	9.0
3137000	Omaha city	318,877	28.6	42.9	382,369	70.3	2.3	49.4	204,135	71,238	15.1	18.5	10.7
32000	**NEVADA**	2,253,253	39.1	28.7	2,594,279	63.5	4.5	68.5	1,224,685	76,364	14.0	19.0	13.9
3223770	Enterprise CDP	171,688	30.4	35.4	198,007	72.9	2.1	52.1	90,011	91,225	7.9	24.4	9.0
3231900	Henderson city	247,576	29.3	38.6	274,663	60.6	2.1	42.9	136,680	82,476	13.6	23.5	9.4
3240000	Las Vegas city	459,087	39.9	28.8	532,885	64.2	3.4	43.2	252,848	73,784	14.7	19.4	16.9
3251800	North Las Vegas city	187,503	48.6	20.4	222,189	64.6	3.0	47.0	92,288	78,949	13.2	16.3	16.1
3254600	Paradise CDP	128,707	45.7	24.1	148,819	67.6	5.3	43.7	74,847	61,680	19.9	12.8	20.2
3260600	Reno city	193,483	32.3	36.9	228,125	67.4	2.8	45.3	114,623	80,365	13.5	21.3	10.7
3268400	Sparks city	77,524	35.0	26.7	89,378	68.1	1.7	47.6	41,595	86,081	9.5	19.6	9.4
3268585	Spring Valley CDP	147,181	39.1	31.9	167,366	68.8	3.5	45.7	82,320	71,988	14.4	16.0	10.4
3271400	Sunrise Manor CDP	134,444	61.1	14.6	160,342	61.7	3.8	42.8	67,326	52,496	20.1	9.3	29.0

Table B-4. Cities — What: Education, Employment, and Income, 2023—*Continued*

STATE and place code	STATE Place	Educational attainment			Employment status				Household income and benefits				
		Total population 25 years and over	Percent with a high school diploma or less	Percent with a bachelor's degree or more	Total population 16 years and over	Labor force participation (percent)	Percent unemployed	Percent of persons age 16 years and over who worked full-time year-round in the past 12 months	Total households	Median household income in the past 12 months (in 2022 inflation-adjusted dollars)	Income less than $25,000 (percent)	Income greater than $150,000 (percent)	Percent who received cash public assistance or food stamps/ SNAP
	ACS table number:	C15003	C15003	C15003	C23001	C23001	C23001	S2402	B19001	B19049	B19001	B19001	B19058
	column number:	1	2	3	4	5	6	7	8	9	10	11	12
33000	**NEW HAMPSHIRE**	1,030,965	32.7	40.7	1,184,596	66.5	2.6	69.8	569,493	96,838	10.7	28.2	7.3
3345140	Manchester city	83,366	39.0	34.7	98,182	72.3	2.0	52.1	50,053	78,825	13.4	19.8	12.3
3350260	Nashua city	65,708	35.8	41.0	73,773	72.8	1.3	54.4	36,451	97,667	8.5	29.8	8.4
34000	**NEW JERSEY**	6,511,081	34.5	43.8	7,520,182	66.9	4.7	68.8	3,538,457	99,781	12.1	31.9	10.4
3403580	Bayonne city	48,751	41.3	38.4	NA	NA	NA	NA	30,335	73,669	22.7	15.7	15.8
3410000	Camden city	47,840	63.3	12.4	57,055	62.7	6.7	NA	27,511	35,129	33.2	4.7	50.5
3413690	Clifton city	64,886	40.0	35.9	71,845	67.7	4.7	47.5	31,968	98,598	15.1	28.1	12.5
3419390	East Orange city	50,770	46.9	22.5	59,051	64.7	5.2	NA	30,360	56,293	21.4	10.7	20.9
3421000	Elizabeth city	83,518	58.4	17.3	102,253	71.5	5.7	49.4	45,491	71,715	14.4	15.9	18.3
3436000	Jersey City city	213,222	26.6	56.8	241,162	71.5	3.3	53.4	130,020	91,286	17.0	31.1	16.2
3438580	Lakewood CDP	25,444	43.6	33.0	NA	NA	NA	NA	13,406	70,483	9.7	15.4	18.2
3451000	Newark city	199,201	59.4	20.9	237,987	64.9	6.3	41.3	114,599	53,818	24.9	10.8	25.4
3456550	Passaic city	40,536	62.6	21.6	50,975	67.7	4.3	38.1	21,234	50,893	28.1	11.3	43.8
3457000	Paterson city	99,621	69.1	11.8	120,941	63.7	2.8	40.3	51,969	56,907	25.3	11.0	35.2
3473110	Toms River CDP	67,709	40.1	34.6	75,843	60.7	1.4	43.2	36,998	90,593	11.6	28.0	6.5
3474000	Trenton city	55,916	63.4	13.8	67,972	62.6	6.2	NA	32,131	49,117	26.2	8.6	23.8
3474630	Union City city	44,975	51.3	32.3	52,904	73.1	4.5	48.7	25,001	86,123	14.6	19.6	24.1
35000	**NEW MEXICO**	1,471,057	37.6	31.6	1,723,938	58.6	4.7	65.7	856,580	62,268	20.5	14.4	20.8
3502000	Albuquerque city	399,150	30.7	39.6	464,550	64.7	2.8	43.1	243,664	67,907	18.1	15.3	19.3
3539380	Las Cruces city	74,364	31.2	38.5	94,437	62.7	3.5	38.4	50,409	55,012	24.6	11.4	24.5
3563460	Rio Rancho city	76,301	27.0	34.1	89,864	60.8	2.0	43.2	42,054	88,366	9.4	21.7	11.7
3570500	Santa Fe city	68,066	33.4	44.1	77,630	60.4	2.5	40.9	42,397	70,940	15.7	17.7	13.0
36000	**NEW YORK**	13,885,155	35.9	40.6	16,085,030	63.0	5.0	67.6	7,809,267	82,095	16.7	25.6	17.2
3601000	Albany city	63,495	28.2	47.5	88,768	62.9	4.8	38.5	44,875	61,390	18.7	11.5	18.0
3611000	Buffalo city	187,364	42.9	31.2	222,075	59.5	3.7	37.9	123,347	46,458	28.8	8.7	30.4
3615000	Cheektowaga CDP	54,901	38.4	28.4	63,932	62.2	1.5	43.7	34,150	61,246	16.0	9.6	16.7
3649121	Mount Vernon city	50,865	42.8	35.4	57,581	66.8	4.6	NA	27,369	77,190	22.5	20.4	19.7
3650617	New Rochelle city	58,503	30.5	53.5	70,348	66.6	5.4	NA	29,052	128,199	13.0	45.7	11.1
3651000	New York city	5,956,052	37.9	42.5	6,800,583	64.0	4.0	42.8	3,394,750	76,577	20.3	25.6	23.1
3663000	Rochester city	141,762	43.2	29.3	171,955	62.7	4.9	38.7	91,471	48,618	27.4	8.5	33.5
3665508	Schenectady city	44,550	46.9	24.1	56,012	56.5	3.7	NA	28,730	54,773	26.3	8.5	29.0
3673000	Syracuse city	88,881	40.6	31.6	119,326	58.2	3.9	32.8	60,652	47,525	30.7	7.3	31.0
3684000	Yonkers city	145,309	43.0	35.1	171,441	66.5	4.8	42.5	79,190	81,097	18.4	23.1	20.3
37000	**NORTH CAROLINA**	7,487,552	33.9	36.8	8,792,430	63.2	4.0	69.1	4,392,669	70,804	15.8	17.7	13.0
3701520	Apex town	46,880	9.5	73.8	NA	NA	NA	NA	27,306	151,386	6.7	50.6	1.8
3702140	Asheville city	71,123	20.8	55.6	81,901	64.0	1.4	42.5	39,811	66,032	21.7	16.2	12.4
3710740	Cary town	125,558	12.9	71.5	144,080	68.4	2.4	49.3	71,248	129,607	7.0	43.1	2.9
3712000	Charlotte city	618,750	25.9	50.1	735,831	72.3	2.5	53.6	375,680	80,581	12.5	23.0	10.6
3714100	Concord city	73,411	28.4	43.6	84,231	72.6	4.8	53.5	42,777	82,262	10.7	23.1	15.5
3719000	Durham city	204,551	22.0	59.3	244,035	70.9	2.2	50.7	127,514	80,064	14.2	23.5	6.4
3722920	Fayetteville city	129,612	30.5	30.8	164,877	68.5	3.4	34.5	83,410	59,732	17.3	11.1	20.2
3725580	Gastonia city	56,083	37.4	29.5	65,295	63.3	2.7	45.3	33,496	63,597	19.0	14.0	19.0
3728000	Greensboro city	195,337	29.7	40.7	245,720	66.3	2.6	45.4	125,752	61,747	18.6	14.8	18.4
3728080	Greenville city	51,321	26.5	40.4	74,120	65.2	6.9	37.2	41,037	51,628	26.6	8.7	15.0
3731400	High Point city	74,840	37.3	31.5	93,929	61.0	2.7	42.6	45,442	57,436	19.7	13.2	19.7
3734200	Jacksonville city	30,975	38.5	23.9	59,830	78.3	2.1	NA	24,538	58,146	19.7	8.1	18.3
3755000	Raleigh city	329,001	20.6	55.7	395,002	73.1	2.2	53.0	211,433	86,309	10.8	24.6	8.2
3774440	Wilmington city	84,440	19.2	50.9	107,109	66.0	2.1	41.5	59,730	71,362	17.4	19.0	11.1
3775000	Winston-Salem city	163,783	29.6	44.6	201,586	62.0	2.8	42.3	107,693	59,189	19.8	13.3	16.1
38000	**NORTH DAKOTA**	520,006	29.8	33.6	622,500	69.4	2.8	68.3	338,059	76,525	14.6	17.9	7.7
3807200	Bismarck city	53,148	25.4	39.6	62,277	65.6	1.6	NA	34,598	75,846	19.6	17.4	7.2
3825700	Fargo city	83,777	22.5	43.9	108,324	74.6	3.4	50.3	60,510	61,422	17.2	13.8	8.4
39000	**OHIO**	8,172,692	39.9	32.0	9,520,298	63.5	4.0	68.7	4,917,309	67,769	16.8	16.3	13.0
3901000	Akron city	126,633	40.3	26.3	153,653	65.3	5.4	41.0	85,349	50,025	25.4	7.1	25.3
3912000	Canton city	46,280	51.4	16.5	55,934	58.2	3.2	NA	29,864	39,692	30.3	3.8	27.7

Table B-4. Cities — What: Education, Employment, and Income, 2023—*Continued*

STATE and place code	STATE Place	Educational attainment			Employment status				Household income and benefits				
		Total population 25 years and over	Percent with a high school diploma or less	Percent with a bachelor's degree or more	Total population 16 years and over	Labor force participation (percent)	Percent unemployed	Percent of persons age 16 years and over who worked full-time year-round in the past 12 months	Total households	Median household income in the past 12 months (in 2022 inflation-adjusted dollars)	Income less than $25,000 (percent)	Income greater than $150,000 (percent)	Percent who received cash public assistance or food stamps/ SNAP
	ACS table number:	C15003	C15003	C15003	C23001	C23001	C23001	S2402	B19001	B19049	B19001	B19001	B19058
	column number:	1	2	3	4	5	6	7	8	9	10	11	12
	OHIO—Cont.												
3915000	Cincinnati city	209,214	30.8	45.0	256,931	66.7	4.2	44.5	149,698	54,314	24.4	14.2	20.0
3916000	Cleveland city	251,031	50.6	22.5	298,141	60.0	5.7	36.4	168,307	39,041	34.2	6.7	31.4
3918000	Columbus city	602,968	35.2	39.6	730,901	70.8	3.1	48.9	394,905	62,350	17.6	13.5	12.9
3921000	Dayton city	84,868	43.0	25.4	108,698	58.1	4.1	35.0	57,882	45,995	32.2	6.9	23.4
3944856	Lorain city	44,395	50.1	17.5	NA	NA	NA	NA	27,930	41,480	30.1	7.8	23.9
3961000	Parma city	59,570	44.4	25.6	66,726	66.5	4.6	45.0	34,406	66,681	13.6	10.8	12.0
3977000	Toledo city	178,481	47.9	21.3	210,520	61.3	5.0	39.4	117,902	46,302	27.1	5.6	24.4
40000	**OKLAHOMA**	2,684,421	40.9	28.7	3,201,739	61.2	4.5	69.6	1,589,105	62,138	19.1	13.1	15.7
4009050	Broken Arrow city	80,865	30.5	34.7	92,576	67.1	2.0	49.5	44,802	84,374	10.7	17.7	8.7
4023200	Edmond city	63,657	15.1	58.7	77,648	65.1	3.0	42.8	39,282	98,524	11.6	28.8	9.5
4041850	Lawton city	57,942	45.1	23.7	71,466	61.1	4.4	29.5	34,205	51,571	21.4	5.8	22.7
4052500	Norman city	78,690	27.0	45.2	113,053	62.0	2.0	37.7	54,715	62,411	18.2	16.6	12.2
4055000	Oklahoma City city	461,858	35.2	36.6	542,511	67.9	3.0	47.8	284,755	67,015	17.2	15.4	15.0
4075000	Tulsa city	272,208	36.7	33.7	325,291	64.4	3.9	43.9	173,905	56,821	21.2	13.2	18.0
41000	**OREGON**	3,050,675	30.1	37.7	3,506,067	62.6	4.1	65.7	1,752,050	80,160	14.8	21.1	17.6
4105350	Beaverton city	71,174	20.2	50.7	80,604	71.5	2.6	49.2	43,874	92,650	10.8	26.3	16.5
4105800	Bend city	77,412	17.6	55.7	86,788	68.1	2.1	42.5	46,318	95,527	15.3	28.8	10.0
4123850	Eugene city	122,540	23.3	43.4	155,454	62.7	4.5	35.1	78,974	65,663	19.9	17.1	18.5
4131250	Gresham city	76,681	41.7	23.6	88,192	65.5	2.2	45.9	42,173	76,205	16.6	16.5	21.6
4134100	Hillsboro city	76,980	28.0	46.8	89,602	73.0	3.4	51.3	42,575	103,439	8.9	27.0	14.2
4147000	Medford city	60,555	36.5	26.1	68,487	57.4	3.1	36.4	34,867	66,186	14.6	11.7	20.9
4159000	Portland city	479,262	20.2	55.3	544,026	70.6	2.7	47.6	292,037	86,057	15.4	26.7	16.9
4164900	Salem city	120,762	37.3	31.5	143,552	63.6	2.5	41.8	68,817	72,827	16.5	17.6	21.4
42000	**PENNSYLVANIA**	9,171,006	40.9	35.3	10,658,635	62.8	4.2	69.3	5,324,209	73,824	16.1	19.3	15.7
4202000	Allentown city	75,316	59.2	20.5	94,839	61.2	4.5	39.9	46,104	47,175	27.0	7.8	32.7
4206088	Bethlehem city	51,793	38.8	33.0	65,613	64.6	5.9	42.1	32,208	68,719	14.6	12.7	20.1
4224000	Erie city	59,608	50.7	21.8	73,860	58.2	3.0	37.2	39,704	41,377	30.3	6.2	30.9
4260000	Philadelphia city	1,072,210	42.3	35.7	1,262,049	64.3	4.0	43.9	688,112	60,302	24.0	14.6	27.7
4261000	Pittsburgh city	205,051	27.1	50.5	265,190	64.6	3.2	41.8	140,615	66,219	20.3	16.6	15.5
4263624	Reading city	55,040	69.5	12.3	68,529	64.7	8.9	38.3	31,358	38,814	32.0	4.6	37.1
4269000	Scranton city	51,849	53.7	22.5	62,507	53.9	2.0	34.9	31,094	41,601	34.0	5.3	30.0
44000	**RHODE ISLAND**	786,493	36.8	39.0	916,988	64.6	4.7	66.4	443,980	84,972	15.0	23.3	14.0
4419180	Cranston city	60,516	29.3	39.1	NA	NA	NA	NA	31,571	92,795	12.5	26.7	10.0
4454640	Pawtucket city	56,682	47.3	28.2	62,249	71.4	6.9	NA	33,667	63,499	24.2	10.7	21.2
4459000	Providence city	121,363	46.4	35.1	158,441	64.0	5.2	40.4	71,374	65,206	20.7	14.2	23.1
4474300	Warwick city	64,493	33.5	38.3	70,507	66.7	1.9	45.3	36,989	86,193	14.0	24.2	15.6
45000	**SOUTH CAROLINA**	3,745,394	38.0	32.9	4,370,726	61.1	4.2	68.7	2,177,733	67,804	17.2	15.4	11.1
4513330	Charleston city	109,712	15.9	61.2	130,995	69.7	1.8	49.1	69,588	95,126	12.2	26.6	4.0
4516000	Columbia city	88,026	29.1	47.4	124,364	65.2	3.6	37.1	58,713	52,943	23.8	16.4	13.2
4530850	Greenville city	50,329	20.5	59.6	61,279	69.6	2.9	49.8	35,609	73,536	20.7	22.1	10.9
4548535	Mount Pleasant town	68,455	7.6	71.6	NA	NA	NA	NA	40,023	127,357	6.2	40.9	1.4
4550875	North Charleston city	82,577	40.3	29.2	99,494	67.7	3.7	45.1	53,710	64,070	17.6	9.7	14.6
4561405	Rock Hill city	53,957	37.3	32.0	64,531	66.7	4.6	45.4	31,189	65,397	13.6	13.6	6.4
46000	**SOUTH DAKOTA**	615,517	34.2	33.3	725,788	67.3	2.6	69.8	378,559	71,810	14.9	15.4	8.2
4652980	Rapid City city	54,625	25.9	37.3	63,949	63.7	1.5	41.2	33,880	70,094	17.1	14.8	10.1
4659020	Sioux Falls city	138,388	31.5	40.7	161,366	73.4	1.7	53.4	90,489	70,925	12.7	16.1	7.4
47000	**TENNESSEE**	4,931,967	40.9	31.7	5,747,865	62.7	3.9	70.4	2,889,226	67,631	17.2	15.8	10.4
4714000	Chattanooga city	129,146	32.7	36.3	150,749	66.6	3.6	43.7	81,086	62,547	17.0	14.7	12.4
4715160	Clarksville city	113,638	35.6	32.9	139,006	65.9	3.4	39.9	71,172	67,246	14.3	9.8	10.4
4727740	Franklin city	61,522	15.1	65.6	72,378	66.7	1.2	NA	35,730	118,156	6.5	36.8	3.8
4737640	Jackson city	46,292	46.8	23.8	55,352	60.3	3.6	NA	28,458	51,343	25.4	11.1	19.3
4738320	Johnson City city	47,721	32.8	42.6	62,001	60.1	2.6	38.0	31,162	55,406	21.9	13.0	8.1
4740000	Knoxville city	127,670	37.3	35.6	167,613	64.1	2.5	40.2	87,036	50,183	25.4	9.8	13.5
4748000	Memphis city	403,455	43.1	28.8	477,049	64.7	4.8	44.5	257,188	51,399	25.3	9.2	19.9

Table B-4. Cities — What: Education, Employment, and Income, 2023—*Continued*

STATE and place code	STATE Place	Educational attainment: Total population 25 years and over	Educational attainment: Percent with a high school diploma or less	Educational attainment: Percent with a bachelor's degree or more	Employment status: Total population 16 years and over	Employment status: Labor force participation (percent)	Employment status: Percent unemployed	Employment status: Percent of persons age 16 years and over who worked full-time year-round in the past 12 months	Household income and benefits: Total households	Household income and benefits: Median household income in the past 12 months (in 2022 inflation-adjusted dollars)	Household income and benefits: Income less than $25,000 (percent)	Household income and benefits: Income greater than $150,000 (percent)	Household income and benefits: Percent who received cash public assistance or food stamps/ SNAP
	ACS table number:	C15003	C15003	C15003	C23001	C23001	C23001	S2402	B19001	B19049	B19001	B19001	B19058
	column number:	1	2	3	4	5	6	7	8	9	10	11	12
	TENNESSEE—Cont.												
4751560	Murfreesboro city	102,461	32.7	43.0	131,435	73.4	2.1	54.4	63,223	78,069	11.6	16.2	6.5
4752006	Nashville-Davidson metropolitan government (balance)	480,095	27.7	50.9	561,819	73.1	2.3	52.7	330,506	80,217	13.2	20.6	8.1
48000	**TEXAS**	20,029,447	37.9	34.2	23,857,262	66.0	4.4	71.1	11,260,645	75,780	14.9	20.4	11.8
4801000	Abilene city	82,118	44.5	27.2	104,353	60.2	1.9	40.3	47,511	57,953	19.8	9.6	11.8
4801924	Allen city	75,441	17.7	56.0	87,675	71.8	3.1	53.4	38,830	126,549	7.3	42.2	1.8
4803000	Amarillo city	133,506	41.4	25.9	159,952	67.3	2.2	47.7	80,754	58,897	18.9	12.9	13.8
4804000	Arlington city	257,587	36.2	32.9	310,417	71.6	2.7	51.3	150,945	69,208	14.7	15.2	10.3
4804462	Atascocita CDP	70,873	29.6	32.4	87,961	66.9	4.2	49.8	38,628	97,244	8.5	25.5	8.1
4805000	Austin city	708,288	19.4	61.7	829,666	75.6	3.0	54.8	475,680	91,501	12.4	29.2	6.5
4806128	Baytown city	55,895	52.0	16.0	65,568	65.0	4.4	NA	31,402	57,421	17.9	11.7	17.5
4807000	Beaumont city	73,343	46.8	20.1	87,009	61.5	3.5	40.6	44,169	60,010	21.0	10.9	21.3
4810768	Brownsville city	117,977	50.3	24.6	147,324	61.9	3.1	42.0	64,083	49,920	23.5	8.4	27.9
4810912	Bryan city	55,648	45.9	28.3	70,708	65.7	3.4	42.4	33,775	53,006	23.3	11.6	18.5
4813024	Carrollton city	93,342	28.2	44.7	108,687	71.6	1.8	53.3	52,503	93,937	6.4	24.3	6.4
4813552	Cedar Park city	51,506	17.9	58.7	61,621	71.7	3.3	51.4	27,998	119,943	7.9	39.3	5.7
4815976	College Station city	55,164	19.6	59.1	106,892	60.9	3.5	32.0	47,029	47,632	29.0	15.2	8.5
4816432	Conroe city	68,598	34.8	36.6	83,921	69.6	2.5	52.0	42,134	77,027	8.3	12.9	10.1
4817000	Corpus Christi city	209,401	41.8	26.3	248,822	63.3	2.5	44.6	118,392	65,138	16.4	14.9	16.1
4819000	Dallas city	872,032	39.5	38.7	1,029,969	69.8	3.1	51.6	536,727	70,121	15.9	19.1	12.2
4819972	Denton city	100,796	25.3	43.8	134,420	66.1	3.7	39.9	59,711	73,051	19.1	19.3	6.6
4822660	Edinburg city	61,857	45.6	27.0	78,949	62.4	2.8	NA	34,958	61,059	20.2	11.9	27.0
4824000	El Paso city	445,650	42.6	28.5	534,903	62.3	2.6	41.9	249,362	57,317	23.1	11.6	19.3
4826232	Flower Mound town	54,620	13.4	64.4	NA	NA	NA	NA	29,171	147,490	4.1	49.6	2.5
4827000	Fort Worth city	621,199	38.7	33.8	752,657	69.8	3.0	49.8	346,392	77,082	13.3	19.5	13.1
4827684	Frisco city	149,598	12.4	67.5	175,101	70.6	3.3	52.6	80,665	141,129	4.7	47.6	4.6
4829000	Garland city	155,038	51.1	24.9	186,021	68.5	2.6	51.2	80,786	71,729	13.3	12.6	7.8
4829336	Georgetown city	73,940	23.8	43.1	79,842	56.9	2.1	NA	42,239	95,160	8.6	26.5	3.5
4830464	Grand Prairie city	129,104	42.5	31.2	153,889	70.2	4.1	50.4	70,750	72,106	12.5	15.9	8.8
4832372	Harlingen city	43,331	46.5	24.0	52,608	64.0	4.3	NA	25,629	60,065	19.6	10.1	17.4
4835000	Houston city	1,543,216	40.2	37.1	1,830,523	68.6	4.3	47.9	942,146	62,637	19.4	17.8	15.1
4837000	Irving city	158,707	38.8	42.3	194,452	71.2	3.3	55.3	95,909	79,335	9.7	19.2	4.8
4839148	Killeen city	99,109	35.2	24.2	120,436	68.1	4.0	42.0	64,777	60,067	15.1	9.1	13.9
4841464	Laredo city	147,275	49.0	23.9	185,157	62.5	2.8	44.2	79,072	60,720	22.1	9.3	23.3
4841980	League City city	76,599	20.6	46.8	86,968	69.1	1.6	53.1	41,978	118,475	6.8	34.9	6.2
4842016	Leander city	52,222	19.6	57.9	NA	NA	NA	NA	28,615	138,938	4.9	44.2	2.7
4842508	Lewisville city	93,412	31.9	38.4	107,981	77.2	2.8	56.5	50,672	88,784	6.4	25.9	7.9
4843888	Longview city	53,777	36.5	21.4	66,039	64.1	2.3	47.6	32,201	57,211	20.7	10.5	14.9
4845000	Lubbock city	157,039	36.4	33.2	210,965	68.5	2.8	45.7	108,609	54,451	20.2	11.9	12.9
4845384	McAllen city	93,030	39.5	32.9	112,337	62.7	2.3	42.0	51,319	60,200	22.8	13.4	18.8
4845744	McKinney city	138,882	20.5	51.4	162,253	70.8	2.2	52.1	74,833	116,654	7.8	36.9	3.4
4846452	Mansfield city	48,405	25.0	47.0	NA	NA	NA	NA	26,245	113,378	5.7	32.1	5.9
4847892	Mesquite city	92,710	48.6	21.3	112,860	67.2	1.9	49.5	49,690	67,333	14.3	13.0	13.5
4848072	Midland city	84,525	36.7	36.3	100,168	70.0	2.0	50.9	53,640	90,699	14.0	24.4	10.3
4848768	Mission city	53,593	47.6	27.6	64,819	61.2	3.3	NA	29,183	60,512	20.9	12.8	18.9
4848804	Missouri City city	50,302	30.2	40.0	NA	NA	NA	NA	26,271	87,072	11.9	19.3	8.9
4850820	New Braunfels city	76,474	28.2	37.0	89,665	71.3	2.8	52.4	42,756	87,778	9.3	24.1	5.7
4852356	North Richland Hills city	49,645	28.0	38.8	NA	NA	NA	NA	27,385	100,327	6.4	26.0	3.4
4853388	Odessa city	76,822	53.0	21.8	NA	NA	NA	NA	54,163	74,562	11.5	16.1	10.7
4856000	Pasadena city	89,090	57.1	17.0	111,276	63.0	4.5	43.8	49,618	59,111	20.0	11.2	21.9
4856348	Pearland city	82,476	23.4	45.6	97,543	69.3	2.1	55.1	45,686	108,454	7.1	34.3	5.5
4857176	Pflugerville city	46,605	23.4	45.2	NA	NA	NA	NA	24,333	108,974	4.9	35.8	3.6
4857200	Pharr city	44,642	57.7	17.9	57,133	64.3	3.9	NA	23,919	57,171	20.9	6.6	28.6
4858016	Plano city	205,670	18.3	60.8	237,578	69.3	1.8	51.8	114,555	108,594	9.0	35.6	4.4
4861796	Richardson city	77,711	18.7	56.0	99,194	69.6	2.9	46.7	45,822	95,170	10.8	27.1	4.5
4863500	Round Rock city	87,881	24.8	45.9	104,788	72.5	2.8	52.9	48,682	102,420	9.8	32.5	4.6
4863572	Rowlett city		44,564	23.7	41.8	52,778	71.3	2.7	NA	23,939	106,199	8.1	29.0
4864472	San Angelo city	63,970	41.2	24.9	76,439	65.7	2.3	43.8	39,231	52,048	23.6	9.1	13.8
4865000	San Antonio city	986,458	41.5	30.5	1,191,672	66.0	3.2	44.8	558,796	62,322	17.3	13.1	15.5
4865600	San Marcos city	34,230	30.1	43.0	63,721	69.8	3.8	NA	28,741	53,516	24.1	10.7	7.6

Table B-4. Cities — What: Education, Employment, and Income, 2023—*Continued*

STATE and place code	STATE Place	Educational attainment: Total population 25 years and over	Percent with a high school diploma or less	Percent with a bachelor's degree or more	Employment status: Total population 16 years and over	Labor force participation (percent)	Percent unemployed	Percent of persons age 16 years and over who worked full-time year-round in the past 12 months	Household income and benefits: Total households	Median household income in the past 12 months (in 2022 inflation-adjusted dollars)	Income less than $25,000 (percent)	Income greater than $150,000 (percent)	Percent who received cash public assistance or food stamps/ SNAP
	ACS table number:	C15003	C15003	C15003	C23001	C23001	C23001	S2402	B19001	B19049	B19001	B19001	B19058
	column number:	1	2	3	4	5	6	7	8	9	10	11	12
	TEXAS—Cont.												
4869596	Spring CDP	43,120	40.8	23.6	NA	NA	NA	NA	22,132	84,489	7.0	18.0	12.0
4870808	Sugar Land city	74,388	18.1	61.4	NA	NA	NA	NA	36,977	133,144	5.3	40.7	2.2
4872176	Temple city	60,313	35.9	27.8	71,267	67.1	3.6	49.4	35,445	74,923	14.8	14.0	12.0
4872656	The Woodlands CDP	81,141	14.3	64.0	90,900	62.3	2.8	45.4	44,480	140,794	6.0	48.7	3.2
4874144	Tyler city	70,691	34.9	29.4	87,077	64.1	2.3	44.6	36,292	68,441	12.8	14.3	13.1
4875428	Victoria city	42,071	46.9	21.2	50,714	61.3	2.5	NA	25,267	66,739	21.5	11.7	13.7
4876000	Waco city	81,990	41.9	28.8	114,315	63.1	2.7	41.4	52,857	52,770	28.4	9.5	17.0
4879000	Wichita Falls city	66,141	43.0	27.2	83,276	62.3	1.5	39.7	38,473	60,772	16.9	13.9	9.5
49000	**UTAH**	2,085,019	29.1	38.4	2,600,950	70.2	3.3	65.3	1,167,591	93,421	9.4	24.5	5.8
4943660	Layton city	52,932	28.6	34.5	62,028	71.2	2.0	NA	28,387	99,866	9.3	25.9	3.8
4944320	Lehi city	47,577	17.4	53.3	59,922	73.6	2.2	NA	25,416	129,274	4.6	41.4	3.0
4955980	Ogden city	54,714	42.2	24.7	68,198	69.0	2.2	46.0	32,848	65,035	17.7	11.1	9.6
4957300	Orem city	52,145	21.8	44.3	75,259	70.6	2.6	42.5	31,948	82,348	9.7	18.6	5.5
4962470	Provo city	46,903	21.9	48.0	93,230	72.4	3.7	26.9	36,198	62,556	15.7	12.0	7.9
4965330	St. George city	70,540	28.0	37.5	83,473	60.8	2.4	36.4	38,886	77,431	13.6	16.0	7.2
4967000	Salt Lake City city	140,566	25.6	52.1	178,850	71.8	3.0	45.3	92,626	72,951	14.9	22.4	6.2
4967440	Sandy city	63,906	22.1	49.7	72,989	68.1	2.4	47.6	35,081	108,926	7.3	34.7	3.6
4970850	South Jordan city	54,039	22.4	46.5	NA	NA	NA	NA	27,610	126,974	5.3	43.2	2.3
4982950	West Jordan city	70,671	35.1	31.4	85,910	75.3	2.2	52.5	36,479	105,396	6.1	28.5	7.3
4983470	West Valley City city	84,539	57.1	15.2	104,013	74.6	4.2	50.1	43,539	80,889	10.9	14.8	9.2
50000	**VERMONT**	471,255	31.6	43.7	547,286	64.9	2.6	66.4	279,612	81,211	14.1	20.4	11.0
51000	**VIRGINIA**	6,037,339	32.6	42.4	7,066,427	65.3	3.6	69.8	3,402,670	89,931	13.0	27.2	10.5
5101000	Alexandria city	117,655	19.8	66.1	129,362	78.6	2.7	57.8	76,890	110,294	9.1	36.2	5.5
5103000	Arlington CDP	172,764	12.1	78.0	196,649	78.3	2.7	60.1	114,097	140,219	8.4	46.9	4.3
5114440	Centreville CDP	48,317	25.0	55.2	57,062	79.3	2.2	57.0	25,109	131,503	5.0	44.3	4.6
5116000	Chesapeake city	172,684	31.2	36.6	199,843	66.1	1.9	44.2	94,056	92,633	12.8	27.9	8.6
5121088	Dale City CDP	44,362	41.9	29.6	54,033	72.7	4.1	NA	19,694	121,763	3.2	36.5	11.5
5135000	Hampton city	93,018	37.0	29.0	110,874	66.5	3.5	39.8	57,645	70,238	15.2	13.2	16.7
5147672	Lynchburg city	44,115	34.3	42.3	65,737	57.4	1.5	34.8	28,916	61,693	22.7	11.8	16.2
5156000	Newport News city	119,123	37.9	30.5	145,834	66.7	3.5	46.5	76,086	64,962	17.4	12.3	15.3
5157000	Norfolk city	150,391	36.8	33.1	188,652	70.2	3.2	39.6	94,056	62,382	19.6	15.0	17.8
5164000	Portsmouth city	65,762	42.2	28.3	77,216	67.0	3.5	44.8	40,661	57,109	23.6	11.0	23.6
5166672	Reston CDP		48,314	12.9	70.9	55,391	74.9	3.8	56.6	29,528	130,635	7.8	42.3
5167000	Richmond city	162,645	31.7	46.7	192,612	67.9	2.6	47.7	104,332	65,650	19.7	18.5	13.1
5168000	Roanoke city	68,568	42.7	29.9	77,529	60.9	1.8	44.5	45,061	51,038	22.0	10.2	17.4
5176432	Suffolk city	70,100	33.4	35.9	80,189	65.5	2.8	43.5	39,203	81,154	15.4	21.2	9.7
5182000	Virginia Beach city	317,353	29.3	40.5	366,903	68.2	2.6	43.4	179,291	91,141	9.6	24.2	8.7
53000	**WASHINGTON**	5,511,197	29.2	40.5	6,357,108	65.1	4.4	66.6	3,101,265	94,605	12.1	28.3	13.0
5303180	Auburn city	56,999	35.6	26.2	67,403	68.0	4.5	47.4	30,938	92,824	11.1	19.3	15.4
5305210	Bellevue city	110,975	9.0	76.4	125,201	68.9	2.9	48.7	62,868	158,253	8.5	53.7	6.0
5305280	Bellingham city	61,444	20.3	48.2	81,715	64.3	4.1	34.6	42,207	54,867	22.9	13.8	16.8
5322640	Everett city	81,798	34.5	32.2	93,237	67.3	3.2	46.8	46,726	74,276	14.9	19.4	17.4
5323515	Federal Way city	69,687	36.6	34.7	80,124	65.9	2.7	41.3	37,759	81,997	14.3	19.4	16.2
5335275	Kennewick city	52,945	42.9	27.7	63,342	58.9	3.2	NA	30,295	65,796	17.7	16.7	19.2
5335415	Kent city	93,893	37.4	33.0	109,237	68.9	3.5	44.1	50,481	85,982	14.0	22.8	18.1
5335940	Kirkland city	67,795	10.5	68.4	75,278	75.2	2.6	58.2	39,893	144,080	7.5	48.6	3.5
5343955	Marysville city	52,573	36.5	26.0	NA	NA	NA	NA	27,002	85,708	13.4	23.2	16.5
5353545	Pasco city	47,407	46.2	23.0	58,931	65.6	3.4	44.4	26,284	84,337	10.5	19.6	17.2
5357535	Redmond city	59,134	8.1	76.4	65,385	78.3	4.4	NA	36,551	172,979	8.2	57.1	4.7
5357745	Renton city	76,059	31.0	38.4	86,014	71.7	2.6	49.4	40,968	100,237	10.8	28.5	16.9
5361115	Sammamish city	42,672	6.6	83.4	49,203	66.7	1.9	NA	21,792	238,750	3.1	70.7	2.3
5363000	Seattle city	568,435	13.2	69.8	657,518	75.3	3.1	52.2	364,627	120,608	11.7	40.8	8.0
5365922	South Hill CDP	43,086	33.2	35.7	52,348	70.9	2.7	49.7	23,059	114,928	5.9	33.6	7.4
5367000	Spokane city	160,358	32.3	33.7	186,063	63.0	2.4	40.9	95,061	65,016	18.0	15.3	19.7
5367167	Spokane Valley city	79,058	35.4	24.0	91,021	66.8	3.0	45.6	45,025	74,787	16.2	12.6	21.9
5370000	Tacoma city	162,113	32.7	35.7	187,370	67.8	3.9	44.7	97,027	89,107	13.9	23.7	17.3
5374060	Vancouver city	140,526	33.4	31.7	162,543	66.0	2.7	42.2	84,778	80,618	11.0	17.3	19.2
5380010	Yakima city	63,489	50.4	22.9	74,668	61.8	3.0	41.8	37,918	61,776	18.2	12.3	24.5

Table B-4. Cities — What: Education, Employment, and Income, 2023—*Continued*

STATE and place code	STATE Place	Educational attainment: Total population 25 years and over	Educational attainment: Percent with a high school diploma or less	Educational attainment: Percent with a bachelor's degree or more	Employment status: Total population 16 years and over	Employment status: Labor force participation (percent)	Employment status: Percent unemployed	Employment status: Percent of persons age 16 years and over who worked full-time year-round in the past 12 months	Household income and benefits: Total households	Household income and benefits: Median household income in the past 12 months (in 2022 inflation-adjusted dollars)	Household income and benefits: Income less than $25,000 (percent)	Household income and benefits: Income greater than $150,000 (percent)	Household income and benefits: Percent who received cash public assistance or food stamps/ SNAP
	ACS table number:	C15003	C15003	C15003	C23001	C23001	C23001	S2402	B19001	B19049	B19001	B19001	B19058
	column number:	1	2	3	4	5	6	7	8	9	10	11	12
54000	**WEST VIRGINIA**	1,259,219	50.7	24.0	1,464,056	54.4	4.5	69.7	743,644	55,948	22.0	10.7	18.9
55000	**WISCONSIN**	4,116,216	35.8	33.8	4,822,901	65.2	2.8	69.8	2,495,539	74,631	14.3	17.2	12.0
5502375	Appleton city	53,131	36.1	36.1	61,824	64.8	1.6	46.0	30,831	73,449	11.5	18.5	11.7
5522300	Eau Claire city	44,495	31.0	33.8	59,783	68.3	2.6	46.4	30,280	68,221	13.2	10.8	12.4
5531000	Green Bay city	70,908	40.1	26.7	84,978	68.3	2.4	48.5	45,483	66,950	18.4	13.4	16.9
5537825	Janesville city	46,232	34.6	29.2	54,426	67.7	3.9	44.2	27,361	71,885	11.8	13.7	16.6
5539225	Kenosha city	66,969	39.6	28.1	80,680	70.5	2.3	49.2	42,461	68,885	18.2	13.0	15.6
5548000	Madison city	180,675	21.2	59.3	243,206	71.8	1.9	45.9	134,512	70,484	16.7	19.1	11.2
5553000	Milwaukee city	354,933	44.7	28.0	438,466	65.6	3.3	42.8	227,173	52,992	23.5	9.8	28.8
5560500	Oshkosh city	44,575	41.2	29.0	55,533	64.4	1.6	43.9	28,147	62,155	14.6	9.4	13.5
5566000	Racine city	50,213	44.8	21.6	NA	NA	NA	NA	31,700	55,065	21.1	5.8	26.3
5584250	Waukesha city	49,447	27.6	40.7	NA	NA	NA	NA	30,668	81,480	17.0	19.7	10.2
56000	**WYOMING**	403,853	33.6	30.4	469,355	63.5	3.2	66.9	247,368	72,415	14.9	15.2	5.8
5613900	Cheyenne city	47,235	29.8	33.4	NA	NA	NA	NA	30,643	74,244	11.5	14.8	7.5
72000	**PUERTO RICO**	2,407,254	45.2	30.8	2,777,060	47.1	9.1	63.3	1,277,486	25,621	49.1	3.1	47.0
7206593	Bayamón zona urbana	124,698	35.6	34.9	141,094	48.4	3.1	32.5	69,470	30,870	43.2	3.4	38.7
7210334	Caguas zona urbana		54,359	42.6	32.0	61,117	49.9	4.2	NA	30,465	27,360	46.8	2.4
7214290	Carolina zona urbana	104,795	35.7	37.1	120,874	52.9	4.1	39.5	58,026	36,427	35.7	3.8	29.9
7232522	Guaynabo zona urbana		52,042	26.8	60.3	NA	NA	NA	NA	26,800	57,861	26.8	20.1
7263820	Ponce zona urbana	79,913	42.4	32.9	91,917	41.6	7.2	23.5	48,343	18,591	59.1	1.4	53.4
7276770	San Juan zona urbana	239,766	30.9	44.2	273,561	51.3	4.8	33.2	143,453	27,770	47.0	6.3	34.4

NA = Not available.

PART C

Where

Migration, Housing, and Transportation

Where: Migration, Housing, and Transportation

Migration

An important question that the ACS can help to answer is how many people have moved recently, and from where to where. Nationally, 87.9 percent of Americans lived in the same home in 2023 as they did one year earlier. However, there was much variation among the smaller geographic areas.

Among the states, North Dakota (16.0 percent) had the highest proportion of movers and New Jersey had the lowest proportion (9.4 percent). The District of Columbia had an even higher proportion of movers at 21.0 percent, as well as the highest percentage of residents who moved from abroad—1.9 percent. Florida had the next-highest proportion of residents who moved from abroad, at 1.4 percent, while Hawaii, Massachusetts, and New Jersey were next at 1.0 percent each.

In 67 metropolitan areas, 90 percent or more of the residents had not moved in the past year. Most of these were smaller metropolitan areas, but among them was New York-Newark-Jersey City, NY-NJ and Los Angeles-Long Beach-Anaheim, CA—the metropolitan areas with the largest populations. In 18 metropolitan areas (a substantial uptick once more, likely due to the same circumstances), 80 percent or less of the population had lived in the same house—most with large student or military populations, including Ithaca, New York; State College, Pennsylvania; Lawrence, Kansas; Ann Arbor, Michigan; College Station-Bryan, Texas; Bloomington, Indiana; and Ames, Iowa, among others.

In two of the counties surveyed in 2023, more than 209 percent of the population had moved into the county within a year or less. The highest proportion was Walker County, Texas (22.1 percent). Among larger counties, 6.6 percent of the residents of Dallas County, Texas (where Dallas is located), moved into the county within the past year. New York County (Manhattan) had a rate of 7.3 percent.

In 36 of the 649 cities surveyed in 2023, more than 93 percent of the residents lived in the same house they had lived in 1 year earlier. With a few exceptions, they were relatively small cities. At the other extreme, less than 67 percent of the

Figure C-1. Residence 1 Year Ago, 2023

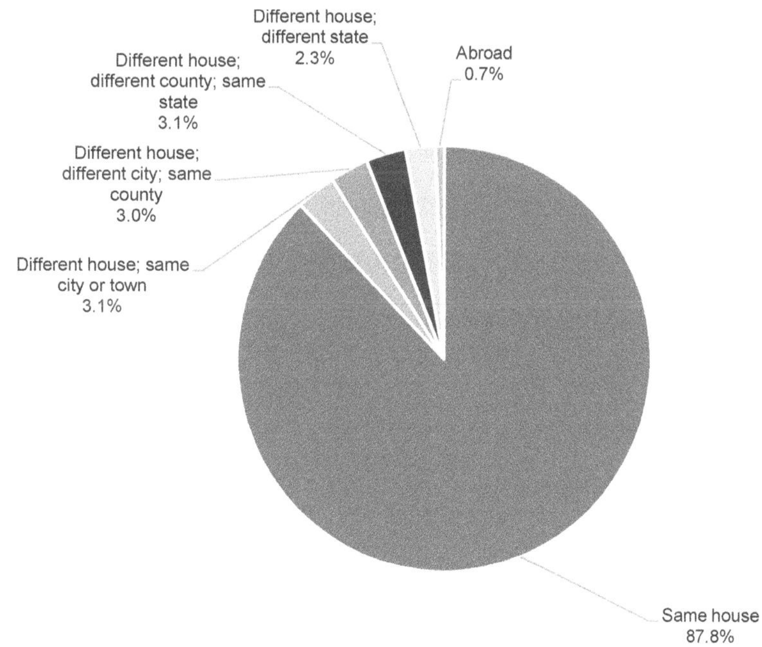

population in 4 cities lived in the same house a year earlier. These were also small cities, all with universities.

(The number of counties and cities in this book is limited due to the fact that the population threshold for the tables used is 65,000 residents.)

Owning and Renting

Homeownership in the United States reached record high levels in the early 2000s before beginning to decline in 2008. In 2023, owners occupied 65.2 percent of American housing units, after hovering around 63.1 percent for much of the latter 2010s. Maine, Michigan, and Delaware had the highest rates of ownership, with all three states above 73.5 percent, followed by 11 states in which more than 70 percent of households owned their homes: West Virginia, Vermont, Idaho, New Hampshire, South Carolina, Minnesota, Iowa, Wyoming, Mississippi, Indiana, and Alabama. The states with the smallest proportion of owner-occupied units were New York and California, both under 56 percent. The District of Columbia (39.1 percent) had a lower rate than any of the states. However, the District of Columbia's homeownership rate was higher than cities like Los Angeles, San Francisco, Boston, New York, and Miami. New York City's relatively low homeownership rate of 32.5 percent brought down the state's overall rate.

Homeownership rates varied considerably by race of householder in 2023. Nationally, 73.1 percent of non-Hispanic White households lived in a home they owned, while fewer than half of Black householders were homeowners. Eight states—led by Mississippi with 57.6 percent—had 50 percent or more of Black householders residing in owner-occupied units. More than 50 percent of Latino households were homeowners in Puerto Rico and in 32 states—including Texas, Arizona, and Florida, which have large Latino populations. Approximately 62.8 percent of Asian and Native Hawaiian and Other Pacific Islander–headed households were homeowners.

Homeownership varied even more by age of householder in 2023. For all householders age 25 to 44 years, 51.9 percent owned their own homes, compared with 72.8 percent of 45- to 64-year-olds and 78.5 percent of householders 65 years old and over. Maine, Wyoming, and Mississippi had the highest proportions of younger homeowners, with more than 26 percent of 25- to 44-year-olds owning homes in these states, while Delaware, Idaho, West Virginia, and South Carolina,

Figure C-2. Counties with the Greatest and Least Numbers of Owner-Occupied Housing Units, 2023

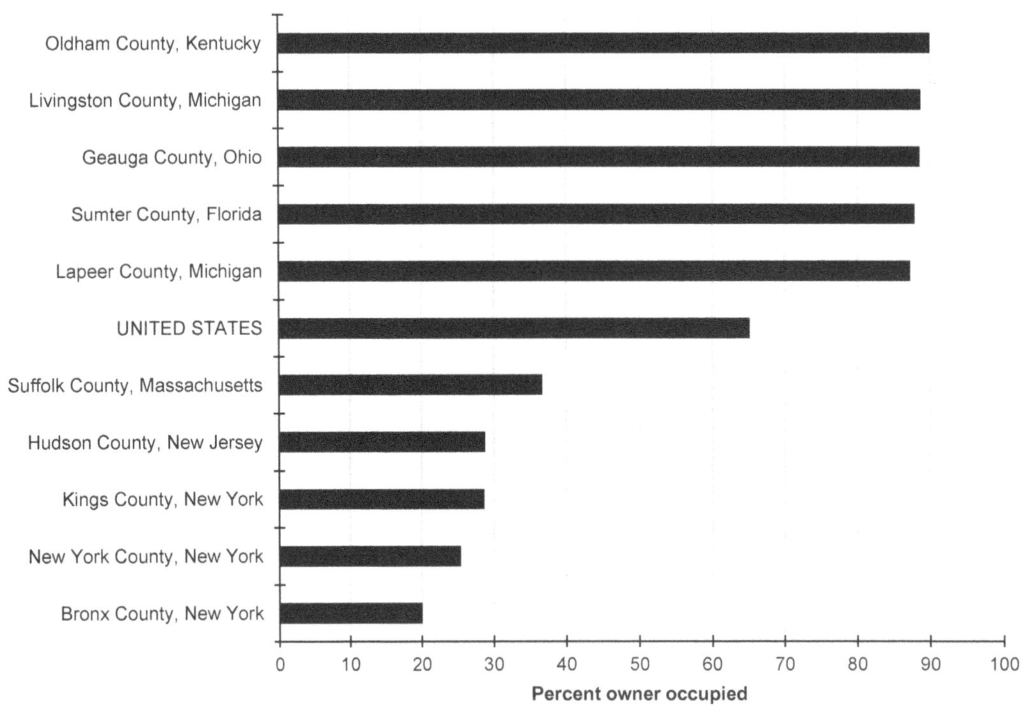

had the highest homeownership rates among householders 65 years old and older, all over 85 percent.

Nearly 82 percent of married-couple family households were homeowners, while just over half of female-headed family households owned their homes. The homeownership rate of nonfamily households was just under half. In West Virginia, 62.1 percent of nonfamily households owned their homes. More than 88 percent of married-couple families in 6 states owned their homes, topped by Michigan, which was just under 90 percent. The lowest homeownership rate for married-couple families was 67.5 percent in the District of Columbia, while California and Hawaii had rates below 72 percent.

In the Wildwood-The Villages, Florida, metropolitan area, 87.9 percent of housing units were owner occupied in 2023. Punta Gorda, Florida; Homosassa Springs, Florida; and Sebring, Florida, also had homeownership rates above 80 percent, as did Traverse City, Michigan; Muskegon-Norton Shores, Michigan; and Monroe, Michigan. Los Angeles-Long Beach-Anaheim, California; Lawrence, Kansas; College Station-Bryan, Texas; Santa Maria-Santa Barbara, California; and Manhattan, Kansas, had the lowest homeownership rate of the metropolitan areas, with less than 51 percent households owning their homes.

Ninety of the counties surveyed in 2023 had homeownership rates of 80 percent or more, most of them counties with populations under 100,000. However, New York's Nassau and Suffolk counties, with nearly half a million households each, were in this group. The three lowest homeownership rates in the country were in the New York City boroughs of Bronx County at 20.1 percent, New York County (Manhattan) at 25.4 percent, and Kings County (Brooklyn) at 28.7 percent.

Twenty-nine small cities—many of them suburban—had homeownership rates higher than 80 percent, and 24 had rates below 35 percent. Many of these were university towns, but they included Newark, New Jersey, with a homeownership rate of 24.6 percent and Miami, Florida, with a homeownership rate of 33.4 percent. New York City's overall homeownership rate was 32.5 percent. Very few of the largest cities exceeded homeownership rates of 60 percent.

Housing Characteristics

In 2023, American households had an average size of 2.49persons per household. Owner-occupied households tended to be slightly larger (2.61) than renter-occupied households (2.25). Utah had the largest size households, with an average of 2.88

Figure C-3. Metropolitan Areas with the Most and Least Access to the Internet, 2023

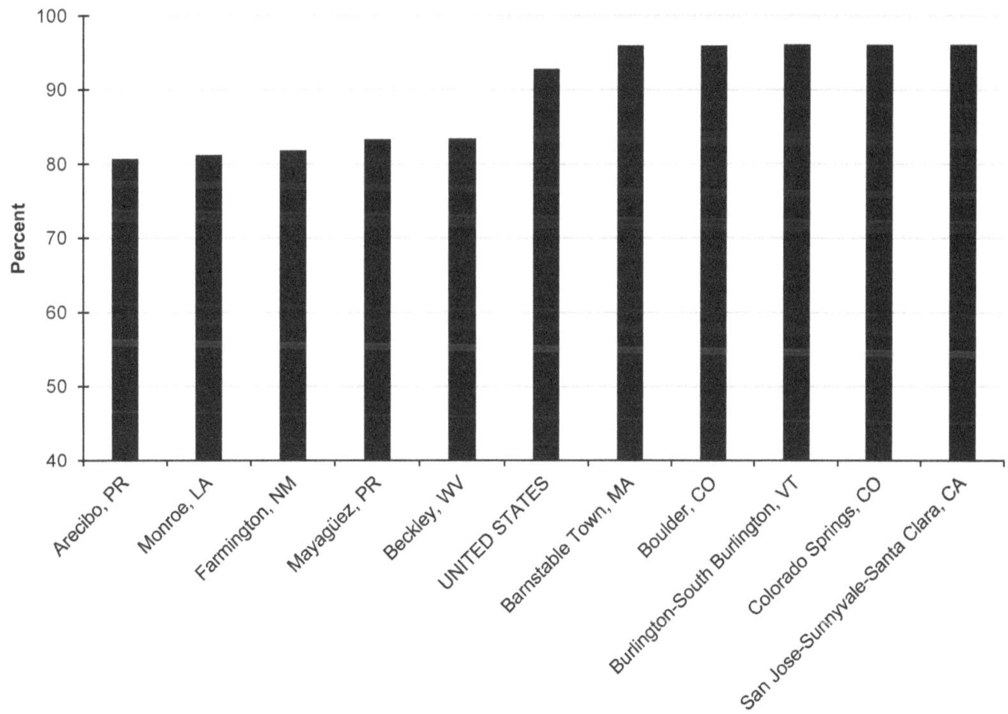

Figure C-4. Median Gross Rent for Renter-Occupied Units, by State, 2023

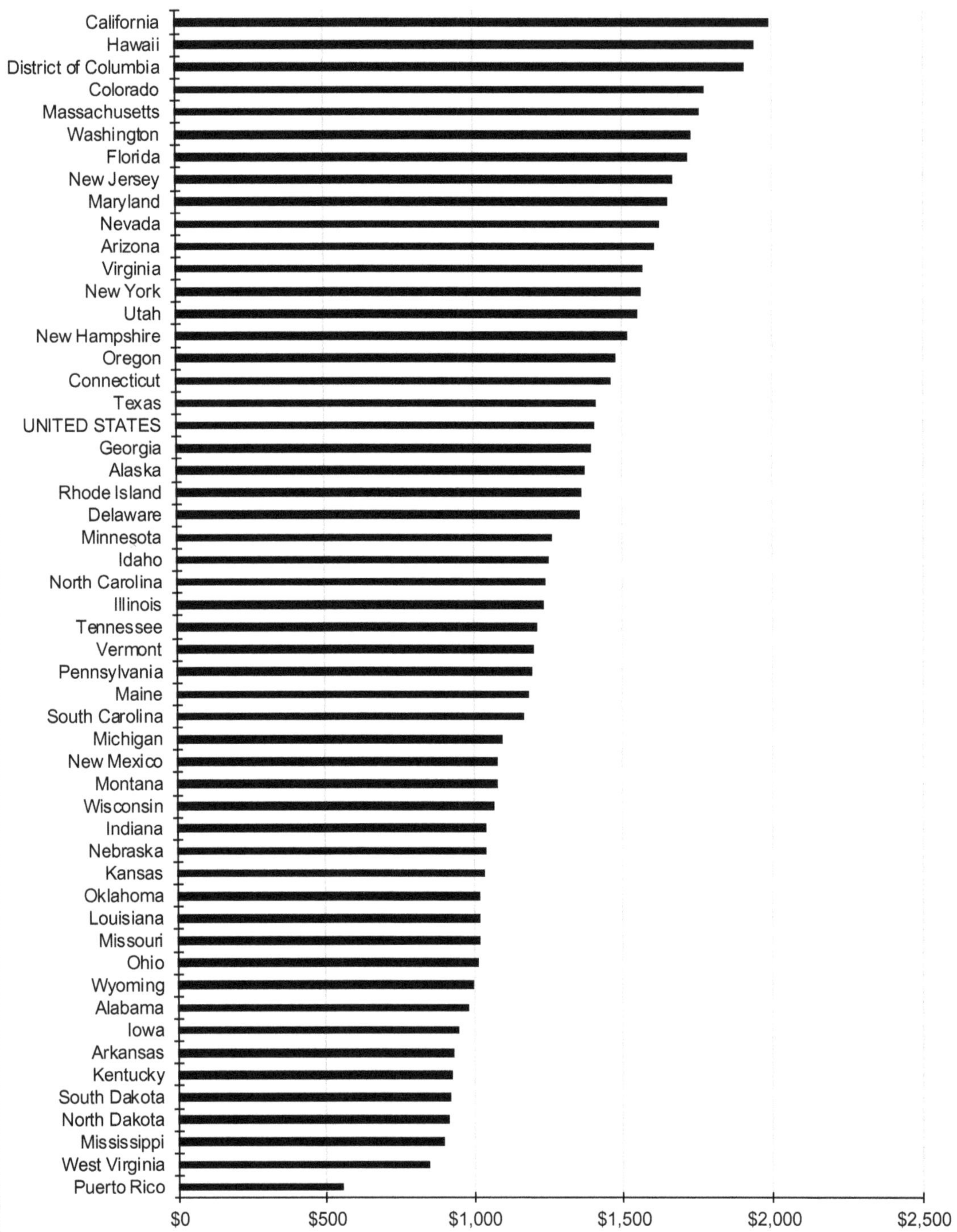

person per household. Maine, North Dakota, and Vermont had the smallest households among the states at under 2.30 persons each, while the District of Columbia had the smallest overall households with an average of 1.92 persons per household.

Housing quality is sometimes measured by crowding (more than one person per room is considered crowded) and/or lack of complete plumbing (which consists of hot and cold piped water, a flush toilet, and a bathtub or shower). Nationally, 3.9 percent of housing units were considered substandard by this definition, but 10.0 percent of housing units in Hawaii did not meet these standards. Alaska and California also had high levels of substandard housing at 9.3 and 8.6 percent respectively.

Approximately 7.8 percent of American households had no access to the Internet in 2023. In 25 metropolitan areas, 5.0 percent or fewer households lacked Internet access. Metropolitan areas with more than 17 percent of households lacking access included Arecibo, Puerto Rico (19.3 percent); Monroe, Louisiana (18.8 percent); and Farmington, New Mexico (18.2 percent). In 644 of the counties surveyed in 2023, less than 10 percent of households lacked Internet access. In three of the counties surveyed in 2023, less than three-quarters of households had Internet access: Apache County, Arizona (34.9 percent); St. Landry Parish, Louisiana (30.4 percent); and McKinley County, New Mexico (27.5 percent). In over two-thirds of the cities surveyed in 2023, more than 90 percent of households had Internet access. The lowest level of Internet availability was 44.0 percent in Lakewood CDP, New Jersey, which has a large Orthodox Jewish community.

Housing Value and Costs

The median value of owner-occupied housing units in the United States was $340,200 in 2023. Hawaii, California, and the District of Columbia had median housing values over $700,000, with Hawaii at $846,400, California at $725,800, and the District of Columbia at $715,500. The median value was under $170,000 in Mississippi and West Virginia. Thirty-four metropolitan areas had median housing values over $550,000—five in Washington; three in Colorado; two each in Hawaii and Massachusetts; one each in Connecticut, Florida, Idaho, Montana, New York, Oregon, Utah, and the District of Columbia; and the remainder in California—with the highest median value in the San Jose-Sunnyvale-Santa Clara, California, metropolitan area at $1.39 million. At the other extreme, 10 metropolitan areas and all of the municipos in Puerto Rico had median housing values below $150,000. Three areas could be found in West Virginia (with one having some of its area located in Ohio); two could be found in Indiana; and one each could be found in Illinois, Michigan, Ohio, New York, and Pennsylvania. Three California cities had median housing values of $2,000,000 or more, and 36 additional cities had median values over $1,000,000. Most of these cities were also in California. Flint, Michigan, had a median value of less than $55,000, while the median value in Detroit was just under $87,000.

Just over 60 percent of owner-occupants held mortgages on their homes. More than 70 percent of homeowners in the District of Columbia and Maryland held mortgages, while less than 50 percent of Mississippi and West Virginia's homeowners did. Just under 8 percent of all owner-occupants held a second mortgage and/or a home equity loan, but 10 percent or more held these mortgages in Hawaii, Utah, and Massachusetts. Fewer than 4 percent had them in Louisiana, Mississippi, Arkansas, Oklahoma, Alaska, and Texas.

For all Americans, the median monthly housing cost was $1,358. For owners, this included mortgages, real estate taxes, insurance, utilities, fuel, and condominium fees, where appropriate. For renters, this included the contract rent, utilities, and fuels if paid by the renter. Median housing costs were highest in the District of Columbia, California, Massachusetts, Hawaii, New Jersey, Washington, Colorado, and Maryland (more than $1,600) and lowest in Mississippi ($819), West Virginia ($710) and Puerto Rico ($412).

On average, renters devoted a relatively high share of their monthly income to rent: a median of 32.6 percent. Even owners with a mortgage spent relatively less on their housing—21.1 percent of monthly household income. (Those with no mortgage spent 11.5 percent.) Homeowners with mortgages in Hawaii paid 25.5 percent of their incomes for owner costs, while those in West Virginia paid only 17.0 percent.

Among the states in 2023, renters in Florida, Louisiana, Massachusetts, and Nevada, paid the highest proportion of their incomes for their rental costs—between 35.0 and 38.5 percent—while renters in North Dakota paid only 23.4 percent of their incomes. Median gross rents were highest in California, the District of Columbia, and Hawaii—all $1,900 or more. The lowest median gross rents (under $900) were in Mississippi, West Virginia, and Puerto Rico.

Property taxes varied widely from the national annual median of $3,507 in 2023. New Jersey residents paid a median of $9,163 per year, with New Hampshire, Connecticut, and New York, all paying more than $6,000. The median was below $1,000 in two states and Puerto Rico, with Alabama households paying only $786 per year.

Transportation

More than 90 percent of households had at least one vehicle. More than half of households had two or more vehicles, and the share of housing units with three or more vehicles was more than double the share without any at all. In the District of Columbia, 36.3 percent of households had no vehicles. New

York had the highest level among the states—29.7 percent. In Idaho, Utah, Montana, and Wyoming, more than 30 percent of households had three or more vehicles.

Commuting patterns have changed due to the global pandemic, with workers working at home roughly tripling between 2019 and 2021 and the return to office not completed as of 2023. For those who commute, more than two out of three drove their cars to work alone, and less than one in ten carpooled. Approximately 3.5 percent took public transportation, while 4.4 percent walked, bicycled, or used "other means." Americans' average commute (excluding those who worked at home) was 23.08 minutes. This ranged from just under 17 minutes in North Dakota and South Dakota to nearly 29 minutes in New York. Nationally, commuting by public transportation averaged just over one and a half times as long as commuting by car, but car trips ranged from an average of 18 and a half minutes in South Dakota to over 30 minutes in Maryland. Public transportation commuting times ranged from under 25 minutes in North Dakota to more than an hour in Connecticut.

Commuting patterns are influenced by local conditions, so broad national averages are not very revealing. Walking or biking are generally more popular in a climate with good weather, and the presence or absence of public transport obviously determines how many people use it. For instance, more people take public transportation in states with cities containing well-developed systems (such as New York, the District of Columbia, and New Jersey)—not many other Americans have this option. Public transportation usage has also not fully recovered from the conditions of the pandemic.

Eight of the 649 cities (all but two located in California) included in this volume had 30 percent or more of its commuters traveling 60 minutes or more to work, including Poinciana CDP, Florida; Brentwood city, California; Murrieta city, California; Lake Elsinore city, California; Tracy city, California; Palmdale city, California; Menifee city, California; and East Orange city, New Jersey. Four cities had more than 30 percent of commuters traveling 30 minutes or less to work: Jacksonville city, North Carolina; Wichita Falls city, Texas; Chico city, California; and Ames city, Iowa.

Figure C-5. Cities with the Greatest Percentage of Commutes of 60 Minutes or Longer, 2023

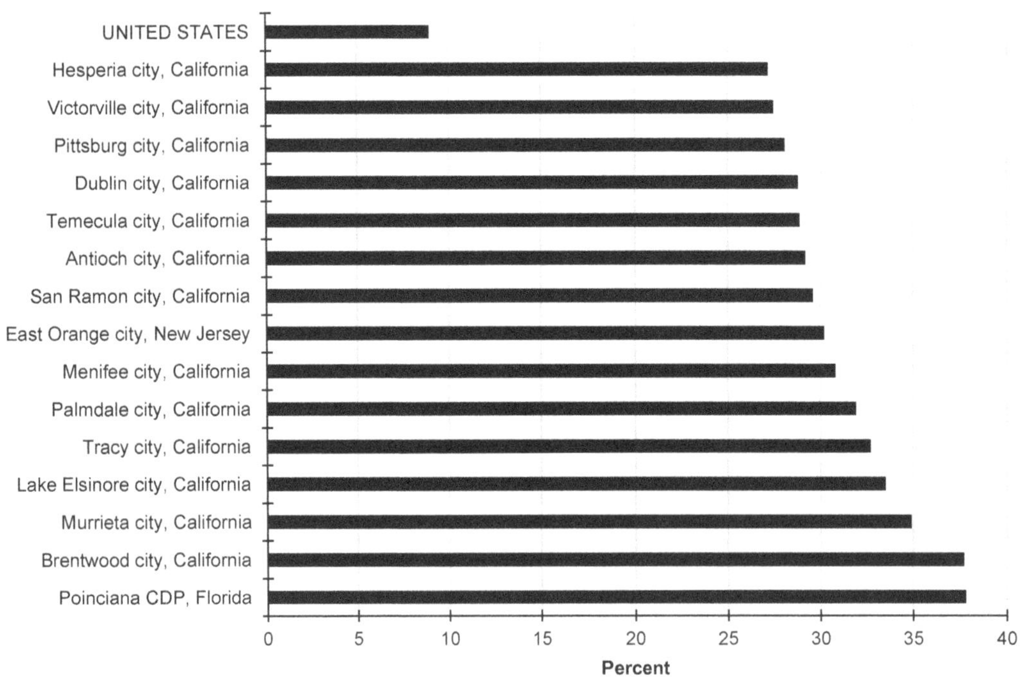

State Rankings, 2023

Selected Rankings

Lived in the same house one year ago rank	State	Percent who lived in the same house one year ago [C-1, col. 2]	Did not live in the state one year ago rank	State	Percent who did not live in the state one year ago [C-1, cols. 6 + 7]	Owner-occupied housing unit rank	State	Percent of owner-occupied housing units [C-1, col. 9]
	UNITED STATES	87.9		**UNITED STATES**	3.0		**UNITED STATES**	65.2
1	New Jersey	90.6	1	District of Columbia	10.4	1	Maine	74.4
2	New York	90.4	2	North Dakota	5.4	2	Michigan	73.7
3	New Hampshire	90.1	3	Hawaii	5.1	3	Delaware	73.6
4	West Virginia	90.0	4	Alaska	4.9	4	West Virginia	73.5
5	California	89.5	5	Nevada	4.8	5	Vermont	73.2
5	Mississippi	89.5	6	Idaho	4.7	6	Idaho	72.5
7	Maine	89.4	7	Colorado	4.6	7	New Hampshire	72.4
7	Pennsylvania	89.4	8	Delaware	4.5	7	South Carolina	72.4
9	Illinois	89.2	8	Vermont	4.5	9	Minnesota	72.0
10	Connecticut	89.1	10	Wyoming	4.4	10	Iowa	71.8
10	Rhode Island	89.1	11	Arizona	4.3	11	Wyoming	71.2
10	Vermont	89.1	11	South Carolina	4.3	12	Mississippi	71.1
13	Louisiana	89.0	13	Florida	4.2	13	Indiana	70.4
13	Maryland	89.0	14	Virginia	3.9	14	Alabama	70.1
13	Michigan	89.0	15	North Carolina	3.8	14	Utah	70.1
16	Delaware	88.8	16	Washington	3.7	16	Pennsylvania	69.5
16	Wisconsin	88.8	16	Rhode Island	3.7	17	South Dakota	69.4
18	Alabama	88.6	16	New Mexico	3.7	18	New Mexico	69.3
18	Ohio	88.6	19	Oregon	3.6	19	Montana	69.2
20	South Dakota	88.5	19	South Dakota	3.6	20	Kentucky	68.8
21	Minnesota	88.4	21	Utah	3.5	20	Missouri	68.8
22	Massachusetts	88.2	21	Montana	3.5	22	Florida	68.1
22	New Mexico	88.2	23	Connecticut	3.4	22	Louisiana	68.1
24	Hawaii	88.1	23	Maryland	3.4	24	Maryland	67.9
25	Arkansas	87.9	23	Kansas	3.4	24	Wisconsin	67.9
25	Missouri	87.9	23	Georgia	3.4	26	Virginia	67.8
27	Kentucky	87.7	27	Tennessee	3.3	27	Arizona	67.7
27	Tennessee	87.7	28	New Hampshire	3.2	28	Illinois	67.4
29	South Carolina	87.6	29	Massachusetts	3.1	29	Tennessee	67.3
30	Indiana	87.5	29	Nebraska	3.1	30	Ohio	67.1
30	Iowa	87.5	29	Oklahoma	3.1	31	Kansas	66.7
32	Georgia	87.4	29	Maine	3.1	32	Alaska	66.3
33	North Carolina	87.1	33	Kentucky	3.0	32	Nebraska	66.3
34	Nebraska	87.0	34	Texas	2.9	32	North Carolina	66.3
34	Virginia	87.0	35	Iowa	2.8	35	Arkansas	66.2
36	Montana	86.9	36	New Jersey	2.7	36	Georgia	66.1
37	Oregon	86.5	36	Alabama	2.7	37	Colorado	65.7
38	Florida	86.4	36	Indiana	2.7	37	Connecticut	65.7
39	Kansas	86.2	36	Missouri	2.7	39	Oklahoma	65.1
39	Wyoming	86.2	36	Arkansas	2.7	40	Rhode Island	64.0
41	Arizona	86.1	41	Mississippi	2.6	41	New Jersey	63.7
42	Utah	86.0	41	West Virginia	2.6	41	North Dakota	63.7
43	Texas	85.9	43	New York	2.4	41	Washington	63.7
44	Idaho	85.8	43	Illinois	2.4	44	Oregon	63.4
44	Oklahoma	85.8	43	Pennsylvania	2.4	45	Texas	62.6
44	Washington	85.8	46	Minnesota	2.3	46	Hawaii	62.4
47	Alaska	85.7	46	Wisconsin	2.3	47	Massachusetts	62.3
48	Nevada	85.4	48	Ohio	2.1	48	Nevada	60.4
49	Colorado	84.3	49	Louisiana	2.0	49	California	55.9
50	North Dakota	84.0	50	California	1.9	50	New York	54.1
51	District of Columbia	79.0	50	Michigan	1.9	51	District of Columbia	39.1

State Rankings, 2023

Selected Rankings

Median value of owner-occupied housing units rank	State	Median value of owner-occupied housing units (dollars) [C-1, col. 45]	Mean travel time to work rank	State	Mean travel time to work (minutes) [C-1, col. 78]	Median selected monthly owner (with a mortgage) costs as a percentage of household income rank	State	Median selected monthly owner (with a mortgage) costs as a percentage of household income [C-1, col. 59]
	UNITED STATES	340,200		**UNITED STATES**	26.37		**UNITED STATES**	21.1
1	Hawaii	846,400	1	New York	32.99	1	New York	28.7
2	California	725,800	2	Maryland	30.84	2	New Jersey	27.0
3	District of Columbia	715,500	3	New Jersey	30.27	3	Maryland	26.1
4	Washington	576,000	4	District of Columbia	30.05	4	West Virginia	25.4
5	Massachusetts	570,800	5	Massachusetts	28.56	5	Massachusetts	25.3
6	Colorado	550,300	6	California	28.34	6	California	24.9
7	Utah	517,700	7	Georgia	28.23	7	Hawaii	24.6
8	Oregon	484,800	8	Florida	28.02	8	Georgia	24.4
9	New Jersey	461,000	9	Illinois	27.85	9	Illinois	24.2
10	Nevada	441,100	10	Virginia	27.07	10	Florida	24.0
11	Idaho	428,600	11	West Virginia	26.86	11	Louisiana	23.6
12	New York	420,200	12	Connecticut	26.79	12	Mississippi	23.6
13	New Hampshire	415,400	13	New Hampshire	26.72	13	Texas	23.5
14	Maryland	413,600	14	Texas	26.71	14	Alabama	23.2
15	Rhode Island	411,800	15	Pennsylvania	26.36	15	Delaware	23.1
16	Arizona	411,200	16	Washington	26.29	16	Connecticut	23.1
17	Montana	392,300	17	Delaware	26.07	17	Virginia	22.9
18	Virginia	382,900	18	Hawaii	26.06	18	Tennessee	22.9
19	Florida	381,000	19	Louisiana	25.61	19	Pennsylvania	22.8
20	Connecticut	367,800	20	South Carolina	25.60	20	New Hampshire	22.7
21	Delaware	359,700	21	Mississippi	25.51	21	Rhode Island	22.5
22	Alaska	347,500	22	Tennessee	25.49	22	Nevada	22.5
23	Vermont	332,000	23	Rhode Island	25.39	23	South Carolina	22.5
24	Minnesota	328,600	24	Alabama	25.36	24	District of Columbia	22.1
25	Georgia	323,000	25	North Carolina	25.06	25	Washington	22.1
26	Maine	310,700	26	Colorado	25.04	26	Kentucky	21.9
27	North Carolina	308,600	27	Arizona	24.94	27	Indiana	21.8
28	Tennessee	307,300	28	Maine	24.70	28	Michigan	21.5
29	Wyoming	298,700	29	Nevada	24.54	29	Arizona	21.2
30	Texas	296,900	30	Michigan	24.21	30	North Carolina	21.2
31	South Carolina	272,900	31	Kentucky	24.09	31	Maine	20.8
32	Wisconsin	272,500	32	Indiana	24.06	32	Arkansas	20.8
33	South Dakota	268,200	33	Missouri	23.71	33	New Mexico	20.7
34	Illinois	263,300	33	New Mexico	23.71	34	Ohio	20.7
35	Pennsylvania	259,900	35	Ohio	23.55	35	Missouri	20.6
36	New Mexico	256,300	36	Vermont	23.24	36	Oklahoma	20.6
37	North Dakota	246,700	37	Oregon	22.81	37	Colorado	20.4
38	Nebraska	245,200	38	Minnesota	22.79	38	Vermont	20.3
39	Michigan	236,100	39	Oklahoma	22.67	39	Wisconsin	19.7
40	Missouri	233,600	40	Arkansas	22.36	40	Oregon	19.1
41	Indiana	225,900	41	Wisconsin	22.18	41	Minnesota	19.1
42	Ohio	220,200	42	Idaho	22.10	42	Idaho	19.0
43	Kansas	219,800	43	Utah	21.61	43	Utah	18.9
44	Alabama	216,600	44	Iowa	19.70	44	Alaska	18.0
45	Louisiana	215,600	45	Kansas	19.65	45	Iowa	17.9
46	Iowa	213,300	46	Alaska	19.36	46	Montana	17.9
47	Kentucky	211,800	47	Montana	19.05	47	Kansas	17.9
48	Oklahoma	208,600	48	Nebraska	18.79	48	Wyoming	17.5
49	Arkansas	195,700	49	North Dakota	18.32	49	Nebraska	17.2
50	Mississippi	169,800	50	South Dakota	18.23	50	North Dakota	17.0
51	West Virginia	163,700	51	Wyoming	17.98	51	South Dakota	16.6

County Rankings, 2023

Selected Rankings

Lived in the same house one year ago rank	County	Percent who lived in the same house one year ago [C-2, col. 2]	Did not live in the county one year ago rank	County	Percent who did not live in the county one year ago [C-2, col. 3]
	UNITED STATES	87.9		**UNITED STATES**	6.0
1	Apache County, Arizona	97.7	1	Walker County, Texas	22.1
2	Jones County, Mississippi	95.8	2	Tompkins County, New York	21.3
3	St. Landry Parish, Louisiana	95.5	3	Payne County, Oklahoma	18.1
4	Tehama County, California	95.3	4	Coryell County, Texas	17.9
5	Iberia Parish, Louisiana	94.8	5	Grand Forks County, North Dakota	17.0
5	Washington County, Wisconsin	94.8	6	Benton County, Oregon	16.4
7	Richmond County, New York	94.7	7	Monroe County, Indiana	16.0
8	Tooele County, Utah	94.4	8	Arlington County, Virginia	15.6
8	DeKalb County, Alabama	94.4	8	Alexandria city, Virginia	15.6
8	Robeson County, North Carolina	94.4	10	Story County, Iowa	15.3
11	Fauquier County, Virginia	94.3	11	Clarke County, Georgia	15.0
12	Livingston County, Michigan	94.2	12	Orange County, North Carolina	14.9
13	Creek County, Oklahoma	94.1	13	Liberty County, Georgia	14.8
13	Nassau County, New York	94.1	14	Leavenworth County, Kansas	14.6
15	Washington County, Rhode Island	94.0	15	Christian County, Kentucky	14.3
15	Kendall County, Illinois	94.0	15	Brazos County, Texas	14.3
15	Rockland County, New York	94.0	17	Centre County, Pennsylvania	14.2
18	Carroll County, Maryland	93.8	18	Norfolk city, Virginia	13.8
18	Northwest Hills Planning Region, Connecticut	93.8	19	Douglas County, Kansas	13.7
18	Sussex County, New Jersey	93.8	20	Riley County, Kansas	13.6
18	Wayne County, Ohio	93.8	21	Boulder County, Colorado	13.3
22	Cole County, Missouri	93.7	22	Broomfield County, Colorado	13.2
23	Hamblen County, Tennessee	93.6	22	Tippecanoe County, Indiana	13.2
23	Nash County, North Carolina	93.6	24	York County, Virginia	13.1
23	Putnam County, New York	93.6	25	Columbia County, Florida	12.9
26	Chatham County, North Carolina	93.5	26	Dougherty County, Georgia	12.8
26	Davidson County, North Carolina	93.5	27	Albemarle County, Virginia	12.6
28	Warren County, New Jersey	93.4	28	Coconino County, Arizona	12.5
29	Suffolk County, New York	93.3	28	Hampshire County, Massachusetts	12.5
29	Martin County, Florida	93.3	28	Montgomery County, Virginia	12.5
31	San Juan County, New Mexico	93.2	31	Onslow County, North Carolina	12.4
31	McHenry County, Illinois	93.2	32	Stafford County, Virginia	12.3
31	Erie County, Ohio	93.2	33	Durham County, North Carolina	12.2
34	Somerset County, Pennsylvania	93.1	34	Hays County, Texas	12.1
34	Henderson County, North Carolina	93.1	34	Bulloch County, Georgia	12.1
36	Imperial County, California	93.0	36	Denver County, Colorado	12.0
36	St. Croix County, Wisconsin	93.0	36	Johnson County, Iowa	12.0
36	Harford County, Maryland	93.0	38	Craven County, North Carolina	11.8
36	Ascension Parish, Louisiana	93.0	38	Richmond city, Virginia	11.8
40	Kauai County, Hawaii	92.8	38	Comanche County, Oklahoma	11.8
40	Will County, Illinois	92.8	38	Blue Earth County, Minnesota	11.8
42	Kankakee County, Illinois	92.7	38	Alachua County, Florida	11.8
43	Lincoln County, North Carolina	92.6	43	Dallas County, Iowa	11.7
43	Livingston Parish, Louisiana	92.6	44	Pickens County, South Carolina	11.5
43	Tulare County, California	92.6	45	Yolo County, California	11.3
43	Licking County, Ohio	92.6	45	Washtenaw County, Michigan	11.3
43	Morris County, New Jersey	92.6	47	Lynchburg city, Virginia	11.2
43	Burke County, North Carolina	92.6	48	Sumter County, Florida	10.9
43	Vermilion County, Illinois	92.6	48	Anderson County, Tennessee	10.9
43	Kershaw County, South Carolina	92.6	48	Greene County, Ohio	10.9
43	Kanawha County, West Virginia	92.6	48	Ingham County, Michigan	10.9
52	Fond du Lac County, Wisconsin	92.5	52	Warren County, Kentucky	10.8
52	Frederick County, Virginia	92.5	52	Richland County, South Carolina	10.8
52	Armstrong County, Pennsylvania	92.5	54	St. Johns County, Florida	10.7
52	Augusta County, Virginia	92.5	54	Montgomery County, Tennessee	10.7
52	Bucks County, Pennsylvania	92.5	54	Nacogdoches County, Texas	10.7
52	Westmoreland County, Pennsylvania	92.5	54	Jefferson County, New York	10.7
52	Carver County, Minnesota	92.5	58	Gallatin County, Montana	10.6
59	Beaver County, Pennsylvania	92.4	58	Boone County, Missouri	10.6
59	Schuylkill County, Pennsylvania	92.4	60	James City County, Virginia	10.4
59	Crawford County, Pennsylvania	92.4	60	District of Columbia, District of Columbia	10.4
59	Geauga County, Ohio	92.4	62	Paulding County, Georgia	10.3
59	Porter County, Indiana	92.4	62	Comal County, Texas	10.3
59	Racine County, Wisconsin	92.4	62	Adams County, Colorado	10.3
59	Anoka County, Minnesota	92.4	62	DeKalb County, Illinois	10.3
66	Mercer County, Pennsylvania	92.3	62	New Hanover County, North Carolina	10.3
66	Medina County, Ohio	92.3	67	Rockwall County, Texas	10.2
66	McCracken County, Kentucky	92.3	67	Manatee County, Florida	10.2
66	Ocean County, New Jersey	92.3	67	Dorchester County, South Carolina	10.2
66	Greenwood County, South Carolina	92.3	67	Cumberland County, North Carolina	10.2
71	Putnam County, Florida	92.2	71	Newport County, Rhode Island	10.1
71	Shiawassee County, Michigan	92.2	71	Charleston County, South Carolina	10.1
71	Roanoke County, Virginia	92.2	71	Pitt County, North Carolina	10.1
71	Calvert County, Maryland	92.2	74	Santa Rosa County, Florida	10.0
71	Chemung County, New York	92.2	74	Virginia Beach city, Virginia	10.0
71	Lenawee County, Michigan	92.2	74	Suffolk County, Massachusetts	10.0
71	Morgan County, Indiana	92.2	74	Chatham County, Georgia	10.0
71	Carbon County, Pennsylvania	92.2	74	Delaware County, Indiana	10.0

County Rankings, 2023

Selected Rankings

Perent with a commute to work of less than 10 minutes rank	County	Perent with a commute to work of less than 10 minutes [C-2. col. 11]	Percent owner-occupied housing units rank	County	Percent owner-occupied housing units [C-2, col. 5]
	UNITED STATES	12.5		**UNITED STATES**	65.2
1	Grand Forks County, North Dakota	35.2	1	Oldham County, Kentucky	89.9
2	Riley County, Kansas	34.5	2	Livingston County, Michigan	88.7
3	Lea County, New Mexico	31.9	3	Geauga County, Ohio	88.5
4	Wichita County, Texas	31.2	4	Sumter County, Florida	87.9
5	Umatilla County, Oregon	30.9	5	Lapeer County, Michigan	87.3
6	Marquette County, Michigan	30.8	6	Calvert County, Maryland	86.4
7	Aroostook County, Maine	30.5	7	Carroll County, Maryland	86.0
8	Navajo County, Arizona	30.1	8	St. Clair County, Alabama	86.0
9	Grant County, Washington	29.2	9	Hunterdon County, New Jersey	85.6
10	Payne County, Oklahoma	28.9	10	Kendall County, Illinois	85.3
10	Manitowoc County, Wisconsin	28.9	11	Bullitt County, Kentucky	85.1
12	Wood County, Wisconsin	28.4	12	Sussex County, New Jersey	85.0
13	Cape Girardeau County, Missouri	28.3	13	Jefferson County, Missouri	84.8
14	Hancock County, Ohio	27.8	14	Wright County, Minnesota	84.8
15	Otero County, New Mexico	27.7	15	Allegan County, Michigan	84.6
15	Chautauqua County, New York	27.7	16	Sherburne County, Minnesota	84.6
17	Rice County, Minnesota	27.6	17	Kershaw County, South Carolina	84.4
18	Cascade County, Montana	27.5	18	Montcalm County, Michigan	84.3
18	Douglas County, Oregon	27.5	19	Hernando County, Florida	84.2
20	Chelan County, Washington	27.4	20	Mason County, Washington	84.1
21	Humboldt County, California	27.1	21	Belknap County, New Hampshire	83.9
21	Mendocino County, California	27.1	22	Forsyth County, Georgia	83.9
23	Ward County, North Dakota	26.8	23	Tooele County, Utah	83.9
23	Eau Claire County, Wisconsin	26.8	24	Georgetown County, South Carolina	83.8
25	Angelina County, Texas	26.7	25	Brunswick County, North Carolina	83.8
26	Christian County, Kentucky	26.6	26	Charlotte County, Florida	83.7
27	Butte County, California	26.4	27	Charles County, Maryland	83.7
27	Story County, Iowa	26.4	28	Pender County, North Carolina	83.4
27	Nacogdoches County, Texas	26.4	29	Chatham County, North Carolina	83.3
30	Cattaraugus County, New York	26.1	30	McHenry County, Illinois	83.2
30	St. Lawrence County, New York	26.1	31	Lancaster County, South Carolina	82.9
32	Grant County, Indiana	25.9	32	Scott County, Minnesota	82.9
33	Monroe County, Florida	25.8	33	Cape May County, New Jersey	82.9
34	Oneida County, New York	25.7	34	Washington County, Minnesota	82.8
34	Fond du Lac County, Wisconsin	25.7	35	Will County, Illinois	82.8
36	Cache County, Utah	25.6	36	Flagler County, Florida	82.8
37	Bannock County, Idaho	25.4	37	Frederick County, Virginia	82.7
37	Coryell County, Texas	25.4	38	Ascension Parish, Louisiana	82.7
39	Clallam County, Washington	25.3	39	Shelby County, Alabama	82.6
40	Jefferson County, New York	24.8	40	Toa Alta Municipio, Puerto Rico	82.6
41	Tehama County, California	24.7	41	Citrus County, Florida	82.5
41	Dubuque County, Iowa	24.7	42	Santa Rosa County, Florida	82.4
43	Blue Earth County, Minnesota	24.6	43	Livingston Parish, Louisiana	82.3
43	Lycoming County, Pennsylvania	24.6	44	St. Johns County, Florida	82.2
43	San Patricio County, Texas	24.6	45	DeSoto County, Mississippi	82.2
46	Cape May County, New Jersey	24.3	46	DeKalb County, Alabama	82.1
47	Blair County, Pennsylvania	24.2	47	Pinal County, Arizona	82.0
48	Coconino County, Arizona	24.1	48	Fauquier County, Virginia	82.0
48	Grays Harbor County, Washington	24.1	49	Bedford County, Virginia	81.9
50	Sauk County, Wisconsin	24.0	50	Wagoner County, Oklahoma	81.9
51	Twin Falls County, Idaho	23.8	51	Warrick County, Indiana	81.8
51	Berrien County, Michigan	23.8	52	Carver County, Minnesota	81.6
51	Josephine County, Oregon	23.8	53	Kaufman County, Texas	81.6
54	Howard County, Indiana	23.5	54	Columbia County, Georgia	81.5
54	Allen County, Ohio	23.5	55	Clinton County, Michigan	81.4
56	Chemung County, New York	23.4	56	St. Charles County, Missouri	81.4
57	Cayuga County, New York	23.3	57	Van Buren County, Michigan	81.3
57	Comanche County, Oklahoma	23.3	58	Putnam County, New York	81.3
59	Walworth County, Wisconsin	23.2	59	Wise County, Texas	81.3
60	Sutter County, California	23.1	60	Shiawassee County, Michigan	81.2
60	Portage County, Wisconsin	23.1	61	Suffolk County, New York	81.2
62	Bonneville County, Idaho	22.8	62	Muskegon County, Michigan	81.2
63	Steuben County, New York	22.7	63	Nassau County, New York	81.1
63	Carteret County, North Carolina	22.7	64	Union County, North Carolina	81.1
65	Dodge County, Wisconsin	22.5	65	Nassau County, Florida	81.1
66	Yamhill County, Oregon	22.4	66	Morgan County, Indiana	81.1
67	Apache County, Arizona	22.2	67	Stafford County, Virginia	81.1
67	Imperial County, California	22.2	68	Guadalupe County, Texas	81.0
67	McCracken County, Kentucky	22.2	69	Sussex County, Delaware	80.9
67	Klamath County, Oregon	22.2	70	Monroe County, Michigan	80.8
67	Mercer County, Pennsylvania	22.2	71	Effingham County, Georgia	80.8
72	Allegany County, Maryland	22.1	72	Liberty County, Texas	80.8
72	Clinton County, New York	22.1	73	Walton County, Florida	80.7
74	Vermilion County, Illinois	22.0	74	Hanover County, Virginia	80.6
74	Madison County, Tennessee	22.0	75	Northwest Hills Planning Region, Connecticut	80.6

County Rankings, 2023

Selected Rankings

Percent owner-occupied housing units with a mortgage, contract to purchase, or similar debt rank	County	Percent owner-occupied housing units with a mortgage, contract to purchase, or similar debt [C-2, col. 6]	Percent of households without Internet access rank	County	Percent of households without Internet access [C-2, col. 9]	Median value of owner-occupied units rank	County	Median value of owner-occupied housing units [C-4, col. 7]
	UNITED STATES	60.2		**UNITED STATES**	7.8		**UNITED STATES**	340,200
1	Stafford County, Virginia	81.5	1	Apache County, Arizona	34.9	1	Marin County, California	1,512,200
2	Charles County, Maryland	81.4	2	St. Landry Parish, Louisiana	30.4	2	San Mateo County, California	1,492,600
3	Spotsylvania County, Virginia	80.3	3	McKinley County, New Mexico	27.5	3	Santa Clara County, California	1,443,100
4	Prince William County, Virginia	79.2	4	San Juan Municipio, Puerto Rico	24.1	4	San Francisco County, California	1,348,000
5	Loudoun County, Virginia	78.5	5	Navajo County, Arizona	21.6	5	Alameda County, California	1,067,800
6	Douglas County, Colorado	77.6	6	Arecibo Municipio, Puerto Rico	19.3	6	Santa Cruz County, California	1,011,300
7	Calvert County, Maryland	77.4	7	Lee County, North Carolina	18.6	7	New York County, New York	1,010,800
8	District of Columbia, District of Columbia	77.3	7	Greene County, Tennessee	18.6	8	Orange County, California	961,400
9	Prince George's County, Maryland	77.2	9	Indiana County, Pennsylvania	18.4	9	Maui County, Hawaii	934,500
10	Kendall County, Illinois	76.0	10	San Juan County, New Mexico	18.2	10	Honolulu County, Hawaii	899,300
11	Suffolk city, Virginia	75.3	11	Marquette County, Michigan	17.8	11	Kauai County, Hawaii	888,500
12	Tooele County, Utah	75.2	12	Randolph County, North Carolina	17.6	12	Kings County, New York	880,300
13	Hamilton County, Indiana	75.1	13	Ouachita Parish, Louisiana	17.3	13	San Diego County, California	864,900
14	Alexandria city, Virginia	74.8	13	Orangeburg County, South Carolina	17.3	14	Arlington County, Virginia	850,900
15	Sherburne County, Minnesota	74.7	15	Robeson County, North Carolina	17.0	15	King County, Washington	848,300
15	Virginia Beach city, Virginia	74.7	15	Raleigh County, West Virginia	17.0	16	Napa County, California	831,800
17	Mecklenburg County, North Carolina	74.6	17	Story County, Iowa	16.8	17	Contra Costa County, California	829,600
18	Douglas County, Georgia	74.4	17	Walker County, Texas	16.8	18	Los Angeles County, California	828,700
19	Union County, Ohio	74.3	19	Marion County, Ohio	16.7	19	Ventura County, California	820,300
19	Paulding County, Georgia	74.3	20	Cattaraugus County, New York	16.6	20	San Luis Obispo County, California	817,600
21	Union County, North Carolina	74.2	21	Dougherty County, Georgia	16.4	21	Monroe County, Florida	806,100
21	Newton County, Georgia	74.2	22	Caddo Parish, Louisiana	16.1	22	Sonoma County, California	784,900
23	Solano County, California	74.1	22	Muskogee County, Oklahoma	16.1	23	Santa Barbara County, California	780,700
24	Portsmouth city, Virginia	73.9	24	Tuscarawas County, Ohio	16.0	24	Williamson County, Tennessee	777,800
25	Sarpy County, Nebraska	73.8	25	Pottawattamie County, Iowa	15.9	25	Boulder County, Colorado	763,600
25	Norfolk city, Virginia	73.8	25	Blue Earth County, Minnesota	15.9	26	San Benito County, California	761,600
27	Frederick County, Maryland	73.7	25	Somerset County, Pennsylvania	15.9	27	Monterey County, California	759,100
28	Arapahoe County, Colorado	73.6	25	Augusta County, Virginia	15.9	28	Alexandria city, Virginia	737,900
29	Anne Arundel County, Maryland	73.5	29	Merced County, California	15.7	29	Loudoun County, Virginia	734,700
29	Wake County, North Carolina	73.5	30	Ector County, Texas	14.9	30	Fairfax County, Virginia	727,200
31	Onslow County, North Carolina	73.4	31	St. Lawrence County, New York	14.8	31	Douglas County, Colorado	725,500
32	Hampton city, Virginia	73.3	31	Nash County, North Carolina	14.8	32	Middlesex County, Massachusetts	716,100
33	Forsyth County, Georgia	73.2	31	Rutherford County, North Carolina	14.8	33	District of Columbia, District of Columbia	715,500
34	Columbia County, Georgia	72.9	34	Garland County, Arkansas	14.7	34	Snohomish County, Washington	697,700
35	Weld County, Colorado	72.8	35	Henderson County, Texas	14.6	35	Queens County, New York	692,500
35	Fulton County, Georgia	72.8	36	Iberia Parish, Louisiana	14.5	36	El Dorado County, California	691,600
37	Utah County, Utah	72.5	37	Jefferson County, Arkansas	14.3	37	Gallatin County, Montana	691,200
37	Henry County, Georgia	72.5	37	Fayette County, Pennsylvania	14.3	38	Norfolk County, Massachusetts	686,500
39	Washington County, Oregon	72.4	39	Roanoke city, Virginia	14.2	39	Suffolk County, Massachusetts	683,900
39	Harnett County, North Carolina	72.4	40	Lauderdale County, Alabama	14.0	40	Nassau County, New York	674,200
39	Arlington County, Virginia	72.4	40	Coconino County, Arizona	14.0	41	Placer County, California	673,900
42	Denver County, Colorado	72.2	42	Valencia County, New Mexico	13.9	42	Richmond County, New York	672,400
43	Cabarrus County, North Carolina	72.1	43	Aroostook County, Maine	13.8	43	Deschutes County, Oregon	662,700
43	Chesterfield County, Virginia	72.1	44	Sebastian County, Arkansas	13.7	44	Broomfield County, Colorado	660,800
43	Clark County, Washington	72.1	44	Grant County, Indiana	13.7	45	Western Connecticut Planning Region, Connecticut	657,900
46	Adams County, Colorado	71.8	46	Lowndes County, Georgia	13.6	46	Nevada County, California	647,200
47	Chesapeake city, Virginia	71.7	47	Jones County, Mississippi	13.4	47	Jefferson County, Colorado	645,900
48	Montgomery County, Maryland	71.2	47	Wood County, West Virginia	13.4	48	Westchester County, New York	645,700
48	Pierce County, Washington	71.2	49	Bibb County, Georgia	13.3	49	Montgomery County, Maryland	636,200
50	El Dorado County, California	71.1	49	Floyd County, Georgia	13.3	50	Barnstable County, Massachusetts	634,700
50	Snohomish County, Washington	71.1	49	Rapides Parish, Louisiana	13.3	51	Newport County, Rhode Island	633,700
50	Kings County, California	71.1	52	Montcalm County, Michigan	13.2	52	Monmouth County, New Jersey	628,000
53	Delaware County, Ohio	71.0	53	Harrison County, Texas	13.1	53	Denver County, Colorado	626,500
53	Wright County, Minnesota	71.0	53	Rockingham County, Virginia	13.1	54	Essex County, Massachusetts	624,700
55	El Paso County, Colorado	70.9	55	Richmond County, Georgia	13.0	55	Solano County, California	621,000
55	Hancock County, Indiana	70.9	55	Kosciusko County, Indiana	13.0	56	Bergen County, New Jersey	615,300
55	Clayton County, Georgia	70.9	55	Cambria County, Pennsylvania	13.0	57	Whatcom County, Washington	611,200
58	Fauquier County, Virginia	70.8	55	San Patricio County, Texas	13.0	58	Yolo County, California	610,000
59	St. Mary's County, Maryland	70.6	59	Lauderdale County, Mississippi	12.9	59	Clackamas County, Oregon	605,400
59	Rockdale County, Georgia	70.6	59	Steuben County, New York	12.9	60	Howard County, Maryland	603,400
61	Oldham County, Kentucky	70.5	59	Schuylkill County, Pennsylvania	12.9	61	Rockland County, New York	600,500
61	Sussex County, New Jersey	70.5	59	Lewis County, Washington	12.9	62	Collier County, Florida	595,500
63	Washington County, Minnesota	70.4	63	Calhoun County, Alabama	12.8	63	Island County, Washington	595,100
63	Davidson County, Tennessee	70.4	63	Calcasieu Parish, Louisiana	12.8	64	Washington County, Oregon	589,000
63	DeKalb County, Illinois	70.4	63	Bay County, Michigan	12.8	65	Forsyth County, Georgia	587,300
66	Cobb County, Georgia	70.3	63	Buchanan County, Missouri	12.8	66	Suffolk County, New York	584,800
66	Larimer County, Colorado	70.3	67	Cullman County, Alabama	12.7	67	Morris County, New Jersey	577,700
66	Denton County, Texas	70.3	67	Orange County, Texas	12.7	68	Riverside County, California	576,000
66	Lincoln County, South Dakota	70.3	69	Vigo County, Indiana	12.5	69	Larimer County, Colorado	574,900
66	Hays County, Texas	70.3	70	McCracken County, Kentucky	12.4	70	Flathead County, Montana	570,800
71	Scott County, Minnesota	70.2	70	Clearfield County, Pennsylvania	12.4	71	Utah County, Utah	570,100
71	Multnomah County, Oregon	70.2	70	Sumter County, South Carolina	12.4	72	Travis County, Texas	569,000
71	Warren County, Ohio	70.2	70	Brazos County, Texas	12.4	73	Plymouth County, Massachusetts	568,500
71	Essex County, Massachusetts	70.2	70	Cabell County, West Virginia	12.4	74	Arapahoe County, Colorado	567,300
71	DeKalb County, Georgia	70.2	75	Burleigh County, North Dakota	12.3	75	Kitsap County, Washington	564,600
71	Kauai County, Hawaii	70.2	75	Columbiana County, Ohio	12.3			
			75	Crawford County, Pennsylvania	12.3			
			75	Liberty County, Texas	12.3			
			75	Starr County, Texas	12.3			

Metropolitan Area Rankings, 2023

Selected Rankings

Lived in the same house one year ago rank	Area name	Percent who lived in the same house one year ago [C-3, col. 2]	Percent owner-occupied housing units rank	Area name	Percent owner-occupied housing units [C-3, col. 5]
	UNITED STATES	87.9		**UNITED STATES**	65.2
1	Farmington, NM	93.2	1	Wildwood-The Villages, FL	87.9
2	El Centro, CA	93.0	2	Punta Gorda, FL	83.7
3	Kankakee, IL	92.7	3	Homosassa Springs, FL	82.5
4	Visalia, CA	92.6	4	Traverse City, MI	81.3
4	Sandusky, OH	92.6	5	Muskegon-Norton Shores, MI	81.2
6	Fond du Lac, WI	92.5	6	Monroe, MI	80.8
6	Charleston, WV	92.5	7	Sebring, FL	80.1
8	Racine-Mount Pleasant, WI	92.4	8	Sebastian-Vero Beach-West Vero Corridor, FL	79.8
9	Elmira, NY	92.2	9	Lexington Park, MD	78.9
10	Traverse City, MI	92.1	10	Myrtle Beach-Conway-North Myrtle Beach, SC	78.7
11	Midland, MI	91.9	10	Slidell-Mandeville-Covington, LA	78.7
12	Johnstown, PA	91.8	12	Port St. Lucie, FL	78.6
12	Rocky Mount, NC	91.8	13	Barnstable Town, MA	78.5
12	Santa Fe, NM	91.8	14	Gettysburg, PA	78.1
12	Paducah, KY-IL	91.8	15	Bay City, MI	77.7
16	Florence, SC	91.6	16	Ocala, FL	77.6
16	Springfield, MA	91.6	17	Midland, MI	77.4
18	Grants Pass, OR	91.5	18	Naples-Marco Island, FL	77.2
18	Canton-Massillon, OH	91.5	19	Jackson, MI	76.8
18	Elkhart-Goshen, IN	91.5	20	Palm Bay-Melbourne-Titusville, FL	76.7
18	Bakersfield-Delano, CA	91.5	21	Houma-Bayou Cane-Thibodaux, LA	76.6
22	Bay City, MI	91.4	21	Kingsport-Bristol, TN-VA	76.6
22	Appleton, WI	91.4	21	Ogden, UT	76.6
22	Decatur, AL	91.4	21	Saginaw, MI	76.6
25	Hickory-Lenoir-Morganton, NC	91.3	25	Johnstown, PA	76.5
25	Roanoke, VA	91.3	26	Chambersburg, PA	76.4
25	Vineland, NJ	91.3	27	Prescott Valley-Prescott, AZ	75.9
28	New York-Newark-Jersey City, NY-NJ	91.2	28	North Port-Bradenton-Sarasota, FL	75.6
28	Merced, CA	91.2	28	Pinehurst-Southern Pines, NC	75.6
28	Glens Falls, NY	91.2	30	Decatur, AL	75.3
31	Sebastian-Vero Beach-West Vero Corridor, FL	91.1	30	Deltona-Daytona Beach-Ormond Beach, FL	75.3
32	Kiryas Joel-Poughkeepsie-Newburgh, NY	91.0	32	Cape Coral-Fort Myers, FL	75.2
33	Punta Gorda, FL	90.9	32	Hilton Head Island-Bluffton-Port Royal, SC	75.2
33	Idaho Falls, ID	90.9	32	Sandusky, OH	75.2
35	Oxnard-Thousand Oaks-Ventura, CA	90.8	35	York-Hanover, PA	75.1
35	Houma-Bayou Cane-Thibodaux, LA	90.8	36	Lake Havasu City-Kingman, AZ	75.0
35	Allentown-Bethlehem-Easton, PA-NJ	90.8	37	Daphne-Fairhope-Foley, AL	74.9
35	Modesto, CA	90.8	38	Grand Rapids-Wyoming-Kentwood, MI	74.8
35	Saginaw, MI	90.8	38	Greeley, CO	74.8
35	McAllen-Edinburg-Mission, TX	90.8	40	Guayama, PR	74.7
41	Los Angeles-Long Beach-Anaheim, CA	90.7	40	Parkersburg-Vienna, WV	74.7
41	Texarkana, TX-AR	90.7	40	Rochester, MN	74.7
41	Dothan, AL	90.7	43	Gadsden, AL	74.6
41	Reading, PA	90.7	44	Peoria, IL	74.5
41	Riverside-San Bernardino-Ontario, CA	90.7	45	Beckley, WV	74.4
41	Waterbury-Shelton, CT	90.7	46	Michigan City-La Porte, IN	74.3
47	York-Hanover, PA	90.6	46	Morristown, TN	74.3
48	Morristown, TN	90.5	48	Dubuque, IA	74.1
48	Sioux City, IA-NE-SD	90.5	49	Grants Pass, OR	73.9
48	Kahului-Wailuku, HI	90.5	50	Cedar Rapids, IA	73.8
51	Port St. Lucie, FL	90.4	51	Niles, MI	73.7
51	Daphne-Fairhope-Foley, AL	90.4	52	Bismarck, ND	73.6
51	Laredo, TX	90.4	53	Winchester, VA-WV	73.5
54	Brownsville-Harlingen, TX	90.3	54	Coeur d'Alene, ID	73.4
54	Utica-Rome, NY	90.3	54	Portland-South Portland, ME	73.4
54	Winchester, VA-WV	90.3	54	Weirton-Steubenville, WV-OH	73.4
54	Mobile, AL	90.3	57	Casper, WY	73.3
58	Kingsport-Bristol, TN-VA	90.2	58	Glens Falls, NY	73.2
58	Peoria, IL	90.2	59	Davenport-Moline-Rock Island, IA-IL	73.1
58	Pittsfield, MA	90.2	59	Lake Charles, LA	73.1
61	Valdosta, GA	90.1	61	Appleton, WI	73.0
61	St. Joseph, MO-KS	90.1	61	Dover, DE	73.0
61	Gainesville, GA	90.1	61	Hickory-Lenoir-Morganton, NC	73.0
61	Fresno, CA	90.1	61	Idaho Falls, ID	73.0
61	Monroe, MI	90.1	61	St. George, UT	73.0
61	Detroit-Warren-Dearborn, MI	90.1	66	Wausau, WI	72.9
67	Jefferson City, MO	90.0	67	Wheeling, WV-OH	72.7
68	Kenosha, WI	89.9	68	Farmington, NM	72.6
68	Florence-Muscle Shoals, AL	89.9	69	Crestview-Fort Walton Beach-Destin, FL	72.5
68	Stockton-Lodi, CA	89.9	69	Duluth, MN-WI	72.5
68	Ogden, UT	89.9	69	Pensacola-Ferry Pass-Brent, FL	72.5
68	Eagle Pass, TX	89.9	69	Racine-Mount Pleasant, WI	72.5
68	Portland-South Portland, ME	89.9	73	Battle Creek, MI	72.4
68	Youngstown-Warren, OH	89.9	73	Huntington-Ashland, WV-KY-OH	72.4
68	Chambersburg, PA	89.9	73	Kingston, NY	72.4
			73	Spartanburg, SC	72.4

Metropolitan Area Rankings, 2023

Selected Rankings

Percent with commute less than 10 minutes rank	Area name	Percent with commute less than 10 minutes [C-3, col. 11]	Median value of owner-occupied units rank	Area name	Median value of owner-occupied housing units [C-3, col. 7]
	UNITED STATES	12.5		**UNITED STATES**	340,200
1	Grand Forks, ND-MN	34.7	1	San Jose-Sunnyvale-Santa Clara, CA	1,393,400
2	Walla Walla, WA	34.5	2	San Francisco-Oakland-Fremont, CA	1,105,100
3	Wichita Falls, TX	30.1	3	Santa Cruz-Watsonville, CA	1,011,300
4	Manhattan, KS	29.5	4	Kahului-Wailuku, HI	934,500
5	Great Falls, MT	27.5	5	Urban Honolulu, HI	899,300
6	Mankato, MN	26.5	6	Los Angeles-Long Beach-Anaheim, CA	867,200
6	Minot, ND	26.5	7	San Diego-Chula Vista-Carlsbad, CA	864,900
8	Chico, CA	26.4	8	Napa, CA	831,800
9	Ames, IA	26.3	9	Oxnard-Thousand Oaks-Ventura, CA	820,300
10	Grand Island, NE	25.8	10	San Luis Obispo-Paso Robles, CA	817,600
11	Cape Girardeau, MO-IL	25.7	11	Santa Rosa-Petaluma, CA	784,900
11	Fond du Lac, WI	25.7	12	Santa Maria-Santa Barbara, CA	780,700
13	Pocatello, ID	25.4	13	Boulder, CO	763,600
14	Logan, UT-ID	25.3	14	Salinas, CA	759,100
15	Watertown-Fort Drum, NY	24.8	15	Seattle-Tacoma-Bellevue, WA	712,200
16	Dubuque, IA	24.7	16	Bozeman, MT	691,200
17	Williamsport, PA	24.6	17	Boston-Cambridge-Newton, MA-NH	646,600
18	Eau Claire, WI	24.3	18	Barnstable Town, MA	634,700
19	Altoona, PA	24.2	19	Bend, OR	622,900
20	Flagstaff, AZ	24.1	20	Vallejo, CA	621,000
21	Wenatchee-East Wenatchee, WA	23.9	21	Denver-Aurora-Centennial, CO	611,300
22	Grants Pass, OR	23.8	22	Bellingham, WA	611,200
22	Niles, MI	23.8	23	New York-Newark-Jersey City, NY-NJ	610,200
24	Kokomo, IN	23.5	24	Naples-Marco Island, FL	595,500
24	Lawton, OK	23.5	25	Sacramento-Roseville-Folsom, CA	587,600
24	Lima, OH	23.5	26	Fort Collins-Loveland, CO	574,900
27	Elmira, NY	23.4	27	Bridgeport-Stamford-Danbury, CT	574,800
28	Utica-Rome, NY	23.0	28	Washington-Arlington-Alexandria, DC-VA-MD-WV	574,000
29	Enid, OK	22.9	29	Provo-Orem-Lehi, UT	566,900
29	Lewiston, ID-WA	22.9	30	Bremerton-Silverdale-Port Orchard, WA	564,600
31	El Centro, CA	22.2	31	Portland-Vancouver-Hillsboro, OR-WA	560,900
32	Lawrence, KS	21.8	32	Mount Vernon-Anacortes, WA	558,300
33	Sierra Vista-Douglas, AZ	21.7	33	Coeur d'Alene, ID	556,500
33	Twin Falls, ID	21.7	34	Riverside-San Bernardino-Ontario, CA	552,000
33	Waterloo-Cedar Falls, IA	21.7	35	Salt Lake City-Murray, UT	547,500
36	Sioux City, IA-NE-SD	21.6	36	Corvallis, OR	538,100
37	Joplin, MO-KS	21.4	37	Stockton-Lodi, CA	531,500
38	La Crosse-Onalaska, WI-MN	21.2	38	St. George, UT	528,100
39	Jacksonville, NC	21.1	39	Reno, NV	509,700
39	San Luis Obispo-Paso Robles, CA	21.1	40	Olympia-Lacey-Tumwater, WA	493,100
41	Idaho Falls, ID	20.9	41	Wenatchee-East Wenatchee, WA	489,300
41	Jonesboro, AR	20.9	42	Missoula, MT	487,700
41	Peoria, IL	20.9	43	Ogden, UT	487,400
44	Bismarck, ND	20.8	44	Austin-Round Rock-San Marcos, TX	487,200
44	Bloomington, IL	20.8	45	Santa Fe, NM	485,300
46	Lake Havasu City-Kingman, AZ	20.7	46	Greeley, CO	475,400
46	Texarkana, TX-AR	20.7	47	Miami-Fort Lauderdale-West Palm Beach, FL	474,000
48	Oshkosh-Neenah, WI	20.6	48	Colorado Springs, CO	472,600
49	Mansfield, OH	20.5	49	Boise City, ID	471,700
50	Jefferson City, MO	20.4	50	Flagstaff, AZ	470,900
51	Medford, OR	20.3	51	Logan, UT-ID	466,900
52	Grand Junction, CO	20.1	52	Phoenix-Mesa-Chandler, AZ	457,400
52	Victoria, TX	20.1	53	Modesto, CA	456,700
54	Sherman-Denison, TX	20.0	54	Carson City, NV	455,100
55	San Angelo, TX	19.9	55	Prescott Valley-Prescott, AZ	454,200
56	Hinesville, GA	19.7	56	Hilton Head Island-Bluffton-Port Royal, SC	453,800
56	Napa, CA	19.7	57	Portland-South Portland, ME	444,600
58	Cedar Rapids, IA	19.6	58	Raleigh-Cary, NC	439,500
58	Corvallis, OR	19.6	59	North Port-Bradenton-Sarasota, FL	438,600
58	Hanford-Corcoran, CA	19.6	60	Eugene-Springfield, OR	438,200
58	Muncie, IN	19.6	61	Las Vegas-Henderson-North Las Vegas, NV	437,900
62	Amarillo, TX	19.4	62	Nashville-Davidson--Murfreesboro--Franklin, TN	437,200
62	Prescott Valley-Prescott, AZ	19.4	62	Salem, OR	437,200
64	Sheboygan, WI	19.3	64	Lexington Park, MD	434,200
64	Terre Haute, IN	19.3	65	Worcester, MA	433,900
64	Topeka, KS	19.3	66	Medford, OR	431,500
67	Pittsfield, MA	19.2	67	Charlottesville, VA	431,200
68	Abilene, TX	19.1	68	Manchester-Nashua, NH	430,300
68	Glens Falls, NY	19.1	69	Providence-Warwick, RI-MA	430,200
70	Bend, OR	19.0	70	Walla Walla, WA	429,700
70	Sandusky, OH	19.0	71	Chico, CA	420,500
72	Midland, MI	18.9	72	Spokane-Spokane Valley, WA	417,000
72	St. George, UT	18.9	73	Kennewick-Richland, WA	416,600
74	Lubbock, TX	18.8	74	Durham-Chapel Hill, NC	414,600
75	Duluth, MN-WI	18.7	75	Wildwood-The Villages, FL	411,000
75	Hot Springs, AR	18.7			
75	Jackson, TN	18.7			
75	St. Joseph, MO-KS	18.7			
75	Wausau, WI	18.7			

Metropolitan Area Rankings, 2023

Selected Rankings

Percent of owners with a mortgage, contract to purchase, or similar debt rank	Area name	Percent of owners with a mortgage, contract to purchase, or similar debt [C-3, col. 6]	Percent of households without Internet access rank	Area name	Percent of households without access to the Internet [C-3, col. 9]
	UNITED STATES	60.2		**UNITED STATES**	7.8
1	Washington-Arlington-Alexandria, DC-VA-MD-WV	74.7	1	Arecibo, PR	19.3
2	Vallejo, CA	74.1	2	Monroe, LA	18.8
3	Lexington Park, MD	73.8	3	Farmington, NM	18.2
4	Jacksonville, NC	73.4	4	Mayagüez, PR	16.7
5	Greeley, CO	72.8	5	Beckley, WV	16.6
6	Denver-Aurora-Centennial, CO	72.4	6	Albany, GA	16.4
7	Provo-Orem-Lehi, UT	72.3	7	Rocky Mount, NC	16.1
8	Raleigh-Cary, NC	72.0	8	Merced, CA	15.7
9	Hanford-Corcoran, CA	71.1	9	Eagle Pass, TX	15.3
10	Virginia Beach-Chesapeake-Norfolk, VA-NC	71.0	10	Ames, IA	15.1
11	Colorado Springs, CO	70.7	11	Odessa, TX	14.9
12	Fort Collins-Loveland, CO	70.3	12	Hot Springs, AR	14.7
13	Portland-Vancouver-Hillsboro, OR-WA	69.8	13	Valdosta, GA	14.5
14	Salt Lake City-Murray, UT	69.6	14	Parkersburg-Vienna, WV	14.3
15	Baltimore-Columbia-Towson, MD	69.5	14	Walla Walla, WA	14.3
16	Visalia, CA	69.4	16	Mankato, MN	14.2
16	Seattle-Tacoma-Bellevue, WA	69.4	17	Aguadilla, PR	14.1
16	Atlanta-Sandy Springs-Roswell, GA	69.4	17	Alexandria, LA	14.1
19	Worcester, MA	69.2	19	Flagstaff, AZ	14.0
20	Dover, DE	69.1	19	San Juan-Bayamón-Caguas, PR	14.0
21	Indianapolis-Carmel-Greenwood, IN	69.0	21	Paducah, KY-IL	13.9
22	Ogden, UT	68.9	22	Lake Charles, LA	13.8
22	San Diego-Chula Vista-Carlsbad, CA	68.9	22	Shreveport-Bossier City, LA	13.8
22	Minneapolis-St. Paul-Bloomington, MN-WI	68.9	24	Guayama, PR	13.6
22	Sacramento-Roseville-Folsom, CA	68.9	24	Kingsport-Bristol, TN-VA	13.6
26	Charlotte-Concord-Gastonia, NC-SC	68.7	26	Florence-Muscle Shoals, AL	13.5
27	Riverside-San Bernardino-Ontario, CA	68.6	26	Wheeling, WV-OH	13.5
28	Pueblo, CO	68.3	28	Harrisonburg, VA	13.3
28	Columbus, OH	68.3	28	Rome, GA	13.3
28	Logan, UT-ID	68.3	30	Terre Haute, IN	13.2
31	Richmond, VA	68.1	30	Weirton-Steubenville, WV-OH	13.2
32	Los Angeles-Long Beach-Anaheim, CA	67.9	32	Johnstown, PA	13.0
32	Des Moines-West Des Moines, IA	67.9	33	Anniston-Oxford, AL	12.8
34	Burlington-South Burlington, VT	67.8	33	Bay City, MI	12.8
34	Stockton-Lodi, CA	67.8	33	Tuscaloosa, AL	12.8
36	San Francisco-Oakland-Fremont, CA	67.7	36	Dalton, GA	12.7
37	Boston-Cambridge-Newton, MA-NH	67.6	36	Longview, TX	12.7
38	Santa Rosa-Petaluma, CA	67.5	36	Staunton-Stuarts Draft, VA	12.7
39	Kenosha, WI	67.4	39	College Station-Bryan, TX	12.5
39	Hinesville, GA	67.4	40	Sumter, SC	12.4
41	Manchester-Nashua, NH	67.3	40	Texarkana, TX-AR	12.4
42	Bend, OR	66.9	42	Huntington-Ashland, WV-KY-OH	12.3
43	Oxnard-Thousand Oaks-Ventura, CA	66.6	42	St. Joseph, MO-KS	12.3
43	Nashville-Davidson--Murfreesboro--Franklin, TN	66.6	44	Kankakee, IL	12.2
45	Las Vegas-Henderson-North Las Vegas, NV	66.5	45	Columbus, GA-AL	12.1
46	Omaha, NE-IA	66.3	45	Sierra Vista-Douglas, AZ	12.1
46	Austin-Round Rock-San Marcos, TX	66.3	47	Altoona, PA	12.0
46	Albany, OR	66.3	47	Auburn-Opelika, AL	12.0
49	Boise City, ID	65.9	47	Dothan, AL	12.0
49	Bakersfield-Delano, CA	65.9	47	Fort Smith, AR-OK	12.0
49	Lawrence, KS	65.9	47	Lewiston, ID-WA	12.0
52	Lexington-Fayette, KY	65.8	47	Macon-Bibb County, GA	12.0
52	Slidell-Mandeville-Covington, LA	65.8	47	Roanoke, VA	12.0
54	San Jose-Sunnyvale-Santa Clara, CA	65.7	47	Springfield, MO	12.0
54	Bremerton-Silverdale-Port Orchard, WA	65.7	55	Gainesville, FL	11.9
54	Charleston-North Charleston, SC	65.7	56	Charleston, WV	11.7
54	Racine-Mount Pleasant, WI	65.7	57	Blacksburg-Christiansburg-Radford, VA	11.6
58	Phoenix-Mesa-Chandler, AZ	65.6	57	Michigan City-La Porte, IN	11.6
58	Olympia-Lacey-Tumwater, WA	65.6	57	Muncie, IN	11.6
60	Providence-Warwick, RI-MA	65.5	60	Decatur, AL	11.5
60	Cincinnati, OH-KY-IN	65.5	60	Youngstown-Warren, OH	11.5
60	Waterbury-Shelton, CT	65.5	62	Hattiesburg, MS	11.4
60	Anchorage, AK	65.5	63	Augusta-Richmond County, GA-SC	11.3
60	Fayetteville, NC	65.5	64	Battle Creek, MI	11.2
65	Madison, WI	65.2	64	Topeka, KS	11.2
66	Modesto, CA	65.1	64	Victoria, TX	11.2
66	Fargo, ND-MN	65.1	67	Enid, OK	11.1
66	Bozeman, MT	65.1	67	Minot, ND	11.1
69	Milwaukee-Waukesha, WI	64.9	67	Tallahassee, FL	11.1
70	Kokomo, IN	64.6	67	Williamsport, PA	11.1
71	Sioux Falls, SD-MN	64.4	71	State College, PA	11.0
71	Redding, CA	64.4	72	Brownsville-Harlingen, TX	10.9
73	Clarksville, TN-KY	64.3	72	Grand Forks, ND-MN	10.9
73	Fresno, CA	64.3	72	Lancaster, PA	10.9
75	Grand Junction, CO	64.2	72	San Angelo, TX	10.9

City Rankings, 2023

Selected Rankings

Lived in the same house one year ago rank	City	Percent who lived in the same house one year ago [C-4, col. 2]
	UNITED STATES	87.9
1	Baldwin Park city, California	96.7
2	Cicero town, Illinois	95.7
3	Tulare city, California	95.3
4	Bayonne city, New Jersey	95.0
5	Rialto city, California	94.8
6	Inglewood city, California	94.6
6	Santa Ana city, California	94.6
8	Mission Viejo city, California	94.5
9	San Leandro city, California	94.4
9	Sunrise city, Florida	94.4
9	Toms River CDP, New Jersey	94.4
12	Livonia city, Michigan	94.1
13	Jurupa Valley city, California	94.0
13	Murrieta city, California	94.0
15	Perris city, California	93.8
16	Downey city, California	93.7
16	Redlands city, California	93.7
16	Fishers city, Indiana	93.7
19	Daly City city, California	93.5
19	Fontana city, California	93.5
19	Haverhill city, Massachusetts	93.5
19	New Rochelle city, New York	93.5
23	Indio city, California	93.4
23	Westminster city, California	93.4
23	The Woodlands CDP, Texas	93.4
26	Brentwood city, California	93.3
26	East Los Angeles CDP, California	93.3
26	Ontario city, California	93.3
26	Whittier city, California	93.3
26	Lakeville city, Minnesota	93.3
31	Palmdale city, California	93.2
31	Clifton city, New Jersey	93.2
33	Corona city, California	93.1
33	Elk Grove city, California	93.1
33	Lancaster city, California	93.1
36	Apple Valley town, California	93.0
36	Brownsville city, Texas	93.0
38	Castro Valley CDP, California	92.9
38	Eastvale city, California	92.9
38	Tamarac city, Florida	92.9
38	Mount Vernon city, New York	92.9
42	Pittsburg city, California	92.8
42	San Bernardino city, California	92.8
42	San Ramon city, California	92.8
42	Kenner city, Louisiana	92.8
42	Rock Hill city, South Carolina	92.8
47	Buena Park city, California	92.5
47	Carson city, California	92.5
47	Richmond city, California	92.5
50	El Monte city, California	92.4
51	West Covina city, California	92.3
51	Danbury city, Connecticut	92.3
51	Shawnee city, Kansas	92.3
54	Livermore city, California	92.2
55	Modesto city, California	92.1
55	Maple Grove city, Minnesota	92.1
57	Kendall CDP, Florida	92.0
57	Johns Creek city, Georgia	92.0
57	Joliet city, Illinois	92.0
57	Naperville city, Illinois	92.0
57	Union City city, New Jersey	92.0
62	Moreno Valley city, California	91.9
62	Rancho Cucamonga city, California	91.9
62	Simi Valley city, California	91.9
62	Sioux City city, Iowa	91.9
62	Missouri City city, Texas	91.9
67	Oxnard city, California	91.8
67	Santa Maria city, California	91.8
69	Bellflower city, California	91.7
69	Torrance city, California	91.7
69	Blaine city, Minnesota	91.7
69	Pasco city, Washington	91.7
73	Springdale city, Arkansas	91.6
73	Lawrence city, Massachusetts	91.6
73	Cheektowaga CDP, New York	91.6
73	Laredo city, Texas	91.6

Percent with commute less than 10 minutes to work rank	City	Percent with commute less than 10 minutes to work [C-4. col. 11]
	UNITED STATES	12.5
1	Jacksonville city, North Carolina	37.5
2	Wichita Falls city, Texas	32.2
3	Chico city, California	31.0
4	Ames city, Iowa	30.9
5	Eau Claire city, Wisconsin	29.7
6	Idaho Falls city, Idaho	29.1
7	Muncie city, Indiana	28.9
8	Jackson city, Tennessee	27.4
9	Lawton city, Oklahoma	27.3
10	Flagstaff city, Arizona	26.1
11	Grand Junction city, Colorado	25.7
12	Tuscaloosa city, Alabama	25.6
13	Oshkosh city, Wisconsin	25.2
14	Lodi city, California	24.9
15	Victoria city, Texas	24.7
16	Medford city, Oregon	24.6
17	Bismarck city, North Dakota	24.0
18	Bloomington city, Illinois	23.9
19	Madera city, California	23.8
20	Kalamazoo city, Michigan	23.6
21	Albany city, Georgia	23.5
22	Lawrence city, Kansas	23.3
22	Topeka city, Kansas	23.3
22	Lake Charles city, Louisiana	23.3
25	Napa city, California	23.1
26	Yuba City city, California	23.0
26	Evansville city, Indiana	23.0
26	Fayetteville city, North Carolina	23.0
29	Peoria city, Illinois	22.8
30	Columbia city, South Carolina	22.7
31	Bowling Green city, Kentucky	22.1
32	Auburn city, Alabama	22.0
33	Yakima city, Washington	21.9
34	Conway city, Arkansas	21.8
34	St. Joseph city, Missouri	21.8
36	Turlock city, California	21.7
37	Decatur city, Illinois	21.5
37	Bloomington city, Indiana	21.5
39	Boulder city, Colorado	21.3
40	Jonesboro city, Arkansas	21.2
40	Merced city, California	21.2
40	Bellingham city, Washington	21.2
43	Ocala city, Florida	21.0
43	Greenville city, South Carolina	21.0
45	Bend city, Oregon	20.9
46	Redding city, California	20.8
46	Wilmington city, North Carolina	20.8
48	Waterloo city, Iowa	20.6
48	Cheyenne city, Wyoming	20.6
50	Lakewood CDP, New Jersey	20.3
50	Abilene city, Texas	20.3
52	Billings city, Montana	20.2
52	Canton city, Ohio	20.2
52	San Angelo city, Texas	20.2
55	Syracuse city, New York	20.1
55	Johnson City city, Tennessee	20.1
57	Greeley city, Colorado	20.0
57	Fargo city, North Dakota	20.0
59	Norman city, Oklahoma	19.9
60	Yuma city, Arizona	19.7
61	Bryan city, Texas	19.6
62	Orem city, Utah	19.5
63	Santa Barbara city, California	19.4
63	Frederick city, Maryland	19.4
63	Ogden city, Utah	19.4
66	Amarillo city, Texas	19.3
67	Cedar Rapids city, Iowa	19.0
67	Columbia city, Missouri	19.0
69	Duluth city, Minnesota	18.9
69	Rochester city, Minnesota	18.9
71	Grand Rapids city, Michigan	18.8
71	Lubbock city, Texas	18.8
73	Harlingen city, Texas	18.7
74	Dothan city, Alabama	18.4
74	Kenosha city, Wisconsin	18.4

Percent owner-occupied housing units rank	City	Percent owner-occupied housing units [C-4, col. 5]
	UNITED STATES	65.2
1	The Villages CDP, Florida	93.7
2	Queen Creek town, Arizona	93.3
3	Lakeville city, Minnesota	87.7
4	Livonia city, Michigan	87.0
5	San Tan Valley CDP, Arizona	86.1
6	Yorba Linda city, California	85.2
6	Blaine city, Minnesota	85.2
8	Tamarac city, Florida	85.0
9	Port St. Lucie city, Florida	84.9
10	Maricopa city, Arizona	84.8
11	South Jordan city, Utah	83.8
12	Buckeye city, Arizona	83.7
12	Sammamish city, Washington	83.7
14	Atascocita CDP, Texas	82.9
15	Dale City CDP, Virginia	82.8
16	O'Fallon city, Missouri	82.5
17	Bolingbrook village, Illinois	82.3
18	Spring Hill CDP, Florida	82.1
19	Brentwood city, California	81.8
20	Riverview CDP, Florida	81.6
21	Commerce City city, Colorado	81.5
21	Toms River CDP, New Jersey	81.5
23	Wesley Chapel CDP, Florida	81.0
23	Maple Grove city, Minnesota	81.0
25	Surprise city, Arizona	80.9
25	Port Charlotte CDP, Florida	80.9
27	Johns Creek city, Georgia	80.6
28	Palm Coast city, Florida	80.4
29	Palm Bay city, Florida	80.3
30	North Port city, Florida	79.6
30	St. Cloud city, Florida	79.6
32	Castle Rock town, Colorado	79.3
32	Cape Coral city, Florida	79.3
34	League City city, Texas	78.7
35	Mission Viejo city, California	78.5
36	Menifee city, California	78.2
36	Deltona city, Florida	78.2
38	Rio Rancho city, New Mexico	78.1
39	Centennial city, Colorado	77.9
39	Waldorf CDP, Maryland	77.9
41	Flower Mound town, Texas	77.7
42	Missouri City city, Texas	77.6
42	Sandy city, Utah	77.6
44	Port Orange city, Florida	77.5
45	Poinciana CDP, Florida	77.4
45	Leander city, Texas	77.4
47	Fishers city, Indiana	77.3
47	Sugar Land city, Texas	77.3
49	Eastvale city, California	77.1
49	Naperville city, Illinois	77.1
49	Lehi city, Utah	77.1
52	Goodyear city, Arizona	76.8
53	Mount Pleasant town, South Carolina	76.6
54	Parma city, Ohio	76.4
55	Pearland city, Texas	75.9
56	Manteca city, California	75.7
57	Rochester Hills city, Michigan	75.5
58	Peoria city, Arizona	75.4
58	Santa Clarita city, California	75.4
58	Boca Raton city, Florida	75.4
58	Woodbury city, Minnesota	75.4
62	Apex town, North Carolina	75.2
63	Sterling Heights city, Michigan	75.1
63	Chesapeake city, Virginia	75.1
63	South Hill CDP, Washington	75.1
66	Murrieta city, California	75.0
67	Weston city, Florida	74.9
68	Roswell city, Georgia	74.6
69	Simi Valley city, California	74.5
70	Elk Grove city, California	74.4
71	Apple Valley town, California	74.3
71	Olathe city, Kansas	74.3
71	West Jordan city, Utah	74.3
74	Highlands Ranch CDP, Colorado	74.2
75	Lakewood city, California	74.0
75	Palm Harbor CDP, Florida	74.0

City Rankings, 2023

Selected Rankings

Percent of owners with a mortgage, contract to purchase, or similar debt rank	City	Percent of owners with a mortgage, contract to purchase, or similar debt [C-4, col. 6]	Median value of owner-occupied units rank	City	Median value of owner-occupied housing units [C-4, col. 7]	Percent of households without Internet access rank	City	Percent of households without access to the Internet [C-4, col. 9]
	UNITED STATES	60.2		**UNITED STATES**	340,200		**UNITED STATES**	7.8
1	Castle Rock town, Colorado	86.0	1	Newport Beach city, California	2,000,000+	1	Lakewood CDP, New Jersey	44.0
2	Leander city, Texas	82.4	1	Palo Alto city, California	2,000,000+	2	San Juan zona urbana, Puerto Rico	23.4
3	Buckeye city, Arizona	82.0	1	Santa Monica city, California	2,000,000+	3	Ames city, Iowa	22.2
4	Temecula city, California	81.6	4	Mountain View city, California	1,963,700	4	Flint city, Michigan	18.9
5	Maricopa city, Arizona	81.1	5	Redwood City city, California	1,815,900	5	Albany city, Georgia	18.8
6	Dublin city, California	79.6	6	Sunnyvale city, California	1,739,100	6	New Britain city, Connecticut	17.8
7	Vacaville city, California	79.3	7	Santa Barbara city, California	1,635,700	7	Trenton city, New Jersey	17.7
8	Fishers city, Indiana	79.2	8	San Mateo city, California	1,562,300	8	Shreveport city, Louisiana	16.9
8	Dale City CDP, Virginia	79.2	9	Pleasanton city, California	1,557,400	9	Gary city, Indiana	16.5
10	Apex town, North Carolina	78.3	10	Santa Clara city, California	1,553,400	10	Waterbury city, Connecticut	16.3
11	Centreville CDP, Virginia	78.1	11	San Ramon city, California	1,540,800	10	San Marcos city, Texas	16.3
12	Antioch city, California	77.9	12	Fremont city, California	1,443,200	12	Lawrence city, Massachusetts	16.1
12	Santa Clarita city, California	77.9	13	Sammamish city, Washington	1,441,300	13	Fort Smith city, Arkansas	15.4
14	Commerce City city, Colorado	77.6	14	Berkeley city, California	1,360,800	13	Allentown city, Pennsylvania	15.4
15	Queen Creek town, Arizona	77.5	15	Carlsbad city, California	1,359,600	15	Muncie city, Indiana	15.3
15	Murrieta city, California	77.5	16	Newton city, Massachusetts	1,350,800	15	Gulfport city, Mississippi	15.3
15	Marysville city, Washington	77.5	17	Bellevue city, Washington	1,349,200	17	College Station city, Texas	15.2
18	Visalia city, California	77.4	18	San Francisco city, California	1,348,000	18	Gainesville city, Florida	14.9
19	Washington city, District of Columbia	77.3	19	Dublin city, California	1,292,900	18	Provo city, Utah	14.9
20	Victorville city, California	77.0	20	Redondo Beach city, California	1,280,000	20	Cleveland city, Ohio	14.6
21	Lehi city, Utah	76.4	21	San Jose city, California	1,217,500	20	Knoxville city, Tennessee	14.6
22	Ontario city, California	76.3	22	Irvine city, California	1,199,600	22	Iowa City city, Iowa	14.5
22	South Hill CDP, Washington	76.3	23	Milpitas city, California	1,164,200	23	Springfield city, Missouri	14.3
24	South Fulton city, Georgia	76.2	24	Yorba Linda city, California	1,152,500	23	Bismarck city, North Dakota	14.3
25	Ankeny city, Iowa	76.1	25	Bethesda CDP, Maryland	1,147,800	23	Odessa city, Texas	14.3
26	Pittsburg city, California	76.0	26	Kirkland city, Washington	1,134,600	26	Roanoke city, Virginia	14.2
27	Lakeville city, Minnesota	75.9	27	Alameda city, California	1,122,200	27	Canton city, Ohio	13.8
28	Enterprise CDP, Nevada	75.8	27	Union City city, California	1,122,200	28	Springfield city, Massachusetts	13.6
29	Avondale city, Arizona	75.7	29	Pasadena city, California	1,105,300	29	Macon-Bibb County, Georgia	13.3
30	Fairfield city, California	75.6	30	Redmond city, Washington	1,103,800	30	Augusta-Richmond County consolidated government (balance), Georgia	13.2
30	Moreno Valley city, California	75.6	31	Costa Mesa city, California	1,099,800	31	Delray Beach city, Florida	13.1
30	Frisco city, Texas	75.6	32	Castro Valley CDP, California	1,074,400	32	Columbia city, South Carolina	13.0
33	San Tan Valley CDP, Arizona	75.5	33	Huntington Beach city, California	1,070,600	32	Victoria city, Texas	13.0
34	Fontana city, California	75.3	34	Glendale city, California	1,062,600	34	Hammond city, Indiana	12.8
34	Deltona city, Florida	75.3	35	Burbank city, California	1,057,100	34	Lake Charles city, Louisiana	12.8
34	Silver Spring CDP, Maryland	75.3	36	Torrance city, California	1,055,700	36	St. Joseph city, Missouri	12.7
34	Suffolk city, Virginia	75.3	37	Livermore city, California	1,052,100	37	Wichita Falls city, Texas	12.6
38	Brentwood city, California	75.2	38	Mission Viejo city, California	1,028,800	38	Detroit city, Michigan	12.5
39	Thornton city, Colorado	75.1	39	Daly City city, California	1,028,400	38	Fargo city, North Dakota	12.5
40	Livermore city, California	75.0	40	Orange city, California	996,800	40	Compton city, California	12.3
40	Aurora city, Colorado	75.0	41	Boulder city, Colorado	989,100	40	Lorain city, Ohio	12.3
40	Riverview CDP, Florida	75.0	42	Cambridge city, Massachusetts	987,400	40	Pawtucket city, Rhode Island	12.3
40	McKinney city, Texas	75.0	43	Thousand Oaks city, California	978,000	43	Hartford city, Connecticut	12.2
44	Lakewood city, California	74.8	44	Walnut Creek city, California	964,800	43	Toledo city, Ohio	12.2
44	Menifee city, California	74.8	45	Tustin city, California	939,300	45	Dayton city, Ohio	11.9
44	Charlotte city, North Carolina	74.8	46	San Diego city, California	923,900	45	Caguas zona urbana, Puerto Rico	11.9
44	West Jordan city, Utah	74.8	47	Los Angeles city, California	919,900	47	Flagstaff city, Arizona	11.7
44	Alexandria city, Virginia	74.8	48	Oakland city, California	915,000	48	Miami city, Florida	11.5
44	Tacoma city, Washington	74.8	49	Lake Forest city, California	910,900	49	Birmingham city, Alabama	11.4
50	O'Fallon city, Missouri	74.7	50	Somerville city, Massachusetts	905,200	49	Deerfield Beach city, Florida	11.4
50	Beaverton city, Oregon	74.7	51	Seattle city, Washington	898,600	49	Tallahassee city, Florida	11.4
50	Virginia Beach city, Virginia	74.7	52	Fullerton city, California	897,100	49	Topeka city, Kansas	11.4
53	Concord city, North Carolina	74.6	53	Chino Hills city, California	886,000	49	Cincinnati city, Ohio	11.4
54	Clovis city, California	74.5	54	Hawthorne city, California	882,900	54	Hemet city, California	11.3
54	Hillsboro city, Oregon	74.5	55	Westminster city, California	875,800	54	El Paso city, Texas	11.3
54	Sammamish city, Washington	74.5	56	San Marcos city, California	859,000	54	Norfolk city, Virginia	11.3
57	Gilbert town, Arizona	74.3	57	San Leandro city, California	855,300	57	Cicero town, Illinois	11.2
57	Vallejo city, California	74.3	58	Arlington CDP, Virginia	850,900	58	Port Charlotte CDP, Florida	11.1
57	Atlanta city, Georgia	74.3	59	Davis city, California	841,000	58	Columbus city, Georgia	11.1
57	North Las Vegas city, Nevada	74.3	60	Buena Park city, California	835,900	58	Brownsville city, Texas	11.1
61	Frederick city, Maryland	74.2	61	Scottsdale city, Arizona	835,100	61	Tuscaloosa city, Alabama	11.0
62	Noblesville city, Indiana	74.0	62	Alhambra city, California	833,000	61	New Bedford city, Massachusetts	11.0
62	Woodbury city, Minnesota	74.0	62	Eastvale city, California	833,000	61	Cheektowaga CDP, New York	11.0
64	Mission Viejo city, California	73.9	64	Hayward city, California	831,900	61	Rochester city, New York	11.0
64	Simi Valley city, California	73.9	65	Urban Honolulu CDP, Hawaii	831,600	61	High Point city, North Carolina	11.0
64	Germantown CDP, Maryland	73.9	66	Napa city, California	829,800	66	Clearwater city, Florida	10.9
64	Portsmouth city, Virginia	73.9	67	Anaheim city, California	826,700	67	Waterloo city, Iowa	10.8
68	Corona city, California	73.8	68	Mount Pleasant town, South Carolina	825,300	68	Ocala city, Florida	10.7
68	Brockton city, Massachusetts	73.8	69	Camarillo city, California	825,100	68	New Orleans city, Louisiana	10.7
68	Norfolk city, Virginia	73.8	70	Garden Grove city, California	824,600	68	Baltimore city, Maryland	10.7
71	Palmdale city, California	73.7	71	Downey city, California	824,300	68	Duluth city, Minnesota	10.7
72	Fort Collins city, Colorado	73.6	72	Long Beach city, California	823,300	68	Buffalo city, New York	10.7
72	Olathe city, Kansas	73.6	73	Lakewood city, California	822,500	73	Bridgeport city, Connecticut	10.6
74	Murfreesboro city, Tennessee	73.5	74	Brentwood city, California	817,700	73	Bryan city, Texas	10.6
75	Fremont city, California	73.4	75	San Buenaventura (Ventura) city, California	817,600	75	Hialeah city, Florida	10.5
75	Bolingbrook village, Illinois	73.4				75	Largo city, Florida	10.5
75	Glen Burnie CDP, Maryland	73.4				75	Urban Honolulu CDP, Hawaii	10.5
75	Lynn city, Massachusetts	73.4						

Table C-1. States — Where: Migration, Housing, and Transportation, 2023

	STATE	Total population 1 year and over	Residence 1 year ago (percent): Same house	Different house; same city or town	Different house; different city; same county	Different house; different county; same state	Different house; different state	Abroad	Total occupied housing units (households)	Percent owner occupied
	ACS table number:	C07204	C07204	C07204	C07204	C07204	C07204	C07204	B25003	B25003
State code	Column number	1	2	3	4	5	6	7	8	9

Table C-1. States — Where: Migration, Housing, and Transportation, 2023

		Homeownership by race and Hispanic origin of householder									
		White alone, not of Hispanic or Latino origin		Black or African American alone		American Indian and Alaska Native alone		Asian and Native Hawaiian and Other Pacific Islander alone		Hispanic or Latino	
	STATE	Number of householders	Percent owner occupied	Number of householders	Percent owner occupied	Number of householders	Percent owner occupied	Number of householders	Percent owner occupied	Number of householders	Percent owner occupied
State code	ACS table number:	B25003H	B25003H	B25003B	B25003B	B25003C	B25003C	B25003D+ B25003E	B25003D + B25003E	B25003I	B25003I
	Column number	10	11	12	13	14	15	16	17	18	19

Table C-1. States — Where: Migration, Housing, and Transportation, 2023

		Homeownership by age of householder							
		Householder 15 to 24 years		Householder 25 to 44 years		Householder 45 to 64 years		Householder 65 years and over	
	STATE	Number of householders	Percent owners	Number of householders	Percent owners	Number of householders	Percent owners	Number of householders	Percent owners
	ACS table number:	B25007	B25007	B25007	B25007	B25007	B25007	B25007	B25007
State code	Column number	20	21	22	23	24	25	26	27

Table C-1. States — Where: Migration, Housing, and Transportation, 2023

		Homeownership by household type								Average household size			Percent of housing units that are crowded and/or lacking complete plumbing
		Married-couple family households		Male householder families, no spouse present		Female householder families, no spouse present		Nonfamily households					
	STATE	Number of householders	Percent owners	Number of householders	Percent owners	Number of householders	Percent owners	Number of householders	Percent owners	All households	Owner-occupied households	Renter-occupied households	
State code	ACS table number:	B25115	B25115	B25115	B25115	B25115	B25115	B25115	B25115	B25010	B25010	B25010	B25016
	Column number	28	29	30	31	32	33	34	35	36	37	38	39

Table C-1. States — Where: Migration, Housing, and Transportation, 2023

		Median household income in the past 12 months (in 2023 inflation-adjusted dollars)					Median housinng value (dollars; owner estimated)		
			Owner-occupied households						
	STATE	All households	All owner-occupied households	Households with a mortgage	Households without a mortgage	Renter-occupied households	All owner-occupied households	Households with a mortgage	Households without a mortgage
	ACS table number:	B25119	B25099	B25099	B25099	B25119	B25097	B25097	B25097
State code	Column number	40	41	42	43	44	45	46	47

Table C-1. States — Where: Migration, Housing, and Transportation, 2023

		Owner-occupied housing units			Median monthly housing costs for all housing units with costs (dollars)	Gross rent for renter-occupied housing units		Median selected monthly owner costs for owner-occupied housing units (dollars)			Median annual real estate taxes paid by owner-occupied housing units (dollars)
	STATE	Total owner-occupied housing units	Percent with a mortgage, contract to purchase, or similar debt	Percent with a second mortgage, or a home equity loan, or both		Median gross rent (dollars)	As a percentage of household income	All owner-occupied households	Households with a mortgage	Households without a mortgage	
	ACS table number:	B25081	B25081	B25081	B25105	B25064	B25071	B25088	B25088	B25088	B25103
State code	Column number	48	49	50	51	52	53	54	55	56	57

Table C-1. States — Where: Migration, Housing, and Transportation, 2023

		Median selected monthly owner costs as a percentage of household income			Households who pay 30 percent or more of income for housing expenses by tenure and age of householder (percent)							
					Owner-occupied households				Renter-occupied households			
	STATE	All owner-occupied households	Households with a mortgage	Households without a mortgage1	Householder 15 to 24 years	Householder 25 to 34 years	Householder 35 to 64 years	Householder 65 years and over	Householder 15 to 24 years	Householder 25 to 34 years	Householder 35 to 64 years	Householder 65 years and over
State code	ACS table number:	B25092	B25092	B25092	C25093	C25093	C25093	C25093	B25072	B25072	B25072	B25072
	Column number	58	59	60	61	62	63	64	65	66	67	68

Table C-1. States — Where: Migration, Housing, and Transportation, 2023

			Means of transportation to work (percent)						
			Car, truck, or van						
	STATE	Total number of workers 16 years and over	Drove alone	Carpooled	Public transportation (excluding taxicab)	Bicycle	Walked	Taxicab, motorcycle, or other means	Worked at home
	ACS table number:	B08301	B08301	B08301	B08301	B08301	B08301	B08301	B08301
State code	Column number	69	70	71	72	73	74	75	76

Table C-1. States — Where: Migration, Housing, and Transportation, 2023

			Mean travel time to work (minutes)					Vehicles available (percent of households)				
	STATE	Number of workers who did not work at home	All workers who did not work at home	By car, truck, or van	Public transportation (excluding taxicab)	Taxicab, motorcycle, bicycle, walked, or by other means	Number of households	No vehicles	One vehicle	Two vehicles	Three or more vehicles	Average vehicles per household
State code	ACS table number:	B08301	C08136/ B08301	C08136/ B08301	C08136/ B08301	C08136/ B08301	B08201	B08201	B08201	B08201	B08201	B25046/ B08201
	Column number	77	78	79	80	81	82	83	84	85	86	87

Table C-2. Counties — Where: Migration, Housing, and Transportation, 2023

	STATE County	Total population 1 year and over	Lived in the same house 1 year ago (percent)	Did not live in the same county 1 year ago (percent)	Total occupied housing units	Owner-occupied units (percent)	Percent with a mortgage, contract to purchase, or similar debt	Median value of owner-occupied units (dollars; owner estimated)	Median gross rent of renter-occupied units paying cash rent	Households without Internet access (percent)	Number of workers who commuted to work	Commute of less than 10 minutes (percent)	Commute of 60 minutes or more (percent)
STATE County code	ACS table number:	C07204	C07204	C07204	B25003	B25003	B25081	B25097	B25064	S2801	B08012	B08012	B08012
	Column number:	1	2	3	4	5	6	7	8	9	10	11	12

Table C-3. Metropolitan Areas — Where: Migration, Housing, and Transportation, 2023

	Metropolitan area / division	Total population 1 year and over	Lived in the same house 1 year ago (percent)	Did not live in the same county 1 year ago (percent)	Total occupied housing units	Owner-occupied units (percent)	Percent with a mortgage, contract to purchase, or similar debt	Median value of owner-occupied units (dollars; owner estimated)	Median gross rent of renter-occupied units paying cash rent	Households without Internet access (percent)	Number of workers who commuted to work	Commute of less than 10 minutes (percent)	Commute of 60 minutes or more (percent)
Metropolitan area / division code	ACS table number:	C07204	C07204	C07204	B25003	B25003	B25081	B25097	B25064	S2801	B08012	B08012	B08012
	column number:	1	2	3	4	5	6	7	8	9	10	11	12

Table C-4. Cities — Where: Migration, Housing, and Transportation, 2023

	STATE Place	Total population 1 year and over	Lived in the same house 1 year ago (percent)	Did not live in the same county 1 year ago (percent)	Total occupied housing units	Owner-occupied units (percent)	Percent with a mortgage, contract to purchase, or similar debt	Median value of owner-occupied units (dollars; owner estimated)	Median gross rent of renter-occupied units paying cash rent	Households without Internet access (percent)	Number of workers who commuted to work	Commute of less than 10 minutes (percent)	Commute of 60 minutes or more (percent)
STATE and place code	ACS table number:	C07204	C07204	C07204	B25003	B25003	B25081	B25097	B25064	S2801	B08012	B08012	B08012
	column number:	1	2	3	4	5	6	7	8	9	10	11	12

Table C-1. States — Where: Migration, Housing, and Transportation, 2023

State code	STATE	Total population 1 year and over	Residence 1 year ago (percent): Same house	Residence 1 year ago (percent): Different house; same city or town	Residence 1 year ago (percent): Different house; different city; same county	Residence 1 year ago (percent): Different house; different county; same state	Residence 1 year ago (percent): Different house; different state	Residence 1 year ago (percent): Abroad	Total occupied housing units (households)	Percent owner occupied
	ACS table number:	C07204	C07204	C07204	C07204	C07204	C07204	C07204	B25003	B25003
	Column number	1	2	3	4	5	6	7	8	9
00	**UNITED STATES**	331,383,809	87.9	3.1	3.0	3.0	2.3	0.7	131,332,360	65.2
01	Alabama	5,058,397	88.6	2.7	3.0	2.9	2.4	0.4	2,051,545	70.1
02	Alaska	725,129	85.7	6.2	1.5	1.7	4.2	0.7	276,852	66.3
04	Arizona	7,362,464	86.1	4.3	3.8	1.6	3.5	0.8	2,907,014	67.7
05	Arkansas	3,034,111	87.9	3.1	3.0	3.4	2.4	0.3	1,232,871	66.2
06	California	38,552,167	89.5	3.2	2.9	2.5	1.1	0.8	13,699,816	55.9
08	Colorado	5,819,109	84.3	4.1	2.3	4.6	4.0	0.6	2,428,261	65.7
09	Connecticut	3,576,682	89.1	2.2	3.3	1.8	2.7	0.8	1,442,969	65.7
10	Delaware	1,022,638	88.8	1.0	4.2	1.5	3.8	0.7	412,048	73.6
11	District of Columbia	670,127	79.0	10.6	0.0	0.0	8.5	1.9	334,673	39.1
12	Florida	22,395,466	86.4	2.4	3.9	3.2	2.8	1.4	8,966,402	68.1
13	Georgia	10,909,651	87.4	2.2	2.8	4.2	2.8	0.6	4,150,138	66.1
15	Hawaii	1,420,012	88.1	2.6	3.7	0.6	4.1	1.0	493,898	62.4
16	Idaho	1,945,004	85.8	3.9	2.8	2.8	4.2	0.5	733,244	72.5
17	Illinois	12,427,191	89.2	3.5	2.7	2.2	1.6	0.8	5,071,288	67.4
18	Indiana	6,783,874	87.5	3.6	2.6	3.6	2.2	0.4	2,754,881	70.4
19	Iowa	3,170,553	87.5	4.1	2.2	3.4	2.3	0.5	1,337,243	71.8
20	Kansas	2,907,735	86.2	4.7	2.6	3.2	2.7	0.7	1,188,340	66.7
21	Kentucky	4,477,307	87.7	3.2	2.8	3.3	2.4	0.6	1,853,603	68.8
22	Louisiana	4,524,085	89.0	3.0	3.0	3.0	1.5	0.5	1,833,915	68.1
23	Maine	1,385,562	89.4	1.5	3.5	2.6	2.7	0.3	616,085	74.4
24	Maryland	6,110,314	89.0	1.9	2.9	2.7	2.7	0.8	2,384,715	67.9
25	Massachusetts	6,936,108	88.2	2.9	2.9	2.9	2.1	1.0	2,800,984	62.3
26	Michigan	9,939,831	89.0	1.9	3.9	3.3	1.4	0.6	4,107,809	73.7
27	Minnesota	5,673,119	88.4	2.8	2.4	4.2	1.8	0.5	2,344,432	72.0
28	Mississippi	2,907,634	89.5	2.0	2.8	3.2	2.2	0.4	1,166,617	71.1
29	Missouri	6,126,390	87.9	2.9	3.1	3.3	2.3	0.4	2,556,271	68.8
30	Montana	1,120,157	86.9	3.6	2.8	3.2	3.3	0.2	472,867	69.2
31	Nebraska	1,956,041	87.0	5.2	1.4	3.2	2.5	0.7	813,864	66.3
32	Nevada	3,159,456	85.4	4.5	4.8	0.6	3.9	0.9	1,224,685	60.4
33	New Hampshire	1,389,863	90.1	2.1	2.4	2.1	2.9	0.4	569,493	72.4
34	New Jersey	9,192,631	90.6	1.5	2.8	2.4	1.7	1.0	3,538,457	63.7
35	New Mexico	2,093,439	88.2	4.5	1.5	2.2	3.1	0.6	856,580	69.3
36	New York	19,365,855	90.4	3.5	1.9	1.9	1.6	0.9	7,809,267	54.1
37	North Carolina	10,719,307	87.1	2.8	2.7	3.7	3.2	0.6	4,392,669	66.3
38	North Dakota	774,985	84.0	5.6	2.3	2.8	4.4	0.9	338,059	63.7
39	Ohio	11,660,232	88.6	3.1	3.2	3.0	1.6	0.5	4,917,309	67.1
40	Oklahoma	4,011,072	85.8	4.6	2.7	3.8	2.7	0.4	1,589,105	65.1
41	Oregon	4,196,830	86.5	4.0	2.8	3.1	3.0	0.6	1,752,050	63.4
42	Pennsylvania	12,829,324	89.4	2.2	3.2	2.7	1.9	0.6	5,324,209	69.5
72	Puerto Rico	NA	NA	NA	NA	NA	NA	NA	1,277,486	68.4
44	Rhode Island	1,086,909	89.1	2.2	3.2	1.8	2.9	0.8	443,980	64.0
45	South Carolina	5,319,249	87.6	1.3	3.8	2.9	3.8	0.5	2,177,733	72.4
46	South Dakota	907,196	88.5	3.6	1.5	2.9	3.3	0.2	378,559	69.4
47	Tennessee	7,046,744	87.7	3.5	2.6	3.0	2.9	0.4	2,889,226	67.3
48	Texas	30,134,547	85.9	4.4	3.1	3.7	2.0	0.9	11,260,645	62.6
49	Utah	3,373,801	86.0	3.2	4.6	2.7	2.7	0.8	1,167,591	70.1
50	Vermont	642,670	89.1	1.2	3.2	2.0	4.2	0.3	279,612	73.2
51	Virginia	8,626,985	87.0	2.4	2.0	4.8	3.2	0.7	3,402,670	67.8
53	Washington	7,727,767	85.8	3.5	4.3	2.8	2.8	0.9	3,101,265	63.7
54	West Virginia	1,753,113	90.0	1.4	3.5	2.4	2.4	0.2	743,644	73.5
55	Wisconsin	5,857,364	88.8	3.2	2.7	3.0	2.0	0.4	2,495,539	67.9
56	Wyoming	577,612	86.2	4.1	2.1	3.2	4.0	0.4	247,368	71.2

Table C-1. States — Where: Migration, Housing, and Transportation, 2023—*Continued*

State code	STATE	Homeownership by race and Hispanic origin of householder: White alone, not of Hispanic or Latino origin — Number of householders	White alone, not of Hispanic or Latino origin — Percent owner occupied	Black or African American alone — Number of householders	Black or African American alone — Percent owner occupied	American Indian and Alaska Native alone — Number of householders	American Indian and Alaska Native alone — Percent owner occupied	Asian, Native Hawaiian, and Other Pacific Islander alone — Number of householders	Asian, Native Hawaiian, and Other Pacific Islander alone — Percent owner occupied	Hispanic or Latino — Number of householders	Hispanic or Latino — Percent owner occupied
	ACS table number:	B25003H	B25003H	B25003B	B25003B	B25003C	B25003C	B25003D+ B25003E	B25003D + B25003E	B25003I	B25003I
	Column number	10	11	12	13	14	15	16	17	18	19
00	**UNITED STATES**	83,259,640	73.1	15,925,324	44.7	1,110,405	53.7	7,238,621	62.8	19,463,074	51.0
01	Alabama	1,339,888	78.2	535,918	52.3	8,684	71.1	28,904	67.8	79,848	57.9
02	Alaska	182,023	72.5	7,891	40.1	29,911	56.6	16,265	57.8	16,141	50.2
04	Arizona	1,783,585	74.0	133,197	37.9	94,914	58.5	105,426	66.2	704,042	59.0
05	Arkansas	873,857	72.9	180,508	43.9	7,346	60.3	19,972	58.9	80,946	54.8
06	California	5,823,156	64.4	824,292	36.6	172,681	48.0	2,177,605	61.1	4,294,300	45.9
08	Colorado	1,734,768	70.3	89,916	39.4	25,612	55.9	74,774	62.7	418,790	54.4
09	Connecticut	971,411	75.1	151,817	40.9	4,786	38.1	62,348	63.2	213,257	40.3
10	Delaware	265,134	81.7	87,021	56.3	1,337	60.9	15,869	72.1	31,144	58.6
11	District of Columbia	137,824	48.7	137,382	31.7	972	13.5	14,454	37.7	29,912	29.7
12	Florida	5,131,296	76.9	1,198,625	50.1	31,577	53.2	245,739	73.9	2,084,392	56.5
13	Georgia	2,191,205	76.5	1,286,341	51.9	15,385	43.9	172,040	70.7	338,609	53.8
15	Hawaii	137,161	58.7	9,879	27.3	948	35.8	228,997	70.1	36,032	43.6
16	Idaho	606,122	74.7	3,866	32.7	7,327	63.5	10,211	57.0	73,514	61.5
17	Illinois	3,234,289	75.3	684,812	41.9	28,769	62.9	288,472	64.2	710,694	58.8
18	Indiana	2,174,909	75.4	245,534	41.5	8,022	61.2	61,873	61.1	176,762	59.6
19	Iowa	1,156,713	75.1	42,809	27.8	4,808	52.9	25,477	61.8	69,278	57.3
20	Kansas	918,953	71.1	61,305	33.0	9,404	54.5	31,208	62.7	121,474	55.1
21	Kentucky	1,562,058	72.9	135,347	40.2	4,495	62.6	23,135	56.3	64,969	43.2
22	Louisiana	1,075,779	78.5	553,793	50.3	12,632	64.2	30,670	60.7	102,721	55.3
23	Maine	563,401	76.2	9,466	21.1	2,349	57.6	5,364	45.4	9,603	52.4
24	Maryland	1,215,782	78.4	725,193	54.5	9,671	56.8	139,573	73.0	211,247	52.2
25	Massachusetts	2,016,235	70.4	170,203	37.5	7,389	39.9	182,522	59.1	299,125	31.7
26	Michigan	3,118,734	79.6	532,669	47.7	18,030	61.5	116,770	65.1	175,942	63.4
27	Minnesota	1,909,035	76.8	135,033	32.3	19,285	46.9	96,875	64.2	104,564	55.9
28	Mississippi	663,410	80.4	415,586	57.6	5,064	48.2	10,721	72.4	33,574	57.6
29	Missouri	2,021,571	73.5	281,481	43.4	7,310	60.7	49,314	56.3	98,609	56.4
30	Montana	411,994	71.2	2,214	20.3	18,208	53.0	2,716	66.0	16,729	51.7
31	Nebraska	654,891	70.4	35,180	32.1	7,028	43.2	17,634	61.8	73,445	53.4
32	Nevada	655,846	68.4	116,904	33.8	14,685	53.6	111,506	67.3	275,393	51.6
33	New Hampshire	508,604	74.3	5,998	43.9	NA	NA	13,638	59.0	18,989	48.3
34	New Jersey	1,988,788	76.6	446,423	41.3	22,580	29.1	332,657	64.5	668,024	40.4
35	New Mexico	375,499	74.4	17,066	46.7	66,743	58.8	14,493	54.7	362,256	67.4
36	New York	4,551,665	66.7	1,068,327	32.8	45,749	31.7	634,878	53.3	1,293,983	27.6
37	North Carolina	2,836,048	74.4	905,010	47.6	44,112	67.3	128,439	67.2	343,777	51.8
38	North Dakota	284,616	69.6	9,624	10.2	12,511	40.1	5,505	29.8	12,919	25.5
39	Ohio	3,864,180	73.2	583,460	37.3	8,351	61.0	107,487	59.9	174,960	49.9
40	Oklahoma	1,083,016	70.1	113,093	35.8	99,395	62.3	31,667	62.1	144,166	56.3
41	Oregon	1,346,909	67.2	33,850	29.9	15,351	50.8	81,614	60.9	184,335	46.5
42	Pennsylvania	4,093,297	75.3	542,960	46.1	11,579	40.2	179,696	63.2	352,525	46.8
72	Puerto Rico	7,747	61.9	73,028	69.0	2,839	57.2	1,934	57.2	1,264,946	68.5
44	Rhode Island	328,145	71.3	24,488	38.3	2,281	37.4	13,607	56.5	57,216	40.7
45	South Carolina	1,434,537	79.9	526,772	55.8	7,192	54.6	37,131	69.0	112,564	58.3
46	South Dakota	322,061	72.9	6,693	23.9	19,370	43.4	5,045	72.2	13,030	40.2
47	Tennessee	2,146,940	74.2	452,829	43.0	6,839	47.7	48,359	63.3	143,336	46.7
48	Texas	5,099,777	70.8	1,475,229	41.8	92,601	58.3	609,467	66.0	3,730,654	59.2
49	Utah	927,821	73.4	10,830	31.9	11,356	57.9	36,190	59.6	148,251	56.9
50	Vermont	256,026	74.3	2,953	29.8	405	60.5	3,647	65.6	5,735	66.3
51	Virginia	2,152,128	75.0	633,638	49.6	11,299	49.9	207,685	70.8	275,553	53.7
53	Washington	2,160,954	68.6	117,563	34.5	32,092	51.0	308,782	61.1	307,140	46.6
54	West Virginia	678,788	75.3	21,449	42.3	427	90.4	4,769	39.0	11,580	56.6
55	Wisconsin	2,076,348	72.6	131,509	28.8	16,938	57.0	60,606	55.7	138,862	46.8
56	Wyoming	212,463	72.9	1,378	27.9	4,362	51.9	2,226	65.8	18,163	56.4

Table C-1. States — Where: Migration, Housing, and Transportation, 2023—*Continued*

		Homeownership by age of householder							
		Householder 15 to 24 years		Householder 25 to 44 years		Householder 45 to 64 years		Householder 65 years and over	
	STATE	Number of householders	Percent owners	Number of householders	Percent owners	Number of householders	Percent owners	Number of householders	Percent owners
	ACS table number:	B25007	B25007	B25007	B25007	B25007	B25007	B25007	B25007
State code	Column number	20	21	22	23	24	25	26	27
00	**UNITED STATES**	5,233,879	16.2	43,342,178	51.9	33,695,706	72.8	28,642,830	78.5
01	Alabama	98,302	21.6	640,088	57.2	554,124	76.7	497,202	84.1
02	Alaska	14,912	17.9	104,545	55.4	69,503	75.1	53,519	82.6
04	Arizona	126,716	14.9	923,253	53.0	726,521	74.8	733,247	82.8
05	Arkansas	64,088	17.3	403,782	54.4	305,015	73.1	280,311	80.5
06	California	392,350	9.7	4,704,788	39.1	3,150,207	63.0	2,632,391	73.1
08	Colorado	125,801	13.7	924,533	53.1	610,369	77.2	475,771	81.1
09	Connecticut	36,625	15.2	441,342	51.9	397,756	73.1	315,791	75.0
10	Delaware	10,914	14.1	118,711	59.6	117,645	78.3	113,177	85.6
11	District of Columbia	20,297	3.7	161,239	30.9	42,677	48.1	37,725	58.6
12	Florida	265,049	16.7	2,595,033	50.4	2,309,409	73.0	2,441,323	82.9
13	Georgia	164,706	15.9	1,406,175	53.0	1,137,738	73.9	833,397	80.1
15	Hawaii	11,463	9.9	146,128	40.7	115,531	69.6	132,206	77.7
16	Idaho	39,439	13.7	241,683	61.3	202,176	82.0	175,849	85.6
17	Illinois	197,869	17.8	1,680,110	55.2	1,346,351	74.8	1,108,525	79.5
18	Indiana	145,589	20.6	904,387	61.5	749,431	78.3	605,002	80.9
19	Iowa	86,309	23.1	434,635	65.8	350,991	79.2	302,800	81.1
20	Kansas	77,662	17.8	400,880	57.4	291,851	76.4	256,654	78.2
21	Kentucky	96,149	20.5	584,035	58.4	493,584	74.5	420,099	82.2
22	Louisiana	76,967	17.7	607,112	56.9	477,742	75.0	411,515	80.3
23	Maine	21,710	29.8	177,360	62.1	179,028	81.7	162,837	82.3
24	Maryland	64,197	16.4	764,696	54.8	675,259	74.7	514,715	79.0
25	Massachusetts	83,636	12.3	902,148	47.6	722,779	71.0	581,592	73.0
26	Michigan	171,358	22.3	1,257,806	64.0	1,166,782	80.3	1,018,837	83.1
27	Minnesota	108,503	18.8	790,908	63.6	659,389	82.2	505,199	78.6
28	Mississippi	48,702	26.4	361,837	58.3	322,503	76.4	282,805	84.6
29	Missouri	128,862	18.3	835,218	58.6	667,324	76.8	577,647	79.9
30	Montana	25,091	15.1	148,583	56.2	121,528	78.1	118,487	82.5
31	Nebraska	54,397	11.2	282,288	58.6	201,777	76.6	166,303	77.8
32	Nevada	39,595	14.7	419,632	45.7	289,105	66.4	253,599	76.9
33	New Hampshire	12,703	16.7	166,531	60.9	171,660	79.2	137,084	79.0
34	New Jersey	68,216	20.2	1,104,862	49.7	949,719	70.1	743,275	73.5
35	New Mexico	39,380	23.1	264,428	54.8	210,780	75.9	228,534	83.1
36	New York	234,379	14.9	2,479,014	39.6	1,732,037	61.1	1,472,219	65.2
37	North Carolina	188,822	16.5	1,445,566	52.2	1,163,845	74.8	963,386	80.1
38	North Dakota	28,488	12.6	125,766	58.0	75,333	75.7	63,548	75.4
39	Ohio	210,967	17.8	1,567,924	55.3	1,278,115	74.5	1,116,751	78.5
40	Oklahoma	91,942	16.2	539,869	54.4	382,620	72.3	343,159	80.1
41	Oregon	74,230	14.9	587,249	49.8	411,462	70.7	396,816	78.0
42	Pennsylvania	178,542	18.0	1,646,705	56.7	1,454,557	77.6	1,277,203	78.6
72	Puerto Rico	21,577	12.4	314,326	46.1	321,730	72.2	404,652	81.6
44	Rhode Island	13,773	17.6	141,678	53.5	109,905	69.7	95,895	73.3
45	South Carolina	83,746	19.7	678,564	59.2	603,407	79.0	555,449	85.3
46	South Dakota	21,710	21.8	125,573	64.1	96,711	77.0	80,723	76.4
47	Tennessee	130,705	14.3	961,496	54.2	753,390	75.1	649,755	81.8
48	Texas	553,208	13.8	4,241,965	49.5	2,861,009	72.7	2,010,866	79.5
49	Utah	80,964	17.7	459,291	62.2	307,150	81.5	210,810	84.2
50	Vermont	11,597	19.7	79,109	62.1	80,106	80.8	73,217	81.6
51	Virginia	116,839	13.8	1,155,613	54.5	911,980	75.1	748,650	81.8
53	Washington	121,808	10.9	1,132,765	50.0	758,410	73.2	637,462	78.6
54	West Virginia	32,139	19.1	200,374	63.0	202,517	77.0	211,930	85.4
55	Wisconsin	129,339	14.3	790,795	57.5	663,966	77.1	557,796	78.1
56	Wyoming	13,124	27.9	84,106	59.2	62,932	79.7	59,777	84.0

Table C-1. States — Where: Migration, Housing, and Transportation, 2023—*Continued*

State code	STATE	Homeownership by household type								Average household size				Percent of housing units that are crowded and/or lacking complete plumbing
		Married-couple family households		Male householder families, no spouse present		Female householder families, no spouse present		Nonfamily households						
		Number of householders	Percent owners	Number of householders	Percent owners	Number of householders	Percent owners	Number of householders	Percent owners	All households	Owner-occupied households	Renter-occupied households		
	ACS table number:	B25115	B25115	B25115	B25115	B25115	B25115	B25115	B25115	B25010	B25010	B25010		C25016
	Column number	28	29	30	31	32	33	34	35	36	37	38		39
00	**UNITED STATES**	61,421,188	81.9	6,750,842	57.7	15,873,654	50.2	47,286,676	49.7	2.49	2.61	2.25		3.9
01	Alabama	949,532	86.7	90,483	64.9	288,839	52.2	722,691	56.1	2.42	2.52	2.19		2.3
02	Alaska	128,090	82.0	15,913	59.6	27,367	53.5	105,482	51.6	2.54	2.70	2.23		9.3
04	Arizona	1,359,887	82.6	154,585	61.2	343,764	52.6	1,048,778	54.2	2.50	2.57	2.34		5.1
05	Arkansas	575,802	83.9	61,867	59.3	159,585	46.7	435,617	50.9	2.42	2.52	2.21		3.2
06	California	6,572,440	70.6	863,837	46.7	1,791,283	43.4	4,472,256	41.1	2.78	2.90	2.62		8.6
08	Colorado	1,160,768	82.9	112,354	60.5	213,501	52.8	941,638	47.9	2.37	2.51	2.10		2.8
09	Connecticut	668,432	84.5	69,202	58.7	185,599	49.2	519,736	48.3	2.44	2.61	2.11		2.9
10	Delaware	196,308	87.9	17,454	66.0	54,734	59.0	143,552	60.4	2.45	2.53	2.21		2.3
11	District of Columbia	85,373	67.5	8,272	40.9	43,859	32.8	197,169	28.2	1.92	2.21	1.73		4.3
12	Florida	4,213,940	81.1	466,260	57.5	1,122,695	53.0	3,163,507	57.7	2.47	2.51	2.38		3.7
13	Georgia	1,925,665	83.0	205,989	60.8	603,531	50.3	1,414,953	50.6	2.60	2.71	2.37		2.9
15	Hawaii	248,739	71.3	30,687	57.7	57,322	57.7	157,150	51.2	2.82	2.98	2.57		10.0
16	Idaho	408,624	84.7	35,369	58.3	66,569	56.8	222,682	57.1	2.61	2.71	2.36		3.6
17	Illinois	2,274,511	85.4	267,917	62.0	591,083	54.1	1,937,777	51.0	2.42	2.59	2.08		2.8
18	Indiana	1,287,098	88.0	138,085	62.5	309,384	55.1	1,020,314	54.0	2.43	2.57	2.09		2.2
19	Iowa	644,904	89.0	56,265	65.9	118,623	57.7	517,451	54.1	2.33	2.46	1.97		2.2
20	Kansas	581,346	84.2	56,382	57.3	115,732	53.2	434,880	48.0	2.40	2.57	2.07		2.5
21	Kentucky	867,100	84.9	96,383	62.0	224,070	50.1	666,050	55.0	2.38	2.48	2.15		2.3
22	Louisiana	767,299	86.5	98,983	63.0	286,114	51.7	681,519	54.8	2.43	2.51	2.24		2.7
23	Maine	294,871	89.3	27,914	73.8	52,592	59.4	240,708	59.5	2.20	2.30	1.91		1.9
24	Maryland	1,092,004	84.3	125,788	61.2	316,123	54.0	850,800	53.1	2.54	2.67	2.27		2.9
25	Massachusetts	1,269,734	82.1	129,354	57.2	331,767	46.4	1,070,129	44.3	2.41	2.60	2.10		2.8
26	Michigan	1,896,709	89.9	203,656	69.5	465,987	59.0	1,541,457	58.9	2.39	2.52	2.04		2.0
27	Minnesota	1,140,240	89.5	107,028	73.0	200,104	57.0	897,060	52.9	2.39	2.56	1.95		2.6
28	Mississippi	507,946	87.7	56,654	71.7	188,639	54.8	413,378	58.0	2.44	2.54	2.20		2.8
29	Missouri	1,190,753	85.9	117,340	65.9	279,178	54.4	969,000	52.2	2.36	2.51	2.04		2.2
30	Montana	228,589	84.7	20,055	60.2	37,625	58.0	186,598	53.6	2.33	2.47	2.04		2.5
31	Nebraska	398,895	86.1	32,582	61.8	76,023	51.0	306,364	44.8	2.37	2.57	1.99		2.7
32	Nevada	528,265	76.4	81,096	52.3	158,321	47.6	457,003	47.9	2.58	2.65	2.47		4.9
33	New Hampshire	292,316	87.8	25,205	64.0	49,814	58.1	202,158	54.6	2.39	2.55	1.98		2.0
34	New Jersey	1,755,631	79.2	184,566	52.1	455,541	47.1	1,142,719	48.4	2.58	2.72	2.32		4.3
35	New Mexico	350,569	83.7	54,573	66.7	119,408	56.5	332,030	59.1	2.42	2.51	2.21		4.6
36	New York	3,290,690	72.9	403,921	48.4	1,057,201	40.3	3,057,455	39.3	2.43	2.62	2.19		5.8
37	North Carolina	2,080,906	83.1	203,257	56.0	542,368	51.0	1,566,138	50.7	2.40	2.51	2.19		2.4
38	North Dakota	155,411	84.8	14,717	63.5	21,869	57.8	146,062	42.1	2.23	2.49	1.78		2.1
39	Ohio	2,172,396	86.9	237,512	60.8	584,204	48.5	1,923,197	51.3	2.34	2.47	2.06		2.0
40	Oklahoma	735,765	82.9	87,124	55.4	195,429	48.8	570,787	49.2	2.48	2.61	2.22		3.5
41	Oregon	810,607	82.4	90,861	53.3	181,635	49.9	668,947	45.5	2.36	2.51	2.11		3.5
42	Pennsylvania	2,446,845	87.0	264,659	66.3	605,371	54.9	2,007,334	52.8	2.35	2.50	2.02		2.1
72	Puerto Rico	434,951	84.0	77,036	65.4	286,215	56.0	479,284	62.1	2.48	2.55	2.33		2.9
44	Rhode Island	193,263	84.8	21,144	58.2	54,424	48.4	175,149	46.5	2.37	2.57	2.02		2.3
45	South Carolina	1,036,532	87.1	93,471	66.1	292,963	56.6	754,767	59.2	2.40	2.48	2.21		2.3
46	South Dakota	182,163	87.7	18,694	61.7	30,833	47.1	146,869	52.3	2.34	2.50	1.99		2.5
47	Tennessee	1,350,430	84.0	137,423	56.4	359,305	49.6	1,042,068	53.1	2.42	2.50	2.24		2.8
48	Texas	5,486,996	79.8	626,843	54.1	1,473,207	49.4	3,673,599	43.6	2.66	2.85	2.33		5.3
49	Utah	679,547	82.3	55,512	60.2	108,103	56.7	324,429	50.5	2.88	3.04	2.50		3.6
50	Vermont	132,173	89.8	12,311	76.7	21,275	61.9	113,853	55.7	2.23	2.39	1.79		2.2
51	Virginia	1,665,817	83.3	158,755	60.7	393,221	50.9	1,184,877	52.6	2.49	2.60	2.26		2.6
53	Washington	1,511,217	80.4	149,669	55.6	293,453	50.9	1,146,926	46.0	2.47	2.61	2.22		3.9
54	West Virginia	336,677	87.7	38,587	71.1	82,034	58.6	286,346	61.5	2.31	2.41	2.04		2.0
55	Wisconsin	1,169,734	88.3	112,784	60.9	220,703	49.2	992,318	48.8	2.31	2.49	1.94		2.0
56	Wyoming	121,639	84.6	11,500	56.5	21,280	58.8	92,949	58.4	2.30	2.40	2.07		2.5

Table C-1. States — Where: Migration, Housing, and Transportation, 2023—*Continued*

State code	STATE	Median household income in the past 12 months (in 2023 inflation-adjusted dollars)					Median housinng value (dollars; owner estimated)		
			Owner-occupied households						
		All households	All owner-occupied households	Households with a mortgage	Households without a mortgage	Renter-occupied households	All owner-occupied households	Households with a mortgage	Households without a mortgage
	ACS table number:	B25119	B25099	B25099	B25099	B25119	B25097	B25097	B25097
State code	Column number	40	41	42	43	44	45	46	47
00	**UNITED STATES**	77,719	95,915	112,834	69,832	51,719	340,200	372,600	282,000
01	Alabama	62,212	76,647	93,987	56,959	37,317	216,600	250,800	168,100
02	Alaska	86,631	104,700	123,085	81,543	59,274	347,500	368,600	309,700
04	Arizona	77,315	90,601	106,413	66,568	55,554	411,200	439,600	351,500
05	Arkansas	58,700	72,934	91,134	55,786	37,431	195,700	225,600	158,800
06	California	95,521	122,776	139,980	89,821	68,804	725,800	745,300	679,200
08	Colorado	92,911	113,483	128,317	81,320	63,023	550,300	563,000	514,500
09	Connecticut	91,665	119,486	135,898	87,511	51,138	367,800	374,700	354,200
10	Delaware	81,361	95,981	108,660	74,590	50,127	359,700	366,500	344,200
11	District of Columbia	108,210	181,363	200,101	116,359	78,034	715,500	728,600	658,400
12	Florida	73,311	85,257	101,722	65,016	53,760	381,000	404,300	344,200
13	Georgia	74,632	92,852	107,321	68,006	48,234	323,000	348,700	266,000
15	Hawaii	95,322	116,579	134,229	90,170	67,101	846,400	859,800	819,900
16	Idaho	74,942	87,979	101,019	66,075	50,675	428,600	437,800	408,800
17	Illinois	80,306	98,752	113,954	74,124	50,095	263,300	283,200	230,800
18	Indiana	69,477	83,638	96,509	63,006	41,757	225,900	238,600	200,100
19	Iowa	71,433	86,520	100,452	67,150	41,557	213,300	227,000	190,400
20	Kansas	70,333	86,867	104,256	66,655	45,750	219,800	249,800	175,700
21	Kentucky	61,118	75,670	93,375	54,408	36,891	211,800	238,900	165,800
22	Louisiana	58,229	74,506	94,627	53,606	33,347	215,600	246,200	171,200
23	Maine	73,733	84,969	101,517	65,771	47,126	310,700	334,200	275,200
24	Maryland	98,678	123,128	136,098	90,358	59,099	413,600	428,100	377,300
25	Massachusetts	99,858	129,479	148,916	91,809	58,686	570,800	581,900	546,100
26	Michigan	69,183	82,155	100,049	61,774	41,178	236,100	256,200	201,800
27	Minnesota	85,086	102,079	117,719	75,637	50,345	328,600	339,600	307,100
28	Mississippi	54,203	66,565	86,301	50,790	33,209	169,800	211,000	124,500
29	Missouri	68,545	84,050	99,908	62,380	42,843	233,600	252,100	203,600
30	Montana	70,804	83,135	99,781	63,757	46,960	392,300	425,400	349,000
31	Nebraska	74,590	94,687	108,328	72,100	46,259	245,200	264,900	214,100
32	Nevada	76,364	95,109	106,098	75,476	55,422	441,100	452,200	417,100
33	New Hampshire	96,838	114,853	133,468	84,618	53,816	415,400	430,000	387,100
34	New Jersey	99,781	127,398	146,962	94,954	61,685	461,000	474,700	433,400
35	New Mexico	62,268	74,692	89,745	57,638	40,700	256,300	290,200	211,900
36	New York	82,095	108,513	129,368	82,967	56,259	420,200	452,100	376,300
37	North Carolina	70,804	86,087	102,228	62,339	48,270	308,600	343,400	245,300
38	North Dakota	76,525	98,769	114,529	79,262	46,907	246,700	274,100	212,400
39	Ohio	67,769	86,288	101,635	63,147	41,615	220,200	237,700	188,500
40	Oklahoma	62,138	79,731	97,438	59,942	40,979	208,600	234,900	168,800
41	Oregon	80,160	100,277	115,458	71,309	53,686	484,800	509,100	441,700
42	Pennsylvania	73,824	90,396	108,129	66,478	45,926	259,900	283,300	227,600
72	Puerto Rico	25,621	31,474	48,878	23,396	16,095	131,500	153,800	114,500
44	Rhode Island	84,972	111,520	124,620	88,877	50,825	411,800	425,300	387,000
45	South Carolina	67,804	80,325	97,380	57,527	42,914	272,900	306,900	212,900
46	South Dakota	71,810	89,645	102,210	72,062	41,661	268,200	293,800	233,200
47	Tennessee	67,631	81,748	98,204	60,213	46,431	307,300	338,200	260,300
48	Texas	75,780	96,818	117,304	70,954	52,180	296,900	341,300	236,900
49	Utah	93,421	110,602	119,939	86,957	61,383	517,700	527,100	496,400
50	Vermont	81,711	96,425	110,607	71,525	47,919	332,000	344,900	310,100
51	Virginia	89,931	107,827	125,721	75,831	60,380	382,900	410,500	321,500
53	Washington	94,605	114,128	132,986	81,732	65,271	576,000	597,700	526,200
54	West Virginia	55,948	66,867	91,698	50,587	33,811	163,700	198,100	125,900
55	Wisconsin	74,631	92,350	106,377	70,110	46,818	272,500	283,400	253,800
56	Wyoming	72,415	85,406	100,712	68,526	47,846	298,700	320,100	275,900

Table C-1. States — Where: Migration, Housing, and Transportation, 2023—*Continued*

State code	STATE	Owner-occupied housing units: Total owner-occupied housing units	Owner-occupied housing units: Percent with a mortgage, contract to purchase, or similar debt	Owner-occupied housing units: Percent with a second mortgage, or a home equity loan, or both	Median monthly housing costs for all housing units with costs (dollars)	Gross rent for renter-occupied housing units: Median gross rent (dollars)	Gross rent for renter-occupied housing units: As a percentage of household income	Median selected monthly owner costs for owner-occupied housing units (dollars): All owner-occupied households	Median selected monthly owner costs for owner-occupied housing units (dollars): Households with a mortgage	Median selected monthly owner costs for owner-occupied housing units (dollars): Households without a mortgage	Median annual real estate taxes paid by owner-occupied housing units (dollars)
	ACS table number:	B25081	B25081	B25081	B25105	B25064	B25071	B25088	B25088	B25088	B25103
State code	Column number	48	49	50	51	52	53	54	55	56	57
00	**UNITED STATES**	85,685,869	60.2	6.1	1,358	1,406	32.6	1,320	1,904	629	3,057
01	Alabama	1,438,756	54.1	4.4	912	982	31.6	858	1,372	438	786
02	Alaska	183,575	57.3	3.0	1,395	1,373	27.8	1,421	2,136	659	3,718
04	Arizona	1,967,704	61.1	5.5	1,381	1,608	34.7	1,218	1,751	499	1,811
05	Arkansas	816,038	52.6	3.3	878	933	29.9	812	1,315	434	1,038
06	California	7,658,458	67.1	6.7	2,055	1,992	34.7	2,137	2,844	834	5,114
08	Colorado	1,594,191	69.1	8.6	1,772	1,771	33.7	1,769	2,289	676	2,604
09	Connecticut	948,121	63.5	8.0	1,668	1,463	34.3	1,846	2,354	1,038	6,388
10	Delaware	303,131	64.6	6.6	1,340	1,358	32.5	1,328	1,747	542	1,715
11	District of Columbia	130,934	77.3	7.9	2,083	1,904	29.3	2,561	3,001	772	4,525
12	Florida	6,103,429	55.7	4.9	1,492	1,719	38.4	1,327	1,950	681	2,793
13	Georgia	2,742,232	63.2	5.3	1,310	1,400	34.8	1,245	1,733	530	2,383
15	Hawaii	308,421	62.2	10.2	1,902	1,940	34.7	1,869	2,739	675	2,283
16	Idaho	531,631	61.5	8.3	1,206	1,256	29.7	1,171	1,686	488	2,101
17	Illinois	3,416,749	60.3	4.9	1,312	1,238	29.7	1,366	1,905	764	5,089
18	Indiana	1,940,443	63.5	6.9	1,025	1,044	30.0	1,012	1,359	511	1,647
19	Iowa	959,743	59.3	7.3	1,012	949	27.4	1,063	1,483	611	2,827
20	Kansas	792,366	57.1	5.2	1,077	1,036	27.2	1,113	1,635	640	2,746
21	Kentucky	1,274,521	56.1	6.4	917	929	30.2	906	1,386	457	1,524
22	Louisiana	1,248,223	51.7	3.6	982	1,020	36.7	938	1,564	453	1,168
23	Maine	458,444	56.1	7.3	1,168	1,189	30.3	1,157	1,688	651	2,886
24	Maryland	1,619,478	70.7	7.5	1,716	1,651	33.5	1,787	2,224	731	3,936
25	Massachusetts	1,744,474	66.4	10.5	1,917	1,757	35.9	2,056	2,629	1,022	5,821
26	Michigan	3,028,591	57.2	5.6	1,074	1,101	32.1	1,058	1,509	593	2,845
27	Minnesota	1,687,695	63.8	7.6	1,364	1,264	30.1	1,424	1,879	689	3,321
28	Mississippi	829,160	48.0	3.5	819	898	32.4	756	1,321	431	1,177
29	Missouri	1,758,041	59.7	4.9	1,029	1,019	28.5	1,036	1,461	532	1,907
30	Montana	327,344	55.2	4.8	1,116	1,083	27.7	1,141	1,754	571	2,658
31	Nebraska	539,532	58.9	6.0	1,140	1,042	27.0	1,222	1,718	681	3,523
32	Nevada	740,187	64.5	5.0	1,521	1,622	35.1	1,407	1,876	555	2,037
33	New Hampshire	412,231	62.5	7.4	1,652	1,517	33.8	1,746	2,303	996	6,285
34	New Jersey	2,255,452	63.9	6.7	1,848	1,667	32.4	2,061	2,676	1,161	9,163
35	New Mexico	593,413	52.2	4.4	985	1,084	32.0	916	1,500	455	1,709
36	New York	4,221,669	57.4	6.6	1,587	1,561	33.3	1,621	2,430	923	6,325
37	North Carolina	2,913,467	61.3	6.9	1,153	1,245	31.0	1,085	1,578	472	1,880
38	North Dakota	215,363	52.8	4.6	972	916	23.4	1,053	1,687	589	2,455
39	Ohio	3,300,279	60.1	7.6	1,045	1,014	29.2	1,068	1,468	579	2,754
40	Oklahoma	1,034,153	52.9	3.3	995	1,020	29.9	970	1,527	534	1,593
41	Oregon	1,111,597	63.8	7.1	1,515	1,481	33.1	1,553	2,089	664	3,750
42	Pennsylvania	3,697,771	57.1	7.5	1,176	1,197	31.3	1,161	1,698	640	3,151
72	Puerto Rico	873,896	37.7	0.7	412	557	41.5	310	899	176	582
44	Rhode Island	283,990	65.7	9.6	1,529	1,365	32.2	1,708	2,175	853	4,644
45	South Carolina	1,577,358	57.5	5.0	1,049	1,170	32.7	972	1,477	425	1,236
46	South Dakota	262,639	55.1	6.0	994	921	26.5	1,081	1,625	604	2,712
47	Tennessee	1,943,282	57.7	5.3	1,078	1,214	31.4	979	1,503	445	1,420
48	Texas	7,048,369	55.8	2.7	1,395	1,413	32.5	1,373	2,071	681	4,274
49	Utah	818,033	68.1	11.4	1,550	1,551	30.3	1,555	1,978	561	2,585
50	Vermont	204,730	60.4	7.3	1,341	1,202	30.1	1,406	1,827	796	4,851
51	Virginia	2,307,077	66.3	7.1	1,513	1,567	31.1	1,474	2,032	576	2,754
53	Washington	1,975,569	65.6	7.5	1,749	1,731	31.8	1,777	2,396	757	4,478
54	West Virginia	546,870	44.4	4.1	710	850	30.2	621	1,208	394	843
55	Wisconsin	1,694,748	60.8	8.8	1,131	1,071	27.5	1,183	1,629	641	3,582
56	Wyoming	176,197	53.2	4.4	1,033	1,000	25.1	1,060	1,653	548	1,793

Table C-1. States — Where: Migration, Housing, and Transportation, 2023—*Continued*

State code	STATE	Median selected monthly owner costs as a percentage of household income			Households who pay 30 percent or more of income for housing expenses by tenure and age of householder (percent)							
					Owner-occupied households				Renter-occupied households			
		All owner-occupied households	Households with a mortgage	Households without a mortgage[1]	Householder 15 to 24 years	Householder 25 to 34 years	Householder 35 to 64 years	Householder 65 years and over	Householder 15 to 24 years	Householder 25 to 34 years	Householder 35 to 64 years	Householder 65 years and over
	ACS table number:	B25092	B25092	B25092	C25093	C25093	C25093	C25093	B25072	B25072	B25072	B25072
	Column number	58	59	60	61	62	63	64	65	66	67	68
00	**UNITED STATES**	17.6	21.1	11.5	36.3	24.1	20.4	27.0	57.4	43.8	45.6	57.3
01	Alabama	14.8	19.0	10.0-	29.4	19.9	14.9	20.5	55.2	42.3	38.9	50.7
02	Alaska	16.8	21.8	10.0-	37.6	27.7	20.8	21.4	45.0	37.4	40.4	43.6
04	Arizona	16.6	20.4	10.0-	40.9	23.5	18.8	24.8	64.5	47.7	45.6	59.4
05	Arkansas	14.6	18.7	10.0-	20.9	16.5	15.9	18.9	42.6	39.6	38.0	51.7
06	California	21.0	24.9	11.8	48.6	34.8	29.0	35.0	65.8	49.3	50.8	63.0
08	Colorado	19.0	22.4	10.4	38.4	30.7	22.1	29.5	65.2	43.8	46.7	65.2
09	Connecticut	19.6	21.9	14.7	30.0	23.7	23.8	32.7	57.9	44.1	46.4	61.7
10	Delaware	16.6	20.0	10.0-	53.9	22.5	18.4	22.8	60.6	40.5	44.6	59.1
11	District of Columbia	17.0	19.0	10.0-	38.9	17.7	16.3	29.1	72.2	35.1	35.6	62.8
12	Florida	19.2	23.9	12.8	42.0	31.7	25.7	30.7	65.6	56.5	55.2	64.0
13	Georgia	16.7	20.3	10.0-	36.5	23.4	19.0	25.1	57.9	48.4	45.5	58.3
15	Hawaii	19.5	25.5	10.0-	64.2	49.5	29.0	29.4	74.6	55.6	47.5	52.9
16	Idaho	16.8	21.0	10.0-	29.9	28.6	19.2	22.5	55.3	43.3	41.9	49.2
17	Illinois	17.8	20.6	12.8	37.6	20.7	19.7	27.5	53.6	36.4	41.3	55.2
18	Indiana	15.5	18.3	10.1	30.0	17.9	14.9	21.4	53.8	39.6	41.8	55.7
19	Iowa	16.4	19.1	11.5	30.3	18.7	15.2	21.5	49.4	35.0	35.3	50.8
20	Kansas	17.0	19.9	12.3	31.6	20.1	16.9	23.4	50.6	32.7	36.5	50.9
21	Kentucky	15.6	18.9	10.2	33.6	19.3	15.7	22.0	47.4	38.1	40.8	48.6
22	Louisiana	16.1	20.8	10.7	34.7	22.5	20.5	22.3	61.5	46.3	46.9	51.8
23	Maine	17.8	21.2	12.7	42.5	27.0	20.2	26.3	47.5	35.7	44.8	53.1
24	Maryland	18.0	20.4	10.1	42.8	23.8	20.0	28.2	63.3	48.0	46.3	60.3
25	Massachusetts	19.5	22.0	14.0	48.7	29.1	22.3	34.5	64.3	42.5	49.1	57.3
26	Michigan	16.6	19.4	12.0	34.1	22.5	17.1	24.3	54.9	41.6	44.4	54.9
27	Minnesota	17.3	19.8	11.5	32.6	20.3	17.2	26.2	53.0	36.9	39.7	61.1
28	Mississippi	15.2	19.8	10.7	21.9	19.9	17.9	22.4	46.6	44.9	42.4	45.9
29	Missouri	15.9	18.8	10.9	30.4	17.5	15.1	22.5	52.4	36.5	39.3	49.5
30	Montana	17.6	22.4	11.3	48.3	29.0	21.0	24.1	54.2	37.5	37.7	48.1
31	Nebraska	16.9	19.7	11.9	31.7	18.3	16.4	23.4	53.9	35.2	33.9	52.3
32	Nevada	18.1	22.1	10.0-	30.1	25.6	20.7	29.4	59.3	54.7	50.0	63.6
33	New Hampshire	19.1	21.7	14.2	27.1	25.6	20.2	32.4	54.3	37.0	48.5	60.5
34	New Jersey	20.0	22.5	14.8	52.6	27.1	24.1	35.3	56.4	41.6	47.1	57.9
35	New Mexico	15.9	20.7	10.0-	23.6	29.8	17.2	23.8	53.2	38.4	40.9	53.9
36	New York	18.9	22.5	13.7	45.6	27.4	25.3	32.0	59.3	42.2	46.4	57.1
37	North Carolina	15.9	19.4	10.0-	31.9	20.8	16.7	23.5	56.3	42.2	41.0	52.4
38	North Dakota	14.7	18.9	10.0-	37.6	18.9	13.2	17.1	42.4	26.2	26.0	53.8
39	Ohio	16.0	18.6	11.4	28.4	17.1	14.5	23.5	52.7	38.6	41.5	53.2
40	Oklahoma	16.2	20.0	11.3	29.9	19.8	17.8	22.0	49.7	38.6	39.5	53.3
41	Oregon	19.0	22.6	11.8	39.5	29.5	23.0	29.2	63.7	44.8	46.6	62.4
42	Pennsylvania	16.8	19.6	12.2	29.7	19.6	17.5	25.5	55.7	38.5	43.4	54.0
72	Puerto Rico	13.8	23.2	10.0-	37.5	22.1	19.6	17.7	30.0	36.8	26.7	27.4
44	Rhode Island	19.4	22.1	12.8	25.9	25.3	22.1	30.2	45.1	41.5	43.4	52.5
45	South Carolina	15.4	19.5	10.0-	41.4	20.1	16.9	20.6	59.1	43.7	43.2	51.8
46	South Dakota	16.8	20.7	11.2	52.8	25.7	15.8	18.9	44.4	39.5	31.6	44.9
47	Tennessee	15.5	19.6	10.0-	35.3	21.4	16.9	20.8	55.1	43.0	41.1	50.5
48	Texas	18.0	22.0	12.2	40.7	26.8	21.6	25.8	59.4	47.0	46.8	59.2
49	Utah	17.4	21.1	10.0-	39.9	26.8	19.0	22.2	51.5	37.4	44.8	54.0
50	Vermont	18.8	20.8	14.2	34.9	28.1	21.1	30.3	66.7	35.1	37.9	55.7
51	Virginia	17.2	20.2	10.0-	34.8	22.4	18.3	24.3	58.7	42.6	42.5	53.8
53	Washington	19.0	22.5	11.7	45.3	28.6	22.2	28.7	61.2	41.6	44.4	63.2
54	West Virginia	13.3	17.0	10.0-	16.5	12.2	13.1	16.7	45.3	35.1	38.1	39.1
55	Wisconsin	16.8	19.4	11.8	34.8	17.2	15.6	25.6	50.1	31.8	37.0	56.6
56	Wyoming	17.0	21.2	10.5	33.1	16.0	20.0	24.5	36.5	36.3	34.8	46.6

Table C-1. States — Where: Migration, Housing, and Transportation, 2023—*Continued*

State code	STATE	Total number of workers 16 years and over	Means of transportation to work (percent): Car, truck, or van: Drove alone	Car, truck, or van: Carpooled	Public transportation (excluding taxicab)	Bicycle	Walked	Taxicab, motorcycle, or other means	Worked at home
	ACS table number:	B08301	B08301	B08301	B08301	B08301	B08301	B08301	B08301
State code	Column number	69	70	71	72	73	74	75	76
00	**UNITED STATES**	162,434,675	69.2	9.0	3.5	0.5	2.4	1.5	13.8
01	Alabama	2,270,651	80.0	8.3	0.3	0.1	1.3	1.2	8.8
02	Alaska	360,378	65.5	11.6	0.8	0.5	7.2	5.4	9.0
04	Arizona	3,462,617	67.1	10.3	1.2	0.6	1.7	1.7	17.5
05	Arkansas	1,360,950	78.3	9.9	0.3	0.2	1.6	1.1	8.7
06	California	18,673,528	67.1	10.2	3.1	0.8	2.5	1.7	14.6
08	Colorado	3,148,372	66.0	7.9	1.6	0.8	2.4	1.3	19.9
09	Connecticut	1,848,443	69.9	8.3	3.7	0.2	2.2	1.4	14.3
10	Delaware	499,912	72.1	8.2	2.3	0.2	2.1	1.4	13.6
11	District of Columbia	383,558	28.6	4.1	22.9	3.5	11.3	2.3	27.3
12	Florida	10,619,674	69.1	9.7	1.4	0.5	1.5	2.0	15.8
13	Georgia	5,288,857	70.8	9.5	1.1	0.2	1.4	1.8	15.2
15	Hawaii	697,762	64.2	15.8	4.1	0.9	3.9	2.5	8.7
16	Idaho	924,144	71.0	10.2	0.6	0.8	2.8	1.1	13.5
17	Illinois	6,228,796	66.2	8.3	6.6	0.6	2.9	1.4	14.0
18	Indiana	3,335,367	76.4	9.4	0.7	0.3	1.8	1.0	10.4
19	Iowa	1,628,327	76.2	8.2	0.8	0.4	2.8	1.2	10.5
20	Kansas	1,477,068	76.6	8.8	0.4	0.2	2.5	1.1	10.4
21	Kentucky	2,062,616	76.7	9.9	0.7	0.2	1.8	1.2	9.5
22	Louisiana	2,012,816	78.7	8.6	0.8	0.4	1.9	1.6	8.1
23	Maine	695,746	72.2	7.8	0.8	0.3	3.3	1.2	14.3
24	Maryland	3,171,852	65.6	8.3	4.9	0.3	2.2	1.8	16.9
25	Massachusetts	3,685,099	62.8	7.2	7.3	1.1	4.2	1.8	15.6
26	Michigan	4,737,965	75.0	8.4	0.9	0.4	2.0	1.0	12.2
27	Minnesota	3,000,271	69.8	8.0	1.7	0.5	2.6	1.2	16.1
28	Mississippi	1,268,449	80.3	10.3	0.2	0.1	1.5	1.1	6.4
29	Missouri	3,034,468	75.0	8.4	0.8	0.3	1.8	1.2	12.5
30	Montana	556,134	72.5	9.4	0.6	0.8	4.2	1.3	11.3
31	Nebraska	1,028,835	76.9	8.6	0.5	0.4	2.3	1.2	10.1
32	Nevada	1,543,818	69.8	12.1	2.3	0.3	1.6	2.3	11.6
33	New Hampshire	754,752	72.1	6.8	0.7	0.2	2.6	1.5	16.1
34	New Jersey	4,687,400	63.3	8.0	9.6	0.3	2.5	2.2	14.0
35	New Mexico	948,156	74.8	10.1	0.7	0.6	1.8	1.3	10.7
36	New York	9,412,279	49.1	6.4	23.5	0.9	5.8	1.9	12.4
37	North Carolina	5,237,672	71.3	8.5	0.6	0.2	1.7	1.4	16.1
38	North Dakota	414,250	76.7	10.1	0.2	0.2	3.1	1.5	8.3
39	Ohio	5,692,277	75.4	8.1	1.1	0.3	2.0	1.2	11.9
40	Oklahoma	1,841,227	77.4	9.9	0.3	0.2	1.8	1.3	9.1
41	Oregon	2,060,890	64.6	9.4	2.2	1.3	3.4	1.4	17.7
42	Pennsylvania	6,289,250	68.5	8.2	3.8	0.5	3.5	1.4	14.1
72	Puerto Rico	1,158,530	83.1	6.8	1.1	0.1	2.3	1.5	5.1
44	Rhode Island	549,317	73.0	7.6	1.9	0.2	3.0	2.5	11.8
45	South Carolina	2,506,678	76.1	8.7	0.4	0.1	1.5	1.4	11.8
46	South Dakota	468,617	76.0	9.1	0.7	0.3	3.1	1.1	9.8
47	Tennessee	3,403,140	75.8	8.3	0.5	0.1	1.4	1.1	12.8
48	Texas	14,801,534	71.7	10.6	0.9	0.2	1.4	1.6	13.7
49	Utah	1,733,596	68.0	10.5	1.6	0.5	1.8	1.2	16.4
50	Vermont	339,587	68.1	8.5	0.9	0.7	4.5	1.0	16.2
51	Virginia	4,377,734	68.4	8.6	2.5	0.3	2.0	1.5	16.7
53	Washington	3,863,532	64.9	8.9	4.0	0.7	3.1	1.2	17.3
54	West Virginia	747,673	77.6	9.8	0.5	0.1	2.3	1.4	8.3
55	Wisconsin	3,015,418	74.9	7.6	1.1	0.5	2.6	1.1	12.2
56	Wyoming	283,223	72.8	10.5	1.2	0.9	3.4	1.0	10.2

Table C-1. States — Where: Migration, Housing, and Transportation, 2023—*Continued*

State code	STATE	Number of workers who did not work at home	Mean travel time to work (minutes): All workers who did not work at home	Mean travel time to work (minutes): By car, truck, or van	Mean travel time to work (minutes): Public transportation	Mean travel time to work (minutes): Taxicab, motorcycle, bicycle, walked, or by other means	Number of households	Vehicles available (percent of households): No vehicles	Vehicles available (percent of households): One vehicle	Vehicles available (percent of households): Two vehicles	Vehicles available (percent of households): Three or more vehicles	Average vehicles per household
	ACS table number:	B08301	C08136/ B08301	C08136/ B08301	C08136/ B08301	C08136/ B08301	B08201	B08201	B08201	B08201	B08201	B25046/ B08201
	Column number	77	78	79	80	81	82	83	84	85	86	87
00	**UNITED STATES**	139,948,165	23.08	26.25	48.92	18.71	131,332,360	8.4	33.3	36.5	21.7	1.82
01	Alabama	2,071,583	23.25	25.67	37.66	17.89	2,051,545	5.5	31.4	36.8	26.3	1.96
02	Alaska	327,931	17.99	18.68	30.05	25.45	276,852	9.2	32.7	34.3	23.8	1.84
04	Arizona	2,857,204	21.24	25.63	42.15	22.76	2,907,014	5.6	34.1	37.3	23.0	1.89
05	Arkansas	1,242,629	20.76	22.93	32.19	15.65	1,232,871	6.1	33.8	37.0	23.2	1.88
06	California	15,937,869	24.93	29.01	50.06	19.45	13,699,816	7.3	31.1	36.1	25.5	1.94
08	Colorado	2,522,855	20.44	25.39	47.13	19.72	2,428,261	5.4	31.0	38.7	24.9	1.96
09	Connecticut	1,584,717	23.10	25.64	64.00	17.55	1,442,969	9.0	33.6	37.5	20.0	1.77
10	Delaware	431,706	23.13	26.56	45.21	20.07	412,048	6.6	32.5	39.0	21.8	1.87
11	District of Columbia	278,932	22.14	29.45	38.87	21.03	334,673	36.3	47.3	13.3	3.1	0.84
12	Florida	8,944,682	23.98	28.51	45.56	21.73	8,966,402	5.8	39.1	38.3	16.9	1.73
13	Georgia	4,484,489	24.36	28.71	48.30	22.52	4,150,138	5.9	32.7	37.3	24.2	1.91
15	Hawaii	637,246	24.63	26.89	45.87	16.92	493,898	8.8	33.0	34.4	23.8	1.89
16	Idaho	799,102	18.98	22.15	49.87	14.79	733,244	3.5	23.8	39.6	33.1	2.21
17	Illinois	5,354,834	24.16	26.98	48.48	17.64	5,071,288	11.1	36.2	35.0	17.7	1.67
18	Indiana	2,989,879	21.79	24.49	45.42	14.75	2,754,881	6.5	32.0	37.9	23.7	1.90
19	Iowa	1,457,641	17.92	20.31	26.38	13.20	1,337,243	5.3	31.2	37.0	26.5	1.99
20	Kansas	1,323,613	17.88	20.13	30.20	14.66	1,188,340	5.0	30.7	38.0	26.3	1.99
21	Kentucky	1,867,279	21.89	24.37	38.92	15.99	1,853,603	6.7	32.7	37.0	23.6	1.89
22	Louisiana	1,850,348	23.64	25.74	42.68	21.89	1,833,915	8.4	37.1	36.8	17.7	1.71
23	Maine	596,229	20.81	24.75	38.11	14.31	616,085	6.4	33.8	39.8	20.0	1.81
24	Maryland	2,635,654	26.13	30.82	53.47	17.01	2,384,715	8.9	34.1	35.5	21.5	1.80
25	Massachusetts	3,110,218	25.26	29.09	48.59	19.24	2,800,984	11.6	37.3	35.2	15.9	1.62
26	Michigan	4,159,103	21.54	24.71	40.31	16.13	4,107,809	7.1	34.9	38.4	19.6	1.79
27	Minnesota	2,516,455	19.06	22.90	34.11	14.88	2,344,432	6.4	31.7	39.5	22.4	1.88
28	Mississippi	1,187,693	23.64	25.46	56.76	15.88	1,166,617	6.1	32.2	35.9	25.8	1.94
29	Missouri	2,654,112	20.59	23.61	47.01	16.57	2,556,271	6.6	33.1	37.5	22.8	1.87
30	Montana	493,140	17.89	20.16	44.56	18.18	472,867	4.7	26.2	36.7	32.4	2.18
31	Nebraska	924,422	17.15	19.33	27.20	12.86	813,864	5.4	29.5	37.4	27.6	2.02
32	Nevada	1,365,439	22.53	24.50	58.68	26.34	1,224,685	7.3	34.4	36.3	22.0	1.84
33	New Hampshire	632,959	22.73	27.55	61.88	13.39	569,493	4.5	31.4	39.8	24.3	1.96
34	New Jersey	4,030,075	27.02	28.68	58.20	19.36	3,538,457	11.4	34.7	35.9	18.0	1.68
35	New Mexico	846,938	20.72	23.16	43.34	20.20	856,580	5.3	32.8	36.0	25.9	1.96
36	New York	8,243,157	28.72	27.66	50.00	18.81	7,809,267	29.7	33.6	25.1	11.6	1.23
37	North Carolina	4,392,673	21.24	25.53	34.73	18.64	4,392,669	5.5	31.1	38.4	25.0	1.95
38	North Dakota	380,033	16.99	18.85	24.39	12.48	338,059	6.9	29.5	38.0	25.6	1.97
39	Ohio	5,015,931	20.68	23.53	40.18	16.35	4,917,309	7.6	34.4	37.1	20.9	1.81
40	Oklahoma	1,673,752	20.58	22.78	35.25	17.99	1,589,105	6.2	32.2	37.5	24.1	1.91
41	Oregon	1,696,954	19.12	23.14	45.34	16.16	1,752,050	7.1	32.5	37.1	23.2	1.88
42	Pennsylvania	5,400,641	22.76	26.25	44.42	17.49	5,324,209	10.6	35.1	35.8	18.5	1.70
72	Puerto Rico	1,099,792	27.31	29.13	38.24	18.00	1,277,486	12.9	40.0	31.1	16.0	1.56
44	Rhode Island	484,372	22.55	25.47	50.89	18.70	443,980	9.2	36.6	36.1	18.0	1.71
45	South Carolina	2,210,448	22.52	25.77	27.39	18.91	2,177,733	6.0	32.0	38.3	23.7	1.91
46	South Dakota	422,763	16.64	18.50	27.93	15.67	378,559	5.3	27.4	37.5	29.8	2.10
47	Tennessee	2,966,891	22.89	26.38	41.49	19.29	2,889,226	5.3	31.3	37.5	25.9	1.98
48	Texas	12,780,053	23.48	27.27	45.65	20.13	11,260,645	5.5	33.3	38.7	22.5	1.88
49	Utah	1,449,487	18.90	22.32	40.72	20.33	1,167,591	4.1	23.8	38.4	33.7	2.22
50	Vermont	284,545	20.29	25.05	32.25	17.85	279,612	5.7	34.9	42.0	17.5	1.78
51	Virginia	3,646,196	22.92	27.34	46.35	18.60	3,402,670	5.9	31.2	37.7	25.2	1.95
53	Washington	3,196,649	22.11	26.25	43.47	20.23	3,101,265	7.2	31.1	36.4	25.4	1.94
54	West Virginia	685,618	25.39	28.09	33.30	17.87	743,644	8.8	34.6	36.4	20.2	1.77
55	Wisconsin	2,646,802	19.74	22.62	40.89	15.00	2,495,539	6.5	33.1	39.4	21.0	1.84
56	Wyoming	254,224	17.48	19.14	48.23	18.46	247,368	4.4	26.8	35.8	32.9	2.16

NA = Not available.
'- = The median falls in the lowest interval of an open-ended distribution.
[1]A value of 10.0 represents the minimum percentage range--10 percent or less.

Table C-2. Counties — Where: Migration, Housing, and Transportation, 2023

State code	STATE County	Total population 1 year and over	Lived in the same house 1 year ago (percent)	Did not live in the same county 1 year ago (percent)	Total occupied housing units	Owner-occupied units (percent)	Percent with a mortgage, contract to purchase, or similar debt	Median value of owner-occupied units (dollars; owner estimated)	Median gross rent of renter-occupied units paying cash rent	Households without Internet access (percent)	Number of workers who commuted to work	Commute of less than 10 minutes (percent)	Commute of 60 minutes or more (percent)
	ACS table number:	C07204	C07204	C07204	B25003	B25003	B25081	B25097	B25064	S2801	B08012	B08012	B08012
	Column number:	1	2	3	4	5	6	7	8	9	10	11	12
00000	**UNITED STATES**	331,383,809	87.9	6.0	131,332,360	65.2	60.2	340,200	1,406	7.8	139,948,165	12.5	8.9
01000	**ALABAMA**	5,058,397	88.6	5.7	2,051,545	70.1	54.1	216,600	982	10.5	2,071,583	12.0	6.7
01003	Baldwin County	252,103	90.4	5.5	105,698	74.9	57.8	307,000	1,286	8.7	103,319	13.6	7.7
01015	Calhoun County	115,152	88.8	5.9	46,310	68.7	50.6	160,900	782	12.8	45,139	12.2	5.3
01043	Cullman County	90,987	86.3	4.9	35,961	79.1	53.8	204,000	788	12.7	38,902	14.7	16.4
01049	DeKalb County	71,509	94.4	1.8	27,182	82.1	34.1	156,800	659	8.5	27,848	12.6	4.6
01051	Elmore County	89,284	91.5	3.6	33,692	76.0	56.0	229,900	933	7.0	37,060	10.3	3.4
01055	Etowah County	101,834	88.8	5.4	40,027	74.6	50.7	188,200	760	8.9	38,542	12.6	8.1
01069	Houston County	107,860	88.7	5.5	44,880	61.9	59.1	187,100	957	10.2	47,521	16.8	3.4
01073	Jefferson County	656,106	87.4	4.3	272,648	62.7	58.9	249,000	1,164	8.4	276,241	8.4	5.0
01077	Lauderdale County	96,004	89.1	6.0	41,199	67.2	52.1	211,700	745	14.0	39,320	17.5	11.2
01081	Lee County	181,761	85.9	9.1	74,799	63.4	60.6	280,900	979	11.5	75,933	15.4	3.7
01083	Limestone County	113,548	86.4	8.8	43,490	77.2	62.9	292,500	999	10.0	45,889	9.9	5.2
01089	Madison County	408,858	86.5	6.9	168,996	68.8	64.1	316,200	1,263	5.6	177,728	10.4	2.2
01095	Marshall County	99,874	90.4	5.5	36,274	74.9	51.3	199,000	724	8.5	40,983	18.1	10.3
01097	Mobile County	408,985	90.3	3.7	163,963	66.8	54.1	191,600	1,022	8.8	165,436	10.5	4.7
01101	Montgomery County	222,832	84.1	7.8	92,816	57.5	62.1	170,700	1,023	7.7	91,410	10.6	3.9
01103	Morgan County	123,986	90.9	5.0	49,759	72.3	55.9	222,000	870	10.2	54,289	11.7	3.6
01115	St. Clair County	94,368	87.5	7.3	35,354	86.0	61.4	223,400	1,027	9.1	38,816	8.1	10.6
01117	Shelby County	230,463	89.6	6.6	88,270	82.6	66.3	326,600	1,363	4.7	100,344	6.1	7.5
01121	Talladega County	80,250	90.4	5.8	34,080	73.5	48.4	154,400	728	9.2	32,426	14.6	10.2
01125	Tuscaloosa County	234,184	82.3	8.6	93,966	62.3	60.7	248,200	975	11.1	101,440	15.0	6.3
02000	**ALASKA**	725,129	85.7	6.6	276,852	66.3	57.3	347,500	1,373	6.8	327,931	25.7	5.4
02020	Anchorage Municipality	282,455	81.3	7.2	109,125	63.0	67.0	385,900	1,474	4.8	136,557	15.9	3.2
02090	Fairbanks North Star Borough	94,002	86.9	8.0	37,510	63.8	57.5	285,700	1,503	5.2	46,089	18.3	2.6
02170	Matanuska-Susitna Borough	113,807	91.1	4.1	39,870	77.7	62.0	341,300	1,195	4.8	45,195	12.5	18.5
04000	**ARIZONA**	7,362,464	86.1	5.8	2,907,014	67.7	61.1	411,200	1,608	7.5	2,857,204	11.8	6.6
04001	Apache County	64690	97.7	1.2	24,010	78.1	NA	52,700	607	34.9	18,440	22.2	11.4
04003	Cochise County	123,587	84.2	9.3	50,919	69.3	47.0	235,200	988	12.1	39,760	21.7	9.9
04005	Coconino County	142,937	79.9	12.5	56,954	60.0	52.2	470,900	1,579	14.0	61,686	24.1	4.2
04013	Maricopa County	4,542,419	86.4	4.8	1,753,589	65.4	66.1	468,700	1,766	6.1	1,839,907	9.8	6.2
04015	Mohave County	221,742	86.9	6.4	98,791	75.0	51.3	293,800	1,077	10.0	67,490	20.7	6.2
04017	Navajo County	107223	91.3	3.9	41,945	71.9	39.3	241,400	869	21.6	30,673	30.1	9.8
04019	Pima County	1,053,319	84.2	6.3	445,471	65.6	58.6	337,800	1,263	7.2	423,811	11.0	4.6
04021	Pinal County	479,466	86.2	9.7	168,479	82.0	61.9	370,600	1,520	7.3	164,982	11.9	13.6
04025	Yavapai County	247,437	84.6	8.4	113,784	75.9	52.8	454,200	1,442	9.2	79,943	19.4	6.6
04027	Yuma County	211,564	85.9	9.1	83,811	70.6	52.1	246,900	1,055	7.4	73,960	16.5	5.2
05000	**ARKANSAS**	3,034,111	87.9	6.1	1,232,871	66.2	52.6	195,700	933	11.5	1,242,629	17.6	5.4
05007	Benton County	306,660	87.3	6.1	117,446	65.1	62.6	367,400	1,365	5.0	137,569	13.4	2.7
05031	Craighead County	112,221	83.3	7.9	47,150	57.0	61.7	189,700	968	9.6	47,884	20.7	3.4
05045	Faulkner County	128,522	90.9	5.7	50,963	65.1	64.9	238,700	1,000	5.4	59,197	19.4	4.1
05051	Garland County	99,536	88.1	6.7	45,243	67.0	NA	220,900	944	14.7	37,807	18.7	10.6
05069	Jefferson County	63,063	87.1	5.7	23,885	60.4	NA	92,000	904	14.3	23,783	9.2	11.6
05085	Lonoke County	75,473	89.3	8.3	29,388	79.7	61.6	189,300	1,065	4.4	31,651	7.2	8.5
05119	Pulaski County	395,877	88.9	4.3	169,230	58.6	60.7	222,500	1,060	9.4	161,312	11.2	2.9
05125	Saline County	128745	91.0	6.1	50,684	76.1	63.7	235,500	965	11.5	54,808	10.5	3.3
05131	Sebastian County	127,384	84.2	7.6	51,596	60.7	56.6	191,500	885	13.7	53,929	14.5	4.0
05143	Washington County	258,237	82.5	9.1	99,630	54.9	60.9	325,700	1,112	7.7	120,382	13.3	3.8
05145	White County	77,218	90.3	5.6	30,920	74.4	NA	175,100	780	11.0	30,680	19.9	6.0
06000	**CALIFORNIA**	38,552,167	89.5	4.5	13,699,816	55.9	67.1	725,800	1,992	5.7	15,937,869	9.5	11.6
06001	Alameda County	1,605,214	87.9	6.0	608,534	53.9	69.9	1,067,800	2,303	5.2	658,192	7.0	14.9
06007	Butte County	205,086	82.6	7.4	86,279	56.5	58.1	420,500	1,434	8.0	83,502	26.4	5.3
06013	Contra Costa County	1,142,180	91.0	4.6	416,172	68.5	70.1	829,600	2,314	3.7	460,715	7.3	23.2
06017	El Dorado County	190,740	88.0	6.5	77,904	76.5	71.1	691,600	1,761	6.1	70,904	13.2	11.4
06019	Fresno County	1,005,417	90.5	3.3	328,895	58.2	64.7	395,500	1,410	9.0	386,256	11.2	5.5
06023	Humboldt County	133,012	82.5	8.6	56,130	54.6	53.4	468,000	1,246	6.7	52,359	27.1	3.3
06025	Imperial County	175,394	93.0	2.4	50,024	56.2	61.8	331,900	1,022	10.1	58,299	22.2	6.7
06029	Kern County	902,357	91.5	3.4	289,845	59.8	65.9	346,600	1,286	7.0	345,017	11.9	8.3
06031	Kings County	149,870	86.3	8.6	44,262	54.9	71.1	348,800	1,220	9.9	53,851	19.6	4.1
06033	Lake County	66166	88.2	4.6	26,092	76.3	NA	336,700	1,544	10.7	20,153	18.6	12.2

Table C-2. Counties — Where: Migration, Housing, and Transportation, 2023—*Continued*

State code	STATE County	Total population 1 year and over	Lived in the same house 1 year ago (percent)	Did not live in the same county 1 year ago (percent)	Total occupied housing units	Owner-occupied units (percent)	Percent with a mortgage, contract to purchase, or similar debt	Median value of owner-occupied units (dollars; owner estimated)	Median gross rent of renter-occupied units paying cash rent	Households without Internet access (percent)	Number of workers who commuted to work	Commute of less than 10 minutes (percent)	Commute of 60 minutes or more (percent)
	ACS table number:	C07204	C07204	C07204	B25003	B25003	B25081	B25097	B25064	S2801	B08012	B08012	B08012
	Column number:	1	2	3	4	5	6	7	8	9	10	11	12
	CALIFORNIA—Cont.												
06037	Los Angeles County	9,569,835	91.0	2.9	3,450,470	45.4	68.5	828,700	1,896	5.8	4,053,687	7.0	13.2
06039	Madera County	161,365	87.6	6.0	46,781	65.7	61.5	398,500	1,477	8.5	55,625	18.1	8.2
06041	Marin County	252,307	90.4	5.8	101,608	65.6	64.3	1,512,200	2,614	3.7	89,456	11.0	12.4
06045	Mendocino County	88,301	88.4	4.8	34,951	61.7	53.0	510,400	1,439	7.8	31,410	27.1	7.7
06047	Merced County	287,778	91.2	3.9	88,053	52.6	62.7	409,000	1,294	15.7	110,084	16.5	18.7
06053	Monterey County	426,437	89.8	4.6	132,170	53.0	62.3	759,100	2,004	5.7	172,408	10.0	8.6
06055	Napa County	132,017	89.1	5.1	51,167	62.7	63.8	831,800	2,239	5.9	59,158	19.7	8.4
06057	Nevada County	101,727	90.9	5.8	42,712	73.6	61.9	647,200	1,782	3.8	32,602	20.2	11.4
06059	Orange County	3,104,970	90.1	3.8	1,092,528	57.0	66.3	961,400	2,382	4.2	1,334,808	7.5	8.4
06061	Placer County	419,091	87.9	6.6	160,315	73.3	67.9	673,900	2,009	4.9	156,988	11.3	8.9
06065	Riverside County	2,465,135	90.6	4.3	791,757	69.1	68.2	576,000	1,871	6.1	988,643	8.3	18.9
06067	Sacramento County	1,566,942	89.4	5.0	573,170	60.2	69.4	533,900	1,762	5.8	611,358	9.3	7.6
06069	San Benito County	67,878	91.4	3.4	20,194	69.0	NA	761,600	1,985	2.2	29,579	10.7	32.2
06071	San Bernardino County	2,170,516	90.7	4.0	682,807	62.8	69.1	515,500	1,831	5.7	893,085	9.7	16.4
06073	San Diego County	3,230,012	87.4	5.1	1,181,259	54.5	68.9	864,900	2,296	4.9	1,407,306	9.1	6.3
06075	San Francisco County	801,259	84.4	7.1	372,027	37.1	63.4	1,348,000	2,356	7.0	348,055	4.5	11.7
06077	San Joaquin County	792,319	89.9	5.4	251,091	63.2	67.8	531,500	1,655	6.5	323,133	11.7	20.7
06079	San Luis Obispo County	279,754	83.2	7.1	110,283	62.5	64.0	817,600	1,922	5.0	112,983	21.1	4.9
06081	San Mateo County	719,859	89.0	6.7	265,124	59.1	64.1	1,492,600	2,797	3.4	308,011	7.2	7.1
06083	Santa Barbara County	437,404	85.7	6.7	150,932	50.8	60.4	780,700	1,988	7.1	174,805	18.1	5.9
06085	Santa Clara County	1,856,575	86.1	6.1	665,549	54.1	65.5	1,443,100	2,781	3.9	821,272	6.4	7.5
06087	Santa Cruz County	259,146	84.6	7.2	99,069	60.1	62.0	1,011,300	2,055	4.9	106,755	13.2	11.2
06089	Shasta County	178,077	89.0	4.8	72,320	68.0	64.4	355,100	1,351	7.6	66,894	18.4	3.7
06095	Solano County	443,482	88.5	6.7	157,766	64.4	74.1	621,000	2,059	5.7	184,288	11.3	15.8
06097	Sonoma County	477,288	88.8	4.4	192,765	64.6	67.5	784,900	2,061	5.0	208,012	13.5	9.0
06099	Stanislaus County	544,477	90.8	3.2	179,152	61.1	65.1	456,700	1,595	5.8	224,795	14.4	14.5
06101	Sutter County	96,394	87.9	4.6	33,325	61.8	67.2	405,100	1,403	7.0	38,650	23.1	10.0
06103	Tehama County	64,211	95.3	2.8	24,919	67.5	53.1	322,800	1,126	5.9	23,306	24.7	2.5
06107	Tulare County	473,858	92.6	2.7	145,442	59.2	69.4	339,800	1,277	9.2	182,357	17.1	7.2
06111	Ventura County	821,563	90.8	4.3	283,718	63.4	66.6	820,300	2,264	4.5	343,832	11.7	9.1
06113	Yolo County	219,198	81.5	11.3	77,230	55.3	64.2	610,000	1,900	5.3	87,975	17.8	5.3
06115	Yuba County	84,706	87.4	7.7	29,253	67.1	60.4	391,400	1,304	8.3	30,665	10.0	12.7
08000	**COLORADO**	5,819,109	84.3	9.3	2,428,261	65.7	69.1	550,300	1,771	5.4	2,522,855	13.5	7.2
08001	Adams County	527,683	83.3	10.3	192,742	68.3	71.8	494,500	1,811	5.6	246,684	7.8	8.0
08005	Arapahoe County	649,126	83.9	8.6	261,161	65.0	73.6	567,300	1,933	4.3	292,355	9.8	6.3
08013	Boulder County	325,389	78.7	13.3	137,425	61.2	63.2	763,600	1,915	4.0	126,056	16.2	7.0
08014	Broomfield County	76,156	82.5	13.2	33,563	59.1	69.3	660,800	2,086	2.5	28,069	8.8	4.6
08031	Denver County	708,432	79.5	12.0	342,996	47.1	72.2	626,500	1,843	6.3	317,805	8.9	5.6
08035	Douglas County	379,803	86.0	9.9	145,551	75.1	77.6	725,500	2,219	1.7	152,472	11.1	7.5
08041	El Paso County	735,467	81.1	9.0	298,973	66.4	70.9	470,900	1,708	3.9	325,000	11.6	6.1
08059	Jefferson County	571,041	86.8	8.8	242,433	69.8	68.9	645,900	1,851	5.6	247,602	10.3	6.5
08069	Larimer County	366,428	84.8	8.9	156,498	63.3	70.3	574,900	1,699	6.4	156,701	15.9	7.4
08077	Mesa County	157,924	88.9	5.9	68,115	69.4	64.2	373,200	1,184	5.5	62,736	20.1	6.6
08101	Pueblo County	167,576	89.5	5.9	68,732	71.3	68.3	313,700	1,165	7.6	67,504	13.7	4.6
08123	Weld County	355504	86.6	7.2	129,057	74.8	72.8	475,400	1,569	6.0	157,934	13.8	10.7
09000	**CONNECTICUT**	3,576,682	89.1	5.3	1,442,969	65.7	63.5	367,800	1,463	7.2	1,584,717	12.6	9.4
09110	Capitol Planning Region	964,264	89.2	4.6	391,422	65.3	64.7	326,700	1,389	8.3	422,821	12.0	4.9
09120	Greater Bridgeport Planning Region	324,197	88.8	6.0	119,505	65.8	61.2	441,400	1,488	8.0	141,730	10.9	16.1
09130	Lower Connecticut River Valley Planning Region	175,062	92.0	4.8	75,959	73.4	61.1	385,300	1,449	7.3	79,453	15.4	8.0
09140	Naugatuck Valley Planning Region	450,191	90.7	4.5	180,851	67.9	65.5	327,000	1,298	8.5	200,158	11.8	8.9
09150	Northeastern Connecticut Planning Region	96,277	91.5	4.0	40,349	75.2	68.5	305,600	1,217	4.7	47,251	10.8	12.3
09160	Northwest Hills Planning Region	111,914	93.8	2.5	50,297	80.6	58.7	331,100	1,141	5.8	48,917	15.4	10.5
09170	South Central Connecticut Planning Region	561,487	86.5	6.5	233,004	58.8	63.6	349,200	1,471	6.7	251,695	14.5	7.0
09180	Southeastern Connecticut Planning Region	277,050	87.5	6.5	114,156	64.8	56.9	323,700	1,348	8.7	123,616	15.1	5.1
09190	Western Connecticut Planning Region	616,240	89.2	5.7	237,426	64.6	65.3	657,900	2,076	4.8	269,076	11.2	17.5

Table C-2. Counties — Where: Migration, Housing, and Transportation, 2023—*Continued*

State code	STATE County	Total population 1 year and over	Lived in the same house 1 year ago (percent)	Did not live in the same county 1 year ago (percent)	Total occupied housing units	Owner-occupied units (percent)	Percent with a mortgage, contract to purchase, or similar debt	Median value of owner-occupied units (dollars; owner estimated)	Median gross rent of renter-occupied units paying cash rent	Households without Internet access (percent)	Number of workers who commuted to work	Commute of less than 10 minutes (percent)	Commute of 60 minutes or more (percent)
	ACS table number:	C07204	C07204	C07204	B25003	B25003	B25081	B25097	B25064	S2801	B08012	B08012	B08012
	Column number:	1	2	3	4	5	6	7	8	9	10	11	12
10000	**DELAWARE**	1,022,638	88.8	6.0	412,048	73.6	64.6	359,700	1,358	7.2	431,706	9.7	8.8
10001	Kent County	188,020	86.7	7.7	74,183	73.0	69.1	325,200	1,320	9.7	84,848	10.3	9.7
10003	New Castle County	572,774	88.6	5.5	226,373	70.2	67.1	357,400	1,393	6.0	248,601	8.4	9.0
10005	Sussex County	261,844	90.9	6.0	111,492	80.9	57.6	397,100	1,236	7.9	98,257	12.7	7.2
11000	**DISTRICT OF COLUMBIA**	670,127	79.0	10.4	334,673	39.1	77.3	715,500	1,904	7.9	278,932	4.1	7.8
11001	District of Columbia	670,127	79.0	10.4	334,673	39.1	77.3	715,500	1,904	7.9	278,932	4.1	7.8
12000	**FLORIDA**	22,395,466	86.4	7.4	8,966,402	68.1	55.7	381,000	1,719	7.0	8,944,682	8.6	9.2
12001	Alachua County	283299	78.7	11.8	121,753	55.7	59.4	307,000	1,370	10.9	123,207	12.3	3.1
12005	Bay County	188,772	84.4	8.3	80,689	68.9	56.8	327,700	1,534	5.2	87,511	16.2	5.1
12009	Brevard County	639,082	88.1	6.3	258,656	76.7	53.9	356,600	1,648	5.6	248,914	10.7	4.8
12011	Broward County	1,940,270	86.6	6.5	758,853	63.9	58.1	439,100	1,961	6.5	856,311	7.0	10.7
12015	Charlotte County	205,423	90.9	5.8	90,367	83.7	45.6	365,900	1,520	8.4	62,385	9.2	13.8
12017	Citrus County	165,476	89.3	8.2	75,745	82.5	46.1	278,800	1,138	9.2	47,740	9.8	9.8
12019	Clay County	228,513	88.0	7.8	86,946	74.5	61.4	338,000	1,619	5.1	94,242	10.0	11.5
12021	Collier County	401,279	88.3	6.8	166,192	77.2	48.4	595,500	2,039	6.7	137,956	11.9	6.8
12023	Columbia County	71,656	83.9	12.9	27,280	75.9	48.3	230,300	998	7.6	27,593	9.8	9.2
12031	Duval County	1,018,988	83.3	7.6	428,020	58.6	64.4	321,400	1,516	7.7	423,005	8.2	3.7
12033	Escambia County	323,180	84.2	9.9	131,375	67.0	58.4	287,000	1,394	5.8	134,826	10.4	6.7
12035	Flagler County	130717	87.0	9.1	56,177	82.8	57.6	400,400	1,749	5.1	42,862	11.6	8.1
12053	Hernando County	211,299	90.8	7.0	85,911	84.2	52.5	305,100	1,392	5.5	70,176	8.9	15.8
12055	Highlands County	106,910	85.1	9.8	47,278	80.1	37.2	208,900	1,073	10.3	32,375	12.2	8.0
12057	Hillsborough County	1,520,571	84.7	8.1	593,029	60.7	63.5	396,200	1,757	4.8	617,318	8.4	9.9
12061	Indian River County	169,236	91.1	4.6	72,833	79.8	44.9	370,600	1,409	9.7	60,173	14.1	4.8
12069	Lake County	420196	87.6	9.1	172,803	76.5	54.9	321,700	1,644	6.5	156,034	9.2	12.6
12071	Lee County	826,292	87.1	6.3	326,338	75.2	52.2	391,700	1,797	6.5	296,186	7.8	10.3
12073	Leon County	294,547	80.1	9.9	124,867	51.7	62.4	311,800	1,284	9.5	132,866	11.7	3.5
12081	Manatee County	438238	84.8	10.2	190,091	74.4	49.2	424,000	1,771	6.9	162,680	9.7	10.1
12083	Marion County	405,722	86.9	8.7	171,369	77.6	47.6	265,100	1,365	7.6	142,091	9.3	6.3
12085	Martin County	161,530	93.3	5.0	69,169	78.4	43.7	438,800	1,585	8.8	56,042	10.3	9.8
12086	Miami-Dade County	2,659,522	87.2	5.1	985,935	54.0	57.3	488,600	1,864	7.9	1,172,869	5.6	11.9
12087	Monroe County	79,751	88.2	6.9	32,559	70.0	47.2	806,100	2,091	4.8	36,710	25.8	7.4
12089	Nassau County	100,959	85.8	9.3	41,045	81.1	56.1	411,500	1,546	2.9	36,298	14.3	8.7
12091	Okaloosa County	215,965	84.6	8.1	86,541	69.1	60.5	363,800	1,710	5.0	96,335	10.9	9.3
12095	Orange County	1,457,041	84.4	7.9	556,557	56.1	65.5	405,700	1,815	5.8	632,756	6.8	6.3
12097	Osceola County	433,858	85.2	9.8	154,722	68.6	65.5	373,300	1,802	6.1	188,315	3.2	16.3
12099	Palm Beach County	1,518,598	87.0	6.3	605,132	71.8	52.8	491,500	1,982	7.6	614,047	8.6	7.3
12101	Pasco County	627,285	86.1	7.9	239,952	77.3	59.0	337,700	1,540	7.2	232,526	9.6	13.3
12103	Pinellas County	954,290	86.9	6.6	439,896	69.2	49.4	382,400	1,776	7.5	375,152	10.7	8.0
12105	Polk County	807,890	87.3	6.9	306,915	71.4	55.4	296,300	1,403	8.9	319,338	7.8	13.9
12107	Putnam County	75,362	92.2	3.6	32,487	77.0	40.4	160,200	964	7.2	24,651	14.2	12.0
12109	St. Johns County	317,193	85.1	10.7	126,240	82.2	67.9	534,600	2,037	4.2	105,916	9.3	5.1
12111	St. Lucie County	371,128	89.2	6.1	145,735	78.7	56.2	371,400	1,729	7.3	142,708	4.1	9.4
12113	Santa Rosa County	200,898	84.4	10.0	72,969	82.4	66.8	342,100	1,269	4.2	81,257	9.9	8.9
12115	Sarasota County	466,409	84.0	8.7	218,010	76.6	47.9	450,300	1,940	5.4	162,414	11.5	5.9
12117	Seminole County	480,163	87.4	8.0	189,580	63.1	65.2	404,100	1,803	6.4	189,902	8.2	5.5
12119	Sumter County	150,512	85.8	10.9	73,238	87.9	43.0	411,000	1,347	4.3	27,704	9.4	7.4
12127	Volusia County	586,140	88.7	6.8	243,904	73.6	55.1	341,900	1,480	7.1	225,251	11.5	11.7
12131	Walton County	85,523	87.2	8.0	35,435	80.7	49.2	438,000	1,720	6.7	34,456	10.1	13.4
13000	**GEORGIA**	10,909,651	87.4	7.6	4,150,138	66.1	63.2	323,000	1,400	7.5	4,484,489	10.0	10.6
13013	Barrow County	90,849	90.8	6.6	32,217	80.1	63.9	300,800	1,285	8.1	43,361	9.8	12.9
13015	Bartow County	113,829	88.7	6.8	42,225	75.3	63.5	309,400	1,383	6.7	49,553	8.3	12.0
13021	Bibb County	154,681	83.1	8.0	60,919	46.6	60.2	199,800	1,038	13.3	55,602	11.7	5.8
13031	Bulloch County	83,317	77.7	12.1	30,988	54.4	NA	240,200	927	11.3	31,843	18.5	6.5
13045	Carroll County	125,541	85.4	8.3	44,515	71.6	60.1	280,800	1,174	12.1	53,245	14.4	19.0
13047	Catoosa County	67,960	88.4	7.6	26,248	77.5	57.5	232,000	971	11.3	29,106	8.4	3.6
13051	Chatham County	300,349	81.2	10.0	123,272	56.6	61.6	320,800	1,485	5.6	129,490	10.7	3.7
13057	Cherokee County	283,125	90.3	6.6	102,811	79.4	69.5	450,800	1,857	3.4	119,092	6.5	12.7
13059	Clarke County	129,089	72.0	15.0	55,505	42.6	58.8	318,700	1,281	6.9	59,924	16.5	4.7
13063	Clayton County	295,094	88.4	8.4	106,914	52.5	70.9	245,900	1,440	6.6	122,021	4.8	15.1
13067	Cobb County	769,446	87.1	8.1	299,074	67.3	70.3	432,000	1,740	3.6	331,795	7.5	10.0
13073	Columbia County	163,949	87.2	8.3	57,807	81.5	72.9	327,700	1,339	7.7	68,508	9.5	6.5
13077	Coweta County	153,541	91.2	4.4	57,325	79.5	63.6	383,000	1,546	5.2	64,262	8.8	10.3

Table C-2. Counties — Where: Migration, Housing, and Transportation, 2023—*Continued*

State code	STATE County	Total population 1 year and over	Lived in the same house 1 year ago (percent)	Did not live in the same county 1 year ago (percent)	Total occupied housing units	Owner-occupied units (percent)	Percent with a mortgage, contract to purchase, or similar debt	Median value of owner-occupied units (dollars; owner estimated)	Median gross rent of renter-occupied units paying cash rent	Households without Internet access (percent)	Number of workers who commuted to work	Commute of less than 10 minutes (percent)	Commute of 60 minutes or more (percent)
	ACS table number:	C07204	C07204	C07204	B25003	B25003	B25081	B25097	B25064	S2801	B08012	B08012	B08012
	Column number:	1	2	3	4	5	6	7	8	9	10	11	12
	GEORGIA—Cont.												
13089	DeKalb County	755,287	86.2	8.0	291,423	60.8	70.2	368,200	1,707	4.4	309,251	6.5	9.3
13095	Dougherty County	82,197	79.3	12.8	35,052	44.2	60.4	144,500	856	16.4	28,895	21.0	5.1
13097	Douglas County	147,873	89.3	7.9	53,350	68.3	74.4	328,400	1,594	6.4	67,262	8.8	16.7
13103	Effingham County	70,804	88.8	8.7	25,452	80.8	NA	282,800	1,170	7.1	32,623	5.0	12.1
13113	Fayette County	122,133	90.5	6.6	45,095	80.4	68.6	462,900	1,712	3.3	46,880	9.4	12.3
13115	Floyd County	99,224	87.9	7.1	37,835	63.3	51.4	221,100	993	13.3	41,134	15.8	8.7
13117	Forsyth County	270,241	91.1	6.0	90,635	83.9	73.2	587,300	2,166	3.1	102,230	7.3	12.0
13121	Fulton County	1,068,289	84.2	8.2	458,812	56.0	72.8	477,500	1,775	5.1	434,058	7.4	9.4
13127	Glynn County	85871	86.9	7.7	37,904	66.2	57.7	337,200	1,267	8.3	33,088	14.5	3.1
13135	Gwinnett County	972,584	87.9	6.6	330,254	67.3	67.5	395,500	1,847	4.1	401,393	5.9	13.8
13139	Hall County	214,819	90.1	6.4	76,413	67.3	59.6	357,600	1,360	4.4	89,444	9.2	9.6
13151	Henry County	252,006	90.1	7.2	89,313	74.4	72.5	334,600	1,838	3.8	106,811	5.6	15.8
13153	Houston County	170,059	86.1	9.9	65,688	66.3	63.3	221,200	1,179	4.8	70,852	10.9	4.5
13157	Jackson County	87,234	91.3	6.8	30,300	75.4	64.3	363,200	1,111	5.9	40,784	6.6	16.3
13179	Liberty County	68,160	80.5	14.8	24,654	55.0	67.3	226,200	1,236	4.8	29,117	21.1	12.2
13185	Lowndes County	118,284	88.2	6.6	48,322	56.5	NA	221,800	1,029	13.6	50,972	19.1	3.4
13215	Muscogee County	199,279	84.1	8.4	82,007	50.5	66.1	198,200	1,004	11.1	76,270	14.4	3.8
13217	Newton County	118,067	90.4	7.1	42,633	74.0	74.2	295,800	1,564	4.7	50,580	6.2	21.1
13223	Paulding County	181,603	87.8	10.3	61,401	78.9	74.3	354,000	1,798	3.5	77,219	3.3	25.3
13245	Richmond County	202,721	79.6	8.5	77,202	52.6	62.1	197,100	1,149	13.0	86,577	12.9	2.1
13247	Rockdale County	95,030	88.5	9.9	35,459	76.1	70.6	328,200	1,553	3.4	40,579	4.3	22.0
13255	Spalding County	69,506	90.2	6.4	26,898	63.5	NA	240,400	1,073	5.6	27,830	6.4	16.7
13285	Troup County	69,663	85.2	6.8	28,232	56.4	NA	241,000	1,126	12.0	30,702	11.6	8.6
13295	Walker County	68,763	88.2	6.7	26,020	78.5	53.6	219,800	796	7.4	26,071	15.5	6.3
13297	Walton County	105,180	89.9	8.9	37,132	79.5	68.8	357,200	1,402	9.0	43,887	10.3	17.2
13313	Whitfield County	102,956	86.8	4.4	37,316	62.6	41.3	243,400	935	12.0	47,056	10.8	4.1
15000	**HAWAII**	1,420,012	88.1	5.6	493,898	62.4	62.2	846,400	1,940	7.3	637,246	10.6	8.7
15001	Hawaii County	204,205	89.3	3.4	73,933	74.5	54.9	528,800	1,492	8.4	77,289	12.9	12.4
15003	Honolulu County	978,959	87.1	6.2	338,496	59.1	63.4	899,300	2,033	7.0	454,017	9.3	8.8
15007	Kauai County	73,497	92.8	4.7	24,621	70.4	70.2	888,500	1,816	6.8	34,408	13.2	5.1
15009	Maui County	163,331	90.5	5.3	56,848	63.1	62.9	934,500	1,828	7.5	71,512	14.7	5.8
16000	**IDAHO**	1,945,004	85.8	7.5	733,244	72.5	61.5	428,600	1,256	7.1	799,102	19.2	5.3
16001	Ada County	520,496	84.2	7.2	209,863	70.0	66.0	525,600	1,599	4.4	218,273	11.8	2.6
16005	Bannock County	89,653	81.9	7.5	33,729	69.5	58.8	341,800	1,068	10.3	35,883	25.4	7.4
16019	Bonneville County	130,245	90.3	5.4	45,245	70.0	61.0	374,800	1,182	5.3	55,828	22.8	9.1
16027	Canyon County	254,398	86.7	7.2	88,688	76.1	67.5	378,600	1,366	5.9	107,248	13.8	4.2
16055	Kootenai County	182,201	88.4	7.7	74,253	73.4	63.1	556,500	1,426	7.8	71,065	14.2	5.2
16083	Twin Falls County	94,507	85.6	5.8	35,050	67.9	60.7	329,000	1,142	8.9	42,202	23.8	1.5
17000	**ILLINOIS**	12,427,191	89.2	4.7	5,071,288	67.4	60.3	263,300	1,238	8.2	5,354,834	12.3	10.1
17019	Champaign County	203,388	83.2	9.5	89,155	54.3	61.8	216,100	987	6.1	87,215	16.3	2.9
17031	Cook County	5,036,429	88.0	3.7	2,117,084	57.8	62.2	313,700	1,386	8.4	2,165,771	7.4	13.1
17037	DeKalb County	99,586	83.2	10.3	40,202	63.8	70.4	244,000	1,037	6.2	46,315	16.3	8.9
17043	DuPage County	912,079	89.8	6.0	353,618	73.4	64.1	383,100	1,672	4.4	383,517	11.4	9.7
17089	Kane County	510,918	92.0	4.7	185,921	77.4	67.1	324,000	1,479	6.7	231,585	10.0	9.1
17091	Kankakee County	104,788	92.7	4.6	41,130	70.8	55.7	182,900	1,058	12.2	44,867	17.7	10.7
17093	Kendall County	138,493	94.0	4.3	44,934	85.3	76.0	326,700	1,714	4.4	65,161	9.3	11.6
17097	Lake County	703,191	90.4	5.6	260,243	76.8	63.7	340,400	1,406	5.1	294,659	9.9	9.8
17099	LaSalle County	107,588	89.3	4.9	44,319	74.8	53.5	154,300	885	10.3	48,992	18.5	14.1
17111	McHenry County	310,228	93.2	3.8	119,150	83.2	67.0	308,300	1,369	4.2	144,284	13.8	14.1
17113	McLean County	168,363	85.4	7.6	71,060	65.5	61.8	211,000	1,013	9.1	73,991	20.8	4.2
17115	Macon County	99,584	89.6	3.8	43,598	69.2	52.6	115,300	822	8.3	39,396	18.0	5.8
17119	Madison County	259,528	88.8	4.3	110,909	74.5	60.6	173,300	999	7.4	117,945	15.0	4.5
17143	Peoria County	175510	88.5	6.9	77,525	70.4	50.6	153,000	938	9.2	71,684	21.3	2.9
17161	Rock Island County	140,179	89.8	4.7	62,396	72.5	56.8	144,100	845	8.9	59,012	16.5	3.9
17163	St. Clair County	248,321	88.9	4.4	102,701	66.0	56.2	185,400	1,077	10.4	103,329	12.1	3.7
17167	Sangamon County	192,224	89.1	4.2	85,477	70.1	55.3	181,700	956	4.8	81,444	12.4	3.0
17179	Tazewell County	128,403	91.5	4.2	54,228	76.4	58.5	162,000	869	10.8	57,976	20.0	2.4
17183	Vermilion County	70,867	92.6	2.1	30,703	65.6	42.8	96,100	850	11.6	25,849	22.0	2.5
17197	Will County	691916	92.8	4.8	246,145	82.8	68.0	322,200	1,527	5.5	313,078	9.8	13.4
17199	Williamson County	66,288	82.4	7.9	29,509	64.8	51.1	155,900	980	11.3	27,323	13.3	5.0
17201	Winnebago County	278,087	87.5	4.0	115,540	64.4	55.2	161,400	988	8.3	119,251	13.8	6.4

Table C-2. Counties — Where: Migration, Housing, and Transportation, 2023—*Continued*

State code	STATE County	Total population 1 year and over	Lived in the same house 1 year ago (percent)	Did not live in the same county 1 year ago (percent)	Total occupied housing units	Owner-occupied units (percent)	Percent with a mortgage, contract to purchase, or similar debt	Median value of owner-occupied units (dollars; owner estimated)	Median gross rent of renter-occupied units paying cash rent	Households without Internet access (percent)	Number of workers who commuted to work	Commute of less than 10 minutes (percent)	Commute of 60 minutes or more (percent)
	ACS table number:	C07204	C07204	C07204	B25003	B25003	B25081	B25097	B25064	S2801	B08012	B08012	B08012
	Column number:	1	2	3	4	5	6	7	8	9	10	11	12
18000	**INDIANA**	6,783,874	87.5	6.3	2,754,881	70.4	63.5	225,900	1,044	9.1	2,989,879	15.2	6.4
18003	Allen County	390,204	86.0	5.7	160,153	67.7	64.5	226,000	957	7.6	172,708	11.3	4.0
18005	Bartholomew County	83,200	86.6	6.7	33,777	69.8	61.4	253,900	1,169	4.9	37,829	13.1	5.2
18011	Boone County	75,458	86.1	8.3	29,659	76.5	69.9	369,300	1,303	5.7	34,012	14.4	2.5
18019	Clark County	123,493	87.5	6.1	52,156	70.7	62.3	232,400	1,109	10.3	56,230	13.6	3.9
18035	Delaware County	111,125	81.2	10.0	44,361	65.8	56.7	139,700	878	11.6	51,919	19.6	10.2
18039	Elkhart County	203649	91.5	4.3	73,439	71.5	63.7	214,000	1,079	10.4	95,133	17.5	3.0
18043	Floyd County	80,103	89.1	6.2	31,833	72.2	66.8	258,700	991	8.4	34,536	7.5	2.6
18053	Grant County	65,845	90.1	4.6	27,670	70.5	55.1	121,800	734	13.7	26,283	25.9	5.3
18057	Hamilton County	367,232	90.7	5.2	140,850	75.9	75.1	419,800	1,510	4.0	152,747	12.5	4.1
18059	Hancock County	85,960	89.4	8.2	34,114	77.0	70.9	288,900	1,166	8.7	37,832	9.0	9.1
18063	Hendricks County	183,881	90.2	7.4	69,367	79.3	69.8	306,100	1,431	6.1	82,440	14.7	5.6
18067	Howard County	83,112	85.4	6.6	35,551	67.3	64.6	169,300	949	8.9	34,161	23.5	6.6
18081	Johnson County	164,956	82.1	9.7	64,079	73.1	68.2	286,900	1,249	6.3	73,147	15.5	4.8
18085	Kosciusko County	79,300	88.3	9.0	32,268	76.6	59.6	227,800	1,010	13.0	36,911	16.2	5.9
18089	Lake County	494,573	90.6	4.8	197,595	73.1	64.9	236,800	1,116	8.5	208,387	12.0	13.1
18091	LaPorte County	110,174	89.6	5.8	45,725	74.3	59.6	196,300	994	11.6	44,010	16.9	8.9
18095	Madison County	131,322	85.4	7.3	54,317	72.0	65.8	163,200	935	9.6	54,535	17.7	10.2
18097	Marion County	954,790	85.3	6.0	408,293	57.4	67.6	238,700	1,187	7.4	436,591	9.1	4.9
18105	Monroe County	138,319	72.3	16.0	61,400	52.0	65.1	301,400	1,130	9.2	60,363	17.1	4.2
18109	Morgan County	72,395	92.2	4.1	29,202	81.1	63.6	262,700	951	6.9	30,339	11.8	10.1
18127	Porter County	174,007	92.4	3.2	68,120	76.4	68.9	280,500	1,127	5.1	78,820	12.8	9.7
18141	St. Joseph County	269,474	88.5	5.8	106,607	69.0	62.7	195,000	1,077	7.4	117,627	14.8	3.9
18157	Tippecanoe County	186,658	76.2	13.2	76,240	54.9	64.5	246,800	1,131	8.0	85,260	12.9	3.5
18163	Vanderburgh County	177,815	85.3	6.8	77,472	64.0	61.4	187,300	938	8.1	80,498	19.6	4.8
18167	Vigo County	104,969	79.7	9.3	42,219	63.2	60.7	142,800	927	12.5	42,618	19.3	4.8
18173	Warrick County	65,335	89.7	7.7	25,278	81.8	64.4	262,200	1,021	5.8	29,411	12.4	4.6
18177	Wayne County	65,894	90.2	4.4	26,843	68.4	59.3	136,100	825	11.2	27,027	15.1	8.8
19000	**IOWA**	3,170,553	87.5	6.2	1,337,243	71.8	59.3	213,300	949	9.8	1,457,641	23.6	4.0
19013	Black Hawk County	128,633	86.7	6.5	53,791	65.3	64.4	180,100	942	8.3	60,287	20.1	2.5
19049	Dallas County	110,000	83.7	11.7	44,043	66.3	68.2	351,100	1,430	4.5	49,000	13.3	1.6
19061	Dubuque County	97575	87.8	7.2	42,889	74.1	60.8	231,700	868	10.3	46,520	24.7	3.7
19103	Johnson County	155,556	74.9	12.0	64,076	58.6	61.3	310,700	1,089	9.8	76,244	15.7	2.7
19113	Linn County	226,480	87.4	5.0	96,058	72.5	63.5	222,900	942	7.6	100,791	19.6	3.4
19153	Polk County	498,849	85.7	5.5	207,757	67.3	69.5	271,300	1,137	7.4	237,321	14.5	2.8
19155	Pottawattamie County	92,145	89.0	6.3	38,289	70.5	63.5	216,200	902	15.9	42,572	16.7	2.9
19163	Scott County	172,393	87.1	4.9	75,239	69.6	65.2	243,000	993	7.7	77,226	13.9	2.0
19169	Story County	98,279	74.6	15.3	38,771	55.8	53.7	260,600	991	16.8	46,956	26.4	3.1
19193	Woodbury County	104,571	91.6	3.5	40,348	67.6	57.6	182,900	1,025	9.4	46,962	17.2	3.1
20000	**KANSAS**	2,907,735	86.2	6.5	1,188,340	66.7	57.1	219,800	1,036	8.3	1,323,613	22.2	3.8
20015	Butler County	67,930	88.8	6.8	25,801	79.1	61.6	222,200	992	6.2	30,033	17.9	1.7
20045	Douglas County	119,666	75.7	13.7	51,013	48.9	65.9	305,600	1,056	5.6	52,364	21.8	3.9
20091	Johnson County	614,377	88.3	5.0	250,337	66.7	68.3	387,700	1,427	3.9	280,173	12.0	2.4
20103	Leavenworth County	83,269	80.2	14.6	30,246	72.7	63.2	275,500	1,175	7.6	34,580	13.2	4.2
20161	Riley County	70,528	76.6	13.6	27,875	46.1	61.1	221,500	1,095	7.5	37,897	34.5	4.6
20173	Sedgwick County	522,816	85.2	4.5	211,238	62.1	60.3	209,700	974	6.8	242,344	14.6	3.4
20177	Shawnee County	175,467	86.3	3.6	73,980	66.4	54.2	183,200	962	10.2	75,147	19.9	4.1
20209	Wyandotte County	163,167	88.3	6.5	62,238	61.1	53.6	177,000	1,113	9.8	71,907	10.9	2.7
21000	**KENTUCKY**	4,477,307	87.7	6.3	1,853,603	68.8	56.1	211,800	929	9.8	1,867,279	14.5	6.2
21015	Boone County	139,408	88.9	6.8	51,702	74.9	70.1	285,600	1,397	4.5	60,881	7.9	5.9
21029	Bullitt County	84,310	91.7	5.9	32,321	85.1	67.4	260,500	907	6.3	39,270	9.2	4.4
21037	Campbell County	93,044	86.6	6.7	40,425	69.3	65.8	268,500	1,292	5.8	44,366	13.5	2.5
21047	Christian County	69,580	80.5	14.3	25,768	53.9	54.0	175,300	1,032	7.8	30,428	26.6	5.3
21059	Daviess County	102,215	88.5	2.9	42,164	62.9	58.2	200,500	904	10.2	48,036	18.6	2.4
21067	Fayette County	315,940	79.6	8.5	141,680	55.8	65.6	294,300	1,145	7.2	149,981	13.2	3.8
21093	Hardin County	111,332	87.0	8.5	45,909	63.7	61.4	237,200	952	5.2	47,933	13.1	5.7
21111	Jefferson County	763,002	86.1	5.4	331,206	63.7	63.5	250,800	1,123	8.1	321,689	10.3	3.7
21117	Kenton County	169,558	89.6	6.2	67,180	70.3	68.4	251,500	1,083	4.7	75,482	8.3	2.9
21145	McCracken County	67,102	92.3	3.0	28,934	64.7	53.6	179,600	764	12.4	30,092	22.2	1.1
21151	Madison County	95,985	86.5	6.7	37,672	61.3	60.8	253,100	804	10.8	45,276	12.7	7.8
21185	Oldham County	69,670	91.0	6.1	23,415	89.9	70.5	387,500	1,032	6.0	29,070	8.9	5.0
21199	Pulaski County	65,409	87.2	3.7	26,203	72.5	51.3	189,500	850	11.8	23,977	18.6	8.0
21227	Warren County	140654	83.3	10.8	57,773	58.3	69.9	268,700	972	7.2	66,611	14.4	8.1

Table C-2. Counties — Where: Migration, Housing, and Transportation, 2023—*Continued*

State code	STATE County	Total population 1 year and over	Lived in the same house 1 year ago (percent)	Did not live in the same county 1 year ago (percent)	Total occupied housing units	Owner-occupied units (percent)	Percent with a mortgage, contract to purchase, or similar debt	Median value of owner-occupied units (dollars; owner estimated)	Median gross rent of renter-occupied units paying cash rent	Households without Internet access (percent)	Number of workers who commuted to work	Commute of less than 10 minutes (percent)	Commute of 60 minutes or more (percent)
	ACS table number:	C07204	C07204	C07204	B25003	B25003	B25081	B25097	B25064	S2801	B08012	B08012	B08012
	Column number:	1	2	3	4	5	6	7	8	9	10	11	12
22000	**LOUISIANA**	4,524,085	89.0	5.1	1,833,915	68.1	51.7	215,600	1,020	11.9	1,850,348	13.4	7.8
22005	Ascension Parish	130,268	93.0	4.2	48,526	82.7	64.3	279,900	1,176	6.0	62,718	10.5	9.0
22015	Bossier Parish	128,403	90.5	4.7	54,151	71.3	57.7	211,500	1,163	8.6	56,973	11.3	5.1
22017	Caddo Parish	224,719	87.8	4.5	98,864	60.9	54.7	170,500	996	16.1	88,893	15.5	3.2
22019	Calcasieu Parish	201,516	88.1	4.2	79,222	72.4	50.1	221,500	1,081	12.8	86,321	17.3	4.2
22033	East Baton Rouge Parish	443,894	83.3	6.2	177,309	57.8	59.4	253,300	1,131	7.9	188,031	10.7	4.4
22045	Iberia Parish	66,515	94.8	1.7	26,439	68.7	38.0	147,500	836	14.5	25,613	16.1	9.8
22051	Jefferson Parish	417,864	89.7	5.0	176,635	63.1	53.8	259,100	1,135	9.3	182,577	11.3	5.5
22055	Lafayette Parish	245,851	89.3	4.4	102,227	66.0	57.7	244,400	972	6.8	108,772	13.0	4.1
22057	Lafourche Parish	94,341	90.8	5.4	38,393	78.4	42.3	195,200	1,088	10.0	38,446	19.6	12.5
22063	Livingston Parish	149,002	92.6	4.9	55,653	82.3	56.3	223,600	1,003	5.7	62,840	7.5	12.5
22071	Orleans Parish	359,843	87.5	5.1	155,005	55.9	56.0	306,400	1,203	10.7	144,366	11.7	5.6
22073	Ouachita Parish	155521	86.0	5.0	63,158	62.3	54.7	195,300	940	17.3	61,546	9.5	6.2
22079	Rapides Parish	125,216	86.5	6.5	50,301	60.3	50.3	170,900	929	13.3	48,658	15.8	6.8
22097	St. Landry Parish	80,157	95.5	2.2	34,635	74.7	31.2	114,100	658	30.4	28,577	15.4	7.7
22103	St. Tammany Parish	272,599	89.1	5.1	106,164	78.7	65.8	286,500	1,259	5.7	116,420	9.4	14.0
22105	Tangipahoa Parish	136,887	87.3	6.5	54,627	69.7	55.2	218,300	987	5.9	55,625	11.5	14.4
22109	Terrebonne Parish	102,450	90.9	4.1	42,203	74.9	47.4	185,300	1,043	10.4	44,210	17.0	6.3
23000	**MAINE**	1,385,562	89.4	5.7	616,085	74.4	56.1	310,700	1,189	8.0	596,229	17.3	6.6
23001	Androscoggin County	112,436	88.4	3.5	48,239	66.0	61.5	263,000	997	8.2	49,811	16.2	5.7
23003	Aroostook County	66,907	91.2	4.0	32,671	76.2	50.0	154,400	859	13.8	27,433	30.5	5.0
23005	Cumberland County	307,515	89.3	6.0	134,326	71.0	61.9	470,600	1,609	7.0	139,845	13.3	4.3
23011	Kennebec County	126,277	86.7	5.4	55,601	72.6	57.3	253,200	1,055	5.2	54,006	17.5	6.1
23019	Penobscot County	154612	88.2	6.5	66,556	71.5	50.3	228,600	1,105	9.5	66,415	18.4	5.8
23031	York County	217,681	91.6	4.6	93,995	75.9	60.9	422,600	1,473	6.4	95,945	13.6	7.3
24000	**MARYLAND**	6,110,314	89.0	6.2	2,384,715	67.9	70.7	413,600	1,651	7.0	2,635,654	8.3	13.1
24001	Allegany County	66,979	88.5	5.2	28,187	74.0	52.3	146,900	841	12.0	23,949	22.1	6.0
24003	Anne Arundel County	587,401	89.2	6.3	226,503	74.7	73.5	460,600	1,998	4.7	266,395	8.0	11.9
24005	Baltimore County	833,092	90.2	5.0	331,624	67.2	67.0	345,900	1,597	7.9	365,632	8.4	9.0
24009	Calvert County	93,731	92.2	5.6	33,642	86.4	77.4	473,400	1,760	4.9	42,936	4.9	25.4
24013	Carroll County	174,556	93.8	3.8	64,081	86.0	69.2	433,300	1,529	5.3	78,525	11.7	14.8
24015	Cecil County	105,037	90.1	7.0	41,195	76.9	67.8	327,500	1,196	9.4	44,598	12.7	13.4
24017	Charles County	170,311	91.8	5.5	62,532	83.7	81.4	410,000	1,815	4.4	77,672	7.3	28.0
24021	Frederick County	289,764	89.8	5.6	107,332	76.7	73.7	462,500	1,719	6.3	123,182	11.8	20.0
24025	Harford County	261,847	93.0	3.0	103,909	79.1	69.4	388,400	1,451	11.3	113,678	7.1	10.3
24027	Howard County	333,726	87.0	8.7	121,399	70.0	70.0	603,400	2,053	4.6	130,591	6.0	8.3
24031	Montgomery County	1,045,295	88.3	6.6	392,629	64.4	71.2	636,200	1,984	3.9	426,373	5.8	13.1
24033	Prince George's County	937,792	87.9	6.7	351,460	64.1	77.2	422,300	1,722	6.5	424,598	4.6	16.4
24037	St. Mary's County	114,625	85.9	8.8	43,227	73.1	70.6	403,900	1,682	8.1	51,352	11.2	13.6
24043	Washington County	153,682	87.0	7.1	59,404	69.3	65.1	283,700	1,135	9.5	65,657	14.2	11.4
24045	Wicomico County	103923	87.7	7.6	39,679	58.6	64.2	257,300	1,311	8.0	48,113	15.0	6.7
24510	Baltimore city	558,241	86.0	6.5	259,385	47.9	68.7	241,900	1,239	10.7	233,519	8.4	10.0
25000	**MASSACHUSETTS**	6,936,108	88.2	6.0	2,800,984	62.3	66.4	570,800	1,757	6.1	3,110,218	10.6	12.8
25001	Barnstable County	231,323	89.7	6.2	109,475	78.5	58.4	634,700	1,604	4.0	96,287	14.7	9.4
25003	Berkshire County	126,384	90.2	4.0	58,807	68.8	58.9	298,200	1,074	6.3	54,626	19.2	6.1
25005	Bristol County	575,233	89.3	5.4	233,990	61.7	65.1	459,700	1,269	8.0	266,984	12.2	13.1
25009	Essex County	801,657	90.9	4.3	313,787	63.8	70.2	624,700	1,726	7.1	358,597	10.9	14.4
25011	Franklin County	70,278	91.6	3.6	32,430	68.2	57.5	329,300	1,164	7.2	31,559	19.1	8.2
25013	Hampden County	456,958	91.6	3.4	184,698	62.3	62.0	302,100	1,136	10.1	197,593	12.5	4.9
25015	Hampshire County	161,377	79.4	12.5	61,802	65.4	57.8	380,800	1,355	6.2	70,657	17.8	4.5
25017	Middlesex County	1,607,797	87.5	6.5	632,721	61.4	66.7	716,100	2,193	4.9	717,123	8.6	12.0
25021	Norfolk County	722,048	89.9	5.6	286,649	68.1	67.8	686,500	2,081	4.6	312,674	8.6	17.5
25023	Plymouth County	530,609	91.8	4.3	203,356	78.0	68.2	568,500	1,762	5.5	236,112	10.8	19.9
25025	Suffolk County	759,629	81.3	10.0	332,924	36.7	69.0	683,900	2,114	6.7	367,257	7.0	11.3
25027	Worcester County	857,961	87.4	5.5	336,660	65.5	69.2	433,900	1,449	5.2	385,528	11.8	14.3
26000	**MICHIGAN**	9,939,831	89.0	5.2	4,107,809	73.7	57.2	236,100	1,101	8.3	4,159,103	14.2	6.3
26005	Allegan County	120,705	90.7	4.2	46,317	84.6	57.2	264,800	1,098	8.7	52,997	11.7	5.4
26017	Bay County	101,761	91.4	3.3	44,417	77.7	55.5	156,200	811	12.8	42,360	14.2	5.6
26021	Berrien County	151,264	89.8	5.2	65,129	73.7	54.0	237,900	936	9.2	61,509	23.8	3.9
26025	Calhoun County	131,501	89.5	5.0	54,568	72.4	58.2	163,500	906	11.2	55,289	18.1	4.3
26037	Clinton County	78,778	91.3	6.6	31,653	81.4	61.5	276,500	1,040	7.5	34,834	11.4	7.4

Table C-2. Counties — Where: Migration, Housing, and Transportation, 2023—*Continued*

State code	STATE County	Total population 1 year and over	Lived in the same house 1 year ago (percent)	Did not live in the same county 1 year ago (percent)	Total occupied housing units	Owner-occupied units (percent)	Percent with a mortgage, contract to purchase, or similar debt	Median value of owner-occupied units (dollars; owner estimated)	Median gross rent of renter-occupied units paying cash rent	Households without Internet access (percent)	Number of workers who commuted to work	Commute of less than 10 minutes (percent)	Commute of 60 minutes or more (percent)
	ACS table number:	C07204	C07204	C07204	B25003	B25003	B25081	B25097	B25064	S2801	B08012	B08012	B08012
	Column number:	1	2	3	4	5	6	7	8	9	10	11	12
	MICHIGAN—Cont.												
26045	Eaton County	108062	90.3	7.2	45,181	75.1	60.4	226,200	997	8.5	47,049	15.5	6.0
26049	Genesee County	397,724	89.2	3.1	164,086	72.0	54.9	181,600	928	9.6	158,078	13.3	11.3
26055	Grand Traverse County	95,370	90.9	4.6	42,544	77.0	57.3	343,200	1,357	6.4	43,452	15.7	4.7
26065	Ingham County	282,639	81.2	10.9	117,197	60.6	65.8	190,900	1,055	8.2	121,395	16.6	6.1
26067	Ionia County	65,964	91.1	4.1	23,600	79.5	58.9	221,500	816	11.3	26,319	15.7	6.1
26075	Jackson County	158,251	88.2	5.7	61,851	76.8	58.9	203,700	964	6.0	62,539	15.5	5.3
26077	Kalamazoo County	259,332	87.2	5.4	107,893	61.7	60.1	251,200	1,058	6.9	117,564	16.5	3.5
26081	Kent County	653,832	87.4	4.9	257,898	70.5	63.2	297,400	1,270	6.2	304,288	14.8	3.8
26087	Lapeer County	88322	91.7	5.9	34,494	87.3	56.0	234,000	988	9.9	39,453	11.9	13.2
26091	Lenawee County	96,748	92.2	3.6	40,142	80.3	59.0	198,200	922	7.2	41,030	16.5	9.7
26093	Livingston County	194,908	94.2	3.2	77,304	88.7	69.9	347,800	1,231	6.3	84,008	8.2	12.4
26099	Macomb County	865,807	90.1	4.5	359,464	76.0	61.5	246,600	1,229	5.7	382,713	9.5	6.8
26103	Marquette County	66,572	85.7	6.8	28,707	66.5	52.1	227,800	842	17.8	28,655	30.8	5.1
26111	Midland County	83,105	91.9	4.5	35,761	77.4	56.9	195,900	894	9.8	34,489	18.9	5.4
26115	Monroe County	153,428	90.1	4.6	62,936	80.8	61.1	245,000	983	8.4	67,410	10.2	6.3
26117	Montcalm County	67,730	90.5	6.1	24,697	84.3	57.7	200,500	924	13.2	28,421	17.7	10.6
26121	Muskegon County	175,708	89.5	4.7	70,042	81.2	56.6	208,700	1,003	7.4	74,657	16.1	5.0
26125	Oakland County	1,257,273	89.5	5.1	533,533	72.8	63.3	338,000	1,349	5.0	546,706	10.0	6.0
26139	Ottawa County	300,840	87.7	6.8	114,316	79.1	58.3	328,400	1,149	6.2	138,937	19.1	2.8
26145	Saginaw County	186,038	90.8	4.2	77,158	76.6	49.8	146,400	917	10.1	74,617	14.5	5.9
26147	St. Clair County	158,489	89.6	3.1	69,234	79.0	59.4	232,300	914	8.0	68,754	18.0	16.3
26155	Shiawassee County	67,340	92.2	4.7	26,950	81.2	53.3	182,600	951	7.3	28,387	19.0	9.1
26159	Van Buren County	74,881	91.7	5.9	31,149	81.3	56.3	213,200	758	10.9	29,922	17.5	6.9
26161	Washtenaw County	363,179	79.7	11.3	149,379	62.6	61.9	360,400	1,451	5.6	149,947	10.6	5.2
26163	Wayne County	1,731,271	89.9	3.6	696,332	66.2	50.5	177,300	1,095	9.2	661,890	9.8	5.1
27000	**MINNESOTA**	5,673,119	88.4	6.5	2,344,432	72.0	63.8	328,600	1,264	7.6	2,516,455	16.2	4.9
27003	Anoka County	367,814	92.4	4.2	138,924	80.3	68.0	349,400	1,294	4.5	169,451	9.6	4.8
27013	Blue Earth County	68883	79.1	11.8	27,037	60.7	59.2	276,300	1,055	15.9	34,545	24.6	3.8
27019	Carver County	109,789	92.5	5.2	42,250	81.6	69.1	456,700	1,583	3.3	47,387	12.1	4.9
27027	Clay County	65,041	85.2	9.4	26,890	63.8	68.8	267,600	1,111	9.6	30,485	13.7	2.4
27035	Crow Wing County	67,589	89.8	4.5	31,463	75.8	57.9	332,400	1,034	10.6	28,159	16.4	6.9
27037	Dakota County	443,809	88.7	7.1	176,865	72.7	68.8	383,600	1,585	5.0	192,745	12.4	3.9
27053	Hennepin County	1,244,776	86.0	6.5	545,627	61.9	69.0	386,600	1,445	6.8	542,608	9.9	2.4
27109	Olmsted County	162,373	86.8	8.9	66,425	71.1	64.2	335,000	1,401	6.0	71,799	16.9	4.1
27123	Ramsey County	528,681	85.1	8.8	225,183	59.0	67.1	319,600	1,367	6.2	225,861	11.2	3.0
27131	Rice County	67,203	87.9	9.3	23,512	75.6	62.0	302,100	1,028	8.9	31,901	27.6	9.6
27137	St. Louis County	199,087	86.4	6.7	87,576	70.8	56.9	236,700	1,004	11.0	90,825	18.3	5.1
27139	Scott County	152,815	90.8	5.6	55,921	82.9	70.2	394,700	1,434	4.7	70,652	13.8	3.9
27141	Sherburne County	101,159	87.3	9.4	35,909	84.6	74.7	366,300	1,105	5.6	46,609	12.0	12.3
27145	Stearns County	158,781	85.6	8.6	60,666	68.8	56.5	288,500	1,129	10.4	74,334	17.6	7.3
27163	Washington County	277,135	90.3	5.4	109,093	82.8	70.4	415,100	1,668	4.5	113,000	12.1	3.2
27171	Wright County	148992	91.3	6.1	55,367	84.8	71.0	355,200	1,272	5.3	72,828	12.6	7.6
28000	**MISSISSIPPI**	2,907,634	89.5	5.8	1,166,617	71.1	48.0	169,800	898	13.4	1,187,693	13.2	7.3
28033	DeSoto County	191,244	88.9	8.4	70,666	82.2	69.4	275,400	1,381	5.6	90,728	7.3	4.9
28035	Forrest County	77,522	85.5	7.7	30,255	60.4	55.3	169,400	1,006	11.1	35,152	17.5	6.1
28047	Harrison County	208,003	87.0	6.7	86,167	62.4	52.4	213,900	1,054	10.2	88,423	13.8	6.5
28049	Hinds County	213,539	88.8	4.3	88,687	59.1	55.7	164,200	992	9.9	88,452	7.4	3.1
28059	Jackson County	144,393	90.1	6.1	59,347	70.9	59.3	198,000	1,021	7.2	64,090	13.8	4.9
28067	Jones County	65,271	95.8	2.3	25,758	76.8	39.2	160,000	749	13.4	27,461	17.5	9.1
28073	Lamar County	65,566	88.0	6.4	26,301	68.5	53.8	232,100	1,041	9.0	26,325	12.0	8.4
28075	Lauderdale County	69,861	88.0	4.1	29,693	67.8	46.1	145,600	840	12.9	29,411	13.1	3.8
28081	Lee County	81,957	91.7	4.6	32,115	75.4	57.2	196,200	877	11.8	36,580	12.8	6.8
28089	Madison County	111,412	85.3	8.9	45,674	72.1	63.2	341,500	1,288	4.2	51,380	6.5	3.0
28121	Rankin County	158,466	88.0	8.1	60,434	77.7	63.8	240,400	1,184	4.5	70,936	8.1	4.9
29000	**MISSOURI**	6,126,390	87.9	6.0	2,556,271	68.8	59.7	233,600	1,019	9.1	2,654,112	15.4	5.4
29019	Boone County	186,880	80.5	10.6	76,762	56.8	60.5	272,400	1,100	7.7	88,765	17.7	3.5
29021	Buchanan County	82,166	88.3	5.3	33,257	68.5	54.8	166,500	889	12.8	35,476	19.9	6.3
29031	Cape Girardeau County	82,227	82.3	9.0	33,624	65.3	59.2	223,300	895	7.0	39,394	28.3	2.2
29037	Cass County	110,442	87.1	7.8	44,422	79.2	67.6	294,400	1,194	5.3	48,274	13.0	6.0
29043	Christian County	93,757	90.4	6.2	35,654	76.7	67.5	310,800	1,024	9.9	37,324	7.6	2.5
29047	Clay County	256,774	90.0	4.6	103,995	69.7	67.5	283,200	1,245	9.1	115,686	9.5	3.9
29051	Cole County	76,371	93.7	4.2	31,874	71.2	61.2	228,700	754	6.2	35,256	20.1	3.6

Table C-2. Counties — Where: Migration, Housing, and Transportation, 2023—*Continued*

State code	STATE County	Total population 1 year and over	Lived in the same house 1 year ago (percent)	Did not live in the same county 1 year ago (percent)	Total occupied housing units	Owner-occupied units (percent)	Percent with a mortgage, contract to purchase, or similar debt	Median value of owner-occupied units (dollars; owner estimated)	Median gross rent of renter-occupied units paying cash rent	Households without Internet access (percent)	Number of workers who commuted to work	Commute of less than 10 minutes (percent)	Commute of 60 minutes or more (percent)
	ACS table number:	C07204	C07204	C07204	B25003	B25003	B25081	B25097	B25064	S2801	B08012	B08012	B08012
	Column number:	1	2	3	4	5	6	7	8	9	10	11	12
	MISSOURI—Cont.												
29071	Franklin County	105,333	90.5	5.3	44,140	70.4	59.0	229,900	895	8.8	46,248	16.3	12.1
29077	Greene County	301,360	83.3	7.7	132,232	56.9	61.5	231,400	1,000	12.1	139,444	13.2	3.0
29095	Jackson County	710,203	87.5	4.7	310,868	60.6	60.1	228,100	1,197	6.3	306,942	11.5	3.5
29097	Jasper County	123,693	80.4	9.2	52,000	60.3	55.4	177,100	915	10.6	55,561	21.9	5.6
29099	Jefferson County	228,780	89.8	5.1	88,836	84.8	65.1	235,100	882	6.9	106,048	7.6	9.1
29165	Platte County	110,068	87.0	8.7	44,751	70.5	69.3	356,500	1,287	5.7	47,152	9.5	3.3
29183	St. Charles County	411,823	91.2	4.5	163,272	81.4	69.6	325,600	1,420	4.5	191,621	11.8	3.7
29187	St. Francois County	66,664	84.3	7.8	25,489	71.0	65.6	181,100	803	11.4	26,211	18.6	12.4
29189	St. Louis County	975,504	89.2	4.6	419,348	70.5	65.6	272,400	1,204	5.8	417,237	9.7	3.5
29510	St. Louis city	278,251	86.0	7.3	150,404	48.1	59.3	192,800	1,011	9.3	132,722	11.8	3.3
30000	**MONTANA**	1,120,157	86.9	6.8	472,867	69.2	55.2	392,300	1,083	8.8	493,140	23.4	5.6
30013	Cascade County	83,741	84.0	6.3	36,414	68.1	60.7	286,500	959	7.7	37,156	27.5	3.6
30029	Flathead County	112,516	88.3	5.3	45,510	74.7	60.9	570,800	1,275	5.9	49,300	17.5	3.2
30031	Gallatin County	124,744	83.1	10.6	54,621	60.4	65.1	691,200	1,790	6.6	66,444	17.1	6.1
30049	Lewis and Clark County	73550	84.8	7.9	30,756	69.0	58.7	379,500	1,078	6.8	31,108	17.4	6.3
30063	Missoula County	121,156	85.0	7.4	55,084	60.3	61.0	488,300	1,172	5.7	57,024	14.5	6.3
30111	Yellowstone County	168,865	85.2	5.4	72,668	66.7	61.4	358,700	999	7.3	78,652	17.0	2.3
31000	**NEBRASKA**	1,956,041	87.0	6.4	813,864	66.3	58.9	245,200	1,042	7.8	924,422	23.3	3.5
31055	Douglas County	582,844	86.2	5.9	242,890	61.4	66.4	274,700	1,178	5.8	266,662	12.2	3.1
31109	Lancaster County	323,591	83.6	6.2	138,006	57.4	63.1	277,700	1,024	6.5	154,187	17.3	3.3
31153	Sarpy County	197,872	86.6	9.4	75,546	70.0	73.8	322,400	1,385	4.5	95,066	11.8	2.3
32000	**NEVADA**	3,159,456	85.4	5.4	1,224,685	60.4	64.5	441,100	1,622	5.9	1,365,439	9.5	6.0
32003	Clark County	2,311,988	84.9	5.4	880,604	57.8	66.5	437,900	1,654	5.8	996,328	7.5	5.3
32031	Washoe County	491,578	86.2	5.0	201,140	62.7	63.3	545,100	1,627	5.9	223,636	10.7	4.4
33000	**NEW HAMPSHIRE**	1,389,863	90.1	5.4	569,493	72.4	62.5	415,400	1,517	5.9	632,959	13.9	9.7
33001	Belknap County	64,525	91.3	5.5	27,150	83.9	62.3	411,900	1,037	5.6	28,322	13.6	9.4
33005	Cheshire County	76,656	89.7	5.7	31,921	71.2	66.1	328,200	1,259	7.2	37,375	19.7	7.8
33009	Grafton County	92,343	87.1	9.6	40,528	70.3	53.5	354,800	1,366	7.3	38,163	21.6	6.4
33011	Hillsborough County	422,992	89.3	4.2	170,761	68.2	67.3	430,300	1,668	4.9	200,278	11.4	10.5
33013	Merrimack County	155,991	90.9	5.6	62,305	71.2	62.3	372,200	1,398	4.7	72,109	13.2	10.0
33015	Rockingham County	318,211	91.8	5.2	127,021	78.1	66.4	518,600	1,664	5.8	143,952	11.2	11.3
33017	Strafford County	132,062	87.4	7.4	53,495	67.2	59.6	379,800	1,505	5.4	60,063	13.1	8.1
34000	**NEW JERSEY**	9,192,631	90.6	5.1	3,538,457	63.7	63.9	461,000	1,667	5.9	4,030,075	9.8	15.1
34001	Atlantic County	272,315	90.2	4.8	111,158	67.4	63.3	303,800	1,307	6.6	122,279	12.5	6.8
34003	Bergen County	947,775	91.0	4.8	356,438	64.8	60.9	615,300	1,870	5.3	432,907	10.9	18.1
34005	Burlington County	464,221	90.0	6.9	179,477	76.6	66.1	358,000	1,671	3.7	204,820	9.1	12.4
34007	Camden County	521285	89.5	5.2	201,670	66.5	64.5	294,900	1,328	6.3	228,002	11.6	11.1
34009	Cape May County	93,777	88.6	6.5	47,516	82.9	60.3	474,800	1,440	4.7	36,879	24.3	7.8
34011	Cumberland County	150,825	91.3	4.6	54,482	66.2	56.8	220,500	1,196	8.1	62,707	17.5	10.3
34013	Essex County	842,542	89.4	5.4	322,456	45.5	69.1	522,800	1,477	5.4	361,007	6.0	21.0
34015	Gloucester County	305,149	89.7	6.1	113,391	79.2	67.7	317,900	1,582	6.5	135,837	10.8	9.3
34017	Hudson County	696,272	89.4	6.0	305,743	28.8	66.6	531,900	1,816	7.4	327,090	4.9	16.7
34019	Hunterdon County	128,254	92	4	51,186	85.6	66.6	506,000	1,573	3.7	55,217	9.6	17.4
34021	Mercer County	378,726	87.8	6.3	146,258	60.3	60.5	390,900	1,466	7.5	154,716	11.3	10.2
34023	Middlesex County	855,071	90.1	5.7	311,100	63.1	64.3	475,200	1,823	4.7	368,841	10.5	16.7
34025	Monmouth County	636,563	91.3	4.4	252,995	74.5	63.3	628,000	1,752	6.0	280,005	10.2	18.7
34027	Morris County	510,256	92.6	4.6	193,192	74.8	62.9	577,700	1,923	3.5	225,220	9.4	12.9
34029	Ocean County	650,974	92.3	3.5	245,827	80.3	57.9	408,000	1,692	9.9	244,467	11.9	14.5
34031	Passaic County	506,767	91.6	4.1	178,277	54.4	64.5	465,700	1,551	5.5	222,555	8.6	10.2
34033	Salem County	65026	89.8	5.3	25,207	72.4	56.4	249,500	1,318	7.1	27,187	13.3	8.1
34035	Somerset County	346,147	92.1	5.7	132,047	74.5	66.4	556,600	1,970	4.1	153,814	9.3	15.9
34037	Sussex County	144,589	93.8	4.6	58,679	85.0	70.5	367,500	1,397	3.7	68,928	10.7	21.5
34039	Union County	565,376	90.9	4.6	206,095	58.9	67.3	522,500	1,744	5.5	262,404	9.3	15.6
34041	Warren County	110,721	93.4	4.1	45,263	75.5	65.3	350,500	1,440	6.5	55,193	12.7	19.4
35000	**NEW MEXICO**	2,093,439	88.2	5.9	856,580	69.3	52.2	256,300	1,084	11.2	846,938	18.4	6.8
35001	Bernalillo County	665,320	87.0	4.9	285,796	64.8	61.7	303,400	1,206	9.3	290,131	11.8	5.1
35013	Doña Ana County	223,005	84.1	8.5	87,688	66.3	53.3	228,000	933	7.6	90,716	15.6	5.9
35025	Lea County	70,827	89.3	5.1	24,812	68.8	NA	197,200	1,173	12.0	32,262	31.9	11.2
35031	McKinley County	null	NA	NA	21,312	65.0	NA	71,000	768	27.5	21,153	15.3	7.5

Table C-2. Counties — Where: Migration, Housing, and Transportation, 2023—*Continued*

State code	STATE County	Total population 1 year and over	Lived in the same house 1 year ago (percent)	Did not live in the same county 1 year ago (percent)	Total occupied housing units	Owner-occupied units (percent)	Percent with a mortgage, contract to purchase, or similar debt	Median value of owner-occupied units (dollars; owner estimated)	Median gross rent of renter-occupied units paying cash rent	Households without Internet access (percent)	Number of workers who commuted to work	Commute of less than 10 minutes (percent)	Commute of 60 minutes or more (percent)
	ACS table number:	C07204	C07204	C07204	B25003	B25003	B25081	B25097	B25064	S2801	B08012	B08012	B08012
	Column number:	1	2	3	4	5	6	7	8	9	10	11	12
	NEW MEXICO—Cont.												
35035	Otero County	68,373	85.1	8.0	25,289	70.3	45.8	154,200	965	11.7	28,686	27.7	4.2
35043	Sandoval County	154,365	91.8	6.1	58,731	80.4	62.3	324,100	1,464	8.8	58,156	12.8	11.2
35045	San Juan County	119,480	93.2	3.5	42,670	72.6	46.2	201,700	965	18.2	45,900	18.3	7.1
35049	Santa Fe County	154,880	91.8	5.7	71,322	68.8	53.1	485,300	1,254	7.3	60,618	13.9	5.0
35061	Valencia County	77,965	92.0	4.9	29,932	76.3	55.4	232,700	1,021	13.9	28,926	14.3	10.4
36000	**NEW YORK**	19,365,855	90.4	4.3	7,809,267	54.1	57.4	420,200	1,561	7.9	8,243,157	10.0	16.9
36001	Albany County	313,923	87.3	7.2	134,971	55.9	61.3	291,300	1,313	8.1	140,962	11.6	3.8
36005	Bronx County	1,342,443	91.9	2.5	537,953	20.1	55.2	498,200	1,352	11.9	506,839	6.1	31.1
36007	Broome County	194,393	88.6	5.6	80,001	65.2	51.1	155,100	935	6.9	77,757	18.0	4.0
36009	Cattaraugus County	74,786	89.5	4.2	32,376	74.9	42.0	105,500	715	16.6	28,443	26.1	7.1
36011	Cayuga County	74,070	88.6	5.3	32,786	78.6	50.4	161,700	925	7.5	33,593	23.3	4.8
36013	Chautauqua County	123735	88.8	4.8	54,284	70.1	50.0	124,600	797	10.7	50,939	27.7	5.6
36015	Chemung County	80,825	92.2	3.2	35,591	70.3	57.6	139,600	1,013	6.7	34,518	23.4	4.9
36019	Clinton County	77,434	88.5	6.5	34,639	64.5	51.6	173,000	948	9.8	34,089	22.1	6.0
36027	Dutchess County	293,855	90.1	4.6	115,529	69.1	59.4	395,400	1,574	5.9	124,606	11.6	13.9
36029	Erie County	937,032	89.1	3.8	410,430	65.4	55.2	241,900	1,067	8.7	410,070	13.6	3.9
36045	Jefferson County	113,609	77.8	10.7	50,542	52.9	56.4	184,200	1,227	9.4	51,476	24.8	4.1
36047	Kings County	2,526,291	90.9	3.2	1,035,549	28.7	60.1	880,300	1,762	9.6	1,037,590	4.4	24.7
36053	Madison County	66,450	89.5	7.5	26,755	76.7	53.8	180,600	869	10.7	27,950	20.8	3.7
36055	Monroe County	741933	85.9	6.1	317,369	62.9	60.9	217,300	1,163	8.8	315,853	13.9	2.8
36059	Nassau County	1,369,887	94.1	3.4	458,162	81.1	61.7	674,200	2,228	4.4	586,156	9.2	23.1
36061	New York County	1,581,522	84.7	7.3	787,747	25.4	50.2	1,010,800	2,169	5.9	710,625	4.8	9.2
36063	Niagara County	208,030	90.4	4.4	91,894	69.4	53.1	189,700	985	8.7	89,035	15.7	3.4
36065	Oneida County	225,595	89.6	4.4	96,767	66.4	51.5	188,300	913	10.0	90,869	25.7	5.4
36067	Onondaga County	462147	85.5	6.6	198,699	65.8	58.2	202,400	1,095	7.3	204,271	14.1	4.4
36069	Ontario County	111,452	89.7	6.1	48,610	76.4	57.7	228,000	1,210	7.4	47,497	18.6	3.5
36071	Orange County	402,212	91.6	4.5	138,856	69.3	65.1	391,800	1,642	9.8	166,651	13.8	19.0
36075	Oswego County	117,053	85.5	8.2	48,010	77.1	57.1	153,500	957	10.2	48,153	15.3	8.1
36079	Putnam County	96955	93.6	4.6	36,405	81.3	62.4	482,300	1,833	5.1	46,013	7.9	24.1
36081	Queens County	2,229,937	91.9	2.7	863,975	44.6	53.6	692,500	1,877	6.0	987,590	3.5	30.7
36083	Rensselaer County	158,115	87.5	7.9	66,583	68.4	62.0	257,600	1,242	7.9	69,747	10.0	4.7
36085	Richmond County	486,338	94.7	1.4	169,526	66.6	63.8	672,400	1,688	9.1	201,610	4.9	34.8
36087	Rockland County	332,963	94.0	2.5	104,325	69.5	60.3	600,500	1,868	11.2	130,891	14.6	13.1
36089	St. Lawrence County	106,223	89.0	2.8	42,945	66.7	46.9	130,200	789	14.8	41,960	26.1	4.7
36091	Saratoga County	236,613	88.8	5.6	103,758	69.9	60.1	348,800	1,362	6.3	101,965	11.1	4.2
36093	Schenectady County	158,589	90.5	5.4	68,172	63.6	63.5	242,700	1,240	9.1	65,486	15.3	3.1
36101	Steuben County	91240	91.3	3.8	38,764	75.1	45.4	137,000	838	12.9	38,019	22.7	6.3
36103	Suffolk County	1,507,367	93.3	2.9	508,809	81.2	62.5	584,800	2,045	5.2	686,307	10.9	15.2
36105	Sullivan County	78,634	89.0	7.0	30,971	69.4	47.4	273,800	1,028	8.7	30,674	16.0	8.6
36109	Tompkins County	102,361	72.5	21.3	43,054	55.1	48.9	263,100	1,383	8.8	41,736	16.5	6.0
36111	Ulster County	180,859	89.1	5.9	73,895	72.4	54.4	373,400	1,363	6.7	71,784	13.4	8.2
36113	Warren County	64,742	91.9	3.6	31,013	69.7	58.4	265,300	1,051	7.7	30,558	20.7	5.5
36117	Wayne County	89,916	91.6	5.6	39,094	80.4	58.4	173,600	996	10.7	39,814	19.4	4.5
36119	Westchester County	980,272	91.8	4.5	374,012	62.0	60.8	645,700	1,873	4.8	421,092	8.2	22.0
37000	**NORTH CAROLINA**	10,719,307	87.1	7.4	4,392,669	66.3	61.3	308,600	1,245	8.3	4,392,673	12.6	6.6
37001	Alamance County	177,309	88.6	7.1	70,911	66.0	58.9	265,200	1,033	7.7	78,215	15.4	3.0
37019	Brunswick County	158,432	87.5	8.4	72,932	83.8	54.2	360,100	1,373	6.9	53,194	10.7	8.4
37021	Buncombe County	272,578	87.5	7.1	104,181	66.0	55.7	426,000	1,368	6.4	108,122	11.3	3.3
37023	Burke County	87,312	92.6	3.8	37,485	73.2	53.9	212,500	786	10.6	38,495	17.2	4.7
37025	Cabarrus County	237,987	86.4	8.1	90,254	67.0	72.1	374,400	1,484	4.4	106,152	6.3	8.7
37027	Caldwell County	79,592	90.9	4.1	34,367	69.5	47.7	205,400	764	8.7	36,296	12.6	6.3
37031	Carteret County	69,355	87.2	8.6	34,497	74.3	55.4	343,000	1,144	5.5	27,969	22.7	4.3
37035	Catawba County	162,748	91.0	6.1	68,126	73.1	59.6	257,100	947	9.4	72,235	11.7	7.2
37037	Chatham County	80,203	93.5	5.5	33,971	83.3	56.3	442,800	1,100	10.7	30,384	8.0	12.2
37045	Cleveland County	100,624	90.4	4.8	39,314	73.7	55.9	228,300	880	10.9	42,867	12.8	10.8
37049	Craven County	101,375	82.3	11.8	41,100	69.3	50.2	229,500	1,039	11.2	41,398	21.2	6.1
37051	Cumberland County	331,890	81.2	10.2	131,421	56.5	65.7	214,600	1,228	6.2	149,176	17.7	4.8
37057	Davidson County	173,357	93.5	4.7	71,400	72.9	55.8	232,100	836	9.7	73,691	12.0	4.6
37063	Durham County	333,287	80.2	12.2	143,466	55.2	69.1	419,200	1,587	4.4	146,927	11.8	3.4
37067	Forsyth County	389,558	86.1	6.6	166,028	62.8	62.0	267,800	1,104	9.1	160,908	14.2	3.5
37069	Franklin County	76072	90.9	6.6	31,057	78.5	62.7	290,600	1,065	7.5	34,017	7.2	15.2
37071	Gaston County	233,862	88.6	4.7	97,287	63.6	65.5	284,400	1,221	8.5	99,730	8.7	8.1
37081	Guilford County	542,253	84.0	6.8	222,927	60.2	64.5	270,000	1,165	8.9	231,564	14.3	5.2

Table C-2. Counties — Where: Migration, Housing, and Transportation, 2023—*Continued*

State code	STATE County	Total population 1 year and over	Lived in the same house 1 year ago (percent)	Did not live in the same county 1 year ago (percent)	Total occupied housing units	Owner-occupied units (percent)	Percent with a mortgage, contract to purchase, or similar debt	Median value of owner-occupied units (dollars; owner estimated)	Median gross rent of renter-occupied units paying cash rent	Households without Internet access (percent)	Number of workers who commuted to work	Commute of less than 10 minutes (percent)	Commute of 60 minutes or more (percent)
	ACS table number:	C07204	C07204	C07204	B25003	B25003	B25081	B25097	B25064	S2801	B08012	B08012	B08012
	Column number:	1	2	3	4	5	6	7	8	9	10	11	12
	NORTH CAROLINA—Cont.												
37085	Harnett County	138,601	89.1	8.6	49,285	76.1	72.4	285,300	1,095	6.6	50,642	11.2	11.4
37089	Henderson County	118,129	93.1	4.5	52,492	75.0	52.4	372,000	1,186	10.9	45,667	11.7	4.9
37097	Iredell County	197,733	87.7	6.6	77,592	71.2	57.8	356,100	1,238	7.1	87,297	11.8	8.8
37101	Johnston County	238,842	88.2	7.4	87,955	74.6	68.6	324,500	1,307	8.0	103,171	8.0	10.8
37105	Lee County	66,828	89.5	8.3	25,961	65.7	59.8	241,200	864	18.6	27,580	20.6	9.5
37109	Lincoln County	94,922	92.6	4.3	37,618	79.7	59.4	350,700	1,082	6.3	39,624	10.1	7.7
37119	Mecklenburg County	1,149,527	85.1	8.4	474,611	54.6	74.6	441,900	1,660	5.4	452,947	8.3	4.8
37125	Moore County	105,416	89.8	6.5	46,385	75.6	56.7	369,100	1,342	5.8	39,900	9.5	7.2
37127	Nash County	95499	93.6	4.0	39,349	59.6	51.1	210,800	937	14.8	38,868	8.4	5.7
37129	New Hanover County	236,327	82.8	10.3	106,358	60.7	67.1	394,100	1,466	7.0	98,039	14.7	3.7
37133	Onslow County	208,726	80.4	12.4	76,788	61.9	73.4	253,100	1,261	5.7	94,326	21.1	5.8
37135	Orange County	149,571	81.2	14.9	59,771	64.0	62.0	470,300	1,425	5.9	60,672	12.3	5.6
37141	Pender County	68,320	89.1	9.1	27,256	83.4	59.8	315,700	1,070	7.7	28,666	12.6	8.7
37147	Pitt County	173,261	81.4	10.1	74,443	53.0	63.2	224,100	1,042	9.4	71,873	13.3	6.2
37151	Randolph County	145,177	90.8	3.9	59,646	70.3	55.0	215,200	964	17.6	64,970	14.6	5.3
37155	Robeson County	115,703	94.4	2.4	43,590	65.3	36.3	87,100	786	17.0	40,149	13.3	6.8
37157	Rockingham County	91,745	89.9	5.0	39,251	74.2	59.0	174,900	790	7.6	39,002	18.4	9.4
37159	Rowan County	150,455	90.2	5.4	60,965	73.7	60.0	273,700	974	9.9	62,769	13.5	9.3
37161	Rutherford County	65,272	89.8	4.1	26,805	73.5	50.5	207,900	794	14.8	27,522	17.1	8.4
37167	Stanly County	65,162	87.5	8.4	25,371	76.9	53.7	235,800	856	7.2	26,170	15.1	9.9
37171	Surry County	70,618	88.5	6.3	30,752	74.3	49.9	181,800	697	11.8	27,713	17.7	7.9
37179	Union County	254,681	89.7	7.6	87,714	81.1	74.2	446,600	1,559	5.7	103,715	8.2	9.7
37183	Wake County	1,178,714	85.7	7.4	481,294	63.9	73.5	482,100	1,652	4.7	464,730	9.2	5.1
37191	Wayne County	117,273	85.5	7.1	47,035	59.8	55.1	181,800	931	10.1	48,493	13.6	9.5
37193	Wilkes County	null	NA	NA	26,154	73.2	45.0	182,600	655	9.7	27,706	20.4	6.5
37195	Wilson County	78,786	90.5	6.7	34,524	59.3	55.5	212,200	1,005	9.3	29,374	16.3	5.9
38000	**NORTH DAKOTA**	774,985	84.0	8.1	338,059	63.7	52.8	246,700	916	10.9	380,033	28.8	5.4
38015	Burleigh County	98,727	88.8	4.2	42,486	71.6	59.2	309,500	926	12.3	47,688	19.9	6.5
38017	Cass County	194,457	78.6	8.9	84,603	52.4	63.7	293,700	968	10.7	100,634	18.2	2.7
38035	Grand Forks County	71,618	71.8	17.0	32,099	54.7	55.6	257,400	949	11.6	39,110	35.2	2.9
38101	Ward County	67,825	83.5	7.7	28,565	60.6	59.1	251,800	1,010	11.1	33,282	26.8	6.0
39000	**OHIO**	11,660,232	88.6	5.1	4,917,309	67.1	60.1	220,200	1,014	8.7	5,015,931	14.2	5.0
39003	Allen County	99,813	88.1	5.2	42,147	68.0	54.9	179,800	941	9.9	44,506	23.5	3.4
39007	Ashtabula County	96,236	92.0	3.9	37,507	77.3	52.8	161,600	721	9.5	39,870	17.2	6.8
39013	Belmont County	64,082	87.7	6.7	27,281	73.7	49.5	151,500	743	10.5	27,372	17.0	7.9
39017	Butler County	388,461	88.0	6.7	148,804	67.5	62.3	275,100	1,139	7.1	167,292	10.3	3.3
39023	Clark County	133,157	88.2	5.0	55,322	68.4	60.3	173,800	785	10.2	52,191	14.3	7.1
39025	Clermont County	209,239	91.1	4.8	87,429	74.9	63.2	279,700	1,076	5.9	90,979	10.1	4.8
39029	Columbiana County	99,179	90.3	6.3	42,415	74.9	53.0	163,700	756	12.3	40,489	20.4	7.2
39035	Cuyahoga County	1,220,025	87.6	3.9	551,306	61.4	58.2	197,900	1,053	9.4	517,527	11.4	3.8
39041	Delaware County	228,804	90.9	5.5	84,413	77.9	71.0	460,600	1,494	4.5	95,605	10.6	5.0
39043	Erie County	73,410	93.2	3.6	33,608	69.6	47.9	197,000	895	8.9	32,914	20.7	6.5
39045	Fairfield County	163,325	90.3	6.1	62,834	74.6	66.4	314,800	1,146	5.0	69,673	10.9	5.6
39049	Franklin County	1,309,302	82.4	5.9	561,634	51.1	69.6	301,000	1,287	5.0	571,677	10.2	3.0
39055	Geauga County	94,584	92.4	4.7	36,405	88.5	58.5	318,800	904	11.9	39,662	16.8	5.7
39057	Greene County	168,477	84.0	10.9	70,169	67.7	65.9	265,500	1,204	6.2	75,474	13.5	4.2
39061	Hamilton County	816,742	86.8	5.3	360,340	58.1	66.5	250,500	1,053	8.1	360,920	12.2	3.2
39063	Hancock County	74,114	90.8	6.3	31,675	71.6	57.2	208,500	989	7.3	35,493	27.8	1.7
39085	Lake County	229,773	91.2	3.7	103,532	75.1	59.1	217,600	1,085	5.9	105,367	11.1	2.4
39089	Licking County	180,877	92.6	4.6	68,568	73.7	65.9	277,400	1,048	7.4	76,766	15.0	6.1
39093	Lorain County	314697	91.2	4.4	128,887	75.5	64.0	223,800	930	7.7	138,949	11.8	4.9
39095	Lucas County	421,528	88.1	4.1	182,625	61.1	57.1	168,400	934	9.9	180,432	13.4	3.7
39099	Mahoning County	223,477	89.8	4.9	98,872	68.8	53.5	154,300	813	11.7	88,334	17.7	7.2
39101	Marion County	64,785	87.3	6.3	24,957	70.0	53.6	153,800	814	16.7	25,381	15.2	8.5
39103	Medina County	182,584	92.3	4.5	73,675	80.0	64.2	284,800	1,128	5.4	80,071	11.8	5.3
39109	Miami County	109,407	92.0	3.4	44,756	69.8	61.1	255,500	884	5.8	45,015	15.1	4.1
39113	Montgomery County	529,067	86.4	5.1	235,734	61.2	60.9	184,100	1,014	8.0	226,068	13.5	3.7
39119	Muskingum County	85,368	89.7	4.2	32,776	69.8	54.5	184,900	840	10.6	33,401	16.2	13.1
39133	Portage County	161,631	86.1	8.2	65,601	69.5	61.0	229,800	1,085	9.0	70,667	11.5	5.5
39139	Richland County	123,880	88.3	5.9	51,046	70.2	52.1	176,800	808	10.1	50,070	20.5	8.9
39141	Ross County	75,838	89.4	6.7	28,870	69.1	59.7	177,200	865	8.3	29,124	16.9	7.5
39145	Scioto County	70,939	90.4	3.9	30,143	67.4	44.6	163,400	805	12.0	28,996	18.7	10.4
39151	Stark County	368,857	91.4	3.4	156,143	69.7	58.5	188,500	891	9.2	160,650	15.2	5.7

Table C-2. Counties — Where: Migration, Housing, and Transportation, 2023—*Continued*

State code	STATE County	Total population 1 year and over	Lived in the same house 1 year ago (percent)	Did not live in the same county 1 year ago (percent)	Total occupied housing units	Owner-occupied units (percent)	Percent with a mortgage, contract to purchase, or similar debt	Median value of owner-occupied units (dollars; owner estimated)	Median gross rent of renter-occupied units paying cash rent	Households without Internet access (percent)	Number of workers who commuted to work	Commute of less than 10 minutes (percent)	Commute of 60 minutes or more (percent)
	ACS table number:	C07204	C07204	C07204	B25003	B25003	B25081	B25097	B25064	S2801	B08012	B08012	B08012
	Column number:	1	2	3	4	5	6	7	8	9	10	11	12
	OHIO—Cont.												
39153	Summit County	530,571	90.5	4.1	232,592	67.8	62.8	210,500	1,007	7.8	229,521	11.2	3.6
39155	Trumbull County	198,680	90.0	4.6	87,955	71.0	49.4	142,900	761	11.4	81,121	16.1	7.3
39157	Tuscarawas County	90,799	91.6	3.6	39,110	68.6	54.9	185,500	850	16.0	38,456	18.1	6.3
39159	Union County	68,682	86.9	9.6	25,554	77.7	74.3	358,900	1,247	3.8	31,471	14.2	4.5
39165	Warren County	250,016	89.8	6.6	93,271	79.7	70.2	364,700	1,453	5.3	107,834	10.8	3.7
39169	Wayne County	114,696	93.8	3.1	44,453	76.4	53.0	218,900	886	12.1	51,686	20.6	5.4
39173	Wood County	131,577	85.7	8.7	54,408	64.6	58.0	229,400	929	6.4	60,200	17.8	2.4
40000	**OKLAHOMA**	4,011,072	85.8	6.9	1,589,105	65.1	52.9	208,600	1,020	9.7	1,673,752	17.1	5.0
40017	Canadian County	173,418	86.0	7.0	58,214	72.5	63.1	260,400	1,329	5.6	75,829	8.5	4.7
40027	Cleveland County	298,694	81.7	9.3	118,062	61.2	57.6	245,700	1,149	6.4	134,303	14.3	4.9
40031	Comanche County	120,673	79.3	11.8	45,945	57.2	55.9	160,900	991	9.7	47,985	23.3	4.0
40037	Creek County	72,429	94.1	3.8	28,988	72.4	47.3	189,400	882	11.8	29,591	17.1	3.4
40101	Muskogee County	65,808	88.1	6.0	26,362	65.9	48.1	157,300	800	16.1	23,565	21.7	7.1
40109	Oklahoma County	798,821	84.1	6.2	335,473	57.6	60.0	242,700	1,143	7.9	348,688	11.4	3.1
40119	Payne County	82,907	72.2	18.1	32,739	53.6	54.6	227,300	953	9.5	36,706	28.9	4.8
40125	Pottawatomie County	73,083	88.2	6.3	27,150	67.0	48.3	175,000	832	10.6	27,683	15.0	8.4
40131	Rogers County	99,410	86.5	8.6	37,082	78.2	64.0	247,500	1,053	10.8	39,957	13.8	4.5
40143	Tulsa County	674,414	85.2	6.0	275,702	58.5	58.1	238,600	1,108	7.7	291,903	12.4	3.1
40145	Wagoner County	88,816	91.7	5.5	31,633	81.9	62.3	240,100	1,088	6.4	37,290	9.1	6.2
41000	**OREGON**	4,196,830	86.5	6.7	1,752,050	63.4	63.8	484,800	1,481	6.6	1,696,954	16.5	6.2
41003	Benton County	97,320	77.9	16.4	38,306	57.5	58.0	538,100	1,368	5.2	40,613	19.6	3.9
41005	Clackamas County	420,385	89.1	6.1	167,319	73.0	65.3	605,400	1,749	4.0	171,365	13.3	6.6
41017	Deschutes County	206,266	87.4	6.4	88,597	70.6	69.0	662,700	1,806	5.8	80,920	17.8	3.3
41019	Douglas County	111,792	85.5	5.0	47,733	73.9	50.1	326,900	1,038	8.6	40,707	27.5	6.3
41029	Jackson County	219,560	86.6	5.7	92,225	66.7	61.1	431,500	1,419	7.2	86,531	20.3	3.0
41033	Josephine County	87,555	91.5	3.2	37,241	73.9	56.2	399,400	1,166	8.5	28,332	23.8	6.4
41035	Klamath County	69,165	90.4	4.5	30,395	67.4	47.8	271,700	987	12.2	23,019	22.2	4.7
41039	Lane County	377,418	83.5	7.1	162,001	59.6	61.1	438,200	1,373	7.9	152,482	15.7	5.0
41043	Linn County	129,903	88.7	6.2	51,636	66.9	66.3	398,300	1,359	8.2	53,310	14.7	8.0
41047	Marion County	343,370	86.7	5.2	129,087	61.0	64.0	429,400	1,416	7.2	144,700	16.5	8.2
41051	Multnomah County	781,245	82.3	8.1	354,646	52.3	70.2	543,700	1,543	6.4	336,214	10.2	6.0
41053	Polk County	88,892	87.5	7.3	33,113	65.0	61.8	466,500	1,201	7.8	32,693	17.8	6.9
41059	Umatilla County	79,701	88.8	5.3	30,821	63.0	54.3	299,200	963	8.8	32,448	30.9	2.6
41067	Washington County	592927	88.5	6.0	237,507	62.1	72.4	589,000	1,818	3.8	253,620	10.2	6.6
41071	Yamhill County	107,979	88.0	8.7	40,380	72.0	63.8	471,900	1,421	6.8	39,517	22.4	7.2
42000	**PENNSYLVANIA**	12,829,324	89.4	5.1	5,324,209	69.5	57.1	259,900	1,197	8.8	5,400,641	13.3	8.2
42001	Adams County	105,794	89.7	5.3	41,810	78.1	62.7	275,300	1,061	10.1	47,933	12.9	13.1
42003	Allegheny County	1,211,235	87.4	4.4	547,396	65.8	57.4	232,300	1,154	7.3	513,658	10.2	5.4
42005	Armstrong County	63,674	92.5	3.4	28,117	79.4	44.7	157,800	724	12.1	26,126	17.4	9.7
42007	Beaver County	164,775	92.4	4.8	73,220	76.2	53.5	191,100	840	9.8	71,230	12.2	7.6
42011	Berks County	427956	90.7	4.6	163,307	72.1	60.4	261,200	1,219	7.7	187,744	13.2	7.8
42013	Blair County	119,253	86.1	4.1	50,651	71.7	51.9	157,000	837	12.0	51,888	24.2	4.9
42017	Bucks County	640,487	92.5	4.3	249,189	77.6	61.5	450,900	1,612	4.6	272,369	11.6	12.0
42019	Butler County	196,653	90.1	4.6	81,535	76.1	56.3	296,300	1,060	9.1	82,758	11.5	8.1
42021	Cambria County	129,635	91.8	4.3	57,282	76.5	45.2	121,800	725	13.0	51,971	17.8	4.6
42025	Carbon County	65,078	92.2	4.9	28,934	78.3	55.4	207,900	1,074	11.2	27,368	12.7	17.0
42027	Centre County	156,545	78.3	14.2	62,175	59.0	56.6	322,900	1,198	11.0	63,398	15.7	2.9
42029	Chester County	544,275	91.1	4.7	205,426	75.5	66.5	489,500	1,719	5.0	229,426	11.9	9.3
42033	Clearfield County	76,354	90.8	4.7	33,554	78.3	47.4	145,100	790	12.4	32,288	19.2	7.1
42037	Columbia County	65,045	88.8	6.8	25,929	72.3	48.8	224,000	870	11.9	28,991	17.9	8.0
42039	Crawford County	81,612	92.4	3.6	34,813	75.1	49.3	150,500	764	12.3	33,217	18.5	7.5
42041	Cumberland County	268,200	88.4	6.8	107,981	74.1	60.3	285,200	1,148	7.1	112,542	16.0	3.6
42043	Dauphin County	285,600	87.7	8.6	121,773	62.1	60.9	239,800	1,244	9.3	119,364	13.4	4.6
42045	Delaware County	569,416	91.4	4.3	215,645	71.5	61.6	333,800	1,307	4.9	231,422	9.0	9.1
42049	Erie County	265,200	87.3	4.6	111,118	69.0	54.4	179,200	894	8.8	111,008	18.2	3.4
42051	Fayette County	122,831	91.9	3.4	55,724	71.2	47.1	144,300	745	14.3	47,667	16.0	9.9
42055	Franklin County	156,168	89.9	5.2	62,966	76.4	59.9	248,900	1,095	8.8	66,888	15.8	6.7
42063	Indiana County	82,319	88.7	6.6	32,454	73.2	48.6	152,600	788	18.4	34,277	18.0	10.6
42069	Lackawanna County	213,557	87.7	5.8	88,871	64.7	48.3	200,900	1,069	9.9	88,811	16.3	3.8
42071	Lancaster County	551,869	88.8	5.1	211,669	68.9	58.4	306,900	1,329	10.9	246,992	15.8	5.5
42073	Lawrence County	83,947	91.7	5.2	36,638	77.4	51.4	150,800	763	10.5	33,735	19.2	7.1
42075	Lebanon County	141,808	89.5	5.8	58,012	71.1	55.8	235,400	1,186	10.8	64,153	16.5	4.5

Table C-2. Counties — Where: Migration, Housing, and Transportation, 2023—*Continued*

State code	STATE County	Total population 1 year and over	Lived in the same house 1 year ago (percent)	Did not live in the same county 1 year ago (percent)	Total occupied housing units	Owner-occupied units (percent)	Percent with a mortgage, contract to purchase, or similar debt	Median value of owner-occupied units (dollars; owner estimated)	Median gross rent of renter-occupied units paying cash rent	Households without Internet access (percent)	Number of workers who commuted to work	Commute of less than 10 minutes (percent)	Commute of 60 minutes or more (percent)
	ACS table number:	C07204	C07204	C07204	B25003	B25003	B25081	B25097	B25064	S2801	B08012	B08012	B08012
	Column number:	1	2	3	4	5	6	7	8	9	10	11	12
	PENNSYLVANIA—Cont.												
42077	Lehigh County	373,419	89.0	5.2	147,524	64.8	62.6	318,700	1,346	9.0	161,399	11.6	7.8
42079	Luzerne County	324,659	87.5	5.3	136,046	68.4	52.9	179,900	1,058	11.2	134,021	15.1	4.8
42081	Lycoming County	111,469	89.5	5.6	46,849	68.9	57.0	205,900	869	11.1	48,716	24.6	5.4
42085	Mercer County	107,695	92.3	4.8	47,517	73.2	49.1	166,800	874	11.0	43,185	22.2	6.9
42089	Monroe County	164,648	90.7	5.5	61,129	79.1	60.2	275,300	1,325	7.1	68,167	11.4	18.8
42091	Montgomery County	860,702	91.3	4.8	338,467	70.7	64.5	445,000	1,674	4.7	358,439	11.4	9.1
42095	Northampton County	316,932	91.7	4.8	123,536	71.3	57.0	312,800	1,390	8.3	133,356	12.2	9.8
42097	Northumberland County	88,974	91.9	5.3	37,343	78.1	51.3	164,300	746	11.9	37,076	17.3	7.1
42101	Philadelphia County	1,530,695	85.6	6.0	688,112	51.8	59.7	246,600	1,390	8.9	623,577	7.7	11.7
42107	Schuylkill County	141,552	92.4	3.6	58,809	75.7	47.4	149,600	801	12.9	57,523	15.3	10.8
42111	Somerset County	71,468	93.1	3.6	29,435	78.5	41.1	144,700	794	15.9	29,641	20.7	8.7
42125	Washington County	208,400	91.4	4.5	89,091	78.0	54.1	233,200	966	7.2	90,920	13.6	8.1
42129	Westmoreland County	347,485	92.5	3.6	155,459	78.8	52.4	203,600	862	9.5	152,406	15.2	8.2
42133	York County	460,777	90.6	4.1	183,864	75.1	62.8	257,600	1,149	8.4	209,755	12.1	8.6
44000	**RHODE ISLAND**	1,086,909	89.1	5.5	443,980	64.0	65.7	411,800	1,365	7.1	484,372	12.6	7.7
44003	Kent County	169,038	90.5	5.7	73,493	72.1	67.7	366,800	1,342	7.8	78,704	9.1	6.4
44005	Newport County	83,256	84.4	10.1	36,932	70.5	59.8	633,700	1,657	3.6	37,329	19.4	7.1
44007	Providence County	655,382	88.2	5.3	259,528	57.1	66.1	377,700	1,369	8.3	289,343	11.8	8.4
44009	Washington County	129,388	94.0	3.9	53,307	78.8	64.8	541,500	1,194	3.0	57,243	13.6	6.7
45000	**SOUTH CAROLINA**	5,319,249	87.6	7.3	2,177,733	72.4	57.5	272,900	1,170	9.0	2,210,448	12.2	6.7
45003	Aiken County	175530	90.6	5.2	70,920	79.0	52.4	223,400	1,022	9.3	70,367	12.9	3.9
45007	Anderson County	211,224	87.7	7.4	86,773	76.1	54.8	250,500	1,053	9.1	92,528	11.0	5.7
45013	Beaufort County	197,289	87.1	9.4	87,165	74.9	59.9	466,600	1,759	5.5	81,000	17.2	5.3
45015	Berkeley County	252,069	87.3	7.3	97,713	76.4	67.3	330,400	1,654	8.7	113,599	8.3	8.7
45019	Charleston County	417,796	83.0	10.1	183,800	64.3	63.9	510,900	1,665	5.6	180,932	10.7	5.7
45035	Dorchester County	168,049	82.7	10.2	65,532	74.1	67.3	327,100	1,505	5.9	73,620	7.1	13.6
45041	Florence County	135,915	90.7	6.7	53,651	63.7	48.1	173,200	1,012	9.3	56,430	9.7	6.4
45043	Georgetown County	64,814	86.9	8.4	28,720	83.8	44.2	322,200	1,517	10.4	22,184	15.6	17.3
45045	Greenville County	551,063	87.1	7.3	226,571	68.1	63.7	326,100	1,295	6.9	239,975	9.9	4.7
45047	Greenwood County	68,880	92.3	3.8	29,676	66.1	52.9	191,300	894	12.0	30,935	14.7	6.1
45051	Horry County	395,640	85.6	8.0	168,080	78.7	55.7	316,800	1,265	6.2	150,836	14.7	4.8
45055	Kershaw County	69,861	92.6	5.2	27,356	84.4	62.3	222,400	1,032	6.9	29,270	12.2	7.5
45057	Lancaster County	107,823	89.7	5.6	42,439	82.9	63.0	334,300	1,097	9.2	40,039	9.5	10.4
45059	Laurens County	68600	90.6	5.0	28,833	71.0	42.0	172,700	876	11.9	28,531	15.1	5.5
45063	Lexington County	307,046	89.4	5.3	126,509	76.5	62.9	243,500	1,166	8.0	131,082	10.0	4.8
45073	Oconee County	80,565	91.2	5.0	34,416	74.3	48.8	255,000	814	10.8	30,040	17.3	7.1
45075	Orangeburg County	81,835	89.2	8.3	34,120	70.6	NA	123,400	838	17.3	29,228	12.2	15.8
45077	Pickens County	134,296	82.4	11.5	54,412	72.2	50.8	240,400	961	10.7	56,800	11.3	6.8
45079	Richland County	419,831	82.6	10.8	169,715	61.6	66.5	246,900	1,198	7.7	181,450	15.5	4.2
45083	Spartanburg County	353,103	87.9	6.0	134,559	72.6	61.2	240,600	1,028	9.7	153,713	10.7	5.0
45085	Sumter County	102,526	88.7	5.7	40,059	66.8	51.9	190,400	931	12.4	41,564	9.1	6.0
45091	York County	296,034	90.5	4.7	113,164	76.7	68.8	383,600	1,360	7.6	124,417	12.1	8.2
46000	**SOUTH DAKOTA**	907,196	88.5	6.4	378,559	69.4	55.1	268,200	921	8.1	422,763	27.6	4.1
46083	Lincoln County	72,003	89.9	4.0	28,842	72.5	70.3	359,800	1,261	3.6	36,897	10.3	5.5
46099	Minnehaha County	203,693	89.2	4.9	87,657	65.5	64.0	297,000	949	6.2	102,094	15.9	2.8
46103	Pennington County	115,011	83.0	8.7	48,946	67.0	59.4	313,000	1,127	5.6	51,222	17.3	5.2
47000	**TENNESSEE**	7,046,744	87.7	6.3	2,889,226	67.3	57.7	307,300	1,214	8.9	2,966,891	11.9	7.7
47001	Anderson County	79,738	85.6	10.9	33,521	72.9	55.9	243,700	927	12.0	31,859	16.9	3.3
47009	Blount County	140,030	90.7	5.8	56,548	78.3	59.5	348,300	1,159	7.1	62,482	8.8	4.2
47011	Bradley County	110,645	84.7	6.1	42,712	66.0	57.3	267,000	983	5.9	43,803	18.7	4.5
47037	Davidson County	701,541	82.0	8.3	341,597	52.8	70.4	437,700	1,620	6.8	327,415	9.4	4.6
47059	Greene County	71,942	89.7	5.5	28,214	77.1	52.0	217,300	737	18.6	27,792	20.9	11.1
47063	Hamblen County	65314	93.6	4.3	27,311	69.8	37.8	238,400	901	11.7	27,795	14.6	6.1
47065	Hamilton County	373,584	85.4	6.4	157,992	63.7	60.1	333,900	1,298	6.3	163,581	11.2	3.1
47093	Knox County	496,955	87.2	6.3	200,022	65.7	59.9	359,000	1,301	9.4	217,889	9.1	3.5
47113	Madison County	98,582	82.7	8.7	40,525	61.0	57.1	225,500	1,152	8.2	41,024	22.0	6.6
47119	Maury County	109,426	89.8	7.7	45,571	67.6	60.8	379,200	1,219	8.8	47,570	9.4	11.9
47125	Montgomery County	236,837	82.8	10.7	91,893	59.6	69.8	305,200	1,376	4.6	102,279	10.3	13.2
47141	Putnam County	82,767	87.1	4.7	34,727	60.0	47.3	290,100	873	10.2	34,147	17.4	6.8
47147	Robertson County	75,364	85.7	6.8	29,522	77.1	60.5	355,800	1,258	8.1	34,895	10.3	12.3
47149	Rutherford County	363,947	86.8	6.0	134,245	63.7	68.5	406,700	1,548	4.2	174,903	8.9	11.1

Table C-2. Counties — Where: Migration, Housing, and Transportation, 2023—*Continued*

State code	STATE County	Total population 1 year and over	Lived in the same house 1 year ago (percent)	Did not live in the same county 1 year ago (percent)	Total occupied housing units	Owner-occupied units (percent)	Percent with a mortgage, contract to purchase, or similar debt	Median value of owner-occupied units (dollars; owner estimated)	Median gross rent of renter-occupied units paying cash rent	Households without Internet access (percent)	Number of workers who commuted to work	Commute of less than 10 minutes (percent)	Commute of 60 minutes or more (percent)
	ACS table number:	C07204	C07204	C07204	B25003	B25003	B25081	B25097	B25064	S2801	B08012	B08012	B08012
	Column number:	1	2	3	4	5	6	7	8	9	10	11	12
	TENNESSEE—Cont.												
47155	Sevier County	98,295	90.7	6.3	42,727	69.4	49.5	302,400	970	11.6	46,081	10.9	7.3
47157	Shelby County	897,676	87.8	3.5	362,776	53.6	63.0	271,000	1,226	7.4	380,308	10.1	2.8
47163	Sullivan County	160,477	90.1	6.3	68,655	75.5	52.2	230,500	879	11.3	64,583	14.8	3.2
47165	Sumner County	206,233	86.3	7.3	80,536	70.4	64.5	411,900	1,424	5.7	90,122	10.5	11.9
47179	Washington County	138,033	84.0	9.6	57,629	66.3	55.4	260,800	1,026	8.1	53,677	17.6	4.8
47187	Williamson County	262,073	90.7	6.1	95,439	79.3	68.0	777,800	1,972	3.8	98,139	8.5	6.6
47189	Wilson County	162,783	87.5	8.9	60,911	79.1	67.8	475,100	1,517	5.8	71,319	8.5	9.4
48000	**TEXAS**	30,134,547	85.9	6.6	11,260,645	62.6	55.8	296,900	1,413	7.4	12,780,053	11.7	8.8
48005	Angelina County	86,455	82.5	6.5	31,996	65.3	NA	167,400	1,068	8.8	34,335	26.7	3.3
48021	Bastrop County	109,691	87.9	7.6	38,591	74.7	NA	317,000	1,605	8.1	41,256	14.5	17.2
48027	Bell County	385,810	80.4	8.8	145,863	58.7	62.6	262,300	1,331	7.8	167,567	13.0	9.4
48029	Bexar County	2,061,995	83.1	6.1	758,070	59.3	60.1	277,000	1,332	6.3	876,243	8.1	6.7
48037	Bowie County	90,734	89.8	4.4	36,110	64.3	NA	160,700	1,026	11.6	34,893	21.5	6.5
48039	Brazoria County	394,725	90.4	5.6	138,692	73.2	62.2	304,700	1,471	3.7	166,687	10.6	10.4
48041	Brazos County	241,516	74.1	14.3	92,216	45.7	NA	309,300	1,188	12.4	108,270	15.7	5.5
48061	Cameron County	422,364	90.3	2.9	143,033	66.2	37.1	154,200	904	10.9	165,141	10.7	4.2
48085	Collin County	1,181,567	84.4	8.6	431,746	63.9	69.3	513,100	1,866	3.3	480,549	9.7	8.5
48091	Comal County	193,050	85.6	10.3	75,234	78.4	66.2	465,900	1,546	5.4	73,773	9.3	8.5
48099	Coryell County	83,855	78.9	17.9	28,070	61.7	NA	216,100	1,181	8.8	33,575	25.4	14.1
48113	Dallas County	2,574,754	85.7	6.6	993,312	50.3	57.2	319,100	1,597	6.6	1,133,870	9.4	8.1
48121	Denton County	997,852	84.3	8.8	370,503	66.1	70.3	460,300	1,747	4.1	434,232	10.3	8.8
48135	Ector County	162,991	86.1	4.8	66,937	64.7	46.5	196,500	1,169	14.9	77,709	12.3	7.4
48139	Ellis County	220,339	88.6	5.8	75,570	74.7	63.2	366,500	1,693	5.2	98,934	10.6	13.9
48141	El Paso County	857,302	87.7	4.8	301,198	63.3	51.0	191,100	1,127	10.2	364,362	8.9	5.0
48157	Fort Bend County	908,352	90.1	6.5	303,900	77.2	62.5	384,100	1,839	3.8	368,261	6.6	12.9
48167	Galveston County	358,427	88.0	5.8	142,199	68.1	58.3	315,000	1,401	6.0	156,800	10.1	13.1
48181	Grayson County	145,720	82.5	9.9	56,267	66.1	47.6	281,700	1,325	9.1	57,099	20.0	12.2
48183	Gregg County	124,313	84.0	7.6	47,550	59.7	46.6	197,700	1,117	11.5	52,638	16.6	6.0
48187	Guadalupe County	186,393	88.2	8.3	69,236	81.0	63.8	325,000	1,598	5.7	81,679	10.1	11.2
48201	Harris County	4,767,957	85.1	5.3	1,791,013	55.2	57.3	287,100	1,403	6.9	2,088,042	7.3	9.5
48203	Harrison County	70,111	89.2	5.3	26,811	72.8	NA	201,900	972	13.1	30,524	14.8	6.9
48209	Hays County	276,664	81.8	12.1	105,917	64.0	70.3	428,400	1,443	6.0	120,087	7.8	12.1
48213	Henderson County	85,538	85.2	6.8	33,957	78.4	38.8	212,500	999	14.6	33,618	14.5	17.3
48215	Hidalgo County	885868	90.8	2.6	277,001	66.5	38.3	151,200	936	9.8	331,794	15.3	4.4
48221	Hood County	67,475	86.6	7.8	25,660	80.5	55.9	350,100	1,514	4.3	25,648	9.1	12.9
48231	Hunt County	111,852	85.2	8.3	40,067	71.7	50.0	259,800	1,214	8.0	46,807	14.5	17.3
48245	Jefferson County	247,388	87.6	5.4	94,005	64.8	42.7	171,000	1,129	9.6	100,367	12.7	4.2
48251	Johnson County	199,923	88.5	7.5	65,934	75.1	62.4	310,900	1,370	6.0	89,841	11.7	9.3
48257	Kaufman County	183,238	90.2	6.9	52,963	81.6	67.1	347,000	1,526	7.2	76,602	7.1	23.7
48291	Liberty County	null	NA	NA	32,959	80.8	NA	201,200	1,099	12.3	39,166	6.6	24.5
48303	Lubbock County	316,734	79.4	8.2	128,053	52.3	50.9	213,900	1,170	9.4	149,998	17.8	3.1
48309	McLennan County	265,084	84.2	7.2	96,965	64.8	52.7	264,100	1,120	9.5	114,116	14.3	5.1
48329	Midland County	174,163	85.5	6.4	70,890	65.7	58.6	314,500	1,328	8.2	84,827	13.4	4.3
48339	Montgomery County	703,327	86.7	7.4	262,273	69.4	63.0	359,800	1,508	4.5	285,443	6.6	15.5
48347	Nacogdoches County	64,415	81.8	10.7	25,074	57.5	NA	201,500	883	11.3	27,857	26.4	4.5
48355	Nueces County	347,813	86.3	5.6	132,759	59.1	51.0	213,500	1,248	8.5	NA	NA	NA
48361	Orange County	85,114	86.0	6.7	33,271	72.0	43.6	180,500	1,067	12.7	37,181	13.9	5.9
48367	Parker County	171,383	87.1	8.2	57,996	80.2	58.3	383,100	1,541	2.9	75,159	12.5	15.2
48375	Potter County	113,840	88.9	4.4	42,674	59.3	43.9	144,800	980	12.0	50,138	18.7	6.9
48381	Randall County	147,225	86.5	4.5	56,279	68.9	57.2	236,900	1,059	8.1	72,120	19.2	3.8
48397	Rockwall County	129,405	87.7	10.2	43,259	80.3	68.3	429,700	2,093	4.1	50,067	9.9	20.5
48409	San Patricio County	69,925	85.9	7.8	25,735	68.4	NA	193,200	1,165	13.0	32,321	24.6	1.7
48423	Smith County	241,184	89.3	5.2	81,987	69.8	50.7	272,700	1,299	7.9	92,859	11.7	5.9
48427	Starr County	65,273	92.0	2.0	19,004	66.9	NA	89,600	747	12.3	23,665	20.6	7.4
48439	Tarrant County	2,156,192	86.3	5.4	801,716	58.5	61.6	336,000	1,569	6.0	968,729	8.7	7.6
48441	Taylor County	144,583	84.0	6.4	54,805	59.3	53.7	200,300	1,269	5.8	63,610	20.0	1.3
48451	Tom Green County	116,863	82.4	7.2	47,638	58.9	NA	198,500	1,128	10.9	53,744	20.0	6.0
48453	Travis County	1,320,664	82.4	8.6	608,921	52.2	67.6	569,000	1,770	4.7	556,516	9.8	4.6
48469	Victoria County	90,193	88.6	6.6	34,484	67.6	NA	202,400	1,164	10.9	38,734	20.0	7.3
48471	Walker County	80,703	72.8	22.1	26,539	58.5	NA	298,600	1,045	16.8	28,059	19.2	12.3
48479	Webb County	265,082	90.4	1.5	83,045	65.3	54.1	200,800	990	9.7	108,694	10.5	5.7
48485	Wichita County	128,657	85.1	9.0	49,403	64.2	46.5	168,100	976	10.9	57,835	31.2	2.3
48491	Williamson County	689903	86.5	7.8	264,986	65.9	68.2	464,800	1,830	4.2	285,462	10.7	8.6
48497	Wise County	null	NA	NA	26,319	81.3	57.3	318,300	1,292	10.7	32,668	9.2	17.1

Table C-2. Counties — Where: Migration, Housing, and Transportation, 2023—*Continued*

State code	STATE County	Total population 1 year and over	Lived in the same house 1 year ago (percent)	Did not live in the same county 1 year ago (percent)	Total occupied housing units	Owner-occupied units (percent)	Percent with a mortgage, contract to purchase, or similar debt	Median value of owner-occupied units (dollars; owner estimated)	Median gross rent of renter-occupied units paying cash rent	Households without Internet access (percent)	Number of workers who commuted to work	Commute of less than 10 minutes (percent)	Commute of 60 minutes or more (percent)
	ACS table number:	C07204	C07204	C07204	B25003	B25003	B25081	B25097	B25064	S2801	B08012	B08012	B08012
	Column number:	1	2	3	4	5	6	7	8	9	10	11	12
49000	**UTAH**	3,373,801	86.0	6.2	1,167,591	70.1	68.1	517,700	1,551	5.8	1,449,487	15.7	5.0
49005	Cache County	139,889	82.0	9.7	46,318	60.3	68.8	468,300	1,275	6.2	60,600	25.6	4.8
49011	Davis County	369,205	89.1	5.3	118,498	77.6	69.8	538,100	1,615	4.9	157,769	13.6	3.1
49035	Salt Lake County	1,174,904	84.7	5.5	436,181	65.4	69.2	556,300	1,651	5.2	522,919	9.4	3.6
49045	Tooele County	81397	94.4	4.2	24,796	83.9	75.2	459,000	1,090	2.9	33,413	15.3	11.6
49049	Utah County	705,649	83.0	7.3	214,806	67.2	72.5	570,100	1,560	6.0	295,252	16.9	7.0
49053	Washington County	199,382	87.8	6.1	72,315	73.0	59.2	528,100	1,624	5.9	79,021	18.9	3.0
49057	Weber County	268,643	90.8	6.0	97,783	74.5	67.5	437,200	1,445	6.2	123,951	14.1	7.4
50000	**VERMONT**	642,670	89.1	6.5	279,612	73.2	60.4	332,000	1,202	7.7	284,545	18.2	6.6
50007	Chittenden County	168,106	85.0	7.8	73,216	66.3	67.6	436,100	1,659	3.2	77,008	14.8	3.9
51000	**VIRGINIA**	8,626,985	87.0	8.7	3,402,670	67.8	66.3	382,900	1,567	7.8	3,646,196	10.1	9.0
51003	Albemarle County	114,679	81.9	12.6	46,900	66.4	66.2	492,800	1,607	8.1	46,808	8.3	3.2
51013	Arlington County	231,669	78.7	15.6	114,097	41.1	72.4	850,900	2,223	5.1	105,078	7.2	4.0
51015	Augusta County	77,566	92.5	4.8	32,169	80.0	54.7	293,600	1,114	15.9	35,215	16.7	4.7
51019	Bedford County	81,199	87.4	7.0	33,205	81.9	60.0	295,100	942	7.9	32,325	8.1	7.0
51041	Chesterfield County	379,580	89.3	6.8	143,255	78.6	72.1	367,000	1,594	2.7	158,569	6.8	3.8
51059	Fairfax County	1,130,102	87.9	6.7	414,946	67.6	69.8	727,200	2,156	2.8	470,925	6.6	7.8
51061	Fauquier County	74,701	94.3	4.6	26,954	82.0	70.8	562,100	1,473	5.4	34,375	9.8	21.0
51069	Frederick County	95,524	92.5	5.2	35,341	82.7	67.6	387,800	1,368	5.6	41,485	9.6	17.9
51085	Hanover County	112,816	91.8	7.1	43,496	80.6	70.0	405,000	1,593	5.8	50,570	8.8	5.6
51087	Henrico County	331,582	84.7	8.2	137,529	63.3	67.7	362,400	1,593	5.1	144,445	11.0	4.1
51095	James City County	82,078	87.5	10.4	33,898	76.3	65.9	449,300	1,646	4.7	31,053	9.7	9.9
51107	Loudoun County	431,154	89.2	6.6	145,601	78.0	78.5	734,700	2,321	3.4	165,347	9.1	12.5
51121	Montgomery County	97,999	78.7	12.5	37,229	55.9	57.9	303,500	1,241	8.2	37,617	15.2	2.6
51153	Prince William County	483,159	89.9	6.1	158,620	76.0	79.2	532,600	2,042	4.3	211,764	4.1	19.1
51161	Roanoke County	95,878	92.2	5.5	40,176	75.5	62.0	296,800	1,161	9.0	38,782	9.2	1.7
51165	Rockingham County	85,799	89.0	6.7	32,827	77.0	57.2	312,700	1,047	13.1	37,969	14.8	5.2
51177	Spotsylvania County	148,000	87.0	8.2	55,487	80.0	80.3	421,800	1,770	4.0	63,777	7.2	27.4
51179	Stafford County	164,397	84.7	12.3	53,938	81.1	81.5	492,500	2,026	1.6	69,875	6.2	27.2
51199	York County	70705	84.7	13.1	27,654	67.3	67.8	414,600	1,845	4.0	30,181	13.1	5.4
51510	Alexandria city	153,790	77.1	15.6	76,890	43.2	74.8	737,900	1,954	5.6	74,818	6.0	7.4
51550	Chesapeake city	251,301	89.4	9.0	94,056	75.1	71.7	380,100	1,628	8.0	108,759	8.1	4.0
51650	Hampton city	135,688	84.8	8.3	57,645	55.7	73.3	258,400	1,455	5.4	62,935	12.2	3.1
51680	Lynchburg city	78,515	82.8	11.2	28,916	48.6	67.3	247,100	1,062	7.0	31,029	16.1	3.0
51700	Newport News city	180,603	86.1	7.6	76,086	48.6	69.9	261,800	1,326	7.7	79,606	10.1	6.1
51710	Norfolk city	226,794	78.2	13.8	94,056	44.6	73.8	298,600	1,314	11.3	113,008	11.5	4.6
51740	Portsmouth city	95,777	88.6	8.8	40,661	55.6	73.9	268,300	1,225	9.5	43,614	9.8	3.0
51760	Richmond city	225,478	81.3	11.8	104,332	45.1	65.3	365,100	1,441	9.7	103,889	9.5	3.7
51770	Roanoke city	96,192	90.2	7.4	45,061	51.9	63.7	215,000	1,110	14.2	39,227	15.0	2.4
51800	Suffolk city	99,653	86.2	9.7	39,203	70.2	75.3	352,000	1,460	6.7	45,133	7.7	7.7
51810	Virginia Beach city	450,178	84.3	10.0	179,291	65.9	74.7	384,200	1,704	5.0	205,017	9.9	3.9
53000	**WASHINGTON**	7,727,767	85.8	6.4	3,101,265	63.7	65.6	576,000	1,731	5.7	3,196,649	12.5	9.1
53005	Benton County	213,184	88.6	5.1	78,748	70.0	62.5	427,200	1,327	6.4	83,491	13.9	4.7
53007	Chelan County	79,377	86.5	6.4	32,915	65.3	53.3	526,200	1,139	7.3	33,523	27.4	4.5
53009	Clallam County	77,180	89.3	4.8	34,807	71.4	49.0	431,000	1,094	5.1	26,315	25.3	4.5
53011	Clark County	513,323	87.1	6.1	202,217	66.7	72.1	542,200	1,731	4.4	210,141	13.2	6.7
53015	Cowlitz County	111,733	86.6	6.9	44,694	68.5	62.9	405,400	1,176	7.0	45,163	18.4	8.4
53021	Franklin County	97,315	90.5	5.6	30,733	66.6	67.5	392,100	1,183	9.5	39,858	11.5	3.8
53025	Grant County	101,543	87.3	4.0	34,911	63.3	57.5	309,500	1,057	7.6	40,879	29.2	5.9
53027	Grays Harbor County	76,356	86.7	6.7	30,498	74.8	52.9	323,200	1,041	10.7	27,484	24.1	10.4
53029	Island County	85,257	90.9	5.9	35,431	76.4	60.7	595,100	1,632	4.1	32,489	19.3	12.4
53033	King County	2,248,046	83.5	6.8	949,792	55.6	68.0	848,300	2,043	4.2	953,105	8.3	8.0
53035	Kitsap County	275,815	86.0	7.2	109,652	70.9	65.7	564,600	1,808	4.4	119,787	11.1	13.8
53041	Lewis County	85,090	91.3	4.3	33,672	75.3	60.8	395,200	1,080	12.9	29,358	15.1	9.5
53045	Mason County	67,680	84.2	9.5	25,161	84.1	58.2	432,400	1,368	9.1	20,340	16.5	18.8
53053	Pierce County	916,974	85.4	6.2	356,066	64.3	71.2	538,000	1,802	4.9	399,933	9.6	14.7
53057	Skagit County	130,236	88.5	6.1	53,087	70.5	60.5	558,300	1,667	5.6	52,835	16.4	11.8
53061	Snohomish County	835,909	86.6	6.6	321,835	67.5	71.1	697,700	1,911	5.0	356,193	9.2	13.2
53063	Spokane County	544,468	85.7	5.1	219,230	64.1	65.2	421,400	1,297	8.1	222,659	12.2	4.7
53067	Thurston County	296,425	84.5	7.7	119,786	66.5	65.6	493,100	1,776	5.7	115,681	12.3	7.7
53073	Whatcom County	230,507	85.8	6.1	93,449	63.0	61.7	611,200	1,497	5.4	98,124	16.3	6.2
53077	Yakima County	252,632	89.4	2.9	89,414	61.8	54.8	318,900	1,119	8.7	104,271	17.6	5.3

Table C-2. Counties — Where: Migration, Housing, and Transportation, 2023—*Continued*

State code	STATE County	Total population 1 year and over	Lived in the same house 1 year ago (percent)	Did not live in the same county 1 year ago (percent)	Total occupied housing units	Owner-occupied units (percent)	Percent with a mortgage, contract to purchase, or similar debt	Median value of owner-occupied units (dollars; owner estimated)	Median gross rent of renter-occupied units paying cash rent	Households without Internet access (percent)	Number of workers who commuted to work	Commute of less than 10 minutes (percent)	Commute of 60 minutes or more (percent)
	ACS table number:	C07204	C07204	C07204	B25003	B25003	B25081	B25097	B25064	S2801	B08012	B08012	B08012
	Column number:	1	2	3	4	5	6	7	8	9	10	11	12
54000	**WEST VIRGINIA**	1,753,113	90.0	5.0	743,644	73.5	44.4	163,700	850	12.9	685,618	13.6	10.8
54003	Berkeley County	130,624	89.6	5.5	51,094	72.7	63.7	271,600	1,269	8.5	59,494	7.4	15.8
54011	Cabell County	91,558	83.4	8.0	39,720	60.6	50.3	175,100	859	12.4	37,851	17.4	5.6
54033	Harrison County	63,955	90.9	3.0	27,161	72.6	45.4	174,900	824	11.9	25,441	13.4	6.8
54039	Kanawha County	172,537	92.6	3.4	76,963	71.2	47.0	138,000	839	12.0	67,569	10.9	7.2
54061	Monongalia County	107,309	79.5	9.7	44,307	57.5	53.8	261,500	913	10.7	50,920	14.6	5.6
54081	Raleigh County	71,403	87.3	5.5	28,275	73.0	42.8	158,800	893	17.0	25,835	11.4	11.8
54107	Wood County	82,312	89.9	3.1	36,936	74.3	46.9	163,700	736	13.4	33,383	12.3	4.0
55000	**WISCONSIN**	5,857,364	88.8	5.3	2,495,539	67.9	60.8	272,500	1,071	8.2	2,646,802	17.7	5.1
55009	Brown County	269,168	86.7	4.5	112,027	64.6	62.9	273,900	1,033	7.2	126,313	12.6	4.5
55017	Chippewa County	66,353	89.7	5.3	27,846	80.0	59.7	260,900	873	6.4	29,466	20.0	6.5
55025	Dane County	571,424	81.4	7.5	257,528	55.3	65.8	393,500	1,378	6.9	266,069	13.0	2.7
55027	Dodge County	87,043	91.9	4.6	35,795	71.7	60.5	242,200	968	8.9	41,781	22.5	7.0
55035	Eau Claire County	106,727	81.0	8.2	44,769	61.2	62.4	269,000	1,041	6.9	49,384	26.8	4.0
55039	Fond du Lac County	103,161	92.5	4.1	44,262	70.7	57.6	232,900	964	8.2	48,756	25.7	6.7
55055	Jefferson County	85,164	91.5	3.8	34,914	75.1	59.4	283,700	953	6.5	40,938	20.2	4.9
55059	Kenosha County	166,244	89.9	5.9	69,907	66.5	67.4	265,500	1,212	5.3	80,162	15.2	7.0
55063	La Crosse County	119,151	84.4	8.0	51,283	61.7	56.8	272,200	1,009	7.5	59,450	21.1	2.7
55071	Manitowoc County	80,704	91.9	3.6	35,669	76.8	55.1	199,800	752	9.3	36,980	28.9	4.5
55073	Marathon County	136,855	89.1	3.5	58,104	72.9	56.8	215,700	977	10.5	62,197	18.7	3.6
55079	Milwaukee County	906,472	87.3	4.5	388,165	51.5	64.8	232,500	1,084	8.3	392,065	11.3	4.5
55087	Outagamie County	191,240	90.9	3.8	78,027	71.8	59.9	276,500	1,101	6.6	91,757	15.4	4.2
55089	Ozaukee County	92,855	91.3	6.3	38,030	74.0	64.4	403,300	988	5.4	41,733	17.9	2.4
55097	Portage County	70,545	85.9	8.1	30,620	67.1	51.3	258,900	948	7.0	34,144	23.1	3.2
55101	Racine County	194,112	92.4	3.2	79,066	72.5	65.7	253,200	1,038	7.2	86,939	13.4	5.2
55105	Rock County	162,507	89.6	5.9	66,220	70.5	62.1	247,500	973	7.5	72,788	16.1	8.2
55109	St. Croix County	95,705	93.0	3.6	38,606	78.5	70.1	375,000	1,478	4.6	44,218	15.9	10.3
55111	Sauk County	65554	90.4	3.7	28,295	70.8	62.8	271,300	1,076	10.8	31,672	24.0	8.1
55117	Sheboygan County	116,939	89.5	5.3	49,852	71.1	61.0	239,700	895	7.7	54,653	19.3	5.0
55127	Walworth County	105,279	88.5	6.4	43,005	70.8	61.0	315,100	1,116	8.6	48,099	23.2	7.8
55131	Washington County	136,392	94.8	3.4	56,641	77.4	64.0	356,800	1,174	5.5	64,216	13.9	6.1
55133	Waukesha County	408,899	91.4	4.8	168,150	75.2	65.5	390,500	1,330	5.6	181,925	13.2	3.0
55139	Winnebago County	170,513	86.3	8.1	71,563	66.2	58.6	222,400	929	7.1	81,523	20.6	3.8
55141	Wood County	73,511	90.9	3.4	32,099	73.5	56.8	174,500	766	8.4	30,547	28.4	3.4
56000	**WYOMING**	577,612	86.2	7.6	247,368	71.2	53.2	298,700	1,000	9.2	254,224	29.0	6.6
56021	Laramie County	99,272	86.9	7.4	44,460	67.9	58.1	357,300	1,143	7.7	45,226	17.8	3.5
56025	Natrona County	79,548	84.2	6.8	34,332	73.3	58.3	267,300	1,063	7.4	35,523	14.0	7.5
72000	**PUERTO RICO**	NA	NA	NA	1,277,486	68.4	37.7	131,500	557	14.2	1,099,792	9.2	11.5
72013	Arecibo Municipio	NA	NA	NA	33,466	68.2	NA	114,600	536	19.3	25,425	9.6	10.0
72021	Bayamón Municipio	NA	NA	NA	76,203	70.3	48.8	144,900	662	9.3	66,469	7.1	10.3
72025	Caguas Municipio	NA	NA	NA	51,579	68.2	NA	152,900	590	11.4	47,183	9.9	10.3
72031	Carolina Municipio	NA	NA	NA	63,447	72.5	NA	155,700	609	8.0	54,492	5.6	19.1
72061	Guaynabo Municipio	NA	NA	NA	34,184	68.3	NA	235,900	1,079	6.6	32,262	8.2	5.9
72097	Mayagüez Municipio	NA	NA	NA	31,111	45.6	NA	107,000	447	8.2	19,806	13.0	3.0
72113	Ponce Municipio	NA	NA	NA	56,772	61.6	NA	100,600	526	8.6	37,748	10.5	6.5
72127	San Juan Municipio	NA	NA	NA	150,969	54.2	45.4	175,300	607	24.1	126,027	5.0	6.1
72135	Toa Alta Municipio	NA	NA	NA	24,486	82.6	NA	176,800	566	10.0	27,634	4.0	19.6
72137	Toa Baja Municipio	NA	NA	NA	30,304	71.7	NA	148,100	772	7.8	29,207	5.1	11.5
72139	Trujillo Alto Municipio	NA	NA	NA	27,299	76.3	NA	167,800	749	11.2	29,881	6.0	12.0

NA = Not available.

Table C-3. Metropolitan Areas — Where: Migration, Housing, and Transportation, 2023

Metropolitan area / division code	Metropolitan area / division	Total population 1 year and over	Lived in the same house 1 year ago (percent)	Did not live in the same county 1 year ago (percent)	Total occupied housing units	Owner-occupied units (percent)	Percent with a mortgage, contract to purchase, or similar debt	Median value of owner-occupied units (dollars; owner estimated)	Median gross rent of renter-occupied units paying cash rent	Households without Internet access (percent)	Number of workers who commuted to work	Commute of less than 10 minutes (percent)	Commute of 60 minutes or more (percent)
	ACS table number:	C07204	C07204	C07204	B25003	B25003	B25081	B25097	B25064	S2801	B08012	B08012	B08012
	column number:	1	2	3	4	5	6	7	8	9	10	11	12
10180	Abilene, TX	177,675	83.4	8.1	66,460	62.3	50.8	180,400	1,221	6.6	75,645	19.1	1.7
10380	Aguadilla, PR	NA	NA	NA	89,374	66.2	NA	136,500	548	14.1	79,315	18.0	8.8
10420	Akron, OH	692,202	89.5	5.1	298,193	68.1	62.3	216,000	1,029	8.1	300,188	11.2	4.1
10500	Albany, GA	146,129	84.4	10.0	59,228	53.2	62.4	164,100	858	16.4	53,750	15.6	5.7
10540	Albany, OR	129,903	88.7	6.2	51,636	66.9	66.3	398,300	1,359	8.2	53,310	14.7	8.0
10580	Albany-Schenectady-Troy, NY	897,238	88.4	6.6	386,690	63.9	61.0	284,000	1,293	7.9	389,903	12.0	4.1
10740	Albuquerque, NM	914,181	88.2	5.3	381,326	68.2	60.9	297,100	1,203	9.8	383,819	12.2	6.8
10780	Alexandria, LA	146,895	86.8	7.1	58,235	62.6	48.5	166,700	915	14.1	56,922	14.9	7.0
10900	Allentown-Bethlehem-Easton, PA-NJ	866,150	90.8	4.9	345,257	69.7	60.2	309,300	1,347	8.6	377,316	12.0	10.9
11020	Altoona, PA	119,253	86.1	4.1	50,651	71.7	51.9	157,000	837	12.0	51,888	24.2	4.9
11100	Amarillo, TX	271,219	87.4	4.8	102,739	65.1	51.8	205,000	1,008	9.7	126,969	19.4	5.2
11180	Ames, IA	124,642	78.2	13.6	49,962	62.1	56.5	246,200	981	15.1	59,335	26.3	3.5
11200	Amherst Town-Northampton, MA	161,377	79.4	12.5	61,802	65.4	57.8	380,800	1,355	6.2	70,657	17.8	4.5
11260	Anchorage, AK	396,262	84.2	6.3	148,995	66.9	65.5	371,600	1,428	4.8	181,752	15.1	7.0
11460	Ann Arbor, MI	363,179	79.7	11.3	149,379	62.6	61.9	360,400	1,451	5.6	149,947	10.6	5.2
11500	Anniston-Oxford, AL	115,152	88.8	5.9	46,310	68.7	50.6	160,900	782	12.8	45,139	12.2	5.3
11540	Appleton, WI	244,129	91.4	4.0	99,606	73.0	60.2	274,600	1,087	6.4	116,191	16.0	4.1
11640	Arecibo, PR	NA	NA	NA	65,668	71.5	NA	112,700	565	19.3	54,705	6.1	9.6
11700	Asheville, NC	412,596	89.4	6.2	164,757	69.5	54.3	398,500	1,286	7.9	163,001	11.7	3.9
12020	Athens-Clarke County, GA	218,278	80.1	11.3	87,635	56.0	58.4	328,000	1,270	6.7	95,062	13.3	6.9
12060	Atlanta-Sandy Springs-Roswell, GA	6,237,031	87.7	7.6	2,341,283	67.1	69.4	383,600	1,701	5.0	2,588,713	7.1	12.8
1206012054	Atlanta-Sandy Springs-Roswell, GA Metro Division	4,855,586	87.6	7.5	1,823,623	65.7	69.3	376,600	1,695	5.2	1,998,152	7.2	12.9
1206031924	Marietta, GA Metro Division	1,381,445	88.1	7.9	517660	71.8	69.7	405,300	1,724	4.2	590,561	6.8	12.8
12100	Atlantic City-Hammonton, NJ	366,092	89.8	5.2	158,674	72.0	62.3	350,000	1,321	6.0	159,158	15.3	7.0
12220	Auburn-Opelika, AL	201,105	86.2	9.1	81,935	64.1	58.1	265,600	966	12.0	83,154	15.0	3.6
12260	Augusta-Richmond County, GA-SC	621,908	86.2	7.4	236,371	70.6	60.2	238,300	1,101	11.3	257,116	12.1	4.5
12420	Austin-Round Rock-San Marcos, TX	2,446,446	83.9	8.7	1,036,074	58.1	66.3	487,200	1,752	4.9	1,023,148	10.0	7.4
12540	Bakersfield-Delano, CA	902,357	91.5	3.4	289,845	59.8	65.9	346,600	1,286	7.0	345,017	11.9	8.3
12580	Baltimore-Columbia-Towson, MD	2,800,999	89.3	5.8	1,127,320	67.0	69.5	385,900	1,557	7.7	1,211,828	8.3	10.4
12620	Bangor, ME	154,612	88.2	6.5	66,556	71.5	50.3	228,600	1,105	9.5	66,415	18.4	5.8
12700	Barnstable Town, MA	231,323	89.7	6.2	109,475	78.5	58.4	634,700	1,604	4.0	96,287	14.7	9.4
12940	Baton Rouge, LA	864,978	88.0	5.3	334,402	69.3	58.2	239,700	1,100	8.0	368,004	10.8	7.7
12980	Battle Creek, MI	131,501	89.5	5.0	54,568	72.4	58.2	163,500	906	11.2	55,289	18.1	4.3
13020	Bay City, MI	101,761	91.4	3.3	44,417	77.7	55.5	156,200	811	12.8	42,360	14.2	5.6
13140	Beaumont-Port Arthur, TX	389,915	87.6	5.5	150,294	68.3	45.2	173,800	1,100	10.3	161,688	12.7	6.1
13220	Beckley, WV	110,379	89.6	4.6	44,847	74.4	40.5	119,900	838	16.6	39,482	11.7	13.2
13380	Bellingham, WA	230,507	85.8	6.1	93,449	63.0	61.7	611,200	1,497	5.4	98,124	16.3	6.2
13460	Bend, OR	258,439	88.1	6.2	107,729	71.8	66.9	622,900	1,725	6.8	102,421	19.0	5.2
13740	Billings, MT	189,331	85.6	5.7	81,750	68.0	60.0	363,100	1,002	7.6	87,907	18.2	4.1
13780	Binghamton, NY	241,751	88.9	5.4	99,826	68.4	50.9	157,300	921	6.5	96,465	17.5	3.7
13820	Birmingham, AL	1,172,121	88.4	4.9	471,767	71.0	58.5	247,900	1,153	8.7	491,303	8.3	7.5
13900	Bismarck, ND	133,805	89.7	4.5	57,951	73.6	57.9	289,400	951	10.8	65,815	20.8	6.5
13980	Blacksburg-Christiansburg-Radford, VA	179,722	83.7	10.2	71,419	63.9	54.5	227,100	1,101	11.6	71,246	15.7	3.6
14010	Bloomington, IL	168,363	85.4	7.6	71,060	65.5	61.8	211,000	1,013	9.1	73,991	20.8	4.2
14020	Bloomington, IN	159,750	74.7	14.8	70,681	55.5	62.4	279,600	1,109	9.8	68,470	16.6	5.4
14260	Boise City, ID	818,645	85.3	7.2	314,846	72.2	65.9	471,700	1,511	5.1	341,312	12.9	3.8
14460	Boston-Cambridge-Newton, MA-NH	4,872,013	88.2	6.2	1,949,953	61.6	67.6	646,600	2,000	5.6	2,195,778	9.2	13.8
1446014454	Boston, MA Metro Division	2,012,286	87.2	6.9	822929	57.9	68.2	648,700	2,050	5.7	916,043	8.5	15.6
1446015764	Cambridge-Newton-Framingham, MA Metro Division	2,409,454	88.6	5.7	946,508	62.2	67.9	681,900	2,026	5.6	1,075,720	9.4	12.8
1446040484	Rockingham County-Strafford County, NH Metro Division	450,273	90.5	5.8	180516	74.9	64.6	474,200	1,605	5.6	204,015	11.8	10.4
14500	Boulder, CO	325,389	78.7	13.3	137,425	61.2	63.2	763,600	1,915	4.0	126,056	16.2	7.0
14540	Bowling Green, KY	190,011	85.7	9.0	77,804	62.3	63.3	241,200	923	9.8	87,964	14.7	8.0
14580	Bozeman, MT	124,744	83.1	10.6	54,621	60.4	65.1	691,200	1,790	6.6	66,444	17.1	6.1
14740	Bremerton-Silverdale-Port Orchard, WA	275,815	86.0	7.2	109,652	70.9	65.7	564,600	1,808	4.4	119,787	11.1	13.8
14860	Bridgeport-Stamford-Danbury, CT	940,437	89.1	5.8	356,931	65.0	63.9	574,800	1,862	5.8	410,806	11.1	17.0
15180	Brownsville-Harlingen, TX	422,364	90.3	2.9	143,033	66.2	37.1	154,200	904	10.9	165,141	10.7	4.2
15260	Brunswick-St. Simons, GA	114,530	88.4	7.4	48,281	68.7	55.3	281,800	1,194	8.2	43,310	13.3	5.3
15380	Buffalo-Cheektowaga, NY	1,145,062	89.4	3.9	502,324	66.1	54.8	233,300	1,054	8.7	499,105	14.0	3.8
15500	Burlington, NC	177,309	88.6	7.1	70,911	66.0	58.9	265,200	1,033	7.7	78,215	15.4	3.0
15540	Burlington-South Burlington, VT	225,649	86.9	7.4	96,541	69.6	67.8	400,000	1,604	3.9	102,966	14.7	5.1

Metropolitan area / division code	Metropolitan area / division	Total population 1 year and over	Lived in the same house 1 year ago (percent)	Did not live in the same county 1 year ago (percent)	Total occupied housing units	Owner-occupied units (percent)	Percent with a mortgage, contract to purchase, or similar debt	Median value of owner-occupied units (dollars; owner estimated)	Median gross rent of renter-occupied units paying cash rent	Households without Internet access (percent)	Number of workers who commuted to work	Commute of less than 10 minutes (percent)	Commute of 60 minutes or more (percent)
	ACS table number:	C07204	C07204	C07204	B25003	B25003	B25081	B25097	B25064	S2801	B08012	B08012	B08012
	column number:	1	2	3	4	5	6	7	8	9	10	11	12
15940	Canton-Massillon, OH	395,171	91.5	3.4	168,115	70.4	58.3	189,000	887	9.9	171,933	15.1	5.9
15980	Cape Coral-Fort Myers, FL	826,292	87.1	6.3	326,338	75.2	52.2	391,700	1,797	6.5	296,186	7.8	10.3
16020	Cape Girardeau, MO-IL	97,168	84.0	7.6	39,485	67.1	56.6	215,500	865	8.6	45,485	25.7	3.9
16180	Carson City, NV	57,199	82.2	5.4	24,562	63.3	59.7	455,100	1,322	4.8	25,541	15.3	6.2
16220	Casper, WY	79,548	84.2	6.8	34,332	73.3	58.3	267,300	1,063	7.4	35,523	14.0	7.5
16300	Cedar Rapids, IA	272,430	88.4	4.7	114,563	73.8	62.3	222,200	922	8.6	121,288	19.6	3.6
16540	Chambersburg, PA	156,168	89.9	5.2	62,966	76.4	59.9	248,900	1,095	8.8	66,888	15.8	6.7
16580	Champaign-Urbana, IL	234,421	84.5	8.8	102,205	57.3	60.5	207,400	982	6.5	100,477	16.8	3.0
16620	Charleston, WV	200,886	92.5	3.4	89,395	70.6	44.9	135,800	863	11.7	76,986	11.2	7.5
16700	Charleston-North Charleston, SC	837,914	84.3	9.3	347,045	69.5	65.7	384,800	1,641	6.5	368,151	9.2	8.2
16740	Charlotte-Concord-Gastonia, NC-SC	2,776,280	87.6	7.0	1,103,360	65.4	68.7	381,200	1,505	6.5	1,136,681	9.4	7.2
16820	Charlottesville, VA	223,040	82.6	12.3	92,687	66.6	63.7	431,200	1,540	7.1	91,266	10.2	4.2
16860	Chattanooga, TN-GA	571,615	86.7	6.6	235,003	68.6	56.9	289,700	1,214	7.7	242,094	11.8	4.0
16940	Cheyenne, WY	99,272	86.9	7.4	44,460	67.9	58.1	357,300	1,143	7.7	45,226	17.8	3.5
16980	Chicago-Naperville-Elgin, IL-IN	9,171,705	89.5	4.4	3,671,659	65.9	64.1	316,500	1,390	7.3	3,978,255	9.2	12.2
1698016984	Chicago-Naperville-Schaumburg, IL Metro Division	7,004,044	89.0	4.1	2856546	63.1	63.4	325,200	1,414	7.5	3,031,099	8.5	12.7
1698020994	Elgin, IL Metro Division	748,997	91.2	5.4	271057	76.7	69.1	310,600	1,354	6.3	343,061	10.8	9.6
1698029404	Lake County, IL Metro Division	703,191	90.4	5.6	260243	76.8	63.7	340,400	1,406	5.1	294,659	9.9	9.8
1698029414	Lake County-Porter County-Jasper County, IN Metro Division	715,473	91.1	4.5	283813	74.6	65.6	244,100	1,104	7.8	309,436	12.9	12.5
17020	Chico, CA	205,086	82.6	7.4	86,279	56.5	58.1	420,500	1,434	8.0	83,502	26.4	5.3
17140	Cincinnati, OH-KY-IN	2,247,597	88.5	5.8	921,306	67.4	65.5	270,100	1,101	7.1	987,630	11.1	4.3
17300	Clarksville, TN-KY	331,024	82.8	11.2	129,593	60.0	64.3	275,900	1,271	7.0	141,675	13.8	11.6
17420	Cleveland, OH	2,137,899	89.3	4.0	931,312	68.0	59.5	217,300	1,032	8.6	921,446	12.0	4.1
17460	Cleveland, TN	128,608	86.2	5.8	50,001	68.9	56.1	258,500	964	7.4	50,023	17.7	5.1
17660	Coeur d'Alene, ID	182,201	88.4	7.7	74,253	73.4	63.1	556,500	1,426	7.8	71,065	14.2	5.2
17780	College Station-Bryan, TX	277,438	76.0	13.8	107,713	50.2	54.4	286,900	1,160	12.5	123,008	16.3	5.4
17820	Colorado Springs, CO	760,007	81.4	9.0	311,530	67.3	70.7	472,600	1,706	3.9	335,746	11.7	6.2
17860	Columbia, MO	213,055	81.7	10.2	87,256	58.8	59.2	259,100	1,084	8.4	100,470	18.2	4.0
17900	Columbia, SC	848,674	86.2	8.2	346,000	70.1	63.1	239,600	1,169	8.4	363,533	13.2	5.0
17980	Columbus, GA-AL	325,204	85.6	8.7	131,169	58.4	61.5	195,100	998	12.1	128,874	13.6	4.5
18020	Columbus, IN	83,200	86.6	6.7	33,777	69.8	61.4	253,900	1,169	4.9	37,829	13.1	5.2
18140	Columbus, OH	2,154,021	85.6	5.9	879,910	60.2	68.3	312,900	1,254	5.6	925,444	11.1	4.4
18580	Corpus Christi, TX	440,603	86.4	6.0	170,701	62.3	50.3	213,600	1,228	9.4	NA	NA	NA
18700	Corvallis, OR	97,320	77.9	16.4	38,306	57.5	58.0	538,100	1,368	5.2	40,613	19.6	3.9
18880	Crestview-Fort Walton Beach-Destin, FL	301,488	85.3	8.1	121,976	72.5	56.9	374,300	1,712	5.5	130,791	10.7	10.4
19100	Dallas-Fort Worth-Arlington, TX	8,003,877	85.8	7.0	2,959,385	59.8	62.8	373,900	1,638	5.5	3,487,458	9.5	9.2
1910019124	Dallas-Plano-Irving, TX Metro Division	5,399,007	85.4	7.6	2007420	59.0	63.5	395,400	1,673	5.4	2,321,061	9.7	9.5
1910023104	Fort Worth-Arlington-Grapevine, TX Metro Division	2,604,870	86.6	5.8	951965	61.6	61.2	337,100	1,552	5.9	1,166,397	9.2	8.5
19140	Dalton, GA	143,599	87.9	4.8	52,722	64.2	41.3	224,700	916	12.7	66,254	9.4	6.2
19300	Daphne-Fairhope-Foley, AL	252,103	90.4	5.5	105,698	74.9	57.8	307,000	1,286	8.7	103,319	13.6	7.7
19340	Davenport-Moline-Rock Island, IA-IL	375,961	88.9	4.5	164,230	73.1	60.2	177,100	919	8.6	166,758	17.1	3.3
19380	Dayton-Kettering-Beavercreek, OH	806,951	86.6	6.1	350,659	63.6	62.0	209,800	1,027	7.4	346,557	13.7	3.9
19460	Decatur, AL	156,961	91.4	5.1	64,526	75.3	52.7	213,500	854	11.5	68,384	10.0	4.7
19500	Decatur, IL	99,584	89.6	3.8	43,598	69.2	52.6	115,300	822	8.3	39,396	18.0	5.8
19660	Deltona-Daytona Beach-Ormond Beach, FL	716,857	88.4	7.2	300,081	75.3	55.6	355,000	1,516	6.7	268,113	11.5	11.2
19740	Denver-Aurora-Centennial, CO	2,973,694	83.7	10.0	1,244,895	63.1	72.4	611,300	1,898	5.0	1,310,265	9.4	6.8
19780	Des Moines-West Des Moines, IA	728,456	86.1	6.5	299,784	69.1	67.9	276,600	1,137	7.1	337,366	15.5	3.0
19820	Detroit-Warren-Dearborn, MI	4,296,070	90.1	4.2	1,770,361	72.1	58.3	251,200	1,183	7.1	1,783,524	10.1	6.7
1982019804	Detroit-Dearborn-Livonia, MI Metro Division	1,731,271	89.9	3.6	696332	66.2	50.5	177,300	1,095	9.2	661,890	9.8	5.1
1982047664	Warren-Troy-Farmington Hills, MI Metro Division	2,564,799	90.1	4.7	1074029	75.9	62.7	290,600	1,264	5.7	1,121,634	10.2	7.6
20020	Dothan, AL	152,575	90.7	4.8	62,401	67.1	54.7	170,600	952	12.0	65,897	15.4	4.6
20100	Dover, DE	188,020	86.7	7.7	74,183	73.0	69.1	325,200	1,320	9.7	84,848	10.3	9.7
20220	Dubuque, IA	97,575	87.8	7.2	42,889	74.1	60.8	231,700	868	10.3	46,520	24.7	3.7
20260	Duluth, MN-WI	279,599	88.0	6.1	120,943	72.5	58.6	232,800	993	10.7	126,845	18.7	5.1
20500	Durham-Chapel Hill, NC	602,374	82.9	11.2	253,951	62.8	63.8	414,600	1,532	5.7	256,085	11.9	5.4
20580	Eagle Pass, TX	57,044	89.9	4.5	18,890	67.6	NA	168,100	770	15.3	20,308	16.0	6.1
20740	Eau Claire, WI	173,080	84.3	7.1	72,615	68.4	61.2	265,700	983	6.7	78,850	24.3	4.9
20940	El Centro, CA	175,394	93.0	2.4	50,024	56.2	61.8	331,900	1,022	10.1	58,299	22.2	6.7

Table C-3. Metropolitan Areas — Where: Migration, Housing, and Transportation, 2023—*Continued*

Metropolitan area / division code	Metropolitan area / division	Total population 1 year and over	Lived in the same house 1 year ago (percent)	Did not live in the same county 1 year ago (percent)	Total occupied housing units	Owner-occupied units (percent)	Percent with a mortgage, contract to purchase, or similar debt	Median value of owner-occupied units (dollars; owner estimated)	Median gross rent of renter-occupied units paying cash rent	Households without Internet access (percent)	Number of workers who commuted to work	Commute of less than 10 minutes (percent)	Commute of 60 minutes or more (percent)
	ACS table number:	C07204	C07204	C07204	B25003	B25003	B25081	B25097	B25064	S2801	B08012	B08012	B08012
	column number:	1	2	3	4	5	6	7	8	9	10	11	12
21060	Elizabethtown, KY	128,295	87.6	7.8	51,413	65.2	60.7	231,500	916	5.3	55,187	12.6	6.1
21140	Elkhart-Goshen, IN	203,649	91.5	4.3	73,439	71.5	63.7	214,000	1,079	10.4	95,133	17.5	3.0
21300	Elmira, NY	80,825	92.2	3.2	35,591	70.3	57.6	139,600	1,013	6.7	34,518	23.4	4.9
21340	El Paso, TX	859,485	87.7	4.8	301,927	63.4	51.0	191,000	1,127	10.2	365,335	8.9	5.0
21420	Enid, OK	61,459	80.1	11.4	23,645	61.2	50.5	160,500	943	11.1	28,001	22.9	3.6
21500	Erie, PA	265,200	87.3	4.6	111,118	69.0	54.4	179,200	894	8.8	111,008	18.2	3.4
21660	Eugene-Springfield, OR	377,418	83.5	7.1	162,001	59.6	61.1	438,200	1,373	7.9	152,482	15.7	5.0
21780	Evansville, IN	268,029	86.8	6.9	113,389	69.2	61.8	210,900	947	7.7	121,474	17.5	4.6
21820	Fairbanks-College, AK	94,002	86.9	8.0	37,510	63.8	57.5	285,700	1,503	5.2	46,089	18.3	2.6
22020	Fargo, ND-MN	259,498	80.2	9.0	111,403	55.1	65.1	287,200	989	10.5	131,119	17.2	2.6
22140	Farmington, NM	119,480	93.2	3.5	42,670	72.6	46.2	201,700	965	18.2	45,900	18.3	7.1
22180	Fayetteville, NC	385,623	82.0	10.2	150,658	58.6	65.5	216,900	1,220	6.4	171,794	16.7	5.0
22220	Fayetteville-Springdale-Rogers, AR	582,476	85.4	7.3	224,357	60.8	61.1	342,100	1,223	6.3	265,155	13.2	3.6
22380	Flagstaff, AZ	142,937	79.9	12.5	56,954	60.0	52.2	470,900	1,579	14.0	61,686	24.1	4.2
22420	Flint, MI	397,724	89.2	3.1	164,086	72.0	54.9	181,600	928	9.6	158,078	13.3	11.3
22500	Florence, SC	197,640	91.6	5.5	78,453	66.7	45.1	160,600	957	10.0	79,987	12.5	5.9
22520	Florence-Muscle Shoals, AL	154,077	89.9	5.1	67,774	67.6	52.5	194,700	758	13.5	62,545	16.6	9.7
22540	Fond du Lac, WI	103,161	92.5	4.1	44,262	70.7	57.6	232,900	964	8.2	48,756	25.7	6.7
22660	Fort Collins-Loveland, CO	366,428	84.8	8.9	156,498	63.3	70.3	574,900	1,699	6.4	156,701	15.9	7.4
22900	Fort Smith, AR-OK	228,538	87.2	6.0	90,483	66.0	55.6	181,900	857	12.0	93,757	14.3	5.6
23060	Fort Wayne, IN	452,494	85.9	5.8	186,586	69.4	64.0	222,700	941	8.0	203,109	13.3	3.9
23420	Fresno, CA	1,166,782	90.1	3.6	375,676	59.2	64.3	396,000	1,418	8.9	441,881	12.0	5.9
23460	Gadsden, AL	101,834	88.8	5.4	40,027	74.6	50.7	188,200	760	8.9	38,542	12.6	8.1
23540	Gainesville, FL	347,124	81.1	10.8	146,910	60.1	55.1	279,300	1,317	11.9	143,495	12.0	4.7
23580	Gainesville, GA	214,819	90.1	6.4	76,413	67.3	59.6	357,600	1,360	4.4	89,444	9.2	9.6
23900	Gettysburg, PA	105,794	89.7	5.3	41,810	78.1	62.7	275,300	1,061	10.1	47,933	12.9	13.1
24020	Glens Falls, NY	124,635	91.2	4.1	55,835	73.2	58.9	233,300	988	8.6	54,269	19.1	7.3
24140	Goldsboro, NC	117,273	85.5	7.1	47,035	59.8	55.1	181,800	931	10.1	48,493	13.6	9.5
24220	Grand Forks, ND-MN	101,804	77.2	13.6	44,443	60.4	56.3	243,100	908	10.9	53,965	34.7	3.4
24260	Grand Island, NE	75,344	89.3	4.8	30,614	67.6	63.2	203,200	947	9.1	35,792	25.8	3.3
24300	Grand Junction, CO	157,924	88.9	5.9	68,115	69.4	64.2	373,200	1,184	5.5	62,736	20.1	6.6
24340	Grand Rapids-Wyoming-Kentwood, MI	1,151,536	88.2	5.4	445,882	74.8	61.3	293,500	1,207	7.0	524,360	16.0	4.1
24420	Grants Pass, OR	87,555	91.5	3.2	37,241	73.9	56.2	399,400	1,166	8.5	28,332	23.8	6.4
24500	Great Falls, MT	83,741	84.0	6.3	36,414	68.1	60.7	286,500	959	7.7	37,156	27.5	3.6
24540	Greeley, CO	355,504	86.6	7.2	129,057	74.8	72.8	475,400	1,569	6.0	157,934	13.8	10.7
24580	Green Bay, WI	329,108	88.0	4.4	137,111	68.3	60.9	264,800	1,007	7.6	152,523	13.3	4.8
24660	Greensboro-High Point, NC	779,175	86.0	6.1	321,824	63.8	61.8	244,000	1,103	10.3	335,536	14.8	5.7
24780	Greenville, NC	173,261	81.4	10.1	74,443	53.0	63.2	224,100	1,042	9.4	71,873	13.3	6.2
24860	Greenville-Anderson-Greer, SC	965,183	86.8	7.7	396,589	70.6	58.2	281,800	1,168	8.3	417,834	10.7	5.3
25020	Guayama, PR	NA	NA	NA	27,480	74.7	NA	97,200	479	13.6	19,720	17.3	9.7
25060	Gulfport-Biloxi, MS	416,822	88.3	6.4	174,612	67.8	51.7	204,700	1,034	9.5	179,542	14.3	7.0
25180	Hagerstown-Martinsburg, MD-WV	300,491	88.4	6.3	117,709	71.4	63.3	276,900	1,162	9.3	131,310	10.8	13.7
25220	Hammond, LA	136,887	87.3	6.5	54,627	69.7	55.2	218,300	987	5.9	55,625	11.5	14.4
25260	Hanford-Corcoran, CA	149,870	86.3	8.6	44,262	54.9	71.1	348,800	1,220	9.9	53,851	19.6	4.1
25420	Harrisburg-Carlisle, PA	599,570	88.4	7.5	248,403	68.6	60.2	259,700	1,195	8.4	250,770	14.2	4.6
25500	Harrisonburg, VA	136,686	84.5	9.2	50,113	63.8	59.3	305,200	1,156	13.3	59,550	16.9	4.7
25540	Hartford-West Hartford-East Hartford, CT	1,139,326	89.6	4.6	467,381	66.6	64.0	336,600	1,397	8.1	502,274	12.5	5.4
25620	Hattiesburg, MS	154,433	87.5	6.7	61,290	65.2	52.5	192,000	997	11.4	66,903	14.6	7.2
25740	Helena, MT	93,611	86.6	7.6	38,384	72.1	60.2	400,100	1,088	7.2	39,414	17.7	7.7
25860	Hickory-Lenoir-Morganton, NC	366,045	91.3	5.2	155,168	73.0	54.2	230,400	828	10.0	162,095	12.7	6.9
25940	Hilton Head Island-Bluffton-Port Royal, SC	230,753	86.5	9.2	100,794	75.2	59.1	453,800	1,687	6.3	93,685	16.3	5.7
25980	Hinesville, GA	87,565	81.1	15.2	31,349	58.5	67.4	235,100	1,193	4.4	36,970	19.7	11.7
26140	Homosassa Springs, FL	165,476	89.3	8.2	75,745	82.5	46.1	278,800	1,138	9.2	47,740	9.8	9.8
26300	Hot Springs, AR	99,536	88.1	6.7	45,243	67.0	NA	220,900	944	14.7	37,807	18.7	10.6
26380	Houma-Bayou Cane-Thibodaux, LA	196,791	90.8	4.7	80,596	76.6	44.9	189,600	1,062	10.2	82,656	18.2	9.2
26420	Houston-Pasadena-The Woodlands, TX	7,415,334	86.4	5.8	2,731,843	61.4	58.8	308,200	1,433	6.4	3,177,856	7.6	11.2
26580	Huntington-Ashland, WV-KY-OH	363,717	88.2	5.8	156,188	72.4	48.2	159,700	831	12.3	147,434	15.5	7.2
26620	Huntsville, AL	522,406	86.5	7.3	212,486	70.5	63.8	311,400	1,240	6.5	223,617	10.3	2.8
26820	Idaho Falls, ID	166,162	90.9	5.2	56,728	73.0	61.3	386,100	1,186	4.7	70,223	20.9	9.4
26900	Indianapolis-Carmel-Greenwood, IN	2,112,452	87.1	6.4	862,092	67.2	69.0	278,200	1,207	6.8	935,820	11.6	5.5

Table C-3. Metropolitan Areas — Where: Migration, Housing, and Transportation, 2023—*Continued*

Metropolitan area / division code	Metropolitan area / division	Total population 1 year and over	Lived in the same house 1 year ago (percent)	Did not live in the same county 1 year ago (percent)	Total occupied housing units	Owner-occupied units (percent)	Percent with a mortgage, contract to purchase, or similar debt	Median value of owner-occupied units (dollars; owner estimated)	Median gross rent of renter-occupied units paying cash rent	Households without Internet access (percent)	Number of workers who commuted to work	Commute of less than 10 minutes (percent)	Commute of 60 minutes or more (percent)
	ACS table number:	C07204	C07204	C07204	B25003	B25003	B25081	B25097	B25064	S2801	B08012	B08012	B08012
	column number:	1	2	3	4	5	6	7	8	9	10	11	12
26980	Iowa City, IA	177,869	77.3	11.0	73,376	60.8	60.7	298,700	1,072	10.0	85,966	17.2	3.4
27060	Ithaca, NY	102,361	72.5	21.3	43,054	55.1	48.9	263,100	1,383	8.8	41,736	16.5	6.0
27100	Jackson, MI	158,251	88.2	5.7	61,851	76.8	58.9	203,700	964	6.0	62,539	15.5	5.3
27140	Jackson, MS	603,542	88.1	6.7	240,218	67.9	55.7	211,000	1,023	9.6	255,869	9.0	4.6
27180	Jackson, TN	180,554	86.0	7.6	73,444	64.2	55.5	199,800	1,002	8.9	73,420	18.7	8.2
27260	Jacksonville, FL	1,693,716	84.5	8.3	693,081	66.7	64.0	361,800	1,564	6.5	671,416	9.0	5.4
27340	Jacksonville, NC	208,726	80.4	12.4	76,788	61.9	73.4	253,100	1,261	5.7	94,326	21.1	5.8
27500	Janesville-Beloit, WI	162,507	89.6	5.9	66,220	70.5	62.1	247,500	973	7.5	72,788	16.1	8.2
27620	Jefferson City, MO	148,622	90.0	5.4	59,911	71.1	55.9	212,600	792	9.6	65,633	20.4	5.1
27740	Johnson City, TN	211,609	86.0	8.2	91,198	69.9	50.6	239,400	934	10.2	81,672	15.0	5.1
27780	Johnstown, PA	129,635	91.8	4.3	57,282	76.5	45.2	121,800	725	13.0	51,971	17.8	4.6
27860	Jonesboro, AR	134,505	82.5	8.4	56,301	58.6	59.8	181,800	940	10.6	57,262	20.9	3.4
27900	Joplin, MO-KS	202,697	81.8	9.0	83,470	67.2	54.9	169,600	890	10.6	88,521	21.4	4.5
27980	Kahului-Wailuku, HI	163,351	90.5	5.3	56,848	63.1	62.9	934,500	1,828	7.5	71,532	14.7	5.8
28020	Kalamazoo-Portage, MI	259,332	87.2	5.4	107,893	61.7	60.1	251,200	1,058	6.9	117,564	16.5	3.5
28100	Kankakee, IL	104,788	92.7	4.6	41,130	70.8	55.7	182,900	1,058	12.2	44,867	17.7	10.7
28140	Kansas City, MO-KS	2,194,249	87.9	5.8	906,504	66.1	63.6	289,200	1,240	6.7	968,742	11.8	3.8
28420	Kennewick-Richland, WA	310,499	89.2	5.3	109,481	69.0	63.9	416,600	1,298	7.3	123,349	13.1	4.4
28450	Kenosha, WI	166,244	89.9	5.9	69,907	66.5	67.4	265,500	1,212	5.3	80,162	15.2	7.0
28660	Killeen-Temple, TX	492,577	80.5	10.1	182,336	60.0	60.3	251,000	1,301	7.8	209,971	15.1	10.3
28700	Kingsport-Bristol, TN-VA	308,516	90.2	6.7	132,975	76.6	48.8	208,100	810	13.6	119,190	15.3	6.1
28740	Kingston, NY	180,859	89.1	5.9	73,895	72.4	54.4	373,400	1,363	6.7	71,784	13.4	8.2
28880	Kiryas Joel-Poughkeepsie-Newburgh, NY	696,067	91.0	4.5	254,385	69.2	62.5	393,400	1,610	8.0	291,257	12.9	16.8
28940	Knoxville, TN	939,118	88.5	6.4	380,978	71.2	56.8	320,700	1,170	9.8	394,934	10.3	5.1
29020	Kokomo, IN	83,112	85.4	6.6	35,551	67.3	64.6	169,300	949	8.9	34,161	23.5	6.6
29100	La Crosse-Onalaska, WI-MN	168,408	87.1	6.4	72,276	68.0	53.2	265,200	970	9.8	79,969	21.2	3.1
29180	Lafayette, LA	408,097	89.8	4.7	166,896	67.9	51.0	219,700	946	8.7	178,092	14.6	6.5
29200	Lafayette-West Lafayette, IN	224,303	78.7	12.3	91,594	59.1	62.3	235,300	1,100	8.3	102,431	14.0	3.5
29340	Lake Charles, LA	237,698	88.6	4.2	93,049	73.1	48.1	215,900	1,057	13.8	101,141	16.1	5.7
29420	Lake Havasu City-Kingman, AZ	221,742	86.9	6.4	98,791	75.0	51.3	293,800	1,077	10.0	67,490	20.7	6.2
29460	Lakeland-Winter Haven, FL	807,890	87.3	6.9	306,915	71.4	55.4	296,300	1,403	8.9	319,338	7.8	13.9
29540	Lancaster, PA	551,869	88.8	5.1	211,669	68.9	58.4	306,900	1,329	10.9	246,992	15.8	5.5
29620	Lansing-East Lansing, MI	469,479	85.0	9.3	194,031	67.4	63.6	219,100	1,042	8.2	203,278	15.4	6.3
29700	Laredo, TX	265,082	90.4	1.5	83,045	65.3	54.1	200,800	990	9.7	108,694	10.5	5.7
29740	Las Cruces, NM	223,005	84.1	8.5	87,688	66.3	53.3	228,000	933	7.6	90,716	15.6	5.9
29820	Las Vegas-Henderson-North Las Vegas, NV	2,311,988	84.9	5.4	880,604	57.8	66.5	437,900	1,654	5.8	996,328	7.5	5.3
29940	Lawrence, KS	119,666	75.7	13.7	51,013	48.9	65.9	305,600	1,056	5.6	52,364	21.8	3.9
30020	Lawton, OK	125,739	79.9	11.5	48,105	58.3	54.6	158,500	984	9.9	50,079	23.5	4.0
30140	Lebanon, PA	141,808	89.5	5.8	58,012	71.1	55.8	235,400	1,186	10.8	64,153	16.5	4.5
30300	Lewiston, ID-WA	64,188	83.5	9.0	26,723	69.3	55.7	332,400	1,105	12.0	25,756	22.9	4.9
30340	Lewiston-Auburn, ME	112,436	88.4	3.5	48,239	66.0	61.5	263,000	997	8.2	49,811	16.2	5.7
30460	Lexington-Fayette, KY	514,004	82.7	8.1	222,167	60.9	65.8	289,200	1,117	7.9	235,331	14.6	4.8
30500	Lexington Park, MD	208,356	88.7	7.3	76,869	78.9	73.8	434,200	1,718	6.7	94,288	8.3	19.0
30620	Lima, OH	99,813	88.1	5.2	42,147	68.0	54.9	179,800	941	9.9	44,506	23.5	3.4
30700	Lincoln, NE	340,320	83.8	6.2	144,767	58.1	62.5	277,300	1,018	6.6	162,603	18.6	3.5
30780	Little Rock-North Little Rock-Conway, AR	757,402	89.6	5.4	310,926	65.2	61.3	220,700	1,031	8.7	319,097	12.3	4.2
30860	Logan, UT-ID	154,509	83.2	9.1	51,478	61.9	68.3	466,900	1,253	6.1	66,850	25.3	5.3
30980	Longview, TX	289,748	86.8	7.1	108,309	69.3	49.1	192,100	1,050	12.7	121,532	15.4	7.2
31020	Longview-Kelso, WA	111,733	86.6	6.9	44,694	68.5	62.9	405,400	1,176	7.0	45,163	18.4	8.4
31080	Los Angeles-Long Beach-Anaheim, CA	12,674,805	90.7	3.1	4,542,998	48.2	67.9	867,200	1,993	5.5	5,388,495	7.1	12.0
3108011244	Anaheim-Santa Ana-Irvine, CA Metro Division	3,104,970	90.1	3.8	1092528	57.0	66.3	961,400	2,382	4.2	1,334,808	7.5	8.4
3108031084	Los Angeles-Long Beach-Glendale, CA Metro Division	9,569,835	91.0	2.9	3450470	45.4	68.5	828,700	1,896	5.8	4,053,687	7.0	13.2
31140	Louisville/Jefferson County, KY-IN	1,349,589	88.1	5.4	563,933	69.7	63.4	253,600	1,083	8.5	579,183	10.8	4.8
31180	Lubbock, TX	355,583	80.3	8.4	143,229	54.4	48.9	204,500	1,149	9.6	165,286	18.8	3.8
31340	Lynchburg, VA	263,563	86.6	9.1	104,544	71.9	59.3	248,600	973	9.7	108,360	12.7	5.8
31420	Macon-Bibb County, GA	230,777	87.3	6.2	89,842	59.6	56.2	195,600	1,022	12.0	87,411	10.5	7.2
31540	Madison, WI	689,486	83.1	7.1	308,244	58.7	65.2	372,700	1,335	7.5	320,553	14.7	3.4
31700	Manchester-Nashua, NH	422,992	89.3	4.2	170,761	68.2	67.3	430,300	1,668	4.9	200,278	11.4	10.5
31740	Manhattan, KS	131,010	78.1	14.2	51,764	50.9	58.5	220,400	1,059	7.1	65,860	29.5	5.3

Table C-3. Metropolitan Areas — Where: Migration, Housing, and Transportation, 2023—*Continued*

Metropolitan area / division code	Metropolitan area / division	Total population 1 year and over	Lived in the same house 1 year ago (percent)	Did not live in the same county 1 year ago (percent)	Total occupied housing units	Owner-occupied units (percent)	Percent with a mortgage, contract to purchase, or similar debt	Median value of owner-occupied units (dollars; owner estimated)	Median gross rent of renter-occupied units paying cash rent	Households without Internet access (percent)	Number of workers who commuted to work	Commute of less than 10 minutes (percent)	Commute of 60 minutes or more (percent)
	ACS table number:	C07204	C07204	C07204	B25003	B25003	B25081	B25097	B25064	S2801	B08012	B08012	B08012
	column number:	1	2	3	4	5	6	7	8	9	10	11	12
31860	Mankato, MN	102,808	82.3	10.8	40,152	63.2	58.5	279,600	1,014	14.2	50,057	26.5	3.9
31900	Mansfield, OH	123,880	88.3	5.9	51,046	70.2	52.1	176,800	808	10.1	50,070	20.5	8.9
32420	Mayagüez, PR	NA	NA	NA	83,931	64.4	NA	109,600	468	16.7	59,805	11.0	5.6
32580	McAllen-Edinburg-Mission, TX	885,868	90.8	2.6	277,001	66.5	38.3	151,200	936	9.8	331,794	15.3	4.4
32780	Medford, OR	219,560	86.6	5.7	92,225	66.7	61.1	431,500	1,419	7.2	86,531	20.3	3.0
32820	Memphis, TN-MS-AR	1,318,807	88.4	4.7	523,295	60.7	62.2	265,200	1,200	8.6	564,797	9.8	4.1
32900	Merced, CA	287,778	91.2	3.9	88,053	52.6	62.7	409,000	1,294	15.7	110,084	16.5	18.7
33100	Miami-Fort Lauderdale-West Palm Beach, FL	6,118,390	87.0	5.8	2,349,920	61.8	56.2	474,000	1,914	7.4	2,643,227	6.8	10.4
3310022744	Fort Lauderdale-Pompano Beach-Sunrise, FL Metro Division	1,940,270	86.6	6.5	758853	63.9	58.1	439,100	1,961	6.5	856,311	7.0	10.7
3310033124	Miami-Miami Beach-Kendall, FL Metro Division	2,659,522	87.2	5.1	985935	54.0	57.3	488,600	1,864	7.9	1,172,869	5.6	11.9
3310048424	West Palm Beach-Boca Raton-Delray Beach, FL Metro Division	1,518,598	87.0	6.3	605132	71.8	52.8	491,500	1,982	7.6	614,047	8.6	7.3
33140	Michigan City-La Porte, IN	110,174	89.6	5.8	45,725	74.3	59.6	196,300	994	11.6	44,010	16.9	8.9
33220	Midland, MI	83,105	91.9	4.5	35,761	77.4	56.9	195,900	894	9.8	34,489	18.9	5.4
33260	Midland, TX	179,487	85.7	6.5	73,012	66.3	58.2	311,700	1,326	8.5	87,238	13.7	4.5
33340	Milwaukee-Waukesha, WI	1,544,618	89.3	4.6	650,986	61.2	64.9	308,100	1,122	7.2	679,939	12.4	4.1
33460	Minneapolis-St. Paul-Bloomington, MN-WI	3,669,532	88.3	6.5	1,501,453	70.2	68.9	369,500	1,427	5.9	1,618,919	11.4	4.3
33500	Minot, ND	74,925	84.7	7.2	31,532	62.7	57.0	237,800	985	11.1	36,388	26.5	6.5
33540	Missoula, MT	125,051	85.0	7.6	56,810	60.6	60.4	487,700	1,166	6.1	58,513	14.5	6.2
33660	Mobile, AL	408,985	90.3	3.7	163,963	66.8	54.1	191,600	1,022	8.8	165,436	10.5	4.7
33700	Modesto, CA	544,477	90.8	3.2	179,152	61.1	65.1	456,700	1,595	5.8	224,795	14.4	14.5
33740	Monroe, LA	219,597	87.3	4.4	87,927	65.5	50.3	175,700	936	18.8	85,010	11.9	6.9
33780	Monroe, MI	153,428	90.1	4.6	62,936	80.8	61.1	245,000	983	8.4	67,410	10.2	6.3
33860	Montgomery, AL	381,652	87.2	6.0	153,926	65.3	57.8	193,200	1,018	7.5	156,732	10.6	3.8
34060	Morgantown, WV	140,949	82.0	8.6	57,621	63.4	49.4	235,000	903	10.6	63,084	13.6	7.7
34100	Morristown, TN	122,788	90.5	7.2	49,910	74.3	40.3	247,800	903	10.5	52,680	11.1	9.2
34580	Mount Vernon-Anacortes, WA	130,236	88.5	6.1	53,087	70.5	60.5	558,300	1,667	5.6	52,835	16.4	11.8
34620	Muncie, IN	111,125	81.2	10.0	44,361	65.8	56.7	139,700	878	11.6	51,919	19.6	10.2
34740	Muskegon-Norton Shores, MI	175,708	89.5	4.7	70,042	81.2	56.6	208,700	1,003	7.4	74,657	16.1	5.0
34820	Myrtle Beach-Conway-North Myrtle Beach, SC	395,640	85.6	8.0	168,080	78.7	55.7	316,800	1,265	6.2	150,836	14.7	4.8
34900	Napa, CA	132,017	89.1	5.1	51,167	62.7	63.8	831,800	2,239	5.9	59,158	19.7	8.4
34940	Naples-Marco Island, FL	401,279	88.3	6.8	166,192	77.2	48.4	595,500	2,039	6.7	137,956	11.9	6.8
34980	Nashville-Davidson--Murfreesboro--Franklin, TN	2,079,619	86.2	7.1	863,464	65.0	66.6	437,200	1,566	6.4	928,801	9.4	8.8
35300	New Haven, CT	561,487	86.5	6.5	233,004	58.8	63.6	349,200	1,471	6.7	251,695	14.5	7.0
35380	New Orleans-Metairie, LA	952,269	89.6	4.8	399,198	63.1	54.2	263,500	1,159	9.5	399,035	11.6	5.9
35620	New York-Newark-Jersey City, NY-NJ	19,284,561	91.2	4.0	7,490,498	51.1	61.0	610,200	1,764	6.7	8,317,168	7.4	20.6
3562029484	Lakewood-New Brunswick, NJ Metro Division	2,488,755	91.2	4.8	941969	72.2	62.5	495,900	1,799	6.3	1,047,127	10.6	16.6
3562035004	Nassau County-Suffolk County, NY Metro Division	2,877,254	93.7	3.1	966971	81.2	62.1	629,100	2,130	4.8	1,272,463	10.1	18.9
3562035084	Newark, NJ Metro Division	2,191,017	91.0	4.9	831608	60.9	66.8	513,800	1,619	4.7	972,776	8.2	17.5
3562035614	New York-Jersey City-White Plains, NY-NJ Metro Division	11,727,535	90.6	4.0	4749950	39.0	58.4	668,400	1,761	7.6	5,024,802	5.9	22.5
35660	Niles, MI	151,264	89.8	5.2	65,129	73.7	54.0	237,900	936	9.2	61,509	23.8	3.9
35840	North Port-Bradenton-Sarasota, FL	904,647	84.4	9.4	408,101	75.6	48.5	438,600	1,854	6.1	325,094	10.6	8.0
35980	Norwich-New London-Willimantic, CT	277,050	87.5	6.5	114,156	64.8	56.9	323,700	1,348	8.7	123,616	15.1	5.1
36100	Ocala, FL	405,722	86.9	8.7	171,369	77.6	47.6	265,100	1,365	7.6	142,091	9.3	6.3
36220	Odessa, TX	162,991	86.1	4.8	66,937	64.7	46.5	196,500	1,169	14.9	77,709	12.3	7.4
36260	Ogden, UT	650,506	89.9	5.6	220,388	76.6	68.9	487,400	1,528	5.4	286,748	14.1	4.9
36420	Oklahoma City, OK	1,461,254	84.7	6.8	581,140	62.4	59.0	244,000	1,140	7.5	638,993	12.5	4.3
36500	Olympia-Lacey-Tumwater, WA	296,425	84.5	7.7	119,786	66.5	65.6	493,100	1,776	5.7	115,681	12.3	7.7
36540	Omaha, NE-IA	973,569	86.9	6.8	397,769	66.1	66.3	278,300	1,168	6.9	449,426	13.2	3.1
36740	Orlando-Kissimmee-Sanford, FL	2,791,258	85.5	8.4	1,073,662	62.4	63.3	383,100	1,799	6.1	1,167,007	6.8	8.6
36780	Oshkosh-Neenah, WI	170,513	86.3	8.1	71,563	66.2	58.6	222,400	929	7.1	81,523	20.6	3.8
36980	Owensboro, KY	110,882	89.0	3.0	45,814	64.2	55.8	195,700	883	10.3	51,990	18.0	3.1
37100	Oxnard-Thousand Oaks-Ventura, CA	821,563	90.8	4.3	283,718	63.4	66.6	820,300	2,264	4.5	343,832	11.7	9.1
37140	Paducah, KY-IL	101,445	91.8	4.0	43,021	70.3	52.6	157,600	754	13.9	44,713	18.3	2.7
37340	Palm Bay-Melbourne-Titusville, FL	639,082	88.1	6.3	258,656	76.7	53.9	356,600	1,648	5.6	248,914	10.7	4.8
37460	Panama City-Panama City Beach, FL	214,368	84.2	8.9	89,699	70.3	54.6	313,100	1,506	5.9	94,980	15.6	5.8

Table C-3. Metropolitan Areas — Where: Migration, Housing, and Transportation, 2023—*Continued*

Metropolitan area / division code	Metropolitan area / division	Total population 1 year and over	Lived in the same house 1 year ago (percent)	Did not live in the same county 1 year ago (percent)	Total occupied housing units	Owner-occupied units (percent)	Percent with a mortgage, contract to purchase, or similar debt	Median value of owner-occupied units (dollars; owner estimated)	Median gross rent of renter-occupied units paying cash rent	Households without Internet access (percent)	Number of workers who commuted to work	Commute of less than 10 minutes (percent)	Commute of 60 minutes or more (percent)
	ACS table number:	C07204	C07204	C07204	B25003	B25003	B25081	B25097	B25064	S2801	B08012	B08012	B08012
	column number:	1	2	3	4	5	6	7	8	9	10	11	12
37620	Parkersburg-Vienna, WV	86,841	89.7	3.6	38,866	74.7	47.4	162,300	735	14.3	35,187	12.1	4.6
37860	Pensacola-Ferry Pass-Brent, FL	524,078	84.3	9.9	204,344	72.5	61.8	308,600	1,374	5.3	216,083	10.3	7.5
37900	Peoria, IL	358,260	90.2	5.4	153,577	74.5	53.8	160,600	899	10.0	152,016	20.9	3.0
37980	Philadelphia-Camden-Wilmington, PA-NJ-DE-MD	6,179,067	89.4	5.3	2,484,152	67.2	63.6	356,700	1,456	6.3	2,604,278	9.9	10.5
3798015804	Camden, NJ Metro Division	1,290,655	89.8	6.0	494538	73.1	65.9	324,800	1,478	5.4	568,659	10.5	11.1
3798033874	Montgomery County-Bucks County-Chester County, PA Metro Division	2,045,464	91.6	4.6	793082	74.1	64.0	458,400	1,667	4.8	860,234	11.6	10.1
3798037964	Philadelphia, PA Metro Division	2,100,111	87.2	5.5	903757	56.5	60.3	267,200	1,375	7.9	854,999	8.1	11.0
3798048864	Wilmington, DE-MD-NJ Metro Division	742,837	88.9	5.7	292775	71.3	66.3	344,700	1,365	6.5	320,386	9.4	9.6
38060	Phoenix-Mesa-Chandler, AZ	5,021,885	86.3	5.3	1,922,068	66.9	65.6	457,400	1,760	6.2	2,004,889	10.0	6.8
38420	Pinehurst-Southern Pines, NC	105,416	89.8	6.5	46,385	75.6	56.7	369,100	1,342	5.8	39,900	9.5	7.2
38300	Pittsburgh, PA	2,399,000	89.6	4.3	1,067,180	71.3	54.8	218,300	1,044	8.5	1,018,500	12.3	6.8
38340	Pittsfield, MA	126,384	90.2	4.0	58,807	68.8	58.9	298,200	1,074	6.3	54,626	19.2	6.1
38540	Pocatello, ID	89,653	81.9	7.5	33,729	69.5	58.8	341,800	1,068	10.3	35,883	25.4	7.4
38660	Ponce, PR	NA	NA	NA	105,603	67.3	NA	98,200	502	8.6	84,553	10.9	8.7
38860	Portland-South Portland, ME	562,504	89.9	5.9	244,997	73.4	61.7	444,600	1,551	6.7	251,263	13.6	5.4
38900	Portland-Vancouver-Hillsboro, OR-WA	2,483,388	86.5	6.8	1,028,651	62.1	69.8	560,900	1,670	5.1	1,034,502	12.0	6.7
38940	Port St. Lucie, FL	532,658	90.4	5.8	214,904	78.6	52.2	385,700	1,679	7.8	198,750	5.8	9.5
39140	Prescott Valley-Prescott, AZ	247,437	84.6	8.4	113,784	75.9	52.8	454,200	1,442	9.2	79,943	19.4	6.6
39300	Providence-Warwick, RI-MA	1,662,142	89.2	5.4	677,970	63.2	65.5	430,200	1,330	7.4	751,356	12.4	9.6
39340	Provo-Orem-Lehi, UT	719,554	83.3	7.2	219,263	67.7	72.3	566,900	1,556	6.2	300,938	17.3	6.9
39380	Pueblo, CO	167,576	89.5	5.9	68,732	71.3	68.3	313,700	1,165	7.6	67,504	13.7	4.6
39460	Punta Gorda, FL	205,423	90.9	5.8	90,367	83.7	45.6	365,900	1,520	8.4	62,385	9.2	13.8
39540	Racine-Mount Pleasant, WI	194,112	92.4	3.2	79,066	72.5	65.7	253,200	1,038	7.2	86,939	13.4	5.2
39580	Raleigh-Cary, NC	1,493,628	86.4	7.4	600,306	66.2	72.0	439,500	1,605	5.4	601,918	8.9	6.6
39660	Rapid City, SD	155,389	84.4	8.6	65,028	69.9	58.8	321,600	1,125	5.7	70,829	17.2	5.6
39740	Reading, PA	427,956	90.7	4.6	163,307	72.1	60.4	261,200	1,219	7.7	187,744	13.2	7.8
39820	Redding, CA	178,077	89.0	4.8	72,320	68.0	64.4	355,100	1,351	7.6	66,894	18.4	3.7
39900	Reno, NV	557,117	86.4	5.4	227,132	64.3	63.0	509,700	1,615	5.7	252,135	11.3	5.0
40060	Richmond, VA	1,335,318	86.0	9.4	536,542	67.6	68.1	357,600	1,491	6.5	579,133	9.9	5.4
40140	Riverside-San Bernardino-Ontario, CA	4,635,651	90.7	4.2	1,474,564	66.2	68.6	552,000	1,850	5.9	1,881,728	9.0	17.7
40220	Roanoke, VA	310,456	91.3	6.1	134,105	68.2	60.0	258,300	1,087	12.0	126,094	13.0	3.1
40340	Rochester, MN	225,981	88.7	7.2	92,141	74.7	62.8	308,900	1,271	7.1	101,053	17.1	4.7
40380	Rochester, NY	1,042,517	87.1	6.2	446,704	67.4	59.6	207,100	1,138	8.8	445,726	15.7	3.5
40420	Rockford, IL	330,924	87.9	4.4	135,255	67.5	57.2	169,500	991	8.2	140,374	13.1	6.8
40580	Rocky Mount, NC	143,383	91.8	4.7	59,997	58.7	52.0	187,500	884	16.1	58,228	12.3	7.3
40660	Rome, GA	99,224	87.9	7.1	37,835	63.3	51.4	221,100	993	13.3	41,134	15.8	8.7
40900	Sacramento-Roseville-Folsom, CA	2,395,971	88.3	6.0	888,619	63.6	68.9	587,600	1,800	5.6	927,225	10.7	7.9
40980	Saginaw, MI	186,038	90.8	4.2	77,158	76.6	49.8	146,400	917	10.1	74,617	14.5	5.9
41060	St. Cloud, MN	200,062	85.8	8.7	77,652	67.9	57.7	287,600	1,038	9.8	93,971	17.2	7.6
41100	St. George, UT	199,382	87.8	6.1	72,315	73.0	59.2	528,100	1,624	5.9	79,021	18.9	3.0
41140	St. Joseph, MO-KS	117,749	90.1	4.5	47,529	70.0	51.6	172,000	898	12.3	50,461	18.7	7.4
41180	St. Louis, MO-IL	2,762,895	89.5	4.8	1,179,884	71.0	63.6	247,900	1,102	7.0	1,228,194	11.5	5.2
41420	Salem, OR	432,262	86.9	5.6	162,200	61.8	63.6	437,200	1,391	7.3	177,393	16.7	8.0
41500	Salinas, CA	426,437	89.8	4.6	132,170	53.0	62.3	759,100	2,004	5.7	172,408	10.0	8.6
41540	Salisbury, MD	128,608	88.2	7.7	48,542	60.8	61.0	248,500	1,270	8.0	55,223	16.9	6.4
41620	Salt Lake City-Murray, UT	1,256,301	85.3	5.4	460,977	66.4	69.6	547,500	1,639	5.1	556,332	9.8	4.1
41660	San Angelo, TX	117,861	82.5	7.2	48,119	59.1	NA	199,000	1,127	10.9	54,077	19.9	6.0
41700	San Antonio-New Braunfels, TX	2,672,642	84.4	6.5	986,961	64.3	60.2	292,700	1,342	6.6	1,114,952	8.9	7.8
41740	San Diego-Chula Vista-Carlsbad, CA	3,230,012	87.4	5.1	1,181,259	54.5	68.9	864,900	2,296	4.9	1,407,306	9.1	6.3
41780	Sandusky, OH	112,939	92.6	4.4	53,716	75.2	49.1	206,800	886	8.0	50,212	19.0	6.5
41860	San Francisco-Oakland-Fremont, CA	4,520,819	88.4	5.9	1,763,465	55.3	67.7	1,105,100	2,397	4.9	1,864,429	6.8	14.9
4186036084	Oakland-Fremont-Berkeley, CA Metro Division	2,747,394	89.2	5.4	1024706	59.9	70.0	951,600	2,307	4.6	1,118,907	7.1	18.3
4186041884	San Francisco-San Mateo-Redwood City, CA Metro Division	1,521,118	86.6	6.9	637151	46.3	63.8	1,424,900	2,526	5.5	656,066	5.8	9.5
4186042034	San Rafael, CA Metro Division	252,307	90.4	5.8	101608	65.6	64.3	1,512,200	2,614	3.7	89,456	11.0	12.4
41940	San Jose-Sunnyvale-Santa Clara, CA	1,924,453	86.3	6.0	685,743	54.6	65.7	1,393,400	2,773	3.9	850,851	6.5	8.4
41980	San Juan-Bayamón-Caguas, PR	NA	NA	NA	827,522	68.4	42.2	145,000	592	14.0	740,590	7.5	12.8
42020	San Luis Obispo-Paso Robles, CA	279,754	83.2	7.1	110,283	62.5	64.0	817,600	1,922	5.0	112,983	21.1	4.9
42100	Santa Cruz-Watsonville, CA	259,146	84.6	7.2	99,069	60.1	62.0	1,011,300	2,055	4.9	106,755	13.2	11.2
42140	Santa Fe, NM	154,880	91.8	5.7	71,322	68.8	53.1	485,300	1,254	7.3	60,618	13.9	5.0

Table C-3. Metropolitan Areas — Where: Migration, Housing, and Transportation, 2023—*Continued*

Metropolitan area / division code	Metropolitan area / division	Total population 1 year and over	Lived in the same house 1 year ago (percent)	Did not live in the same county 1 year ago (percent)	Total occupied housing units	Owner-occupied units (percent)	Percent with a mortgage, contract to purchase, or similar debt	Median value of owner-occupied units (dollars; owner estimated)	Median gross rent of renter-occupied units paying cash rent	Households without Internet access (percent)	Number of workers who commuted to work	Commute of less than 10 minutes (percent)	Commute of 60 minutes or more (percent)
	ACS table number:	C07204	C07204	C07204	B25003	B25003	B25081	B25097	B25064	S2801	B08012	B08012	B08012
	column number:	1	2	3	4	5	6	7	8	9	10	11	12
42200	Santa Maria-Santa Barbara, CA	437,404	85.7	6.7	150,932	50.8	60.4	780,700	1,988	7.1	174,805	18.1	5.9
42220	Santa Rosa-Petaluma, CA	477,288	88.8	4.4	192,765	64.6	67.5	784,900	2,061	5.0	208,012	13.5	9.0
42340	Savannah, GA	420,467	82.9	10.2	165,394	62.4	64.0	318,400	1,482	5.6	181,886	9.4	5.6
42540	Scranton--Wilkes-Barre, PA	563,941	87.7	5.5	236,141	67.4	51.1	189,500	1,057	NA	233,933	15.7	4.4
42660	Seattle-Tacoma-Bellevue, WA	4,000,929	84.6	6.6	1,627,693	59.8	69.4	712,200	1,965	4.5	1,709,231	8.8	10.7
4266021794	Everett, WA Metro Division	835,909	86.6	6.6	321,835	67.5	71.1	697,700	1,911	5.0	356,193	9.2	13.2
4266042644	Seattle-Bellevue-Kent, WA Metro Division	2,248,046	83.5	6.8	949,792	55.6	68.0	848,300	2,043	4.2	953,105	8.3	8.0
4266045104	Tacoma-Lakewood, WA Metro Division	916,974	85.4	6.2	356,066	64.3	71.2	538,000	1,802	4.9	399,933	9.6	14.7
42680	Sebastian-Vero Beach-West Vero Corridor, FL	169,236	91.1	4.6	72,833	79.8	44.9	370,600	1,409	9.7	60,173	14.1	4.8
42700	Sebring, FL	106,910	85.1	9.8	47,278	80.1	37.2	208,900	1,073	10.3	32,375	12.2	8.0
43100	Sheboygan, WI	116,939	89.5	5.3	49,852	71.1	61.0	239,700	895	7.7	54,653	19.3	5.0
43300	Sherman-Denison, TX	145,720	82.5	9.9	56,267	66.1	47.6	281,700	1,325	9.1	57,099	20.0	12.2
43340	Shreveport-Bossier City, LA	380,236	89.2	4.6	164,006	65.6	53.5	181,600	1,029	13.8	156,335	13.9	4.3
43420	Sierra Vista-Douglas, AZ	123,587	84.2	9.3	50,919	69.3	47.0	235,200	988	12.1	39,760	21.7	9.9
43580	Sioux City, IA-NE-SD	142,075	90.5	4.8	55,198	67.2	56.5	192,000	1,019	8.8	64,947	21.6	3.2
43620	Sioux Falls, SD-MN	299,104	89.5	4.8	126,616	68.0	64.4	307,600	988	5.8	150,964	15.4	3.8
43640	Slidell-Mandeville-Covington, LA	272,599	89.1	5.1	106,164	78.7	65.8	286,500	1,259	5.7	116,420	9.4	14.0
43780	South Bend-Mishawaka, IN-MI	320,346	88.5	6.0	128,897	71.1	60.7	201,800	1,058	7.7	138,234	14.6	3.8
43900	Spartanburg, SC	379,292	88.2	6.0	146,672	72.4	59.2	233,400	1,006	10.4	163,818	11.4	5.3
44060	Spokane-Spokane Valley, WA	593,072	85.8	5.4	239,251	65.4	63.7	417,000	1,279	8.4	238,960	12.4	5.0
44100	Springfield, IL	203,719	89.3	4.2	91,114	70.9	54.5	177,200	952	5.2	85,242	12.8	3.2
44140	Springfield, MA	456,958	91.6	3.4	184,698	62.3	62.0	302,100	1,136	10.1	197,593	12.5	4.9
44180	Springfield, MO	486,429	85.3	7.6	200,832	63.8	61.6	242,200	984	12.0	214,168	12.9	3.6
44220	Springfield, OH	133,157	88.2	5.0	55,322	68.4	60.3	173,800	785	10.2	52,191	14.3	7.1
44300	State College, PA	156,545	78.3	14.2	62,175	59.0	56.6	322,900	1,198	11.0	63,398	15.7	2.9
44420	Staunton-Stuarts Draft, VA	125,903	89.5	6.9	54,483	72.3	58.0	273,100	1,083	12.7	54,398	18.2	4.8
44700	Stockton-Lodi, CA	792,319	89.9	5.4	251,091	63.2	67.8	531,500	1,655	6.5	323,133	11.7	20.7
44940	Sumter, SC	102,526	88.7	5.7	40,059	66.8	51.9	190,400	931	12.4	41,564	9.1	6.0
45060	Syracuse, NY	645,650	85.9	7.0	273,464	68.8	57.5	189,400	1,067	8.1	280,374	15.0	5.0
45220	Tallahassee, FL	390,437	81.8	9.1	163,838	56.2	59.8	289,200	1,238	11.1	169,004	10.8	4.0
45300	Tampa-St. Petersburg-Clearwater, FL	3,313,445	86.0	7.5	1,358,788	67.9	57.1	372,100	1,729	6.2	1,295,172	9.3	10.3
4530041304	St. Petersburg-Clearwater-Largo, FL Metro Division	954,290	86.9	6.6	439,896	69.2	49.4	382,400	1,776	7.5	375,152	10.7	8.0
4530045294	Tampa, FL Metro Division	2,359,155	85.6	7.9	918,892	67.2	60.9	368,000	1,707	5.5	920,020	8.8	11.2
45460	Terre Haute, IN	165,422	84.2	7.3	67,572	67.6	58.8	139,800	879	13.2	68,166	19.3	5.4
45500	Texarkana, TX-AR	144,693	90.7	4.2	59,815	65.2	48.1	150,400	953	12.4	55,455	20.7	5.5
45780	Toledo, OH	594,537	87.7	5.2	254,228	62.9	57.4	184,900	927	9.1	261,471	15.4	3.4
45820	Topeka, KS	229,450	87.3	3.9	95,618	70.6	54.9	184,000	953	11.2	100,369	19.3	5.2
45900	Traverse City, MI	155,042	92.1	4.6	69,457	81.3	55.1	333,800	1,288	7.6	66,707	15.3	4.8
45940	Trenton-Princeton, NJ	378,726	87.8	6.3	146,258	60.3	60.5	390,900	1,466	7.5	154,716	11.3	10.2
46060	Tucson, AZ	1,053,319	84.2	6.3	445,471	65.6	58.6	337,800	1,263	7.2	423,811	11.0	4.6
46140	Tulsa, OK	1,032,867	86.9	6.1	411,320	64.5	56.8	230,200	1,075	8.6	433,110	13.3	3.9
46220	Tuscaloosa, AL	267,797	83.8	8.0	108,078	64.3	56.7	229,900	958	12.8	112,847	14.8	6.4
46300	Twin Falls, ID	119,171	85.9	5.3	43,326	69.5	61.3	322,800	1,110	9.1	52,816	21.7	2.2
46340	Tyler, TX	241,184	89.3	5.2	81,987	69.8	50.7	272,700	1,299	7.9	92,859	11.7	5.9
46520	Urban Honolulu, HI	978,959	87.1	6.2	338,496	59.1	63.4	899,300	2,033	7.0	454,017	9.3	8.8
46540	Utica-Rome, NY	284,810	90.3	4.1	124,085	67.8	51.5	173,300	919	10.0	115,692	23.0	5.9
46660	Valdosta, GA	149,409	90.1	5.8	60,298	60.1	57.5	205,900	1,003	14.5	63,642	17.9	3.7
46700	Vallejo, CA	443,482	88.5	6.7	157,766	64.4	74.1	621,000	2,059	5.7	184,288	11.3	15.8
47020	Victoria, TX	98,315	89.1	6.4	37,816	69.5	NA	197,600	1,153	11.2	41,375	20.1	8.0
47220	Vineland, NJ	150,825	91.3	4.6	54,482	66.2	56.8	220,500	1,196	8.1	62,707	17.5	10.3
47260	Virginia Beach-Chesapeake-Norfolk, VA-NC	1,763,525	85.5	9.8	710,613	63.3	71.0	343,700	1,465	7.5	793,336	9.9	5.7
47300	Visalia, CA	473,858	92.6	2.7	145,442	59.2	69.4	339,800	1,277	9.2	182,357	17.1	7.2
47380	Waco, TX	301,323	84.5	7.4	111,745	66.7	50.4	250,500	1,115	9.6	126,696	15.3	6.0
47460	Walla Walla, WA	61,162	85.8	10.6	23,887	65.2	59.2	429,700	1,049	14.3	24,723	34.5	4.9
47580	Warner Robins, GA	198,618	86.0	9.9	77,061	66.6	63.0	223,600	1,152	5.5	83,383	10.8	4.3
47900	Washington-Arlington-Alexandria, DC-VA-MD-WV	6,233,421	86.8	7.8	2,409,575	63.5	74.7	574,000	1,945	5.0	2,652,851	6.5	14.0
4790011694	Arlington-Alexandria-Reston, VA-WV Metro Division	3,120,132	87.1	8.4	1,160,949	67.8	74.3	627,800	2,074	3.9	1,322,094	7.2	13.5

Table C-3. Metropolitan Areas — Where: Migration, Housing, and Transportation, 2023—*Continued*

Metropolitan area / division code	Metropolitan area / division	Total population 1 year and over	Lived in the same house 1 year ago (percent)	Did not live in the same county 1 year ago (percent)	Total occupied housing units	Owner-occupied units (percent)	Percent with a mortgage, contract to purchase, or similar debt	Median value of owner-occupied units (dollars; owner estimated)	Median gross rent of renter-occupied units paying cash rent	Households without Internet access (percent)	Number of workers who commuted to work	Commute of less than 10 minutes (percent)	Commute of 60 minutes or more (percent)
	ACS table number:	C07204	C07204	C07204	B25003	B25003	B25081	B25097	B25064	S2801	B08012	B08012	B08012
	column number:	1	2	3	4	5	6	7	8	9	10	11	12
4790023224	Frederick-Gaithersburg-Bethesda, MD Metro Division	1,335,059	88.6	6.3	499,961	67.1	71.8	587,400	1,947	4.4	549,555	7.2	14.6
4790047764	Washington, DC-MD Metro Division	1,778,230	84.9	8.0	748,665	54.5	77.8	468,900	1,809	6.9	781,202	4.7	14.5
47930	Waterbury-Shelton, CT	450,191	90.7	4.5	180,851	67.9	65.5	327,000	1,298	8.5	200,158	11.8	8.9
47940	Waterloo-Cedar Falls, IA	166,026	87.7	6.4	68,791	67.9	63.5	190,200	929	7.8	77,739	21.7	3.0
48060	Watertown-Fort Drum, NY	113,609	77.8	10.7	50,542	52.9	56.4	184,200	1,227	9.4	51,476	24.8	4.1
48140	Wausau, WI	136,855	89.1	3.5	58,104	72.9	56.8	215,700	977	10.5	62,197	18.7	3.6
48260	Weirton-Steubenville, WV-OH	113,254	89.7	3.4	50,285	73.4	46.1	126,200	760	13.2	45,788	16.4	11.8
48300	Wenatchee-East Wenatchee, WA	123,847	88.7	6.0	49,671	66.0	55.9	489,300	1,133	7.1	52,138	23.9	4.4
48540	Wheeling, WV-OH	133,987	88.7	5.8	59,980	72.7	44.6	161,300	777	13.5	57,587	17.6	7.8
48620	Wichita, KS	646,158	86.1	4.8	260,885	65.0	59.4	207,300	965	7.1	296,501	15.8	3.1
48660	Wichita Falls, TX	148,392	85.6	9.1	57,000	66.6	45.6	171,500	954	10.8	66,624	30.1	2.9
48680	Wildwood-The Villages, FL	150,512	85.8	10.9	73,238	87.9	43.0	411,000	1,347	4.3	27,704	9.4	7.4
48700	Williamsport, PA	111,469	89.5	5.6	46,849	68.9	57.0	205,900	869	11.1	48,716	24.6	5.4
48900	Wilmington, NC	463,079	85.3	9.5	206,546	71.9	60.7	370,400	1,426	7.1	179,899	13.2	5.9
49020	Winchester, VA-WV	147,567	90.3	7.5	56,287	73.5	64.0	354,600	1,279	7.5	61,617	12.9	20.0
49180	Winston-Salem, NC	689,622	88.8	5.9	292,187	68.4	57.6	248,600	994	9.3	289,949	12.9	4.4
49340	Worcester, MA	857,961	87.4	5.5	336,660	65.5	69.2	433,900	1,449	5.2	385,528	11.8	14.3
49420	Yakima, WA	252,632	89.4	2.9	89,414	61.8	54.8	318,900	1,119	8.7	104,271	17.6	5.3
49620	York-Hanover, PA	460,777	90.6	4.1	183,864	75.1	62.8	257,600	1,149	8.4	209,755	12.1	8.6
49660	Youngstown-Warren, OH	422,157	89.9	4.8	186,827	69.8	51.5	149,700	788	11.5	169,455	17.0	7.3
49700	Yuba City, CA	181,100	87.7	6.1	62,578	64.3	63.9	398,200	1,357	7.6	69,315	17.3	11.2
49740	Yuma, AZ	211,564	85.9	9.1	83,811	70.6	52.1	246,900	1,055	7.4	73,960	16.5	5.2

NA = Not available.

Table C-4. Cities — Where: Migration, Housing, and Transportation, 2023

STATE and place code	STATE Place	Total population 1 year and over	Lived in the same house 1 year ago (percent)	Did not live in the same county 1 year ago (percent)	Total occupied housing units	Owner-occupied units (percent)	Percent with a mortgage, contract to purchase, or similar debt	Median value of owner-occupied units (dollars; owner estimated)	Median gross rent of renter-occupied units paying cash rent	Households without Internet access (percent)	Number of workers who commuted to work	Commute of less than 10 minutes (percent)	Commute of 60 minutes or more (percent)
	ACS table number:	C07204	C07204	C07204	B25003	B25003	B25081	B25097	B25064	S2801	B08012	B08012	B08012
	column number:	1	2	3	4	5	6	7	8	9	10	11	12
00000	**UNITED STATES**	331,383,809	87.9	6.0	131,332,360	65.2	60.2	340,200	1,406	7.8	139,948,165	12.5	8.9
01000	**ALABAMA**	5,058,397	88.6	5.7	2,051,545	70.1	54.1	216,600	982	10.5	2,071,583	12.0	6.7
0103076	Auburn city	81,490	80.6	13.0	32,859	49.8	NA	365,500	1,013	8.9	33,553	22.0	4.2
0107000	Birmingham city	195,387	83.1	5.4	91,740	45.0	50.2	157,200	1,102	11.4	84,183	9.8	5.2
0121184	Dothan city	71,275	85.9	7.2	30,920	55.5	58.6	190,000	948	8.7	31,686	18.4	2.9
0135896	Hoover city	90,578	90.4	4.4	38,178	73.9	67.1	415,300	1,379	1.9	44,116	8.3	4.6
0137000	Huntsville city	225,487	84.6	6.9	99,557	59.1	60.5	309,900	1,207	6.0	100,765	11.0	2.0
0150000	Mobile city	181,542	87.6	5.1	79,383	53.0	53.4	189,000	1,051	7.1	75,949	11.3	3.9
0151000	Montgomery city	193,246	82.8	8.2	82,966	54.6	61.1	158,500	1,023	7.7	79,440	11.6	4.1
0177256	Tuscaloosa city	109,081	69.8	14.8	42,870	41.5	61.5	252,200	976	11.0	42,647	25.6	4.1
02000	**ALASKA**	725,129	85.7	6.6	276,852	66.3	57.3	347,500	1,373	6.8	327,931	25.7	5.4
0203000	Anchorage municipality	282,455	81.3	7.2	109,125	63.0	67.0	385,900	1,474	4.8	136,557	15.9	3.2
04000	**ARIZONA**	7,362,464	86.1	5.8	2,907,014	67.7	61.1	411,200	1,608	7.5	2,857,204	11.8	6.6
0404720	Avondale city	92,789	91.4	3.7	32,208	61.3	75.7	404,900	1,904	4.6	38,936	12.6	10.2
0407940	Buckeye city	107,038	90.2	4.9	32,161	83.7	82.0	426,000	1,930	2.2	37,701	6.8	14.4
0410670	Casas Adobes CDP	70107	83.2	5.8	32,025	69.4	65.3	358,000	1,574	3.8	28,834	8.2	8.0
0412000	Chandler city	276,898	86.2	4.8	105,611	68.3	71.8	537,100	1,974	5.0	115,090	10.8	4.8
0423620	Flagstaff city	75,634	69.8	20.5	30,080	39.6	66.3	605,600	1,694	11.7	38,318	26.1	2.0
0427400	Gilbert town	272,764	86.9	4.8	94,016	70.7	74.3	614,200	2,181	2.6	109,005	8.8	5.7
0427820	Glendale city	250,880	89.9	3.7	89,664	60.4	68.4	398,900	1,550	8.5	103,493	7.1	6.4
0428380	Goodyear city	110,133	88.2	5.3	38,956	76.8	72.9	516,200	1,977	1.8	37,496	5.2	9.1
0444410	Maricopa city	NA	NA	NA	23,278	84.8	81.1	386,700	2,194	NA	24,363	17.6	17.5
0446000	Mesa city	506,487	85.5	4.9	203,676	66.2	62.7	424,100	1,695	6.8	200,461	11.2	5.1
0454050	Peoria city	196,792	90.9	3.0	74,637	75.4	70.3	473,400	1,837	4.7	72,117	11.8	8.2
0455000	Phoenix city	1,634,990	85.6	4.8	621,234	56.2	66.4	441,300	1,655	8.1	707,200	8.5	5.6
0458150	Queen Creek town	75,200	91.2	2.6	24,749	93.3	77.5	677,600	2,352	4.3	26,008	12.2	10.5
0464210	San Tan Valley CDP	117,420	87.2	11.0	36,966	86.1	75.5	433,500	2,091	5.2	47,058	6.5	15.3
0465000	Scottsdale city	242,388	82.2	5.3	118,561	66.2	58.5	835,100	2,140	1.9	88,803	13.7	3.9
0471510	Surprise city	156,492	85.4	6.7	59,045	80.9	69.2	443,500	2,110	3.8	60,710	12.5	12.2
0473000	Tempe city	189,217	75.8	10.2	76,512	45.1	63.8	470,200	1,792	4.7	96,151	11.9	3.5
0477000	Tucson city	541,472	80.7	7.1	233,257	52.9	59.8	284,200	1,183	8.4	239,687	12.4	3.2
0485540	Yuma city	99,925	84.9	10.5	41,742	65.8	55.4	256,000	1,194	5.3	40,389	19.7	5.1
05000	**ARKANSAS**	3,034,111	87.9	6.1	1,232,871	66.2	52.6	195,700	933	11.5	1,242,629	17.6	5.4
0515190	Conway city	68,713	89.5	6.7	28,356	52.4	67.5	246,100	989	5.0	31,752	21.8	2.0
0523290	Fayetteville city	100,264	74.3	12.8	42,333	39.7	63.7	376,200	1,069	9.0	46,122	12.7	1.6
0524550	Fort Smith city	88,894	82.7	8.7	36,439	51.1	51.1	181,900	888	15.4	35,264	16.5	3.9
0535710	Jonesboro city	79,225	79.6	9.8	32,817	47.7	63.9	201,000	971	8.5	33,446	21.2	3.8
0541000	Little Rock city	201,111	87.8	4.5	89,358	54.0	58.3	241,600	1,097	8.4	82,031	14.0	2.4
0560410	Rogers city	72,499	88.0	4.5	27,613	57.8	NA	346,300	1,294	5.3	34,584	18.0	2.1
0566080	Springdale city	87,925	91.6	4.5	29,550	53.5	66.2	275,000	1,187	4.1	40,410	12.2	2.5
06000	**CALIFORNIA**	38,552,167	89.5	4.5	13,699,816	55.9	67.1	725,800	1,992	5.7	15,937,869	9.5	11.6
0600562	Alameda city	74,574	87.8	5.9	30,642	52.9	60.4	1,122,200	2,402	5.0	26,866	8.9	20.1
0600884	Alhambra city	79,065	90.7	2.8	30,242	40.1	NA	833,000	1,863	6.1	35,976	5.4	12.2
0602000	Anaheim city	337,347	90.3	3.7	109,885	44.8	69.1	826,700	2,113	5.8	156,302	5.9	7.3
0602252	Antioch city	115,508	89.6	4.6	37,645	67.2	77.9	633,800	2,258	3.8	49,860	5.5	29.2
0602364	Apple Valley town	74,563	93.0	1.8	26,684	74.3	64.9	427,600	1,530	7.0	27,035	9.6	18.7
0602553	Arden-Arcade CDP	90,161	87.5	5.1	37,548	48.3	65.7	584,200	1,582	5.5	35,139	10.8	7.6
0603526	Bakersfield city	407,776	89.9	2.8	130,761	59.9	71.5	375,800	1,431	5.9	162,515	8.9	7.3
0603666	Baldwin Park city	68,252	96.7	0.8	18,805	53.4	68.1	600,900	1,732	5.0	30,028	3.5	14.0
0604982	Bellflower city	74,433	91.7	1.3	23,352	41.3	72.4	752,600	1,829	9.9	35,577	6.9	10.8
0606000	Berkeley city	118,414	73.6	16.5	49,088	40.9	64.0	1,360,800	2,083	6.3	42,504	11.5	14.5
0608142	Brentwood city	64,463	93.3	4.2	22,600	81.8	75.2	817,700	2,541	4.3	22,633	10.4	37.7
0608786	Buena Park city	81,341	92.5	2.7	23,777	56.9	64.1	835,900	2,099	4.0	39,253	6.7	15.2
0608954	Burbank city	101,091	90.7	2.5	43,209	42.0	62.0	1,057,100	2,111	5.4	37,540	12.1	6.1
0610046	Camarillo city	69,199	90.5	3.1	26,253	64.7	NA	825,100	2,823	3.7	28,093	18.1	8.4
0611194	Carlsbad city	112,099	84.9	6.5	43,752	64.3	67.4	1,359,600	2,877	3.1	38,756	8.9	8.4
0611390	Carmichael CDP	75,160	89.6	3.7	30,982	52.9	59.6	580,000	1,631	6.4	30,807	9.2	6.0
0611530	Carson city	90,302	92.5	1.9	27,512	70.2	65.7	672,600	2,014	4.8	36,652	12.0	7.7
0611964	Castro Valley CDP	64,422	92.9	1.7	23,198	69.6	67.0	1,074,400	2,399	2.2	26,748	7.4	16.8
0613014	Chico city	101,063	75.4	9.0	44,270	40.4	65.9	455,100	1,515	6.7	47,808	31.0	4.0

Table C-4. Cities — Where: Migration, Housing, and Transportation, 2023—*Continued*

STATE and place code	STATE Place	Total population 1 year and over	Lived in the same house 1 year ago (percent)	Did not live in the same county 1 year ago (percent)	Total occupied housing units	Owner-occupied units (percent)	Percent with a mortgage, contract to purchase, or similar debt	Median value of owner-occupied units (dollars; owner estimated)	Median gross rent of renter-occupied units paying cash rent	Households without Internet access (percent)	Number of workers who commuted to work	Commute of less than 10 minutes (percent)	Commute of 60 minutes or more (percent)
	ACS table number:	C07204	C07204	C07204	B25003	B25003	B25081	B25097	B25064	S2801	B08012	B08012	B08012
	column number:	1	2	3	4	5	6	7	8	9	10	11	12
	CALIFORNIA—Cont.												
0613210	Chino city	NA	NA	NA	26,314	65.8	67.0	707,000	2,364	3.0	40,540	7.2	17.7
0613214	Chino Hills city	76,249	87.9	5.2	24,476	70.0	65.4	886,000	3,196	1.7	33,382	7.0	18.3
0613392	Chula Vista city	271,658	89.8	3.5	88,029	59.3	71.2	773,100	2,178	5.5	114,955	6.0	9.5
0613588	Citrus Heights city	85,287	86.2	4.8	34,364	62.0	65.4	442,600	1,789	5.9	34,684	10.4	8.9
0614218	Clovis city	124,941	89.4	4.7	44,194	62.4	74.5	500,100	1,839	4.8	47,487	9.1	7.0
0615044	Compton city	NA	NA	NA	23,447	55.8	72.7	593,100	1,637	12.3	38,011	5.8	11.6
0616000	Concord city	120,936	90.2	3.6	47,248	61.9	64.8	795,300	2,194	3.1	53,557	5.0	19.9
0616350	Corona city	159,836	93.1	4.7	51,110	65.6	73.8	690,500	2,270	4.0	68,351	6.9	20.1
0616532	Costa Mesa city	106,748	87.3	3.0	42,336	38.5	67.2	1,099,800	2,458	3.6	49,765	9.8	7.5
0617918	Daly City city	99,553	93.5	4.4	33,137	61.9	56.5	1,028,400	2,392	4.5	47,219	4.4	8.4
0618100	Davis city	65,560	69.0	19.3	25,542	43.6	57.2	841,000	2,102	5.6	28,151	15.5	4.6
0619766	Downey city	107,774	93.7	2.0	33,472	53.1	68.7	824,300	1,845	3.0	50,724	7.9	12.7
0620018	Dublin city	68,371	83.1	8.6	23,439	64.8	79.6	1,292,900	3,136	3.2	26,230	7.7	28.8
0620802	East Los Angeles CDP	105,651	93.3	1.5	29,208	34.0	66.8	633,600	1,437	5.2	44,312	6.5	10.2
0621230	Eastvale city	69,528	92.9	5.2	18,433	77.1	NA	833,000	3,244	NA	30,679	4.0	18.0
0621712	El Cajon city	101,090	85.0	1.7	32,145	39.4	68.3	683,800	1,898	6.5	37,313	9.7	5.4
0622020	Elk Grove city	177,020	93.1	3.6	53,383	74.4	72.8	639,000	2,243	3.1	64,333	8.5	9.0
0622230	El Monte city	102,664	92.4	1.1	29,314	40.9	53.2	648,300	1,673	8.5	42,696	5.8	12.0
0622804	Escondido city	145,156	88.7	2.4	47,740	55.6	69.1	696,700	2,058	6.6	64,768	8.9	6.5
0623182	Fairfield city	119,288	89.4	5.7	38,515	63.5	75.6	622,500	2,196	6.1	53,546	13.1	14.3
0624638	Folsom city	84,134	84.4	8.7	32,761	69.6	67.6	724,700	2,384	4.7	30,166	14.1	6.4
0624680	Fontana city	213,214	93.5	2.8	59,598	68.8	75.3	598,600	1,873	2.3	88,172	5.3	17.8
0626000	Fremont city	223,843	87.5	7.6	81,639	60.8	73.4	1,443,200	2,801	2.7	88,376	3.7	11.3
0627000	Fresno city	539,014	88.9	3.0	180,634	53.1	65.5	385,600	1,427	8.6	213,107	8.3	4.5
0628000	Fullerton city	137,756	87.2	4.9	49,425	52.7	59.9	897,100	2,131	6.0	66,523	9.3	15.7
0629000	Garden Grove city	167,119	91.5	2.6	50,343	53.0	65.2	824,600	1,971	3.9	71,682	3.8	10.0
0630000	Glendale city	185,764	90.5	3.3	76,375	34.3	67.3	1,062,600	2,084	7.2	75,111	6.4	11.9
0632548	Hawthorne city	82,798	88.1	4.0	32,299	28.0	NA	882,900	1,765	7.5	39,518	7.5	11.2
0633000	Hayward city	153,878	91.0	3.5	49,029	58.9	70.9	831,900	2,311	3.8	68,224	5.6	12.7
0633182	Hemet city	91,213	88.0	4.2	33,674	64.0	NA	370,200	1,617	11.3	30,098	13.4	19.0
0633434	Hesperia city	99,224	90.0	1.4	29,608	68.8	69.9	415,000	1,811	6.6	38,117	9.4	27.2
0636000	Huntington Beach city	189,868	90.0	3.6	75,314	56.7	64.6	1,070,600	2,509	2.1	80,204	8.1	8.5
0636448	Indio city	91,946	93.4	1.4	31,048	65.7	62.8	495,700	1,328	4.1	42,269	10.8	3.1
0636546	Inglewood city	102,097	94.6	1.5	37,918	40.0	67.8	801,200	1,686	5.6	45,748	4.0	16.4
0636770	Irvine city	310,752	82.3	7.6	111,471	46.4	66.0	1,199,600	2,970	3.9	121,194	7.6	7.2
0637692	Jurupa Valley city	105,739	94.0	2.8	30,398	70.3	68.3	591,400	1,736	7.7	43,893	5.8	15.8
0639486	Lake Elsinore city	NA	NA	NA	20,252	69.4	71.4	591,400	1,986	6.5	30,382	6.8	33.5
0639496	Lake Forest city	84,138	88.2	5.1	29,721	69.6	73.2	910,900	2,648	1.7	35,555	5.9	6.0
0639892	Lakewood city	77,885	90.2	5.0	25,033	74.0	74.8	822,500	2,441	3.2	33,562	4.7	10.1
0640130	Lancaster city	163,249	93.1	1.1	52,431	61.4	69.3	450,500	1,726	6.3	56,604	8.9	23.2
0641992	Livermore city	81,719	92.2	4.0	29,208	73.1	75.0	1,052,100	2,747	2.5	31,807	14.5	17.9
0642202	Lodi city	66,976	90.8	4.4	23,274	56.2	NA	493,400	1,664	7.2	24,873	24.9	9.0
0643000	Long Beach city	445,466	89.2	3.5	176,407	41.0	71.9	823,300	1,831	6.0	204,143	6.4	12.0
0644000	Los Angeles city	3,783,801	89.4	3.5	1,460,167	35.1	70.1	919,900	1,875	6.3	1,618,024	6.7	12.6
0644574	Lynwood city	NA	NA	NA	16,131	41.1	NA	617,100	1,655	9.0	27,254	2.6	12.3
0645022	Madera city	67,487	87.8	4.6	19,945	54.5	NA	357,700	1,371	10.2	22,129	23.8	8.8
0645484	Manteca city	90,071	90.5	4.6	30,532	75.7	NA	589,500	1,934	7.3	37,106	12.3	24.7
0646842	Menifee city	110,686	89.6	5.2	39,358	78.2	74.8	570,000	2,349	8.9	42,688	5.0	30.8
0646898	Merced city	92,622	85.0	3.9	27,221	48.1	NA	394,900	1,359	3.6	35,190	21.2	11.5
0647766	Milpitas city	76,982	86.2	6.8	25,653	56.2	58.8	1,164,200	3,001	2.4	35,737	5.3	8.9
0648256	Mission Viejo city	89,416	94.5	2.8	34,477	78.5	73.9	1,028,800	2,852	3.7	34,808	6.7	7.3
0648354	Modesto city	215,555	92.1	2.9	76,577	59.4	63.8	449,100	1,645	6.3	88,123	13.1	14.6
0649270	Moreno Valley city	209,971	91.9	3.1	56,294	62.3	75.6	547,800	2,081	6.7	90,847	9.5	15.1
0649670	Mountain View city	80,960	80.8	10.3	35,859	37.6	65.3	1,963,700	3,107	3.4	41,275	7.8	4.8
0650076	Murrieta city	110,621	94.0	2.4	36,867	75.0	77.5	631,500	2,503	2.3	43,427	6.9	34.9
0650258	Napa city	76,423	87.2	5.1	30,838	58.5	65.9	829,800	2,285	6.7	35,628	23.1	6.9
0651182	Newport Beach city	81,689	87.1	5.7	36,300	54.6	62.9	2,000,000+	3,254	2.4	29,831	7.6	3.1
0652526	Norwalk city	NA	NA	NA	27,925	66.6	71.3	648,600	1,981	3.5	47,259	3.4	13.0
0653000	Oakland city	432,324	88.0	4.9	182,014	41.2	71.9	915,000	1,938	8.3	179,403	6.8	12.3
0653322	Oceanside city	168,494	88.0	4.2	63,683	57.9	70.1	786,900	2,293	4.9	78,100	5.9	11.9
0653896	Ontario city	179,466	93.3	4.6	54,719	59.4	76.3	592,900	1,937	4.9	80,056	6.1	14.3
0653980	Orange city	136,924	89.8	4.2	46,584	54.0	71.7	996,800	2,218	5.6	60,701	12.2	7.1
0654652	Oxnard city	195,384	91.8	2.4	55,777	48.1	62.1	659,200	1,962	7.3	84,736	4.4	6.9
0655156	Palmdale city	160,002	93.2	0.9	47,380	68.1	73.7	475,700	1,839	5.9	64,682	7.4	31.9
0655282	Palo Alto city	65,091	83.8	8.4	27,768	44.9	55.7	2,000,000+	3,306	3.2	22,194	12.1	1.8

Table C-4. Cities — Where: Migration, Housing, and Transportation, 2023—*Continued*

STATE and place code	STATE Place	Total population 1 year and over	Lived in the same house 1 year ago (percent)	Did not live in the same county 1 year ago (percent)	Total occupied housing units	Owner-occupied units (percent)	Percent with a mortgage, contract to purchase, or similar debt	Median value of owner-occupied units (dollars; owner estimated)	Median gross rent of renter-occupied units paying cash rent	Households without Internet access (percent)	Number of workers who commuted to work	Commute of less than 10 minutes (percent)	Commute of 60 minutes or more (percent)
	ACS table number:	C07204	C07204	C07204	B25003	B25003	B25081	B25097	B25064	S2801	B08012	B08012	B08012
	column number:	1	2	3	4	5	6	7	8	9	10	11	12
	CALIFORNIA—Cont.												
0656000	Pasadena city	131,806	88.3	3.5	57,025	40.8	68.8	1,105,300	2,284	4.3	52,934	10.7	11.6
0656700	Perris city	78,779	93.8	1.7	20,943	70.6	64.7	496,400	1,931	4.7	33,945	6.0	23.3
0657456	Pittsburg city	75,425	92.8	3.2	24,968	54.6	76.0	618,200	2,202	9.4	34,652	6.2	28.1
0657792	Pleasanton city	74,245	87.2	9.9	26,569	66.9	70.9	1,557,400	3,151	1.0	27,638	9.3	21.4
0658072	Pomona city	143,755	90.7	3.3	42,390	53.4	70.6	614,600	1,816	5.6	65,972	9.0	11.9
0659444	Rancho Cordova city	81,715	88.6	4.2	28,916	55.8	72.0	489,800	1,678	9.0	30,077	10.9	7.0
0659451	Rancho Cucamonga city	172,901	91.9	4.1	58,173	61.4	72.2	739,200	2,308	4.6	75,841	9.3	13.2
0659920	Redding city	91,624	86.8	5.6	37,380	57.1	63.9	359,500	1,386	5.1	35,622	20.8	2.5
0659962	Redlands city	71,638	93.7	3.5	27,161	52.7	67.3	631,600	2,075	3.7	32,746	13.6	8.5
0660018	Redondo Beach city	66,664	90.3	2.7	29,220	52.8	NA	1,280,000	2,565	3.2	26,543	6.3	11.9
0660102	Redwood City city	79,493	83.7	12.2	29,831	51.6	63.9	1,815,900	3,077	3.5	33,566	7.3	7.5
0660466	Rialto city	102,021	94.8	1.4	26,568	72.1	NA	515,700	1,694	9.0	41,442	6.6	15.4
0660620	Richmond city	112,402	92.5	3.2	45,299	58.3	69.5	651,200	1,814	5.9	50,687	6.6	19.5
0662000	Riverside city	316,195	89.6	5.7	96,201	56.3	70.0	597,000	1,903	5.8	140,294	6.5	16.5
0662364	Rocklin city	72,523	87.0	7.5	27,308	69.7	71.1	686,300	2,059	4.7	28,141	9.6	10.6
0662938	Roseville city	157,247	87.3	8.5	61,142	64.6	69.8	652,200	2,158	2.3	57,509	11.7	6.6
0664000	Sacramento city	520,620	88.1	6.0	202,421	53.9	70.9	505,800	1,779	6.8	208,665	8.8	6.5
0664224	Salinas city	157,548	91.2	1.3	43,233	45.6	59.5	643,000	1,969	6.5	63,511	6.3	9.2
0665000	San Bernardino city	220,537	92.8	2.6	64,370	48.9	70.2	432,800	1,561	7.6	89,991	7.6	14.7
0665042	San Buenaventura (Ventura) city	107,952	88.5	5.1	43,032	52.2	60.5	817,600	2,181	5.1	47,655	15.5	10.2
0666000	San Diego city	1,373,641	85.5	6.5	537,532	46.6	69.0	923,900	2,389	4.8	626,898	9.5	4.5
0667000	San Francisco city	801,259	84.4	7.1	372,027	37.1	63.4	1,348,000	2,356	7.0	348,055	4.5	11.7
0668000	San Jose city	959,239	88.3	4.4	331,229	55.6	66.7	1,217,500	2,574	4.6	432,501	5.4	7.7
0668084	San Leandro city	84,280	94.4	1.8	31,539	57.7	60.8	855,300	2,193	5.5	37,807	7.7	15.2
0668196	San Marcos city	92,987	88.2	2.7	31,360	61.1	NA	859,000	2,362	4.1	39,646	6.7	6.7
0668252	San Mateo city	100,540	87.0	8.6	39,795	49.9	71.4	1,562,300	3,002	3.5	46,450	6.5	6.9
0668378	San Ramon city	83,998	92.8	5.5	30,872	73.5	71.1	1,540,800	3,126	3.2	32,086	7.5	29.6
0669000	Santa Ana city	308,340	94.6	1.7	83,498	46.1	64.2	688,200	1,999	6.0	148,316	5.3	5.4
0669070	Santa Barbara city	85,736	86.4	5.2	38,553	38.8	NA	1,635,700	2,285	5.7	36,793	19.4	2.7
0669084	Santa Clara city	129,396	78.7	9.1	51,014	39.0	68.5	1,553,400	2,971	3.8	63,877	7.9	5.4
0669088	Santa Clarita city	221,502	89.4	2.3	76,446	75.4	77.9	777,900	2,597	3.0	91,832	8.4	21.6
0669196	Santa Maria city	109,030	91.8	2.0	28,422	49.6	63.8	536,400	1,801	9.0	44,794	14.7	5.7
0670000	Santa Monica city	89,063	89.6	5.0	48,189	26.6	NA	2,000,000+	2,294	4.9	32,908	9.2	12.1
0670098	Santa Rosa city	173,541	87.9	4.4	70,361	56.4	69.2	697,300	2,072	5.2	80,057	13.8	7.3
0672016	Simi Valley city	123,766	91.9	3.4	44,629	74.5	73.9	817,100	2,406	3.7	50,960	9.8	9.0
0673080	South Gate city	NA	NA	NA	27,422	42.2	NA	623,700	1,469	8.0	42,807	4.9	16.5
0675000	Stockton city	315,727	88.7	5.0	101,924	54.1	67.6	441,300	1,492	6.7	130,215	8.8	15.7
0677000	Sunnyvale city	149,575	77.0	10.6	58,756	41.6	64.5	1,739,100	2,972	1.7	75,467	5.5	6.2
0678120	Temecula city	109,311	88.2	4.6	35,801	62.5	81.6	697,700	2,281	1.4	44,435	10.1	28.9
0678582	Thousand Oaks city	123,019	87.2	8.1	46,158	72.2	69.1	978,000	2,743	1.7	47,834	16.4	11.9
0680000	Torrance city	138,135	91.7	3.2	55,836	57.4	66.1	1,055,700	2,049	3.4	54,438	6.9	11.1
0680238	Tracy city	96,951	90.3	6.4	27,880	67.9	68.4	673,100	2,502	3.3	42,044	10.6	32.7
0680644	Tulare city	70,181	95.3	1.9	20,967	56.1	72.3	331,900	1,382	6.7	30,131	17.4	5.8
0680812	Turlock city	71,756	89.8	2.7	25,660	57.8	70.6	476,200	1,618	3.6	30,145	21.7	10.4
0680854	Tustin city	77,376	89.8	3.4	26,025	52.9	72.5	939,300	2,615	4.9	35,520	7.9	4.5
0681204	Union City city	65,116	87.9	4.0	21,920	66.3	63.3	1,122,200	2,623	2.9	27,074	3.8	15.8
0681344	Upland city	78,128	85.7	7.8	28,043	56.7	70.7	763,800	2,095	2.5	34,889	10.3	16.1
0681554	Vacaville city	100,970	88.1	6.5	35,647	66.8	79.3	624,600	2,155	3.9	40,097	14.7	12.9
0681666	Vallejo city	121,248	89.3	7.1	44,936	57.1	74.3	595,800	1,981	5.6	50,125	7.3	18.3
0682590	Victorville city	137,857	83.4	6.2	38,786	59.8	77.0	397,900	1,589	8.2	50,383	10.5	27.5
0682954	Visalia city	142,809	91.5	4.5	48,446	61.6	77.4	363,300	1,534	5.9	59,073	15.6	5.4
0682996	Vista city	96,516	89.3	3.2	31,866	54.8	71.9	784,700	2,245	3.0	42,166	5.0	8.1
0683346	Walnut Creek city	68,881	84.7	9.2	32,550	63.2	58.3	964,800	2,741	2.5	25,145	8.3	14.5
0684200	West Covina city	105,209	92.3	2.2	31,349	58.4	67.8	781,400	2,143	5.3	46,303	8.3	19.6
0684550	Westminster city	87,674	93.4	1.3	28,524	51.1	60.2	875,800	2,046	5.9	38,434	4.7	9.5
0685292	Whittier city	82,880	93.3	1.6	27,466	58.6	66.9	795,800	1,850	5.6	33,583	5.6	13.6
0686832	Yorba Linda city	NA	NA	NA	22,960	85.2	67.5	1,152,500	2,753	3.3	27,673	8.7	8.9
0686972	Yuba City city	67,543	87.0	3.8	23,521	58.7	71.1	397,500	1,403	6.2	28,676	23.0	9.3
08000	**COLORADO**	5,819,109	84.3	9.3	2,428,261	65.7	69.1	550,300	1,771	5.4	2,522,855	13.5	7.2
0803455	Arvada city	122,177	90.2	6.4	49,987	73.2	71.7	641,900	1,804	4.1	53,624	9.3	7.7
0804000	Aurora city	390,124	82.6	9.4	149,344	63.3	75.0	481,300	1,867	5.8	186,177	8.3	6.1
0807850	Boulder city	105,648	67.0	21.5	44,722	45.1	56.8	989,100	1,932	5.6	38,818	21.3	5.1
0809280	Broomfield city	76,156	82.5	13.2	33,563	59.1	69.3	660,800	2,086	2.5	28,069	8.8	4.6
0812415	Castle Rock town	80,193	86.4	9.1	29,100	79.3	86.0	665,400	2,081	NA	31,457	13.4	10.6

Table C-4. Cities — Where: Migration, Housing, and Transportation, 2023—*Continued*

STATE and place code	STATE Place	Total population 1 year and over	Lived in the same house 1 year ago (percent)	Did not live in the same county 1 year ago (percent)	Total occupied housing units	Owner-occupied units (percent)	Percent with a mortgage, contract to purchase, or similar debt	Median value of owner-occupied units (dollars; owner estimated)	Median gross rent of renter-occupied units paying cash rent	Households without Internet access (percent)	Number of workers who commuted to work	Commute of less than 10 minutes (percent)	Commute of 60 minutes or more (percent)
	ACS table number:	C07204	C07204	C07204	B25003	B25003	B25081	B25097	B25064	S2801	B08012	B08012	B08012
	column number:	1	2	3	4	5	6	7	8	9	10	11	12
	COLORADO—Cont.												
0812815	Centennial city	105,692	89.3	7.1	41,393	77.9	70.8	660,400	2,112	3.0	41,340	13.3	6.5
0816000	Colorado Springs city	482,018	80.0	9.1	208,035	61.8	69.6	460,900	1,648	3.7	209,974	11.3	6.2
0816495	Commerce City city	67,431	85.6	7.7	21,705	81.5	77.6	543,200	1,914	3.5	30,329	4.7	5.2
0820000	Denver city	708,432	79.5	12.0	342,996	47.1	72.2	626,500	1,843	6.3	317,805	8.9	5.6
0827425	Fort Collins city	168,594	78.7	12.8	72,318	50.4	73.6	586,800	1,688	7.6	74,029	17.3	5.3
0831660	Grand Junction city	68,823	86.1	7.7	31,087	62.2	69.1	397,800	1,194	5.7	29,660	25.7	6.0
0832155	Greeley city	111,565	82.6	6.1	42,813	59.6	61.9	367,400	1,486	8.4	47,972	20.0	8.5
0836410	Highlands Ranch CDP	101822	87.3	10.1	39,866	74.2	73.0	731,800	2,439	1.6	40,370	12.0	5.8
0843000	Lakewood city	154,379	82.7	12.5	71,477	58.1	66.6	589,600	1,790	8.3	72,125	10.6	5.2
0845970	Longmont city	98,919	83.0	10.3	42,201	59.9	69.1	602,800	1,865	4.5	42,369	14.4	7.7
0846465	Loveland city	78,316	88.5	6.2	35,134	64.0	69.0	486,000	1,658	6.2	33,941	15.8	7.8
0862000	Pueblo city	110,188	88.6	6.5	46,921	64.9	70.2	278,900	1,107	8.0	45,330	17.4	3.6
0877290	Thornton city	144,233	86.5	8.0	52,600	70.9	75.1	511,300	1,913	3.5	68,739	8.2	10.5
0883835	Westminster city	113783	81.9	11.5	51,565	61.9	69.2	538,200	1,921	3.7	54,442	9.1	6.8
09000	**CONNECTICUT**	3,576,682	89.1	5.3	1,442,969	65.7	63.5	367,800	1,463	7.2	1,584,717	12.6	9.4
0908000	Bridgeport city	146,689	86.7	5.3	54,695	41.8	56.8	307,100	1,408	10.6	67,287	9.6	16.3
0918430	Danbury city	85,153	92.3	3.4	32,993	43.9	69.1	419,900	1,837	7.8	43,446	9.2	19.3
0937000	Hartford city	118,943	84.3	5.5	49,229	24.9	NA	237,500	1,268	12.2	43,975	10.0	5.9
0950370	New Britain city	73,132	89.9	5.7	30,047	47.2	NA	229,700	1,313	17.8	34,365	10.5	4.1
0952000	New Haven city	133,665	81.2	10.5	57,392	29.0	66.5	287,000	1,401	9.6	54,260	16.5	6.5
0955990	Norwalk city	91,083	86.7	5.7	37,777	57.1	68.2	540,200	2,178	4.3	43,834	11.5	7.6
0973000	Stamford city	134,595	84.7	8.7	55,324	51.3	65.1	642,300	2,177	6.2	67,299	14.7	14.7
0980000	Waterbury city	113,021	87.6	6.5	45,898	47.4	65.8	225,400	1,142	16.3	41,030	13.8	7.0
10000	**DELAWARE**	1,022,638	88.8	6.0	412,048	73.6	64.6	359,700	1,358	7.2	431,706	9.7	8.8
1077580	Wilmington city	70,342	84.4	7.7	32,131	45.7	NA	228,600	1,150	9.5	29,775	10.0	4.8
11000	**DISTRICT OF COLUMBIA**	670,127	79.0	10.4	334,673	39.1	77.3	715,500	1,904	7.9	278,932	4.1	7.8
1150000	Washington city	670,127	79.0	10.4	334,673	39.1	77.3	715,500	1,904	7.9	278,932	4.1	7.8
12000	**FLORIDA**	22,395,466	86.4	7.4	8,966,402	68.1	55.7	381,000	1,719	7.0	8,944,682	8.6	9.2
1200410	Alafaya CDP	93,566	88.2	5.3	34,029	65.4	68.9	459,000	1,932	6.0	42,554	6.6	8.4
1207300	Boca Raton city	99,655	86.3	7.5	41,274	75.4	47.2	755,400	2,573	3.6	34,606	15.9	4.4
1207875	Boynton Beach city	80,960	87.8	3.0	31,874	65.6	54.9	363,200	2,078	9.1	35,072	8.0	5.9
1208150	Brandon CDP	115,371	84.5	6.5	44,579	54.4	61.5	360,200	1,890	3.9	49,650	6.4	8.5
1210275	Cape Coral city	222534	88.5	6.3	83,021	79.3	62.8	401,000	1,969	6.2	86,962	5.9	11.7
1212875	Clearwater city	115,632	87.5	6.5	52,536	58.7	47.2	419,100	1,791	10.9	46,542	12.0	4.8
1214400	Coral Springs city	133,760	85.4	4.8	46,223	61.9	60.8	591,300	2,330	2.3	59,991	8.4	10.0
1216475	Davie town	105,728	86.6	7.8	38,969	65.9	57.7	462,400	2,079	5.0	46,736	7.8	10.2
1216525	Daytona Beach city	81,013	83.4	9.5	33,906	49.9	NA	315,000	1,287	9.9	26,246	12.2	6.2
1216725	Deerfield Beach city	86,164	85.8	4.3	34,846	67.1	NA	340,300	1,856	11.4	38,756	6.6	4.5
1217100	Delray Beach city	66,956	84.3	8.9	30,118	64.0	47.5	434,700	1,965	13.1	27,859	10.3	10.0
1217200	Deltona city	98025	89.6	7.3	33,155	78.2	75.3	321,900	1,864	5.4	44,215	8.1	15.7
1217935	Doral city	78,907	84.9	6.8	26,222	49.6	70.8	612,900	2,776	2.7	32,222	6.8	5.1
1224000	Fort Lauderdale city	182,822	85.0	6.4	81,232	52.8	56.0	539,800	1,871	6.2	75,088	11.6	10.9
1224125	Fort Myers city	96271	82.9	8.0	39,447	48.6	55.5	406,800	1,762	8.4	36,359	8.4	6.4
1224581	Four Corners CDP	71,746	84.9	13.1	27,549	55.7	58.5	354,300	1,836	7.6	32,990	5.4	10.7
1225175	Gainesville city	144,686	68.1	18.6	65,576	37.8	58.8	275,500	1,318	14.9	64,048	17.8	2.5
1230000	Hialeah city	219067	86.9	4.8	78,792	46.3	53.2	417,900	1,710	10.5	96,306	6.1	9.5
1232000	Hollywood city	153,093	86.3	8.6	61,197	61.6	48.4	446,700	1,599	8.3	64,238	7.4	10.1
1232275	Homestead city	80,670	91.0	3.6	26,901	51.5	NA	410,500	1,790	7.8	39,680	4.0	24.6
1232610	Horizon West CDP	73520	85.3	9.7	24,678	67.9	NA	603,000	2,437	3.2	28,106	6.2	4.4
1235000	Jacksonville city	974,186	83.1	7.6	409,221	57.9	64.5	312,400	1,508	7.9	406,367	7.8	3.8
1236100	Kendall CDP	72,274	92.0	2.9	28,984	61.7	58.6	672,600	1,826	6.0	30,190	4.3	11.6
1236950	Kissimmee city	80,965	76.6	14.0	28,697	50.6	NA	331,900	1,761	9.0	31,875	3.9	10.3
1238250	Lakeland city	119,839	80.9	11.3	51,663	58.0	52.0	274,400	1,466	7.6	46,093	13.7	10.4
1239425	Largo city	81,268	82.0	9.3	37,626	63.0	44.4	257,900	1,794	10.5	35,884	10.6	5.0
1239550	Lauderhill city	71,850	87.5	3.5	27,832	53.7	NA	284,200	1,772	4.6	29,146	5.4	8.9
1239925	Lehigh Acres CDP	128217	90.5	4.6	40,585	69.8	61.1	321,700	1,718	5.3	46,612	5.9	22.2
1243975	Melbourne city	86,354	86.0	5.5	36,223	58.8	56.2	326,100	1,634	8.6	34,507	12.6	4.6
1245000	Miami city	451,265	82.0	7.3	201,102	33.4	57.5	587,400	1,833	11.5	208,875	6.1	6.2
1245025	Miami Beach city	79139	85.3	6.7	37,894	47.1	39.8	596,700	1,845	6.2	33,525	10.1	7.7
1245060	Miami Gardens city	109,095	90.6	3.6	34,688	66.8	66.8	417,000	1,817	7.9	46,971	2.7	9.6
1245975	Miramar city	135,208	87.9	7.1	44,827	70.4	67.2	521,300	2,252	4.4	57,865	3.0	13.2

Table C-4. Cities — Where: Migration, Housing, and Transportation, 2023—*Continued*

STATE and place code	STATE Place	Total population 1 year and over	Lived in the same house 1 year ago (percent)	Did not live in the same county 1 year ago (percent)	Total occupied housing units	Owner-occupied units (percent)	Percent with a mortgage, contract to purchase, or similar debt	Median value of owner-occupied units (dollars; owner estimated)	Median gross rent of renter-occupied units paying cash rent	Households without Internet access (percent)	Number of workers who commuted to work	Commute of less than 10 minutes (percent)	Commute of 60 minutes or more (percent)
	ACS table number:	C07204	C07204	C07204	B25003	B25003	B25081	B25097	B25064	S2801	B08012	B08012	B08012
	column number:	1	2	3	4	5	6	7	8	9	10	11	12
	FLORIDA—Cont.												
1249675	North Port city	88473	80.1	13.9	35,320	79.6	64.5	381,400	1,982	2.4	34,142	7.0	8.7
1250750	Ocala city		67,756	84.0	8.0	29,755	51.3	54.8	300,800	1,469	10.7	25,599	21.0
1253000	Orlando city	316,702	79.8	8.8	141,669	39.5	61.9	389,100	1,815	6.8	145,179	8.5	3.9
1254000	Palm Bay city	133,709	88.2	5.9	50,448	80.3	59.4	300,600	1,722	6.2	56,874	4.9	6.2
1254200	Palm Coast city	101,837	85.8	9.4	43,003	80.4	62.7	385,000	1,790	5.0	34,476	11.9	9.0
1254350	Palm Harbor CDP		61,943	85.8	6.9	27,659	74.0	52.3	463,900	1,944	5.6	24,384	13.2
1255775	Pembroke Pines city	168,359	86.0	9.9	63,065	73.3	61.8	461,100	2,154	6.3	78,359	4.0	15.0
1256825	Pine Hills CDP	78,329	88.5	5.6	24,671	63.4	69.0	281,500	1,448	3.1	35,617	6.8	8.6
1257425	Plantation city	95,918	85.2	4.8	36,927	64.1	64.9	490,100	2,323	4.4	47,763	5.0	10.0
1257900	Poinciana CDP	77,702	91.5	6.7	26,064	77.4	NA	302,200	2,165	8.0	27,473	2.8	37.8
1258050	Pompano Beach city	113,039	85.0	6.6	51,440	56.2	49.4	355,400	1,718	9.9	50,852	12.1	10.9
1258350	Port Charlotte CDP	64,660	89.0	8.0	26,105	80.9	56.1	310,200	1,551	11.1	27,017	8.9	13.0
1258575	Port Orange city	65,904	90.1	5.3	27,070	77.5	51.7	322,600	1,679	5.7	25,528	15.0	6.8
1258715	Port St. Lucie city	243,641	89.9	5.9	90,069	84.9	63.6	397,500	2,053	4.9	94,621	3.9	10.5
1260950	Riverview CDP	118,401	89.8	5.3	44,076	81.6	75.0	392,100	2,215	1.7	51,324	5.3	16.8
1262625	St. Cloud city	65,762	87.6	8.0	23,749	79.6	NA	379,800	1,491	4.1	29,147	2.1	8.6
1263000	St. Petersburg city	260,711	84.4	7.6	123,605	63.1	56.6	400,200	1,761	5.3	109,155	10.4	11.2
1263650	Sanford city	64,536	89.1	8.0	26,511	47.7	NA	341,700	1,560	4.4	24,104	9.9	5.3
1268350	Spring Hill CDP	121,274	89.4	7.4	47,821	82.1	61.7	315,100	1,511	4.9	43,623	10.9	15.4
1269700	Sunrise city	96,317	94.4	1.8	34,455	68.1	63.9	367,000	2,218	5.5	47,088	4.5	12.1
1270600	Tallahassee city	201,392	74.4	12.8	87,824	39.1	60.2	303,300	1,281	11.4	94,976	14.2	2.7
1270675	Tamarac city	71,319	92.9	2.3	32,913	85.0	51.5	310,900	2,075	8.7	35,609	5.6	12.2
1271000	Tampa city	399,334	79.8	10.8	169,317	47.9	62.8	454,800	1,781	4.8	163,996	10.7	5.4
1271625	The Villages CDP	79,191	90.7	7.3	45,000	93.7	40.3	413,100	1,355	2.8	null	NA	NA
1272145	Town 'n' Country CDP	78,269	80.0	11.4	31,323	58.5	NA	386,900	1,820	3.0	37,410	4.8	12.1
1275875	Wesley Chapel CDP	81,263	82.5	11.5	26,661	81.0	70.1	446,800	2,126	6.6	31,151	5.4	10.6
1276582	Weston city	67,528	91.3	4.2	22,243	74.9	62.6	715,500	3,009	2.4	24,835	7.3	11.9
1276600	West Palm Beach city	123,075	85.3	6.2	50,890	53.3	56.0	458,700	1,869	8.8	60,249	10.5	4.2
13000	**GEORGIA**	10,909,651	87.4	7.6	4,150,138	66.1	63.2	323,000	1,400	7.5	4,484,489	10.0	10.6
1301052	Albany city	67,084	78.2	12.5	28,379	36.1	NA	139,500	851	18.8	23,098	23.5	6.2
1301696	Alpharetta city	66,569	90.4	5.5	26,224	66.8	71.6	670,600	1,930	0.9	23,722	13.4	11.1
1303440	Athens-Clarke County unified government (balance)	127,615	71.8	15.2	54,856	42.2	58.5	319,300	1,283	6.8	59,124	16.6	4.7
1304000	Atlanta city	505,496	78.8	11.3	233,047	48.3	74.3	443,300	1,764	6.7	207,512	8.5	7.9
1304204	Augusta-Richmond County consolidated government (balance)	199,960	79.4	8.6	76,232	52.2	61.7	195,100	1,150	13.2	85,496	13.1	2.1
1319000	Columbus city	199,279	84.1	8.4	82,007	50.5	66.1	198,200	1,004	11.1	76,270	14.4	3.8
1342425	Johns Creek city	80,039	92.0	6.2	28,800	80.6	67.4	640,700	2,350	2.4	28,460	8.3	11.4
1349008	Macon-Bibb County	154,681	83.1	8.0	60,919	46.6	60.2	199,800	1,038	13.3	55,602	11.7	5.8
1367284	Roswell city	90,237	90.2	5.0	35,275	74.6	69.9	617,900	1,782	2.8	35,047	9.5	6.9
1368516	Sandy Springs city	104,836	81.2	8.9	50,453	49.1	66.4	627,000	1,898	4.3	48,346	6.1	6.7
1369000	Savannah city	145,911	76.6	12.2	60,129	43.8	66.4	293,200	1,420	7.1	65,883	12.9	3.5
1372122	South Fulton city	110,139	91.3	4.8	40,298	73.7	76.2	334,100	1,815	4.0	45,810	4.6	14.0
1380508	Warner Robins city	83,411	80.1	14.2	33,527	54.8	65.1	176,000	1,259	5.7	31,872	11.4	4.9
15000	**HAWAII**	1,420,012	88.1	5.6	493,898	62.4	62.2	846,400	1,940	7.3	637,246	10.6	8.7
1571550	Urban Honolulu CDP	339,097	85.9	6.6	137,203	48.6	54.4	831,600	1,737	10.5	164,217	9.1	5.1
16000	**IDAHO**	1,945,004	85.8	7.5	733,244	72.5	61.5	428,600	1,256	7.1	799,102	19.2	5.3
1608830	Boise City city	233,706	82.6	7.1	104,336	62.4	63.3	491,800	1,483	5.1	105,472	14.3	2.6
1612250	Caldwell city		67,684	85.0	7.3	21,765	72.2	71.2	351,500	1,150	8.0	28,821	16.5
1639700	Idaho Falls city	67,425	88.3	6.2	24,008	61.2	70.1	343,800	1,130	3.4	29,227	29.1	5.7
1652120	Meridian city	133,449	82.6	8.6	50,116	72.8	69.2	546,000	1,890	4.9	55,333	9.1	2.3
1656260	Nampa city	112313	86.4	8.0	41,060	71.4	70.3	361,400	1,468	4.5	50,654	12.6	4.4
17000	**ILLINOIS**	12,427,191	89.2	4.7	5,071,288	67.4	60.3	263,300	1,238	8.2	5,354,834	12.3	10.1
1702154	Arlington Heights village	77,284	87.4	3.7	32,370	72.9	57.5	397,000	1,755	2.5	32,511	9.4	11.7
1703012	Aurora city	177,101	87.5	6.7	61,278	65.5	71.1	277,300	1,625	5.7	79,588	9.9	7.6
1706587	Bloomington city	77,776	86.5	5.7	33,447	65.8	66.5	210,400	987	8.3	32,502	23.9	3.3
1707133	Bolingbrook village	74,540	90.9	8.1	25,142	82.3	73.4	326,000	1,794	2.5	37,931	9.9	9.6
1712385	Champaign city	88,488	76.4	12.9	40,599	43.1	62.7	210,800	1,021	5.7	38,102	17.9	3.0
1714000	Chicago city	2,638,357	85.9	4.4	1,179,081	46.3	64.4	318,900	1,391	9.8	1,149,361	6.0	13.7
1714351	Cicero town	80,695	95.7	0.8	24,167	50.3	NA	266,000	1,150	11.2	41,003	12.3	9.2

Table C-4. Cities — Where: Migration, Housing, and Transportation, 2023—*Continued*

STATE and place code	STATE Place	Total population 1 year and over	Lived in the same house 1 year ago (percent)	Did not live in the same county 1 year ago (percent)	Total occupied housing units	Owner-occupied units (percent)	Percent with a mortgage, contract to purchase, or similar debt	Median value of owner-occupied units (dollars; owner estimated)	Median gross rent of renter-occupied units paying cash rent	Households without Internet access (percent)	Number of workers who commuted to work	Commute of less than 10 minutes (percent)	Commute of 60 minutes or more (percent)
	ACS table number:	C07204	C07204	C07204	B25003	B25003	B25081	B25097	B25064	S2801	B08012	B08012	B08012
	column number:	1	2	3	4	5	6	7	8	9	10	11	12
1718823	Decatur city	65,760	87.2	4.5	30,783	60.9	49.9	89,400	823	8.7	24,636	21.5	3.2
1723074	Elgin city	118,292	90.7	5.4	41,062	73.3	70.1	272,500	1,445	7.5	54,497	9.8	9.6
1724582	Evanston city	74,269	80.0	9.2	31,310	56.7	65.4	449,600	1,741	4.8	26,549	11.5	10.6
1738570	Joliet city	146,642	92.0	4.2	52,512	73.9	68.3	269,900	1,340	6.5	71,625	10.5	11.2
1751622	Naperville city	150,268	92.0	5.1	55,580	77.1	67.0	558,100	1,920	2.6	56,658	10.1	17.3
1757225	Palatine village	64555	85.2	5.0	27,531	63.3	68.7	369,600	1,344	5.1	31,007	8.9	9.3
1759000	Peoria city	111705	86.1	8.6	49,577	61.8	50.3	146,700	915	9.3	44,724	22.8	2.4
1765000	Rockford city	144787	85.4	4.7	62,552	53.8	54.5	136,200	956	9.4	59,384	14.0	4.9
1768003	Schaumburg village	75,364	85.2	6.8	31,791	60.2	60.0	323,100	1,841	4.1	32,701	8.1	12.8
1770122	Skokie village	63,866	88.8	2.9	23,942	73.9	58.7	365,700	1,504	4.6	24,383	6.5	10.6
1772000	Springfield city	111698	86.1	5.2	51,843	63.6	54.9	165,000	945	5.1	46,461	12.8	1.7
1779293	Waukegan city	88,646	87.2	4.5	31,784	57.3	58.1	203,200	1,144	10.0	40,819	7.8	7.4
18000	**INDIANA**	6,783,874	87.5	6.3	2,754,881	70.4	63.5	225,900	1,044	9.1	2,989,879	15.2	6.4
1805860	Bloomington city	73,532	57.4	25.0	33,738	27.4	65.9	342,000	1,124	9.8	31,463	21.5	3.1
1810342	Carmel city	100,583	89.2	5.2	38,523	73.8	69.6	476,900	1,641	2.9	40,522	12.6	4.4
1822000	Evansville city	112,019	83.6	7.1	51,696	53.7	62.0	149,000	922	9.9	49,802	23.0	3.7
1823278	Fishers city	100,276	93.7	4.3	38,270	77.3	79.2	407,500	1,450	4.4	39,841	11.4	2.0
1825000	Fort Wayne city	268,483	84.3	6.1	115,195	60.4	64.5	199,900	948	7.6	118,390	11.3	4.8
1827000	Gary city		66752	84.1	6.2	27,688	48.9	40.0	89,900	990	16.5	21,182	13.8
1831000	Hammond city	75,537	89.6	5.1	29,271	64.3	61.5	162,800	1,209	12.8	28,976	12.0	9.0
1836003	Indianapolis city (balance)	861,634	85.1	6.0	368,064	57.0	67.5	238,400	1,188	7.2	394,010	9.1	5.0
1840788	Lafayette city	66,601	80.9	9.3	31,331	49.7	64.0	190,100	1,023	7.9	30,534	15.0	3.2
1851876	Muncie city		64,226	72.8	15.0	26,505	52.7	47.2	102,100	867	15.3	30,010	28.9
1854180	Noblesville city	75,172	90.1	6.5	28,543	72.1	74.0	352,000	1,387	4.1	32,824	15.6	3.6
1871000	South Bend city	98,849	88.6	5.1	42,331	59.8	60.5	148,800	1,062	7.6	44,926	17.1	3.1
19000	**IOWA**	3,170,553	87.5	6.2	1,337,243	71.8	59.3	213,300	949	9.8	1,457,641	23.6	4.0
1901855	Ames city	65,676	67.0	20.3	26,633	44.9	51.5	273,000	993	22.2	31,903	30.9	2.4
1902305	Ankeny city	73,588	82.1	8.6	30,257	71.5	76.1	334,500	1,211	6.4	38,155	15.4	0.6
1912000	Cedar Rapids city	134560	83.3	7.0	58,123	65.7	64.6	191,100	971	7.4	62,866	19.0	3.6
1919000	Davenport city	98,891	83.6	6.0	44,171	63.7	66.0	172,300	956	6.4	46,567	13.8	1.5
1921000	Des Moines city	207,196	86.7	3.6	90,465	59.5	70.0	194,700	1,074	8.7	103,709	15.6	3.7
1938595	Iowa City city	74729	61.9	18.5	30,588	43.4	61.5	291,500	1,051	14.5	38,560	17.0	0.4
1973335	Sioux City city	83,992	91.9	4.1	32,278	63.8	60.4	174,100	1,021	9.6	38,133	16.9	3.1
1982425	Waterloo city	65,505	89.9	4.8	28,471	59.8	65.4	153,600	885	10.8	29,582	20.6	2.8
1983910	West Des Moines city	71,407	76.9	16.3	33,094	56.8	66.5	306,100	1,284	6.8	31,272	14.6	2.6
20000	**KANSAS**	2,907,735	86.2	6.5	1,188,340	66.7	57.1	219,800	1,036	8.3	1,323,613	22.2	3.8
2036000	Kansas City city	147,958	88.1	6.5	57,487	59.9	51.3	169,300	1,117	10.3	65,565	10.2	2.8
2038900	Lawrence city	95,687	72.0	16.3	41,551	43.5	NA	294,300	1,033	5.9	42,383	23.3	3.6
2052575	Olathe city	145610	88.8	2.9	53,252	74.3	73.6	360,200	1,361	5.4	67,790	12.5	1.6
2053775	Overland Park city	194,671	86.5	7.2	85,022	56.5	65.0	420,000	1,475	3.5	84,489	10.8	2.2
2064500	Shawnee city	68,504	92.3	3.3	28,168	72.8	70.1	357,000	1,332	3.5	33,711	10.8	4.4
2071000	Topeka city	123875	84.1	4.4	55,148	59.4	53.3	148,400	937	11.4	54,008	23.3	2.8
2079000	Wichita city	392,189	85.3	4.7	163,555	59.0	58.2	198,100	963	7.2	182,656	14.6	3.7
21000	**KENTUCKY**	4,477,307	87.7	6.3	1,853,603	68.8	56.1	211,800	929	9.8	1,867,279	14.5	6.2
2108902	Bowling Green city	75,963	78.3	14.1	32,904	38.0	NA	244,000	950	7.8	36,777	22.1	5.2
2146027	Lexington-Fayette urban county	315,940	79.6	8.5	141,680	55.8	65.6	294,300	1,145	7.2	149,981	13.2	3.8
2148006	Louisville/Jefferson County metro government (balance)	614,982	86.0	5.1	264,694	62.9	63.8	233,900	1,084	8.7	258,600	9.8	3.9
22000	**LOUISIANA**	4,524,085	89.0	5.1	1,833,915	68.1	51.7	215,600	1,020	11.9	1,850,348	13.4	7.8
2205000	Baton Rouge city	217,327	80.3	7.1	86,978	46.6	53.0	227,800	1,001	9.0	87,452	11.4	3.2
2239475	Kenner city	62,743	92.8	3.3	23,924	69.5	57.0	268,000	1,091	8.7	25,319	5.6	2.4
2240735	Lafayette city	119,694	87.8	5.3	53,953	54.1	53.9	252,100	985	6.1	55,969	17.1	4.7
2241155	Lake Charles city	78,950	82.8	4.8	33,140	57.9	50.5	217,300	1,102	12.8	36,275	23.3	2.5
2250115	Metairie CDP	134,723	87.5	6.7	61,486	58.9	52.6	319,700	1,143	9.3	63,228	14.0	4.9
2255000	New Orleans city	359,843	87.5	5.1	155,005	55.9	56.0	306,400	1,203	10.7	144,366	11.7	5.6
2270000	Shreveport city	175,739	86.9	4.8	78,443	53.4	53.9	168,300	1,013	16.9	69,328	16.9	3.2
23000	**MAINE**	1,385,562	89.4	5.7	616,085	74.4	56.1	310,700	1,189	8.0	596,229	17.3	6.6
2360545	Portland city	67,931	83.6	8.3	34,067	49.1	61.5	494,400	1,571	6.2	32,448	17.0	3.0

Table C-4. Cities — Where: Migration, Housing, and Transportation, 2023—*Continued*

STATE and place code	STATE Place	Total population 1 year and over	Lived in the same house 1 year ago (percent)	Did not live in the same county 1 year ago (percent)	Total occupied housing units	Owner-occupied units (percent)	Percent with a mortgage, contract to purchase, or similar debt	Median value of owner-occupied units (dollars; owner estimated)	Median gross rent of renter-occupied units paying cash rent	Households without Internet access (percent)	Number of workers who commuted to work	Commute of less than 10 minutes (percent)	Commute of 60 minutes or more (percent)
	ACS table number:	C07204	C07204	C07204	B25003	B25003	B25081	B25097	B25064	S2801	B08012	B08012	B08012
	column number:	1	2	3	4	5	6	7	8	9	10	11	12
24000	**MARYLAND**	6,110,314	89.0	6.2	2,384,715	67.9	70.7	413,600	1,651	7.0	2,635,654	8.3	13.1
2404000	Baltimore city	558,241	86.0	6.5	259,385	47.9	68.7	241,900	1,239	10.7	233,519	8.4	10.0
2407125	Bethesda CDP	69692	83.3	12.9	28,973	62.5	63.9	1,147,800	2,578	1.6	26,613	8.1	9.0
2419125	Columbia CDP	100,668	84.3	11.4	42,978	60.5	68.6	475,300	2,021	5.2	41,889	8.3	6.9
2426000	Ellicott City CDP	74,122	90.6	7.5	25,715	72.9	65.1	669,600	1,868	6.7	25,144	5.0	6.6
2430325	Frederick city	84,671	84.8	8.6	34,562	58.5	74.2	404,900	1,744	6.4	37,960	19.4	15.8
2431175	Gaithersburg city	68,433	86.2	7.4	25,813	48.0	72.7	481,800	2,076	2.5	26,143	6.7	17.2
2432025	Germantown CDP	94,892	86.6	4.5	34,372	65.7	73.9	407,200	1,918	3.8	44,905	6.8	17.1
2432650	Glen Burnie CDP	78,478	88.5	6.2	29,159	64.4	73.4	331,600	1,660	5.3	34,529	13.0	8.0
2467675	Rockville city	66,435	79.2	14.6	26,261	52.9	NA	665,600	2,206	5.5	26,313	8.3	14.2
2472450	Silver Spring CDP	84000	87.1	7.0	35,086	36.9	75.3	620,800	1,887	4.8	37,921	4.8	13.5
2481175	Waldorf CDP	82,316	91.4	5.7	31,345	77.9	NA	399,800	1,902	3.7	37,017	6.8	24.6
25000	**MASSACHUSETTS**	6,936,108	88.2	6.0	2,800,984	62.3	66.4	570,800	1,757	6.1	3,110,218	10.6	12.8
2507000	Boston city	645,761	80.6	10.1	288,129	35.9	69.9	703,600	2,128	6.6	312,870	6.8	10.7
2509000	Brockton city	103807	88.1	8.3	35,485	60.4	73.8	443,100	1,608	9.4	45,592	9.0	21.5
2511000	Cambridge city	116,843	77.1	15.5	49,310	34.5	55.2	987,400	2,930	3.6	53,167	8.9	7.0
2523000	Fall River city	92,985	87.7	3.4	43,425	32.3	63.0	402,100	1,217	8.4	43,321	14.4	9.6
2524960	Framingham city	70,965	85.0	4.4	25,727	54.8	72.1	624,800	2,034	4.5	32,774	9.8	15.4
2529405	Haverhill city	66,523	93.5	2.1	27,274	63.8	67.4	449,300	1,742	5.9	30,612	10.3	12.2
2534550	Lawrence city	86,636	91.6	3.3	32,631	30.8	NA	399,800	1,559	16.1	41,853	14.4	7.2
2537000	Lowell city	112,814	86.5	6.3	43,220	45.8	66.0	453,400	1,662	10.1	53,744	10.4	8.3
2537490	Lynn city	100,298	89.9	6.0	36,403	52.3	73.4	524,800	1,636	7.7	46,357	8.2	15.2
2537875	Malden city	64,295	87.7	6.3	27,716	40.4	70.2	624,700	2,071	3.4	31,814	3.2	14.6
2545000	New Bedford city	98289	84.2	7.1	41,300	42.9	63.7	366,600	1,156	11.0	40,855	14.5	8.5
2545560	Newton city	87,826	88.1	7.1	32,074	71.6	59.7	1,350,800	2,503	2.5	35,643	9.8	5.8
2555745	Quincy city	101,398	85.7	8.4	46,448	45.6	63.0	610,200	1,973	4.8	44,647	3.8	24.4
2562535	Somerville city	79,851	77.9	12.8	37,108	35.6	69.7	905,200	2,341	5.1	41,227	3.7	9.2
2567000	Springfield city	152,295	90.3	3.6	56,229	50.1	63.6	264,100	1,187	13.6	59,524	13.4	2.4
2582000	Worcester city	204601	82.2	8.6	81,973	43.7	67.0	378,900	1,605	7.0	93,453	13.4	11.1
26000	**MICHIGAN**	9,939,831	89.0	5.2	4,107,809	73.7	57.2	236,100	1,101	8.3	4,159,103	14.2	6.3
2603000	Ann Arbor city	118825	67.2	18.9	49,077	47.8	59.9	437,400	1,652	5.8	46,039	11.9	3.1
2621000	Dearborn city	104,109	89.9	4.4	38,777	65.2	48.3	223,200	1,371	7.2	34,856	12.7	1.1
2622000	Detroit city	625,759	89.6	3.5	255,857	53.8	31.3	86,400	1,043	12.5	209,110	8.4	5.9
2627440	Farmington Hills city	81,902	90.9	6.6	37,173	62.3	58.7	363,200	1,545	8.1	35,130	8.3	4.7
2629000	Flint city	78,519	84.5	3.1	33,879	55.7	NA	53,600	831	18.9	27,578	14.1	11.0
2634000	Grand Rapids city	193,940	81.4	8.3	80,311	54.4	64.5	260,000	1,297	7.6	93,906	18.8	4.9
2642160	Kalamazoo city	71,905	79.0	9.2	30,482	43.5	55.9	172,400	1,075	9.5	33,818	23.6	3.2
2646000	Lansing city	110,391	85.6	7.5	52,849	56.8	66.8	128,200	960	9.2	50,270	17.3	5.8
2649000	Livonia city	90229	94.1	3.4	38,023	87.0	65.0	283,400	1,460	4.9	37,298	9.2	4.5
2659440	Novi city	65,272	88.6	7.2	26,962	64.6	55.9	420,100	1,795	4.8	24,864	7.0	4.8
2669035	Rochester Hills city	75,509	90.1	5.6	28,914	75.5	62.2	389,100	1,675	3.4	30,756	10.0	6.4
2674900	Southfield city	75104	90.8	5.3	35,348	60.6	62.0	234,200	1,213	8.4	32,724	12.5	2.8
2676460	Sterling Heights city	131,942	90.4	5.4	52,105	75.1	60.3	274,000	1,271	4.7	54,423	8.9	5.0
2680700	Troy city	86,520	86.3	9.4	34,743	66.6	57.2	410,900	1,672	5.0	38,105	9.7	4.6
2684000	Warren city	134,684	89.5	4.9	54,644	71.5	59.7	197,600	1,209	7.5	55,970	9.8	4.1
2686000	Westland city	82101	84.1	4.4	35,723	62.7	61.5	188,400	1,089	7.4	37,901	7.9	6.8
2688940	Wyoming city	76,151	85.9	3.1	30,586	65.4	65.9	235,000	1,258	7.7	38,603	11.7	1.4
27000	**MINNESOTA**	5,673,119	88.4	6.5	2,344,432	72.0	63.8	328,600	1,264	7.6	2,516,455	16.2	4.9
2706382	Blaine city	72,809	91.7	5.1	25,670	85.2	68.5	345,500	1,743	4.5	29,624	10.1	3.9
2706616	Bloomington city	86,270	88.0	3.8	39,370	63.0	58.2	357,200	1,640	8.9	36,529	13.0	2.1
2707966	Brooklyn Park city	80,923	89.8	7.3	29,325	72.9	71.3	340,200	1,206	7.2	35,773	7.5	1.2
2717000	Duluth city	87,237	82.7	9.2	38,843	58.9	61.6	252,700	1,057	10.7	42,190	18.9	2.7
2717288	Eagan city	67,068	87.8	6.0	27,978	67.6	62.8	406,600	1,678	4.1	27,899	16.2	3.6
2735180	Lakeville city	75,323	93.3	4.5	25,289	87.7	75.9	464,300	1,726	2.1	33,610	10.4	4.4
2740166	Maple Grove city	70,345	92.1	1.8	29,987	81.0	69.6	405,600	1,909	4.8	29,761	11.9	4.4
2743000	Minneapolis city	419,780	78.3	10.7	198,866	45.8	72.8	355,600	1,343	9.1	193,989	8.9	2.3
2751730	Plymouth city	76596	90.7	5.2	29,393	72.7	72.1	522,600	1,712	3.1	32,004	12.0	1.0
2754880	Rochester city	120289	84.1	10.8	51,184	65.9	66.4	324,200	1,445	5.8	54,524	18.9	3.9
2756896	St. Cloud city	67,907	80.8	11.2	25,769	51.2	61.7	251,100	1,002	6.7	31,102	16.6	7.4
2758000	St. Paul city	299,516	83.1	9.8	126,409	52.4	70.5	293,500	1,314	7.7	132,635	11.9	2.6
2771428	Woodbury city	78,999	89.7	5.7	31,280	75.4	74.0	441,500	1,875	2.3	32,540	9.1	3.8

Table C-4. Cities — Where: Migration, Housing, and Transportation, 2023—*Continued*

STATE and place code	STATE Place	Total population 1 year and over	Lived in the same house 1 year ago (percent)	Did not live in the same county 1 year ago (percent)	Total occupied housing units	Owner-occupied units (percent)	Percent with a mortgage, contract to purchase, or similar debt	Median value of owner-occupied units (dollars; owner estimated)	Median gross rent of renter-occupied units paying cash rent	Households without Internet access (percent)	Number of workers who commuted to work	Commute of less than 10 minutes (percent)	Commute of 60 minutes or more (percent)
	ACS table number:	C07204	C07204	C07204	B25003	B25003	B25081	B25097	B25064	S2801	B08012	B08012	B08012
	column number:	1	2	3	4	5	6	7	8	9	10	11	12
28000	**MISSISSIPPI**	2,907,634	89.5	5.8	1,166,617	71.1	48.0	169,800	898	13.4	1,187,693	13.2	7.3
2829700	Gulfport city	72,006	84.2	5.2	31,011	56.6	52.6	175,600	989	15.3	27,776	18.0	2.5
2836000	Jackson city	142758	88.9	3.2	60,636	50.8	51.6	110,600	988	9.2	57,451	8.2	2.7
29000	**MISSOURI**	6,126,390	87.9	6.0	2,556,271	68.8	59.7	233,600	1,019	9.1	2,654,112	15.4	5.4
2915670	Columbia city	127,743	74.1	13.9	53,894	48.5	59.9	281,100	1,118	8.1	60,640	19.0	3.4
2935000	Independence city	119,809	85.8	4.2	51,311	64.9	57.2	180,700	1,057	7.7	48,949	8.3	3.2
2938000	Kansas City city	504,509	86.8	5.8	227,773	56.4	60.4	243,200	1,215	7.8	224,882	10.6	3.4
2941348	Lee's Summit city	102,524	89.6	3.1	40,435	68.7	72.8	344,500	1,446	2.3	44,242	14.1	2.9
2954074	O'Fallon city	92,666	91.3	4.0	34,714	82.5	74.7	340,400	1,564	3.1	46,370	10.5	3.6
2964082	St. Charles city	70,884	87.2	6.3	31,316	70.9	68.3	310,700	1,321	4.6	32,002	13.7	2.2
2964550	St. Joseph city	70,033	88.0	5.3	28,196	64.3	55.2	156,000	886	12.7	29,980	21.8	6.4
2965000	St. Louis city	278,251	86.0	7.3	150,404	48.1	59.3	192,800	1,011	9.3	132,722	11.8	3.3
2970000	Springfield city	167875	77.6	9.9	79,707	44.6	59.2	199,800	962	14.3	79,334	16.8	2.1
30000	**MONTANA**	1,120,157	86.9	6.8	472,867	69.2	55.2	392,300	1,083	8.8	493,140	23.4	5.6
3006550	Billings city	119,133	84.7	6.0	52,878	62.4	65.0	346,500	1,033	7.3	55,789	20.2	1.7
3050200	Missoula city	77,169	82.0	8.7	35,775	48.2	60.3	493,600	1,178	5.7	36,348	18.2	6.3
31000	**NEBRASKA**	1,956,041	87.0	6.4	813,864	66.3	58.9	245,200	1,042	7.8	924,422	23.3	3.5
3128000	Lincoln city	291,913	82.7	6.8	126,828	54.1	63.4	265,700	1,024	6.7	141,356	18.0	3.3
3137000	Omaha city	478300	85.5	6.2	204,135	57.2	63.6	255,500	1,161	6.1	222,077	13.1	3.3
32000	**NEVADA**	3,159,456	85.4	5.4	1,224,685	60.4	64.5	441,100	1,622	5.9	1,365,439	9.5	6.0
3223770	Enterprise CDP	241557	85.9	4.9	90,011	64.2	75.8	484,800	1,894	2.4	121,706	7.5	5.2
3231900	Henderson city	334,461	86.0	4.8	136,680	64.7	64.8	493,800	1,852	4.3	130,665	7.8	4.7
3240000	Las Vegas city	654,018	84.0	5.6	252,848	56.8	66.7	434,200	1,590	6.3	278,878	7.0	5.2
3251800	North Las Vegas city	282,600	85.9	4.9	92,288	65.1	74.3	411,200	1,722	7.3	122,072	5.8	4.9
3254600	Paradise CDP	176,030	83.0	6.3	74,847	43.5	61.2	378,300	1,401	7.1	79,974	8.3	7.1
3260600	Reno city	271,297	82.3	6.4	114,623	51.8	64.9	546,500	1,594	7.0	128,926	11.1	4.0
3268400	Sparks city	108,101	87.7	3.5	41,595	65.6	65.8	478,100	1,716	4.7	51,878	12.3	4.1
3268585	Spring Valley CDP	195,786	80.8	7.9	82,320	48.4	65.2	441,000	1,757	4.3	93,376	5.7	4.2
3271400	Sunrise Manor CDP	209,786	87.3	2.8	67,326	52.4	60.8	329,700	1,411	10.0	85,608	5.8	4.9
33000	**NEW HAMPSHIRE**	1,389,863	90.1	5.4	569,493	72.4	62.5	415,400	1,517	5.9	632,959	13.9	9.7
3345140	Manchester city	115,055	81.2	5.7	50,053	48.5	67.1	369,300	1,638	6.4	59,891	13.3	6.5
3350260	Nashua city	89,608	89.8	4.1	36,451	58.5	67.2	415,300	1,750	4.9	42,204	12.2	11.2
34000	**NEW JERSEY**	9,192,631	90.6	5.1	3,538,457	63.7	63.9	461,000	1,667	5.9	4,030,075	9.8	15.1
3403580	Bayonne city	69,437	95.0	3.3	30,335	32.8	62.9	489,300	1,638	6.9	27,910	9.3	19.4
3410000	Camden city	70,329	90.2	6.0	27,511	37.1	45.4	103,500	1,114	9.7	29,025	12.1	2.9
3413690	Clifton city	87410	93.2	4.4	31,968	62.7	60.6	445,100	1,551	3.8	38,210	8.1	14.5
3419390	East Orange city	69,293	87.8	6.0	30,360	31.6	NA	384,000	1,360	5.0	31,428	7.1	30.2
3421000	Elizabeth city	133,008	91.3	3.6	45,491	29.1	62.1	468,200	1,511	7.9	62,438	8.4	10.7
3436000	Jersey City city	288,042	87.7	6.2	130,020	27.6	71.0	556,900	1,984	6.2	132,493	2.6	17.2
3438580	Lakewood CDP	NA	NA	NA	13,406	31.3	NA	660,100	1,668	44.0	16,644	20.3	10.6
3451000	Newark city	300969	88.8	4.9	114,599	24.6	70.4	403,500	1,341	6.3	124,441	4.7	16.9
3456550	Passaic city	NA	NA	NA	21,234	26.7	NA	440,500	1,417	3.7	28,891	12.2	10.7
3457000	Paterson city	153,627	89.5	4.0	51,969	26.2	NA	415,100	1,512	9.3	66,761	8.3	5.2
3473110	Toms River CDP	94,701	94.4	1.5	36,998	81.5	61.1	414,000	1,723	8.1	38,606	16.8	15.9
3474000	Trenton city	88,997	81.7	7.3	32,131	32.4	NA	182,300	1,210	17.7	35,627	12.7	4.8
3474630	Union City city	64,048	92.0	5.7	25,001	24.2	NA	440,100	1,553	9.4	33,190	5.9	13.6
35000	**NEW MEXICO**	2,093,439	88.2	5.9	856,580	69.3	52.2	256,300	1,084	11.2	846,938	18.4	6.8
3502000	Albuquerque city	555,391	86.7	5.1	243,664	61.7	63.8	300,100	1,203	8.5	247,598	12.2	5.0
3539380	Las Cruces city	113,884	82.9	7.4	50,409	58.7	61.1	246,200	965	7.3	49,012	14.8	4.8
3563460	Rio Rancho city	109,366	90.6	7.2	42,054	78.1	71.0	326,800	1,557	5.1	44,379	11.7	11.3
3570500	Santa Fe city	88,415	90.9	6.3	42,397	58.8	57.0	457,400	1,273	7.0	38,425	16.0	3.9
36000	**NEW YORK**	19,365,855	90.4	4.3	7,809,267	54.1	57.4	420,200	1,561	7.9	8,243,157	10.0	16.9
3601000	Albany city	100,098	84.4	8.9	44,875	42.4	57.7	231,500	1,264	7.6	46,384	14.0	2.6
3611000	Buffalo city	272,138	84.7	5.2	123,347	43.3	50.5	174,200	1,022	10.7	108,492	11.2	4.4
3615000	Cheektowaga CDP	74,368	91.6	3.9	34,150	69.6	58.9	202,000	1,059	11.0	34,093	12.7	1.2
3649121	Mount Vernon city	70,421	92.9	2.5	27,369	45.4	NA	506,600	1,628	9.2	32,226	7.6	13.2
3650617	New Rochelle city	82,315	93.5	4.6	29,052	57.1	59.9	629,900	1,859	5.6	35,765	8.6	14.9

Table C-4. Cities — Where: Migration, Housing, and Transportation, 2023—*Continued*

STATE and place code	STATE Place	Total population 1 year and over	Lived in the same house 1 year ago (percent)	Did not live in the same county 1 year ago (percent)	Total occupied housing units	Owner-occupied units (percent)	Percent with a mortgage, contract to purchase, or similar debt	Median value of owner-occupied units (dollars; owner estimated)	Median gross rent of renter-occupied units paying cash rent	Households without Internet access (percent)	Number of workers who commuted to work	Commute of less than 10 minutes (percent)	Commute of 60 minutes or more (percent)
	ACS table number:	C07204	C07204	C07204	B25003	B25003	B25081	B25097	B25064	S2801	B08012	B08012	B08012
	column number:	1	2	3	4	5	6	7	8	9	10	11	12
	NEW YORK—Cont.												
3651000	New York city	8166531	90.3	3.6	3,394,750	32.5	55.9	743,000	1,748	8.2	3,444,254	4.5	24.8
3663000	Rochester city	205,820	79.6	8.2	91,471	37.0	61.3	133,200	1,043	11.0	87,885	16.1	3.8
3665508	Schenectady city	67988	87.4	6.3	28,730	43.5	63.4	170,800	1,239	10.3	27,163	15.2	4.1
3673000	Syracuse city	143659	75.7	12.2	60,652	39.3	54.2	135,400	1,060	10.3	56,745	20.1	5.0
3684000	Yonkers city	206139	91.0	4.4	79,190	44.3	61.3	541,200	1,671	7.5	95,420	7.3	21.6
37000	**NORTH CAROLINA**	10,719,307	87.1	7.4	4,392,669	66.3	61.3	308,600	1,245	8.3	4,392,673	12.6	6.6
3701520	Apex town		71,471	90.8	4.3	27,306	75.2	78.3	608,300	1,947	2.3	23,175	10.8
3702140	Asheville city	94,221	84.3	8.9	39,811	52.8	59.3	465,800	1,377	7.3	38,756	14.6	2.8
3710740	Cary town	177,110	88.1	6.6	71,248	64.7	71.4	600,900	1,771	3.2	65,975	10.0	4.2
3712000	Charlotte city	899,656	85.1	8.4	375,680	50.2	74.8	413,800	1,656	5.5	355,196	8.6	4.5
3714100	Concord city	109,295	84.6	10.7	42,777	58.0	74.6	374,700	1,524	3.4	46,806	6.8	9.2
3719000	Durham city	292,429	79.2	12.5	127,514	51.5	71.1	417,400	1,589	4.3	129,442	11.8	3.5
3722920	Fayetteville city	206,091	79.7	11.1	83,410	49.1	65.3	201,100	1,252	5.8	96,958	23.0	3.9
3725580	Gastonia city	82,413	88.7	4.4	33,496	53.1	71.2	293,500	1,255	7.9	33,549	9.4	10.5
3728000	Greensboro city	298,516	82.3	7.1	125,752	51.3	67.4	262,300	1,199	8.8	131,887	14.7	6.6
3728080	Greenville city	89,036	75.4	14.3	41,037	36.7	70.7	239,700	1,016	10.1	37,146	17.3	6.0
3731400	High Point city	114645	82.4	7.4	45,442	54.3	62.4	252,700	1,088	11.0	49,431	17.7	2.8
3734200	Jacksonville city	71,710	69.4	20.6	24,538	35.1	NA	240,300	1,320	5.7	37,246	37.5	1.6
3755000	Raleigh city	477,712	82.3	9.5	211,433	50.0	71.6	445,500	1,591	5.9	210,707	10.2	5.1
3774440	Wilmington city	121,626	77.8	12.4	59,730	47.7	65.1	389,100	1,437	9.2	53,255	20.8	2.7
3775000	Winston-Salem city	251112	82.7	8.4	107,693	55.7	62.5	256,700	1,114	10.4	102,119	17.6	2.4
38000	**NORTH DAKOTA**	774,985	84.0	8.1	338,059	63.7	52.8	246,700	916	10.9	380,033	28.8	5.4
3807200	Bismarck city	74,264	86.9	4.4	34,598	66.4	NA	280,400	929	14.3	36,584	24.0	6.3
3825700	Fargo city	130,895	73.9	10.7	60,510	44.5	61.6	282,700	954	12.5	69,029	20.0	2.6
39000	**OHIO**	11,660,232	88.6	5.1	4,917,309	67.1	60.1	220,200	1,014	8.7	5,015,931	14.2	5.0
3901000	Akron city	187,106	87.2	5.1	85,349	53.0	63.0	131,600	903	10.2	78,953	12.1	3.9
3912000	Canton city	68083	88.9	2.4	29,864	49.1	46.3	96,600	798	13.8	28,116	20.2	4.4
3915000	Cincinnati city	307,941	81.1	7.0	149,698	37.9	67.7	247,300	1,013	11.4	138,962	12.3	3.2
3916000	Cleveland city	358,939	82.7	4.9	168,307	43.1	49.7	107,100	939	14.6	143,089	12.8	4.2
3918000	Columbus city	897,432	79.4	6.7	394,905	42.4	69.0	265,800	1,273	5.3	406,014	10.0	3.0
3921000	Dayton city	133,549	79.1	7.4	57,882	48.2	55.1	108,100	892	11.9	52,031	13.8	3.6
3944856	Lorain city	64,771	91.3	3.9	27,930	62.4	59.7	140,500	790	12.3	26,093	5.4	4.7
3961000	Parma city	77725	85.1	4.1	34,406	76.4	62.8	180,700	1,142	8.1	35,719	8.3	3.3
3977000	Toledo city	262,966	86.6	4.5	117,902	52.1	52.4	108,200	901	12.2	108,621	13.0	3.3
40000	**OKLAHOMA**	4,011,072	85.8	6.9	1,589,105	65.1	52.9	208,600	1,020	9.7	1,673,752	17.1	5.0
4009050	Broken Arrow city	118,329	89.9	3.9	44,802	73.8	61.8	256,100	1,330	6.4	53,225	13.0	2.9
4023200	Edmond city	96,929	87.5	4.8	39,282	70.8	63.1	367,600	1,284	2.2	42,323	10.3	4.4
4041850	Lawton city	89,485	76.8	13.0	34,205	47.3	58.4	140,000	989	9.8	35,592	27.3	3.1
4052500	Norman city	129188	76.8	12.7	54,715	49.0	55.6	270,300	1,049	7.2	60,388	19.9	5.5
4055000	Oklahoma City city	693,309	83.4	6.5	284,755	57.0	61.1	248,100	1,166	7.5	310,359	10.0	2.7
4075000	Tulsa city	405,937	82.3	7.0	173,905	50.0	54.6	214,200	1,055	9.0	172,118	13.6	3.2
41000	**OREGON**	4,196,830	86.5	6.7	1,752,050	63.4	63.8	484,800	1,481	6.6	1,696,954	16.5	6.2
4105350	Beaverton city	95,435	85.6	7.8	43,874	47.3	74.7	566,500	1,789	5.7	40,034	8.9	7.0
4105800	Bend city	103619	84.4	8.0	46,318	61.5	69.5	720,500	1,868	4.9	40,631	20.9	1.0
4123850	Eugene city	176,620	77.6	10.7	78,974	47.6	62.0	468,100	1,439	9.9	74,418	14.6	3.1
4131250	Gresham city	108,211	88.9	6.1	42,173	57.8	68.1	454,900	1,481	9.0	48,537	10.9	11.2
4134100	Hillsboro city	106,947	85.6	6.2	42,575	53.3	74.5	521,800	1,974	2.1	49,977	13.8	6.6
4147000	Medford city	84,852	83.6	5.8	34,867	55.4	62.9	404,400	1,430	6.5	32,783	24.6	2.0
4159000	Portland city	624,727	81.1	8.4	292,037	50.8	71.4	570,300	1,556	6.0	269,891	10.0	5.1
4164900	Salem city	175,177	83.2	6.8	68,817	57.2	66.7	434,600	1,425	7.0	72,940	18.1	7.5
42000	**PENNSYLVANIA**	12,829,324	89.4	5.1	5,324,209	69.5	57.1	259,900	1,197	8.8	5,400,641	13.3	8.2
4202000	Allentown city	123,307	83.6	7.5	46,104	38.5	52.9	211,400	1,296	15.4	49,849	12.2	8.3
4206088	Bethlehem city	76,884	89.1	7.0	32,208	51.6	57.3	259,400	1,434	8.0	32,993	12.7	7.2
4224000	Erie city	91,640	83.6	6.6	39,704	55.4	55.5	117,200	885	7.6	36,989	18.3	5.4
4260000	Philadelphia city	1530695	85.6	6.0	688,112	51.8	59.7	246,600	1,390	8.9	623,577	7.7	11.7
4261000	Pittsburgh city	300,292	77.4	9.1	140,615	48.6	54.6	214,100	1,260	7.5	130,637	10.1	5.0
4263624	Reading city	93,310	85.7	8.1	31,358	38.9	49.9	136,800	1,159	7.1	35,087	15.9	7.8
4269000	Scranton city	74,448	83.1	8.9	31,094	50.5	41.2	164,700	1,088	NA	28,668	15.6	3.6

Table C-4. Cities — Where: Migration, Housing, and Transportation, 2023—*Continued*

STATE and place code	STATE Place	Total population 1 year and over	Lived in the same house 1 year ago (percent)	Did not live in the same county 1 year ago (percent)	Total occupied housing units	Owner-occupied units (percent)	Percent with a mortgage, contract to purchase, or similar debt	Median value of owner-occupied units (dollars; owner estimated)	Median gross rent of renter-occupied units paying cash rent	Households without Internet access (percent)	Number of workers who commuted to work	Commute of less than 10 minutes (percent)	Commute of 60 minutes or more (percent)
	ACS table number:	C07204	C07204	C07204	B25003	B25003	B25081	B25097	B25064	S2801	B08012	B08012	B08012
	column number:	1	2	3	4	5	6	7	8	9	10	11	12
44000	**RHODE ISLAND**	1,086,909	89.1	5.5	443,980	64.0	65.7	411,800	1,365	7.1	484,372	12.6	7.7
4419180	Cranston city	81,693	91.4	3.7	31,571	70.0	72.5	384,900	1,278	4.0	38,459	9.9	5.1
4454640	Pawtucket city	75155	86.8	5.6	33,667	50.7	62.5	332,500	1,216	12.3	36,381	8.1	6.0
4459000	Providence city	189885	82.5	9.7	71,374	39.2	64.8	359,900	1,501	8.4	80,623	16.9	7.6
4474300	Warwick city	81,823	91.1	6.5	36,989	71.1	71.9	359,500	1,322	8.5	39,358	11.7	7.6
45000	**SOUTH CAROLINA**	5,319,249	87.6	7.3	2,177,733	72.4	57.5	272,900	1,170	9.0	2,210,448	12.2	6.7
4513330	Charleston city	153,947	79.7	12.0	69,588	57.2	72.1	515,800	1,728	6.3	68,689	11.0	5.6
4516000	Columbia city	140,457	73.2	18.9	58,713	46.8	61.4	269,100	1,205	13.0	66,383	22.7	1.0
4530850	Greenville city	71,954	75.5	14.7	35,609	40.4	71.1	496,400	1,451	8.4	33,569	21.0	5.1
4548535	Mount Pleasant town	93976	90.4	5.0	40,023	76.6	69.4	825,300	2,179	2.3	36,390	10.1	5.2
4550875	North Charleston city	119,378	76.8	14.6	53,710	49.0	65.5	306,800	1,534	5.2	55,132	11.4	6.1
4561405	Rock Hill city	74,782	92.8	3.6	31,189	59.5	68.5	315,900	1,301	6.9	35,219	14.9	7.1
46000	**SOUTH DAKOTA**	907,196	88.5	6.4	378,559	69.4	55.1	268,200	921	8.1	422,763	27.6	4.1
4652980	Rapid City city	79,009	80.0	10.6	33,880	60.6	63.2	312,200	1,123	5.6	35,567	17.5	5.7
4659020	Sioux Falls city	203,230	88.2	5.2	90,489	62.2	65.3	302,500	986	5.9	103,216	12.9	2.5
47000	**TENNESSEE**	7,046,744	87.7	6.3	2,889,226	67.3	57.7	307,300	1,214	8.9	2,966,891	11.9	7.7
4714000	Chattanooga city	183,978	84.3	5.7	81,086	51.9	59.7	311,300	1,296	7.6	81,813	15.8	1.6
4715160	Clarksville city	178,291	79.5	12.1	71,172	53.0	71.1	290,800	1,381	4.7	79,315	11.4	12.6
4727740	Franklin city	87,669	87.8	8.3	35,730	68.1	67.7	738,300	1,944	4.7	33,739	12.1	5.0
4737640	Jackson city	67651	84.8	8.3	28,458	51.7	53.5	238,900	1,185	7.1	28,061	27.4	5.7
4738320	Johnson City city	73,308	81.1	12.8	31,162	55.5	53.7	271,600	1,084	8.4	30,723	20.1	5.2
4740000	Knoxville city	196,571	84.4	6.5	87,036	48.4	58.7	282,300	1,193	14.6	87,802	11.9	2.3
4748000	Memphis city	609,736	86.1	3.7	257,188	44.9	57.6	200,900	1,175	8.6	255,135	11.0	2.0
4751560	Murfreesboro city	163683	81.6	8.0	63,223	51.2	73.5	419,200	1,536	4.3	79,456	10.3	10.1
4752006	Nashville-Davidson metropolitan government (balance)	677,047	81.9	8.2	330,506	52.5	70.6	433,500	1,626	6.8	318,153	9.4	4.6
48000	**TEXAS**	30,134,547	85.9	6.6	11,260,645	62.6	55.8	296,900	1,413	7.4	12,780,053	11.7	8.8
4801000	Abilene city	128424	81.8	8.3	47,511	56.2	53.7	195,200	1,268	6.0	54,789	20.3	1.4
4801924	Allen city	110,797	86.3	7.2	38,830	66.9	66.7	535,600	2,064	3.5	46,384	10.7	10.7
4803000	Amarillo city	201,686	88.3	3.0	80,754	61.6	51.0	190,700	1,002	10.2	96,153	19.3	5.1
4804000	Arlington city	392,803	84.6	6.6	150,945	53.2	59.1	312,700	1,495	5.8	182,727	8.5	8.0
4804462	Atascocita CDP	116820	91.3	3.9	38,628	82.9	NA	311,300	1,847	3.9	48,367	5.0	18.2
4805000	Austin city	970,338	79.6	9.4	475,680	43.5	66.5	600,600	1,764	5.0	424,865	10.5	4.0
4806128	Baytown city	84,698	86.3	4.0	31,402	54.8	NA	210,300	1,167	7.1	35,975	11.4	3.3
4807000	Beaumont city	110,413	86.4	4.5	44,169	59.1	NA	169,200	1,115	9.5	47,455	15.0	2.4
4810768	Brownsville city	187,797	93.0	2.8	64,083	65.6	NA	154,800	897	11.1	77,874	7.1	3.6
4810912	Bryan city	87,707	79.6	11.5	33,775	46.6	NA	231,000	1,176	10.6	40,011	19.6	6.7
4813024	Carrollton city	130,748	88.6	6.0	52,503	58.0	59.5	388,300	1,770	4.0	63,121	9.8	4.0
4813552	Cedar Park city	78,090	89.2	7.0	27,998	65.2	71.2	562,300	1,832	5.1	31,612	9.6	4.5
4815976	College Station city	124,450	65.8	19.2	47,029	34.9	NA	355,200	1,185	15.2	54,913	14.2	4.4
4816432	Conroe city	107,087	83.2	8.6	42,134	50.8	NA	323,800	1,441	3.7	50,826	7.8	12.1
4817000	Corpus Christi city	312,450	85.3	6.0	118,392	57.3	52.7	218,600	1,277	7.7	null	NA	NA
4819000	Dallas city	1287866	84.6	6.8	536,727	41.9	53.0	329,700	1,512	8.0	583,156	9.5	6.8
4819972	Denton city	156,696	78.5	11.8	59,711	47.8	59.0	380,000	1,411	7.7	71,200	14.9	5.6
4822660	Edinburg city	104164	86.7	3.3	34,958	51.1	NA	197,900	965	6.0	43,151	14.0	5.7
4824000	El Paso city	669744	87.3	4.4	249,362	60.4	51.2	194,100	1,122	11.3	286,328	8.9	5.1
4826232	Flower Mound town	78048	84.5	8.6	29,171	77.7	72.6	590,500	2,275	3.3	31,459	13.5	3.6
4827000	Fort Worth city	965,536	85.5	5.7	346,392	56.9	63.6	318,300	1,547	7.1	427,330	8.0	8.6
4827684	Frisco city	222,628	83.4	9.8	80,665	66.3	75.6	687,900	2,099	1.6	77,164	11.1	6.8
4829000	Garland city	240,267	91.0	4.7	80,786	59.1	54.4	280,900	1,678	3.5	106,108	5.7	8.6
4829336	Georgetown city	95503	86.1	9.2	42,239	66.7	NA	428,000	1,719	4.9	33,789	8.3	9.2
4830464	Grand Prairie city	199,293	83.5	9.0	70,750	54.3	57.2	314,800	1,612	6.7	87,360	7.1	6.2
4832372	Harlingen city	70,678	84.3	4.7	25,629	52.9	NA	170,700	922	6.8	27,096	18.7	2.0
4835000	Houston city	2,276,308	82.0	6.8	942,146	42.4	51.3	282,400	1,362	8.9	1,014,280	7.9	8.1
4837000	Irving city	251,669	84.6	8.2	95,909	38.6	58.7	341,500	1,650	6.9	104,695	8.1	3.6
4839148	Killeen city	156,121	80.0	7.1	64,777	52.4	NA	227,000	1,280	7.7	70,302	11.7	13.8
4841464	Laredo city	249,438	91.6	1.6	79,072	64.5	55.6	204,900	994	9.0	102,521	10.5	4.2
4841980	League City city	116824	91.1	4.7	41,978	78.7	70.3	359,300	1,621	3.1	50,828	7.0	13.4
4842016	Leander city	79,154	89.2	5.1	28,615	77.4	82.4	528,000	1,988	1.8	29,925	10.6	10.4
4842508	Lewisville city	132,883	84.0	7.4	50,672	51.7	65.4	377,800	1,678	3.3	66,369	14.0	6.9
4843888	Longview city	82,924	81.3	8.1	32,201	53.2	52.9	188,700	1,107	10.1	37,181	18.1	6.6

Table C-4. Cities — Where: Migration, Housing, and Transportation, 2023—*Continued*

STATE and place code	STATE Place	Total population 1 year and over	Lived in the same house 1 year ago (percent)	Did not live in the same county 1 year ago (percent)	Total occupied housing units	Owner-occupied units (percent)	Percent with a mortgage, contract to purchase, or similar debt	Median value of owner-occupied units (dollars; owner estimated)	Median gross rent of renter-occupied units paying cash rent	Households without Internet access (percent)	Number of workers who commuted to work	Commute of less than 10 minutes (percent)	Commute of 60 minutes or more (percent)
	ACS table number:	C07204	C07204	C07204	B25003	B25003	B25081	B25097	B25064	S2801	B08012	B08012	B08012
	column number:	1	2	3	4	5	6	7	8	9	10	11	12
	TEXAS—Cont.												
4845000	Lubbock city	263,071	78.0	9.0	108,609	48.5	52.3	217,800	1,180	9.3	127,149	18.8	3.3
4845384	McAllen city	144,149	88.4	3.4	51,319	58.7	48.2	203,900	1,016	6.1	56,940	13.6	3.2
4845744	McKinney city	209,647	82.6	8.9	74,833	60.8	75.0	497,700	1,862	3.9	83,166	9.9	5.5
4846452	Mansfield city	NA	NA	NA	26,245	65.9	NA	432,500	2,039	3.7	34,644	9.2	6.9
4847892	Mesquite city	145272	87.9	4.5	49,690	64.6	58.3	252,000	1,487	3.8	65,114	9.1	18.3
4848072	Midland city	135,512	84.3	7.1	53,640	66.7	61.0	316,600	1,253	7.7	63,655	15.3	3.6
4848768	Mission city	85,854	87.6	4.2	29,183	65.7	NA	169,500	945	9.4	33,482	12.7	4.5
4848804	Missouri City city	71,019	91.9	3.9	26,271	77.6	59.3	316,900	1,888	1.9	30,997	3.6	8.6
4850820	New Braunfels city	110657	83.9	9.6	42,756	66.6	66.9	356,200	1,737	5.8	47,476	10.9	8.1
4852356	North Richland Hills city	69,618	86.0	4.4	27,385	58.8	NA	368,300	1,759	3.8	33,429	11.3	7.3
4853388	Odessa city	120,702	85.4	5.9	54,163	57.1	NA	233,300	1,269	14.3	64,540	12.3	7.1
4856000	Pasadena city	145,384	86.8	3.3	49,618	57.9	47.4	219,000	1,206	7.3	59,791	10.8	11.9
4856348	Pearland city	125,687	89.4	7.6	45,686	75.9	NA	349,200	1,805	1.9	54,059	6.4	8.9
4857176	Pflugerville city	63,818	87.7	5.4	24,333	66.3	72.0	433,000	2,120	2.8	27,343	10.7	10.0
4857200	Pharr city	79233	90.3	2.7	23,919	56.6	NA	126,700	1,042	6.8	32,428	9.3	7.7
4858016	Plano city	285,839	84.2	9.3	114,555	56.7	58.2	472,500	1,848	3.9	119,161	10.4	6.0
4861796	Richardson city	116516	79.2	11.5	45,822	52.5	60.3	435,400	1,834	4.0	49,743	14.3	4.3
4863500	Round Rock city	130,493	87.1	7.8	48,682	56.6	67.3	439,400	1,809	4.0	56,846	11.1	4.8
4863572	Rowlett city		66,130	89.9	5.9	23,939	72.6	NA	390,100	2,188	NA	29,089	5.7
4864472	San Angelo city	95,014	79.8	8.1	39,231	53.8	NA	181,500	1,107	10.3	45,016	20.2	5.6
4865000	San Antonio city	1,477,259	82.2	5.5	558,796	53.2	55.6	250,000	1,284	6.6	639,956	8.4	6.2
4865600	San Marcos city	70,571	69.5	19.4	28,741	29.1	NA	298,200	1,263	16.3	36,401	12.8	10.2
4869596	Spring CDP	NA	NA	NA	22,132	72.7	NA	246,600	1,754	3.1	28,802	4.0	11.1
4870808	Sugar Land city	107702	90.7	7.1	36,977	77.3	56.6	433,600	2,108	2.7	41,847	6.7	9.7
4872176	Temple city	91,386	77.3	9.4	35,445	56.1	NA	255,700	1,359	8.9	40,496	17.8	6.9
4872656	The Woodlands CDP	120,604	93.4	4.2	44,480	69.7	64.2	572,500	1,919	2.6	43,269	7.9	11.9
4874144	Tyler city	108,779	88.0	5.4	36,292	51.1	NA	251,600	1,385	8.7	45,235	13.2	3.3
4875428	Victoria city	64,735	86.1	8.4	25,267	60.8	NA	195,900	1,184	13.0	27,550	24.7	4.7
4876000	Waco city	142,299	78.8	9.3	52,857	51.1	NA	233,000	1,123	10.0	64,549	15.1	3.9
4879000	Wichita Falls city	101281	83.2	10.2	38,473	61.4	47.0	168,800	977	12.6	45,794	32.2	2.4
49000	**UTAH**	3,373,801	86.0	6.2	1,167,591	70.1	68.1	517,700	1,551	5.8	1,449,487	15.7	5.0
4944320	Lehi city	88,426	88.2	4.9	25,416	77.1	76.4	619,100	1,944	1.6	32,580	8.7	9.4
4955980	Ogden city	86258	87.7	7.4	32,848	59.0	69.0	360,800	1,332	8.0	41,533	19.4	8.9
4957300	Orem city	94,464	83.6	7.7	31,948	56.8	57.6	492,700	1,591	5.9	42,796	19.5	6.8
4962470	Provo city	111,363	66.9	15.7	36,198	39.2	66.6	495,300	1,206	14.9	52,742	18.2	3.2
4965330	St. George city	102,530	87.4	7.2	38,886	70.7	60.2	512,100	1,546	6.1	42,497	16.6	2.7
4967000	Salt Lake City city	207,084	78.2	9.1	92,626	46.5	64.1	566,400	1,492	7.5	98,625	13.1	2.5
4967440	Sandy city	91153	88.0	7.5	35,081	77.6	65.4	629,700	1,848	5.9	37,674	8.4	3.5
4970850	South Jordan city	83,828	89.8	5.0	27,610	83.8	72.5	678,200	1,997	4.8	34,994	10.4	3.0
4982950	West Jordan city	114,209	83.8	4.1	36,479	74.3	74.8	536,600	1,880	4.1	52,219	7.7	4.3
4983470	West Valley City city	133,601	87.4	5.2	43,539	69.1	71.4	427,300	1,469	4.4	63,673	6.3	4.2
50000	**VERMONT**	642,670	89.1	6.5	279,612	73.2	60.4	332,000	1,202	7.7	284,545	18.2	6.6
51000	**VIRGINIA**	8,626,985	87.0	8.7	3,402,670	67.8	66.3	382,900	1,567	7.8	3,646,196	10.1	9.0
5101000	Alexandria city	153790	77.1	15.6	76,890	43.2	74.8	737,900	1,954	5.6	74,818	6.0	7.4
5103000	Arlington CDP	231,669	78.7	15.6	114,097	41.1	72.4	850,900	2,223	5.1	105,078	7.2	4.0
5114440	Centreville CDP	70,740	88.0	4.8	25,109	68.1	78.1	586,800	2,318	NA	35,865	8.4	5.5
5116000	Chesapeake city	251,301	89.4	9.0	94,056	75.1	71.7	380,100	1,628	8.0	108,759	8.1	4.0
5121088	Dale City CDP	69,968	90.0	5.9	19,694	82.8	79.2	437,400	1,822	3.0	32,402	2.4	20.8
5135000	Hampton city	135,688	84.8	8.3	57,645	55.7	73.3	258,400	1,455	5.4	62,935	12.2	3.1
5147672	Lynchburg city	78,515	82.8	11.2	28,916	48.6	67.3	247,100	1,062	7.0	31,029	16.1	3.0
5156000	Newport News city	180,603	86.1	7.6	76,086	48.6	69.9	261,800	1,326	7.7	79,606	10.1	6.1
5157000	Norfolk city	226,794	78.2	13.8	94,056	44.6	73.8	298,600	1,314	11.3	113,008	11.5	4.6
5164000	Portsmouth city	95,777	88.6	8.8	40,661	55.6	73.9	268,300	1,225	9.5	43,614	9.8	3.0
5166672	Reston CDP		65,618	80.3	11.7	29,528	59.2	70.5	647,200	2,040	2.1	28,499	5.4
5167000	Richmond city	225478	81.3	11.8	104,332	45.1	65.3	365,100	1,441	9.7	103,889	9.5	3.7
5168000	Roanoke city	96,192	90.2	7.4	45,061	51.9	63.7	215,000	1,110	14.2	39,227	15.0	2.4
5176432	Suffolk city	99653	86.2	9.7	39,203	70.2	75.3	352,000	1,460	6.7	45,133	7.7	7.7
5182000	Virginia Beach city	450,178	84.3	10.0	179,291	65.9	74.7	384,200	1,704	5.0	205,017	9.9	3.9
53000	**WASHINGTON**	7,727,767	85.8	6.4	3,101,265	63.7	65.6	576,000	1,731	5.7	3,196,649	12.5	9.1
5303180	Auburn city	83,853	88.5	4.3	30,938	60.1	66.3	555,900	1,772	8.1	35,412	6.6	14.2
5305210	Bellevue city	149,955	79.8	8.9	62,868	54.9	56.6	1,349,200	2,442	1.6	60,075	10.0	6.9

Table C-4. Cities — Where: Migration, Housing, and Transportation, 2023—*Continued*

STATE and place code	STATE Place	Total population 1 year and over	Lived in the same house 1 year ago (percent)	Did not live in the same county 1 year ago (percent)	Total occupied housing units	Owner-occupied units (percent)	Percent with a mortgage, contract to purchase, or similar debt	Median value of owner-occupied units (dollars; owner estimated)	Median gross rent of renter-occupied units paying cash rent	Households without Internet access (percent)	Number of workers who commuted to work	Commute of less than 10 minutes (percent)	Commute of 60 minutes or more (percent)
	ACS table number:	C07204	C07204	C07204	B25003	B25003	B25081	B25097	B25064	S2801	B08012	B08012	B08012
	column number:	1	2	3	4	5	6	7	8	9	10	11	12
	WASHINGTON—Cont.												
5305280	Bellingham cityc	93888	79.1	10.4	42,207	40.3	52.3	628,000	1,484	5.6	40,596	21.2	3.9
5322640	Everett city	109,679	85.2	7.9	46,726	51.7	69.5	565,500	1,658	7.9	51,092	14.5	12.8
5323515	Federal Way city	96,053	85.9	5.3	37,759	57.8	61.0	565,700	1,855	4.8	43,640	9.1	13.5
5335275	Kennewick city	84,090	90.1	3.6	30,295	63.8	61.7	401,700	1,246	7.4	31,157	12.7	3.8
5335415	Kent city	130,814	81.1	6.1	50,481	56.8	67.7	608,900	1,865	5.0	60,432	7.1	14.0
5335940	Kirkland city	90,477	81.5	7.8	39,893	57.3	71.0	1,134,600	2,392	2.7	38,796	11.4	6.3
5343955	Marysville city	71,824	83.4	4.8	27,002	65.5	77.5	594,100	1,776	3.9	33,008	10.4	13.6
5353545	Pasco city	80,053	91.7	4.3	26,284	66.7	69.7	392,100	1,208	7.2	33,284	10.2	3.1
5357535	Redmond city	79,832	81.8	9.4	36,551	41.6	NA	1,103,800	2,366	3.4	35,586	9.1	5.9
5357745	Renton city	103,374	85.3	5.9	40,968	53.9	NA	665,700	1,952	4.4	46,931	7.9	9.1
5361115	Sammamish city	64,342	91.4	3.7	21,792	83.7	74.5	1,441,300	2,756	1.6	21,668	9.6	9.3
5363000	Seattle city	747884	78.9	9.3	364,627	43.7	70.6	898,600	1,948	4.6	333,650	8.0	4.9
5365922	South Hill CDP	66,992	80.5	12.2	23,059	75.1	76.3	557,100	1,946	NA	29,918	5.9	17.1
5367000	Spokane city	226,436	84.3	5.0	95,061	60.7	67.3	375,900	1,291	8.3	93,544	11.4	4.7
5367167	Spokane Valley city	106,207	83.9	4.3	45,025	55.2	66.2	392,800	1,325	8.9	49,015	10.7	4.2
5370000	Tacoma city	220,476	82.1	7.9	97,027	54.8	74.8	474,100	1,696	6.9	99,304	12.5	12.5
5374060	Vancouver city	193,173	85.7	6.9	84,778	48.9	70.4	469,300	1,683	5.2	84,091	14.5	5.1
5380010	Yakima city	94,654	87.1	3.9	37,918	54.0	54.6	311,600	1,132	7.6	40,469	21.9	3.5
54000	**WEST VIRGINIA**	1,753,113	90.0	5.0	743,644	73.5	44.4	163,700	850	12.9	685,618	13.6	10.8
55000	**WISCONSIN**	5,857,364	88.8	5.3	2,495,539	67.9	60.8	272,500	1,071	8.2	2,646,802	17.7	5.1
5502375	Appleton city	75,267	89.4	4.5	30,831	67.3	58.8	237,300	989	7.1	34,631	16.7	3.3
5522300	Eau Claire city	69503	75.1	10.5	30,280	53.3	65.1	257,800	1,008	6.1	33,919	29.7	4.7
5531000	Green Bay city	104,628	83.0	3.6	45,483	57.2	64.8	221,700	902	8.9	49,441	12.7	5.0
5537825	Janesville city	65,578	90.3	4.1	27,361	63.9	63.2	241,500	1,000	3.8	29,787	17.6	8.9
5539225	Kenosha city	97,889	91.4	4.4	42,461	60.1	67.8	222,900	1,139	5.9	49,376	18.4	6.1
5548000	Madison city	278,318	74.1	11.3	134,512	43.1	65.2	379,100	1,386	7.6	136,636	14.1	2.0
5553000	Milwaukee city	555,962	86.1	4.4	227,173	43.8	65.4	183,700	1,046	8.8	235,115	11.1	5.4
5560500	Oshkosh city	65,518	79.9	12.1	28,147	55.9	59.2	173,900	946	7.1	30,560	25.2	2.3
5566000	Racine city	NA	NA	NA	31,700	61.8	62.0	163,000	962	7.7	32,194	13.4	2.2
5584250	Waukesha city	69,867	88.5	6.6	30,668	63.0	71.8	320,200	1,168	8.4	33,701	13.5	3.4
56000	**WYOMING**	577,612	86.2	7.6	247,368	71.2	53.2	298,700	1,000	9.2	254,224	29.0	6.6
5613900	Cheyenne city	64,131	86.5	8.8	30,643	64.2	62.0	340,800	1,113	8.0	31,019	20.6	2.6
72000	**PUERTO RICO**	NA	NA	NA	1,277,486	68.4	37.7	131,500	557	14.2	1,099,792	9.2	11.5
7206593	Bayamón zona urbana	NA	NA	NA	69,470	69.4	50.8	145,000	661	8.9	59,140	7.7	8.9
7210334	Caguas zona urbana		NA	NA	NA	30,465	57.9	NA	141,700	578	11.9	26,702	13.1
7214290	Carolina zona urbana	NA	NA	NA	58,026	72.1	NA	157,100	602	7.4	51,602	5.1	19.1
7232522	Guaynabo zona urbana		NA	NA	NA	26,800	67.1	NA	265,900	1,150	5.0	25,540	5.6
7263820	Ponce zona urbana	NA	NA	NA	48,343	59.6	NA	103,200	544	9.0	29,866	10.8	6.8
7276770	San Juan zona urbana	NA	NA	NA	143,453	54.3	47.4	180,400	602	23.4	119,449	5.1	5.7

NA = Not available.
+ = The median falls in the highest interval of an open-ended distribution.

Appendixes

A: Geographic Concepts and Codes

B: Source Notes and Explanations

C: Metropolitan Statistical Areas, Metropolitan Divisions, and Components

APPENDIX A: GEOGRAPHIC CONCEPTS AND CODES

Geographic Areas Covered

The Who, What, and Where of America presents American Community Survey (ACS) data for the United States, all states, all metropolitan areas, and all counties and cities with populations of 65,000 or more. ACS population sizes are based on the most recent population estimates from the Census Bureau's Population Estimates Program. A few counties and cities may show populations below the 65,000 threshold. If a geographic area met the threshold for a previous period but dropped below the threshold for the current period, it will continue to be published as long as the population does not drop more than five percent below the threshold. Additionally, the Census Bureau uses housing unit estimates to distribute the county population among subcounty areas within the county (cities.) Housing unit estimates use building permits, mobile home shipments, and estimates of housing unit loss to update housing unit change since the last census. The Census Bureau does use vital statistics data in producing the initial county estimates, but not for the town and city numbers, so the estimates do not always seem consistent. All estimates are based on the geographic boundaries as they existed on January 1 of the sample year.

States and Counties

Data are presented for each of the 50 states, the District of Columbia, and the United States as a whole. The states are arranged alphabetically and counties are arranged alphabetically within each state. Data are presented for 854 counties and county equivalents with populations of 65,000 or more.

County Equivalents

In Louisiana, the primary divisions of the state are known as parishes rather than counties. In Alaska, the county equivalents are the organized boroughs, together with the census areas that were developed for general statistical purposes by the state of Alaska and the U.S. Census Bureau. Four states—Maryland, Missouri, Nevada, and Virginia—have one or more incorporated places that are legally independent of any county and thus constitute primary divisions of their states. Within each state, independent cities are listed alphabetically following the list of counties. The District of Columbia is not divided into counties or county equivalents—data for the entire district are presented as a county equivalent. New York City contains five counties: Bronx, Kings, New York, Queens, and Richmond.

Metropolitan Areas

Data are included for 393 metropolitan statistical areas and 31 metropolitan divisions, which are located within 13 of the largest metropolitan statistical areas. The metropolitan statistical areas are listed alphabetically, and the metropolitan divisions are listed alphabetically under the metropolitan statistical area of which they are components.

Appendix C is an alphabetical listing of the metropolitan areas, together with their metropolitan divisions and component counties and their 2010 census populations.

The U.S. Office of Management and Budget (OMB) defines metropolitan and micropolitan statistical areas according to published standards. The major purpose of defining these areas is to enable all U.S. government agencies to use the same geographic definitions in tabulating and publishing data. The general concept of a metropolitan or micropolitan statistical area is that of a core area containing a substantial population nucleus, together with adjacent communities that have a high degree of economic and social integration with the core.

New delineations of these Core Based Statistical Areas (CBSAs) based on the 2010 census were first released in February 2013. Standard definitions of metropolitan areas were first issued in 1949 by the Bureau of the Budget (the predecessor of OMB), under the designation "standard metropolitan area" (SMA). The term was changed to "standard metropolitan statistical area" (SMSA) in 1959, and to "metropolitan statistical area" (MSA) in 1983. The term "metropolitan area" (MA) was adopted in 1990 and referred collectively to metropolitan statistical areas (MSAs), consolidated metropolitan statistical areas (CMSAs), and primary metropolitan statistical areas (PMSAs). The term "core based statistical area" (CBSA) became effective in 2000 and refers collectively to metropolitan and micropolitan statistical areas.

The 2010 standards provide that each CBSA must contain at least one urban area of 10,000 or more population. Each metropolitan statistical area must have at least one urbanized area of 50,000 or more inhabitants. Each micropolitan statistical area must have at least one urban cluster of at least 10,000 but less than 50,000 people.

Under the standards, A metro area contains a core urban area of 50,000 or more population, and a micro area contains an urban core of at least 10,000 (but less than 50,000) population. Each metro or micro area consists of one or more counties and includes the counties containing the core urban area, as well as any adjacent counties that have a high degree of social and economic integration (as measured by commuting to work) with the urban core.

If specified criteria are met, a metropolitan statistical area containing a single core with a population of 2.5 million or more may be subdivided to form smaller groupings of counties referred to as "metropolitan divisions."

The largest city in each metropolitan or micropolitan statistical area is designated a "principal city." Additional cities qualify if specified requirements are met concerning population size and employment. The title of each metropolitan statistical area consists of the names of up to three of its principal cities and the name of each state into which the metropolitan or micropolitan statistical area extends. Titles of metropolitan divisions also typically are based on principal city names, but in certain cases consist of county names. The principal city need not be an incorporated place if it meets the requirements of population size and employment. Usually such a principal city is a census designated place (CDP.)

In view of the importance of cities and towns in New England, the 2010 standards also provide for a set of geographic areas that are defined using cities and towns in the six New England states. These New England city and town areas (NECTAs) are not included in this volume.

Cities

This book presents data for 649 cities (called "places") with estimated populations of 65,000 or more in 2023. Corresponding data for states are also provided. The states are arranged alphabetically and the cities are ordered alphabetically within each state.

As used in this volume, the term *city* refers to *places* as defined by the Census Bureau. These include places that have been incorporated as cities, boroughs, towns, or villages under the laws of their respective states, as well as census designated places (CDPs). CDPs are delineated by the Census Bureau, in cooperation with states and localities, as statistical counterparts of incorporated places for purposes of the decennial census and the ACS. CDPs comprise densely settled concentrations of population that are identifiable by name but are not legally incorporated places.

Included with the incorporated cities are the principal portions of seven consolidated cities. A consolidated city is an incorporated place that has combined its government functions with a county or subcounty entity but contains one or more other semi-independent incorporated places that continue to function as local governments within the consolidated government. Consolidated cities are not included in this book, but the "consolidated city (balance)" portions are treated as incorporated places in the ACS data. Consolidated city (balance) portions included in this volume are Athens-Clarke County, Georgia; Augusta-Richmond County, Georgia; Macon-Bibb County, Georgia; Indianapolis, Indiana; Lexington-Fayette County, Kentucky; Louisville-Jefferson County, Kentucky; and Nashville-Davidson, Tennessee.

Towns in the New England states and New York are treated as minor civil divisions (MCDs) and are not included in this book.

Geographic Codes

The tables in this book provide a geographic code or codes for each area.

For counties, a five-digit state and county code is given for each state and county. The first two digits indicate the state; the remaining three represent the county. Within each state, the counties are listed in order, beginning with 001, with even numbers usually omitted. Independent cities follow the counties and begin with the number 510. In the state-level tables, a two-digit state code is provided. The state code is a sequential numbering, with some gaps, of the states and the District of Columbia in alphabetical order from Alabama (01) to Wyoming (56).

These codes have been established by the U.S. government as Federal Information Processing Standards and are often referred to as *FIPS codes*. They are used by U.S. government agencies and many other organizations for data presentation. The codes are provided in this volume for use in matching the data given here with other data sources in which counties are identified by FIPS code.

The metropolitan area tables provide metro area codes for each metropolitan area, as well as metropolitan division codes where appropriate.

For cities, a seven-digit state and place code is included. The first two digits identify the state and are the same as the FIPS codes described above. The remaining five digits are the place FIPS codes established by the U.S. government.

Independent Cities

The following independent cities are not included in any county; their data are presented separately in this volume.

MARYLAND

Baltimore (separate from Baltimore County)

MISSOURI

St. Louis (separate from St. Louis County)

VIRGINIA

Alexandria
Chesapeake
Hampton
Lynchburg
Newport News
Norfolk
Portsmouth
Richmond
Roanoke
Suffolk
Virginia Beach

APPENDIX B: SOURCE NOTES AND EXPLANATIONS

With one exception, all data in this book are from the American Community Survey (ACS). The sole exception is the population change between 2010 and 2023, which come from the Census Bureau's Population Estimates Program, the official source for population totals.

Annual ACS data are released for all geographic entities with populations of 65,000 or more. Until 2014, 3-year estimates were released for counties and cities with populations between 20,000 and 65,000, while only 5-year estimates were available for smaller areas. In the first four editions of this book, the county and city tables included the 3-year data. Beginning with the 2014 data, the 3-year releases were discontinued and replaced by 1-year Supplemental Estimates which were used for the county and city tables in this book. These 1-year Supplemental Estimates have less precise categories but are more timely than the 5-year estimates also available for these areas. This is the third edition of this book to use the 1-year Supplemental Estimates.

This section of source notes is generally excerpted from https://www2.census.gov/programs-surveys/acs/tech_docs/subject_definitions/2021_ACSSubjectDefinitions.pdf.

The data were assembled from the ACS detailed tables and the following notes reference the numbers of those detailed tables. Also included with each table number and title is the table's universe, which is the total number of units (e.g., individuals, households, businesses, in the population of interest). Many of the data items can also be found in ACS profiles, subject tables, geographic comparison tables, and other formats available on the ACS website.

Symbols

A "-" in a cell indicates that either there were no sample cases or the number of sample cases was too small.

Part A: Who

Table A-1. Who — Age, Race/Ethnicity, and Household Structure

Table A-1 presents 61 items for the United States as a whole and for each individual state and the District of Columbia.

POPULATION AND POPULATION CHANGE, Items 1 and 2
Source: Table B01003. Total Population
Universe: Total Population

In the 2022 1-year ACS, the total population for states is the official estimate from the Population Estimates Program. The 2010 1-year ACS used the total population from the 2010 census.

RACE, Items 3–8, 10–11
Sources: Table B02001. Race; Table B02008. White Alone or in Combination with One or More Other Races; Table B02009. Black or African American Alone or in Combination with One or More Other Races; Table B02010. American Indian and Alaska Native alone or in Combination with One or More Other Races; Table B02011. Asian Alone or in Combination with One or More Other Races; Table B02012. Native Hawaiian and Other Pacific Islander Alone or in Combination with One or More Other Races; Table B02013. Some Other Race Alone or in Combination with One or More Other Races; and Table B01001H. Sex by Age (White Alone, not Hispanic or Latino)
Universe: Total Population

The concept of race, as used by the Census Bureau, reflects self-identification by people according to the race or races with which they most closely identify. These categories are socio-political constructs and should not be interpreted as being scientific or anthropological in nature. Furthermore, the race categories include both racial and national-origin groups. The racial classifications used by the Census Bureau adhere to the October 30, 1997, *Federal Register Notice* entitled, "Revisions to the Standards for the Classification of Federal Data on Race and Ethnicity," issued by the Office of Management and Budget (OMB). These standards govern the categories used to collect and present federal data on race and ethnicity. The OMB requires five minimum categories (White, Black or African American, American Indian or Alaska Native, Asian, and Native Hawaiian or Other Pacific Islander) for race. The race categories are described below with a sixth category, "Some other race," added with OMB approval. In addition to the five race groups, the OMB also states that respondents should be offered the option of selecting one or more races.

The concept "race alone or in combination" includes people who reported a single race alone (e.g., Asian) and people who reported that race in combination with one or more of the other

major race groups (e.g., White, Black or African American, American Indian and Alaska Native, Native Hawaiian and Other Pacific Islander, and Some Other Race). The "race alone or in combination" concept, therefore, represents the maximum number of people who reported as that race group, either alone, or in combination with another race(s). The sum of the six individual race "alone or in combination" categories may add to more than the total population because people who reported more than one race were tallied in each race category.

The **White** population includes persons having origins in any of the original peoples of Europe, the Middle East, or North Africa. It includes people who indicate their race as "White" or report entries such as Irish, German, Italian, Lebanese, Near Easterner, Arab, or Polish.

The **Black or African American** population includes persons having origins in any of the Black racial groups of Africa. It includes people who indicate their race as "Black, African American, or Negro," or provide written entries such as African American, Afro-American, Kenyan, Nigerian, or Haitian.

The **American Indian or Alaska Native** population includes persons having origins in any of the original peoples of North and South America (including Central America) and who maintain tribal affiliation or community attachment. It includes people who classified themselves as Canadian Indian, French-American Indian, Spanish-American Indian, Eskimo, Aleut, Alaska Indian, or any of the American Indian or Alaska Native tribes.

The **Asian** population includes persons having origins in any of the original peoples of the Far East, Southeast Asia, or the Indian subcontinent including, for example, Cambodia, China, India, Japan, Korea, Malaysia, Pakistan, the Philippine Islands, Thailand, and Vietnam. It includes Asian Indian, Chinese, Filipino, Korean, Japanese, Vietnamese, and Other Asian.

The **Native Hawaiian or Other Pacific Islander** population includes persons having origins in any of the original peoples of Hawaii, Guam, Samoa, or other Pacific Islands. It includes people who indicate their race as Native Hawaiian, Guamanian or Chamorro, Samoan, and Other Pacific Islander.

Some Other Race includes all other responses not included in the "White," "Black or African American," "American Indian or Alaska Native," "Asian," and "Native Hawaiian or Other Pacific Islander" race categories described above. Respondents providing write-in entries such as multiracial, mixed, interracial, or a Hispanic/Latino group (for example, Mexican, Puerto Rican, or Cuban) in the "Some other race" write-in space are included in this category.

Two or More Races. People may have chosen to provide two or more races either by checking two or more race response check boxes, by providing multiple write-in responses, or by some combination of check boxes and write-in responses. These people are included in each of the "race alone or in combination" categories that they selected.

HISPANIC ORIGIN, Item 9

Source: Table B03003. Hispanic or Latino Origin
Universe: Total Population

The data on the **Hispanic or Latino** population was asked of all people. The terms "Spanish," "Hispanic," and "Latino" are used interchangeably. Some respondents identify with all three terms, while others may identify with only one of these three specific terms. Hispanics or Latinos who identify with the terms "Spanish," "Hispanic," or "Latino" are those who classify themselves in one of the specific Hispanic or Latino categories listed on the questionnaire—"Mexican," "Puerto Rican," or "Cuban"—as well as those who indicate that they are "other Spanish/Hispanic/Latino." People who do not identify with one of the specific origins listed on the questionnaire but indicate that they are "other Spanish/Hispanic/Latino" are those whose origins are from Spain, the Spanish-speaking countries of Central or South America, the Dominican Republic, or people identifying themselves generally as Spanish, Spanish-American, Hispanic, Hispano, Latino, and so on.

AGE, Items 12–21, 23–31

Sources: Table B01001. Sex by Age; Table B01002. Median Age by Sex; Table B01002H. Median Age by Sex (White Alone, not Hispanic or Latino); Table B01002B. Median Age by Sex (Black or African American Alone); Table B01002C. Median Age by Sex (American Indian and Alaska Native); Table B01002D. Median Age by Sex (Asian Alone); Table B01002E. Median Age by Sex (Native Hawaiian and Other Pacific Islander Alone); Table B01002F. Median Age by Sex (Some Other Race Alone); Table B01002G. Median Age by Sex (Two or More Races); and Table B01002I. Median Age by Sex (Hispanic or Latino)
Universe: Total Population

The age classification is based on the age of the person in complete years at the time of interview. Both age and date of birth are used in combination to calculate the most accurate age at the time of the interview. Inconsistently reported and missing values are assigned or imputed based on the values of other variables for that person, from other people in the household, or from people in other households ("hot deck" imputation). Data on age are used to determine the applicability of other questions for a particular individual and to classify other characteristics in tabulations. Age data are needed to interpret most social and economic characteristics used to plan and analyze programs and policies. Therefore, age data are tabulated by many different age groupings, such as 5-year age groups.

The median age is the age that divides the population into two equal-size groups. Half of the population is older than the median age and half is younger. Median age is based on a standard distribution of the population by single years of age and is shown to the nearest tenth of a year.

PERCENT FEMALE, Item 22

Source: Table B01001. Sex by Age
Universe: Total Population
The female population is shown as a percentage of the total population.

MARITAL STATUS, Items 32–36

Source: Table B12001. Sex by Marital Status for the Population 15 Years and Over
Universe: Population 15 Years and Over

The **marital status** classification refers to the status at the time of interview. Data on marital status are tabulated only for people 15 years old and over. All people were asked whether they were "now married," "widowed," "divorced," "separated," or "never married." Couples who live together (unmarried people, people in common-law marriages) were allowed to report the marital status they considered the most appropriate. When marital status was not reported, it was imputed according to the relationship to the householder and sex and age of the person. Differences in the number of currently married males and females occur because there is no step in the weighting process to equalize the weighted estimates of husbands and wives.

Never married includes all people who have never been married, including people whose only marriage(s) was annulled.

Now married includes all people whose current marriage has not ended by widowhood or divorce. This category includes people defined as "separated" and "spouse absent." The category may also include couples who live together or people in common-law marriages if they consider this category the most appropriate. Beginning in 2013, same-sex married couples are included in the married spouse present category.

Widowed includes widows and widowers who have not remarried.

Divorced includes people who are legally divorced and who have not remarried.

Differences between the number of currently married males and the number of currently married females occur because of reporting differences, because some husbands and wives have their usual residence in different areas, and because husbands and wives do not have the same weights.

FOREIGN BORN, Item 37

Source: Table C05002. Place of Birth by Citizenship Status
Universe: Total Population

The **foreign-born** population includes anyone who was not a U.S. citizen or a U.S. national at birth. This includes respondents who indicated they were a U.S. citizen by naturalization or not a U.S. citizen.

LANGUAGES SPOKEN, Items 38–41

Source: Table C16002. Household Language by Household Limited English Speaking Status
Universe: Households

Language Spoken at Home. Questions on language spoken at home were asked only of persons 5 years of age and older. Instructions mailed with the American Community Survey questionnaire instructed respondents to mark "Yes" if they sometimes or always spoke a language other than English at home, and "No" if a language was spoken only at school—or if speaking was limited to a few expressions or slang. Respondents printed the name of the non-English language they spoke at home. If the person spoke more than one non-English language, they reported the language spoken most often. If the language spoken most frequently could not be determined, the respondent reported the language learned first.

The questions referred to languages spoken at home in an effort to measure the current use of languages other than English. This category excluded respondents who spoke a language other than English exclusively outside of the home.

Most respondents who reported speaking a language other than English also spoke English. The questions did not permit a determination of the primary language of persons who spoke both English and another language.

Household Language. In households where one or more people spoke a language other than English, the household language assigned to all household members was the non-English language spoken by the first person with a non-English language. This assignment scheme ranked household members in the following order: householder, spouse, parent, sibling, child, grandchild, other relative, stepchild, unmarried partner, housemate or roommate, and other nonrelatives. Therefore, a person who spoke only English may have had a non-English household language assigned during tabulations by household language.

Ability to Speak English. Respondents who reported speaking a language other than English were asked to indicate their English ability based on one of the following categories: "Very well," "Well," "Not well," or "Not at all." Ideally, the data on ability to speak English represented a person's perception of their own ability. However, because one household member usually completes American Community Survey questionnaires, the responses may have represented the perception of another household member.

Limited English Speaking Household. A "limited English speaking household" is one in which no member 14 years old and over (1) speaks only English or (2) speaks a non-English language and speaks English "very well." In other words, all members 14 years old and over have at least some difficulty with English. By definition, English-only households cannot belong to this group. Previous Census Bureau data products referred to these households as "linguistically isolated" and "Household where no one age 14 and over speaks English only or speaks English 'very well.'"

HOUSEHOLDS AND HOUSEHOLD TYPE, Item 42–61

Sources: Table B11001. Household Type (Including Living Alone); Table B11006. Households by Presence of People 60 Years and Over by Household Type; Table B11009. Unmarried-Partner Households by Sex of Partner; B11010. Nonfamily Households by Sex of Householder by Living Alone by Age of Householder; Table C11005. Households by Presence of People Under 18 Years by Household Type; and Table B25010. Average Household Size of Occupied-Housing Units by Tenure
Universe: Households

A **household** includes all the people who occupy a housing unit. (People not living in households are classified as living in group quarters.) A housing unit is a house, an apartment, a mobile home, a group of rooms, or a single room that is occupied (or if vacant, is intended for occupancy) as separate living quarters. Separate living quarters are those in which the occupants live separately from any other people in the building and which have direct access from the outside of the building or through a common hall. The occupants may be a single family, one person living alone, two or more families living together, or any other group of related or unrelated people who share living arrangements.

A **family household** consists of a householder and one or more other people living in the same household who are related to the householder by birth, marriage, or adoption. All people in a household who are related to the householder are regarded as members of his or her family. A family household may contain people not related to the householder, but those people are not included as part of the householder's family in tabulations. Thus, the number of family households is equal to the number of families, but family households may include more members than do families. A household can contain only one family for purposes of tabulations.

A **married-couple family** is one in which the householder and his or her spouse are listed as members of the same household.

The category **male family households** includes only male-headed family households with no spouse present. Similarly, the category **female family households** includes only female-headed family households with no spouse present.

A **nonfamily household** consists of a group of unrelated people or of one person living alone.

An unmarried-partner household is a household other than a "married-couple household" that includes a householder and an "unmarried partner." An "unmarried partner" can be of the same sex or of the opposite sex as the householder. An "unmarried partner" in an "unmarried-partner household" is an adult who is unrelated to the householder, but shares living quarters and has a close personal relationship with the householder. An unmarried-partner household also may be a family household or a nonfamily household, depending on the presence or absence of another person in the household who is related to the householder. There may be only one unmarried partner per household, and an unmarried partner may not be included in a married-couple household, as the householder cannot have both a spouse and an unmarried partner.

Tables A-2, A-3, and A-4. Who—Age, Race/Ethnicity, and Household Structure

Table A-2 presents 24 items for the United States as a whole, each individual state and the District of Columbia, and 848 counties, county equivalents, and independent cities with a 2022 population of 65,000 or more. This table is from the 2022 1-year file, from ACS tables beginning with "B" and "C," as the supplemental estimates were not available.

Table A-3 presents 24 items for 384 Metropolitan Statistical Areas and 31 Metropolitan Divisions within the 12 largest Metropolitan Statistical Areas. This table is from the 2022 1-year file, from ACS tables beginning with "B" and "C".

Table A-4 presents 24 items for 646 cities, Census Designated Places, and the principal portions of consolidated cities with a 2022 estimated population of 65,000 or more. This table is from the 2012 1-year file, from ACS tables beginning with "B" and "C," as the supplemental estimates were not available.

POPULATION, Item 1
Source: Table B01003. Total Population; Table K200104. Population by Age.
Universe: Total Population

In the 2022 ACS, the total population is based on the official estimate from the Population Estimates Program .

POPULATION CHANGE, Item 2
Source: U.S. Census Bureau—Population Estimates Program
The population change data for 2010 through 2022 are from the official estimates of the Population Estimates Program which estimates the population as of July 1 each year.

AGE, Items 3–8
Sources: Table B01001. Sex by Age; Table B01002. Median Age by Sex; Table K200104. Population by Age; Table K200103. Median Age by Sex.
Universe: Total Population

The age classification is based on the age of the person in complete years at the time of interview. Both age and date of birth are used in combination to calculate the most accurate age at the time of the interview. Inconsistently reported and missing values are assigned or imputed based on the values of other variables for that person, from other people in the household, or from people in other households ("hot deck" imputation). Data on age are used to determine the applicability of other questions for a particular individual and to classify other characteristics in tabulations. Age data are needed to interpret most social and economic characteristics used to plan and analyze programs and policies. Therefore, age data are tabulated by many different age groupings, such as 5-year age groups.

The median age is the age that divides the population into two equal-size groups. Half of the population is older than the median age and half is younger. Median age is based on a standard distribution of the population by single years of age and is shown to the nearest tenth of a year.

RACE, Items 9–12
Sources: Table B02008. White Alone or in Combination with One or More Other Races; Table B02009. Black or African American Alone or in Combination with One or More Other Races; Table B02010. American Indian and Alaska Native alone or in Combination with One or More Other Races; Table B02011. Asian Alone or in Combination with One or More Other Races; Table B02012. Native Hawaiian and Other Pacific Islander Alone or in Combination with One or More Other Races; and Table B02013. Some Other Race Alone or in Combination with One or More Other Races; Table K200201. Race.
Universe: Total Population

The concept of race, as used by the Census Bureau, reflects self-identification by people according to the race or races with which they most closely identify. These categories are socio-political constructs and should not be interpreted as being scientific or anthropological in nature. Furthermore, the race categories include both racial and national-origin groups. The racial classifications used by the Census Bureau adhere to the October 30, 1997, *Federal Register Notice* entitled, "Revisions to the Standards for the Classification of Federal Data on Race and Ethnicity," issued by the Office of Management and Budget (OMB). These standards govern the categories used to collect and present federal data on race and ethnicity. The OMB requires five minimum categories (White, Black or African American, American Indian or Alaska Native, Asian, and Native Hawaiian or Other Pacific Islander) for race. The race categories are described below with a sixth category, "Some other race," added with OMB approval. In addition to the five race groups, the OMB also states that respondents should be offered the option of selecting one or more races.

There are several concepts used to display and tabulate race information for the six major race categories (White; Black or African American; American Indian or Alaska Native; Asian; Native Hawaiian or Other Pacific Islander; and Some Other Race) and the various details within these groups.

The concept "race alone" includes people who reported a single entry (e.g., Korean) and no other race, as well as people who reported two or more entries within the same major race group (e.g., Asian). For example, respondents who reported Korean and Vietnamese are part of the larger "Asian alone" race group. Items 9 through 12 in Tables A-2 and A-4 use the concept of "race alone."

The concept "race alone or in combination" includes people who reported a single race alone (e.g., Asian) and people who reported that race in combination with one or more of the other

major race groups (e.g., White, Black or African American, American Indian and Alaska Native, Native Hawaiian and Other Pacific Islander, and Some Other Race). The "race alone or in combination" concept, therefore, represents the maximum number of people who reported as that race group, either alone, or in combination with another race(s). The sum of the six individual race "alone or in combination" categories may add to more than the total population because people who reported more than one race were tallied in each race category. Items 9 through 12 in Table A-3 use the concept of "race alone or in combination."

The **White** population includes persons having origins in any of the original peoples of Europe, the Middle East, or North Africa. It includes people who indicate their race as "White" or report entries such as Irish, German, Italian, Lebanese, Near Easterner, Arab, or Polish.

The Black or African American population includes persons having origins in any of the Black racial groups of Africa. It includes people who indicate their race as "Black, African American, or Negro," or provide written entries such as African American, Afro-American, Kenyan, Nigerian, or Haitian.

The **American Indian or Alaska Native** population includes persons having origins in any of the original peoples of North and South America (including Central America) and who maintain tribal affiliation or community attachment. It includes people who classified themselves as Canadian Indian, French-American Indian, Spanish-American Indian, Eskimo, Aleut, Alaska Indian, or any of the American Indian or Alaska Native tribes.

The **Asian and Pacific Islander** population combines two census groupings: Asian and Native Hawaiian or Other Pacific Islander. The **Asian** population includes persons having origins in any of the original peoples of the Far East, Southeast Asia, or the Indian subcontinent including, for example, Cambodia, China, India, Japan, Korea, Malaysia, Pakistan, the Philippine Islands, Thailand, and Vietnam. It includes Asian Indian, Chinese, Filipino, Korean, Japanese, Vietnamese, and Other Asian. The **Native Hawaiian or Other Pacific Islander** population includes persons having origins in any of the original peoples of Hawaii, Guam, Samoa, or other Pacific Islands. It includes people who indicate their race as Native Hawaiian, Guamanian or Chamorro, Samoan, and Other Pacific Islander. Because Table A-3 uses the "race alone or in combination" concept, this combination results in double-counting of individuals who combine these two racial groups. While the groups are combined in Tables A-2, A-3, and A-4, the separate populations are shown in Table A-1, States.

Some Other Race. Includes all other responses not included in the "White," "Black or African American," "American Indian or Alaska Native," "Asian," and "Native Hawaiian or Other Pacific Islander" race categories described above. Respondents reporting entries such as multiracial, mixed, interracial, or a Hispanic, Latino, or Spanish group (for example, Mexican, Puerto Rican, Cuban, or Spanish) in response to the race question are included in this category. In Tables A-2 through A-4, this group is combined with the **American Indian or Alaska Native** group. The **Some Other Race** alone or in combination is shown separately in Table A-1, States.

HISPANIC ORIGIN, Item 13

Source: Table B03003. Hispanic or Latino Origin; Table K200301. Hispanic or Latino Origin.
Universe: Total Population

The data on the **Hispanic or Latino** population was asked of all people. The terms "Spanish," "Hispanic," and "Latino" are used interchangeably. Some respondents identify with all three terms, while others may identify with only one of these three specific terms. Hispanics or Latinos who identify with the terms "Spanish," "Hispanic," or "Latino" are those who classify themselves in one of the specific Hispanic or Latino categories listed on the questionnaire—"Mexican," "Puerto Rican," or "Cuban"—as well as those who indicate that they are "other Spanish/Hispanic/Latino." People who do not identify with one of the specific origins listed on the questionnaire but indicate that they are "other Spanish/Hispanic/Latino" are those whose origins are from Spain, the Spanish-speaking countries of Central or South America, the Dominican Republic, or people identifying themselves generally as Spanish, Spanish-American, Hispanic, Hispano, Latino, and so on.

BORN IN STATE OF RESIDENCE, Item 14.

Source: Table B05002. Place of Birth by Nativity and Citizenship Status; Table K200503. Place of Birth in the United States.
Universe: Total Population

Respondents were asked to select one of two categories: (1) in the United States, or (2) outside the United States. In the ACS, respondents selecting category (1) were then asked to report the name of the state while respondents selecting category (2) were then asked to report the name of the foreign country, or Puerto Rico, Guam, etc. People not reporting a place of birth were assigned the state or country of birth of another family member, or were allocated the response of another individual with similar characteristics. People born outside the United States were asked to report their place of birth according to current international boundaries.

FOREIGN-BORN, Item 15

Source: Table B05002. Place of Birth by Nativity and Citizenship Status; Table K200503. Place of Birth in the United States.
Universe: Total Population

The **foreign-born** population includes anyone who was not a U.S. citizen or a U.S. national at birth. This includes respondents who indicated they were a U.S. citizen by naturalization or not a U.S. citizen.

NON-CITIZENS, Item 16

Source: Table B05002. Place of Birth by Nativity and Citizenship; Table K200501. Citizenship Status in the United States.
Universe: Total Population

Respondents who indicated that they were born in the United States, Puerto Rico, a U.S. Island Area (such as Guam), or abroad of American (U.S. citizen) parent or parents are considered U.S. citizens at birth. Foreign-born people who indicated that they were U.S. citizens through naturalization also are considered U.S. citizens. Respondents who indicated that they were not U.S. citizens at the time of the survey were considered **non-citizens**.

HOUSEHOLDS AND HOUSEHOLD TYPE, Items 17–24

Sources: Table B11001. Household Type (Including Living Alone); Table B11006. Households by Presence of People 60 Years and Over by Household Type; Table K200901. Household Type; Table K201102. Households by Presence of People 60 Years and Over by Household Type
Universe: Households

A **household** includes all the people who occupy a housing unit. (People not living in households are classified as living in group quarters.) A housing unit is a house, an apartment, a mobile home, a group of rooms, or a single room that is occupied (or if vacant, is intended for occupancy) as separate living quarters. Separate living quarters are those in which the occupants live separately from any other people in the building and which have direct access from the outside of the building or through a common hall. The occupants may be a single family, one person living alone, two or more families living together, or any other group of related or unrelated people who share living arrangements.

A **family household** consists of a householder and one or more other people living in the same household who are related to the householder by birth, marriage, or adoption. All people in a household who are related to the householder are regarded as members of his or her family. A family household may contain people not related to the householder, but those people are not included as part of the householder's family in tabulations. Thus, the number of family households is equal to the number of families, but family households may include more members than do families. A household can contain only one family for purposes of tabulations.

A **married-couple family** is one in which the householder and his or her spouse are listed as members of the same household.

The category **male family households** includes only male-headed family households with no spouse present. Similarly, the category **female family households** includes only female-headed family households with no spouse present.

A **nonfamily household** consists of a group of unrelated people or of one person living alone.

Part B: What

Table B-1. What — Education, Employment, and Income

Table B-1 presents 158 items for the United States as a whole and for each individual state and the District of Columbia.

EDUCATIONAL ATTAINMENT, Items 1–6

Source: Table C15003. Educational Attainment for the Population 25 Years and Over
Universe: Population 25 Years and Over

Data on **educational attainment** were derived from a question that asked respondents for the highest level of school completed or the highest degree received. Persons currently enrolled in school are instructed to report the level of the previous grade attended or the highest degree received. Persons who had passed a high school equivalency examination were considered high school graduates. Schooling received in foreign schools was to be reported as the equivalent grade or years in the regular American school system.

Specifically excluded are vocational and technical training, such as barber school training; business, trade, technical, and vocational schools; or other training for a specific trade.

No high school diploma includes all persons who have not received a high school diploma.

High school graduate includes persons whose highest degree was a high school diploma or its equivalent, including those who passed a high school equivalency examination.

Some college or associate degree includes people who attended college but did not receive a degree or received an associate degree.

Bachelor's degree includes persons who have received bachelor's degrees.

Graduate or professional degree includes persons who have received master's degrees, professional school degrees (such as law school or medical school degrees), or doctoral degrees.

SCHOOL ENROLLMENT, Items 7–17

Source: Table C14002. School Enrollment by Level of School by Type of School by for the Population 3 Years and Over
Universe: Population 3 Years and Over

People were classified as **enrolled in school** if they were attending a "regular" public or private school or college at any time during the 3 months prior to the time of interview. The question included instructions to "include only nursery or preschool, kindergarten, elementary school, and schooling that leads to a high school diploma, or a college degree" as regular school or college. Respondents who did not answer the enrollment question were assigned the enrollment status and type of school of a person with the same age, sex, race, and Hispanic or Latino origin whose residence was in the same or nearby area.

A regular school advances a person toward an elementary school certificate, a high school diploma, or a college, university, or professional school (such as law or medicine) degree. Tutoring or correspondence schools are included if credit can be obtained in a "regular school." People enrolled in "vocational, technical, or business school" were not reported as enrolled in regular school. Field interviewers were instructed to classify individuals who were home schooled as enrolled in private school. The guide sent out with the mail questionnaire does not include explicit instructions for how to classify home schoolers.

Enrolled in public and private school includes people who attended school in the reference period and indicated they were enrolled by marking one of the questionnaire categories for "public school, public college," or "private school, private college." The instruction guide defines a public school as "any school or college controlled and supported primarily by a local, county, state, or federal government." Private schools are defined as schools supported and controlled primarily by religious organizations or other private groups. Respondents who marked both the "public" and "private" boxes are edited to the first entry, "public."

Grade in which enrolled. Since 1999, in the American Community Survey, people reported to be enrolled in "public school, public college" or "private school, private college" were classified by grade or level according to responses to the question "What grade or level was this person attending?" Seven levels were identified: **nursery school, preschool**; **kindergarten**; **elementary grade 1 to grade 4** or **grade 5 to grade 8**; **high school grade 9 to grade 12**; **college undergraduate** years (freshman to senior); and **graduate or professional school** (*for example: medical, dental, or law school*).

EMPLOYMENT STATUS, Items 18–40

Sources: Table C23001. Sex by Age by Employment status for the Population 16 Years and Over
Universe: Population 16 Years and Over

Table B23006. Educational Attainment by Employment Status for the Population 25 to 64 Years
Universe: Population 25 to 64 Years;

Table C14005. Sex by School Enrollment by Educational Attainment by Employment Status for the Population 16 to 19 Years
Universe: Population 16 to 19 Years

Table C23022. Sex by Full-Time Work Status in the Past 12 Months for the Population 16 To 64 Years
Universe: Population 16 to 64 Years

Table B08202. Household Size by Number of Workers in Household
Universe: Households

Total employment includes all civilians 16 years old and over who were either (1) "at work"—those who did any work at all during the reference week as paid employees, worked in either their own business or profession, worked on their own farm, or worked 15 hours or more as unpaid workers in a family farm or business; or were (2) "with a job, but not at work"—those who had a job but were not at work that week due to illness, weather, industrial dispute, vacation, or other personal reasons.

The **labor force** consists of all persons 16 years old and over who are either employed or unemployed, including those in the armed forces.

The **unemployment rate** represents the number of unemployed people as a percentage of the labor force.

Unemployment includes all persons who did not work during the survey week, made specific efforts to find a job during the previous four weeks, and were available for work during the survey week (except for temporary illness). Persons waiting to be called back to a job from which they had been laid off and those waiting to report to a new job within the next 30 days are included in unemployment figures.

Full-time, year-round includes all persons 16 years old and over who usually worked 35 hours or more per week for 50 to 52 weeks in the past 12 months.

Households with no worker. The term "worker" as used here refers to work status in the past 12 months.

Not enrolled, not high school graduate. This category includes people of compulsory school attendance age or slightly above (ages 16 to 19) who were not enrolled in school and were not high school graduates. These people may be referred to as "high school dropouts." There is no restriction on when they "dropped out" of school; therefore, they may have dropped out before high school and never attended high school.

CHILDREN IN FAMILIES BY LIVING ARRANGEMENTS AND EMPLOYMENT STATUS OF PARENTS, Items 41–60

Sources: Table C23008. Age of Own Children Under 18 Years in Families and Subfamilies by Living Arrangements by Employment Status of Parents
Universe: Own Children Under 18 Years in Families and Subfamilies

Table C23007. Presence of Own Children Under 18 Years by Family Type by Employment Status
Universe: Families

Table B23003. Presence of Own Children Under 18 Years by Age of Own children Under 18 Years by Employment Status for Females 20 to 64 Years
Universe: Females 20 to 64 Years in Households

An **own child** is a never-married child under 18 years who is a son or daughter by birth, a stepchild, or an adopted child of the householder. Own children are further classified as living with two parents or with one parent only. Own children of the householder living with two parents are by definition found only in married-couple families. In the employment status tabulations in this book, own child refers to a never married child under the age of 18 in a family or a subfamily who is a son or daughter, by birth, marriage, or adoption, of a member of the householder's family, but not necessarily of the householder.

CLASS OF WORKER, Items 61–64

Source: Table C24080. Sex by Class of Worker for the Civilian Employed Population 16 Years and Over
Universe: Civilian Employed Population 16 Years and Over

For employed people, the data on **class of worker** refer to the person's job during the previous week. For those who worked two or more jobs, the data refer to the job where the person worked the greatest number of hours. The information on **class of worker** refers to the same job as a respondent's industry and occupation and categorizes people according to the type of ownership of the employing organization. The class of worker categories are defined as follows:

Private wage and salary workers includes people who worked for wages, salary, commission, tips, pay-in-kind, or piece rates for a private for-profit employer or a private not-for-profit, tax-exempt or charitable organization. Self-employed people whose business was incorporated are included with private wage and salary workers because they are paid employees of their own companies.

Government workers includes people who were employees of any local, state, or federal governmental unit, regardless of the activity of the particular agency. Employees of foreign governments, the United Nations, or other formal international organizations controlled by governments were classified as "federal government workers." The class of worker government categories includes all government workers, though government workers may work in different industries. For example, people who work in a public elementary or secondary school are coded as local government class of workers.

Self-employed includes people who worked for profit or fees in their own unincorporated business, profession, or trade, or who operated a farm.

Unpaid family workers includes people who worked 15 hours or more a week without pay in a business or on a farm operated by a relative.

OCCUPATION, Items 65–70

Source: Table C24060. Occupation by Class of Worker for the Civilian Employed Population 16 Years and Over
Universe: Civilian Employed Population 16 Years and Over

For employed people, the data on **occupation** refer to the person's job during the previous week. For those who worked two or more jobs, the data refer to the job where the person worked the greatest number of hours.

Written responses to the occupation questions are coded using the occupational classification system developed for the 2000 census and modified in 2010. This system consists of 539 specific occupational categories, including military, for employed people, arranged into 23 major occupational groups. This classification was developed based on the *Standard Occupational Classification (SOC) Manual: 2010*, published by the Executive Office of the President, Office of Management and Budget.

This table uses the standard ACS groupings of occupations.

INDUSTRY, Items 71–83

Source: Table C24070. Industry by Class of Worker for Civilian Employed Population 16 Years and Over
Universe: Civilian Employed Population 16 Years and Over

For employed people, the data on **industry** refer to the person's job during the previous week. For those who worked two or more jobs, the data refer to the job where the person worked the greatest number of hours.

Written responses to the industry questions are coded using the industry classification system developed for Census 2000. This system consists of 269 categories for employed people, including military, classified into 20 sectors. The NAICS was developed to increase comparability in industry definitions between the United States, Mexico, and Canada. It provides industry classifications that group establishments into industries based on the activities in which they are primarily engaged. The NAICS was created for establishment designations and provides detail about the smallest operating establishment, while the American Community Survey data are collected from households and differ in detail and nature from those obtained from establishment surveys. Because of disclosure issues, ACS data cannot be released in great detail, and the industry classification system, while defined in NAICS terms, cannot reflect the full detail for all categories.

The industry category, "Public administration," is limited to regular government functions such as legislative, judicial, administrative, and regulatory activities. Other government organizations such as public schools, public hospitals, liquor stores, and bus lines are classified by industry according to the activity in which they are engaged.

This table uses the standard ACS groupings of industries. The detailed NAICS industry code list, together with the corresponding NAICS codes can be found at https://www2.census.gov/programs-surveys/acs/tech_docs/code_lists/2021_ACS_Code_Lists.pdf?#.

VETERAN STATUS, Item 84

Source: Table B21001. Sex by Age by Veteran Status for the Civilian Population 18 Years and Over
Universe: Civilian Population 18 Years and Over

A "civilian veteran" is a person 18 years old or over who has served (even for a short time), but is not now serving, on active duty in the U.S. Army, Navy, Air Force, Marine Corps, or the Coast Guard, or who served in the U.S. Merchant Marines during World War II. People who served in the National Guard or military Reserves are classified as veterans only if they were ever called or ordered to active duty, not counting the 4–6 months for initial training or yearly summer camps. All other civilians 18 years old and over are classified as nonveterans.

HOUSEHOLD INCOME, Items 85–98, 112–137

Sources: Table B19049. Median Household Income in the Past 12 Months (in 2022 Inflation -Adjusted Dollars) By Age of Householder; Table B19013A through B19013I Median Household Income in the Past 12 Months (in 2023 Inflation-Adjusted Dollars) for 9 Race and Hispanic Origin Groups; Table B19052. Wage or Salary Income in the Past 12 Months for Households; Table B19053. Self-Employment Income in the Past 12 Months for Households; Table B19054. Interest, Dividends, or Net Rental Income in the Past 12 Months for Households; Table B19055. Social Security Income in the Past 12 Months for Households; Table B19056. Supplemental Security Income (SSI) in the Past 12 Months for Households; Table B19057. Public Assistance Income in the Past 12 Months for Households; Table B19058. Public Assistance Income or Food Stamps in the Past 12 Months for Households; Table B19059. Retirement Income in the Past 12 Months for Households; Table B19060. Other Types of Income in the Past 12 Months for Households; Table B19001. Household Income in the Past 12 Months (in 2023 Inflation-Adjusted Dollars); and Table C19037. Age of Householder by Household Income in the Past 12 Months (in 2023 Inflation-Adjusted Dollars)
Universe: Households

Income of households includes the income of the householder and all other individuals 15 years old and over in the household, whether they are related to the householder or not. Because many households consist of only one person, average household income is usually less than average family income. Although the household income statistics cover the past 12 months, the characteristics of individuals and the composition of households refer to the time of interview. Thus, the income of the household does not include amounts received by individuals who were members of the household during all or part of the past 12 months if these individuals no longer resided in the household at the time of interview. Similarly, income amounts reported by individuals who did not reside in the household during the past 12 months but who were members of the household at the time of interview are included. However, the composition of most households was the same during the past 12 months as at the time of interview.

Income components were reported for the 12 months preceding the interview month. Monthly Consumer Price Indices (CPI) factors were used to inflation-adjust these components to a reference calendar year (January through December). For example, a household interviewed in March 2022 reports their income for March 2021 through February 2022. Their income is adjusted to the 2022 reference calendar year by multiplying their reported income by 2022 average annual CPI (January–December 2022) and then dividing by the average CPI for March 2021–February 2022.

In order to inflate income amounts from previous years, the dollar values on individual records are inflated to the latest year's dollar values by multiplying by a factor equal to the average annual CPI-U-RS factor for the current year, divided by the average annual CPI-U-RS factor for the earlier/earliest year.

Median income divides the income distribution into two equal parts, with half of all cases below the median income level and half of all cases above the median income level. For households and families, the median income is based on the distribution of the total number of households and families, including those with no income. Median income for households is computed on the basis of a standard distribution with a minimum value of less than $2,500 and a maximum value of $250,000 or more and is rounded to the nearest whole dollar.

The eight types of income reported in the American Community Survey are defined as follows:

1. **Wage or salary income:** Wage or salary income includes total money earnings received for work performed as an employee during the past 12 months. It includes wages, salary, armed forces pay, commissions, tips, piece-rate payments, and cash bonuses earned before deductions were made for taxes, bonds, pensions, union dues, etc.

2. **Self-employment income:** Self-employment income includes both farm and non-farm self-employment income.

Farm self-employment income includes net money income (gross receipts minus operating expenses) from the operation of a farm by a person on his or her own account, as an owner, renter, or sharecropper. Gross receipts include the value of all products sold, government farm programs, money received from the rental of farm equipment to others, and incidental receipts from the sale of wood, sand, gravel, etc. Operating expenses include cost of feed, fertilizer, seed, and other farming supplies, cash wages paid to farmhands, depreciation charges, cash rent, interest on farm mortgages, farm building repairs, farm taxes (not state and federal personal income taxes), etc. The value of fuel, food, or other farm products used for family living is not included as part of net income.

Non-farm self-employment income includes net money income (gross receipts minus expenses) from one's own business, professional enterprise, or partnership. Gross receipts include the value of all goods sold and services rendered. Expenses include costs of goods purchased, rent, heat, light, power, depreciation charges, wages and salaries paid, business taxes (not personal income taxes), etc.

3. **Interest, dividends, or net rental income:** Interest, dividends, or net rental income includes interest on savings or bonds, dividends from stockholdings or membership in associations, net income from rental of property to others and receipts from boarders or lodgers, net royalties, and periodic payments from an estate or trust fund.

4. **Social Security income:** Social Security income includes Social Security pensions and survivor benefits, permanent disability insurance payments made by the Social Security Administration prior to deductions for medical insurance, and railroad retirement insurance checks from the U.S. government. Medicare reimbursements are not included.

5. **Supplemental Security Income (SSI):** Supplemental Security Income (SSI) is a nationwide U.S. assistance program administered by the Social Security Administration that guarantees a minimum level of income for needy aged, blind, or disabled individuals.

6. **Public assistance income:** Public assistance income includes general assistance and Temporary Assistance to Needy Families (TANF). Separate payments received for hospital or other medical care, (vendor payments) are excluded. This does not include Supplemental Security Income (SSI) or noncash benefits such as Food Stamps. The terms "public assistance income" and "cash public assistance" are used interchangeably in the ACS data products.

7. **Retirement, survivor, or disability income:** Retirement income includes: (1) retirement pensions and survivor benefits from a former employer; labor union; or federal, state, or local government; and the U.S. military; (2) disability income from companies or unions; federal, state, or local government; and the U.S. military; (3) periodic receipts from annuities and insurance; and (4) regular income from IRA and Keogh plans. This does not include Social Security income.

8. **All other income:** All other income includes unemployment compensation, Veterans' Administration (VA) payments, alimony and child support, contributions received periodically from people not living in the household, military family allotments, and other kinds of periodic income other than earnings.

Receipts from the following sources are not included as income: capital gains, money received from the sale of property (unless the recipient was engaged in the business of selling such property); the value of income "in kind" from food stamps, public housing subsidies, medical care, employer contributions for individuals, etc.; withdrawal of bank deposits; money borrowed; tax refunds; exchange of money between relatives living in the same household; gifts and lump-sum inheritances, insurance payments, and other types of lump-sum receipts.

Although receipt of **food stamps** is included in an income table, the data on Food Stamp benefits were obtained from a Housing Question in the 2023 American Community Survey. The Food Stamp Act of 1977 defines this federally funded program as one intended to "permit low-income households to obtain a more nutritious diet" (from Title XIII of Public Law 95-113, The Food Stamp Act of 1977, declaration of policy). Food purchasing power is increased by providing eligible households with coupons or cards that can be used to purchase food. The Food and Nutrition Service (FNS) of the U.S. Department of Agriculture (USDA) administers the Food Stamp Program through state and local welfare offices. The Food Stamp Program is the major national income support program to which all low-income and low-resource households, regardless of household characteristics, are eligible. In 2008, the Federal Food Stamp program was renamed SNAP (Supplemental Nutrition Assistance Program). Respondents were asked if one or more of the current members received food stamps or a food stamp benefit card during the past 12 months. Respondents were also asked to include benefits from the Supplemental Nutrition Assistance Program (SNAP) in order to incorporate the program name change.

The questions on participation in the Food Stamp Program were designed to identify households in which one or more of the current members received food stamps during the past 12 months. Once a food stamp household was identified, a question was asked about the total value of all food stamps received for the household during that 12-month period.

FAMILY INCOME, Items 99–105

Source: Table B19126. Median Family Income in the Past 12 Months (in 2023 Inflation-Adjusted Dollars) by Family Type by Presence of Own Children Under 18 Years
Universe: Families

In compiling statistics on **family income**, the incomes of all members 15 years old and over related to the householder are summed and treated as a single amount. Although the family income statistics cover the past 12 months, the characteristics of individuals and the composition of families refer to the time of interview. Thus, the income of the family does not include amounts received by individuals who were members of the family during all or part of the past 12 months if these individuals no longer resided with the family at the time of interview. Similarly, income amounts reported by individuals who did not reside with the family during the past 12 months but who were members of the family at the time of interview are included. However, the composition of most families was the same during the past 12 months as at the time of interview.

NONFAMILY HOUSEHOLD INCOME, Items 106–108

Source: Table B19215. Median Nonfamily Household Income in the Past 12 Months (in 2023 Inflation-Adjusted Dollars) by Sex of Householder by Living Alone by Age of Householder
Universe: Nonfamily Households

Nonfamily household income includes the income of the householder and all other individuals 15 years old and over in the nonfamily household. Although the household income statistics cover the past 12 months, the characteristics of individuals and the composition of households refer to the time of interview. Thus, the income of the household does not include amounts received by individuals who were members of the household during all or part of the past 12 months if these individuals no longer resided in the household at the time of interview. Similarly, income amounts reported by individuals who did not reside in the household during the past 12 months but who were members of the household at the time of interview are included. However, the composition of most households was the same during the past 12 months as at the time of interview.

INCOME OF INDIVIDUALS, Items 109–110

Source: Table B19326. Median Income in the Past 12 Months (in 2023 Inflation-Adjusted Dollars) by Sex by Work Experience in the Past 12 Months for the Population 15 Years and Over with Income
Universe: Population 15 Years and Over with Income in the Past 12 Months

Income of individuals. Income for individuals is obtained by summing the eight types of income for each person 15 years old and over. The characteristics of individuals are based on the time of interview even though the amounts are for the past 12 months.

PER CAPITA INCOME, Item 111

Source: Table B19301. Per Capita Income in the Past 12 Months (in 2023 Inflation-Adjusted Dollars)
Universe: Total Population

Per capita income is the mean income computed for every man, woman, and child in a particular group including those living in group quarters. It is derived by dividing the aggregate income of a particular group by the total population in that group. Per capita income is rounded to the nearest whole dollar.

POVERTY STATUS, Items 138–153

Sources: Table C17017. Poverty Status in the Past 12 Months by Household Type
Universe: Households

Table C17001. Poverty Status in the Past 12 Months by Sex by Age: Table C17001H, C17001B, C17001D, and C17001I. Poverty Status in the Past 12 Months by Sex by Age for specific race/Hispanic origin groups.
Universe: Population for Whom Poverty Status is Determined

The **poverty status** data were derived from data collected on the number of persons in the household, from questionnaire item 3, which provides data on each person's relationship to the householder, and items 47 and 48, the same questions used to derive the income data. The Social Security Administration

(SSA) developed the original poverty definition in 1964, which federal interagency committees subsequently revised in 1969 and 1980. The Office of Management and Budget's (OMB) *Directive 14* prescribes the SSA's definition as the official poverty measure for federal agencies to use in their statistical work. Poverty statistics presented in American Community Survey products adhere to the standards defined by OMB in *Directive 14*.

The poverty thresholds vary depending on three criteria: size of family, number of children, and, for one- and two-person families, age of householder. In determining the poverty status of families and unrelated individuals, the Census Bureau uses thresholds (income cutoffs) arranged in a two-dimensional matrix. The matrix consists of family size (from one person to nine or more persons), cross-classified by presence and number of family members under 18 years old (from no children present to eight or more children present). Unrelated individuals and two-person families are further differentiated by age of reference person (under 65 years old and 65 years old and over). To determine a person's poverty status, the person's total family income in the last 12 months is compared to the poverty threshold appropriate for that person's family size and composition. If the total income of that person's family is less than the threshold appropriate for that family, then the person is considered poor or "below the poverty level," together with every member of his or her family. If a person is not living with anyone related by birth, marriage, or adoption, then the person's own income is compared with his or her poverty threshold. The average poverty threshold for a four-person family was $29,950 in 2022.

Since ACS is a continuous survey, people respond throughout the year. Because the income questions specify a period covering the last 12 months, the appropriate poverty thresholds are determined by multiplying the base-year poverty thresholds (1982) by the average of the monthly inflation factors for the 12 months preceding the data collection.

HEALTH INSURANCE, Items 154–158

Source: Table C27010. Types of Health Insurance Coverage by Age
Universe: Civilian Non-institutionalized Population

In 2022, respondents were instructed to report their current health insurance coverage and to mark "yes" or "no" for each of the eight types listed:

a. Insurance through a current or former employer or union (of this person or another family member)
b. Insurance purchased directly from an insurance company (by this person or another family member)
c. Medicare, for people 65 and older, or people with certain disabilities
d. Medicaid, Medical Assistance, or any kind of government-assistance plan for those with low incomes or a disability
e. TRICARE or other military health care
f. VA (including those who have ever used or enrolled for VA health care)
g. Indian Health Service
h. Any other type of health insurance or health coverage plan (Respondents who answered "yes" were asked to provide their other type of coverage type in a write-in field.)

Health insurance coverage in the ACS and other Census Bureau surveys define coverage to include plans and programs that provide comprehensive health coverage. Plans that provide insurance for specific conditions or situations such as cancer and long-term care policies are not considered coverage. Likewise, other types of insurance like dental, vision, life, and disability insurance are not considered health insurance coverage.

In defining types of coverage, write-in responses were reclassified into one of the first seven types of coverage or determined not to be a coverage type. Write-in responses that referenced the coverage of a family member were edited to assign coverage based on responses from other family members. As a result, only the first seven types of health coverage are included in the four categories in this table.

An eligibility edit was applied to give Medicaid, Medicare, and TRICARE coverage to individuals based on program eligibility rules. TRICARE or other military health care was given to active-duty military personnel and their spouses and children. Medicaid or other means-tested public coverage was given to foster children, certain individuals receiving Supplementary Security Income or Public Assistance, and the spouses and children of certain Medicaid beneficiaries. Medicare coverage was given to people 65 and older who received Social Security or Medicaid benefits.

People were considered insured if they reported at least one "yes". People who had no reported health coverage, or those whose only health coverage was Indian Health Service, were considered uninsured. For reporting purposes, the Census Bureau broadly classifies health insurance coverage as private health insurance or public coverage. Private health insurance is a plan provided through an employer or union, a plan purchased by an individual from a private company, or TRICARE or other military health care. Respondents reporting a "yes" to the types listed in parts a, b, or e were considered to have private health insurance. Public health coverage includes the federal programs Medicare, Medicaid, and VA Health Care (provided through the Department of Veterans Affairs); the Children's Health Insurance Program (CHIP); and individual state health plans. Respondents reporting a "yes" to the types listed in c, d, or f were considered to have public coverage. The types of health insurance are not mutually exclusive; people may be covered by more than one at the same time.

Tables B-2, B-3, and B-4. What — Education, Employment, and Income

Table B-2 presents 12 items for the United States as a whole, each individual state and the District of Columbia, and 848 counties, county equivalents, and independent cities with a 2022 population of 65,000 or more. This table is from the 2022 1-year file, from ACS tables beginning with "B" and "C," as the supplemental estimates were not available.

Table B-3 presents 12 items for 384 Metropolitan Statistical Areas and 31 Metropolitan Divisions within the 12 largest Metropolitan Statistical Areas. This table is from the 2022 1-year file, from ACS tables beginning with "B".

Table B-4 presents 12 items for 646 cities, Census Designated Places, and the principal portions of consolidated cities with a 2022 population of 65,000 or more. This table is from the 2022 1-year file, from ACS tables beginning with "B" and "C," as the supplemental estimates were not available.

EDUCATIONAL ATTAINMENT, Items 1–3

Source: Table C15002. Sex by Educational Attainment for the Population 25 Years and Over; Table K201501. Educational Attainment for the Population 25 Years and Over.
Universe: Population 25 Years and Over

Data on **educational attainment** were derived from a question that asked respondents for the highest level of school completed or the highest degree received. Persons currently enrolled in school are instructed to report the level of the previous grade attended or the highest degree received. Persons who had passed a high school equivalency examination were considered high school graduates. Schooling received in foreign schools was to be reported as the equivalent grade or years in the regular American school system.

Specifically excluded are vocational and technical training, such as barber school training; business, trade, technical, and vocational schools; or other training for a specific trade.

High school diploma or less. This category includes persons whose highest degree was a high school diploma or its equivalent, and those who reported any level lower than a high school diploma.

Bachelor's degree or more. This category includes persons who have received bachelor's degrees, master's degrees, professional school degrees (such as law school or medical school degrees), or doctoral degrees.

EMPLOYMENT STATUS, Items 4–8

Sources: Table B23025. Employment Status for the Population 16 Years and Over;
Table K202301. Employment Status for the Population 16 Years and Over
Universe: Population 16 Years and Over

Table B23022. Sex By Work Status In The Past 12 Months By Usual Hours Worked Per Week In The Past 12 Months By Weeks Worked In The Past 12 Months For The Population 16 To 64 Years;

Table K202302. Sex By Full-Time Work Status In The Past 12 Months For The Population 16 To 64 Years
Universe: Population 16 to 64 Years

Total employment includes all persons 16 years old and over who were either (1) "at work"—those who did any work at all during the reference week as paid employees, worked in either their own business or profession, worked on their own farm, or worked 15 hours or more as unpaid workers in a family farm or business; or were (2) "with a job, but not at work"—those who had a job but were not at work that week due to illness, weather, industrial dispute, vacation, or other personal reasons.

The **labor force** consists of all persons 16 years old and over who are either employed or unemployed, including those in the armed forces.

The **unemployment rate** represents the number of unemployed people as a percentage of the labor force.

Unemployment includes all persons who did not work during the survey week, made specific efforts to find a job during the previous four weeks, and were available for work during the survey week (except for temporary illness). Persons waiting to be called back to a job from which they had been laid off and those waiting to report to a new job within the next 30 days are included in unemployment figures.

Full-time, year-round includes all persons 16 to 64 years old who usually worked 35 hours or more per week for 50 to 52 weeks in the past 12 months.

INCOME AND BENEFITS, Items 9–12

Sources: Table B19013. Median Household Income in the Past 12 Months (in 2023 Inflation-Adjusted Dollars); Table K201902. Median Household Income in the Past 12 Months (in 2023 Inflation-Adjusted Dollars); B19001. Household Income in the Past 12 Months (in 2023 Inflation-Adjusted Dollars); Table K201901. Household Income in the Past 12 Months (in 2023 Inflation-Adjusted Dollars); Table C22001.

Receipt Of Food Stamps/Snap In The Past 12 Months For Households; Table K202201. Receipt Of Food Stamps/Snap In The Past 12 Months By Presence Of Children Under 18 Years For Households
Universe: Households

Household income includes the income of the householder and all other individuals 15 years old and over in the household, whether or not they are related to the householder. Since many households consist of only one person, average household income is usually less than average family income. Although the household income statistics cover the past 12 months, the characteristics of individuals and the composition of households refer to the time of enumeration. Thus, the income of the household does not include amounts received by individuals who were members of the household during all or part of the past 12 months if these individuals no longer resided in the household at the time of enumeration. Similarly, income amounts reported by individuals who did not reside in the household during the past 12 months but who were members of the household at the time of enumeration are included. However, the composition of most households was the same during the past 12 months as at the time of enumeration.

Median income divides the income distribution into two equal parts, with half of all cases below the median income level and half of all cases above the median income level. For households and families, the median income is based on the distribution of the total number of households and families, including those with no income. Median income for households is computed on the basis of a standard distribution with a minimum value of less than $2,500 and a maximum value of $250,000 or more and is rounded to the nearest whole dollar.

Income in the American Community Survey is for the past 12 months as opposed to a single reference year.

Part C: Where

Table C-1. Where — Migration, Housing, and Transportation

Table C-1 presents 87 items for the United States as a whole and for each individual state and the District of Columbia.

PLACE OF RESIDENCE, Items 1–7

Source: Table C07204. Geographical Mobility in the Past Year for Current Residence—State, County, and Place Level in the United States
Universe: Population 1 Year and Over in the United States

Residence one year ago is used in conjunction with location of current residence to determine the extent of residential mobility of the population and the resulting redistribution of the population across the various states, metropolitan areas, and regions of the country.

Same house includes all people 1 year and over who did not move during the 1 year as well as those who had moved and returned to their residence 1 year ago.

Different house in the United States includes people who lived in the United States 1 year ago but in a different house or apartment from the one they occupied at the time of interview. These movers are then further subdivided according to the type of move. Movers within the U.S. are divided into groups according to their previous residence: Different house, same city or town; Different house, different city, same county; Different house, different county, same state; and Different state.

Abroad includes those whose previous residence was in a foreign country, Puerto Rico, American Samoa, Guam, the Northern Marianas, or the U.S. Virgin Islands, including members of the armed forces and their dependents.

HOME-OWNERSHIP BY RACE, HISPANIC ORIGIN, AGE OF HOUSEHOLDER, AND HOUSEHOLD TYPE, Items 8–35

Sources: Table B25003. Tenure; Table B25003H. Tenure (White alone, Not Hispanic or Latino Householder); Table B25003B. Tenure (Black or African American Alone Householder); Table B25003C. Tenure (American Indian and Alaska Native Alone Householder); Table B25003D. Tenure (Asian Alone Householder); Table B25003E. Tenure (Native Hawaiian and Other Pacific Islander Alone Householder); Table B25003I. Tenure (Hispanic or Latino Householder); Table B25007. Tenure by Age of Householder; and Table B25115. Tenure by Household Type And Presence And Age Of Own Children
Universe: Occupied Housing Units

A **housing unit** is a house, apartment, mobile home or trailer, group of rooms, or single room occupied or, if vacant, intended for occupancy as separate living quarters. Separate living quarters are those in which the occupants do not live and eat with any other person in the structure and which have direct access from the outside of the building or through a common hall. For vacant units, the criteria of separateness and direct access are applied to the intended occupants whenever possible. If that information cannot be obtained, the criteria are applied to the previous occupants.

The occupants of a housing unit may be a single family, one person living alone, two or more families living together, or any other group of related or unrelated persons who share living arrangements. Both occupied and vacant housing units are included in the housing inventory, although recreational vehicles, tents, caves, boats, railroad cars, and the like are included only if they are occupied as a person's usual place of residence.

Occupied housing units are classified as either owner occupied or renter occupied. A housing unit is classified as occupied if it is the usual place of residence of the person or group of persons living in it at the time of enumeration, or if the occupants are only temporarily absent from the residence for two months or less, that is, away on vacation or a business trip. If all the people staying in the unit at the time of the interview are staying there for two months or less, the unit is considered to be temporarily occupied and classified as "vacant."

A housing unit is **owner occupied** if the owner or co-owner lives in the unit even if it is mortgaged or not fully paid for. The owner or co-owner must live in the unit and usually is Person 1 on the questionnaire. The unit is "Owned by you or someone in this household with a mortgage or loan" if it is being purchased with a mortgage or some other debt arrangement such as a deed of trust, trust deed, contract to purchase, land contract, or purchase agreement. The unit also is considered owned with a mortgage if it is built on leased land and there is a mortgage on the unit. Mobile homes occupied by owners with installment loan balances also are included in this category.

All occupied housing units which are not owner occupied, whether they are rented for cash rent or occupied without payment of cash rent, are classified as **renter occupied**. "No cash rent" units are separately identified in the rent tabulations. Such units are generally provided free by friends or relatives or in exchange for services such as resident manager, caretaker, minister, or tenant farmer. Housing units on military bases also are classified in the "No cash rent" category. "Rented for cash rent" includes units in continuing care, sometimes called life care arrangements. These arrangements usually involve a contract between one or more individuals and a health services provider guaranteeing the individual shelter, usually a house or apartment, and services, such as meals or transportation to shopping or recreation.

HOUSEHOLD SIZE, Items 36–38

Source: Table B25010. Average Household Size of Occupied Housing Units by Tenure
Universe: Occupied Housing Units

Household size is based on the count of people in occupied housing units. All people occupying the housing unit are counted, including the householder, occupants related to the householder, and lodgers, roomers, boarders, and so forth.

Average household size of occupied units is obtained by dividing the number of people living in occupied housing units by the total number of occupied housing units. This measure is rounded to the nearest hundredth.

Average household size of owner-occupied units is obtained by dividing the number of people living in owner-occupied housing units by the total number of owner-occupied housing units. This measure is rounded to the nearest hundredth.

Average household size of renter-occupied units is obtained by dividing the number of people living in renter-occupied housing units by the total number of renter-occupied housing units. This measure is rounded to the nearest hundredth.

UNITS THAT ARE CROWDED OR LACKING COMPLETE PLUMBING, Item 39

Source: Table C25016. Tenure by Plumbing Facilities by Occupants per Room
Universe: Occupied Housing Units

Item 39 shows the percentage of housing units in the state that are **crowded** or **lacking complete plumbing facilities.**

Occupants per room is obtained by dividing the number of people in each occupied housing unit by the number of rooms in the unit. Although the Census Bureau has no official definition of **crowded** units, many users consider units with more than one occupant per room to be crowded, the measure used in this item.

The question on plumbing facilities was asked at both occupied and vacant housing units. Complete plumbing facilities include: (1) hot and cold piped water, (2) a flush toilet, and (3) a bathtub or shower. All three facilities must be located inside the house, apartment, or mobile home, but not necessarily in the same room. Housing units are classified as **lacking complete plumbing facilities** when any of the three facilities is not present.

MEDIAN HOUSEHOLD INCOME IN THE PAST 12 MONTHS, Items 40–44

Sources: Table B25119. Median Household Income the Past 12 Months (in 2023 Inflation-Adjusted Dollars) by Tenure
Universe: Occupied Housing Units

Table B25099. Mortgage Status by Median Household Income in the Past 12 Months (in 2023 Inflation-Adjusted Dollars)
Universe: Owner-Occupied Housing Units

The data on **mortgage status** were obtained from questions that were asked at owner-occupied units. The category **with a mortgage** refers to all forms of debt where the property is pledged as security for repayment of the debt, including deeds of trust; trust deeds; contracts to purchase; land contracts; junior mortgages; and home equity loans.

The category **without a mortgage** comprises housing units owned free and clear of debt.

A detailed definition of income and types of income is included above under Table B-1.

HOUSING VALUES AND COSTS, Items 45–51, 54–64

Sources: Table B25097. Mortgage Status by Median Value (Dollars); Table B25081. Mortgage Status; Table B25092. Median Selected Monthly Owner Costs as a Percentage of Household Income in the Past 12 Months; Table B25088. Median Selected Monthly Owner Costs (Dollars) by Mortgage Status; Table B25103. Mortgage Status by Median Real Estate Taxes Paid (Dollars); and Table C25093. Age of Householder by Selected Monthly Owner costs as a Percentage of Household Income in the Past 12 Months
Universe: Owner-Occupied Housing Units
Table B25105. Median Monthly Housing Costs (Dollars)
Universe: Occupied Housing Units with Monthly Housing Cost

Median value is the dollar amount that divides the distribution of specified owner-occupied housing units into two equal parts, with half of all units below the median value and half above the median value. Value is defined as the respondent's estimate of what the house would sell for if it were for sale. If the house or mobile home was owned or being bought, but the land on which it sits was not, the respondent was asked to estimate the combined value of the house or mobile home and the land. For vacant units, value was the price asked for the property. Value was tabulated separately for all owner-occupied and vacant-for-sale housing units, as well as owner-occupied and vacant-for-sale mobile homes.

Housing cost, as a percentage of income, is shown separately for owners with mortgages, owners without mortgages, and renters. Selected owner costs include utilities and fuels, mortgage payments, insurance, taxes, etc. In each case, the ratio of housing cost to income is computed separately for each housing unit. The housing cost ratios for half of all units are above the median shown in this book, and half are below the median shown in the book.

The data for monthly housing costs in item 51 are developed from a distribution of **selected monthly owner costs** for owner-occupied units and **gross rent** for renter-occupied units.

Selected monthly owner costs are the sum of payments for mortgages, deeds of trust, contracts to purchase, or similar debts on the property (including payments for the first mortgage, second mortgages, home equity loans, and other junior mortgages); real estate taxes; fire, hazard, and flood insurance on the property; utilities (electricity, gas, and water and sewer); and fuels (oil, coal, kerosene, wood, etc.). It also includes, where appropriate, the monthly condominium fee for condominiums and mobile home costs (installment loan payments, personal property taxes, site rent, registration fees, and license fees). Selected monthly owner costs were tabulated for all owner-occupied units, and usually are shown separately for units "with a mortgage" and for units "not mortgaged."

Real estate taxes include state, local, and all other real estate taxes even if delinquent, unpaid, or paid by someone who is not a member of the household. However, taxes due from prior years are not included. If taxes are paid on other than a yearly basis, the payments are converted to a yearly basis.

RENT, Items 52–53, 65–68

Sources: Table B25064. Median Gross Rent (Dollars); and Table B25071. Median Gross Rent as a Percentage of Household Income in the Past 12 Months (Dollars)
Universe: Renter-Occupied Housing Units Paying Cash Rent

Table B25072. Age of Householder by Gross Rent as a Percentage of Household Income in the Past 12 Months
Universe: Renter-Occupied Housing Units

Median gross rent divides the distribution of renter-occupied housing units into two equal parts: one-half of the cases falling below the median gross rent and one-half above the median.

Gross rent is the **contract ren**t plus the estimated average monthly cost of **utilities** (electricity, gas, and water and sewer) and fuels (oil, coal, kerosene, wood, etc.) if these are paid by the renter (or paid for the renter by someone else). Gross rent is intended to eliminate differentials that result from varying practices with respect to the inclusion of utilities and fuels as part of the rental payment. The estimated costs of water and sewer, and fuels are reported on a 12-month basis but are converted to monthly figures for the tabulations. Renter units occupied without payment of cash rent are not included in the tabulations.

Gross rent as a percentage of household income is a computed ratio of monthly gross rent to monthly household income (total household income divided by 12). Median gross rent divides the gross rent as a percentage of household income distribution into two equal parts: one-half of the cases falling below the median gross rent as a percentage of household income and one-half above the median.

MEANS OF TRANSPORTATION TO WORK, ITEMS 69–76

Source: Table B08301. Means of Transportation to Work
Universe: Workers 16 Years and Over

Means of transportation to work refers to the principal mode of travel or type of conveyance that the worker usually used to get from home to work during the reference week. People who used different means of transportation on different days of the week were asked to specify the one they used most often, that is, the greatest number of days. People who used more than one means of transportation to get to work each day were asked to report the one used for the longest distance during the work trip.

The category, **car, truck, or van**, includes workers using a car (including company cars but excluding taxicabs), a truck of one-ton capacity or less, or a van. A question on vehicle occupancy was asked of people who indicated that they worked at some time during the reference week and who reported that their means of transportation to work was **car, truck, or van**. The category, **drove alone**, includes people who usually drove alone to work as well as people who were driven to work by someone who then drove back home or to a nonwork destination. The category, **carpooled**, includes workers who reported that two or more people usually rode to work in the vehicle during the reference week.

The category, **public transportation**, includes workers who used a bus or trolley bus, streetcar or trolley car, subway or elevated, railroad, or ferryboat, even if each mode is not shown separately in the tabulation. The category, "Other means," includes workers who used a mode of travel that is not identified separately within the data distribution.

MEAN TRAVEL TIME TO WORK, Items 77–81

Sources: Table C08301. Means of Transportation to Work
Universe: Workers 16 Years and Over

Table C08136. Aggregate Travel Time to Work (in Minutes) of Workers by Means of Transportation to Work
Universe: Workers 16 Years and Over Whom Did Not Work at Home

Travel time to work refers to the total number of minutes that it usually took the worker to get from home to work during the reference week. The elapsed time includes time spent waiting for public transportation, picking up passengers in carpools, and time spent in other activities related to getting to work.

Mean travel time to work (in minutes) is the average travel time that workers usually took to get from home to work (one way) during the reference week. This measure is obtained by dividing the total number of minutes taken to get from home to work (the aggregate travel time) by the number of workers 16 years old and over who did not work at home.

VEHICLES AVAILABLE, Items 83–87

Sources: Table B08201. Household Size by Vehicles Available; and Table B25046. Aggregate Number of Vehicles Available by Tenure
Universe: Occupied Housing Units

The data on vehicles available show the number of passenger cars, vans, and pickup or panel trucks of one-ton capacity or less kept at home and available for the use of household members. Vehicles rented or leased for one month or more, company vehicles, and police and government vehicles are included if kept at home and used for non-business purposes. Dismantled or immobile vehicles are excluded. Vehicles kept at home but used only for business purposes also are excluded.

Tables C-2, C-3, and C-4. Where — Migration, Housing, and Transportation

Table C-2 presents 12 items for the United States as a whole, each individual state and the District of Columbia, and 848 counties, county equivalents, and independent cities with a 2022 population of 65,000 or more. This table is from the 2022 1-year file, from ACS tables beginning with "B" and "C," as the supplemental estimates were not available.

Table C-3 presents 12 items for 384 Metropolitan Statistical Areas and 31 Metropolitan Divisions within the 12 largest Metropolitan Statistical Areas. This table includes data from the 2021 1-year file, from ACS tables beginning with "B" and "C".

Table C-4 presents 12 items for 646 cities, Census Designated Places, and the principal portions of consolidated cities with a 2022 population of 65,000 or more. This table is from the 2022 1-year Supplemental file, from ACS tables beginning with "K". This table is from the 2022 1-year file, from ACS tables beginning with "B" and "C," as the supplemental estimates were not available.

PLACE OF RESIDENCE, Items 1-3

Sources: Table B07201. Geographical Mobility in the Past Year for Current Residence--Metropolitan Statistical Area Level in the United States
Universe: Population 1 year and over living in a Metropolitan Statistical Area in the United States

Table K200701. Geographical Mobility in the Past Year in the United States
Universe: Population 1 Year and Over in the United States

Residence one year ago is used in conjunction with location of current residence to determine the extent of residential mobility of the population and the resulting redistribution of the population across the various states, metropolitan areas, and regions of the country. **Same house** includes all people 1 year old and over who, a year earlier, lived in the same house or apartment that they occupied at the time of interview.

Did not live in same county one year ago includes all persons who did not live in the same county 1 year ago, whether their previous residence was in the same metropolitan area, the same state, a different state, Puerto Rico, or abroad. Persons who moved within the county but to a new city cannot be identified as movers in Table C-4.

Did not live in same metropolitan area one year ago includes all persons who did not live in the same metropolitan area 1 year ago, whether their previous residence was in the same state, a different state, Puerto Rico, or abroad.

OCCUPIED HOUSING UNITS, Items 4-5

Source: Table B25003. Housing Tenure; Table K202502. Housing Tenure
Universe: Occupied Housing Units

A **housing unit** is a house, apartment, mobile home or trailer, group of rooms, or single room occupied or, if vacant, intended for occupancy as separate living quarters. Separate living quarters are those in which the occupants do not live and eat with any other person in the structure and which have direct access from the outside of the building or through a common hall. For vacant units, the criteria of separateness and direct access are applied to the intended occupants whenever possible. If that information cannot be obtained, the criteria are applied to the previous occupants.

The occupants of a housing unit may be a single family, one person living alone, two or more families living together, or any other group of related or unrelated persons who share living arrangements. Both occupied and vacant housing units are included in the housing inventory, although recreational vehicles, tents, caves, boats, railroad cars, and the like are included only if they are occupied as a person's usual place of residence.

Occupied housing units are classified as either owner occupied or renter occupied. A housing unit is classified as occupied if it is the usual place of residence of the person or group of persons living in it at the time of enumeration, or if the occupants are only temporarily absent from the residence for two months or less, that is, away on vacation or a business trip. If all the people staying in the unit at the time of the interview are staying there for two months or less, the unit is considered to be temporarily occupied and classified as "vacant."

A housing unit is **owner occupied** if the owner or co-owner lives in the unit even if it is mortgaged or not fully paid for. The owner or co-owner must live in the unit and usually is Person 1 on the questionnaire. The unit is "Owned by you or someone in this household with a mortgage or loan" if it is being purchased with a mortgage or some other debt arrangement such as a deed of trust, trust deed, contract to purchase, land contract, or purchase agreement. The unit also is considered owned with a mortgage if it is built on leased land and there is a mortgage on the unit. Mobile homes occupied by owners with installment loan balances also are included in this category.

All occupied housing units that are not owner occupied, whether they are rented for cash rent or occupied without payment of cash rent, are classified as **renter occupied**. "No cash rent" units are separately identified in the rent tabulations. Such units are generally provided free by friends or relatives or in exchange for services such as resident manager, caretaker, minister, or tenant farmer. Housing units on military bases also are classified in the "No cash rent" category. "Rented for cash rent" includes units in continuing care, sometimes called life care arrangements. These arrangements usually involve a contract between one or more individuals and a health services provider guaranteeing the individual shelter, usually a house or apartment, and services, such as meals or transportation to shopping or recreation.

HOUSING VALUES AND COSTS, Items 6-7

Sources: Table B25081. Mortgage Status; Table B25077. Median Value (dollars); Table K202508. Mortgage Status; Table K202510. Median Value (dollars).
Universe: Owner-Occupied Housing Units

The data on **mortgage status** were obtained from questions that were asked at owner-occupied units. The category **with a mortgage** refers to all forms of debt where the property is pledged as security for repayment of the debt, including deeds of trust; trust deeds; contracts to purchase; land contracts; junior mortgages; and home equity loans.

Housing value is defined as the respondent's estimate of what the house would sell for if it were for sale. If the house or mobile home was owned or being bought, but the land on which it sits was not, the respondent was asked to estimate the combined value of the house or mobile home and the land. For vacant units, value was the price asked for the property. Value was tabulated separately for all owner-occupied and vacant-for-sale housing units, as well as owner-occupied and vacant-for-sale mobile homes.

Median value is the dollar amount that divides the distribution of specified owner-occupied housing units into two equal parts, with half of all units below the median value and half above the median value. Value is defined as the respondent's estimate of what the house would sell for if it were for sale. If the house or mobile home was owned or being bought, but the land on which it sits was not, the respondent was asked to estimate the combined value of the house or mobile home and the land. For vacant units, value was the price asked for the property. Value was tabulated separately for all owner-occupied and vacant-for-sale housing units, as well as owner-occupied and vacant-for-sale mobile homes.

RENT, Item 8
Table K202511. Median Gross Rent (dollars). Table B25064. Median Gross Rent (dollars)
Universe: Renter-Occupied Housing Units

Gross rent is the contract rent plus the estimated average monthly cost of utilities (electricity, gas, and water and sewer) and fuels (oil, coal, kerosene, wood, etc.) if these are paid by the renter (or paid for the renter by someone else). Gross rent is intended to eliminate differentials that result from varying practices with respect to the inclusion of utilities and fuels as part of the rental payment. The estimated costs of water and sewer, and fuels are reported on a 12-month basis but are converted to monthly figures for the tabulations. Renter units occupied without payment of cash rent are not included in the tabulations.

Median gross rent divides the distribution of renter-occupied housing units into two equal parts: one-half of the cases falling below the median gross rent and one-half above the median.

Gross rent is the **contract ren**t plus the estimated average monthly cost of **utilities** (electricity, gas, and water and sewer) and fuels (oil, coal, kerosene, wood, etc.) if these are paid by the renter (or paid for the renter by someone else). Gross rent is intended to eliminate differentials that result from varying practices with respect to the inclusion of utilities and fuels as part of the rental payment. The estimated costs of water and sewer, and fuels are reported on a 12-month basis but are converted to monthly figures for the tabulations. Renter units occupied without payment of cash rent are not included in the tabulations.

INTERNET ACCESS, Item 9
Source: Table K202801. Presence Of A Computer And Type Of internet Subscription In Household; B28003. Presence Of A Computer And Type Of internet Subscription In Household.
Universe: Households

The computer use question asked if anyone in the household owned or used a computer and included three response categories for a desktop/laptop, a handheld computer, or some other type of computer. The Category **Households with Internet Access** includes housing units where someone pays to access the internet through a service such as a data plan for a mobile phone, a cable modem, DSL or other type of service. This will normally refer to a service that someone is billed for directly for internet alone or sometimes as part of a bundle. Not included in this category are those respondents who may live in a city or town that provides free internet services for their residents, or attend a university that provides internet services. These persons may be able to access the internet without a subscription, but are not included in the total in Item 9.

TRAVEL TIME TO WORK, Items 10-12
Sources: Table K200802. Travel Time to Work; B08303. Travel Time to Work.
Universe: Workers 16 Years and Over Who Did Not Work at Home

Travel time to work refers to the total number of minutes that it usually took the worker to get from home to work during the reference week. The elapsed time includes time spent waiting for public transportation, picking up passengers in carpools, and time spent in other activities related to getting to work.

APPENDIX C:
METROPOLITAN STATISTICAL AREAS, METROPOLITAN DIVISIONS, AND COMPONENTS (AS DEFINED JULY 2015)

Core based statistical area	State/ County FIPS code	Title and Geographic Components	2010 Census Population
CBSA	FIPS	AREANAME	C0021
10180		Abilene, TX	165252
10180	48059	Callahan County	13544
10180	48253	Jones County	20202
10180	48441	Taylor County	131506
10420		Akron, OH	703200
10420	39133	Portage County	161419
10420	39153	Summit County	541781
10500		Albany, GA	157308
10500	13007	Baker County	3451
10500	13095	Dougherty County	94565
10500	13177	Lee County	28298
10500	13273	Terrell County	9315
10500	13321	Worth County	21679
10540		Albany, OR	116672
10540	41043	Linn County	116672
10580		Albany-Schenectady-Troy, NY	870716
10580	36001	Albany County	304204
10580	36083	Rensselaer County	159429
10580	36091	Saratoga County	219607
10580	36093	Schenectady County	154727
10580	36095	Schoharie County	32749
10740		Albuquerque, NM	887077
10740	35001	Bernalillo County	662564
10740	35043	Sandoval County	131561
10740	35057	Torrance County	16383
10740	35061	Valencia County	76569
10780		Alexandria, LA	153922
10780	22043	Grant Parish	22309
10780	22079	Rapides Parish	131613
10900		Allentown-Bethlehem-Easton, PA-NJ	821173
10900	34041	Warren County	108692
10900	42025	Carbon County	65249
10900	42077	Lehigh County	349497
10900	42095	Northampton County	297735
11020		Altoona, PA	127089
11020	42013	Blair County	127089
11100		Amarillo, TX	251933
11100	48011	Armstrong County	1901
11100	48065	Carson County	6182
11100	48359	Oldham County	2052
11100	48375	Potter County	121073
11100	48381	Randall County	120725
11180		Ames, IA	89542
11180	19169	Story County	89542
11260		Anchorage, AK	380821
11260	02020	Anchorage Municipality	291826
11260	02170	Matanuska-Susitna Borough	88995
11460		Ann Arbor, MI	344791
11460	26161	Washtenaw County	344791
11500		Anniston-Oxford-Jacksonville, AL	118572
11500	01015	Calhoun County	118572
11540		Appleton, WI	225666
11540	55015	Calumet County	48971
11540	55087	Outagamie County	176695
11700		Asheville, NC	424858
11700	37021	Buncombe County	238318
11700	37087	Haywood County	59036
11700	37089	Henderson County	106740
11700	37115	Madison County	20764
12020		Athens-Clarke County, GA	192541
12020	13059	Clarke County	116714
12020	13195	Madison County	28120
12020	13219	Oconee County	32808
12020	13221	Oglethorpe County	14899
12060		Atlanta-Sandy Springs-Roswell, GA	5286728
12060	13013	Barrow County	69367
12060	13015	Bartow County	100157
12060	13035	Butts County	23655
12060	13045	Carroll County	110527
12060	13057	Cherokee County	214346
12060	13063	Clayton County	259424
12060	13067	Cobb County	688078
12060	13077	Coweta County	127317
12060	13085	Dawson County	22330
12060	13089	DeKalb County	691893
12060	13097	Douglas County	132403
12060	13113	Fayette County	106567
12060	13117	Forsyth County	175511
12060	13121	Fulton County	920581
12060	13135	Gwinnett County	805321
12060	13143	Haralson County	28780
12060	13149	Heard County	11834
12060	13151	Henry County	203922
12060	13159	Jasper County	13900
12060	13171	Lamar County	18317
12060	13199	Meriwether County	21992
12060	13211	Morgan County	17868
12060	13217	Newton County	99958
12060	13223	Paulding County	142324
12060	13227	Pickens County	29431
12060	13231	Pike County	17869
12060	13247	Rockdale County	85215
12060	13255	Spalding County	64073
12060	13297	Walton County	83768
12100		Atlantic City-Hammonton, NJ	274549
12100	34001	Atlantic County	274549
12220		Auburn-Opelika, AL	140247
12220	01081	Lee County	140247
12260		Augusta-Richmond County, GA-SC	564873
12260	13033	Burke County	23316
12260	13073	Columbia County	124053
12260	13181	Lincoln County	7996
12260	13189	McDuffie County	21875
12260	13245	Richmond County	200549
12260	45003	Aiken County	160099
12260	45037	Edgefield County	26985
12420		Austin-Round Rock, TX	1716289
12420	48021	Bastrop County	74171
12420	48055	Caldwell County	38066
12420	48209	Hays County	157107
12420	48453	Travis County	1024266
12420	48491	Williamson County	422679
12540		Bakersfield, CA	839631
12540	06029	Kern County	839631
12580		Baltimore-Columbia-Towson, MD	2710489
12580	24003	Anne Arundel County	537656
12580	24005	Baltimore County	805029
12580	24013	Carroll County	167134

Appendix C: Metropolitan Statistical Areas, Metropolitan Divisions, and Components (as defined July 2015)—*Continued*

Core based statistical area	State/ County FIPS code	Title and Geographic Components	2010 Census Population
12580	24025	Harford County	244826
12580	24027	Howard County	287085
12580	24035	Queen Anne's County	47798
12580	24510	Baltimore city	620961
12620		Bangor, ME	153923
12620	23019	Penobscot County	153923
12700		Barnstable Town, MA	215888
12700	25001	Barnstable County	215888
12940		Baton Rouge, LA	802484
12940	22005	Ascension Parish	107215
12940	22033	East Baton Rouge Parish	440171
12940	22037	East Feliciana Parish	20267
12940	22047	Iberville Parish	33387
12940	22063	Livingston Parish	128026
12940	22077	Pointe Coupee Parish	22802
12940	22091	St. Helena Parish	11203
12940	22121	West Baton Rouge Parish	23788
12940	22125	West Feliciana Parish	15625
12980		Battle Creek, MI	136146
12980	26025	Calhoun County	136146
13020		Bay City, MI	107771
13020	26017	Bay County	107771
13140		Beaumont-Port Arthur, TX	403190
13140	48199	Hardin County	54635
13140	48245	Jefferson County	252273
13140	48351	Newton County	14445
13140	48361	Orange County	81837
13220		Beckley, WV	124898
13220	54019	Fayette County	46039
13220	54081	Raleigh County	78859
13380		Bellingham, WA	201140
13380	53073	Whatcom County	201140
13460		Bend-Redmond, OR	157733
13460	41017	Deschutes County	157733
13740		Billings, MT	158934
13740	30009	Carbon County	10078
13740	30037	Golden Valley County	884
13740	30111	Yellowstone County	147972
13780		Binghamton, NY	251725
13780	36007	Broome County	200600
13780	36107	Tioga County	51125
13820		Birmingham-Hoover, AL	1128047
13820	01007	Bibb County	22915
13820	01009	Blount County	57322
13820	01021	Chilton County	43643
13820	01073	Jefferson County	658466
13820	01115	St. Clair County	83593
13820	01117	Shelby County	195085
13820	01127	Walker County	67023
13900		Bismarck, ND	114778
13900	38015	Burleigh County	81308
13900	38059	Morton County	27471
13900	38065	Oliver County	1846
13900	38085	Sioux County	4153
13980		Blacksburg-Christiansburg-Radford, VA	178237
13980	51063	Floyd County	15279
13980	51071	Giles County	17286
13980	51121	Montgomery County	94392
13980	51155	Pulaski County	34872
13980	51750	Radford city	16408
14010		Bloomington, IL	186133
14010	17039	De Witt County	16561
14010	17113	McLean County	169572
14020		Bloomington, IN	159549
14020	18105	Monroe County	137974
14020	18119	Owen County	21575
14100		Bloomsburg-Berwick, PA	85562
14100	42037	Columbia County	67295
14100	42093	Montour County	18267
14260		Boise City, ID	616561
14260	16001	Ada County	392365
14260	16015	Boise County	7028
14260	16027	Canyon County	188923
14260	16045	Gem County	16719
14260	16073	Owyhee County	11526
14460		Boston-Cambridge-Newton, MA-NH	4552402
14460		.Boston, MA Div 14454	1887792
14460	25021	Norfolk County	670850
14460	25023	Plymouth County	494919
14460	25025	Suffolk County	722023
14460		.Cambridge-Newton-Framingham, MA Div 15764	2246244
14460	25009	Essex County	743159
14460	25017	Middlesex County	1503085
14460		.Rockingham County-Strafford County, NH Div 40484	418366
14460	33015	Rockingham County	295223
14460	33017	Strafford County	123143
14500		Boulder, CO	294567
14500	08013	Boulder County	294567
14540		Bowling Green, KY	158599
14540	21003	Allen County	19956
14540	21031	Butler County	12690
14540	21061	Edmonson County	12161
14540	21227	Warren County	113792
14740		Bremerton-Silverdale, WA	251133
14740	53035	Kitsap County	251133
14860		Bridgeport-Stamford-Norwalk, CT	916829
14860	09001	Fairfield County	916829
15180		Brownsville-Harlingen, TX	406220
15180	48061	Cameron County	406220
15260		Brunswick, GA	112370
15260	13025	Brantley County	18411
15260	13127	Glynn County	79626
15260	13191	McIntosh County	14333
15380		Buffalo-Cheektowaga-Niagara Falls, NY	1135509
15380	36029	Erie County	919040
15380	36063	Niagara County	216469
15500		Burlington, NC	151131
15500	37001	Alamance County	151131
15540		Burlington-South Burlington, VT	211261
15540	50007	Chittenden County	156545
15540	50011	Franklin County	47746
15540	50013	Grand Isle County	6970
15680		California-Lexington Park, MD	105151
15680	24037	St. Mary's County	105151
15940		Canton-Massillon, OH	404422
15940	39019	Carroll County	28836
15940	39151	Stark County	375586
15980		Cape Coral-Fort Myers, FL	618754
15980	12071	Lee County	618754
16020		Cape Girardeau, MO-IL	96275
16020	17003	Alexander County	8238
16020	29017	Bollinger County	12363
16020	29031	Cape Girardeau County	75674
16060		Carbondale-Marion, IL	126575
16060	17077	Jackson County	60218
16060	17199	Williamson County	66357
16180		Carson City, NV	55274
16180	32510	Carson City	55274
16220		Casper, WY	75450
16220	56025	Natrona County	75450
16300		Cedar Rapids, IA	257940
16300	19011	Benton County	26076
16300	19105	Jones County	20638
16300	19113	Linn County	211226
16540		Chambersburg-Waynesboro, PA	149618
16540	42055	Franklin County	149618
16580		Champaign-Urbana, IL	231891
16580	17019	Champaign County	201081
16580	17053	Ford County	14081
16580	17147	Piatt County	16729
16620		Charleston, WV	227078
16620	54005	Boone County	24629

Appendix C: Metropolitan Statistical Areas, Metropolitan Divisions, and Components (as defined July 2015)—*Continued*

Core based statistical area	State/ County FIPS code	Title and Geographic Components	2010 Census Population
16620	54015	Clay County	9386
16620	54039	Kanawha County	193063
16700		Charleston-North Charleston, SC	664607
16700	45015	Berkeley County	177843
16700	45019	Charleston County	350209
16700	45035	Dorchester County	136555
16740		Charlotte-Concord-Gastonia, NC-SC	2217012
16740	37025	Cabarrus County	178011
16740	37071	Gaston County	206086
16740	37097	Iredell County	159437
16740	37109	Lincoln County	78265
16740	37119	Mecklenburg County	919628
16740	37159	Rowan County	138428
16740	37179	Union County	201292
16740	45023	Chester County	33140
16740	45057	Lancaster County	76652
16740	45091	York County	226073
16820		Charlottesville, VA	218705
16820	51003	Albemarle County	98970
16820	51029	Buckingham County	17146
16820	51065	Fluvanna County	25691
16820	51079	Greene County	18403
16820	51125	Nelson County	15020
16820	51540	Charlottesville city	43475
16860		Chattanooga, TN-GA	528143
16860	13047	Catoosa County	63942
16860	13083	Dade County	16633
16860	13295	Walker County	68756
16860	47065	Hamilton County	336463
16860	47115	Marion County	28237
16860	47153	Sequatchie County	14112
16940		Cheyenne, WY	91738
16940	56021	Laramie County	91738
16980		Chicago-Naperville-Elgin, IL-IN-WI	9461105
16980		.Chicago-Naperville-Arlington Heights, IL Div 16974	7262718
16980	17031	Cook County	5194675
16980	17043	DuPage County	916924
16980	17063	Grundy County	50063
16980	17093	Kendall County	114736
16980	17111	McHenry County	308760
16980	17197	Will County	677560
16980		.Elgin, IL Div 20994	620429
16980	17037	DeKalb County	105160
16980	17089	Kane County	515269
16980		.Gary, IN Div 23844	708070
16980	18073	Jasper County	33478
16980	18089	Lake County	496005
16980	18111	Newton County	14244
16980	18127	Porter County	164343
16980		.Lake County-Kenosha County, IL-WI Div 29404	869888
16980	17097	Lake County	703462
16980	55059	Kenosha County	166426
17020		Chico, CA	220000
17020	06007	Butte County	220000
17140		Cincinnati, OH-KY-IN	2114580
17140	18029	Dearborn County	50047
17140	18115	Ohio County	6128
17140	18161	Union County	7516
17140	21015	Boone County	118811
17140	21023	Bracken County	8488
17140	21037	Campbell County	90336
17140	21077	Gallatin County	8589
17140	21081	Grant County	24662
17140	21117	Kenton County	159720
17140	21191	Pendleton County	14877
17140	39015	Brown County	44846
17140	39017	Butler County	368130
17140	39025	Clermont County	197363
17140	39061	Hamilton County	802374
17140	39165	Warren County	212693
17300		Clarksville, TN-KY	260625
17300	21047	Christian County	73955
17300	21221	Trigg County	14339
17300	47125	Montgomery County	172331
17420		Cleveland, TN	115788
17420	47011	Bradley County	98963
17420	47139	Polk County	16825
17460		Cleveland-Elyria, OH	2077240
17460	39035	Cuyahoga County	1280122
17460	39055	Geauga County	93389
17460	39085	Lake County	230041
17460	39093	Lorain County	301356
17460	39103	Medina County	172332
17660		Coeur d'Alene, ID	138494
17660	16055	Kootenai County	138494
17780		College Station-Bryan, TX	228660
17780	48041	Brazos County	194851
17780	48051	Burleson County	17187
17780	48395	Robertson County	16622
17820		Colorado Springs, CO	645613
17820	08041	El Paso County	622263
17820	08119	Teller County	23350
17860		Columbia, MO	162642
17860	29019	Boone County	162642
17900		Columbia, SC	767598
17900	45017	Calhoun County	15175
17900	45039	Fairfield County	23956
17900	45055	Kershaw County	61697
17900	45063	Lexington County	262391
17900	45079	Richland County	384504
17900	45081	Saluda County	19875
17980		Columbus, GA-AL	294865
17980	01113	Russell County	52947
17980	13053	Chattahoochee County	11267
17980	13145	Harris County	32024
17980	13197	Marion County	8742
17980	13215	Muscogee County	189885
18020		Columbus, IN	76794
18020	18005	Bartholomew County	76794
18140		Columbus, OH	1901974
18140	39041	Delaware County	174214
18140	39045	Fairfield County	146156
18140	39049	Franklin County	1163414
18140	39073	Hocking County	29380
18140	39089	Licking County	166492
18140	39097	Madison County	43435
18140	39117	Morrow County	34827
18140	39127	Perry County	36058
18140	39129	Pickaway County	55698
18140	39159	Union County	52300
18580		Corpus Christi, TX	428185
18580	48007	Aransas County	23158
18580	48355	Nueces County	340223
18580	48409	San Patricio County	64804
18700		Corvallis, OR	85579
18700	41003	Benton County	85579
18880		Crestview-Fort Walton Beach-Destin, FL	235865
18880	12091	Okaloosa County	180822
18880	12131	Walton County	55043
19060		Cumberland, MD-WV	103299
19060	24001	Allegany County	75087
19060	54057	Mineral County	28212
19100		Dallas-Fort Worth-Arlington, TX	6426214
19100		.Dallas-Plano-Irving, TX Div 19124	4230520
19100	48085	Collin County	782341
19100	48113	Dallas County	2368139
19100	48121	Denton County	662614
19100	48139	Ellis County	149610
19100	48231	Hunt County	86129
19100	48257	Kaufman County	103350
19100	48397	Rockwall County	78337
19100		.Fort Worth-Arlington, TX Div 23104	2195694

Appendix C: Metropolitan Statistical Areas, Metropolitan Divisions, and Components (as defined July 2015)—*Continued*

Core based statistical area	State/ County FIPS code	Title and Geographic Components	2010 Census Population
19100	48221	Hood County	51182
19100	48251	Johnson County	150934
19100	48367	Parker County	116927
19100	48425	Somervell County	8490
19100	48439	Tarrant County	1809034
19100	48497	Wise County	59127
19140		Dalton, GA	142227
19140	13213	Murray County	39628
19140	13313	Whitfield County	102599
19180		Danville, IL	81625
19180	17183	Vermilion County	81625
19300		Daphne-Fairhope-Foley, AL	182265
19300	01003	Baldwin County	182265
19340		Davenport-Moline-Rock Island, IA-IL	379690
19340	17073	Henry County	50486
19340	17131	Mercer County	16434
19340	17161	Rock Island County	147546
19340	19163	Scott County	165224
19380		Dayton, OH	799232
19380	39057	Greene County	161573
19380	39109	Miami County	102506
19380	39113	Montgomery County	535153
19460		Decatur, AL	153829
19460	01079	Lawrence County	34339
19460	01103	Morgan County	119490
19500		Decatur, IL	110768
19500	17115	Macon County	110768
19660		Deltona-Daytona Beach-Ormond Beach, FL	590289
19660	12035	Flagler County	95696
19660	12127	Volusia County	494593
19740		Denver-Aurora-Lakewood, CO	2543482
19740	08001	Adams County	441603
19740	08005	Arapahoe County	572003
19740	08014	Broomfield County	55889
19740	08019	Clear Creek County	9088
19740	08031	Denver County	600158
19740	08035	Douglas County	285465
19740	08039	Elbert County	23086
19740	08047	Gilpin County	5441
19740	08059	Jefferson County	534543
19740	08093	Park County	16206
19780		Des Moines-West Des Moines, IA	569633
19780	19049	Dallas County	66135
19780	19077	Guthrie County	10954
19780	19121	Madison County	15679
19780	19153	Polk County	430640
19780	19181	Warren County	46225
19820		Detroit-Warren-Dearborn, MI	4296250
19820		.Detroit-Dearborn-Livonia, MI Div 19804	1820584
19820	26163	Wayne County	1820584
19820		.Warren-Troy-Farmington Hills, MI 47664	2475666
19820	26087	Lapeer County	88319
19820	26093	Livingston County	180967
19820	26099	Macomb County	840978
19820	26125	Oakland County	1202362
19820	26147	St. Clair County	163040
20020		Dothan, AL	145639
20020	01061	Geneva County	26790
20020	01067	Henry County	17302
20020	01069	Houston County	101547
20100		Dover, DE	162310
20100	10001	Kent County	162310
20220		Dubuque, IA	93653
20220	19061	Dubuque County	93653
20260		Duluth, MN-WI	279771
20260	27017	Carlton County	35386
20260	27137	St. Louis County	200226
20260	55031	Douglas County	44159
20500		Durham-Chapel Hill, NC	504357
20500	37037	Chatham County	63505
20500	37063	Durham County	267587
20500	37135	Orange County	133801
20500	37145	Person County	39464
20700		East Stroudsburg, PA	169842
20700	42089	Monroe County	169842
20740		Eau Claire, WI	161151
20740	55017	Chippewa County	62415
20740	55035	Eau Claire County	98736
20940		El Centro, CA	174528
20940	06025	Imperial County	174528
21060		Elizabethtown-Fort Knox, KY	148338
21060	21093	Hardin County	105543
21060	21123	Larue County	14193
21060	21163	Meade County	28602
21140		Elkhart-Goshen, IN	197559
21140	18039	Elkhart County	197559
21300		Elmira, NY	88830
21300	36015	Chemung County	88830
21340		El Paso, TX	804123
21340	48141	El Paso County	800647
21340	48229	Hudspeth County	3476
21420		Enid, OK	60580
21420	40047	...Garfield County	60580
21500		Erie, PA	280566
21500	42049	Erie County	280566
21660		Eugene, OR	351715
21660	41039	Lane County	351715
21780		Evansville, IN-KY	311552
21780	18129	Posey County	25910
21780	18163	Vanderburgh County	179703
21780	18173	Warrick County	59689
21780	21101	Henderson County	46250
21820		Fairbanks, AK	97581
21820	02090	Fairbanks North Star Borough	97581
22020		Fargo, ND-MN	208777
22020	27027	Clay County	58999
22020	38017	Cass County	149778
22140		Farmington, NM	130044
22140	35045	San Juan County	130044
22180		Fayetteville, NC	366383
22180	37051	Cumberland County	319431
22180	37093	Hoke County	46952
22220		Fayetteville-Springdale-Rogers, AR-MO	463204
22220	05007	Benton County	221339
22220	05087	Madison County	15717
22220	05143	Washington County	203065
22220	29119	McDonald County	23083
22380		Flagstaff, AZ	134421
22380	04005	Coconino County	134421
22420		Flint, MI	425790
22420	26049	Genesee County	425790
22500		Florence, SC	205566
22500	45031	Darlington County	68681
22500	45041	Florence County	136885
22520		Florence-Muscle Shoals, AL	147137
22520	01033	Colbert County	54428
22520	01077	Lauderdale County	92709
22540		Fond du Lac, WI	101633
22540	55039	Fond du Lac County	101633
22660		Fort Collins, CO	299630
22660	08069	Larimer County	299630
22900		Fort Smith, AR-OK	280467
22900	05033	Crawford County	61948
22900	05131	Sebastian County	125744
22900	40079	Le Flore County	50384
22900	40135	Sequoyah County	42391
23060		Fort Wayne, IN	416257
23060	18003	Allen County	355329
23060	18179	Wells County	27636
23060	18183	Whitley County	33292
23420		Fresno, CA	930450
23420	06019	Fresno County	930450
23460		Gadsden, AL	104430
23460	01055	Etowah County	104430

Appendix C: Metropolitan Statistical Areas, Metropolitan Divisions, and Components (as defined July 2015)—*Continued*

Core based statistical area	State/ County FIPS code	Title and Geographic Components	2010 Census Population
23540		Gainesville, FL	264275
23540	12001	Alachua County	247336
23540	12041	Gilchrist County	16939
23580		Gainesville, GA	179684
23580	13139	Hall County	179684
23900		Gettysburg, PA	101407
23900	42001	Adams County	101407
24020		Glens Falls, NY	128923
24020	36113	Warren County	65707
24020	36115	Washington County	63216
24140		Goldsboro, NC	122623
24140	37191	Wayne County	122623
24220		Grand Forks, ND-MN	98461
24220	27119	Polk County	31600
24220	38035	Grand Forks County	66861
24260		Grand Island, NE	81850
24260	31079	Hall County	58607
24260	31081	Hamilton County	9124
24260	31093	Howard County	6274
24260	31121	Merrick County	7845
24300		Grand Junction, CO	146723
24300	08077	Mesa County	146723
24340		Grand Rapids-Wyoming, MI	988938
24340	26015	Barry County	59173
24340	26081	Kent County	602622
24340	26117	Montcalm County	63342
24340	26139	Ottawa County	263801
24420		Grants Pass, OR	82713
24420	41033	Josephine County	82713
24500		Great Falls, MT	81327
24500	30013	Cascade County	81327
24540		Greeley, CO	252825
24540	08123	Weld County	252825
24580		Green Bay, WI	306241
24580	55009	Brown County	248007
24580	55061	Kewaunee County	20574
24580	55083	Oconto County	37660
24660		Greensboro-High Point, NC	723801
24660	37081	Guilford County	488406
24660	37151	Randolph County	141752
24660	37157	Rockingham County	93643
24780		Greenville, NC	168148
24780	37147	Pitt County	168148
24860		Greenville-Anderson-Mauldin, SC	824112
24860	45007	Anderson County	187126
24860	45045	Greenville County	451225
24860	45059	Laurens County	66537
24860	45077	Pickens County	119224
25060		Gulfport-Biloxi-Pascagoula, MS	370702
25060	28045	Hancock County	43929
25060	28047	Harrison County	187105
25060	28059	Jackson County	139668
25180		Hagerstown-Martinsburg, MD-WV	251599
25180	24043	Washington County	147430
25180	54003	Berkeley County	104169
25220		Hammond, LA	121097
25220	22105	Tangipahoa Parish	121097
25260		Hanford-Corcoran, CA	152982
25260	06031	Kings County	152982
25420		Harrisburg-Carlisle, PA	549475
25420	42041	Cumberland County	235406
25420	42043	Dauphin County	268100
25420	42099	Perry County	45969
25500		Harrisonburg, VA	125228
25500	51165	Rockingham County	76314
25500	51660	Harrisonburg city	48914
25540		Hartford-West Hartford-East Hartford, CT	1212381
25540	09003	Hartford County	894014
25540	09007	Middlesex County	165676
25540	09013	Tolland County	152691
25620		Hattiesburg, MS	142842
25620	28035	Forrest County	74934
25620	28073	Lamar County	55658
25620	28111	Perry County	12250
25860		Hickory-Lenoir-Morganton, NC	365497
25860	37003	Alexander County	37198
25860	37023	Burke County	90912
25860	37027	Caldwell County	83029
25860	37035	Catawba County	154358
25940		Hilton Head Island-Bluffton-Beaufort, NC	187010
25940	45013	Beaufort County	162233
25940	45053	Jasper County	24777
25980		Hinesville, GA	77917
25980	13179	Liberty County	63453
25980	13183	Long County	14464
26140		Homosassa Springs, FL	141236
26140	12017	Citrus County	141236
26300		Hot Springs, AR	96024
26300	05051	Garland County	96024
26380		Houma-Thibodaux, LA	208178
26380	22057	Lafourche Parish	96318
26380	22109	Terrebonne Parish	111860
26420		Houston-The Woodlands-Sugar Land, TX	5920416
26420	48015	Austin County	28417
26420	48039	Brazoria County	313166
26420	48071	Chambers County	35096
26420	48157	Fort Bend County	585375
26420	48167	Galveston County	291309
26420	48201	Harris County	4092459
26420	48291	Liberty County	75643
26420	48339	Montgomery County	455746
26420	48473	Waller County	43205
26580		Huntington-Ashland, WV-KY-OH	364908
26580	21019	Boyd County	49542
26580	21089	Greenup County	36910
26580	39087	Lawrence County	62450
26580	54011	Cabell County	96319
26580	54043	Lincoln County	21720
26580	54079	Putnam County	55486
26580	54099	Wayne County	42481
26620		Huntsville, AL	417593
26620	01083	Limestone County	82782
26620	01089	Madison County	334811
26820		Idaho Falls, ID	133265
26820	16019	Bonneville County	104234
26820	16023	Butte County	2891
26820	16051	Jefferson County	26140
26900		Indianapolis-Carmel-Anderson, IN	1887877
26900	18011	Boone County	56640
26900	18013	Brown County	15242
26900	18057	Hamilton County	274569
26900	18059	Hancock County	70002
26900	18063	Hendricks County	145448
26900	18081	Johnson County	139654
26900	18095	Madison County	131636
26900	18097	Marion County	903393
26900	18109	Morgan County	68894
26900	18133	Putnam County	37963
26900	18145	Shelby County	44436
26980		Iowa City, IA	152586
26980	19103	Johnson County	130882
26980	19183	Washington County	21704
27060		Ithaca, NY	101564
27060	36109	Tompkins County	101564
27100		Jackson, MI	160248
27100	26075	Jackson County	160248
27140		Jackson, MS	567122
27140	28029	Copiah County	29449
27140	28049	Hinds County	245285
27140	28089	Madison County	95203
27140	28121	Rankin County	141617
27140	28127	Simpson County	27503
27140	28163	Yazoo County	28065
27180		Jackson, TN	130011

Core based statistical area	State/ County FIPS code	Title and Geographic Components	2010 Census Population
27180	47023	Chester County	17131
27180	47033	Crockett County	14586
27180	47113	Madison County	98294
27260		Jacksonville, FL	1345596
27260	12003	Baker County	27115
27260	12019	Clay County	190865
27260	12031	Duval County	864263
27260	12089	Nassau County	73314
27260	12109	St. Johns County	190039
27340		Jacksonville, NC	177772
27340	37133	Onslow County	177772
27500		Janesville-Beloit, WI	160331
27500	55105	Rock County	160331
27620		Jefferson City, MO	149807
27620	29027	Callaway County	44332
27620	29051	Cole County	75990
27620	29135	Moniteau County	15607
27620	29151	Osage County	13878
27740		Johnson City, TN	198716
27740	47019	Carter County	57424
27740	47171	Unicoi County	18313
27740	47179	Washington County	122979
27780		Johnstown, PA	143679
27780	42021	Cambria County	143679
27860		Jonesboro, AR	121026
27860	05031	Craighead County	96443
27860	05111	Poinsett County	24583
27900		Joplin, MO	175518
27900	29097	Jasper County	117404
27900	29145	Newton County	58114
27980		Kahului-Wailuku-Lahaina, HI	154924
27980	15005	Kalawao County	90
27980	15009	Maui County	154834
28020		Kalamazoo-Portage, MI	326589
28020	26077	Kalamazoo County	250331
28020	26159	Van Buren County	76258
28100		Kankakee, IL	113449
28100	17091	Kankakee County	113449
28140		Kansas City, MO-KS	2009342
28140	20091	Johnson County	544179
28140	20103	Leavenworth County	76227
28140	20107	Linn County	9656
28140	20121	Miami County	32787
28140	20209	Wyandotte County	157505
28140	29013	Bates County	17049
28140	29025	Caldwell County	9424
28140	29037	Cass County	99478
28140	29047	Clay County	221939
28140	29049	Clinton County	20743
28140	29095	Jackson County	674158
28140	29107	Lafayette County	33381
28140	29165	Platte County	89322
28140	29177	Ray County	23494
28420		Kennewick-Richland, WA	253340
28420	53005	Benton County	175177
28420	53021	Franklin County	78163
28660		Killeen-Temple, TX	405300
28660	48027	Bell County	310235
28660	48099	Coryell County	75388
28660	48281	Lampasas County	19677
28700		Kingsport-Bristol-Bristol, TN-VA	309544
28700	47073	Hawkins County	56833
28700	47163	Sullivan County	156823
28700	51169	Scott County	23177
28700	51191	Washington County	54876
28700	51520	Bristol city	17835
28740		Kingston, NY	182493
28740	36111	Ulster County	182493
28940		Knoxville, TN	837571
28940	47001	Anderson County	75129
28940	47009	Blount County	123010
28940	47013	Campbell County	40716
28940	47057	Grainger County	22657
28940	47093	Knox County	432226
28940	47105	Loudon County	48556
28940	47129	Morgan County	21987
28940	47145	Roane County	54181
28940	47173	Union County	19109
29020		Kokomo, IN	82752
29020	18067	Howard County	82752
29100		La Crosse-Onalaska, WI-MN	133665
29100	27055	Houston County	19027
29100	55063	La Crosse County	114638
29180		Lafayette, LA	466750
29180	22001	Acadia Parish	61773
29180	22045	Iberia Parish	73240
29180	22055	Lafayette Parish	221578
29180	22099	St. Martin Parish	52160
29180	22113	Vermilion Parish	57999
29200		Lafayette-West Lafayette, IN	201789
29200	18007	Benton County	8854
29200	18015	Carroll County	20155
29200	18157	Tippecanoe County	172780
29340		Lake Charles, LA	199607
29340	22019	Calcasieu Parish	192768
29340	22023	Cameron Parish	6839
29420		Lake Havasu City-Kingman, AZ	200186
29420	04015	Mohave County	200186
29460		Lakeland-Winter Haven, FL	602095
29460	12105	Polk County	602095
29540		Lancaster, PA	519445
29540	42071	Lancaster County	519445
29620		Lansing-East Lansing, MI	464036
29620	26037	Clinton County	75382
29620	26045	Eaton County	107759
29620	26065	Ingham County	280895
29700		Laredo, TX	250304
29700	48479	Webb County	250304
29740		Las Cruces, NM	209233
29740	35013	Dona Ana County	209233
29820		Las Vegas-Henderson-Paradise, NV	1951269
29820	32003	Clark County	1951269
29940		Lawrence, KS	110826
29940	20045	Douglas County	110826
30020		Lawton, OK	130291
30020	40031	Comanche County	124098
30020	40033	Cotton County	6193
30140		Lebanon, PA	133568
30140	42075	Lebanon County	133568
30300		Lewiston, ID-WA	60888
30300	16069	Nez Perce County	39265
30300	53003	Asotin County	21623
30340		Lewiston-Auburn, ME	107702
30340	23001	Androscoggin County	107702
30460		Lexington-Fayette, KY	472099
30460	21017	Bourbon County	19985
30460	21049	Clark County	35613
30460	21067	Fayette County	295803
30460	21113	Jessamine County	48586
30460	21209	Scott County	47173
30460	21239	Woodford County	24939
30620		Lima, OH	106331
30620	39003	Allen County	106331
30700		Lincoln, NE	302157
30700	31109	Lancaster County	285407
30700	31159	Seward County	16750
30780		Little Rock-North Little Rock-Conway, AR	699757
30780	05045	Faulkner County	113237
30780	05053	Grant County	17853
30780	05085	Lonoke County	68356
30780	05105	Perry County	10445
30780	05119	Pulaski County	382748
30780	05125	Saline County	107118
30860		Logan, UT-ID	125442

Appendix C: Metropolitan Statistical Areas, Metropolitan Divisions, and Components (as defined July 2015)—*Continued*

Core based statistical area	State/ County FIPS code	Title and Geographic Components	2010 Census Population
30860	16041	Franklin County	12786
30860	49005	Cache County	112656
30980		Longview, TX	214369
30980	48183	Gregg County	121730
30980	48401	Rusk County	53330
30980	48459	Upshur County	39309
31020		Longview, WA	102410
31020	53015	Cowlitz County	102410
31080		Los Angeles-Long Beach-Anaheim, CA	12828837
31080		.Anaheim-Santa Ana-Irvine, CA Div 11244	3010232
31080	06059	Orange County	3010232
31080		.Los Angeles-Long Beach-Glendale, CA Div 31084	9818605
31080	06037	Los Angeles County	9818605
31140		Louisville/Jefferson County, KY-IN	1235708
31140	18019	Clark County	110232
31140	18043	Floyd County	74578
31140	18061	Harrison County	39364
31140	18143	Scott County	24181
31140	18175	Washington County	28262
31140	21029	Bullitt County	74319
31140	21103	Henry County	15416
31140	21111	Jefferson County	741096
31140	21185	Oldham County	60316
31140	21211	Shelby County	42074
31140	21215	Spencer County	17061
31140	21223	Trimble County	8809
31180		Lubbock, TX	290805
31180	48107	Crosby County	6059
31180	48303	Lubbock County	278831
31180	48305	Lynn County	5915
31340		Lynchburg, VA	252634
31340	51009	Amherst County	32353
31340	51011	Appomattox County	14973
31340	51019	Bedford County	68676
31340	51031	Campbell County	54842
31340	51515	Bedford city	6222
31340	51680	Lynchburg city	75568
31420		Macon, GA	232293
31420	13021	Bibb County	155547
31420	13079	Crawford County	12630
31420	13169	Jones County	28669
31420	13207	Monroe County	26424
31420	13289	Twiggs County	9023
31460		Madera, CA	150865
31460	06039	Madera County	150865
31540		Madison, WI	605435
31540	55021	Columbia County	56833
31540	55025	Dane County	488073
31540	55045	Green County	36842
31540	55049	Iowa County	23687
31700		Manchester-Nashua, NH	400721
31700	33011	Hillsborough County	400721
31740		Manhattan, KS	92719
31740	20149	Pottawatomie County	21604
31740	20161	Riley County	71115
31860		Mankato-North Mankato, MN	96740
31860	27013	Blue Earth County	64013
31860	27103	Nicollet County	32727
31900		Mansfield, OH	124475
31900	39139	Richland County	124475
32580		McAllen-Edinburg-Mission, TX	774769
32580	48215	Hidalgo County	774769
32780		Medford, OR	203206
32780	41029	Jackson County	203206
32820		Memphis, TN-MS-AR	1324829
32820	05035	Crittenden County	50902
32820	28009	Benton County	8729
32820	28033	DeSoto County	161252
32820	28093	Marshall County	37144
32820	28137	Tate County	28886
32820	28143	Tunica County	10778
32820	47047	Fayette County	38413
32820	47157	Shelby County	927644
32820	47167	Tipton County	61081
32900		Merced, CA	255793
32900	06047	Merced County	255793
33100		Miami-Fort Lauderdale-West Palm Beach, FL	5564635
33100		.Fort Lauderdale-Pompano Beach-Deerfield Beach, FL Div 22744	1748066
33100	12011	Broward County	1748066
33100		.Miami-Miami Beach-Kendall, FL Div 33124	2496435
33100	12086	Miami-Dade County	2496435
33100		.West Palm Beach-Boca Raton-Delray Beach, FL Div 48424	1320134
33100	12099	Palm Beach County	1320134
33140		Michigan City-La Porte, IN	111467
33140	18091	LaPorte County	111467
33220		Midland, MI	83629
33220	26111	Midland County	83629
33260		Midland, TX	141671
33260	48317	Martin County	4799
33260	48329	Midland County	136872
33340		Milwaukee-Waukesha-West Allis, WI	1555908
33340	55079	Milwaukee County	947735
33340	55089	Ozaukee County	86395
33340	55131	Washington County	131887
33340	55133	Waukesha County	389891
33460		Minneapolis-St. Paul-Bloomington, MN	3348859
33460	27003	Anoka County	330844
33460	27019	Carver County	91042
33460	27025	Chisago County	53887
33460	27037	Dakota County	398552
33460	27053	Hennepin County	1152425
33460	27059	Isanti County	37816
33460	27079	Le Sueur County	27703
33460	27095	Mille Lacs County	26097
33460	27123	Ramsey County	508640
33460	27139	Scott County	129928
33460	27141	Sherburne County	88499
33460	27143	Sibley County	15226
33460	27163	Washington County	238136
33460	27171	Wright County	124700
33460	55093	Pierce County	41019
33460	55109	St. Croix County	84345
33540		Missoula, MT	109299
33540	30063	Missoula County	109299
33660		Mobile, AL	412992
33660	01097	Mobile County	412992
33700		Modesto, CA	514453
33700	06099	Stanislaus County	514453
33740		Monroe, LA	176441
33740	22073	Ouachita Parish	153720
33740	22111	Union Parish	22721
33780		Monroe, MI	152021
33780	26115	Monroe County	152021
33860		Montgomery, AL	374536
33860	01001	Autauga County	54571
33860	01051	Elmore County	79303
33860	01085	Lowndes County	11299
33860	01101	Montgomery County	229363
34060		Morgantown, WV	129709
34060	54061	Monongalia County	96189
34060	54077	Preston County	33520
34100		Morristown, TN	113951
34100	47063	Hamblen County	62544
34100	47089	Jefferson County	51407
34580		Mount Vernon-Anacortes, WA	116901
34580	53057	Skagit County	116901
34620		Muncie, IN	117671
34620	18035	Delaware County	117671
34740		Muskegon, MI	172188
34740	26121	Muskegon County	172188

Appendix C: Metropolitan Statistical Areas, Metropolitan Divisions, and Components (as defined July 2015)—*Continued*

Core based statistical area	State/ County FIPS code	Title and Geographic Components	2010 Census Population
34820		Myrtle Beach-Conway-North Myrtle Beach, NC-SC	376722
34820	37019	Brunswick County	107431
34820	45051	Horry County	269291
34900		Napa, CA	136484
34900	06055	Napa County	136484
34940		Naples-Immokalee-Marco Island, FL	321520
34940	12021	Collier County	321520
34980		Nashville-Davidson--Murfreesboro--Franklin, TN	1670890
34980	47015	Cannon County	13801
34980	47021	Cheatham County	39105
34980	47037	Davidson County	626681
34980	47043	Dickson County	49666
34980	47081	Hickman County	24690
34980	47111	Macon County	22248
34980	47119	Maury County	80956
34980	47147	Robertson County	66283
34980	47149	Rutherford County	262604
34980	47159	Smith County	19166
34980	47165	Sumner County	160645
34980	47169	Trousdale County	7870
34980	47187	Williamson County	183182
34980	47189	Wilson County	113993
35100		New Bern, NC	126802
35100	37049	Craven County	103505
35100	37103	Jones County	10153
35100	37137	Pamlico County	13144
35300		New Haven-Milford, CT	862477
35300	09009	New Haven County	862477
35380		New Orleans-Metairie, LA	1189866
35380	22051	Jefferson Parish	432552
35380	22071	Orleans Parish	343829
35380	22075	Plaquemines Parish	23042
35380	22087	St. Bernard Parish	35897
35380	22089	St. Charles Parish	52780
35380	22093	St. James Parish	22102
35380	22095	St. John the Baptist Parish	45924
35380	22103	St. Tammany Parish	233740
35620		New York-Newark-Jersey City, NY-NJ-PA	19567410
35620		.Dutchess County-Putnam County, NY Div 20524	397198
35620	36027	Dutchess County	297488
35620	36079	Putnam County	99710
35620		.Nassau County-Suffolk County, NY Div 35004	2832882
35620	36059	Nassau County	1339532
35620	36103	Suffolk County	1493350
35620		.Newark, NJ-PA Div 35084	2471171
35620	34013	Essex County	783969
35620	34019	Hunterdon County	128349
35620	34027	Morris County	492276
35620	34035	Somerset County	323444
35620	34037	Sussex County	149265
35620	34039	Union County	536499
35620	42103	Pike County	57369
35620		.New York-Jersey City-White Plains, NY-NJ Div 35614	13866159
35620	34003	Bergen County	905116
35620	34017	Hudson County	634266
35620	34023	Middlesex County	809858
35620	34025	Monmouth County	630380
35620	34029	Ocean County	576567
35620	34031	Passaic County	501226
35620	36005	Bronx County	1385108
35620	36047	Kings County	2504700
35620	36061	New York County	1585873
35620	36071	Orange County	372813
35620	36081	Queens County	2230722
35620	36085	Richmond County	468730
35620	36087	Rockland County	311687
35620	36119	Westchester County	949113

Core based statistical area	State/ County FIPS code	Title and Geographic Components	2010 Census Population
35660		Niles-Benton Harbor, MI	156813
35660	26021	Berrien County	156813
35840		North Port-Sarasota-Bradenton, FL	702281
35840	12081	Manatee County	322833
35840	12115	Sarasota County	379448
35980		Norwich-New London, CT	274055
35980	09011	New London County	274055
36100		Ocala, FL	331298
36100	12083	Marion County	331298
36140		Ocean City, NJ	97265
36140	34009	Cape May County	97265
36220		Odessa, TX	137130
36220	48135	Ector County	137130
36260		Ogden-Clearfield, UT	597159
36260	49003	Box Elder County	49975
36260	49011	Davis County	306479
36260	49029	Morgan County	9469
36260	49057	Weber County	231236
36420		Oklahoma City, OK	1252987
36420	40017	Canadian County	115541
36420	40027	Cleveland County	255755
36420	40051	Grady County	52431
36420	40081	Lincoln County	34273
36420	40083	Logan County	41848
36420	40087	McClain County	34506
36420	40109	Oklahoma County	718633
36500		Olympia-Tumwater, WA	252264
36500	53067	Thurston County	252264
36540		Omaha-Council Bluffs, NE-IA	865350
36540	19085	Harrison County	14928
36540	19129	Mills County	15059
36540	19155	Pottawattamie County	93158
36540	31025	Cass County	25241
36540	31055	Douglas County	517110
36540	31153	Sarpy County	158840
36540	31155	Saunders County	20780
36540	31177	Washington County	20234
36740		Orlando-Kissimmee-Sanford, FL	2134411
36740	12069	Lake County	297052
36740	12095	Orange County	1145956
36740	12097	Osceola County	268685
36740	12117	Seminole County	422718
36780		Oshkosh-Neenah, WI	166994
36780	55139	Winnebago County	166994
36980		Owensboro, KY	114752
36980	21059	Daviess County	96656
36980	21091	Hancock County	8565
36980	21149	McLean County	9531
37100		Oxnard-Thousand Oaks-Ventura, CA	823318
37100	06111	Ventura County	823318
37340		Palm Bay-Melbourne-Titusville, FL	543376
37340	12009	Brevard County	543376
37460		Panama City, FL	184715
37460	12005	Bay County	168852
37460	12045	Gulf County	15863
37620		Parkersburg-Vienna, WV	92673
37620	54105	Wirt County	5717
37620	54107	Wood County	86956
37860		Pensacola-Ferry Pass-Brent, FL	448991
37860	12033	Escambia County	297619
37860	12113	Santa Rosa County	151372
37900		Peoria, IL	379186
37900	17123	Marshall County	12640
37900	17143	Peoria County	186494
37900	17175	Stark County	5994
37900	17179	Tazewell County	135394
37900	17203	Woodford County	38664
37980		Philadelphia-Camden-Wilmington, PA-NJ-DE-MD	5965343
37980		.Camden, NJ Div 15804	1250679
37980	34005	Burlington County	448734
37980	34007	Camden County	513657

Appendix C: Metropolitan Statistical Areas, Metropolitan Divisions, and Components (as defined July 2015)—*Continued*

Core based statistical area	State/ County FIPS code	Title and Geographic Components	2010 Census Population
37980	34015	Gloucester County	288288
37980		.Montgomery County-Bucks County-Chester County, PA Div 33874	1924009
37980	42017	Bucks County	625249
37980	42029	Chester County	498886
37980	42091	Montgomery County	799874
37980		.Philadelphia, PA Div 37964	2084985
37980	42045	Delaware County	558979
37980	42101	Philadelphia County	1526006
37980		.Wilmington, DE-MD-NJ Div 48864	705670
37980	10003	New Castle County	538479
37980	24015	Cecil County	101108
37980	34033	Salem County	66083
38060		Phoenix-Mesa-Scottsdale, AZ	4192887
38060	04013	Maricopa County	3817117
38060	04021	Pinal County	375770
38220		Pine Bluff, AR	100258
38220	05025	Cleveland County	8689
38220	05069	Jefferson County	77435
38220	05079	Lincoln County	14134
38300		Pittsburgh, PA	2356285
38300	42003	Allegheny County	1223348
38300	42005	Armstrong County	68941
38300	42007	Beaver County	170539
38300	42019	Butler County	183862
38300	42051	Fayette County	136606
38300	42125	Washington County	207820
38300	42129	Westmoreland County	365169
38340		Pittsfield, MA	131219
38340	25003	Berkshire County	131219
38540		Pocatello, ID	82839
38540	16005	Bannock County	82839
38860		Portland-South Portland, ME	514098
38860	23005	Cumberland County	281674
38860	23023	Sagadahoc County	35293
38860	23031	York County	197131
38900		Portland-Vancouver-Hillsboro, OR-WA	2226009
38900	41005	Clackamas County	375992
38900	41009	Columbia County	49351
38900	41051	Multnomah County	735334
38900	41067	Washington County	529710
38900	41071	Yamhill County	99193
38900	53011	Clark County	425363
38900	53059	Skamania County	11066
38940		Port St. Lucie, FL	424107
38940	12085	Martin County	146318
38940	12111	St. Lucie County	277789
39140		Prescott, AZ	211033
39140	04025	Yavapai County	211033
39300		Providence-Warwick, RI-MA	1600852
39300	25005	Bristol County	548285
39300	44001	Bristol County	49875
39300	44003	Kent County	166158
39300	44005	Newport County	82888
39300	44007	Providence County	626667
39300	44009	Washington County	126979
39340		Provo-Orem, UT	526810
39340	49023	Juab County	10246
39340	49049	Utah County	516564
39380		Pueblo, CO	159063
39380	08101	Pueblo County	159063
39460		Punta Gorda, FL	159978
39460	12015	Charlotte County	159978
39540		Racine, WI	195408
39540	55101	Racine County	195408
39580		Raleigh, NC	1130490
39580	37069	Franklin County	60619
39580	37101	Johnston County	168878
39580	37183	Wake County	900993
39660		Rapid City, SD	134598
39660	46033	Custer County	8216
39660	46093	Meade County	25434
39660	46103	Pennington County	100948
39740		Reading, PA	411442
39740	42011	Berks County	411442
39820		Redding, CA	177223
39820	06089	Shasta County	177223
39900		Reno, NV	425417
39900	32029	Storey County	4010
39900	32031	Washoe County	421407
40060		Richmond, VA	1208101
40060	51007	Amelia County	12690
40060	51033	Caroline County	28545
40060	51036	Charles City County	7256
40060	51041	Chesterfield County	316236
40060	51053	Dinwiddie County	28001
40060	51075	Goochland County	21717
40060	51085	Hanover County	99863
40060	51087	Henrico County	306935
40060	51101	King William County	15935
40060	51127	New Kent County	18429
40060	51145	Powhatan County	28046
40060	51149	Prince George County	35725
40060	51183	Sussex County	12087
40060	51570	Colonial Heights city	17411
40060	51670	Hopewell city	22591
40060	51730	Petersburg city	32420
40060	51760	Richmond city	204214
40140		Riverside-San Bernardino-Ontario, CA	4224851
40140	06065	Riverside County	2189641
40140	06071	San Bernardino County	2035210
40220		Roanoke, VA	308707
40220	51023	Botetourt County	33148
40220	51045	Craig County	5190
40220	51067	Franklin County	56159
40220	51161	Roanoke County	92376
40220	51770	Roanoke city	97032
40220	51775	Salem city	24802
40340		Rochester, MN	206877
40340	27039	Dodge County	20087
40340	27045	Fillmore County	20866
40340	27109	Olmsted County	144248
40340	27157	Wabasha County	21676
40380		Rochester, NY	1079671
40380	36051	Livingston County	65393
40380	36055	Monroe County	744344
40380	36069	Ontario County	107931
40380	36073	Orleans County	42883
40380	36117	Wayne County	93772
40380	36123	Yates County	25348
40420		Rockford, IL	349431
40420	17007	Boone County	54165
40420	17201	Winnebago County	295266
40580		Rocky Mount, NC	152392
40580	37065	Edgecombe County	56552
40580	37127	Nash County	95840
40660		Rome, GA	96317
40660	13115	Floyd County	96317
40900		Sacramento--Roseville--Arden-Arcade, CA	2149127
40900	06017	El Dorado County	181058
40900	06061	Placer County	348432
40900	06067	Sacramento County	1418788
40900	06113	Yolo County	200849
40980		Saginaw, MI	200169
40980	26145	Saginaw County	200169
41060		St. Cloud, MN	189093
41060	27009	Benton County	38451
41060	27145	Stearns County	150642
41100		St. George, UT	138115
41100	49053	Washington County	138115
41140		St. Joseph, MO-KS	127329
41140	20043	Doniphan County	7945

Appendix C: Metropolitan Statistical Areas, Metropolitan Divisions, and Components (as defined July 2015)—*Continued*

Core based statistical area	State/ County FIPS code	Title and Geographic Components	2010 Census Population
41140	29003	Andrew County	17291
41140	29021	Buchanan County	89201
41140	29063	DeKalb County	12892
41180		St. Louis, MO-IL	2787701
41180	17005	Bond County	17768
41180	17013	Calhoun County	5089
41180	17027	Clinton County	37762
41180	17083	Jersey County	22985
41180	17117	Macoupin County	47765
41180	17119	Madison County	269282
41180	17133	Monroe County	32957
41180	17163	St. Clair County	270056
41180	29071	Franklin County	101492
41180	29099	Jefferson County	218733
41180	29113	Lincoln County	52566
41180	29183	St. Charles County	360485
41180	29189	St. Louis County	998954
41180	29219	Warren County	32513
41180	29510	St. Louis city	319294
41420		Salem, OR	390738
41420	41047	Marion County	315335
41420	41053	Polk County	75403
41500		Salinas, CA	415057
41500	06053	Monterey County	415057
41540		Salisbury, MD-DE	373802
41540	10005	Sussex County	197145
41540	24039	Somerset County	26470
41540	24045	Wicomico County	98733
41540	24047	Worcester County	51454
41620		Salt Lake City, UT	1087873
41620	49035	Salt Lake County	1029655
41620	49045	Tooele County	58218
41660		San Angelo, TX	111823
41660	48235	Irion County	1599
41660	48451	Tom Green County	110224
41700		San Antonio-New Braunfels, TX	2142508
41700	48013	Atascosa County	44911
41700	48019	Bandera County	20485
41700	48029	Bexar County	1714773
41700	48091	Comal County	108472
41700	48187	Guadalupe County	131533
41700	48259	Kendall County	33410
41700	48325	Medina County	46006
41700	48493	Wilson County	42918
41740		San Diego-Carlsbad, CA	3095313
41740	06073	San Diego County	3095313
41860		San Francisco-Oakland-Hayward, CA	4335391
41860		.Oakland-Hayward-Berkeley, CA Div 36084	2559296
41860	06001	Alameda County	1510271
41860	06013	Contra Costa County	1049025
41860		.San Francisco-Redwood City-South San Francisco, CA Div 41884	1523686
41860	06075	San Francisco County	805235
41860	06081	San Mateo County	718451
41860		.San Rafael, CA Div 42034	252409
41860	06041	Marin County	252409
41940		San Jose-Sunnyvale-Santa Clara, CA	1836911
41940	06069	San Benito County	55269
41940	06085	Santa Clara County	1781642
42020		San Luis Obispo-Paso Robles-Arroyo Grande, CA	269637
42020	06079	San Luis Obispo County	269637
42100		Santa Cruz-Watsonville, CA	262382
42100	06087	Santa Cruz County	262382
42140		Santa Fe, NM	144170
42140	35049	Santa Fe County	144170
42200		Santa Maria-Santa Barbara, CA	423895
42200	06083	Santa Barbara County	423895
42220		Santa Rosa, CA	483878
42220	06097	Sonoma County	483878
42340		Savannah, GA	347611
42340	13029	Bryan County	30233

Core based statistical area	State/ County FIPS code	Title and Geographic Components	2010 Census Population
42340	13051	Chatham County	265128
42340	13103	Effingham County	52250
42540		Scranton--Wilkes-Barre--Hazleton, PA	563631
42540	42069	Lackawanna County	214437
42540	42079	Luzerne County	320918
42540	42131	Wyoming County	28276
42660		Seattle-Tacoma-Bellevue, WA	3439809
42660		.Seattle-Bellevue-Everett, WA Div 42644	2644584
42660	53033	King County	1931249
42660	53061	Snohomish County	713335
42660		.Tacoma-Lakewood, WA Div 45104	795225
42660	53053	Pierce County	795225
42680		Sebastian-Vero Beach, FL	138028
42680	12061	Indian River County	138028
42700		Sebring, FL	98786
42700	12055	Highlands County	98786
43100		Sheboygan, WI	115507
43100	55117	Sheboygan County	115507
43300		Sherman-Denison, TX	120877
43300	48181	Grayson County	120877
43340		Shreveport-Bossier City, LA	439811
43340	22015	Bossier Parish	116979
43340	22017	Caddo Parish	254969
43340	22031	De Soto Parish	26656
43340	22119	Webster Parish	41207
43420		Sierra Vista-Douglas, AZ	131346
43420	04003	Cochise County	131346
43580		Sioux City, IA-NE-SD	168563
43580	19149	Plymouth County	24986
43580	19193	Woodbury County	102172
43580	31043	Dakota County	21006
43580	31051	Dixon County	6000
43580	46127	Union County	14399
43620		Sioux Falls, SD	228261
43620	46083	Lincoln County	44828
43620	46087	McCook County	5618
43620	46099	Minnehaha County	169468
43620	46125	Turner County	8347
43780		South Bend-Mishawaka, IN-MI	319224
43780	18141	St. Joseph County	266931
43780	26027	Cass County	52293
43900		Spartanburg, SC	313268
43900	45083	Spartanburg County	284307
43900	45087	Union County	28961
44060		Spokane-Spokane Valley, WA	527753
44060	53051	Pend Oreille County	13001
44060	53063	Spokane County	471221
44060	53065	Stevens County	43531
44100		Springfield, IL	210170
44100	17129	Menard County	12705
44100	17167	Sangamon County	197465
44140		Springfield, MA	621570
44140	25013	Hampden County	463490
44140	25015	Hampshire County	158080
44180		Springfield, MO	436712
44180	29043	Christian County	77422
44180	29059	Dallas County	16777
44180	29077	Greene County	275174
44180	29167	Polk County	31137
44180	29225	Webster County	36202
44220		Springfield, OH	138333
44220	39023	Clark County	138333
44300		State College, PA	153990
44300	42027	Centre County	153990
44420		Staunton-Waynesboro, VA	118502
44420	51015	Augusta County	73750
44420	51790	Staunton city	23746
44420	51820	Waynesboro city	21006
44700		Stockton-Lodi, CA	685306
44700	06077	San Joaquin County	685306
44940		Sumter, SC	107456
44940	45085	Sumter County	107456

Core based statistical area	State/ County FIPS code	Title and Geographic Components	2010 Census Population
45060		Syracuse, NY	662577
45060	36053	Madison County	73442
45060	36067	Onondaga County	467026
45060	36075	Oswego County	122109
45220		Tallahassee, FL	367413
45220	12039	Gadsden County	46389
45220	12065	Jefferson County	14761
45220	12073	Leon County	275487
45220	12129	Wakulla County	30776
45300		Tampa-St. Petersburg-Clearwater, FL	2783243
45300	12053	Hernando County	172778
45300	12057	Hillsborough County	1229226
45300	12101	Pasco County	464697
45300	12103	Pinellas County	916542
45460		Terre Haute, IN	172425
45460	18021	Clay County	26890
45460	18153	Sullivan County	21475
45460	18165	Vermillion County	16212
45460	18167	Vigo County	107848
45500		Texarkana, TX-AR	149198
45500	05081	Little River County	13171
45500	05091	Miller County	43462
45500	48037	Bowie County	92565
45540		The Villages, FL	93420
45540	12119	Sumter County	93420
45780		Toledo, OH	610001
45780	39051	Fulton County	42698
45780	39095	Lucas County	441815
45780	39173	Wood County	125488
45820		Topeka, KS	233870
45820	20085	Jackson County	13462
45820	20087	Jefferson County	19126
45820	20139	Osage County	16295
45820	20177	Shawnee County	177934
45820	20197	Wabaunsee County	7053
45940		Trenton, NJ	366513
45940	34021	Mercer County	366513
46060		Tucson, AZ	980263
46060	04019	Pima County	980263
46140		Tulsa, OK	937478
46140	40037	Creek County	69967
46140	40111	Okmulgee County	40069
46140	40113	Osage County	47472
46140	40117	Pawnee County	16577
46140	40131	Rogers County	86905
46140	40143	Tulsa County	603403
46140	40145	Wagoner County	73085
46220		Tuscaloosa, AL	230162
46220	01065	Hale County	15760
46220	01107	Pickens County	19746
46220	01125	Tuscaloosa County	194656
46340		Tyler, TX	209714
46340	48423	Smith County	209714
46520		Urban Honolulu, HI	953207
46520	15003	Honolulu County	953207
46540		Utica-Rome, NY	299397
46540	36043	Herkimer County	64519
46540	36065	Oneida County	234878
46660		Valdosta, GA	139588
46660	13027	Brooks County	16243
46660	13101	Echols County	4034
46660	13173	Lanier County	10078
46660	13185	Lowndes County	109233
46700		Vallejo-Fairfield, CA	413344
46700	06095	Solano County	413344
47020		Victoria, TX	94003
47020	48175	Goliad County	7210
47020	48469	Victoria County	86793
47220		Vineland-Bridgeton, NJ	156898
47220	34011	Cumberland County	156898
47260		Virginia Beach-Norfolk-Newport News, VA-NC	1676822
47260	37053	Currituck County	23547
47260	37073	Gates County	12197
47260	51073	Gloucester County	36858
47260	51093	Isle of Wight County	35270
47260	51095	James City County	67009
47260	51115	Mathews County	8978
47260	51199	York County	65464
47260	51550	Chesapeake city	222209
47260	51650	Hampton city	137436
47260	51700	Newport News city	180719
47260	51710	Norfolk city	242803
47260	51735	Poquoson city	12150
47260	51740	Portsmouth city	95535
47260	51800	Suffolk city	84585
47260	51810	Virginia Beach city	437994
47260	51830	Williamsburg city	14068
47300		Visalia-Porterville, CA	442179
47300	06107	Tulare County	442179
47380		Waco, TX	252772
47380	48145	Falls County	17866
47380	48309	McLennan County	234906
47460		Walla Walla, WA	62859
47460	53013	Columbia County	4078
47460	53071	Walla Walla County	58781
47580		Warner Robins, GA	179605
47580	13153	Houston County	139900
47580	13225	Peach County	27695
47580	13235	Pulaski County	12010
47900		Washington-Arlington-Alexandria, DC-VA-MD-WV	5636232
47900		.Silver Spring-Frederick-Rockville, MD Div 43524	1205162
47900	24021	Frederick County	233385
47900	24031	Montgomery County	971777
47900		.Washington-Arlington-Alexandria, DC-VA-MD-WV Div 47894	4431070
47900	11001	District of Columbia	601723
47900	24009	Calvert County	88737
47900	24017	Charles County	146551
47900	24033	Prince George's County	863420
47900	51013	Arlington County	207627
47900	51043	Clarke County	14034
47900	51047	Culpeper County	46689
47900	51059	Fairfax County	1081726
47900	51061	Fauquier County	65203
47900	51107	Loudoun County	312311
47900	51153	Prince William County	402002
47900	51157	Rappahannock County	7373
47900	51177	Spotsylvania County	122397
47900	51179	Stafford County	128961
47900	51187	Warren County	37575
47900	51510	Alexandria city	139966
47900	51600	Fairfax city	22565
47900	51610	Falls Church city	12332
47900	51630	Fredericksburg city	24286
47900	51683	Manassas city	37821
47900	51685	Manassas Park city	14273
47900	54037	Jefferson County	53498
47940		Waterloo-Cedar Falls, IA	167819
47940	19013	Black Hawk County	131090
47940	19017	Bremer County	24276
47940	19075	Grundy County	12453
48060		Watertown-Fort Drum, NY	116229
48060	36045	Jefferson County	116229
48140		Wausau, WI	134063
48140	55073	Marathon County	134063
48260		Weirton-Steubenville, WV-OH	124454
48260	39081	Jefferson County	69709
48260	54009	Brooke County	24069
48260	54029	Hancock County	30676
48300		Wenatchee, WA	110884
48300	53007	Chelan County	72453

Appendix C: Metropolitan Statistical Areas, Metropolitan Divisions, and Components (as defined July 2015)—*Continued*

Core based statistical area	State/ County FIPS code	Title and Geographic Components	2010 Census Population
48300	53017	Douglas County	38431
48540		Wheeling, WV-OH	147950
48540	39013	Belmont County	70400
48540	54051	Marshall County	33107
48540	54069	Ohio County	44443
48620		Wichita, KS	630919
48620	20015	Butler County	65880
48620	20079	Harvey County	34684
48620	20095	Kingman County	7858
48620	20173	Sedgwick County	498365
48620	20191	Sumner County	24132
48660		Wichita Falls, TX	151306
48660	48009	Archer County	9054
48660	48077	Clay County	10752
48660	48485	Wichita County	131500
48700		Williamsport, PA	116111
48700	42081	Lycoming County	116111
48900		Wilmington, NC	254884
48900	37129	New Hanover County	202667
48900	37141	Pender County	52217
49020		Winchester, VA-WV	128472
49020	51069	Frederick County	78305
49020	51840	Winchester city	26203
49020	54027	Hampshire County	23964
49180		Winston-Salem, NC	640595
49180	37057	Davidson County	162878
49180	37059	Davie County	41240
49180	37067	Forsyth County	350670
49180	37169	Stokes County	47401
49180	37197	Yadkin County	38406
49340		Worcester, MA-CT	916980
49340	09015	Windham County	118428
49340	25027	Worcester County	798552
49420		Yakima, WA	243231
49420	53077	Yakima County	243231
49620		York-Hanover, PA	434972
49620	42133	York County	434972
49660		Youngstown-Warren-Boardman, OH-PA	565773
49660	39099	Mahoning County	238823
49660	39155	Trumbull County	210312
49660	42085	Mercer County	116638
49700		Yuba City, CA	166892
49700	06101	Sutter County	94737
49700	06115	Yuba County	72155
49740		Yuma, AZ	195751
49740	04027	Yuma County	195751

www.ingramcontent.com/pod-product-compliance
Ingram Content Group UK Ltd.
Pitfield, Milton Keynes, MK11 3LW, UK
UKHW050951290926
15470UKWH00005B/1754

9 781636 714318